Asteroid Goddesses

The Mythology, Psychology and Astrology of the Reemerging Feminine

by **Demetra George**

with **Douglas Bloch**

ACS Publications
San Diego, California

Asteroid Goddesses

International Standard Book Number 0-935127-15-1

Cover illustration based upon an original drawing by Terrence Stark,
commissioned by Tony Joseph for his work "The Archetypal Universe."
Used with permission of the artist.

Author Photography by Cathleen Rountree

Published by ACS Publications
P.O. Box 34487
San Diego, CA 92163-4487

First Printing, May 1986
Second Printing, May 1987
Third Printing, August 1988
Fourth Printing, September 1990
Fifth Printing, September 1992
Sixth Printing, May 1994

Dedication

To the Mother Goddess in her emanation as Tara

May this offering bring compassionate understanding
and benefit to all beings.

Acknowledgments

Of the many individuals who assisted me in the production of *The Asteroid Goddesses*, my heartfelt gratitude goes to my editor and writer Douglas Bloch whose dedication and expertise made this work a physical reality.

Other writer-editors include Polly Mitchell, Beth-Hedva, Maritha Pottenger, and Tom Bol Guta who provided the mandala concept.

For their financial support, thanks goes to Carolyn Cavalier and Sam Mills.

My ocean view of the beautiful Oregon coast continually inspired me during the conception and writing of this book.

Dharma Dan sustained a vision.

Emotional support was provided by my parents John and Jean Canner, my children Daniel and Reina Frankfort, Jim Frankfort, Michelle Frankfort, Charlie Tabasko who kept the home fires burning, Susan Swift, Robert Rubin, Joan Cypress, Aaron Greenberg, Signe Haynes, Bill Bisignano, Christiane Carruth, Dennis Conroy, Yeshe Nyingpo and the Newport Sangha, Papa John, and A.B.A.T.E.

Appreciation goes to Christa Bax and Rodney Derrick for the gracious use of their homes and to Dennis Riordin for the use of his computer.

My gratitude also extends to the astrological community, particularly to Eleanor Bach for starting me on my journey. My astrological colleagues Judy Franzen, Tsering Everest, Stash, Diana Stone, Yana Breeze, Mary Works, and Babette Cabral gave me feedback and encouragement. My astrological teachers Dane Rudhyar, Alan Oken, Virginia Dayan, Joanne Wickenburg, and Zipporah Dobyns imparted their inspiration.

Many productive hours were spent at the Archive for Research in Archetypal Symbolism of the C. G. Jung Institute of San Francisco.

And finally, for his teachings on motivation and compassion, I give special thanks to my spiritual teacher Lama Chagdud Tulku Rinpoche.

Demetra George
November 9, 1984
Waldport, Oregon

To begin, I would like to thank my astrological mentor, Richard, who introduced me to the sacred science of astrology 13 years ago.

I am also indebted to Demetra for asking me to collaborate with her on this pioneering work.

Finally, I give special thanks to my wife Joan (a gift from the goddesses whom I married while writing this book) for her unconditional devotion and support.

Douglas Bloch
November 11, 1984
Portland, Oregon

Contents

Please refer to the last pages of this book for information on additional titles and astrological reports and calculation services available from Astro Communications Services, Inc.

Preface to the First Edition

My godmother named me Demetra, a name that had been in our family for generations. My roots are in the Arcadian mountains of Greece, an ancient cult site of the worship of Demeter.

In the spring of 1973, I attended my first astrological conference and there met Eleanor Bach who had just published the first asteroid ephemeris. Discovering that my name was Demetra (Greek for Ceres) and that I had Ceres opposite my Sun, she gave me a copy of the tables of asteroid positions. After returning to my home in Oregon where I pursued my studies outside of the mainstream of astrological thought, I became inspired to place the asteroids—Ceres, Pallas Athene, Vesta, and Juno—in the charts of my clients and to study their meanings. Ten years and thousands of charts later, I have developed an understanding of these magical messengers that I wish to share with the astrological community in the hopes that it will add to your understanding and appreciation of this divine science.

"Why include the asteroids in the horoscope? Aren't we doing just fine with the ten planets?" As an astrologer or student of astrology, you have probably asked that question since you first heard of the emergence of asteroids into natal astrology, Yet the inclusion of asteroids adds a depth, richness, and accuracy into horoscope interpretations that have previously been missing from astrology.

When placed in the birth chart, the asteroids accomplish a great deal. First, they provide the astrologer with essential information that simply is not available through the use of the traditional planets. For example, Ceres symbolizes the role of parental bonding in family structures and the development of self-worth as the foundation for healthy relationships. Vesta indicates our need for personal commitment and focus to work or to an ideal. Juno depicts our need for intimate relationships and our capacity to commit ourselves to them. Pallas Athene governs the ability of the mind to create our reality and to formulate and attain our goals.

Aside from providing us with the new astrological archetypes, the asteroids help to clarify and enhance the horoscope's existing astrological themes. It is not unusual for the asteroids to group around the major points of focus in the chart and complete major aspect patterns. Thus, by using the asteroids, the astrological counselor can give the client a more fine-tuned astrological interpretation as well as more relevant insights into his or her life.

The following chapters will fully describe the teachings of the asteroid goddesses so that you may successfully employ them in astrological interpretations. We will begin each study by exploring the mythology of the asteroid goddesses. From the mythology, we will derive the ways the essential archetypal principles are expressed in modern-day psychological terms. Finally, each asteroid will be delineated according to its sign, house, and aspects with the other planets and asteroids. And, to further demonstrate the relevance of these deities, they will be placed in the horoscopes of famous men and women so that you may see how they manifest in real life situations.

Preface to the Second Edition

It has been four years now since *Asteroid Goddesses* was first published and its impact in the astrological community continues to parallel the public's expansion of interest in mythology, transpersonal psychology and women's studies. *Asteroid Goddesses* was one of the first books to describe the astrological counterpart to the reemergence of the feminine in society and the rebirth of the Goddess in women's spirituality. This counterpart is found in the symbolism of the four asteroids, Ceres, Pallas Athena, Juno and Vesta—named after four of the great goddesses of antiquity.

As more and more astrologers integrate the asteroids into the wholeness of the birthchart, they are experiencing the depth of insights that the asteroids lend to the new and often confusing social and interpersonal issues of our times. Many astrologers have written and spoken to me of how the asteroids explain dimensions of themselves and their relationships that could not be explained in the ten planet chart.

In keeping with the bridging of astrology with transpersonal psychology, mythology and women's spirituality, Maria Kay Simms, Douglas Bloch and I are proud to present a new second edition of *Asteroid Goddesses*, reborn after transiting Pluto squared its natal Moon in 15° of Leo. We have given it a new subtitle, "The Mythology, Psychology and Astrology of the Reemerging Feminine," have redone the cover with a classic Greek portrayal of Ceres, the Great Mother Goddess, and have added another twelve years of ephemerides up to 2002.

In the way of the Goddess, the beautiful new cover was provided by Terry Stark whose drawing of Ceres first appeared in Tony Joseph's unpublished manuscript, *The Archetypal Universe*. Tony was a mentor of mine and it was in discussions with him that I realized the link between planetary bodies, mythological archetypes, and their expression in the lives of individuals.

So with thanksgiving to all the midwives who have helped in the rebirthing of *Asteroid Goddesses*, and a wish that this work continue to benefit all beings, Blessed Be.

Demetra George
October 2, 1990

CHAPTER ONE

THE ASTEROIDS — AGENTS OF TRANSFORMATION

The Asteroids and Cultural Transformation

From a historical perspective the discoveries, naming, and recognition of planetary bodies in outer space has coincided with leaps in the evolution of human consciousness and corresponding cultural changes. For example, just before and after the discovery of Uranus, planet of equality and freedom, in 1781, humanity witnessed the American and French Revolutions. When Neptune, planet of mysticism and illusion, was discovered in 1846, idealist movements such as transcendentalism and spiritualism emerged. In 1930 with the sighting of Pluto, planet of mass transformation, the awakening of a sense of collective welfare and the dawning of the Atomic Age brought humanity face-to-face with a choice of life or death. The discovery of each new outer body indicated that humanity was ready to activate and integrate the archetypal principle inherent in the mythology of that planet. As we shall see, the same process is occurring through the discovery of the asteroids.

The asteroids, a belt of planetary bodies largely between the orbits of Mars and Jupiter, were discovered in the early 1800s. The first four sighted were named after the great goddesses of antiquity: Ceres, Pallas Athene, Juno and Vesta. Mythologically, these goddesses were co-equivalent in rank with the gods Jupiter, Neptune, and Pluto. Vesta, Ceres, and Juno were the three sisters of Jupiter,

Neptune, and Pluto, all born from the union of the Titan god Saturn (Cronus) and Rhea. Pallas Athene, the favorite daughter of the new sky god Jupiter, was conceived by himself and birthed from his head. Symbolically, these four asteroids represent aspects of the archetypal feminine principle that are now emerging into mass consciousness. (An archetype is a universal thought form, prototype, primordial pattern, deeply imprinted in the collective human psyche.)

Before the use of the asteroids, the only significators of the feminine in traditional chart interpretation were the Moon and Venus. The socially acceptable roles for women were the Moon as mother and Venus as mate. This began to change when the first four feminine named asteroids were discovered in the nineteenth century as the women's movement, led by Susan B. Anthony and Elizabeth Cady Stanton, sought to increase women's participation in society. These seeds did not bear fruit, however, until the early 1970s at the same time that Eleanor Bach published the first asteroid ephemeris. At this point, the new aspects of feminine expression fully entered into the consciousness of humanity. Women became imbued with the seed possibilities of feminine creativity and intelligence that transcended the traditional roles of mother and wife. Consequently, society saw the widespread entrance of women into the fields of politics, arts, education, sports, and other professional careers. It also marked a time of the rediscovery of women's history and the revival of the Goddess in women's spirituality.

Eleanor Bach, the woman who published the asteroid ephemeris, stated,

> Women are saying today, we are not just vehicles of pleasure (Venus), or emotional weather vanes, utterly dominated by our menstrual cycles (Moon). What about our resourcefulness, our productivity, our ingenuity, efficiency, our nurturing concern for life, our capacity for dedication, our humanity?[1]

Ceres, Pallas Athene, Juno, and Vesta represent these new voices of the dormant feminine, recently activated and now demanding power, recognition, justice, and equality in our society.

It is important to emphasize that this phenomenon is not solely limited to women. The awakening of new aspects of feminine expression has had an equally profound effect on men. As women are

1. Eleanor Bach, "Preface," in *The Asteroid Ephemeris* by Zipporah Dobyns with Rique Pottenger and Neil Michelsen providing calculations (Los Angeles: TIA Publications, 1977), 3.

altering their traditional role expressions, men are developing new responses to the transformed women. Old patterns are no longer acceptable, and new sets of expectations and roles are now required of them.

In the past, men had projected their feminine qualities of emotion, nurturance, and sensitivity onto women. With the recent activation of the feminine centers represented by the asteroids, men have been pressured and encouraged to both "own" and develop these qualities. Consequently, an increasing number of men have rejected the "macho" stereotype image and have acknowledged and expressed their intuitive and feeling selves. Men are now moving into traditional women's territory through their roles as house husbands, nurses, telephone operators, and secretaries. Men have also increased their involvement in the raising of their children, as well as sharing prenatal childbirth training and assisting in the birth process. This emerging participation has prompted men to request and be awarded custody of their children — a previously unacceptable option — and to apply as single male parents for child adoption. The increase in homosexuality is another forefront area of men's liberation where the acknowledgment and expression of the feminine polarity has surfaced in many men.

On a level that goes beyond male and female, the upsurge of the feminine has become the foundation of the general consciousness-expansion movement that is reflected in the human brain. Psychologists define the mind as having left- and right-brain functions. The left brain organizes and structures information within a linear conceptual frame of reference. This rational logical activity is the masculine or *yang* polarity and has been most prevalent in the analytical, technological intellectualism of modern times. The right brain, on the other hand, accesses and processes information which is based on experiences that have no causal relationship. It has been called the intuitive, artistic, and relational part of the brain — the feminine or *yin* polarity. During the last decade, we have witnessed an emergence of right-brain functions in the disciplines of holistic health, healing, education and therapy, and increased psychic awareness.

The Asteroids and Planetary Transformation

The asteroids correspond to the feminine archetype embodied in their mythological namesakes. In essence, the feminine relates to the all-pervading force in the universe which receives, gestates, and gives birth to life. On a global level the discovery of the asteroids points to the birth pangs that humanity is now experiencing as we approach the Aquarian Age.

Aquarius is the sign of group consciousness and planetary awareness. We are presently in a period that astrologers call the Cusp of the Ages. This transition between the Piscean and Aquarian Ages is a time of intense transformation. During this phase, the basic energy of the former 2200-year cycle is changing over into the energy of the latter. To better understand how this transformation works, imagine that the energy which constitutes our experience of history travels in a wave we call time. During cusp periods, a shift occurs in the amplitude and frequency of the wave (see Figure 1-1). Just as the ocean has the cyclic rhythm of waves, history has cycles. As certain multiples of ocean waves are exceptionally large ones, so, at certain periods in history, we get an "extra big" wave of change — known as a quantum leap. This shift in intensity is experienced by society as an increase in pressure, tension, and the rate of change until enough energy is generated to provoke a quantum shift in consciousness.

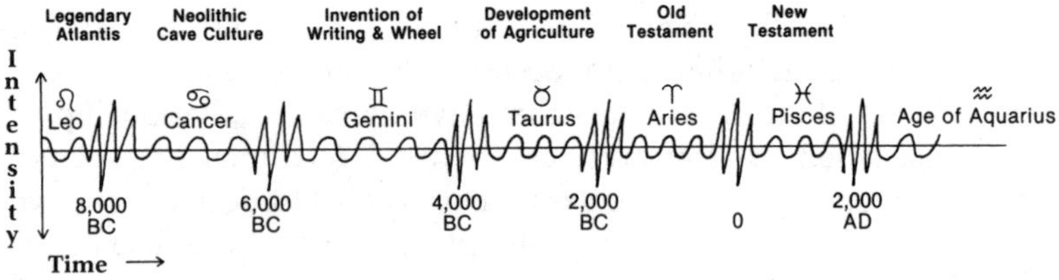

Figure 1.1

This phenomenon is producing marked changes in our social order and paving the way for new cultural experiences. Not only astrologers but philosophers and theorists of human potential are proposing that humanity is on the brink of a quantum leap in consciousness. For example, the computer (ruled by Aquarius) is heralding an information explosion that is physically affecting the human brain's capacity to process information. Up until now, humans had perhaps 13% of their brain cells in active use. With this information explosion, some people are beginning to process information at a rate which is far greater than the brain's present ability. They are "awakening" new centers which in turn builds neuronal patterns of thought on the electrochemical level that increase the brain's capacity for psychic awareness. These changes and new centers in brain functioning correspond to the emergence of the asteroids into human consciousness.

We are living in historic times of global transformation. As we come closer to the Age of Aquarius, humanity as a whole will experience the opportunity to become reborn into collective awareness. During this time we can realize the Aquarian ideals of brotherhood, sisterhood, and planetary family (or the Aquarian confusion of anarchy, chaos, and headlong rush into the new without a sensible incorporation of the old; excessive emphasis on individuality which denies the connection to others).

Emotional transformative crises are changing our psychospiritual vibrations so that we may attune our individual frequency to the spiritual core which resonates with the whole of creation. The positions of Ceres, Pallas Athene, Juno, and Vesta in our charts describe a personal way whereby we can effect this change.

That is why there is such a crucial need today for good therapists and counselors; we are in a transitional stage of history. And, astrologers **need** the asteroids because the traditional planets simply do not and cannot fully explain the issues which are emerging — simply because they are new. (It is true that some individuals in the past have gone through these issues in a limited way, but not on such a **mass level** as now.) The very fact that issues about the balance between the feminine and the masculine are important to many people now, makes the transformation both an individual and societal issue.

The Asteroids as Agents of Personal Transformation

The essence of the feminine principle is symbolized by the moon. As the motion of the physical moon is cyclical in nature, phases of waxing and waning affecting the ebbs and flows of the tides, so essential teachings of the asteroid goddesses relate to the cycle of coming and going. This is also known as the cycle of transformation. Not only do the asteroids relate to new archetypal principles that are currently being activated and integrated into the psyche, but also they serve as active agents in the transformative process of individuals.

The asteroids function as links between personal and collective awareness. This relationship manifests through three symbolic systems: the cycle of zodiacal signs, the planetary positions in the solar system, and the constellations of the stars.

1) The first mode occurs through the cycle of signs of the zodiac. On an esoteric level, the cycle describes the growth and development of human consciousness. This evolutionary process begins in Aries with the birth of individualized awareness — "I" as a separate, unique, free entity — and ends in Pisces with the intuitive awareness that the individual is a cellular component of a greater whole. The intermediate signs describe the progressive stages from Aries to Pisces.

   In the first five personal signs, the germinal life spark of Aries manifests through the physical body in Taurus, the mental body in Gemini, the emotional body in Cancer, and finds its fulfillment in the creative expression and reproductive power of Leo. The last four collective signs — Sagittarius, Capricorn, Aquarius, and Pisces describe the individual functioning within the context of the larger society. Sagittarius provides access to collective knowledge, Capricorn to participation in collective structures, Aquarius to collective ideals and visions, and Pisces to the compassion and empathy that arise from the experience of oneness.

   The intermediary signs Virgo, Libra, and Scorpio are the transitional signs of the transformative process that bring a person from individualized consciousness (Aries-Leo) into collective consciousness (Sagittarius-Pisces).

   In Virgo the evolving entity perfects and integrates itself so that it may enter into the sign of partnership, Libra, as a whole and complete individual. In Libra the person becomes aware of the other for the first time. Communication that leads to sustained interaction is the groundwork for the final transmutation in Scorpio, where the personal sense of "I" dies and totally submerges, interpenetrates, and unifies with the other. The union of "I" into "we" becomes the gateway into the collective awareness symbolized by Sagittarius (see Figure 1-2).

The asteroids Ceres, Pallas Athene, Juno, and Vesta have strong rulership associations with the transitional signs Virgo, Libra, and Scorpio. Therefore, we may postulate that they function as the active agents in these signs that facilitate the transformation from individual to collective awareness.

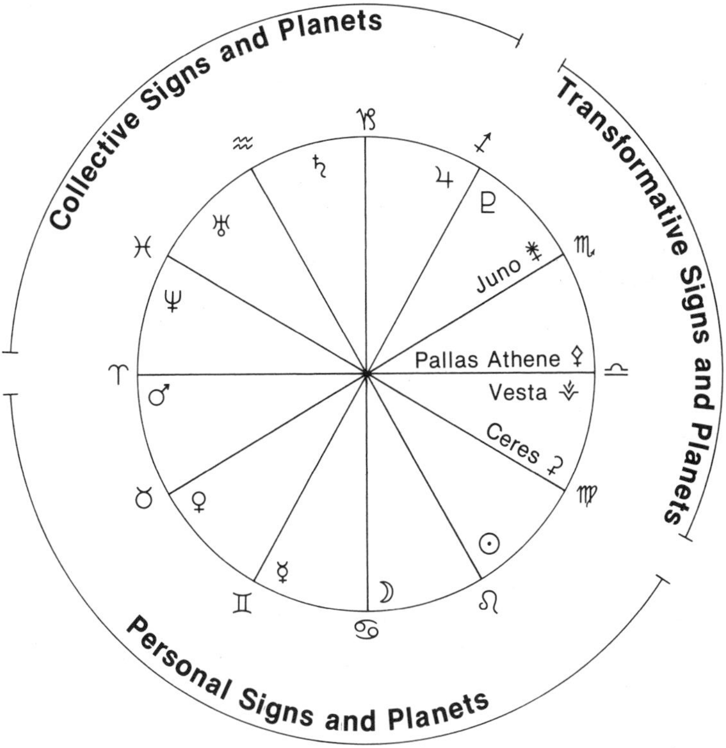

Figure 1-2

2) The second symbolic mode of human unfoldment occurs through the planets of the solar system. The Sun, Mercury, Venus, Moon, and Mars are known as the personal planets because they rule the personal qualities of identity, intellect, values, emotions and drives. Jupiter and Saturn function as the social planets, signifying the ethics and laws by which a society operates. Uranus, Neptune, and Pluto are the universal planets or ambassadors of the galaxy, vibrating to large-scale cosmic forces. The asteroids mostly

occupy the belt between Mars and Jupiter, thereby forming a physical and spiritual bridge that links the personal to the social and collective (see Figure 1-3).

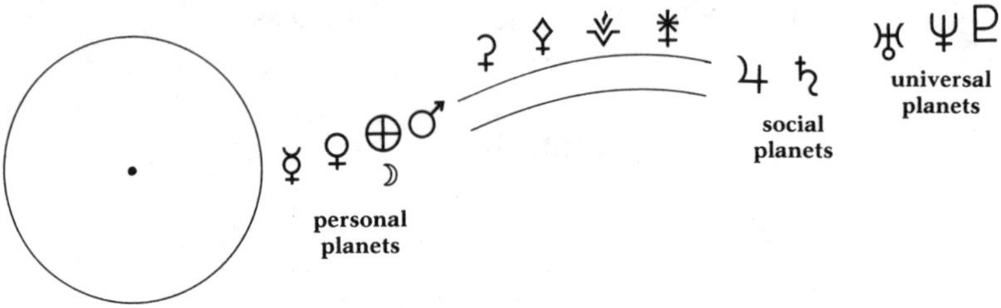

Figure 1-3

3) The final mode uses the constellations of the stars to diagram the evolutionary process. In particular the two snake constellations Serpens and Hydra run along each side of the constellation groups associated with the asteroids — Virgo, Libra and Scorpio. The snake, often associated with the goddesses Ceres, Pallas Athene, Juno, and Vesta, has long existed as a primary symbol of feminine transformative power (see Figure 1-4).

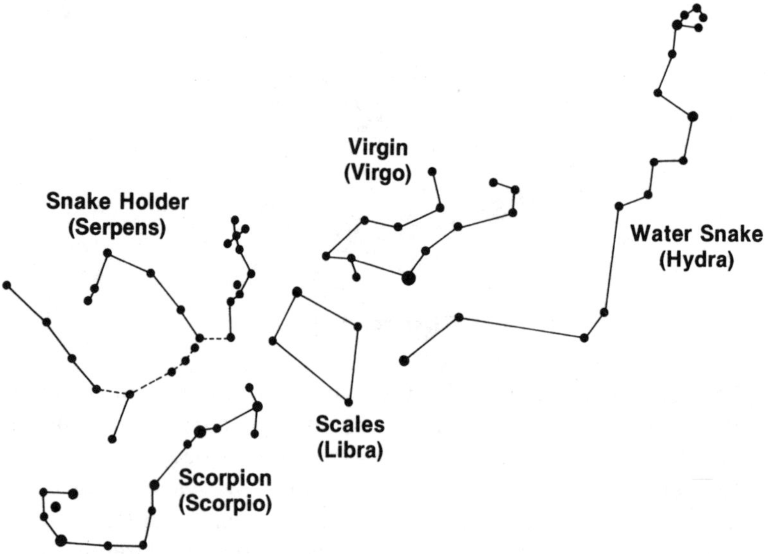

Figure 1-4

Thus in all three systems — the cycle of the signs, the planets of the solar system, and the stellar constellations — the asteroids Ceres, Pallas Athene, Juno and Vesta and their corresponding signs Virgo, Libra, and Scorpio form the stages of the transformative process from the personal to the collective.

Today, activation of the feminine psychic centers is causing the release of a great amount of unconscious archetypal material in both men and women. Unfortunately, the prior repression of the feminine principle throughout recorded history is affecting the way in which this material is being released. Imagine that a ray of light is filtered through a smudged, dirty windowpane. When we look through the window, the obstructions prevent us from seeing a clear image. So it is with our pictures and images of the feminine nature. Suppression has created twisted beliefs and attitudes through which the pure power of the feminine is filtered. Thus we have interpreted our experiences and created our concepts of the feminine based upon these unrecognized and blurry distortions.

Because of the power of subliminal conditioning, modern men and women tend to live out these distorted archetypal forms. Classical Juno is an excellent example. The story is told that Juno is a jealous and vindictive wife. This encourages women to look upon members of their own sex as potential threats or rivals. It also promoted the belief that men feel a sense of territoriality, ownership and possession toward "their" women, causing men to feel distrustful of other men. Juno (or Hera as she was known in earlier times) had been the special goddess of women and had promoted feminine bonding among them. How ironic that this feeling of special connection with the same sex has been distorted into jealousy, competitiveness, and suspicion. (We will discover why when we explore Juno's mythology.) The psychic energy of the archetype is now locked into a distorted mental image ("false god"). The breaking of the idol can liberate the true archetypal force within. One way this can occur is through the process of transformation — an experience that we shall now explore in greater detail.

THE THREE STAGES OF PERSONAL TRANSFORMATION

In any transformative process, a certain force or momentum is needed to overcome the existing inertia and propel us to the next spiral of the evolutionary cycle. As indicated in Figure 1-1, the planetary evolution of the changing of ages receives its momentum through the intensification of the wave vibration of psychic energy. Likewise in personal transformation the momentum is produced through a compression of the emotions.

Let us employ the analogy of taking a coil and pushing it down tightly until it has acquired enough tension to spring forward. This **intensification** or **compressing action** is the first stage of the transformative process and is symbolized by the asteroid Vesta whose energy of self-containment pulls us inward. We experience Vesta on the psychological level as the compression of our emotions. This often produces the experience of "hitting bottom" through separation, loss, grief, pain, despair, failure, frustration, and rejection.

The second stage of the transformative process, the **stage of dissolution**, is symbolized by the asteroid Pallas Athene who governs the use of creative energy. In this period, the compressed emotional energy generated by Vesta succeeds in breaking through and shattering the limiting structures. The result can take many forms — the ending of a relationship, family, job, attitude, or a certain way of life. At this point, the individual experiences a great deal of free-floating energy, but none of it has coalesced. Being in a state of limbo, the individual may thus experience panic, free-floating anxiety, or chaos. On the other hand, he or she may feel the liberation and excitement of formulating new possibilities, dreams, or visions.

The third stage of the transformative process is called the **renewal stage** and is symbolized by the asteroid Juno whose urge toward union draws us from isolation into participation. Now, we may take the liberated energy and restructure it to create new forms that will facilitate expanded growth and continual unfoldment. During this stage all facets of our interpersonal life — our jobs, our relationships, the groups we associate with, the schools we attend — are healed and renewed.

This brings us to Ceres, the largest of the asteroids and the first to be discovered. Some astronomers theorize that Ceres might have been the core of a planet before it exploded and formed the asteroids. Ceres, the Great Mother, symbolizes the matrix out of which the other asteroids operate. The goddess Ceres, through her mythology and participation in the Eleusinian Mysteries, symbolizes the process of birth, death, and renewal that is represented by all of the asteroids. In this sense Ceres provides the foundation for the entire transformational process.

When asteroid themes are prominent in an individual's chart, they denote a personality in which the power of the transformative principle can be operative. Often these persons become vehicles in the general society through which old, crystallized structures, attitudes and values are destroyed, then renewed and regenerated.

Consequently, their lives are marked by crises of individuality challenging the established path of mass consciousness.

The extent to which psychological issues represented by the asteroids are acknowledged and experienced in an individual's life indicates the degree to which he/she will enter into the transformative process. Consciously experiencing these transformations is extremely important because the process enables the individual to pass through the Virgo-Libra-Scorpio transition and enter into the collective vision of the last four signs. They allow the individual to extend boundaries of consciousness and perceive a reality beyond the illusion of separateness, to truly find oneness. In this manner, the individual and all of humankind can evolve side by side.

The asteroid goddesses, therefore, are literally "vehicles" of rapidly vibrating birthing energy. They are both agents of transformation and symbolic keys to our transformation. They represent those experiences/crises which can lead to changes in brain functioning and ultimately open the individual to tuning into more collective or cosmic frequencies. As a part of the universe, certain vibratory, planetary changes among the asteroids also symbolize the reawakening of the feminine from the deep slumber in each of our psyches in order to effect an equilibrium in the planetary biosphere. Ceres, Pallas Athene, Juno and Vesta, with their essential generative qualities, are the "carriers over the bridge" into the birthing of the Aquarian ideal of the equality of all people. They point us to the archetypal images we need to face to make the transition between personal ego and collective understanding. Together, the asteroids are the magical agents transforming each and every one of us. They are the keys to our rites of initiation — the experiences that will unlock the doors to universal understanding.

CHAPTER TWO

THE ASTEROIDS — HARBINGERS OF A NEW MYTHOLOGY

The Meaning of Myth

Carl Jung called myths the "great dreams of humanity" and "the archetypes of the collective unconscious." Archetypes are the essential universal thought forms available to human consciousness during all periods of time. The planets and asteroids are named after the deities that correspond to these primal forces. To understand how the asteroid archetypes operate, we need to explore the myths associated with them.

The meaning of myth may be interpreted on several levels. On an outer level, myth is the oral transmission of the teachings of our origins and history as they have been passed down over generations. Before writing and certainly before the invention of the printing press, myth and oral teachings served as the primary record of accumulated knowledge. Tracing the development and change of a myth reveals much about ancient historical times. Different versions of the same myth occur due to periods of growth and change in a culture. Though scholars have gotten lost in endless debates over which version of the myth is correct, the fact is that usually all of the accounts are true and no one is exclusive.

Within the development of a myth that portrays the current events of a given era, we find that the retelling of the myth describes progressive development of human consciousness at those points in time. Critical changes in the unfolding character of the deities point to significant developments in the expression of human potential. For example, one story depicts the wisdom goddess Pallas Athene as emerging from the crown chakra of her father Jupiter. This myth tell us that the expression of the feminine principle was then shifting from the procreative function of the fertility goddess, whose creative divine energy is channeled solely through the genitals, to an outpouring of feminine energy through the head. This change personified the emergence of the new ability of feminine functioning to express creative intelligence and the birth of ideas.

THE DISTORTION OF MYTH

Historically, as mythological deities have been molded by the needs of successive political or religious dynasties, their presentation to humanity changed accordingly. Their earlier attributes were either forgotten or consciously suppressed especially if they posed a threat to the security of the current order. It is one thing for an archetypal energy to go through change in its normal evolutionary development, but quite another situation when the change is defined by a distortion of expediency. An example of this distortion can be seen in the transition from the precessional Age of Taurus to that of Aries. At this time, the lunar-based (the Moon is exalted in Taurus), matriarchal, agricultural societies shifted into solar-based (the Sun is exalted in Aries) patriarchal and nomadic societies. The dominion of the earth goddess gave way to the dominion of the sky god. The functions and activities of the goddesses diminished as their power declined. When Olympian mythology emerged around 1100 BC and Jupiter became supreme god of the heavens, the goddesses became faint shadows of their former grandeur. In many cases their new roles were defined as contrary to their original nature. For example, the virgin priestesses of ancient Sumer, enacting ritual sexuality as religious devotion, mutated through the patriarchal culture to the Roman vestal virgins, oathbound to celibacy as religious commitment.

These distorted images of the feminine deities have unfortunately become imprinted in the modern psyche. Consequently, the expression of the original archetype has become repressed or distorted. This pathology has resulted in the frustration, unhappiness, and dis-ease that exist in the modern psyche especially as they relate to the feminine nature. For example, the asteroid Vesta may express itself in the personality as sexual fear, withdrawal, and alienation. This fear is explained when we discover that, at a certain time, virgin priestesses of the temple were forbidden their sexual devotions and upon violation were buried alive.

Although the earlier versions of the original goddess nature are buried deeply in historical strata and are relatively inaccessible to the conscious mind, they continue to exist in the collective unconscious mind.

> "The unconscious contains, as it were, two layers: the personal and the collective. The personal layer ends at the earliest memories of infancy, but the collective layer comprises the pre-infantile period, that is, the residues of ancestral life. Whereas the memory-images of the personal unconscious are, as it were, filled out, because they are images personally experienced by the individual, the archetypes of the collective unconscious are not filled out because they are forms not personally experienced. On the other hand, when psychic energy regresses, going even beyond the period of early infancy, and breaks into the legacy of ancestral life, then mythological images are awakened: these are archetypes,"[1]

This is not to suggest that we go back to what was. Not only is regression not possible, it is not desirable. However, a clear vision of the pure or original essence of the archetypal image can reawaken the soul work of the present transformative process during this cusp age.

THE FUNCTION OF MYTH IN THE THERAPEUTIC PROCESS

Probing the deeper or "secret" meaning of the myth illustrates the process of archetypal patterns as they unconsciously direct the dramas of human life. The myths depict the basic life scripts that humanity has available through which to express itself. As individuals live out these myths, they bring the unconscious energies of the archetypes into their awareness. Jung referred to this process as individuation, known to the ancients as "initiation." Therefore, insight into one's personal mythology, gained by an understanding of planetary themes in the birth chart, can enable the individual to more consciously live out his or her destiny.

For example, the myth of Ceres describes the loss of her daughter Persephone and the subsequent sharing of Persephone part-time with Pluto. Hence, Ceres-Pluto aspects in a person's chart often indicate life lessons of losing or sharing one's children. The activation of this theme through a transit or progression can point to a time of child custody decisions. Here we see that the critical point in the myth

1. Carl G. Jung, "On the Psychology of the Unconscious," in *Two Essays on Analytic Psychology* (Cleveland: Meridian Books, 1965), 87.

corresponds to the points in an individual's life that necessitate decision making or action taking.

Oftentimes, however, an individual may become fixated at a certain point in the mythological process by repeating habitual patterns that are negative or nonproductive. Each time a conscious decision is foregone, instinctive unconscious patterns are deepened. In the words of Alexander Ruperti, author of *Cycles of Becoming*, "What was a groove in childhood, later becomes a rut, and finally a grave."[2]

For example we can look at the psychic development of the feminine in the role of consort or mate. Initial-stage Lilith (a minor feminine asteroid) encountered a relationship, found it unsatisfactory, and left it. Intermediary-stage Juno encountered relationship, also found it unsatisfactory, but continued to participate in it. Completion-stage Psyche encountered relationship and through the transformative process perfected the form to soul-mate union. Oftentimes, a block in this process occurs at the Lilith stage. Here, the individual avoids working through relationship conflicts by running away. Such avoidance prevents movement through the succeeding unfoldments and the final resolution in the Psyche stage.

Thus, through a knowledge of mythology, the therapist, astrologer, or counselor can recognize archetypal fixations and point the way to liberation. Using the planetary myths as a guide, the therapist can discover the nature of the client's blockages and facilitate the healing process to its natural and harmonious conclusion. Hence, the birth chart provides the diagnosis, the myth and the cure.

The power of the Goddess has been in a state of deep sleep for the last four to five thousand years. With the discovery of the asteroids, the power of the feminine has at last been activated and released into our conscious awareness. By studying and working with the asteroids and restoring the true archetypal imagery, astrologers can assist evolving humanity in regaining the inner balance of the male and female principles within both sexes.

2. Alexander Ruperti, *Cycles of Becoming* (Vancouver, Wash.: CRCS Publications, 1978), 8.

CHAPTER THREE

THE MANDALA OF THE ASTEROID GODDESSES

Within the brilliant clear light of the Sun

The silver light of the Moon reflects the ground of lunar energy — the undifferentiated feminine prior to manifestation with her powers of fertilization and transformation.

Arising from the center is Venus Aphrodite, core essence of the feminine nature in her manifest form. Through her powers of divine beauty and magnetic desirability as love, she awakens the impulse to life.

In her emanation to the north, the feminine appears as Ceres representing her procreative aspect as mother in her propagation and nurturing of the species.

In her emanation to the south, the feminine appears as Pallas Athene, representing her creative aspect as daughter giving rise to mental and artistic progeny.

In her emanation to the east, the feminine appears as Vesta representing the self-containment of the feminine nature as Virgin and sister, complete in-one-self, belonging to no man.

In her emanation to the west, the feminine appears as Juno representing the union of the feminine nature with the masculine as consort and wife through the Sacred Marriage, Conjunctio.

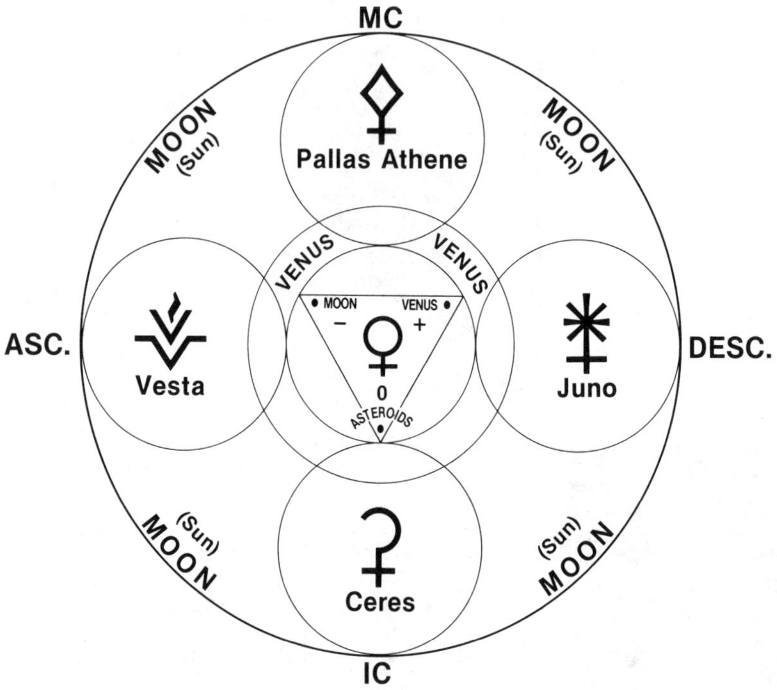

Figure 3-1

In his explorations into the human psyche, C. G. Jung determined that there exist basic unifying symbols which describe the nature and relationship of archetypal energies. One such symbol is the **mandala**, the Sanskrit word for "circle." The key feature of a circle is that it possesses both a circumference and a center. "The center or innermost point is surrounded by a periphery containing everything that belongs to the self — the paired opposites that make up the total personality."[1] The asteroid mandala (see Figure 3-1) is a visual image that integrates the primary components of the feminine principle of **human** expression. The feminine principle represented here manifests in both men and women. Feminine is **not** a synonym for female or woman, but indicates one half of a human polarity — and

1. Carl G. Jung, *Mandala Symbolism* (New Jersey: Princeton University Press, 1972), M.73.

neither half, masculine or feminine, exists without the other. Both sides exist within both human sexes. While in the past the feminine principle has been expressed primarily by women, due to the present rebalancing of masculine and feminine energies signified by the emergence of the asteroids, men are now identifying and expressing their feminine nature.

The foundation or ground of the feminine principle is represented by the potential power of the moon. In the center, the core essence of the feminine nature in active form is depicted by Venus Aphrodite. At the periphery, the paired opposite asteroids Ceres-Pallas Athene and Vesta-Juno describe the basic differentiated functions of feminine activity. In this manner the asteroid mandala illustrates the principle of "wholeness." Each celestial body defines the characteristic relationships between the self in the center and the components of the self on the periphery, thereby creating a unified image of feminine consciousness.

Within the Brilliant Clear Light of the Sun

Feminine expression as symbolized by the moon in the mandala presupposes the existence of masculine expression symbolized by the sun. Masculine and feminine are polar manifestations of the same force which, when unified, forms what mystics have defined as "oneness." Feminine in and of itself does not exist; it is the feminine end of the polarity.

Figure 3-2

In Chinese philosophy, the feminine principle, *yin*, stands in direct opposition to the masculine principle *yang*. *Yang* is the bright, hot, powerful creative energy, while *yin* is the dark, moist, shadowy and receptive power which is also creative because it brings to birth and manifestation the creative stirrings of the *yang* energy. The *yin* is said to be of equal power with the *yang* because it brings all his stirrings into manifestation.[2]

2. Esther Harding, *Woman's Mysteries: Ancient and Modern* (New York: Harper and Row, 1976), 105.

In the mandala the moon/sun serve as symbolic representations of the undifferentiated divine force of Goddess/God awareness. Symbolically, the sun emanates its light and projects its creative energy outward. The reflective quality of the moon returns the light back toward the source, thereby completing the soli-lunar circuit. This creates an ongoing cycle in which the sun and moon continuously interact with and interpenetrate each other.

The Silver Light of the Moon Reflects the Ground of Lunar Energy — the Undifferentiated Feminine Prior to Manifestation with Her Powers of Fertilization and Transformation.

The moon is the primary symbol of the feminine polarity personified by the ancients as the Goddess. The moon, in her phases of waxing and waning, symbolizes the many goddesses that represent the various facets of her changing face. The moon contains the totality of the potential of feminine expression. Combined within her are all of the possible expressions of the Goddess in their ethereal forms prior to manifestation.

The feminine lunar principle manifests in human biology, for like the moon's waxing and waning, a woman's body becomes full with child. When not swelling with new life, she menstruates in attunement to the lunar cycle.

The cyclic nature of the moon reveals two principles of feminine power. The first principle that manifests through the feminine polarity is the power of **growth and fertilization** — forces that quicken the life impulse to recreate and sustain itself. According to the beliefs of the ancients, the moon was the force that fertilized all new life. Symbolically, animal mating cycles and the seasonal nature of crop production, as well as women's menstrual cycles and pregnancies represent the rhythmic ebbs and flows of the moon's power of fertilization.

The second principle that manifests through the feminine polarity is the power of **transformation**. Feminine energy is transformative in that it possesses the ability to change one thing into another. From antiquity women have presided over the food mysteries whereby through cooking grain, grass becomes bread. And when they internalize this power within their own bodies, women transform their blood into the milk that nourishes and sustains life. The feminine was venerated for this awesome power to transform.

The serpent, who like the waxing and waning of the moon sheds its skin and renews itself, was believed to embody the mysteries of rebirth and renewal. Thus the serpent became a symbol of the transformative power of the feminine energy of the moon.

Subsequently, the moon goddess became refined and revered in a symbology known as the triple moon goddess. In her phase of the waxing new crescent moon, she displayed herself as *Artemis*, who symbolized the first virginal budding strength of the maiden, ruling the season of spring and the upper air. Upon reaching the full moon, she became *Selene*, who depicted the middle phase of a woman's life — that of mother, who embodies the qualities of fertility and productivity, ruling the season of summer and the earth. As the waning dark moon she became *Hecate*, symbolizing the final phase of life as crone, wise-old-one, distilling wisdom essence into the seed, ruling the season of winter and the Underworld. The crone, having passed through maternity, cyclically emerges anew as the maiden.

SELENE

Terra-cotta Vessel
Hellenic Era: Greek Early Classical Period: ca. 500-475 B.C. Selene wearing cap with pointed tip having loop or tassel, holding rod, moon disc above head, seated on chariot drawn by two winged horses, sinking into sea.

Mus. Staatliche, Berlin
Photograph permission: Columbia University Press

In summation, the large silver circle of the moon contained within the golden sun's light represents the entirety of the potential powers of feminine expression, including the powers of fertilization and transformation. Its phase changes symbolize the many different goddesses who are unique expressions of the ever-changing face of the Great Goddess. Each of the goddesses of the moon, as they periodically withdraw into their waning dark phase, teach the mysteries and initiations of the intermediary passage between death and rebirth.

Arising from the Center Is Venus Aphrodite,
Core Essence of the Feminine Nature in Her Manifest Form.
Through Her Powers of Divine Beauty
and Magnetic Desirability as Love,
She Awakens the Impulse to Life.

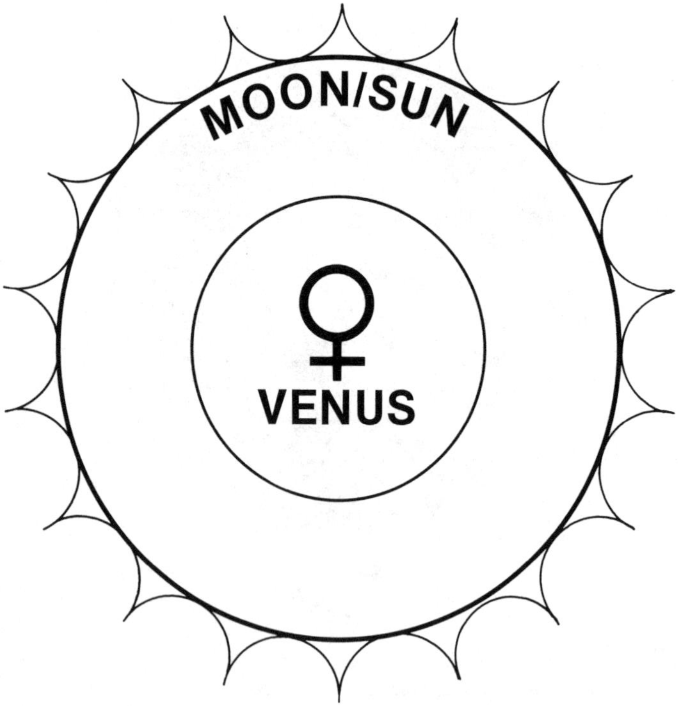

Figure 3-3

From the center of the basic realm of primal, lunar energy emerges Venus Aphrodite, symbol of the active, magnetic, reproductive force of the feminine nature.

The first feminine expression to differentiate from the lunar ground of all possibilities is symbolized in the myth of Venus Aphrodite. According to Hesiod, the oldest story of the birth of Aphrodite, she is born from the "sea foam" (*aphros*), which billowed up when the dismembered genitals of Uranus were cast into the sea by the insurgent Cronus. The gentle breath of the Western Wind carried this lovely figure on a mussel shell across the sea until she landed on the shores of Cyprus. There Aphrodite was greeted by the *Horae*, the divine nature-guardians, whose cyclic and life-giving showers identify them as seasons. With each step, fresh green grass sprouted beneath her feet, and Aphrodite's other companions, *Eros*/Love and *Himeros*/Tender Desire, joined the *Horae* to accompany the beautiful new goddess to the assembly of the immortals. According to Homer, each god upon seeing Aphrodite wished in his heart to take her as wife and lead her to his abode.[3] Indeed, many there were, both mortal and god alike, whose desire to make love with the Goddess was fulfilled. Though later tales marry her to *Hephaestus*, she was never possessed by him, and stories of the *Graces* bathing her and annointing her with an immortal oil remind us that she renews her virginity.[4]

The archetypal feminine energy as Aphrodite also subdivides into a trinity, where she is identified with the names *Aphrodite Pandemos, Aphrodite Ourania*, and *Apostrophia*. In the *Symposium*, Plato makes a clear distinction between the "common love" which is *Aphrodite Pandemos* and the idealized spiritual or platonic love of *Aphrodite Ourania* (literally, "heavenly love"). *Apostrophia*, the third form, translates as "she who turns herself away."

VENUS AS THE EXPRESSION OF REPRODUCTION

In the story of Venus, the primary potential of fertilization and transformation symbolized as cyclic possibilities in the moon becomes activated as a vital reproductive force. Refer ing again to the image of the mandala, from the center of the lunar ground arises the core of feminine expression — Venus Aphrodite —

3. *New Larousse Encyclopedia of Mythology*, trans. R. Aldington and D. Ames (New York and London: Hamlym Publishing Group, Ltd., 1983), 130.
4. For more on this concept of virginity, see Esther Harding's *Woman's Mysteries*, "The Virgin Goddess" (New York: Harper and Row, 1971).

VENUS APHRODITE

Parian marble statue
Greco-Roman Era: Hellenistic Period: ca. 100 B.C.
Crouching Aphrodite of Rhodes; Aphrodite, just emerged from bath, crouching and raising hair to top of head.

Mus. of Rhodes
Photograph permission: Hirmer Verlag, Munich

the essential reproductive force which manifests through the feminine polarity as divine beauty, magnetic desirability, and love.

Venus Aphrodite as creatress is the wellspring of feminine expression and as such represents the vessel which contains and emits reproductive energy. This is the magnetic energy which activates the transformation of a flaccid phallus into an erection so that the potential power of fertilization can be activated through sexual intercourse.

As goddess of love she recreates life through the arousal of sexuality. The impulse to love is brought forth as magnetic desirability through the irresistible attractive power of her divine beauty. Because she is the source of all the reproductive energy in the universe, Empedocles called her the "giver of life."[5]

Aphrodite originally came from Asia, associated with *Ishtar*, *Astarte*, as a fertility goddess of all of nature and life forms. In later Greek times, Aphrodite became recognized chiefly through her outer attributes of love and erotic desirability. The fertility goddess's function as "primal mother of all ongoing creation"[6] was repressed and forgotten. Consequently, in her patriarchal form, her essence was filtered and distorted into being simply an alluring, beautiful woman whose associations with the cyclic fertilizing and transforming principles of nature were denied expression.

VENUS AND THE LESSONS OF LOVE

Using her magnetic energy, Venus Aphrodite can either affect an attractive force between people, or she can "turn away" and create a repelling force. The ability to stir love and arouse erotic impulses in others but not to take responsibility for what one has awakened sets into motion the *karmic* causes which yield the future experiences of being "rejected in love." As *Apostrophia*, "she who turns herself away," the dark side of Venus Aphrodite initiates us into the painful experiences of rejection and loss in love. She teaches us the meaning of responsibility so that we may learn to be sensitive to the emotional impact of arousing affections in others.

Through experiencing the sorrow of rejection and loss, we learn the spiritual lessons associated with the transitory nature of love. As goddess of mourning, Venus Aphrodite annually weeps and grieves over the death of her beautiful young lover *Adonis*. Through her pain and suffering, Venus Aphrodite comes to realize the impossibility of possessing love. Love and passion are by their very nature impermanent. Through the recognition of the transient nature of earthly love, Venus Aphrodite nevertheless is able to express, with heightened intensity, the ecstatic bliss of the divine love which begets and renews life.

---

5. Christine Downing, *The Goddess: Mythological Images of the Feminine* (New York: The Crossroad Publishing Co., 1981), 190.
6. E. O. James, *The Cult of the Mother Goddess: An Archeological and Documentary Study* (New York: Frederick A. Praeger, Inc., 1959), 147.

In summation, Venus Aphrodite symbolizes the core essence of the feminine nature as beauty and desirability. She is the magnetic force which activates the sexual and reproductive energy. Venus Aphrodite resides at the center of the mandala of feminine expression, "a center of personality, a kind of central point within the psyche, to which everything is related, by which everything is arranged, and which is in itself a source of energy."[7]

THE ASTEROIDS — THE COMPLETION OF THE MANDALA

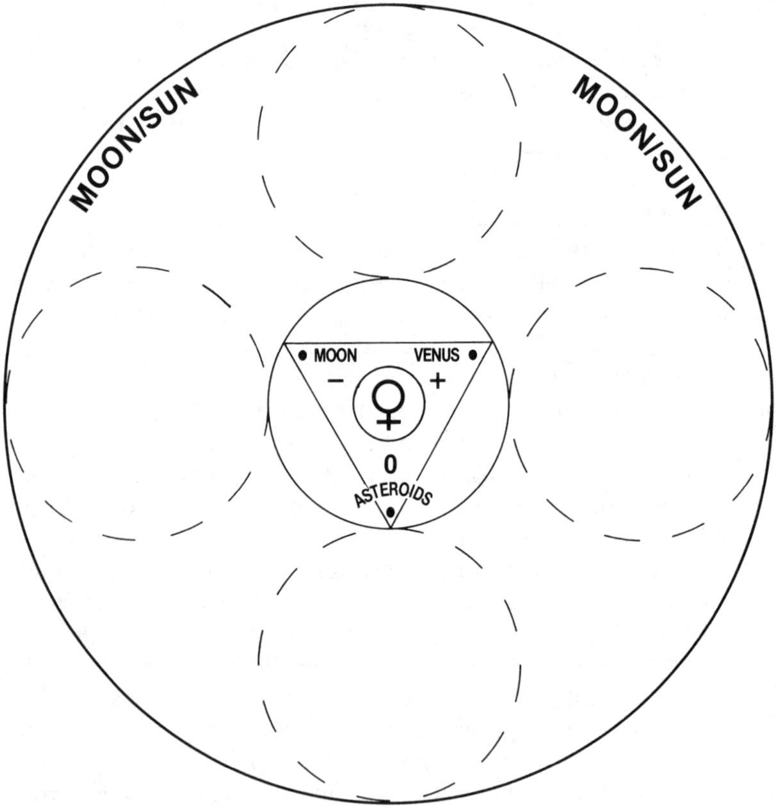

Figure 3-4

7. Jung, *Mandala Symbolism*, 72.

Referring to the above mandala we see that the outer circle of sun/moon represents the domain of the feminine polarity of consciousness, while a smaller circle identifies Venus as the center and active source of this feminine potential. Within the mandala there exists a triangle containing the electrical symbols "+ charge," "– charge," and "0 ground." These distinguish the activating kinetic (+) energy of Venus from the passive potential (–) energy of the moon. The circuitry of feminine consciousness uses the asteroids as a (0) ground through which the feminine energy can flow and thus differentiate into unique patterns of activity. The asteroids Ceres, Pallas Athene, Vesta, and Juno each utilize the sexual energy of Venus in their own particular way. They represent the various functions and activities of the feminine nature.

In the past, people have confused women's relationships with her feminine functions and thus denied the feminine functions of men. Moreover, certain stereotyped visions of women's relationships have narrowed the expression of women's feminine functions as well, allowing only certain manifestations as societally approved. On a biological level, mother, daughter, sister and wife are the primary **relationships** a woman has, based on ties of blood and kin. However, the **feminine functions** are much more varied than the stereotyped activities of women as mother, daughter, sister and wife. The feminine functions include a range of activities and accomplishments which flow from the feminine polarity energy (manifesting in both men and women).

The relationship between the center and the circumference of the mandala creates two distinct axes. From an astrological perspective the "y" axis is the meridian, connecting the Midheaven with the IC. It depicts one's outer public personality role (MC) versus one's inner private nature and domain (IC). The "x" axis, known as the horizon, connects the Ascendant with the Descendant and describes the polarity between one's self-identity (Ascendant) and one's relationship to the "other" (Descendant).

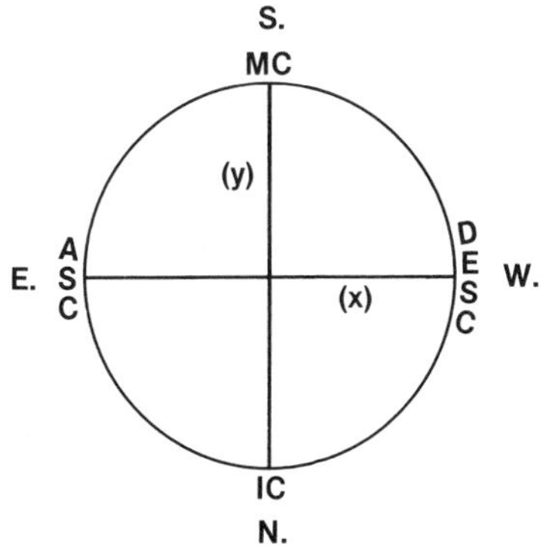

Figure 3-5

The four asteroids Ceres, Pallas Athene, Vesta, and Juno also lie along these cardinal points of north-south and east-west (see Figure 3-6), thereby creating a mandala of relatedness and unification. Hence the essence of the potential generative and transformative power of the Great Goddess (Moon) in her active, reproductive energy (Venus) differentiates into four functions of feminine activity. Ceres, at the IC, utilizes the sexual-creative energy to generate physical beings and the food for their survival. Pallas Athene, at the MC, utilizes the sexual-creative energy to birth mental and artistic forms. Vesta, at the Ascendant, utilizes the sexual-creative energy to renew and regenerate the self. Juno, at the Descendant, utilizes the sexual creative energy to renew and regenerate others.

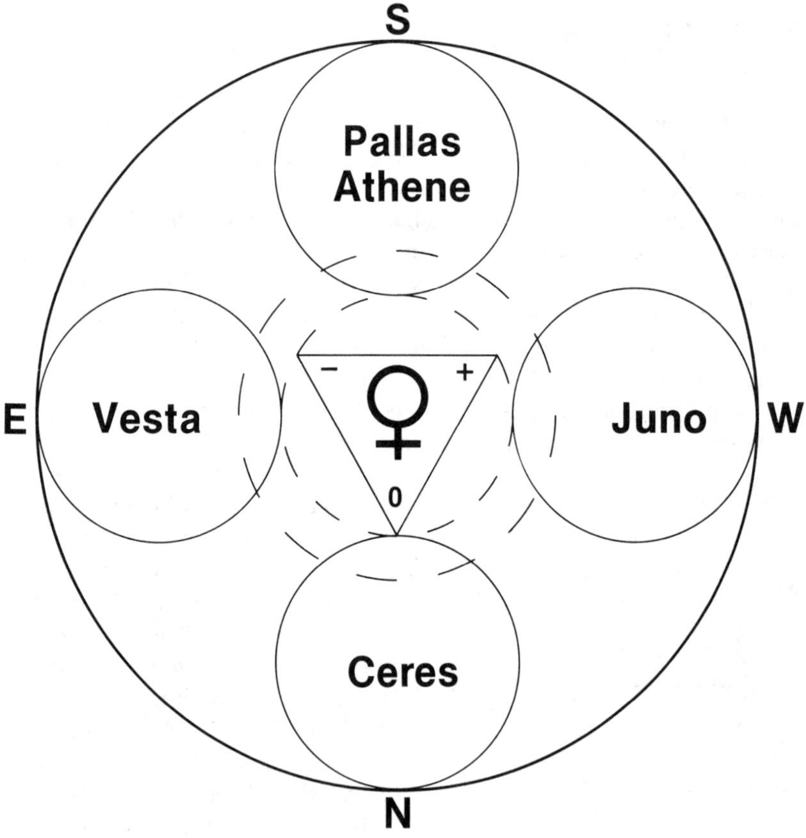

Figure 3-6

In Her Emanation to the North, the Feminine Appears as Ceres Representing Her Procreative Aspect as Mother in Her Propagation and Nurturing of the Species.

The feminine archetype first manifests at the nadir (IC) as Ceres the mother. As such, she goes beyond Venus' sexual magnetism which activates the potential for life, by utilizing the creative energy for the procreative generation of physical forms. The mother nurtures the embryonic new life within her and then gives birth to the child. This nurturance continues until the child becomes independent and self-sufficient in its own right. Thus, the mother is also responsible for producing the foodstuffs which feed and nourish the propagation of the species.

CERES

Terra-cotta relief
Greco-Roman Era: Hellenistic Period
Ceres rising from ground holding poppy capsules, lilies, and ears of barley, with snakes on either side, coiled around her forearms, with heads raised toward her.

Museo Nazionale delle Terme, Rome
Photograph permission: Museo Nazionale Romano

As mother, Ceres also symbolizes the principle of unconditional love, sustaining and nourishing newly created life forms. (It is important to note that in mythology, Ceres was both the compassionate, nurturing mother and the angry, withholding mother.) Through her association with the Eleusinian Mysteries, Ceres also contains the secret of the great mystery of birth, death and renewal, which speaks to the feeding and nourishment of the soul and spirit.

Ceres' outer color is green, symbolizing the abundant display of the vegetation of cultivated soil. Her inner color is blue-black, the color of the underworld where seeds lie dormant within the earth during winter incubation. Ceres' practical qualities also associate her with the element of earth.

In the symbolism of the astrological wheel, Ceres corresponds to the north position of the IC, representing the principles of foundation, roots, and family. Astrologically, Ceres represents the ability to unconditionally love and accept yourself and others. When a person becomes excessively attached to their children, creations, or possessions, Ceres' cycle takes them through the transformative process of loss and return. She teaches the wisdom that sharing and letting go lead to reunion. If one is fixated on the Ceres process, he or she may experience abandonment and rejection in the life, until learning to transform grasping into generosity.

In summation, Ceres is the lunar energy grounded through the physical reproductive organs where it procreatively regenerates and provides for fundamental human needs.

In Her Emanation to the South, the Feminine Appears as Pallas Athene, Representing Her Creative Aspect as Daughter, Giving Rise to Mental and Artistic Progeny.

Opposite from Ceres, located at the south position on the mandala, is Pallas Athene, the daughter. As goddess of wisdom born from the crown of her father Jupiter's head, she is active, creative intelligence that gives birth to thought forms. Here the reproductive energy of Venus is released not through the genitals, but rises like the *kundalini* serpent to the head, where the creative generation of ideas (mental progeny) is born. Hence, Pallas Athene represents the principle of creative wisdom.

Pallas is mythologically related to the regenerative properties of the *Gorgon Medusa* whose head is brandished upon her breastplate. Pallas Athene's visible face is that of self-confidence and courage;

her hidden face, however, holds the fears of success that thwart creativity. Her color is yellow, symbolizing the mastery of the intellectual domain, and her mental qualities link her to the element of air.

PALLAS ATHENE

Bronze statue
Greco-Roman Era: Hellenistic Period: II B.C., Roman copy of IV B.C. Greek original. Athena wearing helmet, breastplate in form of snake-skin aegis at center of which is affixed gorgoneum.

Museo Archeologico, Florence
Photograph permission: Bruckmann, Munich

In the symbolism of the astrological wheel, Pallas Athene corresponds to the Midheaven where visible, socially useful accomplishments are realized. Astrologically, Pallas Athene represents one's mental creativity and the capacity to create and control one's reality. When a person becomes clouded by ignorance, Pallas Athene's cycle takes them through the transformative process of destruction and renewal of their life structures. She teaches the wisdom that the mind's eye contains the seed of manifested form. If one is fixated in the Pallas Athene process, he or she may experience inadequacy and inability to influence the life, until learning to utilize the creative mind to transform ideas into reality.

In summation, Pallas Athene depicts the lunar energy grounded through the mentally creative organ (brain/mind), where through exercising her knowledge of the laws of manifestation she births image to form.

The bipolar relationship between Ceres and Pallas Athene is symbolized by the IC-MC polarity, forming an axis of creative energy and power. The reproductive-creative energy of Venus is expressed through Ceres as the procreative generation of physical forms, and through Pallas Athene as the creative generation of mental forms.

In Her Emanation to the East, the Feminine Appears as Vesta Representing the Self Containment of the Feminine Nature as Virgin and Sister, Complete-in-One-Self, Belonging to No Man.

At the eastern position of the mandala on the Ascendant lies Vesta, the sister. Her virgin nature is defined in the ancient sense as being complete and whole in herself. Here Vesta uses the reproductive energy of Venus for self-regeneration. Vesta is the principle of focus and commitment which utilizes the creative energy in a one-pointed devotion and dedication toward specific goals and aspirations.

In her original function and nature, Vesta ruled the virgin priestesses of the temple and esoteric orders of sisterhoods who, in sacred sexual rites, brought the fertilizing power of the Moon into effective contact with the lives of human beings. In later times, as the concept of virgin came to signify sexual chastity, Vesta's outer face expressed itself through sexual denial, celibacy and barrenness. On an occult level the sexual energy was internalized in order to attain inner spiritual union. Vesta's outer color is white/crystal, symbolizing the purity that gives rise to luminosity as seen in her symbol of the torch. Her aspirational qualities link her with the element of fire; her glyph is the symbol for fire itself — the eternal flame and secret, sexual fires.

VESTA

Pentalic marble statue
Hellenic Era: Greek Early Classical Period: ca. 480-460 B.C., based on bronze original. So called Hestia Guistiniani, standing female goddess, veil over head, right hand resting on hip, left arm missing.

Museo Capitolini, Rome
Photograph permission: Mansell Collection, London

In the symbolism of the astrological wheel, Vesta corresponds to the Ascendant, which relates to self-identity and autonomy. Astrologically, Vesta represents the ability to focus energy and experience wholeness of self. When a person becomes fragmented, overly dependent upon others, or without personal direction, Vesta's cycle takes them through the transformative process of the renewal of their virginity (essential self). She teaches the wisdom that periodic retreat from others in order to cleanse and regenerate the self can lead to a clarity of vision and purpose. If one is fixated in Vesta's process, he or she may experience aimlessness, alienation, or depletion of vital force, until learning to transform confusion into commitment.

In summation, Vesta is the lunar energy grounded through the vessel of the self, where it is used to purify and integrate personal circuitry, and to devote oneself to a mission or ideal.

In Her Emanation to the West, the Feminine Appears as Juno Representing the Union of the Feminine Nature with the Masculine as Consort and Wife through the Sacred Marriage, Conjunctio.

Opposite from Vesta, at the western position of Descendant, lies Juno the wife. As goddess of marriage, Juno symbolizes the union of the feminine and masculine through the vehicle of committed relationship. The reproductive energy of Venus is utilized to foster relationship and consummate union with the Other. On an occult level, Juno holds the secret teachings of sexual *tantric* practices where perfected relationship is used as a path to spiritual realization.

Juno is the principle of relatedness and commitment to the other. In her longing for union, Juno's gifts of intimacy and sharing are often expressed as jealousy and manipulation. This occurs when she feels powerless and tries to regain her lost influence through covert means. Juno's outer color of red describes her passion and her desire to possess. Her inner color is blue-violet, symbolizing the transcendence of deep union. Her emotional qualities link her to the element of water, a medium which dissolves separate forms and unifies their essences.

In the symbolism of the astrological wheel, Juno corresponds to the Descendant as awareness of and cooperation with the other. Astrologically, Juno represents one's capacity for meaningful relationship and commitment to another person. When a person becomes jealous and dishonest with others, Juno's cycle takes them through the transformative process of consummation and separation in relationships. She teaches the wisdom that forgiveness and fair play lead to depth and renewal with others. If one is fixated in the Juno process, he or she may experience isolation, loneliness and superficial interactions, until learning to transform selfish desire into cooperative union.

JUNO AS HERA WITH ZEUS

Relief sculpture
Hellenic Era: Greek Early Classical Period: ca. 450-425 B.C.
Wedding of Zeus and Hera (from Temple of Hera at Selinus); Zeus grasping Hera's wrist in gesture of possession as she raises veil over her head.

Museo Nazionale, Palermo
Photograph permission: Hirmer Verlag, Munich

In summation, Juno symbolizes the lunar energy grounded through the vehicle of relationship, where the connection to the masculine is affirmed and regenerated. She functions as a link to the "other," thereby completing the circuitry of conscious union.

The bipolar relationship between Vesta and Juno, symbolized by the Ascendant-Descendant polarity, depicts the line of relationship energy of the feminine. Although Vesta interacts with the masculine, she remains autonomous and becomes reabsorbed back into herself. Juno, on the other hand, unifies with the masculine principle. The symbolic union completes the circle of the mandala of feminine expression.

Asteroid Centers

Thus, the four asteroids — Ceres the mother, Pallas Athene the daughter, Vesta the sister, and Juno the wife — symbolize the four primary activities and relationships of Venus Aphrodite, the vessel of the reproductive energy, who in turn arises from the Moon, our original feminine source.

The awakening of asteroid centers has affected consciousness in both men and women. In the past, the feminine energy has been contained in stereotypes. These socially determined traditional role forms by which men and women have been defined have limited their ranges of expression. For example, Ceres represents the mothering function within the human psyche which expresses in both men and women. (Women and men also have a fathering function, symbolized by Saturn.) Until the 1960s the only "acceptable" expression of the mothering function for women was a full-time mother and wife, staying at home, looking after the household and putting the emotional needs of the family before her own. The only "acceptable" expression of the fathering function for men was going out into the world and becoming "successful" (i.e., earning money) in order to bring material goods and reflected success back to his wife and children.

To the extent that these human (masculine and feminine) functions have polarized in sexual role stereotyping, women have largely expressed only Ceres (as mother) and projected Saturn. Likewise, men have only expressed Saturn (as father) and projected Ceres. In the same way, women have largely manifested the emotional commitment and caretaking of the partnership relationship symbolized by Juno, leaving to men more of the outer world expressions denoted by the Sun and Jupiter.

Until recently, Ceres and Juno have been primarily concerned with relating and emotions while Vesta and Pallas have been more involved with individual accomplishment. Partially this is because Ceres and Juno require another person (child or partner) to express their meanings, while Vesta and Pallas do not necessarily need anyone else. It seems that women's accomplishments, beyond mothering and mating, have emerged more through Vesta and Pallas.

Now with the awakening of the asteroid centers, women are breaking out of stereotypic confines and enlarging their scope of expression of feminine energy. For men, the activation of these centers makes it increasingly difficult to continue to repress or project their feminine aspects. This energy is demanding release from its confined inner structures, which is manifesting as new personal issues for men.

The following table helps to distinguish between:

(1) feminine functions
(2) woman's relationships
(3) stereotyped roles into which these feminine functions were locked
(4) alternative ways for women to express this feminine energy
(5) how men can develop and use the feminine more fully in their lives.

	Ceres	**Pallas Athene**
Feminine Function	creating, supporting, sustaining physical progeny, physical nurturing — food	creating mental progeny, mental nurturing — visions
Woman's Relationship	mother	daughter
Woman's Stereotype	"Mom" at home cooking in kitchen, cleaning the house, nursing the family living for and through children	asexual comrade/friend, Amazon: "mannish," tomboy, professional career woman *puella*: behind-the-scene supporter of a man's success, "Daddy's girl"
Alternative Modes of Expression for Women and Men	teachers and educators of children children's services, issues of pro-choice/pro-life midwifery and humane childbirth farming, gardening food-related services, nutrition, health awareness single parenting as a conscious choice world hunger & relief organizations death, dying, hospice work	development of talents, artistic creativity, intelligence educational & career potential political and social awareness, depolarizing male/female role typing integrating love and creativity

	Ceres	Pallas Athene
Practice of the Magical Life	rituals for transformation & dying women's blood mysteries — menstruation, menopause, menarche	creative visualization, ceremony and ritual psychic development
Especially for Men in Order to Activate and Utilize Their Centers/powers	increased participation in childbirth/child rearing/child sharing developing active role of nurturer (as opposed to nurturee) developing attitudes of compassion/acceptance/empathy single father issues and responsibilities	development of imagination/creativity integrating values of emotional concerns with worldly success developing **holistic** understanding in education, health and all areas

	Vesta	Juno
Feminine Function	self-renewal & regeneration, inner union with self	relationship renewal & regeneration, outer union with other
Woman's Relationship	Sister	Wife
Woman's Stereotype	old maid/spinster/ workaholic/ fanatic priest/nun	wife as woman who gives economic responsibility and decision making to husband 1:1 solo, monogamous, heterosexual relationship husband as sole/major source of identity, fulfillment

	Vesta	Juno
Alternative Modes of Expression for Women and Men	commitment to a cause, idea, belief system (for women apart from and in addition to family responsibilities as wife and mother) spiritual/devotional paths acknowledging value and active practice of periodic retreat from outer world liberation from sexual inhibitions and complexes work on "self" — health/fitness integration	dissolving illusion of ego separateness, "I don't need anyone else" attitude advocate for women's rights in economic/political/ educational/sports arenas enlarged scope of intimate relationships, gay/lesbian cutting through jealousy & attachments in relationships, creating new forms of relating
Practice of the Magical Life	creative visualization, ceremony and ritual psychic development	*tantric* sexual practices
Especially for Men in Order to Activate and Utilize Their Centers/Powers	learning to recognize that sexuality belongs only to oneself and no one else has rights of ownership over it acknowledgments of "inner life" developing nonjudgmental attitudes and morality concerning sexuality development of sexual sensitivity and skill in pleasing partner	house husband ability and willingness to adapt to changing women and rules of relationships accepting idea of equality/work/values of women's input (apart from sex/food/physical comfort) development of sexual sensitivity and skill in pleasing partner

CHAPTER FOUR

CERES: THE GREAT MOTHER

And, now let me sing
Demeter,
that awesome goddess,
with her beautiful hair,
her
and her daughter
with slender feet,
whom Aedoneus
carried away,
and Zeus
who sees far
in his deep voice
allowing it.[1]
Homer

The Mythology of Ceres

The Roman goddess Ceres was originally known to the ancient Greeks as Demeter. Her name was derived from the ancient form *da mater* meaning earth mother. In the Olympian pantheon, Ceres was the daughter of Saturn and Rhea. Along with her sisters Vesta and Juno and her brothers Jupiter, Neptune and Pluto, Ceres was swallowed by her father. Freed by Jupiter after his victory over Saturn and the Titans, these deities became the ruling family of ancient Greece.

1. Homer, "The Hymn to Demeter," *The Homeric Hymns*, trans. Charles Boer (Irving Texas: Spring Publications, 1979), 89.

As time passed Ceres came to live not only in the heavens but on the earth with humanity to whom she gave two gifts: grain and the Eleusinian Rites.[2] As goddess of agriculture and the harvest, Ceres symbolized the cultivated, fertile soil that fed and provided for humanity. Hence, she was worshipped as the all-nourishing mother, crowned with a wreath composed of ears of corn and wheat, holding grain or poppies in one hand and a lighted torch in the other.

It was, however, as devoted and loving mother to the maiden Kore/Persephone that Ceres assumed her greatest importance among the Greeks. Their story — Persephone's abduction by Pluto to the Underworld, Ceres' subsequent grief and suffering, and her search to become reunited with her daughter — became a major myth of the ancient world. This drama of loss and return was reenacted for close to two thousand years (1600 BC to AD 400) as the initiation rites of the Eleusinian Mysteries.

The Story of Ceres and Persephone

Long ago, Ceres and her beloved daughter Persephone wandered the earth together. So happy were they in each other's presence that they blessed the earth with a perpetual season of harvest. In this Golden Age, the world knew no deprivation, no winter.

THE ABDUCTION OF PERSEPHONE

Persephone grew to be as beautiful as her mother and was greatly desired by men and gods alike. The love between mother and daughter was so strong, however, that they had no desire to be parted from one another. Thus, all suitors were rebuffed and sent away.

One day, away from Ceres' ever-watchful gaze, Persephone wandered with her companions into the Nysian fields. There, she was irresistibly drawn to the lovely, fragrant beauty of the hundred-bloomed narcissus. As Persephone plucked it and inhaled its intoxicating fragrance, the earth suddenly split open and formed a deep abyss from which emerged Pluto, god of the Underworld, who had long been covetous of the fair Persephone. Riding in his golden, fiery chariot drawn by four screeching black horses, Pluto seized the screaming maiden, ravished her, and carried her off to the realm of the dead to become his bride and queen. The torn earth then immediately healed itself, leaving behind no evidence of the incident.

2. Jane E. Harrison, *The Religion of Ancient Greece* (London: Archibald Constable and Co., 1905), 51.

When Ceres returned to the now-peaceful meadow, she could find no trace of her daughter. Racing over fields and hills, calling Persephone's name, Ceres' anxiety turned to desperation and panic as she realized that no one knew of the whereabouts of her daughter. For nine days and nights, the grief-stricken Ceres refused to eat or bathe. Instead, she wandered the earth with blazing torches, searching everywhere for her daughter. On the tenth day, Ceres encountered the crone goddess *Hecate* who suggested that she consult the sun god and seer, *Helios*.

From Helios, Ceres learned of the abduction by Pluto who had acted with the approval of their brother Zeus. It seems that Zeus had considered Pluto a worthy husband for Persephone whom he wished to see rule as queen of the Underworld. Upon hearing this news, Ceres angrily tore the diadem from her head and wrapped herself in mourning clothes. Full of hatred toward Zeus for his betrayal, she withdrew from Mt. Olympus to avoid him and his compatriots. Disguising her true identity, she then wandered as a bereaved old woman seeking refuge in the cities of men.

CERES IN ELEUSIS

After what must have seemed an eternity, Ceres, brokenhearted and weary, sought refuge in a town called Eleusis where she was met at the well by the four daughters of *King Celeus* who invited her to return with them to his palace. There she met *Queen Metaneira* who welcomed the stranger and gave her the care of the royal infant son *Demophoon*.

Under the care of Ceres, the child grew as a god. In her desire to make the young prince immortal like Persephone, Ceres anointed him with ambrosia by day and placed him in the fire's embers each night in order to burn off his mortality. One evening, *Queen Metaneira* caught Ceres in the act of holding *Demophoon* in the flames and screamed out in terror. Ceres, outraged at being thwarted in her attempt to give the child eternal youth, snatched the boy from the fire and cast him to the ground. She then revealed her true identity as a goddess and ordered that a temple and altar be built for her where mortals could be initiated into her rites and offer her worship.

THE RETURN OF PERSEPHONE

Ceres now retired to her temple where she continued to mourn the loss of her beloved daughter. In her rage, she prepared for mankind a cruel and terrible year: the earth would refuse to give forth any crop, crops in the ground would be destroyed, and fruit would rot on the trees. If she, the goddess of fertility, must live without her child, then humanity would suffer famine and starvation.

In desperation, the people of the earth prayed to Zeus to intervene. Zeus, realizing that if humanity died out there would be none to worship the gods, sent *Iris* to summon Ceres to Olympus. Ceres refused to go. Each of the gods then offered Ceres a gift and implored her to show mercy, but she refused. Only if her daughter were freed would she relent.

Realizing his defeat, Zeus commanded Hermes to descend into the Underworld and command Pluto to release Persephone. Persephone, in her frozen beauty, had been following her mother's mourning fast, refusing food or drink. Pluto, in sly kindness, agreed to let Persephone go but first tempted her great thirst by offering her several pomegranate seeds. Since the pomegranate was the symbol of sexual consummation, Persephone's consent rendered her marriage union with him indissoluble.

Upon returning to the world of light, Persephone was joyfully reunited with her mother at Eleusis. Ceres immediately inquired whether her daughter had consumed any food of the dead while in the Underworld. When Persephone revealed what had occurred, Ceres realized that she had been tricked; her daughter was still Pluto's prisoner. Once more, she refused to lift her curse from the land.

To prevent Ceres and Pluto from destroying the world he had created, Zeus, with the assistance of their mother Rhea, demanded that they compromise. His edict commanded that for each pomegranate seed ingested by Persephone, she would spend a portion of each year as Pluto's bride of the Underworld. The remaining months could then be spent with her mother upon the earth.

And so it has come to pass that each spring Persephone emerges above ground and rejoins Ceres who allows the earth to become fruitful. Seeds sprout, flowers bloom, plants grow, and crops fill the fields. Summer follows, and the earth continues to flourish until the arrival of autumn when Persephone must return to Pluto's Underworld. After her daughter's departure, Ceres lays her sorrowful hand upon the earth and makes it barren. And desolate it will stay throughout the winter until Persephone's arrival the following spring.

Thus, the world alternately blooms and dies each year as Ceres rejoices at Persephone's return and weeps at her leaving. On an outer level, the story of Persephone's annual disappearance and return is an allegory of spring sprouting from the dormant winter seed that explained the changing of the seasons to the peasants. On an inner level, the reenactment of this drama gave humanity access to the archetypal themes of loss and return. On the esoteric level taught by the initiates of the Eleusinian Mysteries, this ritual revealed the great transformation mystery — the cycle of birth, death, and renewal.

Before leaving Eleusis, Ceres expressed her gratitude to the city by giving *Triptolemus*, oldest son of the king and queen, the first grain of corn. She then instructed him to convey her sacred art of agriculture to all humanity. Finally, she taught the people of Eleusis her sacred rites and initiated them into her divine worship:

> . . . which may be neither revealed nor heard, nor even spoken aloud, for sacred awe of the goddess chokes the utterance. Blessed is the man on earth who has seen such things. But, he who remains uninitiated and has no share in them will when he is dead have no portion in the like blessings in the musty darkness down below.[3]

These rites formed the heart of the Eleusinian Mysteries and became the major initiation rites of the ancient world. They addressed humanity's fears and concerns about death by allowing the initiates to traverse the passage between death and rebirth during their earthly lives. The direct experience of the eternal continuity of life in its visible and invisible forms, symbolized by the secret of the seed, offered the participants "a guarantee of life without fear of death, of confidence in the face of death."[4]

THE PRE-HELLENIC ORIGINS OF CERES MYTHOLOGY

The preceding tale, derived from Homer's *Hymn to Demeter* written in the seventh century BC, is the most popular source of information concerning the mythos of Ceres. There is, however, additional evidence that describes Ceres/Demeter as a universal archetype of the Great Goddess that emerged in the nuclear area of the Near East and Egypt, and migrated to Minoan Crete and Classical Greece.[5] In the myths associated with these cultures, we find a recurring theme of the great fertility/mother goddess (e.g., Sumeria's *Inanna*, the Semitic *Ishtar*, and Egypt's *Isis*) who enters the realm of the dead, returns to the land of the living, and is associated with a resurrected vegetation god.

---

3. Carl Kerenyi, *The Gods of the Greeks*, trans. Norman Cameron (London: G. B. Billings and Son, Ltd., 1982), 240.
4. Carl Kerenyi, *Eleusis: Archetype Image of Mother and Daughter*, trans. Ralph Manheim (New York: Schocken Books, 1967), 15.
5. Joseph Campbell, *The Masks of the Gods: Occidental Mythology* (New York: Penguin Books, 1981), 50.

As Great Mother of Crete, Ceres participated in ancient fertility rites that were created to insure a good harvest. At the autumnal equinox, she, the corn priestess, would lie with her lover *Iasion* on a thrice-plowed field and give birth to *Plutus*, god of the earth's wealth. *Plutus* became a symbol of that rich bounty that the earth produced when it was so honored by the Sacred Marriage.

The archetype of Ceres/Demeter also expressed itself through the Egyptian *Isis*, the Hesiodic *Gaia* (used in many New Age writings to name our planet Earth), the Minoan *Rhea*, and the Buddhist *Tara*, whose dominion over the Earth also extended into the Underworld (They all received the dead and nourished the living).

Homer's *Hymn to Demeter* eventually gained fame through its portrayal of the rape of Persephone, a later adjunct to the story having no precedent in the earlier cult versions. Historically, Persephone's rape symbolizes the power struggle that was occurring between the patriarchal cultures (Pluto) and the indigenous matriarchal goddess cults (represented by Ceres). The final outcome of the story points to a clear victory for the northern Zeus worshippers. The Great Mother not only had to stand by and watch her daughter being raped and abducted, Ceres was also forced to share her beloved Persephone with the enemy. Hence, she had to abdicate a portion of her powers over the birth and death rituals, a dominion that was eventually wrested from her in its entirety.

In summation, Ceres is the symbol of the all-nourishing mother, from whose name we derive our word "cereal." As mother goddess, Ceres embodied a mythos that symbolized the continuity of life. As corn goddess, she gave to humanity the gift of agriculture and the secret of the seed that nourishes the living. And, as goddess of the mysteries, Ceres, in her aspect as Persephone, received the dead for rebirth.

Within the framework of this archetypal drama, the Eleusinian Mysteries led their initiates through the drama of Ceres and Persephone, of loss and return. First, the story was retold; then, in the Lesser Mysteries, the participants identified with the story's action; finally, in the Greater Mysteries, they received a vision and revelation that the great mythic drama took place within themselves. These rites are still taking place today, as reported by psychotherapists who have observed the symbols of the ancient initiatory process emerging in their patients' dreams and fantasies.[6] Thus, Ceres' rites of passage are now being lived out on the inner planes as stages of psychic transformation.

6. Nor Hall, *The Moon and the Virgin* (New York: Harper and Row, 1980), 23.

CERES

Greek Demeter

Character

Goddess of Agriculture and the Eleusinian Rites
Earth Mother

Principle of Unconditional Love

Glyph: ⚳

Sickle — gift of agriculture

Symbols

sickle/plow
ears of wheat or corn
cornucopia
poppy flower - solace for human grief
pig
torch
crane bird

Associated Rulerships

Cancer
Taurus - Scorpio polarity
Virgo

Polarities

Compassion/Anger

The Astrology of Ceres

"To enter into the figure of Ceres means to be pursued, to be robbed, to be raped, to fail to understand, to rage and grieve, but then to get everything back and be born again."[7]

In symbolizing the function of mother in psychology, Ceres governs a number of psychological qualities that cannot be described

7. Carl Kerenyi, and C. G. Jung, "Kore," *Essays on a Science of Mythology*, trans. R. F. C. Hall (New Jersey: Princeton University Press, 1973), 123.

by any one zodiacal sign. After spending a number of years observing how Ceres functions in the horoscope, the author has concluded that Ceres' attributes are best depicted by the signs Cancer, Taurus-Scorpio and Virgo. As ruler of Cancer, Ceres addresses the issues of how we give and receive nurturance, how we develop feelings of self-worth, how we provide for and care for others, and how we respond neurotically if these needs are not met. As the ruler of the Taurus-Scorpio polarity, Ceres governs the lessons of attachment and aversion, the pathology of loss and rejection, the capacity for grief and sorrow, and the principle of sharing. And, as the ruler of Virgo, she addresses the issues of productivity, growth, self-reliance, and work. In the pages that follow, we shall explore these processes in greater detail.

Ceres as a Ruler of Cancer

CERES: THE UNIVERSAL MOTHER

Ceres, as the ruler of Cancer and the maternal instinct, primarily symbolizes the need to nurture and care for others. This desire is most often fulfilled through becoming a mother or father. The Ceres-type individual feels a powerful need to become a parent and nurture, raise, and provide for his or her children. Ceres' transits and progressions are timers for pregnancy and childbirth as well as for difficulties in conception, the birth process, and nursing. In her role as provider, Ceres nurtures others on physical (she supplies food and shelter), emotional (she gives love and support), and spiritual (she offers guidance and wisdom) levels.

As a symbol of the maternal function, Ceres in the horoscope describes the quality of the mothering experience that we received as a child and express as a parent. Though the provider of this nurturance is usually the physical mother, it can actually be any family member — the father, grandparents, aunts, uncles, close family friends, or foster/step/adoptive parents. Whoever takes primary responsibility for the nurturance and early development of the child acts out the archetype of Ceres.

As goddess of fertility and agriculture, Ceres personifies the all-nourishing earth mother. An infant's first experience of love and security comes through being fed by its mother. Through receiving love in the form of food, the child develops the feeling that s/he deserves nourishment which in turn provides the foundation for his or her self-worth. Because these early experiences become the basis for a healthy self-acceptance and self-esteem in adulthood, if the

Ceres mother-love is absent or lacking, then a poor self-image and low self-esteem are likely to develop in the later years. It is necessary to note here that the child's perception and interpretation of his or her nurturing experience is as important as what actually occurred.

Ideally, the type of love imparted by the mother or nurturing figure will be unconditional — i.e., without expectations. When this is not the case, Ceres' astrological position will point to what the child has to do in order to gain parental approval and receive love. If love and approval continue to be given on a conditional basis, the individual will experience him- or herself as being unworthy of love. For example, a child with Ceres in Aries receives nurturance through being granted independence. Distortion of this need may occur in two ways. First, the child may be denied autonomy by an over-domineering parent. In this instance, the child will cope through denying his or her assertive impulses. Second, the child may be pushed toward autonomy before he/she is ready to take on this responsibility, thereby creating feelings of fear and self-doubt. In each case, the fact that the child's independence needs were not adequately nurtured hinders the development of its self-assertion skills.

CERES LOVE AS THE BASIS FOR LOVING OTHERS

The ability to love oneself which originates in a positive Ceres mother-love and the child's receptivity to it also generates the ability to love others and to rejoice in their accomplishmets. In cases where Ceres energy is either distorted or insufficient, a child can become self-rejecting instead of self-accepting. This produces a critical, judgmental attitude toward others and resentment over their achievements. Buddhist philosophy teaches that to heal this attitude, one must develop compassion for others, a compassion that originates in the mothering experience. As taught by this belief system, through countless lifetimes each of us has mothered or has been mothered by all those whom we encounter in the present incarnation. Thus, we must always remember and honor the inestimable service our mother performed in bearing, nurturing, and sustaining us by loving and accepting others.

From an astrological perspective, this evolution from personal to universal love is symbolized by the three water signs — Cancer, Scorpio, and Pisces. The initial stage of love associated with Cancer is the unconditional mother-love that gives rise to a strong sense of self-worth. When this self-esteem is operating, the person becomes able to successfully enter into the more complex sexual and conditional interactions of the second water sign Scorpio. This ability to unite on a one-to-one level provides the basis for the love of humanity developed in the third sign Pisces.

What occurs if this process is somehow disrupted? One such incident occurred in the 1930s when children began to be born en masse in hospitals. As a result, they were severed from the initial Ceres imprint of being held and nursed by mother. After being spanked under glaring lights, they were put in sterile cribs and given rubber-nippled bottles of sugar water as their food. This denial of the primary bonding experience is one of the factors that has contributed to this generation's relationship difficulties and frustrations.

Yet, the individual who received a weak Ceres foundation is by no means doomed to loneliness or unfulfilling relationships. In order to heal the isolation and depression (two common Ceres ailments), he or she should seek counseling in order to build self-esteem and thereby lay the groundwork for future successful interactions. These relationships, however, need not be limited to heterosexual interactions. Indeed, Cerès mother-love may be given and received through a variety of forms — e.g., homosexual and lesbian relationships, men's and women's support groups, and/or nurturing, platonic friendships.

CERES PSYCHOLOGICAL COMPLEXES

Because Ceres governs the entire mothering experience, she also rules the many psychological problems that result from negative, early parental conditioning. Here we will briefly enumerate the most important of these complexes so as to give the reader a direction for further inquiry and astrological investigation.

PASSIVITY COMPLEXES

When the Ceres mother-love given to the child is experienced as primarily conditional, he or she will respond by either living up to parental expectations or by failing to do so. In the latter case, the child's experience of repeated failure will usually breed a "why bother?" attitude. Thus, when confronted with a difficult or challenging task, the individual will muse, "I know that I can't succeed, so why bother trying?" This defeatist attitude, when carried into adult life, creates a number of psychological complexes: fear of competition, the inability to take action, and prolonged feelings of powerlessness and dependency. Overcompensatory behavior can also manifest as the compulsive need to excel simply to feel adequate.

FOOD COMPLEXES

Because Ceres governs the care and feeding of the human organism, she also rules the entire range of food complexes and eating disorders. It is no coincidence, therefore, that since the publication of the Ceres ephemeris in 1973, a great deal of attention has been given to these previously ignored eating malfunctions.

In her anger over her daughter's abduction, Ceres punished her enemies by halting all food production upon the earth. Thus, challenging aspects to Ceres often indicate a parent punishing the child by withholding nourishment, e.g., sending him or her to bed without dinner. This socially accepted form of parenting lays the foundation for many food-related illnesses. Two such maladies — anorexia (starvation) and bulemia (bingeing-purging) — are cited by physicians and therapists as currently being at epidemic levels. The psychological roots of these disorders are clearly related to Ceres — deep feelings of unworthiness, a poor self-image, and the need to live up to standards of perfection set by the parents.

These complexes affect, in a less pernicious manner, the millions of women for whom obsessive dieting has become a way of life. Fortunately, the remedy for these imbalances may also be found in Ceres psychology — developing an unconditional love for oneself and others.

Other eating complexes are created when food is used as a substitution for love and approval. Two common injunctions that exemplify this strategy are "Eat! — to make me happy" and "Finish all your dinner if you want dessert" (a reward for your efforts). This type of conditioning encourages the child to ignore its bodily instincts of hunger and appetite and instead to respond to external cues that ignore or contradict the body's needs. Such unconscious programming lies at the root of the overeating compulsions that afflict so many members of our society.

A final Ceres food disorder arises when an individual with a low self-image uses food to insulate him/herself from having to perform (sexually or otherwise) in the outside world. Thus, food is used to defend the person from forming relationships with others. Ceres, therefore, is clearly one astrological significator of all weight and body-image disorders. Ceres aspects to other planets and asteroids reveal additional information as to what parts of the personality are involved in these stressful and often painful conditions.

RELATIONSHIP COMPLEXES

Because the Ceres mother-imprint leaves such a strong impression on the human psyche, its significance spills over into the realm of interpersonal relationships. Conflict aspects to Ceres can signify an individual who is unwilling or unable to nurture and emotionally support others. In turn, his or her need to receive nurturance is often denied.

In the horoscope, when Ceres is in the seventh house or aspected to Venus, Mars, or Juno, the parental relationships become the role model for future adult partnerships. When the child's initial love experience is positive, then he or she will experience supportive love relationships. When, however, the mother or "nurturing figure" is perceived by the child as dominating, controlling , or smothering, the child will set up defense mechanisms to hold back the destructive power of the parent. This resistance to receiving nurturance will then be projected onto the adult partner.

For example, men who have conflicting aspects to Ceres in their horoscope may initially be drawn to women who appear to be nurturing and comforting. As the relationship progresses, however, subconscious patterns of early conditioning begin to surface, and the man will have to struggle against his ensuing feelings of dependency. The compassionate mother-wife is then experienced in her dark form as demanding and controlling . Often the woman's means of gaining this influence is food, i.e., "the best way to a man's heart is through his stomach." In a similar fashion, women whose charts contain Ceres imbalances often attract a nurturing father figure to support and protect them only to discover that they soon take on the identity of "Daddy's little girl" and become imprisoned in a childlike identity like Persephone.

Clearly, the key to expressing a psychologically healthy Ceres in our relationships is to be maternal toward our partner while simultaneously supporting his or her independence and self- sufficiency. When instead, we nurture in order to fulfill power and control needs or validate our purpose, the Ceres mother-love becomes neurotic and self-defeating.

PARENT-CHILD COMPLEXES

> "Every mother contains her daughter in herself and every daughter her mother; every woman extends backward into her mother and forward into her daughter."[8]
>
> C. G. Jung

Ceres is the significator of the secret unrealized hopes, dreams, anxieties, fears, and disillusionments that are transferred from

8. Carl G. Jung, "Psychological Aspects of Kore," *Essays on a Science of Mythology*, 162.

mother to child. These messages are conveyed, not through words and actions, but subliminally, through the unconscious emotional bond that is forged between parent and offspring.[9] Oftentimes this bond serves as a conduit by which the parents' visions and aspirations (or fears and inadequacies) are projected onto the child who then takes them on as his or her own. Thus, the astrologer who encounters this complex in a Ceres-type client should suggest therapeutic counseling to enable the client to break free of the symbiotic dependency.

Before we conclude our analysis of Ceres as the ruler of Cancer, we need to address an important point. If you, the reader, are an astrologer, you are probably asking yourself, "How is this definition of Ceres different from that of the Moon?" The answer is simple. On one level, a correspondence does exist between Ceres and the Moon because the Moon represents the matrix out of which Ceres and the other three asteroids emerge. Ceres, however, is a more specific differentiation of the Moon in her feminine role as Mother. Thus, Ceres in the horoscope provides additional information about the mothering function that cannot be gained from an analysis of the Moon sign alone.

Ceres as a Ruler of the Taurus-Scorpio Polarity

The powerful correspondence between Ceres and the zodiacal polarity of Taurus and Scorpio may be observed in four distinct ways:

1) The Moon, "parent" of Ceres, is exalted in the sign of Taurus. Ceres was the goddess of agriculture who grounded the lunar energy onto the physical plane to create the fertile earth (Taurus).
2) The Eleusinian Mysteries of Ceres were officiated by a sacred priest called the Hierophant. The Hierophant is also the card in the *tarot* deck that corresponds to the astrological sign Taurus.
3) In her mythology, Ceres' adversary was none other than Pluto, ruler of Taurus' opposing sign Scorpio.
4) The Buddha was born, attained enlightenment and died during Taurus-Scorpio full Moons. His teachings focused upon the issues of attachment (Taurus) and death and letting go (Scorpio). In being

9. Nancy Friday, *My Mother My Self* (New York: Dell Publishing Co., 1977).

forced to release her attachment to her daughter and presiding over the rites of the dead, Ceres likewise addresses these Taurus-Scorpio themes.

To sum up, as ruler of the Taurus-Scorpio polarity, Ceres in the horoscope describes the psychological experiences of attachment, separation and loss, death and renewal, the capacity for grief and sorrow, and the need to learn how to share. Her mythos contains the guideposts for traversing these paths of death and regeneration.

THE LESSONS OF ATTACHMENT AND SEPARATION

For individuals whose charts contain a prominent Ceres, the need to transform their attachments to the people they love and the objects or ideas they value can become a major life lesson. Perhaps their parents clung to them or they attempted to possess their own children. Yet, because our holistic universe ever strives toward balance, a strongly polarized attachment sets into motion the very causes and conditions that separate the person from his object of desire. Obsessive attachment, therefore, generates the lesson of nonattachment. This, of course, was the exact experience of Ceres and Persephone. Ceres' unwillingness to give Persephone the freedom of self-determination, and the equally strong attachment of Persephone to her mother unconsciously attracted Persephone's rape and abduction.

After being violently separated from her daughter, Ceres retaliated by halting the productivity of mankind's life-giving crops. Thus, the dark side of Ceres symbolizes the experience of being denied and cut off from life-sustaining nourishment. Therefore, when Ceres is prominent in the chart or aspected to Pluto, separations may become a constant theme in the native's life. Examples of such deprivations include: the loss of one's parents through death, rejection, abandonment, or illness; the loss of one's children through death, custodial award to the other parent or state, or abduction; and separations from relationships, one's pets, work, or a secure environment.

In addition, the growing awareness of the prevalence of child abuse, incest, and other forms of child molestation are related to the kidnapping of Persephone and her subsequent violation by Pluto.

Even when no actual losses occur, the Ceres-Pluto individual can be plagued on the subconscious plane by the fear of being rejected, cut off, or separated from his or her loved ones. This anxiety will, of course, magnetize the very situations that reinforce the negative programming. Consequently, these client types should enter into in-depth therapy in order to resolve and heal their deep-seated fears.

Following the loss of her child, Ceres entered into a prolonged period of grief and sorrow. Hence, Ceres transits often depict those times when we mourn the loss of a loved one or anything to which we were emotionally bonded — a job, relationship, home, cigarettes, or alcohol. In her mythos, Ceres passed through the stages of the normal grieving process — shock, depression, guilt, anger, and, finally, acceptance. Hence, she provides us with a metaphor for our own losses and transitions.

The most important stage that Ceres had to experience was that of anger. Anger provides one with the force to break free of the immobilizing quality of sorrow. Consequently, in counseling Ceres clients who are grieving, the astrologer must offer them a healthy means of expressing anger. Primal scream therapies, bioenergetics, meditation, or even intense physical exercise can break up the blocked energies and get the people moving forward so that they may return to their normal, productive activities. This process is especially important in a society that encourages us to repress our grief and anger when we experience a loss. Yet, these destructive energies, if not expressed through normal channels, can ultimately manifest through chronic depression (a common complaint of Ceres clients) or through such degenerative diseases as heart disease and cancer.

Ceres is divine in her suffering and transforms us through her pain and sorrow. Those who pass through the Ceres initiation emerge tempered, stronger, deeper, and more compassionate. As the ruler of the cycles of the seasons, Ceres also teaches that pain, like the winter, is impermanent and passes with time. Or, as God told Job, "Thou shalt forget thy misery and remember it as waters that pass away."

DEATH AND DYING

Persephone's abduction into the Underworld is a "metaphor of the descent we must all make — into the darkness and terror of the unconscious where fears of abandonment and death reside."[10] As teacher of the Eleusinian rites of death, Ceres governs our need to fully understand the death process and thereby resolve our fears about dying. Her astrological entrance into the human psyche has

---

10. Anthony M. Joseph, "Zodiacal Virgo and the Ceres Complex," *Geocosmic Research Monographs* (No. 2, 1981), 17.

brought a resurgence of interest in death and dying. This is clearly evidenced by the rediscovery of Eastern teachings on reincarnation, the proliferation of books on "life after death," and the emergence of hospices as centers of passage for the terminally ill.

To prepare for the moment of death, one must learn to experience "little deaths" every day through the process of letting go. While letting go may seem frightening at first, it is actually a necessary part of the cycle of life/death/renewal. In this transformative process, nothing new can be reborn until something old first dies. Thus, whenever we cling to a person, thing, or situation that has outlived its purpose, we only prevent ourselves from experiencing the abundance of renewal. At this point, a Ceres transit will inevitably come along, denoting our need to confront our fears of dying and to realize the truth of the Ceres-Scorpio death secret — that release is the precursor to rebirth. Given the appropriate preparation, this placement may also point to entering into the work of guiding the dying through their death passage.

CERES AS THE PRINCIPLE OF SHARING

In ancient mythology, Ceres was portrayed as the great mother who possessed exclusive control over productivity and growth. This preemption of male participation created a significant imbalance. In this light, Pluto's outrageous act of raping and abducting the daughter of Ceres may be seen not as a villainous act but as the catalyst that was needed to break up Ceres' monopoly over her child. Pluto's essential message, therefore, was a call for Ceres to share the offspring of the union of masculine and feminine energies. This, indeed, came to pass when Ceres and Pluto agreed to share their wife-daughter, Persephone.

Astrologically, individuals who have strong Ceres-Pluto aspects will often experience lifelong lessons concerning the sharing of children. These people will commonly find themselves in the midst of ugly custody struggles as each parent battles to maintain control of the child, with Ceres transits chronicling the timing of such events. Yet, no matter how much each partner may want that child, the only sane resolution is to follow the example of Ceres and Pluto: share the offspring. Otherwise, the partner who is unwilling to share will undoubtedly attract one of two situations: either s/he will have sole responsibility of the child but will lack the necessary financial and emotional support, or s/he will be totally denied access to the children (through custody or abduction).

In a similar fashion, Ceres teaches us to share our mental

children — our creative ideas, projects, and creations — instead of jealously guarding them in the hopes that no one else will receive credit for them. Strong Ceres-Pluto connections also indicate the need to share and delegate authority.

On a planetary level, Ceres has brought to humanity an awareness of the need to share food among its peoples. Hence, in the past decade, we have witnessed the formation of the Hunger Project and various movements that seek to redistribute foodstuffs from the wealthier to the poorer nations.

CERES AND RENEWAL

Ceres' secret teaching is that death is the gateway to rebirth. Loss is necessary in order that something new may emerge. At the end of Ceres' passageway lies the hope of renewal, regeneration, and the promise of eternal return.

Ceres as a Ruler of Virgo

GROWTH AND PRODUCTIVITY

In her pictograph, Ceres, goddess of the grain, carries a stalk of grain and wears a crown of wheat/corn. This image, of course, is identical to the one displayed in the image of Virgo the Virgin. This visual correspondence depicts the strong affinity between these two earth goddesses.

As ruler of Cancer, Ceres provides food as a means of communicating love and acceptance. As ruler of Virgo, the food of the all-nourishing mother becomes the actual physical nourishment that builds, sustains, and repairs the cellular structure of the corporeal body. This nutritional nourishment fosters growth and enables the individual to work and function efficiently (Virgoan attributes). Ceres, the grain goddess, gave infant humanity the gift of agriculture. During the harvest season of Virgo, Ceres utilizes the resources of the earth sign Taurus to produce and distribute the vital life-sustaining foodstuffs to humankind. Thus, in the horoscope, Ceres is the significator of any and all vocations that involve the growing, distribution, preparation, and serving of food. (Hence, the charts of many farmers, cooks, and waiters-waitresses have Ceres/Virgo emphasized).

The maternal concern of Ceres insures the proper functioning of the body by instilling a personal concern for the health and hygienic well-being of the body. Ceres also signifies the therapeutic use of food in healing. Hence, Ceres-Virgo types will be drawn to healing techniques that employ vitamins, diet, and herbs. In medical astrology, since Cancer rules the stomach and Virgo the intestines, Ceres-related illnesses include: digestive imbalances, gastrointestinal disorders, and assimilation difficulties.

CERES AND EFFICIENT FUNCTIONING

Through physically nourishing and sustaining the body, Ceres imparts to it the capacity for work. This ability, coupled with the Virgo urge toward efficient functioning, produces a personality type marked by a strong sense of competency and self-reliance. These individuals will often devote themselves to some standard of excellence or excel at mastering the details of a chosen vocation.

When such a personality type becomes a parent, it becomes transformed into Super-Mom or Super-Dad — the strong, devoted, capable, and reliable parent. This individual identifies with both mother and father — nurturer and provider — and is capable of doing whatever is necessary to insure the survival of the offspring. Thus, it follows that the arrival of Ceres into the astrological arena (1973) corresponded to a marked rise in the number of individuals who consciously chose single parenthood.

For example, certain women are now opting for motherhood without becoming involved in a relationship or marriage. They will decide to conceive the child without informing the father, and raise it alone. The growing fields of genetic engineering and artificial insemination are further decreasing the need for a relationship involvement in order for a woman to parent. On the other hand, an increasing number of men are feeling capable of assuming sole responsibility for raising their offspring. This has prompted many of them to apply for sole custody of children in relationship separations, to adopt children, or to stay at home and care for their children while the spouse works (e.g., John Lennon had Ceres square the Moon).

Astrologically, therefore, a prominent Ceres indicates the potential for one to consciously become a competent and effective single parent.

CERES AND WORK

Ceres, in her Virgoan expression, depicts the ability and capacity to work (Virgo, sociologically, rules the working class). Ceres symbolizes concern for the workers, social service organizations, labor unions, and labor productivity as reflected in the G.N.P. In her extreme anger, Ceres halted all productivity of the land; hence she rules strikes and other expressions of the "refusal to work."

Therefore, challenging aspects to Ceres, natally or in current patterns, can point to the inability to work or hold a job, disability, prolonged unemployment, or being the recipient of workers' compensation. When this complex polarizes into its opposite, we of course have the individual who is completely obsessed with work. Hence, the Ceres/Virgo archetype can manifest either as the workaholic or the professional loafer, with hints given by the other factors in the horoscope.

Ceres' cyclic nature points to understanding the alternation of cycles of work and rest — that there is a time to plant and a time to let the fields lie fallow and regenerate. Thus, the individual with a healthy Ceres expression learns the wisdom of combining periods of hard work with times of relaxation and play. In this way he/she attains a balanced work life and avoids the pitfalls of either "burning out" or "dropping out."

The Occult Teachings of Ceres

DEATH PASSAGE

Ceres gave the ancient Greeks the Eleusinian Mystery Rites which instructed the initiates in the death passage transition. These rites were passed down from the Egyptian cult of Isis.

BLOOD MYSTERIES

Ceres as a goddess of death functions as the matrix which receives the dead for rebirth. The entrance to rebirth is through the womb. Thus Ceres as Mother, whose blood provides the nourishment for the fertilized egg and fetus, rules over the women's "blood transformation mysteries."

The first mystery is that of menstruation, indicating the ripening of the womb whereby a girl becomes capable of becoming a mother. In earlier times a girl's first menstrual period was an occasion for great rejoicing. The second blood mystery is pregnancy. To the primitive mind, pregnancy meant that the menstrual blood ceased its monthly flow and instead formed and nourished the embryo. The third and final mystery, the transformation of the mother's blood into child-nourishing milk, provides the foundation for the primordial mysteries of food transformation.[11]

In the earliest offerings to the Great Goddess, menstrual blood,

---

11. Erich Neumann, *The Great Mother*, trans. Ralph Manheim (Princeton, New Jersey: Princeton University Press, 1974), 31-32.

not human blood, was sacrificed. When the esoteric teachings became denigrated, menstrual blood was replaced by animal and human sacrifice. Today, *tantric* mystery teachings still believe that the menstrual blood and semen are the true elixir offerings for rejuvenation and enlightenment. Ironically, this tradition also survives through the initiation rites of the Hell's Angels motorcycle club. To become a member, the novitiate may have to "eat his old lady while she's on the rag." Little are they aware that in the lineage of an ancient tradition, they are paying homage to the great mother goddess.

Summary

In summation, we have observed the depth and complexity of the mythology and psychology of Ceres. So rich is her meaning that she corresponds to two earth and two water signs of the zodiac. In the chapter on chart delineation, we will examine more precisely how the Great Mother expresses herself in the signs, the houses, and with other planets.

Ceres Psychological Themes

Principle of Unconditional Love and Acceptance
nurturing care and concern • self-image • self-worth • self-esteem • love matrix

Pathology of Loss
rejection • abandonment • grief • suffering •anger

Attachment and Aversion
attempting to maintain sole control over children, possessions or creations

Principle of Sharing and Letting Go

Themes of Transformation
birth • death • and renewal cycles • death and dying • hospice work

Single Parenting and Responsibility

Relationship with Nature and Natural Earth Energies

Growth, Productivity, Work, and Efficient Functioning

Occult Themes
death passage • blood mysteries

Further Reading on Ceres

Berry, Patricia. "The Rape of Demeter/Persephone and Neurosis." *Spring* (1975).

Bolen, Jean Shinoda. "Demeter: Goddess of Grain, Nurturer, and Mother." In *Goddesses in Everywoman*. San Francisco: Harper and Row, 1984.

Friday, Nancy. *My Mother My Self*. New York: Dell Publishing Co., 1977.

Hall, Nor. "Mothers and Daughters." In *The Moon and the Virgin*. New York: Harper and Row, 1980.

Homer. "The Hymn to Demeter." In *The Homeric Hymns*, translated by Charles Boer. Irving Texas: Spring Publications, Inc., 1979.

Joseph, Anthony M. "Zodiacal Virgo and the Ceres Complex." *Geocosmic Research Monographs* no. 2 (1981).

Jung, Carl G., and Carl Kerenyi. *Essays on a Science of Mythology: The Myth of the Divine Child and the Mysteries of Eleusis*. Translated by R. F. Hull. New Jersey: Princeton University Press, 1969.

Kerenyi, Karl. *Eleusis: Archetypal Image of Mother and Daughter*. Translated by Ralph Manheim. New York: Schocken Books, 1977.

Mylonas, George. *Eleusis and the Eleusinian Mysteries*. New Jersey: Princeton University Press, 1961.

Schure, Edouard. *The Mysteries of Ancient Greece: Orpheus/Plato*. New York: Rudolf Steiner Publications, 1971.

Spignesi, Angelyn. *Starving Women: A Psychology of Anorexia Nervosa*. Texas: Spring, 1983.

Spretnak, Charlene. "Demeter/Persephone." In *Lost Goddesses of Early Greece*. Berkeley: Moon Books, 1978.

Stone, Merlin. "Demeter and Kore." In *Ancient Mirrors of Womanhood Vol. II*. New York: New Sibylline Books, 1979.

Wasson, R. Gordon, Carl A. Ruck, and Albert Hofmann. *The Road to Eleusis: Unveiling the Secret of the Mysteries*. New York: Harcourt Brace Jovanovich, 1978.

Woodman, Marion. *Addiction to Perfection: The Still Unravished Bride*. Toronto: Inner City Books, 1982.

CHAPTER FIVE

CERES IN THE HOROSCOPE

The Greeks worshiped Ceres (as earth mother) as goddess of agriculture who worked unceasingly to bring food and nourishment to the people of the earth.

Ceres' tie to her daughter Persephone was so strong that it constituted her primary relationship. The story of Persephone's abduction by Pluto to become queen of the Underworld, Ceres' grief and suffering in her loss, and her search for reunion with her child became a major myth of the ancient world. This drama was enacted regularly for several thousand years as the initiation rites of the Eleusinian Mysteries. Ceres' pathology of repeated loss stems from grasping and over-attachment.

In her relationship as mother, Ceres is the principle of unconditional love — sustaining and nourishing newly created life forms. She functions as matrix-womb and umbilical cord transmitting life-sustaining nourishment.

Astrologically Ceres describes the ways in which we face the issues of self-worth and self-esteem, relationship to our parents and children, attachment, dependency, loss, separation, rejection, grief, sharing, work and productivity.

Ceres in the signs describes twelve styles of nurturing. Ceres shows how we meet our needs to give and receive nurturance, and what we need from ourselves and others to feel unconditionally loved and accepted.

Ceres in the houses shows where we most readily experience the need to give and receive nurturing. Ceres also indicates what types of experiences will foster feelings of self-love and self-acceptance, or self-rejection and critical attitudes.

Ceres aspects to the planets describe how the nurturing/mothering function may be integrated with other areas of the personality. Harmonious aspects indicate an easy blending, while stressful ones signify potential conflicts between nurturing needs and other psychic requirements of the individual. When the varying needs are mastered and integrated, an individual with conflict aspects in the horoscope no longer needs stress in order to learn balance.

Ceres Astrological Rulerships

Ceres, as mother, is an indicator and timer of all phases of procreative sexuality.

pregnancy • birth • miscarriage • abortion •nursing • ovulation • onset of menstruation and menopause • women's gynecological health • birth control

Ceres is a significator of the various parental relationships.

parent/child • child/parent • single parent (mother or father) • grandparent • foster/step/adoptive parent •nanny/governess

Ceres is concerned with child care and children's education.

prenatal care • childbirth training • children's rights • mothers' rights • child abuse •preschools • primary education

Ceres values the family.

deep family roots and ties • extended family systems • communes • clanship systems • tribes

Ceres vocations center around nurturing and helping professions.

nursing • social services • child care and education • midwifery • hospices

As goddess of the grain, Ceres is involved with agriculture and growing cycles.

cultivation of the land • farming • gardening •ecology • botany • seasons • relation to Nature •"green thumb" plants • nurseries • seeds • harvest

Ceres, as all-nourishing mother, is an indicator of food and food-related services.

farmers • organic gardeners • cooks • bakers •waiters-waitresses • restaurants • co-ops • nutritional counselors • health/healing through food, diet, and herbs •food complexes: overweight, anorexia, bulemia • food-related disorders in physical health

Ceres has a nurturing concern and sensitivity for animals.
animal care and domestication • veterinarians •trainers • breeders • caretakers

Ceres as worker is involved in labor and productivity.
labor workers • labor unions • producers •consumers • commodities • GNP • strikes •unemployment • disability • workers' compensation

Ceres symbolizes the principle of adaptation and survival of the species.

Ceres in the Signs

The source of the data for charts cited in the following sections is indicated by a number in parentheses.

(1) Lois Rodden's *The American Book of Charts*
(2) Lois Rodden's *Profiles of Women*
(3) Marc Penfield's *An Astrological Who's Who*

Ceres in Aries people identify nurturance with autonomy and being granted independence. In turn, the Ceres in Aries individual nurtures others through promoting their self-determination and self-sufficiency. To feel truly loved, this person must receive these experiences from his or her significant others. Pathology or imbalance can occur when the child feels either dominated by the nurturer or pushed toward autonomy before he or she is ready to take on this responsibility.

Chart Example: Janis Joplin had Ceres in Aries in the first house. She nurtured the youth culture through providing them with a symbol of freedom. (2)

Ceres in Taurus individuals receive nurturance through physical substance, a sense of stability, and being touched and held. In turn, they can nurture others by fostering their physical security and providing for them in tangible ways. Feelings of self-worth and acceptance are derived from learning how to provide materially for themselves. Imbalance results when the individual overidentifies with substance, and feelings of material lack promote excessive hoarding of possessions.

Chart Example: Pearl Buck portrays her Ceres-Vesta conjunction in the earth sign Taurus in her Pulitzer prize novel *The Good Earth*, a story describing the life of a Chinese peasant whose love of the land sustains him through years of hardship. (2)

Ceres in Gemini persons receive nurturance through being educated, talked to, and listened to. These people nurture others mentally through communicating knowledge to them. Self-acceptance is based on feeling smart or intellectually competent. Imbalance occurs when feelings of mental inadequacy lead to learning difficulties or to attempts to intellectually impress or verbally manipulate others.

Chart Example: Alan Leo, founder of the Theosophical Lodge and astrological and occult writer, has Ceres in Gemini conjunct Uranus in the tenth house. (1)

Ceres in Cancer individuals receive nurturance through bonding with the mother, feeling loved, and being fed. If these needs are met at an early age, these people will excel at caring for others physically and emotionally. Self-acceptance is based on one's ability to express feelings and master emotions. Imbalance occurs when the child is either deprived of nurturance or smothered with love and affection. Excessive neediness or emotional dependency are the resulting psychological afflictions.

Chart Example: A positive expression of Ceres in Cancer was given by Albert Schweitzer. With his Ceres placed in the ninth house, he nurtured others by being a clergyman and missionary whose philosophy was based on the sacredness of life. (1)

Ceres in Leo people identify nurturance with self-expression. Ideally, the parents will foster in the child a sense of pride, confidence in his/her abilities, and an appreciation for the creative efforts of others. These people can nurture others by helping them to express their creativity — thereby making a unique impression upon the outer world. Self-acceptance is based upon one's ability to create and share something he/she takes pride in. The inability to do so may bring self-rejection and lack of self-confidence.

Chart Example: Shakespearean actor Richard Burton, born with Ceres conjunct Neptune in Leo, nurtured the world through his creative acting. (1)

Ceres in Virgo persons identify nurturance with perfection or with service. Ideally, the mothering experience can foster the child's sense of competence, discrimination, and self-discipline which gives the ability to extend skills to others. Nurturing is expressed through teaching others to achieve excellence by right application of skills and talents. Feelings of self-worth arise through mastering a skill or technique and expressing it in the work world, or through feeling useful to others. Imbalance often results when the children are constantly criticized for their efforts, no matter how good they were. This can lead to an obsessive need to be perfect and to be critical of the imperfections in others.

Chart Example: An example of Ceres in Virgo in its highest expression is found in the horoscope of Elisabeth Kubler-Ross. With her seventh-house placement of Ceres in Virgo, she dedicates her life to the service of others by counseling those in need of physical and psychological healing. (2)

Ceres in Libra individuals identify nurturing with cooperation. Ideally, the mothering experience fosters a sensitivity to others and a positive attitude toward relationships. Nurturing is expressed through imparting instructions on how to interact, cooperate, and exhibit right conduct in egalitarian relationships. Self-acceptance may be based upon one's demonstrated ability to create harmony in one's relationships and environment. Imbalances occur when one is so other-directed that he or she places being accepted above a need for self-determination.

Chart Example: Paul Cezanne, with Ceres in Libra in the twelfth house, spent his solitary life nurturing the world through expressing his ideals of beauty and harmony. (1)

Ceres in Scorpio natives identify nurturance with intense and deep emotional bonding. Ideally, the mothering experience was intimate and fostered a sense of emotional self-control. Nurturance is expressed through emotional commitments to others and through acting as a catalytic agent that transforms or heals them. Self-acceptance may be gained through transforming one's own inner negativity and lack of trust into the healing power of love. Imbalance occurs when feelings of isolation are expressed as selfishness, jealousy, envy, anger and revenge.

Chart Example: Sybil Leek, with her twelfth-house Ceres in Scorpio trining Pluto, was naturally inclined to studying the hidden mysteries of the occult. She is the author of *Diary of a Witch*. (2)

Ceres in Sagittarius people identify nurturance with the freedom to explore and expand their horizons. Ideally, the mothering experience encouraged and fostered these needs. Nurturing is expressed through teaching others how to expand their mental and physical horizons (e.g., the *guru* or spiritual teacher). In addition, the Ceres in Sagittarius individual may help others to develop a philosophy or belief system that gives meaning to their lives. Self-acceptance may be based on the ability to find purpose in one's life and constantly move forward in consciousness. The failure to do so may lead to the belief that life is meaningless and purposeless ("a tale told by an idiot, signifying nothing" — *Hamlet*). Feelings of aimlessness that cause the person to wander without direction may result.

Chart Example: The great humanitarian Tom Dooley, with his Ceres in Sagittarius in the first house, was impelled to dedicate his life to nurturing the sick through setting up hospitals in the distant land of Laos. (1)

Ceres in Capricorn individuals identify nurturance with achievement. Ideally, the mothering experience taught the child how to be responsible, organize his/her time, and to carry out plans that would lead to the accomplishment of specific goals. Nurturing others takes the form of teaching them to be responsible for themselves, as well as giving them practical tools that they can use to succeed in the outer world. Self-acceptance is derived from tangible accomplishments that the individual attains through his or her own efforts. Imbalances occur when the person equates feeling loved with how well he or she performs in the world. This leads to the syndrome of using outer achievements to impress others in order to gain their recognition.

Chart Example: David Ben-Gurion, founder and first prime minister of Israel, expressed his responsibility to serve his people denoted by Ceres in Capricorn. (1)

Ceres in Aquarius persons identify nurturing with individuality. Ideally, the mothering experience fostered self-determination and a recognition of the rights of others. Nurturing is expressed through teaching others to accept their eccentricities and themselves, even if they "follow the beat of a different drummer." Self-acceptance can be gained through following one's own original and unique path. Imbalances may occur if the child was not given limits and guidelines, and therefore received more freedom than he or she was prepared to cope with. This would manifest as the "rebel without a cause," the individual who needs to gain inner control and self-discipline so that he/she can handle the responsibilities of freedom.

Chart Example: Multifaceted David Bowie, with Ceres in Aquarius in the fifth house, has demonstrated success in his unique and original approach in his artistic endeavors. (1)

Ceres in Pisces people identify nurturing with compassion. Such a person receives nurturance through feeling connected to and unified with a reality beyond him or herself. Nurturance is expressed through alleviating the suffering of others — either through empathy or inspiring in them the qualities of faith, universal love, and recognition of a transcendent reality. Self-acceptance may be based upon the ability to serve others selflessly without expecting anything in return. Imbalances occur when the individual does not receive the proper reassurance and emotional support as a child. This often leads to feelings of helplessness and powerlessness which in turn promote the victim-martyr syndrome.

Chart Example: Former Secretary-General of the United Nations Dag Hammarskjold was awarded the Nobel Peace prize for establishing and keeping a peace force in the Middle East. He was born with Ceres in Pisces trine Mars in Scorpio. (1)

Ceres in the Houses

Ceres in the first house implies the projection of one's personality as nurturing, sympathetic, and concerned for others. One may identify one's role as being a parent or provider. It may be necessary for this person to nurture themselves.

Chart Example: George Washington, "Father of His Country," was born with Ceres in Gemini in the first house. (3)

Ceres in the second house represents an urge to nurture by providing fundamental needs — shelter, food, and money for loved ones. There can also be an obsessive attachment to what/whom one loves, creating struggle for independence on the other end. Nurturing oneself may take the form of buying things, indulging, or pampering oneself.

Chart Example: With Ceres conjunct the Moon in Libra in the second house, Patty Hearst was nurtured by being provided for (second house) in style. She was kidnapped by the Symbionese Liberation Army and became involved in bank robberies. (2)

Ceres in the third house suggests nurturing through feeding ideas, teaching, and exposure to a variety of ideas and stimuli. Nurturing is expressed through creating networks that link together one's friends and associates.

Chart Example: Anthropologist Margaret Mead's Ceres in the third house mirrored her recognition through writings on the roles of women, adolescents, and family structures. (2)

Ceres in the fourth house can signify an idealized image of mother nurturing in the home and family. One's role as a parent is the foundation of the chart and life. In a universal sign this may manifest as mother to the world or whoever comes into the home. When Ceres is near the IC, the mythos of Ceres is especially predominant as a psychological foundation — an emotional connection with the themes of loss and return of loved ones, or of rejection and acceptance.

Chart Example: With Ceres in Sagittarius conjunct Neptune in the fourth house, Prince Albert provided his wife Queen Victoria with nine children and the emotional support she needed to rule the British Empire. (1)

Ceres in the fifth house denotes the experiencing of nurturing issues through a strong involvement with children or the creative arts. One is nourished through play or through putting oneself in risky situations.

Chart Example: With Ceres in Leo in the fifth house (a double dose), Percy Bysshe Shelley spent his life writing love poetry and being denied his children through death and custody loss. (1)

Ceres in the sixth house symbolizes fulfilling one's needs through engaging in the day-to-day activities of maintaining the efficient functioning of one's family. There is a strong service aspect here especially in the areas of nutrition and health. A parent who works, or has values of the work ethic is also symbolized by this position.

Chart Example: Saint Bernadette of Lourdes, who was born with Ceres in Scorpio in the sixth house, was inspired with a vision of the Holy Mother (Ceres), and discovered the healing (Virgo) waters (Scorpio). (2)

Ceres in the seventh house points to a need to nurture or be nurtured and protected by their mate. One's parent is often a role model for one's relationship needs. There is sometimes difficulty in outgrowing a dependent relationship with one's partner. Unconditional love provides an essential foundation for egalitarian functioning.

Chart Example: Jane Fonda, with Ceres in Aquarius in the seventh house, whose father was a powerful influence in her upbringing, has created just such an egalitarian relationship with her husband Tom Hayden. Her and her father's roles in *On Golden Pond* aptly express this link between parental and mating relationships. (2)

Ceres in the eighth house indicates receiving nurturing through intense peak experiences and through deep emotional involvements. Sexuality is often an essential component in giving and receiving nurturance. Nurturance may also be expressed through assisting the dying in hospice settings.

Chart Example: Sigmund Freud, with Ceres conjunct the Moon in the eighth house, probed the issues of sexuality and mother love and projected his own experiences in his theory of the Oedipal Complex. (1)

Ceres in the ninth house suggests nurturing oneself and others through the pursuit of knowledge, freedom, truth, and travel. There can emerge the development of philosophies that address the question of providing for fundamental human needs, e.g., Marxism. This placement can also denote philosophies that are based upon the worship of the all-nurturing mother such as those that revere the Virgin Mary or other goddesses.

Chart Example: Anne Morrow Lindberg, pilot, writer of women's feelings, and mother of six children, was born with Ceres in Taurus in the ninth house. (2)

Ceres in the tenth house connotes expressing the nurturing urge by caring and providing for others through one's profession or social destiny. Careers and public work in children services, health care, and food-related businesses can fulfill one's sense of social responsibility. This position of Ceres may indicate that love is given conditionally, based upon the performance or achievement of the child. When, however, the child fails to live up to parental or societal expectations, he or she may feel either rejected or abandoned. Hence, many individuals with Ceres in the tenth house must learn to love themselves for what they are, not what they do.

Chart Example: Clara Barton fully expressed her Ceres in Capricorn in the tenth house through devoting her life to helping others. She founded the American Red Cross, as well as serving as a nurse in three wars and headed relief work after several disasters. (2)

Ceres in the eleventh house symbolizes extending the nurturing urge into the collective — extended families, mothers' support groups, child-care co-ops, and communes. This position can also show giving birth to humanitarian visions and ideals. One may express or receive mothering through one's friendships.

Chart Example: Attorney Gloria Allred, with Ceres in Sagittarius in the eleventh house, is politically active in protecting and securing women's rights. (2)

Ceres in the twelfth house denotes *karmic* themes in the responsibilities of parenthood and in the development of empathy and understanding for the suffering of others. This position may symbolize experiences such as loss, illness, rejection, and denial of one's parents or children. The key to relieving one's own grief is to extend love and assistance to those in pain or need. This position of Ceres denotes the potential for nurturing the entire universe, and connection to higher reality through unconditional love.

Chart Example: Maria Montessori fulfilled her Ceres in Leo in the twelfth house beautifully through becoming an educator of impoverished and disadvantaged children. (2)

Ceres Aspects to the Planets

CERES-SUN ASPECTS

The nurturing principle combines with identity and purpose. This combination suggests that one's identity and self-image will center around being a parent or nurturer.

Harmonious aspects signify the desire to love and care for others. These individuals may become intensely involved with their families, growing or preparing food, or serving the needs of humankind. In some instances, this aspect indicates work with the dying, or the capacity to be productive and fruitful in one's endeavors.

Stressful aspects point to potential conflicts between being one's own person and taking care of others. This can lead to self-sacrifice for the benefit of family or the denial of intimacy and closeness with loved ones. Excessive attachment can produce smothering relationships or separation and loss. Other problems may include a low self-image, the thwarting of one's nurturing needs, or reoccurring themes of depression and rejection.

The resolution of these challenges lies in developing a positive sense of self-worth so that one may extend and receive loving, non-judgmental support. Counseling and therapy can clearly facilitate this process.

Chart Examples: The USSR, also known as Mother Russia, has Ceres conjunct the Sun in Scorpio. Feeding her people is the greatest national challenge, and the Ceres symbol of the sickle is on her flag.

Yoko Ono, with Ceres conjunct the Sun in Aquarius/Pisces, suffered the denial of her first child, lost her husband, and now as a single parent has given much of her inheritance from John Lennon to feed poor and hungry children. (2)

Queen Victoria, with Ceres conjunct the Sun, Moon, and Ascendant in Gemini, was the matriarch of the expanding British Empire and the mother of nine children. Known as the Widow of Windsor, she extensively mourned her husband. (2)

Napoleon Bonaparte, Emperor of France, had Ceres conjunct the Sun in Leo. He founded an empire, and after his downfall at Waterloo was exiled and died of cancer. (1)

CERES-MOON ASPECTS

The nurturing principle combines with emotional responsiveness.

Ceres-Moon configurations describe a personality type who has a deep longing to be needed by others and to exchange emotional energy with them. With harmonious aspects, this need is fulfilled through selflessly giving to others and nurturing one's surroundings.

Stressful aspects point to the conflict between meeting one's own personal needs and those of the family. Other problems that may arise are separation anxieties, fears of rejection, and feelings of isolation.

This denial of emotional fulfillment can be healed if the individual becomes sensitive to the emotional needs of others and strives to forge an emotional bond/bridge with them which is mutually supportive.

Chart Examples: Queen Elizabeth, with Ceres conjunct the Moon in Leo, devoted herself to serving "our great imperial family." (2)

Adelle Davis, with Ceres in Sagittarius in the twelfth house opposed to the Moon in Gemini, taught people how to "eat right" and "have healthy children." (2)

Luther Burbank, with Ceres in Capricorn trine a Virgo Moon, developed over 800 new varieties of plants. (3)

Civil rights martyr Martin Luther King, with Ceres conjunct the Moon in Pisces, dedicated himself to spiritually nurturing his race and all humankind. (3)

CERES-MERCURY ASPECTS

The nurturing principle combines with mental expression.

Here we have people who can nurture through their minds and receive nurturance through intellectual stimulation. These people associate being loved with being understood.

Harmonious aspects signify the ability to communicate empathetically with others and have rapport with beings who exhibit various levels of intelligence: children, the mentally disabled, plants, and animals.

Stressful aspects indicate difficulties in communicating one's nurturance needs to others, especially the family. A common example is the person who expects others to know what he or she needs without having to say so, and becomes angry when the other person doesn't "come through."

Integration can be achieved if the individual develops new communication skills that enable them to clearly articulate their needs and actively listen to and receive the responses of others.

Chart Examples: Sri Meher Baba, the silent *guru*, had Ceres conjunct Vesta in Virgo opposed to Mercury in Pisces. He spent thirteen years in complete silence, communicating in finger/sign language, in spiritual devotions to a mother goddess. (1)

Joan of Arc, French heroine, had Ceres conjunct Mercury in Capricorn. In her prayers she heard secret mystical voices that inspired her to attempt to save France. (2)

CERES-VENUS ASPECTS

The nurturing principle combines with the feminine principle of love and sexuality. The individual with a Ceres-Venus contact may link the feeling of being attractive and loved to subconscious images of self-worth.

Harmonious aspects depict the ability to nurture others through expressing sensual tenderness or erotic sexuality. These individuals have an aesthetic appreciation that enables them to create nurturing and harmonious environments. This is an extremely fertile aspect for physical and artistic creativity.

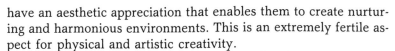

Stressful aspects point to potential conflict between personal needs for intimacy and the needs of family. These individuals may experience feelings of being undesirable and sexually unattractive; hence, unsatisfactory relationships and painful rejections may result. Because Ceres represents the parental imprint, one may also project a negative parental experience onto his or her partner.

The key to transforming the above challenges lies in balancing parent/child needs and roles with equality/relationship needs. It may also be helpful to redefine one's inner feminine self-image in order to magnetize nurturing and supportive sexual interactions.

Finally, stressful aspects of Ceres to both the Moon and Venus can often point to food complexes. When Saturn is involved, starvation (e.g., anorexia nervosa) will possibly occur; when Jupiter comes into play, the individual may overindulge and substitute food for love. In such cases, the individual needs to find security, love, and acceptance through channels other than food. Therapy may be helpful to catalyze this transformation.

Chart Examples: Princess Caroline of Monaco, with Ceres in Aries square Venus in Capricorn, has had conflicting needs between her personal love life and her prominent family's expectations. (2)

Isadora Duncan had Ceres conjunct Venus in Aries in the first house. She established schools of dance for children which emphasized an individual form of expression. (2)

CERES-MARS ASPECTS

The nurturing principle combines with the masculine principle of action and assertion. The individual with Ceres-Mars contacts links the ability to act and to be effective in the outer world to subconscious images of self-worth.

Harmonious aspects denote a productive individual whose drive and energy are channeled into caring for or defending others. This person may also take on the role of single or primary nurturing parent.

Stressful aspects may indicate that the child's needs for independence and autonomy felt thwarted by a dominating parent. As an adult, this person could feel inadequate, incompetent, or powerless. When Saturn or Pluto are involved, the individual may experience harsh discipline as a child or may embody these qualities as a parent. There may also exist the tendency to overdo caretaking of others.

The resolution of these challenges lies in balancing self-will with the desire to nurture and be nurtured. It may also be helpful to transform one's subconscious self-image and replace thoughts of fear and inadequacy with those of confidence, courage, and self-reliance.

Chart Examples: Joan Baez, with Ceres conjunct Mars in Sagittarius' crusades against injustice and protests against war and prejudice. (2)

Moshe Dayan, a general in the Israeli army, had Ceres conjunct Mars in Aries in the twelfth house. (3)

Marquis de Sade, notorious sadist, had Ceres conjunct Mars in Aries. (1)

CERES-JUNO ASPECTS

The nurturing principle combines with relationship needs.

These contacts signify themes of blending the unconditional acceptance of Ceres with the conditional relating of Juno. In some instances, the partner will become the primary recipient of one's unconditional love and nurturance; in others, parenting may serve as the focal point of the relationship.

Harmonious aspects signify an ability to develop nurturing and egalitarian partnerships in which the "children" of the union (whether physical or mental/creative) are accepted and integrated.

Stressful contacts may point to potential disagreements with one's mate over childrearing. If the children are from a previous marriage, then conflicting pulls of loyalty will be intensified. In addition, the individual may experience conflicts between his/her responsibilities as a partner and as a mate; or a general dissatisfaction with one's marital role, whether it be husband, wife, mother, or father.

The key to integrating these aspects lies in the formulation of new role models. Therapy can be helpful in deconditioning the subconscious images and social imprinting that keep us locked in old response patterns. In this way, one can meet the challenge of creating nurturing and supportive relationships denoted by the Ceres-Juno aspects.

Chart Examples: Betty Friedan, author of *The Feminine Mystique*, wrote about the discontent of women as mothers and wives. She was born with Ceres in Gemini conjunct the Descendant opposed to Juno in Sagittarius on the Ascendant. (2)

Ronald Reagan, who has Ceres in Aries opposed to Juno in Libra, has had family conflicts between his wife Nancy and his children from his first marriage. (1)

CERES-VESTA ASPECTS

The nurturing principle combines with the dedication and focusing urges.

Harmonious aspects can indicate an intense devotion to family, or the ability to experience nurturing through one's work, vision quest, or spiritual practice. In some instances, the Ceres-Vesta individual may become inspired to dedicate his/her life to serving and nurturing others.

Stressful aspects can point to an alienation from the parenting role, barrenness, or sterility. There may exist a conflict between family demands and one's personal need to seek solitude or to be engrossed in work.

Resolution of these challenges can be achieved through learning to balance the needs of the self with the obligations and responsibilities one has for others. That this integration is possible is evidenced by the many parents who combine a rich family life with a fulfilling career focus.

Chart Examples: Mao Tse-tung, first chairman of the People's Republic of China, was born with Ceres conjunct Vesta in Virgo. He dedicated his life to reorganizing China's agricultural and sociocultural systems. (1)

Princess Diana was born with Ceres conjunct Vesta in Taurus and will dedicate her life to raising her children for the throne of England.

Geraldine Ferraro's family was caught up in the political stresses of her vice-presidential campaign, testing her dedication to them and their dedication to her. She has Ceres in Virgo opposing Vesta in Pisces.

CERES-PALLAS ASPECTS

The nurturing principle combines with the mental-creative urge. This combination shows the potential to bring powerful creative forces into play.

Harmonious aspects describe the successful channeling of procreative energy into mental and artistic creations as well as political activity. There may exist a positive identification with the primary nurturing figure. In many instances, a high regard for education and learning will be imparted from parent to child.

Stressful aspects can point to a denial or rejection of the mother and an overidentification with the father. Psychologically, this can manifest as the alienation from one's feminine origins and nature which in turn can block one's creative abilities. Women in particular may feel forced to thwart their mental/educational development in order to serve the needs or expectations of their family.

The resolution of these challenges lies in successfully reintegrating the empathetic values of Ceres with the intellectual pragmatism of Pallas. This more holistic integration can give the individual a new and freer expression of his or her creative abilities and perceptions.

Chart Examples: Earl Warren, as implied by his Ceres conjunct Pallas in the first house, became a liberal and compassionate justice of the Supreme Court. (1)

Mary Baker Eddy, with Ceres conjunct Pallas in Scorpio in the eleventh house Scorpio was the founder of the Christian Science religion . She spread the doctrine of mental and spiritual healing. (2)

CERES-JUPITER ASPECTS

The nurturing principle combines with the expansive, broadening urge. This combination combines a social vision and exploratory urge with the values of Ceres.

Harmonious aspects indicate the desire to nurture generously which is best expressed through education, philosophy, religion, and travel. Involvement with the large-scale production, provision, and distribution of food and other basic services is often possible.

Stressful aspects can denote the exaggerated experience of nurturing (the smothering parent) or an overidentification with the parental role. The inability to say "no" to other people's needs can deplete one's own nurturing reserves or lead to personal overindulgences such as overeating.

The resolution of these challenges lies in balancing personal and transpersonal nurturance. It is also helpful to expand one's vision of nurturing to encompass social and cultural forms of providing for others — e.g., becoming involved in world hunger programs, etc.

Chart Examples: Edna St. Vincent Millay, with Ceres conjunct Jupiter in Pisces, was a poet and spokeswoman for the human spirit in her world travels and political protests. (2)

Emmeline Pankhurst, a militant suffrage leader, protested her imprisonment by hunger-striking. She was born with Ceres in Sagittarius on the Midheaven opposed to Jupiter in Gemini. (2)

CERES-SATURN ASPECTS

The nurturing principle combines with the urge to create form and structure. This combination can signify a solid and realistic foundation for nurturing activities.

Harmonious aspects enhance stability, longevity, and depth in one's nurturing relationships. Traditional family values are strengthened and strong emotional support systems are formed.

Stressful aspects suggest potential thwarting or blocking of the nurturing function due to a variety of causes. One's parents may have withheld love and validation, demanded certain behaviors in exchange for their approval, administered harsh disciplines, or simply may have been absent. In other cases the parents may have been too responsible, doing everything for the child who had trouble discovering his/her own strength. In addition, this individual may feel overly obligated and constrained by the responsibilities of caring for his/her children or elderly parents.

The resolution of these conflicts lies in learning how to be one's own parent by nurturing and caring for the child within. In this way, the Ceres-Saturn individual can learn to care for himself or herself as well as for others.

Chart Examples: Albert Camus, with Ceres in Sagittarius in the third house opposing Saturn in Gemini in the ninth, philosophically nurtured the world through his writings stressing humanity's responsibility to fight social evils. (1)

Fidel Castro, Communist dictator of Cuba, repressed individual freedom but improved education, housing and health facilities for his people. He has Ceres conjunct Saturn in Sagittarius. (3)

CERES-URANUS ASPECTS

The nurturing principle combines with individuality and intuition. This combination has the potential to universalize the nurturing impulse into humanitarian activities.

Harmonious aspects can suggest original and innovative approaches toward caring for others and developing family structures. Ceres-Uranus individuals are often advocates of human rights and especially support children's individuality. This aspect can connote a highly developed intuition concerning human nature that enables the person to establish rapport with people of various races and nationalities.

Stressful aspects may signify unreliable and erratic nurturing experiences which might lead to difficulty in forming emotional bonds. The child who is raised in a "broken" home or who rebels against his or her parents may later experience the conflict between personal freedom and family closeness. In addition, this aspect could point to difficulties in listening to and trusting one's own thoughts and intuitions.

The resolution of these challenges lies in integrating one's individuality and visions of change with one's concern and need for loved ones.

Chart Examples: India's first prime minister Jawaharlal Nehru had Ceres conjunct Pallas and Uranus in Libra, and thus fought side by side with Gandi for India's freedom. (3)

Helen Keller, with Ceres conjunct Uranus at the Virgo Midheaven, revolutionized the techniques of teaching the handicapped. (2)

Alice Bailey (2), Helena P. Blavatsky (2), and Alan Leo (1) all have Ceres-Uranus conjunctions. Each of these teachers emphasized the development of one's intuitive faculties.

CERES-NEPTUNE ASPECTS

The nurturing principle combines with the transcendent urge. This combination can indicate a sensitizing of the nurturing impulse to create a depth of compassion and empathy for all beings.

Harmonious aspects can signify the desire to selflessly give, based upon the experience of unconditional and absolute love obtained through spiritual devotions. This aspect may also symbolize psychic sensitivity to the emotions of others that enables these individuals to serve as healer-helpers in their chosen roles or professions. Artistic and acting abilities may also be indicated by this aspect.

Stressful aspects can point to unrealistic perceptions of loved ones and consequent feelings of disappointment or deception. The resulting emotional neediness may predispose the individual to playing victim as a way of receiving attention in the form of nurturing. Or, unable to bear the emotional pain and isolation, this person may seek refuge in various forms of escapism — drugs, alcohol, or withdrawal.

The resolution of these challenges lies in finding one's source of nourishment through the experience of oneness and unity that connects all beings. Ministering to the needs of others, without self-sacrifice, also enables the Ceres-Neptune individual to fulfill his/her deep longing for wholeness and unity.

Chart Examples: Marilyn Monroe, with Ceres conjunct Neptune in Leo, nurtured the world through creatively expressing her beauty, but her inability to form a positive self-image and emotional neediness led to her tragic demise. (2)

Anthropologist Carlos Castaneda, with Ceres conjunct Neptune in Leo, served as an apprentice to a Yaqui Indian sorcerer and offers humanity visions transcending our limited physical realm in *A Separate Reality*. (1)

CERES-PLUTO ASPECTS

The nurturing principle combines with the transformative urge. This combination emphasizes the archetypal Ceres-Pluto theme of loss and return which teaches that one cannot become attached to the life that one has created and nurtured.

Harmonious aspects denote the ability to share one's physical and mental/emotional/creative offspring. There may exist a deep understanding of the human psyche and physical world that enables the individual to facilitate others in their life/death passages. Becoming a parent can transform one's values and create greater tolerance and acceptance of others.

Stressful aspects may signify intense emotional crises brought about through the loss or separation of loved ones. Intense grief, sorrow, and depression may result. If the person tends to grasp or attempts to possess his or her creations, power struggles may result.

The resolution of these challenges lies in transforming one's attachments through accepting the teaching of the Ceres-Pluto myth — that return and renewal follow letting go, that every death is followed by a birth, and that every loss is replenished by a gain. Thus, a real understanding of this truth permanently erases the fear of loss from one's subconscious mind and replaces it with trust, acceptance and joy.

Chart Examples: Timothy Leary, with Ceres conjunct Pluto in Cancer, used LSD to experience transformational states including the death passage. (1)

Scientist Albert Einstein was born with Ceres conjunct Pluto in Taurus in the eleventh house. He founded the theory of relativity which totally transformed the preexisting concepts about the nature of the universe. (1)

CHAPTER SIX

PALLAS ATHENE: THE WARRIOR QUEEN

I'll start this singing with
that grand goddess,
Pallas Athena,
bright-eyes,
so shrewd,
her heart inexorable,
as virgin, redoubtable,
protectress of cities,
powerful,
Tritogene,
whom shrewd Zeus himself
produced
out of his sacred head —
bedecked in that
spangly gold war armor
she wears — [1]

The Mythology of Pallas Athene

Pallas Athene, virgin goddess of wisdom, was second only to Jupiter, king of the heavens, in her importance to classical Greece. Athene's name was given to the city of Athens, the intellectual center of Greek civilization. As the goddess of war and victory, Pallas, a master

1. Homer, "The Hymn to Athena," *The Homeric Hymns*, trans. Charles Boer (Texas: Spring Publications, Inc., 1979), 137.

tactician and strategist, was invincible in battle. And, as protectress and guardian of Athens, Pallas used her wisdom to teach the populace how to peacefully settle disputes and uphold the law by pacific means. Ever compassionate in her wisdom, she was a firm advocate of merciful justice.

Pallas Athene was represented as a majestic woman sheathed in tight draperies and clad in armor. In her hands she held a spear and shield, a helmet upon her head, with her breast covered by a breastplate called the *aegis*, made of the skin of a goat, bordered with snakes, in the center of which was the head of the Gorgon Medusa. She was often accompanied by an owl representing wisdom and with a snake for prophecy.

Pallas Athene is credited with advancing the civilizing influence of culture upon humanity, and her gifts are numerous. She invented the flute, the trumpet, the potter's wheel, the first earthenware vases, the plough, rake, and ox-yoke. As goddess of the arts and crafts, Pallas served as the patroness of artists, artisans, architects, and sculptors. She instructed humanity in the trades of smithing and metal founding as well as the arts of cooking, embroidery, woolworking, and weaving. Finally, as goddess of health and healing, Pallas Athene taught a variety of medical practices, including the secret of regeneration through the *Medusa's* blood.

MYTHS OF THE BIRTH OF ATHENE

Homeric legend describes Pallas Athene's parthenogenetic birth from the head of her father Jupiter (Zeus). According to the poet-historian, Pallas sprung from Zeus' forehead as a full-grown warrior queen, clad in a suit of armor and shouting a triumphant cry of victory. This account is actually a foreshortening of an earlier version developed around *Metis*, Pallas' mother, which describes the transition from matriarchy to patriarchy in the Mediterranean cultures.

The true inception of Pallas, however, occurred in Libya 6,000 years ago where she was born on the shores of Lake Triton, home of several tribes of African Amazons. Her ancient title "*Tritogenia*" refers to her origins from water.[2] After her birth, Pallas was found and nurtured by three Libyan nymphs dressed in goat skins. During this period she was known as the Libyan Triple Goddess Neith.[3]

---

2. H. J. Rose, *A Handbook of Greek Mythology* (New York: E. P. Dutton and Co., 1959), 108.
3. Robert Graves, *The White Goddess* (New York: Farrar, Straus and Giroux, 1978), 231.

Around 4000 BC, Libyan refugees brought their goddess to Crete where her worship was adopted and passed on to Thrace and Greece in the first Minoan age. From this era arose the transitional version of Pallas' birth through her Titan sea goddess mother *Metis* (Wise Counsel), daughter of *Oceanus*. Metis helped Zeus-Jupiter achieve victory over his father, Cronus, by giving him an emetic that forced him to cough up his swallowed children. Although Metis changed into many shapes to avoid Zeus' lustful advances, she was finally ravished and got with child. Gaia and Uranus warned Jupiter that Metis would bear a child after Pallas Athene who would become king of gods and men. To maintain his sovereignty, Jupiter consumed Metis whole while she was pregnant with Athene. The blinding headache that resulted when Jupiter walked the shores of Lake Triton could only be relieved through having his head cleft with a double-edged axe (a matriarchal symbol). Amidst the rumbling of the earth and raging of the sea, out sprang Pallas Athene in armor of gleaming gold. She immediately became her father's favorite.

From a sociological perspective, the myth of Pallas Athene's birth from Jupiter's head marks the ingestion and adaptation of the feminine wisdom principle to the needs of the new patriarchal order.

THE SERPENT WISDOM OF PALLAS ATHENE

Throughout Pallas Athene's historical unfoldment she is accompanied by serpent symbolism. Her gift of prophecy is derived from her essential relationship with the qualities of the serpent. Secret tradition tells that the ingestion of minute amounts of certain snake venoms causes divinatory visions. For this reason the serpents became symbols of wisdom and the guardians of prophecy.

Affirming her origins with the Libyan snake goddess Neith, Pallas Athene wears in the center of her breastplate the head of serpent-haired Medusa, queen of an Amazon tribe from Pallas Athene's birthplace in Libya.

In Minoan Crete, Pallas Athene was worshiped as "Lady of Athana," protectress of the palace and city, whose emblems were the house-guarding serpent and the bird.[4]

Then in later Athens upon the Acropolis stood a huge statue of Athene with a snake of equal size considered to be the fate or guardian genius of the city. The goddess and divine snake were regarded as one. When Athens was besieged by the Persians, and the guardian

4. Joseph Campbell, *The Masks of the Gods: Occidental Mythology* (New York: Penguin Books, 1981), 149.

snake refused to eat its sacrificial food, the people believed that the goddess had abandoned her city.

Athene was also known as mother to the serpent child *Erichthonius* who became a king of Athens and instituted the worship of Athene. An older tradition invoking her as mother preserves a memory where she bore her son to Hephaestus.[5] The Athenians, in order to defend their goddess maidenhood — a symbol of their city's invincibility — tell the following tale. Lustfully attacked by the smith god Hephaestus, Pallas Athene defended herself and struggled away. She wiped off his ejaculation against her thigh with a bit of wool which fell near Athens and fertilized the earth. Gaia, Mother Earth, then bore the child. Athene secretly raised her serpent child in her holy temple of Erechtheum. Here the serpent of wisdom was ceremonially fed cakes of honey by the priestesses, and Erichthonius, represented as a snake with a human head, made known the prophecies of the oracles.[6]

A final example of Athene's serpent — connected oracular gifts is portrayed in the myth of a Thebean named *Tiresias*. One day he inadvertently glimpsed Athene bathing and was blinded by the angry goddess. Despite the pleas of Tiresias' mother, Athene was unable to restore his sight. Instead, she removed the serpent Erichthonius from her breastplate and gave the order, "Cleanse Tiresias' ears with your tongue that he may understand the language of prophetic birds." Hence, Tiresias became endowed with prophetic powers and oracular insight that he carried into the Underworld after his death.

PALLAS THE WARRIOR GODDESS

On Mt. Olympus, Pallas Athene's immense respect was due in part to her quality of manliness. Virgin goddess, not even born of woman, she was described by a number of martial epithets — "leader of the war-host," "raiser of battle," "driver of armies," and "she who repulses the enemy." Invincible in battle, she became a symbol of strategic and well-planned warfare. As protectress of heroes, Pallas Athene aided Hercules in his labors, assisted Odysseus in his return voyage from Troy, and enabled Perseus to kill Medusa, whose head of coiled serpents Athene wears brandished in the center of her breastplate.

The clues to Athene's warrior origins may be found in her surname Pallas. The word Pallas may be accented or inflected so as to

5. Carl Kerenyi, *The Gods of the Greeks*, trans. Norman Cameron (Great Britain: Billings and Sons, Ltd., 1982), 123.
6. Robert Graves, *The Greek Myths*, vol. I (Maryland: Penguin Books, 1964), 99.

express either a masculine or a feminine meaning. In the masculine, it means "a strong young man"; in the feminine, she is "a strong virgin."[7] Athene was honored annually in a Libyan festival of maidens in armed combat, reminiscent of the virgin priestesses of Neith competing for the position of high-priestess. The Greeks copied their Libyan garments of goat skins and shield with the image of Athene,[8] and retold the patriarchal version of this tale as follows. One day, as the story goes, Athene was engaged in friendly combat with her foster sister Pallas, daughter of a local sea-god *Triton*. Suddenly, Jupiter interposed his *aegis* (breastplate), thereby distracting Athene's attention so that she accidentally killed her sister. In her sorrow and grief, Athene set Pallas' name before her own and fashioned an image of her dead sister, endowing it with the fatal, power-bearing *aegis*. This image, known as the *Palladium*, was wrought with magical qualities that granted invulnerability to the beholder.

In her original nature, the warrior attributes of Athene were embodied in her aspect as Pallas — a strong maiden protectress of the matriarchal Amazon tribes of her Libyan cult. This is the true derivation of the Pallas prefix. In the Olympian version Athene kills her own earlier defensive nature and takes on the violent, aggressive, warlike qualities of the new patriarchal order. However she leaves behind a legacy in the *Palladium* as a testimony guaranteeing her presence and protection. The Roman Temple of Vesta was said to be the secret repository of the genuine *Palladium*.

THE SEPARATION OF PALLAS ATHENE FROM HER MATRIARCHAL HERITAGE

Pallas, Athene, and Medusa as maiden, mother, and crone were the triple Moon emanations of the Libyan snake goddess Neith. Originally, Athene was one and the same with Pallas and Medusa. However by the time she entered Greek culture, she had become a symbol of the new patriarchal order and is hence portrayed as assisting in the destruction of her matriarchal antecedents.

THE SLAYING OF MEDUSA

From a historical perspective the classical myth of Perseus' triumph over Medusa, with the aid of Athene, represents actual events during the reign of the historical King Perseus (circa 1290 BC), founder of the new dynasty in Mycenae. During this period the early Moon

7. Kerenyi, *The Gods of the Greeks*, 121.
8. Graves, *The Greek Myths*, 44.

goddess powers were usurped by patriarchally dominated invaders of mainland Greece. The Hellenes overran the goddess's chief shrines, stripped her priestesses of their Gorgon masks, and took possession of the sacred horse.[9] This historical rupture and sociological trauma registered itself in the following myth.[10]

Medusa, the third aspect of the triple-goddess triad, was a queen of the Gorgon Amazons who lived near Lake Triton, the very spot of Athene's origins. Renowned for her loveliness, she was greatly desired by her suitors. Poseidon, lord of the sea, whose original form was "*Hippios*," the horse deity, violated Medusa in Athene's temple and begot her with twins. Athene was outraged at this act; yet, she punished not Poseidon, but Medusa by turning her loveliest possession, her hair, into hissing snakes and causing her glance to turn men into stone. Athene then assisted Perseus by lending him her great shield which he could use as a mirror against Medusa, thereby avoiding direct contact with her terrifying face. Using the shield and Hermes' magical blade, Perseus was able to cut off Medusa's head and present it to Athene.

Out of Medusa's severed head sprang the two children of Poseidon: *Chrysaor*, the hero of the golden sword, and the winged horse *Pegasus*, symbol of poetry. As Perseus flew away, drops of blood from Medusa's neck fell to the ground, causing oases to grow in the desert. Athene also procured some of Medusa's blood and gave a portion to her son Erichthonius and the remainder to *Asclepius*, god of healing, who used it to heal the living and regenerate the dead.

Athene and Medusa were originally two aspects of the Libyan snake goddess Neith. Yet, as we just witnessed, she was portrayed in Olympian times as having helped to destroy her matriarchal roots. Yet, for all who have eyes to see, Athene still flaunts the mark of her authentic nature, the head of Medusa, in the center of her breastplate.

ATHENE'S CONTEST WITH POSEIDON

The following contest arose out of a dispute between the Greek (Ionian) people who migrated across the sea and the native Athenians who worshipped the Minoan goddess. According to the rules, whoever could bestow the better gift to the people of Athens would govern the city. To answer the challenge, Poseidon thrust his trident into a rock of the Acropolis and generated a salt spring.

9. Graves, *The Greek Myths*, 17.
10. Campbell, *The Masks of the Gods*, 152.

According to another account, he created the first horse. Athene, however, offered the olive tree (the cultivated olive was originally imported from Libya, thus supporting her Libyan origins). By either a divine court or a vote of all the citizens, men and women alike, the olive tree was chosen as the more useful gift as it could be used for food, fuel, shelter, and shade. Athene, therefore, was declared the victor. In his anger, Poseidon revengefully flooded the Thriasian Plain and would not be satisfied until the Olympian gods honored him in Athens. The gods succumbed and appeased him by depriving the Athenian women of their citizenship, their vote, and the right to give their surnames to their children. Thus, for daring to prove her superiority, Pallas Athene won the battle, but lost the war. From that time on, the position, power, and rights of women were decreased and ultimately denied.

THE TRIAL OF ORESTES

The final renouncement of Athene's matriarchal origins occurred at the trial of Orestes when she cast the deciding vote in favor of his innocence. Orestes was accused of matricide. He had murdered his mother Clytemnestra who had killed his father Agamemnon. Under the ancient law, killing a person unrelated by blood was no crime. Thus, Clytemnestra bore no guilt for dutifully killing Agamemnon after he had sacrificed their innocent daughter Iphigenia. Murdering blood kin, however, was taboo, and a son's slaying of his mother was the ultimate crime.

Consequently, Orestes was pursued and hounded by the avenging *Errinyes* (the Furies). Driven to the brink of madness, he sought sanctuary at the altar of Apollo where Athene appeared in time to arrange a trial by jury. Apollo acted as counsel for the accused and in his famous speech justifying Orestes' act, Apollo denied the sanctity of the blood relationship to the mother.

> The mother is not the true parent of the child
> Which is called hers. She is a nurse who tends the growth
> Of young seed planted by its true parent, the male.
> So, if Fate spares the child, she keeps it as one might
> Keep for some friend a growing plant.[11]

11. Aeschylus, *The Orestian Trilogy*, trans. Philip Vellacott (Maryland: Penguin Books, 1962), 169.

To prove his assertion, he pointed to Athene who was presiding over the trial and stated:

And of this truth
That father without the mother beget we have
Present, as proof, the daughter of Olympian Zeus:
One never nursed in the dark cradle of the womb.[12]

When the case was put to a vote, the verdict of the judges was tied. Then, in an unexpected move, Athene cast the deciding ballot in favor of Orestes' acquittal. In validating male superiority, she stated,

My duty is to give the final vote. When yours
Are counted, mine goes to uphold Orestes' plea.
No mother gave me birth. Therefore the father's claim
And male supremacy in all things, save to give
Myself in marriage, wins my heart's loyalty.[13]

The fertility goddesses *Errinyes*, furious at this traitorous violation of matriarchal law, threatened to curse Greece with blight and famine. However, Athene persuaded them to accept the new rule, change their ways, and be worshipped at Athens as the *Eumenides* — pacific and docile protectoresses who offered their blessings of fruitfulness to the triumphant patriarchal order.

Thus, Pallas Athene was instrumental in catalyzing the transition between the matriarchal and patriarchal cultures by declaring victory for father-right. She was made to forswear her feminine origins and to destroy the earlier aspects of her feminine nature — Pallas and Medusa. By becoming virgin in the new sense — isolate and chaste — she denied the expression of the goddess fertility principle. Credited to Pallas Athene was the loss of women's rights as citizens and mothers. And finally, her wisdom nature was now used in the service of the masculine outlet of war. Such was the transformation of Pallas Athene by the new patriarchal society.

12. Aeschylus, *The Orestian Trilogy*. 170.
13. Aeschylus, *The Orestian Trilogy*. 172.

PALLAS ATHENE

Principle of Creative Intelligence

Character
Goddess of Wisdom and Justice
Protectress of the State

Glyph: ⚴

Spear of the Protectress

Symbols
owl
serpent
olive tree
shield and spear
distaff
aegis with Gorgon's head

Associated Rulerships
Libra
Leo
Aquarius

Polarities
Courage/Fear

The Astrology of Pallas Athene

As the principle of creative intelligence, Pallas Athene utilizes Venus' sexual, reproductive energy to generate mental progeny. She is the vehicle through which thoughts take form, and thus represents the spark of intelligence that initiates the creative act. Astrologically, her essence brings together the mental qualities of the air element and the creative attributes of fire. Pallas, therefore, governs the air signs of Libra and Aquarius and the fire sign Leo. Together, they form an aspect pattern that combines opposition, trine, and sextile. This aspect configuration in the kite family stabilizes the inherent power of the Libra-Aquarius trine while the Leo-Aquarius opposition provides a focal point for the release of creative tension. Pallas Athene's essence thus lies in the interplay between the creative impulse of Leo, the transpersonal social concern of Aquarius, and the balance and cohesion of Libra.

THE WISDOM ASPECT OF PALLAS

From a sociological perspective, the myth of the birth of Pallas from Jupiter's head marks the ingestion and adaptation of the feminine wisdom principle to the needs of the patriarchal state. In terms of the evolution of consciousness, however, this myth also describes the growth of wisdom from the instinctive to the conscious (the primordial knowing of the sea goddess Metis was grounded through Jupiter to produce the active aspect of a feminine intelligence through Pallas). Thus, by elevating the procreative urge to the level of creative intelligence, the patriarchal birth of Pallas Athene heralded a historical turning point in the development of the human psyche.

As the goddess invoked by weavers and artisans, Pallas Athene bestows the wisdom of inner vision that endows perception of whole patterns. This mental image is the seed whose fruit is the creative act. Thus, Pallas symbolizes the process of creative visualization and the knowledge of the laws of manifestation.

PALLAS AS THE SIGNIFICATOR OF CREATIVE INTELLIGENCE

Astrologically, Pallas Athene represents a type of intelligence that extends far beyond the mental synthesis of the Gemini-Sagittarius polarity. Instead, she symbolizes creative intelligence — the flash of insight (Aquarius) that spawns new and original formulations of preexisting possibilities (Leo).

Pallas Athene is the indicator of our intelligence and style of perception. In the horoscope, she describes one's capacities for inspired vision, intuition, curiosity, genius, and exceptional perception. When the Thebean Tiresias was blinded by the sight of Pallas bathing naked, the goddess bestowed upon him the miraculous powers of insight and oracular prophecy.

Stressful aspects to Pallas, however, can point to a number of possible problems in both visual and auditory perception — color blindness, dyslexia, poor hand-eye coordination, limited vision and hearing, difficulties in learning, and mental retardation. To the degree that one's outer reality is shaped by inner thoughts, therapies that revise these misperceptions (e.g., guided fantasy and visualization) can greatly benefit the individual dealing with issues symbolized by Pallas Athene.

Finally, because of their capacity for whole pattern perception, Pallas types possess the ability to conceive and coordinate the schema for systems. Pallas Athene represents the wisdom of strategy, foresight, and planning which leads to concrete achievements and tangible results. Thus, by utilizing their rational thinking, intellect, and will, these individuals can achieve success in the business, political, academic, or scientific worlds.

PALLAS AS SIGNIFICATOR OF THE ARTS

Pallas Athene's wisdom-ray of creative intelligence expressed itself in three primary areas of human activity — the arts, healing, and political activism. In classical Greece, Pallas served as patroness of artisans and craftspeople. She also taught the practical arts and crafts that enabled humanity to develop a more civilized culture. Her wisdom inspired artistic vision, thus enabling the artist to infuse image into form and soul into art.

Astrologically, Pallas Athene signifies that artistic ability which utilizes clear sight and the perception of whole patterns. She figures prominently in the charts of individuals involved in the visual arts — drawing, painting, graphics, design, photography, and film. She is also the astrological ruler of all crafts — pottery, embroidery, woolworking, weaving, etc.

PALLAS AS SIGNIFICATOR OF THE HEALING ARTS

One of Pallas Athene's many aspects was that of *Hygeia*, goddess of miraculous healing. Legend has it that she gave Aesclepius a vial of blood from Medusa's severed head and instructed him to use it to revive the dead and regenerate the living.

Astrologically, Pallas governs those healing techniques that integrate mind and body. Such "holistic" health therapies have gained a large following since the activation of the asteroid functions in 1973. Specifically, Pallas governs all mental self-healing techniques — visualization, affirmation, meditation, mind control, guided imagery, and hypnosis.

In the psychological area, Pallas Athene rules those psychotherapies which integrate and balance whole patterns of the psyche. These include gestalt therapy, transactional analysis, bioenergetics, and psychodrama.

In physical healing, Pallas acts to activate, balance, and redirect the vital energy currents that flow through the body. Hence, she heals through such sciences as polarity therapy, acupuncture, homeopathy, macrobiotics, and cellular regeneration.

Astrologically, a prominent or well-aspected Pallas will indicate a potential for working with these therapies, either as a healer or as a healee. Stressful aspects may denote the presence of diseases that are rooted in the mind, or the existence of major imbalances in body functioning, until the person learns to see clearly on all levels.

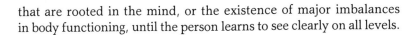

PALLAS AS SIGNIFICATOR OF THE POLITICAL ARTS

As warrior queen, Pallas Athene played the role of protectress who defended the people and state in times of war. Although she did not like violence and bloodshed, when her homeland was attacked Pallas became a fierce, courageous, and aggressive fighter. Athene fashioned the image of her dead sister and imbued it with magical properties that granted invulnerability to the beholder.

Astrologically, then, Pallas Athene symbolizes a feminine-defined quality of heroism, bravery, courage, and sensible toughness. In the birth chart, she describes the political activist, militant feminist, or champion of oppressed minorities. She also rules the martial arts, particularly those defenses which deflect the attack using balance and poise — e.g., *t'ai chi, aikido*, and fencing.

As protectress of the state, Pallas extended her political domain into the laws and political life of the *polis*. The judicial ability of Pallas is rooted in her association with the sign Libra, scales of justice, where the issues of war-and-peace and strife-and-harmony are paramount. Like Libra, Pallas serves as the fair mediator who, because she is able to see the whole picture, uses wise counsel and diplomacy in arriving at her decisions. In the horoscope, stressful aspects to Pallas may point to weakness in character, a lack of tact and diplomacy, ruthless aggressiveness, or the inability to resist attack.

PALLAS: A WOMAN IN A MAN'S WORLD

Pallas Athene, goddess of wisdom and courage, functions as the prototype for the creative, intelligent woman. Like Vesta, she was a virgin goddess in that she was sexually chaste and had no husband or lovers. But while Vesta sublimated her sexuality into religious devotion and personal integration, Pallas Athene fashioned it into mental and artistically creative works.

As the deity who stood closest to Jupiter/Zeus, Pallas attained a high degree of prestige and status in Olympus. She was accepted as sister, colleague, and equal in the world of men, and was allowed to express her intellectual competence in governing the Greek state. In addition, Pallas' virginity enabled her to cultivate many male friendships without the complication of sexual entanglement. Pallas, however, paid a substantial price in achieving this privileged position — the denial of her femininity and feminine origins. In her lament she cried, "No mother gave me birth. Therefore, the father's claim and male supremacy in all things, save to give myself in marriage, wins my whole heart's loyalty."[14]

This repudiation lies at the source of her pathology as the unconscious masculine side of a woman takes over and dominates the personality. Yet, it was this very sacrifice that enabled Pallas to enter the patriarchal world and provide a forum for harmonious communication between men and women. Thus, the ancient voice of the matriarchy was able to adapt and grow within the changing times rather than fade away into a past that was no more. However there are those who perceive Pallas Athene as a symbol of a feminine goddess who sold out to the patriarchy. Astrologically, this archetype can signify those women who support and defend a male-ordered world, or align themselves as the right hand to successful and powerful men.

In addition, Pallas can signify putting aside one's sexual nature (consciously or unconsciously) in order to relate harmoniously in a platonic manner with those of the opposite sex.

PALLAS AND ANDROGYNY

Because Pallas powerfully expressed both her male and female sides, she symbolized the movement of soul development toward androgyny. Her association with the sign Libra points to her role in balancing the internal male-female polarities. Astrologically, individuals with a prominent Pallas will seek companionship rather than passion in their heterosexual relationships. The fruits of such a path are usually an abundance of friends and a concurrent scarcity of lovers. In some instances, the same individual can function as both friend and lover.

Another result of androgyny is the deconditioning of sex-role typing. As Pallas ever strives toward balance and wholeness, she permits us to express and blend our male and female sides within one unified and integrated self. As a result of her Aquarian influence, Pallas can help us to recognize the indwelling humanity of another person rather than judge him or her according to a sexual stereotype.

PALLAS AND SEXUAL IDENTITY IMBALANCES

In the movement toward androgyny, individuals sometimes hurtle past the balance point and polarize to one end of the spectrum. Pallas, in donning Jupiter's *aegis*, overly identified with the father.

---

14. Aeschylus, *The Orestian Trilogy*, trans. Philip Vellacott (Maryland: Penguin Books, 1962), 169.

> Thus the force of the masculine is absorbed and converted into a kind of masculine forcefulness of the father's daughter. To defend herself from him, she becomes like him; in his pride, then, he may protect rather than attack her. . . But because she has used the defense of identification with the aggressor, she has no means open for full expression of her womanhood.[15]

Astrologically, therefore, Pallas-type women tend to overidentify with the masculine and develop "animus ridden" personalities. In pure form, this archetype can manifest as the Amazon, a pre-Hellenic personification of Pallas. In modern society, it can depict a competitive, combative, and aggressive woman who has lost touch with her softness and receptivity. Achievement, impregnability, power, and success become the goals of fulfillment, and preclude the emotional and sensual life of this woman.

In a man's horoscope, a strong Pallas can denote the reverse situation — the "anima ridden" personality. The anima is a man's unconscious feminine side. When this is dominant at an extreme range, it may express as excessive passivity, dependence, moodiness, and a hesitancy to assert his will. In both cases, Pallas' overidentification can lead to an estrangement from one's intrinsic nature, giving rise to a personality expression that alienates others and prevents intimacy with the opposite sex.

The protective suit of armor that Pallas Athene wore to ease her entry into the masculine world later becomes the barrier that prevents access to the world of emotions. The defense system of intellectualizing and rationalizing acts to put distance between the self and others and keeps one from experiencing feeling and pain.

In summary, Pallas Athene represents the need to balance the male and female polarities within us as well as the difficulties that result when this harmony is not achieved.

PALLAS AND FATHER COMPLEXES

During matriarchal times, daughters did not relate to their fathers and in most instances did not even know them. Pallas Athene's birth from her father Jupiter symbolized the need for women to relate to the paternal authority in their lives. While Ceres signifies the maternal imprint (the IC), Pallas represents the paternal imprint that instructs us how to function in the world (the MC). Just as Ceres types bond with their mothers, Pallas types identify with fathers. When

15. Murray Stein, "Translator's Afterthoughts," in *Athene*, by Carl Kerenyi (Switzerland: Spring Publications, 1978), 77.

the Pallas father-bond is impaired, a number of psychological complexes emerge. Two such archetypes are the *puella* and the "armored amazon."[16]

The *puella* (Latin for "girl"), often dubbed "Daddy's little girl," is the dutiful daughter who passively submits to her father's patriarchal power. She validates herself by seeking her father's approval and actively competes with her mother for his love and attention. The intensity of the father-daughter relationship may be accompanied by incestuous undertones. In marriage, the *puella* woman functions as a behind-the-scenes supporter of her husband's success, an indispensable second in command. For the *puella*, her outer submissiveness hides her natural strength and inner need to rebel and fight.

At the other extreme we find the Amazon who seeks to absorb and imitate the masculine power of the father. In her early years, she may act out the "tomboy" archetype and disdain the silly pastimes of her feminine counterparts. Once again, she looks to the father for validation, but this time emulates his drive to succeed, perform, and accomplish. The outer world, similar to the actual father, may be perceived as a threatening power. Like the *puella*, the Amazon has her repressed side — the helpless and dependent girl. In order to protect her vulnerable half, she simply denies her feelings and strong emotions.

Astrologically, therefore, Pallas Athene is the significator of father complexes for both men and women. In some cases the mother either plays a small part in the child's upbringing or the child rejects the mother's influence.

PALLAS AND THE FEAR OF SUCCESS

While Pallas was respected and admired in the world of men, she was never validated for being a woman. Her mental and creative abilities, while highly praised, were not recognized as feminine qualities. Hence, her womanly needs for love, tenderness, and closeness were denied. Likewise in our culture, "the brain," while applauded for her debate-team victories, is not asked to the prom. Women are taught that their worldly success will threaten a man's ego and highlight his own failings. For example, due to the commonly held belief that book learning in women makes for uppity wives, daughters are taught to play dumb as a means of attracting men. In a 1984 issue of a prominent men's magazine, many men were most

16. Linda S. Leonard, *The Wounded Woman* (Colorado: Shambala Press, 1982).

attracted to a woman "who has enough brains not to act smarter than me." Thus, the bitter irony for a Pallas woman is that the more she expresses her creative potential, the more she threatens her opportunity to form a conventional relationship with a man.

The consequence of this propaganda is all too clear: women have been conditioned to stifle their mental and creative expression in order to avoid rejection from men. And, "since what you don't use, you lose," these women soon begin to lose their intellectual abilities.

In a man's horoscope, a similar situation exists. Here Pallas depicts a highly developed intellectual or artistic male who fears being rejected for not being macho or manly enough. Hence, these men will often block their softness and sensitivity in order to conform to the norm of women's expectations.

WINNING AND LOSING

When Pallas Athene won the rulership of Athens in a contest with Poseidon, she was punished for her victory. Athenian women subsequently lost the right to vote, remain citizens, and give their name to their children. Thus, Pallas themes can denote "winning the battle but losing the war." Based on Pallas' experience, many women hesitate to compete with men for fear that if they give their best and emerge victorious, they will be punished or abandoned. Women report that they feel intimidated to compete and would rather acquiesce than fight.

This "competitiveness phobia" blocks an individual from expressing his or her potential to the maximum. On a social level, when half the population does not contribute their gifts and talents, everyone suffers. Hence, women and men (but especially women) with strong Pallas themes need to find the courage to stand up for their rights and express their wisdom without fearing the potential consequences. At the other extreme, Pallas themes can signify an obsessive need for victory at any cost, ruthless competition, and the destruction of a relationship in order to prove one's own point.

CREATIVITY VERSUS LOVE

As a virgin warrior goddess, Pallas Athene often counseled others to refrain from sexual intercourse before combat in order to conserve their strength and vitality. This edict symbolizes a fundamental split in the Pallas archetype between creativity and relationship, or the head versus the heart. Astrologically, individuals with strong Pallas themes feel torn between their intimate relationships and their work and ambitions. Often they will sacrifice one of these focuses in order to further the other. For example, a Pallas woman may find that her need for a vocation supersedes her commitment to a family. Her children will not be her physical progeny, but, instead, her ideas and accomplishments. In this respect, emergence of the Pallas archetype in modern society accounts for the remarkable rise in "career women" that has occurred over the past decade. Pallas themes here can signify the difficulties that women working in the outer world experience in balancing the other parts of their lives, as well as the discrimination and sexism they encounter in the professional world.

SOUL WORK

The suffering and alienation that are found in today's Pallas archetype are rooted in the assumption that femininity and mental creativity are mutually exclusive. In a world that considers strength, courage, and intellectual prowess to be masculine, a woman who expresses these qualities is expected to divorce herself from her femininity. Thus, the soul work for the Pallas Athene woman is to recover her lost feminine origins; "to see her not as a goddess who has renounced her femininity, but as one who teaches us to recognize courage and vulnerability, creativity and receptivity, as equally feminine qualities."[17]

In the center of her breastplate, Pallas wore the emblem of the Gorgon's Head, which according to legend, would turn men into stone. Freud believed that the head symbolized the terrifying genitals of the Great Mother and the horror and dread of her feminine sexuality. Because of this association, modern men and women have feared the dark, primal, instinctive, feminine nature and have dissociated it from the intellect. Yet, the instinctual power of the Medusa, the intuitive wisdom of Metis, and the courage and valor of Pallas herself are Pallas Athene's heritage from her matriarchal lineage. Recognizing this source of feminine power and integrating it with the intellect and mental functions is the key to synthesizing the feminine and masculine qualities of Pallas. This redemption of the feminine will in turn resolve the arbitrary separation between a woman's love nature and her mental/spiritual creativity.

17. Christine Downing, *The Goddess: Mythological Images of the Feminine* (New York: The Crossroad Publishing Co., 1981), 103.

The Occult Teachings of Pallas Athene

Pallas Athene's occult teachings are derived from the serpent-haired Gorgon Medusa whose face she wears on her breastplate. The serpent aspect of the Medusa represented the wisdom of the oracles and granted the ability to hear the voices of prophecy. The blood from the Medusa's severed head became the tonic elixir that revived the dead and regenerated the living. Pallas therefore governs the *yogic* techniques that activate the *kundalini* force that leads to cellular regeneration and the illumination gained through the opening of the crown chakra.

Pallas Athene also embodies the magical will that enables us to create and control our own reality. Rather than depending upon ceremony and ritual, Pallas spontaneously manifests whatever is needed through the mode of creative visualization. Thus she is the occultist rather than the mystic, the scientist opposed to the psychic, who uses natural laws to manifest ideas onto the physical plane.

Pallas Athene's Psychological Themes

Principle of Creative Wisdom

intelligence • social justice • artistic ability • healing power • political activism • confidence • courage • strength • valor

Androgyny

Imbalances in Sexual Identity

denial of femininity • overidentification with men • sexual alienation • father-daughter complexes • conflicts between love and creativity

Occult Themes

kundalini • prophecy and oracle • magical will • creative visualization

Further Reading on Pallas Athene

Aeschylus. *The Orestian Trilogy*. Translated by Philip Vellacott. Maryland: Penguin Books, 1962.

Bolen, Jean Shinoda. "Athena: Goddess of Wisdom and Crafts, Strategist and Father's Daughter." In *Goddesses in Everywoman*.

San Francisco: Harper and Row, 1984.

Downing, Christine. "Dear Grey Eyes: A Revaluation of Pallas Athene." In *The Goddess: Mythological Images of the Feminine*. New York: Crossroad, 1981.

Hillman, James. "On the Necessity of Abnormal Psychology: Anake and Athene." In *Facing the Gods*, edited by James Hillman. Irving Texas: Spring Publications, Inc., 1980.

Homer. "The Hymn to Athena I" and "The Hymn to Athena II." In *The Homeric Hymns*, translated by Charles Boer. Irving Texas: Spring Publications, Inc., 1979.

Kerenyi, Carl. *Athene: Virgin and Mother*. Zurich Switzerland: Spring Publications, 1978.

______. "Metis and Pallas Athene." In *The Gods of the Greeks*, translated by Norman Cameron. Great Britain: Billings and Sons, Ltd., 1981.

Leonard, Linda S. *The Wounded Woman*. Colorado: Shambala Press, 1982.

Spretnak, Charlene. "Athena." In *Lost Goddesses of Early Greece*. Berkeley: Moon Books, 1978.

Stein, Murray. "Translator's Afterthoughts." In *Athene: Virgin and Mother* by Carl Kerenyi. Switzerland: Spring Publications, 1978.

Stone, Merlin. "Athena." In *Ancient Mirrors of Womanhood* Vol II. New York: New Sibylline Books, 1979.

Walton, Evangeline. *The Sword is Forged*. New York: Pocket Books, 1983.

CHAPTER SEVEN

PALLAS ATHENE IN THE HOROSCOPE

The Greeks worshipped Pallas Athene, goddess of wisdom and justice, as patroness of the arts and protectress of the state. Through her all-encompassing perception, she gave wise counsel to the people of the earth.

Originally an ancient Libyan amazon queen, Pallas Athene was known by the Olympian Greeks as the parthenogenetic daughter of their sky god Jupiter — born from the crown of his head. This account is a foreshortening of an earlier version where Jupiter swallowed whole his first consort Metis, a primordial sea goddess who was pregnant with Athene. On an outer level this myth marks the ingestion and adaptation of the feminine wisdom principle to the needs of the state. On an inner level this myth traces the evolution of consciousness where the procreative urge of sexual energy becomes polarized to release the mentally creative impulse. Pallas Athene's pathology of the fear of success stems from the culturally conditioned divorce of mental creativity from femininity.

In her role as daughter, Pallas Athene symbolizes the principle of creative intelligence giving birth to thought forms. Through her knowledge of the natural laws of manifestation, she functions as one's capacity for realization and accomplishment.

Astrologically, Pallas Athene describes how we face the issues of learning, creativity, the arts, politics, healing, alienation from relationships, competition, and the fears of success.

Pallas Athene in the signs describes twelve styles of perception through which the creative mind operates.

Pallas Athene in the houses tells us where the creative-mental urge is expressed and where fears of success may block that urge.

Pallas Athene aspects to the planets describe how the mental-creative urge may be integrated with other parts of the personality. Harmonious contacts indicate an easy blending, while stressful contacts point to potential conflicts between the creative needs and other requirements of the individual. When the varying needs are mastered and integrated, an individual with conflicting aspects in the horoscope no longer needs stress in order to learn balance.

Pallas Athene's Astrological Rulerships

Pallas, as goddess of wisdom, is an indicator of wisdom and intelligence.

range of intelligence — genius to mongoloid • learning problems • mental retardation • difficulties in perception • dyslexia • color blindness • hand-eye coordination • perception of whole picture patterns and systems • problem solving • troubleshooting • skill • precision • planning • foresight • practicality • technology • coordination

Pallas, as patroness of artisans, values the arts.

artistically creative • visual arts • drawing • painting • graphics • design • photography • domestic crafts • spinning • weaving • knitting • sewing • pottery • smithing • metallurgy • musical instruments

Pallas, in her aspect as *Hygeia*, signifies healing powers.

mental healing • visualization • hypnosis • affirmation • physical healing through balance • polarity • macrobiotics • acupuncture • homeopathy • cellular regeneration • energy healing through channeling, purifying, and polarizing currents • psychological healing through balance and integration • gestalt • transactional analysis • psychodrama

Pallas, as goddess of justice and protectress of the state, rules over political activism.

defender of justice • law • legal matters • People's Champion • defender of minority groups • nukes • sprays • whales • aged • young • racial/ethnic • arts of peace • mediator • diplomacy

• counselor • fair witness • martial arts • *kung fu* • *t'ai chi* • *aikido* • fencing • militant feminism

Pallas supports excellence in the professional world.
career training • vocational guidance • discrimination and sexism in the professional world

Pallas Athene in the Signs

The source of the data for charts cited in the following sections is indicated by a number in parentheses.
(1) Lois Rodden's *The American Book of Charts*
(2) Lois Rodden's *Profiles of Women*
(3) Marc Penfield's *An Astrological Who's Who*

Pallas Athene in Aries shows a perception that seeks to activate or initiate. "Seeing" is in terms of how to get something going. Because of Aries' strong connection to vital energy, Pallas Athene in healing shows the vision which activates the vital force expressed in techniques such as homeopathy and acupuncture. Pallas Athene expresses aesthetically in athletes using their bodies as vehicles for the creative impulse, or in the pioneering field of kinetic art. Politically, Pallas Athene is a very militant warrior, mobilizing the vital energy into fighting for what the person believes in. The wisdom of Pallas Athene is that of sudden inspiration — the "brainstorm" or the sudden pioneering urge.

Chart Examples: Magician Harry Houdini, with Pallas in Aries, won world fame with his dangerous feats as an escape artist. (3)

Markswoman Annie Oakley, an expert shot with pistol, rifle and shotgun, was born with Pallas in Aries. (1)

Pallas Athene in Taurus represents perceiving through the physical-sense organs. One continually "sees" the beauty of the physical world of nature through visual, auditory, and tactile senses. Because of Taurus' strong connection to the earth and physical substance, Pallas Athene can work through nature or by the laying on of hands in healing. Aesthetically, Pallas Athene is strong in Taurus — skilled in using color, form, and texture to reproduce beauty through art, music, and landscaping. Politically, Pallas Athene in Taurus is concerned with fighting for the land — earth ecology or land reform. The wisdom of Pallas in Taurus is "common sense" — the practical suggestions of folk remedies or streetwise knowledge.

Chart Example: Actress Katharine Hepburn's sensuality is partially described by her Pallas-Moon conjunction in Taurus in the seventh house. (2)

Pallas Athene in Gemini denotes perceiving through the written and spoken language. One "sees" the world through a plethora of words. In healing, Pallas Athene uses the power of words through such techniques as affirmations, neurolinguistic programming, and speech therapy. As an analyst, Pallas in Gemini uses words to elicit unconscious feelings. Aesthetically this is the strength of a writer and poet, creating images with words, or of the storyteller who creates through oral tradition. Politically, Pallas Athene in Gemini is a warrior with words — orator, debater, political writer — where inner truth is translated to language. The wisdom of Pallas in Gemini is knowledge — knowing, which comes from one's inner personal mind. Paradox can play a role in the understanding.

Chart Examples: Pioneering astrologer and writer Marc Edmund Jones was born with Pallas in Gemini in the seventh house. (1)

Comedian Lenny Bruce, known for his controversial social satire, has Pallas in Gemini in the seventh house. (1)

Pallas Athene in Cancer suggests perceiving essentially through the emotions. One "sees" through "feeling out" one's way in the world. Pallas Athene heals through creating healing environments that provide for the satisfaction of basic biological needs: warmth, comfort, food, and security. Aesthetically, the creative talents express easily through the home arts (e.g., gourmet chef), becoming the host/hostess, or creating feeling environments. Politically, Pallas Athene is a defender of home and family, a patriot of one's country, as well as an advocate for children, the elderly, the disabled or needy. The wisdom of Pallas in Cancer is that of empathy — a knowing gained through one's hypersensitive emotional antennae.

Chart Examples: Astronaut Neil Armstrong, the first person to set foot on the Moon, has Pallas conjunct Jupiter in the lunar sign Cancer. (3)

Patriot Nathan Hale, "I regret that I have but one life to give for my country," was born with a Pallas-Ceres conjunction in Cancer. (3)

Pallas Athene in Leo represents a creative perception that is especially strong. One "sees" in terms of how one can impress one's unique vision upon the world. As a healer, Pallas Athene works with art therapy, psychodrama, play (sand tray) therapy, dance therapy, and stress reduction through pleasure. Pallas in Leo people create through drama, acting, performing, courtship, and romance as an art form, and through solar inventions. Individuals with Pallas Athene in Leo have charisma and the ability to stand up in the public eye as a front person for causes, and to sway the masses through political comedy and drama. The wisdom of Pallas Athene in Leo is the wisdom of the Creative Impulse that gives birth to new forms of expression.

Chart Examples: Charismatic and courageous vice presidential nominee Geraldine Ferraro was born with Pallas in Leo conjunct her Virgo Sun.

Simon Bolivar, "El Libertador" of South America, has Pallas conjunct Ceres in Leo. (3)

Pallas Athene in Virgo indicates an analytical perception. One has the ability to see the essence of things in their simplest forms apart from the surrounding superfluous complications. In healing, Pallas Athene is skilled in *Hatha-Yoga* techniques, and in purification of the body through food (nutritionist or herbalist) and through exercise. Aesthetically, she brings an image to earth-form through the integrity of detailed craftsmanship for practical use (pottery, woodworking, sewing, computer programming). Politically, she fights for perfection, high quality and standards in any field. The wisdom of Pallas in Virgo is the wisdom of discrimination — separating the wheat from the chaff.

Chart Example: Healer Ellen Yoakum, born with Pallas in Virgo in the fourth house, diagnosed patients by simply looking at them, and then healed by laying on of hands. (2)

Pallas Athene in Libra mirrors a perception that seeks to reconcile opposites. One sees in terms of spatial relations, bringing balance, composition, and cohesion into view. As a healer, Pallas Athene works here with techniques of energy balancing such as polarity therapy and macrobiotics (*yin-yang*), *t'ai chi*, marital counseling, conflict management, and gestalt techniques. Aesthetically she is very strong, skilled in creating harmonious designs in graphics, interior design, and fashion. Politically, she is a defender of justice, seeking to implement the arts of peace — mediation, diplomacy, and legal action. The wisdom of Pallas in Libra is the wisdom of balance — the ability to harmonize and integrate polarities.

Chart Example: Television anchorwoman Barbara Walters, with Pallas in Libra at the Ascendant, has been a groundbreaker for women in the media profession. (5)

Pallas Athene in Scorpio points to a penetrating perception. One is able to see through, under, and beneath the surface of things, as in an X-ray vision. As a healer, Pallas Athene in Scorpio is very strong — piercing to the core of the difficulty and getting to the root of the problem. In addition, she employs the techniques of depth psychology that bring the unconscious to conscious awareness — i.e., primal scream, past-life regressions, and hypnosis. As part of her healing repertoire, Pallas Athene in Scorpio also uses the techniques of sexual therapy and cellular regeneration. Aesthetically Pallas expresses the vision of symbolic art, such as mandalas, meanings within meanings, or sex as an art form, as in *tantric* practices or the *Kama Sutra*. Politically, this is a fearless and ruthless warrior, controlling the power of the masses, and skilled in strategy and espionage. The wisdom of Pallas Athene in Scorpio is the wisdom of insight — penetrating to the core and grasping the essence.

Chart Examples: Surgeon Christiaan Barnard who performed the first human heart transplant in history has Pallas conjunct his Sun in Scorpio. (3)

Agatha Christie, imaginative writer of detective story mysteries, has Pallas in Scorpio in the second house. (2)

Pallas Athene in Sagittarius implies conceptual perception. One is able to see in terms of the broad-scale vision — the "big picture." As a healer this is expressed as mental healing — using the power of clear imagery of a perfect, whole body to resonate change and attunement. Sagittarius' connection to religion can indicate the *shaman* or *guru*, who heals through spiritual knowledge. Aesthetically, the urge is to create art that conveys the meaning of universal principles (the *tarot*), or emphasizes unique ethnic and cultural qualities. Politically, Pallas Athene in Sagittarius is a defender of truth and righteousness, fighting for ideologies. This can depict the sage or adviser to the ruler (as the Merlin to Arthur), or religious warriors such as the Crusaders and the *jihad* (in the holy wars of the Muslims). The wisdom of Pallas in Sagittarius is the wisdom of unification — forging the cohesive links of the parts to form the whole.

Chart Examples: Writer Bertrand Russell, defender of humanity and freedom of thought, was born with Pallas in Sagittarius. (1)

The Reverend Jesse Jackson, whose political campaign was based on religious ideologies, has Pallas in Sagittarius. (5)

Pallas Athene in Capricorn denotes structural perception. One "sees" through a comprehension of the structural foundation which supports form. As a healer, this expresses by healing through the skeleton, such as chiropractic, posture therapy, rolfing, deep-tissue massage, and dentistry. Aesthetically, Pallas Athene is very strong in Capricorn representing the ability to formulate precise structures (molds) into which raw creative energy can coalesce. Instant manifestation is often possible and can be seen as a magical process. Here, Pallas excels in the arts of architecture, drafting, and sculpture. Capricorn's association with time connects Pallas Athene with the art of timing — being in the right place at the right time. Politically, this is a defender of law and order. There is a strong power drive for authority over others in political and social institutions. The wisdom of Pallas in Capricorn is the wisdom of order — putting things in their proper sequence.

Chart Example: Renowned sculptor Auguste Rodin who manifested his beautiful images in physical forms was born with Pallas in Capricorn in the twelfth house. (1)

Pallas Athene in Aquarius represents a futuristic perception. One can "see" in terms of all the various possibilities of the future. As a healer, she works with vibration, healing with color, sound, crystals, and white light (as reflector of the Sun's Leo rays). Aesthetically, she expresses through creating the new. As inventor or genius, she creates science fiction art, computer graphics, new-wave music, rock video, and radical art. These artists are out on the forefront of the future, translating the tone of what is coming in for the masses. Politically, Pallas Athene in Aquarius is the political revolutionary, advocating and defending humanitarian causes and organizing grass roots protests.The wisdom of Pallas Athene in Aquarius is the wisdom of the future — creating forms that will benefit generations to come.

Chart Examples: Political mavericks and humanitarians Abraham Lincoln (1), Earl Warren (1), and Martin Luther King (1) were all born with Pallas in Aquarius.

Lois Rodden, astrologer, pilot, and member of Mensa, was born with Pallas rising in Aquarius. (2)

Pallas Athene in Pisces shows a diffuse perception. One "sees" through merging oneself in between the spaces of dense reality and experiencing a direct contact with the object. As a healer, she excels in psychic and faith healing. Success can be achieved through the psychological techniques of guided imagery, fantasy, and dream interpretation, as well as meditation, devotion, spirit guides, and spiritual practices. Aesthetically, she brings out the poetic, inspirational, and illusory qualities in artistic expression. There exists creative skill in the media of film and photography, which play with light and illusion, and in ethereal music (synthesizer), which evokes feeling. Politically, Pallas Athene in Pisces can be a proponent of nonviolent resistance: turning the other cheek or refusing to fight. She is also the enlightened warrior, the *bodhisattva*, and the martyr. The wisdom of Pallas in Pisces is the wisdom of compassion — the recognition of the universal suffering and desire for happiness that permeates humanity.

Chart Examples: Walt Disney, creator of famous cartoon characters such as Mickey Mouse and Donald Duck, has Pallas in Pisces.

Johann Sebastian Bach, born with Pallas in Pisces conjunct his Aries Sun, infused deep religious feeling into his musical compositions. (3)

Pallas Athene in the Houses

Pallas Athene in the first house suggests a strong personal identification with intelligence, power and/or creativity. There can be a tendency to express androgynous qualities or to defy conventional male/female stereotypes.

Chart Example: Pilot Amelia Earhart, with Pallas conjunct her Taurus Ascendant stated, "Women must try to do things as men have tried. When they fail, their failure must be looked on as a challenge to others."(2)

Pallas Athene in the second house points to a strong practical sense and creative skill in acquiring resources. One can manifest an abundance of material possessions or value in one's life through creative visualization.

Chart Example: Poet Jack Kerouac, with Pallas conjunct the north node in his second house, protested against the materialism of middle-class values. (1)

Pallas Athene in the third house is an indicator of strong intuitive abilities. One can create with words and communications, revolutionize educational techniques, be an environmental activist. There exists a personal intelligence and a strong thirst for knowledge.

Chart Example: With Pallas conjunct Neptune in Virgo in his third house, Richard Alpert was naturally drawn to investigating alternative states of mind. (1)

Pallas Athene in the fourth house suggests the native can be highly psychic or empathetic. The subconscious is the source of the wisdom nature. There is a strong talent for creating home and holiday atmospheres.

Chart Example: Writer and chef Julia Child has Pallas conjunct her fourth-house Sun in Leo. (4)

Pallas Athene in the fifth house shows a person who can be highly talented in giving birth to original ideas. There can be sexual isolation through the diversion of the reproductive energy into creative works, or through the sacrifice of passion for friendship.

Chart Example: Helen Frankenthaler, with Pallas in Aquarius in the fifth house, is considered one of the foremost contemporary abstract painters. (2)

Pallas Athene in the sixth house individuals use their intelligence to integrate and perfect systems. This creative ability can express itself through one's work or job, or through powerful mental healing of the physical body. It can manifest as an advocate for workers' rights.

Chart Example: Edgar Cayce expressed his Pallas in Capricorn in the sixth house by serving people as a prophet and healer. (3)

Pallas Athene in the seventh house people possess strong mediating and counseling abilities. One's creative wisdom and skills can be used to improve interpersonal relations. There may be difficulty here with the intimate personal and sexual domain as some see a conflict between relationship and creativity. Often such people function better in impersonal relationships than in personal ones.

Chart Example: Shirley MacLaine, with Pallas-Mercury in Aries in the seventh house, was a forerunner in being an outspoken advocate of women's rights. (5)

Pallas Athene in the eighth house represents strong psychic and oracular intelligence. These people have creative skill with joint business and money affairs, the power of sexual magic, and using *kundalini yoga* as a spiritual transformer. One can experience limitations and restrictions in traditional sexual expressions, and instead sublimate sexuality into the field of creativity and transformation.

Chart Example: Spiritual leader Paramahansa Yogananda, founder of the Self-Realization Movement, with Pallas in Pisces in the eighth house was a lifelong celibate and mystic. (1)

Pallas Athene in the ninth house indicates that the individual's creative thought can emerge as political, philosophical, or social ideologies which can revolutionize through education. This is also an indicator of legal involvement and activism.

Chart Examples: Jefferson Davis, champion of the constitutional rights of the Southern States during the Civil War, was born with Pallas in Aquarius in the ninth house. (3)

Madalyn Murray O'Hair, with Pallas in Aquarius in the ninth house opposing Saturn, waged war against organized religion, and as a lawyer won her court case to outlaw prayer in public schools. (2)

Pallas Athene in the tenth house suggests a strong destiny to accomplish and receive recognition in the professional world. One can use one's wisdom-nature to advance one's career. With women this position can emphasize the archetypal situation of high professional success at the cost of the denial of their femininity unless integrated with emotional needs.

Chart Example: Helen Gurley Brown, editor-in-chief of *Cosmopolitan* magazine which encourages women's liberation, has Pallas conjunct Jupiter in Libra in the tenth house. (2)

Pallas Athene in the eleventh house individuals can conceive and birth new social visions. Working with the group format, one can implement new concepts in societal organizations. One's creative ideals can be enhanced through working with fraternal and sororal organizations. There also exists a strong political nature that ardently works for social change. Creative wisdom is expressed through becoming an advocate or spokesperson.

Chart Example: Musician Bob Dylan, who wrote protest songs of social reform, was born with Pallas in Sagittarius in the eleventh house opposing his Sun. (1)

Pallas Athene in the twelfth house indicates intelligence that is linked to the collective unconscious. There can be a mastery of spiritual teachings. This position also suggests *karma* associated with the use of one's mind, intelligence, and belief system. One may experience limitations in mind and intelligence (retardation, mental breakdown). On the positive level, it depicts dedicating the use of one's mind to the benefit of others, or as a spiritual service.

Chart Examples: With Pallas in their twelfth houses of confinement, Angela Davis (2) was imprisoned and Patty Hearst (2) was kidnapped because of their respective political affiliations.

Pallas Aspects to the Planets

PALLAS-SUN ASPECTS

The mental-creative principle combines with identity and purpose. This combination indicates that the transformation of sexual-creative energy into artistic and mental accomplishments is central to the life purpose.

Harmonious aspects point to strength of character, intelligence, and courage. These individuals tend to create through artistic, political, or healing forms. Due to the depolarization of male/female roles, the individual usually feels at ease in all types of sexual relationships.

Stressful aspects may symbolize a fear of one's power to accomplish which can lead to blocks in the mental and creative processes. Difficulties may arise in relating to one's father. These individuals may feel alienated from their own sexual identity. Consequently, they can experience confusion in their sexual interactions with others until they clarify their inner confusion.

The resolution of these conflicts lies in learning to harmoniously integrate one's creative aspirations into one's basic life purpose.

Chart Examples: John Lennon, with Pallas conjunct the Sun in Libra, gave a vision of world unity and peace through his songs *Give Peace a Chance*, *Imagine*, and *Power to the People*. (1)

Queen Beatrix of Holland was born with Pallas conjunct her Sun in Aquarius in the eleventh house. She is an independent, intelligent woman with a law degree who has spent her life training for her civic position as Queen of the Netherlands. (2)

Naturalist Charles Darwin,ho has Pallas conjunct the Sun in Aquarius, caused a revolution in biological science with his original theories of evolution through natural selection.

Scientist and writer Rachel Carson, with Pallas conjunct the Sun in Gemini, called public attention to the wasteful and destructive use of pesticides through her book *Silent Spring*. (1)

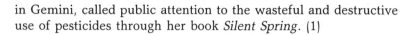

PALLAS-MOON ASPECTS

The mental-creative principle combines with emotions and feelings. This combination can show a fusion of intellect and emotion, producing a clear perception of the world of feelings.

Harmonious aspects can denote a highly intuitive and fertile mind as well as overall psychic ability. One's female powers and abilities will be strongly experienced and clearly expressed. These individuals may become involved with the protection and defense of minority groups.

Stressful aspects may signify an ongoing conflict between mind and feelings, between meeting one's emotional versus one's achievement needs. These people may experience alienation from their mothers and consequently from their own female identity. Other difficulties may include feelings of dependency and powerlessness due to a lack of education and self-confidence.

The resolution of these conflicts lies in acknowledging a feminine-defined intelligence which integrates the mind and heart, logical thought with intuition, warmth, and feeling.

Chart Examples: Simone de Beauvoir, who was born with Pallas in Virgo in the tenth house opposing a Pisces Moon, was a brilliant philosopher of existentialism. Along with Jean-Paul Sartre she presided over avant-garde Parisian intelligentsia. (2)

Frederic Chopin, a master of piano composition known for his romantic, haunting melodies, has Pallas in Aries opposed to the Moon in Libra. (3)

Powerful ruler of Russia, Catherine the Great, with Pallas on a Sagittarius Midheaven opposed to Moon, encouraged science, literature, art, and the development of national culture. (2)

Scientist Willy Ley who has Pallas conjunct the Moon in Aries is a prolific writer on space travel and rocketry. (1)

PALLAS-MERCURY ASPECTS

The mental-creative principle combines with the intellect. This combination greatly heightens the creative intelligence symbolized by Pallas Athene.

Harmonious aspects depict strong creative-intellectual capacities. These individuals often display power and skill in the use of words and the communications media. They may be adept in the arts of mediation, negotiation, affirmation, and positive thinking.

Stressful aspects signify potential blockages in one's ability to reason, create, and verbally express one's ideas. This aspect may point to learning problems or to perceptual, auditory, or mental dysfunctions.

The resolution of these challenges lies in aligning one's rational faculties with the creative-impulsive so that one can successfully communicate one's original ideas.

Chart Examples: Marie Curie, the only person to win a Nobel Prize in both chemistry and physics, has Pallas conjunct Mercury at her Sagittarius Midheaven. Yet, she was never admitted to the Academy of Sciences because she was a woman. (2)

Chiang Kai-shek, political and military leader of the Nationalist Chinese government, has Pallas conjunct Mercury in Scorpio in the ninth house. (3)

PALLAS-VENUS ASPECTS

The mental-creative principle combines with the feminine principle of love and sensuality.

Since Venus is the goddess of beauty, this blend highlights the aesthetic qualities of Pallas Athene.

Harmonious aspects indicate the ability to channel sexual energy into artistic expression. One's feminine sexual identity can also be integrated with outer world accomplishments. Because of the internal sexual balance that is present, the individual may be androgynous and experience ease in a variety of sexual interactions. There may be a desire to become an advocate and protector of women's equal rights.

Stressful aspects can signify a blockage in sexual-creative expression. Conflicting choices between intimate relating and creative accomplishment may lead to a sacrifice of one for the benefit of the other. Confusion over the nature of one's female sexual identity may also exist.

The resolution of these conflicts lies in learning not only to actively create in the outer world, but also to become receptive and open so that one can attract the necessary inspiration. In a general sense, this represents balancing one's internal male and female energies.

Chart Examples: Singer Elton John's androgynous orientation and creative productivity is portrayed by his Pallas-Venus conjunction in the seventh house. (1)

Yoko Ono's Pallas-Venus conjunction in Aquarius in the fifth house depicts her avant-garde artistic creativity as well as her independent love-life style. (2)

PALLAS-MARS ASPECTS

The mental-creative principle combines with the masculine principle of action and assertion. This combination emphasizes the valor and activism of Pallas Athene.

Harmonious aspects denote the ability to execute well-thought plans with strategic skill and confidence. One has the capacity to actively fight for cherished ideas and emerge victorious. The masculine energies are very well developed and expressed.

Stressful aspects can signify a blockage in sexual-creative expression or the inability to actualize creative ideas. The sexual frustration can lead to feelings of sexual inadequacy and compensatory militant behavior. There may also exist confusion over one's masculine sexual identity with either too little or too much masculine expression.

The resolution of these challenges lies in aligning one's creative thought processes with will and execution. Learning to access one's inner strength and courage appropriately will facilitate this process.

Chart Examples: Consumer crusader and protector Ralph Nader has been true to his calling of Pallas conjunct Mars in Pisces. (4)

Billy Graham, charismatic and aggressive evangelist, has Pallas conjunct Mars in Sagittarius. (4)

PALLAS-VESTA ASPECTS

The focusing principle combines with creative self-expression. This is a powerful combination for focusing and manifesting one's visions.

Harmonious aspects can depict the capacity to become inspired by an idea or dedicated to a cause. These individuals have the ability to sublimate sexual energy into artistic, political, intellectual, or spiritual pursuits. This aspect can also signify a talent for the healing arts.

Stressful aspects can point to blocks in the expression of one's intellect or creativity. Moreover, excessive involvement in one's personal creative process can lead to social and sexual alienation from others. In some instances, the potential for political fanaticism may be present.

The resolution of these challenges lies in using Vesta's self-integrated and focused energies for the transmission and actualization of creative ideas.

Chart Examples: Carrie Nation, who had Vesta in Virgo opposing Pallas in Pisces, saw visions and felt destined in her crusade against alcoholic beverages. (1)

Rudolf Nureyev expressed the tension of his Vesta in Sagittarius squaring Pallas in Pisces by defecting from Russia in order to pursue his dance career. (3)

PALLAS-JUNO ASPECTS

The mental-creative principle combines with the relating urge. This combination uses partnerships to enhance the creative process.

Harmonious aspects denote the capacity to work with others to produce creative accomplishments. The male and female polarities within can be balanced, thereby bringing harmony and cooperation in one's outer relationships. These individuals often encourage and support the creative development of their partners.

Stressful aspects point to potential for conflict between creativity needs and relationship needs. Perhaps the partner may place limitations on one's creativity and intellectual accomplishments. In addition, imbalances in one's own male/female polarity may cause difficulties in relating to others (e.g., early father complexes may be carried over into adult relationships).

The resolution of these challenges lies in acknowledging the value of others in one's creative process and finding a way to incorporate their contributions while still being true to oneself.

Chart Examples: Mary Shelley's wonderfully creative relationship with her husband Percy is depicted by her Pallas-Juno conjunction in Virgo in the fourth house. (2)

Occultist Aleister Crowley, who was born with Pallas conjunct Juno in Virgo opposed to a Pisces Moon, wrote of the power of creative visualization in sexual rites with partners. (1)

Elizabeth Arden, born with Pallas conjunct Juno in Capricorn, created a successful cosmetic empire. (2)

PALLAS-JUPITER ASPECTS

The mental-creative principle combines with the expansive broadening urge.

As Jupiter symbolizes the search for truth and meaning, this combination emphasizes and enhances the wisdom activity of Pallas Athene.

Harmonious aspects signify the potential for exceptional intelligence. These individuals are likely to possess a broad, farseeing mind that grasps the implications of the large social issues that face humanity. They may engage in philosophical, judicial, or educational pursuits, or become involved in fighting for justice or defending the truth.

Stressful aspects may point to potential conflicts between one's ambition and ethics, especially if the individual has inflated achievement needs. These may be caused by the high expectations communicated by the father to the child. This aspect may also signify mental blocks in expressing or understanding concepts and ideas.

The resolution of these challenges lies in giving ones mental-creative powers an expanded scope of social expression, one that benefits the highest social good.

Chart Examples: Metaphysical writer Paul Foster Case, founder of the B.O.T.A. arcane school of the *Tarot* and Qabalah, was born with Pallas conjunct Jupiter in Leo. (4)

Sir Winston Churchill, Prime Minister of Great Britain throughout World War II and one of the great statesmen of world history, aptly portrayed his Pallas in Aries opposed to Jupiter in Libra. (1)

Actress Vanessa Redgrave's statement, "I choose my roles very carefully, so that when my career is finished, I will have covered all our recent history of oppression," depicts her Pallas-Jupiter conjunction in Capricorn in the fifth house. (2)

PALLAS-SATURN ASPECTS

The mental-creative principle combines with the consolidation urge. This combination can lead to the concrete realization of one's creative ideas that arises from the ability to infuse self-discipline and structure into one's creative process.

Harmonious aspects signify the capacity for mental concentration and focus. These individuals may experience a sense of social responsibility and campaign against unjust social laws. The attributes of strength and success may strongly contribute to the feminine identity.

Stressful aspects point to potential conflicts between the need for pragmatism and freedom of artistic expression which can lead to the blocking of the creative process. Parental pressure and high expectations for success may cause these individuals to lack confidence in their own creative-mental abilities.

The resolution of these challenges lies in using Saturn to develop a strong structural and stable foundation which will support and help to realize one's mental and creative processes.

Chart Examples: Revolutionary thinker Karl Marx focused his idealistic political views through his Pallas-Saturn conjunction in Pisces in the first house. (1)

Eva Braun with Pallas conjunct Saturn in the seventh house portrayed the sacrifice of her creative potentials in the years of friendship, loyalty, and loneliness as Hitler's mistress. (2)

PALLAS-URANUS ASPECTS

The mental-creative principle combines with individuality and intuition.

People with this combination can universalize the creative impulse to produce a visionary and humanitarian perception.

Harmonious aspects may describe an original and intuitive mind that is especially creative in the fields of science and technology. There may exist the ability to work with electrical fields in healing. These individuals may become involved in social reform, human rights struggles, or revolutionary causes. This aspect can also depict an inclination toward androgyny with the capacity to befriend all types of people.

Stressful aspects point to the tendency for erratic thinking and an overloaded nervous system to inhibit the full expression of mental creativity. The need to be unconventional may also lead to excessively rebellious ideas and behavior.

The resolution of these challenges lies in aligning one's mental-creative impulses with the higher channels of intuition and transpersonal thought.

Chart Examples: Iconoclast Alan Watts manifested unconventional values represented by his Pallas-Uranus conjunction in Aquarius in the second house. (1)

Pilot Helen Boucher set seven world speed records and specialized in aviation acrobatics displaying her first-house Pallas trining a fifth-house Uranus. (2)

PALLAS-NEPTUNE ASPECTS

The mental-creative principle combines with the transcendent urge.

Individuals with this combination can sensitize their perceptions and allow access to more subtle realms and dimensions.

Harmonious aspects can describe telepathic abilities and the capacity for psychic healing using color and music. Special talents may manifest in the fine arts, film, and photography. These individuals may possess a high degree of faith and spirituality.

Stressful aspects can point to confusion in one's perception of reality with the inability to distinguish between the real and unreal.

In some instances, mental delusions and hallucinations may occur. Due to the impressionality symbolized by Neptune, these individuals may attract negative psychic influences. They may also experience a dissolution of their belief system or become inculcated with blind faith.

The resolution of these conflicts lies in using one's mental creativity to develop a holistic and realistic perception of subtle dimensions as they interact with earthbound reality.

Chart Examples: Saint Francesca Cabrini, who sublimated her sexual and relationship needs toward divine service, was born with Pallas conjunct Neptune in Pisces in the seventh house. (2)

Other metaphysicians who have Pallas-Neptune aspects include Alice Bailey (2), Helena P. Blavatsky (2), Richard Alpert (1), Marc Edmund Jones (1), and Nostradamus (3).

Minette Lenier, magician creating illusion for entertainment, has Pallas conjunct Neptune in the fifth house. (2)

PALLAS-PLUTO ASPECTS

The mental-creative principle combines with the transformative urge. This combination emphasizes the power of ideas to transform reality.

Harmonious aspects can point to the power of the mind to create ideas that will influence and transform others. There may exist the capacity to work with regenerative healing techniques, as well as inventive and artistic processes. In addition, one's inner and outer male/female identity and roles may be subject to far-reaching changes.

Stressful aspects can signify deep unconscious blockages in the expression of one's sexual identity and creative potential. There may also exist powerful mental obsessions and fixations that dominate one's thinking.

The resolution of these conflicts lies in releasing the negative aspects of our mental expression and replacing them with faith, hope, and optimism. As an ancient spiritual proverb puts it, "Be ye transformed through the renewing of your mind."

Chart Examples: Alexander Graham Bell, with Pallas conjunct Pluto and Uranus in Aries, transformed the world through his ideas and inventions. He also taught music and speech for deaf children. (1)

Investigator of the unconscious Sigmund Freud was born with Pallas conjunct Vesta and Pluto in Taurus in the sixth house. (1)

CHAPTER EIGHT

VESTA: THE ETERNAL FLAME

And third, the things that Aphrodite does are not
pleasing to that venerable virgin Hestia,
Whom Cronus in his craftiness first gave
birth to (and also last - thanks to Zeus
who carries the aegis), the lady that
Poseidon and Apollo were both after. She
didn't want them, she refused them firmly.
And she swore a great oath on it, one that
was fulfilled, touching the head of father
Zeus who carries the aegis, that she would
be a virgin every day, a divine goddess.
And father Zeus gave her a wedding gift: he has
her sit in the center of the house to receive the
best in offerings. In all temples
of the gods she is honored, and among all
mortals she is a venerated goddess.[1]

The Mythology of Vesta

Vesta, known to the ancient Greeks as Hestia, is symbolized by the Virgin who appears in the Virgo pictograph. The Romans worshipped her as goddess of the hearth and keeper of the sacred flame (her name is derived from the Sanskrit root *vas*, meaning "shining"). While not the largest of the asteroids, Vesta is the brightest and the only one

1. Homer,"The Hymn to Aphrodite," *The Homeric Hymns*, trans. Charles Boer (Texas: Spring Publications, Inc., 1979), 70.

that can be seen with the naked eye. This is due to the fact that Vesta is composed of an unusual type of volcanic surface rock, caused by extremely high internal temperatures, that reflects a remarkable amount of sunlight.[2] Thus, Vesta's association with the element of fire aptly corresponds to her luminous astronomical qualities.

As goddess of the hearth fire, Vesta had a shrine placed at the center of every household and at the central public hearth of every city. She became the symbol of the guardian of the home and community, thereby insuring the cohesion of family and state. Vesta's priestesses of Rome were known as the vestal virgins. Sworn to celibacy, their duty was to tend the sacred flame.

Because few artistic representations or legends concerning Vesta exist, she is the most difficult to understand of all goddesses. Consequently, Vesta is dismissed by many mythological writers as bland, dull, and unworthy of serious study. Yet, Vesta's meaning and significance are available to us if we pay close attention to her story, a tale that will carry us through Greece, Rome, and the pre-Hellenic civilizations.

THE STORY OF VESTA

In Greek mythology, Vesta was the first Olympian to be born to Cronus (Saturn) and Rhea and the last to be reborn when Zeus (Jupiter) freed his siblings from Saturn's stomach. Subsequently, Vesta chose to remain a virgin, refusing to marry either Apollo or Poseidon.

Hestia emigrated to Greece from Mycenaean Crete at a very early period. Although there existed no images of her at time, she was worshipped in all Greek towns where an altar to Hestia was placed at the *prythaneum*, the public hearth which contained the sacred fire. This fire symbolized the unity and cohesion of the family and state. Thus, when emigrating to foreign lands, Greek colonists brought a portion of the fire with them in order to link their new community with their homeland. Likewise, women leaving home brought fire from their mothers' hearths in order to begin their own.

Because she was the first of the Olympians, the Greeks initiated a tradition that ceremonies and new enterprises would begin with an offering to the altar of Hestia. In addition, she received the best parts of the sacrifices offered at the temples of the other gods. With every burnt offering, her presence was acknowledged as the goddess

2. William K. Hartman, "Vesta, A World of Its Own," *Astronomy*, vol. 77, no. 2 (February 1983).

of the sacred hearth and altar flame.

Hestia embodied the meaning of honest and faithful dealings; hence, her name was used to seal oaths and social contracts. Hestia also governed the sacred law of hospitality, with her offerings of the warmth of the hearth fire, food, and shelter to strangers. Her hearth therefore became known as a sanctuary of protection.

THE VESTAL VIRGINS

Following the Greeks, the Romans absorbed Hestia and renamed her Vesta. In tribute to her, *Numa Pompilius*, the second king of Rome, built a temple designed to ensure the safety of the Roman Empire whose center contained Vesta's eternal fire. The sacred responsibility of tending the flames was given to the priestesses of the goddess Vesta, the vestal virgins. First two, then four, then six in number, these divine servants were chosen from the loveliest and noblest of all Roman maidens. Admitted into the temple at the age of six, they took vows of chastity and celibacy which lasted for the duration of their 30-year service. Aside from tending the sacred flame, their duties included purifying the shrine with holy water each morning, performing daily devotions and offerings, and guarding sacred relics. Upon completing their term, the priestesses were granted the liberty to leave and marry. Apparently few did.

The *Pontifex Maximus* who chose the virgins had absolute authority over their lives and inflicted harsh punishments for their offenses. Since the sacred fire's extinction was considered a threat to the safety of the state, the priestess who allowed it to go out would be severely whipped. Moreover, those who broke the primary vow of chastity were meted out a cruel death. After being publicly whipped, the condemned priestess was bound and carried via procession to a subterranean crypt. There she was walled up alive with a light, a few provisions, and left to die a slow, agonizing death.

Perhaps to compensate for the severity of their lifestyle, the vestal virgins were granted many privileges in Rome. The priestesses were free from paternal control and possessed the right to own and dispose of their property. The best seats in the theater were reserved for them. During processions, the virgins were preceded by a *lictor*, a symbol honoring their sovereign power, while consuls and proctors bowed before them. If a priestess met a criminal on his way to execution, she had the power to set him free. Wills and solemn contracts were placed in the hands of the virgins for safekeeping. Finally, the vestals could choose to be buried within city limits, a privilege normally reserved for a select few.

Statues of Vesta from this period portray a woman of majestic beauty clad in long, white robes, holding a lighted torch or candle in one hand and a votive bowl in the other. In this pose, she embodies the qualities of purity, safety, divine protection, and security.

Festivals honoring Vesta were celebrated on March 1 of each year when the vestals doused and relit their sacred fire. On June 9 (the *Vestalia*) the temple was opened to the matrons of the city who brought plates of food baked on their own hearths. After a week of offerings, the temple was closed, cleansed, and purified. The vestals continued their rituals until the fifth century AD when the Christian Emperor Theodosius abolished the worship of Vesta, dispersed the vestals, and extinguished the sacred flame. This was the same ruler who had ended the Eleusinian Mysteries of Ceres/Demeter.

THE PRE-HELLENIC ORIGINS OF VESTA

The story of Vesta ends here. Due to the lack of tales that describe her legend, it is difficult to unravel her origins prior to Hellenic times; yet, the clues to her essence point to the center. The guarding and tending of the original altar, the hearth fire, was the center of the feminine mysteries which were conspicuously preserved in ancient Rome as the cult of Vesta, and its round temple.[3] At Delphi, Vesta was worshipped as a heap of glowing charcoals which became known as the *omphalos* (navel) or center of the Greek world.[4] By tracing back the path of the priestesses who kept Vesta alive through tending her sacred flame, we are able to arrive at the place of her throne.

In the ancient world of pre-Hellenic Greece, the chief deity was the Great Mother Goddess who was worshipped in the form of the moon. The women priestesses of this time fostered the fertilizing power of the moon through caring for the water supply and tending a sacred flame which could not be allowed to die.[5] Aside from representing the light of the moon, the sacred flame symbolized the *kundalini* fires of Indian *yogic* practice and the secret powers of sexual transmutation. The women who tended the perpetual fires were known as virgins, not because they were sexually chaste, but because

3. Erich Neumann, *The Great Mother*, trans. Ralph Manheim (Princeton, New Jersey: Princeton University Press, 1974), 284.
4. Barbara Koltuv, "Hestia/Vesta," *Quadrant 10* (Winter 1977), 57.
5. M. Esther Harding, *Woman's Mysteries: Ancient and Modern* (New York: Harper and Row, 1976), 127.

they remained unmarried and belonged to no man. Thus, the virgins existed as whole and complete unto themselves; they had no need of being defined or controlled by a man.

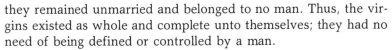

These vestals also served as sacred harlots who sexually gave of themselves to strangers — men who came to the temple to honor the goddess and partake of the sacred union. They used their sexuality not to satisfy their own needs, attract a husband, nor to procreate; "their woman's nature was dedicated to a higher purpose, that of bringing the fertilizing power of the goddess into effective contact with the lives of human beings."[6] Moreover, any child born of a virgin priestess who had been conceived during the sacred union was called divine and took on a special destiny in the royal succession.

The vestals, it seems, transmitted the royal line of descent in the following manner. Each year at midsummer a marriage feast of the oak-queen and oak-king was arranged in which six vestals coupled with six of the oak-king's twelve companions. This promiscuous lovemaking took place in the darkness of a sacred cave so that nobody knew who lay with whom nor who was the father of any child. The rite was again repeated at the midwinter feast of *Saturnalia*. Subsequently, if the oak-queen failed to have a son, the new king was chosen from a child born to a vestal and served only one year.[7]

The above tale explains the origins of the legends that describe how Latin kings were born of a virgin mother with no known father or to be the son of the god.[8] In fact, many of the kings of early Rome were the sons of vestal virgins. The most famous of these was Romulus, first king of Rome, who was born to the vestal virgin Rhea Silvia. Consequently, the community's religious and political focus centered around the hearth fire of the royal house which was tended by the princesses of the royal line, namely the vestal virgins.

As time passed, however, and the patriarchal culture began to assume prominence, the line of descent shifted away from the vestals to the kings-by-marriage who implemented ways to retain their throne. Gradually, they extended the kingship from one year, to four years, to eight, to nineteen, until finally it became a life tenure. To further insure that the line of descent remained on the male side,

---

6. Harding, *Women's Mysteries*. 132.
7. Robert Graves, *The White Goddess* (New York: Farrar, Straus and Giroux, 1978), 357.
8. Graves, *The White Goddess*, 357.

the king, on the death of his wife, married either his own daughter or her heir; or arranged for his son to marry them. This phenomenon accounts for the widespread custom of brother-sister marriages within royal families during this era.

As a result of the rise of the patriarchal culture, the vestal love nymphs were eventually reduced to the barren spinster nuns of the Middle Ages. This process began when the Roman King Tarquin the Elder, to prevent the vestals from breeding claimants to the throne, ordered that the virgins remain sexually chaste or be punished by death. The college of vestal virgins was then founded to contain the heiresses and nullify any attempts made to reestablish the matrilineal throne. Likewise, King David of Palestine established the royal harem for the same purpose — to isolate the women of the royal house of Saul and to preserve the monarchy in his own family.[9]

The essence of Vesta's original tradition consisted of the sexual rites honoring the fertilizing and generative powers of the Moon goddess which provided for a divinely blessed rulership. It was for this reason that Vesta was venerated as idealized maternity. Patriarchal rule obscured Vesta's functions and transformed her into the virgin goddess of purity and sexual chastity. In this light the hidden meaning of Homer's hymn concerning Vesta's virginity becomes apparent. By virtue of her seniority Vesta was granted her request to remain virgin — that is, not to be violated by being owned by Poseidon or Apollo in monogamous marriage. In return she swore a great oath to be a virgin in the new sense — denying her sacred sexual customs so that the transition of power from matrilineal to patrilineal descent could be smoothly effected.

Although the sexual rites of the pre-Hellenic vestal virgins were completely lost by Imperial Roman times, they were nevertheless observed on a sacred symbolic level. The Temple of Vesta contained a cupboard near the hearth called the *Penus*. Within the *Penus*, hidden from sight, lay a phallic statue known as the *Palladium*, named after the gods *Pales, Pallas*, and *Priapus*. This phallic symbol became united with the Moon goddess, symbolized by the glowing coals of the hearth, and created the deity *Pabulum* from which we derive the word pabulum signifying food).[10] This union was considered to be of such importance that the safekeeping of the *Palladium* was believed to insure the safety and continuity of the Roman state.

9. Robert Graves, *The Greek Myths* Vol. I (Maryland: Penguin Books, 1955), 20.
10. Harding, *Women's Mysteries*, 33.

THE TRUE MEANING OF VESTA

Based upon the preceding mythology, we can see that the deeper significance of Vesta is revealed through her central symbol, the hearth — the place in the center where the fire is maintained. This fire, central to the survival of ancient cultures, served as a gathering point for the community (the Latin word for hearth is *focus*). Because the fires were so necessary yet difficult to procure and maintain, they and their keepers were venerated. Ovid states, "Conceive of Vesta as naught but the living flame"; and "Vesta is the same as the earth. . . under both of them is a perpetual fire."[11] This eternal fire also contained the spark of fertility. Hence, behind the veil of chastity and barrenness, the inner nature of Vesta is the sexuality and fertilizing power of the Goddess. Hence, Vesta's two central themes focus on her fire and sexual symbology. We shall discover how these themes express themselves in the horoscope through exploring Vesta's astro-psychology.

VESTA

Greek Hestia

Principle of Focus and Commitment

Character
Goddess of the Hearth Fire
Priestess

Glyph ⚶

Fire of the Hearth

Symbols
eternal flame
torch
altar fire
donkey

Associated Rulerships
Virgo
Scorpio

Polarities
Devotion/Fanaticism

11. Ovid, *Fasti*, trans. Sir James Frazer (Cambridge: Harvard University Press), 341.

The Astrology of Vesta

Because Vesta, the keeper of the vestal virgins, is depicted as the Virgin in the Virgo pictograph, most astrologers have given it rulership over that sign. Vesta, however, also has a strong affinity with the sign of Scorpio. Vesta's dual rulership over Scorpio and Virgo becomes clearer when we examine the astronomical origins of these signs.

In the original zodiacal belt outlined by the Assyrian and Babylonian cultures, Scorpio was symbolized by a serpent and directly followed the sign Virgo. What is today called Libra was contained within the constellation Scorpio and was designated as "the Chelae," the claws of the scorpion. The Virgo and Scorpio glyphs were similar in design but contained subtle distinctions. In the Virgo glyph, the "M" of matter (mother) was turned inward (♍) while the Scorpio "M" of matter (mother) was turned outward (♏). Hence, her reign of supremacy, the ancient Great Mother Goddess simultaneously manifested as both Virgo virgin and Scorpio consort. Only with the ascent of the patriarchal culture was Libra, sign of marriage, placed between Virgo and Scorpio by Greek astronomers whose society created an artificial duality in a woman's sexual identity. From then on, a woman was either virgin-chaste before marriage (Virgo) or a sexual consort after marriage (Scorpio). The recent discovery of Vesta has given us a means of healing this unhealthy split by reuniting the Virgo-Scorpio themes of this archetype. In the following pages, we shall examine how Vesta's essential meaning can give astrologers greater insight into the nature of these two sister signs.

Vesta as a Ruler of Scorpio

VESTA AS SEXUALITY

As we witnessed in the mythology section, the vestal virgin of the Roman era later evolved into the archetype of the nun — a woman whose sole function was that of work and religious devotion and whose life was totally devoid of sexual intimacy and personal relationships. This image has come down to us as the barren spinster or old maid. The only difficulty with this description of Vesta is that it does not always hold true in actual chart interpretations. Repeatedly, we have found prominent Vestas in the horoscopes of sexually active men and women. Their sexuality, however, is not confined within the boundaries of traditional, monogamous relationships.

For example, women, married or single, with strong Vesta emphases in their horoscopes may engage in sexual encounters with a variety of men. Yet, the nature of these sexual unions is by no means profane; on the contrary, the participants describe them as transcendent, spiritual, and healing. It is as if these women are unconsciously recreating the ancient sexual rituals of the original vestal virgins. In those rituals, the virgins used their sexuality not to capture a husband but to serve the Moon goddess and bless the lives of her human devotees. Yet, modern society ignores the purity of these motivations and condemns such open sexual expression as immoral and wicked. All too often this condemnation is internalized, and our modern-day vestals experience guilt and shame over their sexual responses.

In a similar manner, Vesta-type men possess a high degree of sensitivity to the sexual needs of women and a strong desire to enter into sexual union with them. At the same time, their "virgin" nature causes them to remain whole unto themselves and avoid long-term commitment. Consequently, these men are labeled gigolos, heartbreakers, users, or "only after one thing."

Thus, a strong Vesta points to a variety of possible sexual expressions that include sexual denial, sexual union outside the marriage, and, at an extreme, promiscuity and prostitution. In these latter cases, the individuals who outwardly express rebellion and defiance against traditional mores may subliminally feel a sense of shame and guilt over their actions.

SEX AS SIN

From the preceding paragraphs, it should be evident that Vesta in the chart can symbolize either sexual freedom or sexual repression. In our culture, the latter pathology is far more prevalent due to the fact that women's sexuality has been stifled in order to effect the patrilineal inheritance of land by demanding unquestionable assurance of paternity. As we observed through studying Vesta's mythology, as the patriarchy gained power, powerful taboos for women were issued against premarital sex, postmarital infidelity, illegitimate children, and abortion. In short, sex without marriage (Libra) became an unforgivable sin. This in turn created an artificial separation between spirituality (Virgo) and sexuality (Scorpio) that has endured for millennia in the collective psyche. It comes as no surprise, therefore, that many individuals with prominent Vestas experience shame, guilt, and self-denial over their sexuality. In working with these clients, it is helpful to give them an understanding of the origin of these sexual taboos and to show them that their sexual desires, in light of Vesta's ancient practices, are not sinful or wicked. Sex is, however, a powerful force that can be abused if not used responsibly. Thus, Vesta types need to find a balance in their sexual expression that avoids the two extremes of promiscuity and total repression.

SEX AS FEAR

The second major pathological expression of Vesta's sexuality is the association of sex with fear. The root cause of this complex is once again to be found in the cruel practices that occurred during the transition between the matriarchal and patriarchal cultures. The sacred sexual customs of the goddess were denigrated and prohibited, and men assumed the right to sexual satisfaction with no thought of women's pleasures. As detailed in the mythology section, a slow and tortuous live burial was given to any vestal virgin who broke the vow of chastity. These racial imprints carry over today in the psyches of many contemporary men and women. Even after marriage many individuals continue to experience fears of sexuality, intimacy, alienation from relationships, and the inability to conceive — typical Vesta challenges. Although the negative consequences of the repression of sexual energy were uncovered by Sigmund Freud, their effects are still bringing frustrations and disappointments into the sexual lives of many individuals.

SEXUAL REPRESSION

In the Olympian family, Vesta was the eldest child of Saturn. Vesta's affinity with Saturn is also evidenced by the fact that they rule the earth signs of Virgo and Capricorn. Vesta and Saturn both express the principles of limitation, boundaries, focus, and commitment. Thus, the sexual restrictions depicted by Vesta are similar to those described by hard aspects of Saturn to the sexual planets of Venus and Mars. These configurations can indicate a blockage or restriction of the sexual response that often arises from painful memories associating sex with death and dishonor.

When Vesta adversely aspects Mars and other masculine planets, the sexual blockage can manifest as physical or psychological impotence. The ability to act and be effective might be impaired, and subsequent feelings of failure and the inability to pursue other "masculine" activities often follow. Aggressive and macho behavior may be expressed in order to compensate for the inner experience of inadequacy.

When Vesta aspects the classic female planets or asteroids (Venus or Juno), the woman may feel unable to love or relate meaningfully. This in turn may lead to physical or psychological frigidity. In order to compensate for her inadequacies, she may adopt a false veneer of independence, claiming she doesn't need men while inwardly longing for a relationship.

In each of the above cases the blockage of the sexual principle leads to a thwarting of intimate and fulfilling relationships in the life of the individual. This inability to fully share oneself with others is one of the most painful possibilities shown by an afflicted Vesta.

VESTA AND PROJECTION

When the restrictive principle of Vesta contacts the male principle in a woman's chart (Vesta aspecting the Sun or Mars) or the female principle in a man's chart (Vesta aspecting the Moon or Venus), the inner fear and lack of trust are often projected outward. As a result, the potential partner will be perceived as brutal, tyrannical, demanding, or manipulating. Ironically, this type of paranoia often becomes a self-fulfilling prophecy as the individual attracts the very mate he or she is afraid of ("The thing that I feared most has come upon me"). Responses of self-protection often manifest as detachment, coolness, withdrawal, and giving oneself physically but withholding emotionally. These attitudes become a means of maintaining distance, control, and power over the feared other. For such people, ongoing therapy may be needed to transform their neurotic fear patterns into those of love and trust.

VESTA AND SEXUAL DISCRIMINATION

Because Vesta types carry the subconscious memories of sex as an experience of heightened spiritual intensity, they embrace extremely high standards concerning sex. Unfortunately, this attitude brings with it an inevitable disappointment with most sexual couplings which they regard as mundane, unfulfilling, and even degrading. Their subsequent inability to participate in ordinary sex in order to hold out for ecstatic sex generally results in not much sex at all. Unfortunately, this kind of sexual idealism is often misunderstood by their thwarted mates who will accuse the Vesta individual of being cold, unfeeling, and devoid of sexual interest. Ironically many Vesta types who do not understand their own motives for being sexually discriminating will accept these negative judgments as valid. There is a particularly poignant pathos to this kind of Vesta alienation.

In summation, Vesta, in its original and true meaning, represents sexuality as an expression of spiritual devotion. However, she has come to be distorted in the modern psyche and too often represents sexual inadequacy, denial, fear of intimacy and commitment, celibacy, barrenness, promiscuity, and a vast range of sexual difficulties resulting from the repression of natural instincts.

Vesta as a Ruler of Virgo

The development of sexual energy traced through the cycle of the signs goes through a critical change from Leo to Virgo. Leo embodies the instinctive spontaneous expression of the sexual energy as the creative principle through physical or mental children. It is the impulse of the evolving life entity to reproduce itself. In Virgo, the reproductive energy of Venus is used spiritually to transform and regenerate the self so that it may become a channel of service and healing.

Vesta is the means by which this transition from Leo to Virgo takes place. Astrologically, therefore, individuals with prominent Vestas can sublimate and transform their sexual energy into one-pointed focus, unobstructed commitment, and dedication to work. On the inner planes, the transmuted energy brings about personal integration and wholeness. Clearly, these are all well-known characteristics of the sign Virgo.

VESTA AND VIRGINITY

In her original nature, the virginal quality of Vesta did not mean that she was sexually chaste. Quite the contrary, Vesta freely expressed her sexuality. Being a virgin meant that she was whole and complete unto herself — self-contained, self-possessed, and self-fulfilled. A virgin, therefore, was not barren, but especially fertile as in a virgin forest that has not been violated or depleted.

In order to renew their virginity, the vestals bathed in a number of sacred springs. After their sexual encounters, they would withdraw back into themselves to regenerate their inner wholeness. Therefore, transits to and from Vesta signify times when we need to retreat from the outer world to purify, replenish, and reintegrate ourselves. These withdrawals often follow times when we have depleted our resources due to excessive involvement with people or events. Perhaps this explains why many Vesta transits point to relationship separations. During these periods, the need exists to seek out aloneness in order to renew one's virginity and rebuild the self in preparation for the next cycle of relating. Astrologically, Vesta denotes the capacity to be self-identified, whole, and fertile.

When Vesta is stressfully aspected in the natal chart, the personality may be unable to integrate itself and remains depleted of its vital energy. Infertility, barrenness, or sterility are other responses to these patterns. Alienation may be experienced until the individual learns to manifest a healthy focus on self and an ability to stand alone, when appropriate, with a sense of inner strength.

VESTA AND CENTEREDNESS

The Greeks portrayed Vesta as the *omphalos*, navel, or center of the world. As the hearth fire at the center of the home, Vesta provided a gathering place for the family. Likewise, Vesta functions as the center of the psyche, coordinating various facets of the personality. Astrologically, Vesta symbolizes individuals who are "centered" in their own identity and thus self-determined in their activities. Stressful aspects to the planets may portray a person who is off-center, off-base, or not yet able to find a place.[12]

VESTA AND FOCUS

As we have seen, the essence of Vesta was embodied in the fire of the hearth. The Latin word for hearth is *focus*. As the principle of focus, Vesta gathers energy and brings it to a single point, thereby bringing clarity and illumination. Astrologically, individuals with strong Vestas possess the ability to concentrate their energies to a point of focus and give their undivided attention to whatever they are doing. When Vesta is stressfully aspected, the focus could be too vague, unclear and spacey. At the other extreme, the focus may be too tight, causing one to have a narrow-minded and restricted view of the world.

VESTA AND COMMITMENT

By the constructive use of Vesta's attributes, a person can become self-determined, integrated, intact, centered, and focused. Through this process, people gain the ability to dedicate and commit themselves to some goal or aspiration. A stressful Vesta, therefore, might indicate someone who fears to make commitments or is unable to keep them.

---

12. Barbara Kirksey, "Hestia: A Background of Psychological Focusing," in *Facing the Gods*, ed. James Hillman (Texas: Spring Publications, Inc., 1980), 105.

VESTA AND WORK

Vesta also signifies a person's work in terms of the path that one must take in order to fulfill his or her *dharma*. This focus goes beyond the personal and extends outward to the society and the planet. If individuals are denied the opportunity to perform this type of work, they will become frustrated and discontent. Thus, the Vesta individual must truly "do his/her own thing." In our patriarchal culture, women have had to put aside meeting this fundamental need. Fortunately, this inequity is slowly being remedied.

VESTA, ALIENATION AND SACRIFICE

The act of concentrating on one thing implies the need to withdraw one's focus from other areas of life. This in turn brings about a certain estrangement and alienation from the world. Astrologically, Vesta indicates the type of severe alienation that occurs when an individual becomes too absorbed in his or her personal quest. Vesta also suggests the sacrifices one must make in order follow a self-directed path. These sacrifices may include the giving up of family, children, relationships, friends, and home. When carried to an extreme, these activities produce martyrs who totally deny themselves everything and attempt to make others guilty for what they have sacrificed.

Summary

It is these qualities of being self-determined, centered, focused, and immersed in one's identity that describe the true and original meaning of the word virgin. Those who have studied astrology recognize that these qualities are to be found in the Virgo type. With the sextile between Virgo and Scorpio, the element of water nourishes and fructifies the earth element. As we stated at the beginning of this section, Virgo and Scorpio are derived from the same root essence. Thus, the fertile virgin cyclically withdraws in order to prepare herself for the devotional merging that sanctifies the process of creation.

The Occult Teachings of Vesta

Vesta, the Elder keeper of tradition, preserves and hands down ancient ceremonies and rituals which provide forms for the descent of magical energy into the world. Denied the practice of her sexual devotions outwardly with the "other" (♏), Vesta turned the sexual energy inward (♍) to realize the divine through inner union with the self. Her most important occult teachings describe how one may transform sexual energy for the purposes of enlightenment and liberation. Vesta governs the sexual fires known as the *kundalini* force that reside in the etheric body at the base of the spine. When this force is awakened and consciously channeled to higher centers, one gains an increased psychic awareness, ecstatic bliss, and eventual illumination known as "adeptship." The psi circuits running through the etheric body travel along the same circuits as the sexual currents. Thus, while following this particular path, it is usually necessary to abstain from sexual intercourse during the discipleship period in order to avoid overloading these circuits.

In the *tarot*, Vesta corresponds to the Hermit card, also Virgo ruled, who symbolizes ascetic retreat. The Hermit also corresponds to the root letter of the Hebrew alphabet known as the yod. The yod is traditionally depicted as a luminous flame, the very flame that was tended to by the vestal priestesses.

In terms of astrological analysis, individuals who experience a constriction of normal sexual outlets may be doing so in order to commit themselves to psychic and spiritual development. If ordinary outlets were available, there would be no motivation to discover other ways of expressing this powerful and relentless force. Instead, the modern day vestal virgin will often sacrifice personal pleasure in order to obtain a deeper relationship with his or her own soul.

Vesta Psychological Themes

Vesta represents the principle of focus and commitment. She functions as an autonomous being to transform sexual energies and bring about personal integration.

Principle of Focus and Commitment:

dedication and aspiration toward a path or goal • sacrifices that are made to attain that goal

Sexual Themes:

liberated sexuality, sex outside of committed relationships • sexual fears, guilt and inadequacies • frustration, alienation, denial and separation from personal relationships • fears of intimacy and commitment • avoidance of marriage and children

Sublimation of Sexual Energies:

Bhakti Yoga — devotional
Hatha Yoga — physical
Gnani Yoga — intellectual
Raja Yoga — mental
Karma Yoga — work

Principle of Virginity:

one-in-selfness, unmarried, self-contained, self-reliant • personal integration, centeredness, focus • purification, inner strength, self-discipline, asceticism, voluntary simplicity

Occult Themes:

transmutation of the sexual force • union with or the regeneration of the self • psychic development of the psi currents

Further Reading on Vesta

Bolen, Jean Shinoda. "Hestia: Goddess of the Hearth and Temple." In *Goddesses in Everywoman*. San Francisco: Harper and Row, 1984.

Bradley, Marion Zimmer. *The Forbidden Tower*. New York: Daw Books, 1977.

Demetrakopoulus, Stephanie. "Hestia, Goddess of the Hearth." *Spring* (1979).

Graves, Robert. *The White Goddess*. New York: Farrar, Straus and Giroux, 1948.

Harding, Esther M. *Woman's Mysteries: Ancient and Modern*. New York: Harper Colophon Books, 1976.

Homer. "The Hymn to Hestia," "The Second Hymn to Hestia" and "The Hymn to Aphrodite." In *The Homeric Hymns*, translated by Charles Boer. Irving, Texas: Spring Publications, Inc., 1979.

Kirksey, Barbara. "Hestia: Backround of Psychological Focusing." In *Facing the Gods*, edited by James Hillman. Irving, Texas: Spring Publications, Inc., 1980.

Koltuv, Barbara. "Hestia/Vesta." *Quadrant 10* (Winter 1977).

Luke, Helen M. *Woman: Earth and Spirit*. New York: Crossroad, 1981.

CHAPTER NINE

VESTA IN THE HOROSCOPE

As Goddess of the Hearth, the Greeks worshipped Vesta as the keeper of both the sacred fire and the home fire. She was a symbol of protection which insured the cohesion of the state and family for the people of the earth.

Vesta was associated with unmarried temple virgin priestesses who, through sacred sexual religious devotions, brought the fertilizing power of the moon into effective contact with the lives of human beings. Yet, by Roman times, Vesta became the divinity of the vestal virgins who were venerated for their purity in sexual chastity. Vesta's pathology of alienation in intimate relationships stems from the thwarting of natural instincts.

In her role as sister, Vesta represents the principle of focus and commitment. She functions as autonomous self-identity transforming creative energies into purifying and integrating personal circuitry.

Astrologically Vesta describes the ways in which we face the issues of personal integration, work, devotion, commitment, sacrifice, alienation from personal relationships, and a range of sexual complexes based on denial and fear of intimacy.

Vesta in the signs describes twelve styles of focus and commitment, and what we have to exclude from our lives in order to achieve that purpose. Vesta also describes the way in which we deal with personal sexual energy — either through free expression, sublimation, or repression.

Vesta in the houses shows the area of one's dedication and commitment, as well as where one is most likely to experience limitation.

Vesta's aspects to the planets describes how the focusing, self-involvement principle may be integrated with other parts of the personality. Harmonious aspects indicate an easy blending, while stressful contacts signify potential conflicts between needs for self-containment and other psychic requirements of the individual. When the varying needs are mastered and integrated, an individual with conflicting aspects in the horoscope no longer needs stress in order to learn balance.

Vesta Astrological Rulerships

Vesta rules over personal integration.
disciplined personal routines • health • nutrition • exercise • meditation

Vesta is an indicator of sexuality and sexual complexes.
frigidity • barrenness • impotence • sterility • virginity • chastity • purity • celibacy • fertility • promiscuity • prostitution • pornography • discrimination in sexuality

Vesta signifies devotional and religious activities.
prayer • meditation • devotion • solitary *sadhana* • retreat • religious orders • nuns, priests, priestesses, holy men and women • esoteric orders • religious and magical ceremony and ritual • initiation • vows • commitment • *samaya* • altars and ceremonial objects • altar flames • hearth fires

Vesta is associated with scholastic interests.
scholar • scribe, illuminator • teacher • professor • *guru* • light bearer • keeper of esoteric and religious teachings

Vesta indicates one's work or path of service.
workaholic • sacrifice to reach goals • personal dedication to service, career or cause • transmuting *karma* through *dharma* • fanatic-zealot

Vesta binds together groups sharing a common belief.
fraternal and sororal orders • social or service groups • hospitality • secret societies and orders

Vesta represents the principle of conservatism and safety.
seniority • heritage • tradition • sanctuary • security • protection • contracts • treaties • credibility • locks • keys • safes • fences

Vesta in the Signs

The source of the data for charts cited in the following sections is indicated by a number in parentheses.

(1) Lois Rodden's *The American Book of Charts*
(2) Lois Rodden's *Profiles of Women*
(3) Marc Penfield's *An Astrological Who's Who*

Vesta in Aries people work with a high degree of self-involvement. Motivation arises within the self and these individuals perform best working by themselves or from their own ideas. There exist strong independence needs of not being possessed or dominated by another. Alienation occurs if one becomes excessively self-centered in the vortex of one's own activities, so that there is no space left for the participation of others. Remaining one's own person and retaining individual identity is an important sexual need. However, this individualism can prevent being able to maintain ongoing relationships. This placement can be a key to marked personal accomplishments.

Chart Example: Mary Wells Lawrence, with Vesta conjunct Mars and Uranus in Aries in the eighth house, focused her energies to create her own highly successful advertising agency. (2)

Vesta in Taurus individuals best focus their work energy by becoming firmly anchored and grounded in a stable space. Their performance can then be persistent and "steady as a rock" as they produce the necessary tangible results of their efforts. Alienation can occur through becoming excessively fixed or inflexible in their process. Sexuality is based on the organic release of natural instincts. If sexual gratification is frustrated, the accumulated tension can cause physical stress and supersede sensitivity to the partner's desires. A pragmatic, yet accepting, approach to sensuality and comfort yields great dividends.

Chart Example: Xaviera Hollander with Vesta in Taurus in the eleventh house opposed to a Scorpio Moon is the author of *The Happy Hooker* and counsels individuals on their sexual problems in her magazine column. (2)

Vesta in Gemini individuals focus their work ability through words and conveying information. Skills are best utilized through networking and coordinating. Alienation can occur through getting so caught up in the words that the conveyance of meaning is lost, or through excessive intellectualism. Communication and mental interchange are important components for sexually fulfilled relationships. However these individuals are vulnerable to using words and rationalizations to create an emotional distance from others. The mind can be a professional asset but must not be allowed to dominate the emotional experiences.

Chart Example: Astrologer Evangeline Adams, with Vesta in Gemini at the IC, devoted her life to delineating nearly 100,000 charts in true Gemini fashion — in brief 30-minute intervals that left her clients with a taste of what astrology could offer. (2)

Vesta in Cancer people require the feeling of being needed in order to activate commitment. Sympathetic extension to their family or dependent individuals enables them to tap into the reservoir of work energy. Because of emotional hypersensitivity, alienation can occur through withdrawal in order to gain protection from the real or imagined harshness of others. Sexual fulfillment comes from the feeling of being loved and cherished. However, excessive emotional neediness can produce insecurity and paranoia which then can drain the relationship. A practical approach to empathy can lead to emotional stability.

Chart Example: Zelda Fitzgerald's Vesta conjunct the Moon in Cancer exemplified her strong emotionalism and ties to her family. These can be seen as primary causes of her instability in later years. (2)

Vesta in Leo individuals work best when allowed a creative free rein in their efforts. The capacity to have pride in one's work focuses the lens of aesthetic output. Because of the quality of brilliant shining that exudes from this person, alienation can occur through "burning out" those in close proximity. Alienation can also occur through excessive pride or arrogance. Romanticism and admiration inspire sexual response. However, sexuality here can also be inhibited if the reproductive energy is diverted/sublimated solely to one's personal creative effort.

Chart Example: Marie Antoinette, prideful and haughty queen of France who devoted herself to extravagant court entertainment, was born with Vesta in Leo. (3)

Vesta in Virgo placements emphasize the work focus. The drive to be perfect fuels the need to concentrate and to perform. Tendencies toward being a workaholic and toward an overly-critical attitude can alienate one from relating to others. Sex can be seen as a service to comfort the partner or as a duty. Because of the high degree of sexual discrimination, these individuals can inhibit their natural response through obsessing on the imperfections of others. Much productive accomplishment and efficiency is possible with this placement.

Chart Example: Martin Luther, priest, reformationist, and founder of the Puritans and their work ethic, was born with Vesta in Virgo in the first house. (1)

Vesta in Libra individuals prefer to work with others rather than alone. These individuals like to bring other people into their work and gain from their input. Yet, because of the Libran need to compare oneself to others, extreme competitiveness can result in the work situation. The need to be recognized as an equal and to exchange a reciprocal give-and-take is an important factor in sexual response. However due to the need to be accepted and admired, individuals here are prone to giving up their own needs and desires. Achieving a sensible balance between personal preferences and those of others is vital.

Chart Example: Designer Coco Chanel who devoted her life to establishing a worldwide standard of fashion and style has Vesta in Libra in the ninth house. (2)

Vesta in Scorpio expresses itself in an intense and penetrating manner. People with this placement seek depth and thoroughness in all of their commitments. Sexuality is regarded as a peak experience to be had regardless of the existing social taboos. On the other hand, these individuals may experience feelings of guilt, sin, and shame in sexual affairs, which cause them to become sexually inhibited or repressed. Tremendous concentration and dedication are available.

Chart Example: Theosophist Annie Besant, with Vesta in Scorpio opposed to Mars, was an avid proponent of birth control and was arrested on a morals charge for distributing information about it. (2)

Vesta in Sagittarius individuals focus best when they are working for something they can believe in. An ideal or cause is the motivation which can generate their work energy. Alienation can occur if they become totally consumed with spreading or elaborating their own vision until there is no consideration for the beliefs of others.

A sense of high adventure and truth-seeking stimulates sexual receptivity, yet lack of honesty and loyalty can undermine the foundation of trust in relationships. These individuals can also sublimate the sexual drive into their causes. An integrated blending reveals practical idealists and mystics who affect the material world.

Chart Examples: Alice Bailey, visionary writer and founder of the Arcane Society, was born with Vesta in Sagittarius in the fifth house. (2)

Mohandas Gandhi, spiritual and political leader of India, has Vesta conjunct Saturn in Sagittarius. Though married, he remained celibate for many years and tried to impose celibacy upon his sons. (1)

Vesta in Capricorn individuals work best in a structured and disciplined fashion. The work effort is often motivated by personal ambition and the drive to succeed. The ability to formulate and execute plans leads to success in administrative work. Yet Vesta in Capricorn's strict adherence to rules and regulations can denote excessive rigidity in the individual. The presence of commitment and honor in the relationship is often necessary for sexual fulfillment.These individuals may fear sexual intimacy and emotional involvement if they associate it with criticism, judgment, or loss of power or control. Discipline is marked, and great attainments can be reached. These people expect success through "paying their dues" (obliging the system).

Chart Example: Hard working Walter Mondale has Vesta in Capricorn in the eleventh house. (1)

Vesta in Aquarius individuals work best through humanitarian, social, or political motivations. The ideal of freedom for oneself and others is paramount. Because of Aquarius' strong detachment from the personal, alienation can occur through insufficient focus on the needs of loved ones. Rebellion against authority figures is often present. Sexual response is activated through the unusual, and one can engage in sexuality with friends on a nonpossessive and noncommittal basis.

Chart Example: Germaine Greer, author of *The Female Eunuch* and promoter of unconventional sexual lifestyles, has Vesta in Aquarius conjunct her Ascendant. (2)

Vesta in Pisces souls can best focus their work energy by serving others. Because of the diffuse, scattered nature of Pisces, Vesta here can point to difficulty in finding a focus or maintaining a commitment. This person can play the role of a martyr and attempt to make others feel guilty and responsible for his or her suffering. One can serve to heal others through sexual interaction, or sublimate sexuality into spiritual realization. This person may feel that his or her sexuality belongs to whoever has need of it, and that no one person has sole rights to it. Integration includes a blending of dreams and reality, the poetic and the practical.

Chart Example: Writer Robert Graves, whose inspiration is reflected by his Vesta in Pisces opposing his Moon, focused his visions and ideals in poetic works such as *The White Goddess*. (1)

Vesta in the Houses

Vesta in the first house shows dedication to experiencing a primary relationship with oneself. Because of this intense focus on finding one's own identity or commitment to one's own goals, this person may tend to exclude long-term relationships from his or her life. Single-minded focus and perseverance can lead to great achievements.

Chart Example: Saint Teresa of Avila, who sought and found ecstatic inner union, was born with Vesta conjunct her Aries Ascendant. (2)

Vesta in the second house represents dedication to generating resources to provide for and support oneself and/or loved ones. One may experience limitations in money, comfort, and sensuality so that pressure will be brought to learn the skill of manifesting.

Chart Example: Catherine the Great, with Vesta conjunct Mars in Taurus in the second house, acquired new provinces for Russia and replenished the state economy. (2)

Vesta in the third house signifies a dedication to one's mind — furthering personal understanding and disseminating information to others. One may experience limitations in communication as one is pressured to focus on clarifying one's ideas. Also this person may experience a sense of inferiority about his or her intellect and ability to communicate if the critical faculties are self-directed. Working with the mind is common with this placement.

Chart Example: Hermann Hesse, spiritual writer, had Vesta in the third house conjunct the Moon in Pisces. (1)

Vesta in the fourth house denotes dedication to one's family and home. There is often a pattern of added responsibility and work in one's home when young that continues into duty and obligation to one's family later on. This person may experience deprivations or curtailment of personal freedom because of family obligations. An efficient approach to domestic needs is suggested.

Chart Example: Actress Eleonora Duse, with Vesta in Sagittarius in the fourth house, was born into and toured with her theatrical family as they devoted their lives to the stage. (2)

Vesta in the fifth house suggests a dedication to one's personal creative expressions — children or artistic forms. Alienation from children, romance, and pleasure or creative blockage can often result. Sexual inhibition occurs through excessive sublimation of sexual energy into fifth-house affairs, or a painstaking focus on flaws may sabotage spontaneity. This placement can denote a creative profession and/or one which brings attention and limelight.

Chart Example: Tennis champion Billy Jean King utilized her Vesta-Mars conjunction in Gemini in the fifth house to focus and concentrate her athletic energy. (2)

Vesta in the sixth house reveals a dedication to work and efficient functioning. Because of Vesta's association with the sign Virgo, her significance is very marked in this house. Limitations in health will often lead one to focus on self-healing and proper care of the body through nutrition, exercise, and positive thinking. A drive for perfection, if not overdone, can lead to doing things very well.

Chart Example: Elizabeth Taylor, despite her six marriages and health problems, has made her main focus her work in film. Her horoscope reveals Vesta in Pisces in her sixth house. (2)

Vesta in the seventh house points to a dedication to working on one's relationships. Yet, because Vesta strives for self-sufficiency and independence, conflict may arise when seventh-house compromise and cooperative efforts are required. Often this person will become overly focused upon or obsessed with his or her primary relationship.

Chart Example: First Lady Pat Nixon, with Vesta in Leo in the seventh house, has remained a devoted and loyal wife in the face of her husband's political upheavals.

Vesta in the eighth house individuals have a dedication to the psychic/occult fields or to depth interactions with others. It may also be difficult for them to find someone to meet their sexual intensity, and so they may experience limitations here. Complications with others over shared resources — money and sexuality — put pressure on one to learn the skill of letting go of personal desire and on learning how to share possessions.

Chart Example: Disappointed in love and religion, Vincent van Gogh's artistic intensity and numerous transformations are described by his Vesta in the eighth house squaring Venus and Saturn. (1)

Vesta in the ninth house symbolizes a dedication to seeking the truth and conveying wisdom. An overly extreme focus on one's belief system, however, may result in political or religious fanaticism. Limitations may arise that challenge a wide scope of vision. Ideal images can be given form in the material world.

Chart Example: Religious visionary William Blake was born with Vesta in Aquarius in the ninth house. (1)

Vesta in the tenth house indicates a dedication to one's career or position in society. When close to the MC it can indicate a spiritual destiny. One may experience limitations in finding a fulfilling vocational path, if the critical faculties are overly developed. Tremendous discipline, thoroughness, and willingness to work hard are potential talents.

Chart Example: Pope John Paul I was born with a Vesta-Mercury conjunction in Scorpio in the tenth house. (1)

Vesta in the eleventh house connotes a dedication to group interactions. Working with collectives (land, business, political living) fulfills the need to participate in larger wholes. One may experience limitations in friendships or groups in order that one may learn the importance of others in one's life. There exists the need to define and focus one's hopes and aspirations so that one can dedicate oneself to an ideal.

Chart Example: Social worker and humanitarian Jane Addams was born with Vesta in Cancer in the eleventh house opposing Mars. She set up "neighborhood houses" for immigrants, as well as contributing to reforms in child labor, public health, and social insurance. (3)

Vesta in the twelfth house implies a dedication to selfless service and to the pursuit of spiritual values.There exist strong unconscious needs for isolation and retreat, as well as for a focus of deep faith. Persecution for one's religious beliefs in a past life, anxieties concerning public exposure or making mistakes may produce a fear of exploring one's spiritual nature. In addition, there may exist deep, unconscious, sexual fears and inhibitions which can be overcome by balancing faith and fear, yearning for the infinite with a practical assessment of the physical world and its limitations.

Chart Example: Renowned spiritualist Helena Blavatsky was born with Vesta in Cancer in her mystical twelfth house. (2)

Vesta Aspects to the Planets

VESTA-SUN ASPECTS

The focusing principle combines with identity and purpose. This combination indicates that one's work, self-involvement, and sense of commitment become a major part of life's purpose.

Harmonious aspects describe an individual who is self-identified and demonstrates a high level of personal integration. There exists the dedication to an ideal and seriousness of commitment. These people may live out their individually determined sexual values and avoid possessive relationships.

Stressful aspects indicate possible conflicts between one's work focus and life purpose which can result in the inability to find a fulfilling career. Other problems may include frustrations and denials in sexuality, and fears of intimacy and commitment. A general sense of confusion and aimlessness about one's life direction may produce mental anxiety and stress; excessive self-absorption may lead to alienation from others.

The resolution of these challenges lies in developing a purposeful focus and then integrating and aligning one's personal energies to harmonize with the vision.

Chart Examples: Isadora Duncan, self-identified woman who was devoted to her career and defied sexual taboos, had Vesta conjunct the Sun in Taurus/Gemini. (2)

Anne Frank, whose diary of confinement in Germany has brought spiritual uplift to millions, was born with Vesta conjunct the Sun and Mercury in Gemini. (2)

Carl G. Jung, whose analytic psychology stressed integration with the concept of self, had Vesta conjunct the Sun in Leo. (3)

English novelist Charles Dickens focused his unusual mental energy through prolific writings observing the human condition. He was born with Vesta conjunct the Sun in Aquarius at the IC. (3)

Atomic scientist Enrico Fermi who discovered uranium fission and invented the atomic reactor had Vesta conjunct the Sun in Libra in the sixth house. (1)

VESTA-MOON ASPECTS

The focusing principle combines with emotional responsiveness. This combination indicates that one's emotional world may become the field of self-involvement and integration.

Harmonious aspects indicate a fertile nature, both physically and mentally. There can exist a devotion to one's family or a strong desire to care for others. These individuals can display a sympathetic understanding and emotional rapport in responding to a variety of sexual situations. They may also have a free and open attitude about sex.

Stressful aspects may signify an alienation from one's own emotional needs. This can produce a fear of intimacy and of commitment to family ties. Potential difficulties in sexual performance or in fertility (being sterile) may also exist. Excessive emotional introspection may also occur in these people.

The resolution of these challenges lies in understanding and deconditioning socially imposed morality concerning sexual standards. Therapy can be useful in helping the individual to release blocked energies — both sexual and emotional — so that free and open self-expression may occur. Releasing unnecessary judgments can help balance one's need for emotional closeness with obsession over shortcomings and flaws.

Chart Examples: Charles Baudelaire, with his Vesta-Moon conjunction in Cancer square an Aries Sun, expressed his sexual torment in his poetic writings, and he died from syphilis. (1)

Maria Montessori, with Vesta at the Midheaven opposing a fourth-house Scorpio Moon, dedicated herself to rehabilitating the lives of underprivileged children. (2)

Nurse Florence Nightingale, the lady with the lamp, was born with Vesta conjunct the Moon and Sun in Taurus opposing Juno in Scorpio. She turned away from marriage in order to devote herself to the service of the wounded soldiers in the Crimea, and brought about worldwide reforms in hospital administration and nursing. (3)

Writer Virginia Woolf, with Vesta conjunct the Moon and Saturn in Taurus, focused her emotional sensitivity into psychologically perceptive and precise character portrayals. She suffered from reoccurring mental breakdowns. (1)

VESTA-MERCURY ASPECTS

The focusing principle combines with mental expression. This combination emphasizes the need to focus one's thought and communication processes.

Harmonious aspects can indicate a highly developed mind which can powerfully focus and direct its thoughts. There can exist an overpowering drive to express one's ideas or to dedicate oneself to the transmission of teachings. This person can excel in research or in the media.

Stressful aspects may point to communications difficulties: either by being overly precise with words or the opposite, vague and noncommittal. There may exist excessive mental self-introspection, vagaries of the mind, or poor concentration in learning situations. Some individuals may experience sexual problems due to a lack of communication with their partner.

The resolution of these challenges lies in clarifying one's personal objectives and thoughts and eliminating unessential mental baggage. Once one's mental processes are sharpened and focused, then clear communication can result.

Chart Examples: Physicist Werner Heisenberg, famous for his studies in theoretical atomic physics, focused his penetrating mental abilities through his Vesta-Mercury conjunction in Scorpio. (1)

Princess Margaret of England has Vesta conjunct Mercury in Virgo in the sixth house. (3)

VESTA-VENUS ASPECTS

The focusing principle combines with the feminine principle of love and sexuality. This aspect can indicate a self-determined and independent attitude concerning intimate relationships.

Harmonious aspects signify the ability to integrate one's femininity with one's individual identity. There can exist a devotion to sexual expression and the sensitive understanding of feminine psychology. These individuals may also choose to sublimate their sexual expression into artistic expression or a spiritual path.

Stressful aspects may point to conflicts between independence/work needs and relationship needs, often resulting in alienation from people. This may manifest as psychological or physical frigidity, fear and withdrawal from intimacy, puritanical attitudes toward sexuality, or the opposite expression: promiscuity.

The resolution of these challenges lies in the integration of one's independence and work energies within the context of intimate relationships. Developing an individually determined sexual code can facilitate this process.

Chart Examples: Anais Nin, whose Venus conjuncts Vesta in Pisces, was able to integrate her femininity with her independence, and wrote intimate and psychologically perceptive novels on the nature of women. (2)

Dante Gabriel Rossetti, English painter and poet, expressed his Vesta-Venus conjunction in Cancer through his hauntingly beautiful portraits and poems of women. (1)

VESTA-MARS ASPECTS

The focusing principle combines with the masculine principle of action and assertion. This combination emphasizes the ability to concentrate and direct one's energy at will.

Harmonious aspects signify the ability to integrate autonomy and self-determination in intimate relationships as well as the possession of skill and sensitivity in sexual expression. These individuals have the capacity to sublimate sexual energy into fighting for a cause — e.g., the spiritual warrior or crusader.

Stressful aspects depict restrictions in the expression of masculine energies which can lead to physical or psychological impotence, or to alienation from intimate relationships. Blocks may exist in taking action and following through on commitments. Some individuals may attempt to compensate for feelings of masculine inadequacy by becoming overly aggressive in their sexual expression.

The resolution of these challenges lies in learning to align energy, drive, and will with clearly conceived/focused direction and purpose.

Chart Examples: Franciscan missionary Junipero Serra, born with Vesta conjunct Mars in Capricorn, became famous as a preacher and made long journeys on foot in spite of his lameness. (3)

Harriet Beecher Stowe, with Vesta conjunct Mars in Scorpio, is best known for her antislavery novel *Uncle Tom's Cabin*. (1)

Heavyweight boxer Rocky Marciano was born with Vesta conjunct Mars in Aquarius. (1)

VESTA-JUNO ASPECTS

The focusing principle combines with the relating urge. This combination suggests an evolutionary path that begins with the autonomy of the self and ends with a joining together with others.

Harmonious aspects indicate the ability to make a serious

commitment to another. These individuals dedicate themselves to purifying and perfecting their partnerships which often take on the form of sexually fulfilled, spiritual relationships.

Stressful aspects can symbolize a conflict between personal needs and relationship needs. These people may feel alienated from relationships or may experience isolation within them. In other instances, they may sacrifice themselves for their partners or become obsessively involved with them. Sexual domination and control may also exist as part of the interaction.

The resolution of these challenges lies in integrating the role of the autonomous individual within the context of a committed partnership.

Chart Examples: Comedienne Lucille Ball, with Vesta at her Cancer Ascendant squaring a fourth-house Juno in Libra, devoted much of her life to sharing an acting career with her husband Desi Arnez.

French author Colette portrayed her Vesta-Juno conjunction in Sagittarius in the third house as she collaborated with all three of her husbands in her writings of women's love and jealousy. (2)

Prince Albert, husband of Queen Victoria, with Vesta conjunct Juno in Cancer placed in the tenth house, exemplified a devotion to his wife. (1)

VESTA-JUPITER ASPECTS

The focusing principle combines with the expansive/broadening urge. This combination can indicate enlargement and a social vision within one's field of dedication and commitment.

Harmonious aspects can point to a dedication to the pursuit of truth and knowledge. These individuals possess the ability to focus on and synthesize the details of broad-scale issues. The sexual force of Vesta may be sublimated into the areas of politics, teaching, the ministry, or spiritual devotion.

Stressful aspects indicate potential conflicts between one's personal philosophy and that which is beneficial for the larger whole. These individuals may believe that their philosophy is the only valid truth, e.g., religious fundamentalists. In some cases, the person may tend to overcommit himself and hence be unable to deliver on his promises. Other difficulties may include the exaggeration of sexual fears or an overemphasis on sexual power.

The resolution of these challenges lies in expanding one's focus to include social and cultural forms as well as infusing one's vision with the qualities of faith, hope, and optimism.

Chart Examples: Elizabeth I of England, also known as the ageless "Virgin Queen," aptly expresses her Vesta in Gemini opposing Jupiter in Sagittarius. She remained single throughout her reign, took many lovers, initiated England's colonial expansion, and attempted to resolve the religious conflicts of her country. (3)

Leonard Bernstein's ability to compose and conduct emotionally moving symphonies, musical comedies, film scores, chamber music, and ballets is depicted by his Vesta-Jupiter conjunction in Cancer. (1)

VESTA-SATURN ASPECTS

The focusing principle combines with the urge to create form and structure. This combination can signify intensely focused and committed energies.

Harmonious aspects depict an individual who possesses self-discipline, seriousness of purpose, and the ability to actualize goals and aspirations through dedication and hard work. Once realized, these aspirations will be grounded in a solid and secure foundation. There can also exist a devotion to one's duties and obligations.

Stressful aspects describe conflicts between one's personal needs and one's obligations toward others. The result may manifest either as an avoidance of commitment or as suffering under the burden of too much responsibility. These individuals may set harsh standards of perfection for themselves and others. Other problems may include workaholism, extreme ambition, and sexual fears and restrictions.

The resolution of these challenges lies in developing a balanced approach to fulfilling one's responsibilities in the world so that personal enjoyment and fulfillment may also be experienced.

Chart Examples: Paul Gauguin, whose Vesta-Saturn conjunction in Pisces opposed his Ceres in Virgo, left his wife and five children to follow his artistic calling in Polynesia. (1)

Philosopher Friedrich Nietzsche, with his second-house Vesta-Saturn conjunction in Aquarius, believed the time had come for people to critically examine their traditional values and the origin of these values. (1)

VESTA-URANUS ASPECTS

The focusing urge combines with individuality and intuition. People with this combination have the potential to infuse original and universal impulses into personal dedication.

Harmonious aspects indicate a mind that can focus and

concentrate on innovative and intuitive ideas. Hence, these individuals may become involved in the pursuit of scientific and occult studies. In addition, there may exist the capacity to dedicate oneself to new political, spiritual, and revolutionary visions. These people sometimes advocate sexual liberation and implement nonpossessive behavior in sexual relationships.

Stressful aspects may point to potential conflicts between a desire to focus oneself versus the desire for innovation and change. This may lead to a rebellion from obligation or erratic behavior that thwarts long-term commitment. Politically, this aspect can manifest as the "rebel without a cause." In some instances, these individuals may express deviant forms of behavior from the traditional sexual/ethical codes.

The resolution of these challenges lies in committing and dedicating oneself to a type of innovation and reform that promotes constructive and healing changes in the old order, or building functional structures of a new order.

Chart Examples: Scientist George Washington Carver who had Vesta-Uranus conjunct in Gemini revolutionized the agriculture of the South through his research in agricultural chemistry. (3)

Leonardo da Vinci, with his Vesta-Uranus opposition, was one of the most versatile geniuses in history. (3)

Statesman Charles de Gaulle was born with Vesta in Scorpio conjunct Uranus in Libra. He led French resistance against Germany in World War II and guided his country as France's overseas empire won independence. (3)

VESTA-NEPTUNE ASPECTS

The focusing principle combines with the transcendent urge. This combination emphasizes a devotion to spiritual or artistic ideals.

Harmonious aspects denote a depth of compassion that can lead one to participate as a universal world-server. There may be a long-term commitment to a spiritual path or a focused devotion to the fine arts. Some individuals may use sexual union as the means of experiencing Neptune's mystic unity.

Stressful aspects may point to a diffusion of focus and confusion about one's commitments. There may be a misperception of reality that leads to inappropriate self-denial and self-sacrifice. Other problems may include a disillusionment with sexuality or spirituality, or escapism from work.

The resolution of these challenges lies in using Vesta's powers of focus and concentration to effectively deal with physical reality and other dimensions.

Chart Examples: Spanish artist Francisco Goya drew upon the inspiration of his Vesta-Neptune opposition as he portrayed in his paintings his search for a deeper reality in human emotions and the subconscious. (3)

Salvador Dali, a surrealist painter, also drew upon the talents indicated by his Vesta-Neptune conjunction to produce "hand-painted dream photographs," many of which have strong sexual associations. (3)

Astrologer Doris Chase Doane, with Vesta in Capricorn in the first house opposing Neptune in Cancer the seventh house, worked with her husband as an ordained minister and teacher. (2)

VESTA-PLUTO ASPECTS

The focusing principle combines with the transformative urge. This combination can signify a sense of destiny and personal commitment to the transformation of society.

Harmonious aspects describe an individual who can focus and direct large amounts of energy to penetrate hidden and unknown realms. There may exist the ability to transmute sexuality for regeneration, healing, and illumination. This aspect can signify a dedication to use personal power in the service of spiritual or social ideals.

Stressful aspects may point to conflicts between using one's power for personal versus transpersonal ends. This may lead to the blocking of one's power needs or releasing them destructively on a mass scale. Obsessive sexual compulsions, exaggerated fears of death, paranoia, and excessive self-absorption may also occur. One may also feel overly isolated from society.

The resolution of these challenges lies in focusing power into constructive social change and transformation.

Chart Examples: Plutonian dictator Adolf Hitler was born with Vesta semisquare Pluto. (3)

Anarchist Emma Goldman expressed her Vesta in Scorpio opposed to Pluto in Taurus through her revolutionary activities, as well as in advocating free love, birth control, and atheism. (1)

CHAPTER TEN

JUNO: THE DIVINE CONSORT

Here I sing of Hera
She has a golden throne
Rhea was her mother
She is an immortal queen
Hers is the most eminent of figures
She is the sister
she is even the wife
of Zeus thunderer
She is glorious
All the gods on vast Olympus
revere her,
They honor her
even equal to Zeus
the lover of lightning[1]

The Mythology of Juno

Juno, goddess of marriage, was one of the two legally married women in Olympus, the other being Venus Aphrodite. But while Venus totally disregarded her marriage vows, Juno, as wife of Zeus/Jupiter, was revered for her loyalty and fidelity. Juno was known to the Greeks as Hera, derived from the roots *he era*, meaning "the earth," and also translated as "lady," the feminine form of "hero." She was portrayed as a beautiful and majestic woman with her hair bound with

1. Homer, "The Hymn to Hera," *The Homeric Hymns*, trans. Charles Boer (Irving Texas: Spring Publications, Inc., 1979), 7.

a diadem (a crown depicting *Horae* and the Graces) and a veil hanging from the back of her head. Accompanied by a peacock and frequently attended by a rainbow, she held a pomegranate in her left hand (identifying her as an earlier goddess of the dead) and a scepter surmounted by a cuckoo in the right.

According to the Romans, each man possessed an indwelling reproductive power, called his *genius*, and similarly, each woman had her *juno*, her conceiving and bearing power. The virtues of this *juno* developed into the goddess Juno, the guardian of childbirth and motherhood. As *Juno Lucretia*, she became the feminine principle of celestial light, and as *Juno Lucina*, she personified the birth goddess who leads the child into the light.

Juno's most important function, however, was as patroness of married women. Juno presided over all rites and arrangements of legal marriage. The sixth month of June was sacred to her, and even today many women seek her blessings as "June/Juno brides." Juno also governed the female reproductive cycle, and as goddess of the calendar, she used the menstrual cycle to symbolize the orderly passage of time. Accordingly, she was worshipped by the Roman women on the *Calends*, the first day of each lunar month.

THE STORY OF ZEUS AND HERA

In the Olympic pantheon, Hera, Zeus' sister, was swallowed along with her siblings by her father Cronus. After being released from Cronus' stomach, she was raised by *Oceanus* and *Tethys* while the Gods fought the Titans. Meanwhile, Zeus had developed a romantic interest in his sister. One day, he spotted Hera walking alone by Mt. *Thronax* (now called Cuckoo Mountain) in the country of Argos and disguised himself as a cuckoo bird. The cuckoo, whose cries announced the rain that yielded forth food and fruits, was considered a harbinger of fertility to the ancients. Zeus then caused a mighty rainstorm to fall and flew, shivering and frozen from the cold, into the lap of Hera. Taking pity upon the bedraggled and frightened bird, Hera drew it to her breast and warmed it with her cloak. At once Zeus resumed his true shape and ravished her. Shamed by her violation, Hera married Zeus out of guilt and obligation.

Another legend has it that the sacred marriage occurred in complete secrecy on the isle of Samos and lasted for three hundred years. The secrecy is perhaps explained by the fact that Zeus' mother Rhea had enjoined him not to marry. Because the tale recounts the forcing of monogamy on the indigenous cults, the three hundred years may refer to the time it took the conquering Hellenes to subdue Hera's people.[2]

After Zeus married Hera, he took her to Olympus to share the throne he had won by subduing the Titans. The wedding ceremony was celebrated by all the gods who brought various gifts. Gaia (Mother Earth) gave Hera a tree of golden apples. All the immortals took part in the bridal procession, and the *Fates* chanted the hymnal chorus. Thus, the forced marriage between the two predominant divinities initiated the merging of their respective cultures.

At first, the divine bride and bridegroom exchanged much love and tenderness. In the *Iliad*, Homer recounts their lovemaking on Mt. Ida. Zeus, comparing Hera to his previous lovers, praises her thus: "Never has such desire, for goddess or woman, flooded and overwhelmed my heart. . . never have I felt such love, such sweet desire, as fills me now for you."[3] Unfortunately, aside from such transitory encounters of sexual ecstasy, the couple's marital bliss rapidly faded.

THE TRIALS OF HERA AND ZEUS

For the remainder of the marriage, Zeus and Hera lived in a continual state of tension and perpetual combat. Although Zeus did consult Hera for advice, he never fully trusted her. According to some tales, Zeus would punish Hera by angrily hurling thunderbolts at her. In retaliation, Hera covertly worked to defeat and humiliate Zeus. When she could no longer bear his infidelities and arrogance, she avenged herself, with the assistance of Athene and Apollo, by binding Zeus to his bed with knotted leather thongs, where a host of gods mocked and insulted him. Freed by the hundred-handed *Briareus*, Zeus then punished Hera by hanging her from the heavens with her wrists bound by golden bracelets and heavy anvils weighting her ankles.

Through her monogamous marriage, Hera was deprived of her sacred sexual customs that honored the goddess and was locked into a chastity belt. Her fidelity to her husband was exemplary. Zeus, on the other hand, constantly embarked upon amorous adventures with both goddesses and mortals. Hera's deepest pain and rage occurred through helplessly watching Zeus and his worshippers destroy her goddess cults. Forced into obedience and submission, Hera's only means of striking back at Zeus was by taking revenge on his lovers

2. Robert Graves, *The Greek Myths Vol. 1* (Maryland: Penguin Books, 1964), 53.
3. Homer, *The Iliad*, trans. E. V. Riev (Maryland: Penguin Books, 1961), 265.

and their children. Among the women who Hera believed betrayed her and therefore persecuted were *Leto, Io, Callisto, Lamia*, and *Alcmene*. In each case, Hera either arranged for their death or visited a horrible curse upon them.

HERA AS THE IDEALIZED WIFE

Despite her stormy marriage, Hera became worshipped as the model bride and wife who had sought fulfillment through her relationship. In classical mythology, her ability to remain faithful to Zeus despite his infidelity was considered her greatest gift. Those who attempted to seduce her such as the giant *Porphyrion, Ephialtes*, and *Ixion*, were violently rejected by Hera and severely punished by Zeus. In living up to her reputation for chastity, Hera repeatedly refused to dishonor her husband's bed. "The form of marriage that Hera protected as marriage goddess was monogamy, or, as seen from the woman's point of view, the fulfillment of herself through a single husband, to whom she could be a single wife."[4] Ironically, this lawful union of the male and female polarities was notably unprolific. Not more than four offspring are attributed to the divine couple — *Ares*, war god; *Hephaestus*, smith god; *Eileithyia*, childbirth goddess; and *Hebe*, flower of youth — and traditions abound in which none of them were the result of the union between Zeus and Hera. Meanwhile, Zeus generated many of the Greek heroes through his sexual assaults upon Hera's priestesses and worshippers.

HERA AND HER CHILDREN

In order to fulfill her desire for children and still maintain her fidelity, Hera birthed several parthenogenetic children. In order to match Zeus' feat of creating Pallas Athene, she implored the imprisoned Titans to assist her in bringing forth a son who was as strong as Zeus himself. After spending a year in solitary retreat, Hera bore the *Typhaon of Delphi*, a creature with a hundred burning snake heads, who later became a fearsome enemy of Zeus. Later, Hera conceived Ares, god of war and strife, when she touched the fertility-inducing May blossom administered to her by the goddess *Flora*. Zeus came to hate Ares for taking delight in violence and destruction, just like his mother. Finally, Hera bore Hephaestus, skilled artisan and smith god. Conceived in anger, he was born lame and crippled, and Hera, embarrassed at having created a deformed child, sought to conceal

4. Carl Kerenyi, *The Gods of the Greeks*, trans. Norman Cameron (Great Britain: Billings and Sons Limited, 1982), 158.

her maternity by casting him from Olympus into the sea. (An older tradition maintains that Hephaestus' disfigurement was due to his premature birth during the three-hundred-year secrecy of his parents' relationship,[5] with Hera herself hiding the child to protect him and to conceal her defection.) This callous act came back upon her as Hephaestus gained revenge by imprisoning his mother in a throne that he had fashioned.

The sexual tensions that plagued Hera and Zeus' infertile marriage symbolized the struggle between the customs of matrilineal and patrilineal descent. By withholding his sexuality, Zeus denied Hera both sexual and emotional fulfillment and the experience of birthing a divine child, who, under the tradition of mother-descent would have usurped his claim to sovereignty. Hera, on the other hand, refused to bear Zeus a legitimate male heir to carry on his title — the *de facto* reason for the monogamous marriage — and so resisted participating in the patrilineal transference. Yet, their marriage remained at the core of Hera's cult and was finally consummated only by Hera's acceptance of Heracles, also known as Hercules.

Heracles, whose name means "Hera's Glory," may originally have been Hera's divine consort and protector against the Achaean enemy Perseus in times before her cultic association with Zeus. Heracles later emerged as Zeus' mighty son born of the beautiful mortal *Alcmene*. One legend states that when Hera realized the glory to which Heracles was destined, she sought to rob him of his birthright as ruler of the noble house of Perseus. This led to a lifetime of fierce hostility between the two. A tale was told that Hera was tricked into suckling Heracles in her sleep in order to make him immortal. When she suddenly awakened to this, she thrust him from her breast, and the divine milk spurting from her breast showered the heavens, creating the Milky Way. However, other legends tell of a profound transformation that occurred in Hera when Zeus persuaded her to adopt Hercules in a ceremony of rebirth. In the ceremony, Hera retired to her bed, clasped the burly hero to her bosom, and pushed him through her robes in an imitation of birth (an adoption ritual still practiced by primitive tribes).[6] Now that he was accepted and loved as a son, Hera welcomed Heracles as an Olympian god and married him to her daughter *Hebe*, "flower of youth," a maiden aspect of Hera herself. Thus, through her acceptance of Hercules, Hera reconciled herself to Zeus. By the sixth

5. Kerenyi, *The Gods of the Greeks*, 155.
6. Sir James Frazer, *The Golden Bough* (New York: The Macmillan Company, 1960), 17.

century BC, they began to share an altar that had been barred to the older female divinities.

HERA'S SOLITUDE

The sacred marriage of Zeus and Hera became the prototype of human marriage. The myths of leaving and returning were incorporated as an essential aspect of their relationship. "There are special tales concerning Hera's solitude, her separation from other gods and from her husband. . . Hera's wanderings during which she was wrapped in deepest darkness, that repeatedly ended in her returning to her husband."[7] According to one legend, when Hera was humiliated by Zeus' infidelities and shamed by her now-hateful nature, she left him and retreated to the place of her maidenhood on the isle of Euboea. Zeus could not persuade her to return and so devised a ruse in which he announced his imminent marriage to a local princess. The day of the marriage, he marched in a bridal procession to Mt. Chitaeron with a veiled wooden statue as his bride. Upon seeing this, Hera rushed out with the women of Plataiai at her heels and snatched the image from the litter. Even though she realized Zeus' trickery, amidst the laughter she reconciled herself to her husband.

Greek mythology repeatedly emphasizes the need for Hera's periodic retreat into solitude. At Argos, she annually bathed in the spring of Kanathos to renew her virginity and prepare for her reunion with Zeus.

Thus, we have told the story of Hera, the pre-Hellenic great goddess who initiated womenhood into the rites of marriage and yet never realized the fulfillment she sought with her husband.

THE PRE-HELLENIC ORIGINS OF JUNO

In the days before classical Greece, Hera was worshipped in a variety of forms by the indigenous goddess cults. Early sculptures portray Hera as beautiful, poised, and vibrant. An Orphic hymn to her sings, "May you, O blessed Goddess and many named Queen of all, come with kindness and joy on your lovely face."[8] During the age of Taurus, Hera was worshipped as the cow-eyed sky queen who presided over all phases of feminine existence, from childhood to

7. Kerenyi, *The Gods of the Greeks*, 98.
8. *The Orphic Hymns*, trans. Apostoious N. Athanassakis (Montana: Scholars Press, 1977), 27.

old age. As an embodiment of the triple moon goddess, Hera symbolized three universal, female life stages:

"*Hera Parthenia*," child-maiden of the new Moon and budding spring

"*Hera Telia*," fulfilled bride of the full Moon and fertile summer; and

"*Hera Chera*," solitary widow of the dark Moon and desolate winter.

Hera's birthplace was reputed to be the isle of Samos, where she was raised by the seasons. As the pre-Hellenic great goddess, Hera reigned alone at many religious centers — Argos, Samos, and Euboea, as well as at Tiryns and Mycenae. Symbols of Hera also remain in Crete and the western coast of Anatolia. Her temple at Olympia is far older than that of Zeus.

Celebrated in Hera's honor was the *Heraea*, a festival of women's foot races which predated the Olympics. The three winners of the races, one from each life stage, received crowns of olives, symbolizing peace and fertility, and a share of a cow sacrificed to Hera. By partaking of her sacred cow, they became one with the goddess. In later times, the chosen virgin of the *Heraea* and the victor of the men's Olympic chariot race became the heavenly bride and bridegroom of the ancient, midsummer, sacred marriage.[9]

Originally, Hera reigned alone and had no consort. But, when the invading Achaean tribes descended upon Greece from the north, Hera's cult became an obstacle that had to be reckoned with. Hence, the Achaeans made Hera the divine partner of their own chief god Zeus. Hera's forced marriage to Zeus thus symbolized the overthrow of her supremacy in both Crete and Mycenaean Greece.[10] The subsequent strife between the divine couple as told in myth literally described the racial conflict between the Achaean followers of Zeus and the Argive worshippers of Hera. And while Homer has traditionally depicted Hera as the jealous and quarrelsome wife, in reality she is the image of the turbulent nation princess coerced, but never really subdued, by an alien conqueror.[11]

9. Jane E. Harrison, *Epilegomena to the Study of Greek Religion and Themis* (New York: University Books, 1966), 226.
10. Graves, *The Greek Myths Vol. 1*, 53.
11. Jane E. Harrison, *Mythology* (Massachusetts: Marshall Jones Company, 1924), 95.

JUNO

Greek Hera

Principle of Relatedness

Character

Goddess of Marriage
Queen of the Heavens
Triple Moon Goddess

Glyph: ⚵

Scepter for Royalty

Symbols

diadem (crown)
veil
scepter
peacock/cuckoo
pomegranate
cow (holy heifer)
rainbow (winds and atmosphere)

Associated Rulerships

Libra
Scorpio

Polarities

Intimacy/Manipulation

The Astrology of Juno

As the point on the mandala where the feminine principle unifies with the masculine, Juno symbolizes the principle of relatedness. Through the vehicle of committed partnership, she strives to realize a perfected and balanced union with another. Juno therefore exhibits strong rulership associations with Libra and Scorpio, the signs of marriage and consummation.

The semisextile aspect between Libra and Scorpio links the two signs, but also implies friction in attempting to join and utilize their different resources. Likewise, Juno's major frustration came in her inability to actualize the full potential inherent in her marriage to Jupiter.

Juno's psychological function can be better understood when contrasted with that of her companion, Vesta. Both goddesses utilize the sexual energy of Venus, but for very different purposes. Vesta, after her sexual encounters, becomes reabsorbed back into her own identity. She is the Virgin, complete unto herself. Juno, on the other hand, uses her sexuality to transcend personal identity through committed relationship. Juno thus represents the emergence of the maiden into the full essence of womanhood. She is the transition from the one-in-selfness of the virgin to "*Hera Telia*," the perfected state of the bride and consort.

Juno symbolizes the yearning for full mystic union that is emotionally, sexually, and psychologically fulfilling. Some versions of her story suggest that Juno was coerced into marrying Jupiter, but others indicate she voluntarily relinquished her power in order to experience the deep fulfillment of *gamos* (marriage). However, Jupiter did not live up to her ideals and expectations. Instead Jupiter accepted her power and sovereignty, and then imprisoned Juno in monogamy, forbade her religious practices, helped to destroy her goddess cults, flaunted his infidelities, and created his children without her. "Zeus is no longer Teleius, 'Bringer to perfection,' for Hera but rather her Ateleius, 'Thwarter of fulfillment.' "[12] Juno's suffering lies in the denial of deep union in her marriage. She subsequently expresses the pathology of jealousy, a distorted expression of the healthy Juno archetype that has been passed down to the modern psyche.

Astrologically, therefore, Juno describes the need for a deeply committed and just relationship as well as for the range of suffering and neurotic complexes that arise when this union is denied or frustrated.

JUNO AS THE SIGNIFICATOR OF RELATIONSHIP

In the horoscope, Juno represents the emotional and psychological needs that motivate us to seek marital union. The other feminine functions of fertility, sexuality, child bearing, and rearing are far less important to Juno than her need to merge with another. Therefore, those individuals, both men and women, with prominent Junos in

12. Murray Stein, "Hera, Bound and Unbound," *Spring* (1977), 111.

their charts are drawn to the path of committed relationship. Invariably, they spend their lifetimes experiencing the seventh-house lessons of learning to develop cooperation, compromise, understanding, and harmony with other people.

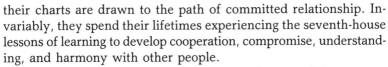

Juno generally represents the mate (or those qualities we project onto the mate), but depending on other factors, this asteroid can describe any close one-to-one relationship such as teacher-disciple, therapist-client, business partners or close friends. In addition, when Juno refers to the "significant other," it is not necessary that the couple be legally married as was the case in the myth. In today's world of changing social mores, any living-together union, heterosexual or homosexual, qualifies as a Juno relationship.

By transit, Juno describes the timings for the inception of relationships as well as periods of crisis and separation. She governs the rituals of courtship, engagement, marriage, wedding anniversaries, and divorce. In synastry, Juno is a primary indicator of compatibility and *karmic* connection. Thus, the use of Juno as a relationship significator simplifies the process of chart comparison and provides essential information that could not be gained from the traditional relationship rulers (Venus, Mars, Sun, Moon, and the signs on the fifth-, seventh-, and eighth-house cusps).

Astrologers may perceive similarities between the delineations of Juno and those of Moon and Venus as given in traditional chart interpretation. This correspondence exists because the Moon is the ground of feminine energy and Venus is the Moon's active sexual expression from which Juno emerges. Juno, however, is the specific differentiation of the Moon-Venus energy as expressed through her role as wife and mate.

THE PATHOLOGY OF RELATIONSHIPS

When the relationship needs of Juno are not fulfilled, then Juno's horoscope position indicates the variety of complexes that arise from the denial of these needs. These pathologies usually are associated with the sign Scorpio; they include jealousy, possessiveness, infidelity, subjugation, manipulation, emotional and sexual power games, projection, betrayal, and abandonment. Let us examine these behaviors in greater detail.

INFIDELITY

The root cause of jealousy that undermines relationships is the issue of sexual fidelity that in our present culture is linked with monogamy. Fidelity, as loyalty, is ultimately determined by sexual boundaries.

This pattern was established for humanity through the marriage of Juno and Jupiter in which Juno took on a vow of fidelity.

Sexual fidelity can be a valuable tool when used to sustain the bonds of a committed relationship. However, if this fidelity is maintained by force and oppression, or if a double standard exists, then the ensuing feelings of unfairness, deception, and mistrust begin to erode the foundations of the relationship.

The most common response to a breach of sexual fidelity is anger. While this anger should naturally be directed toward the unfaithful partner, it is more often unleashed at the accomplice. Juno, for example, took out her revenge on Jupiter's lovers and their children. Consequently, Juno came to symbolize the suspicious wife, cut off from her feminine roots, who engages in female rivalry, competition, backbiting, and cattiness toward other women. Likewise, Jupiter came to represent the type of man who views his wife as personal property to be jealously protected from any potential male trespasser.

Astrologically, therefore, Juno depicts the issue of sexual fidelity as well as the patterns of oppression and force that are often used to maintain it. Juno also represents the humiliation, shame, anger, and revenge that erupt when the slighted partner finally retaliates.

SACRIFICE IN RELATIONSHIPS

An important aspect of the monogamous bargain is the implied message that a person be loved for what he or she has sacrificed for the marriage. Because of this assumption that love implies sacrifice, many women have been pressured to give up careers, educational opportunities, desire for children, proximity to family, religious faith, political beliefs, or material assets in order to demonstrate love for their mate.

When an individual renounces a great deal for their partner, they naturally expect some type of reciprocation — usually in the form of love, gratitude, or appreciation. If this reciprocity does not occur, then Juno's flowers of resentment, regret, and bitterness emerge. In addition, the Juno partner will become increasingly jealous of anything else that attracts the mate's attention — potential lovers, friends, career, family, and hobbies.

Astrologically, therefore, Juno is the significator for the jealousy and resentment that emerge when a partner does not feel adequately acknowledged for the sacrifices he or she has made. This discontent will emerge as silent embitterment or as aggressive demands for tit-for-tat reciprocation.

FEARS IN RELATIONSHIPS

1) **The Fear of Abandonment** — One of the strongest fears that Juno individuals face is the fear of abandonment. Just as Juno's childhood was spent inside her father's (Cronus) stomach, women in patriarchal culture have been conditioned to seek essential support and protection from men. Thus, many women believe that if their husbands left them, they would not know how to provide for themselves.

In a similar fashion, men who are conditioned to receive nurturance exclusively from their mothers or wives fear the emotional deprivation that would arise from the departure of their spouses. Living with this insecurity, they often react by becoming overly possessive to protect themselves from losing their sustenance.

Thus, for both men and women, Juno is the astrological significator for the fear of losing their significant other and the grasping, possessive attitude that arises from this insecurity.

2) **The Fear of Betrayal** — Many individuals with strong Junos live out her myth by being consumed with the anxiety that their partner, like Jupiter, will be faithless. In some instances, their fears are based on solid evidence. In other cases, however, an individual will project a repressed need for sexual or psychic freedom onto his or her mate. Through indulging in fantasies about their partner being with someone else, these people actually visualize their fears into existence. The intensity and passion of their jealousy are directly related to the repression of their own freedom needs.

Astrologically, then, Juno is an indicator of the fear of betrayal that arises from the partner's real or imagined faithlessness.

3) **The Fear of Sexuality** — Unlike Pallas Athene who hid her femininity and thus gained the trust of a male-ordered world, Juno retained and expressed her feminine qualities. This inspired tremendous fear among the Greeks, for in the tradition of the Great Goddess, male year-kings were sacrificed as lover/victims. Hence, in their collective unconscious, men continued to associate memories of deep sex with the loss of life. In the realm of the subconscious these memories manifested as the fear of being consumed and devoured by the sexual power of the feminine. To defend themselves from these fears, men in modern society have adopted a "macho" attitude — desiring a variety and abundance of shallow sex in order to avoid the potential consequences of deep sexual union.

Astrologically, Juno is an indicator of the tension and fears that exist concerning the depth of sexual and emotional encounters within relationships.

POWER IN RELATIONSHIPS

In the search for ideal Libran partnership, Juno individuals aspire to create a relationship that is equal, fair, and reciprocal. However, what they often experience are the imbalances of unjust relationships. Juno themes indicate the power struggles, disappointments, and conflicts encountered in the attempt to align ideals with reality.

1) **The Giving Away of Power** — Juno gave her power over to Jupiter and then raged and retaliated when he used it to oppress her. Likewise, many wives give themselves over to their husbands and then struggle to overcome their feelings of powerlessness or resign themselves to their captive state.

   Juno and Jupiter also engaged in a variety of sadomasochistic punishments. Juno tied and bound Jupiter to his bed with leather thongs and mocked him; he retaliated by suspending her by her wrists from the heavens and weighting her ankles with heavy anvils. Men and women use both physical and emotional devices to imprison and torture each other. Astrologically, Juno is an indicator of the subjugation and revenge that follows the relinquishing of personal power and can predispose an individual to participate in self-defeating power struggles.

2) **Subtle Manipulation** — If a Juno individual is denied overt access to power, he or she may attempt to gain control of their life covertly through the use of subtle manipulation. Such tactics may include the withholding of food or sex; using guilt, children, family, or flattery; or attempting to foil, trick, or deceive one's partner. Historically, women have most often had to resort to these tactics; hence Juno wives have been labeled, somewhat appropriately, as sneaky, conniving, manipulative, and dishonest. Once the Juno person addresses the power imbalance in his or her relationship, however, these tactics are no longer the only means for control.

3) **Children as Power** — Because Jupiter created his children independently of Juno, she retaliated by also birthing her children alone and by persecuting Jupiter's children. Astrologically, therefore, Juno individuals are prone to using children as pawns

in their power struggles. Juno can indicate a denial of children through marriage, using children to exert power over the partner, or taking out aggression on the partner's children from previous marriages. As Juno's sons Ares and Hephaestus symbolized her frustrated expressions of assertion and creativity, Juno individuals may live out their repressed identity needs through their children. And as guardian of legal marriage, Juno signifies the rights of legitimate children and society's ostracism of illegitimate children.

4) **Projection and Repression** — In projecting their power onto the mate, Juno types will take on their partner's identity as their own. Hence, they are prone to measuring their own success, validation, and status through the marriage partner — e.g., becoming the doctor's wife or marrying the boss' daughter.

If an individual simply represses his need for power and equality in a relationship, he/she will either withdraw into numbness and apathy or smolder with resentment and bitterness. The former approach leads to a living death; the latter to psychosomatic illness and martyrdom.

5) **Juno and the Powerless** — As the ruler of those who lack power in relationships, Juno acts as a universal symbol for the classes of powerless individuals — abused women and children, victims of seduction, rape and incest, minorities, and the disabled. And because she never ceased to fight against injustice, Juno rules those who fight for the rights of the underdog (particularly women) in the political, economic, educational, and judicial arenas.

In conclusion, Juno symbolizes both the need for relationship and the refusal to accept the inequality and injustice that can result from poor communication between the partners. The weapons she uses to fight her battle are rage, revenge, plotting, and being a shrew. In essence, "what Hera means is the strength not to pretend that some lesser gift is the fulfillment nor to deny the longing."[13]

---

13. Christine Downing, *The Goddess: Mythological Images of the Feminine* (New York: The Crossroad Publishing Co., 1981), 95.

Juno as the Capacity for Meaningful Relationships

We have just witnessed that Juno's suffering has the capacity to induce dissatisfaction and conflict in the best intentioned of relationships. There is, however, another side to her nature that brings refinement, fulfillment, and intimacy into that same realm. Such relationships are founded on the principles of empathy, mutual trust, equality, and balance of power. It is this vision, and not the neuroses of the Juno-Jupiter marriage, that can serve as the new model for creating forms that can contain harmonious and joyful relationships.

JUNO COMMITMENT

As depicted in the mythology section, Juno describes a universal, three-fold cycle of relating that embodies the inherent rhythm of uniting with and separating from a mate. In addition to the three separate life stages of a woman, Juno's three aspects as *Parthenia* (maiden), *Teleia* (bride), and *Chera* (widow) refer to a natural rhythm that exists within her marital state. Juno cyclically restores her virginity in the bridal bath or sacred spring in preparation for consummation as a bride. The cycle culminates in an argument and separation with Jupiter, and then Juno retreats into hiding.[14] Contained within Juno's separation is the promise of return and reconciliation.

The psychic development of the feminine as consort and wife can be symbolized by the progressive stages of the goddesses Lilith, Juno, and Psyche. While Lilith embarked upon marriage with Adam, she chose to leave it when conflicts arose, prefering isolation and loneliness to subjugation. Juno entered into a relationship, and while she never derived true happiness and fulfillment from it, she demonstrated her willingness to return from her separations in order to resolve the conflicts. This dedication laid the foundation for Psyche to realize soul-mate union with her lover, Eros.

Juno, therefore, is the astrological significator of commitment, steadfastness, loyalty, devotion, and the willingness to remain in a relationship within the context of separation and return.

14. Stein, *Spring* (1977), 108.

JUNO ENHANCEMENT

Renowned for her beauty and her fidelity, Juno is an indicator of the many devices that can be employed to enhance the quality of a relationship. In Libran fashion, she used the aesthetics of Venus to beautify herself and her home for her partner. Hence, Juno governs women's (and men's) beauty and adornment — dress, jewels, scents, make-up, coquetry — the means by which one arouses and pleases her partner. The talent for enhancement extends into the home where Juno uses her instinct for style and decoration to create a harmonious and pleasing living environment. Moreover, Juno's expertise in the art of hospitality makes her a charming hostess to friends and guests.

Astrologically, therefore, an individual with a prominent Juno has the capacity to improve and enhance a relationship through bringing beauty, harmony, and pleasure into the union.

Juno as an Indicator of Women's Cycles and Functions

Juno is the general ruler of female development and represents the preparation for, culmination of, and separation from the married state.

In the first stage, girls learn how to attract men and to be good wives as opposed to mothers. Juno is the timer of menstruation, an experience that indicates a ripeness for sexual intercourse and subsequent marriage.

In the second stage, Juno becomes the bride, wife, matriarch, and emotional supporter of the husband's goals. (Ideally, he also supports her goals.) Here, she functions as the patroness of the nuclear family, home, and community.

In the final stage of widowhood, Juno signifies loss or separation, and the need for the woman to regain her sense of self. If she has lived primarily through her husband, the Juno woman will now face the challenge of establishing her own identity and inner purpose.

The Occult Teachings of Juno

On an occult level, Juno suggests the spiritual use of sexual energy within the marriage commitment. The bed in the center of Juno's temple symbolizes the ritual enactment of sexual consummation following the marriage bond. Juno holds the secret teachings of sexual *tantric* practices and the state of perfection that can be realized from following this path.

SEX AS BLISS

When two individuals unify their separate vibratory rates through mutual orgasm, they attune themselves to the cosmic rhythm of the whole and enter into the "one mind." While this state may last only for a moment, it provides the partners with a true experience of ecstatic bliss, cosmic union, and personal transcendence.

SEX AS MAGIC

The sex act contains the necessary forces to create life. Hence, at the moment of sexual union one can direct this creative energy into visual images that will later manifest as physical forms in the real world. This is the true meaning of magic — bringing invisible ideas into visible manifestation.

SEX AS REJUVENATION

The sexual energy released through orgasm can also be used to heal. Through repolarizing the cells, one can activate the vital force, purify the system, and regenerate the life energy. This process is similar to that of recharging a battery.

MARRIAGE AS ALCHEMICAL UNION

In true occult terms, marriage is a path of transcendence that transforms the ego's separateness into the larger whole. The marriage ceremony is a sacred ritual that merges the separate selves into a third essence; and, like many chemical reactions, the process is irreversible. Juno's spiritual gift enables each partner to use the marriage union as a vehicle to enter into the unity of the Divine Love that permeates all of life.

Juno Psychological Themes

Principle of Relatedness

relationship as self-expression • freedom and equality • intimacy and sharing • mutual trust and understanding • creating new forms of relationships

Pathology in Relationship

infidelity • jealousy • subjugation • betrayal • emotional attachment and possessiveness • emotional and sexual power games • projection and reflection • giving away power • attempt to regain power • identification through partner or children • woman as malcontent • subtle manipulation • feminine wiles

Occult Themes

tantric sexuality • soul mates • marriage as alchemical union • spiritual relationships

Themes of Transformation

separation and return

Further Reading on Juno

Bolen, Jean Shinoda. "Hera: Goddess of Marriage Commitment Maker and Wife." In *Goddesses in Everywoman.* San Francisco: Harper and Row, 1984.

Downing, Christine. "Coming to Terms With Hera." In *The Goddess: Mythological Images of the Feminine.* New York: Crossroad, 1981.

Kerenyi, Carl. "Zeus and Hera" and "Hera, Ares and Hephaistus." In *Gods of the Greeks*, translated by Norman Cameron. Great Britain: Billings and Sons, Ltd., 1981.

Kerenyi, Carl. *Zeus and Hera: Archetypal Image of Father, Husband, and Wife*, translated by Christopher Holme. New Jersey: Princeton University Press, 1975.

Spretnak, Charlene. "Hera." In *Lost Goddesses of Early Greece.* Berkeley: Moon Books, 1978.

Stein, Murray. "Hera: Bound and Unbound." *Spring* (1977).

Stone, Merlin. "Hera." In *Ancient Mirrors of Womanhood Vol. II.* New York: New Sibylline Books, 1979.

Zabriski, Philip. "Goddesses in Our Midst." *Quadrant* (Fall 1974).

CHAPTER ELEVEN

JUNO IN THE HOROSCOPE

Juno, goddess of marriage, was revered by the Greeks for her beauty and fidelity. As idealized wife, she exemplified the duties and attitudes of a proper mate within the institution of marriage.

Originally known as Hera, triple moon goddess and queen of the heavens, she ruled women's sexuality. Hera passed through the three life stages of women — maiden, mother and widow, corresponding to the new Moon, full Moon, and dark Moon. When she wedded the new sky god Jupiter, ancient Hera became the Olympian Juno and initiated women into the rites of marriage. Juno's pathology of jealousy and malcontentment mate stemmed from her subsequent unhappiness in her marriage.

In her role as wife, Juno symbolizes the principle of relatedness. She represents our capacity for meaningful relationship and the degree of awareness and sensitivity that we bring to another person.

Astrologically, Juno describes the ways in which we face the issues of compatibility, receptivity to others, mutual sharing, trust, jealousy, possessiveness, and power struggles.

Juno in the signs describes twelve styles of relating and meeting our intimacy needs. If these needs are denied, then Juno signifies the subsequent neurotic interactions that we will experience.

Juno in the houses shows where we are most likely to experience the need to relate and in what area of life experiences we will encounter our most important relationship lessons.

Juno's aspects to the planets describe how the relatedness function may be integrated with other parts of the personality. Harmonious aspects point to an easy blending, while stressful contacts signify potential conflicts between the relating urge and other psychic requirements of the individual.

Juno's sign and house position also describes those qualities that we seek in our ideal mate. When the varying needs are mastered and integrated, an individual with conflicting aspects in the horoscope no longer needs stress in order to learn balance.

Juno Astrological Rulerships

Juno is an indicator of all one-to-one relationships.
marriage • business • friendship • partner • mate • equality and freedom • balance of power • compatibility • marriage and relationship counseling

Juno rules over marriage rituals and institutions.
chastity and feminine virtue • courtship • betrothal • engagement • marriage • separation • divorce • legal marriage • freemate union • weddings and anniversaries • childbirth • legitimate and illegitimate children

Juno is a significator of protocol and social ritual.
host/hostess • hospitality• entertainment • etiquette • charm

Juno enhances feminine beauty.
adornment • dress style • makeup• scents • glamour • decor

Juno represents creative talent in the arts.
women's arts • performing arts • projection of image • masks • dance • drama • vocal

Juno stands up for women's rights.
E.R.A. • the matriarch • women's support groups

Juno is a symbol for the powerless.
women • battered wives • abused children • victims • minorities • disabled • crimes of sexual violence • seduction • rape • incest

Juno is associated with the atmosphere.
weather • climate • meteorology • storms • quality of environment • clean and pure air

Juno in the Signs

The source of the data for charts cited in the following sections is indicated by a number in parentheses.
(1) Lois Rodden's *The American Book of Charts*
(2) Lois Rodden's *Profiles of Women*
(3) Marc Penfield's *An Astrological Who's Who*

Juno in Aries individuals need independence and freedom in relationships. Outbursts of temper and anger are the release mechanisms for the frustrated need for autonomy. The suppression of identity needs can give rise to illnesses such as migraine headaches (a common housewife's ailment). Attraction to a domineering and assertive individual is possible when one projects one's power onto the partner.

Chart Example: Anita Bryant, whose opposition to gay rights stirred controversy, was born with Juno in Aries conjunct Saturn. She later recanted and said it was all her husband's idea. (2)

Juno in Taurus people need to have stability and groundedness in their relationships. The partner must be dependable, reliable , and exude the sensual contact of "being there." Nagging, complaining about money, and excessive need to possess tangible assets can result from fears of abandonment, financial impoverishment, and physical insecurity. People might either experience these traits or attract partners who express the malcontent.

Chart Example: Wallis Simpson, Duchess of Windsor, with Juno in Taurus in the second house opposing Saturn was unacceptable as a queen to the British government. She and her husband led a life of high-society luxury and travel in their self-imposed exile. (2)

Juno in Gemini indicates the need to have verbal stimulation and exchange in the relationship. The capacity to discuss day-to-day plans and having a variety of activities in which to participate together are essential ingredients. A lack of daily communication can lead to nervous tension, inner mental agitation of imagined dialogues, or continual verbal monologues. There can exist the desire for more than one mate and an ability to handle multiple relationships.

Chart Example: Jean-Paul Sartre, with Juno in Gemini in the eighth house, sought intense intellectual companionship from his partner Simone de Beauvoir. (2)

Juno in Cancer people desire emotional closeness and nurturing from their relationship. Sharing food as ritual and a strong emphasis on home life are essential. Moodiness, withdrawal, clinging, and dependent behavior arise when these emotional needs are not secured.

Chart Example: Raquel Welch, born with Juno conjunct Venus and Vesta in Cancer in the fifth house, has projected her sensuous beauty as a warm, caring, and desirable mate in her entertainment career. (2)

Juno in Leo individuals need admiration and excitement in their relationship. The romantic rites of courtship need to continue into the marriage, and the person must take pride in the partner. Being taken for granted, rejected, or ignored can produce egocentric, selfish behavior, and inappropriate means of gaining attention.

Chart Example: Ballerina Margot Fonteyn, with Juno conjunct Neptune in Leo, has had an artistically creative partnership with Rudolf Nureyev. (2)

Juno in Virgo people desire to achieve perfection in the relationship. A willingness of the partner to engage in analyzing day-to-day functioning and adjusting daily habit patterns contributes to the sense of a working relationship. This individual may become overly critical, faultfinding, and compulsive when his or her partner is unwilling to make these adjustments.

Chart Example: Glamorous actress Zsa Zsa Gabor was born with Juno in Virgo at her Ascendant. Unsatisfied with her six marriages, she is the author of *How to Catch a Man - Keep a Man - Get Rid of a Man*. (1)

Juno in Libra individuals need to feel as an equal and require a fair give-and-take in their relationship. Consultation from their partner on decision making and respect and approval for their ideas are required. When equality needs are not being met, this individual can become uncooperative, excessively competitive, or can even engage in direct combat.

Chart Example: Cher, with Juno conjunct Jupiter in Libra in the fourth house, has striven, unsuccessfully, to form equal and supportive relationships with her numerous husbands in her entertainment career. (2)

Juno in Scorpio people crave emotional and sexual intensity and intimate bonding with the partner. There can exist the tendency to attempt to control the partner, or to desire exclusive attention from him. Jealousy, manipulation, and territoriality or sexual withdrawal are reactions to the thwarting or denial of these needs.

Chart Example: Sensuality therapist Sylvia Kars has expressed her Juno-Venus conjunction in Scorpio in the ninth house through teaching, lecturing, and demonstrating new methods of sexual rehabilitation. (2)

Juno in Sagittarius individuals require intellectual stimulation with their partner. Consensus on a belief system or a mutually shared vision of the future is required. Rigid insistence on one's own beliefs, religious fanaticism, or inflated expectations of the future can result when a unifying vision is not shared.

Chart Example: Sirimavo Bandaranaike, with Juno in Sagittarius in the third house, succeeded her assassinated husband to become the first woman prime minister of Ceylon. (2)

Juno in Capricorn people seek depth and the assurance of long-term commitment in their relationship, and therefore may need the security of traditional and legally sanctioned forms. These individuals may attempt to control their partners and demand obedience or withdraw emotionally if their need for respect and stability is threatened.

Chart Example: Poet Robert Browning's marriage and devotion to an older and invalid woman, Elizabeth Barrett Browning, is one of the world's most famous romances. He was born with Juno conjunct Saturn in Capricorn. (3)

Juno in Aquarius persons require the freedom to be an individual and have a life apart from the relationship. These individuals need to have the opportunity to experiment with new relationship forms such as open marriage or role reversals. When the Juno in Aquarius partners are denied their freedom, they may engage in non-committal, unreliable, or erratic behavior.

Chart Example: Gertrude Stein's Juno in Aquarius conjunct the Sun reflected her assortment of intellectual, artistic, and offbeat friendships. (2)

Juno in Pisces people desire to realize their highest ideals through their relationship. Complete faith, commitment, and reverence toward/from their partner is what gives meaning and value. Disillusionment, withdrawal, escapism into fantasy and self-deception, martyrdom and victimization result when these idealistic expectations are not met.

Chart Example: Many of William Butler Yeats' poems and plays were inspired by his idealized love for beautiful Irish nationalist leader Maud Gonne. He was born with Juno in Pisces in the first house. (1)

Juno in the Houses

Juno in the first house correlates personal identity with being a partner to someone else. Relationship is self-expression, and this individual may feel more secure to be themselves when they have the support of a partner. This individual must learn the lessons of how to initiate relationship encounters, how to approach others, and how to get along with them. The most important relationship interactions will occur in how one presents oneself to others.

Chart Example: Foreign ambassador and diplomat Clare Boothe Luce was born with Juno rising in the sign of Sagittarius. (2)

Juno in the second house implies that value is placed on the financial and material security derived from their relationship. Mutual interdependency in providing for each other's needs is an important factor in compatibility. This person's most important relationship interactions will occur in the area of attachments and possessions.

Chart Example: Elvis Presley's provision of a lavish home, Graceland, and generosity to his mate may be described by his Juno in Aquarius conjunct the north node in the second house. (1)

Juno in the third house suggests that intellectual and verbal communication are required for fulfillment of relationship needs. The partner often serves as a catalyst for one's own self-understanding. The most important relationship interactions will occur in the area of daily communication and networking with others.

Chart Example: Sally Struthers, with Juno-Moon conjunction in Sagittarius in the third house, has made many media presentations on behalf of the Christian Children's Fund. (2)

Juno in the fourth house represents the need for a secure relationship as the foundation for the rest of life's activities. This can be an idealized version of "mate as nurturer" — one who provides (or needs providing for) home, food, comfort, and support. The most important relationship interactions will occur in the area of one's personal, private domain or with the family.

Chart Example: Margaret Trudeau, with Juno in Aries in the fourth house, was unable to bear the strain of the public protocol and duties of a politician's wife. (2)

Juno in the fifth house indicates that the relationship can be used to inspire and support one's personal creativity. Children often contribute to the sense of creative fulfillment. Thus, the major focus of the partnership can often center on parenting. The most important relationship interactions will occur with one's children, lovers, or creative endeavors.

Chart Example: James Dean, with Juno in Pisces in the fifth house opposing Neptune, became a film idol famous for his brooding portrayals of disillusioned young men. (1)

Juno in the sixth house people desire to be able to work efficiently and constructively with their partner, and may feel that a large part of the relationship function consists of keeping the day-to-day details of life in order. The most important relationship interactions will occur with employers and coworkers in one's job, or with health or service-related issues.

Chart Example: With Juno in Aquarius in the sixth house, Indira Gandhi worked with her husband for political causes. With the opposition to a twelfth house Saturn and Neptune, the couple was imprisoned by the British for their community work. (2)

Juno in the seventh house persons place primary emphasis on the value of marital, business or other intimate partnerships. The need to cooperate with others and form lifelong primary relationships becomes a major focus throughout the lifetime. The most important relationship interactions will occur in one-to-one encounters with others.

Chart Example: Edward Kennedy, with Juno in Cancer in the seventh house opposing Ceres, has experienced strong feelings of commitment to his marriage and family. It was this bond that partially contributed to his decision not to run for president in 1984. (2)

Juno in the eighth house individuals thrive on the intensity of emotional peak experiences in their relationship. Partners often put each other through continual changes and transformations. The most important relationship interactions will concern mutual finances and possessions, as well as the issues of trust, power, and sexuality.

Chart Example: Columnist Hedda Hopper, with Juno in Libra in the eighth house, exposed the private lives, romances, and incomes of Hollywood stars. (2)

Juno in the ninth house people seek meaning and truth through their relationships. There needs to exist a mutual respect for each other's mind. Oftentimes a person "marries" his or her teacher or vision quest. The most important relationship interactions will occur in the area of ideas, philosophical concepts, or foreign contacts.

Chart Example: Actress and Ambassador to Ghana Shirley Temple Black, with Juno in Virgo in the ninth house, has served as an articulate delegate to the United Nations. (2)

Juno in the tenth house can signify the person who "marries" his or her career. In addition, one's relationship may be on public display or provide a role model for other people to emulate (e.g., the political wife). Partnership may become the means for gaining social status. The most important relationship interactions occur through one's profession or career.

Chart Example: Actress and singer Judy Garland, with Juno in Aries in the tenth house, was essentially married to her career. A top star at the age of 13, she made 34 movies in the next 27 years. (2)

Juno in the eleventh house individuals need friendship and acceptance from the partner. One's "relationship unit" needs to be able to extend into friends and group associations, e.g., extended family forms, social and political activism, and group marriage. There is a visionary dimension represented by Juno in the eleventh house that revolutionizes old relationship forms. The most important relationship interactions will occur with friends and social associates.

Chart Example: Angela Davis, with Juno in Aquarius in the eleventh house, is known for her activism in many radical group activities. (2)

Juno in the twelfth house is significant in the *karmic* aspect of relationships. Often the partnerships one magnetizes have a destined quality to them. There may seem to be no visible reason for the union, but underlying the surface is an emotional power that one cannot deny. The visible relationship is only the tip of an iceberg whose antecedent causes go back into past lifetimes. Yet, it is these unconscious aspects that surface and dominate the relationship interplay. Sometimes the partner may be disabled or ill, so that one needs to selflessly serve and make amends to them. In other cases the partner may be a victim, and one must learn to release them and let them evolve on their own. Juno in the twelfth house individuals may experience loss, denial, or death of their partner. On a spiritual level, partnership is connected to a desire to merge with the infinite. Where mysticism, dreams, ideals, and yearnings are shared, this placement can signify an ecstatic union.

Chart Example: French cabaret singer Edith Piaf, with Juno in Scorpio in the twelfth house, was born in her grandmother's house of prostitution and experienced many personal tragedies including death and desertion in her relationships. (2)

Juno Aspects to the Planets

JUNO-SUN ASPECTS

The relating principle combines with identity and purpose. This combination indicates that learning to harmoniously interact with others becomes a major life theme.

Harmonious aspects depict a sensitivity to others and a gift for developing harmony and intimacy in a partnership. Because they see relationships as fundamental to a fulfilled life, these individuals will be committed to perfecting relationships as well as supporting their partners' individuality.

Stressful aspects point to potential conflicts between one's need for individuality and the need for relatedness. This could lead either to the stifling of personal expression or to a blockage in forming ongoing relationships. In the latter case, the desire for a meaningful relationship may become a lifelong challenge. Jealousy, mistrust, or power struggles with the partner are some of the obstacles that may have to be transformed for the harmonious relationship to occur.

Juno-Sun individuals are often attracted to solar, magnetic types. If the projection is overdone, the partner may be egocentric, grandiose, or childish.

The resolution of these challenges lies in developing a relationship structure that provides equality, honesty, and mutual support.

Chart Examples: Elizabeth Barrett Browning, with a twelfth house Juno in Virgo opposed to a Pisces Sun, was an invalid spinster until she found her true love at the age of 40. "How do I love thee? Let me count the ways," etc. (2)

Gloria Steinem's stressful square of Juno in Capricorn to the Sun in Aries fits her response when asked why she never married, "I don't mate well in captivity." (2)

Transsexual Christine Jorgensen's desire to become a woman is partially explained by her Juno in Pisces squaring a Gemini Sun. (3)

Paul Simon's musical partnership with Art Garfunkle is depicted by his Sun-Juno conjunction in Libra.

JUNO-MOON ASPECTS

The relatedness principle combines with emotional responsiveness. This combination indicates that the fulfillment of one's emotional needs is linked to having a meaningful relationship.

Harmonious aspects imply the capacity for sensitivity and empathy toward others. These individuals have the ability to be nurturing, supportive, and understanding of their partners. This aspect is particularly appropriate for counselors and performing artists who can feel the emotions of others and respond to them.

Stressful aspects point to potential conflicts between meeting one's emotional needs and those of the partner. The tendency may exist to project unconscious needs onto the partner or to become a reflection of the partner's own desires. Feelings of insecurity in either of the partners may bring out possessiveness, jealousy, or dependency. In addition, this individual may use emotional outbursts such as crying or throwing temper tantrums to manipulate and control the mate.

Juno-Moon individuals are often attracted to sympathetic and feeling (lunar) types. If the projection is overdone, the partner may manifest as moody, dependent, or smothering.

The resolution of these challenges lies in learning to find emotional security and fulfillment within oneself as well as through the partnership.

Chart Examples: Soraya of Iran, with a tenth-house Juno in Leo opposing the Moon in Aquarius, was divorced by the Shah because she could not fulfill her lunar role of bearing him any children. (2)

Hans Christian Andersen, with Juno conjunct the Moon in Taurus opposing Neptune in Scorpio, idealized relationships in his fairy tales, but in reality was rejected in love and remained lonely throughout his life. (3)

Writer Sylvia Plath's longing for and alienation from meaningful human relationships, which resulted in mental breakdown and suicide is symbolized by her Juno-Moon conjunction in Libra in the seventh house. (2)

JUNO-MERCURY ASPECTS

The relatedness principle combines with mental expression. This combination emphasizes the importance of mental and verbal communication in one's relationships.

Harmonious aspects indicate the capacity to articulate important ideas, concerns, and feelings to one's partner. Such clarity in daily communications contributes to sharing and intimacy. This is an excellent aspect for those in the communications professions such as teachers, counselors, salespeople, etc.

Stressful aspects point to potential communications difficulties between partners which can result in frequent arguments, disputes, and mental games. The individual with this aspect may also experience communication problems in daily interactions with others. In some instances, words may be used to manipulate and denigrate other people.

Juno-Mercury individuals are often attracted to mental and intellectual (i.e., mercurial) types. If the projection is overdone, the partner may manifest as rationalizing, detached, or cold.

The resolution of these challenges lies in learning how to listen without judgment to another's point of view. Then you can clearly and impartially express your own response, thereby engaging in meaningful communication.

Chart Examples: Victoria Woodhull, with Juno in Sagittarius squaring Mercury in Virgo, was the first woman to run for US president on the Equal Rights Party. Along with her sister, she established a brokerage business and published a feminist periodical. (1)

Former First Lady Eleanor Roosevelt expressed her Juno-Mercury conjunction in Libra in the tenth house through her diplomatic and communicative skills promoting civil rights and other liberties across the world. (3)

Dr. Marjorie Weinzweig, with Juno conjunct Mercury in Aquarius in the twelfth house, has written a college textbook entitled *A Philosophical Approach to Women's Liberation*. (2)

JUNO-VENUS ASPECTS

The relatedness principle combines with the feminine principle of love and sexuality. This combination emphasizes the romantic and aesthetic dimensions of relationship.

Harmonious aspects indicate the ability to infuse love and the appreciation of beauty into one's relationships. As part of creating a fulfilling relationship, these individuals can make themselves beautiful and sexually desirable to their partner. They may also engage in artistically creative partnerships.

Stressful aspects can point to potential conflicts between love and relationships. These people may experience difficulties in living with the person they love, may find the sexual and romantic aspects of relating frustrating, or may vainly attempt to validate their femininity through a relationship. Other problems can include jealousy, fear of sexual betrayal, or competitive rivalry.

Juno-Venus individuals can be attracted to artistic and sensual (Venusian) types. If the projection is overdone, the partner may manifest as overly accommodating, self-indulgent, or superficial (beauty's only skin deep).

The resolution of these challenges lies in learning to develop an inner appreciation of one's beauty and self-worth which is not dependent upon the opinions of others.

Chart Examples: Ringo Starr's commitment to his marriage is described by the conjunction of Juno to Venus at the IC. (4)

Clark Gable, with Juno in Aries square Venus in Capricorn, projected himself as a romantic ideal in his film career. (1)

Adrienne Hirt, with Juno conjunct Venus in Capricorn in the first house opposing Vesta, is a professional sex therapist and surrogate partner. (2)

JUNO-MARS ASPECTS

The relatedness principle combines with the masculine principle of action and assertion. This combination emphasizes the challenge of cooperation versus competition that arises in relationships.

Harmonious aspects link energy, dynamism, and productivity to a relationship. Intense passion and sexual finesse may contribute to relationship fulfillment. These individuals may experience the desire to protect and defend their intimate partners.

Stressful aspects point to potential conflicts between the assertion and cooperation urges, leading to the problem of domination/subjugation in the partnership. These individuals may express anger, aggression, or insensitivity in their relationships. In some cases, the need to prove one's masculinity through sexual performance may be present.

Juno-Mars individuals may attract willful, assertive, and

energetic (martial) types. If the projection is overdone, the partner can manifest as violent, self-centered, or abusive.

The resolution of these challenges lies in integrating the competitive, ego-oriented will of Mars with Juno's desire for cooperative union and harmony.

Chart Examples: Body-builder Charles Atlas titled the "world's most perfectly developed man" was born with Juno conjunct Mars in Libra. (1)

Mary Stuart, Queen of Scots, was the center of plots, intrigues, and destructive violence in her intimate relationships, as well as lifelong competition with her cousin Queen Elizabeth I for the English throne. She was born with Juno conjunct Mars in Aquarius. (3)

JUNO-JUPITER ASPECTS

The relatedness principle combines with the expansive/broadening urge. This combination emphasizes the mythic process symbolized by Juno and Jupiter as idealized husband and wife.

Harmonious aspects describe a search for truth and meaning in and through relationships. Often, these individuals will experience the desire for a complete "meeting of the minds" on mental, emotional, sexual, and spiritual levels. They may also choose to work with a partner for the advancement of a shared philosophical, educational, or religious belief system.

Stressful aspects point to potential conflict between the ideals and the reality of one's relationship. These individuals, like Juno herself, may experience frustration, resentment, and despair in their intimate partnerships and may subsequently strive to correct the inequalities and injustices. This aspect may also depict an exaggerated emphasis on the importance of relationships.

Juno-Jupiter individuals are attracted to philosophical and adventuresome types. If the projection is overdone, the partner may be arrogant, self-righteous, and extravagant.

The resolution of these challenges lies in the development of a mutually agreeable moral and philosophical code which allows for balance and equality within a partnership. For the health of the planet, this balance should extend to relationships between all men and women.

Chart Examples: Grace Kelly, with Juno in Sagittarius opposing Jupiter in Gemini, clearly experienced an expansion in lifestyle through her marriage to a foreign prince. (2)

Other individuals whose marriages have emulated the royal prominence of Jupiter and Juno include:

Queen Elizabeth II with Juno conjunct Jupiter in a first-house Aquarius (2)

Catherine the Great with Juno in Capricorn opposed to Jupiter in Cancer (2)

Soraya of Iran with Juno conjunct Jupiter in Leo (2)

Eva Braun (Hitler's mistress) with Juno conjunct Jupiter in Sagittarius (2)

First Lady Pat Nixon with Juno conjunct Jupiter in Sagittarius (2)

President George Washington with Juno conjunct Jupiter in Libra (3)

President Thomas Jefferson with Juno in Pisces opposed to Jupiter in Virgo (3)

President Abraham Lincoln with Juno conjunct Jupiter in Pisces. (1)

JUNO-SATURN ASPECTS

The relatedness principle combines with the urge to create form and structure. This combination can signify a solid, grounded, and realistic approach toward relationships.

Harmonious aspects represent the capacity for loyalty, longevity, and commitment in one's relationships. These individuals can work to build structures of lasting value for themselves and others. They also have the ability to work with others in business partnerships and other financial concerns.

Stressful aspects denote that one's limiting belief systems, personal insecurities, or fears of commitment may become obstacles to forming meaningful relationships. These individuals may remain with a partner out of social pressure, a sense of duty, or due to the desire for material security. This in turn can lead to feelings of oppression, frustration, and dependency. In some instances, fears of closeness and intimacy may block the formation of lasting unions.

Juno-Saturn individuals can be attracted to serious, older, responsible, parental types who can provide safety and security; or, they may also attract people who expect them to fill this role. If this projection is overdone, the partner may be authoritarian, cold, or may function exclusively as a parent or child.

The resolution of these challenges lies in building realistic steps to create a secure relationship which supports each partner's development. It may be necessary to transform one's limiting belief systems about partnerships in order to release past fears and insecurities.

Chart Examples: Emily Dickenson's Juno in Pisces at the IC opposing Saturn in Virgo at the MC describes her unfulfilled love for a married preacher. Subsequently, she lived alone with her domineering father, an unfortunate manifestation of her Saturn theme. (2)

George Sand, with Juno in a first-house Pisces opposing Saturn in seventh-house Virgo, refused to tolerate a stifling and restrictive marriage. She left her husband and two children to live a bohemian life and pursue her passion for writing. (2)

JUNO-URANUS ASPECTS

The relatedness principle combines with individuality and intuition. This combination shows the potential to revolutionize traditional relationship role models by universalizing the relating urge to include any and all types of relationships.

Harmonious aspects can symbolize the ability to bring new visions and formulations to relationship roles and functions. These partners have the capacity to create changes, excitement, and encourage individual freedom in their interactions. Their relationships may be seen as innovative, unusual, or radical.

Stressful aspects point to potential conflicts between one's need for personal freedom and the demands of the relationship. Fears of confinement and restriction can lead to erratic and unreliable commitments that produce frequent separations. These individuals may experience discomfort in participating in "traditional" role expectations and thus have a difficult time conforming to social norms of how a relationship should be.

Juno-Uranus individuals may be attracted to unconventional, original, or rebellious types. If the projection is overdone, the partner may be erratic, irresponsible, or just plain weird.

The resolution of these challenges lies in integrating one's individuality and independence into a committed partnership. This can occur when each partner acknowledges and supports the other's need for freedom while maintaining a loving bond.

Chart Examples: Marianne Alireza became the first American woman to marry and raise her children in a harem. Suddenly, without warning her husband divorced her, and she later won custody of her children — unheard of in Moslem law. This unconventional act is described by her Juno conjunct Uranus in Pisces trining Ceres in Scorpio. (2)

The Duke of Windsor with his Juno-Uranus conjunction in

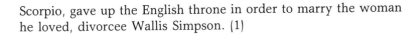

Scorpio, gave up the English throne in order to marry the woman he loved, divorcee Wallis Simpson. (1)

JUNO-NEPTUNE ASPECTS

The relatedness principle combines with the transcendent urge. This combination can symbolize psychic sensitivity and idealism in relationships.

Harmonious aspects may point to the capacity for telepathic rapport, empathy, and compassion in relationships. These people may project high ideals onto their relationships, desiring a mystical, spiritual union or dedicating the relationship to a social cause. They may also work harmoniously with others in artistic pursuits, or can infuse fantasy and imagination into their relationships.

Stressful aspects point to potential discrepancies between one's ideals and the reality of relationships. Unrealistic perceptions and expectations can lead to disillusionment and disappointment. Other problems may include deception, inappropriate self-sacrifice, or victimization.

Juno-Neptune individuals may attract mystical, poetic, or artistic types in relationships. If the projection is overdone, however, the partner may be deluded, chronically ill, or deceitful.

The resolution of these challenges lies in learning to seek the infinite from one's spiritual communion rather than from another human being.

Chart Examples: F. Scott Fitzgerald's partner, Zelda, may certainly be described as Neptunian, from her artistic imagination to her tragic schizophrenia that forced her in and out of sanitariums. Fitzgerald's attraction to his wife is depicted by the conjunction of Juno and Neptune in the air sign Gemini in the fifth house of romance and creativity. (1)

Marcia Moore, born with Juno in Virgo conjunct Neptune in Leo, experienced drug-induced, transcendent states of awareness with her anesthesiologist husband. These are rumored to be connected to her mysterious death. (2)

JUNO-PLUTO ASPECTS

The relatedness principle combines with the transformative urge. This combination symbolizes the personal and social transformation of relationship attitudes and roles.

Harmonious aspects can indicate the capacity to experience deep personal transformation through a partnership. These individuals can transmute the emotional and sexual intensity of their interactions for healing, strengthening, and personal regeneration. They also may exert a powerful influence over others or use the partnership energies to engage in Plutonian activities, e.g., peak experiences, research, healing, etc.

Stressful aspects point to potential conflicts between personal power and relationship needs. These individuals may experience violent or compulsive power struggles with the partner that may lead to his domination or destruction. Deep-seated resentments may continue long after the relationship has ended. Other problems may include sexual difficulties, intense jealousy, or prolonged attachment.

Juno-Pluto individuals may be attracted to intense, secretive, powerful, or occult types. If the projection is overdone, the partner may be dictatorial, violent, or destructive.

The resolution of these challenges lies in transforming personal power into mutual trust and fusion. Learning to forgive oneself and one's partner will bring about the much-needed healing.

Chart Examples: Debbie Reynolds, with Juno conjunct Pluto in Cancer in the tenth house, has undergone a number of painful transformations through her marriages, e.g., being publicly left for another woman by her first husband Eddie Fisher, and inheriting massive debts from her second husband. (2)

CHAPTER TWELVE

THE MINOR ASTEROIDS: AN OVERVIEW

The Asteroids as Octave Transformers

As defined in music theory, octaves are two notes that possess the identical harmonic structure but differ in pitch. If a particular note contains a certain number of vibrations per second, the higher octave (e.g., "high C") contains exactly twice the vibrations; the lower octave, half as many.

Astrology, the systematic study of the music of the spheres, likewise contains its version of the octave principle. The planetary pairs Mercury-Uranus, Venus-Neptune, and Mars-Pluto have similar energy patterns, but express at different levels. Lower octave planets — Mercury, Venus, and Mars — represent the forces that govern personal growth and awareness. The higher octave planets — Uranus, Neptune, and Pluto — denote a more rapid, finely tuned vibration and symbolize cosmic energy that affects humanity as a whole. Their primary meaning is a speeding up of the evolutionary process of the solar system.

The asteroids, in occupying primarily the space between Mars and Jupiter, forge a link between the lower and higher octave planets.

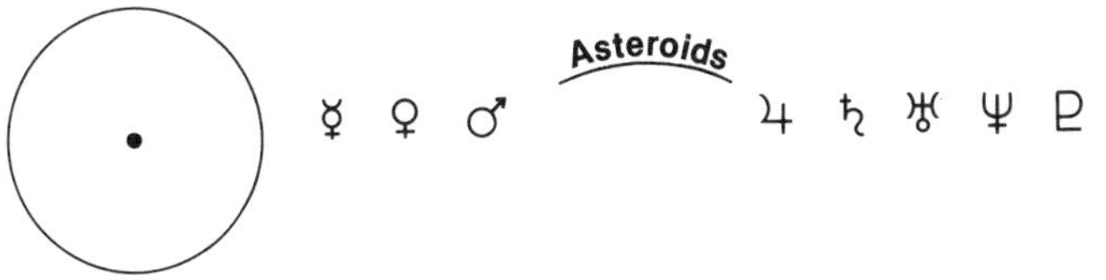

Figure 12-1

The asteroids are symbolic transformers between these two energy systems and point to the techniques by which the lower octave vibrations may be raised to their higher octave correspondences.

The advent of asteroid usage in astrology at this point in history clearly depicts the accelerating number of individuals who are responding en masse to the collective theme of planetary awareness and unity.

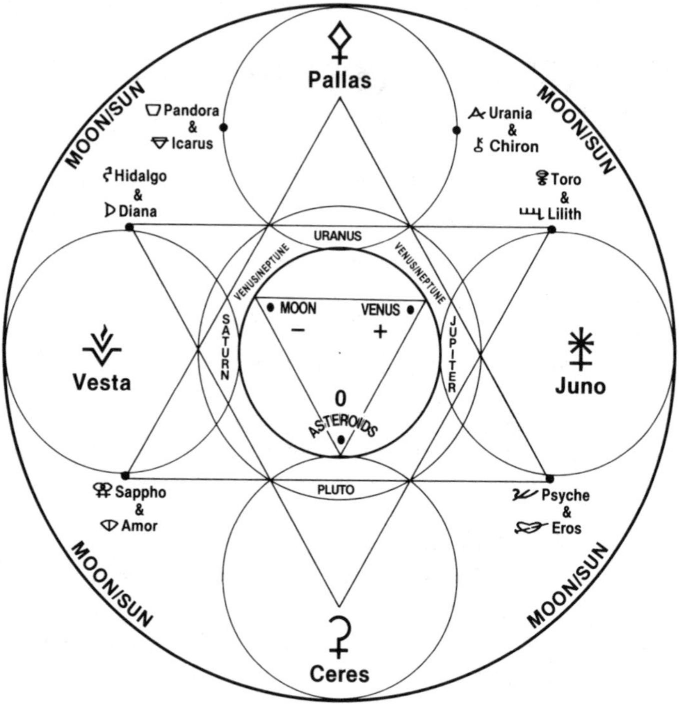

Figure 12-2

Table 12-1 provides a comprehensive overview of how each asteroid serves as a bridge between lower and higher octave functions.

Table 12-1

Lower Octave Planet	Transformer	Higher Octave Planet	Principle
Mercury	Icarus, Pandora, Urania	Uranus	Wisdom
Venus	Psyche, Sappho, Amor	Neptune	Love
Mars	Eros, Lilith, Toro	Pluto	Power
Mars	Diana, Hidalgo	Jupiter	Protection
Saturn	Chiron	Outer Planets	Knowledge

In the following pages, we will learn about the minor asteroids by viewing them as a series of bipolar functions. As portrayed in the table below, each asteroid pair contains a masculine and a feminine body, each of which represents one pole of the bipolar principle.

Table 12-2

Asteroid Pair		Polarity Principle
Psyche	Eros	The Lovers
Lilith	Toro	The Warriors
Sappho	Amor	The Empaths
Pandora	Icarus	The Liberators
Diana	Hidalgo	The Protectors
Urania	Chiron ⚷	The Knowledge Holders

Table 12-3

ASTEROID KEYPHRASES

Symbol	Asteroid	Keyphrase
	Psyche	Capacity to be psychically sensitive to another person
	Eros	Capacity for vitality and passion
	Lilith	Capacity to constructively release repressed anger and resolve conflict
	Toro	Capacity to use and control power
	Sappho	Capacity for romantic and artistic sensitivity
	Amor	Capacity for spiritual or platonic love and compassion
	Pandora	Capacity for curiosity which initiates change
	Icarus	Capacity for liberation and risk-taking
	Diana	Capacity for survival and self-protection
	Hidalgo	Capacity for self-assertion in defense of principles
	Urania	Capacity for inspired knowledge
⚷	Chiron	Capacity for wholistic understanding

Let us now explore these agents of transformation in greater detail.

The Lovers: Psyche and Eros

PSYCHE

The asteroid Psyche represents the principle of being psychically attuned and bonded to another human being. Often portrayed as a butterfly maiden, Psyche was born as a beautiful mortal, who in her search for reunion with her lover Eros, mastered heroic tasks set upon her by a wrathful Aphrodite. Through each undertaking, Psyche sensitized her internal telepathic channels. Depicting the soul's journey from mortality to divinity, Psyche successfully transformed her earthly nature into that of a deity so that she could become the heavenly bride of Eros, god of erotic love. Their union produced children named *Bliss, Pleasure*, and *Ecstasy*. Together, their love has come to symbolize soul-mate union.

In perfecting the relationship progression of Lilith and Juno, Psyche represents the completion stage of the development of the feminine as consort. Astrologically, Psyche is a higher octave of Venus, expressing a refinement of personal love and psychic attunement to another. Through following the path of Psyche, conscious relationship provides a path to spiritual illumination.

In chart analysis, a prominent Psyche symbolizes the capacity for psychic sensitivity to the mind and feelings of another person (her glyph is the Greek letter *psi*). This heightened awareness can produce the yearning for mystic, soul-mate union. Stressful placements of Psyche can indicate a total lack of sensitivity to others, a blocked psychic awareness or the inability to enter personal relationships. Because of their need for deep, intuitive communication, Psyche individuals may often decline to enter into superficial or short-term relationships. Thus, they may have many admirers but remain essentially alone.

When analyzed according to element, Psyche in an air sign depicts mental telepathy; in water, she implies empathy; in fire, she suggests the ability to control and direct energy fields; and in earth she points to achievements in physical manifestation.

Psyche aspects connect the meaning of the contacted planet with a heightened awareness. For example, Psyche-Uranus denotes precognition; Psyche-Chiron connotes abilities in psychic healing; and Psyche-Ceres can mirror skills in communicating with children or plant life.

In synastry, Psyche contacts describe points of intuitive knowing — and understanding — or total lack thereof — between individuals. Psyche-Eros contacts indicate the potential for soul-mate union.

EROS

Eros, god of erotic love, represents the principle of passionate desire. Mythologically, Eros was a primal, phallic god born out of *Chaos* (the Void) at the beginning of time. Embodying the masculine sexual force, he served as the generative masculine power which brought the world into creation. Thus, he manifested as the son of Mars and Venus in the later Olympic pantheon.

Astrologically, Eros functions as a higher octave of Mars. Eros was able to refine and transform his unconscious, instinctual sexual drive into erotic love as a path to spiritual illumination through his romance with Psyche. In classical Greece, Eros became a patron of homosexual love and can be one indicator of sexual preference. Beyond sexuality, Eros' passion is experienced as simply "whatever turns you on," excites, or arouses. Eros is also the powerful emotional force that motivates one toward consummating desires and visions.

In chart analysis, Eros serves as an indicator of one's passion, sexual attraction, sexual preference, and vital energy. The Eros personality is marked by the need to continuously recreate the excitement of falling in and being in love. Hence, Eros by transit is a timer of sexual activity.

Stressful placements of Eros in the chart may describe potential difficulties in sexual potency and activity, frustrated passion, a depletion of vital force, or obsessive-compulsive attitudes toward love until the individual channels passion positively. Planetary contacts indicate that the individual will be "turned on" by the aspected planet. For example, with Eros-Ceres, the passion is food; Eros-Urania loves astrology and music; Eros-Saturn is excited by work, etc.

In synastry, Eros aspects signify sexual compatibility and the reciprocation of passion.

The Warriors: Lilith and Toro

LILITH

Lilith, portrayed as goddess of the night who tames the wild beasts, represents the principle of repressed anger and conflict resolution. Originally Lilith was a handmaiden of the great goddess *Inanna* from

Sumeria who brought in the men from the fields to the holy temple at Erech for the sacred, sexual customs. According to Hebraic tradition, as the first wife of Adam, Lilith depicts the first stage of the feminine as consort. In this encounter, she found herself in conflict with Adam who wished to rule over her, despite her belief that "we are both equal because we both come from the same earth." Eventually, Lilith left Adam, choosing exile and loneliness rather than domination and subjugation. As punishment for rejecting her husband, Lilith became regarded as the personification of feminine evil — a dark demoness who threatened pregnant women, killed children, and seduced and destroyed men. Her image embodied men's worst fears concerning their sexuality and potency.

Astrologically, Lilith, linked with Toro, forms an intermediary step in the octave progression between Mars and Pluto and addresses the issues of personal, sexual power and repressed anger. In interpersonal relationships, her responses range from complete withdrawal to bickering and sexual manipulation to skillful negotiation and compromise. Because of the primal resentment that arises from being rejected, Lilith contains a tremendous amount of repressed anger. This suppressed rage, when activated, has the potential to erupt in sexual domination and violence. On the positive side, Lilith teaches us the art of consensus by which the transformative energy of Mars-Pluto can be used to fuse rather than destroy relationships.

In chart analysis, a prominent Lilith displays the quality of personal independence and a refusal to submit to another or compromise one's beliefs as well as the potential for resolution. Stressful placements of Lilith point to the perception of the feminine as evil (the vamp), potential rape and sexual abuse (especially when aspected to Toro or Saturn), or the inability to reach agreement until power issues are resolved.

Lilith's aspects to the planets depict how the contacted planet deals with the issue of conflict resolution. For example, Lilith-Ceres focuses on resolving conflict in family matters; Lilith-Jupiter contacts may involve religious beliefs; with Lilith-Venus the focus is on love and sex, etc.

In synastry, Lilith contacts signify the need for the individuals to learn negotiation as well as potential problems involving sexual fear, rejection, anger, and suspicion.

TORO

Toro, the Spanish word for bull, represents the principle of boundless strength and power. From the Stone Age to modern times, the bull has impressed all as the supreme embodiment of power and fertility. Early Paleolithic cave paintings depict humanity's belief in the special magic derived from the bull. Veneration of a bull deity took hold of the Sumerians, Hittites, Cannanites, Hebrews, and in India, where it continues today. The bull-leaping spectacles of the Creteans and the secret religious rites of the cults of Dionysus and Mithras attempted to extract the *manna*, or concentrated essence of the bull's fertile potency, for the benefit of mankind.

Astrologically, Toro symbolizes an intermediary in the octave progression between Mars and Pluto, transforming the raw, instinctive desire of Mars into the controlled, focused, and penetrating power of Pluto. Toro also describes how we confront and handle the onslaught of violent or negative influences that we experience either from without or from within our own minds.

When expressed unconsciously, Toro energy can manifest as brute force or ruthless aggression. When this power is repressed or projected, one may become the passive victim of outside attack or assault. More skillful applications of Toro include the mastery of the martial arts that seek to deflect and reverse aggression, the application of nonviolent resistance, and the ability to transmute potentially harmful forces into protective ones. Knowing how to turn one's enemy into an ally is indeed a potent power, especially when the "enemy" lies within your own being! Thus, Toro's secret teaching involves taming the inner power of the bull that resides in each of us and directing it for constructive purposes.

In chart analysis, a prominent Toro indicates that the proper channeling of one's inner power will become a lifelong theme. When this force is correctly handled, the Toro individual displays strength, power, and unusual vitality. Stressful placements of Toro point to the potential for violent or destructive outbursts until inner strength is harnessed for good. If this power is projected, the person will experience fear, paranoia, and victimization.

Aspects of Toro to the planets suggest intensified strength and power for the themes indicated by the contacted planet. For example, Mercury-Toro can represent forceful communications; Toro-Moon, emotional power; Toro-Neptune, spiritual power, etc.

In synastry, Toro contacts depict the areas where power struggles and confrontations are likely to arise.

The Empaths: Sappho and Amor

SAPPHO

The Greek poetess Sappho represents the principle of romantic and artistic sensitivity. While dwelling on the island of Lesbos in the sixth century BC, Sappho presided over a young woman's academy of fine arts where she composed love poetry and lyrical verse. Evidence now exists that Sappho's school was a mystery temple of Aphrodite where the sexual teachings of the ancient goddess-religion were briefly rekindled after 1,500 years of suppression.

Sappho's love poetry evokes intimate, personal feelings of yearning, desolation, jealousy and rapture. She speaks of a variety of loves — single and multiple, conjugal and nonconjugal, heterosexual and lesbian, and maternal. Her vision rests on empathy and attraction between persons as being, in a sense, all we've got.[1] Referred to as the tenth muse, Sappho delicately and subtly probed the agony and ecstasy of being in love. She writes, "Once again, Love, the loosener of limbs, the bittersweet, the irresistible, insinuous thing snakes me like a tree in the wind."[2]

Astrologically, Sappho serves as an intermediary in the octave progression that links Venus and Neptune. Sappho refines the Venus vibration and sensitizes individuals to the emotions associated with their sexuality. Recognizing that all of humanity has the same need to love, Sappho taught of the need to love both men and women, and to honor the healing power of love in whatever form it presents itself (such teachings sparked controversy as to her possible lesbian nature).

In chart analysis, Sappho is a significator of sensuality and sexuality, emotional extremes in love, poetic ability, and feminine education in the fine arts. The Sappho personality is characterized by a high degree of aesthetic refinement and romantic sensitivity. While Sappho can function as an indicator of sexual preference, it more commonly suggests a sensitivity and bonding with one's same sex that may or may not result in sexual activity.

Stressful placements of Sappho point to potential difficulties in understanding or expressing love and sexuality as the individual learns to balance intimacy needs with other sides to the nature.

---

1. Maurice Hill, *The Poems of Sappho* (New York: Philosophical Library,1954), 37.
2. Paul Frederick, *The Meaning of Aphrodite* (Chicago: University of Chicago Press, 1978), 128.

In synastry, Sappho contacts depict sexual/sensual attractions or repulsions.

AMOR

Amor, Roman god of love, represents the principle of compassion and loving kindness. Amor is frequently confused with Cupid, the mischievous prankster of love games and Eros, god of sexual passion. Amor, however expresses his own quality of love — a state of loving as opposed to "falling" in love.

Astrologically, Amor, like Sappho, functions as an intermediary in the progression from the personal love of Venus to the transpersonal love of Neptune. Amor expresses a loving kindness that is given without judgment or expectation of return. He teaches us to develop what is loving in ourselves and others, to let go of what is negative, and to rejoice in the good fortune of others. Esoterically, Amor is exalted in Pisces where his love, pure motivation, compassion, and selfless service find their ultimate fulfillment.

In chart analysis, a prominent Amor signifies a personality marked by kindness, goodwill, and a desire to selflessly serve. Stressful aspects suggest possible difficulties in expressing one's compassionate and empathetic side or in combining compassion with other psychic needs. Amor's aspects to the planets show an all-abiding love and concern in the realm of their activities. For example, Amor-Jupiter indicates a love of learning; Amor-Venus shows a love of beauty; Amor-Toro denotes the enlightened warrior, etc.

In synastry, Amor contacts signify that a loving, caring bond and deep affection may exist between individuals. Eros-Amor interchart contacts often symbolize the transmutation of erotic desire into platonic love and friendship.

The Liberators: Pandora and Icarus

PANDORA

Pandora, ancestress of mortal women and opener of the forbidden box, represents the principle of curiosity that initiates change. In her earlier form, Pandora was the all-giving *Anesidora* who arose from the earth bearing gifts of food for people and animals. In later Olympian mythology, Pandora was fashioned by the gods out of earth and water, the first woman to be created. According to Hesiod, Zeus sent her as his malicious gift to punish humanity for using Prometheus' gift of fire. Upon opening the jar, Pandora released a host of sorrows, miseries, and plagues upon the earth and closed it just before

Hope could escape. Thus, she became regarded, like the biblical Eve, as the personification of feminine evil.

Astrologically, Pandora serves as an intermediary in the octave progression between Mercury and Uranus. Through her curiosity, Pandora acts an an agent of change, inviting the unexpected and opening up new possibilities. By rising from the earth, she brings to light what had previously been hidden. Pandora may signify a process of deep cleansing, purification, and healing. Pandora is a Gemini-Scorpio blend who through her unorthodox actions raises the rational intellect of Mercury to the intuitive and revolutionary vibration of Uranus.

In chart analysis, a prominent Pandora denotes an affinity for innovation, unexpected discovery, and controversy. The Pandora personality is marked by a curious, restless, and rebellious nature. Stressful placements of Pandora can depict a meddling troublemaker or its opposite — the individual who resists change ("don't rock the boat") or who covers up anything unpleasant. Conflicting aspects can be integrated by encouraging creative changes.

Pandora's aspects connect curiosity and change to the planet involved. For example, this author has Pandora conjunct Urania, the ruler of astrology. Hence, her research into the asteroids has stirred up established modes of thought in astrology, unleashing a new array of archetypes to be considered.

In synastry, Pandora contacts signify those areas where we stir up others and put them through a variety of changes.

ICARUS

My Icarus! he says; I warn thee fly.
Along the middle track: nor high, nor low
If low, thy plumes may flag with oceans spray
If high, the sun may dart his fiery ray.[3]
Ovid (Elton's tr.)

Icarus, the winged youth who flew too close to the sun, represents the principle of liberation and risk-taking. Imprisoned with his father, the inventor *Daedalus*, in the Cretean labyrinth of the *Minotaur*, Icarus escaped the island with wings constructed from the feathers of birds. Although terrified at first to leap into the unknown, Icarus overcame his fear and flew off. Soaring ever upward, Icarus became

3. H. A. Guerber, *Myths of Greece and Rome* (New York: American Book Company, 1893), 255.

exhilarated with the freedom of flight and forgot his father's warning to follow the middle path. As he approached the sun, the wax binding his feathers melted, and Icarus crashed into what is now known as the Icarian Sea.

Astrologically, Icarus, like Pandora, serves as an intermediary in the octave progression between Mercury and Uranus. As Icarus comes closer to the Sun than any planet, including Mercury, he represents the most direct, but also the most dangerous path to liberation. Icarus' teaching involves the necessity of maintaining self-discipline and mindfulness during free flight so as to avoid going to extremes and crashing. The Icarus' symbol of upward-soaring wings is the literal emblem for motorcycle enthusiasts (e.g., Honda and Harley-Davidson) where a sense of freedom is experienced at high speeds but requires concentration and skillful control in order to avoid disaster. And in meditation, another technique offering liberation, the same means of disciplining the mind is employed.

On the physical plane, Icarus symbolizes the opportunity to achieve liberation from confining or restrictive situations. On the psychological plane, Icarus can show the individual gaining freedom from social conditioning and conformity. On the spiritual plane, Icarus depicts liberating the mind from *samsara* — the attachment to earthbound reality.

In chart analysis, Icarus denotes an affinity for freedom, risk-taking (especially through the sports of aviation, motorcycling, car-racing, and skiing), and meditation. The Icarus personality rebels against confinement, continually tests and attempts to go beyond his or her limits, and strives for freedom, with various degrees of skill and success. Stressful placements of Icarus can indicate recklessness, extremism, overreach, and fear of flight or the unknown until one's risk-taking side is blended with other inner needs.

Aspects to planets associate them with a desire for freedom (e.g., Icarus-Mercury desires freedom of speech; Icarus-Mars/Venus wants sexual freedom; Icarus-Jupiter wants religious freedom, etc.).

In synastry, Icarus contacts show how we tend to support or repress another's individuality.

The Protectors: Diana and Hidalgo

DIANA

Diana, goddess of untamed nature, represents the principle of survival and self-protection. Known to the Greeks as Artemis, Diana assumed many forms. As the virgin new-moon goddess, she roamed the remote forests and mountains with her band of chaste nymphs antagonistic toward men. As Lady of the Wild Things, she protected all young life forms, both animal and human. For her fierce, warlike nature, she was venerated by the Amazons. And, as the many-breasted Artemis of Ephesus, she became a symbol of fertility and childbirth. Later Olympian mythology transformed Artemis into the goddess of the hunt, armed with a bow and quiver, twin sister of Apollo the sun god.

Astrologically, Diana represents the first stage of the feminine as virgin, and as such depicts the inviolateness of the maiden stage. Thus, Diana protected the virginity of young girls and safely guided them into puberty. Diana symbolizes the vitality, strength, and aspirations of young womanhood. This stage of development corresponds to the waxing, crescent moon.

Diana also signifies the wisdom that comes from an instinctual understanding of nature and natural laws. Residing in the distant wilderness, Diana spent much of her time in solitude. Here, covered by privacy and darkness, the germinal budding maiden could emerge from the seed pod of the wise old crone, dark moon Hecate.

In chart analysis, a prominent Diana signifies an attunement to natural as opposed to civilized laws, and to the instinct to protect those in need. The Diana personality is private, self-identified, strong, independent, and concerned with personal survival. Stressful placements can indicate a desire to remain in perpetual youth, or the fear of intimacy and closeness.

Aspects to planets denote a protective concern for the activities of the contacted planet. For example, Diana-Ceres protects children; Diana-Eros protects the sexual encounter; Diana-Neptune protects the faith, etc.

In synastry, Diana contacts point to sister-sister camaraderie or brother-sister relationships.

HIDALGO

Hidalgo, a Mexican priest and revolutionary, represents the principle of self-assertion and fighting for one's beliefs. Miguel Hidalgo y Costilla, the father of Mexican independence, was born into the Spanish upper class in 1753. As a Catholic priest, he worked to improve the economic conditions of his impoverished Indian parishoners, and joined a secret revolutionary group whose purpose was to free the Indians from the oppression of the Spanish colonial government. To achieve this end, he led an army of thousands of Mexican natives in revolt against the Spanish. After many courageous battles, Hidalgo was captured, tried, excommunicated, and shot as a rebel on July 31, 1811. After his execution, his fame quickly spread as a hero, martyr, and saint. Today, Mexico's Independence Day is celebrated on the day (September 16) that Hidalgo proclaimed his nation's freedom.

Astrologically, Hidalgo, like Diana, serves as an intermediary between Mars and Jupiter. Hidalgo symbolizes the courage and dedication to act (Mars) on one's beliefs (Jupiter). He uses the forms of political involvement, protest, and radical movements to challenge the authority of the established religion and government. Because Hidalgo works to correct injustices, he is considered to be a "protector" of the weak and oppressed. The politics of Liberation Theology in Latin America are an expression of Hidalgo issues.

In chart analysis, a prominent Hidalgo can indicate involvement in political causes, an affinity with Spanish-speaking countries (especially Latin America), or a desire to protect and defend minorities. The personality is characterized by an assertive, rugged, willful or rebellious nature. Stressful placements of Hidalgo may point to conflicts with authority, recklessness, fanatical adherence to one's own vision, defiance, and possible incarceration.

Hidalgo's aspects show how the protective theme combines with the activity of the contacted planet. For example, a Hidalgo-Ceres individual may dedicate himself to defending abused children; Hidalgo-Venus indicates protecting loved ones; Hidalgo-Mercury will defend his ideas.

In synastry, Hidalgo contacts depict areas of potential protection or domination between people.

The Knowledge Holders: Urania and Chiron

URANIA

Urania, the "Heavenly One," represents the principle of inspired knowledge. Mythologically, Urania was one of the nine muses (from whom we derive the word "museum") whose tasks were to serve as sources of divine inspiration for their respective spheres of knowledge. Urania presided over the domains of astrology, astronomy, music, and number. Associated with the Harmony of the Spheres, she gave birth to the great musician Linus, inventor of melody and rhythm. Urania's symbols are the celestial globe and compass (⚹), the instruments that she uses to measure the heavens.

In the *tarot*, Isis-Urania is the woman depicted in the Star key. She symbolizes truth gained through meditation as well as the ability to bring wisdom and insight into one's creative work. Astrologically, Urania represents the principle of cosmic knowledge. She is a deep thinker who draws upon her inspiration to uncover mental treasures. In her search for celestial truths, Urania uses her mental astuteness to probe both the microcosm and the macrocosm.

In chart analysis, a prominent Urania indicates an affinity for astrology, astronomy, music (more theory and composition than performance), pure sciences, mathematics, measurement, or numerology. The Urania personality type is introspective, thoughtful, and serious. Stressful placements can point to learning difficulties, and blocked access to intuition and insight.

Aspects with planets blend inspirational understanding with the activities of the contacted planet. For example, Urania-Venus denotes inspired love; Urania-Neptune can imply inspired music, poetry, or devotion; Urania-Uranus suggests inspired genius and revolutionary ideas.

In synastry, Urania contacts symbolize individuals who can share a common source of inspiration — especially, music, astrology, or any abstract symbol system.

CHIRON

Discovered in 1977 by astronomer Charles Kowal, Chiron is not an asteroid but a planetoid (a body resembling a planet) traveling between the orbits of Saturn and Uranus. Astronomers believe that Chiron originated outside our solar system and will eventually leave it. Likewise, mythological Chiron came from another realm and left the human kingdom after he had completed his teachings. Thus, Chiron serves as a link between our solar system and the galaxy, between the known (Saturn) and the unknown (Uranus).

Chiron the Centaur represents the principle of wholistic understanding. His 49-year orbit symbolizes the number of higher wisdom (7x7), as well as the number of days in the Bardo passage of the Egyptian and Tibetan Books of the Dead. Half horse, half man, Chiron emerged from the elemental nature kingdom to the human sphere where he became foster parent to many a Greek hero. His students included *Achilles*, *Jason*, and *Asclepius*, god of healing who learned of medicinal herbs and surgery.

One day, Chiron became wounded in battle when a poison arrow was shot into his knee. For all his healing knowledge, he was unable to cure himself. In order to relieve his agony, Chiron gave up his immortality. Subsequently, Zeus transformed him into the constellation Sagittarius in honor of his devoted service to the human kingdom.

Astrologically, Chiron is a knowledge holder who transmits higher teachings either as an outer teacher (Saturn) or as an inner teacher or spirit guide (Uranus). Embodying the archetype of "wounded healer," Chiron stresses the importance of going within to find a cure or answer — and then sharing it with others. In his two primary subjects of education and medicine, Chiron unites the body and mind, instinct and intellect. We see his ancient teachings now emerging through the recent advent of holistic health and education.

In chart analysis, a prominent Chiron indicates the potential to be an educator or healer, one who challenges established limited views. The Chiron personality can be wise, yet grounded in practical reality. Stressful placements might point to limited understanding, reliance on authority or dogma, self-doubt, or spiritual unrest.

Aspects to the planets associate an intuitive, higher knowledge with the activities of the contacted planet. For example, Chiron-Jupiter denotes the enlightened spiritual teacher or political ruler; Chiron-Mars describes the physician or surgeon; Chiron-Juno can describe the spiritual counselor or partner.

In synastry, Chiron contacts suggest healing and educational exchange between the individuals.

Summary

As you can see by now, the "minor asteroids" are by no means minor or secondary. Their symbology and value to astrology take on as much importance as do Ceres, Pallas, Vesta, and Juno. Only through future research and study will these archetypes assume their rightful place in astrological interpretation.

Further Reading on the Minor Asteroids

Addey, John M. "Urania: The Astrologer's Asteroid." In *Ephemeris of Urania 1900-2000.* New York: C.A.O. Times, 1981.

Apuleius. *The Golden Ass.* Translated by William Adlington. New York: Collier Books, 1972.

Association for Studying Chiron, 158 Poplar, Ambler, PA 19002.

Barnard, Mary. *Sappho: A New Translation.* Berkeley and Los Angeles, California: University of California Press, 1958.

Bolen, Jean Shinoda. "Artemis: Goddess of the Hunt and Moon,

Competitor and Sister." In *Goddesses in Everywoman*. San Francisco: Harper and Row, 1984.
Bradley, Marion Zimmer. Darkover novels mostly published by DAW. A series of science fiction novels.
Brindel, June R. *Ariadne*. New York: St. Martin's Press, 1980.
Conrad, Jack Randolph. *The Horn and The Sword: The History of the Bull as a Symbol of Power and Fertility*. New York: E. P. Dutton and Company, Inc., 1957.
Dobyns, Zipporah. *Expanding Astrology's Universe*. San Diego: ACS Publications, Inc., 1983.
Downing, Christine. "Artemis: The Goddess Who Comes from Afar." In *The Goddess: Mythological Images of the Feminine*. New York: Crossroad Publishing Company, 1981.
Frederick, Paul. *The Meaning of Aphrodite*. Chicago: University of Chicago Press, 1978.
Graves, Robert. *The White Goddess*. New York: Farrar, Straus and Giroux, 1948.
Graves, Robert, and Raphael Patai. *Hebrew Myths: The Book of Genesis*. New York: McGraw-Hill Book Co., 1966.
Hall, Nor. *The Moon and the Virgin*. New York: Harper and Row, 1980.
Hallett, Judith P. "Sappho and Her Social Context: Sense and Sensuality." *Signs* (Spring 1979): 447-469.
Hesiod. *Theogony* 570-612, and *Works and Days* 47-105.
Hill, Maurice. *The Poems of Sappho*. New York: Philosophical Library, 1954.
Johnson, Robert A. *She: Understanding Feminine Psychology*. New York: Harper and Row, 1977.
Joseph, Anthony M. "Chiron: Archetypal Image of Teacher and Healer." In *Ephemeris of Chiron 1890-2000*. Toronto, Canada: Phenomena Publications, 1978.
Kerenyi, Carl. "A Mythological Image of Girlhood: Artemis." In *Facing the Gods*. Edited by James Hillman. Irving, Texas: Spring Publications, Inc., 1980.
Lantero, Ermine. *The Continuing Discovery of Chiron*. York, Maine: Samuel Weiser, Inc., 1983.
Lehman, J. Lee. "*Amor* Introduction." In *Ephemeris of Amor 1900-2000*. New York: C.A.O. Times, 1981.
Lehman, J. Lee. "*Eros* Introduction," and Al H. Morrison, "Commentary: *Eros and Our Culture*." In *Ephemeris of Eros 1900-2000*. New York: C.A.O. Times, 1980.
Lehman, J. Lee. "Interpreting Diana"; Nona Press, "Introduction

to Diana''; and Diana Rosenberg, ''The Mythology of Diana.'' In *Ephemeris of Diana 1900-2000*. National Council for Geocosmic Research, Inc., 1981.

Lehman, J. Lee, ''Introduction to the Asteroid Hidalgo''; Al H. Morrison, ''Commentary on the Asteroid Hidalgo''; and Zane B. Stein, ''Thoughts About Hidalgo.'' In *Ephemeris of Hidalgo 1900-2000*. New York: C.A.O. Times, 1980.

Lehman, J. Lee. ''Introduction to the Asteroid Sappho,'' and Al H. Morrison, ''Perspective on the Asteroid Sappho.'' In *Ephemeris of Sappho 1900-2000*. New York: C.A.O. Times, 1980.

Lehman, J. Lee, ''*Lilith* Introduction,'' and Al H. Morrison, ''Comment.'' In *Ephemeris of Lilith 1900-2000*. New York: C.A.O. Times, 1980.

Lehman, J. Lee. ''*Pandora* Introduction.'' In *Ephemeris of Pandora 1900-2000*. New York: C.A.O. Times, 1980.

Lehman, J. Lee. ''*Psyche* Introduction,'' and Al H. Morrison, ''Commentary: *Psyche and Our Culture.'' In Ephemeris of Psyche 1900-2000*. New York: C.A.O. Times, 1980.

Lewis, C. S. *Till We Have Faces: A Myth Retold*. New York: Harcourt, Brace and World, 1956.

MacDonald, George. *Phantasies and Lilith*. Michigan: Wm. B. Eerdmans Publishing Co., 1975.

Morrison, Al H., ''Commentary on *Icarus*,'' and Zane B. Stein, ''Icarus.'' *Ephemeris of Icarus*. New York: C.A.O. Times, 1980.

Neumann, Erich. *Amor and Psyche: The Psychic Development of the Feminine*. Translated by Ralph Manheim. Princeton, New Jersey: Princeton University Press, 1973.

Noelle, Richard. *Chiron*: New Planet in the Horoscope. Tempe, Arizona: American Federation of Astrologers, 1983.

Panofsky, Dora and Edwin. *Pandora's Box*. Princeton, New Jersey: Princeton University Press, 1962.

Rivlin, Lily. ''Lilith.'' *Ms.* vol. 6 (December 1972).

Robinson, David M. *Sappho and Her Influence*. New York: Michael Jones Company, 1925.

Stein, Zane B. *Interpreting Chiron*. Lansdale, Pennsylvania: Association for Studying Chiron, 1983.

———., editor. *The Chiron Booklet #1* and *The Chiron Booklet #2*. Lansdale, Pennsylvania: Association for Studying Chiron, 1983.

Stein, Zane B., and Al H. Morrison, ''Toro.'' *Ephemeris of Toro 1900-2000*. New York: C.A.O. Times, 1981.

Tenzin Gyatso, The Fourteenth Dalai Lama. *Kindness, Clarity and Insight*. Translated by Jeffrey Hopkins and Elizabeth Napper. New

York: Snow Lions Publications, 1984.
Thompson, William Irwin. *The Time Falling Bodies Take to Light*. New York: St. Martin's Press, 1981.
Von Franz, Maria-Louise. *The Interpretation of Apuleius' Golden Ass*. Irving, Texas: Spring Publications, Inc., 1980.
Weigall, Arthur. *Sappho of Lesbos*. New York: Frederick A. Stokes Company, 1932.
Weinberg, Judy. "Lilith Sources." *Lilith* vol. 1, no. 1 (June 1976).
Zuckoff, Avina Cantor. "The Lilith Question." *Lilith* vol.1, no. 1 (June 1976).

CHAPTER THIRTEEN

AN ASTRONOMICAL PORTRAIT OF THE ASTEROIDS

Positioned largely between the orbits of Mars and Jupiter, thousands of minor planetary bodies known as the asteroids revolve around the sun. Varying in size and shape, composition and orbital patterns, the asteroids are believed to contain clues about the formation and evolution of our solar system. Numbering up to 100,000, their total combined mass is less than that of our moon. Because they are so tiny, it is very difficult to see their discs, even with a fine telescope. The absence of apparent discs suggested the name asteroid, meaning ''star-like.''

In the following pages, we will present an overview of the astronomical data that has been accumulated on these enigmatic wanderers since their discovery in 1801.

The Discovery of the Asteroids

As early as 1596, astronomer Johannes Kepler wrote, ''Between Mars and Jupiter I place a planet.'' A century and a half later, Titius of Wittenburg published an empirical law of planetary distances that proposed a geometrical spacing of the six known planets from the sun. The only exception to this progression was the space between Mars and Jupiter, an area large enough to contain the missing planet. In 1772, Johann Bode, a contemporary of Titius, publicized the progression, and consequently it became known as Bode's Law.

Most astronomers dismissed Bode's Law as idle speculation until 1781 when William Herschel sighted a new planet beyond the orbit of Saturn right where Bode's Law predicted it would be. In spired by the discovery of Uranus, astronomer Baron von Zach and his ''celestial police'' organized a search to locate the missing planet between Mars and Jupiter. It was not until New Year's Day of 1801, however, that the Italian astronomer Father Guiseppe Piazzi, while attempting to correct an error in a star catalog, spotted a new body in the constellation Taurus. It was located in the precise position between Mars and Jupiter that Bode's Law predicted a planetary body to be. Thus, Piazzi named his planet Ceres after the guardian divinity of his native Sicily.

After observing the planet for six weeks, Piazzi became ill. When he returned to the telescope, Ceres was lost in the luminous night sky. However the brilliant mathematical genius Karl Frederich Gauss had just invented a simplified formula for calculating planetary orbits from a few observations. He computed an orbit that enabled astronomers to permanently locate Ceres on December 31, 1801.

Compared to the other planets, Ceres was extremely small in size and possessed an unusually tilted and elliptical orbit. Hence, questions arose as to whether it was a true planet. Then, several months later on March 28, 1802, German astronomer Wilhelm Olbers discovered a second asteroid. He named the asteroid Pallas and speculated that Pallas and Ceres were the debris of a former planet which had previously exploded. Olbers predicted that many more pieces would be found in similar odd-shaped orbits. Eighteen months later, on September 1, 1804, his prediction was validated when Karl Harding discovered the asteroid Juno in the constellation of Aries. Finally, on March 29, 1807, Olbers located a fourth asteroid in the constellation of Virgo. He named it Vesta.

All four orbits of these new ''planets'' approximated the 2.8 AU (astronomical units) distance from the sun as predicted by Bode's Law. As the nineteenth century progressed, the asteroid search became increasingly popular so that by 1890, three hundred of them had been discovered. After the introduction of photographic searches, the location of new asteroids accelerated even more rapidly.

When an asteroid is first spotted, it is identified by a number and a letter indicating the month and year of its discovery. After its orbit has been determined and proven to be that of a new asteroid, the body is officially listed in the asteroid catalog. The discoverer then has the privilege of naming the object. Generally, those objects with regular orbits have been given feminine names while those with unusual or irregular orbits have been supplied with masculine ones. Today, over 2,000 asteroids have been named, numbered, and charted.

Table 13-1

Bode's Law

Bodies	Bode's Formula	Distance Predicted from Sun Astronomical Units (AU)	Actual Distance (AU)
Mercury	.4+0	.4	.39
Venus	.4+.3	.7	.72
Earth	.4+.6	1.0	1.0
Mars	.4+1.2	1.6	1.52
Asteroids	.4+2.4	2.8	2.1-3.5
Jupiter	.4+4.8	5.2	5.2
Saturn	.4+9.6	10.0	9.5
Uranus	.4+19.2	19.2	19.8
Neptune	.4+38.4	38.8	30.1
Pluto	.4+76.8	77.2	39.5

The Physical Properties of the Asteroids

SIZE AND SHAPE

Most asteroids measure just a few miles in diameter. However, Ceres, the largest, is 620 miles across. Pallas measures 350 miles, Vesta 310 miles, and Juno 140 miles. The largest asteroids, those 100 miles and over, are spherical in shape because the force of their own gravity smooths them into balls. The smaller asteroids have irregular, jagged, or lumpy shapes, suggesting that they are fragments of violent collisions.

COMPOSITION AND BRIGHTNESS

The asteroids vary greatly in size and composition, both from the planets and each other. Spectroscopic analysis reveals that the larger asteroids are composed of dark carbon compounds and reflect little light. The smaller asteroids are more reflective due to the presence of iron-rich metals called silicates. Exceptions include Vesta's surface of volcanic basalt that induces maximum reflectivity, and Psyche's nickel-iron, reddish tinge. Albedos (the measure of reflectivity) vary from extremely low (2.8% for Hector) to as bright as 26.4% for Vesta, with the majority of asteroids falling in the 7-18% range.

Recently, a fascinating relationship between the composition of an asteroid and its distance from the sun has emerged. The inner part of the belt near the orbit of Mars contains mostly reflective, silicate asteroids. On the outer edge of the belt, more than 3 AU from the sun, 80% of the asteroids are of the carbonaceous type. One suggested explanation for this correlation may be that the differences in melting temperatures at various distances from the sun caused this distinct compositional stratification of the asteroids.[1]

ORBITAL PATTERNS OF THE ASTEROID GROUPS

The asteroids have been classified into three groups based upon their orbital travel: the main belt, the Apollo and Amor group, and the Trojans.

1) The main belt contains 95% of the known asteroids. They revolve in slightly elliptical orbits with periods of two to six years. Their distribution is irregular, containing distinct spaces called the Kirkwood gaps. These gaps are due to regular perturbations caused by Jupiter's gravitational pull.
2) The Apollo and Amor group have highly elliptical and more sharply inclined orbits. The Amor asteroids cross the orbit of Mars but do not reach our orbit. The tiny asteroid Eros (8x9x22 miles) approaches the Earth every few years to become one of the brightest asteroids in the night sky.

   The Apollo group, on the other hand, does cross the Earth's orbit. The asteroid Apollo, discovered in 1932, was named for the sun god because it came closer to that star than any previous asteroid. A few years later, however, the mile-long Icarus was discovered. Like the legendary hero who flew into the Sun, this asteroid travels to a point inside Mercury's orbit. Finally, Toro, also in the Apollo group, resonates like a Ping Pong ball between the orbits of Venus and the Earth.
3) The Trojans, named after the heroes in Homer's *Iliad*, are comprised of two groups of asteroids in Jupiter's orbit. One moves 60° ahead of Jupiter while the other travels 60°behind. Together with Jupiter, they form an equilateral triangle with the Sun. Each body possesses a period and mean distance nearly identical to that of the giant planet.

   In 1920, the distance record held by the Trojans was broken by the discovery of Hidalgo whose aphelion from the Sun receded back to Saturn's orbit. Hidalgo's 14-year period (2x7) symbolically links it to the period of Saturn (4x7 years), Chiron (7x7 years), and Uranus (12x7 years).

A final grouping of asteroids with similar orbit patterns was

1. Dr. David Morrison, "Asteroids," *Astronomy*, vol. 4, no. 6 (June 1976), 15.

discovered by the Japanese astronomer Hirayama Seiji in 1920. He determined that 25% of the asteroids could be placed in ten so-called "Hirayama families." These groupings are suspected to be the fragments from collisions between two major asteroids. Some families are compact while others are dispersed, suggesting that the collisions occurred at widely different times in the solar system's history.

TABLE 13-2

THE ASTEROIDS' ASTRONOMICAL DATA

Disc* No.	Name	Period (Years)	Diameter (km)	Brightness (Albedo %)	Perihelion (AU)	Surface Type	Group
1	Ceres	4.60	955	7.2	2.55	Carbonaceous	Main Belt
2	Pallas	4.61	538	10.3	2.11	Carbonaceous	Main Belt
3	Juno	4.36	226	19.0	1.99	Siliceous	Main Belt
4	Vesta	3.63	503	26.4	2.55	Basaltic	Main Belt
1566	Icarus	1.12	1.4	17.8	0.187	Siliceous	Apollo
433	Eros	1.76	7 x 16 x 35 km	14.2	1.13	Siliceous	Amor
944	Hidalgo	13.70	—	—	1.98 (9.6 apihelion)	—	Unique Body
16	Psyche	—	249	—	2.9	Nickle-Iron	—

* Discovery Number

Orbital Groups of the Asteroids

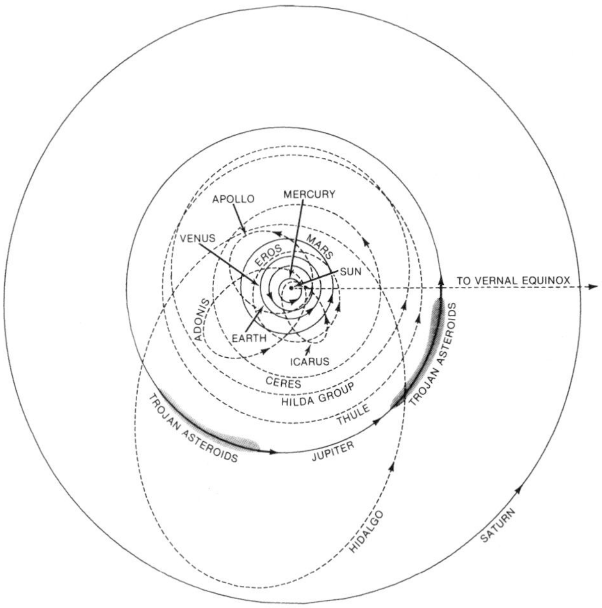

Figure 13-1

The Origin of the Asteroids

The origin of the 100,000 asteroids is a subject that has spawned a number of intriguing theories. Wilhelm Olbers, pioneer discoverer of Pallas and Vesta, first proposed that the asteroids were remnants from the explosion of an ancient planet. An alternate theory suggests that the asteroids are material from a planet that never formed, due to conflicting gravitational pulls of Jupiter and the sun. Evidence for the latter theory is seen by the stratification of the asteroids by composition into two distinct belts. Had a giant explosion occurred, its fragments would not have been evenly mixed.

The theory most in vogue today suggests that during the formation of the solar system, a nebula cloud formed an original family of about 15-50 asteroids with diameters of 60-100 miles. Due to Jupiter's gravitational pull, these bodies collided among themselves, and their fragments scattered throughout the solar system. The original cores are believed to have formed the metallic asteroids, with Vesta being the only body that remained completely intact.

Recently, the exploding-planet theory has been revived by proposing the destruction of a giant object the size of Saturn. According to this account, most of the debris was destroyed through colliding with Jupiter and the other planets, except for the pieces between Mars and Jupiter which remained intact to form the current asteroid belt.

This theory also seeks to explain the origin of the comets by postulating that the explosion's energy might have hurled some fragments trillions of miles into space. Eventually the sun's gravity would have pulled them back into the solar system, thereby creating the vast orbits of these enigmatic messengers. By applying the laws of gravitation to comets, it has been found that all comets seem to have originated from a common point between Mars and Jupiter 4 million years ago.[2]

COLLISIONS WITH THE EARTH

Asteroids are a major source of the estimated 500 meteorites that fall each year to the earth's surface. Heated by the friction of our atmosphere, they create brilliant fireballs whose remains provide one source of information for asteroid analysis.

2. Thomas Van Flandern, "Exploding Planets," *Science Digest* (April 1982).

Occasionally, a very large piece weighing thousands of tons will release the energy equivalent of a large hydrogen bomb. A current theory suggests that such an asteroid collided with the Earth at the close of the dinosaur age. This impact would have released tens of quadrillions of bits of pulverized rock into the stratosphere, creating a veil that would block out Sun's rays for several years. The catastrophic effects would have included the death of land and sea plants, the shattering of food chains, and the subsequent extinction of life forms.[3]

In conclusion, the asteroid riddle — "What are these tiny celestial bodies and where did they come from?" — continues to remain a major astronomical mystery. Unraveling the answers to these and related questions promises to supply us with a greater understanding of the origins of our solar system.

3. Richard A. Kerr, "Asteroid Theory of Extinctions Strengthened," *Science*, vol. 210, no. 4469 (October 31, 1980).

CHAPTER FOURTEEN

EPILOGUE

The asteroids or "minor planets" are by no means minor in their powers of expression. Situated largely between the orbits of Mars and Jupiter, the asteroids are octave transformers between the personal and the collective planets. The asteroids symbolize the techniques by which an individual can raise the vibrations of the lower octave planets which indicate the personal parts of the personality to higher octave correspondences. In this way, individuals can respond to higher-frequency cosmic forces.

The emergence of the asteroids also coincides with the awakening of new centers of awareness in the evolution of consciousness. The first four sighted, named after great goddesses of antiquity (⚳ ⚴ ⚵ ⚶), represent a rediscovery and renewed strengthening of the feminine principle in the collective psyche. As the vibratory rate of the feminine polarity in the energy field of the physical world has intensified, new issues concerning feminine and masculine roles and functioning are affecting women, men, and society as a whole.

Historically, to the extent that subconscious images of the feminine have been repressed and distorted by cultural conditioning, the energy contained in these twisted forms has manifested in destructive and self-defeating ways. Men's and women's experiences of their own feminine natures, and of the feminine as they perceive it in others, have resulted in much misunderstanding and suffering. As these centers are currently being activated, their toxic contents are erupting into the conscious psyches of individuals, causing chaos and confusion in their lives. The transformative process is now facilitating the purification of these blockages (cancers) so that the regenerated and clarified inner images can manifest in healthy and harmonious expressions.

Traditionally, Pluto has been considered the significator of the transformative process. On a subtle level, the feminine aspect of this process has been implied by the Moon's waxing and waning cycles. Now, the inclusion of the asteroids, Ceres, Pallas Athene, Juno, and Vesta, has expanded the scope and power of the feminine aspect of the metamorphosing principle. In addition, both masculine and feminine asteroids (including the minor ones) symbolize the opportunities and techniques now available by which individuals can transmute, regenerate, and evolve.

In the evolution of human consciousness, the meaning of the asteroids is being expressed at several levels. On the physiological level, the asteroids correspond to the activation of new brain cells and nerve centers that result in "quantum leaps" in growth processes. On the psychological level, the asteroids are manifesting as the appearance of previously potential or slumbering (and for many people, repressed and distorted) aspects of personality. The majority of this work is devoted to these psychological functions symbolized by the archetypes embodied in the mythology of these deities. Finally, on a spiritual level, the asteroids correlate to the catalytic forces that are transforming individuals, enabling them to perceive the essential interdependence and unity of all life forms.

The issues contained within all of the asteroid symbolism provide the transformational pathways between personal and universal awareness. As men and women break down and cleanse the old images and attitudes which govern the interaction between feminine and masculine, they can then rebalance and integrate the conflicting polarities. The illusion of duality spawns an artificial separation between object/subject, me/you, male/female, us/them. Responding to the possibilities inherent in the asteroid symbolism can lead individuals to a more inclusive and wholistic awareness of all sentient beings.

Take these new ideas and apply them by placing the asteroids in your own charts and those of your clients. During this process, you should realize that the asteroids, like all astrological archetypes, manifest on a number of different levels. Hence, the delineations presented in the book are but suggestions of the many variations that emerge in the lives of individuals. Nevertheless, by blending the asteroid key words with your basic knowledge of the signs, houses, and aspects, you will be able to fine-tune and add depth to the quality of your astrological understanding and interpretations.

As you use the asteroids, new insights and new questions will no doubt arise. If you would like to share them, please do send your letters and comments (to ACS Publications, Inc., PO Box 16430, San Diego, CA 92116, to be forwarded to the authors). We hope that this dialogue, and ones like it among astrologers across the country, will further increase our understanding of the timely teachings of these light-bearing deities.

APPENDIX ONE

CERES IN THE CHARTS OF FAMOUS PEOPLE

Ceres in Aspect to the Planets

CERES-SUN ASPECTS

Neil Armstrong - Ceres conjunct the Sun in Leo at the IC.
Clara Barton - Ceres conjunct the Sun in Capricorn in the tenth house
Helena P. Blavatsky - Ceres and Uranus in Aquarius in the eighth house opposing the Sun in Leo in the second house
Napoleon Bonaparte - Ceres conjunct the Sun and Pallas in Leo
Richard Burton - Ceres in Leo square the Sun in Scorpio
Kit Carson - Ceres in Taurus trine the Sun in Capricorn
Charles Chaplin - Ceres in Cancer square the Sun in Aries
Zipporah Dobyns - Ceres conjunct the Sun in Virgo in the fifth house
Werner Erhard - Ceres conjunct the Sun in Virgo
F. Scott Fitzgerald - Ceres in Pisces in the second house opposing the Sun in Libra in the eighth house
Indira Gandhi - Ceres conjunct the Sun in Scorpio at the IC
Andre Gide - Ceres in Taurus opposing the Sun in Scorpio
Ken Kesey - Ceres conjunct the Sun in Virgo
Princess Margaret - Ceres conjunct the Sun in Leo in the sixth house
Rudolf Nureyev - Ceres in Aries conjunct the Sun in Pisces
Yoko Ono - Ceres conjunct the Sun in Pisces/Aquarius in the fifth house
Fritz Perls - Ceres conjunct the Sun and Vesta in Cancer
Pierre-Auguste Renoir - Ceres conjunct the Sun in Pisces in the first house
Dante Gabriel Rossetti - Ceres conjunct the Sun in Taurus

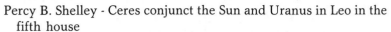

Percy B. Shelley - Ceres conjunct the Sun and Uranus in Leo in the fifth house
Sally Struthers - Ceres in Taurus in the eighth house square the Sun in Leo in the tenth house
Noel Tyl - Ceres conjunct the Sun in Capricorn in the seventh house opposing Vesta in Cancer in the first house
Vincent van Gogh - Ceres in Capricorn square the Sun in Aries
Queen Victoria - Ceres conjunct the Sun, Moon, and Ascendant in Gemini
Virginia Woolf - Ceres conjunct the Sun in Aquarius

CERES-MOON ASPECTS

Hans Christian Andersen - Ceres conjunct the Moon in Taurus in the fourth house
Johann Sebastian Bach - Ceres in Aries opposing the Moon in Libra
Lucille Ball - Ceres in Cancer in the twelfth house opposing the Moon in Capricorn in the sixth house
Clara Barton - Ceres conjunct the Moon in Capricorn in the tenth house
Ludwig van Beethoven - Ceres conjunct the Moon, Pallas, Sun and Mercury in Sagittarius
Luther Burbank - Ceres in Capricorn trine the Moon in Virgo
Saint Francesca Cabrini - Ceres in Aries in the eighth house opposing the Moon in Libra in the third house
Buffalo Bill Cody - Ceres conjunct the Moon in Pisces
Colette - Ceres conjunct the Moon in Aquarius on the fourth-fifth cusp
Aleister Crowley - Ceres in Virgo opposing the Moon in Pisces
Leonardo da Vinci - Ceres in Leo opposing the Moon and Jupiter in Pisces
Adelle Davis - Ceres in Sagittarius in the twelfth house opposing the Moon and Pluto
Charles Dickens - Ceres conjunct the Moon in Sagittarius
Queen Elizabeth II - Ceres conjunct the Moon in Leo in the seventh house
Jane Fonda - Ceres in Aquarius in the seventh house opposing the Moon in Leo in the first house
Sigmund Freud - Ceres conjunct the Moon in Gemini in the eighth house
Francoise Gauquelin - Ceres in Taurus opposing the Moon in Scorpio
Kahlil Gibran - Ceres in Pisces square the Moon in Sagittarius
Patty Hearst - Ceres conjunct the Moon in Libra in the second house

Alfred Hitchcock - Ceres conjunct the Moon and Jupiter in Scorpio in the eighth house
Michael Jackson - Ceres in Virgo in the tenth house opposing the Moon in Pisces in the fourth house
Martin Luther King - Ceres conjunct the Moon in Pisces
John F. Kennedy - Ceres conjunct the Moon in Virgo
Linda Ronstadt - Ceres conjunct the Moon in Aquarius in the second house
Gloria Steinem - Ceres in Taurus in the sixth house square the Moon in Leo in the ninth house

CERES-MERCURY ASPECTS

John Lennon - Ceres conjunct Mercury in Scorpio
Emily Dickenson - Ceres conjunct Mercury and the Sun in Sagittarius in the second house
Zelda Fitzgerald - Ceres in Aquarius at the Descendant opposing Mercury in Leo
Adolf Eichmann - Ceres conjunct Mercury in Aries in the twelfth house
George Gershwin - Ceres conjunct Mercury in Virgo in the ninth house
Joan of Arc - Ceres conjunct Mercury in Capricorn
Rudolf Nureyev - Ceres conjunct Mercury, Venus and Saturn in Aries
Sri Meher Baba - Ceres and Vesta in Virgo opposing Mercury in Pisces
Dr. Joyce Brothers - Ceres in Pisces trine Mercury in Scorpio
Vanessa Redgrave - Ceres conjunct Mercury in Capricorn in the fifth house
Bette Midler - Ceres conjunct Mercury and Vesta in Sagittarius in the ninth house
Sylvia Kars - Ceres in Aries in the second house opposing Mercury in Libra in the eighth house
Xaviera Hollander - Ceres in Taurus conjunct Mercury and Uranus in Gemini in the twelfth house
Geraldine Ferraro - Ceres conjunct Mercury and Neptune in Virgo

CERES-VENUS ASPECTS

Maria Montessori - Ceres conjunct Venus in Leo in the twelfth house
Princess Caroline - Ceres in Aries square Venus in Capricorn
Isadora Duncan - Ceres conjunct Venus in Aries in the first house
Christiaan Barnard - Ceres conjunct Venus in Sagittarius
Carrie Nation - Ceres in Taurus opposing Venus in Scorpio

Barbra Streisand - Ceres conjunct Venus in Pisces in the twelfth house
Marlon Brando - Ceres in Pisces sextile Venus in Taurus
Taylor Caldwell - Ceres in Aquarius opposing Venus in Cancer
Sirimavo Bandaranaike - Ceres conjunct Venus in Gemini in the ninth house
Ellen Yoakum - Ceres conjunct Venus in Virgo on the fourth-fifth cusp
Julia Child - Ceres conjunct Venus in Virgo in the fourth house
Victoria Woodhull - Ceres conjunct Venus in Virgo
Sylvia Porter - Ceres in Scorpio in the first house opposing Venus in Taurus in the sixth house

CERES-MARS ASPECTS

Joan Baez - Ceres conjunct Mars in Sagittarius in the eighth house opposing the Moon in Gemini
Jane Fonda - Ceres in Aquarius conjunct Mars in Pisces in the seventh house opposing the Moon in Leo
Elton John - Ceres conjunct Mars in Pisces in the eighth house
Dag Hammarskjold - Ceres in Pisces trine Mars in Scorpio
Moshe Dayan - Ceres conjunct Mars in Aries in the twelfth house
Hugh Hefner - Ceres in Leo in the seventh house opposing Mars in Aquarius in the first house
Sir Winston Churchill - Ceres in Cancer in the tenth house square Mars in Libra in the first house
Aleister Crowley - Ceres in Virgo trine Mars in Capricorn
Marquis de Sade - Ceres conjunct Mars in Aries
Florence Nightingale - Ceres conjunct Mars in Leo in the eleventh house
Orson Wells - Ceres conjunct Mars in Aries in the eleventh house
Barbara Walters - Ceres conjunct Mars in Scorpio in the first house
Anwar Sadat - Ceres in Capricorn conjunct Mars in Aquarius
Cher - Ceres in Aquarius in the eighth house opposing Mars and Pluto in Leo in the second house
Rudolph Valentino - Ceres in Capricorn opposing Mars in Cancer

CERES-PALLAS ASPECTS

Earl Warren - Ceres conjunct Pallas and Juno in Aquarius in the first house
Saint Teresa of Avila - Ceres conjunct Pallas and Mercury in Taurus in the first house
William Blake - Ceres conjunct Pallas and Venus in Capricorn in the

seventh house
Paul Cezanne - Ceres conjunct Pallas and Jupiter in Libra in the twelfth house
Simon Bolivar - Ceres conjunct Pallas in Leo
Robert Browning - Ceres conjunct Pallas in Sagittarius
Luther Burbank - Ceres in Capricorn conjunct Pallas, the Moon and Neptune in Sagittarius
Charles Dickens - Ceres conjunct Pallas in Sagittarius
Mary Baker Eddy - Ceres conjunct Pallas in Scorpio in the eleventh house
Nathan Hale - Ceres conjunct Pallas in Cancer
Mary Stuart, Queen of Scots - Ceres conjunct Pallas in Taurus opposing Uranus in Scorpio
Isaac Newton - Ceres conjunct Pallas and Juno in Aquarius
Friedrich Nietzsche - Ceres conjunct Pallas in Sagittarius in the first house
Florence Nightingale - Ceres conjunct Pallas and Mars in Leo in the eleventh house
Mark Twain - Ceres conjunct Pallas in Capricorn in the third house opposing Jupiter in Cancer in the ninth house
Victoria Woodhull - Ceres conjunct Pallas in Virgo
Harriet Beecher Stowe - Ceres conjunct Pallas in Virgo
Daniel Boone - Ceres conjunct Pallas in Capricorn
Saint Bernadette of Lourdes - Ceres conjunct Vesta in Scorpio in the sixth house
Mary Shelley - Ceres conjunct Pallas, Mercury and Juno in Virgo in the sixth house

CERES-VESTA ASPECTS

Pearl Buck - Ceres conjunct Vesta in Taurus in the eighth house
Karl Marx - Ceres in Aries in the first house opposing Vesta in Libra in the seventh house
Paul Gauguin - Ceres in Virgo in the second house opposing Vesta and Saturn in Pisces in the eighth house
Paramahansa Yogananda - Ceres conjunct Vesta in Taurus in the ninth house
Geraldine Ferraro - Ceres in Virgo opposing Vesta in Pisces
Mao Tse-tung - Ceres conjunct Vesta in Virgo
Francisco Franco - Ceres conjunct Vesta in Taurus on the eighth-ninth cusp
Henry David Thoreau - Ceres in Capricorn opposing Vesta in Cancer
Shirley MacLaine - Ceres in Taurus in the eighth house trine Vesta

in Virgo in the twelfth house
Duke of Windsor - Ceres conjunct Vesta in Virgo in the seventh house trine Venus in Taurus
Charles Atlas - Ceres conjunct Vesta in Virgo
Sri Meher Baba - Ceres conjunct Vesta in Virgo
Emma Goldman - Ceres conjunct Jupiter and Pluto in Taurus opposing Vesta in Scorpio
Princess Diana - Ceres conjunct Vesta in Taurus
Henry Winkler - Ceres conjunct Vesta in Sagittarius in the tenth house
John Calvin - Ceres in Pisces opposing Vesta and Juno in Virgo
Walter Mondale - Ceres conjunct Vesta in Capricorn in the eleventh house opposing Pluto in Cancer in the fifth house

CERES-JUNO ASPECTS
Betty Friedan - Ceres in Gemini at the Descendant opposing Juno in Sagittarius at the Ascendant
Elizabeth Taylor - Ceres in Capricorn in the fourthhouse opposing Juno and Pluto in Cancer in the tenth house
Grace Kelly - Ceres in Gemini in the eighth house opposing Juno in Sagittarius in the second house
D. H. Lawrence - Ceres conjunct Juno in Scorpio
Debbie Reynolds - Ceres in Capricorn in the fourth house opposing Juno and Pluto in Cancer in the tenth house
Ronald Reagan - Ceres in Aries opposing Juno in Libra
Frank Sinatra - Ceres in Taurus opposing Juno in Scorpio
Marianne Alireza - Ceres in Scorpio in the tenth house trine Juno and Uranus in Pisces in the second house
Edith Piaf - Ceres in Taurus in the sixth house opposing Juno in Scorpio in the twelfth house
Queen Victoria - Ceres in Gemini at the Ascendant square Juno in Virgo in the fifth house
Shirley Temple Black - Ceres in Pisces in the third house opposing Juno in Virgo in the ninth house
Louisa May Alcott - Ceres in Taurus in the eighth house opposing Juno in Scorpio in the second house
Agatha Christie - Ceres conjunct Juno in Sagittarius in the third house opposing Neptune and Pluto in Gemini in the ninth house
Henry Miller - Ceres conjunct Juno in Pisces on the eleventh-twelfth cusp
Richard Alpert (Ram Dass) - Ceres in Libra in the fourth house opposing Juno in Aries in the tenth house

Elisabeth Kubler-Ross - Ceres in Virgo in the seventh house opposing Juno in Pisces in the first house
Anne Frank - Ceres in Taurus in the eleventh house opposing Juno in Scorpio in the fourth house
Edward Kennedy - Ceres in Capricorn in the twelfth house opposing Juno in Cancer in the seventh house
Charles de Gaulle - Ceres conjunct Juno in Sagittarius
Chiang Kai-shek - Ceres conjunct Juno in Scorpio at the Midheaven
Jefferson Davis - Ceres conjunct Juno in Aquarius in the ninth house
Coco Chanel - Ceres conjunct Juno in Gemini in the sixth house
Helen Keller - Ceres conjunct Juno in Virgo in the tenth house
Edna Ferber - Ceres conjunct Juno in Libra in the eleventh house
Earl Warren - Ceres conjunct Juno in Aquarius in the first house

CERES-JUPITER ASPECTS

Elizabeth Barrett Browning - Ceres in Cancer in the tenth house opposing Jupiter in Capricorn in the fourth house
Edna St. Vincent Millay - Ceres conjunct Jupiter in Pisces in the eleventh house
Grace Kelly - Ceres conjunct Jupiter in the eighth house opposing Juno in Sagittarius in the second house
Henry Miller - Ceres conjunct Jupiter and Juno in Pisces in the twelfth house
Emmeline Pankhurst - Ceres in Sagittarius at the Midheaven opposing Jupiter in Gemini in the third house
Galileo - Ceres in Capricorn opposing Jupiter and Saturn in Cancer
Al Capone - Ceres conjunct Jupiter in Scorpio
Rachel Carson - Ceres conjunct Jupiter and Neptune in Cancer
Mao Tse-tung - Ceres and Vesta in Virgo trine Jupiter in Taurus
Billy Graham - Ceres in Capricorn opposing Jupiter in Cancer
Ernest Hemingway - Ceres conjunct Jupiter in Scorpio in the third house
Leonardo da Vinci - Ceres in Leo opposing Jupiter in Pisces
Babe Ruth - Ceres in Sagittarius opposing Jupiter in Gemini
Rudolph Valentino - Ceres in Capricorn opposing Jupiter and Mars in Cancer
Immanuel Velikovsky - Ceres in Capricorn opposing Jupiter and Mercury in Cancer
Sri Meher Baba - Ceres in Virgo trine Jupiter in Taurus
Eleonora Duse - Ceres in Sagittarius in the fourth house opposing Jupiter in Gemini in the tenth house
The Reverend Jesse Jackson - Ceres in Capricorn opposing Jupiter

in Cancer

Jacqueline Kennedy Onnasis - Ceres conjunct Jupiter in Gemini

Emma Goldman - Ceres conjunct Jupiter and Pluto in Taurus opposing Vesta in Scorpio

Alan Ginsberg - Ceres in Leo opposing Jupiter in Aquarius

Ellen Yoakum - Ceres in Virgo in the fourth house opposing Jupiter in Pisces in the eleventh house

Katharine Hepburn - Ceres conjunct Jupiter in Cancer in the eighth house

CERES-SATURN ASPECTS

Dr. Tom Dooley - Ceres conjunct Saturn in Sagittarius in the first house

Albert Camus - Ceres in Sagittarius in the third house opposing Saturn in Gemini in the ninth house

Fidel Castro - Ceres conjunct Saturn in Sagittarius

Prince Albert - Ceres and Neptune in Sagittarius in the fourth house square Saturn in Pisces in the seventh house

David Ben-Gurion - Ceres in Capricorn opposing Saturn in Cancer

George Bush - Ceres in Aries opposing Saturn and the Moon in Libra

Jefferson Davis - Ceres in Aquarius in the ninth house square Saturn in Scorpio in the sixth house

Carl G. Jung - Ceres in Leo opposing Saturn in Aquarius

Helen Boucher - Ceres in Libra in the second house opposing Saturn in Aries in the eighth house

Joan Crawford - Ceres in Leo in the ninth house opposing Saturn and the Moon in Aquarius in the third house

Doris Chase Doane - Ceres in Sagittarius in the tenth house opposing Saturn in Gemini in the fourth house

Clare Boothe Luce - Ceres in Leo in the ninth house opposing Saturn in Aquarius in the second house

Angela Davis - Ceres conjunct Saturn in Gemini in the second house

CERES-URANUS ASPECTS

Alice Bailey - Ceres conjunct Uranus and Juno in Virgo in the second house

Germaine Greer - Ceres conjunct Uranus and the Moon in Taurus in the fourth house

Helen Keller - Ceres conjunct Uranus in Virgo at the Midheaven

Helena P. Blavatsky - Ceres conjunct Uranus and Jupiter in Aquarius in the eighth house

Alan Leo - Ceres conjunct Uranus in Gemini in the tenth house

Jawaharlal Nehru - Ceres conjunct Uranus and Pallas in Libra in the third house
James Dean - Ceres in Libra in the first house opposing Uranus in Aries in the seventh house
Jane Addams - Ceres conjunct Uranus in Gemini in the tenth house
Frederic Chopin - Ceres in Taurus opposing Uranus in Scorpio
Marie Antoinette - Ceres in Virgo opposing Uranus in Pisces
Annie Oakley - Ceres conjunct Uranus in Gemini
Maxfield Parrish - Ceres conjunct Uranus in Cancer
Victoria Woodhull - Ceres in Virgo opposing Uranus in Pisces
Andy Warhol - Ceres in Libra opposing Uranus in Aries
Tennessee Williams - Ceres conjunct Uranus and Jupiter in Aquarius
Robert J. Oppenheimer - Ceres conjunct Uranus in Sagittarius opposing Pluto in Gemini
George Sand - Ceres in Aries in the first house opposing Uranus in Libra in the seventh house
Mick Jagger - Ceres conjunct Uranus in Gemini in the eleventh house
Ralph Nader - Ceres conjunct Uranus in Aries
Rollo May - Ceres conjunct Uranus in Capricorn in the eleventh house
Kahlil Gibran - Ceres in Pisces opposing Uranus in Virgo
George Washington - Ceres in Gemini opposing Uranus in Sagittarius

CERES-NEPTUNE ASPECTS

Marilyn Monroe - Ceres conjunct Neptune in Leo in the first house opposing Jupiter in Aquarius in the seventh house
Janis Joplin - Ceres in Aries in the first house opposing Neptune in Libra in the seventh house
Annie Besant - Ceres in Leo in the sixth house opposing Neptune in Aquarius in the twelfth house
Eva Braun - Ceres conjunct Neptune in Cancer in the ninth house
Catherine the Great - Ceres in Sagittarius opposing Neptune in Gemini
Prince Albert - Ceres conjunct Neptune in Sagittarius in the fourth house
Richard Burton - Ceres conjunct Neptune in Leo
Rachel Carson - Ceres conjunct Neptune and Jupiter in Cancer
Ingrid Bergman - Ceres conjunct Neptune in Leo
Charles Dickens - Ceres conjunct Neptune and Pallas in Sagittarius
Christine Jorgensen - Ceres conjunct Neptune in Leo in the twelfth house
Alan Ginsberg - Ceres conjunct Neptune in Leo in the twelfth house

Paul McCartney - Ceres in Pisces opposing Neptune in Virgo
Henry Kissinger - Ceres in Aquarius in the ninth house opposing Neptune in Leo in the third house
Nancy Reagan - Ceres conjunct Neptune in Leo
Pat Nixon - Ceres conjunct Neptune in Cancer in the sixth house
Ringo Starr - Ceres conjunct Neptune in Virgo in the sixth house
Carlos Castaneda - Ceres conjunct Neptune in Leo

CERES-PLUTO ASPECTS

Timothy Leary - Ceres conjunct Pluto in Cancer
Albert Einstein - Ceres conjunct Pluto in Taurus in the eleventh house
Abraham Lincoln - Ceres conjunct Pluto in Pisces in the first house
Soraya of Iran - Ceres in Capricorn at the IC opposing Pluto in Cancer in the tenth house
Karl Marx - Ceres in Aries conjunct Pluto in Pisces in the first house
Marianne Alireza - Ceres in Scorpio in the tenth house trine Pluto in Cancer in the seventh house
Brigitte Bardot - Ceres conjunct Pluto in Cancer on the seventh-eighth cusp
Muhammad Ali (Cassius Clay) - Ceres in Aquarius opposing Pluto in Leo
Salvador Dali - Ceres in Sagittarius opposing Pluto in Gemini
Charles Darwin - Ceres conjunct Pluto in Pisces
Prince Charles - Ceres conjunct Pluto in Leo in the first house
Pearl Bailey - Ceres in Capricorn in the ninth house opposing Pluto in Cancer in the third house
Willie Ley - Ceres conjunct Pluto in Gemini
Sylvia Plath - Ceres in Capricorn in the eleventh house opposing Pluto in Cancer in the fifth house
Billy Joel - Ceres conjunct Pluto in Leo
Vanessa Redgrave - Ceres in Capricorn in the fifth house opposing Pluto in Cancer in the twelfth house
Dr. Marjorie Weinzweig - Ceres conjunct Pluto in Cancer in the sixth house opposing the Sun in Capricorn in the twelfth house
Amelia Earhart - Ceres conjunct Pluto, the Moon, and Venus in Gemini in the second house
Uri Geller - Ceres in Aquarius in the fourth house opposing Pluto in Leo in the tenth house
Elvis Presley - Ceres conjunct Pluto in Cancer in the eighth house opposing Venus in Capricorn in the second house

Ceres in the Houses

CERES
IN THE FIRST HOUSE

George Washington
Queen Victoria (Asc)
Janis Joplin
James Dean
Princess Caroline
Isadora Duncan (Asc)
Robert Browning
Gertrude Stein
Sylvia Porter (Asc)
Saint Teresa of Avila
George Sand
Marilyn Monroe
Anita Bryant
Bob Dylan
Lois Rodden
Karl Marx
Enrico Fermi (Asc)
Dr. Tom Dooley
Abraham Lincoln
Earl Warren
Barbara Walters
Friedrich Nietzsche
Carol Burnett (Asc)
Duchess of Windsor
Auguste Rodin (Asc)
Prince Charles
Pierre-Auguste Renoir

CERES
IN THE SECOND HOUSE

Amelia Earhart
Angela Davis
Alice Bailey
Patty Hearst
Alexander Graham Bell
Paul Gauguin
Hermann Hesse
F. Scott Fitzgerald
Alan Watts
Linda Ronstadt
John Dillinger
Sylvia Kars
Helen Boucher
Sissy Spacek
Emily Dickenson
F. Scott Fitzgerald
Joyce Carol Oates

CERES
IN THE THIRD HOUSE

Margaret Mead
Indira Gandhi (IC)
Jack Kerouac
Albert Camus
Bertrand Russell
Jimi Hendrix
Mark Twain
Ernest Hemingway
Agatha Christie
Diane Von Furstenberg
Adrienne Hirt
Shirley Temple Black

CERES
IN THE FOURTH HOUSE

Germaine Greer
Mary Shelley
Debbie Reynolds
Soraya of Iran
Elizabeth Taylor
Richard Alpert (Ram Dass)
Prince Albert
Charles Baudelaire (IC)
Uri Geller
Jean-Paul Sartre
Marlon Brando

Ellen Yoakum
Julia Child
Leonard Bernstein
Queen Margrethe II of Denmark (IC)
Hans Christian Andersen
Eleonora Duse
William Butler Yeats
Neil Armstrong (IC)

CERES IN THE FIFTH HOUSE

Zipporah Dobyns
Percy B. Shelley
Warren Beatty
David Bowie
Louis Pasteur
Yoko Ono
Vivien Kellems
Judy Garland
Vanessa Redgrave
Colette

CERES IN THE SIXTH HOUSE

Gloria Steinem (Desc)
Princess Margaret
Annie Besant
Saint Bernadette of Lourdes
Ringo Starr
Vincent van Gogh
Edgar Cayce
Zsa Zsa Gabor
Kahlil Gibran
Billy Jean King
Helen Frankenthaler
Pat Nixon
Dr. Marjorie Weinzweig
Minette Lenier
Edith Piaf
Coco Chanel

CERES IN THE SEVENTH HOUSE

Betty Friedan (Desc)
Brigitte Bardot
Elisabeth Kubler-Ross
Mary Wells Lawrence
Raquel Welch
Jane Fonda
Zelda Fitzgerald (Desc)
Pierre Teilhard de Chardin
William Blake
Alice Cooper
Queen Elizabeth II
Jack Nicholson
Hedda Hopper
Duke of Windsor
Hugh Hefner
Noel Tyl

CERES IN THE EIGHTH HOUSE

Saint Francesca Cabrini
Marlene Dietrich
Pearl Buck
Sally Struthers
Louisa May Alcott
Grace Kelly
Katharine Hepburn
Joan Baez
Shirley MacLaine
Helena P. Blavatsky
Sigmund Freud
Elvis Presley
Elton John
Walt Disney
Andre Gide
Margaret Trudeau
Lenny Bruce
Michel Gauquelin
Adlai Stevenson
Cher
R. D. Laing
Robert Redford

CERES
IN THE NINTH HOUSE

Anne Morrow Lindbergh
Eva Braun
Clare Boothe Luce
Catherine the Great
Albert Schweitzer
John Paul I
Cheiro
Henry Kissinger
Francisco Franco
Farrah Fawcett
Marc Edmund Jones
George Gershwin
Jefferson Davis
Paramahansa Yogananda
Pearl Bailey
Joan Crawford (MC)
Emmeline Pankhurst (MC)
Sirimavo Bandaranaike
Bette Midler
Eleanor Roosevelt

CERES
IN THE TENTH HOUSE

Elizabeth Barrett Browning
Helen Keller (MC)
Simone de Beauvoir
Marie Curie
Clara Barton
Alan Leo
Bobby Fischer
Mary Todd Lincoln
Judy Collins
Sir Winston Churchill
Napoleon Bonaparte
Chiang Kai-shek
Madalyn Murray O'Hair
Doris Chase Doane
Marianne Alireza
Farah Diba Pahlavi (MC)
Michael Jackson
Jean Houston
Henry Winkler
Taylor Caldwell
Jane Addams

CERES
IN THE ELEVENTH HOUSE

Anais Nin
Edna St. Vincent Millay
Albert Einstein
Walter Mondale
Henry Miller
Florence Nightingale
Anne Frank
Edna Ferber
Gloria Allred
Mary Baker Eddy
Charles de Gaulle
Thomas Jefferson
Helen Gurley Brown
Evangeline Adams
Mick Jagger
Elizabeth Arden
Sylvia Plath
Ira Progoff
Rollo May
Orson Wells

CERES
IN THE TWELFTH HOUSE

Xaviera Hollander
Maria Montessori
Adelle Davis
Queen Beatrix
Martin Luther
Paul Cezanne
Edward Kennedy (Asc)
Adolf Eichmann
Sybil Leek (Asc)
Christine Jorgensen
Lucille Ball
Barbra Streisand

Francoise Gauquelin
Adelle Davis

Ceres in the Signs

CERES IN ARIES
Margaret Mead
Janis Joplin
Princess Caroline of Monaco
Isadora Duncan
Saint Francesca Cabrini
Gertrude Stein
Marlene Deitrich
Karl Marx
Bobby Fischer
George Bush
Werner Heisenberg
Walt Disney
Adolf Eichmann
Johann Sebastian Bach
Marquis de Sade
Mary Todd Lincoln
Rudolf Nureyev
Ronald Reagan
Orson Wells
Duchess of Windsor
George Sand
Federico Fellini
Moshe Dayan
Adrienne Hirt
Sylvia Kars
Ralph Nader

CERES IN TAURUS
Gloria Steinem
Xaviera Hollander
Anne Morrow Lindbergh
Pearl Buck
Sally Struthers
Edith Piaf
Germaine Greer
Saint Teresa of Avila
Louisa May Alcott
Anne Frank
Enrico Fermi
Alexander Graham Bell
Albert Einstein
Alice Cooper
Francisco Franco
Joyce Carol Oates
Hans Christian Andersen
Kit Carson
Frederic Chopin
Andre Gide
Harry Houdini
Empress Josephine
Mary Stuart, Queen of Scots
Carrie Nation
Dante Gabriel Rossetti
Shirley MacLaine
Frank Sinatra
Emma Goldman
Princess Diana
Farah Diba Pahlavi
Francoise Gauquelin
Paramahansa Yogananda

CERES IN GEMINI
Amelia Earhart
Grace Kelly
Angela Davis
Betty Friedan
Queen Victoria
Coco Chanel
Sigmund Freud
Alan Leo
William Butler Yeats
Jane Addams
Queen Elizabeth I of England

Mohandas Gandhi
Francisco Goya
Annie Oakley
George Washington
Willie Ley
Mick Jagger
Jean Houston
Jacqueline Kennedy Onassis
Judy Collins
Sirimavo Bandaranaike

CERES IN CANCER
Katharine Hepburn
Eva Braun
Elizabeth Barrett Browning
Marc Edmund Jones
Elvis Presley
Albert Schweitzer
Rachel Carson
Charles Chaplin
Lucille Ball
Brigitte Bardot
Sir Winston Churchill
Nathan Hale
Maxfield Parrish
Junipero Serra
Adolf Hitler
Fritz Perls
Dr. Marjorie Weinzweig
Pat Nixon
Margaret Trudeau
Timothy Leary
Billy Jean King

CERES IN LEO
Clare Boothe Luce
Marilyn Monroe
Princess Margaret of England
Anais Nin
Maria Montessori
Annie Besant
Martin Luther
Percy B. Shelley
Lenny Bruce
Prince Charles of England
Richard Burton
Neil Armstrong
Ingrid Bergman
Hugh Hefner
Simon Bolivar
Leonardo da Vinci
Queen Elizabeth II
Jesse James
Carl G. Jung
Napoleon Bonaparte
Florence Nightingale
Christine Jorgensen
Alan Ginsberg
Nancy Reagan
Billy Joel
Joan Crawford
Ira Progoff
Carlos Castaneda

CERES IN VIRGO
Anita Bryant
Elisabeth Kubler-Ross
Zipporah Dobyns
Alice Bailey
Helen Keller
Mary Shelley
Queen Margrethe II of Denmark
Ringo Starr
Paul Gauguin
John Dillinger
Mao Tse-tung
George Gershwin
Aleister Crowley
Marie Antoinette
Charles Atlas
Victoria Woodhull
Sri Meher Baba
Duke of Windsor

Werner Erhard
Michael Jackson
Harriet Beecher Stowe
John F. Kennedy
Julia Child
Ellen Yoakum
Eleanor Roosevelt
Geraldine Ferraro

CERES IN LIBRA
Raquel Welch
Simone de Beauvoir
Patty Hearst
Helen Boucher
Richard Alpert (Ram Dass)
John Paul I
Paul Cezanne
Cheiro
James Dean
Edna Ferber
Andy Warhol
Minette Lenier
Judy Garland
Hedda Hopper
Jawaharlal Nehru

CERES IN SCORPIO
Indira Gandhi
Sybil Leek
Saint Bernadette of Lourdes
Marianne Alireza
Jack Kerouac
John Lennon
Al Capone
D. H. Lawrence
Chiang Kai-shek
Ernest Hemingway
Alfred Hitchcock
Mary Baker Eddy
Barbara Walters
Helen Gurley Brown
Sylvia Porter
Sissy Spacek
Robert Redford
Benjamin Franklin

CERES IN SAGITTARIUS
Doris Chase Doane
Joan Baez
Adelle Davis
Catherine the Great
Marie Curie
Emily Dickenson
Albert Camus
Dr. Tom Dooley
Prince Albert of England
Charles Baudelaire
Pierre Teilhard de Chardin
Christiaan Barnard
Leonard Bernstein
Salvador Dali
Gloria Allred
Charles de Gaulle
Ludwig van Beethoven
R. D. Laing
Robert Browning
Charles Dickens
Friedrich Nietzsche
Nostradamus
Pablo Picasso
Fidel Castro
Babe Ruth
Robert Graves
Robert J. Oppenheimer
Eleanora Duse
Henry Winkler
Bette Midler
Emmeline Pankhurst
Agatha Christie

CERES IN CAPRICORN
Debbie Reynolds
Soraya of Iran
Elizabeth Taylor

Clara Barton
Pearl Bailey
Bob Dylan
Walter Mondale
William Blake
Galileo Galilei
Auguste Rodin
Bertrand Russell
Vincent van Gogh
Edward Kennedy
David Ben-Gurion
Billy Graham
Luther Burbank
Thomas Jefferson
Joan of Arc
Henry David Thoreau
Mark Twain
Rudolph Valentino
Immanuel Velikovsky
The Reverend Jesse Jackson
Anwar Sadat
Paul Simon
Noel Tyl
Adlai Stevenson
Vanessa Redgrave
Sylvia Plath
Evangeline Adams

CERES IN AQUARIUS

Zelda Fitzgerald
Jane Fonda
Helena P. Blavatsky
Taylor Caldwell
Warren Beatty
David Bowie
Uri Geller
Earl Warren
Hermann Hesse
Louis Armstrong
Muhammad Ali (Cassius Clay)
Edgar Cayce
Jefferson Davis
Isaac Newton
Virginia Woolf
Shelley Winters
Tennessee Williams
Colette
Jack Nicholson
Elizabeth Arden
Diane Von Furstenberg
Cher
Linda Ronstadt
Maria Callas
Henry Kissinger

CERES IN PISCES

Lois Rodden
Yoko Ono
Edna St. Vincent Millay
Queen Beatrix
Farrah Fawcett
Marlon Brando
F. Scott Fitzgerald
Jimi Hendrix
Elton John
Henry Miller
Jean-Paul Sartre
Alan Watts
Abraham Lincoln
Louis Pasteur
Zsa Zsa Gabor
Clark Gable
Dag Hammarskjold
Martin Luther King
Kahlil Gibran
Howard Hughes
John Calvin
Buffalo Bill Cody
Charles Darwin
Edgar Allan Poe
Pierre-Auguste Renoir
Barbra Streisand
Paul McCartney
Vivien Kellems

Dr. Joyce Brothers
Michel Gauquelin
Shirley Temple Black
Madalyn Murray O'Hair
Mary Wells Lawrence
Marcia Moore
Margot Fonteyn
Helen Frankenthaler
Carol Burnett

APPENDIX TWO

PALLAS IN THE CHARTS OF FAMOUS PEOPLE

Pallas in Aspect to the Planets

PALLAS-SUN ASPECTS

John Lennon - Pallas conjunct the Sun in Libra

Bob Dylan - Pallas in Sagittarius in the eleventh house opposing the Sun in Gemini

Clara Barton - Pallas conjunct the Sun and Uranus in Capricorn in the tenth house

Amelia Earhart - Pallas in Taurus at the Ascendant square the Sun in Leo

Edna St. Vincent Millay - Pallas conjunct the Sun in Pisces in the tenth house

Emily Dickinson - Pallas conjunct the Sun and Venus in Sagittarius in the first house

Abraham Lincoln - Pallas conjunct the Sun in Aquarius in the first house

George Harrison - Pallas conjunct the Sun in Pisces

Rachel Carson - Pallas conjunct the Sun in Gemini opposing the Moon in Sagittarius

Clark Gable - Pallas conjunct the Sun and Mercury in Aquarius

Mao Tse-tung - Pallas in Virgo trine the Sun in Capricorn

Walt Disney - Pallas in Pisces square the Sun in Sagittarius

Hans Christian Andersen - Pallas conjunct the Sun and Vesta in Aries in the third house

Johann Sebastian Bach - Pallas in Pisces conjunct the Sun in Aries

Buffalo Bill Cody - Pallas conjunct the Sun in Pisces

Bobby Fischer - Pallas conjunct the Sun in Pisces in the ninth house
Paul McCartney - Pallas in Aquarius trine the Sun in Gemini
Queen Beatrix - Pallas conjunct the Sun in Aquarius in the eleventh house
Farrah Fawcett - Pallas conjunct the Sun in Aquarius in the eighth house
Immanuel Velikovsky - Pallas in Sagittarius opposing the Sun in Gemini
Nancy Reagan - Pallas conjunct the Sun, Mercury and Mars in Cancer
Mary Baker Eddy - Pallas in Scorpio in the eleventh house trine the Sun in Cancer
Carl G. Jung - Pallas conjunct the Sun and Vesta in Leo
Napoleon Bonaparte - Pallas conjunct the Sun and Ceres in Leo
Annie Oakley - Pallas in Aries trine the Sun and Saturn in Leo
Julia Child - Pallas conjunct the Sun in Leo in the fourth house
Patty Hearst - Pallas in Leo in the twelfth house opposing the Sun in Pisces in the sixth house
Timothy Leary - Pallas in Aries opposing the Sun in Libra
Colette - Pallas conjunct the Sun in Aquarius in the fourth house
Geraldine Ferraro - Pallas in Leo conjunct the Sun in Virgo
Henry David Thoreau - Pallas in Capricorn opposing the Sun in Cancer
Charles Darwin - Pallas conjunct the Sun in Aquarius
Emma Goldman - Pallas in Aries square the Sun in Cancer
Leonard Bernstein - Pallas in Sagittarius in the fourth house square the Sun in Virgo at the Ascendant
Ira Progoff - Pallas conjunct the Sun in Leo in the eleventh house
Christiaan Barnard - Pallas conjunct the Sun in Scorpio

PALLAS-MOON ASPECTS

Catherine the Great - Pallas in Sagittarius opposing the Moon and Venus in Gemini
Princess Margaret - Pallas conjunct the Moon in Cancer
Grace Kelly - Pallas conjunct the Moon in Pisces in the fifth house
Alan Leo - Pallas conjunct the Moon in Aries in the ninth house
Martin Luther - Pallas in Libra opposing the Moon in Aries
Albert Schweitzer - Pallas conjunct the Moon in Aries in the seventh house
Paul Gauguin - Pallas conjunct the Moon in Virgo in the first house
Anais Nin - Pallas in Cancer in the ninth house opposing the Moon in Cancer in the third house
Simone de Beauvoir - Pallas in Virgo in the tenth house opposing

the Moon and Mars in Pisces in the fourth house
Jean Paul Sartre - Pallas conjunct the Moon in Aquarius in the fourth house
Al Capone - Pallas in Libra opposing the Moon in Aries
Frederic Chopin - Pallas in Aries opposing the Moon in Libra
Duke of Windsor - Pallas in Virgo in the seventh house opposing the Moon in Pisces in the first house
Helen Boucher - Pallas in Virgo in the first house opposing the Moon in Pisces in the seventh house
Willie Ley - Pallas conjunct the Moon in Aries
Katharine Hepburn - Pallas conjunct the Moon in Taurus in the seventh house
Billy Jean King - Pallas in Aries in the second house opposing the Moon and Neptune in Libra in the eighth house
Adolf Hitler - Pallas in Cancer opposing the Moon in Capricorn
Adrienne Hirt - Pallas conjunct the Moon in Pisces in the second house
Ellen Yoakum - Pallas in Virgo in the fourth house square the Moon in Sagittarius in the sixth house
Cher - Pallas conjunct the Moon in Capricorn in the seventh house
Friedrich Nietzsche - Pallas conjunct the Moon in Sagittarius in the first house
D. H. Lawrence - Pallas conjunct the Moon and Venus in Libra
Maxfield Parrish - Pallas conjunct the Moon and Mars in Cancer
Charles Dickens - Pallas conjunct the Moon, Ceres, and Neptune in Sagittarius

PALLAS-MERCURY ASPECTS

Albert Camus - Pallas conjunct Mercury in Sagittarius in the third house
Saint Teresa of Avila - Pallas conjunct Mercury and Ceres in Taurus in the first house
Queen Victoria - Pallas conjunct Mercury in Taurus in the twelfth house
Marie Curie - Pallas conjunct Mercury in Sagittarius at the Midheaven
Clark Gable - Pallas conjunct Mercury and the Sun in Aquarius
Chiang Kai-shek - Pallas conjunct Mercury and the Sun in Scorpio
Ludwig van Beethoven - Pallas conjunct Mercury in Sagittarius
Shirley MacLaine - Pallas conjunct Mercury in Aries in the seventh house
Michael Jackson - Pallas conjunct Mercury in Leo in the ninth house

Sirimavo Bandaranaike - Pallas in Taurus conjunct Mercury in Aries in the eighth house
Clare Boothe Luce - Pallas in Cancer in the eighth house square Mercury in Aries in the fourth house
Walter Mondale - Pallas conjunct Mercury in Capricorn on the tenth-eleventh cusp
Carlos Castaneda - Pallas in Gemini opposing Mercury in Sagittarius
Mary Shelley - Pallas conjunct Mercury, Ceres, and Juno in Virgo in the fourth house

PALLAS-VENUS ASPECTS

Elton John - Pallas conjunct Venus in Aquarius in the seventh house
Yoko Ono - Pallas conjunct Venus and Saturn in Aquarius on the fourth-fifth cusp
Ken Kesey - Pallas conjunct Venus in Virgo
Eleanor Roosevelt - Pallas conjunct Venus in Virgo in the ninth house
Hermann Hesse - Pallas in Capricorn in the first house opposing Venus in Cancer in the seventh house
Percy B. Shelley - Pallas conjunct Venus in Leo in the fifth house
Charles de Gaulle - Pallas conjunct Venus in Sagittarius in the tenth house
Ernest Hemingway - Pallas in Libra in the second house square Venus in Cancer in the eleventh house
John Dillinger - Pallas conjunct Venus in Leo in the first house
Alice Cooper - Pallas conjunct Venus in Pisces in the sixth house
Sri Meher Baba - Pallas in Leo opposing Venus in Aquarius
Doris Chase Doane - Pallas in Scorpio in the ninth house opposing Venus in Taurus in the third house
Bette Midler - Pallas conjunct Venus in Scorpio in the eighth house
Virginia Woolf - Pallas conjunct Venus in Capricorn
Rudolph Valentino - Pallas in Sagittarius opposing Venus in Gemini
Zelda Fitzgerald - Pallas in Capricorn in the sixth house opposing Venus, Vesta, and the Moon in Cancer in the eleventh house
Louis Armstrong - Pallas in Capricorn opposing Venus in Cancer

PALLAS-MARS ASPECTS

Xaviera Hollander - Pallas conjunct Mars in Aries in the tenth house
Annie Besant - Pallas in Leo in the fifth house square Mars in Taurus in the first house
Billy Graham - Pallas conjunct Mars and the Moon in Sagittarius
Ralph Nader - Pallas conjunct Mars and Mercury in Pisces
Lucille Ball - Pallas conjunct Mars in Taurus on the tenth-eleventh cusp

Salvador Dali - Pallas in Scorpio opposing Mars in Taurus
Francisco Franco - Pallas conjunct Mars in Pisces in the sixth house
Nostradamus - Pallas and Neptune in Capricorn opposing Mars in Cancer
Maxfield Parrish - Pallas conjunct Mars in Cancer
Andy Warhol - Pallas conjunct Mars in Libra in the first house
Emmeline Pankhurst - Pallas conjunct Mars in Scorpio in the eighth house
Sally Struthers - Pallas in Pisces in the sixth house square Mars in Gemini in the ninth house
Carol Burnett - Pallas in Pisces in the twelfth house opposing Mars in Virgo in the sixth house
Adrienne Hirt - Pallas in Pisces in the second house opposing Mars in Virgo in the eighth house
Maria Montessori - Pallas conjunct Mars and Uranus in Cancer in the twelfth house

PALLAS-VESTA ASPECTS

Jimi Hendrix - Pallas conjunct Vesta in Aquarius in the second house
Alexander Graham Bell - Pallas in Aries in the first house opposing Vesta in Libra in the seventh house
Queen Elizabeth II - Pallas conjunct Vesta in Cancer in the sixth house
Fidel Castro - Pallas conjunct Vesta in Scorpio square the Sun in Leo
Adelle Davis - Pallas in Sagittarius in the eleventh house opposing Vesta in Gemini in the fifth house
Elizabeth Barrett Browning - Pallas conjunct Vesta in Gemini in the ninth house opposing Neptune in Sagittarius in the third house
Gertrude Stein - Pallas conjunct Vesta in Pisces in the first house opposing the Moon in Virgo in the seventh house
Sigmund Freud - Pallas conjunct Vesta and Pluto in Taurus in the sixth house
Henry Miller - Pallas conjunct Vesta in Aquarius in the eleventh house
Louis Pasteur - Pallas conjunct Vesta in Aquarius in the fourth house
Gloria Steinem - Pallas in Pisces in the fifth house opposing Vesta in Virgo in the eleventh house
Brigitte Bardot - Pallas in Taurus in the fifth house opposing Vesta in Scorpio in the eleventh house
James Dean - Pallas in Virgo in the twelfth house square Vesta in Sagittarius in the third house
George Gershwin - Pallas in Virgo in the ninth house square Vesta

in Sagittarius in the first house
Hugh Hefner - Pallas in Cancer at the Descendant conjunct Vesta in the sixth house
Alfred Hitchcock - Pallas in Libra opposing Vesta in Aries
Elizabeth I of England - Pallas conjunct Vesta in Gemini
Carrie Nation - Pallas in Pisces opposing Vesta in Virgo
Rudolf Nureyev - Pallas in Pisces square Vesta in Sagittarius
Gertrude Stein - Pallas conjunct Vesta in Pisces in the first house
Federico Fellini - Pallas in Pisces square Vesta in Sagittarius
Vanessa Redgrave - Pallas in Capricorn in the fifth house opposing Vesta in Cancer in the eleventh house
Sylvia Kars - Pallas in Aquarius in the first house opposing Vesta in Leo in the seventh house
Eleonora Duse - Pallas conjunct Vesta in Sagittarius in the fourth house
Pierre-Auguste Renoir - Pallas conjunct Vesta in Aquarius in the first house
Benjamin Franklin - Pallas conjunct Vesta in Sagittarius
R. D. Laing - Pallas conjunct Vesta and Saturn in Sagittarius in the eighth house

PALLAS-JUNO ASPECTS

Mary Shelley - Pallas conjunct Juno and Mercury in Virgo in the fourth house
Kahlil Gibran - Pallas conjunct Juno in Aquarius
Howard Hughes - Pallas in Aquarius opposing Juno in Leo
Luther Burbank - Pallas in Sagittarius opposing Juno in Gemini
Aleister Crowley - Pallas conjunct Juno in Virgo opposing the Moon in Pisces
Jefferson Davis - Pallas conjunct Juno in Aquarius in the ninth house
Junipero Serra - Pallas conjunct Juno in Leo
Shirley MacLaine - Pallas in Aries in the seventh house square Juno in Capricorn in the fourth house
Princess Diana - Pallas conjunct Juno in Pisces
Princess Margaret - Pallas and the Moon in Cancer in the fifth house opposing Juno in Capricorn in the eleventh house
Elizabeth Arden - Pallas conjunct Juno in Capricorn in the eleventh house
Richard Burton - Pallas in Gemini opposing Juno in Sagittarius
Carl G. Jung - Pallas conjunct Juno in Leo

PALLAS-JUPITER ASPECTS

Jane Fonda - Pallas conjunct Jupiter in Aquarius in the sixth house
Sybil Leek - Pallas conjunct Jupiter in Libra in the eleventh house
Paul Foster Case - Pallas conjunct Jupiter in Leo
Paul Cezanne - Pallas conjunct Jupiter in Libra in the twelfth house
Vincent van Gogh - Pallas in Sagittarius in the sixth house opposing Jupiter in Gemini in the twelfth house
Warren Beatty - Pallas conjunct Jupiter in Capricorn in the fourth house
Neil Armstrong - Pallas conjunct Jupiter in Cancer in the second house
Moshe Dayan - Pallas conjunct Jupiter in Pisces
Sir Winston Churchill - Pallas in Aries in the eighth house opposing Jupiter in Libra in the first house
Francisco Goya - Pallas in Gemini opposing Jupiter in Sagittarius
Frank Sinatra - Pallas conjunct Jupiter in Pisces
Orson Wells - Pallas conjunct Jupiter in Pisces in the tenth house
Edith Piaf - Pallas conjunct Jupiter in Pisces in the fourth house
Anwar Sadat - Pallas in Capricorn opposing Jupiter in Cancer
Helen Gurley Brown - Pallas conjunct Jupiter in Libra in the tenth house
Vanessa Redgrave - Pallas conjunct Jupiter and Mercury in Capricorn in the fifth house
Louisa May Alcott - Pallas conjunct Jupiter in Pisces on the sixth-seventh cusp
Jack Kerouac - Pallas conjunct Jupiter in Libra in the second house

PALLAS-SATURN ASPECTS

Madalyn Murray O'Hair - Pallas in Aquarius in the ninth house opposing Saturn in Leo in the third house
Eva Braun - Pallas conjunct Saturn in Taurus in the seventh house
Karl Marx - Pallas conjunct Saturn in Pisces in the first house
Lucille Ball - Pallas conjunct Saturn and Mars in Taurus in the eleventh house
John Calvin - Pallas in Pisces opposing Saturn in Virgo
Mary Todd Lincoln - Pallas conjunct Saturn in Pisces in the ninth house
Werner Erhard - Pallas in Virgo opposing Saturn in Pisces
Marianne Alireza - Pallas conjunct Saturn in Libra in the ninth house opposing the Sun and the Moon
Adlai Stevenson - Pallas conjunct Saturn in Capricorn in the eighth house

Judy Garland - Pallas in Virgo conjunct Saturn in Libra in the fourth house
Gloria Allred - Pallas in Scorpio in the ninth house opposing Saturn in Taurus in the third house
Albert Einstein - Pallas conjunct Saturn in Aries in the tenth house
David Bowie - Pallas in Aquarius in the fourth house opposing Saturn in Leo in the tenth house
Adolf Eichmann - Pallas conjunct Saturn in Pisces in the eleventh house

PALLAS-URANUS ASPECTS

Anne Frank - Pallas conjunct Uranus in Aries at the Midheaven
Joan Baez - Pallas in Scorpio in the seventh house opposing Uranus in Taurus in the first house
Maria Montessori - Pallas conjunct Uranus and Mars in Cancer in the twelfth house
Elvis Presley - Pallas conjunct Uranus in Aries in the fifth house
Alan Watts - Pallas conjunct Uranus in Aquarius in the second house
Jawaharlal Nehru - Pallas conjunct Uranus in Libra
George Bush - Pallas conjunct Uranus in Pisces
Andre Gide - Pallas in Pisces in the sixth house trine Uranus in Cancer in the tenth house
Joan of Arc - Pallas conjunct Uranus in Aquarius
Mary Stuart, Queen of Scots- Pallas in Taurus opposing Uranus in Scorpio
Pablo Picasso - Pallas in Sagittarius square Uranus in Virgo
Dante Gabriel Rossetti - Pallas in Aries square Neptune in Capricorn
Francoise Gauquelin - Pallas conjunct Uranus in Aries in the eleventh house
John F. Kennedy - Pallas in Leo opposing Uranus in Aquarius
Jacqueline Kennedy Onassis - Pallas conjunct Uranus in Aries
Dr. Marjorie Weinzweig - Pallas in Taurus conjunct Uranus in Aries in the second house
Margot Fonteyn - Pallas conjunct Uranus in Aquarius opposing Saturn in Leo
Mary Stuart, Queen of Scots- Pallas and Ceres in Taurus opposing Uranus in Scorpio
Barbara Walters - Pallas in Libra in the first house opposing Uranus in Aries in the seventh house

PALLAS-NEPTUNE ASPECTS

Richard Alpert (Ram Dass) - Pallas conjunct Neptune in Virgo in the third house

Marc Edmund Jones - Pallas conjunct Neptune and Pluto in Gemini in the seventh house

Alice Bailey - Pallas in Leo in the first house square Neptune in Taurus in the tenth house

Saint Francesca Cabrini - Pallas conjunct Neptune in Pisces in the seventh house opposing Mars in Virgo in the first house

Helena P. Blavatsky - Pallas conjunct Neptune in Capricorn in the seventh house

Zipporah Dobyns - Pallas conjunct Neptune in Leo in the fourth house

Anais Nin - Pallas conjunct Neptune in Cancer in the ninth house

Bertrand Russell - Pallas in Sagittarius in the second house trine Neptune in Aries in the sixth house

Paul Gauguin - Pallas in Virgo in the first house opposing Neptune in Pisces in the seventh house

Sir Winston Churchill - Pallas conjunct Neptune in Aries in the eighth house

Thomas Jefferson - Pallas in Capricorn opposing Neptune in Cancer

Ronald Reagan - Pallas in Pisces trine Neptune in Cancer

Tennessee Williams - Pallas in Capricorn opposing Neptune in Cancer

Fritz Perls - Pallas conjunct Neptune and Pluto in Gemini

Minette Lenier - Pallas conjunct Neptune in Libra in the fifth house

Rollo May - Pallas in Capricorn in the eleventh house opposing Neptune in Cancer in the fifth house

Nostradamus - Pallas conjunct Neptune in Capricorn opposing Jupiter, Saturn, and Mars in Cancer

Elisabeth Kubler-Ross - Pallas conjunct Neptune in Leo in the sixth house

Germaine Greer - Pallas in Pisces in the second house opposing Neptune in Virgo in the eighth house

Raquel Welch - Pallas conjunct Neptune in Virgo in the seventh house

Cheiro - Pallas in Libra in the ninth house opposing Neptune in Aries in the third house

PALLAS-PLUTO ASPECTS

Alexander Graham Bell - Pallas conjunct Pluto and Uranus in Aries in the first house

Sigmund Freud - Pallas conjunct Pluto and Vesta in Taurus in the sixth house

Queen Elizabeth II - Pallas conjunct Pluto in Cancer in the sixth house

Ingrid Bergman - Pallas conjunct Pluto in Cancer

Edgar Cayce - Pallas in Capricorn in the sixth house trine Pluto in Taurus in the tenth house

Babe Ruth - Pallas in Sagittarius opposing Pluto in Gemini

Robert Graves - Pallas in Sagittarius opposing Pluto in Gemini

Princess Margaret - Pallas conjunct Pluto in Cancer in the fifth house

Marc Edmund Jones - Pallas conjunct Pluto and Neptune in Gemini in the seventh house

William Butler Yeats - Pallas conjunct Pluto in Taurus on the second-third cusp

Pallas in the Houses

PALLAS IN THE FIRST HOUSE

Princess Caroline (Asc)
Alice Bailey
Barbara Walters (Asc)
George Sand
Emily Dickenson
Lois Rodden (Asc)
Margaret Mead
Alexander Graham Bell
Paul Gauguin
Hermann Hesse
F. Scott Fitzgerald
Earl Warren
Abraham Lincoln (Asc)
Karl Marx
Amelia Earhart (Asc)
John Dillinger
Sylvia Kars
Robert Browning
Linda Ronstadt
Duchess of Windsor
Helen Boucher
Queen Margrethe II of Denmark
Gertrude Stein
Saint Teresa of Avila
Friedrich Nietzsche
Auguste Rodin
Joyce Carol Oates

PALLAS IN THE SECOND HOUSE

Germaine Greer
William Butler Yeats
Jack Kerouac
Martin Luther
Bertrand Russell
Jimi Hendrix
Alan Watts
Ernest Hemingway
Billy Jean King
Sissy Spacek
Agatha Christie
Adrienne Hirt

Dr. Marjorie Weinzweig
Neil Armstrong

PALLAS
IN THE THIRD HOUSE

Indira Gandhi
Soraya of Iran
Elizabeth Taylor
Debbie Reynolds (IC)
Richard Alpert (Ram Dass)
Albert Camus
Prince Albert (IC)
Charles Baudelaire (IC)
Uri Geller
Marlon Brando
Coco Chanel
Shirley Temple Black
Diane Von Furstenberg
Hans Christian Andersen
Mark Twain

PALLAS
IN THE FOURTH HOUSE

Betty Friedan
Julia Child
Mary Shelley
David Bowie
Jean-Paul Sartre (IC)
Zipporah Dobyns
Colette
Eleonora Duse
Pat Nixon
Vivien Kellems
Ellen Yoakum
Judy Garland
Leonard Bernstein
Edith Piaf
Warren Beatty
Louis Pasteur

PALLAS
IN THE FIFTH HOUSE

Princess Margaret
Annie Besant
Gloria Steinem
Grace Kelly
Percy B. Shelley
Zza Zza Gabor
Helen Frankenthaler
Vanessa Redgrave
Minette Lenier
Brigitte Bardot
Yoko Ono
Elvis Presley

PALLAS
IN THE SIXTH HOUSE

Elisabeth Kubler-Ross
Saint Bernadette of Lourdes
Zelda Fitzgerald
Jane Fonda
Sally Struthers
Lousia May Alcott (Desc)
Sigmund Freud
Ringo Starr
Pierre Teilhard de Chardin
Vincent van Gogh
Edgar Cayce
Marlene Dietrich (Desc)
Alice Cooper
Francisco Franco
Noel Tyl
Michel Gauquelin
Walt Disney
Mary Wells Lawrence
Queen Elizabeth II
Andre Gide
Hugh Hefner (Desc)

**PALLAS
IN THE SEVENTH HOUSE**

Anne Morrow Lindbergh
Robert Redford
Pearl Buck (Desc)
Jack Nicholson (Desc)
Katharine Hepburn
Eva Braun
Raquel Welch
Joan Baez
Helena P. Blavatsky
Saint Francesca Cabrini
Albert Schweitzer
Marc Edmund Jones
William Blake
Elton John
Lenny Bruce (Desc)
Duke of Windsor
Shirley MacLaine
Margaret Trudeau (Desc)
Cher
Hedda Hopper
Farah Diba Pahlavi

**PALLAS
IN THE EIGHTH HOUSE**

Clare Boothe Luce
Frederic Chopin
Pearl Bailey
Farrah Fawcett
Henry Kissinger
Paramahansa Yogananda
Adlai Stevenson
Joan Crawford
Bette Midler
Sirimavo Bandaranaike
Emmeline Pankhurst
Sir Winston Churchill
R. D. Laing

**PALLAS
IN THE NINTH HOUSE**

Marianne Alireza
Elizabeth Barrett Browning
Anais Nin
Taylor Caldwell
Helen Keller
Doris Chase Doane
Alan Leo
Henry Winkler
John Paul I
Michael Jackson
Cheiro
Jane Addams
George Gershwin
Madalyn Murray O'Hair
Bobby Fischer
Mary Todd Lincoln
Jefferson Davis
Judy Collins
Gloria Allred
Jean Houston
Chiang Kai-shek
Eleanor Roosevelt

**PALLAS
IN THE TENTH HOUSE**

Catherine the Great (MC)
Marie Curie (MC)
Simone de Beauvoir
Clara Barton
Edna St. Vincent Millay
Albert Einstein
Walter Mondale
Sylvia Plath
Charles de Gaulle
Helen Gurley Brown (MC)
Anne Frank (MC)
Xaviera Hollander
Nick Jagger
Orson Wells

PALLAS IN THE ELEVENTH HOUSE

Anita Bryant
Sybil Leek
Adelle Davis
Bob Dylan
Henry Miller
Enrico Fermi
Lucille Ball
Prince Charles
Florence Nightingale
Edna Ferber
Mary Baker Eddy
Christine Jorgensen
Barbra Streisand
Elizabeth Arden
Evangeline Adams
Queen Beatrix
Adolf Eichmann
Francoise Gauquelin
Ira Progoff
Rollo May

PALLAS IN THE TWELFTH HOUSE

Angela Davis
Queen Victoria
Marilyn Monroe
Patty Hearst
Isadora Duncan
Paul Cezanne
Dr. Tom Dooley (Asc)
George Washington
James Dean
Thomas Jefferson
Auguste Rodin (Asc)
Carol Burnett
Sylvia Porter
Maria Montessori
Edward Kennedy

Pallas in the Signs

PALLAS IN ARIES

Xaviera Hollander
Anne Morrow Lindbergh
Pearl Buck
Angela Davis
Betty Friedan
Coco Chanel
Anne Frank
Francoise Gauquelin
Jane Addams
Hans Christian Andersen
Frederic Chopin
Sir Winston Churchill
Marquis de Sade
Harry Houdini
Empress Josephine
Annie Oakley
Dante Gabriel Rossetti
Shirley MacLaine
Timothy Leary
Willie Ley
Emma Goldman
Billy Jean King
Jacqueline Kennedy Onassis
Elvis Presley
Alexander Graham Bell
Albert Einstein
Alan Leo
Albert Schweitzer
Mick Jagger

PALLAS IN TAURUS

Katharine Hepburn
Amelia Earhart
Eva Braun
Saint Teresa of Avila
Queen Victoria
Jean Houston

Sigmund Freud
William Butler Yeats
Lucille Ball
Brigitte Bardot
Mary Stuart, Queen of Scots
Judy Collins
Dr. Marjorie Weinzweig
Sirimavo Bandaranaike

PALLAS IN GEMINI
Elizabeth Barrett Browning
Marc Edmund Jones
Lenny Bruce
Prince Charles of England
Richard Burton
Rachel Carson
Charles Chaplin
Elizabeth I of England
Francisco Goya
George Washington
Carlos Castaneda
Fritz Perls
Pat Nixon
Margaret Trudeau

PALLAS IN CANCER
Anita Bryant
Clare Boothe Luce
Princess Margaret of England
Anais Nin
Maria Montessori
Queen Margrethe II of Denmark
Joan Crawford
Nancy Reagan
Neil Armstrong
Ingrid Bergman
Hugh Hefner
Nathan Hale
Maxfield Parrish
Adolf Hitler
Billy Joel
Queen Elizabeth II

PALLAS IN LEO
Marilyn Monroe
Elisabeth Kubler-Ross
Julia Child
Zipporah Dobyns
Patty Hearst
Alice Baiiey
Helen Keller
Annie Besant
Percy B. Shelley
John Dillinger
Simon Bolivar
Jesse James
Carl G. Jung
Napoleon Bonaparte
Florence Nightingale
Junipero Serra
Sri Meher Baba
Michael Jackson
John F. Kennedy
Christine Jorgensen
Ira Progoff
Charles Atlas
Alan Ginsberg
Geraldine Ferraro

PALLAS IN VIRGO
Raquel Welch
Simone de Beauvoir
Mary Shelley
Helen Boucher
Richard Alpert (Ram Dass)
John Paul I
Ringo Starr
Paul Gauguin
James Dean
Ellen Yoakum
Mao Tse-tung
George Gershwin
Aleister Crowley
Eleanor Roosevelt
Marie Antoinette

Victoria Woodhull
Judy Garland
Duke of Windsor
Werner Erhard
Harriet Beecher Stowe
Hedda Hopper

PALLAS IN LIBRA
Sybil Leek
Marianne Alireza
Jack Kerouac
John Lennon
Paul Cezanne
Cheiro
Martin Luther
Edna Ferber
Al Capone
Ernest Hemingway
Alfred Hitchcock
Andy Warhol
Barbara Walters
Minette Lenier
Sylvia Porter
Helen Gurley Brown
Robert Redford
D. H. Lawrence
Jawaharlal Nehru

PALLAS IN SCORPIO
Doris Chase Doane
Indira Gandhi
Joan Baez
Saint Bernadette of Lourdes
Dr. Tom Dooley
Christiaan Barnard
Chiang Kai-shek
Salvador Dali
Gloria Allred
Mary Baker Eddy
Fidel Castro
Henry Winkler
Emmeline Pankhurst
Bette Midler
Agatha Christie
Sissy Spacek

PALLAS IN SAGITTARIUS
Soraya of Iran
Adelle Davis
Elizabeth Taylor
Catherine the Great
Marie Curie
Emily Dickenson
Pearl Bailey
Eleonora Duse
Albert Camus
Bob Dylan
Prince Albert
Charles Baudelaire
Bertrand Russell
Pierre Teilhard de Chardin
Vincent van Gogh
Paul Simon
Noel Tyl
Leonard Bernstein
Charles de Gaulle
Billy Graham
Ludwig van Beethoven
Robert Browning
Luther Burbank
Leonardo da Vinci
Charles Dickens
Friedrich Nietzsche
Pablo Picasso
R. D. Laing
Babe Ruth
Rudolph Valentino
Robert Graves
Immanuel Velikovsky
Robert J. Oppenheimer
The Reverend Jesse Jackson
Benjamin Franklin
Edward Kennedy

PALLAS IN CAPRICORN

Debbie Reynolds
Zelda Fitzgerald
Clara Barton
Helena P. Blavatsky
Taylor Caldwell
Adlai Stevenson
Warren Beatty
Uri Geller
Walter Mondale
William Blake
Hermann Hesse
Auguste Rodin
Henry Kissinger
Louis Armstrong
Muhammad Ali (Cassius Clay)
Edgar Cayce
Thomas Jefferson
Nostradamus
Henry David Thoreau
Mark Twain
Virginia Woolf
Rollo May
Shelley Winters
Tennessee Williams
Diane Von Furstenberg
Evangeline Adams
Cher
Linda Ronstadt
Vanessa Redgrave
Elizabeth Arden
Sylvia Plath
Maria Callas
David Ben-Gurion
Anwar Sadat
Daniel Boone

PALLAS IN AQUARIUS

Madalyn Murray O'Hair
Lois Rodden
Jane Fonda
Janis Joplin
Yoko Ono
Queen Beatrix
Farah Fawcett
Colette
David Bowie
F. Scott Fitzgerald
Jimi Hendrix
Elton John
Henry Miller
Jean-Paul Sartre
Earl Warren
Alan Watts
Galileo Galilei
Abraham Lincoln
Louis Pasteur
Jack Nicholson
Martin Luther King
Marcia Moore
Margot Fonteyn
Sylvia Kars
Shirley Temple Black
Madalyn Murray O'Hair
Helen Frankenthaler
Charles Darwin
Barbra Streisand
Mary Wells Lawrence
Zsa Zsa Gabor
Michel Gauquelin
Clark Gable
Dag Hammarskjold
Howard Hughes
Paul McCartney
Edgar Allan Poe
Auguste Rodin
Joan of Arc
Jefferson Davis
Kahlil Gibran
Isaac Newton
Dr. Joyce Brothers

PALLAS IN PISCES

Gloria Steinem
Sally Struthers
Grace Kelly
Margaret Mead
Princess Caroline
Germaine Greer
Edna St. Vincent Millay
Isadora Duncan
Saint Francesca Cabrini
Louisa May Alcott
Gertrude Stein
Marlene Dietrich
Joyce Carol Oates
Farah Diba Pahlavi
Edith Piaf
Princess Diana
Marlon Brando
Enrico Fermi
Karl Marx
Federico Fellini
Ronald Reagan
Orson Wells
Ralph Nader
George Sand
Paramahansa Yogananda
Frank Sinatra
Alice Cooper
Bobby Fischer
Francisco Franco
Rudolf Nureyev
George Bush
Werner Heisenberg
Moshe Dayan
Walt Disney
Adolf Eichmann
Johann Sebastian Bach
John Calvin
Kit Carson
Buffalo Bill Cody
Mohandas Gandhi
Andre Gide
Mary Todd Lincoln
Carrie Nation
Vivien Kellems
Adrienne Hirt
Carol Burnett
Duchess of Windsor

APPENDIX THREE

VESTA IN THE CHARTS OF FAMOUS PEOPLE

Vesta in Aspect to the Planets

VESTA-SUN ASPECTS

Isadora Duncan - Vesta in Taurus conjunct the Sun in Gemini in the second house

Anne Frank - Vesta conjunct the Sun and Mercury in Gemini in the eleventh house

Princess Caroline - Vesta conjunct the Sun in Aquarius in the twelfth house

Yoko Ono - Vesta in Taurus in the eighth house square the Sun in Aquarius in the fifth house

Joan Crawford - Vesta conjunct the Sun in Aries in the fifth house

Marc Edmund Jones - Vesta in Aries in the fifth house opposing the Sun in Libra in the eleventh house

Enrico Fermi - Vesta conjunct the Sun and Mercury in Libra in the sixth house

Richard Alpert - Vesta in Capricorn in the sixth house square the Sun in Aries in the tenth house

Albert Schweitzer - Vesta in Taurus in the eighth house trine the Sun in Capricorn in the fourth house

Charles Baudelaire - Vesta in Cancer in the eleventh house square the Sun in Aries in the eighth house

Al Capone - Vesta in Aquarius conjunct the Sun in Capricorn

D. H. Lawrence - Vesta in Gemini square the Sun in Virgo

Ernest Hemingway - Vesta in Aries in the ninth house square the Sun in Cancer in the eleventh house

Howard Hughes - Vesta conjunct the Sun in Capricorn
Sir Winston Churchill - Vesta in Gemini in the ninth house opposing the Sun in Sagittarius in the third house
Charles Dickens - Vesta conjunct the Sun in Aquarius at the IC
Noel Tyl - Vesta in Cancer in the first house opposing the Sun, Jupiter, and Ceres in Capricorn in the seventh house
Harry Houdini - Vesta conjunct the Sun in Aries
Carl G. Jung - Vesta conjunct the Sun in Leo
Mary Stuart, Queen of Scots- Vesta conjunct the Sun in Sagittarius
Florence Nightingale - Vesta conjunct the Sun and Moon in Taurus in the ninth house
Pierre-Auguste Renoir - Vesta in Aquarius conjunct the Sun in Pisces
Werner Erhard - Vesta and Neptune in Pisces opposing the Sun in Virgo
Madalyn Murray O'Hair - Vesta in Cancer in the second house square Sun and Mars in Aries in the eleventh house
Margaret Trudeau - Vesta conjunct the Sun in Virgo in the ninth house
Agatha Christie - Vesta conjunct the Sun in Virgo in the twelfth house
Maria Callas - Vesta conjunct the Sun and Jupiter in Sagittarius
Clark Gable - Vesta in Leo opposing the Sun in Aquarius
Uri Geller - Vesta in Pisces in the fifth house square the Sun in Sagittarius in the third house
F. Scott Fitzgerald - Vesta in Cancer in the fifth house square the Sun in Libra in the eighth house
Warren Beatty - Vesta in Cancer in the tenth house square the Sun in Aries in the fifth house
Fritz Perls - Vesta conjunct the Sun and Ceres in Cancer
Frederic Chopin - Vesta in Cancer trine the Sun in Pisces
Yoko Ono - Vesta in Taurus in the eighth house square the Sun in Aquarius in the fifth house
Germaine Greer - Vesta conjunct the Sun in Aquarius at the Ascendant
Katharine Hepburn - Vesta conjunct the Sun in Taurus in the seventh house

VESTA-MOON ASPECTS

Elton John - Vesta conjunct the Moon in Taurus at the Midheaven
Clara Barton - Vesta in Scorpio in the eighth house sextile the Moon in Capricorn in the tenth house
Helena P. Blavatsky - Vesta in Cancer in the twelfth house square the Moon in Libra in the fourth house

Xaviera Hollander - Vesta in Taurus in the eleventh house opposing the Moon in Scorpio in the fifth house
Zelda Fitzgerald - Vesta conjunct the Moon and Venus in Cancer in the eleventh house
Maria Montessori - Vesta in Taurus at the Midheaven opposing the Moon in Scorpio at the IC
Jawaharlal Nehru - Vesta conjunct the Moon in Leo
Hermann Hesse - Vesta conjunct the Moon and Saturn in Pisces in the third house
Charles Baudelaire - Vesta conjunct the Moon in Cancer in the eleventh house
Robert Browning - Vesta conjunct the Moon in Aries in the third house
Andre Gide - Vesta in Capricorn at the IC opposing the Moon in Cancer in the ninth house
Mary Todd Lincoln - Vesta and Mercury in Capricorn opposing the Moon in Cancer
Isaac Newton - Vesta conjunct the Moon in Cancer
Sirimavo Bandaranaike - Vesta conjunct the Moon in Libra on the first-second cusp
Helen Gurley Brown - Vesta in Taurus in the fifth house opposing the Moon in Scorpio in the eleventh house
Diane Von Furstenberg - Vesta conjunct the Moon in Aries in the fifth house
Christine Jorgensen - Vesta in Cancer in the eleventh house opposing the Moon in Capricorn in the fifth house
Virginia Woolf - Vesta conjunct the Moon, Saturn, and Neptune in Taurus
Annie Oakley - Vesta conjunct the Moon in Cancer
Robert Graves - Vesta in Pisces opposing the Moon in Virgo
Gertrude Stein - Vesta and Pallas in Pisces in the first house opposing the Moon in Virgo in the seventh house

VESTA-MERCURY ASPECTS

Pope John Paul I - Vesta conjunct Mercury in Scorpio in the tenth house
Percy B. Shelley - Vesta conjunct Mercury in Virgo in the sixth house
Paul Cezanne - Vesta in Cancer in the eighth house opposing Mercury in Capricorn in the third house
Werner Heisenberg - Vesta conjunct Mercury in Scorpio
Walt Disney - Vesta conjunct Mercury in Scorpio on the second-third cusp

Johann Sebastian Bach - Vesta conjunct Mercury in Pisces
Marquis de Sade - Vesta conjunct Mercury in Taurus
Mary Baker Eddy - Vesta conjunct Mercury and Venus in Leo in the eighth house
Princess Margaret - Vesta conjunct Mercury in Virgo in the sixth house
Bette Midler - Vesta conjunct Mercury in Sagittarius in the ninth house
Judy Garland - Vesta conjunct Mercury in Cancer in the twelfth house
Hedda Hopper - Vesta conjunct Mercury in Taurus in the second house
Elisabeth Kubler-Ross - Vesta conjunct Mercury in Leo in the sixth house
Thomas Jefferson - Vesta conjunct Mercury in Pisces in the second house
Mary Todd Lincoln - Vesta conjunct Mercury in Capricorn
Clare Boothe Luce - Vesta conjunct Mercury in Aries in the fourth house opposing the Moon in Libra in the tenth house
Amelia Earhart - Vesta conjunct Mercury in Leo on the fourth-fifth cusp
Nathan Hale - Vesta conjunct Mercury in Gemini

VESTA-VENUS ASPECTS

Anais Nin - Vesta conjunct Venus in Pisces in the sixth house
Abraham Lincoln - Vesta conjunct Venus in Aries in the first house
Vincent van Gogh - Vesta in Aquarius in the eighth house square Venus in Taurus and Saturn in Scorpio
Richard Burton - Vesta in Cancer opposing Venus in Capricorn
Charles Chaplin - Vesta conjunct Venus and Mars in Taurus
Kahlil Gibran - Vesta in Virgo square Venus in Sagittarius
Ludwig van Beethoven - Vesta in Libra square Venus in Capricorn
Charles Darwin - Vesta conjunct Venus in Aries
Mary Baker Eddy - Vesta conjunct Venus in Leo in the eighth house
Dante Gabriel Rossetti - Vesta conjunct Venus and Saturn in Cancer
Tennessee Williams - Vesta conjunct Venus and the Sun in Aries
Taylor Caldwell - Vesta conjunct Venus in Cancer in the fourth house
Adrienne Hirt - Vesta in Cancer in the seventh house opposing Venus in Capricorn in the first house
Pat Nixon - Vesta in Leo in the seventh house opposing Moon and Venus in Aquarius in the first house
Judy Collins - Vesta conjunct Venus in Aries on the eighth-ninth cusp

Chiang Kai-shek - Vesta in Gemini opposing Venus in Sagittarius
Alan Watts - Vesta in Gemini in the sixth house opposing Venus in Sagittarius in the twelfth house
Shirley MacLaine - Vesta in Virgo in the twelfth house opposing Venus in Pisces in the sixth house
Saint Francesca Cabrini - Vesta conjunct Venus in Leo in the first house

VESTA-MARS ASPECTS

Catherine the Great - Vesta conjunct Mars in Taurus in the second house
Shirley Temple Black - Vesta conjunct Mars in Pisces at the IC
Angela Davis - Vesta conjunct Mars and Uranus in Gemini in the first house
Jane Addams - Vesta in Cancer in the eleventh house opposing Mars in Capricorn in the fifth house
Frederic Chopin - Vesta in Cancer square Mars in Aries
Jesse James - Vesta in Scorpio opposing Mars in Taurus
Dante Gabriel Rossetti - Vesta and Venus in Cancer opposing Mars in Capricorn
Junipero Serra - Mars conjunct Vesta in Capricorn
Adolf Hitler - Vesta conjunct Mars in Taurus
Harriet Beecher Stowe - Vesta conjunct Mars in Scorpio
Billy Jean King - Vesta conjunct Mars in Gemini in the fifth house
Anwar Sadat - Vesta in Leo opposing Mars in Aquarius
Lois Rodden - Vesta conjunct Mars and Uranus in Aries in the first house
William Blake - Vesta in Aquarius in the ninth house opposing Mars in Leo in the second house

VESTA-JUNO ASPECTS

Helen Keller - Vesta in Sagittarius in the first house square Juno in Virgo in the tenth house
Bob Dylan - Vesta conjunct Juno in Leo in the eighth house
John Lennon - Vesta conjunct Juno in Leo
Prince Albert - Vesta conjunct Juno in Cancer in the tenth house
Lucille Ball - Vesta in Cancer at the Ascendant square Juno in Libra in the fourth house
Billy Graham - Vesta conjunct Juno in Leo
John Calvin - Vesta conjunct Juno in Virgo
Colette - Vesta conjunct Juno in Sagittarius in the third house
Ellen Yoakum - Vesta in Taurus in the twelfth house opposing Juno

in Scorpio in the sixth house
Gloria Allred - Vesta conjunct Juno in Virgo in the seventh house
Helena P. Blavatsky - Vesta conjunct Juno in Cancer in the twelfth house
Adolf Eichmann - Vesta in Aquarius in the tenth house opposing Juno in Leo in the fourth house
Alan Leo - Vesta in Cancer in the eleventh house opposing Juno in Capricorn in the fifth house
William Butler Yeats - Vesta in Virgo in the seventh house opposing Juno in Pisces in the first house
Florence Nightingale - Vesta in Taurus opposing Juno in Scorpio
Barbara Walters - Vesta in Capricorn in the third house opposing Juno in Cancer in the ninth house
Cheiro - Vesta in Pisces in the second house opposing Juno and the Moon in Virgo in the eighth house

VESTA-JUPITER ASPECTS

Hermann Hesse - Vesta and the Moon in Pisces in the third house square Jupiter in Sagittarius in the first house
Ingrid Bergman - Vesta in Scorpio opposing Jupiter in Taurus
Leonard Bernstein - Vesta conjunct Jupiter in Cancer in the eleventh house
Chiang Kai-shek - Vesta in Gemini square Jupiter in Virgo
Muhammad Ali (Cassius Clay) - Vesta in Sagittarius opposing Jupiter in Gemini
Jefferson Davis - Vesta conjunct Jupiter and Pluto in Pisces in the tenth house
Queen Elizabeth I - Vesta and Pallas in Gemini opposing Jupiter in Sagittarius
Sissy Spacek - Vesta conjunct Jupiter in Aquarius in the fifth house
Jean Houston - Vesta in Aries conjunct Jupiter in Pisces in the seventh house
Noel Tyl - Vesta in Cancer in the first house opposing Jupiter, the Sun, and Ceres in Capricorn in the seventh house
Judy Collins - Vesta in Aries conjunct Jupiter in Pisces in the eighth house
Anne Morrow Lindbergh - Vesta in Pisces at the Descendant square Jupiter in Gemini at the Midheaven

VESTA-SATURN ASPECTS

Janis Joplin - Vesta in Pisces in the first house square Saturn in Gemini at the IC

Ken Kesey - Vesta conjunct Saturn in Pisces
Hermann Hesse - Vesta conjunct Saturn and the Moon in Pisces in the third house
Vincent van Gogh - Vesta in Aquarius in the eighth house square Saturn in Scorpio in the fifth house
Paul Gauguin - Vesta conjunct Saturn in Pisces in the eighth house
George Gershwin - Vesta conjunct Saturn in Sagittarius at the Ascendant
Mohandas Gandhi - Vesta conjunct Saturn in Sagittarius
Friedrich Nietzsche - Vesta conjunct Saturn in Aquarius in the second house
Pablo Picasso - Vesta conjunct Saturn in Taurus
Virginia Woolf - Vesta conjunct Saturn and the Moon in Taurus
Ronald Reagan - Vesta conjunct Saturn in Taurus
Shelley Winters - Vesta conjunct Saturn in Libra in the fifth house
Willie Ley - Vesta conjunct Saturn in Pisces opposing Mars in Virgo
Billy Jean King - Vesta conjunct Saturn and Mars in Gemini in the fifth house
Barbara Walters - Vesta conjunct Saturn in Capricorn in the third house

VESTA-URANUS ASPECTS
Martin Luther - Vesta in Virgo in the first house square Uranus in Sagittarius in the fourth house
Jean-Paul Sartre - Vesta in Libra in the eleventh house square Uranus in Capricorn in the second house
Marie Curie - Vesta conjunct Uranus in Cancer in the fifth house
Richard Alpert - Vesta in Capricorn in the sixth house square Uranus in Aries in tenth house
Betty Friedan - Vesta conjunct Uranus in Pisces in the second house
Anita Bryant - Vesta conjunct Uranus in Taurus in the tenth house
Christiaan Barnard - Vesta in Virgo opposing Uranus in Pisces
Charles de Gaulle - Vesta in Scorpio conjunct Uranus in Libra in the eighth house
Edgar Cayce - Vesta in Aquarius in the sixth house opposing Uranus in Leo in the first house
Leonardo da Vinci - Vesta in Capricorn opposing Uranus in Cancer
Nostradamus - Vesta conjunct Uranus in Pisces
Mick Jagger - Vesta conjunct Uranus in Gemini in the eleventh house
Queen Margrethe II - Vesta conjunct Uranus in Taurus in the eleventh house
Eleonora Duse - Vesta in Sagittarius in the fourth house opposing

Uranus in Gemini in the tenth house

Michel Gauquelin - Vesta conjunct Uranus in Aries in the ninth house

Elizabeth Arden - Vesta conjunct Uranus in Libra in the seventh house

Vivien Kellems - Vesta in Taurus in the seventh house opposing Uranus in Scorpio in the first house

Mary Wells Lawrence - Vesta conjunct Uranus and Mars in Aries in the eighth house

Sally Struthers - Vesta conjunct Uranus in Gemini in the ninth house

Francisco Franco - Vesta in Taurus in the eighth house opposing Uranus in Scorpio in the second house

Paramahansa Yogananda - Vesta in Taurus in the ninth house opposing Uranus in Scorpio in the third house

Jane Fonda - Vesta in Scorpio at the IC opposing Uranus in Scorpio in the tenth house

Saint Teresa of Avila - Vesta conjunct Uranus in Aries at the Ascendant

VESTA-NEPTUNE ASPECTS

Simone de Beauvoir - Vesta conjunct Neptune and the north node in Cancer in the eighth house

Elizabeth Barrett Browning - Vesta and Pallas in Gemini in the ninth house opposing Neptune in Sagittarius in the third house

Charles Darwin - Vesta and Venus in Aries trine Neptune in Sagittarius

Louis Armstrong - Vesta conjunct Neptune in Gemini

Salvador Dali - Vesta in Gemini conjunct Neptune in Cancer

Francisco Goya - Vesta in Capricorn opposing Neptune in Cancer

Empress Josephine - Vesta conjunct Neptune in Leo

Werner Erhard - Vesta conjunct Neptune in Pisces opposing Sun and Ceres in Virgo

Farrah Fawcett - Vesta in Aries in the tenth house opposing Neptune in Libra in the fourth house

Princess Diana - Vesta and Ceres in Taurus opposing Neptune in Scorpio

Doris Chase Doane - Vesta in Capricorn at the Ascendant opposing Neptune in Cancer in the seventh house

Bobby Fischer - Vesta in Aries in the ninth house opposing Neptune in Libra in the third house

Linda Ronstadt - Vesta in Aries in the third house opposing Neptune in Libra in the ninth house

Lucille Ball - Vesta conjunct Neptune in Cancer in the twelfth house
Maxfield Parrish - Vesta conjunct Neptune in Aries

VESTA-PLUTO ASPECTS

Sigmund Freud - Vesta conjunct Pluto and Pallas in Taurus in the sixth house
Mary Shelley - Vesta conjunct Pluto in Aquarius at the Midheaven
Adolf Hitler - Vesta semisquare Pluto
Queen Victoria - Vesta conjunct Pluto and Saturn in Pisces in the eleventh house
Isadora Duncan - Vesta conjunct Pluto in Taurus in the second house
Timothy Leary - Vesta in Capricorn opposing Pluto and Ceres in Cancer
Bertrand Russell - Vesta in Leo at the Midheaven square Pluto in Taurus in the seventh house
Emily Dickenson - Vesta conjunct Pluto in Aries in the fifth house
Moshe Dayan - Vesta conjunct Pluto in Cancer in the second house
Simon Bolivar - Vesta in Taurus square Pluto in Aquarius
Luther Burbank - Vesta conjunct Pluto and Uranus in Aries
Thomas Jefferson - Vesta in Pisces trine Pluto in Scorpio
Christine Jorgensen - Vesta conjunct Pluto in Cancer on the tenth-eleventh cusp
Barbra Streisand - Vesta in Aquarius in the eleventh house opposing Pluto in Cancer in the fifth house
Orson Wells - Vesta conjunct Pluto in Cancer in the first house
Robert J. Oppenheimer - Vesta conjunct Pluto in Gemini
Emma Goldman - Vesta in Scorpio opposing Pluto in Taurus
Martin Luther King - Vesta in Aries square Pluto in Cancer
Albert Schweitzer - Vesta conjunct Pluto in Taurus in the eighth house
Daniel Boone - Vesta conjunct Pluto in Libra

Vesta in the Houses

VESTA IN THE FIRST HOUSE

Saint Teresa of Avila (Asc)
Angela Davis
Saint Francesca Cabrini (Asc)
Helen Keller
Doris Chase Doane
Germaine Greer (Asc)
Gertrude Stein
Noel Tyl
Janis Joplin
Abraham Lincoln
Martin Luther
Elvis Presley
Pearl Bailey
Alfred Hitchcock

Lois Rodden
Francoise Gauquelin (Asc)
Orson Wells
Pierre-Auguste Renoir

**VESTA
IN THE SECOND HOUSE**

Catherine the Great
Isadora Duncan
Louisa May Alcott
Betty Friedan
Jimi Hendrix
Cheiro
Friedrich Nietzsche
Thomas Jefferson
Walt Disney
Sirimavo Bandaranaike
Marlon Brando
Madalyn Murray O'Hair
Edward Kennedy
Hedda Hopper

**VESTA
IN THE THIRD HOUSE**

Hermann Hesse
Robert Browning
James Dean
Marlene Dietrich
Colette
Barbara Walters
Sylvia Plath
Sylvia Porter
Linda Ronstadt
Carol Burnett
Duchess of Windsor
Hans Christian Andersen
Robert Redford (IC)
Eleanor Roosevelt

**VESTA
IN THE FOURTH HOUSE**

Ringo Starr
Louis Pasteur
Andre Gide
Taylor Caldwell (IC)
Charles Dickens (IC)
Eleonora Duse
Henry Kissinger
Shirley Temple Black (IC)
Farah Diba Pahlavi
Clare Boothe Luce
Jane Fonda (IC)
Evangeline Adams (IC)
Prince Charles

**VESTA
IN THE FIFTH HOUSE**

Adelle Davis
Raquel Welch
Amelia Earhart
Joan Baez
Alice Bailey
Marc Edmund Jones
Albert Camus
Uri Geller
Billy Jean King
Joan Crawford
Helen Gurley Brown
Diane Von Furstenberg
Julia Child
Sissy Spacek
Marianne Alireza
Marie Curie
Emily Dickenson
F. Scott Fitzgerald
Neil Armstrong
Chiang Kai-shek

VESTA
IN THE SIXTH HOUSE

Elisabeth Kubler-Ross
Princess Margaret
Anais Nin
Elizabeth Taylor
David Bowie
Sigmund Freud
Alan Watts
Percy B. Shelley
Enrico Fermi
Richard Alpert (Ram Dass)
Hugh Hefner
Edgar Cayce
Minette Lenier
Queen Elizabeth I

VESTA
IN THE SEVENTH HOUSE

Debbie Reynolds (Desc)
Soraya of Iran
Sybil Leek
Saint Bernadette of Lourdes (Desc)
William Butler Yeats
Alexander Graham Bell
Karl Marx
Anne Morrow Lindbergh (Desc)
Edna Ferber
Lenny Bruce
Jean Houston
Adrienne Hirt
Elizabeth Arden
Sylvia Kars
Pat Nixon
Vivien Kellems
Gloria Allred
Helen Frankenthaler
Duke of Windsor
Queen Beatrix
Katharine Hepburn

VESTA
IN THE EIGHTH HOUSE

Patty Hearst
Pearl Buck
Yoko Ono
Simone de Beauvoir
Clara Barton
Annie Besant
Indira Gandhi
Albert Schweitzer
Paul Cezanne
Bob Dylan
Vincent van Gogh
Paul Gauguin
Francisco Franco
Michael Jackson
Emmeline Pankhurst
Judy Collins
Mary Wells Lawrence
Ernest Hemingway
Ira Progoff
R. D. Laing
Mary Baker Eddy
Charles de Gaulle

VESTA
IN THE NINTH HOUSE

Sally Struthers
Elizabeth Barrett Browning
Jack Kerouac
Bertrand Russell (MC)
William Blake
Bobby Fischer
Zsa Zsa Gabor
Sir Winston Churchill
Michel Gauquelin
Paramahansa Yogananda
Florence Nightingale
Bette Midler
Coco Chanel
Cher

Margaret Trudeau
Joyce Carol Oates

VESTA
IN THE TENTH HOUSE
Grace Kelly (MC)
Farrah Fawcett
Eva Braun
Margaret Mead
Mary Shelley (MC)
Edna St. Vincent Millay
Anita Bryant
Warren Beatty
Prince Albert
Pope John Paul I
Henry Winkler
Elton John (MC)
John Dillinger
Alice Cooper (MC)
Jefferson Davis
George Washington
Maria Montessori (MC)
Adolf Eichmann
Rollo May (MC)

VESTA
IN THE ELEVENTH HOUSE
Xaviera Hollander
Zelda Fitzgerald
Gloria Steinem
Queen Victoria
Pierre Teilhard de Chardin
Charles Baudelaire
Alan Leo
Jean-Paul Sartre
Walter Mondale
Henry Miller
Christine Jorgensen
Jane Addams
Helen Boucher
George Sand
Barbra Streisand
Dr. Marjorie Weinzweig
Vanessa Redgrave
Brigitte Bardot
Queen Margrethe II of Denmark
Leonard Bernstein
Mick Jagger
Mark Twain

VESTA
IN THE TWELFTH HOUSE
Marilyn Monroe
Helena P. Blavatsky
Zipporah Dobyns
Princess Caroline
Albert Einstein (Asc)
Dr. Tom Dooley
Earl Warren
Auguste Rodin
Lucille Ball
Shirley MacLaine
Jack Nicholson
Adlai Stevenson
Ellen Yoakum
Judy Garland
Agatha Christie

Vesta in the Signs

VESTA IN ARIES
Debbie Reynolds
Lois Rodden
Patty Hearst
Saint Teresa of Avila
Emily Dickenson
Farrah Fawcett
Adlai Stevenson
David Bowie
Marc Edmund Jones

Abraham Lincoln
Pierre Teilhard de Chardin
Michel Gauquelin
Bobby Fisher
Martin Luther King
Ernest Hemingway
Alfred Hitchcock
Hans Christian Andersen
Robert Browning
Luther Burbank
Charles Darwin
Harry Houdini
Maxfield Parrish
Tennessee Williams
Jean Houston
Dr. Joyce Brothers
Joan Crawford
Diane Von Furstenberg
Mary Wells Lawrence
Judy Collins
Linda Ronstadt
Helen Frankenthaler
Clare Boothe Luce

VESTA IN TAURUS

Queen Margrethe II of Denmark
Anita Bryant
Katharine Hepburn
Xaviera Hollander
Soraya of Iran
Pearl Buck
Pearl Bailey
Zipporah Dobyns
Yoko Ono
Sybil Leek
Catherine the Great
Isadora Duncan
Maria Montessori
Elton John
Jack Kerouac
Sigmund Freud
Albert Schweitzer
Ira Progoff
Nancy Reagan
Ronald Reagan
Paramahansa Yogananda
John Dillinger
Francisco Franco
Rachel Carson
Charles Chaplin
Simon Bolivar
Marquis de Sade
Florence Nightingale
Pablo Picasso
Virginia Woolf
Duchess of Windsor
Princess Diana
Adolf Hitler
Helen Gurley Brown
Vivien Kellems
Ellen Yoakum
Hedda Hopper

VESTA IN GEMINI

Sally Struthers
Angela Davis
Adelle Davis
Elizabeth Barrett Browning
Marianne Alireza
Anne Frank
Mick Jagger
Alan Watts
Edna Ferber
Zza Zza Gabor
D. H. Lawrence
Louis Armstrong
Chiang Kai-shek
Salvador Dali
Francoise Gauquelin
Sir Winston Churchill
Buffalo Bill Cody
Queen Elizabeth I
Nathan Hale

Napoleon Bonaparte
Robert Redford
Robert J. Oppenheimer
Billy Jean King
Sylvia Plath
Evangeline Adams
Carlos Castaneda
Carol Burnett

VESTA IN CANCER
Marilyn Monroe
Zelda Fitzgerald
Raquel Welch
Simone de Beauvoir
Helena P. Blavatsky
Marie Curie
Helen Boucher
Taylor Caldwell
Michael Jackson
Warren Beatty
F. Scott Fitzgerald
Ringo Starr
Prince Albert
Charles Baudelaire
Paul Cezanne
Albert Einstein
Alan Leo
Fritz Perls
Lenny Bruce
Alice Cooper
Jack Nicholson
Richard Burton
Lucille Ball
Leonard Bernstein
Moshe Dayan
Hugh Hefner
Jane Addams
Kit Carson
Frederic Chopin
Isaac Newton
Annie Oakley
Dante Gabriel Rossetti
Henry David Thoreau
Queen Elizabeth II
Victoria Woodhull
Christine Jorgensen
Orson Wells
Adrienne Hirt
Vanessa Redgrave
Madalyn Murray O'Hair
Judy Garland
Noel Tyl
Alan Ginsberg
Jacqueline Kennedy Onassis

VESTA IN LEO
Elisabeth Kubler-Ross
Amelia Earhart
Grace Kelly
Joan Baez
Eva Braun
Saint Francesca Cabrini
Bob Dylan
John Lennon
Bertrand Russell
Anwar Sadat
Clark Gable
Billy Graham
Mary Baker Eddy
Empress Josephine
Carl G. Jung
Marie Antoinette
Sylvia Kars
Pat Nixon
Margot Fonteyn
Jawaharlal Nehru

VESTA IN VIRGO
Gloria Steinem
Princess Margaret
Martin Luther
Percy B. Shelley
William Butler Yeats
Henry Kissinger

Mao Tse-tung
Neil Armstrong
Christiaan Barnard
Kahlil Gibran
John Calvin
Aleister Crowley
Carrie Nation
Mark Twain
Gloria Allred
Shirley MacLaine
Agatha Christie
Charles Atlas
Duke of Windsor
Sri Meher Baba
Margaret Trudeau
David Ben-Gurion

VESTA IN LIBRA
Julia Child
Coco Chanel
Edith Piaf
Enrico Fermi
Jean-Paul Sartre
Alexander Graham Bell
Karl Marx
Prince Charles
Dag Hammarskjold
Ludwig van Beethoven
Frank Sinatra
Shelley Winters
Paul Simon
Elizabeth Arden
Sirimavo Bandaranaike
Minette Lenier
Emmeline Pankhurst
Galileo Galilei
Daniel Boone
Ralph Nader
The Reverend Jesse Jackson

VESTA IN SCORPIO
Margaret Mead
Jane Fonda
Clara Barton
Annie Besant
Louisa May Alcott
Queen Beatrix
Joyce Carol Oates
Dr. Tom Dooley
John Paul I
Werner Heisenberg
Brigitte Bardot
Ingrid Bergman
Charles de Gaulle
Walt Disney
Jesse James
Emma Goldman
Harriet Beecher Stowe
Fidel Castro

VESTA IN SAGITTARIUS
Alice Bailey
Helen Keller
Saint Bernadette of Lourdes
Marlene Dietrich
Farah Diba Pahlavi
Colette
Eleonora Duse
Federico Fellini
James Dean
Muhammad Ali (Cassius Clay)
George Gershwin
Mohandas Gandhi
Joan of Arc
Mary Stuart, Queen of Scots
Rudolf Nureyev
Billy Joel
Henry Winkler
Bette Midler
Maria Callas
Rollo May
R. D. Laing
Benjamin Franklin

VESTA IN CAPRICORN
Doris Chase Doane
George Sand
Richard Alpert (Ram Dass)
Walter Mondale
Elvis Presley
Earl Warren
Auguste Rodin
Jacqueline Kennedy Onassis
Howard Hughes
Leonardo da Vinci
Andre Gide
Francisco Goya
Mary Todd Lincoln
Junipero Serra
Babe Ruth
Andy Warhol
Barbara Walters
Dr. Marjorie Weinzweig
Timothy Leary

VESTA IN AQUARIUS
Princess Caroline
Germaine Greer
Mary Shelley
Marlon Brando
Albert Camus
Jimi Hendrix
Henry Miller
William Blake
Louis Pasteur
Vincent van Gogh
Al Capone
Adolf Eichmann
Edgar Cayce
Charles Dickens
Friedrich Nietzsche
Pierre-Auguste Renoir
George Washington
Barbra Streisand
Rudolph Valentino
Eleanor Roosevelt
Paul McCartney
Sylvia Porter
Sissy Spacek

VESTA IN PISCES
Anne Morrow Lindbergh
Indira Gandhi
Janis Joplin
Betty Friedan
Anais Nin
Edna St. Vincent Millay
Elizabeth Taylor
Gertrude Stein
Queen Victoria
Uri Geller
Cheiro
Paul Gauguin
Hermann Hesse
George Bush
Johann Sebastian Bach
Jefferson Davis
Thomas Jefferson
Nostradamus
Edgar Allan Poe
Robert Graves
Werner Erhard
Immanuel Velikovsky
Willie Ley
John F. Kennedy
Shirley Temple Black
Edward Kennedy
Geraldine Ferraro
Cher

APPENDIX FOUR

JUNO IN THE CHARTS OF FAMOUS PEOPLE

Juno in Aspect to the Planets

JUNO-SUN ASPECTS

Marie Curie - Juno conjunct the Sun in Scorpio in the eighth house

Gertrude Stein - Juno conjunct the Sun and Mercury in Aquarius in the twelfth house

Elizabeth Barrett Browning - Juno in Virgo in the twelfth house opposing the Sun in Pisces in the sixth house

Annie Besant - Juno in Capricorn in the tenth house square the Sun in Libra in the seventh house

Anais Nin - Juno in Sagittarius in the third house square the Sun in Pisces in the fifth house

Gloria Steinem - Juno in Capricorn in the second house square the Sun in Aries in the fifth house

Isadora Duncan - Juno in Pisces in the twelfth house square the Sun in Gemini in the second house

Paul Cezanne - Juno in Aquarius conjunct the Sun in Capricorn in the third house

Christiaan Barnard - Juno in Taurus opposing the Sun in Scorpio

Carrie Nation - Juno conjunct the Sun in Sagittarius

Florence Nightingale - Juno in Scorpio in the third house opposing the Sun, Moon, and Vesta in Taurus in the ninth house

Christine Jorgensen - Juno in Pisces in the sixth house square the Sun in Gemini in the ninth house

Shelley Winters - Juno conjunct the Sun in Leo

Marilyn Monroe - Juno in Pisces in the eighth house square the Sun

in Gemini in the tenth house
Marlon Brando - Juno in Libra in the tenth house opposing the Sun and Moon in Aries in the fourth house
Alice Cooper - Juno conjunct the Sun in Aquarius in the fourth house opposing Pluto in the tenth
Pearl Bailey - Juno conjunct the Sun in Aries in the twelfth house
Michael Jackson - Juno conjunct the Sun in Virgo at the Midheaven
Paul Simon - Juno conjunct the Sun in Libra
Dr. Joyce Brothers - Juno conjunct the Sun in Libra
The Reverend Jesse Jackson - Juno conjunct the Sun in Libra opposing Mars in Aries
Eleonora Duse - Juno conjunct the Sun in Libra in the second house
Carlos Castaneda - Juno conjunct the Sun in Capricorn
Queen Victoria - Juno in Virgo in the fifth house square the Sun, Moon, and Ceres in Gemini in the twelfth house
Elton John - Juno in Capricorn in the fifth house square the Sun in Aries in the ninth house
Robert Redford - Juno conjunct the Sun in Leo in the sixth house

JUNO-MOON ASPECTS

Janis Joplin - Juno in Capricorn in the eleventh house opposing the Moon in Cancer in the fifth house
Angela Davis - Juno conjunct the Moon in Aquarius on the tenth-eleventh cusp
Zelda Fitzgerald - Juno in Aries in the ninth house square the Moon, Venus, and Vesta in Cancer in the eleventh house
Annie Besant - Juno in Capricorn in the tenth house opposing the Moon in Cancer in the fourth house
Louis Armstrong - Juno in Aries opposing the Moon in Libra
Hans Christian Andersen - Juno conjunct the Moon in Taurus opposing Neptune in Scorpio
Pablo Picasso - Juno conjunct the Moon in Sagittarius
Annie Oakley - Juno in Capricorn opposing the Moon and Vesta in Cancer
John Dillinger - Juno in Scorpio in the fourth house opposing the Moon in Taurus in the tenth house
Immanuel Velikovsky - Juno in Capricorn opposing the Moon and Mars in Cancer
Jack Nicholson - Juno conjunct the Moon in Virgo in the third house opposing Saturn in Pisces in the ninth house
Sylvia Plath - Juno conjunct the Moon in Libra in the seventh house

Vivien Kellems - Juno conjunct the Moon in Taurus in the seventh house
Sally Struthers - Juno conjunct the Moon in Sagittarius in the third house
Saint Francesca Cabrini - Juno conjunct the Mon in Libra in the third house
Soraya of Iran - Juno and Jupiter in Leo in the tenth house opposing the Moon in Aquarius in the fifth house
Babe Ruth - Juno in Capricorn opposing the Moon in Cancer
Emma Goldman - Juno conjunct the Moon in Aquarius
Alan Ginsberg - Juno conjunct the Moon in Pisces
Cheiro - Juno conjunct the Moon in Virgo in the eighth house opposing Vesta in Pisces
Helen Keller - Juno in Virgo in the tenth house opposing the Moon in Pisces in the fourth house
Charles Baudelaire - Juno in Capricorn in the fifth house opposing the Moon in Cancer in the eleventh house

JUNO-MERCURY ASPECTS

Mary Shelley - Juno conjunct Mercury in Virgo in the fourth house
Germaine Greer - Juno conjunct Mercury in Capricorn in the twelfth house
Eleanor Roosevelt - Juno conjunct Mercury in Libra and Uranus in Virgo in the tenth house
Katharine Hepburn - Juno in Scorpio in the twelfth house opposing Mercury in Taurus in the seventh house
Michel Gauquelin - Juno conjunct Mercury in Scorpio at the IC
Nathan Hale - Juno in Sagittarius opposing Mercury in Gemini
Victoria Woodhull - Juno in Sagittarius square Mercury in Virgo
Dr. Marjorie Weinzweig - Juno conjunct Mercury and Venus in Aquarius in the twelfth house
Helen Gurley Brown - Juno conjunct Mercury and the Sun in Aquarius in the second house
Uri Geller - Juno conjunct Mercury in Sagittarius in the second house
Timothy Leary - Juno conjunct Mercury and Venus in Scorpio
Jawaharlal Nehru - Juno conjunct Mercury in Scorpio

JUNO-VENUS ASPECTS

Edna St. Vincent Millay - Juno conjunct Venus in Aries in the eleventh house
Raquel Welch - Juno conjunct Venus and Vesta in Cancer in the fifth house

Ringo Starr - Juno conjunct Venus in Gemini at the IC
Jimi Hendrix - Juno conjunct Venus in Sagittarius in the twelfth house opposing Saturn in Gemini
Karl Marx - Juno conjunct Venus in Taurus in the third house
Clark Gable - Juno in Aries square Venus in Capricorn
Mary Baker Eddy - Juno in Aquarius in the second house opposing Venus in Leo in the eighth house
Francisco Goya - Juno in Sagittarius trine Venus and the Sun in Aries
Edgar Allan Poe - Juno conjunct Venus and Pluto in Pisces
Adrienne Hirt - Juno conjunct Venus in Capricorn in the first house
Sylvia Kars - Juno conjunct Venus in Scorpio in the ninth house
Francoise Gauquelin - Juno in Scorpio in the sixth house opposing Venus and Ceres in Taurus in the twelfth house
Pierre Teilhard de Chardin - Juno in Scorpio in the sixth house opposing Venus in Taurus in the twelfth house
Rachel Carson - Juno in Scorpio opposing Venus in Taurus
Clara Barton - Juno conjunct Venus in Aquarius on the tenth-eleventh cusp
Paul Cezanne - Juno conjunct Venus in Aquarius in the third house
Elvis Presley - Juno in Aquarius conjunct Venus in Capricorn in the second house

JUNO-MARS ASPECTS

Alexander Graham Bell - Juno conjunct Mars in Capricorn in the eleventh house
Louis Pasteur - Juno in Cancer in the ninth house opposing Mars in Capricorn in the third house
Johann Sebastian Bach - Juno conjunct Mars in Sagittarius
Kit Carson - Juno in Leo opposing Mars in Aquarius
Buffalo Bill Cody - Juno in Scorpio opposing Mars in Taurus
Mary Stuart, Queen of Scots- Juno conjunct Mars in Aquarius
Napoleon Bonaparte - Juno in Pisces opposing Mars in Virgo
Charles Atlas - Juno conjunct Mars in Libra
Adlai Stevenson - Juno conjunct Mars in Aquarius in the ninth house
Hedda Hopper - Juno in Libra in the eighth house opposing Mars in Aries in the second house
Joan of Arc - Juno in Pisces opposing Mars in Virgo
Howard Hughes - Juno in Leo opposing Mars in Aquarius
Daniel Boone - Juno conjunct Mars in Aquarius
Sissy Spacek - Juno in Libra conjunct Mars in Virgo at the Ascendant
Auguste Rodin - Juno conjunct Mars in Virgo in the eighth house opposing Uranus in Pisces in the second house

JUNO-JUPITER ASPECTS

Grace Kelly - Juno in Sagittarius in the second house opposing Jupiter in Gemini in the eighth house
Queen Elizabeth II - Juno conjunct Jupiter in Aquarius in the first house opposing Neptune in Leo in the seventh house
Eva Braun - Juno conjunct Jupiter in Sagittarius in the second house
Soraya of Iran - Juno conjunct Jupiter in Leo on the tenth-eleventh cusp
Catherine the Great - Juno in Capricorn opposing Jupiter in Cancer
Martin Luther - Juno conjunct Jupiter in Libra in the second house
Abraham Lincoln - Juno conjunct Jupiter in Pisces in the first house
Hugh Hefner - Juno conjunct Jupiter in Aquarius in the second house
Charles Darwin - Juno conjunct Jupiter in Pisces
Jesse James - Juno in Capricorn opposing Jupiter in Cancer
Thomas Jefferson - Juno in Pisces opposing Jupiter in Virgo
Carrie Nation - Juno in Sagittarius opposing Jupiter in Gemini
Maxfield Parrish - Juno conjunct Jupiter in Gemini
Mark Twain - Juno conjunct Jupiter in Cancer
Julia Child - Juno conjunct Jupiter in Sagittarius at the Descendant
George Washington - Juno conjunct Jupiter in Libra
Robert Graves - Juno in Capricorn opposing Jupiter and Mercury in Cancer
Xaviera Hollander - Juno in Capricorn in the eighth opposing Jupiter in Cancer in the second house
Bette Midler - Juno conjunct Jupiter in Libra in the seventh house
Cher - Juno conjunct Jupiter in Libra in the fourth house
Linda Ronstadt - Juno conjunct Jupiter in Libra in the tenth house
Pat Nixon - Juno conjunct Jupiter in Sagittarius in the eleventh house
Angela Davis - Juno in Aquarius in the eleventh house opposing Jupiter in Leo in the fourth house
Henry Miller - Juno conjunct Jupiter in Pisces in the twelfth house

JUNO-SATURN ASPECTS

Emily Dickenson - Juno in Pisces at the IC opposing Saturn in Virgo in the ninth house
Simone de Beauvoir - Juno in Sagittarius in the first house square Saturn in Pisces in the fourth house
Yoko Ono - Juno in Scorpio in the first house square Saturn in Aquarius in the fourth house
Saint Teresa of Avila - Juno conjunct Saturn in Sagittarius in the eighth house
Jimi Hendrix - Juno in Sagittarius in the twelfth house opposing

Saturn in Gemini in the sixth house
Muhammad Ali (Cassius Clay) - Juno in Scorpio opposing Saturn in Taurus
Salvador Dali - Juno conjunct Saturn in Aquarius
Ernest Hemingway - Juno conjunct Saturn in Sagittarius in the fourth house opposing Pluto in the tenth house
Alfred Hitchcock - Juno conjunct Saturn in Sagittarius in the ninth house
Charles Dickens - Juno in Sagittarius conjunct Saturn in Capricorn
Mary Todd Lincoln - Juno in Virgo opposing Saturn and Pallas in Pisces
Duchess of Windsor - Juno in Taurus in the second house opposing Saturn in Scorpio in the eighth house
Queen Margrethe II - Juno conjunct Saturn in Taurus in the eleventh house
Robert J. Oppenheimer - Juno conjunct Saturn in Aquarius
George Sand - Juno in Pisces in the first house opposing Saturn in Virgo in the seventh house
Saint Francesca Cabrini - Juno in Libra in the third house opposing Saturn in Aries in the ninth house
Al Capone - Juno conjunct Saturn in Sagittarius
George Washington - Juno in Libra opposing Saturn in Aries

JUNO-URANUS ASPECTS

Marianne Alireza - Juno conjunct Uranus in Pisces in the second house
Ken Kesey - Juno conjunct Uranus in Taurus
Simon Bolivar - Juno conjunct Uranus in Cancer
Queen Elizabeth I - Juno in Capricorn opposing Uranus in Cancer
Mohandas Gandhi - Juno in Capricorn opposing Uranus in Cancer
Carl G. Jung - Juno conjunct Uranus in Leo
Duke of Windsor - Juno conjunct Uranus in Scorpio on the eighth-ninth cusp
Werner Erhard - Juno conjunct Uranus in Taurus
Helen Boucher - Juno conjunct Uranus in Capricorn in the fifth house
Farrah Fawcett - Juno and Venus in Sagittarius in the sixth house opposing Uranus in the twelfth house
Carol Burnett - Juno in Libra in the seventh house opposing Uranus in Aries in the first house
Alice Bailey - Juno conjunct Uranus and Ceres in Virgo in the second house
Amelia Earhart - Juno in Leo in the fifth house square Uranus in

Scorpio in the seventh house

Zelda Fitzgerald - Juno in Aries in the ninth house trine Uranus in Sagittarius in the fifth house

Debbie Reynolds - Juno in Cancer in the tenth house square Uranus in Aries in the seventh house

Gertrude Stein - Juno in Aquarius in the twelfth house opposing Uranus in Leo in the sixth house

Elizabeth Taylor - Juno in Cancer in the tenth house square Uranus and Venus in Aries in the seventh house

William Blake - Juno in Virgo at the IC opposing Uranus in Pisces at the MC

Dr. Tom Dooley - Juno conjunct Uranus in Pisces in the fourth house

Mao Tse-tung - Juno conjunct Uranus in Scorpio

Sri Meher Baba - Juno conjunct Uranus in Scorpio opposing Jupiter in Taurus

JUNO-NEPTUNE ASPECTS

Indira Gandhi - Juno in Aquarius in the sixth house opposing Neptune and Saturn in Leo in the twelfth house

F. Scott Fitzgerald - Juno conjunct Neptune and Mars in Gemini in the fifth house

Bertrand Russell - Juno in Libra in the twelfth house opposing Neptune in Aries in the sixth house

Alice Bailey - Juno in Virgo in the second house trine Neptune in Taurus in the tenth house

Pearl Bailey - Juno in Aries in the twelfth house trine Neptune and Saturn in Leo in the fourth house

Helena P. Blavatsky - Juno in Cancer in the twelfth house opposing Neptune in Capricorn in the sixth house

Colette - Juno in Sagittarius in the third house trine Neptune in Aries in the seventh house

Queen Elizabeth II - Juno in Aquarius in the first house opposing Neptune in Leo in the seventh house

Katharine Hepburn - Juno in Scorpio in the twelfth house trine Neptune in Cancer in the ninth house

George Sand - Juno in Pisces in the first house trine Neptune in Scorpio in the eighth house

Grace Kelly - Juno in Sagittarius in the second house square Neptune in Virgo in the tenth house

James Dean - Juno in Pisces in the fifth house opposing Neptune in Virgo in the eleventh house

Ludwig van Beethoven - Juno conjunct Neptune in Virgo

Anwar Sadat - Juno conjunct Neptune and Vesta in Leo
Henry Winkler - Juno conjunct Neptune in Libra in the eighth house
Janis Joplin - Juno in Capricorn in the eleventh house square Neptune in Libra in the seventh house
Gloria Steinem - Juno in Capricorn in the second house trine Neptune in Virgo in the tenth house
Margot Fonteyn - Juno conjunct Neptune in Leo
Margaret Trudeau - Juno in Aries in the fourth house opposing Neptune and Mercury in Libra in the tenth house
Lois Rodden - Juno in Virgo conjunct Neptune in Leo in the seventh house
Marcia Moore - Juno in Virgo conjunct Neptune in Libra
R. D. Laing - Juno conjunct Neptune in Leo in the sixth house
Billy Graham - Juno conjunct Neptune in Leo
Benjamin Franklin - Juno in Libra opposing Neptune in Aries

JUNO-PLUTO ASPECTS

Elizabeth Taylor - Juno conjunct Pluto in Cancer in the tenth house
Debbie Reynolds - Juno conjunct Pluto in Cancer in the tenth house
Simone de Beauvoir - Juno in Sagittarius in the first house opposing Pluto in Gemini in the seventh house
Princess Margaret - Juno in Capricorn in the eleventh house opposing Pluto and the Moon in Cancer in the fifth house
Paul Gauguin - Juno conjunct Pluto and Uranus in Aries in the ninth house
Al Capone - Juno in Sagittarius opposing Pluto in Gemini
Leonard Bernstein - Juno conjunct Pluto in Cancer in the eleventh house
Pat Nixon - Juno in Sagittarius in the eleventh house opposing Pluto and Mars in Gemini in the fifth house
Pearl Bailey - Juno in Aries in the twelfth house square Pluto in Cancer in the third house
Patty Hearst - Juno conjunct Pluto in Leo in the twelfth house
Catherine the Great - Juno in Capricorn square Pluto in Libra
Elisabeth Kubler-Ross - Juno in Pisces in the first house trine Pluto and the Sun in Cancer in the fifth house
Marilyn Monroe - Juno in Pisces in the eighth house trine Pluto in Cancer in the eleventh house
Edward Kennedy - Juno conjunct Pluto in Cancer in the seventh house
Fidel Castro - Juno conjunct Pluto in Cancer
Francisco Goya - Juno conjunct Pluto in Sagittarius

Henry Kissinger - Juno conjunct Pluto in Cancer in the first house
Paramahansa Yogananda - Juno in Virgo in the first house square Pluto and Neptune in Gemini in the tenth house
Nathan Hale - Juno conjunct Pluto in Gemini
Dag Hammarskjold - Juno conjunct Pluto in Gemini

Juno in the Houses

JUNO IN THE FIRST HOUSE

Clare Boothe Luce
Simone de Beauvoir
Betty Friedan (Asc)
Adelle Davis
Elisabeth Kubler-Ross
Brigitte Bardot
Warren Beatty (Asc)
John Paul I (Asc)
Abraham Lincoln
Henry Kissinger
William Butler Yeats
Paramahansa Yogananda
Walt Disney
Robert Browning
Thomas Jefferson
Marlene Dietrich
George Sand
Billy Jean King (Asc)
Doris Chase Doane
Joan Crawford
Adrienne Hirt
Diane Von Furstenberg
Sissy Spacek (Asc)
Mary Wells Lawrence
Queen Elizabeth II
Rollo May
Earl Warren

JUNO IN THE SECOND HOUSE

Alice Bailey
Yoko Ono
Louisa May Alcott
Grace Kelly
Eva Braun
Gloria Steinem
Uri Geller
Elvis Presley
Marianne Alireza
Hugh Hefner
Mary Baker Eddy
Charles Darwin
Eleonora Duse
Helen Gurley Brown
Madalyn Murray O'Hair
Helen Frankenthaler
Duchess of Windsor
Martin Luther

JUNO IN THE THIRD HOUSE

Saint Francesca Cabrini
Sally Struthers
Anais Nin
Karl Marx
William Blake (IC)
Martin Luther
David Bowie
Paul Cezanne
Sigmund Freud
Ringo Starr (IC)
Florence Nightingale
Colette
Jack Nicholson
Vanessa Redgrave
Sirimavo Bandaranaike

Emily Dickenson (IC)
Agatha Christie

JUNO
IN THE FOURTH HOUSE

Mary Shelley
Jane Fonda
Sybil Leek (IC)
Shirley MacLaine
Cher
Dr. Tom Dooley
Farah Diba Pahlavi
Noel Tyl
Michel Gauquelin (IC)
Lucille Ball
John Dillinger
Ernest Hemingway
Edgar Cayce
Alice Cooper
Andre Gide
Minette Lenier
Margaret Trudeau
Anne Frank
Adolf Eichmann
Ira Progoff (IC)
Orson Wells
Sylvia Porter

JUNO
IN THE FIFTH HOUSE

James Dean
Raquel Welch
Amelia Earhart
Joan Baez
Queen Victoria
F. Scott Fitzgerald
Percy B. Shelley
Enrico Fermi
Elton John
Charles Baudelaire
Alan Leo
Helen Boucher
Hans Christian Andersen
Jane Addams
George Washington

JUNO
IN THE SIXTH HOUSE

Indira Gandhi
Pierre Teilhard de Chardin
Jack Kerouac
Albert Camus
Christine Jorgensen
Francoise Gauquelin
Jean Houston
Mick Jagger
Ellen Yoakum
Farrah Fawcett
Coco Chanel
Bobby Fischer
R. D. Laing
Robert Redford

JUNO
IN THE SEVENTH HOUSE

Lois Rodden
Albert Schweitzer
Walter Mondale
Vincent van Gogh (Desc)
Julia Child
Pierre-Auguste Renoir
Edward Kennedy (Desc)
Bette Midler
Sylvia Plath
Vivien Kellems (Desc)
Judy Collins
Gloria Allred
Emmeline Pankhurst
Carol Burnett

JUNO
IN THE EIGHTH HOUSE

Margaret Mead
Marie Curie

Zipporah Dobyns
Saint Teresa of Avila
Xaviera Hollander
Jean-Paul Sartre
Cheiro
Auguste Rodin
Duke of Windsor
Henry Winkler
Evangeline Adams
Hedda Hopper
Barbra Streisand
Queen Beatrix of Holland
Marilyn Monroe
Sir Winston Churchill
Bob Dylan

JUNO IN THE NINTH HOUSE

Anita Bryant
Zelda Fitzgerald
Pearl Buck
Paul Gauguin
Louis Pasteur
Alan Watts
Prince Charles
Barbara Walters
Adlai Stevenson
Sylvia Kars
Shirley Temple Black
Friedrich Nietzsche
Mark Twain
Joyce Carol Oates
Neil Armstrong
Jefferson Davis

JUNO IN THE TENTH HOUSE

Debbie Reynolds
Elizabeth Taylor
Soraya of Iran
Helen Keller
Catherine the Great
Annie Besant
Saint Bernadette of Lourdes
Richard Alpert (Ram Dass)
Prince Albert
Marc Edmund Jones
Marlon Brando
Chiang Kai-shek (MC)
Eleanor Roosevelt
Michael Jackson
Judy Garland
Linda Ronstadt

JUNO IN THE ELEVENTH HOUSE

Edna St. Vincent Millay
Maria Montessori
Princess Margaret
Angela Davis
Albert Einstein
Alexander Graham Bell
Edna Ferber
Charles de Gaulle
Elizabeth Arden
Pat Nixon
Janis Joplin
Queen Margrethe II of Denmark
Leonard Bernstein

JUNO IN THE TWELFTH HOUSE

Helena P. Blavatsky (Asc)
Anne Morrow Lindbergh
Patty Hearst
Elizabeth Barrett Browning
Germaine Greer
Princess Caroline
Clara Barton
Gertrude Stein
Isadora Duncan
Bertrand Russell
Jimi Hendrix

Hermann Hesse
Edith Piaf
Henry Miller
Francisco Franco
Zsa Zsa Gabor (Asc)
Lenny Bruce
Pearl Bailey
Dr. Marjorie Weinzweig
Taylor Caldwell
Katharine Hepburn (Asc)

Juno in the Signs

JUNO IN ARIES
Anita Bryant
Zelda Fitzgerald
Edna St. Vincent Millay
Pearl Bailey
Taylor Caldwell
Richard Alpert (Ram Dass)
Albert Einstein
Paul Gauguin
Prince Charles
Clark Gable
Louis Armstrong
Judy Garland
Margaret Trudeau

JUNO IN TAURUS
Queen Margrethe II of Denmark
Karl Marx
Christiaan Barnard
Hans Christian Andersen
Duchess of Windsor
Tennessee Williams
Werner Erhard
Vivien Kellems
Sir Winston Churchill
Albert Schweitzer
Geraldine Ferraro

JUNO IN GEMINI
Pearl Buck
Coco Chanel
F. Scott Fitzgerald
Jean-Paul Sartre
Ringo Starr
Dag Hammarskjold
Luther Burbank
Maxfield Parrish
Andy Warhol
Billy Joel

JUNO IN CANCER
Debbie Reynolds
Raquel Welch
Elizabeth Taylor
Helena P. Blavatsky
Maria Montessori
Prince Albert
Louis Pasteur
Barbara Walters
Leonard Bernstein
Simon Bolivar
Leonardo da Vinci
Henry Kissinger
Mark Twain
Fidel Castro
Edward Kennedy

JUNO IN LEO
Anne Morrow Lindbergh
Soraya of Iran
Amelia Earhart
Patty Hearst
Bob Dylan
John Lennon
Percy B. Shelley
Adolf Eichmann
Billy Graham

Howard Hughes
Kit Carson
Frederic Chopin
Marquis de Sade
Carl G. Jung
Friedrich Nietzsche
Junipero Serra
Shelley Winters
Anwar Sadat
Madalyn Murray O'Hair
Minette Lenier
Margot Fonteyn
R. D. Laing
Robert Redford

JUNO IN VIRGO
Lois Rodden
Marcia Moore
Margaret Mead
Joan Baez
Alice Bailey
Helen Keller
Mary Shelley
Elizabeth Barrett Browning
Queen Victoria
Marlene Dietrich
Paramahansa Yogananda
Enrico Fermi
Marc Edmund Jones
Walter Mondale
Alan Watts
William Blake
Cheiro
Auguste Rodin
Francisco Franco
Zsa Zsa Gabor
Charles Chaplin
Werner Heisenberg
Moshe Dayan
Walt Disney
John Calvin
Aleister Crowley
Mary Todd Lincoln
Dante Gabriel Rossetti
Orson Wells
Michael Jackson
Adolf Hitler
Jack Nicholson
Fritz Perls
Ludwig van Beethoven
Shirley Temple Black
Gloria Allred
Emmmaline Pankhurst
Mary Wells Lawrence

JUNO IN LIBRA
Saint Francesca Cabrini
Warren Beatty
Marlon Brando
Martin Luther
Bertrand Russell
Dr. Joyce Brothers
Edna Ferber
Ronald Reagan
George Bush
Lucille Ball
Empress Josephine
Pierre-Auguste Renoir
George Washington
Henry Winkler
Willie Ley
Charles Atlas
Eleonora Duse
Harriet Beecher Stowe
The Reverend Jesse Jackson
Paul Simon
Henry Winkler
Noel Tyl
Vanessa Redgrave
Bette Midler
Sylvia Plath
Cher
Linda Ronstadt
Hedda Hopper

Maria Callas
Sissy Spacek
Carol Burnett
Benjamin Franklin
Eleanor Roosevelt

JUNO IN SCORPIO
Katharine Hepburn
Jane Fonda
Yoko Ono
Marie Curie
Louisa May Alcott
Anne Frank
Edith Piaf
Francoise Gauquelin
Jacqueline Kennedy Onassis
Michel Gauquelin
Martin Luther King
Pierre Teilhard de Chardin
Mick Jagger
John Dillinger
Paul McCartney
Rachel Carson
D. H. Lawrence
Mao Tse-tung
Ingrid Bergman
Muhammad Ali (Cassius Clay)
George Gershwin
Buffalo Bill Cody
Florence Nightingale
Sri Meher Baba
Frank Sinatra
Barbra Streisand
Duke of Windsor
Federico Fellini
Sylvia Kars
Evangeline Adams
Ellen Yoakum
Chiang Kai-shek
Helen Frankenthaler
Timothy Leary
Jawaharlal Nehru
Dr. Joyce Brothers

JUNO IN SAGITTARIUS
Clare Boothe Luce
Sally Struthers
Julia Child
Zipporah Dobyns
Grace Kelly
Simone de Beauvoir
Betty Friedan
Anais Nin
Saint Teresa of Avila
Queen Beatrix of Holland
Farah Diba Pahlavi
David Bowie
Uri Geller
Jimi Hendrix
John Paul I
Hermann Hesse
Lenny Bruce
Richard Burton
Al Capone
Brigitte Bardot
Charles de Gaulle
Ernest Hemingway
Alfred Hitchcock
Johann Sebastian Bach
Farrah Fawcett
Edgar Cayce
Charles Dickens
Francisco Goya
Nathan Hale
Marie Antoinette
Carrie Nation
Pablo Picasso
Victoria Woodhull
Rudolf Nureyev
Joan Crawford
Sirimavo Bandaranaike
Diane Von Furstenberg
Pat Nixon

Eva Braun
Agatha Christie
Ralph Nader
Joyce Carol Oates
David Ben-Gurion
Dr. Marjorie Weinzweig
Ira Progoff
Colette

JUNO IN CAPRICORN
Gloria Steinem
Xaviera Hollander
Janis Joplin
Germaine Greer
Adelle Davis
Catherine the Great
Annie Besant
Helen Boucher
Princess Margaret
Elton John
Charles Baudelaire
Alexander Graham Bell
Alan Leo
Vincent van Gogh
Bobby Fischer
Neil Armstrong
Robert Browning
Queen Elizabeth I
Mohandas Gandhi
Jesse James
Annie Oakley
Virginia Woolf
Shirley MacLaine
Babe Ruth
Rudolph Valentino
Robert Graves
Immanuel Velikovsky
Billy Jean King
Nancy Reagan
Adrienne Hirt
Elizabeth Arden
Mick Jagger
Carlos Castaneda
Jane Addams

JUNO IN AQUARIUS
Indira Gandhi
Princess Caroline
Angela Davis
Sybil Leek
Clara Barton
Gertrude Stein
Elvis Presley
Earl Warren
Paul Cezanne
Sigmund Freud
Alice Cooper
Salvador Dali
Kahlil Gibran
Hugh Hefner
Jefferson Davis
Mary Baker Eddy
Andre Gide
Doris Chase Doane
Mary Stuart, Queen of Scots
Isaac Newton
Queen Elizabeth II
Robert J. Oppenheimer
Emma Goldman
Jean Houston
John F. Kennedy
Adlai Stevenson
Dr. Marjorie Weinzweig
Helen Gurley Brown
Galileo Galilei
Judy Collins
Daniel Boone

JUNO IN PISCES
Marilyn Monroe
Elisabeth Kubler-Ross
Isadora Duncan
Emily Dickenson
Saint Bernadette of Lourdes

Marianne Alireza
George Sand
Albert Camus
Dr. Tom Dooley
Jack Kerouac
Henry Miller
Abraham Lincoln
William Butler Yeats
James Dean
Charles Darwin
Harry Houdini
Thomas Jefferson
Napoleon Bonaparte
Nostradamus
Edgar Allan Poe
Henry David Thoreau
Christine Jorgensen
Princess Diana
Alan Ginsberg
Rollo May
Sylvia Porter
Joan of Arc

APPENDIX FIVE

EPHEMERIDES OF 16 ASTEROIDS 1931-2002

These ephemerides are calculated for 0 hours ET (the beginning of the day) in Greenwich. Longitude positions are given every 10 days. Declinations are supplied for every 20 days. The 16 asteroids included are grouped four at a time. Pages 281 through 304 includes Ceres, Pallas, Juno and Vesta from 1931-2002. Pages 305 through 328 include Psyche, Eros, Lilith and Toro from 1931-2002. Pages 329 through 352 include Sappho, Amor, Pandora and Icarus from 1931-2002. Pages 353 through 376 include Diana, Hidalgo, Urania and Chiron. (Positions in this 1990 edition differ slightly from those in the 1986 printing thanks to updated astronomical information.)

A complete ephemeris for Ceres, Pallas, Juno and Vesta listing their daily longitude and declination positions from 1883 to 1999 can be found in *The Asteroid Ephemeris* by Zipporah Dobyns (through ACS Publications, PO Box 34487, San Diego, CA 92163).

Ephemerides for Psyche, Eros, Lilith, Toro, Sappho, Amor, Icarus, Pandora, Urania, Chiron, Hidalgo, Apollo, Bacchus, America and Atlantis (and more asteroids), listing longitude positions for every 10 days from 1890 to 1999 are available from CAO Times, Box 75, Old Chelsea Station, New York, NY 10113.

Astro Computing Services will calculate the positions of any existing asteroid in the current century for 100 years. Astro Computing Services, PO Box 16430, San Diego, CA 92176.

1931		Ceres 1	Pallas 2	Juno 3	Vesta 4
JAN	1	09♎40.5	18♍25.9	20♒11.6	01♐12.9
	11	11 57.7	19 00.0	24 37.9	06 18.0
	21	13 44.3	18R34.1	29 13.7	11 18.1
	31	14 55.5	17 06.5	03♓58.0	16 11.9
FEB	10	15 27.2	14 43.6	08 49.5	20 57.8
	20	15R16.1	11 40.2	13 47.7	25 34.2
MAR	2	14 22.0	08 21.2	18 51.8	29 59.0
	12	12 49.3	05 14.0	24 01.1	04♑10.3
	22	10 47.4	02 41.6	29 15.1	08 05.1
APR	1	08 31.1	00 58.5	04♈33.2	11 40.2
	11	06 18.1	00 08.9	09 54.8	14 52.0
	21	04 24.4	00D10.2	15 19.9	17 36.1
MAY	1	03 02.9	00 57.5	20 47.6	19 47.4
	11	02 20.1	02 23.8	26 17.5	21 20.6
	21	02D18.0	04 22.6	01♉49.3	22 10.2
	31	02 55.0	06 48.0	07 22.5	22R12.3
JUN	10	04 07.3	09 35.3	12 56.4	21 25.8
	20	05 50.8	12 40.7	18 30.3	19 53.8
	30	08 01.0	16 01.1	24 03.3	17 47.3
JUL	10	10 33.6	19 33.5	29 35.1	15 23.6
	20	13 25.5	23 16.4	05♊04.2	13 03.6
	30	16 33.3	27 07.9	10 29.3	11 07.7
AUG	9	19 54.4	01♎06.5	15 49.0	09 50.2
	19	23 26.8	05 11.2	21 02.0	09 18.5
	29	27 08.6	09 21.1	26 05.8	09D34.5
SEP	8	00♏58.1	13 35.2	00♋58.0	10 35.1
	18	04 54.2	17 52.9	05 35.7	12 15.7
	28	08 55.4	22 13.3	09 55.6	14 30.6
OCT	8	13 00.9	26 35.8	13 53.4	17 14.8
	18	17 09.8	00♏59.8	17 23.8	20 23.7
	28	21 21.1	05 24.5	20 21.2	23 53.1
NOV	7	25 33.9	09 49.2	22 39.3	27 39.2
	17	29 47.5	14 13.2	24 10.6	01♒39.6
	27	04♐00.9	18 35.5	24 49.3	05 51.7
DEC	7	08 13.5	22 55.4	24R31.6	10 13.3
	17	12 24.3	27 11.7	23 18.4	14 42.7
	27	16 32.4	01♐23.2	21 20.1	19 18.3
JAN	6	20♐36.8	05♐28.8	18♋54.7	23♒58.8
JAN	1	06N42.4	20S24.7	12S14.4	15S50.7
	21	06 27.6	19 10.5	10 14.1	17 36.4
FEB	10	07 12.8	14 46.7	07 41.0	18 40.8
MAR	2	08 50.6	07 11.7	04 43.1	19 07.5
	22	10 46.0	01N27.7	01 29.8	19 05.8
APR	11	12 02.0	08 30.9	01N48.5	18 50.5
MAY	1	11 56.5	12 58.1	05 00.9	18 41.6
	21	10 28.7	15 09.1	07 55.7	19 02.5
JUN	10	08 01.6	15 40.8	10 21.3	20 11.5
	30	04 58.4	15 04.6	12 06.5	22 04.1
JUL	20	01 35.3	13 43.7	13 02.4	24 03.6
AUG	9	01S56.6	11 55.5	13 02.8	25 32.9
	29	05 29.3	09 53.6	12 07.1	26 23.8
SEP	18	08 55.7	07 50.0	10 20.1	26 40.9
OCT	8	12 09.8	05 55.2	07 53.3	26 25.4
	28	15 05.8	04 19.0	05 05.7	25 34.6
NOV	17	17 38.6	03 10.5	02 25.9	24 06.4
DEC	7	19 44.2	02 38.2	00 35.8	22 01.2
	27	21S20.2	02N48.8	00N23.2	19S22.4

1932		Ceres 1	Pallas 2	Juno 3	Vesta 4
JAN	1	18♐35.1	03♐26.8	20R09.3	21♒38.0
	11	22 37.3	07 28.9	17♋39.3	26 20.6
	21	26 34.1	11 22.5	15 18.8	01♓06.4
	31	00♑24.4	15 06.1	13 29.6	05 54.3
FEB	10	04 07.0	18 37.4	12 25.0	10 43.8
	20	07 40.1	21 54.0	12D10.2	15 33.8
MAR	1	11 02.3	24 53.0	12 42.7	20 23.5
	11	14 11.6	27 31.2	13 57.7	25 12.5
	21	17 05.6	29 44.4	15 49.2	00♈00.0
	31	19 42.1	01♑28.7	18 10.4	04 45.5
APR	10	21 58.2	02 38.8	20 55.7	09 28.4
	20	23 50.5	03 09.9	24 00.3	14 08.0
	30	25 16.0	02R58.2	27 20.1	18 43.9
MAY	10	26 11.0	02 00.7	00♌52.1	23 15.5
	20	26 32.3	00 18.7	04 33.5	27 42.0
	30	26R18.0	27♐58.6	08 22.1	02♉02.7
JUN	9	25 27.5	25 12.6	12 16.5	06 16.9
	19	24 03.6	22 18.1	16 15.1	10 23.3
	29	22 12.8	19 34.0	20 16.6	14 21.1
JUL	9	20 05.1	17 16.4	24 20.4	18 08.8
	19	17 54.0	15 36.6	28 25.5	21 44.7
	29	15 52.9	14 39.1	02♍31.2	25 06.8
AUG	8	14 13.7	14D24.3	06 37.0	28 12.6
	18	13 05.0	14 49.2	10 42.2	00♊59.2
	28	12 31.0	15 49.1	14 46.3	03 23.2
SEP	7	12D32.9	17 19.7	18 48.8	05 20.3
	17	13 09.2	19 16.0	22 48.9	06 46.0
	27	14 17.1	21 33.9	26 46.1	07 35.5
OCT	7	15 53.3	24 10.0	00♎39.8	07R43.9
	17	17 54.3	27 00.9	04 28.9	07 08.6
	27	20 16.5	00♑04.1	08 12.8	05 49.5
NOV	6	22 57.1	03 17.3	11 50.3	03 51.2
	16	25 53.4	06 38.5	15 20.1	01 25.5
	26	29 02.7	10 06.1	18 41.0	28♉48.6
DEC	6	02♒23.3	13 38.5	21 51.1	26 19.8
	16	05 53.0	17 14.2	24 48.5	24 16.7
	26	09 30.3	20 52.0	27 31.2	22 51.3
JAN	5	13♒13.8	24♑30.9	29♎56.4	22♉09.9
JAN	1	21S39.6	02N58.8	00N39.1	18S38.1
	21	22 39.1	04 09.8	02 51.8	15 25.5
FEB	10	23 13.1	06 11.2	06 08.2	11 54.5
MAR	1	23 28.3	09 00.7	09 22.8	08 13.4
	21	23 34.8	12 30.9	11 56.9	04 30.1
APR	10	23 45.1	16 26.0	13 37.6	00 52.4
	30	24 13.7	20 18.0	14 24.2	02N32.5
MAY	20	25 13.3	23 25.1	14 20.9	05 38.4
JUN	9	26 47.9	25 01.0	13 34.2	08 19.9
	29	28 41.9	24 37.5	12 11.3	10 32.4
JUL	19	30 21.0	22 24.2	10 19.8	12 12.9
AUG	8	31 17.1	19 00.2	08 07.4	13 19.9
	28	31 29.6	15 09.5	05 41.5	13 53.8
SEP	17	31 12.6	11 25.0	03 09.5	13 57.3
OCT	7	30 35.8	08 06.9	00 38.5	13 36.1
	27	29 41.5	05 26.1	01S44.0	12 59.3
NOV	16	28 28.1	03 27.6	03 50.5	12 21.8
DEC	6	26 53.8	02 12.9	05 33.6	12 04.9
	26	24S58.6	01N41.2	06S45.2	12N27.5

1933		Ceres 1	Pallas 2	Juno 3	Vesta 4
JAN	1	11♒43.7	23♑03.4	29♎00.6	22R21.0
	11	15 30.2	26 42.2	01♏14.0	22D06.5
	21	19 20.6	00♒20.2	03 05.2	22♉35.0
	31	23 14.1	03 56.4	04 30.8	23 42.6
FEB	10	27 09.4	07 29.5	05 27.3	25 24.5
	20	01♓05.4	10 58.5	05 51.7	27 35.4
MAR	2	05 01.5	14 22.3	05R41.2	00♊10.8
	12	08 56.5	17 39.6	04 55.2	03 06.7
	22	12 49.6	20 49.1	03 35.2	06 19.5
APR	1	16 39.9	23 49.5	01 46.1	09 46.5
	11	20 26.3	26 38.9	29♎36.8	13 25.1
	21	24 08.0	29 15.7	27 18.8	17 13.4
MAY	1	27 43.9	01♓37.8	25 05.0	21 09.7
	11	01♈12.5	03 42.7	23 07.7	25 12.7
	21	04 32.8	05 27.9	21 35.7	29 21.3
	31	07 43.1	06 50.2	20 34.6	03♋34.5
JUN	10	10 41.4	07 46.5	20 06.6	07 51.5
	20	13 25.8	08 13.6	20D11.0	12 11.6
	30	15 53.7	08R08.2	20 45.9	16 34.3
JUL	10	18 02.2	07 28.5	21 48.2	20 58.9
	20	19 48.1	06 14.2	23 14.6	25 25.0
	30	21 07.6	04 27.5	25 02.1	29 52.1
AUG	9	21 57.1	02 14.8	27 07.8	04♌19.8
	19	22 13.1	29♒45.5	29 29.0	08 47.5
	29	21R52.8	27 12.2	02♏03.5	13 14.6
SEP	8	20 56.0	24 48.4	04 49.2	17 40.6
	18	19 25.3	22 45.5	07 44.5	22 04.8
	28	17 27.4	21 12.2	10 47.8	26 26.4
OCT	8	15 14.0	20 13.0	13 57.7	00♍44.3
	18	12 59.0	19 49.1	17 12.9	04 57.6
	28	10 57.5	19D59.6	20 32.5	09 04.8
NOV	7	09 22.1	20 41.7	23 55.0	13 04.3
	17	08 20.8	21 52.0	27 19.6	16 54.1
	27	07 57.9	23 27.3	00♐45.2	20 31.8
DEC	7	08D13.4	25 24.1	04 10.6	23 54.6
	17	09 05.1	27 39.3	07 34.9	26 59.1
	27	10 29.6	00♓10.2	10 56.8	29 40.9
JAN	6	12♈22.8	02♓54.4	14♐15.0	01♎55.4
JAN	1	24S20.1	01N39.7	06S59.3	12N42.9
	21	22 00.6	01 59.1	07 18.2	13 59.5
FEB	10	19 26.8	02 52.2	06 48.3	15 43.5
MAR	2	16 44.3	04 13.0	05 26.1	17 38.7
	22	13 59.3	05 54.3	03 17.7	19 31.1
APR	11	11 18.4	07 48.0	00 47.2	21 09.3
MAY	1	08 48.4	09 45.0	01N24.5	22 24.5
	21	06 36.5	11 33.6	02 41.2	23 10.1
JUN	10	04 50.2	12 59.1	02 52.2	23 22.2
	30	03 37.1	13 41.2	02 07.2	22 59.2
JUL	20	03 04.8	13 15.1	00 42.7	22 01.9
AUG	9	03 19.5	11 20.5	01S06.1	20 33.2
	29	04 21.4	08 00.8	03 07.2	18 37.9
SEP	18	05 57.2	03 54.9	05 11.2	16 22.8
OCT	8	07 32.5	00S02.5	07 10.2	13 56.0
	28	08 22.2	03 12.9	08 57.6	11 27.6
NOV	17	07 59.8	05 22.1	10 27.5	09 09.1
DEC	7	06 28.8	06 32.2	11 34.9	07 14.5
	27	04S08.1	06S51.5	12S16.2	05N59.9

1934		Ceres 1	Pallas 2	Juno 3	Vesta 4
JAN	1	11♈22.9	01♓30.8	12♐36.4	00♎51.8
	11	13 28.9	04 20.7	15 52.3	02 50.8
	21	15 57.8	07 20.9	19 02.6	04 14.0
	31	18 46.0	10 29.6	22 05.5	04 55.7
FEB	10	21 50.4	13 45.1	24 59.5	04 R51.4
	20	25 08.4	17 06.3	27 42.6	03 58.7
MAR	2	28 37.8	20 31.9	00♑12.5	02 20.6
	12	02♉16.4	24 01.0	02 26.9	00 06.5
	22	06 02.7	27 32.5	04 22.8	27♍33.2
APR	1	09 55.2	01♈05.7	05 57.4	25 02.8
	11	13 52.7	04 39.6	07 07.3	22 55.6
	21	17 54.3	08 13.7	07 49.0	21 27.5
MAY	1	21 58.7	11 46.8	07 R 59.6	20 47.1
	11	26 05.4	15 18.6	07 36.9	20 D55.8
	21	00♊13.6	18 48.0	06 40.0	21 51.3
	31	04 22.5	22 14.0	05 11.3	23 28.8
JUN	10	08 31.5	25 35.7	03 15.9	25 42.3
	20	12 40.1	28 51.7	01 03.1	28 26.9
	30	16 47.4	02♉00.7	28♐45.1	01♎37.6
JUL	10	20 52.9	05 00.8	26 34.6	05 10.3
	20	24 55.7	07 49.5	24 43.9	09 01.6
	30	28 54.9	10 24.5	23 21.9	13 08.6
AUG	9	02♋49.8	12 42.1	22 33.5	17 28.9
	19	06 39.0	14 37.9	22 D 20.8	22 00.7
	29	10 21.2	16 06.9	22 43.2	26 42.1
SEP	8	13 55.0	17 03.4	23 38.2	01♏31.9
	18	17 18.2	17 R 20.2	25 02.9	06 29.0
	28	20 28.6	16 51.3	26 54.1	11 32.2
OCT	8	23 23.4	15 32.1	29 08.4	16 40.6
	18	25 59.1	13 22.8	01♑43.1	21 53.6
	28	28 12.2	10 31.9	04 35.5	27 10.1
NOV	7	29 57.9	07 16.6	07 43.3	02♐29.6
	17	01♌11.5	04 02.7	11 04.4	07 51.5
	27	01 48.4	01 17.2	14 37.2	13 14.8
DEC	7	01 R 44.5	29♈20.4	18 20.0	18 39.2
	17	00 58.0	28 24.0	22 11.5	24 03.9
	27	29♋31.5	28 D 30.2	26 10.4	29 28.1
JAN	6	27♋32.2	29♈35.3	00♒15.8	04♑51.4
JAN	1	03 S 27.4	06 S 49.6	12 S 22.1	05 N49.6
	21	00 29.6	06 19.5	12 27.5	05 49.7
FEB	10	02 N 42.9	05 21.2	12 04.0	07 05.1
MAR	2	06 00.4	04 04.5	11 13.7	09 27.9
	22	09 14.6	02 38.8	10 00.7	12 07.7
APR	11	12 18.8	01 13.3	08 32.4	13 47.1
MAY	1	15 07.1	00 N 02.4	06 59.6	13 43.9
	21	17 34.5	00 58.4	05 38.2	12 08.5
JUN	10	19 37.2	01 23.9	04 48.3	09 28.5
	30	21 12.5	01 06.6	04 47.0	06 06.5
JUL	20	22 19.8	00 S 07.3	05 37.7	02 18.7
AUG	9	23 00.7	02 32.8	07 06.9	01 S42.7
	29	23 19.6	06 23.0	08 54.2	05 47.2
SEP	18	23 24.1	11 39.9	10 41.2	09 44.6
OCT	8	23 25.8	17 55.8	12 14.8	13 24.5
	28	23 40.4	23 55.9	13 25.7	16 37.0
NOV	17	24 26.4	27 58.6	14 07.3	19 12.3
DEC	7	25 59.0	29 04.6	14 15.4	21 02.5
	27	28 N 15.5	27 S 30.6	13 S 48.2	22 S02.3

1935		Ceres 1	Pallas 2	Juno 3	Vesta 4
JAN	1	28 R 35.2	28♈55.7	28♑12.4	02♑09.9
	11	26♋24.2	00♉28.1	02♒20.6	07 32.4
	21	24 02.7	02 49.7	06 33.7	12 52.8
	31	21 48.7	05 52.8	10 50.9	18 10.3
FEB	10	19 58.8	09 31.4	15 11.5	23 24.4
	20	18 45.3	13 39.5	19 34.7	28 34.0
MAR	2	18 13.9	18 11.9	23 59.7	03♒38.6
	12	18 D 25.7	23 04.7	28 26.0	08 37.1
	22	19 18.2	28 13.8	02♓52.9	13 28.3
APR	1	20 47.2	03♊36.2	07 19.8	18 11.5
	11	22 48.0	09 09.1	11 46.1	22 45.2
	21	25 15.8	14 49.7	16 10.8	27 07.7
MAY	1	28 06.3	20 35.9	20 33.5	01♓17.8
	11	01♌16.1	26 26.0	24 53.3	05 12.9
	21	04 41.8	02♋17.9	29 09.1	08 50.8
	31	08 20.8	08 10.3	03♈19.8	12 08.7
JUN	10	12 11.1	14 01.9	07 24.0	15 02.7
	20	16 10.6	19 51.4	11 20.1	17 29.1
	30	20 17.8	25 38.1	15 06.0	19 23.0
JUL	10	24 31.6	01♌21.4	18 38.9	20 39.3
	20	28 50.7	07 00.3	21 55.9	21 13.4
	30	03♍14.3	12 34.7	24 53.5	21 R01.5
AUG	9	07 41.4	18 04.2	27 26.1	20 02.5
	19	12 11.3	23 28.3	29 28.6	18 20.8
	29	16 43.3	28 46.9	00♉54.8	16 06.2
SEP	8	21 16.7	03♍59.7	01 38.7	13 35.5
	18	25 50.8	09 06.4	01 R 35.1	11 09.0
	28	00♎25.0	14 06.8	00 41.8	09 05.4
OCT	8	04 58.6	19 00.4	29♈03.8	07 39.1
	18	09 30.7	23 46.6	26 55.2	06 57.3
	28	14 00.7	28 25.1	24 35.9	07 D01.4
NOV	7	18 27.5	02♎54.8	22 31.4	07 49.3
	17	22 50.2	07 14.7	21 03.8	09 16.3
	27	27 07.8	11 23.6	20 26.9	11 17.0
DEC	7	01♏18.9	15 19.8	20 D 46.6	13 46.6
	17	05 21.9	19 01.3	22 01.2	16 40.1
	27	09 15.5	22 25.8	24 05.1	19 53.5
JAN	6	12♏57.3	25♎29.8	26♈51.7	23♓23.4
JAN	1	28 N 52.8	26 S 48.6	13 S 35.9	22 S09.1
	21	31 08.6	23 12.7	12 25.1	22 04.7
FEB	10	32 27.8	18 53.1	10 42.8	21 13.3
MAR	2	32 41.5	14 21.3	08 33.9	19 43.4
	22	32 08.9	09 58.6	06 04.8	17 46.3
APR	11	31 05.3	06 00.8	03 22.9	15 35.3
MAY	1	29 35.5	02 40.6	00 37.0	13 25.1
	21	27 39.4	00 06.9	02 N 03.2	11 31.8
JUN	10	25 17.0	01 N 35.2	04 26.7	10 12.4
	30	22 29.8	02 25.2	06 20.5	09 45.6
JUL	20	19 21.1	02 26.9	07 28.8	10 28.3
AUG	9	15 55.5	01 47.7	07 33.1	12 25.2
	29	12 18.7	00 37.6	06 13.2	15 07.8
SEP	18	08 37.1	00 S 51.9	03 16.0	17 28.5
OCT	8	04 57.3	02 28.3	00 S 59.7	18 26.7
	28	01 26.3	03 58.3	05 13.1	17 52.2
NOV	17	01 S 48.8	05 07.2	07 38.8	16 06.4
DEC	7	04 41.7	05 39.3	07 37.0	13 32.2
	27	07 S 06.7	05 S 16.6	05 S 37.5	10 S26.0

1936		Ceres 1	Pallas 2	Juno 3	Vesta 4
JAN	1	11♏08.0	24♎00.6	25♈23.5	21♓36.6
	11	14 43.3	26 53.2	28 28.9	25 13.5
	21	18 03.6	29 20.1	02♉06.6	29 02.6
	31	21 06.1	01♏16.3	06 10.8	03♈01.6
FEB	10	23 47.6	02 36.5	10 35.8	07 08.4
	20	26 04.7	03 15.2	15 17.4	11 21.6
MAR	1	27 53.2	03 R 07.2	20 12.3	15 39.7
	11	29 09.2	02 09.5	25 17.2	20 01.4
	21	29 49.0	00 22.6	00♊29.0	24 25.8
	31	29 R 49.2	27♎53.3	05 46.2	28 52.1
APR	10	29 09.4	24 56.4	11 06.8	03♉19.3
	20	27 51.7	21 51.6	16 29.3	07 46.8
	30	26 02.6	19 00.6	21 52.5	12 14.1
MAY	10	23 53.9	16 42.0	27 15.1	16 40.4
	20	21 39.9	15 06.9	02♋36.7	21 05.3
	30	19 36.2	14 19.8	07 56.6	25 28.3
JUN	9	17 56.1	14 D 19.4	13 13.7	29 48.7
	19	16 48.3	15 01.6	18 27.9	04♊06.0
	29	16 17.4	16 21.4	23 38.9	08 19.6
JUL	9	16 D 24.1	18 13.0	28 46.1	12 28.6
	19	17 06.0	20 31.4	03♌49.1	16 32.4
	29	18 20.1	23 12.5	08 47.8	20 29.8
AUG	8	20 02.5	26 12.2	13 41.7	24 19.8
	18	22 09.3	29 27.6	18 30.6	28 01.1
	28	24 37.3	02♏56.2	23 13.9	01♋31.7
SEP	7	27 22.9	06 35.5	27 51.2	04 49.7
	17	00♐23.8	10 23.9	02♍22.1	07 52.7
	27	03 37.5	14 19.8	06 45.8	10 37.4
OCT	7	07 02.0	18 21.6	11 01.4	13 00.4
	17	10 35.5	22 28.4	15 08.0	14 57.5
	27	14 16.7	26 38.9	19 04.4	16 23.6
NOV	6	18 03.9	00♐51.9	22 49.2	17 13.9
	16	21 56.2	05 06.7	26 20.5	17 R23.6
	26	25 52.4	09 22.1	29 36.3	16 49.1
DEC	6	29 51.4	13 37.2	02♎34.2	15 30.6
	16	03♑52.3	17 51.1	05 11.3	13 32.3
	26	07 54.1	22 02.5	07 24.1	11 05.7
JAN	5	11♑55.7	26♐10.6	09♎09.1	08♋27.6
JAN	1	07 S 38.0	05 S 00.1	04 S 55.0	09 S35.8
	21	09 22.3	03 01.6	01 34.3	06 05.4
FEB	10	10 32.4	00 N 34.1	02 N 09.9	02 25.7
MAR	1	11 09.9	05 52.1	05 51.1	01 N15.2
	21	11 19.8	12 21.0	09 10.0	04 50.1
APR	10	11 10.9	18 36.0	11 52.0	08 12.3
	30	10 56.4	22 55.5	13 47.7	11 16.0
MAY	20	10 54.1	24 36.1	14 52.2	13 56.1
JUN	9	11 20.7	24 04.1	15 05.0	16 08.5
	29	12 23.3	22 08.0	14 29.5	17 50.6
JUL	19	13 57.6	19 27.6	13 12.0	19 01.6
AUG	8	15 53.0	16 28.6	11 20.8	19 42.6
	28	17 58.0	13 28.2	09 04.8	19 57.6
SEP	17	20 02.0	10 38.1	06 33.7	19 53.6
OCT	7	21 55.9	08 07.5	03 57.3	19 41.2
	27	23 32.2	06 03.9	01 25.4	19 34.8
NOV	16	24 44.7	04 33.7	00 S 51.4	19 50.4
DEC	6	25 29.5	03 41.9	02 41.6	20 38.8
	26	25 S 44.8	03 N 31.5	03 S 52.4	21 N53.6

1937	Ceres 1	Pallas 2	Juno 3	Vesta 4
JAN 1	10♑19.1	24♐31.8	08♎30.7	09R31.0
11	14 20.4	28 37.4	09 57.1	06♋55.3
21	18 20.1	02♑37.6	10 49.2	04 38.9
31	22 17.2	06 31.3	11R03.8	02 56.8
FEB 10	26 10.9	10 17.1	10 38.6	01 57.3
20	00♒00.0	13 53.3	09 33.5	01D43.5
MAR 2	03 43.4	17 18.2	07 52.8	02 13.5
12	07 19.9	20 29.8	05 44.5	03 23.2
22	10 48.1	23 25.8	03 21.0	05 07.9
APR 1	14 06.4	26 03.5	00 57.4	07 22.2
11	17 13.3	28 20.0	28♍47.9	10 01.8
21	20 06.7	00♒11.6	27 04.2	13 02.6
MAY 1	22 44.2	01 34.6	25 53.3	16 21.1
11	25 03.5	02 25.2	25 18.0	19 54.6
21	27 01.3	02R39.1	25D18.1	23 40.9
31	28 34.7	02 13.8	25 50.9	27 37.9
JUN 10	29 40.1	01 07.8	26 52.9	01♌44.1
20	00♓14.1	29♑23.1	28 20.6	05 58.3
30	00R14.1	27 06.5	00♎10.1	10 19.2
JUL 10	29♒38.6	24 28.7	02 18.2	14 46.2
20	28 28.6	21 44.6	04 42.1	19 18.5
30	26 48.5	19 10.2	07 19.2	23 55.2
AUG 9	24 46.5	16 58.8	10 07.4	28 36.1
19	22 34.7	15 20.3	13 05.0	03♍20.4
29	20 26.6	14 19.3	16 10.1	08 07.7
SEP 8	18 35.3	13 56.5	19 21.6	12 57.7
18	17 11.4	14D10.1	22 38.2	17 49.7
28	16 21.0	14 56.5	25 58.7	22 43.3
OCT 8	16D06.9	16 11.8	29 22.1	27 38.0
18	16 28.8	17 52.0	02♏47.5	02♎33.2
28	17 24.1	19 53.3	06 13.8	07 28.3
NOV 7	18 49.8	22 12.4	09 40.0	12 22.5
17	20 42.4	24 46.5	13 05.2	17 15.0
27	22 58.0	27 32.7	16 28.2	22 05.0
DEC 7	25 33.5	00♒29.1	19 47.9	26 51.2
17	28 25.9	03 33.6	23 02.9	01♏32.3
27	01♓32.4	06 44.5	26 12.0	06 07.1
JAN 6	04♓50.9	10♒00.2	29♏13.6	10♏33.7
JAN 1	25S43.7	03N36.7	04S03.8	22N17.5
21	25 22.6	04 21.7	04 02.3	23 29.5
FEB 10	24 38.3	05 47.6	02 51.0	24 23.1
MAR 2	23 37.7	07 50.4	00 30.8	25 01.1
22	22 29.9	10 23.6	02N29.0	25 24.7
APR 11	21 25.6	13 17.5	05 13.7	25 29.5
MAY 1	20 37.1	16 17.4	06 57.7	25 09.2
21	20 18.1	19 01.2	07 29.5	24 18.5
JUN 10	20 42.1	20 57.6	07 00.0	22 54.9
30	21 58.3	21 31.0	05 45.8	20 58.4
JUL 20	24 01.9	20 18.4	04 01.3	18 30.9
AUG 9	26 22.6	17 28.8	01 58.0	15 36.8
29	28 10.4	13 41.3	00S15.2	12 21.4
SEP 18	28 48.8	09 42.6	02 30.7	08 51.2
OCT 8	28 16.4	06 06.8	04 41.7	05 13.6
28	26 51.1	03 12.1	06 41.9	01 36.8
NOV 17	24 49.5	01 05.2	08 25.5	01S50.8
DEC 7	22 21.9	00S13.6	09 47.1	05 00.2
27	19S34.4	00S47.6	10S42.4	07S43.0

1938	Ceres 1	Pallas 2	Juno 3	Vesta 4
JAN 1	03♓10.3	08♒21.8	27♏43.9	08♏21.6
11	06 34.0	11 39.5	00♐41.0	12 43.2
21	10 06.6	14 59.8	03 27.9	16 53.4
31	13 46.5	18 21.8	06 02.6	20 49.8
FEB 10	17 32.2	21 44.1	08 22.5	24 28.9
20	21 22.4	25 05.7	10 25.2	27 47.0
MAR 2	25 15.9	28 25.5	12 07.8	00♐39.9
12	29 11.8	01♓42.5	13 27.0	03 02.5
22	03♈09.0	04 55.3	14 19.7	04 49.3
APR 1	07 06.6	08 03.2	14 42.9	05 54.4
11	11 03.8	11 04.6	14R34.0	06R12.5
21	14 59.8	13 58.2	13 52.0	05 41.8
MAY 1	18 53.8	16 42.7	12 37.7	04 23.2
11	22 44.9	19 16.2	10 55.1	02 25.3
21	26 32.2	21 36.9	08 51.5	00 04.2
31	00♉14.8	23 42.4	06 37.2	27♏40.6
JUN 10	03 51.6	25 30.2	04 24.3	25 36.4
20	07 21.4	26 57.3	02 24.8	24 08.7
30	10 42.9	28 00.5	00 48.0	23 26.8
JUL 10	13 54.3	28 36.2	29♏40.9	23D34.0
20	16 53.8	28R41.1	29 06.3	24 27.9
30	19 39.0	28 12.3	29D04.8	26 04.2
AUG 9	22 07.1	27 08.3	29 35.0	28 17.4
19	24 15.2	25 30.2	00♐34.3	01♐01.6
29	25 59.5	23 22.3	01 59.7	04 12.1
SEP 8	27 15.9	20 53.2	03 48.4	07 44.9
18	28 00.5	18 15.3	05 57.3	11 35.9
28	28R09.4	15 42.4	08 23.8	15 42.2
OCT 8	27 40.2	13 28.3	11 05.6	20 01.5
18	26 32.9	11 43.3	14 00.5	24 31.5
28	24 51.2	10 33.8	17 06.9	29 10.5
NOV 7	22 44.2	10 02.6	20 22.9	03♑56.8
17	20 25.3	10D08.9	23 47.2	08 49.2
27	18 10.3	10 50.4	27 18.6	13 46.8
DEC 7	16 14.9	12 03.8	00♑55.6	18 48.2
17	14 50.8	13 45.3	04 37.3	23 52.4
27	14 05.0	15 51.5	08 22.7	28 59.0
JAN 6	14D00.0	18♓19.1	12♑10.6	04♒06.8
JAN 1	18S49.9	00S49.7	10S51.6	08S18.6
21	15 43.9	00 35.3	11 09.1	10 17.8
FEB 10	12 28.4	00N10.4	10 54.5	11 36.9
MAR 2	09 08.6	01 19.8	10 08.2	12 15.1
22	05 49.7	02 45.0	08 53.2	12 16.5
APR 11	02 36.8	04 17.7	07 16.7	11 51.3
MAY 1	00N24.9	05 48.8	05 32.7	11 17.6
21	03 10.6	07 08.2	04 03.4	11 00.8
JUN 10	05 36.0	08 03.9	03 13.3	11 26.0
30	07 37.3	08 20.7	03 16.5	12 42.8
JUL 20	09 11.6	07 39.7	04 09.2	14 40.8
AUG 9	10 16.9	05 41.4	05 35.9	17 00.7
29	10 53.2	02 17.5	07 19.9	19 22.9
SEP 18	11 02.2	02S07.3	09 07.1	21 31.0
OCT 8	10 49.4	06 32.4	10 46.8	23 11.1
28	10 25.2	09 58.6	12 10.6	24 12.6
NOV 17	10 07.7	12 02.3	13 12.0	24 28.3
DEC 7	10 18.3	12 49.7	13 46.2	23 55.0
27	11N10.4	12S37.1	13S50.4	22S33.9

1939	Ceres 1	Pallas 2	Juno 3	Vesta 4
JAN 1	13R57.4	17♓02.8	10♑16.4	01♒32.8
11	14D12.4	19 39.9	14 05.2	06 41.0
21	15♉05.2	22 34.2	17 55.3	11 49.5
31	16 32.4	25 43.5	21 45.5	16 57.5
FEB 10	18 29.3	29 05.6	25 35.0	22 04.3
20	20 51.7	02♈39.0	29 22.7	27 09.5
MAR 2	23 36.0	06 22.3	03♒07.6	02♓12.3
12	26 38.3	10 14.2	06 48.5	07 12.1
22	29 56.0	14 14.0	10 24.4	12 08.4
APR 1	03♊26.6	18 20.7	13 53.7	17 00.4
11	07 07.8	22 33.7	17 15.0	21 47.5
21	10 57.9	26 52.6	20 26.5	26 29.1
MAY 1	14 55.5	01♉16.9	23 26.0	01♈04.3
11	18 59.1	05 46.1	26 11.2	05 32.2
21	23 07.9	10 20.2	28 39.2	09 51.9
31	27 21.0	14 58.8	00♓46.4	14 02.1
JUN 10	01♋37.3	19 41.6	02 29.2	18 01.6
20	05 56.4	24 28.5	03 42.9	21 48.6
30	10 17.4	29 19.0	04 23.2	25 20.9
JUL 10	14 39.9	04♊12.9	04R26.1	28 36.4
20	19 03.3	09 09.7	03 48.4	01♉32.1
30	23 26.9	14 08.5	02 30.4	04 04.3
AUG 9	27 50.0	19 08.8	00 37.0	06 09.2
19	02♌12.3	24 09.5	28♒18.3	07 42.0
29	06 32.8	29 08.9	25 50.3	08 37.8
SEP 8	10 50.6	04♋05.2	23 31.3	08R52.4
18	15 05.1	08 56.1	21 38.2	08 22.2
28	19 14.8	13 38.4	20 24.4	07 07.3
OCT 8	23 18.7	18 08.3	19 55.9	05 12.8
18	27 15.1	22 20.3	20D14.4	02 49.2
28	01♍02.0	26 08.3	21 18.4	00 13.8
NOV 7	04 37.6	29 25.2	23 03.5	27♈45.6
17	07 58.9	02♌00.7	25 25.4	25 42.5
27	11 02.9	03 44.2	28 19.4	24 17.4
DEC 7	13 46.0	04 25.4	01♓41.0	23 36.2
17	16 03.8	03R55.2	05 26.8	23D39.7
27	17 51.5	02 12.1	09 33.3	24 25.5
JAN 6	19♍04.4	29♋27.5	13♓57.5	25♈48.7
JAN 1	11N30.0	12S26.5	13S46.6	22S06.7
21	13 10.5	11 21.4	13 12.0	19 53.5
FEB 10	15 15.9	09 49.6	12 08.2	17 07.9
MAR 2	17 32.6	08 02.8	10 38.7	13 59.7
22	19 48.0	06 11.5	08 49.0	10 39.3
APR 11	21 51.7	04 25.3	06 46.4	07 16.7
MAY 1	23 35.0	02 53.7	04 40.0	04 01.3
21	24 51.3	01 46.2	02 41.5	01 02.1
JUN 10	25 35.9	01 12.1	01 06.4	01N32.6
30	25 46.3	01 20.1	00 15.2	03 35.3
JUL 20	25 22.8	02 18.1	00 32.9	04 58.5
AUG 9	24 28.1	04 12.1	02 18.8	05 35.6
29	23 07.3	07 04.5	05 21.3	05 21.7
SEP 18	21 28.0	10 52.7	08 45.9	04 17.6
OCT 8	19 40.0	15 27.4	11 29.6	02 38.4
28	17 55.4	20 30.3	13 01.1	01 02.6
NOV 17	16 28.5	25 29.4	13 17.0	00 18.4
DEC 7	15 36.0	29 32.6	12 25.1	00 48.9
27	15N35.4	31S25.5	10S35.8	02N24.6

1940		Ceres 1	Pallas 2	Juno 3	Vesta 4
JAN	1	18♍32.6	00 R 56.2	11♓43.3	25♈02.7
	11	19 26.1	27♋49.9	16 15.6	26 42.8
	21	19 R 37.9	24 27.5	21 02.6	28 52.9
	31	19 05.9	21 26.7	26 01.9	01♉27.9
FEB	10	17 51.4	19 16.0	01♈12.2	04 23.9
	20	16 01.2	18 10.0	06 31.8	07 37.2
MAR	1	13 48.3	18 D 08.4	11 59.5	11 04.5
	11	11 29.6	19 04.6	17 34.2	14 43.5
	21	09 23.8	20 49.2	23 14.8	18 32.1
	31	07 46.2	23 12.2	29 00.1	22 28.3
APR	10	06 46.4	26 04.9	04♉49.4	26 30.8
	20	06 D 29.1	29 21.2	10 41.9	00♊38.4
	30	06 53.5	02♌55.4	16 36.4	04 49.8
MAY	10	07 56.5	06 43.5	22 32.4	09 04.4
	20	09 33.7	10 42.2	28 28.9	13 21.3
	30	11 40.3	14 49.0	04♊25.1	17 39.7
JUN	9	14 11.8	19 02.4	10 20.4	21 59.4
	19	17 04.3	23 20.9	16 13.8	26 19.4
	29	20 14.1	27 42.9	22 04.4	00♋39.5
JUL	9	23 38.6	02♍08.1	27 51.9	04 59.1
	19	27 15.3	06 35.8	03♋35.0	09 17.6
	29	01♎01.9	11 05.2	09 13.1	13 34.5
AUG	8	04 57.1	15 36.1	14 45.3	17 49.2
	18	08 59.2	20 08.0	20 10.5	22 00.9
	28	13 06.9	24 40.6	25 28.0	26 08.9
SEP	7	17 19.4	29 13.8	00♌36.5	00♌12.2
	17	21 35.6	03♎46.9	05 34.5	04 09.5
	27	25 54.5	08 19.7	10 20.9	07 59.7
OCT	7	00♏15.7	12 51.9	14 53.8	11 40.8
	17	04 38.0	17 22.9	19 11.0	15 10.8
	27	09 00.8	21 52.3	23 10.3	18 27.4
NOV	6	13 23.5	26 19.4	26 48.7	21 27.4
	16	17 45.1	00♏43.5	00♍02.7	24 07.2
	26	22 04.9	05 03.9	02 48.4	26 22.6
DEC	6	26 22.0	09 19.4	05 00.7	28 08.5
	16	00♐35.4	13 28.8	06 35.0	29 19.5
	26	04 44.2	17 31.0	07 26.4	29 50.4
JAN	5	08♐47.2	21♏24.3	07 R 30.5	29 R 36.3

1940		Ceres 1	Pallas 2	Juno 3	Vesta 4
JAN	1	15 N 45.2	31 S 23.7	10 S 00.8	02 N 56.2
	21	17 07.7	28 51.6	07 16.1	05 23.5
FEB	10	19 28.1	22 46.0	04 00.9	08 10.5
MAR	1	21 59.2	14 44.0	00 28.5	11 02.9
	21	23 30.9	06 45.9	03 N 07.5	13 49.7
APR	10	23 24.0	00 09.2	06 33.0	16 21.8
	30	21 49.3	04 N 39.9	09 34.7	18 32.1
MAY	20	19 15.9	07 45.1	12 00.4	20 14.8
JUN	9	16 06.1	09 21.5	13 40.2	21 25.9
	29	12 34.0	09 47.3	14 28.0	22 03.4
JUL	19	08 48.1	09 19.9	14 22.3	22 07.2
AUG	8	04 55.4	08 15.2	13 26.0	21 39.5
	28	01 01.8	06 47.2	11 46.6	20 44.8
SEP	17	02 S 47.0	05 08.9	09 34.6	19 30.2
OCT	7	06 25.4	03 32.4	07 03.0	18 05.2
	27	09 47.6	02 09.3	04 26.6	16 42.3
NOV	16	12 48.6	01 11.0	02 02.7	15 37.8
DEC	6	15 24.0	00 48.3	00 11.9	15 11.3
	26	17 S 30.9	01 N 11.4	00 S 40.6	15 N 44.0

1941		Ceres 1	Pallas 2	Juno 3	Vesta 4
JAN	1	07♐10.7	19♏52.2	07♍34.7	29 R 47.5
	11	11 09.6	23 39.0	07 R 09.5	29♌05.6
	21	15 00.6	27 13.7	05 56.8	27 38.3
	31	18 42.2	00♐33.7	04 02.3	25 31.8
FEB	10	22 12.6	03 35.8	01 39.0	23 00.0
	20	25 29.9	06 16.8	29♌04.4	20 22.2
MAR	2	28 31.9	08 32.3	26 37.8	17 58.8
	12	01♑16.0	10 17.5	24 36.6	16 07.8
	22	03 39.3	11 27.5	23 11.8	14 59.9
APR	1	05 38.4	11 56.5	22 28.3	14 D 39.6
	11	07 09.9	11 R 40.0	22 D 26.2	15 06.2
	21	08 10.4	10 35.7	23 02.2	16 15.5
MAY	1	08 36.4	08 44.7	24 11.9	18 02.6
	11	08 R 25.6	06 14.9	25 50.4	20 22.3
	21	07 37.8	03 20.7	27 52.8	23 09.5
	31	06 15.4	00 21.4	00♍15.3	26 20.2
JUN	10	04 25.1	27♏37.7	02 54.4	29 50.7
	20	02 17.4	25 26.0	05 46.8	03♍37.8
	30	00 05.5	23 56.4	08 50.2	07 39.3
JUL	10	28♐03.7	23 13.0	12 02.7	11 53.1
	20	26 24.1	23 D 14.0	15 22.5	16 17.3
	30	25 14.9	23 55.9	18 48.1	20 50.9
AUG	9	24 41.0	25 13.4	22 18.4	25 32.5
	19	24 D 42.8	27 01.1	25 52.1	00♎21.1
	29	25 19.1	29 14.4	29 28.7	05 16.0
SEP	8	26 27.1	01♐49.1	03♎06.8	10 16.3
	18	28 03.1	04 41.2	06 46.0	15 21.4
	28	00♑03.7	07 48.0	10 25.3	20 30.7
OCT	8	02 25.6	11 06.7	14 03.8	25 43.5
	18	05 05.6	14 35.1	17 40.9	00♏59.2
	28	08 01.2	18 11.4	21 15.6	06 17.5
NOV	7	11 09.9	21 53.8	24 46.8	11 37.5
	17	14 29.6	25 40.9	28 13.6	16 58.7
	27	17 58.6	29 31.6	01♏34.7	22 20.5
DEC	7	21 35.2	03♑24.3	04 48.7	27 42.2
	17	25 18.0	07 18.1	07 54.1	03♐03.1
	27	29 05.7	11 12.0	10 49.0	08 22.4
JAN	6	02♒57.1	15♑04.6	13♏31.5	13♐39.1

1941		Ceres 1	Pallas 2	Juno 3	Vesta 4
JAN	1	18 S 03.2	01 N 28.6	00 S 40.9	16 N 07.8
	21	19 32.0	03 03.7	00 N 20.8	18 12.2
FEB	10	20 34.8	05 40.1	02 55.4	20 55.5
MAR	2	21 17.7	09 16.7	06 18.1	23 09.4
	22	21 50.3	13 42.4	09 19.0	24 05.4
APR	11	22 24.8	18 29.7	11 16.4	23 43.3
MAY	1	23 13.1	22 50.1	12 04.7	22 21.7
	21	24 21.6	25 43.7	11 54.4	20 15.2
JUN	10	25 42.5	26 28.8	10 58.1	17 32.4
	30	26 55.1	25 07.8	09 27.3	14 19.5
JUL	20	27 44.3	22 18.4	07 31.2	10 42.4
AUG	9	28 13.9	18 45.3	05 18.0	06 47.4
	29	28 34.1	15 03.1	02 55.0	02 41.4
SEP	18	28 48.6	11 34.0	00 29.0	01 S 27.8
OCT	8	28 54.4	08 31.4	01 S 53.6	05 31.8
	28	28 45.9	06 03.5	04 06.2	09 21.8
NOV	17	28 17.5	04 15.0	06 02.5	12 48.4
DEC	7	27 26.0	03 08.5	07 36.3	15 43.0
	27	26 S 10.2	02 N 44.0	08 S 41.7	17 S 58.2

1942		Ceres 1	Pallas 2	Juno 3	Vesta 4
JAN	1	01♒01.0	13♑08.5	12♏11.9	11♐01.1
	11	04 53.8	17 00.2	14 47.4	16 16.4
	21	08 48.7	20 49.4	17 06.8	21 28.0
	31	12 44.6	24 34.7	19 07.4	26 34.6
FEB	10	16 40.6	28 15.2	20 46.3	01♑35.3
	20	20 35.7	01♒49.7	22 00.1	06 28.9
MAR	2	24 29.0	05 16.8	22 45.6	11 13.7
	12	28 19.4	08 35.2	23 R 00.0	15 48.3
	22	02♓06.2	11 43.4	22 41.0	20 10.6
APR	1	05 48.1	14 39.6	21 48.2	24 18.4
	11	09 24.1	17 22.0	20 23.8	28 09.3
	21	12 53.0	19 48.2	18 32.7	01♒39.9
MAY	1	16 13.4	21 55.6	16 23.9	04 46.5
	11	19 23.7	23 41.5	14 08.6	07 25.0
	21	22 22.2	25 02.6	11 58.8	09 30.3
	31	25 06.7	25 55.4	10 06.1	10 57.0
JUN	10	27 35.0	26 16.8	08 38.7	11 40.4
	20	29 44.0	26 R 03.6	07 41.7	11 R 36.1
	30	01♈30.8	25 14.3	07 17.1	10 43.5
JUL	10	02 51.9	23 49.5	07 D 24.3	09 06.9
	20	03 43.5	21 52.6	08 01.5	06 56.7
	30	04 02.5	19 31.5	09 06.0	04 30.8
AUG	9	03 R 46.3	16 57.3	10 34.4	02 09.7
	19	02 54.0	14 23.5	12 24.0	00 13.3
	29	01 28.1	12 03.7	14 31.9	28♑55.7
SEP	8	29♓34.8	10 08.6	16 55.6	28 23.5
	18	27 24.2	08 45.4	19 33.0	28 D 38.3
	28	25 10.2	07 57.6	22 22.0	29 37.5
OCT	8	23 06.8	07 D 45.0	25 20.8	01♒15.8
	18	21 26.8	08 05.9	28 28.1	03 28.1
	28	20 19.1	08 57.2	01♐42.3	06 09.2
NOV	7	19 47.9	10 15.2	05 02.3	09 14.4
	17	19 D 54.6	11 56.6	08 26.9	12 39.9
	27	20 37.3	13 57.8	11 54.8	16 21.8
DEC	7	21 52.7	16 16.0	15 25.2	20 17.4
	17	23 37.3	18 48.5	18 56.8	24 24.4
	27	25 47.2	21 32.8	22 28.6	28 40.6
JAN	6	28♓18.6	24♒26.9	25♐59.7	03♓04.0

1942		Ceres 1	Pallas 2	Juno 3	Vesta 4
JAN	1	25 S 47.6	02 N 44.3	08 S 52.9	18 S 25.1
	21	24 04.1	03 10.0	09 15.3	19 44.7
FEB	10	22 03.2	04 11.6	08 58.7	20 19.6
MAR	2	19 50.8	05 43.7	08 00.9	20 15.0
	22	17 33.9	07 39.5	06 24.7	19 40.9
APR	11	15 20.5	09 50.9	04 21.6	18 52.0
MAY	1	13 18.9	12 07.7	02 16.9	18 07.5
	21	11 38.4	14 16.5	00 44.4	17 50.3
JUN	10	10 28.7	15 58.3	00 08.1	18 24.7
	30	09 59.9	16 47.8	00 30.2	20 05.2
JUL	20	10 21.3	16 16.8	01 38.0	22 34.6
AUG	9	11 35.9	14 09.1	03 15.0	24 56.3
	29	13 31.9	10 40.5	05 06.9	26 18.5
SEP	18	15 32.8	06 36.8	07 02.3	26 33.6
OCT	8	16 48.4	02 46.7	08 52.3	25 54.9
	28	16 47.1	00 S 19.4	10 29.5	24 33.6
NOV	17	15 31.5	02 30.6	11 47.8	22 34.9
DEC	7	13 20.8	03 47.8	12 42.4	20 03.1
	27	10 S 34.0	04 S 16.9	13 S 09.9	17 S 02.8

1943		Ceres 1	Pallas 2	Juno 3	Vesta 4
JAN	1	27♓00.4	22♒58.7	24♐14.3	00♓51.4
	11	29 41.4	25 57.1	27 44.5	05 18.1
	21	02♈39.2	29 02.7	01♑12.0	09 49.9
	31	05 50.9	02♓13.8	04 35.7	14 25.6
FEB	10	09 14.5	05 29.4	07 54.3	19 04.2
	20	12 47.8	08 47.9	11 06.1	23 44.7
MAR	2	16 28.9	12 08.4	14 09.8	28 26.1
	12	20 16.6	15 29.9	17 03.3	03♈08.0
	22	24 09.3	18 51.2	19 44.5	07 49.4
APR	1	28 06.0	22 11.5	22 11.3	12 29.8
	11	02♉05.7	25 29.8	24 20.7	17 08.6
	21	06 07.4	28 45.1	26 09.6	21 45.2
MAY	1	10 10.4	01♈56.4	27 34.9	26 19.0
	11	14 13.9	05 02.5	28 32.6	00♉49.5
	21	18 17.2	08 02.1	28 59.2	05 16.1
	31	22 19.6	10 53.9	28R51.9	09 38.1
JUN	10	26 20.4	13 36.1	28 08.4	13 55.0
	20	00♊18.7	16 06.6	26 50.0	18 05.6
	30	04 13.9	18 23.3	25 00.5	22 09.4
JUL	10	08 05.1	20 22.9	22 48.4	26 05.0
	20	11 51.1	22 02.4	20 26.5	29 51.1
	30	15 31.0	23 17.8	18 08.8	03♊26.2
AUG	9	19 03.1	24 04.5	16 09.5	06 48.3
	19	22 25.9	24R17.9	14 39.8	09 54.9
	29	25 37.5	23 53.7	13 46.2	12 43.5
SEP	8	28 35.3	22 48.6	13D31.9	15 10.3
	18	01♋16.6	21 02.7	13 56.3	17 11.5
	28	03 38.1	18 40.1	14 57.0	18 42.6
OCT	8	05 35.6	15 51.4	16 30.9	19 38.4
	18	07 05.1	12 53.0	18 34.2	19R54.5
	28	08 01.8	10 03.5	21 03.2	19 27.4
NOV	7	08 21.2	07 40.9	23 55.0	18 16.0
	17	08R00.4	05 58.7	27 06.4	16 24.5
	27	06 58.6	05 03.4	00♒35.1	14 02.5
DEC	7	05 19.3	04D57.1	04 18.8	11 25.9
	17	03 12.1	05 37.4	08 15.5	08 53.7
	27	00 50.9	07 00.2	12 23.7	06 43.8
JAN	6	28♊33.6	09♈01.0	16♒42.1	05♊09.9
JAN	1	09S48.4	04S17.6	13S12.3	16S14.0
	21	06 35.0	03 57.9	13 03.6	12 46.7
FEB	10	03 10.8	03 09.0	12 26.7	09 06.0
MAR	2	00N17.0	01 59.6	11 24.4	05 19.3
	22	03 42.0	00 38.7	10 01.6	01 34.1
APR	11	06 58.6	00N44.8	08 25.6	02N02.5
MAY	1	10 01.6	02 01.5	06 46.9	05 24.2
	21	12 46.6	03 01.6	05 19.6	08 25.4
JUN	10	15 09.9	03 33.7	04 22.3	11 01.3
	30	17 09.2	03 24.7	04 15.5	13 08.3
JUL	20	18 43.4	02 18.5	05 10.3	14 44.4
AUG	9	19 53.7	00S02.2	06 56.3	15 49.3
	29	20 43.8	03 51.2	09 05.3	16 25.1
SEP	18	21 20.8	09 01.5	11 08.9	16 36.7
OCT	8	21 55.4	14 41.5	12 48.3	16 31.8
	28	22 41.0	19 21.1	13 53.2	16 19.8
NOV	17	23 49.1	21 53.3	14 18.3	16 10.2
DEC	7	25 18.9	22 15.5	14 01.3	16 10.7
	27	26N49.4	21S02.1	13S02.3	16N30.0

1944		Ceres 1	Pallas 2	Juno 3	Vesta 4
JAN	1	29R40.6	07♈56.2	14♒31.8	05R51.8
	11	27♊31.8	10 14.1	18 54.7	04♊39.0
	21	25 50.5	13 02.8	23 25.9	04 10.7
	31	24 47.0	16 18.4	28 04.5	04D26.3
FEB	10	24D26.0	19 57.6	02♓49.7	05 22.6
	20	24 47.2	23 57.1	07 40.5	06 54.5
MAR	1	25 47.9	28 14.8	12 36.5	08 57.1
	11	27 23.8	02♉48.3	17 36.7	11 25.7
	21	29 30.0	07 36.2	22 41.1	14 16.0
	31	02♋02.2	12 36.8	27 49.0	17 24.4
APR	10	04 56.4	17 48.7	02♈59.7	20 48.0
	20	08 08.9	23 10.6	08 13.1	24 24.1
	30	11 36.8	28 41.8	13 28.8	28 10.8
MAY	10	15 17.7	04♊20.6	18 46.2	02♋06.3
	20	19 09.3	10 06.2	24 04.9	06 09.1
	30	23 10.1	15 57.4	29 24.3	10 18.3
JUN	9	27 18.4	21 53.0	04♉44.2	14 32.7
	19	01♌33.0	27 51.9	10 03.7	18 51.6
	29	05 53.1	03♋52.8	15 21.8	23 14.3
JUL	9	10 17.5	09 54.4	20 37.6	27 40.1
	19	14 45.6	15 55.6	25 50.6	02♌08.6
	29	19 16.5	21 55.2	00♊58.7	06 39.3
AUG	8	23 49.6	27 51.7	06 00.2	11 11.5
	18	28 24.4	03♌44.1	10 53.1	15 45.0
	28	03♍00.1	09 31.4	15 35.3	20 19.3
SEP	7	07 36.1	15 12.1	20 03.3	24 53.6
	17	12 11.8	20 45.5	24 13.3	29 27.7
	27	16 46.4	26 10.1	28 00.2	04♍00.7
OCT	7	21 19.1	01♍24.9	01♋19.4	08 31.9
	17	25 49.2	06 28.7	04 04.1	13 00.6
	27	00♎15.5	11 19.8	06 06.5	17 25.6
NOV	6	04 37.0	15 56.6	07 19.9	21 45.6
	16	08 52.5	20 17.3	07R38.4	25 59.5
	26	13 00.4	24 19.4	06 59.5	00♎05.2
DEC	6	16 58.9	28 00.0	05 28.8	04 00.8
	16	20 46.2	01♎15.6	03 19.9	07 43.8
	26	24 19.7	04 01.9	00 55.5	11 11.0
JAN	5	27♎36.8	06♎14.1	28♊42.8	14♎19.1
JAN	1	27N08.8	20S33.3	12S41.3	16N38.8
	21	28 08.2	18 09.8	10 53.9	17 30.9
FEB	10	28 45.1	15 18.0	08 33.4	18 45.9
MAR	1	29 11.0	12 14.9	05 47.1	20 12.5
	21	29 28.3	09 13.4	02 43.3	21 37.3
APR	10	29 31.1	06 24.8	00N28.5	22 48.6
	30	29 11.9	03 59.1	03 38.1	23 37.0
MAY	20	28 24.4	02 05.3	06 34.6	23 55.7
JUN	9	27 05.5	00 50.7	09 06.3	23 40.8
	29	25 14.8	00 19.7	11 01.9	22 51.0
JUL	19	22 54.9	00 33.5	12 10.6	21 27.2
AUG	8	20 10.4	01 29.5	12 24.1	19 32.6
	28	17 07.2	03 01.2	11 37.9	17 12.3
SEP	17	13 52.6	04 59.0	09 53.6	14 32.6
OCT	7	10 34.4	07 11.1	07 20.3	11 41.4
	27	07 21.0	09 23.6	04 18.1	08 47.6
NOV	16	04 21.2	11 20.3	01 23.3	06 01.4
DEC	6	01 43.9	12 41.7	00S28.3	03 34.4
	26	00S22.3	13S03.0	00S21.9	01N39.3

1945		Ceres 1	Pallas 2	Juno 3	Vesta 4
JAN	1	26♎20.1	05♎25.6	29R32.9	13♎06.4
	11	29 26.0	07 14.6	27♊38.2	16 00.9
	21	02♏10.0	08 19.8	26 26.7	18 28.7
	31	04 28.4	08R35.6	26D06.0	20 24.7
FEB	10	06 16.9	07 57.6	26 36.0	21 43.2
	20	07 30.9	06 24.8	27 52.6	22 18.0
MAR	2	08 06.5	04 03.0	29 49.1	22R05.3
	12	08R00.7	01 05.4	02♋17.8	21 03.9
	22	07 12.7	27♍52.9	05 13.0	19 18.0
APR	1	05 46.3	24 50.2	08 29.2	17 00.0
	11	03 49.8	22 18.1	12 01.8	14 28.2
	21	01 36.3	20 30.1	15 47.2	12 05.0
MAY	1	29♎22.5	19 32.1	19 42.3	10 10.7
	11	27 24.2	19D23.1	23 44.9	08 58.8
	21	25 54.2	19 59.3	27 53.3	08D35.9
	31	25 00.4	21 14.5	02♌05.6	09 02.3
JUN	10	24D45.4	23 02.7	06 20.7	10 14.1
	20	25 08.9	25 19.0	10 37.9	12 06.5
	30	26 07.7	27 58.5	14 56.0	14 33.7
JUL	10	27 37.8	00♎57.1	19 14.5	17 30.1
	20	29 35.3	04 12.0	23 32.7	20 51.5
	30	01♏56.0	07 40.2	27 50.1	24 33.7
AUG	9	04 36.5	11 19.7	02♍06.4	28 33.4
	19	07 33.8	15 08.8	06 20.9	02♏48.0
	29	10 45.0	19 05.7	10 33.0	07 14.9
SEP	8	14 08.1	23 09.4	14 42.6	11 52.5
	18	17 41.3	27 18.8	18 48.8	16 39.2
	28	21 22.5	01♏32.5	22 51.1	21 33.3
OCT	8	25 10.8	05 50.0	26 48.8	26 34.1
	18	29 04.7	10 10.3	00♎41.0	01♐40.3
	28	03♐03.1	14 32.4	04 26.9	06 51.0
NOV	7	07 05.0	18 55.8	08 05.2	12 05.5
	17	11 09.5	23 19.3	11 34.6	17 22.9
	27	15 15.5	27 42.2	14 53.7	22 42.4
DEC	7	19 22.4	02♐03.6	18 00.6	28 03.6
	17	23 29.1	06 22.4	20 53.1	03♑25.4
	27	27 34.8	10 37.6	23 28.9	08 47.4
JAN	6	01♑38.5	14♐48.0	25♎45.2	14♑09.0
JAN	1	00S52.9	12S53.0	00N05.5	01N13.0
	21	02 07.3	11 05.9	02 41.8	00 20.2
FEB	10	02 35.8	06 55.7	06 04.8	00 30.2
MAR	2	02 17.8	00 11.5	09 19.2	01 49.1
	22	01 22.5	07N47.8	11 55.7	03 59.9
APR	11	00 15.0	14 31.3	13 42.6	06 08.3
MAY	1	00N25.6	18 30.9	14 37.4	07 05.4
	21	00 07.7	19 59.7	14 42.6	06 22.2
JUN	10	01S12.9	19 44.0	14 03.1	04 15.4
	30	03 21.4	18 22.9	12 45.6	01 13.5
JUL	20	05 59.5	16 23.0	10 57.7	02S19.7
AUG	9	08 52.6	14 02.8	08 47.1	06 07.4
	29	11 49.5	11 35.8	06 21.5	09 55.7
SEP	18	14 41.4	09 12.9	03 48.6	13 32.8
OCT	8	17 20.6	07 03.7	01 16.1	16 47.1
	28	19 40.9	05 17.1	01S08.2	19 28.2
NOV	17	21 36.8	04 00.9	03 16.4	21 26.9
DEC	7	23 04.5	03 21.7	05 00.3	22 36.2
	27	24S02.1	03N24.8	06S11.0	22S52.9

1946	Ceres 1	Pallas 2	Juno 3	Vesta 4
JAN 1	29♐36.9	12♐43.5	24♎39.7	11♑28.3
11	03♑39.4	16 51.0	26 44.9	16 49.4
21	07 38.3	20 51.6	28 25.7	22 08.9
31	11 32.8	24 44.0	29 38.7	27 26.2
FEB 10	15 21.8	28 26.2	00♏20.1	02♒40.8
20	19 03.8	01♑56.2	00R27.2	07 51.7
MAR 2	22 37.9	05 11.9	29♎58.2	12 58.5
12	26 02.2	08 10.5	28 53.2	18 00.2
22	29 15.1	10 48.8	27 15.9	22 56.0
APR 1	02♒14.7	13 03.6	25 13.4	27 45.2
11	04 58.7	14 50.4	22 56.4	02♓26.6
21	07 24.7	16 05.0	20 38.2	06 59.1
MAY 1	09 29.7	16 42.9	18 31.4	11 21.6
11	11 10.5	16R39.8	16 47.0	15 32.4
21	12 23.8	15 53.3	15 32.1	19 29.5
31	13 06.2	14 23.4	14 50.0	23 11.1
JUN 10	13R14.7	12 14.7	14D41.4	26 34.3
20	12 47.8	09 37.7	15 04.4	29 36.1
30	11 45.8	06 47.2	15 56.1	02♈12.8
JUL 10	10 12.2	04 01.0	17 13.6	04 19.9
20	08 14.9	01 35.7	18 53.3	05 52.9
30	06 04.6	29♐43.0	20 52.3	06 46.7
AUG 9	03 54.8	28 30.0	23 07.8	06R56.7
19	01 59.1	27 58.1	25 37.3	06 20.7
29	00 28.0	28D05.4	28 18.7	04 59.2
SEP 8	29♑29.2	28 48.6	01♏10.2	02 59.1
18	29 05.9	00♑02.9	04 10.1	00 33.5
28	29D18.1	01 43.9	07 17.1	28♓00.2
OCT 8	00♒04.4	03 47.7	10 29.9	25 39.8
18	01 21.4	06 10.4	13 47.1	23 49.1
28	03 05.7	08 49.0	17 07.8	22 39.1
NOV 7	05 14.0	11 40.6	20 30.8	22D14.5
17	07 42.7	14 42.7	23 55.1	22 35.0
27	10 28.9	17 53.6	27 19.8	23 37.0
DEC 7	13 30.0	21 11.2	00♐43.5	25 15.7
17	16 43.5	24 34.0	04 05.3	27 25.6
27	20 07.6	28 00.7	07 24.0	00♈02.1
JAN 6	23♒40.2	01♒29.8	10♐38.1	03♈00.6
JAN 1	24S11.8	03N32.6	06S22.4	22S48.8
21	24 33.1	04 32.6	06 39.1	22 01.7
FEB 10	24 29.7	06 18.3	06 03.4	20 30.2
MAR 2	24 08.8	08 46.6	04 31.4	18 23.9
22	23 39.9	11 50.6	02 11.8	15 54.4
APR 11	23 15.2	15 17.9	00N25.5	13 14.2
MAY 1	23 08.6	18 47.9	02 35.4	10 36.3
21	23 34.8	21 48.5	03 44.5	08 13.8
JUN 10	24 45.3	23 39.1	03 47.1	06 20.4
30	26 39.3	23 43.8	02 55.6	05 10.7
JUL 20	28 52.6	21 55.2	01 26.7	04 59.4
AUG 9	30 41.1	18 41.4	00S25.3	05 57.6
29	31 31.0	14 47.9	02 29.0	08 01.3
SEP 18	31 21.4	10 54.8	04 35.4	10 32.7
OCT 8	30 28.4	07 27.6	06 37.2	12 24.9
28	29 05.7	04 39.9	08 27.5	12 49.1
NOV 17	27 19.6	02 37.0	10 00.8	11 45.2
DEC 7	25 12.6	01 19.9	11 11.9	09 36.7
27	22S46.6	00N46.6	11S57.1	06S46.7

1947	Ceres 1	Pallas 2	Juno 3	Vesta 4
JAN 1	21♒52.9	29♑45.0	09♐01.7	01♈28.8
11	25 29.3	03♒14.8	12 13.0	04 36.9
21	29 11.8	06 45.3	15 17.7	08 01.3
31	02♓59.4	10 15.4	18 13.9	11 39.3
FEB 10	06 50.6	13 43.8	21 00.0	15 28.3
20	10 44.4	17 09.6	23 33.7	19 26.2
MAR 2	14 39.8	20 31.7	25 52.8	23 31.3
12	18 35.7	23 48.8	27 54.5	27 41.9
22	22 31.4	26 59.8	29 36.0	01♉56.9
APR 1	26 25.9	00♓03.5	00♑54.0	06 15.3
11	00♈18.3	02 58.3	01 45.3	10 35.8
21	04 07.9	05 42.8	02 06.7	14 58.0
MAY 1	07 53.6	08 15.1	01R55.6	19 21.1
11	11 34.5	10 33.1	01 10.9	23 44.3
21	15 09.5	12 34.6	29♐53.6	28 07.2
31	18 37.3	14 16.8	28 07.8	02♊29.2
JUN 10	21 56.5	15 36.8	26 01.3	06 49.7
20	25 05.7	16 31.4	23 44.7	11 08.3
30	28 02.8	16 57.1	21 31.0	15 24.2
JUL 10	00♉45.7	16R51.1	19 32.3	19 37.0
20	03 11.7	16 11.2	17 58.4	23 45.9
30	05 17.6	14 56.7	16 56.1	27 50.1
AUG 9	07 00.3	13 10.1	16 28.1	01♋48.6
19	08 15.8	10 57.1	16D34.7	05 40.4
29	09 00.0	08 27.4	17 14.3	09 24.0
SEP 8	09R09.7	05 53.5	18 24.0	12 57.8
18	08 42.3	03 28.6	20 00.9	16 19.9
28	07 37.6	01 24.8	22 01.8	19 27.7
OCT 8	05 59.4	29♒50.7	24 23.5	22 18.4
18	03 55.5	28 51.2	27 03.6	24 48.4
28	01 38.7	28 27.8	29 59.6	26 53.4
NOV 7	29♈24.3	28D39.4	03♑09.3	28 29.0
17	27 26.9	29 23.2	06 31.0	29 29.7
27	25 58.9	00♓36.3	10 03.0	29 50.4
DEC 7	25 07.5	02 14.8	13 43.9	29R27.6
17	24D55.5	04 15.5	17 32.5	28 19.6
27	25 22.6	06 35.4	21 27.4	26 30.0
JAN 6	26♈25.5	09♓11.6	25♑27.7	24♋08.6
JAN 1	22S07.5	00N44.6	12S03.9	05S59.8
21	19 21.7	01 00.1	12 13.1	02 40.4
FEB 10	16 24.6	01 48.3	11 53.0	00N49.2
MAR 2	13 21.1	03 02.6	11 05.3	04 19.9
22	10 16.7	04 35.3	09 53.9	07 43.7
APR 11	07 17.2	06 18.5	08 26.0	10 53.7
MAY 1	04 28.4	08 03.1	06 52.6	13 43.8
21	01 56.0	09 38.5	05 30.5	16 08.8
JUN 10	00N14.2	10 51.5	04 40.4	18 04.9
30	01 56.9	11 24.8	04 38.9	19 29.7
JUL 20	03 06.9	10 56.6	05 27.9	20 22.6
AUG 9	03 39.5	09 05.9	06 54.0	20 45.3
29	03 32.3	05 49.4	08 38.1	20 41.9
SEP 18	02 47.9	01 39.1	10 23.5	20 19.9
OCT 8	01 40.0	02S27.4	11 57.5	19 50.0
28	00 38.2	05 43.6	13 11.2	19 26.9
NOV 17	00 18.5	07 52.0	13 58.0	19 28.7
DEC 7	01 00.6	08 55.5	14 13.4	20 12.4
27	02N39.7	09S05.0	13S55.1	21N42.2

1948	Ceres 1	Pallas 2	Juno 3	Vesta 4
JAN 1	25♈49.8	07♓51.6	23♑26.9	25R22.4
11	27 09.3	10 35.1	27 29.6	22♋50.5
21	28 59.0	13 31.5	01♒36.4	20 12.3
31	01♉14.5	16 38.8	05 46.2	17 47.7
FEB 10	03 52.0	19 55.4	09 58.3	15 53.2
20	06 48.2	23 19.8	14 12.0	14 40.1
MAR 1	09 59.9	26 50.8	18 26.5	14 12.8
11	13 24.7	00♈27.4	22 41.1	14D30.6
21	17 00.3	04 08.5	26 55.0	15 30.3
31	20 44.8	07 53.3	01♓07.3	17 06.8
APR 10	24 36.8	11 41.3	05 17.5	19 15.0
20	28 35.0	15 31.7	09 24.5	21 50.3
30	02♊38.0	19 23.9	13 27.2	24 48.2
MAY 10	06 45.1	23 17.4	17 24.6	28 05.2
20	10 55.3	27 11.7	21 15.3	01♌38.6
30	15 07.9	01♉06.1	24 57.7	05 25.5
JUN 9	19 22.3	05 00.2	28 29.7	09 24.2
19	23 37.7	08 53.0	01♈48.8	13 33.1
29	27 53.6	12 44.0	04 52.6	17 50.5
JUL 9	02♋09.4	16 32.1	07 37.1	22 15.5
19	06 24.4	20 15.9	09 57.9	26 47.2
29	10 38.0	23 54.1	11 50.1	01♍24.7
AUG 8	14 49.5	27 24.9	13 08.5	06 07.4
18	18 58.0	00♊45.3	13 46.8	10 54.7
28	23 02.5	03 52.5	13R40.5	15 45.8
SEP 7	27 02.0	06 42.1	12 47.0	20 40.6
17	00♌55.1	09 09.0	11 10.7	25 38.4
27	04 40.3	11 06.7	09 01.5	00♎38.7
OCT 7	08 15.6	12 26.6	06 37.3	05 41.2
17	11 38.7	12 59.9	04 21.6	10 45.0
27	14 47.0	12R38.4	02 36.5	15 49.8
NOV 6	17 37.1	11 15.1	01 37.2	20 55.1
16	20 05.0	08 52.4	01D32.0	25 59.8
26	22 06.7	05 44.6	02 21.2	01♏03.4
DEC 6	23 36.9	02 20.3	04 01.5	06 05.2
16	24 30.8	29♉15.4	06 27.3	11 03.8
26	24R44.0	27 00.8	09 31.9	15 58.3
JAN 5	24♌13.6	25♉54.8	13♈09.4	20♏47.4
JAN 1	03N11.5	09S00.4	13S45.2	22N09.5
21	05 38.7	08 19.5	12 44.9	23 58.8
FEB 10	08 26.5	07 10.9	11 13.7	25 20.3
MAR 1	11 22.2	05 45.2	09 16.1	26 02.4
21	14 15.4	04 12.1	06 58.1	26 11.8
APR 10	16 57.7	02 41.2	04 27.0	25 53.4
30	19 22.0	01 22.0	01 51.4	25 06.1
MAY 20	21 22.5	00 24.2	00N39.1	23 47.7
JUN 9	22 54.6	00N01.8	02 52.6	21 56.7
29	23 55.9	00S15.0	04 34.7	19 34.2
JUL 19	24 25.6	01 26.3	05 26.8	16 42.6
AUG 8	24 25.6	03 43.6	05 06.0	13 26.7
28	24 00.6	07 16.4	03 08.5	09 51.9
SEP 17	23 18.0	12 07.4	00S30.2	06 05.0
OCT 7	22 28.6	18 03.3	04 58.8	02 13.4
27	21 46.7	24 21.4	08 33.4	01S34.8
NOV 16	21 30.1	29 42.1	10 01.7	05 11.1
DEC 6	21 58.8	32 31.1	09 24.0	08 26.9
26	23N29.2	31S57.2	07S13.6	11S14.3

1949	Ceres 1	Pallas 2	Juno 3	Vesta 4
JAN 1	24R31.0	26R12.4	11♈38.8	18♏52.5
11	23♌34.7	25D50.8	15 33.2	23 37.6
21	21 59.1	26♉40.0	19 51.9	28 15.0
31	19 53.5	28 31.5	24 30.6	02♐42.5
FEB 10	17 33.5	01♊15.3	29 25.8	06 57.9
20	15 17.8	04 40.9	04♉33.6	10 58.9
MAR 2	13 23.6	08 39.4	09 51.8	14 42.4
12	12 04.4	13 03.6	15 18.2	18 04.3
22	11 27.0	17 46.8	20 50.5	21 00.7
APR 1	11D32.8	22 44.2	26 26.7	23 26.6
11	12 20.0	27 51.8	02♊05.7	25 16.5
21	13 44.4	03♋06.2	07 46.0	26 24.9
MAY 1	15 41.1	08 25.0	13 26.7	26 46.5
11	18 05.4	13 46.0	19 06.5	26R18.8
21	20 52.9	19 07.7	24 44.6	25 03.7
31	23 59.8	24 29.1	00♋20.6	23 08.7
JUN 10	27 23.0	29 49.3	05 53.8	20 49.5
20	00♍59.5	05♌07.2	11 23.3	18 26.8
30	04 47.3	10 22.8	16 48.9	16 21.8
JUL 10	08 44.5	15 35.7	22 10.2	14 52.1
20	12 49.4	20 45.7	27 26.8	14 07.4
30	17 00.7	25 52.5	02♌38.3	14D10.7
AUG 9	21 17.4	00♍56.2	07 44.2	15 00.9
19	25 38.2	05 56.6	12 44.1	16 33.1
29	00♎02.6	10 53.9	17 37.8	18 42.1
SEP 8	04 29.5	15 47.6	22 24.3	21 22.4
18	08 58.2	20 37.8	27 03.3	24 28.7
28	13 28.1	25 24.4	01♍33.9	27 57.3
OCT 8	17 58.5	00♎06.9	05 55.2	01♑44.3
18	22 28.6	04 45.0	10 06.0	05 46.4
28	26 57.7	09 18.3	14 04.9	10 01.2
NOV 7	01♏25.0	13 45.9	17 50.3	14 26.7
17	05 49.7	18 07.4	21 20.4	19 00.8
27	10 10.9	22 21.5	24 32.4	23 42.1
DEC 7	14 27.4	26 26.9	27 23.7	28 29.1
17	18 38.3	00♏22.4	29 51.0	03♒20.7
27	22 42.2	04 06.0	01♎50.5	08 16.0
JAN 6	26♏37.6	07♏35.2	03♎18.0	13♒13.6
JAN 1	24N08.9	31S09.6	06S21.7	11S57.9
21	26 49.6	26 58.3	03 01.4	13 59.2
FEB 10	29 26.8	21 20.6	00N42.2	15 21.7
MAR 2	30 53.5	15 17.8	04 27.3	16 07.5
22	30 47.0	09 31.7	07 56.0	16 24.1
APR 11	29 27.9	04 28.8	10 53.4	16 24.6
MAY 1	27 21.4	00 25.1	13 08.0	16 27.0
21	24 42.3	02N32.2	14 32.6	16 49.1
JUN 10	21 38.1	04 23.0	15 04.5	17 38.4
30	18 14.1	05 12.8	14 45.3	18 49.7
JUL 20	14 34.9	05 10.7	13 40.3	20 14.6
AUG 9	10 45.4	04 28.1	11 57.4	21 46.2
29	06 51.1	03 17.3	09 46.1	23 14.6
SEP 18	02 57.9	01 50.9	07 16.6	24 27.4
OCT 8	00S48.5	00 21.6	04 39.4	25 12.5
28	04 22.0	00S57.9	02 05.8	25 20.4
NOV 17	07 36.6	01 54.2	00S12.5	24 45.5
DEC 7	10 27.4	02 13.6	02 02.5	23 26.2
27	12S50.5	01S42.2	03S09.5	21S25.1

1950	Ceres 1	Pallas 2	Juno 3	Vesta 4
JAN 1	24♏41.0	05♏52.5	02♎38.5	10♒44.6
11	28 31.7	09 13.7	03 48.6	15 43.1
21	02♐11.4	12 16.5	04 20.8	20 43.1
31	05 38.1	14 57.1	04R12.0	25 43.6
FEB 10	08 49.5	17 11.6	03 21.7	00♓43.8
20	11 43.0	18 54.7	01 51.8	05 43.2
MAR 2	14 15.3	20 01.0	29♍49.7	10 41.1
12	16 23.5	20 25.4	27 27.4	15 36.8
22	18 03.5	20R02.8	24 59.7	20 29.9
APR 1	19 11.6	18 50.8	22 42.6	25 19.6
11	19 44.5	16 52.0	20 49.2	00♈05.4
21	19R39.4	14 14.8	19 28.2	04 46.7
MAY 1	18 55.6	11 15.2	18 43.8	09 22.8
11	17 35.9	08 13.8	18D36.0	13 52.9
21	15 46.5	05 31.6	19 02.5	18 16.4
31	13 38.5	03 25.2	20 00.0	22 32.1
JUN 10	11 25.7	02 03.6	21 24.3	26 39.1
20	09 22.5	01 29.5	23 11.6	00♉36.0
30	07 42.0	01D41.1	25 18.5	04 21.2
JUL 10	06 32.5	02 33.6	27 41.6	07 52.9
20	05 58.6	04 01.8	00♎18.6	11 08.8
30	06D01.4	06 00.3	03 07.1	14 06.0
AUG 9	06 38.8	08 24.1	06 05.0	16 41.4
19	07 48.1	11 09.2	09 10.9	18 50.9
29	09 25.7	14 11.9	12 23.3	20 30.2
SEP 8	11 27.6	17 29.1	15 40.8	21 34.6
18	13 50.9	20 58.4	19 02.5	21 59.0
28	16 32.2	24 37.6	22 27.2	21R40.0
OCT 8	19 28.9	28 24.9	25 53.9	20 36.5
18	22 38.7	02♐18.8	29 21.8	18 51.4
28	25 59.4	06 17.7	02♏49.8	16 34.0
NOV 7	29 29.4	10 20.5	06 17.1	13 59.4
17	03♑07.1	14 26.1	09 42.6	11 26.3
27	06 51.0	18 33.2	13 05.0	09 13.6
DEC 7	10 39.9	22 40.8	16 23.4	07 35.2
17	14 32.7	26 48.2	19 36.3	06 39.4
27	18 28.2	00♑53.9	22 42.2	06D28.5
JAN 6	22♑25.5	04♑57.2	25♏39.7	07♉00.4
JAN 1	13S21.6	01S24.8	03S17.5	20S49.0
21	15 07.4	00N29.2	03 07.4	18 04.2
FEB 10	16 24.8	03 41.1	01 40.6	14 53.7
MAR 2	17 18.4	08 12.3	00N57.1	11 26.9
22	17 55.8	13 43.9	04 05.8	07 52.9
APR 11	18 26.5	19 24.3	06 45.5	04 20.8
MAY 1	18 58.8	23 54.5	08 17.1	00 58.6
21	19 35.2	26 09.8	08 36.9	02N06.0
JUN 10	20 13.1	26 00.8	07 58.8	04 46.3
30	20 52.5	24 04.7	06 38.9	06 56.5
JUL 20	21 39.7	21 08.5	04 50.5	08 31.5
AUG 9	22 38.3	17 47.6	02 44.0	09 27.4
29	23 45.6	14 25.2	00 28.0	09 41.8
SEP 18	24 53.7	11 16.3	01S50.3	09 15.1
OCT 8	25 54.2	08 30.8	04 04.2	08 13.8
28	26 38.9	06 16.2	06 07.5	06 57.0
NOV 17	27 01.5	04 37.7	07 54.3	05 59.9
DEC 7	26 58.1	03 39.2	09 19.1	05 56.0
27	26S27.4	03N22.5	10S17.3	06N54.0

1951	Ceres 1	Pallas 2	Juno 3	Vesta 4
JAN 1	20♑26.7	02♑55.9	24♏12.1	06D39.4
11	24 24.5	06 57.6	27 04.7	07♉31.3
21	28 22.5	10 55.0	29 45.7	08 59.9
31	02♒19.7	14 47.2	02♐13.1	10 59.6
FEB 10	06 15.4	18 32.9	04 24.4	13 25.7
20	10 08.4	22 10.6	06 16.8	16 14.1
MAR 2	13 57.8	25 39.1	07 47.3	19 20.5
12	17 42.5	28 56.5	08 52.6	22 42.2
22	21 21.4	02♒01.0	09 29.6	26 16.4
APR 1	24 53.3	04 50.5	09R35.7	00♊00.7
11	28 16.9	07 22.5	09 08.8	03 53.5
21	01♓30.4	09 34.1	08 09.0	07 53.2
MAY 1	04 32.4	11 22.3	06 38.8	11 58.5
11	07 20.6	12 43.5	04 43.8	16 08.4
21	09 52.7	13 33.9	02 33.3	20 21.9
31	12 06.2	13R50.2	00 18.6	24 38.2
JUN 10	13 58.0	13 29.1	28♏11.7	28 57.0
20	15 24.6	12 29.5	26 23.7	03♋17.2
30	16 22.8	10 52.9	25 02.1	07 38.6
JUL 10	16 49.0	08 44.2	24 11.7	12 00.7
20	16R40.7	06 13.3	23D54.2	16 22.7
30	15 56.8	03 33.3	24 08.7	20 44.4
AUG 9	14 38.8	00 58.8	24 53.2	25 05.2
19	12 52.1	28♑43.6	26 05.0	29 24.4
29	10 45.8	26 57.6	27 40.8	03♌41.4
SEP 8	08 32.6	25 46.8	29 38.0	07 55.5
18	06 26.7	25 12.9	01♐53.7	12 05.5
28	04 40.7	25D14.8	04 25.4	16 10.7
OCT 8	03 24.4	25 49.7	07 11.0	20 09.5
18	02 43.5	26 54.1	10 08.4	24 00.4
28	02D39.4	28 23.9	13 16.1	27 41.5
NOV 7	03 11.3	00♒15.9	16 32.5	01♍10.5
17	04 16.6	02 26.4	19 56.2	04 24.5
27	05 51.6	04 52.5	23 25.9	07 20.3
DEC 7	07 52.7	07 31.7	27 00.6	09 53.5
17	10 16.2	10 21.7	00♑39.0	11 59.6
27	12 58.7	13 20.3	04 20.2	13 33.3
JAN 6	15♓57.6	16♒26.1	08♑03.2	14♍28.7
JAN 1	26S15.6	03N24.8	10S27.2	07N16.8
21	25 12.8	03 59.7	10 46.8	09 12.6
FEB 10	23 49.4	05 13.0	10 33.2	11 33.1
MAR 2	22 11.6	07 00.2	09 46.2	14 02.0
22	20 27.6	09 14.7	08 28.6	16 26.5
APR 11	18 46.7	11 48.0	06 47.8	18 36.5
MAY 1	17 19.1	14 27.9	04 59.6	20 24.0
21	16 16.4	16 57.5	03 28.2	21 42.9
JUN 10	15 50.7	18 51.9	02 39.3	22 29.3
30	16 13.5	19 39.5	02 45.1	22 41.2
JUL 20	17 31.4	18 51.8	03 39.8	22 18.9
AUG 9	19 35.7	16 23.5	05 07.6	21 24.8
29	21 51.7	12 43.9	06 52.3	20 03.7
SEP 18	23 27.9	08 41.4	08 40.7	18 22.3
OCT 8	23 48.6	04 57.6	10 22.3	16 29.6
28	22 53.9	01 56.0	11 49.1	14 37.0
NOV 17	21 02.8	00S14.9	12 54.7	12 58.6
DEC 7	18 33.5	01 35.2	13 34.4	11 51.5
27	15S38.7	02S09.3	13S45.0	11N36.1

1952		Ceres 1	Pallas 2	Juno 3	Vesta 4
JAN	1	14♓26.3	14♒52.5	06♑11.6	14♍06.2
	11	17 32.2	18 01.1	09 55.0	14 40.5
	21	20 50.3	21 14.3	13 38.7	14R29.5
	31	24 18.8	24 31.0	17 21.7	13 30.9
FEB	10	27 55.8	27 49.7	21 02.9	11 48.0
	20	01♈39.4	01♓09.3	24 41.1	09 30.3
MAR	1	05 28.6	04 28.9	28 15.3	06 54.3
	11	09 22.0	07 47.2	01♒44.0	04 21.3
	21	13 18.4	11 03.2	05 06.0	02 11.7
	31	17 17.0	14 16.0	08 19.7	00 40.5
APR	10	21 16.8	17 24.3	11 23.0	29♌56.4
	20	25 16.9	20 27.1	14 14.1	00D00.6
	30	29 16.8	23 23.1	16 50.3	00♍50.9
MAY	10	03♉15.4	26 10.6	19 08.8	02 22.7
	20	07 12.2	28 48.3	21 06.2	04 30.3
	30	11 06.3	01♈14.1	22 38.7	07 08.6
JUN	9	14 56.7	03 25.8	23 42.1	10 13.0
	19	18 42.7	05 21.0	24 12.4	13 39.1
	29	22 23.3	06 56.5	24R05.6	17 24.0
JUL	9	25 57.0	08 08.9	23 19.7	21 24.5
	19	29 22.7	08 54.8	21 55.8	25 38.5
	29	02♊38.5	09 09.9	19 58.5	00♎04.1
AUG	8	05 42.6	08R51.0	17 38.8	04 39.6
	18	08 32.6	07 55.6	15 11.5	09 23.7
	28	11 05.7	06 23.4	12 54.0	14 15.5
SEP	7	13 18.6	04 18.0	11 02.3	19 13.7
	17	15 07.7	01 47.0	09 47.3	24 17.7
	27	16 28.5	29♓02.9	09 15.6	29 26.6
OCT	7	17 16.9	26 21.2	09D28.9	04♏39.7
	17	17R28.8	23 56.9	10 25.0	09 56.4
	27	17 01.4	22 02.6	12 00.6	15 16.1
NOV	6	15 54.7	20 46.4	14 11.3	20 38.0
	16	14 12.6	20 11.5	16 53.0	26 01.6
	26	12 04.3	20D17.8	20 01.8	01♐26.4
DEC	6	09 44.2	21 02.7	23 33.8	06 51.4
	16	07 28.5	22 22.6	27 26.1	12 16.2
	26	05 33.5	24 13.6	01♓36.3	17 40.1
JAN	5	04♊11.4	26♓31.9	06♓01.9	23♐02.3
JAN	1	14S52.0	02S11.3	13S43.0	11N42.8
	21	11 36.6	01 56.6	13 15.9	12 58.0
FEB	10	08 11.9	01 11.4	12 20.0	15 24.6
MAR	1	04 43.8	00 03.8	10 58.8	18 15.1
	21	01 17.5	01N17.9	09 17.6	20 13.1
APR	10	02N01.5	02 45.0	07 23.7	20 36.2
	30	05 08.6	04 08.4	05 26.4	19 32.8
MAY	20	07 59.2	05 18.2	03 38.2	17 26.4
JUN	9	10 29.6	06 02.8	02 15.8	14 35.3
	29	12 37.1	06 08.2	01 40.6	11 11.4
JUL	19	14 19.9	05 17.0	02 16.0	07 23.8
AUG	8	15 38.3	03 10.4	04 11.7	03 20.6
	28	16 34.5	00S23.1	07 03.7	00S50.0
SEP	17	17 13.4	05 06.7	09 59.6	04 59.4
OCT	7	17 42.3	10 00.2	12 15.4	08 58.5
	27	18 09.2	13 49.3	13 31.9	12 37.9
NOV	16	18 39.3	15 57.8	13 46.4	15 47.9
DEC	6	19 12.9	16 32.6	13 02.6	18 19.8
	26	19N51.6	15S57.1	11S26.7	20S06.8

1953		Ceres 1	Pallas 2	Juno 3	Vesta 4
JAN	1	04R39.7	25♓33.6	04♓14.0	20♐53.7
	11	03♊40.8	28 06.3	08 47.8	26 14.4
	21	03D23.2	01♈01.0	13 34.2	01♑32.3
	31	03 46.7	04 14.7	18 31.6	06 46.3
FEB	10	04 48.2	07 45.0	23 38.7	11 55.6
	20	06 23.8	11 30.1	28 54.4	16 59.2
MAR	2	08 28.8	15 28.1	04♈17.5	21 55.8
	12	10 58.9	19 38.0	09 47.3	26 44.5
	22	13 50.3	23 58.5	15 22.9	01♒23.8
APR	1	16 59.6	28 28.7	21 03.4	05 51.9
	11	20 23.7	03♉07.8	26 48.2	10 07.1
	21	24 00.4	07 55.6	02♉36.6	14 07.2
MAY	1	27 47.6	12 51.1	08 27.9	17 49.4
	11	01♋43.5	17 54.0	14 21.3	21 10.8
	21	05 46.8	23 04.1	20 16.1	24 07.5
	31	09 56.3	28 20.8	26 11.6	26 35.2
JUN	10	14 10.8	03♊43.8	02♊07.2	28 29.3
	20	18 29.7	09 12.5	08 01.9	29 44.2
	30	22 51.9	14 46.3	13 54.8	00♓15.3
JUL	10	27 16.9	20 24.8	19 45.3	29R59.2
	20	01♌44.1	26 06.9	25 32.3	28♒55.4
	30	06 12.7	01♋51.6	01♋14.8	27 09.7
AUG	9	10 42.3	07 38.0	06 51.7	24 53.4
	19	15 12.2	13 24.6	12 21.8	22 24.3
	29	19 41.8	19 09.7	17 43.8	20 03.6
SEP	8	24 10.4	24 51.7	22 56.4	18 09.5
	18	28 37.2	00♌28.2	27 57.6	16 55.1
	28	03♍01.3	05 57.2	02♌45.6	16 26.5
OCT	8	07 22.0	11 16.2	07 18.4	16D44.0
	18	11 37.8	16 21.6	11 33.0	17 44.8
	28	15 47.6	21 10.2	15 26.4	19 24.0
NOV	7	19 49.8	25 38.4	18 54.8	21 35.9
	17	23 42.4	29 41.1	21 53.7	24 15.9
	27	27 23.5	03♍12.9	24 18.3	27 19.2
DEC	7	00♎50.3	06 07.4	26 03.0	00♓41.9
	17	03 59.9	08 17.3	27 02.0	04 20.6
	27	06 48.7	09 35.1	27R11.3	08 12.3
JAN	6	09♎12.8	09R52.8	26♌28.9	12♓14.7
JAN	1	20N05.4	15S36.2	10S48.9	20S29.5
	21	21 01.9	14 02.0	08 17.3	21 13.3
FEB	10	22 15.1	12 01.8	05 14.2	21 10.2
MAR	2	23 38.2	09 48.6	01 50.7	20 27.0
	22	25 00.3	07 33.4	01N41.0	19 14.3
APR	11	26 10.1	05 26.4	05 08.0	17 46.6
MAY	1	26 58.0	03 37.1	08 17.2	16 21.0
	21	27 17.1	02 14.6	10 56.1	15 17.5
JUN	10	27 03.0	01 27.1	12 53.5	14 58.4
	30	26 14.4	01 21.5	14 01.0	15 45.2
JUL	20	24 52.7	02 02.5	14 14.3	17 45.8
AUG	9	23 01.6	03 31.5	13 33.9	20 31.7
	29	20 47.1	05 45.7	12 05.7	22 55.1
SEP	18	18 16.6	08 38.6	09 59.5	23 59.9
OCT	8	15 39.1	11 59.1	07 28.9	23 41.1
	28	13 04.8	15 32.8	04 50.4	22 18.4
NOV	17	10 44.9	19 00.5	02 24.1	20 09.5
DEC	7	08 51.8	21 55.2	00 35.1	17 25.7
	27	07N38.5	23S37.2	00S05.6	14S15.2

1954		Ceres 1	Pallas 2	Juno 3	Vesta 4
JAN	1	08♎04.1	09♍51.9	26R56.5	10♓12.3
	11	10 14.0	09R37.3	25♌48.9	14 19.4
	21	11 52.1	08 17.6	23 56.7	18 34.2
	31	12 53.9	05 57.9	21 32.8	22 55.0
FEB	10	13 14.9	02 53.8	18 56.6	27 20.8
	20	12R52.8	29♌32.0	16 29.8	01♈50.1
MAR	2	11 48.3	26 21.8	14 30.2	06 21.9
	12	10 06.7	23 48.1	13 09.4	10 55.4
	22	07 59.4	22 06.3	12 32.8	15 29.7
APR	1	05 42.2	21 20.4	12D39.2	20 04.1
	11	03 32.5	21D27.4	13 25.2	24 38.0
	21	01 46.5	22 21.0	14 45.4	29 10.7
MAY	1	00 34.8	23 53.9	16 34.6	03♉41.7
	11	00 03.1	25 59.4	18 48.0	08 10.5
	21	00D12.2	28 31.3	21 21.0	12 36.5
	31	00 59.5	01♍24.4	24 10.0	16 59.0
JUN	10	02 21.4	04 35.2	27 12.2	21 17.6
	20	04 13.3	08 00.3	00♍24.9	25 31.4
	30	06 30.7	11 37.0	03 46.1	29 39.9
JUL	10	09 09.9	15 23.4	07 14.1	03♊41.8
	20	12 07.3	19 17.8	10 47.5	07 36.3
	30	15 19.9	23 19.1	14 25.1	11 22.1
AUG	9	18 45.4	27 26.1	18 06.0	14 57.5
	19	22 21.5	01♎37.7	21 49.0	18 20.6
	29	26 06.5	05 53.4	25 33.6	21 29.4
SEP	8	29 59.0	10 12.5	29 18.9	24 20.8
	18	03♏57.6	14 34.1	03♎04.1	26 51.6
	28	08 01.2	18 57.8	06 48.6	28 57.9
OCT	8	12 08.8	23 23.0	10 31.5	00♋35.0
	18	16 19.5	27 48.9	14 12.1	01 38.3
	28	20 32.4	02♏15.2	17 49.5	02 02.6
NOV	7	24 46.6	06 40.9	21 22.6	01R44.2
	17	29 01.4	11 05.3	24 50.3	00 41.5
	27	03♐16.0	15 27.8	28 11.5	28♊57.2
DEC	7	07 29.5	19 47.2	01♏24.6	26 39.8
	17	11 40.9	24 02.5	04 28.0	24 04.4
	27	15 49.6	28 12.6	07 19.9	21 29.3
JAN	6	19♐54.3	02♐16.0	09♏58.0	19♊13.7
JAN	1	07N27.9	23S44.8	00S01.4	13S24.2
	21	07 21.8	22 29.2	01N22.1	09 50.6
FEB	10	08 16.9	17 41.4	04 17.3	06 06.7
MAR	2	10 02.9	09 41.5	07 43.2	02 19.9
	22	12 00.6	00 55.9	10 33.7	01N22.7
APR	11	13 11.0	06N08.7	12 19.5	04 54.5
MAY	1	12 55.7	10 45.4	13 00.5	08 09.5
	21	11 18.6	13 12.4	12 46.6	11 02.5
JUN	10	08 44.8	14 02.1	11 48.9	13 29.3
	30	05 36.8	13 42.6	10 17.2	15 26.7
JUL	20	02 09.9	12 36.0	08 20.1	16 53.4
AUG	9	01S25.2	10 59.4	06 05.4	17 50.1
	29	05 00.6	09 06.9	03 40.4	18 20.0
SEP	18	08 29.7	07 10.6	01 11.9	18 29.4
OCT	8	11 46.4	05 21.5	01S13.5	18 27.8
	28	14 44.9	03 49.8	03 29.2	18 27.3
NOV	17	17 20.2	02 45.3	05 28.5	18 39.1
DEC	7	19 28.2	02 16.9	07 05.0	19 06.9
	27	21S06.6	02N32.1	08S12.3	19N45.2

1955	Ceres 1	Pallas 2	Juno 3	Vesta 4
JAN 1	17♐52.5	00♐15.3	08♏40.9	20R18.0
11	21 54.9	04 14.8	11 11.2	18♊18.0
21	25 51.8	08 05.2	13 24.1	16 56.8
31	29 42.0	11 44.6	15 16.5	16 20.0
FEB 10	03♑24.0	15 10.6	16 45.3	16D27.9
20	06 56.5	18 20.7	17 47.3	17 17.2
MAR 2	10 17.5	21 11.5	18 19.0	18 43.5
12	13 25.2	23 39.4	18R18.0	20 41.7
22	16 17.5	25 40.3	17 42.9	23 06.9
APR 1	18 51.5	27 09.3	16 34.2	25 54.8
11	21 04.5	28 01.3	14 55.6	29 01.7
21	22 53.4	28R11.7	12 54.0	02♋24.5
MAY 1	24 14.4	27 36.4	10 39.7	06 00.8
11	25 04.4	26 15.0	08 25.1	09 48.1
21	25R20.2	24 10.7	06 21.9	13 45.0
31	24 59.8	21 33.3	04 40.3	17 50.0
JUN 10	24 03.6	18 38.8	03 27.2	22 01.7
20	22 34.6	15 45.9	02 45.9	26 19.3
30	20 39.9	13 13.5	02D37.0	00♌42.1
JUL 10	18 30.8	11 15.4	02 59.2	05 09.1
20	16 20.2	09 59.0	03 49.9	09 39.9
30	14 22.2	09 26.7	05 06.2	14 13.9
AUG 9	12 47.9	09D36.3	06 44.8	18 50.6
19	11 45.0	10 23.6	08 43.0	23 29.6
29	11 17.5	11 44.1	10 58.1	28 10.3
SEP 8	11D25.8	13 32.5	13 27.6	02♍52.3
18	12 07.9	15 44.5	16 09.6	07 35.3
28	13 21.3	18 16.3	19 02.2	12 18.5
OCT 8	15 02.2	21 04.3	22 03.6	17 01.3
18	17 07.2	24 05.8	25 12.5	21 43.1
28	19 33.1	27 18.3	28 27.7	26 23.0
NOV 7	22 16.8	00♑39.7	01♐47.8	01♎00.2
17	25 15.6	04 08.1	05 11.7	05 33.6
27	28 27.2	07 42.1	08 38.4	10 01.6
DEC 7	01♒49.5	11 20.0	12 06.7	14 23.1
17	05 20.8	15 00.8	15 35.7	18 36.1
27	08 59.5	18 43.1	19 04.0	22 38.3
JAN 6	12♒43.9	22♑25.7	22♐30.8	26♎27.1
JAN 1	21S26.5	02N43.5	08S23.9	19N55.8
21	22 28.3	04 01.1	08 46.4	20 42.3
FEB 10	23 04.6	06 11.3	08 27.8	21 37.2
MAR 2	23 22.2	09 12.2	07 25.3	22 37.2
22	23 31.0	12 55.6	05 41.9	23 33.3
APR 11	23 43.9	17 03.4	03 31.6	24 14.9
MAY 1	24 15.3	21 03.7	01 23.3	24 33.1
21	25 17.5	24 10.1	00N07.2	24 21.4
JUN 10	26 53.6	25 35.0	00 38.1	23 36.0
30	28 46.4	24 56.2	00 10.6	22 16.2
JUL 20	30 21.3	22 31.2	01S01.1	20 23.5
AUG 9	31 13.0	19 02.4	02 40.9	18 01.4
29	31 23.6	15 12.1	04 34.9	15 15.2
SEP 18	31 06.9	11 30.7	06 32.3	12 11.2
OCT 8	30 31.8	08 16.2	08 24.6	08 57.1
28	29 39.6	05 38.5	10 04.6	05 41.2
NOV 17	28 28.3	03 42.5	11 26.4	02 32.6
DEC 7	26 56.0	02 30.0	12 24.9	00S18.5
27	25S02.4	02N00.3	12S56.8	02S42.0

1956	Ceres 1	Pallas 2	Juno 3	Vesta 4
JAN 1	10♒51.0	20♑34.4	20♐47.7	24♎34.5
11	14 37.9	24 16.8	24 13.2	28 15.6
21	18 28.9	27 58.1	27 35.2	01♏38.6
31	22 22.5	01♒36.9	00♑52.4	04 39.2
FEB 10	26 18.0	05 12.4	04 03.5	07 12.8
20	00♓14.3	08 43.4	07 06.7	09 13.9
MAR 1	04 10.4	12 08.6	10 00.2	10 37.0
11	08 05.4	15 26.9	12 42.2	11 16.2
21	11 58.4	18 37.0	15 10.2	11R06.9
31	15 48.5	21 37.3	17 21.6	10 08.8
APR 10	19 34.7	24 26.2	19 13.6	08 26.3
20	23 16.1	27 01.7	20 42.8	06 11.1
30	26 51.3	29 21.7	21 45.8	03 42.8
MAY 10	00♈19.5	01♓23.8	22 19.1	01 23.0
20	03 39.0	03 05.1	22R19.4	29♎32.2
30	06 48.4	04 22.6	21 44.9	28 24.2
JUN 9	09 45.8	05 13.1	20 35.4	28D04.8
19	12 28.8	05 33.0	18 54.2	28 34.6
29	14 55.3	05R19.8	16 48.6	29 49.7
JUL 9	17 02.2	04 31.7	14 29.3	01♏44.8
19	18 46.1	03 08.8	12 10.0	04 14.6
29	20 03.5	01 14.8	10 04.7	07 13.3
AUG 8	20 50.7	28♒56.5	08 24.8	10 36.4
18	21R04.1	26 24.6	07 18.4	14 20.2
28	20 41.4	23 52.3	06 49.2	18 21.1
SEP 7	19 42.2	21 32.4	06D57.8	22 36.4
17	18 09.4	19 36.2	07 42.7	27 03.9
27	16 10.5	18 11.0	09 00.7	01♐41.5
OCT 7	13 56.5	17 20.4	10 48.4	06 27.8
17	11 42.2	17D05.2	13 02.6	11 21.4
27	09 42.2	17 23.6	15 39.7	16 20.8
NOV 6	08 08.5	18 12.7	18 36.9	21 25.4
16	07 09.6	19 29.1	21 51.7	26 34.0
26	06D48.7	21 09.3	25 21.7	01♑45.6
DEC 6	07 06.1	23 10.1	29 05.2	06 59.7
16	07 59.5	25 28.4	03♒00.2	12 15.5
26	09 25.3	28 01.6	07 05.4	17 32.0
JAN 5	11♈19.4	00♓47.3	11♒19.6	22♑48.9
JAN 1	24S30.9	01N59.2	13S00.4	03S12.3
21	22 13.7	02 18.9	12 56.5	04 46.9
FEB 10	19 42.0	03 13.0	12 24.5	05 32.2
MAR 1	17 01.3	04 35.6	11 26.8	05 22.3
21	14 17.7	06 19.6	10 08.4	04 19.0
APR 10	11 38.0	08 17.1	08 36.4	02 42.6
30	09 09.2	10 18.6	07 01.3	01 19.4
MAY 20	06 58.5	12 12.5	05 37.6	01 02.6
JUN 9	05 13.4	13 43.2	04 44.3	02 11.5
29	04 01.8	14 29.4	04 40.3	04 28.9
JUL 19	03 31.3	14 05.6	05 33.8	07 27.8
AUG 8	03 48.2	12 11.5	07 12.8	10 45.5
28	04 52.7	08 52.0	09 12.0	14 04.2
SEP 17	06 30.8	04 47.0	11 07.6	17 09.4
OCT 7	08 07.0	00 50.2	12 43.3	19 48.6
27	08 56.1	02S20.9	13 49.2	21 50.8
NOV 16	08 32.4	04 32.8	14 19.4	23 07.6
DEC 6	07 00.5	05 46.8	14 10.8	23 33.6
26	04S39.0	06S10.3	13S22.6	23S07.5

1957	Ceres 1	Pallas 2	Juno 3	Vesta 4
JAN 1	10♈30.6	29♒39.6	09♒36.9	20♑42.2
11	12 40.0	02♓31.9	13 56.0	25 58.8
21	15 11.5	05 33.4	18 22.2	01♒14.5
31	18 01.8	08 42.6	22 54.8	06 28.9
FEB 10	21 08.0	11 58.0	27 32.8	11 41.1
20	24 27.2	15 18.3	02♓15.6	16 50.3
MAR 2	27 57.4	18 42.5	07 02.8	21 56.3
12	01♉36.7	22 09.3	11 53.4	26 58.2
22	05 23.3	25 37.9	16 47.0	01♓55.2
APR 1	09 15.9	29 07.5	21 43.5	06 46.7
11	13 13.4	02♈37.1	26 42.1	11 31.8
21	17 14.5	06 05.9	01♈42.3	16 09.7
MAY 1	21 18.5	09 33.1	06 43.9	20 39.4
11	25 24.6	12 57.9	11 46.5	24 59.5
21	29 31.9	16 19.2	16 49.4	29 08.8
31	03♊39.9	19 36.0	21 52.1	03♈05.8
JUN 10	07 47.7	22 47.0	26 53.7	06 48.1
20	11 54.9	25 50.8	01♉54.1	10 13.7
30	16 00.8	28 45.8	06 51.9	13 19.6
JUL 10	20 04.5	01♉29.6	11 45.7	16 02.4
20	24 05.3	03 59.8	16 34.3	18 18.1
30	28 02.5	06 13.2	21 16.5	20 02.3
AUG 9	01♋54.9	08 05.8	25 49.3	21 09.7
19	05 41.3	09 33.2	00♊10.1	21 36.1
29	09 20.5	10 29.5	04 15.4	21R17.6
SEP 8	12 50.5	10 49.2	08 01.5	20 13.4
18	16 09.6	10R26.4	11 22.9	18 27.6
28	19 15.2	09 16.3	14 13.1	16 09.7
OCT 8	22 04.3	07 18.7	16 24.9	13 36.2
18	24 33.9	04 39.6	17 52.0	11 06.5
28	26 39.5	01 32.7	18 26.5	08 58.9
NOV 7	28 16.7	28♈20.2	18R05.0	07 27.9
17	29 20.9	25 26.5	16 50.4	06 40.5
27	29 47.2	23 12.9	14 53.9	06D38.4
DEC 7	29R32.3	21 53.0	12 37.6	07 19.5
17	28 35.4	21D31.3	10 28.1	08 39.2
27	26 59.4	22 06.9	08 49.8	10 32.5
JAN 6	24♋53.9	23♈35.1	07♊58.7	12♈54.4
JAN 1	03S49.8	06S09.0	13S00.6	22S49.8
21	00 50.5	05 41.3	11 23.7	21 21.2
FEB 10	02N23.0	04 45.4	09 14.4	19 12.9
MAR 2	05 41.0	03 30.8	06 38.8	16 35.2
22	08 55.6	02 06.8	03 44.7	13 39.2
APR 11	12 00.4	00 42.6	00 40.6	10 36.5
MAY 1	14 49.3	00N32.3	02N23.7	07 38.3
21	17 17.5	01 27.9	05 18.1	04 55.6
JUN 10	19 21.2	01 53.3	07 51.1	02 39.3
30	20 58.0	01 35.9	09 51.1	01 00.3
JUL 20	22 07.2	00 21.2	11 06.0	00 09.9
AUG 9	22 50.5	02S06.6	11 25.1	00 18.2
29	23 12.2	06 00.8	10 39.8	01 29.9
SEP 18	23 20.1	11 21.5	08 47.5	03 32.0
OCT 8	23 26.0	17 33.9	05 54.5	05 40.3
28	23 45.3	23 14.0	02 25.4	06 54.5
NOV 17	24 36.4	26 44.7	00S46.0	06 42.3
DEC 7	26 13.1	27 26.5	02 23.3	05 12.8
27	28N29.6	25S49.2	01S39.0	02S49.6

1958	Ceres 1	Pallas 2	Juno 3	Vesta 4
JAN 1	25 R 59.5	22 ♈ 44.8	08 R 17.7	11 ♈ 40.2
11	23 ♋ 44.5	24 36.8	07 D 53.3	14 14.4
21	21 22.9	27 11.6	08 ♊ 23.0	17 10.3
31	19 13.2	00 ♉ 23.5	09 43.3	20 24.3
FEB 10	17 31.3	04 06.6	11 46.7	23 52.9
20	16 27.3	08 16.4	14 25.6	27 33.5
MAR 2	16 D 06.2	12 48.9	17 34.0	01 ♉ 24.0
12	16 27.8	17 40.2	21 05.4	05 22.3
22	17 29.1	22 47.7	24 54.5	09 27.0
APR 1	19 05.9	28 08.5	28 57.3	13 36.7
11	21 13.3	03 ♊ 40.1	03 ♋ 10.6	17 50.3
21	23 46.6	09 20.5	07 31.9	22 06.8
MAY 1	26 42.0	15 07.5	11 58.8	26 25.4
11	29 55.5	20 59.4	16 29.4	00 ♊ 45.3
21	03 ♌ 24.5	26 54.5	21 02.8	05 06.1
31	07 06.3	02 ♋ 51.2	25 37.8	09 27.0
JUN 10	10 58.7	08 48.1	00 ♌ 13.3	13 47.5
20	15 00.2	14 44.1	04 48.7	18 07.2
30	19 09.1	20 38.0	09 23.5	22 25.4
JUL 10	23 24.3	26 28.8	13 57.0	26 41.5
20	27 44.7	02 ♌ 15.9	18 29.0	00 ♋ 55.2
30	02 ♍ 09.3	07 58.5	22 58.8	05 05.5
AUG 9	06 37.2	13 36.0	27 26.1	09 11.8
19	11 08.0	19 08.1	01 ♍ 50.8	13 13.2
29	15 40.6	24 34.2	06 12.1	17 08.4
SEP 8	20 14.5	29 53.9	10 29.7	20 56.3
18	24 49.2	05 ♍ 06.9	14 43.1	24 35.3
28	29 23.7	10 12.7	18 51.7	28 03.2
OCT 8	03 ♎ 57.5	15 10.8	22 54.7	01 ♌ 18.1
18	08 29.9	20 00.6	26 51.3	04 16.9
28	12 59.8	24 41.3	00 ♎ 40.5	06 56.2
NOV 7	17 26.6	29 12.0	04 21.2	09 12.0
17	21 49.1	03 ♎ 31.6	07 52.0	10 59.6
27	26 06.1	07 38.3	11 11.1	12 13.6
DEC 7	00 ♏ 16.5	11 30.7	14 16.7	12 49.1
17	04 18.6	15 06.2	17 06.5	12 R 41.2
27	08 10.7	18 22.0	19 37.8	11 47.6
JAN 6	11 ♏ 50.9	21 ♎ 14.9	21 ♎ 47.7	10 ♌ 10.3
JAN 1	29 N 05.9	25 S 09.4	01 S 07.7	02 S 08.0
21	31 13.7	21 50.7	01 N 49.0	00 N 52.9
FEB 10	32 23.8	17 55.7	05 21.3	04 07.1
MAR 2	32 33.4	13 49.9	08 43.7	07 23.5
22	32 01.9	09 51.4	11 31.2	10 32.8
APR 11	31 02.3	06 14.3	13 31.9	13 27.5
MAY 1	29 37.4	03 09.9	14 41.1	16 01.1
21	27 46.2	00 47.4	14 59.5	18 08.4
JUN 10	25 28.4	00 N 47.5	14 30.9	19 45.4
30	22 45.2	01 33.1	13 21.6	20 49.9
JUL 20	19 39.8	01 31.8	11 38.9	21 21.7
AUG 9	16 16.9	00 49.8	09 31.1	21 22.7
29	12 42.3	00 S 23.7	07 06.2	20 57.4
SEP 18	09 02.4	01 57.6	04 32.5	20 13.0
OCT 8	05 23.9	03 39.5	01 58.0	19 20.1
28	01 53.9	05 15.9	00 S 29.0	18 32.9
NOV 17	01 S 20.4	06 31.9	02 39.9	18 09.3
DEC 7	04 12.5	07 10.6	04 25.9	18 29.7
27	06 S 36.3	06 S 52.5	05 S 37.3	19 N 49.3

1959	Ceres 1	Pallas 2	Juno 3	Vesta 4
JAN 1	10 ♏ 02.4	19 ♎ 51.5	20 ♎ 45.6	11 R 04.2
11	13 35.8	22 31.4	22 43.6	09 ♌ 07.3
21	16 53.6	24 41.6	24 14.8	06 40.9
31	19 53.0	26 17.4	25 15.9	04 02.4
FEB 10	22 30.7	27 12.7	25 43.3	01 31.8
20	24 42.9	27 R 22.3	25 R 34.3	29 ♋ 27.9
MAR 2	26 25.9	26 42.2	24 48.2	28 03.6
12	27 35.3	25 11.3	23 26.5	27 25.0
22	28 07.3	22 54.1	21 34.7	27 D 33.0
APR 1	27 R 59.6	20 03.2	19 22.1	28 24.5
11	27 11.5	16 56.8	17 01.1	29 54.7
21	25 46.3	13 57.8	14 45.6	01 ♌ 58.6
MAY 1	23 52.0	11 25.8	12 47.9	04 31.1
11	21 40.5	09 34.9	11 17.2	07 27.8
21	19 27.4	08 31.9	10 18.8	10 45.0
31	17 28.0	08 D 16.8	09 54.4	14 19.4
JUN 10	15 54.4	08 46.1	10 D 03.0	18 08.5
20	14 55.0	09 54.9	10 42.3	22 10.3
30	14 33.1	11 37.3	11 48.8	26 22.7
JUL 10	14 D 48.4	13 48.4	13 19.3	00 ♍ 44.6
20	15 38.6	16 23.3	15 10.6	05 14.6
30	17 00.1	19 18.1	17 19.4	09 51.8
AUG 9	18 49.2	22 29.7	19 43.4	14 35.3
19	21 01.9	25 55.2	22 20.2	19 24.4
29	23 34.8	29 32.2	25 07.7	24 18.4
SEP 8	26 24.9	03 ♏ 19.0	28 04.4	29 16.9
18	29 29.6	07 13.9	01 ♏ 08.5	04 ♎ 19.1
28	02 ♐ 46.6	11 15.4	04 18.9	09 24.5
OCT 8	06 14.0	15 22.3	07 34.3	14 32.9
18	09 50.0	19 33.5	10 53.5	19 43.4
28	13 33.2	23 47.9	14 15.5	24 55.6
NOV 7	17 22.4	28 04.6	17 39.3	00 ♏ 08.9
17	21 16.3	02 ♐ 22.5	21 03.7	05 22.7
27	25 13.8	06 40.8	24 27.8	10 36.3
DEC 7	29 14.0	10 58.5	27 50.5	15 48.9
17	03 ♑ 15.8	15 14.5	01 ♐ 10.5	20 59.7
27	07 18.2	19 27.8	04 26.6	26 07.9
JAN 6	11 ♑ 20.6	23 ♐ 37.5	07 ♐ 37.6	01 ♐ 12.3
JAN 1	07 S 07.3	06 S 36.6	05 S 48.5	20 N 18.2
21	08 50.0	04 36.1	06 02.6	22 34.2
FEB 10	09 57.7	00 49.1	05 20.4	24 39.6
MAR 2	10 31.9	04 N 50.7	03 38.2	25 51.2
22	10 37.4	11 43.8	01 07.8	26 04.6
APR 11	10 23.7	18 08.1	01 N 34.8	25 32.1
MAY 1	10 05.6	22 18.7	03 41.4	24 22.0
21	10 02.8	23 47.5	04 42.5	22 37.3
JUN 10	10 32.6	23 11.7	04 37.1	20 19.8
30	11 40.8	21 19.4	03 39.6	17 31.9
JUL 20	13 21.2	18 46.4	02 06.5	14 17.3
AUG 9	15 22.3	15 55.9	00 11.6	10 41.2
29	17 32.3	13 03.3	01 S 54.6	06 49.7
SEP 18	19 40.7	10 19.8	04 03.5	02 49.7
OCT 8	21 38.5	07 54.6	06 07.7	01 S 11.1
28	23 18.2	05 55.6	08 00.7	05 04.2
NOV 17	24 33.9	04 29.2	09 36.9	08 40.9
DEC 7	25 21.7	03 40.8	10 51.1	11 52.7
27	25 S 39.7	03 N 34.0	11 S 39.3	14 S 31.8

1960	Ceres 1	Pallas 2	Juno 3	Vesta 4
JAN 1	09 ♑ 19.5	21 ♐ 33.2	06 ♐ 02.9	28 ♏ 40.7
11	13 21.3	25 40.6	09 10.6	03 ♐ 42.8
21	17 21.4	29 42.3	12 10.8	08 39.3
31	21 19.1	03 ♑ 37.4	15 01.7	13 29.1
FEB 10	25 13.0	07 23.9	17 41.3	18 10.4
20	29 02.3	11 00.5	20 07.4	22 41.4
MAR 1	02 ♒ 45.9	14 25.4	22 17.5	27 00.0
11	06 22.4	17 36.2	24 08.8	01 ♑ 03.6
21	09 50.4	20 30.6	25 38.3	04 49.5
31	13 08.7	23 05.8	26 42.6	08 14.1
APR 10	16 15.1	25 18.5	27 18.6	11 13.0
20	19 07.9	27 05.2	27 R 23.6	13 41.9
30	21 44.8	28 21.6	26 55.5	15 35.3
MAY 10	24 03.0	29 03.8	25 54.1	16 47.6
20	25 59.8	29 R 08.0	24 22.2	17 14.3
30	27 31.8	28 31.3	22 25.4	16 R 51.8
JUN 9	28 35.4	27 13.2	20 13.2	15 41.7
19	29 07.7	25 17.4	17 57.4	13 50.9
29	29 R 05.5	22 51.3	15 50.3	11 33.3
JUL 9	28 27.8	20 08.2	14 03.3	09 09.2
19	27 15.9	17 23.8	12 44.3	06 59.7
29	25 34.1	14 53.7	11 57.9	05 22.5
AUG 8	23 31.2	12 51.2	11 D 45.9	04 29.1
18	21 19.2	11 24.2	12 07.0	04 D 22.8
28	19 11.7	10 35.9	12 59.5	05 02.9
SEP 7	17 22.0	10 D 26.1	14 20.2	06 25.8
17	15 59.9	10 52.0	16 05.9	08 25.6
27	15 11.6	11 49.8	18 13.8	10 57.3
OCT 7	14 D 59.8	13 15.4	20 40.9	13 55.8
17	15 23.6	15 04.6	23 24.8	17 16.5
27	16 20.9	17 13.9	26 23.3	20 56.2
NOV 6	17 48.3	19 40.1	29 34.3	24 51.2
16	19 42.1	22 20.2	02 ♑ 56.2	28 58.9
26	21 59.0	25 11.9	06 27.4	03 ♒ 17.4
DEC 6	24 35.5	28 12.9	10 06.6	07 44.5
16	27 28.6	01 ♒ 21.3	13 52.5	12 18.6
26	00 ♓ 36.0	04 35.7	17 44.1	16 58.4
JAN 5	03 ♓ 55.0	07 ♒ 54.4	21 ♑ 40.3	21 ♒ 42.5
JAN 1	25 S 39.7	03 N 39.0	11 S 47.0	15 S 05.8
21	25 22.4	04 26.3	11 59.1	16 56.4
FEB 10	24 41.6	05 55.6	11 41.3	18 06.4
MAR 1	23 44.2	08 03.2	10 55.1	18 39.2
21	22 39.0	10 42.5	09 44.3	18 43.7
APR 10	21 37.1	13 43.6	08 15.6	18 34.6
30	20 50.9	16 50.9	06 40.8	18 31.8
MAY 20	20 34.0	19 40.4	05 17.4	18 58.2
JUN 9	21 00.1	21 39.0	04 26.9	20 09.1
29	22 18.3	22 10.1	04 25.5	21 55.5
JUL 19	24 23.1	20 52.5	05 14.1	23 42.8
AUG 8	26 43.6	17 58.6	06 38.9	25 04.5
28	28 29.7	14 09.6	08 21.6	25 57.1
SEP 17	29 06.1	10 11.1	10 06.4	26 22.4
OCT 7	28 32.6	06 35.8	11 41.4	26 17.5
27	27 07.4	03 41.0	12 57.7	25 37.7
NOV 16	25 06.8	01 33.4	13 48.6	24 19.6
DEC 6	22 40.5	00 13.3	14 09.6	22 23.1
26	19 S 54.2	00 S 22.0	13 S 58.1	19 S 51.5

1961	Ceres 1	Pallas 2	Juno 3	Vesta 4
JAN 1	02♓34.1	06♒34.5	20♑05.3	19♒48.4
11	05 59.2	09 55.1	24 03.7	24 34.6
21	09 33.0	13 17.9	28 05.3	29 23.6
31	13 13.8	16 41.8	02♒09.1	04♓14.3
FEB 10	17 00.2	20 05.4	06 14.2	09 05.9
20	20 51.0	23 27.9	10 19.9	13 57.8
MAR 2	24 44.9	26 48.0	14 25.2	18 49.2
12	28 40.9	00♓04.7	18 29.5	23 39.3
22	02♈38.2	03 17.0	22 31.8	28 27.8
APR 1	06 35.7	06 23.4	26 31.1	03♈13.8
11	10 32.6	09 22.9	00♓26.5	07 57.0
21	14 28.3	12 14.0	04 16.9	12 36.7
MAY 1	18 21.6	14 55.0	08 00.9	17 12.2
11	22 12.0	17 24.4	11 37.0	21 43.0
21	25 58.4	19 39.9	15 03.3	26 08.5
31	29 39.8	21 39.2	18 17.9	00♉27.6
JUN 10	03♉15.3	23 19.7	21 18.1	04 39.7
20	06 43.6	24 38.2	24 00.6	08 43.7
30	10 03.1	25 31.4	26 21.6	12 38.2
JUL 10	13 12.3	25 56.1	28 17.2	16 21.9
20	16 09.2	25R48.7	29 41.8	19 52.9
30	18 51.2	25 07.2	00♈30.2	23 08.9
AUG 9	21 15.8	23 50.8	00R37.6	26 07.5
19	23 19.6	22 01.7	00 01.0	28 45.4
29	24 59.0	19 46.0	28♓40.8	00♊58.7
SEP 8	26 10.0	17 13.4	26 42.9	02 43.4
18	26 48.3	14 36.8	24 20.9	03 54.3
28	26R50.6	12 10.4	21 55.4	04 27.0
OCT 8	26 14.7	10 06.2	19 46.6	04R17.2
18	25 00.9	08 33.4	18 13.3	03 22.9
28	23 14.3	07 36.9	17 27.8	01 46.4
NOV 7	21 04.3	07D17.8	17D34.5	29♉34.8
17	18 45.0	07 35.1	18 33.0	27 02.0
27	16 32.6	08 25.9	20 19.2	24 26.6
DEC 7	14 41.7	09 46.6	22 47.3	22 07.0
17	13 23.8	11 34.1	25 52.2	20 19.0
27	12 44.8	13 44.5	29 28.1	19 12.3
JAN 6	12D46.2	16♓14.8	03♈30.3	18D50.0
JAN 1	19S01.2	00S24.6	13S48.3	18S59.9
21	15 55.8	00 09.4	12 54.5	15 51.4
FEB 10	12 41.1	00N37.1	11 30.6	12 23.5
MAR 2	09 22.0	01 47.8	09 41.0	08 44.5
22	06 03.8	03 14.8	07 31.4	05 02.9
APR 11	02 51.7	04 49.7	05 09.2	01 26.5
MAY 1	00N09.0	06 23.5	02 43.0	01N57.4
21	02 53.8	07 46.1	00 23.1	05 02.5
JUN 10	05 18.0	08 45.1	01N37.9	07 42.9
30	07 17.8	09 04.9	03 03.5	09 54.2
JUL 20	08 50.3	08 26.0	03 32.5	11 32.9
AUG 9	09 53.4	06 28.5	02 39.1	12 37.1
29	10 26.8	03 05.7	00 04.2	13 06.9
SEP 18	10 32.3	01S15.4	03S54.6	13 04.5
OCT 8	10 15.6	05 34.3	07 58.7	12 35.4
28	09 47.9	08 55.8	10 39.9	11 49.7
NOV 17	09 28.9	10 58.9	11 25.6	11 06.0
DEC 7	09 41.0	11 49.3	10 29.6	10 49.8
27	10N36.7	11S41.7	08S18.1	11N19.5

1962	Ceres 1	Pallas 2	Juno 3	Vesta 4
JAN 1	12D40.4	14♓57.3	01♈26.2	18R55.5
11	13♉01.7	17 36.6	05 40.0	18D55.5
21	14 00.3	20 31.8	10 14.1	19♉37.6
31	15 32.3	23 40.8	15 04.9	20 57.0
FEB 10	17 33.3	27 01.7	20 10.1	22 49.1
20	19 59.3	00♈33.0	25 26.8	25 08.8
MAR 2	22 46.2	04 13.2	00♉52.8	27 51.4
12	25 51.0	08 01.3	06 26.3	00♊53.4
22	29 10.5	11 56.4	12 05.7	04 11.3
APR 1	02♊42.4	15 57.6	17 49.5	07 42.3
11	06 24.7	20 04.4	23 36.2	11 24.3
21	10 15.6	24 16.1	29 24.6	15 15.4
MAY 1	14 13.6	28 32.5	05♊13.7	19 13.9
11	18 17.7	02♉53.0	11 02.8	23 18.7
21	22 26.6	07 17.4	16 50.5	27 28.6
31	26 39.5	11 45.5	22 36.3	01♋42.7
JUN 10	00♋55.8	16 16.8	28 19.7	06 00.4
20	05 14.4	20 51.0	03♋59.8	10 20.7
30	09 35.0	25 28.0	09 36.0	14 43.4
JUL 10	13 56.9	00♊07.3	15 07.9	19 07.7
20	18 19.4	04 48.1	20 34.9	23 33.2
30	22 42.1	09 30.0	25 56.6	27 59.5
AUG 9	27 04.3	14 11.9	01♌12.4	02♌26.0
19	01♌25.3	18 52.7	06 21.7	06 52.1
29	05 44.4	23 30.7	11 24.2	11 17.5
SEP 8	10 00.6	28 03.6	16 19.0	15 41.4
18	14 13.1	02♋28.9	21 05.2	20 02.9
28	18 20.8	06 43.2	25 42.1	24 21.5
OCT 8	22 22.2	10 41.1	00♍08.6	28 36.0
18	26 15.7	14 16.9	04 23.3	02♍45.1
28	29 59.6	17 23.3	08 24.7	06 47.5
NOV 7	03♍31.3	19 50.8	12 10.7	10 41.4
17	06 48.2	21 28.4	15 39.1	14 24.6
27	09 47.1	22 04.6	18 47.3	17 54.6
DEC 7	12 24.1	21R30.5	21 31.8	21 08.3
17	14 34.9	19 44.9	23 48.8	24 02.0
27	16 14.7	16 58.4	25 34.5	26 31.4
JAN 6	17♍18.2	13♋39.6	26♍44.1	28♍30.9
JAN 1	10N57.3	11S32.5	07S36.3	11N34.4
21	12 41.7	10 33.5	04 24.2	12 58.9
FEB 10	14 50.6	09 07.8	00 46.8	14 50.6
MAR 2	17 10.3	07 26.8	02N57.4	16 53.4
22	19 28.5	05 40.8	06 31.9	18 53.0
APR 11	21 34.9	03 59.4	09 41.4	20 38.2
MAY 1	23 20.9	02 32.2	12 13.4	22 00.4
21	24 40.0	01 28.6	13 58.7	22 53.3
JUN 10	25 27.6	00 58.2	14 51.9	23 12.8
30	25 41.3	01 10.5	14 52.5	22 57.2
JUL 20	25 21.3	02 14.1	14 03.9	22 07.2
AUG 9	24 30.2	04 16.4	12 33.3	20 45.6
29	23 13.2	07 21.1	10 29.9	18 57.3
SEP 18	21 38.1	11 27.3	08 04.3	16 48.9
OCT 8	19 54.5	16 25.4	05 28.1	14 28.9
28	18 14.8	21 53.3	02 53.4	12 07.4
NOV 17	16 53.8	27 10.8	00 33.3	09 56.6
DEC 7	16 08.4	31 12.9	01S17.3	08 11.1
27	16N16.3	32S36.6	02S21.1	07N07.6

1963	Ceres 1	Pallas 2	Juno 3	Vesta 4
JAN 1	16♍51.3	15R20.6	26♍14.1	27♍35.2
11	17 35.0	12♋00.4	27 04.2	29 17.9
21	17R36.6	09 06.0	27R12.7	00♎22.9
31	16 54.1	07 06.5	26 37.3	00 44.1
FEB 10	15 30.3	06 15.7	25 19.7	00R18.0
20	13 33.4	06D32.1	23 25.6	29♍04.2
MAR 2	11 17.2	07 47.7	21 05.7	27 08.1
12	08 59.9	09 52.3	18 35.7	24 42.9
22	06 59.3	12 35.2	16 12.4	22 07.5
APR 1	05 29.7	15 47.9	14 10.6	19 43.7
11	04 39.8	19 22.8	12 40.9	17 51.2
21	04D32.4	23 14.8	11 48.3	16 42.0
MAY 1	05 06.3	27 19.8	11D34.0	16D21.6
11	06 18.0	01♌34.3	11 55.9	16 50.0
21	08 02.6	05 55.6	12 50.0	18 02.8
31	10 15.8	10 22.3	14 12.6	19 55.2
JUN 10	12 52.9	14 52.8	15 59.2	22 21.5
20	15 50.0	19 26.1	18 06.2	25 16.5
30	19 04.0	24 01.2	20 30.3	28 35.9
JUL 10	22 31.9	28 37.7	23 08.6	02♎15.7
20	26 11.4	03♍15.1	25 58.6	06 12.7
30	00♎00.8	07 53.2	28 58.6	10 24.6
AUG 9	03 58.0	12 31.3	02♎06.5	14 48.8
19	08 02.0	17 09.5	05 21.1	19 23.7
29	12 11.4	21 47.5	08 41.0	24 08.0
SEP 8	16 25.3	26 25.0	12 05.1	29 00.0
18	20 42.6	01♎01.7	15 32.3	03♏58.9
28	25 02.7	05 37.3	19 01.8	09 03.7
OCT 8	29 24.6	10 11.6	22 32.4	14 13.4
18	03♏47.7	14 44.2	26 03.6	19 27.4
28	08 11.1	19 14.3	29 34.1	24 44.9
NOV 7	12 34.1	23 41.5	03♏03.1	00♐05.0
17	16 56.0	28 05.1	06 29.7	05 27.5
27	21 15.9	02♏24.3	09 52.5	10 51.4
DEC 7	25 32.9	06 37.8	13 10.4	16 16.0
17	29 46.1	10 44.6	16 22.1	21 40.9
27	03♐54.5	14 43.2	19 26.0	27 05.3
JAN 6	07♐56.8	18♏31.8	22♏20.3	02♑28.4
JAN 1	16N28.5	32S24.1	02S27.5	07N00.6
21	18 00.1	29 12.0	02 06.0	07 16.0
FEB 10	20 26.8	22 54.0	00 21.1	08 48.4
MAR 2	22 56.7	15 11.2	02N33.9	11 23.3
22	24 19.8	07 41.7	05 47.4	14 01.0
APR 11	24 03.2	01 24.8	08 18.0	15 25.8
MAY 1	22 22.1	03N17.0	09 35.9	15 07.3
21	19 45.4	06 23.8	09 44.5	13 22.2
JUN 10	16 34.1	08 06.5	08 58.7	10 37.2
30	13 01.2	08 40.2	07 33.6	07 13.1
JUL 20	09 14.9	08 20.4	05 41.6	03 24.0
AUG 9	05 21.8	07 22.1	03 32.0	00S38.9
29	01 27.6	05 59.3	01 13.1	04 45.6
SEP 18	02S22.0	04 25.0	01S08.1	08 46.3
OCT 8	06 01.2	02 51.5	03 25.1	12 31.1
28	09 24.5	01 30.6	05 31.7	15 49.9
NOV 17	12 26.7	00 34.2	07 21.8	18 33.1
DEC 7	15 03.4	00 13.7	08 49.8	20 32.5
27	17S11.6	00N40.1	09S50.7	21S42.4

1964	Ceres 1	Pallas 2	Juno 3	Vesta 4
JAN 1	05♐56.4	16♏38.9	20♏54.4	29♐47.0
11	09 55.3	20 21.8	23 43.3	05♑09.4
21	13 46.1	23 51.5	26 19.6	10 29.5
31	17 27.3	27 05.3	28 41.0	15 46.6
FEB 10	20 57.3	00♐00.1	00♐44.9	21 00.0
20	24 13.9	02 31.9	02 28.4	26 08.9
MAR 1	27 14.9	04 36.3	03 48.2	01♒12.2
11	29 57.8	06 08.6	04 41.3	06 09.2
21	02♑19.4	07 03.0	05 04.4	10 58.7
31	04 16.6	07R14.4	04R55.3	15 39.4
APR 10	05 45.9	06 38.7	04 13.0	20 10.1
20	06 43.4	05 14.5	02 58.3	24 29.2
30	07 06.2	03 05.9	01 15.6	28 34.6
MAY 10	06R52.0	00 23.2	29♏12.0	02♓24.4
20	06 00.6	27♏23.3	26 58.0	05 55.7
30	04 35.2	24 27.3	24 45.8	09 05.3
JUN 9	02 42.6	21 54.5	22 46.7	11 49.6
19	00 33.7	19 59.3	21 10.5	14 03.9
29	28♐22.3	18 49.2	20 03.4	15 43.7
JUL 9	26 22.2	18D25.1	19 28.4	16 43.9
19	24 45.3	18 44.9	19D25.9	16R59.5
29	23 39.8	19 43.6	19 54.4	16 28.3
AUG 8	23 09.5	21 15.9	20 51.4	15 11.0
18	23D15.2	23 16.7	22 13.9	13 14.1
28	23 55.2	25 41.3	23 58.9	10 51.1
SEP 7	25 06.2	28 25.6	26 03.6	08 20.1
17	26 45.2	01♐26.5	28 25.4	06 01.7
27	28 48.4	04 40.7	01♐01.9	04 13.5
OCT 7	01♑12.4	08 06.0	03 51.0	03 06.2
17	03 54.4	11 40.4	06 51.1	02D45.0
27	06 51.5	15 21.9	10 00.4	03 09.1
NOV 6	10 01.6	19 09.2	13 17.5	04 15.0
16	13 22.7	23 00.7	16 41.1	05 58.1
26	16 52.7	26 55.2	20 10.0	08 12.7
DEC 6	20 30.2	00♑51.5	23 43.0	10 53.9
16	24 13.9	04 48.7	27 19.2	13 57.6
26	28 02.2	08 45.4	00♑57.3	17 19.5
JAN 5	01♒54.2	12♑40.8	04♑36.5	20♓56.6
JAN 1	17S39.1	00N55.2	10S01.2	21S51.9
21	19 10.8	02 33.2	10 22.5	21 58.1
FEB 10	20 16.2	05 15.5	10 09.2	21 17.1
MAR 1	21 01.4	09 01.5	09 20.7	19 57.0
21	21 35.6	13 39.6	07 59.5	18 08.8
APR 10	22 10.9	18 38.9	06 13.7	16 06.3
30	22 59.0	23 05.6	04 20.9	14 04.5
MAY 20	24 06.0	25 56.6	02 47.9	12 20.2
JUN 9	25 24.0	26 33.6	02 01.0	11 11.5
29	26 33.3	25 05.7	02 10.3	10 58.2
JUL 19	27 20.8	22 14.1	03 08.0	11 56.8
AUG 8	27 51.3	18 42.9	04 37.9	14 07.9
28	28 14.4	15 04.3	06 24.4	16 54.2
SEP 17	28 32.9	11 38.8	08 14.6	19 04.0
OCT 7	28 43.3	08 39.1	09 58.5	19 45.3
27	28 39.4	06 13.0	11 28.3	18 57.8
NOV 16	28 15.7	04 25.6	12 37.8	17 04.6
DEC 6	27 28.5	03 19.6	13 22.1	14 26.8
26	26S16.8	02N55.6	13S38.0	11S18.6

1965	Ceres 1	Pallas 2	Juno 3	Vesta 4
JAN 1	00♒21.1	11♑06.9	03♑08.7	19♓28.1
11	04 14.7	15 01.0	06 48.0	23 13.0
21	08 10.2	18 51.9	10 26.6	27 08.7
31	12 06.5	22 38.8	14 03.4	01♈13.3
FEB 10	16 02.8	26 20.3	17 37.4	05 25.1
20	19 58.0	29 55.3	21 07.3	09 42.3
MAR 2	23 51.2	03♒22.6	24 31.8	14 03.8
12	27 41.5	06 40.6	27 49.5	18 28.5
22	01♓27.7	09 47.6	00♒58.6	22 55.4
APR 1	05 09.1	12 42.1	03 57.6	27 23.6
11	08 44.3	15 21.7	06 44.1	01♉52.5
21	12 12.1	17 44.2	09 15.7	06 21.3
MAY 1	15 31.2	19 47.0	11 29.7	10 49.5
11	18 39.8	21 26.9	13 22.7	15 16.4
21	21 36.3	22 40.6	14 51.0	19 41.6
31	24 18.4	23 24.8	15 50.8	24 04.5
JUN 10	26 43.7	23R35.8	16 17.9	28 24.5
20	28 49.3	23 11.4	16R09.2	02♊41.0
30	00♈32.1	22 10.2	15 22.7	06 53.4
JUL 10	01 48.4	20 33.8	13 59.0	11 00.9
20	02 34.8	18 27.2	12 03.5	15 02.5
30	02R48.0	15 59.4	09 45.9	18 57.3
AUG 9	02 25.6	13 23.0	07 20.3	22 44.0
19	01 27.5	10 51.8	05 03.0	26 21.1
29	29♓56.4	08 38.6	03 08.7	29 46.7
SEP 8	27 59.4	06 53.5	01 49.2	02♋58.6
18	25 47.4	05 42.1	01 10.3	05 54.2
28	23 34.2	05 06.5	01D13.9	08 30.1
OCT 8	21 34.1	05D05.9	01 59.0	10 42.4
18	19 59.2	05 37.9	03 22.4	12 26.9
28	18 57.3	06 39.0	05 20.0	13 38.4
NOV 7	18 32.8	08 05.8	07 47.9	14 11.9
17	18D45.6	09 54.5	10 42.2	14R03.3
27	19 34.0	12 02.1	13 59.6	13 10.0
DEC 7	20 54.7	14 25.6	17 37.2	11 33.8
17	22 43.7	17 02.4	21 32.0	09 22.3
27	24 57.3	19 50.2	25 42.2	06 48.6
JAN 6	27♓32.1	22♒47.2	00♓06.0	04♋11.6
JAN 1	25S50.7	02N56.5	13S37.0	10S17.8
21	24 09.7	03 25.0	13 14.5	06 45.3
FEB 10	22 11.1	04 29.7	12 23.7	03 03.9
MAR 2	20 00.8	06 05.5	11 07.9	00N38.7
22	17 46.1	08 05.7	09 32.6	04 15.3
APR 11	15 34.9	10 22.0	07 45.2	07 39.3
MAY 1	13 35.9	12 43.8	05 55.5	10 44.9
21	11 58.3	14 56.9	04 16.7	13 27.0
JUN 10	10 52.2	16 41.3	03 06.3	15 41.6
30	10 27.9	17 30.0	02 46.1	17 26.1
JUL 20	10 54.5	16 54.3	03 35.7	18 39.5
AUG 9	12 14.5	14 40.6	05 35.1	19 23.1
29	14 13.8	11 08.5	08 13.7	19 40.9
SEP 18	16 14.1	07 04.9	10 46.9	19 39.9
OCT 8	17 24.9	03 16.9	12 43.4	19 30.7
28	17 17.6	00 12.8	13 50.0	19 27.6
NOV 17	15 56.9	01S57.4	14 03.5	19 45.7
DEC 7	13 42.9	03 14.5	13 25.3	20 33.3
27	10S54.1	03S44.2	11S59.4	21N41.6

1966	Ceres 1	Pallas 2	Juno 3	Vesta 4
JAN 1	26♓12.3	21♒17.7	27♒52.6	05R29.3
11	28 56.2	24 18.5	02♓22.3	02♋58.1
21	01♈56.4	27 25.8	07 03.1	00 51.2
31	05 10.4	00♓38.2	11 53.7	29♊21.8
FEB 10	08 35.7	03 54.3	16 53.0	28 36.8
20	12 10.3	07 12.9	22 00.0	28D36.7
MAR 2	15 52.7	10 33.0	27 13.9	29 19.5
12	19 41.2	13 53.3	02♈33.8	00♋40.3
22	23 34.6	17 13.1	07 59.2	02 34.2
APR 1	27 31.8	20 31.3	13 29.5	04 56.4
11	01♉31.8	23 46.8	19 03.8	07 42.3
21	05 33.7	26 58.8	24 41.8	10 48.1
MAY 1	09 36.7	00♈05.9	00♉22.9	14 10.8
11	13 40.0	03 07.1	06 06.6	17 47.5
21	17 43.1	06 01.0	11 52.2	21 36.1
31	21 45.0	08 46.0	17 39.1	25 34.9
JUN 10	25 45.1	11 20.2	23 26.6	29 42.3
20	29 42.7	13 41.6	29 14.3	03♌57.2
30	03♊36.9	15 47.4	05♊01.0	08 18.5
JUL 10	07 26.8	17 34.8	10 45.8	12 45.4
20	11 11.4	19 00.2	16 28.1	17 17.2
30	14 49.5	19 59.3	22 06.5	21 53.3
AUG 9	18 19.5	20 28.1	27 39.8	26 33.1
19	21 39.9	20R21.9	03♋06.6	01♍16.1
29	24 48.5	19 37.3	08 25.2	06 01.9
SEP 8	27 42.9	18 12.7	13 34.0	10 49.9
18	00♋20.2	16 09.9	18 30.7	15 39.9
28	02 36.9	13 36.0	23 12.5	20 31.1
OCT 8	04 29.1	10 44.0	27 36.8	25 23.0
18	05 52.2	07 50.6	01♌40.0	00♎15.3
28	06 41.7	05 14.1	05 17.7	05 07.0
NOV 7	06R53.4	03 09.6	08 25.4	09 57.5
17	06 24.5	01 47.1	10 57.0	14 46.0
27	05 15.1	01 11.1	12 46.6	19 31.2
DEC 7	03 29.8	01D21.2	13 48.5	24 12.3
17	01 18.6	02 14.8	13R57.5	28 47.7
27	28♊57.1	03 47.7	13 11.8	03♏15.8
JAN 6	26♊42.5	05♈55.2	11♌36.0	07♏34.9
JAN 1	10S08.1	03S45.1	11S31.0	21N59.2
21	06 53.5	03 26.2	09 13.7	23 03.2
FEB 10	03 28.5	02 37.9	06 24.2	23 54.3
MAR 2	00 00.2	01 29.0	03 12.1	24 35.2
22	03N25.2	00 08.1	00N11.8	25 04.7
APR 11	06 42.1	01N15.8	03 36.0	25 16.9
MAY 1	09 45.5	02 33.5	06 48.3	25 04.4
21	12 30.9	03 35.0	09 36.5	24 21.8
JUN 10	14 54.7	04 08.9	11 48.9	23 06.0
30	16 54.4	04 01.7	13 15.6	21 17.0
JUL 20	18 29.2	02 57.3	13 49.8	18 56.7
AUG 9	19 40.2	00 37.6	13 29.0	16 09.2
29	20 31.2	03S10.4	12 16.2	12 59.8
SEP 18	21 09.2	08 16.7	10 19.6	09 35.0
OCT 8	21 44.8	13 45.2	07 52.3	06 02.2
28	22 31.1	18 08.1	05 12.0	02 29.5
NOV 17	23 38.8	20 28.5	02 42.3	00S54.5
DEC 7	25 05.9	20 49.6	00 54.2	04 00.7
27	26N31.3	19S43.7	00N25.7	06S40.4

1967	Ceres 1	Pallas 2	Juno 3	Vesta 4
JAN 1	27R47.9	04♈47.4	12R29.6	05♏26.6
11	25♊43.1	07 10.6	10♌32.5	09 40.4
21	24 08.2	10 02.2	08 05.7	13 41.3
31	23 12.4	13 18.4	05 31.6	17 26.6
FEB 10	22D59.0	16 56.2	03 11.7	20 53.3
20	23 27.5	20 53.1	01 25.2	23 56.6
MAR 2	24 34.7	25 06.7	00 22.6	26 32.0
12	26 16.0	29 35.2	00D06.4	28 34.2
22	28 27.0	04♉17.4	00 34.4	29 57.4
APR 1	01♋03.1	09 11.6	01 42.0	00♐36.2
11	04 00.3	14 16.8	03 23.3	00R26.3
21	07 15.5	19 32.1	05 32.7	29♏27.1
MAY 1	10 45.4	24 56.4	08 04.7	27 44.6
11	14 27.8	00♊28.9	10 55.1	25 30.5
21	18 20.7	06 08.6	14 00.7	23 04.5
31	22 22.3	11 54.5	17 18.0	20 49.0
JUN 10	26 31.3	17 45.9	20 44.8	19 02.9
20	00♌46.4	23 41.4	24 19.2	18 00.0
30	05 06.6	29 39.9	27 59.4	17D45.6
JUL 10	09 31.1	05♋40.4	01♍44.3	18 19.5
20	13 59.1	11 41.7	05 32.7	19 38.0
30	18 29.7	17 42.3	09 23.5	21 35.9
AUG 9	23 02.5	23 41.0	13 16.1	24 07.5
19	27 36.7	29 36.3	17 09.7	27 07.7
29	02♍11.7	05♌27.1	21 03.4	00♐31.6
SEP 8	06 47.0	11 12.1	24 56.9	04 15.5
18	11 21.7	16 49.6	28 49.3	08 16.3
28	15 55.3	22 18.3	02♎40.0	12 31.0
OCT 8	20 26.9	27 37.1	06 28.2	16 57.3
18	24 55.5	02♍43.9	10 13.2	21 33.5
28	29 20.3	07 37.1	13 54.0	26 17.8
NOV 7	03♎40.0	12 14.8	17 29.7	01♑09.0
17	07 53.3	16 34.5	20 59.1	06 05.7
27	11 58.8	20 33.6	24 20.9	11 06.8
DEC 7	15 54.7	24 08.4	27 33.6	16 11.6
17	19 38.6	27 14.9	00♏35.3	21 19.0
27	23 08.4	29 48.5	03 24.2	26 28.1
JAN 6	26♎21.1	01♎43.3	05♏57.9	01♒38.4
JAN 1	26N49.4	19S17.7	00N35.2	07S15.2
21	27 45.4	17 06.9	02 23.4	09 11.0
FEB 10	28 22.7	14 29.0	05 33.3	10 25.4
MAR 2	28 51.7	11 39.5	08 54.9	10 56.5
22	29 13.0	08 50.7	11 34.0	10 47.5
APR 11	29 20.3	06 13.6	13 12.2	10 08.6
MAY 1	29 05.4	03 58.0	13 51.0	09 20.5
21	28 22.1	02 12.7	13 38.2	08 55.5
JUN 10	27 07.1	01 05.2	12 42.3	09 23.4
30	25 20.3	00 40.8	11 12.1	10 51.0
JUL 20	23 03.9	01 01.1	09 15.5	13 02.9
AUG 9	20 22.7	02 04.3	07 00.4	15 36.9
29	17 22.7	03 44.7	04 33.9	18 13.3
SEP 18	14 11.0	05 53.2	02 03.0	20 35.5
OCT 8	10 55.7	08 17.9	00S25.5	22 29.8
28	07 45.3	10 44.7	02 44.5	23 45.5
NOV 17	04 48.6	12 57.3	04 47.3	24 15.1
DEC 7	02 14.6	14 35.1	06 26.8	23 54.9
27	00N12.5	15S11.1	07S36.0	22S45.6

1968	Ceres 1	Pallas 2	Juno 3	Vesta 4
JAN 1	24♎47.1	00♎51.2	04♏43.2	29♑03.2
11	27 50.0	02 24.2	07 08.2	04♒13.7
21	00♏30.8	03 09.3	09 14.1	09 24.2
31	02 45.4	03R00.8	10 57.6	14 34.1
FEB 10	04 29.4	01 55.4	12 15.3	19 42.6
20	05 38.4	29♍55.8	13 04.1	24 49.1
MAR 1	06 08.4	27 11.5	13 20.8	29 53.2
11	05R56.5	24 00.8	13R03.1	04♓54.0
21	05 02.9	20 48.5	12 10.7	09 50.9
31	03 31.5	17 58.2	10 45.7	14 43.5
APR 10	01 31.5	15 48.2	08 53.4	19 30.8
20	29♎16.9	14 27.4	06 43.0	24 12.3
30	27 04.1	13 57.2	04 25.9	28 47.0
MAY 10	25 09.2	14D15.0	02 15.1	03♈14.1
20	23 44.2	15 14.8	00 21.9	07 32.5
30	22 55.9	16 50.3	28♎54.5	11 41.0
JUN 9	22D47.1	18 56.1	27 58.2	15 37.8
19	23 16.2	21 26.9	27 34.7	19 21.5
29	24 20.1	24 18.5	27D43.0	22 49.9
JUL 9	25 55.0	27 27.4	28 21.4	26 00.0
19	27 56.5	00♎50.5	29 26.6	28 49.2
29	00♏20.8	04 25.7	00♏55.6	01♉13.5
AUG 8	03 04.4	08 11.2	02 45.4	03 08.5
18	06 04.2	12 05.0	04 53.1	04 29.8
28	09 17.8	16 06.0	07 16.1	05 12.3
SEP 7	12 43.0	20 13.0	09 52.4	05R11.7
17	16 17.7	24 25.0	12 39.8	04 26.1
27	20 00.6	28 41.2	15 36.8	02 56.5
OCT 7	23 50.1	03♏00.5	18 41.7	00 50.3
17	27 45.1	07 22.3	21 53.2	28♈20.7
27	01♐44.6	11 45.8	25 10.1	25 45.7
NOV 6	05 47.3	16 10.1	28 31.2	23 25.1
16	09 52.5	20 34.4	01♐55.3	21 34.9
26	13 59.4	24 57.9	05 21.6	20 25.5
DEC 6	18 06.7	29 19.6	08 48.7	20D01.3
16	22 13.9	03♐38.6	12 15.7	20 21.1
26	26 20.0	07 53.8	15 41.4	21 21.6
JAN 5	00♑24.0	12♐03.8	19♐04.7	22♈58.1
JAN 1	00S12.1	15S06.5	07S47.9	22S21.1
21	01 23.5	13 32.2	08 10.1	20 17.4
FEB 10	01 47.7	09 23.0	07 48.2	17 39.5
MAR 1	01 24.3	02 25.9	06 39.1	14 37.4
21	00 23.0	05N49.9	04 46.4	11 21.6
APR 10	00N48.8	12 44.5	02 27.4	08 02.5
30	01 29.8	16 54.7	00 16.0	04 49.8
MAY 20	01 08.9	18 37.0	01N10.8	01 53.0
JUN 9	00S16.2	18 36.0	01 34.7	00N39.2
29	02 29.2	17 28.8	01 00.3	02 38.5
JUL 19	05 11.5	15 41.0	00S16.7	03 56.8
AUG 8	08 08.6	13 30.5	02 00.3	04 26.6
28	11 09.3	11 11.0	03 57.4	04 02.6
SEP 17	14 05.0	08 53.7	05 57.8	02 46.6
OCT 7	16 48.4	06 48.6	07 53.1	00 57.9
27	19 12.9	05 04.7	09 36.5	00S38.7
NOV 16	21 13.4	03 50.3	11 02.0	01 14.4
DEC 6	22 45.7	03 12.6	12 04.6	00 32.2
26	23S48.1	03N17.1	12S40.9	01N14.2

1969	Ceres 1	Pallas 2	Juno 3	Vesta 4
JAN 1	28♐46.7	10♐24.5	17♐43.8	22♈15.5
11	02♑49.0	14 30.9	21 05.0	24 10.9
21	06 47.8	18 30.1	24 21.8	26 33.8
31	10 41.8	22 20.3	27 32.6	29 20.0
FEB 10	14 30.0	25 59.8	00♑36.0	02♉25.2
20	18 11.2	29 26.5	03 30.2	05 46.2
MAR 2	21 43.9	02♑37.7	06 13.1	09 20.3
12	25 06.6	05 30.8	08 42.7	13 04.8
22	28 17.6	08 02.4	10 56.4	16 57.9
APR 1	01♒14.7	10 08.5	12 51.2	20 58.1
11	03 55.9	11 45.0	14 24.2	25 03.8
21	06 18.3	12 47.2	15 31.9	29 14.0
MAY 1	08 19.1	13 10.4	16 10.8	03♊27.6
11	09 55.1	12R51.0	16R17.9	07 43.8
21	11 02.7	11 47.0	15 50.9	12 02.1
31	11 38.6	10 00.1	14 49.4	16 21.5
JUN 10	11R40.3	07 37.6	13 16.0	20 41.6
20	11 06.3	04 51.6	11 16.3	25 02.0
30	09 57.5	01 59.4	09 00.6	29 21.9
JUL 10	08 18.6	29♐18.9	06 41.5	03♋40.9
20	06 17.5	27 05.3	04 32.3	07 58.6
30	04 06.3	25 28.8	02 45.4	12 14.3
AUG 9	01 58.5	24 33.5	01 29.1	16 27.3
19	00 07.0	24D19.5	00 48.2	20 36.9
29	28♑42.3	24 43.9	00D44.2	24 42.2
SEP 8	27 50.6	25 42.4	01 15.7	28 42.2
18	27D34.7	27 10.5	02 20.5	02♌35.6
28	27 54.3	29 03.8	03 55.2	06 20.8
OCT 8	28 47.1	01♑18.0	05 56.4	09 56.2
18	00♒10.2	03 50.0	08 20.9	13 19.4
28	01 59.9	06 36.5	11 05.8	16 27.6
NOV 7	04 12.6	09 35.0	14 08.3	19 17.8
17	06 45.3	12 43.3	17 26.4	21 45.9
27	09 34.9	15 59.4	20 57.9	23 47.2
DEC 7	12 38.8	19 21.6	24 41.0	25 16.9
17	15 54.9	22 48.5	28 34.5	26 09.2
27	19 21.0	26 18.4	02♒36.7	26R19.2
JAN 6	22♒55.3	29♑50.4	06♒46.6	25♌43.4
JAN 1	24S00.9	03N27.4	12S46.3	01N55.2
21	24 25.4	04 32.1	12 45.5	04 31.7
FEB 10	24 25.3	06 23.8	12 16.5	07 25.9
MAR 2	24 07.7	08 59.4	11 21.6	10 24.2
22	23 42.3	12 11.7	10 05.6	13 15.9
APR 11	23 21.4	15 47.4	08 35.9	15 52.5
MAY 1	23 19.1	19 23.7	07 03.2	18 07.0
21	23 50.0	22 25.7	05 42.8	19 53.8
JUN 10	25 05.0	24 10.7	04 53.7	21 09.2
30	27 01.8	24 04.7	04 53.8	21 51.0
JUL 20	29 13.7	22 05.9	05 48.1	21 59.3
AUG 9	30 56.4	18 46.8	07 23.0	21 36.3
29	31 40.0	14 52.9	09 15.7	20 46.7
SEP 18	31 26.6	11 02.1	11 05.7	19 37.6
OCT 8	30 32.8	07 38.1	12 38.4	18 19.0
28	29 11.0	04 53.3	13 44.6	17 03.9
NOV 17	27 26.5	02 52.7	14 18.2	16 09.0
DEC 7	25 21.3	01 37.4	14 15.5	15 54.7
27	22S57.0	01N05.6	13S35.3	16N41.6

1970	Ceres 1	Pallas 2	Juno 3	Vesta 4
JAN 1	21♒07.2	28♑04.2	04♒40.7	26 R07.1
11	24 45.2	01♒36.8	08 54.1	25♌08.0
21	28 29.1	05 09.5	13 13.7	23 25.2
31	02♓17.7	08 41.2	17 38.6	21 07.8
FEB 10	06 09.8	12 11.0	22 08.0	18 31.2
20	10 04.3	15 37.6	26 41.2	15 56.1
MAR 2	14 00.2	19 00.0	01♓17.5	13 42.4
12	17 56.5	22 17.1	05 56.6	12 05.2
22	21 52.4	25 27.6	10 37.6	11 13.4
APR 1	25 46.9	28 30.1	15 20.0	11 D09.0
11	29 39.2	01♓23.3	20 03.6	11 49.9
21	03♈28.4	04 05.3	24 47.6	13 12.0
MAY 1	07 13.5	06 34.5	29 31.5	15 09.7
11	10 53.6	08 48.6	04♈14.7	17 38.0
21	14 27.5	10 45.1	08 56.7	20 32.3
31	17 54.1	12 21.4	13 36.8	23 48.4
JUN 10	21 11.8	13 34.3	18 13.9	27 23.2
20	24 19.0	14 20.5	22 46.7	01♍13.7
30	27 13.8	14 37.0	27 14.6	05 17.5
JUL 10	29 53.8	14 R20.6	01♉35.6	09 33.1
20	02♉16.3	13 29.9	05 47.4	13 58.6
30	04 18.4	12 05.1	09 47.8	18 32.8
AUG 9	05 56.3	10 09.5	13 33.7	23 14.7
19	07 06.3	07 50.4	17 01.3	28 03.3
29	07 44.6	05 18.2	20 05.5	02♎57.7
SEP 8	07 R47.5	02 45.9	22 40.1	07 57.5
18	07 13.3	00 26.8	24 39.6	13 01.7
28	06 02.3	28♒31.6	25 56.6	18 09.9
OCT 8	04 18.7	27 07.9	26 23.9	23 21.5
18	02 11.7	26 19.4	25 R58.5	28 35.9
28	29♈54.4	26 D06.5	24 42.9	03♏52.5
NOV 7	27 42.0	26 27.7	22 47.7	09 11.0
17	25 49.4	27 20.0	20 33.7	14 30.3
27	24 27.5	28 40.0	18 26.5	19 50.1
DEC 7	23 43.1	00♓24.4	16 50.7	25 09.7
17	23 D38.3	02 29.8	16 03.8	00♐28.2
27	24 11.7	04 53.1	16 D12.4	05 45.0
JAN 6	25♈20.6	07♓31.8	17♉16.1	10♐59.0
JAN 1	22 S18.2	01 N04.0	13 S19.5	17 N04.4
21	19 33.9	01 21.0	11 54.3	19 15.6
FEB 10	16 38.1	02 10.9	09 57.3	21 55.1
MAR 2	13 35.9	03 27.2	07 33.9	23 56.0
22	10 32.6	05 02.5	04 51.1	24 40.1
APR 11	07 34.3	06 48.7	01 57.1	24 12.8
MAY 1	04 46.9	08 36.6	00 N59.2	22 51.6
21	02 16.1	10 15.6	03 47.9	20 48.4
JUN 10	00 07.7	11 31.9	06 18.2	18 10.1
30	01 N32.5	12 07.4	08 18.0	15 02.0
JUL 20	02 39.3	11 39.5	09 34.0	11 29.2
AUG 9	03 08.0	09 47.3	09 52.4	07 37.9
29	02 56.1	06 29.4	09 00.1	03 34.8
SEP 18	02 06.7	02 20.2	06 48.0	00 S32.7
OCT 8	00 55.2	01 S43.3	03 21.4	04 36.4
28	00 S06.6	04 57.1	00 S40.7	08 27.4
NOV 17	00 22.6	07 05.1	03 53.2	11 56.7
DEC 7	00 N24.5	08 10.3	04 51.8	14 55.7
27	02 N08.3	08 S22.6	03 S26.2	17 S16.8

1971	Ceres 1	Pallas 2	Juno 3	Vesta 4
JAN 1	24♈42.0	06♓10.7	16♉37.6	08♐22.4
11	26 07.1	08 56.2	18 06.9	13 34.7
21	28 01.4	11 53.7	20 21.5	18 43.0
31	00♉20.8	15 01.5	23 14.7	23 46.2
FEB 10	03 01.7	18 17.7	26 39.6	28 42.8
20	06 00.5	21 41.1	00♊29.0	03♑31.6
MAR 2	09 14.4	25 10.5	04 37.6	08 11.3
12	12 40.9	28 44.7	09 01.5	12 39.6
22	16 17.8	02♈22.8	13 36.8	16 54.8
APR 1	20 03.5	06 04.1	18 20.6	20 54.2
11	23 56.2	09 47.7	23 10.2	24 35.0
21	27 54.8	13 33.1	28 03.9	27 53.8
MAY 1	01♊58.2	17 19.6	03♋00.4	00♒46.3
11	06 05.3	21 06.5	07 58.1	03 07.9
21	10 15.4	24 53.3	12 55.9	04 53.7
31	14 27.7	28 39.3	17 53.4	05 57.9
JUN 10	18 41.5	02♉23.6	22 49.7	06 R16.1
20	22 56.3	06 05.6	27 44.2	05 46.0
30	27 11.4	09 44.2	02♌36.6	04 28.6
JUL 10	01♋26.1	13 18.1	07 26.3	02 32.4
20	05 39.9	16 46.0	12 13.2	00 11.8
30	09 52.1	20 05.8	16 56.9	27♑46.5
AUG 9	14 01.8	23 15.3	21 36.8	25 37.7
19	18 08.4	26 11.4	26 12.9	24 02.0
29	22 10.7	28 50.0	00♍44.8	23 10.0
SEP 8	26 07.6	01♊06.5	05 11.8	23 D05.2
18	29 57.9	02 54.9	09 33.5	23 45.8
28	03♌39.7	04 07.5	13 49.4	25 08.3
OCT 8	07 11.0	04 36.1	17 58.6	27 07.4
18	10 29.6	04 R12.8	22 00.4	29 37.5
28	13 32.6	02 51.7	25 53.6	02♒33.7
NOV 7	16 16.5	00 33.7	29 36.9	05 51.9
17	18 37.5	27♉30.1	03♎09.0	09 28.3
27	20 30.8	24 05.5	06 27.8	13 19.8
DEC 7	21 51.7	20 53.7	09 31.3	17 23.5
17	22 35.3	18 24.7	12 17.1	21 37.5
27	22 R37.1	16 59.3	14 42.1	25 59.8
JAN 6	21♌55.7	16 D45.0	16♎43.2	00♓28.7
JAN 1	02 N41.2	08 S18.7	02 S47.7	17 S45.5
21	05 12.0	07 41.0	00 N25.7	19 12.8
FEB 10	08 02.6	06 35.6	04 06.1	19 56.4
MAR 2	11 00.4	05 12.8	07 38.4	20 01.2
22	13 55.5	03 42.4	10 40.7	19 36.8
APR 11	16 39.6	02 13.7	13 00.0	18 58.2
MAY 1	19 05.6	00 56.4	14 29.3	18 24.8
21	21 07.9	00 00.1	15 06.9	18 20.2
JUN 10	22 42.2	00 N24.4	14 54.8	19 07.8
30	23 45.9	00 05.9	13 58.5	20 57.4
JUL 20	24 18.3	01 S08.0	12 25.1	23 23.4
AUG 9	24 21.5	03 30.0	10 22.8	25 29.2
29	24 00.1	07 10.9	08 00.5	26 36.8
SEP 18	23 21.6	12 13.3	05 26.8	26 47.0
OCT 8	22 37.1	18 20.7	02 50.7	26 11.4
28	22 01.0	24 40.9	00 21.1	24 56.6
NOV 17	21 51.3	29 43.2	01 S52.7	23 05.2
DEC 7	22 28.1	31 57.1	03 40.7	20 39.8
27	24 N06.7	30 S54.3	04 S52.2	17 S44.6

1972	Ceres 1	Pallas 2	Juno 3	Vesta 4
JAN 1	22 R21.8	16 R43.3	15♎45.9	28♒13.5
11	21♌19.1	17 D03.8	17 33.6	02♓45.1
21	19 37.9	18♉29.4	18 51.7	07 21.3
31	17 29.0	20 51.2	19 36.6	12 01.0
FEB 10	15 08.4	23 59.2	19 R45.2	16 43.0
20	12 54.5	27 44.9	19 15.3	21 26.6
MAR 1	11 04.7	02♊00.7	18 07.6	26 10.9
11	09 50.9	06 39.6	16 26.0	00♈55.1
21	09 19.3	11 36.7	14 18.5	05 38.7
31	09 D31.2	16 47.3	11 57.3	10 20.9
APR 10	10 23.6	22 07.4	09 36.3	15 01.2
20	11 52.6	27 34.5	07 29.1	19 39.2
30	13 53.3	03♋05.7	05 47.0	24 14.0
MAY 10	16 20.8	08 38.9	04 36.4	28 45.2
20	19 11.0	14 12.8	04 00.4	03♉12.3
30	22 20.2	19 46.0	03 D58.9	07 34.3
JUN 9	25 45.1	25 17.4	04 29.3	11 50.9
19	29 23.3	00♌46.4	05 28.6	16 01.0
29	03♍12.3	06 12.4	06 53.3	20 03.5
JUL 9	07 10.5	11 35.0	08 39.7	23 57.5
19	11 16.3	16 54.2	10 44.9	27 41.4
29	15 28.3	22 09.4	13 05.9	01♊13.5
AUG 8	19 45.5	27 20.8	15 40.3	04 31.9
18	24 06.9	02♍28.2	18 26.0	07 33.8
28	28 31.6	07 31.6	21 21.2	10 16.4
SEP 7	02♎58.8	12 30.8	24 24.3	12 36.1
17	07 27.9	17 25.8	27 34.0	14 28.5
27	11 57.9	22 16.2	00♏48.8	15 49.1
OCT 7	16 28.5	27 02.0	04 07.8	16 32.9
17	20 58.7	01♎42.6	07 30.0	16 R35.4
27	25 27.7	06 17.5	10 54.0	15 54.0
NOV 6	29 55.0	10 46.2	14 19.1	14 29.1
16	04♏19.6	15 07.8	17 44.2	12 26.3
26	08 40.5	19 21.1	21 08.2	09 57.9
DEC 6	12 56.8	23 25.1	24 30.1	07 20.7
16	17 07.3	27 17.9	27 48.5	04 54.1
26	21 10.6	00♏57.8	01♐02.2	02 55.2
JAN 5	25♏05.4	04♏22.2	04♐09.9	01♊35.0
JAN 1	24 N41.0	30 S11.9	05 S03.0	16 S56.8
21	27 23.1	26 07.8	05 12.4	13 33.0
FEB 10	29 56.6	20 52.8	04 20.2	09 54.4
MAR 1	31 17.2	15 17.5	02 23.3	06 08.7
21	31 07.2	09 56.1	00 N20.5	02 23.4
APR 10	29 48.2	05 11.4	03 07.2	01 N14.0
30	27 44.2	01 18.2	05 07.3	04 37.1
MAY 20	25 08.6	01 N35.2	05 57.1	07 40.1
JUN 9	22 08.1	03 26.6	05 41.4	10 18.0
29	18 47.4	04 19.3	04 36.4	12 26.9
JUL 19	15 10.9	04 20.8	02 58.0	14 04.7
AUG 8	11 23.6	03 41.4	00 58.9	15 10.7
28	07 30.8	02 32.6	01 S10.7	15 46.7
SEP 17	03 38.3	01 06.9	03 22.8	15 57.1
OCT 7	00 S07.9	00 S23.0	05 30.2	15 48.8
27	03 41.8	01 44.2	07 26.7	15 31.1
NOV 16	06 57.5	02 43.0	09 06.4	15 14.0
DEC 6	09 49.7	03 05.2	10 24.2	15 08.4
26	12 S14.2	02 S35.8	11 S15.9	15 N26.6

1973		Ceres 1	Pallas 2	Juno 3	Vesta 4
JAN	1	23♏32.6	03♏02.4	02♐55.6	02R01.9
	11	27 21.4	06 16.2	05 58.9	01♊08.1
	21	00♐58.7	09 09.5	08 53.3	00D59.3
	31	04 22.7	11 38.6	11 37.2	01 33.0
FEB	10	07 30.7	13 38.8	14 08.2	02 45.3
	20	10 20.0	15 04.8	16 24.0	04 31.3
MAR	2	12 47.6	15 51.3	18 22.1	06 45.7
	12	14 49.9	15R52.7	19 59.2	09 24.2
	22	16 23.1	15 05.5	21 12.4	12 22.8
APR	1	17 23.5	13 29.1	21 58.3	15 38.0
	11	17 47.6	11 08.7	22 14.0	19 07.2
	21	17R33.4	08 17.2	21R57.2	22 47.9
MAY	1	16 40.7	05 13.2	21 07.2	26 38.3
	11	15 12.9	02 18.3	19 45.3	00♋36.8
	21	13 17.8	29♎52.1	17 56.6	04 42.0
	31	11 07.1	28 07.2	15 48.8	08 52.8
JUN	10	08 55.3	27 09.7	13 33.2	13 08.6
	20	06 56.8	26D59.4	11 22.2	17 28.2
	30	05 23.3	27 32.5	09 27.2	21 51.3
JUL	10	04 22.8	28 44.4	07 57.5	26 17.1
	20	03 58.5	00♏29.2	06 58.8	00♌45.1
	30	04D10.4	02 41.8	06 33.5	05 14.9
AUG	9	04 56.7	05 17.8	06D41.8	09 46.1
	19	06 13.9	08 13.1	07 21.5	14 17.9
	29	07 58.3	11 24.5	08 30.2	18 50.2
SEP	8	10 06.5	14 49.4	10 04.7	23 22.3
	18	12 34.9	18 25.1	12 02.0	27 53.4
	28	15 20.8	22 10.1	14 19.2	02♍23.1
OCT	8	18 21.5	26 02.5	16 53.9	06 50.4
	18	21 34.6	00♐00.7	19 43.4	11 14.5
	28	24 58.3	04 03.6	22 46.0	15 34.3
NOV	7	28 30.8	08 10.0	25 59.9	19 48.2
	17	02♑10.6	12 18.7	29 23.2	23 54.8
	27	05 56.4	16 28.6	02♑54.9	27 52.4
DEC	7	09 46.9	20 38.9	06 33.5	01♎38.2
	17	13 41.0	24 48.3	10 17.7	05 09.6
	27	17 37.6	28 56.1	14 06.8	08 23.5
JAN	6	21♑35.7	03♑01.0	17♑59.5	11♎15.6
JAN	1	12S51.8	02S14.6	11S25.8	15N38.1
	21	14 37.6	00 15.7	11 39.3	16 37.0
FEB	10	15 54.7	03N06.0	11 22.1	18 00.4
MAR	2	16 47.5	07 52.2	10 35.4	19 35.1
	22	17 23.4	13 40.7	09 22.7	21 07.3
APR	11	17 51.7	19 31.2	07 51.1	22 25.3
MAY	1	18 20.2	23 57.4	06 13.3	23 19.9
	21	18 52.1	25 58.8	04 48.5	23 44.6
JUN	10	19 26.5	25 37.8	03 59.6	23 35.5
	30	20 05.9	23 37.0	04 01.6	22 51.3
JUL	20	20 56.6	20 42.0	04 53.0	21 33.1
AUG	9	22 00.8	17 25.6	06 19.0	19 44.2
	29	23 14.0	14 08.6	08 02.1	17 29.6
SEP	18	24 28.0	11 04.9	09 47.4	14 55.8
OCT	8	25 33.9	08 24.0	11 23.5	12 10.8
	28	26 23.5	06 13.1	12 42.0	09 23.8
NOV	17	26 50.8	04 38.0	13 36.2	06 45.6
DEC	7	26 51.6	03 42.4	14 01.7	04 28.0
	27	26S24.8	03N28.5	13S55.9	02N44.9

1974		Ceres 1	Pallas 2	Juno 3	Vesta 4
JAN	1	19♑36.5	00♑59.0	16♑02.7	09♎52.5
	11	23 35.0	05 02.1	19 56.9	12 32.1
	21	27 33.5	09 00.7	23 53.3	14 42.7
	31	01♒31.2	12 53.7	27 51.1	16 18.4
FEB	10	05 27.0	16 39.8	01♒49.4	17 13.9
	20	09 19.9	20 17.6	05 47.2	17R23.9
MAR	2	13 09.1	23 45.4	09 43.7	16 45.0
	12	16 53.2	27 01.6	13 37.9	15 19.1
	22	20 31.4	00♒04.4	17 28.9	13 14.1
APR	1	24 02.2	02 51.1	21 15.4	10 45.4
	11	27 24.3	05 19.4	24 56.3	08 14.4
	21	00♓36.2	07 26.4	28 30.2	06 02.1
MAY	1	03 35.9	09 08.4	01♓55.5	04 26.5
	11	06 21.4	10 22.0	05 10.2	03 37.4
	21	08 50.5	11 03.4	08 12.2	03D37.7
	31	11 00.1	11R08.9	10 58.5	04 25.8
JUN	10	12 47.3	10 36.2	13 26.3	05 57.0
	20	14 08.8	09 24.5	15 31.6	08 05.6
	30	15 00.9	07 36.2	17 09.8	10 46.5
JUL	10	15 20.5	05 18.3	18 16.3	13 54.4
	20	15R05.3	02 41.6	18 46.4	17 24.9
	30	14 14.3	00 00.6	18R35.5	21 14.8
AUG	9	12 50.3	27♑30.3	17 42.1	25 20.8
	19	10 58.9	25 23.2	16 07.6	29 40.4
	29	08 50.3	23 48.3	14 00.5	04♏11.7
SEP	8	06 37.8	22 50.0	11 35.0	08 52.8
	18	04 35.0	22 28.8	09 09.7	13 42.3
	28	02 54.5	22D42.9	07 04.8	18 39.2
OCT	8	01 45.1	23 29.0	05 36.7	23 41.9
	18	01 11.4	24 43.2	04 54.8	28 49.9
	28	01D14.7	26 22.0	05D03.1	04♐02.3
NOV	7	01 53.4	28 21.4	06 00.2	09 18.0
	17	03 04.7	00♒38.5	07 42.5	14 36.6
	27	04 45.0	03 10.2	10 05.2	19 57.2
DEC	7	06 50.5	05 54.1	13 02.7	25 19.1
	17	09 17.8	08 48.1	16 30.2	00♑41.8
	27	12 03.5	11 50.1	20 23.7	06 04.4
JAN	6	15♓04.8	14♒58.5	24♓39.0	11♑26.4
JAN	1	26S13.8	03N31.6	13S49.4	02N26.3
	21	25 14.6	04 09.7	13 03.8	01 47.3
FEB	10	23 54.5	05 26.9	11 48.5	02 15.2
MAR	2	22 19.8	07 18.5	10 07.6	03 53.6
	22	20 38.9	09 38.2	08 06.7	06 17.8
APR	11	19 01.3	12 17.0	05 53.3	08 24.0
MAY	1	17 37.4	15 02.2	03 35.9	09 06.0
	21	16 39.0	17 35.6	01 25.6	08 06.9
JUN	10	16 18.4	19 30.6	00N23.9	05 49.0
	30	16 47.3	20 14.5	01 34.3	02 40.4
JUL	20	18 11.1	19 19.6	01 41.9	00S57.8
AUG	9	20 19.1	16 44.4	00 21.3	04 49.9
	29	22 34.2	13 01.6	02S35.6	08 43.3
SEP	18	24 04.4	08 59.5	06 28.5	12 26.6
OCT	8	24 17.8	05 17.9	09 56.2	15 48.8
	28	23 17.6	02 18.4	11 58.7	18 39.4
NOV	17	21 23.4	00 08.9	12 24.2	20 49.2
DEC	7	18 52.8	01S10.6	11 25.7	22 10.8
	27	15S57.5	01S44.3	09S21.6	22S40.3

1975		Ceres 1	Pallas 2	Juno 3	Vesta 4
JAN	1	13♓32.4	13♒23.6	22♓28.8	08♑45.5
	11	16 40.5	16 34.6	26 53.9	14 07.0
	21	20 00.6	19 49.8	01♈36.4	19 26.9
	31	23 30.5	23 07.8	06 33.5	24 44.3
FEB	10	27 08.4	26 27.4	11 43.1	29 58.9
	20	00♈53.0	29 47.5	17 03.3	05♒09.7
MAR	2	04 42.6	03♓07.0	22 32.2	10 16.0
	12	08 36.2	06 24.8	28 08.4	15 17.1
	22	12 32.7	09 40.0	03♉50.4	20 12.1
APR	1	16 31.0	12 51.2	09 37.0	24 59.8
	11	20 30.3	15 57.6	15 27.0	29 39.6
	21	24 29.9	18 57.8	21 19.5	04♓09.8
MAY	1	28 28.8	21 50.4	27 13.0	08 29.3
	11	02♉26.4	24 34.1	03♊07.2	12 36.3
	21	06 21.8	27 07.0	09 00.9	16 28.8
	31	10 14.3	29 27.2	14 53.2	20 04.5
JUN	10	14 03.0	01♈32.3	20 43.5	23 20.5
	20	17 46.8	03 19.6	26 31.1	26 13.3
	30	21 24.8	04 46.2	02♋15.2	28 39.2
JUL	10	24 55.8	05 48.4	07 55.3	00♈33.3
	20	28 18.1	06 22.6	13 30.6	01 50.7
	30	01♊30.2	06R25.2	19 00.4	02 26.7
AUG	9	04 30.0	05 53.0	24 24.5	02R17.4
	19	07 14.8	04 44.4	29 41.6	01 21.4
	29	09 42.1	03 00.8	04♌51.2	29♓42.2
SEP	8	11 48.4	00 46.6	09 52.7	27 29.2
	18	13 29.6	28♓11.4	14 44.9	24 58.3
	28	14 41.8	25 28.7	19 26.7	22 29.3
OCT	8	15 20.5	22 53.3	23 56.8	20 21.0
	18	15R21.9	20 39.8	28 13.5	18 48.6
	28	14 44.1	18 58.5	02♍15.2	18 00.1
NOV	7	13 27.6	17 55.6	05 59.5	17D57.3
	17	11 37.8	17 33.5	09 23.5	18 38.4
	27	09 25.3	17D50.7	12 24.2	19 59.0
DEC	7	07 04.6	18 44.5	14 57.7	21 53.8
	17	04 52.8	20 11.4	16 59.7	24 18.0
	27	03 05.0	22 07.2	18 25.7	27 06.4
JAN	6	01♊51.7	24♓28.6	19♍11.1	00♈15.1
JAN	1	15S10.9	01S46.2	08S42.4	22S39.5
	21	11 55.7	01 31.4	05 40.9	22 04.9
FEB	10	08 31.5	00 45.9	02 11.9	20 45.1
MAR	2	05 04.0	00N22.2	01N28.7	18 49.2
	22	01 38.4	01 44.8	05 05.5	16 28.7
APR	11	01N40.0	03 13.1	08 23.8	13 56.4
MAY	1	04 46.2	04 38.1	11 10.2	11 25.9
	21	07 36.1	05 49.9	13 13.9	09 11.1
JUN	10	10 05.7	06 36.8	14 27.6	07 26.6
	30	12 12.3	06 44.4	14 48.2	06 28.1
JUL	20	13 54.3	05 55.1	14 17.2	06 31.4
AUG	9	15 11.6	03 49.8	13 00.3	07 46.8
	29	16 06.3	00 18.2	11 06.2	10 04.9
SEP	18	16 43.2	04S20.5	08 45.7	12 38.5
OCT	8	17 09.1	09 05.1	06 11.1	14 17.7
	28	17 31.6	12 45.6	03 35.7	14 23.9
NOV	17	17 55.8	14 50.8	01 14.3	13 05.6
DEC	7	18 24.0	15 27.9	00S36.3	10 47.6
	27	19N00.9	14S58.4	01S35.7	07S51.3

1976		Ceres 1	Pallas 2	Juno 3	Vesta 4
JAN	1	02R23.5	23♓14.9	18♍53.8	28♓38.4
	11	01♊30.2	25 47.7	19 17.3	01♈55.9
	21	01D18.2	28 41.0	18R55.7	05 28.5
	31	01 46.7	01♈52.3	17 48.8	09 13.4
FEB	10	02 52.8	05 19.4	16 01.5	13 08.4
	20	04 32.1	09 00.1	13 44.6	17 11.4
MAR	1	06 40.1	12 53.1	11 13.2	21 20.8
	11	09 12.7	16 57.1	08 45.2	25 35.3
	21	12 06.0	21 11.0	06 37.4	29 53.5
	31	15 16.6	25 33.8	05 01.4	04♉14.6
APR	10	18 42.0	00♉05.0	04 03.9	08 37.7
	20	22 19.4	04 44.0	03D46.0	13 01.8
	30	26 07.0	09 30.3	04 05.6	17 26.5
MAY	10	00♋03.3	14 23.5	04 59.3	21 51.0
	20	04 06.7	19 23.1	06 22.4	26 14.8
	30	08 16.1	24 29.2	08 10.4	00♊37.4
JUN	9	12 30.5	29 41.2	10 19.5	04 58.1
	19	16 49.0	04♊58.6	12 46.1	09 16.5
	29	21 10.9	10 21.2	15 27.2	13 32.1
JUL	9	25 35.4	15 48.4	18 20.4	17 44.0
	19	00♌01.9	21 19.6	21 23.3	21 51.6
	29	04 30.0	26 53.8	24 34.4	25 54.2
AUG	8	08 58.9	02♋30.0	27 52.1	29 50.4
	18	13 27.9	08 07.2	01♎15.0	03♋39.4
	28	17 56.7	13 43.8	04 42.2	07 19.6
SEP	7	22 24.3	19 17.6	08 12.5	10 49.1
	17	26 50.1	24 46.9	11 45.0	14 06.0
	27	01♍13.2	00♌09.2	15 18.8	17 07.6
OCT	7	05 32.5	05 21.4	18 53.2	19 50.8
	17	09 46.9	10 20.1	22 27.0	22 11.9
	27	13 55.1	15 01.0	25 59.7	24 06.5
NOV	6	17 55.4	19 19.7	29 30.0	25 29.6
	16	21 46.0	23 10.7	02♏57.0	26 16.3
	26	25 24.7	26 26.7	06 19.6	26R21.5
DEC	6	28 48.6	29 00.2	09 36.4	25 42.3
	16	01♎54.8	00♍43.3	12 46.1	24 19.0
	26	04 39.6	01 26.8	15 47.0	22 16.6
JAN	5	06♎58.7	01R03.9	18♏37.1	19♋47.6
JAN	1	19N12.4	14S43.1	01S39.9	07S03.0
	21	20 11.3	13 18.3	01 04.2	03 39.3
FEB	10	21 29.1	11 27.1	01N00.8	00 05.8
MAR	1	22 57.8	09 22.2	04 10.7	03N28.5
	21	24 26.0	07 14.4	07 23.3	06 56.0
APR	10	25 42.5	05 13.7	09 41.2	10 09.9
	30	26 37.7	03 29.8	10 45.9	13 04.1
MAY	20	27 04.3	02 11.6	10 45.1	15 33.5
JUN	9	26 58.1	01 27.8	09 53.9	17 34.3
	29	26 17.3	01 25.7	08 25.7	19 03.9
JUL	19	25 03.1	02 11.0	06 31.4	20 01.8
AUG	8	23 19.1	03 46.0	04 19.9	20 29.6
	28	21 11.1	06 09.5	01 58.9	20 31.4
SEP	17	18 46.4	09 15.9	00S24.7	20 14.7
OCT	7	16 14.2	12 54.9	02 44.4	19 50.1
	27	13 44.5	16 51.7	04 53.9	19 32.3
NOV	16	11 29.1	20 45.4	06 47.0	19 39.2
DEC	6	09 40.7	24 05.7	08 18.0	20 26.3
	26	08N32.8	26S05.8	09S21.5	21N54.0

1977		Ceres 1	Pallas 2	Juno 3	Vesta 4
JAN	1	06♎06.4	01R21.2	17♏30.5	20R49.4
	11	08 08.1	00♍17.4	20 13.3	18♋12.4
	21	09 36.6	28♌08.6	22 42.1	15 37.8
	31	10 27.2	25 09.8	24 54.1	13 24.9
FEB	10	10R36.2	21 47.5	26 46.8	11 47.9
	20	10 01.7	18 33.0	28 16.9	10 54.4
MAR	2	08 45.5	15 54.6	29 21.2	10D47.0
	12	06 55.0	14 08.8	29 56.6	11 23.2
	22	04 42.7	13 21.0	00R00.3	12 38.8
APR	1	02 25.7	13D28.7	29♏30.6	14 28.9
	11	00 21.7	14 24.6	28 28.0	16 48.3
	21	28♍44.9	16 00.8	26 54.9	19 32.6
MAY	1	27 45.4	18 10.4	24 57.9	22 38.0
	11	27D26.7	20 46.6	22 46.4	26 00.8
	21	27 48.5	23 44.2	20 31.8	29 38.7
	31	28 47.9	26 59.1	18 26.5	03♌29.2
JUN	10	00♎20.4	00♍27.9	16 40.9	07 30.4
	20	02 21.8	04 08.2	15 22.3	11 41.0
	30	04 47.7	07 57.7	14 35.1	15 59.6
JUL	10	07 34.1	11 54.8	14D20.4	20 25.2
	20	10 37.8	15 58.3	14 37.2	24 57.0
	30	13 56.1	20 07.2	15 23.5	29 34.2
AUG	9	17 26.3	24 20.4	16 36.1	04♍16.0
	19	21 06.8	28 37.3	18 12.1	09 02.2
	29	24 55.7	02♎57.3	20 08.8	13 52.0
SEP	8	28 51.5	07 19.7	22 23.0	18 45.0
	18	02♏53.1	11 44.2	24 52.8	23 40.7
	28	06 59.4	16 09.9	27 35.7	28 38.7
OCT	8	11 09.4	20 36.6	00♐29.9	03♎38.3
	18	15 22.3	25 03.7	03 33.9	08 39.2
	28	19 37.1	29 30.3	06 45.9	13 40.7
NOV	7	23 53.0	03♏56.0	10 04.8	18 42.2
	17	28 09.3	08 20.1	13 29.2	23 42.9
	27	02♐25.1	12 41.6	16 58.0	28 41.9
DEC	7	06 39.6	16 59.6	20 30.1	03♏38.4
	17	10 52.1	21 13.0	24 04.6	08 31.5
	27	15 01.3	25 20.5	27 40.1	13 19.6
JAN	6	19♐06.5	29♏20.8	01♑15.7	18♏01.4
JAN	1	08N22.4	26S16.3	09S34.4	22N24.9
	21	08 26.4	24 48.0	09 55.3	24 03.1
FEB	10	09 32.7	19 34.0	09 39.7	25 13.0
MAR	2	11 27.6	11 21.9	08 46.7	25 50.2
	22	13 26.8	02 43.5	07 18.8	26 01.2
APR	11	14 29.2	04N14.6	05 25.5	25 47.6
MAY	1	14 02.0	08 55.2	03 27.8	25 06.5
	21	12 14.7	11 33.2	01 55.6	23 54.6
JUN	10	09 33.3	12 36.2	01 14.4	22 10.3
	30	06 19.7	12 29.7	01 30.8	19 54.1
JUL	20	02 48.7	11 34.5	02 34.0	17 08.8
AUG	9	00S49.9	10 07.4	04 07.7	13 58.7
	29	04 28.6	08 22.5	05 56.7	10 29.3
SEP	18	08 00.8	06 32.2	07 49.0	06 47.3
OCT	8	11 20.4	04 47.7	09 35.0	03 00.0
	28	14 21.8	03 19.8	11 07.4	00S44.4
NOV	17	16 59.8	02 18.5	12 19.8	04 17.6
DEC	7	19 10.6	01 53.4	13 07.5	07 30.9
	27	20S51.7	02N12.6	13S27.4	10S16.3

1978		Ceres 1	Pallas 2	Juno 3	Vesta 4
JAN	1	17♐04.4	27♏21.6	29♐27.9	15♏41.4
	11	21 07.2	01♐17.7	03♑03.3	20 19.5
	21	25 04.1	05 03.7	06 37.2	24 48.9
	31	28 54.0	08 37.8	10 08.4	29 07.4
FEB	10	02♑35.6	11 57.5	13 35.8	03♐12.6
	20	06 07.2	14 59.6	16 58.0	07 01.2
MAR	2	09 27.0	17 40.9	20 13.5	10 30.4
	12	12 33.1	19 57.5	23 21.0	13 35.9
	22	15 23.1	21 44.4	26 18.3	16 12.6
APR	1	17 54.4	22 57.1	29 03.5	18 15.5
	11	20 04.1	23 30.0	01♒34.3	19 38.9
	21	21 48.7	23R18.7	03 47.7	20 17.3
MAY	1	23 05.0	22 20.8	05 40.9	20R07.2
	11	23 49.3	20 36.9	07 10.1	19 07.7
	21	23R58.9	18 13.7	08 11.7	17 25.1
	31	23 32.2	15 24.5	08 41.9	15 12.2
JUN	10	22 29.5	12 27.2	08R37.2	12 47.8
	20	20 55.1	09 42.0	07 55.7	10 34.4
	30	18 56.9	07 25.4	06 38.1	08 50.8
JUL	10	16 46.2	05 48.3	04 48.1	07 49.7
	20	14 37.1	04 55.7	02 34.8	07D37.0
	30	12 42.6	04D46.7	00 11.1	08 12.1
AUG	9	11 13.7	05 18.3	27♑52.1	09 30.9
	19	10 17.5	06 25.6	25 52.8	11 28.8
	29	09 56.7	08 03.5	24 24.5	13 59.8
SEP	8	10D11.6	10 07.4	23 34.2	16 59.1
	18	11 00.1	12 32.9	23D25.1	20 21.7
	28	12 18.8	15 16.2	23 56.0	24 03.9
OCT	8	14 04.7	18 14.5	25 04.7	28 02.6
	18	16 14.0	21 25.0	26 47.5	02♑15.1
	28	18 43.3	24 45.3	29 00.5	06 38.6
NOV	7	21 30.1	28 13.7	01♒40.2	11 11.8
	17	24 31.5	01♑48.3	04 42.9	15 52.8
	27	27 45.2	05 27.6	08 05.8	20 40.1
DEC	7	01♒09.3	09 10.5	11 46.4	25 32.5
	17	04 42.0	12 55.5	15 42.3	00♒29.0
	27	08 21.7	16 41.5	19 51.6	05 28.5
JAN	6	12♒07.1	20♑27.5	24♒12.8	10♒30.3
JAN	1	21S12.3	02N25.1	13S27.8	10S52.5
	21	22 16.6	03 48.5	13 11.2	12 54.2
FEB	10	22 55.4	06 06.7	12 26.4	14 17.3
MAR	2	23 15.4	09 18.0	11 16.6	15 03.1
	22	23 26.9	13 13.4	09 47.0	15 18.0
APR	11	23 42.5	17 32.6	08 05.1	15 14.4
MAY	1	24 16.8	21 39.2	06 21.1	15 09.3
	21	25 21.7	24 42.6	04 48.5	15 20.2
JUN	10	26 59.0	25 55.7	03 45.6	15 58.0
	30	28 49.8	25 02.8	03 33.6	17 04.5
JUL	20	30 19.8	22 28.5	04 28.1	18 35.4
AUG	9	31 07.1	18 57.0	06 23.2	20 20.6
	29	31 15.8	15 08.6	08 47.8	22 05.9
SEP	18	30 59.9	11 30.8	11 05.2	23 36.4
OCT	8	30 26.9	08 20.2	12 51.5	24 39.0
	28	29 37.2	05 45.9	13 55.4	25 03.6
NOV	17	28 28.4	03 52.8	14 12.9	24 44.0
DEC	7	26 58.5	02 42.6	13 43.6	23 38.3
	27	25S07.2	02N14.9	12S29.3	21S48.6

1979		Ceres 1	Pallas 2	Juno 3	Vesta 4
JAN	1	10♒13.8	18♑34.6	22♒00.8	07♒59.2
	11	14 01.4	22 20.1	26 27.4	13 01.6
	21	17 52.8	26 03.9	01♓03.7	18 04.9
	31	21 46.8	29 44.9	05 48.8	23 08.5
FEB	10	25 42.4	03♒22.1	10 41.4	28 11.7
	20	29 38.5	06 54.2	15 40.9	03♓13.5
MAR	2	03♓34.4	10 20.3	20 46.6	08 13.7
	12	07 28.9	13 38.8	25 57.7	13 11.5
	22	11 21.2	16 48.4	01♈13.4	18 06.3
APR	1	15 10.4	19 47.7	06 33.6	22 57.6
	11	18 55.5	22 34.7	11 57.7	27 44.6
	21	22 35.5	25 07.7	17 25.0	02♈26.8
MAY	1	26 09.2	27 24.2	22 55.1	07 03.6
	11	29 35.4	29 21.6	28 27.6	11 34.0
	21	02♈52.7	00♓57.2	04♉02.2	15 57.2
	31	05 59.5	02 07.7	09 38.2	20 12.4
JUN	10	08 53.7	02 49.6	15 14.7	24 18.1
	20	11 33.3	02R59.9	20 51.4	28 13.2
	30	13 55.6	02 36.0	26 27.7	01♉55.9
JUL	10	15 57.7	01 36.6	02♊02.3	05 24.0
	20	17 36.2	00 03.1	07 34.4	08 35.4
	30	18 47.4	27♒59.9	13 02.7	11 26.9
AUG	9	19 27.7	25 35.6	18 25.9	13 55.0
	19	19R33.9	23 01.8	23 42.4	15 55.8
	29	19 03.6	20 31.7	28 49.9	17 24.4
SEP	8	17 57.3	18 18.5	03♋46.3	18 16.1
	18	16 18.8	16 31.7	08 29.3	18R26.4
	28	14 15.9	15 17.6	12 54.9	17 52.2
OCT	8	12 01.0	14 38.8	16 59.4	16 33.8
	18	09 48.5	14D34.9	20 38.3	14 36.3
	28	07 52.7	15 03.6	23 46.0	12 10.9
NOV	7	06 25.4	16 02.0	26 16.3	09 34.8
	17	05 33.3	17 26.3	28 02.5	07 07.2
	27	05D19.5	19 13.3	28 57.6	05 05.5
DEC	7	05 43.6	21 19.6	28R57.6	03 42.1
	17	06 42.7	23 42.4	28 01.6	03 02.6
	27	08 13.6	26 19.2	26 16.1	03D07.9
JAN	6	10♈12.0	29♒07.6	23♋56.6	03♉54.9

1979		Ceres 1	Pallas 2	Juno 3	Vesta 4
JAN	1	24S36.2	02N14.4	12S04.1	21S15.0
	21	22 21.1	02 36.3	10 00.0	18 38.8
FEB	10	19 51.4	03 33.0	07 23.3	15 34.7
MAR	2	17 12.5	04 58.6	04 22.4	12 12.4
	22	14 31.0	06 46.2	01 07.0	08 41.5
APR	11	11 53.4	08 47.8	02N12.4	05 11.2
MAY	1	09 27.0	10 53.7	05 24.6	01 50.2
	21	07 19.0	12 51.8	08 17.9	01N13.7
JUN	10	05 37.3	14 25.6	10 40.5	03 53.3
	30	04 29.8	15 12.8	12 21.8	06 02.3
JUL	20	04 04.3	14 46.7	13 12.9	07 34.9
AUG	9	04 27.0	12 48.0	13 08.7	08 26.7
	29	05 37.2	09 25.1	12 09.3	08 34.6
SEP	18	07 18.9	05 20.1	10 20.3	07 58.6
OCT	8	08 54.6	01 25.5	07 53.8	06 46.6
	28	09 39.2	01S43.8	05 08.4	05 22.6
NOV	17	09 09.8	03 55.0	02 31.9	04 26.4
DEC	7	07 33.2	05 09.4	00 43.2	04 30.7
	27	05S08.8	05S34.3	00N28.5	05N39.1

1980		Ceres 1	Pallas 2	Juno 3	Vesta 4
JAN	1	09♈09.6	27♒42.1	25R09.4	03♉26.5
	11	11 20.3	00♓35.5	22♋40.7	04 32.6
	21	13 52.9	03 37.8	20 12.6	06 13.4
	31	16 44.0	06 47.2	18 09.0	08 23.8
FEB	10	19 50.5	10 02.2	16 45.8	10 58.9
	20	23 10.0	13 21.7	16 10.0	13 54.6
MAR	1	26 40.3	16 44.5	16D22.9	17 07.5
	11	00♉19.4	20 09.5	17 20.2	20 34.4
	21	04 05.8	23 35.8	18 55.8	24 12.9
	31	07 58.0	27 02.5	21 03.2	28 00.8
APR	10	11 54.8	00♈28.6	23 36.5	01♊56.5
	20	15 55.4	03 53.3	26 31.0	05 58.5
	30	19 58.7	07 15.7	29 42.3	10 05.6
MAY	10	24 03.8	10 34.9	03♌06.6	14 16.8
	20	28 10.3	13 49.8	06 41.4	18 31.4
	30	02♊17.1	16 59.2	10 24.4	22 48.3
JUN	9	06 23.7	20 01.8	14 13.8	27 07.1
	19	10 29.7	22 56.0	18 07.9	01♋27.4
	29	14 34.0	25 39.8	22 05.7	05 48.3
JUL	9	18 36.1	28 10.9	26 06.0	10 09.4
	19	22 35.2	00♉26.4	00♍08.2	14 30.4
	29	26 30.3	02 23.0	04 11.3	18 50.5
AUG	8	00♋20.5	03 56.6	08 14.7	23 09.4
	18	04 04.5	05 02.2	12 17.9	27 26.3
	28	07 40.8	05 34.5	16 20.2	01♌40.5
SEP	7	11 07.9	05R28.2	20 21.1	05 51.3
	17	14 23.5	04 38.2	24 20.0	09 57.6
	27	17 25.1	03 02.8	28 16.2	13 58.1
OCT	7	20 09.9	00 44.3	02♎09.1	17 51.7
	17	22 34.2	27♈52.5	05 57.8	21 36.6
	27	24 34.0	24 44.7	09 41.3	25 10.5
NOV	6	26 04.7	21 42.6	13 18.8	28 31.2
	16	27 01.4	19 08.1	16 48.9	01♍35.4
	26	27 19.8	17 18.2	20 10.3	04 19.6
DEC	6	26R56.8	16 21.1	23 21.3	06 39.6
	16	25 51.8	16D19.3	26 20.1	08 30.0
	26	24 09.6	17 10.1	29 04.5	09 45.6
JAN	5	21♋59.9	18♈48.4	01♏32.0	10♍21.1

1980		Ceres 1	Pallas 2	Juno 3	Vesta 4
JAN	1	04S27.4	05S33.8	00N43.5	06N04.5
	21	01 27.5	05 09.5	02 52.8	08 09.5
FEB	10	01N46.5	04 16.5	06 09.2	10 37.9
MAR	1	05 05.2	03 04.0	09 24.8	13 13.7
	21	08 20.8	01 41.4	11 58.5	15 44.7
APR	10	11 26.9	00 17.7	13 37.1	18 00.8
	30	14 17.6	00N57.6	14 20.6	19 54.6
MAY	20	16 48.2	01 54.6	14 14.0	21 20.0
JUN	9	18 54.8	02 22.3	13 24.1	22 13.1
	29	20 35.1	02 07.8	11 58.6	22 31.9
JUL	19	21 48.1	00 56.5	10 05.2	22 16.6
AUG	8	22 35.6	01S28.0	07 51.5	21 29.7
	28	23 01.7	05 19.7	05 24.9	20 15.9
SEP	17	23 14.1	10 37.2	02 52.7	18 42.0
OCT	7	23 24.4	16 41.4	00 22.1	16 57.2
	27	23 47.9	22 05.0	01S59.7	15 13.2
NOV	16	24 42.5	25 17.7	04 05.4	13 44.5
DEC	6	26 20.8	25 52.1	05 47.4	12 49.2
	26	28N35.0	24S21.8	06S58.2	12N48.3

1981		Ceres 1	Pallas 2	Juno 3	Vesta 4
JAN	1	22R54.2	18♈03.7	00♏35.2	10♍12.1
	11	20♋35.2	20 07.9	02 51.2	10R20.8
	21	18 15.2	22 50.5	04 45.5	09 42.9
	31	16 11.8	26 06.0	06 15.0	08 18.8
FEB	10	14 39.4	29 50.1	07 16.1	06 14.6
	20	13 47.1	03♉58.6	07 45.4	03 44.4
MAR	2	13D37.7	08 28.0	07R40.6	01 07.0
	12	14 10.6	13 15.5	07 00.3	28♌43.5
	22	15 22.2	18 18.4	05 45.6	26 52.5
APR	1	17 07.8	23 34.5	04 01.0	25 44.7
	11	19 22.8	29 01.9	01 54.4	25D25.0
	21	22 02.7	04♊38.4	29♎37.3	25 52.8
MAY	1	25 03.3	10 22.5	27 22.2	27 03.8
	11	28 21.6	16 12.6	25 21.5	28 53.2
	21	01♌54.5	22 06.8	23 45.1	01♍15.6
	31	05 39.6	28 03.9	22 38.6	04 05.8
JUN	10	09 35.0	04♋02.5	22 05.0	07 19.7
	20	13 39.0	10 01.2	22D04.1	10 53.7
	30	17 50.1	15 58.8	22 33.9	14 44.5
JUL	10	22 07.3	21 54.3	23 31.6	18 49.9
	20	26 29.3	27 46.6	24 54.1	23 07.6
	30	00♍55.5	03♌35.0	26 38.1	27 36.0
AUG	9	05 24.9	09 18.6	28 40.8	02♎13.7
	19	09 56.8	14 56.7	00♏59.5	06 59.4
	29	14 30.7	20 28.8	03 31.8	11 52.1
SEP	8	19 05.7	25 54.3	06 15.8	16 51.1
	18	23 41.1	01♍12.4	09 09.5	21 55.3
	28	28 16.5	06 22.8	12 11.5	27 04.2
OCT	8	02♎51.0	11 24.7	15 20.4	02♏17.2
	18	07 23.8	16 17.2	18 34.8	07 33.5
	28	11 54.3	20 59.6	21 53.7	12 52.5
NOV	7	16 21.3	25 30.6	25 15.9	18 13.8
	17	20 43.7	29 48.9	28 40.3	23 36.4
	27	25 00.7	03♎52.8	02♐05.8	29 00.1
DEC	7	29 10.6	07 40.1	05 31.5	04♐24.0
	17	03♏11.9	11 08.3	08 56.0	09 47.3
	27	07 03.0	14 14.1	12 18.5	15 09.6
JAN	6	10♏41.6	16♎53.5	15♐37.5	20♐30.0

1981		Ceres 1	Pallas 2	Juno 3	Vesta 4
JAN	1	29N16.8	23S37.8	07S12.2	13N01.6
	21	31 14.7	20 35.2	07 31.1	14 36.1
FEB	10	32 15.3	17 00.8	07 02.2	17 14.0
MAR	2	32 21.6	13 16.5	05 42.4	19 57.1
	22	31 52.4	09 38.0	03 37.0	21 33.8
APR	11	30 57.9	06 18.2	01 09.0	21 37.8
MAY	1	29 38.9	03 27.9	01N02.1	20 24.3
	21	27 53.6	01 16.1	02 20.0	18 14.7
JUN	10	25 40.9	00N11.2	02 32.6	15 24.1
	30	23 02.1	00 51.3	01 48.8	12 02.2
JUL	20	20 00.4	00 45.6	00 25.2	08 17.0
AUG	9	16 40.3	00S00.7	01S22.8	04 15.8
	29	13 07.8	01 19.2	03 23.2	00 06.5
SEP	18	09 29.4	02 59.3	05 26.2	04S02.7
OCT	8	05 52.0	04 48.7	07 24.1	08 03.0
	28	02 22.8	06 33.6	09 10.0	11 45.0
NOV	17	00S50.9	07 58.9	10 38.2	14 59.4
DEC	7	03 42.3	08 46.8	11 43.8	17 37.5
	27	06S05.3	08S36.3	12S23.1	19S32.2

1982	Ceres 1	Pallas 2	Juno 3	Vesta 4
JAN 1	08♏54.0	15♎37.4	13♐58.5	17♐50.1
11	12 25.5	18 02.0	17 15.3	23 09.2
21	15 41.0	19 53.4	20 26.6	28 25.1
31	18 37.3	21 05.6	23 31.0	03♑37.0
FEB 10	21 11.0	21 33.0	26 26.6	08 43.8
20	23 18.6	21 R11.2	29 11.7	13 44.6
MAR 2	24 55.6	19 57.4	01♑44.1	18 38.1
12	25 58.1	17 54.7	04 01.3	23 22.9
22	26 22.5	15 12.3	06 00.7	27 57.6
APR 1	26 R06.3	12 07.4	07 39.1	02♒20.4
11	25 10.0	09 02.4	08 53.4	06 29.1
21	23 37.6	06 18.9	09 40.2	10 21.3
MAY 1	21 38.0	04 12.8	09 56.3	13 54.1
11	19 24.7	02 53.7	09 R39.2	17 03.9
21	17 13.2	02 23.2	08 48.2	19 46.9
31	15 18.6	02 D38.9	07 24.3	21 58.0
JUN 10	13 52.5	03 35.7	05 32.8	23 32.3
20	13 01.7	05 07.9	03 22.1	24 24.8
30	12 D48.9	07 10.6	01 03.8	24 R30.7
JUL 10	13 13.2	09 38.5	28♐51.2	23 48.8
20	14 11.6	12 27.3	26 56.4	22 21.2
30	15 40.7	15 34.0	25 29.0	20 16.9
AUG 9	17 36.3	18 55.4	24 35.1	17 52.0
19	19 54.7	22 29.1	24 D16.6	15 26.1
29	22 32.7	26 13.3	24 33.5	13 19.5
SEP 8	25 27.2	00♏05.9	25 23.7	11 48.2
18	28 35.6	04 05.9	26 44.1	11 00.9
28	01♐56.0	08 11.9	28 31.6	11 D00.7
OCT 8	05 26.2	12 22.5	00♑43.0	11 45.1
18	09 04.7	16 37.0	03 15.1	13 10.1
28	12 50.1	20 54.3	06 05.4	15 10.8
NOV 7	16 41.1	25 13.4	09 11.5	17 41.5
17	20 36.6	29 33.5	12 31.3	20 37.2
27	24 35.4	03♐53.6	16 03.2	23 54.2
DEC 7	28 36.7	08 12.8	19 45.2	27 28.6
17	02♑39.4	12 30.1	23 36.2	01♓17.4
27	06 42.6	16 44.4	27 35.1	05 17.9
JAN 6	10♑45.4	20♐54.6	01♒40.4	09♓27.9
JAN 1	06 S 36.0	08 S 21.7	12 S 28.5	19 S 53.6
21	08 17.0	06 22.3	12 32.2	20 49.1
FEB 10	09 22.3	02 26.5	12 07.1	20 58.5
MAR 2	09 53.0	03 N 33.3	11 15.7	20 27.7
22	09 54.0	10 46.9	10 02.3	19 27.3
APR 11	09 35.5	17 15.9	08 34.1	18 11.8
MAY 1	09 14.0	21 17.6	07 02.1	16 59.0
21	09 11.3	22 39.6	05 42.0	16 09.9
JUN 10	09 45.0	22 05.3	04 53.4	16 07.9
30	10 59.2	20 20.6	04 53.4	17 13.6
JUL 20	12 45.8	17 57.4	05 45.3	19 29.0
AUG 9	14 52.6	15 16.5	07 15.5	22 14.3
29	17 07.5	12 32.5	09 03.2	24 20.0
SEP 18	19 20.2	09 56.2	10 50.0	25 04.9
OCT 8	21 21.8	07 36.9	12 22.5	24 34.7
28	23 04.9	05 42.5	13 31.6	23 08.5
NOV 17	24 23.7	04 20.1	14 10.9	20 59.9
DEC 7	25 14.3	03 35.4	14 16.3	18 17.7
27	25 S 35.1	03 N 32.5	13 S 46.1	15 S 08.5

1983	Ceres 1	Pallas 2	Juno 3	Vesta 4
JAN 1	08♑44.1	18♐50.1	29♑37.0	07♓21.9
11	12 46.4	22 57.8	03♒45.3	11 35.9
21	16 46.8	26 59.7	07 58.8	15 57.1
31	20 44.4	00♑54.1	12 16.5	20 23.5
FEB 10	24 38.3	04 39.8	16 37.9	24 54.0
20	28 27.3	08 14.7	21 02.0	29 27.6
MAR 2	02♒10.2	11 37.0	25 28.2	04♈03.2
12	05 46.0	14 44.5	29 55.9	08 40.0
22	09 13.0	17 34.3	04♓24.5	13 17.3
APR 1	12 29.7	20 03.4	08 53.2	17 54.2
11	15 34.6	22 08.5	13 21.6	22 30.3
21	18 25.2	23 45.5	17 49.0	27 05.0
MAY 1	20 59.5	24 50.2	22 14.6	01♉37.5
11	23 14.8	25 18.6	26 37.6	06 07.5
21	25 07.8	25 R06.6	00♈57.1	10 34.4
31	26 35.5	24 12.6	05 12.1	14 57.4
JUN 10	27 34.4	22 37.4	09 21.4	19 16.1
20	28 01.1	20 26.0	13 23.1	23 29.7
30	27 R53.2	17 49.4	17 15.4	27 37.3
JUL 10	27 09.8	15 02.0	20 56.2	01♊38.2
20	25 52.4	12 20.7	24 22.3	05 30.9
30	24 06.6	10 00.8	27 30.0	09 14.2
AUG 9	22 01.3	08 13.1	00♉14.9	12 46.6
19	19 49.1	07 03.8	02 31.6	16 05.8
29	17 43.8	06 34.2	04 14.5	19 09.5
SEP 8	15 57.9	06 D42.4	05 16.6	21 54.8
18	14 41.1	07 25.2	05 R31.7	24 18.1
28	13 58.8	08 38.1	04 57.7	26 15.3
OCT 8	13 D52.7	10 17.0	03 36.3	27 41.8
18	14 22.1	12 18.2	01 37.1	28 32.5
28	15 24.4	14 37.8	29♈19.5	28 R43.0
NOV 7	16 56.1	17 12.9	27 08.0	28 09.8
17	18 53.8	20 00.8	25 27.0	26 52.6
27	21 13.8	22 59.2	24 33.5	24 56.2
DEC 7	23 52.9	26 06.0	24 D35.4	22 30.9
17	26 48.3	29 19.6	25 33.4	19 53.5
27	29 57.3	02♒38.2	27 22.9	17 23.2
JAN 6	03♓17.8	06♒00.5	29♈57.3	15♊17.4
JAN 1	25 S 35.7	03 N 38.6	13 S 33.0	14 S 17.8
21	25 20.9	04 30.5	12 19.3	10 44.8
FEB 10	24 42.5	06 05.4	10 34.2	07 00.7
MAR 2	23 47.5	08 20.0	08 22.7	03 12.9
22	22 44.9	11 07.4	05 51.3	00 N 31.4
APR 11	21 45.8	14 17.0	03 07.7	04 05.5
MAY 1	21 02.8	17 31.6	00 20.5	07 23.1
21	20 49.9	20 25.1	02 N 20.7	10 19.1
JUN 10	21 20.4	22 21.4	04 44.9	12 48.9
30	22 43.1	22 43.7	06 39.2	14 49.5
JUL 20	24 50.7	21 15.0	07 48.6	16 19.3
AUG 9	27 10.0	18 13.3	07 55.3	17 18.8
29	28 51.1	14 21.9	06 40.3	17 50.9
SEP 18	29 21.6	10 25.0	03 50.6	18 01.7
OCT 8	28 44.1	06 52.6	00 S 18.3	18 00.2
28	27 17.2	04 00.6	04 33.1	17 58.0
NOV 17	25 16.2	01 55.0	07 07.8	18 05.1
DEC 7	22 50.4	00 36.4	07 13.1	18 25.5
27	20 S 04.9	00 N 02.2	05 S 16.0	18 N 57.0

1984	Ceres 1	Pallas 2	Juno 3	Vesta 4
JAN 1	01♓36.2	04♒19.0	28♈34.9	16 R16.3
11	05 01.7	07 42.7	01♉29.2	14♊28.1
21	08 35.6	11 08.0	04 58.0	13 21.5
31	12 16.5	14 34.0	08 53.9	12 D59.5
FEB 10	16 03.0	17 59.5	13 12.6	13 21.3
20	19 53.6	21 23.2	17 49.0	14 23.2
MAR 1	23 47.3	24 44.2	22 39.2	16 00.1
11	27 43.2	28 01.5	27 39.5	18 07.3
21	01♈40.0	01♓13.6	02♊47.6	20 39.8
31	05 37.1	04 19.7	08 01.4	23 33.6
APR 10	09 33.6	07 18.2	13 19.0	26 45.4
20	13 28.6	10 07.7	18 38.2	00♋11.9
30	17 21.3	12 46.7	23 58.4	03 50.9
MAY 10	21 10.9	15 13.2	29 18.7	07 40.4
20	24 56.4	17 25.2	04♋37.8	11 38.7
30	28 36.9	19 20.1	09 54.9	15 44.5
JUN 9	02♉11.2	20 55.2	15 09.8	19 56.7
19	05 38.0	22 07.4	20 21.8	24 14.2
29	08 56.1	22 53.5	25 30.7	28 36.4
JUL 9	12 03.5	23 09.8	00♌35.8	03♌02.6
19	14 58.4	22 R53.7	05 37.0	07 32.2
29	17 38.3	22 03.1	10 34.0	12 04.6
AUG 8	20 00.2	20 38.1	15 26.5	16 39.5
18	22 01.2	18 42.1	20 13.8	21 16.1
28	23 37.4	16 21.7	24 56.0	25 54.4
SEP 7	24 44.7	13 47.9	29 32.3	00♍33.5
17	25 19.2	11 13.9	04♍02.3	05 13.1
27	25 R17.4	08 53.1	08 25.4	09 52.7
OCT 7	24 37.3	06 57.0	12 40.6	14 31.4
17	23 20.1	05 33.4	16 47.1	19 08.6
27	21 30.7	04 45.9	20 43.9	23 43.4
NOV 6	19 19.3	04 D35.5	24 29.1	28 14.9
16	17 00.3	05 00.1	28 01.5	02♎41.8
26	14 49.3	05 56.8	01♎18.9	07 02.8
DEC 6	13 01.3	07 22.4	04 18.9	11 15.9
16	11 46.8	09 13.0	06 58.7	15 19.5
26	11 11.2	11 25.6	09 15.1	19 11.0
JAN 5	11 D16.1	13♓57.0	11♎04.3	22♎47.3
JAN 1	19 S 21.0	00 N 00.1	04 S 33.5	19 N 06.5
21	16 17.1	00 14.6	01 11.9	19 52.6
FEB 10	13 03.7	01 01.0	02 N 32.8	20 51.9
MAR 1	09 45.7	02 12.4	06 13.5	21 58.8
21	06 28.4	03 40.9	09 30.1	23 02.7
APR 10	03 16.9	05 18.4	12 08.5	23 52.5
30	00 16.6	06 55.7	13 59.4	24 19.0
MAY 20	02 N 27.7	08 22.8	14 58.5	24 15.7
JUN 9	04 51.5	09 27.1	15 05.9	23 38.9
29	06 50.9	09 52.6	14 25.6	22 27.6
JUL 19	08 22.7	09 19.2	13 04.0	20 43.2
AUG 8	09 24.7	07 26.7	11 09.6	18 29.2
28	09 56.3	04 08.4	08 51.5	15 50.7
SEP 17	09 59.0	00 S 07.9	06 19.1	12 54.2
OCT 7	09 38.4	04 23.0	03 42.1	09 47.0
27	09 06.8	07 44.1	01 10.2	06 38.0
NOV 16	08 45.2	09 50.8	01 S 06.2	03 36.3
DEC 6	08 56.9	10 47.2	02 56.0	00 52.4
26	09 N 54.0	10 S 46.9	04 S 06.9	01 S 22.9

1985		Ceres 1	Pallas 2	Juno 3	Vesta 4
JAN	1	11D09.3	12♓54.4	10♎24.1	21♎22.8
	11	11♉37.6	15 35.7	11 55.4	24 48.5
	21	12 42.4	18 31.9	12 53.4	27 53.5
	31	14 19.8	21 40.9	13 14.3	00♏33.0
FEB	10	16 25.3	25 00.7	12R56.1	02 41.9
	20	18 54.8	28 29.9	11 58.2	04 14.4
MAR	2	21 44.8	02♈07.3	10 23.6	05 04.7
	12	24 51.8	05 51.6	08 19.8	05R08.3
	22	28 13.1	09 42.1	05 58.5	04 22.6
APR	1	01♊46.5	13 37.9	03 34.0	02 50.2
	11	05 29.8	17 38.4	01 21.2	00 41.7
	21	09 21.4	21 43.0	29♍31.9	28♎13.6
MAY	1	13 20.0	25 51.3	28 14.4	25 47.9
	11	17 24.1	00♉02.7	27 32.2	23 46.1
	21	21 33.1	04 17.1	27D25.1	22 23.4
	31	25 45.9	08 33.9	27 51.5	21 48.8
JUN	10	00♋01.7	12 52.8	28 47.7	22D03.8
	20	04 19.9	17 13.5	00♎10.1	23 05.4
	30	08 39.8	21 35.3	01 55.1	24 48.9
JUL	10	13 00.8	25 58.0	03 59.4	27 08.5
	20	17 22.5	00♊20.6	06 19.9	29 58.8
	30	21 44.0	04 42.1	08 54.2	03♏15.2
AUG	9	26 04.8	09 01.7	11 39.9	06 53.0
	19	00♌24.4	13 17.8	14 35.3	10 49.1
	29	04 41.8	17 28.1	17 38.8	15 00.7
SEP	8	08 56.1	21 30.1	20 48.7	19 25.0
	18	13 06.5	25 20.5	24 04.1	24 00.2
	28	17 11.7	28 54.7	27 23.6	28 44.6
OCT	8	21 10.3	02♋07.0	00♏46.2	03♐36.8
	18	25 00.6	04 49.7	04 11.0	08 35.6
	28	28 40.5	06 54.0	07 36.9	13 39.8
NOV	7	02♍07.9	08 09.6	11 02.9	18 48.4
	17	05 19.8	08R25.0	14 28.1	24 00.8
	27	08 12.5	07 32.1	17 51.2	29 16.0
DEC	7	10 42.6	05 31.4	21 11.3	04♑33.1
	17	12 45.2	02 35.9	24 27.0	09 51.7
	27	14 15.3	29♊16.2	27 36.9	15 10.8
JAN	6	15♍08.3	26♊11.2	00♐39.6	20♑29.9
JAN	1	10N19.7	10S37.8	04S18.5	01S56.1
	21	12 08.2	09 44.2	04 18.5	03 17.3
FEB	10	14 20.9	08 24.1	03 10.2	03 45.1
MAR	2	16 43.9	06 48.3	00 53.8	03 12.8
	22	19 05.1	05 07.0	02N03.6	01 45.4
APR	11	21 14.5	03 29.9	04 49.0	00N07.6
MAY	1	23 03.7	02 06.5	06 35.6	01 28.3
	21	24 26.2	01 06.3	07 09.7	01 26.2
JUN	10	25 17.5	00 39.2	06 41.5	00S04.5
	30	25 35.2	00 55.1	05 27.9	02 39.6
JUL	20	25 19.5	02 03.8	03 43.8	05 52.2
AUG	9	24 32.9	04 13.6	01 40.7	09 21.3
	29	23 20.7	07 30.5	00S32.2	12 50.7
SEP	18	21 50.4	11 54.1	02 47.0	16 06.7
OCT	8	20 12.2	17 14.4	04 57.0	18 57.2
	28	18 38.5	23 04.0	06 56.0	21 11.4
NOV	17	17 24.2	28 30.8	08 38.2	22 40.5
DEC	7	16 47.0	32 15.4	09 58.4	23 18.7
	27	17N04.9	32S55.6	10S52.0	23S04.4

1986		Ceres 1	Pallas 2	Juno 3	Vesta 4
JAN	1	14♍46.8	27R39.5	29♏09.2	17♑50.4
	11	15 19.4	24♊55.4	02♐07.7	23 09.3
	21	15R08.9	23 12.4	04 56.2	28 27.1
	31	14 14.8	22D41.1	07 32.7	03♒43.2
FEB	10	12 40.9	23 18.8	09 55.1	08 57.1
	20	10 36.9	24 56.9	12 00.5	14 08.0
MAR	2	08 18.6	27 23.5	13 46.3	19 15.1
	12	06 03.8	00♋28.5	15 09.5	24 18.0
	22	04 10.3	04 03.1	16 06.5	29 15.7
APR	1	02 51.0	07 59.5	16 34.5	04♓07.6
	11	02 12.4	12 12.0	16R30.8	08 52.9
	21	02D16.8	16 36.8	15 54.0	13 30.3
MAY	1	03 01.8	21 10.0	14 44.7	17 59.1
	11	04 23.3	25 49.3	13 06.2	22 17.8
	21	06 16.9	00♌32.5	11 05.3	26 24.9
	31	08 37.5	05 18.3	08 52.0	00♈18.7
JUN	10	11 21.2	10 05.9	06 38.0	03 57.1
	20	14 24.1	14 54.2	04 35.5	07 17.3
	30	17 42.8	19 42.4	02 54.6	10 16.4
JUL	10	21 15.0	24 30.5	01 42.3	12 50.8
	20	24 58.3	29 18.2	01 02.5	14 56.0
	30	28 50.7	04♍04.9	00D55.8	16 27.6
AUG	9	02♎50.9	08 50.7	01 21.1	17 20.2
	19	06 57.4	13 35.3	02 16.2	17R29.7
	29	11 09.0	18 18.6	03 37.8	16 53.5
SEP	8	15 25.0	23 00.6	05 23.1	15 32.1
	18	19 44.1	27 40.8	07 29.2	13 32.0
	28	24 05.7	02♎19.0	09 53.3	11 06.1
OCT	8	28 29.1	06 55.1	12 33.1	08 31.9
	18	02♏53.4	11 28.5	15 26.4	06 09.8
	28	07 17.9	15 58.7	18 31.3	04 16.6
NOV	7	11 41.9	20 25.2	21 46.3	03 03.5
	17	16 04.5	24 47.2	25 09.8	02 35.8
	27	20 25.0	29 03.8	28 40.4	02D52.9
DEC	7	24 42.5	03♏13.9	02♑17.1	03 51.4
	17	28 55.9	07 16.1	05 58.6	05 26.8
	27	03♐04.3	11 09.0	09 43.8	07 33.5
JAN	6	07♐06.4	14♏50.6	13♑31.9	10♈06.8
JAN	1	17N19.7	32S31.2	11S00.9	22S52.7
	21	19 01.7	28 45.2	11 17.1	21 36.6
FEB	10	21 34.5	22 30.9	11 01.7	19 39.0
MAR	2	24 01.5	15 20.3	10 15.1	17 10.1
	22	25 14.0	08 27.5	09 00.7	14 21.1
APR	11	24 46.5	02 37.1	07 25.8	11 24.0
MAY	1	22 58.4	01N51.7	05 43.9	08 30.7
	21	20 18.0	04 56.2	04 16.4	05 52.7
JUN	10	17 05.1	06 42.7	03 27.3	03 41.7
	30	13 31.2	07 22.7	03 30.8	02 09.8
JUL	20	09 44.2	07 09.8	04 23.4	01 29.1
AUG	9	05 50.2	06 17.8	05 49.8	01 50.5
	29	01 55.0	05 00.0	07 33.2	03 17.2
SEP	18	01S55.7	03 29.4	09 19.5	05 30.6
OCT	8	05 36.2	01 58.4	10 57.8	07 38.5
	28	09 01.0	00 39.2	12 19.7	08 40.2
NOV	17	12 04.8	00S15.9	13 19.0	08 12.6
DEC	7	14 43.1	00 34.7	13 50.8	06 30.3
	27	16S53.0	00S05.4	13S52.4	03S58.0

1987		Ceres 1	Pallas 2	Juno 3	Vesta 4
JAN	1	05♐06.2	13♏01.4	11♑37.6	08♈47.1
	11	09 04.7	16 36.4	15 26.7	11 32.0
	21	12 54.9	19 56.5	19 17.1	14 36.8
	31	16 35.3	22 58.9	23 08.1	17 58.2
FEB	10	20 03.9	25 39.7	26 58.3	21 33.3
	20	23 18.7	27 55.0	00♒47.0	25 19.3
MAR	2	26 17.6	29 39.8	04 33.3	29 14.3
	12	28 57.6	00♐48.6	08 15.8	03♉16.5
	22	01♑15.8	01 16.4	11 53.4	07 24.3
APR	1	03 08.8	00R58.1	15 25.0	11 36.6
	11	04 32.9	29♏51.2	18 48.9	15 52.3
	21	05 24.8	27 57.7	22 03.4	20 10.5
MAY	1	05R41.1	25 25.1	25 06.5	24 30.4
	11	05 20.0	22 28.6	27 55.9	28 51.3
	21	04 22.0	19 28.4	00♓28.8	03♊12.5
	31	02 50.7	16 44.8	02 41.9	07 33.7
JUN	10	00 53.9	14 35.1	04 31.1	11 54.0
	20	28♐43.3	13 08.8	05 52.6	16 13.1
	30	26 32.8	12 29.2	06 41.5	20 30.5
JUL	10	24 36.4	12D35.1	06R53.5	24 45.5
	20	23 05.3	13 21.8	06 25.4	28 57.4
	30	22 06.5	14 44.2	05 16.4	03♋05.7
AUG	9	21 43.7	16 37.2	03 30.2	07 09.5
	19	21D56.5	18 55.5	01 15.8	11 07.7
	29	22 43.1	21 35.3	28♒47.8	14 59.3
SEP	8	24 00.5	24 32.8	26 25.2	18 42.7
	18	25 44.8	27 44.7	24 25.5	22 16.5
	28	27 52.6	01♐08.9	23 02.5	25 38.5
OCT	8	00♑20.8	04 42.9	22 24.6	28 45.9
	18	03 06.3	08 24.8	22D34.3	01♌36.2
	28	06 06.5	12 13.2	23 30.3	04 05.4
NOV	7	09 19.3	16 06.4	25 08.9	06 09.3
	17	12 42.4	20 03.3	27 25.1	07 43.1
	27	16 14.5	24 02.7	00♓14.8	08 41.3
DEC	7	19 53.6	28 03.4	03 33.4	08R59.1
	17	23 38.5	02♑04.3	07 16.6	08 32.7
	27	27 28.1	06 04.6	11 21.4	07 20.7
JAN	6	01♒21.0	10♑02.9	15♓44.8	05♌27.6
JAN	1	17S20.8	00N10.7	13S47.9	03S14.6
	21	18 54.2	01 55.2	13 10.9	00 07.3
FEB	10	20 01.1	04 48.0	12 04.6	03N12.1
MAR	2	20 47.7	08 49.1	10 32.9	06 33.0
	22	21 23.3	13 44.9	08 41.4	09 46.8
APR	11	21 59.7	18 58.3	06 37.2	12 46.0
MAY	1	22 48.5	23 27.0	04 29.6	15 24.3
	21	23 54.8	26 05.5	02 29.9	17 36.5
JUN	10	25 10.2	26 24.1	00 53.5	19 18.9
	30	26 16.0	24 42.9	00 00.8	20 29.4
JUL	20	27 01.5	21 47.3	00 16.6	21 07.5
AUG	9	27 32.5	18 18.9	02 00.6	21 14.9
	29	27 58.1	14 46.3	05 04.0	20 56.0
SEP	18	28 20.0	11 27.4	08 33.0	20 18.4
OCT	8	28 33.9	08 33.5	11 21.7	19 32.6
	28	28 33.3	06 12.4	12 55.5	18 53.1
NOV	17	28 12.6	04 29.0	13 10.8	18 38.0
DEC	7	27 28.0	03 26.4	12 16.4	19 07.2
	27	26S18.6	03N05.6	10S23.7	20N32.7

1988	Ceres 1	Pallas 2	Juno 3	Vesta 4
JAN 1	29♑24.2	08♑04.1	13♓31.0	06 R28.8
11	03♒18.4	12 01.1	18 02.6	04♌18.6
21	07 14.4	15 54.8	22 49.3	01 45.0
31	11 11.2	19 44.0	27 48.9	29♋07.2
FEB 10	15 07.8	23 27.5	02♈59.5	26 45.0
20	19 03.3	27 04.1	08 20.0	24 54.8
MAR 1	22 56.7	00♒32.4	13 48.8	23 47.3
11	26 47.0	03 50.8	19 24.6	23 D26.0
21	00♓33.4	06 57.9	25 06.4	23 50.0
31	04 14.6	09 51.4	00♉53.2	24 55.9
APR 10	07 49.6	12 29.4	06 43.9	26 38.1
20	11 17.2	14 49.4	12 37.8	28 51.9
30	14 35.8	16 48.3	18 33.6	01♌32.4
MAY 10	17 43.9	18 23.2	24 30.8	04 35.4
20	20 39.7	19 30.5	00♊28.6	07 57.5
30	23 20.9	20 06.6	06 25.9	11 35.8
JUN 9	25 45.1	20 R08.4	12 22.1	15 27.7
19	27 49.4	19 33.4	18 16.3	19 31.4
29	29 30.5	18 21.3	24 07.8	23 45.3
JUL 9	00♈45.1	16 34.5	29 55.8	28 07.8
19	01 29.5	14 19.3	05♋39.5	02♍38.2
29	01 R40.4	11 46.4	11 17.9	07 15.2
AUG 8	01 15.8	09 09.1	16 50.5	11 58.2
18	00 15.5	06 41.4	22 16.3	16 46.6
28	28♓42.6	04 35.9	27 34.2	21 39.5
SEP 7	26 44.4	03 00.9	02♌43.2	26 36.6
17	24 32.0	02 01.0	07 42.1	01♎37.3
27	22 19.4	01 37.4	12 29.5	06 41.1
OCT 7	20 20.6	01 D48.2	17 03.9	11 47.4
17	18 47.4	02 30.8	21 23.1	16 55.9
27	17 47.9	03 41.4	25 24.8	22 05.9
NOV 6	17 25.4	05 16.4	29 06.6	27 16.7
16	17 D40.4	07 12.4	02♍24.9	02♏27.9
26	18 30.6	09 26.2	05 15.8	07 38.6
DEC 6	19 52.7	11 54.8	07 35.1	12 48.1
16	21 43.1	14 36.1	09 17.6	17 55.6
26	23 57.9	17 27.5	10 18.7	22 59.9
JAN 5	26♓33.3	20♒27.3	10 R33.8	28♏00.2
JAN 1	25 S 57.6	03 N 06.9	09 S 47.8	21 N01.9
21	24 19.6	03 37.0	06 59.6	23 12.4
FEB 10	22 23.6	04 44.1	03 41.5	25 04.0
MAR 1	20 15.6	06 23.4	00 06.9	26 03.9
21	18 02.7	08 28.3	03 N 30.0	26 13.4
APR 10	15 53.1	10 50.3	06 55.2	25 43.5
30	13 55.6	13 18.7	09 55.0	24 39.2
MAY 20	12 19.4	15 38.3	12 17.3	23 02.0
JUN 9	11 14.9	17 27.7	13 52.7	20 52.2
29	10 52.5	18 18.3	14 35.3	18 11.8
JUL 19	11 21.2	17 41.2	14 24.3	15 04.1
AUG 8	12 43.3	15 24.6	13 23.3	11 34.1
28	14 44.3	11 50.9	11 39.9	07 47.5
SEP 17	16 44.7	07 47.7	09 25.2	03 51.3
OCT 7	17 54.1	04 00.6	06 52.0	00 S06.9
27	17 45.0	00 56.4	04 15.1	03 59.0
NOV 16	16 23.2	01 S 15.2	01 51.1	07 36.3
DEC 6	14 08.7	02 34.6	00 00.2	10 50.2
26	11 S 19.7	03 S 06.8	00 S 53.8	13 S33.0

1989	Ceres 1	Pallas 2	Juno 3	Vesta 4
JAN 1	25♓28.8	19♒14.5	10♍33.5	26♏00.7
11	28 15.2	22 18.6	10 R19.6	00♐58.0
21	01♈17.6	25 28.4	09 17.9	05 48.9
31	04 33.0	28 42.5	07 33.2	10 32.2
FEB 10	07 59.6	01♓59.7	05 15.7	15 06.1
20	11 35.3	05 18.8	02 42.2	19 28.4
MAR 2	15 18.2	08 38.6	00 12.0	23 36.9
12	19 07.3	11 58.3	28♌02.7	27 28.4
22	23 01.0	15 16.6	26 27.2	00♑59.9
APR 1	26 58.2	18 32.6	25 31.8	04 07.4
11	00♉58.2	21 45.3	25 D17.8	06 46.1
21	04 59.8	24 53.6	25 43.1	08 50.7
MAY 1	09 02.3	27 56.3	26 42.8	10 16.1
11	13 05.2	00♈52.2	28 12.6	10 56.6
21	17 07.3	03 39.6	00♍07.7	10 R48.7
31	21 08.3	06 17.0	02 23.7	09 52.0
JUN 10	25 07.4	08 42.4	04 57.1	08 11.4
20	29 03.6	10 53.2	07 44.8	05 59.8
30	02♊56.4	12 47.0	10 44.2	03 35.8
JUL 10	06 44.5	14 20.4	13 53.2	01 20.8
20	10 27.1	15 29.7	17 09.9	29♐34.4
30	14 02.8	16 10.9	20 32.9	28 29.2
AUG 9	17 30.1	16 R19.7	24 00.9	28 D11.4
19	20 47.3	15 52.5	27 32.8	28 41.3
29	23 52.3	14 46.9	01♎07.6	29 54.6
SEP 8	26 42.5	13 03.0	04 44.5	01♑46.8
18	29 14.8	10 45.6	08 22.5	04 12.5
28	01♋25.8	08 04.2	12 00.9	07 06.2
OCT 8	03 11.3	05 13.3	15 38.9	10 23.5
18	04 27.0	02 30.2	19 15.4	14 00.5
28	05 08.2	00 10.5	22 49.9	17 53.7
NOV 7	05 R10.9	28♓26.6	26 21.2	22 00.8
17	04 33.0	27 25.4	29 48.2	26 18.8
27	03 15.3	27 D08.7	03♏09.8	00♒46.0
DEC 7	01 23.5	27 35.3	06 24.6	05 21.0
17	29♊09.0	28 41.8	09 31.0	10 02.0
27	26 47.5	00♈23.9	12 27.5	14 47.7
JAN 6	24♊36.6	02♈37.6	15♏11.9	19♒37.2
JAN 1	10 S 24.4	03 S 08.3	00 S 54.9	14 S14.8
21	07 09.2	02 50.1	00 N 02.8	16 08.8
FEB 10	03 43.9	02 02.3	02 33.6	17 23.0
MAR 2	00 15.5	00 53.4	05 56.1	18 00.6
22	03 N 10.0	00 N 27.9	09 00.4	18 10.5
APR 11	06 26.9	01 52.9	11 01.0	18 07.2
MAY 1	09 30.2	03 12.2	11 50.6	18 10.8
21	12 15.6	04 15.9	11 39.9	18 42.5
JUN 10	14 39.6	04 52.6	10 42.7	19 53.3
30	16 39.6	04 48.5	09 10.7	21 30.0
JUL 20	18 14.9	03 46.8	07 13.5	23 04.3
AUG 9	19 26.5	01 29.5	04 59.6	24 21.7
29	20 18.3	02 S 15.7	02 36.3	25 20.4
SEP 18	20 57.2	07 15.2	00 10.4	25 57.0
OCT 8	21 33.8	12 29.5	02 S 11.6	26 04.8
28	22 20.7	16 35.1	04 23.4	25 36.8
NOV 17	23 27.5	18 45.6	06 18.6	24 29.0
DEC 7	24 50.8	19 08.1	07 51.1	22 40.9
27	26 N 10.1	18 S 12.0	08 S 55.4	20 S15.7

1990	Ceres 1	Pallas 2	Juno 3	Vesta 4
JAN 1	25 R39.7	01♈27.1	13♏51.4	17♒12.1
11	23♊40.3	03 54.9	16 28.8	22 03.0
21	22 12.9	06 48.3	18 50.9	26 56.1
31	21 25.3	10 04.1	20 54.7	01♓50.6
FEB 10	21 D20.5	13 39.6	22 37.2	06 45.6
20	21 56.7	17 32.2	23 55.5	11 40.4
MAR 2	23 10.6	21 40.2	24 46.0	16 34.5
12	24 57.9	26 02.0	25 05.8	21 27.0
22	27 13.5	00♉36.2	24 R52.7	26 17.5
APR 1	29 53.5	05 21.8	24 05.8	01♈05.3
11	02♋54.0	10 17.6	22 46.7	05 49.9
21	06 11.4	15 23.0	21 00.0	10 30.7
MAY 1	09 43.3	20 37.4	18 53.5	15 07.1
11	13 27.2	25 59.7	16 38.5	19 38.3
21	17 21.1	01♊29.4	14 27.0	24 03.8
31	21 23.5	07 05.9	12 30.5	28 22.7
JUN 10	25 32.9	12 48.3	10 58.1	02♉33.9
20	29 48.3	18 35.8	09 55.3	06 36.5
30	04♌08.6	24 27.4	09 24.7	10 29.1
JUL 10	08 32.9	00♋22.1	09 D26.4	14 10.0
20	13 00.6	06 18.9	09 58.2	17 37.6
30	17 30.9	12 16.4	10 57.9	20 49.1
AUG 9	22 03.1	18 13.1	12 22.3	23 42.0
19	26 36.6	24 07.9	14 08.2	26 13.0
29	01♍10.9	29 59.3	16 13.1	28 17.8
SEP 8	05 45.2	05♌45.5	18 34.2	29 52.2
18	10 18.9	11 24.9	21 09.3	00♊51.3
28	14 51.3	16 55.7	23 56.5	01 10.3
OCT 8	19 21.5	22 16.1	26 53.8	00 R45.9
18	23 48.7	27 24.1	29 59.8	29♉37.2
28	28 11.8	02♍17.2	03♐13.1	27 47.7
NOV 7	02♎29.5	06 52.8	06 32.3	25 27.5
17	06 40.7	11 08.4	09 56.3	22 51.8
27	10 43.6	14 59.8	13 24.0	20 19.6
DEC 7	14 36.3	18 23.0	16 54.2	18 09.5
17	18 16.8	21 13.1	20 26.0	16 34.6
27	21 42.5	23 24.0	23 58.2	15 42.8
JAN 6	24♎50.3	24♍49.4	27♐29.7	15 D35.7
JAN 1	26 N 26.7	17 S 49.0	09 S 06.4	19 S34.2
21	27 19.0	15 52.4	09 28.1	16 31.3
FEB 10	27 56.9	13 29.4	09 11.5	13 07.2
MAR 2	28 29.3	10 54.6	08 15.0	09 30.5
22	28 55.2	08 19.7	06 41.1	05 50.1
APR 11	29 07.4	05 55.1	04 41.0	02 14.0
MAY 1	28 57.5	03 50.6	02 38.6	01 N10.3
21	28 19.2	02 15.2	01 06.8	04 15.9
JUN 10	27 09.1	01 16.4	00 29.7	06 57.0
30	25 26.8	00 59.9	00 50.7	09 08.6
JUL 20	23 14.9	01 28.6	01 57.5	10 46.9
AUG 9	20 37.8	02 41.6	03 33.6	11 49.7
29	17 41.6	04 34.1	05 24.5	12 16.4
SEP 18	14 33.5	06 57.7	07 18.7	12 08.7
OCT 8	11 21.6	09 40.8	09 07.2	11 31.9
28	08 14.4	12 29.4	10 42.6	10 37.6
NOV 17	05 21.1	15 06.2	11 58.9	09 48.6
DEC 7	02 51.1	17 09.3	12 51.2	09 33.5
27	00 N 53.4	18 S 08.7	13 S 16.3	10 N09.6

1991		Ceres 1	Pallas 2	Juno 3	Vesta 4
JAN	1	23♎18.8	24♍12.8	25♐44.1	15R33.8
	11	26 16.5	25 13.0	29 14.9	15D48.3
	21	28 51.0	25R17.9	02♑43.3	16♉43.5
	31	00♏58.2	24 23.9	06 08.2	18 14.7
FEB	10	02 33.9	22 32.3	09 28.1	20 16.4
	20	03 33.1	19 51.7	12 41.8	22 44.2
MAR	2	03 52.4	16 41.2	15 47.5	25 33.8
	12	03R29.6	13 25.3	18 43.5	28 41.2
	22	02 25.3	10 29.7	21 27.8	02♊03.6
APR	1	00 45.1	08 14.4	23 58.0	05 38.3
	11	28♎39.6	06 49.2	26 11.5	09 23.2
	21	26 23.5	06 16.0	28 05.3	13 16.5
MAY	1	24 14.1	06D31.6	29 35.9	17 16.7
	11	22 26.3	07 30.2	00♒40.0	21 22.6
	21	21 11.0	09 05.5	01 13.5	25 33.3
	31	20 33.9	11 11.2	01R13.4	29 47.7
JUN	10	20D36.0	13 41.9	00 37.6	04♋05.3
	20	21 15.7	16 33.6	29♑26.0	08 25.3
	30	22 29.4	19 42.5	27 42.1	12 47.1
JUL	10	24 12.7	23 05.5	25 33.6	17 10.4
	20	26 21.7	26 40.5	23 12.1	21 34.6
	30	28 52.5	00♎25.4	20 52.1	25 59.0
AUG	9	01♏41.7	04 18.7	18 47.9	00♌23.4
	19	04 46.5	08 19.1	17 11.4	04 47.1
	29	08 04.3	12 25.4	16 10.6	09 09.5
SEP	8	11 33.1	16 36.7	15 48.7	13 30.1
	18	15 11.2	20 52.2	16D06.0	17 47.8
	28	18 56.9	25 10.9	17 00.7	22 01.9
OCT	8	22 48.9	29 32.2	18 29.1	26 11.4
	18	26 46.2	03♏55.5	20 28.0	00♍14.8
	28	00♐47.5	08 19.8	22 53.5	04 10.5
NOV	7	04 51.9	12 44.5	25 42.3	07 56.8
	17	08 58.6	17 08.8	28 51.7	11 31.1
	27	13 06.6	21 31.9	02♒18.7	14 50.8
DEC	7	17 15.1	25 52.8	06 01.1	17 52.5
	17	21 23.1	00♐10.4	09 57.3	20 32.0
	27	25 29.8	04 23.7	14 05.3	22 44.9
JAN	6	29♐34.4	08♐31.5	18♒23.7	24♍25.5
JAN	1	00N30.0	18S08.8	13S18.0	10N26.5
	21	00S35.4	16 45.5	13 07.1	11 59.1
FEB	10	00 52.3	12 28.3	12 28.0	13 58.7
MAR	2	00 20.4	05 08.5	11 23.9	16 08.6
	22	00N48.7	03N21.7	09 59.7	18 15.0
APR	11	02 03.8	10 19.2	08 22.9	20 06.9
MAY	1	02 41.5	14 36.1	06 43.8	21 36.0
	21	02 12.8	16 32.7	05 16.5	22 35.9
JUN	10	00 39.2	16 49.5	04 19.5	23 02.8
	30	01S41.2	15 59.7	04 13.2	22 54.8
JUL	20	04 29.5	14 27.4	05 09.1	22 12.5
AUG	9	07 31.5	12 30.0	06 57.3	20 58.7
	29	10 36.6	10 21.2	09 08.8	19 18.3
SEP	18	13 36.2	08 12.5	11 14.0	17 17.8
OCT	8	16 23.3	06 14.1	12 53.4	15 05.9
	28	18 51.4	04 35.7	13 56.8	12 53.1
NOV	17	20 55.3	03 25.8	14 19.3	10 52.0
DEC	7	22 31.0	02 52.4	13 58.9	09 17.9
	27	23S36.7	03N01.7	12S56.1	08N28.9

1992		Ceres 1	Pallas 2	Juno 3	Vesta 4
JAN	1	27♐32.4	06♐28.4	16♒13.3	23♍39.6
	11	01♑35.5	10 32.9	20 36.5	25 01.9
	21	05 34.8	14 29.4	25 08.3	25 43.4
	31	09 29.3	18 16.6	29 47.8	25R39.8
FEB	10	13 17.9	21 52.1	04♓34.2	24 47.9
	20	16 59.3	25 13.9	09 26.4	23 10.7
MAR	1	20 32.1	28 19.2	14 23.9	20 57.1
	11	23 54.7	01♑04.7	19 26.4	18 23.1
	21	27 05.4	03 27.0	24 32.9	15 50.3
	31	00♒02.1	05 22.0	29 43.0	13 39.2
APR	10	02 42.4	06 44.8	04♈56.5	12 05.9
	20	05 03.7	07 30.7	10 12.9	11 19.6
	30	07 03.1	07R35.3	15 31.8	11D22.2
MAY	10	08 37.2	06 55.2	20 52.6	12 11.5
	20	09 42.6	05 30.1	26 14.9	13 43.0
	30	10 16.1	03 24.1	01♉38.5	15 50.9
JUN	9	10R14.8	00 46.9	07 02.6	18 30.3
	19	09 37.9	27♐54.3	12 26.4	21 36.0
	29	08 26.4	25 04.5	17 49.3	25 03.9
JUL	9	06 45.0	22 35.1	23 10.7	28 50.9
	19	04 42.6	20 39.3	28 29.0	02♎53.7
	29	02 31.1	19 24.1	03♊43.0	07 10.1
AUG	8	00 24.3	18 51.5	08 51.0	11 38.3
	18	28♑35.1	18D59.6	13 51.4	16 16.4
	28	27 13.2	19 44.4	18 41.7	21 03.1
SEP	7	26 24.9	21 01.5	23 18.4	25 57.4
	17	26D12.6	22 46.0	27 38.4	00♏58.0
	27	26 35.4	24 53.7	01♋37.9	06 04.2
OCT	7	27 31.5	27 20.8	05 10.8	11 15.3
	17	28 57.4	00♑03.8	08 11.5	16 30.3
	27	00♒49.4	03 00.2	10 32.9	21 48.7
NOV	6	03 04.4	06 07.4	12 07.9	27 09.8
	16	05 38.9	09 23.3	12 49.9	02♐32.9
	26	08 30.1	12 46.2	12R34.6	07 57.4
DEC	6	11 35.5	16 14.5	11 23.5	13 22.6
	16	14 52.7	19 46.6	09 27.2	18 47.9
	26	18 19.8	23 21.4	07 04.9	24 12.6
JAN	5	21♒55.1	26♑57.6	04♋42.7	29♐36.1
JAN	1	23S48.4	03N11.3	12S34.1	08N25.9
	21	24 17.5	04 19.9	10 42.8	09 00.0
FEB	10	24 21.6	06 17.4	08 18.7	10 51.5
MAR	1	24 07.8	09 01.1	05 29.2	13 36.6
	21	23 45.8	12 23.9	02 22.7	16 06.7
APR	10	23 27.9	16 11.0	00N50.9	17 12.4
	30	23 28.3	19 56.9	04 01.4	16 37.4
MAY	20	24 01.6	23 02.8	06 57.5	14 43.2
JUN	9	25 18.6	24 43.7	09 27.9	11 54.7
	29	27 16.0	24 28.4	11 20.8	08 29.5
JUL	19	29 26.6	22 21.2	12 26.2	04 40.0
AUG	8	31 06.2	18 58.8	12 36.1	00 36.3
	28	31 47.0	15 06.3	11 47.3	03S32.2
SEP	17	31 32.6	11 18.8	10 02.1	07 36.3
OCT	7	30 39.6	07 57.8	07 30.7	11 26.3
	27	29 19.7	05 15.0	04 33.0	14 52.2
NOV	16	27 37.5	03 15.5	01 43.0	17 44.4
DEC	6	25 34.8	02 00.5	00S07.7	19 54.6
	26	23S12.9	01N28.7	00S05.5	21S16.7

1993		Ceres 1	Pallas 2	Juno 3	Vesta 4
JAN	1	20♒28.1	25♑31.0	05R37.8	27♐26.9
	11	24 07.5	29 07.4	03♋28.0	02♑49.1
	21	27 52.6	02♒43.4	01 53.6	08 09.0
	31	01♓42.2	06 17.9	01 07.5	13 25.7
FEB	10	05 35.1	09 49.7	01D13.1	18 38.3
	20	09 30.1	13 17.9	02 07.0	23 46.0
MAR	2	13 26.4	16 41.2	03 42.9	28 47.8
	12	17 22.8	19 58.5	05 54.3	03♒42.7
	22	21 18.7	23 08.5	08 34.6	08 29.6
APR	1	25 13.1	26 09.8	11 38.2	13 07.1
	11	29 04.9	29 00.8	14 59.8	17 33.6
	21	02♈53.6	01♓39.9	18 35.6	21 47.6
MAY	1	06 38.0	04 04.9	22 22.8	25 46.7
	11	10 17.0	06 13.6	26 18.4	29 28.5
	21	13 49.7	08 03.6	00♌20.4	02♓50.1
	31	17 14.7	09 31.6	04 27.3	05 47.7
JUN	10	20 30.5	10 34.8	08 37.7	08 17.5
	20	23 35.5	11 09.8	12 50.5	10 14.5
	30	26 27.5	11R13.3	17 04.8	11 33.5
JUL	10	29 04.4	10 43.1	21 19.8	12 10.0
	20	01♉23.3	09 38.2	25 35.1	12R00.0
	30	03 20.9	08 00.0	29 49.9	11 02.6
AUG	9	04 53.8	05 53.8	04♍03.7	09 22.0
	19	05 58.2	03 27.9	08 16.1	07 08.4
	29	06 30.0	00 54.3	12 26.5	04 38.9
SEP	8	06R26.2	28♒26.5	16 34.5	02 13.9
	18	05 45.2	26 16.5	20 39.4	00 12.1
	28	04 27.8	24 34.1	24 40.7	28♒48.0
OCT	8	02 39.5	23 25.0	28 37.6	28 08.9
	18	00 29.7	22 51.3	02♎29.5	28D15.9
	28	28♈12.3	22D52.6	06 15.1	29 06.8
NOV	7	26 02.7	23 26.4	09 53.6	00♓36.7
	17	24 14.8	24 29.7	13 23.7	02 40.5
	27	22 59.3	25 59.1	16 43.7	05 13.2
DEC	7	22 21.6	27 51.1	19 52.0	08 09.7
	17	22D23.2	00♓02.5	22 46.6	11 26.2
	27	23 02.9	02 30.5	25 24.8	14 59.3
JAN	6	24♈16.9	05♓12.5	27♎44.3	18♓45.7
JAN	1	22S26.9	01N27.1	00N20.7	21S31.4
	21	19 43.9	01 46.2	02 54.3	21 47.8
FEB	10	16 49.2	02 38.7	06 17.6	21 17.0
MAR	2	13 48.1	03 58.1	09 31.8	20 06.6
	22	10 46.0	05 37.1	12 06.0	18 28.1
APR	11	07 49.0	07 27.8	13 48.9	16 35.2
MAY	1	05 02.9	09 20.8	14 38.8	14 43.7
	21	02 33.8	11 05.1	14 38.9	13 11.4
JUN	10	00 27.4	12 26.2	13 54.7	12 18.0
	30	01N10.3	13 04.7	12 33.3	12 24.1
JUL	20	02 14.0	12 37.0	10 42.3	13 44.7
AUG	9	02 38.7	10 42.3	08 29.5	16 12.8
	29	02 22.1	07 22.2	06 02.6	18 58.2
SEP	18	01 28.1	03 14.4	03 29.1	20 47.9
OCT	8	00 13.7	00S45.4	00 56.7	21 05.2
	28	00S47.8	03 56.4	01S27.1	20 00.7
NOV	17	01 00.3	06 04.4	03 34.5	17 57.9
DEC	7	00 08.4	07 11.6	05 17.4	15 14.6
	27	01N39.4	07S27.2	06S27.6	12S03.0

1994		Ceres 1	Pallas 2	Juno 3	Vesta 4
JAN	1	23♈35.8	03♓49.9	26♎37.1	16♓51.0
	11	25 05.7	06 38.2	28 46.0	20 43.2
	21	27 04.1	09 37.5	00♏31.2	24 45.4
	31	29 26.9	12 45.8	01 49.3	28 55.5
FEB	10	02♉10.4	16 01.8	02 36.9	03♈11.9
	20	05 11.4	19 24.0	02R50.7	07 33.3
MAR	2	08 26.9	22 51.2	02 28.8	11 58.3
	12	11 54.5	26 22.5	01 31.0	16 26.0
	22	15 32.4	29 56.9	29♎59.9	20 55.6
APR	1	19 18.5	03♈33.4	28 02.0	25 25.9
	11	23 11.4	07 11.5	25 47.3	29 56.6
	21	27 10.1	10 50.3	23 28.4	04♉26.9
MAY	1	01♊13.2	14 29.1	21 18.6	08 56.1
	11	05 19.9	18 07.2	19 28.8	13 23.9
	21	09 29.4	21 43.9	18 07.4	17 49.5
	31	13 40.9	25 18.3	17 18.3	22 12.5
JUN	10	17 53.8	28 49.5	17D02.4	26 32.3
	20	22 07.4	02♉16.4	17 18.8	00♊48.2
	30	26 21.0	05 37.8	18 04.6	04 59.5
JUL	10	00♋34.3	08 52.2	19 16.6	09 05.6
	20	04 46.3	11 57.4	20 51.7	13 05.3
	30	08 56.5	14 51.2	22 46.6	16 57.6
AUG	9	13 04.2	17 30.6	24 58.6	20 41.2
	19	17 08.2	19 51.7	27 25.2	24 14.5
	29	21 07.7	21 49.8	00♏04.1	27 35.5
SEP	8	25 01.5	23 19.3	02 53.5	00♋41.8
	18	28 48.0	24 13.3	05 51.8	03 30.6
	28	02♌25.7	24R24.8	08 57.3	05 58.4
OCT	8	05 52.4	23 46.5	12 08.9	08 01.3
	18	09 05.5	22 14.5	15 25.4	09 34.3
	28	12 02.3	19 51.2	18 45.4	10 32.9
NOV	7	14 39.0	16 47.4	22 08.2	10 51.9
	17	16 51.5	13 26.0	25 32.4	10R27.6
	27	18 35.3	10 16.4	28 57.1	09 19.0
DEC	7	19 45.3	07 45.9	02♐21.3	07 29.4
	17	20 16.7	06 13.9	05 43.7	05 08.3
	27	20R06.1	05D47.5	09 03.2	02 31.5
JAN	6	19♌12.2	06♉26.0	12♐18.5	29♊57.8
JAN	1	02N13.1	07S24.3	06S39.0	11S11.8
	21	04 46.7	06 50.5	06 56.2	07 37.6
FEB	10	07 39.3	05 49.0	06 22.3	03 54.5
MAR	2	10 38.7	04 29.7	04 53.8	00 09.9
	22	13 35.2	03 02.1	02 38.2	03N29.0
APR	11	16 20.6	01 35.7	00 03.4	06 55.6
MAY	1	18 48.1	00 20.0	02N06.7	10 04.2
	21	20 52.3	00N35.2	03 17.9	12 49.5
JUN	10	22 28.7	00 59.0	03 22.7	15 07.7
	30	23 35.0	00 39.7	02 32.8	16 55.8
JUL	20	24 10.6	00S36.0	01 05.0	18 13.1
AUG	9	24 17.4	03 02.1	00S46.1	19 00.5
	29	24 00.1	06 50.5	02 48.9	19 22.0
SEP	18	23 26.5	12 03.6	04 54.4	19 24.5
OCT	8	22 47.6	18 18.5	06 54.8	19 18.4
	28	22 18.2	24 29.3	08 43.6	19 17.4
NOV	17	22 16.4	28 56.2	10 15.0	19 35.6
DEC	7	23 02.2	30 25.1	11 24.1	20 19.3
	27	24N49.1	28S57.2	12S07.1	21N19.2

1995		Ceres 1	Pallas 2	Juno 3	Vesta 4
JAN	1	19R44.5	05D58.9	10♐41.5	01R13.0
	11	18♌30.0	07♉08.0	13 54.1	28♊48.2
	21	16 39.7	09 12.3	17 00.4	26 53.0
	31	14 25.6	12 03.3	19 58.7	25 37.9
FEB	10	12 04.7	15 33.7	22 47.2	25 07.8
	20	09 55.9	19 36.2	25 23.7	25D22.3
MAR	2	08 14.7	24 05.0	27 46.3	26 17.7
	12	07 11.9	28 55.1	29 52.0	27 49.6
	22	06D52.1	04♊01.9	01♑38.1	29 52.8
APR	1	07 14.9	09 21.8	03 01.5	02♋22.4
	11	08 17.6	14 51.6	03 58.7	05 14.5
	21	09 55.5	20 28.5	04 26.7	08 25.2
MAY	1	12 03.7	26 10.1	04R22.8	11 51.6
	11	14 37.7	01♋54.6	03 45.2	15 31.3
	21	17 33.3	07 40.0	02 34.6	19 22.1
	31	20 47.0	13 25.2	00 54.3	23 22.4
JUN	10	24 15.8	19 09.0	28♐51.1	27 30.9
	20	27 57.1	24 50.1	26 35.8	01♌46.2
	30	01♍48.9	00♌28.2	24 20.3	06 07.6
JUL	10	05 49.5	06 02.7	22 17.5	10 34.3
	20	09 57.2	11 33.0	20 37.9	15 05.4
	30	14 11.0	16 58.9	19 28.7	19 40.6
AUG	9	18 29.7	22 20.2	18 53.7	24 19.2
	19	22 52.3	27 36.6	18D53.5	29 00.7
	29	27 18.1	02♍48.2	19 26.8	03♍44.8
SEP	8	01♎46.3	07 54.5	20 31.1	08 30.8
	18	06 16.1	12 55.4	22 03.2	13 18.4
	28	10 47.0	17 50.9	23 59.9	18 07.1
OCT	8	15 18.1	22 40.3	26 18.3	22 56.1
	18	19 48.7	27 23.4	28 55.5	27 45.2
	28	24 18.1	01♎59.6	01♑49.1	02♎33.4
NOV	7	28 45.5	06 28.1	04 57.0	07 20.0
	17	03♏10.1	10 48.1	08 17.2	12 04.0
	27	07 30.9	14 58.2	11 48.1	16 44.5
DEC	7	11 46.7	18 56.9	15 28.2	21 19.9
	17	15 56.6	22 42.7	19 16.1	25 49.1
	27	19 59.1	26 13.1	23 10.9	00♏10.1
JAN	6	23♏52.5	29♎25.2	27♑11.3	04♏20.9
JAN	1	25N25.1	28S13.6	12S13.5	21N34.5
	21	28 08.8	24 22.5	12 20.8	22 31.1
FEB	10	30 34.6	19 39.5	11 59.1	23 20.8
MAR	2	31 43.3	14 42.6	11 10.4	24 05.6
	22	31 25.0	09 57.4	09 58.8	24 41.8
APR	11	30 03.7	05 41.9	08 31.5	25 01.8
MAY	1	28 01.0	02 09.5	06 59.7	24 57.8
	21	25 28.1	00N31.3	05 39.6	24 23.7
JUN	10	22 30.7	02 16.4	04 51.3	23 16.6
	30	19 12.8	03 06.9	04 51.2	21 35.9
JUL	20	15 38.6	03 08.2	05 41.3	19 23.5
AUG	9	11 53.0	02 28.8	07 08.1	16 43.4
	29	08 01.5	01 19.5	08 52.3	13 40.7
SEP	18	04 09.7	00S07.8	10 36.9	10 22.0
OCT	8	00 23.8	01 40.6	12 09.5	06 54.6
	28	03S10.2	03 05.7	13 20.9	03 26.6
NOV	17	06 26.1	04 08.9	14 04.8	00 06.8
DEC	7	09 18.7	04 35.0	14 16.9	02S55.6
	27	11S43.8	04S07.5	13S55.1	05S31.5

1996		Ceres 1	Pallas 2	Juno 3	Vesta 4
JAN	1	21♏57.0	27♎51.6	25♑10.4	02♏16.9
	11	25 45.4	00♏53.5	29 13.2	06 21.8
	21	29 22.2	03 32.0	03♒20.3	10 12.7
	31	02♐45.2	05 42.7	07 30.8	13 46.0
FEB	10	05 51.9	07 20.6	11 43.7	16 58.3
	20	08 39.6	08 20.3	15 58.5	19 45.2
MAR	1	11 04.9	08R36.0	20 14.4	22 01.0
	11	13 04.4	08 03.7	24 30.4	23 40.4
	21	14 34.3	06 41.6	28 46.2	24 37.6
	31	15 30.6	04 32.9	03♓00.9	24R47.6
APR	10	15 50.2	01 48.5	07 13.5	24 08.4
	20	15R31.0	28♎45.3	11 23.4	22 41.9
	30	14 33.3	25 45.1	15 29.6	20 38.0
MAY	10	13 01.3	23 08.4	19 31.0	18 13.9
	20	11 03.0	21 10.1	23 26.3	15 50.5
	30	08 51.2	19 58.4	27 13.8	13 49.8
JUN	9	06 40.5	19D34.4	00♈52.0	12 27.7
	19	04 44.9	19 55.3	04 18.7	11 52.6
	29	03 16.1	20 56.6	07 30.8	12D07.1
JUL	9	02 21.1	22 32.5	10 25.2	13 08.2
	19	02D02.6	24 37.8	12 57.7	14 51.0
	29	02 20.4	27 07.8	15 03.8	17 10.0
AUG	8	03 12.1	29 58.3	16 37.9	19 59.6
	18	04 34.2	03♏06.1	17 33.7	23 15.2
	28	06 23.3	06 28.1	17R46.1	26 52.4
SEP	7	08 35.3	10 01.9	17 12.3	00♐47.5
	17	11 07.3	13 45.7	15 52.2	04 57.8
	27	13 56.3	17 37.6	13 53.9	09 21.0
OCT	7	16 59.5	21 36.0	11 33.5	13 54.6
	17	20 15.1	25 39.7	09 12.9	18 37.2
	27	23 40.9	29 47.5	07 15.6	23 27.2
NOV	6	27 15.2	03♐58.3	05 59.8	28 23.4
	16	00♑56.7	08 11.1	05D36.2	03♑24.6
	26	04 43.9	12 24.8	06 08.3	08 29.8
DEC	6	08 35.6	16 38.4	07 33.1	13 38.2
	16	12 30.9	20 51.0	09 45.6	18 49.0
	26	16 28.4	25 01.5	12 39.3	24 01.2
JAN	5	20♑27.4	29♐08.9	16♈07.4	29♑14.1
JAN	1	12S15.4	03S50.2	13S44.3	06S05.3
	21	14 02.9	01 51.0	12 40.5	07 56.3
FEB	10	15 21.3	01N39.1	11 06.0	09 04.1
MAR	1	16 14.5	06 43.4	09 05.4	09 25.9
	21	16 49.6	12 55.5	06 44.9	09 03.5
APR	10	17 15.6	19 01.3	04 11.8	08 08.2
	30	17 40.5	23 25.0	01 34.6	07 06.1
MAY	20	18 08.2	25 14.1	00N57.0	06 37.5
JUN	9	18 39.7	24 45.4	03 11.4	07 14.0
	29	19 19.4	22 46.3	04 54.7	08 56.0
JUL	19	20 13.3	19 59.3	05 49.2	11 23.1
AUG	8	21 22.5	16 52.9	05 33.1	14 11.8
	28	22 41.4	13 45.7	03 43.3	17 02.3
SEP	17	24 01.2	10 50.1	00 12.9	19 38.3
OCT	7	25 12.7	08 15.4	04S14.5	21 46.7
	27	26 08.0	06 09.0	07 57.3	23 16.4
NOV	16	26 40.6	04 36.9	09 34.8	23 59.7
DEC	6	26 46.7	03 43.6	09 01.1	23 52.4
	26	26S24.6	03N31.9	06S50.5	22S54.7

1997		Ceres 1	Pallas 2	Juno 3	Vesta 4
JAN	1	18♑51.7	27♐30.3	14♈40.4	27♑08.8
	11	22 51.0	01♑35.4	18 26.6	02♒22.0
	21	26 50.2	05 35.4	22 38.9	07 34.8
	31	00♒48.2	09 29.2	27 12.2	12 46.5
FEB	10	04 44.2	13 15.5	02♉02.3	17 56.7
	20	08 37.1	16 52.8	07 06.3	23 04.6
MAR	2	12 25.9	20 19.3	12 21.0	28 09.6
	12	16 09.7	23 33.2	17 44.3	03♓11.2
	22	19 47.0	26 32.3	23 13.4	08 08.5
APR	1	23 16.8	29 14.2	28 46.8	13 01.0
	11	26 37.5	01♒35.9	04♊23.2	17 48.0
	21	29 47.5	03 34.2	10 01.2	22 28.6
MAY	1	02♓45.1	05 05.5	15 39.1	27 02.0
	11	05 28.0	06 05.9	21 16.5	01♈27.3
	21	07 53.7	06 31.4	26 52.4	05 43.1
	31	09 59.5	06R19.1	02♋26.1	09 48.2
JUN	10	11 42.3	05 26.6	07 56.8	13 41.1
	20	12 58.4	03 55.1	13 24.1	17 19.4
	30	13 44.8	01 49.3	18 47.7	20 41.3
JUL	10	13R57.9	29♑18.2	24 07.2	23 43.6
	20	13 35.8	26 35.8	29 21.8	26 22.9
	30	12 38.5	23 57.1	04♌31.4	28 35.5
AUG	9	11 08.6	21 36.8	09 35.8	00♉16.6
	19	09 13.1	19 46.0	14 34.5	01 21.4
	29	07 02.8	18 30.9	19 26.7	01 45.4
SEP	8	04 51.0	17 53.7	24 12.4	01R24.7
	18	02 51.7	17D53.5	28 50.6	00 18.8
	28	01 16.4	18 27.2	03♍20.8	28♈31.7
OCT	8	00 13.2	19 31.1	07 41.8	26 12.7
	18	29♒46.4	21 01.2	11 52.7	23 38.5
	28	29D56.1	22 53.7	15 52.4	21 08.0
NOV	7	00♓40.8	25 05.3	19 38.9	18 59.8
	17	01 57.5	27 32.7	23 10.4	17 27.7
	27	03 42.2	00♒13.4	26 24.7	16 39.0
DEC	7	05 51.7	03 05.0	29 19.0	16D35.6
	17	08 22.1	06 05.4	01♎50.1	17 15.1
	27	11 10.4	09 12.8	03 54.4	18 33.0
JAN	6	14♓13.9	12♒25.8	05♎27.7	20♈24.5

JAN	1	26S12.7	03N36.7	05S58.3	22S28.1
	21	25 16.5	04 19.8	02 36.2	20 32.0
FEB	10	23 59.2	05 42.9	01N08.4	18 00.3
MAR	2	22 27.3	07 41.8	04 53.3	15 03.3
	22	20 49.2	10 10.0	08 20.0	11 51.7
APR	11	19 14.6	12 58.0	11 13.8	08 36.2
MAY	1	17 54.1	15 52.0	13 23.5	05 27.1
	21	16 59.8	18 31.4	14 42.6	02 34.1
JUN	10	16 44.1	20 27.0	15 08.8	00 06.4
	30	17 18.5	21 04.1	14 44.4	01N47.0
JUL	20	18 47.8	19 57.5	13 34.9	02 57.2
AUG	9	20 58.9	17 12.3	11 48.4	03 16.2
	29	23 12.4	13 25.5	09 34.6	02 38.6
SEP	18	24 36.7	09 24.8	07 03.6	01 08.3
OCT	8	24 43.4	05 46.6	04 25.8	00S48.4
	28	23 38.6	02 50.3	01 52.3	02 20.5
NOV	17	21 42.0	00 43.0	00S25.7	02 42.2
DEC	7	19 10.6	00S35.4	02 15.4	01 44.7
	27	16S15.4	01S08.6	03S22.6	00N13.8

1998		Ceres 1	Pallas 2	Juno 3	Vesta 4
JAN	1	12♓40.4	10♒48.7	04♎45.1	19♈24.9
	11	15 50.5	14 03.8	06 01.5	21 31.2
	21	19 11.9	17 22.2	06 41.0	24 03.3
	31	22 43.0	20 42.7	06R40.4	26 57.1
FEB	10	26 21.8	24 04.0	05 58.1	00♉08.9
	20	00♈06.8	27 25.1	04 36.2	03 35.2
MAR	2	03 56.8	00♓44.9	02 40.2	07 13.7
	12	07 50.4	04 02.3	00 21.3	11 01.9
	22	11 46.7	07 16.2	27♍53.9	14 58.1
APR	1	15 44.8	10 25.5	25 33.6	19 00.7
	11	19 43.6	13 29.0	23 34.6	23 08.4
	21	23 42.5	16 25.4	22 06.4	27 20.1
MAY	1	27 40.6	19 13.4	21 13.8	01♊34.9
	11	01♉37.1	21 51.0	20D58.1	05 52.0
	21	05 31.2	24 16.8	21 17.1	10 10.6
	31	09 22.3	26 28.4	22 07.8	14 30.2
JUN	10	13 09.2	28 23.3	23 26.2	18 50.1
	20	16 51.2	29 58.8	25 08.3	23 10.0
	30	20 27.0	01♈11.5	27 10.7	27 29.2
JUL	10	23 55.2	01 58.0	29 30.2	01♋47.2
	20	27 14.6	02 14.8	02♎03.9	06 03.4
	30	00♊23.3	01R58.5	04 49.6	10 17.3
AUG	9	03 18.9	01 07.1	07 45.4	14 28.2
	19	05 59.3	29♓40.4	10 49.3	18 35.2
	29	08 21.1	27 41.3	14 00.1	22 37.5
SEP	8	10 21.0	25 17.2	17 16.4	26 33.8
	18	11 55.2	22 39.2	20 37.1	00♌23.0
	28	12 59.2	20 01.4	24 01.0	04 03.3
OCT	8	13 28.9	17 38.4	27 27.3	07 32.7
	18	13R21.0	15 41.7	00♏54.9	10 49.1
	28	12 33.5	14 19.7	04 22.9	13 49.2
NOV	7	11 08.5	13 36.4	07 50.2	16 29.7
	17	09 12.4	13D31.7	11 16.0	18 46.6
	27	06 56.4	14 04.0	14 39.1	20 34.8
DEC	7	04 36.6	15 10.0	17 58.3	21 49.2
	17	02 29.0	16 45.9	21 12.3	22 24.5
	27	00 48.3	18 48.3	24 19.8	22R15.8
JAN	6	29♉44.1	21♓13.5	27♏18.9	21♌21.1

JAN	1	15S28.8	01S10.5	03S30.9	00N50.3
	21	12 14.2	00 55.3	03 22.7	03 33.7
FEB	10	08 50.7	00 09.3	01 59.6	06 33.5
MAR	2	05 23.9	00N59.9	00N34.1	09 36.7
	22	01 59.2	02 24.1	03 41.4	12 33.2
APR	11	01N18.4	03 54.8	06 22.8	15 14.6
MAY	1	04 23.9	05 23.1	07 57.3	17 34.3
	21	07 12.9	06 38.7	08 19.0	19 26.7
JUN	10	09 41.8	07 29.9	07 41.6	20 48.0
	30	11 47.6	07 41.8	06 21.7	21 36.0
JUL	20	13 28.6	06 56.1	04 33.0	21 50.9
AUG	9	14 44.7	04 53.5	02 26.4	21 34.7
	29	15 37.9	01 25.3	00 10.4	20 52.0
SEP	18	16 12.6	03S05.7	02S07.5	19 50.1
OCT	8	16 35.2	07 37.8	04 20.7	18 39.0
	28	16 53.1	11 08.0	06 23.0	17 32.1
NOV	17	17 11.9	13 10.6	08 08.5	16 46.7
DEC	7	17 35.8	13 52.4	09 31.9	16 43.2
	27	18N12.1	13S32.0	10S28.6	17N41.3

1999		Ceres 1	Pallas 2	Juno 3	Vesta 4
JAN	1	00R11.3	19♓58.3	25♏50.5	21R54.2
	11	29♉27.2	22 33.7	28 44.9	20♌36.9
	21	29D24.3	25 27.6	01♐28.3	18 38.5
	31	00♊01.5	28 37.7	03 58.5	16 11.2
FEB	10	01 15.1	02♈01.6	06 13.1	13 32.8
	20	03 00.9	05 37.8	08 09.4	11 03.4
MAR	2	05 14.6	09 24.8	09 44.3	09 02.1
	12	07 51.8	13 21.2	10 54.8	07 41.4
	22	10 49.0	17 26.4	11 37.6	07 07.1
APR	1	14 02.9	21 39.2	11R49.8	07D19.9
	11	17 30.7	25 59.1	11 29.4	08 16.3
	21	21 10.3	00♉25.7	10 35.9	09 51.5
MAY	1	24 59.8	04 58.3	09 11.3	12 00.5
	11	28 57.4	09 36.7	07 20.6	14 37.9
	21	03♋02.0	14 20.7	05 12.2	17 39.6
	31	07 12.3	19 09.8	02 57.4	21 01.9
JUN	10	11 27.4	24 03.9	00 48.2	24 41.3
	20	15 46.4	29 02.7	28♏55.7	28 35.6
	30	20 08.6	04♊05.7	27 28.7	02♍42.5
JUL	10	24 33.4	09 12.8	26 32.2	07 00.2
	20	29 00.1	14 23.4	26 08.4	11 27.5
	30	03♌28.1	19 36.5	26D17.0	16 02.9
AUG	9	07 56.8	24 51.5	26 56.1	20 45.6
	19	12 25.7	00♋07.5	28 03.1	25 34.7
	29	16 53.9	05 22.6	29 34.9	00♎29.4
SEP	8	21 21.1	10 35.2	01♐28.5	05 29.1
	18	25 46.2	15 42.8	03 41.2	10 33.1
	28	00♍08.3	20 43.0	06 10.3	15 40.9
OCT	8	04 26.6	25 32.2	08 53.8	20 52.0
	18	08 39.7	00♌05.5	11 49.6	26 05.8
	28	12 46.2	04 18.0	14 55.8	01♏21.6
NOV	7	16 44.7	08 03.6	18 11.1	06 39.0
	17	20 32.9	11 14.0	21 34.0	11 57.4
	27	24 08.5	13 40.0	25 03.2	17 16.0
DEC	7	27 29.0	15 11.8	28 37.4	22 34.1
	17	00♎30.9	15R39.6	02♑15.8	27 51.2
	27	03 10.5	14 56.7	05 57.1	03♐06.2
JAN	6	05♎23.6	13♌03.2	09♑40.4	08♐18.4

JAN	1	18N24.2	13S19.3	10S38.1	18N06.5
	21	19 26.9	12 05.8	10 56.6	20 22.7
FEB	10	20 50.0	10 26.2	10 42.3	22 55.1
MAR	2	22 24.4	08 32.3	09 55.5	24 40.9
	22	23 58.2	06 34.9	08 39.1	25 13.2
APR	11	25 20.1	04 43.8	07 00.6	24 41.9
MAY	1	26 20.5	03 08.4	05 15.0	23 22.1
	21	26 52.5	01 58.0	03 45.7	21 23.2
JUN	10	26 51.5	01 21.6	02 57.6	18 50.1
	30	26 15.8	01 27.3	03 03.4	15 47.1
JUL	20	25 06.5	02 21.8	03 57.7	12 19.0
AUG	9	23 27.1	04 09.5	05 25.0	08 31.5
	29	21 23.4	06 51.2	07 09.1	04 31.0
SEP	18	19 02.9	10 23.0	08 56.3	00 25.0
OCT	8	16 34.5	14 35.2	10 36.4	03S38.5
	28	14 09.0	19 11.4	12 01.2	07 30.8
NOV	17	11 57.9	23 45.3	13 04.5	11 03.2
DEC	7	10 14.6	27 35.2	13 41.5	14 06.6
	27	09N13.2	29S37.6	13S49.3	16S33.8

2000	Ceres 1	Pallas 2	Juno 3	Vesta 4
JAN 1	04♎20.7	14 R 08.3	07♑48.6	05♐42.7
11	06 18.6	11♌43.4	11 32.5	10 53.1
21	07 42.6	08 33.2	15 16.8	15 58.9
31	08 28.3	05 10.2	19 00.6	20 59.3
FEB 10	08 R 31.6	02 08.7	22 42.9	25 52.8
20	07 51.3	29♋56.1	26 22.5	00♑37.8
MAR 1	06 30.0	28 44.0	29 58.3	05 12.9
11	04 35.3	28 D 33.3	03♒29.1	09 36.1
21	02 21.2	29 18.1	06 53.4	13 44.8
31	00 04.9	00♌49.3	10 09.8	17 36.5
APR 10	28♍03.8	02 58.0	13 16.5	21 08.0
20	26 32.3	05 36.6	16 11.4	24 15.4
30	25 38.8	08 38.7	18 52.3	26 54.6
MAY 10	25 D 26.6	11 59.6	21 16.1	29 00.0
20	25 54.9	15 35.0	23 19.7	00♒26.6
30	27 00.2	19 21.6	24 59.6	01 09.4
JUN 9	28 38.3	23 17.7	26 11.3	01 R 04.1
19	00♎44.6	27 21.0	26 50.8	00 10.4
29	03 14.7	01♍30.1	26 R 54.2	28♑32.6
JUL 9	06 05.0	05 44.0	26 18.6	26 22.0
19	09 12.2	10 01.8	25 04.1	23 57.1
29	12 33.3	14 22.7	23 14.5	21 38.4
AUG 8	16 06.4	18 46.3	20 59.0	19 45.5
18	19 49.2	23 11.7	18 32.1	18 32.3
28	23 40.1	27 38.9	16 10.6	18 D 05.2
SEP 7	27 37.9	02♎07.4	14 11.0	18 25.3
17	01♏41.3	06 36.5	12 46.6	19 29.5
27	05 49.1	11 06.1	12 04.5	21 12.5
OCT 7	10 00.6	15 35.7	12 D 07.6	23 29.5
17	14 14.6	20 04.7	12 54.4	26 15.1
27	18 30.6	24 32.6	14 21.8	29 24.5
NOV 6	22 47.6	28 58.8	16 25.8	02♒53.9
16	27 04.8	03♏22.5	19 01.9	06 39.9
26	01♐21.5	07 43.0	22 05.8	10 39.5
DEC 6	05 36.8	11 59.2	25 34.1	14 50.4
16	09 49.8	16 09.9	29 23.6	19 10.4
26	13 59.6	20 14.0	03♓31.3	23 37.9
JAN 5	18♐05.2	24♏09.8	07♓55.1	28♒11.5
JAN 1	09 N 06.0	29 S 42.1	13 S 46.5	17 S 04.2
21	09 15.3	27 42.2	13 16.6	18 39.0
FEB 10	10 27.7	21 56.9	12 18.2	19 31.0
MAR 1	12 27.9	13 48.9	10 54.7	19 44.4
21	14 28.5	05 34.7	09 11.6	19 28.9
APR 10	15 27.8	01 N 11.2	07 16.3	18 59.4
30	14 55.2	05 58.9	05 18.1	18 35.8
MAY 20	13 03.0	08 55.9	03 29.2	18 41.9
JUN 9	10 17.9	10 21.8	02 05.9	19 39.9
29	07 01.5	10 37.3	01 29.5	21 34.4
JUL 19	03 27.9	10 01.0	02 03.4	23 53.4
AUG 8	00 S 13.1	08 49.3	03 58.7	25 44.3
28	03 54.2	07 16.2	06 53.2	26 42.0
SEP 17	07 29.0	05 34.5	09 53.8	26 51.4
OCT 7	10 51.4	03 55.9	12 12.8	26 21.0
27	13 55.7	02 31.7	13 29.9	25 13.3
NOV 16	16 36.9	01 32.9	13 42.6	23 29.1
DEC 6	18 51.0	01 09.9	12 55.6	21 10.0
26	20 S 35.4	01 N 32.0	11 S 16.0	18 S 20.0

2001	Ceres 1	Pallas 2	Juno 3	Vesta 4
JAN 1	16♐27.6	22♏36.6	06♓07.8	26♒21.4
11	20 30.1	26 26.6	10 40.2	00♓57.9
21	24 26.7	00♐05.2	15 25.5	05 38.1
31	28 16.1	03 30.0	20 22.3	10 21.3
FEB 10	01♑56.7	06 38.2	25 29.0	15 06.3
20	05 27.1	09 26.7	00♈44.3	19 52.5
MAR 2	08 45.4	11 51.2	06 07.7	24 38.9
12	11 49.4	13 47.4	11 37.6	29 24.9
22	14 37.0	15 10.2	17 13.5	04♈09.8
APR 1	17 05.3	15 54.2	22 54.5	08 53.2
11	19 11.3	15 R 54.4	28 39.8	13 34.2
21	20 51.9	15 07.6	04♉28.7	18 12.5
MAY 1	22 03.2	13 33.2	10 20.6	22 47.5
11	22 42.0	11 17.0	16 14.3	27 18.4
21	22 R 45.7	08 30.4	22 09.7	01♉44.8
31	22 12.7	05 31.4	28 05.8	06 05.9
JUN 10	21 04.4	02 40.7	04♊01.7	10 20.8
20	19 25.2	00 16.2	09 56.7	14 28.9
30	17 23.8	28♏30.8	15 50.0	18 28.9
JUL 10	15 12.5	27 30.2	21 40.7	22 19.6
20	13 04.8	27 D 14.7	27 28.0	25 59.5
30	11 14.0	27 41.5	03♋10.6	29 26.6
AUG 9	09 50.4	28 45.5	08 47.7	02♊38.8
19	08 59.9	00♐21.6	14 18.2	05 33.5
29	08 D 45.3	02 24.9	19 40.7	08 07.1
SEP 8	09 06.1	04 50.8	24 53.8	10 16.1
18	09 59.8	07 35.4	29 56.0	11 56.0
28	11 23.4	10 35.7	04♌45.4	13 01.7
OCT 8	13 13.2	13 48.7	09 19.8	13 28.8
18	15 25.9	17 12.2	13 36.9	13 R 13.3
28	17 58.3	20 44.2	17 33.3	12 13.3
NOV 7	20 47.4	24 22.8	21 05.7	10 31.8
17	23 50.7	28 06.6	24 10.1	08 16.6
27	27 06.1	01♑54.3	26 41.2	05 42.2
DEC 7	00♒31.4	05 44.4	28 33.9	03 07.4
17	04 05.1	09 36.1	29 42.8	00 50.6
27	07 45.5	13 28.0	00 R 03.0	29♉06.9
JAN 6	11♒31.3	17♑19.0	29♌32.2	28♉05.0
JAN 1	21 S 00.8	01 N 48.8	10 S 37.1	17 S 23.8
21	22 07.0	03 21.1	08 02.0	14 02.4
FEB 10	22 47.5	05 52.4	04 56.0	10 25.4
MAR 2	23 09.4	09 21.3	01 30.6	06 40.7
22	23 22.9	13 37.4	02 N 01.9	02 56.2
APR 11	23 40.8	18 15.6	05 28.5	00 N 41.0
MAY 1	24 17.5	22 31.6	08 36.1	04 04.1
21	25 24.5	25 28.3	11 12.1	07 07.0
JUN 10	27 02.2	26 21.5	13 05.7	09 44.8
30	28 50.6	25 07.9	14 08.8	11 53.6
JUL 20	30 16.0	22 21.6	14 17.6	13 30.9
AUG 9	30 59.3	18 47.7	13 33.3	14 35.8
29	31 06.8	15 02.9	12 02.0	15 10.0
SEP 18	30 52.0	11 30.8	09 53.9	15 17.3
OCT 8	30 21.1	08 25.8	07 22.6	15 04.3
28	29 33.9	05 56.2	04 44.4	14 40.1
NOV 17	28 27.7	04 06.8	02 18.9	14 15.9
DEC 7	27 00.3	02 59.7	00 30.5	14 06.3
27	25 S 11.3	02 N 35.0	00 S 11.2	14 N 26.4

2002	Ceres 1	Pallas 2	Juno 3	Vesta 4
JAN 1	09♒37.8	15♑23.7	29 R 54.0	28 R 30.4
11	13 25.8	19 14.0	28♌57.8	27♉50.8
21	17 17.4	23 01.9	27 14.7	27 D 55.6
31	21 11.4	26 46.4	24 57.1	28 42.0
FEB 10	25 06.8	00♒26.4	22 22.4	00♊05.3
20	29 02.6	04 00.7	19 51.4	02 00.6
MAR 2	02♓57.8	07 28.0	17 43.5	04 23.0
12	06 51.6	10 47.1	16 12.1	07 07.9
22	10 43.1	13 56.4	15 23.6	10 11.8
APR 1	14 31.1	16 54.2	15 D 18.6	13 31.4
11	18 15.0	19 38.9	15 53.7	17 04.0
21	21 53.5	22 08.0	17 04.6	20 47.5
MAY 1	25 25.4	24 19.2	18 45.8	24 40.1
11	28 49.6	26 09.8	20 52.0	28 40.1
21	02♈04.5	27 36.6	23 19.0	02♋46.5
31	05 08.5	28 36.2	26 03.0	06 58.2
JUN 10	07 59.6	29 05.4	29 00.8	11 14.2
20	10 35.5	29 R 01.0	02♍09.9	15 34.0
30	12 53.6	28 21.1	05 28.0	19 56.7
JUL 10	14 50.9	27 05.3	08 53.3	24 21.9
20	16 23.7	25 16.5	12 24.6	28 49.1
30	17 28.7	23 01.3	16 00.3	03♌17.7
AUG 9	18 02.2	20 29.9	19 39.5	07 47.3
19	18 R 00.8	17 55.2	23 21.4	12 17.5
29	17 23.3	15 31.1	27 04.9	16 47.5
SEP 8	16 10.2	13 28.9	00♎49.4	21 17.1
18	14 26.0	11 57.2	04 34.0	25 45.5
28	12 19.9	11 00.0	08 18.1	00♍11.8
OCT 8	10 04.3	10 38.3	12 00.9	04 35.4
18	07 54.2	10 D 50.7	15 41.5	08 55.2
28	06 03.4	11 34.3	19 19.1	13 09.9
NOV 7	04 42.2	12 45.6	22 52.7	17 18.3
17	03 57.3	14 21.3	26 21.2	21 18.3
27	03 D 50.7	16 17.8	29 43.4	25 08.2
DEC 7	04 21.3	18 32.1	02♏57.8	28 45.3
17	05 26.5	21 01.4	06 02.9	02♎06.5
27	07 02.4	23 43.2	08 56.8	05 08.2
JAN 6	09♈05.1	26♒35.6	11♏37.4	07♎46.1
JAN 1	24 S 40.9	02 N 35.2	00 S 07.6	14 N 37.1
21	22 27.9	03 00.4	01 N 12.7	15 41.6
FEB 10	20 00.3	04 01.0	04 05.9	17 12.0
MAR 2	17 23.7	05 31.4	07 33.5	18 54.0
22	14 44.2	07 24.8	10 26.8	20 33.4
APR 11	12 09.0	09 32.9	12 13.8	21 58.6
MAY 1	09 45.1	11 45.9	12 54.4	23 00.6
21	07 40.1	13 50.8	12 39.0	23 32.8
JUN 10	06 01.8	15 29.4	11 39.3	23 31.4
30	04 58.6	16 17.5	10 05.6	22 54.9
JUL 20	04 38.3	15 47.3	08 06.9	21 44.3
AUG 9	05 06.8	13 41.5	05 51.1	20 02.8
29	06 22.7	10 13.3	03 25.3	17 55.3
SEP 18	08 07.9	06 08.0	00 56.5	15 28.5
OCT 8	09 42.6	02 15.9	01 S 28.7	12 50.4
28	10 22.3	00 S 51.1	03 43.9	10 10.4
NOV 17	09 47.1	03 01.7	05 42.4	07 39.6
DEC 7	08 06.0	04 17.2	07 18.0	05 30.6
27	05 S 38.5	04 S 44.0	08 S 24.4	03 N 58.1

1931		Psyche 16	Eros 433	Lilith 1181	Toro 1685
JAN	1	02R09.1	27♌32.8	10R24.9	29♑03.8
	11	01♊32.4	02♍35.6	09♊32.6	08♒32.2
	21	01D35.9	06 17.4	09D29.1	18 44.7
	31	02 18.1	08 24.6	10 13.7	29 43.3
FEB	10	03 34.9	08 59.0	11 41.5	11♓27.8
	20	05 21.9	08R20.1	13 46.5	23 54.1
MAR	2	07 34.8	07 15.4	16 22.8	06♈52.8
	12	10 09.0	06D34.0	19 24.5	20 10.4
	22	13 01.0	06 46.6	22 46.9	03♉31.9
APR	1	16 07.7	08 07.1	26 26.0	16 41.6
	11	19 26.0	10 29.4	00♋18.1	29 25.5
	21	22 54.0	13 42.0	04 20.7	11♊33.5
MAY	1	26 29.6	17 34.2	08 31.5	22 58.7
	11	00♋11.1	21 54.6	12 48.5	03♋38.3
	21	03 57.3	26 35.3	17 10.3	13 33.2
	31	07 46.9	01♎31.0	21 35.7	22 46.3
JUN	10	11 39.0	06 36.5	26 03.4	01♌21.7
	20	15 32.7	11 49.1	00♌32.8	09 24.3
	30	19 27.2	17 07.0	05 03.1	16 58.5
JUL	10	23 21.6	22 27.9	09 33.4	24 08.3
	20	27 15.4	27 51.5	14 03.6	00♍57.8
	30	01♌07.8	03♏17.0	18 32.7	07 30.0
AUG	9	04 58.0	08 43.5	23 00.4	13 47.4
	19	08 45.5	14 11.5	27 26.2	19 52.7
	29	12 29.1	19 40.5	01♍49.6	25 47.6
SEP	8	16 08.2	25 10.4	06 09.9	01♎33.6
	18	19 41.6	00♐41.6	10 26.6	07 12.4
	28	23 08.0	06 14.0	14 38.8	12 44.6
OCT	8	26 26.1	11 47.6	18 46.0	18 11.5
	18	29 34.2	17 22.8	22 47.1	23 33.7
	28	02♍30.4	22 59.5	26 40.9	28 51.8
NOV	7	05 12.5	28 38.0	00♎26.3	04♏06.2
	17	07 37.8	04♑18.5	04 01.8	09 17.4
	27	09 43.3	10 00.8	07 25.4	14 25.4
DEC	7	11 25.9	15 45.4	10 35.3	19 30.6
	17	12 41.9	21 32.3	13 29.0	24 33.0
	27	13 27.9	27 21.6	16 03.5	29 32.5
JAN	6	13R40.9	03♒13.6	18♎15.8	04♐29.3
JAN	1	16N19.9	27N03.9	21N42.5	16S54.3
	21	16 44.7	07 26.9	20 38.9	11 04.3
FEB	10	17 38.1	13S30.0	20 18.7	03 00.7
MAR	2	18 46.3	24 31.7	20 25.1	06N11.3
	22	19 54.8	26 20.1	20 36.3	14 18.4
APR	11	20 51.9	24 29.9	20 34.8	19 08.4
MAY	1	21 29.2	22 13.3	20 08.8	20 02.0
	21	21 41.0	20 44.7	19 12.2	17 57.7
JUN	10	21 24.9	20 19.7	17 43.1	14 16.4
	30	20 40.6	20 47.7	15 42.9	09 52.7
JUL	20	19 30.0	21 50.3	13 15.3	05 14.3
AUG	9	17 56.8	23 08.2	10 25.3	00 34.6
	29	16 05.9	24 23.5	07 18.5	03S59.8
SEP	18	14 03.7	25 21.0	04 00.9	08 24.1
OCT	8	11 57.7	25 47.9	00 38.9	12 34.2
	28	09 56.8	25 34.1	02S41.2	16 25.7
NOV	17	08 11.2	24 32.6	05 52.9	19 53.6
DEC	7	06 53.3	22 39.9	08 49.3	22 52.6
	27	06N16.2	19S55.7	11S22.8	25S17.4

1932		Psyche 16	Eros 433	Lilith 1181	Toro 1685
JAN	1	13♍38.7	00♒17.3	17♎12.6	02♐01.2
	11	13R34.4	06 10.7	19 12.5	06 56.6
	21	12 55.0	12 07.0	20 44.6	11 48.8
	31	11 42.3	18 06.4	21 45.4	16 37.9
FEB	10	10 01.2	24 09.3	22 11.1	21 23.7
	20	08 00.6	00♓16.0	21R59.4	26 05.7
MAR	1	05 52.6	06 26.8	21 09.7	00♑43.8
	11	03 49.7	12 42.3	19 44.4	05 17.7
	21	02 04.1	19 02.9	17 50.0	09 46.8
	31	00 44.4	25 29.1	15 37.2	14 11.0
APR	10	29♌55.7	02♈01.8	13 19.2	18 29.5
	20	29D40.1	08 41.5	11 10.4	22 41.6
	30	29 56.5	15 29.0	09 22.8	26 47.2
MAY	10	00♍42.6	22 25.2	08 04.7	00♒45.2
	20	01 55.4	29 30.7	07 20.8	04 35.1
	30	03 31.5	06♉46.6	07D11.5	08 17.3
JUN	9	05 27.7	14 13.6	07 35.5	11 52.0
	19	07 41.2	21 52.2	08 29.8	15 22.8
	29	10 09.1	29 43.1	09 50.8	18 59.0
JUL	9	12 49.5	07♊46.7	11 35.2	23 01.8
	19	15 40.3	16 02.9	13 39.7	28 36.6
	29	18 39.8	24 31.6	16 01.1	09♓39.4
AUG	8	21 46.5	03♋12.4	18 37.2	18♈58.0
	18	24 59.2	12 03.9	21 25.5	06♋03.1
	28	28 16.7	21 05.1	24 24.1	28 14.8
SEP	7	01♎38.0	00♌14.2	27 31.5	06♌54.1
	17	05 01.9	09 29.2	00♏46.1	12 57.4
	27	08 27.7	18 48.0	04 06.6	18 47.9
OCT	7	11 54.4	28 08.2	07 32.1	25 03.0
	17	15 20.9	07♍27.2	11 01.2	01♍45.1
	27	18 46.4	16 42.9	14 33.0	08 43.1
NOV	6	22 09.7	25 52.7	18 06.6	15 40.5
	16	25 29.6	04♎54.2	21 40.9	22 23.9
	26	28 44.9	13 45.5	25 15.0	28 44.2
DEC	6	01♏54.2	22 24.4	28 47.9	04♎34.0
	16	04 55.7	00♏48.9	02♐18.3	09 48.1
	26	07 47.8	08 57.9	05 45.2	14 21.6
JAN	5	10♏28.3	16♏49.5	09♐07.4	18♎07.6
JAN	1	06N14.7	19S06.9	11S56.6	25S47.6
	21	06 43.7	15 22.6	13 49.2	27 22.8
FEB	10	08 03.9	10 55.9	14 56.3	28 14.4
MAR	1	09 51.1	05 53.4	15 04.3	28 20.8
	21	11 26.6	00 22.5	14 05.5	27 41.5
APR	10	12 21.5	05N28.3	12 14.1	26 16.4
	30	12 27.5	11 28.2	10 11.5	24 02.6
MAY	20	11 49.6	17 22.3	08 40.6	20 48.7
JUN	9	10 35.8	22 48.7	08 02.2	15 58.0
	29	08 53.5	27 14.9	08 15.9	07 35.6
JUL	19	06 49.3	29 57.7	09 12.1	11N16.5
AUG	8	04 28.9	30 11.1	10 39.3	63 09.8
	28	01 57.6	27 26.2	12 27.0	62 39.0
SEP	17	00S39.3	21 48.5	14 26.0	38 46.3
OCT	7	03 16.6	13 57.3	16 28.4	23 39.0
	27	05 49.0	04 49.2	18 26.9	11 33.8
NOV	16	08 11.0	04S38.0	20 15.3	01 25.4
DEC	6	10 17.5	13 34.3	21 48.4	07S04.2
	26	12S03.4	21S20.9	23S02.4	14S08.5

1933		Psyche 16	Eros 433	Lilith 1181	Toro 1685
JAN	1	09♏25.6	13♏43.1	07♐47.2	16♎43.4
	11	11 58.1	21 23.5	11 05.7	19 57.3
	21	14 15.2	28 44.8	14 17.2	22 10.6
	31	16 14.2	05♐45.6	17 20.0	23 11.0
FEB	10	17 52.0	12 24.2	20 12.1	22R45.7
	20	19 05.5	18 39.6	22 51.6	20 44.1
MAR	2	19 51.5	24 29.7	25 15.9	17 03.7
	12	20 07.3	29 51.8	27 22.6	12 02.9
	22	19R51.1	04♑43.5	29 08.6	06 23.6
APR	1	19 02.6	09 00.0	00♑30.8	01 00.5
	11	17 44.2	12 36.1	01 25.7	26♍40.2
	21	16 01.4	15 25.3	01 50.5	23 43.9
MAY	1	14 02.5	17 18.5	01R42.4	22 12.6
	11	11 59.0	18 06.2	01 00.5	21D56.4
	21	10 02.4	17R39.3	29♐45.8	22 40.9
	31	08 23.2	15 51.4	28 02.7	24 14.2
JUN	10	07 09.6	12 47.4	25 59.2	26 25.8
	20	06 26.2	08 46.8	23 46.3	29 07.4
	30	06D14.7	04 25.1	21 36.8	02♎13.2
JUL	10	06 34.9	00 25.2	19 43.1	05 38.5
	20	07 24.6	27♐19.7	18 14.8	09 19.8
	30	08 41.2	25 25.7	17 18.3	13 14.9
AUG	9	10 22.0	24D45.6	16 56.4	17 21.6
	19	12 23.7	25 11.9	17D09.1	21 38.8
	29	14 44.1	26 35.2	17 54.7	26 05.5
SEP	8	17 20.4	28 45.7	19 10.5	00♏41.0
	18	20 10.6	01♑34.6	20 53.1	05 24.9
	28	23 12.9	04 55.3	22 59.6	10 17.2
OCT	8	26 25.5	08 42.3	25 26.9	15 17.5
	18	29 46.9	12 51.2	28 12.3	20 26.4
	28	03♐15.8	17 19.3	01♑13.6	25 44.0
NOV	7	06 51.0	22 03.8	04 28.5	01♐10.8
	17	10 31.3	27 02.8	07 55.3	06 47.4
	27	14 15.8	02♒15.2	11 32.3	12 34.8
DEC	7	18 03.3	07 39.7	15 18.2	18 33.9
	17	21 53.0	13 15.6	19 11.6	24 46.3
	27	25 43.8	19 02.4	23 11.4	01♑13.4
JAN	6	29♐34.6	24♒59.6	27♑16.6	07♑57.2
JAN	1	12S30.5	23S23.1	23S20.4	16S00.7
	21	13 43.1	29 03.4	24 06.5	21 23.8
FEB	10	14 25.8	32 58.0	24 31.6	25 07.4
MAR	2	14 35.9	35 16.4	24 38.4	25 58.4
	22	14 12.0	36 22.2	24 31.7	22 41.5
APR	11	13 16.3	36 47.3	24 16.8	16 58.6
MAY	1	12 00.4	37 04.3	23 57.7	12 08.5
	21	10 47.6	37 29.2	23 34.4	09 26.7
JUN	10	10 03.9	37 26.6	23 02.8	08 37.5
	30	10 03.1	35 27.7	22 22.3	09 09.2
JUL	20	10 43.9	31 35.4	21 42.8	10 35.6
AUG	9	11 56.8	27 47.2	21 17.0	12 37.3
	29	13 30.0	25 00.3	21 08.9	14 59.0
SEP	18	15 12.6	22 59.4	21 12.7	17 27.9
OCT	8	16 54.9	21 13.5	21 18.2	19 51.8
	28	18 28.7	19 17.1	21 14.9	21 57.7
NOV	17	19 46.5	16 53.2	20 53.6	23 31.6
DEC	7	20 42.6	13 51.7	20 07.7	24 17.5
	27	21S13.1	10S08.4	18S53.0	23S57.5

1934	Psyche 16	Eros 433	Lilith 1181	Toro 1685
JAN 1	27♐39.2	21♒59.8	25♑13.4	04♑33.1
11	01♑29.7	28 02.1	29 20.9	11 26.2
21	05 18.9	04♓14.9	03♒32.4	18 40.0
31	09 05.4	10 37.9	07 46.9	26 17.4
FEB 10	12 48.4	17 11.1	12 03.7	04♒21.9
20	16 26.4	23 55.0	16 22.1	12 57.6
MAR 2	19 58.0	00♈49.5	20 41.2	22 08.1
12	23 21.9	07 55.0	25 00.3	01♓57.5
22	26 36.2	15 11.9	29 18.7	12 28.4
APR 1	29 39.0	22 40.3	03♓35.4	23 41.6
11	02♒28.2	00♉20.4	07 49.9	05♈35.4
21	05 01.0	08 12.4	12 01.1	18 03.8
MAY 1	07 14.6	16 16.1	16 07.8	00♉56.4
11	09 05.7	24 31.4	20 09.2	13 59.5
21	10 30.7	02♊58.0	24 03.7	26 57.5
31	11 25.9	11 34.7	27 49.6	09♊35.3
JUN 10	11 48.0	20 21.1	01♈25.3	21 41.7
20	11R34.5	29 15.7	04 48.1	03♋09.9
30	10 45.3	08♋17.1	07 55.3	13 57.1
JUL 10	09 23.0	17 23.7	10 43.5	24 03.6
20	07 34.6	26 33.7	13 08.5	03♌31.7
30	05 31.4	05♌45.2	15 05.8	12 24.3
AUG 9	03 27.1	14 56.4	16 30.1	20 45.3
19	01 36.4	24 05.3	17 15.8	28 38.1
29	00 11.7	03♍09.9	17R18.8	06♍06.0
SEP 8	29♑20.9	12 08.7	16 37.0	13 12.2
18	29D08.5	21 00.1	15 12.6	19 59.3
28	29 34.9	29 42.6	13 15.0	26 29.4
OCT 8	00♒38.0	08♎15.4	10 59.7	02♎44.7
18	02 14.8	16 37.4	08 47.3	08 46.7
28	04 21.5	24 47.8	06 58.4	14 36.3
NOV 7	06 54.1	02♏46.6	05 48.3	20 14.9
17	09 49.5	10 33.3	05D26.2	25 42.9
27	13 04.2	18 07.9	05 54.1	01♏00.6
DEC 7	16 35.4	25 30.6	07 09.5	06 08.5
17	20 20.7	02♐41.3	09 07.9	11 06.1
27	24 17.9	09 40.2	11 43.2	15 53.2
JAN 6	28♒25.1	16♐27.8	14♈50.0	20♏29.1
JAN 1	21S16.4	09S06.0	18S29.6	23S40.0
21	21 12.5	04 31.8	16 37.1	21 30.7
FEB 10	20 42.2	00N37.2	14 15.9	17 32.2
MAR 2	19 49.6	06 11.2	11 29.3	11 29.4
22	18 41.0	11 55.5	08 22.2	03 21.9
APR 11	17 25.2	17 28.1	05 00.3	06N13.7
MAY 1	16 13.5	22 17.6	01 29.7	15 34.8
21	15 19.0	25 43.1	02N02.7	22 03.2
JUN 10	14 56.1	27 00.2	05 29.6	23 49.3
30	15 15.6	25 37.6	08 42.4	21 23.7
JUL 20	16 15.6	21 34.3	11 30.9	16 33.1
AUG 9	17 34.8	15 21.5	13 40.3	10 45.1
29	18 43.7	07 48.4	14 50.1	04 47.1
SEP 18	19 23.4	00S15.0	14 37.0	00S59.2
OCT 8	19 28.2	08 05.7	12 57.1	06 24.3
28	18 57.2	15 10.6	10 35.8	11 23.7
NOV 17	17 50.3	21 05.4	08 45.6	15 54.3
DEC 7	16 08.1	25 33.1	08 08.9	19 53.7
27	12S52.9	28S24.7	08N47.6	23S19.9

1935	Psyche 16	Eros 433	Lilith 1181	Toro 1685
JAN 1	26♒20.3	13♐05.4	13♈13.0	18♏12.6
11	00♓32.0	19 47.3	16 33.6	22 42.5
21	04 51.1	26 17.9	20 18.1	26 59.4
31	09 16.5	02♑37.4	24 22.1	01♐01.8
FEB 10	13 47.0	08 45.9	28 42.4	04 47.4
20	18 21.3	14 43.2	03♉15.7	08 13.3
MAR 2	22 58.4	20 29.4	07 59.5	11 15.9
12	27 37.7	26 04.2	12 51.9	13 50.0
22	02♈18.0	01♒26.9	17 50.7	15 49.6
APR 1	06 58.7	06 37.1	22 54.6	17 06.9
11	11 39.0	11 33.8	28 02.3	17R32.1
21	16 18.2	16 15.5	03♊12.5	16 54.8
MAY 1	20 55.6	20 40.8	08 24.4	15 05.6
11	25 30.5	24 47.1	13 37.3	11 59.6
21	00♉02.0	28 31.2	18 50.1	07 45.0
31	04 29.4	01♓49.4	24 02.5	02 46.1
JUN 10	08 51.9	04 35.8	29 13.8	27♏43.0
20	13 08.3	06 43.7	04♋23.5	23 18.7
30	17 17.7	08 04.8	09 31.0	20 02.7
JUL 10	21 18.6	08R28.6	14 36.1	18 08.1
20	25 09.4	07 45.8	19 38.0	17D33.7
30	28 48.5	05 49.2	24 36.4	18 11.1
AUG 9	02♊13.5	02 40.7	29 30.7	19 51.3
19	05 21.9	28♒38.2	04♌20.3	22 24.8
29	08 10.7	24 15.1	09 04.7	25 44.6
SEP 8	10 36.1	20 14.4	13 43.1	29 45.7
18	12 34.2	17 12.1	18 14.4	04♐24.4
28	14 00.5	15 27.0	22 37.9	09 38.8
OCT 8	14 50.6	15D03.4	26 52.0	15 28.6
18	15R01.0	15 55.0	00♍55.5	21 53.7
28	14 29.6	17 51.8	04 46.6	28 55.8
NOV 7	13 18.1	20 44.4	08 23.1	06♑36.8
17	11 33.2	24 23.6	11 42.5	14 58.4
27	09 26.3	28 42.5	14 42.0	24 02.7
DEC 7	07 13.5	03♓36.0	17 17.7	03♒52.4
17	05 12.1	08 59.3	19 26.1	14 31.3
27	03 36.3	14 49.5	21 02.6	26 11.6
JAN 6	02♊36.2	21♓04.3	22♍02.8	09♓16.8
JAN 1	13S14.2	28S52.3	09N07.1	24S06.1
21	10 23.3	29 43.8	10 55.0	26 49.8
FEB 10	07 10.9	29 09.2	13 14.1	29 00.9
MAR 2	03 44.1	27 23.6	15 44.6	30 43.6
22	00 10.7	24 44.8	18 09.0	32 03.5
APR 11	03N21.5	21 29.9	20 12.4	33 02.5
MAY 1	06 44.8	17 54.1	21 42.9	33 22.5
21	09 52.1	14 11.2	22 31.8	32 02.7
JUN 10	12 37.2	10 33.4	22 34.5	28 12.8
30	14 54.6	07 14.3	21 50.3	23 27.1
JUL 20	16 40.6	04 32.0	20 21.9	20 00.2
AUG 9	17 53.6	02 50.7	18 15.0	18 19.8
29	18 34.0	02 26.2	15 37.1	17 52.6
SEP 18	18 45.2	02 51.6	12 36.9	17 56.8
OCT 8	18 32.4	03 11.7	09 23.7	17 52.9
28	18 02.4	02 49.3	06 07.5	17 02.8
NOV 17	17 22.6	01 29.5	02 58.9	14 50.7
DEC 7	16 45.1	00N50.8	00 09.8	10 59.2
27	16N27.7	04N08.0	02S05.4	05S51.3

1936	Psyche 16	Eros 433	Lilith 1181	Toro 1685
JAN 1	03R01.4	17♓54.0	21♍37.5	02♓31.7
11	02♊21.2	24 20.1	22 18.0	16 31.5
21	02D21.1	01♈07.8	22R17.0	02♈43.6
31	03 00.0	08 16.0	21 32.9	21 07.8
FEB 10	04 14.1	15 43.2	20 08.4	10♉27.6
20	05 58.8	23 28.1	18 10.7	28 36.4
MAR 1	08 09.6	01♉30.0	15 51.9	14♊09.9
11	10 42.3	09 47.1	13 28.5	26 58.3
21	13 32.9	18 18.2	11 16.6	07♋32.2
31	16 38.4	27 01.9	09 30.0	16 29.2
APR 10	19 55.8	05♊56.0	08 17.9	24 17.8
20	23 22.9	14 58.6	07 43.6	01♌18.8
30	26 57.8	24 08.1	07D47.4	07 46.6
MAY 10	00♋38.8	03♋21.7	08 26.5	13 50.6
20	04 24.4	12 37.3	09 36.8	19 37.1
30	08 13.7	21 53.1	11 14.4	25 11.3
JUN 9	12 05.4	01♌06.2	13 15.1	00♍35.9
19	15 58.8	10 14.9	15 35.1	05 53.4
29	19 53.0	19 17.2	18 11.6	11 05.8
JUL 9	23 47.2	28 11.1	21 01.5	16 14.1
19	27 40.8	06♍55.5	24 02.7	21 19.6
29	01♌33.1	15 29.1	27 13.4	26 23.1
AUG 8	05 23.2	23 51.0	00♎31.7	01♎25.2
18	09 10.6	02♎01.0	03 56.3	06 26.6
28	12 54.3	09 59.0	07 26.1	11 27.9
SEP 7	16 33.5	17 44.9	10 59.8	16 29.4
17	20 07.1	25 19.5	14 36.7	21 31.5
27	23 33.8	02♏43.1	18 15.7	26 34.7
OCT 7	26 52.3	09 56.2	21 55.8	01♏39.2
17	00♍01.0	16 59.8	25 36.4	06 45.5
27	02 57.9	23 54.5	29 16.6	11 53.8
NOV 6	05 40.9	00♐40.9	02♏55.2	17 04.4
16	08 07.4	07 19.8	06 31.5	22 17.7
26	10 14.3	13 51.9	10 04.3	27 34.1
DEC 6	11 58.6	20 17.5	13 32.5	02♐54.0
16	13 16.7	26 37.4	16 54.8	08 17.9
26	14 05.0	02♑51.9	20 09.7	13 46.4
JAN 5	14♍20.6	09♑01.4	23♏15.5	19♐20.1
JAN 1	16N28.4	05N05.1	02S31.9	04S27.5
21	16 52.2	09 17.9	03 40.3	01N23.9
FEB 10	17 44.5	13 52.6	03 37.1	06 38.5
MAR 1	18 51.3	18 18.1	02 23.3	08 55.6
21	19 58.5	21 52.3	00 31.8	09 05.9
APR 10	20 54.3	23 48.0	01N08.1	08 20.2
30	21 30.2	23 27.4	02 03.7	06 55.5
MAY 20	21 40.7	20 40.0	02 06.9	04 56.9
JUN 9	21 23.2	15 47.9	01 22.7	02 29.1
29	20 37.6	09 33.3	00 00.1	00S21.9
JUL 19	19 25.9	02 41.1	01S52.2	03 30.2
AUG 8	17 51.7	04S11.6	04 06.1	06 49.5
28	15 59.9	10 37.3	06 34.6	10 13.8
SEP 17	13 56.9	16 16.5	09 10.9	13 36.6
OCT 7	11 50.1	20 55.6	11 49.1	16 51.2
27	09 48.2	24 24.5	14 23.3	19 50.1
NOV 16	08 01.7	26 36.6	16 48.3	22 24.6
DEC 6	06 42.4	27 29.2	18 59.4	24 25.6
26	06N03.6	27S03.7	20S52.6	25S42.8

1937	Psyche 16	Eros 433	Lilith 1181	Toro 1685
JAN 1	14♍18.4	06♑34.2	22♏02.3	17♐05.9
11	14R13.4	12 41.0	25 01.9	22 43.3
21	13 33.1	18 43.4	27 49.3	28 27.6
31	12 19.8	24 41.6	00♐22.3	04♑20.0
FEB 10	10 38.2	00♒36.1	02 38.3	10 22.3
20	08 37.3	06 27.0	04 34.5	16 36.5
MAR 2	06 29.2	12 14.5	06 07.7	23 05.1
12	04 26.5	17 59.0	07 14.8	29 51.7
22	02 41.1	23 40.6	07 52.4	07♒00.0
APR 1	01 21.8	29 19.4	07R57.9	14 35.1
11	00 33.4	04♓55.9	07 29.7	22 42.9
21	00D18.0	10 30.0	06 28.0	01♓29.8
MAY 1	00 34.7	16 02.1	04 56.1	11 02.7
11	01 20.9	21 32.4	03 00.4	21 27.7
21	02 33.7	27 00.9	00 50.7	02♈47.7
31	04 09.8	02♈27.8	28♏39.3	15 00.6
JUN 10	06 05.9	07 53.3	26 38.2	27 57.6
20	08 19.3	13 17.1	24 58.1	11♉22.1
30	10 47.2	18 39.4	23 46.4	24 55.1
JUL 10	13 27.4	24 00.1	23 06.8	08♊18.7
20	16 18.0	29 18.4	23D00.6	21 19.1
30	19 17.3	04♉34.1	23 26.5	03♋47.6
AUG 9	22 23.8	09 46.2	24 22.1	15 38.4
19	25 36.4	14 53.1	25 44.5	26 47.8
29	28 53.6	19 53.3	27 30.6	07♌14.6
SEP 8	02♎14.7	24 43.9	29 37.4	17 00.1
18	05 38.5	29 20.7	02♐02.4	26 06.3
28	09 04.0	03♊39.2	04 42.8	04♍36.5
OCT 8	12 30.4	07 31.0	07 36.8	12 34.3
18	15 56.7	10 46.5	10 42.4	20 02.6
28	19 21.9	13 13.9	13 57.9	27 04.2
NOV 7	22 44.9	14 37.1	17 22.0	03♎41.4
17	26 04.5	14R44.3	20 53.1	09 55.7
27	29 19.5	13 33.6	24 30.2	15 48.5
DEC 7	02♏28.4	11 22.6	28 12.2	21 20.2
17	05 29.4	09 01.7	01♑57.9	26 30.5
27	08 21.1	07 30.7	05 46.4	01♏19.0
JAN 6	11♏01.1	07D35.5	09♑36.8	05♏44.1
JAN 1	06N01.7	26S41.7	21S22.6	25S55.9
21	06 31.5	24 44.5	22 48.9	26 00.4
FEB 10	07 52.4	21 47.7	23 53.4	24 56.1
MAR 2	09 40.0	18 02.1	24 36.0	22 31.0
22	11 15.6	13 37.8	24 56.6	18 30.3
APR 11	12 10.2	08 43.6	24 52.3	12 35.7
MAY 1	12 15.8	03 26.3	24 17.6	04 29.2
21	11 37.3	02N09.2	23 11.0	05N45.0
JUN 10	10 23.0	07 59.6	21 47.1	16 45.2
30	08 40.3	14 03.5	20 33.4	25 16.0
JUL 20	06 35.7	20 20.9	19 51.0	28 03.4
AUG 9	04 15.1	26 53.6	19 44.3	24 57.0
29	01 43.9	33 44.3	20 06.1	18 24.0
SEP 18	00S52.9	40 55.4	20 44.8	10 46.7
OCT 8	03 29.8	48 22.3	21 28.6	03 18.4
28	06 01.5	55 36.2	22 07.1	03S33.9
NOV 17	08 22.7	61 03.5	22 31.7	09 42.6
DEC 7	10 28.2	61 19.1	22 35.7	15 06.9
27	12S13.1	53N11.0	22S14.7	19S48.4

1938	Psyche 16	Eros 433	Lilith 1181	Toro 1685
JAN 1	09♏42.7	07D19.0	07♑41.4	03♏34.6
11	12 16.0	08♊21.9	11 32.3	07 47.2
21	14 34.1	11 19.8	15 23.5	11 32.5
31	16 34.4	15 56.9	19 14.3	14 46.9
FEB 10	18 13.6	21 55.6	23 03.4	17 24.7
20	19 28.8	28 53.9	26 49.9	19 19.7
MAR 2	20 16.8	06♋31.7	00♒32.8	20 23.5
12	20 34.7	14 34.8	04 10.8	20R26.5
22	20R20.7	22 48.9	07 42.6	19 20.2
APR 1	19 34.3	01♌03.8	11 06.9	16 58.7
11	18 17.8	09 13.8	14 21.7	13 25.4
21	16 36.3	17 13.3	17 25.3	08 58.6
MAY 1	14 38.3	24 59.7	20 15.5	04 10.2
11	12 34.6	02♍33.0	22 49.3	29♎39.9
21	10 37.1	09 52.3	25 04.0	26 00.4
31	08 56.3	16 58.3	26 55.9	23 29.0
JUN 10	07 40.8	23 52.6	28 21.0	22 09.8
20	06 55.2	00♎35.7	29 15.2	21D56.9
30	06D41.5	07 09.0	29 34.4	22 41.5
JUL 10	06 59.6	13 34.0	29R15.6	24 14.7
20	07 47.4	19 51.3	28 18.3	26 27.8
30	09 02.3	26 02.3	26 44.7	29 14.5
AUG 9	10 41.6	02♏08.1	24 42.9	02♏29.7
19	12 42.1	08 09.1	22 25.7	06 09.3
29	15 01.4	14 06.5	20 09.1	10 10.8
SEP 8	17 36.9	20 01.0	18 10.2	14 32.0
18	20 26.4	25 52.9	16 42.5	19 11.6
28	23 28.1	01♐43.1	15 54.6	24 09.1
OCT 8	26 40.3	07 32.0	15D50.7	29 24.3
18	00♐01.3	13 20.0	16 30.1	04♐57.3
28	03 30.1	19 07.7	17 50.0	10 49.2
NOV 7	07 05.2	24 55.3	19 46.6	17 01.0
17	10 45.5	00♑43.0	22 15.3	23 34.4
27	14 30.1	06 31.4	25 12.0	00♑31.8
DEC 7	18 17.9	12 20.6	28 32.9	07 55.7
17	22 07.8	18 10.6	02♓14.4	15 49.4
27	25 59.0	24 02.1	06 13.7	24 17.0
JAN 6	29♐50.3	29♑55.0	10♓28.2	03♒22.1
JAN 1	12S35.5	49N52.4	22S05.2	20S52.4
21	13 48.3	33 42.1	21 10.2	24 43.5
FEB 10	14 31.6	17 54.7	19 48.8	27 56.7
MAR 2	14 42.5	06 43.2	18 04.1	30 28.4
22	14 19.7	00S10.9	16 01.1	31 55.7
APR 11	13 25.3	04 30.9	13 46.3	31 20.0
MAY 1	12 10.2	07 39.3	11 27.7	27 52.3
21	10 57.4	10 23.4	09 15.3	22 53.7
JUN 10	10 12.8	13 04.3	07 21.2	18 50.8
30	10 10.7	15 46.9	06 00.2	16 41.2
JUL 20	10 50.3	18 27.3	05 27.9	16 10.0
AUG 9	12 02.1	20 57.1	05 51.8	16 46.1
29	13 34.4	23 06.6	06 58.2	18 01.8
SEP 18	15 16.2	24 46.0	08 12.5	19 33.9
OCT 8	16 58.0	25 45.8	09 01.3	21 01.2
28	18 31.1	25 58.3	09 06.9	22 01.9
NOV 17	19 48.3	25 18.1	08 24.2	22 11.7
DEC 7	20 43.9	23 42.7	06 54.1	21 02.8
27	21S13.7	21S12.8	04S40.8	18S05.6

1939	Psyche 16	Eros 433	Lilith 1181	Toro 1685
JAN 1	27♐54.7	26♑58.4	08♓19.2	28♑44.6
11	01♑45.8	02♒52.0	12 40.3	08♒10.0
21	05 35.6	08 47.5	17 13.4	18 19.2
31	09 23.0	14 45.1	21 56.9	29 14.4
FEB 10	13 06.8	20 45.0	26 48.8	10♓55.5
20	16 45.9	26 47.7	01♈48.1	23 18.8
MAR 2	20 18.8	02♓53.4	06 53.6	06♈15.3
12	23 44.0	09 02.5	12 04.1	19 31.8
22	27 00.0	15 15.8	17 18.7	02♉53.0
APR 1	00♒04.7	21 33.6	22 36.6	16 03.5
11	02 55.9	27 56.5	27 56.9	28 49.0
21	05 31.2	04♈25.5	03♉19.0	10♊59.3
MAY 1	07 47.5	11 01.0	08 42.3	22 27.3
11	09 41.7	17 44.0	14 05.9	03♋09.8
21	11 10.2	24 35.5	19 29.5	13 07.7
31	12 09.2	01♉36.1	24 52.3	22 23.8
JUN 10	12 35.4	08 47.0	00♊13.7	01♌01.8
20	12R26.2	16 09.1	05 33.3	09 06.8
30	11 40.9	23 42.9	10 50.1	16 43.2
JUL 10	10 22.1	01♊29.4	16 03.7	23 54.9
20	08 36.0	09 29.1	21 13.2	00♍46.1
30	06 33.7	17 42.1	26 17.7	07 19.7
AUG 9	04 28.9	26 08.4	01♋16.4	13 38.4
19	02 36.0	04♋47.6	06 08.1	19 44.8
29	01 08.2	13 38.5	10 51.3	25 40.6
SEP 8	00 13.9	22 40.1	15 24.7	01♎27.4
18	29D57.7	01♌50.5	19 46.4	07 06.7
28	00♒20.6	11 07.4	23 53.9	12 39.6
OCT 8	01 20.6	20 28.7	27 45.0	18 06.9
18	02 54.7	29 51.7	01♌16.1	23 29.5
28	04 59.3	09♍13.5	04 23.4	28 47.8
NOV 7	07 30.2	18 31.7	07 02.8	04♏02.4
17	10 24.2	27 43.6	09 08.8	09 13.7
27	13 37.9	06♎46.2	10 36.1	14 21.7
DEC 7	17 08.3	15 37.6	11 19.7	19 26.8
17	20 53.2	24 15.2	11R15.4	24 29.1
27	24 50.1	02♏36.6	10 22.7	29 28.4
JAN 6	28♒57.2	10♏40.3	08♌46.0	04♐24.8
JAN 1	21S16.8	20S27.1	04S01.4	17S01.0
21	21 12.1	16 54.3	01 03.3	11 14.1
FEB 10	20 41.0	12 37.5	02N21.1	03 13.1
MAR 2	19 47.3	07 43.6	06 01.8	05N59.1
22	18 37.4	02 19.7	09 47.9	14 10.6
APR 11	17 20.1	03N26.2	13 28.3	19 07.4
MAY 1	16 06.6	09 25.1	16 51.4	20 06.5
21	15 10.1	15 25.1	19 46.5	18 04.8
JUN 10	14 45.0	21 08.7	22 03.6	14 23.7
30	15 02.6	26 09.8	23 35.1	09 59.1
JUL 20	16 01.9	29 50.1	24 16.4	05 19.6
AUG 9	17 22.3	31 22.3	24 07.1	00 38.7
29	18 33.4	30 03.9	23 11.3	03S56.7
SEP 18	19 15.0	25 39.6	21 37.1	08 21.7
OCT 8	19 20.8	18 32.7	19 36.6	12 32.4
28	18 50.0	09 34.6	17 24.8	16 24.4
NOV 17	17 42.9	00S14.0	15 19.5	19 52.7
DEC 7	16 00.0	09 55.4	13 40.6	22 52.0
27	13S43.8	18S43.0	12N46.2	25S17.0

1940		Psyche 16	Eros 433	Lilith 1181	Toro 1685
JAN	1	26♒52.5	06♏40.8	09R39.4	01♐56.9
	11	01♓04.0	14 34.8	07♌44.2	06 51.9
	21	05 23.4	22 07.7	05 24.0	11 43.6
	31	09 49.0	29 17.9	02 58.4	16 32.0
FEB	10	14 19.8	06♐03.6	00 47.2	21 17.0
	20	18 54.5	12 22.0	29♋07.0	25 58.0
MAR	1	23 32.2	18 11.0	28 07.5	00♑35.0
	11	28 12.0	23 26.9	27D51.9	05 07.4
	21	02♈53.0	28 05.0	28 19.0	09 34.7
	31	07 34.3	02♑00.2	29 24.5	13 56.6
APR	10	12 15.4	05 04.9	01♌03.2	18 12.2
	20	16 55.5	07 09.8	03 10.1	22 20.8
	30	21 33.7	08 05.3	05 40.1	26 21.7
MAY	10	26 09.5	07R40.7	08 29.2	00♒13.8
	20	00♉42.0	05 50.8	11 34.0	03 55.8
	30	05 10.5	02 41.5	14 51.4	07 27.4
JUN	9	09 34.2	28♐34.5	18 19.0	10 47.4
	19	13 51.9	24 09.9	21 54.9	13 56.9
	29	18 02.6	20 11.8	25 37.3	17 01.2
JUL	9	22 05.1	17 12.7	29 25.1	20 12.2
	19	25 57.7	15 28.5	03♍16.8	24 11.7
	29	29 38.8	14D58.3	07 11.6	01♓34.8
AUG	8	03♊06.2	15 34.0	11 08.7	01♈05.2
	18	06 17.2	17 05.3	15 07.2	11♋51.1
	28	09 09.1	19 21.7	19 06.4	02♌49.7
SEP	7	11 38.2	22 14.8	23 05.7	09 48.3
	17	13 40.4	25 38.0	27 04.2	14 49.2
	27	15 11.7	29 25.5	01♎01.4	19 58.7
OCT	7	16 07.2	03♑33.7	04 56.5	25 46.7
	17	16R23.4	07 59.3	08 48.6	02♍10.9
	27	15 58.2	12 39.7	12 37.0	08 57.6
NOV	6	14 52.2	17 33.6	16 20.5	15 48.3
	16	13 11.5	22 39.4	19 58.0	22 27.7
	26	11 06.8	27 55.8	23 28.2	28 45.6
DEC	6	08 53.6	03♒22.6	26 49.7	04♎34.0
	16	06 49.3	08 58.8	00♏00.6	09 46.8
	26	05 08.7	14 44.0	02 59.1	14 19.2
JAN	5	04♊02.5	20♒38.4	05♏42.8	18♎03.9
JAN	1	13S05.0	20S42.3	12N40.8	25S47.3
	21	10 13.2	27 38.5	12 48.5	27 22.9
FEB	10	06 59.9	32 50.5	13 25.0	28 15.1
MAR	1	03 32.3	36 24.3	14 02.3	28 22.4
	21	00N01.7	38 42.3	14 21.7	27 44.6
APR	10	03 34.3	40 17.3	14 14.2	26 21.7
	30	06 57.7	41 37.3	13 36.0	24 11.6
MAY	20	10 04.9	42 31.1	12 26.6	21 03.7
JUN	9	12 49.6	41 29.2	10 47.4	16 23.4
	29	15 06.3	37 28.3	08 41.7	08 22.1
JUL	19	16 51.6	32 29.1	06 13.6	09N35.1
AUG	8	18 03.8	28 37.1	03 28.0	59 39.4
	28	18 43.6	26 04.7	00 29.9	64 11.3
SEP	17	18 54.5	24 18.2	02S35.4	39 29.4
OCT	7	18 42.3	22 44.1	05 42.6	24 02.2
	27	18 13.9	20 57.5	08 46.4	11 47.0
NOV	16	17 36.6	18 42.2	11 41.3	01 32.6
DEC	6	17 01.2	15 48.8	14 22.4	07S01.0
	26	16N44.0	12S13.4	16S44.8	14S08.0

1941		Psyche 16	Eros 433	Lilith 1181	Toro 1685
JAN	1	04R24.4	18♒15.6	04♏39.3	16♎40.2
	11	03♊41.7	24 15.2	07 12.8	19 52.5
	21	03D39.2	00♓23.5	09 27.3	22 03.7
	31	04 15.6	06 40.7	11 19.5	23 01.4
FEB	10	05 27.3	13 07.0	12 46.0	22R32.2
	20	07 09.8	19 42.4	13 43.6	20 26.2
MAR	2	09 18.6	26 27.5	14 08.8	16 41.0
	12	11 49.4	03♈22.5	13R59.3	11 36.1
	22	14 38.3	10 27.7	13 14.6	05 54.9
APR	1	17 42.1	17 43.8	11 56.1	00 32.4
	11	20 58.1	25 10.8	10 09.2	26♍14.7
	21	24 23.7	02♉49.2	08 02.9	23 22.0
MAY	1	27 57.3	10 39.2	05 48.8	21 54.3
	11	01♋37.0	18 40.8	03 40.1	21D41.3
	21	05 21.4	26 53.9	01 48.6	22 28.7
	31	09 09.5	05♊18.3	00 23.0	24 04.2
JUN	10	13 00.1	13 53.2	29♎29.0	26 17.6
	20	16 52.3	22 37.8	29 08.1	29 00.6
	30	20 45.5	01♋31.1	29D20.0	02♎07.6
JUL	10	24 38.7	10 31.5	00♏02.5	05 33.8
	20	28 31.3	19 37.6	01 12.4	09 15.9
	30	02♌22.6	28 47.7	02 46.7	13 11.5
AUG	9	06 11.8	07♌59.6	04 42.2	17 18.7
	19	09 58.2	17 11.7	06 55.9	21 36.2
	29	13 41.0	26 21.9	09 25.5	26 03.1
SEP	8	17 19.2	05♍28.2	12 08.6	00♏38.8
	18	20 51.9	14 29.0	15 03.1	05 22.7
	28	24 17.7	23 22.7	18 07.5	10 14.9
OCT	8	27 35.2	02♎07.4	21 20.1	15 15.2
	18	00♍43.0	10 42.4	24 39.6	20 23.9
	28	03 38.9	19 06.5	28 04.9	25 41.2
NOV	7	06 20.9	27 18.8	01♐34.6	01♐07.6
	17	08 46.3	05♏19.0	05 07.8	06 43.7
	27	10 52.2	13 06.7	08 43.6	12 30.6
DEC	7	12 35.4	20 41.5	12 20.7	18 29.0
	17	13 52.4	28 03.7	15 58.3	24 40.5
	27	14 39.5	05♐13.1	19 35.2	01♑06.6
JAN	6	14R54.0	12♐09.7	23♐10.5	07♑49.3
JAN	1	16N44.6	11S00.5	17S23.1	16S00.9
	21	17 08.1	06 31.5	19 14.2	21 25.5
FEB	10	17 58.6	01 26.7	20 35.5	25 09.1
MAR	2	19 03.1	04N05.5	21 20.5	25 56.8
	22	20 07.4	09 52.6	21 20.1	22 34.5
APR	11	21 00.1	15 36.4	20 27.0	16 49.6
MAY	1	21 32.7	20 50.4	18 48.7	12 01.1
	21	21 40.0	24 58.1	16 56.3	09 21.4
JUN	10	21 19.6	27 15.4	15 28.2	08 34.0
	30	20 31.4	27 02.5	14 45.8	09 06.9
JUL	20	19 17.4	24 03.0	14 50.4	10 34.1
AUG	9	17 41.3	18 34.4	15 32.8	12 36.4
	29	15 48.2	11 20.1	16 41.0	14 58.5
SEP	18	13 44.3	03 12.6	18 03.7	17 27.6
OCT	8	11 37.1	05S00.1	19 30.8	19 51.6
	28	09 35.2	12 39.1	20 53.7	21 57.6
NOV	17	07 49.0	19 14.7	22 04.8	23 31.7
DEC	7	06 30.4	24 26.0	22 58.5	24 18.0
	27	05N52.5	28S00.6	23S30.4	23S58.8

1942		Psyche 16	Eros 433	Lilith 1181	Toro 1685
JAN	1	14♍51.0	08♐43.0	21♐23.1	04♑25.7
	11	14R48.4	15 33.4	24 57.1	11 17.6
	21	14 10.7	22 11.3	28 27.8	18 29.9
	31	12 59.7	28 36.5	01♑53.6	26 05.5
FEB	10	11 20.1	04♑49.2	05 13.5	04♒08.0
	20	09 20.5	10 49.2	08 25.9	12 41.4
MAR	2	07 12.5	16 36.2	11 28.9	21 49.3
	12	05 09.0	22 09.8	14 20.9	01♓35.8
	22	03 21.7	27 29.3	16 59.5	12 03.8
APR	1	02 00.0	02♒33.6	19 22.3	23 14.0
	11	01 09.0	07 21.8	21 26.5	05♈04.9
	21	00 50.6	11 51.7	23 09.0	17 31.0
MAY	1	01D04.5	16 01.0	24 26.1	00♉22.1
	11	01 48.0	19 46.7	25 14.7	13 24.8
	21	02 58.5	23 04.3	25 31.1	26 23.5
	31	04 32.5	25 48.4	25R13.0	09♊03.0
JUN	10	06 26.7	27 52.4	24 19.8	21 11.8
	20	08 38.4	29 07.2	22 53.3	02♋42.9
	30	11 04.9	29R23.6	20 59.5	13 33.0
JUL	10	13 43.8	28 32.4	18 48.3	23 42.3
	20	16 33.4	26 27.5	16 32.6	03♌13.1
	30	19 31.8	23 13.8	14 26.8	12 08.2
AUG	9	22 37.5	19 10.0	12 43.1	20 31.3
	19	25 49.3	14 50.3	11 30.9	28 26.0
	29	29 06.0	10 56.4	10 55.4	05♍55.6
SEP	8	02♎26.6	08 00.1	10D57.8	13 03.2
	18	05 50.0	06 18.9	11 37.1	19 51.6
	28	09 15.3	05D55.6	12 50.8	26 22.8
OCT	8	12 41.6	06 43.1	14 35.3	02♎39.1
	18	16 07.8	08 32.8	16 47.2	08 41.8
	28	19 33.0	11 14.8	19 23.1	14 32.1
NOV	7	22 56.1	14 40.7	22 19.8	20 11.3
	17	26 16.0	18 44.1	25 34.8	25 39.7
	27	29 31.2	23 19.5	29 05.6	00♏57.9
DEC	7	02♏40.5	28 22.8	02♒50.1	06 06.0
	17	05 42.3	03♓51.3	06 46.6	11 03.9
	27	08 34.6	09 42.2	10 53.4	15 51.1
JAN	6	11♏15.6	15♓54.0	15♒09.1	20♏27.1
JAN	1	05N50.8	28S38.6	23S34.7	23S41.5
	21	06 18.7	30 08.8	23 36.9	21 33.5
FEB	10	07 38.2	30 07.9	23 15.9	17 37.1
MAR	2	09 25.7	28 51.4	22 35.0	11 37.1
	22	11 02.5	26 38.5	21 39.8	03 32.4
APR	11	11 59.1	23 48.5	20 37.9	06N01.8
MAY	1	12 06.6	20 39.7	19 38.5	15 24.9
	21	11 29.6	17 28.5	18 51.1	21 59.4
JUN	10	10 16.4	14 31.0	18 22.9	23 52.1
	30	08 34.5	12 03.5	18 14.6	21 30.3
JUL	20	06 30.6	10 20.9	18 18.8	16 40.3
AUG	9	04 10.5	09 27.0	18 26.5	10 51.4
	29	01 39.6	09 05.0	18 33.0	04 52.1
SEP	18	00S56.9	08 48.1	18 34.8	00S55.5
OCT	8	03 33.6	08 14.3	18 26.0	06 21.7
	28	06 05.2	07 06.5	17 58.8	11 21.9
NOV	17	08 26.5	05 13.3	17 06.2	15 53.2
DEC	7	10 32.1	02 29.1	15 43.1	19 53.0
	27	12S17.1	01N05.8	13S47.1	23S19.6

1943		Psyche 16	Eros 433	Lilith 1181	Toro 1685
JAN	1	09♏56.6	12♓45.6	13♒00.2	18♏10.5
	11	12 31.1	19 07.4	17 20.0	22 40.5
	21	14 50.4	25 48.3	21 47.0	26 57.3
	31	16 52.1	02♈47.1	26 20.1	00♐59.6
FEB	10	18 33.0	10 03.4	00♓58.6	04 44.9
	20	19 50.1	17 36.2	05 41.4	08 10.4
MAR	2	20 40.2	25 24.7	10 27.9	11 12.4
	12	21 00.4	03♉28.5	15 17.4	13 45.9
	22	20R48.7	11 46.2	20 09.2	15 44.5
APR	1	20 04.7	20 16.8	25 02.7	17 00.7
	11	18 50.2	28 59.2	29 57.4	17R24.5
	21	17 10.2	07♊51.5	04♈52.5	16 45.5
MAY	1	15 13.0	16 52.1	09 47.7	14 54.5
	11	13 09.2	25 59.3	14 42.1	11 46.8
	21	11 10.9	05♋10.7	19 35.1	07 30.9
	31	09 28.7	14 24.4	24 26.1	02 31.9
JUN	10	08 11.1	23 38.5	29 14.1	27♏29.7
	20	07 23.4	02♌50.5	03♉58.1	23 07.1
	30	07D07.7	11 58.6	08 37.1	19 53.3
JUL	10	07 23.7	21 01.1	13 09.5	18 00.7
	20	08 09.9	29 55.9	17 33.8	17D28.1
	30	09 23.4	08♍41.7	21 48.2	18 07.0
AUG	9	11 01.4	17 17.6	25 49.9	19 48.1
	19	13 01.1	25 42.5	29 36.2	22 22.4
	29	15 19.6	03♎56.0	03♊03.6	25 42.6
SEP	8	17 54.6	11 57.8	06 07.5	29 44.0
	18	20 43.8	19 48.0	08 43.2	04♐22.7
	28	23 45.3	27 26.7	10 44.8	09 36.9
OCT	8	26 57.5	04♏54.6	12 06.1	15 26.4
	18	00♐18.7	12 11.9	12 41.6	21 51.2
	28	03 47.7	19 19.4	12R27.6	28 52.7
NOV	7	07 23.2	26 17.6	11 24.3	06♑33.1
	17	11 04.0	03♐07.1	09 39.5	14 54.2
	27	14 49.2	09 48.7	07 27.9	23 58.2
DEC	7	18 37.7	16 22.8	05 10.9	03♒47.7
	17	22 28.5	22 49.8	03 11.5	14 26.5
	27	26 20.6	29 10.4	01 47.6	26 05.6
JAN	6	00♑13.1	05♑25.0	01♊10.2	09♓07.2

1943		Psyche 16	Eros 433	Lilith 1181	Toro 1685
JAN	1	12S39.7	02N06.8	13S12.9	24S05.9
	21	13 53.0	06 34.9	10 36.6	26 49.8
FEB	10	14 36.9	11 28.5	07 31.5	29 01.3
MAR	2	14 48.7	16 22.7	04 02.7	30 44.2
	22	14 27.1	20 41.7	00 16.6	32 04.4
APR	11	13 33.9	23 40.5	03N39.7	33 03.6
MAY	1	12 19.8	24 34.8	07 38.6	33 23.2
	21	11 07.0	22 58.6	11 32.1	32 01.9
JUN	10	10 21.5	18 58.4	15 12.3	28 10.9
	30	10 18.3	13 09.4	18 31.3	23 26.0
JUL	20	10 56.7	06 18.1	21 21.8	20 00.7
AUG	9	12 07.6	00S52.0	23 38.2	18 21.5
	29	13 39.2	07 46.9	25 16.9	17 55.3
SEP	18	15 20.6	14 01.7	26 16.9	18 00.2
OCT	8	17 01.9	19 18.8	26 38.2	17 57.1
	28	18 34.6	23 25.5	26 17.7	17 07.8
NOV	17	19 51.3	26 13.3	25 07.8	14 56.6
DEC	7	20 46.1	27 38.1	23 15.4	11 04.9
	27	21S15.0	27S40.5	21N23.1	05S53.8

1944		Psyche 16	Eros 433	Lilith 1181	Toro 1685
JAN	1	28♐16.9	02♑18.5	01R22.7	02♓24.3
	11	02♑09.1	08 30.0	01D10.2	16 18.3
	21	06 00.1	14 36.0	01♊46.5	02♈18.8
	31	09 49.0	20 36.8	03 07.7	20 26.6
FEB	10	13 34.4	26 32.5	05 08.2	09♉32.3
	20	17 15.2	02♒23.5	07 41.4	27 35.8
MAR	1	20 50.1	08 09.9	10 41.9	13♊12.7
	11	24 17.6	13 51.8	14 04.5	26 08.8
	21	27 36.1	19 29.5	17 44.6	06♋50.9
	31	00♒43.5	25 03.1	21 39.0	15 55.0
APR	10	03 37.8	00♓32.4	25 44.5	23 49.8
	20	06 16.7	05 57.9	29 58.7	00♌55.6
	30	08 37.0	11 19.2	04♋19.8	07 27.4
MAY	10	10 35.6	16 36.2	08 46.0	13 34.6
	20	12 09.1	21 49.0	13 15.9	19 23.8
	30	13 13.6	26 57.1	17 48.7	25 00.0
JUN	9	13 45.6	01♈59.9	22 23.1	00♍26.4
	19	13R42.4	06 57.1	26 58.6	05 45.3
	29	13 02.9	11 47.2	01♌34.4	10 58.9
JUL	9	11 49.1	16 29.1	06 09.9	16 08.3
	19	10 06.8	21 01.1	10 44.6	21 14.6
	29	08 06.0	25 19.9	15 18.0	26 18.8
AUG	8	06 00.7	29 22.2	19 49.6	01♎21.5
	18	04 05.4	03♉03.1	24 18.8	06 23.5
	28	02 33.4	06 15.0	28 45.3	11 25.2
SEP	7	01 34.3	08 49.2	03♍08.2	16 26.9
	17	01D12.9	10 33.2	07 27.2	21 29.4
	27	01 30.9	11 11.5	11 41.4	26 32.8
OCT	7	02 26.5	10R29.8	15 49.9	01♏37.4
	17	03 56.7	08 17.6	19 51.9	06 43.8
	27	05 58.0	04 43.6	23 46.1	11 52.1
NOV	6	08 26.2	00 26.8	27 31.2	17 02.7
	16	11 17.9	26♈27.8	01♎05.7	22 15.9
	26	14 29.9	23 48.4	04 27.6	27 32.2
DEC	6	17 58.9	23D01.8	07 34.6	02♐51.9
	16	21 42.5	24 11.9	10 24.4	08 15.6
	26	25 38.6	27 08.8	12 53.7	13 43.7
JAN	5	29♒45.0	01♉34.6	14♎59.3	19♐17.0

1944		Psyche 16	Eros 433	Lilith 1181	Toro 1685
JAN	1	21S17.9	27S28.9	21N01.0	04S28.7
	21	21 12.1	25 57.3	20 06.8	01N28.3
FEB	10	20 39.5	23 21.8	20 01.3	06 48.6
MAR	1	19 44.2	19 54.1	20 22.8	09 09.7
	21	18 32.4	15 45.5	20 48.3	09 19.1
APR	10	17 12.9	11 05.7	20 59.8	08 30.7
	30	15 56.7	06 02.4	20 45.5	07 03.5
MAY	20	14 57.2	00 41.0	19 59.0	05 02.8
JUN	9	14 28.9	04N55.3	18 38.3	02 33.5
	29	14 43.8	10 45.6	16 44.8	00S18.7
JUL	19	15 42.1	16 51.6	14 21.9	03 27.9
AUG	8	17 04.1	23 17.0	11 34.9	06 47.9
	28	18 18.3	30 06.0	08 29.7	10 12.7
SEP	17	19 02.6	37 09.5	05 12.6	13 35.9
OCT	7	19 09.8	43 24.8	01 50.1	16 50.8
	27	18 39.3	46 06.4	01S31.2	19 49.8
NOV	16	17 31.6	43 14.7	04 44.1	22 24.5
DEC	6	15 47.7	37 28.4	07 41.4	24 25.7
	26	13S30.4	32N05.5	10S15.1	25S43.1

1945		Psyche 16	Eros 433	Lilith 1181	Toro 1685
JAN	1	28♒05.3	29♈38.7	14♎12.1	17♐03.0
	11	02♓17.0	04♉49.7	16 01.8	22 40.0
	21	06 36.6	11 05.8	17 21.6	28 23.8
	31	11 02.5	18 14.5	18 07.9	04♑15.5
FEB	10	15 33.3	26 04.6	18R17.6	10 17.1
	20	20 08.3	04♊28.7	17 48.5	16 30.5
MAR	2	24 46.0	13 18.3	16 41.7	22 58.1
	12	29 25.9	22 25.6	15 01.3	29 43.5
	22	04♈06.9	01♋44.5	12 56.0	06♒50.5
APR	1	08 48.2	11 07.9	10 38.3	14 24.0
	11	13 29.2	20 29.4	08 22.5	22 30.0
	21	18 09.2	29 44.5	06 22.4	01♓15.0
MAY	1	22 47.2	08♌48.3	04 48.6	10 45.9
	11	27 22.9	17 37.7	03 47.3	21 09.0
	21	01♉55.2	26 11.3	03 21.2	02♈27.3
	31	06 23.5	04♍27.8	03D29.8	14 39.0
JUN	10	10 46.9	12 27.2	04 10.3	27 35.5
	20	15 04.4	20 10.5	05 19.6	11♉00.5
	30	19 14.9	27 38.3	06 54.0	24 34.4
JUL	10	23 17.2	04♎51.9	08 50.0	07♊59.5
	20	27 09.7	11 53.1	11 04.6	21 01.5
	30	00♊50.6	18 42.9	13 34.8	03♋31.6
AUG	9	04 18.0	25 22.9	16 18.3	15 24.2
	19	07 29.1	01♏54.4	19 13.0	26 35.3
	29	10 21.1	08 18.4	22 17.1	07♌03.9
SEP	8	12 50.5	14 36.1	25 29.1	16 51.1
	18	14 53.3	20 48.7	28 47.6	25 58.8
	28	16 25.2	26 56.7	02♏11.3	04♍30.4
OCT	8	17 21.8	03♐01.1	05 39.2	12 29.3
	18	17R39.1	09 02.6	09 10.4	19 58.6
	28	17 15.1	15 01.6	12 43.6	27 01.0
NOV	7	16 10.5	20 59.0	16 18.1	03♎39.0
	17	14 30.6	26 54.9	19 52.8	09 53.9
	27	12 26.6	02♑49.9	23 26.7	15 47.1
DEC	7	10 13.3	08 44.3	26 58.9	21 19.1
	17	08 08.1	14 38.4	00♐28.0	26 29.7
	27	06 26.1	20 32.5	03 53.1	01♏18.4
JAN	6	05♊17.8	26♑27.0	07♐12.7	05♏43.7

1945		Psyche 16	Eros 433	Lilith 1181	Toro 1685
JAN	1	12S43.3	30N42.9	10S55.1	25S56.3
	21	09 49.3	26 38.2	12 43.1	26 01.2
FEB	10	06 34.3	22 41.7	13 41.3	24 57.7
MAR	2	03 05.7	18 17.7	13 36.0	22 33.6
	22	00N28.6	13 24.2	12 23.0	18 34.3
APR	11	04 00.7	08 18.1	10 24.4	12 41.7
MAY	1	07 22.9	03 14.3	08 25.9	04 37.2
	21	10 28.4	01S39.7	07 07.1	05N36.0
JUN	10	13 10.6	06 20.6	06 42.6	16 37.9
	30	15 24.7	10 45.1	07 08.7	25 13.7
JUL	20	17 07.1	14 48.8	08 15.1	28 06.5
AUG	9	18 16.4	18 26.0	09 50.6	25 02.8
	29	18 53.8	21 30.1	11 45.3	18 29.9
SEP	18	19 03.1	23 53.9	13 50.3	10 51.4
OCT	8	18 50.3	25 30.1	15 58.1	03 21.7
	28	18 22.6	26 12.6	18 01.7	03S31.8
NOV	17	17 47.4	25 57.0	19 55.1	09 41.4
DEC	7	17 14.5	24 41.7	21 33.3	15 06.4
	27	16N58.7	22S28.4	22S52.4	19S48.3

1946		Psyche 16	Eros 433	Lilith 1181	Toro 1685
JAN	1	05 R 47.3	23 ♑ 29.7	05 ♐ 33.7	03 ♏ 34.1
	11	04 ♊ 58.3	29 24.4	08 50.0	07 46.8
	21	04 D 49.7	05 ♒ 19.6	11 58.6	11 32.0
	31	05 19.9	11 15.9	14 57.8	14 46.3
FEB	10	06 26.0	17 13.5	17 45.6	17 23.9
	20	08 03.6	23 12.6	20 19.8	19 18.4
MAR	2	10 07.9	29 13.6	22 38.1	20 21.8
	12	12 34.8	05 ♓ 17.1	24 37.5	20 R 24.0
	22	15 20.4	11 23.3	26 15.1	19 16.8
APR	1	18 21.2	17 32.9	27 27.7	16 54.4
	11	21 34.7	23 46.5	28 11.9	13 20.2
	21	24 58.1	00 ♈ 04.5	28 R 24.8	08 52.8
MAY	1	28 29.6	06 28.1	28 04.5	04 04.4
	11	02 ♋ 07.6	12 57.9	27 10.3	29 ♎ 34.4
	21	05 50.5	19 34.6	25 44.8	25 55.7
	31	09 37.2	26 19.4	23 53.5	23 25.2
JUN	10	13 26.6	03 ♉ 13.2	21 45.4	22 06.8
	20	17 17.8	10 17.0	19 32.8	21 D 54.7
	30	21 10.0	17 32.1	17 27.8	22 39.9
JUL	10	25 02.4	24 59.0	15 42.3	24 13.5
	20	28 54.3	02 ♊ 38.9	14 24.7	26 27.0
	30	02 ♌ 45.0	10 32.7	13 39.8	29 13.9
AUG	9	06 33.7	18 40.4	13 D 29.5	02 ♏ 29.3
	19	10 19.7	27 02.5	13 53.0	06 08.9
	29	14 02.3	05 ♋ 38.8	14 48.1	10 10.3
SEP	8	17 40.4	14 28.2	16 12.1	14 31.4
	18	21 12.9	23 29.5	18 01.5	19 10.8
	28	24 38.9	02 ♌ 41.2	20 13.4	24 08.0
OCT	8	27 56.7	12 00.3	22 45.0	29 22.9
	18	01 ♍ 04.8	21 24.7	25 33.6	04 ♐ 55.5
	28	04 01.4	00 ♍ 51.3	28 37.0	10 46.8
NOV	7	06 44.2	10 16.6	01 ♑ 53.4	16 58.0
	17	09 10.7	19 37.9	05 20.7	23 30.6
	27	11 18.0	28 52.0	08 57.7	00 ♑ 27.0
DEC	7	13 02.7	07 ♎ 55.4	12 42.9	07 49.9
	17	14 21.7	16 45.7	16 35.1	15 42.3
	27	15 11.2	25 19.8	20 33.2	24 08.4
JAN	6	15 ♍ 28.2	03 ♏ 34.7	24 ♑ 36.1	03 ♒ 11.8
JAN	1	16 N 59.2	21 S 46.4	23 S 08.9	20 S 52.4
	21	17 20.7	18 26.7	24 01.4	24 43.8
FEB	10	18 08.6	14 21.1	24 33.1	27 57.2
MAR	2	19 10.5	09 36.9	24 46.4	30 28.8
	22	20 12.6	04 21.2	24 45.6	31 55.8
APR	11	21 03.2	01 N 18.4	24 35.3	31 19.3
MAY	1	21 34.0	07 14.1	24 18.2	27 50.6
	21	21 39.8	13 16.6	23 52.6	22 51.8
JUN	10	21 18.1	19 12.7	23 14.5	18 49.5
	30	20 28.8	24 42.3	22 26.6	16 40.6
JUL	20	19 13.9	29 14.4	21 42.8	16 09.9
AUG	9	17 37.1	32 05.3	21 16.5	16 46.3
	29	15 43.4	32 24.9	21 10.5	18 02.2
SEP	18	13 38.9	29 36.5	21 18.0	19 34.4
OCT	8	11 31.1	23 39.3	21 28.2	21 01.8
	28	09 28.5	15 11.0	21 30.4	22 02.7
NOV	17	07 41.3	05 11.6	21 15.5	22 12.9
DEC	7	06 21.5	05 S 14.9	20 36.7	21 04.8
	27	05 N 41.8	15 S 11.8	19 S 29.7	18 S 08.7

1947		Psyche 16	Eros 433	Lilith 1181	Toro 1685
JAN	1	15 ♍ 23.9	29 ♎ 29.8	22 ♑ 34.1	28 ♑ 35.2
	11	15 R 23.9	07 ♏ 34.3	26 39.0	07 ♒ 58.9
	21	14 49.0	15 16.1	00 ♒ 47.5	18 06.0
	31	13 40.5	22 31.8	04 58.5	28 59.2
FEB	10	12 03.0	29 18.7	09 11.3	10 ♓ 38.3
	20	10 04.7	05 ♐ 33.5	13 25.1	22 59.9
MAR	2	07 56.9	11 11.4	17 39.1	05 ♈ 55.2
	12	05 52.8	16 07.7	21 52.4	19 11.1
	22	04 03.9	20 15.7	26 04.4	02 ♉ 32.4
APR	1	02 39.9	23 26.4	00 ♓ 14.0	15 43.6
	11	01 46.3	25 30.2	04 20.5	28 30.3
	21	01 25.2	26 15.4	08 22.8	10 ♊ 42.2
MAY	1	01 D 36.4	25 R 31.7	12 19.6	22 12.1
	11	02 17.6	23 17.0	16 09.8	02 ♋ 56.6
	21	03 25.8	19 42.3	19 51.8	12 56.4
	31	04 57.9	15 20.0	23 23.5	22 14.3
JUN	10	06 50.5	10 57.4	26 42.9	00 ♌ 54.1
	20	09 00.7	07 18.2	29 47.3	09 00.6
	30	11 26.0	04 50.2	02 ♈ 33.2	16 38.2
JUL	10	14 03.9	03 40.8	04 57.0	23 51.1
	20	16 52.6	03 D 43.9	06 54.3	00 ♍ 43.2
	30	19 50.3	04 49.5	08 19.7	07 17.7
AUG	9	22 55.5	06 45.5	09 08.5	13 37.1
	19	26 06.9	09 22.1	09 R 16.0	19 44.1
	29	29 23.3	12 31.5	08 39.6	25 40.4
SEP	8	02 ♎ 43.6	16 07.0	07 21.2	01 ♎ 27.6
	18	06 07.0	20 03.9	05 27.7	07 07.4
	28	09 32.3	24 18.8	03 13.6	12 40.5
OCT	8	12 58.6	28 48.5	00 58.2	18 08.1
	18	16 25.0	03 ♑ 31.3	29 ♓ 01.3	23 30.9
	28	19 50.5	08 25.5	27 40.2	28 49.4
NOV	7	23 14.0	13 29.7	27 04.6	04 ♏ 04.1
	17	26 34.4	18 43.3	27 D 18.3	09 15.5
	27	29 50.2	24 05.4	28 20.2	14 23.6
DEC	7	03 ♏ 00.3	29 35.6	00 ♈ 05.8	19 28.7
	17	06 03.1	05 ♒ 13.5	02 29.9	24 31.0
	27	08 56.5	10 59.0	05 27.0	29 30.3
JAN	6	11 ♏ 38.7	16 ♒ 51.7	08 ♈ 51.8	04 ♐ 26.6
JAN	1	05 N 39.7	17 S 31.0	19 S 08.3	17 S 04.6
	21	06 05.6	25 52.9	17 24.1	11 19.4
FEB	10	07 23.6	32 35.8	15 11.3	03 19.9
MAR	2	09 10.9	37 41.6	12 33.4	05 N 52.4
	22	10 49.0	41 30.1	09 34.9	14 06.4
APR	11	11 47.5	44 28.5	06 21.7	19 06.9
MAY	1	11 56.8	46 37.9	02 59.9	20 08.8
	21	11 21.2	46 37.6	00 N 23.4	18 08.1
JUN	10	10 08.9	42 44.9	03 40.4	14 26.8
	30	08 27.6	36 44.3	06 41.8	10 01.5
JUL	20	06 24.1	31 41.9	09 15.5	05 21.1
AUG	9	04 04.3	28 27.7	11 04.2	00 39.5
	29	01 33.5	26 30.6	11 45.4	03 S 56.4
SEP	18	01 S 02.9	25 10.0	11 00.7	08 21.9
OCT	8	03 39.6	23 54.1	09 03.4	12 32.9
	28	06 11.3	22 20.9	06 53.0	16 25.1
NOV	17	08 32.7	20 16.1	05 32.3	19 53.4
DEC	7	10 38.5	17 31.4	05 26.7	22 52.7
	27	12 S 23.9	14 S 03.5	06 N 30.8	25 S 17.7

1948		Psyche 16	Eros 433	Lilith 1181	Toro 1685
JAN	1	10 ♏ 19.1	13 ♒ 54.4	07 ♈ 06.3	01 ♐ 58.8
	11	12 54.9	19 50.9	10 43.2	06 53.7
	21	15 15.9	25 54.9	14 41.4	11 45.3
	31	17 19.5	02 ♓ 06.2	18 57.0	16 33.5
FEB	10	19 02.6	08 25.3	23 26.9	21 18.2
	20	20 22.1	14 52.4	28 08.7	25 59.0
MAR	1	21 14.9	21 27.7	02 ♉ 59.8	00 ♑ 35.5
	11	21 38.1	28 11.8	07 58.4	05 07.4
	21	21 R 29.3	05 ♈ 05.1	13 03.2	09 34.1
	31	20 48.3	12 08.0	18 12.3	13 55.1
APR	10	19 36.5	19 21.1	23 24.9	18 09.9
	20	17 58.5	26 44.9	28 39.8	22 17.2
	30	16 02.5	04 ♉ 19.6	03 ♊ 56.1	26 16.4
MAY	10	13 58.8	12 05.9	09 13.2	00 ♒ 06.4
	20	11 59.5	20 03.6	14 30.2	03 45.5
	30	10 15.6	28 13.0	19 46.4	07 13.2
JUN	9	08 55.6	06 ♊ 33.8	25 01.6	10 27.8
	19	08 05.4	15 05.5	00 ♋ 14.9	13 29.4
	29	07 47.0	23 47.3	05 26.0	16 21.5
JUL	9	08 D 00.5	02 ♋ 38.4	10 34.4	19 12.9
	19	08 44.4	11 37.3	15 39.5	22 35.5
	29	09 56.0	20 42.4	20 40.8	28 31.1
AUG	8	11 32.3	29 52.4	25 37.9	22 ♓ 07.2
	18	13 30.7	09 ♌ 05.0	00 ♌ 30.0	14 ♋ 44.1
	28	15 48.1	18 18.3	05 16.4	04 ♌ 55.7
SEP	7	18 22.2	27 30.6	09 56.4	11 07.3
	17	21 10.8	06 ♍ 39.5	14 28.9	15 40.6
	27	24 11.8	15 43.3	18 52.8	20 31.9
OCT	7	27 23.7	24 40.3	23 06.9	26 07.8
	17	00 ♐ 44.8	03 ♎ 28.6	27 09.4	02 ♍ 24.0
	27	04 13.7	12 07.1	00 ♍ 58.5	09 05.5
NOV	6	07 49.3	20 34.7	04 31.8	15 53.3
	16	11 30.4	28 50.0	07 46.4	22 30.9
	26	15 15.9	06 ♏ 52.8	10 39.4	28 47.9
DEC	6	19 04.9	14 42.4	13 06.7	04 ♎ 35.8
	16	22 56.2	22 18.4	15 04.1	09 48.4
	26	26 48.9	29 40.6	16 27.4	14 20.4
JAN	5	00 ♑ 42.2	06 ♐ 49.1	17 ♍ 11.6	18 ♎ 04.8
JAN	1	12 S 46.5	13 S 04.8	06 N 55.9	25 S 48.0
	21	14 00.3	08 44.4	09 03.1	27 23.4
FEB	10	14 45.0	03 46.8	11 39.4	28 15.6
MAR	1	14 57.9	01 N 40.6	14 26.8	28 22.8
	21	14 37.7	07 27.5	17 08.8	27 45.2
APR	10	13 46.3	13 18.7	19 31.0	26 22.8
	30	12 33.4	18 53.0	21 21.3	24 13.6
MAY	20	11 20.8	23 39.4	22 30.4	21 07.5
JUN	9	10 34.4	26 57.1	22 52.6	16 30.9
	29	10 29.8	28 01.9	22 26.2	08 38.0
JUL	19	11 06.8	26 22.6	21 13.3	08 N 53.7
AUG	8	12 16.4	21 58.4	19 19.0	57 35.8
	28	13 47.0	15 21.5	16 51.0	64 49.8
SEP	17	15 27.5	07 22.3	13 58.1	39 51.5
OCT	7	17 08.0	01 S 06.5	10 50.3	24 14.1
	27	18 39.7	09 19.3	07 38.3	11 53.5
NOV	16	19 55.4	16 40.1	04 33.6	01 35.7
DEC	6	20 49.1	22 42.7	01 49.3	07 S 00.2
	26	21 S 16.8	27 S 09.9	00 S 18.8	14 S 08.9

1949	Psyche 16	Eros 433	Lilith 1181	Toro 1685
JAN 1	29♐08.9	03♐59.4	16♍58.9	16♎41.3
11	03♑01.9	10 59.4	17 18.0	19 53.2
21	06 53.7	17 45.4	16R53.7	22 03.6
31	10 43.3	24 17.5	15 46.4	23 00.3
FEB 10	14 29.5	00♑35.1	14 01.3	22R29.8
20	18 11.2	06 38.1	11 49.1	20 21.9
MAR 2	21 47.0	12 26.3	09 24.7	16 34.9
12	25 15.3	17 58.5	07 05.6	11 28.2
22	28 34.7	23 14.2	05 07.4	05 46.3
APR 1	01♒43.3	28 12.1	03 41.1	00 24.0
11	04 38.7	02♒49.9	02 53.0	26♍07.2
21	07 18.6	07 05.7	02D43.7	23 16.1
MAY 1	09 40.3	10 55.9	03 11.5	21 49.9
11	11 40.2	14 16.3	04 12.8	21D38.2
21	13 15.2	17 01.6	05 43.0	22 26.7
31	14 21.4	19 04.5	07 38.0	24 03.1
JUN 10	14 55.0	20 16.5	09 53.9	26 17.4
20	14R53.7	20R28.6	12 27.2	29 01.1
30	14 15.9	19 31.4	15 15.0	02♎08.5
JUL 10	13 03.6	17 21.0	18 14.9	05 35.2
20	11 22.5	14 03.2	21 24.7	09 17.6
30	09 22.4	09 58.0	24 42.7	13 13.5
AUG 9	07 17.1	05 41.3	28 07.4	17 21.0
19	05 21.4	01 52.1	01♎37.5	21 38.6
29	03 48.5	29♑00.8	05 12.0	26 05.6
SEP 8	02 48.2	27 23.4	08 49.8	00♏41.4
18	02 25.6	27D00.4	12 30.0	05 25.4
28	02D42.2	27 45.7	16 11.7	10 17.6
OCT 8	03 36.6	29 30.3	19 54.1	15 17.9
18	05 05.7	02♒04.4	23 36.4	20 26.5
28	07 05.8	05 20.3	27 17.6	25 43.8
NOV 7	09 33.2	09 11.5	00♏56.8	01♐10.1
17	12 24.0	13 32.5	04 33.0	06 46.1
27	15 35.1	18 19.9	08 05.3	12 32.8
DEC 7	19 03.4	23 30.3	11 32.2	18 31.0
17	22 46.2	29 01.5	14 52.5	24 42.2
27	26 41.5	04♓52.1	18 04.6	01♑08.1
JAN 6	00♓47.1	11♓00.5	21♏06.8	07♑50.4
JAN 1	21S19.6	28S10.1	00S47.5	16S02.2
21	21 10.9	30 24.4	01 41.1	21 27.7
FEB 10	20 35.5	31 02.7	01 21.1	25 11.5
MAR 2	19 37.3	30 20.5	00N03.0	25 58.1
22	18 23.0	28 38.2	01 50.6	22 33.5
APR 11	17 01.2	26 18.1	03 15.4	16 47.5
MAY 1	15 43.1	23 41.5	03 53.0	11 59.3
21	14 42.2	21 08.6	03 40.2	09 20.5
JUN 10	14 13.1	18 58.3	02 43.4	08 33.7
30	14 27.8	17 24.8	01 10.8	09 07.1
JUL 20	15 26.9	16 26.2	00S49.4	10 34.7
AUG 9	16 50.6	15 36.1	03 09.9	12 37.2
29	18 06.5	14 36.1	05 44.0	14 59.4
SEP 18	18 51.5	13 30.9	08 25.3	17 28.6
OCT 8	18 58.3	12 16.9	11 08.2	19 52.5
28	18 26.5	10 39.5	13 46.9	21 58.5
NOV 17	17 17.0	08 25.5	16 16.1	23 32.4
DEC 7	15 31.2	05 26.9	18 31.3	24 18.5
27	13S12.1	01S41.9	20S28.6	23S59.2

1950	Psyche 16	Eros 433	Lilith 1181	Toro 1685
JAN 1	28♒43.1	07♓54.2	19♏37.0	04♑27.1
11	02♓53.2	14 11.1	22 33.6	11 18.5
21	07 11.2	20 44.9	25 17.2	18 30.4
31	11 35.6	27 34.7	27 45.4	26 05.5
FEB 10	16 05.1	04♈40.0	29 55.7	04♒07.4
20	20 38.7	12 00.7	01♐45.0	12 40.1
MAR 2	25 15.2	19 36.3	03 10.0	21 47.4
12	29 53.8	27 26.1	04 07.7	01♓33.0
22	04♈33.6	05♉29.9	04 34.7	12 00.0
APR 1	09 13.8	13 46.8	04R28.7	23 09.3
11	13 53.6	22 15.9	03 48.9	04♈59.3
21	18 32.4	00♊56.3	02 36.1	17 24.6
MAY 1	23 09.4	09 46.4	00 54.8	00♉15.3
11	27 43.9	18 44.7	28♏52.9	13 17.7
21	02♉15.3	27 49.6	26 41.0	26 16.5
31	06 42.5	06♋59.1	24 31.8	08♊56.4
JUN 10	11 04.8	16 11.2	22 37.0	21 05.9
20	15 21.4	25 24.1	21 06.0	02♋37.8
30	19 31.0	04♌35.5	20 05.1	13 28.8
JUL 10	23 32.4	13 43.5	19 37.0	23 39.0
20	27 24.2	22 46.5	19D41.8	03♌10.6
30	01♊04.4	01♍42.6	20 18.0	12 06.4
AUG 9	04 31.2	10 30.4	21 22.6	20 30.2
19	07 41.9	19 08.8	22 52.9	28 25.6
29	10 33.6	27 36.7	24 45.6	05♍55.8
SEP 8	13 03.1	05♎53.5	26 57.9	13 03.9
18	15 06.2	13 59.1	29 27.3	19 52.7
28	16 38.6	21 53.1	02♐11.3	26 24.4
OCT 8	17 36.1	29 35.8	05 07.9	02♎40.9
18	17 54.6	07♏07.6	08 15.5	08 44.0
28	17R31.9	14 28.5	11 32.3	14 34.6
NOV 7	16 28.9	21 39.3	14 56.9	20 13.9
17	14 50.4	28 40.5	18 28.2	25 42.6
27	12 47.2	05♐32.5	22 04.9	01♏00.9
DEC 7	10 34.2	12 15.8	25 45.9	06 09.2
17	08 28.1	18 51.2	29 30.3	11 07.2
27	06 44.7	25 18.7	03♑16.8	15 54.5
JAN 6	05♊34.5	01♑39.0	07♑04.8	20♏30.5
JAN 1	12S32.7	00S38.7	20S54.7	23S41.9
21	09 38.7	03N57.9	22 25.8	21 34.0
FEB 10	06 24.0	09 02.9	23 34.5	17 37.8
MAR 2	02 55.9	14 16.4	24 20.1	11 38.2
22	00N37.6	19 08.5	24 41.2	03 34.2
APR 11	04 08.8	22 59.0	24 33.6	05N59.6
MAY 1	07 30.0	25 02.0	23 51.4	15 23.2
21	10 34.3	24 40.1	22 36.0	21 59.1
JUN 10	13 15.4	21 43.1	21 06.8	23 53.4
30	15 28.4	16 33.6	19 53.5	21 32.1
JUL 20	17 10.0	09 55.9	19 15.5	16 42.0
AUG 9	18 18.7	02 37.4	19 14.6	10 52.5
29	18 55.8	04S41.4	19 42.6	04 52.5
SEP 18	19 05.0	11 29.5	20 27.3	00S55.6
OCT 8	18 52.4	17 24.6	21 17.4	06 22.3
28	18 25.2	22 10.7	22 02.5	11 22.8
NOV 17	17 50.5	25 36.8	22 34.2	15 54.3
DEC 7	17 17.9	27 36.8	22 45.8	19 54.2
27	17N01.9	28S10.3	22S33.0	23S20.7

1951	Psyche 16	Eros 433	Lilith 1181	Toro 1685
JAN 1	06R05.0	28♐29.7	05♑10.7	18♏13.9
11	05♊13.8	04♑46.6	08 59.0	22 44.0
21	05D02.7	10 56.6	12 47.1	27 00.8
31	05 30.7	17 00.1	16 34.1	01♐03.0
FEB 10	06 34.5	22 57.5	20 19.0	04 48.4
20	08 10.0	28 48.7	24 00.5	08 13.8
MAR 2	10 12.5	04♒34.1	27 37.7	11 15.7
12	12 37.7	10 13.7	01♒09.3	13 49.0
22	15 21.8	15 47.5	04 33.7	15 47.4
APR 1	18 21.3	21 15.5	07 49.5	17 03.3
11	21 33.6	26 37.8	10 54.7	17R26.7
21	24 56.1	01♓53.8	13 47.2	16 47.3
MAY 1	28 26.7	07 03.7	16 24.6	14 55.9
11	02♋03.9	12 06.7	18 44.0	11 47.7
21	05 46.1	17 02.2	20 41.9	07 31.5
31	09 32.2	21 49.6	22 15.0	02 32.5
JUN 10	13 21.1	26 27.4	23 18.8	27♏30.4
20	17 11.8	00♈53.9	23 49.6	23 08.3
30	21 03.6	05 07.2	23R44.0	19 55.0
JUL 10	24 55.7	09 03.7	23 00.1	18 02.8
20	28 47.3	12 39.4	21 39.4	17D30.7
30	02♌37.7	15 49.0	19 47.4	18 09.8
AUG 9	06 26.4	18 24.3	17 34.4	19 51.1
19	10 12.3	20 15.8	15 15.7	22 25.5
29	13 54.7	21 11.2	13 07.3	25 45.7
SEP 8	17 32.8	20R55.9	11 24.1	29 46.9
18	21 05.4	19 18.4	10 17.2	04♐25.6
28	24 31.4	16 15.5	09 51.8	09 39.6
OCT 8	27 49.4	12 04.0	10D09.5	15 28.8
18	00♍57.7	07 28.7	11 08.6	21 53.3
28	03 54.6	03 26.4	12 45.3	28 54.5
NOV 7	06 37.8	00 45.8	14 55.8	06♑34.6
17	09 04.6	29D50.4	17 35.8	14 55.4
27	11 12.5	00♈39.2	20 41.4	23 59.0
DEC 7	12 57.8	03 02.3	24 09.1	03♒48.2
17	14 17.4	06 45.0	27 55.8	14 26.7
27	15 07.7	11 33.4	01♓58.8	26 04.9
JAN 6	15♍25.5	17♈17.5	06♓16.0	09♓05.0
JAN 1	17N02.2	28S05.7	22S25.7	24S07.0
21	17 22.8	26 59.2	21 39.5	26 50.8
FEB 10	18 09.8	24 44.5	20 27.4	29 02.0
MAR 2	19 10.9	21 34.4	18 52.5	30 44.8
22	20 12.5	17 41.4	16 59.8	32 04.8
APR 11	21 03.0	13 16.3	14 56.1	33 03.8
MAY 1	21 33.8	08 28.0	12 49.7	33 23.3
21	21 39.9	03 22.6	10 51.1	32 01.7
JUN 10	21 18.5	01N56.0	09 12.7	28 10.6
30	20 29.7	07 26.1	08 09.2	23 26.1
JUL 20	19 15.2	13 07.9	07 53.4	20 01.4
AUG 9	17 38.8	19 01.1	08 26.5	18 22.7
29	15 45.5	24 52.7	09 29.0	17 56.6
SEP 18	13 41.2	29 43.7	10 29.3	18 01.7
OCT 8	11 33.5	31 23.5	11 02.4	17 58.7
28	09 30.9	28 54.6	10 56.0	17 09.5
NOV 17	07 43.6	24 57.3	10 05.9	14 58.4
DEC 7	06 23.3	22 11.1	08 32.1	11 06.6
27	05N43.2	21N10.5	06S17.3	05S54.9

1952		Psyche 16	Eros 433	Lillith 1181	Toro 1685
JAN	1	15♍20.9	14♈19.1	04♓05.8	02♓23.0
	11	15R21.6	20 27.4	08 29.2	16 15.0
	21	14 47.6	27 17.7	13 03.7	02♈12.0
	31	13 39.8	04♉44.1	17 47.9	20 16.0
FEB	10	12 02.9	12 41.3	22 40.3	09♉19.5
	20	10 05.1	21 03.7	27 39.5	27 23.6
MAR	1	07 57.5	29 47.6	02♈44.7	13♊02.8
	11	05 53.2	08♊48.6	07 54.7	26 01.9
	21	04 04.1	18 01.9	13 08.6	06♋46.7
	31	02 39.6	27 24.0	18 25.8	15 53.0
APR	10	01 45.5	06♋50.6	23 45.5	23 49.5
	20	01 24.1	16 17.0	29 06.9	00♌56.6
	30	01D34.8	25 39.7	04♉29.5	07 29.3
MAY	10	02 15.8	04♌55.0	09 52.5	13 37.3
	20	03 23.8	13 59.5	15 15.5	19 27.1
	30	04 55.8	22 51.3	20 37.9	25 03.8
JUN	9	06 48.4	01♍28.6	25 58.8	00♍30.6
	19	08 58.7	09 50.3	01♊17.8	05 49.8
	29	11 24.1	17 56.7	06 34.2	11 03.6
JUL	9	14 02.2	25 47.8	11 47.2	16 13.2
	19	16 51.1	03♎24.2	16 55.9	21 19.6
	29	19 49.0	10 47.2	21 59.5	26 24.0
AUG	8	22 54.5	17 57.8	26 56.8	01♎26.9
	18	26 06.2	24 57.0	01♋46.7	06 28.9
	28	29 23.0	01♏46.4	06 27.5	11 30.6
SEP	7	02♎43.7	08 26.9	10 57.6	16 32.5
	17	06 07.4	14 59.6	15 15.0	21 34.9
	27	09 33.2	21 25.8	19 17.0	26 38.4
OCT	7	13 00.0	27 46.2	23 00.6	01♏43.0
	17	16 27.0	04♐01.6	26 22.4	06 49.3
	27	19 53.1	10 12.9	29 17.8	11 57.7
NOV	6	23 17.1	16 20.6	01♌42.0	17 08.2
	16	26 38.2	22 25.4	03 29.8	22 21.4
	26	29 54.9	28 27.9	04 35.1	27 37.7
DEC	6	03♏05.7	04♑28.3	04R53.5	02♐57.3
	16	06 09.3	10 27.1	04 22.5	08 20.9
	26	09 03.7	16 24.8	03 03.8	13 48.9
JAN	5	11♏47.0	22♑21.4	01♌06.4	19♐22.1
JAN	1	05N40.9	21N08.7	05S37.7	04S29.6
	21	06 06.2	21 31.3	02 39.0	01N28.1
FEB	10	07 23.8	21 57.2	00N46.7	06 49.1
MAR	1	09 10.9	21 29.2	04 30.1	09 11.1
	21	10 49.2	19 30.0	08 21.2	09 20.1
APR	10	11 48.1	15 54.6	12 09.5	08 30.9
	30	11 57.7	11 05.9	15 43.7	07 03.1
MAY	20	11 22.3	05 36.2	18 53.2	05 01.8
JUN	9	10 10.0	00S05.7	21 27.7	02 32.1
	29	08 28.7	05 38.9	23 19.0	00S20.4
JUL	19	06 25.1	10 49.7	24 21.4	03 29.7
AUG	8	04 05.0	15 28.2	24 33.3	06 49.9
	28	01 34.0	19 26.5	23 57.5	10 14.7
SEP	17	01S02.7	22 37.6	22 41.8	13 37.9
OCT	7	03 39.8	24 55.0	20 57.8	16 52.6
	27	06 11.9	26 13.0	19 01.1	19 51.4
NOV	16	08 33.7	26 27.7	17 10.1	22 25.8
DEC	6	10 40.0	25 38.1	15 44.3	24 26.5
	26	12S25.9	23S46.2	14N58.9	25S43.5

1953		Psyche 16	Eros 433	Lillith 1181	Toro 1685
JAN	1	10♏43.1	19♑58.8	01R57.2	17♐08.2
	11	13 18.7	25 55.0	29♋43.2	22 45.0
	21	15 39.3	01♒50.9	27 17.2	28 28.6
	31	17 42.3	07 46.5	25 00.6	04♑20.2
FEB	10	19 24.8	13 42.2	23 11.4	10 21.5
	20	20 43.5	19 38.4	22 01.6	16 34.5
MAR	2	21 35.2	25 35.4	21D36.5	23 01.8
	12	21 57.2	01♓33.5	21 55.4	29 46.8
	22	21R47.1	07 33.3	22 54.7	06♒53.3
APR	1	21 04.7	13 35.1	24 29.3	14 26.1
	11	19 51.7	19 39.6	26 33.5	22 31.5
	21	18 12.7	25 47.3	29 02.5	01♓15.7
MAY	1	16 16.1	01♈58.9	01♌51.7	10 45.6
	11	14 12.5	08 15.2	04 57.2	21 07.8
	21	12 13.7	14 37.1	08 16.2	02♈25.2
	31	10 30.9	21 05.3	11 45.9	14 36.2
JUN	10	09 12.4	27 41.0	15 24.1	27 32.3
	20	08 23.7	04♉25.2	19 09.4	10♉57.3
	30	08D07.2	11 18.9	23 00.0	24 31.5
JUL	10	08 22.4	18 23.5	26 54.7	07♊57.0
	20	09 07.9	25 40.0	00♍52.8	20 59.7
	30	10 21.0	03♊09.5	04 53.1	03♋30.5
AUG	9	11 58.8	10 53.3	08 54.9	15 23.8
	19	13 58.3	18 51.9	12 57.6	26 35.8
	29	16 16.9	27 05.8	17 00.3	07♌05.2
SEP	8	18 52.0	05♋35.6	21 02.5	16 53.1
	18	21 41.5	14 20.1	25 03.6	26 01.6
	28	24 43.3	23 18.7	29 02.7	04♍33.8
OCT	8	27 55.8	02♌29.6	02♎59.3	12 33.3
	18	01♐17.5	11 49.9	06 52.3	20 03.1
	28	04 47.0	21 16.9	10 41.0	27 06.0
NOV	7	08 23.0	00♍47.1	14 24.2	03♎44.3
	17	12 04.5	10 16.1	18 00.9	09 59.6
	27	15 50.3	19 40.3	21 29.5	15 53.1
DEC	7	19 39.5	28 55.8	24 48.6	21 25.5
	17	23 31.0	07♎58.2	27 56.2	26 36.4
	27	27 23.8	16 44.0	00♏50.4	01♏25.3
JAN	6	01♑17.1	25♎09.4	03♏28.7	05♏50.9
JAN	1	12S52.9	23S01.2	14N53.8	25S56.5
	21	14 05.9	19 56.0	14 59.0	26 01.0
FEB	10	14 49.6	16 02.7	15 21.5	24 57.1
MAR	2	15 01.6	11 29.0	15 42.0	22 32.7
	22	14 40.7	06 22.6	15 47.8	18 33.4
APR	11	13 48.8	00 50.7	15 30.8	12 41.1
MAY	1	12 36.0	04N59.8	14 46.2	04 37.2
	21	11 24.3	11 01.4	13 32.1	05N35.4
JUN	10	10 39.3	17 04.4	11 49.2	16 37.3
	30	10 36.0	22 54.8	09 40.3	25 14.1
JUL	20	11 14.1	28 09.8	07 09.2	28 07.8
AUG	9	12 24.4	32 14.0	04 20.7	25 04.1
	29	13 55.3	34 18.4	01 19.8	18 30.4
SEP	18	15 35.5	33 30.6	01S48.4	10 50.8
OCT	8	17 15.2	29 19.5	04 58.4	03 20.3
	28	18 45.9	21 55.7	08 04.8	03S33.7
NOV	17	20 00.1	12 07.0	11 02.2	09 43.7
DEC	7	20 52.1	00 59.8	13 45.4	15 08.8
	27	21S17.8	10S17.6	16S09.3	19S50.8

1954		Psyche 16	Eros 433	Lillith 1181	Toro 1685
JAN	1	29♐20.5	20♎59.5	02♏11.7	03♏41.2
	11	03♑13.6	29 12.9	04 40.9	07 54.2
	21	07 05.5	06♏59.6	06 49.9	11 39.7
	31	10 55.2	14 15.8	08 35.5	14 54.3
FEB	10	14 41.6	20 56.1	09 54.1	17 32.3
	20	18 23.4	26 54.9	10 42.4	19 27.3
MAR	2	21 59.5	02♐05.8	10R57.3	20 31.1
	12	25 28.2	06 19.2	10 36.7	20R33.9
	22	28 48.0	09 25.1	09 40.7	19 27.2
APR	1	01♒57.1	11 11.3	08 12.2	17 05.5
	11	04 53.1	11R24.2	06 17.4	13 31.7
	21	07 33.8	09 57.2	04 06.7	09 04.5
MAY	1	09 56.4	06 55.2	01 52.5	04 16.1
	11	11 57.5	02 44.6	29♎47.7	29♎45.7
	21	13 33.7	28♏15.1	28 03.7	26 06.5
	31	14 41.4	24 17.7	26 47.9	23 35.4
JUN	10	15 16.7	21 29.4	26 04.8	22 16.4
	20	15R17.2	20 03.5	25D55.1	22D04.0
	30	14 41.4	19D55.1	26 17.5	22 48.8
JUL	10	13 30.7	20 53.6	27 09.5	24 22.1
	20	11 50.9	22 46.0	28 28.0	26 35.4
	30	09 51.6	25 20.6	00♏09.6	29 22.1
AUG	9	07 46.1	28 29.0	02 11.5	02♏37.3
	19	05 49.6	02♐03.8	04 30.6	06 16.9
	29	04 14.9	05 59.6	07 04.6	10 18.1
SEP	8	03 12.5	10 12.8	09 51.4	14 39.2
	18	02 47.6	14 40.2	12 48.8	19 18.5
	28	03D01.6	19 19.5	15 55.5	24 15.7
OCT	8	03 53.7	24 09.3	19 09.9	29 30.5
	18	05 20.7	29 08.1	22 30.7	05♐03.0
	28	07 18.8	04♑15.0	25 56.7	10 54.3
NOV	7	09 44.4	09 29.4	29 26.8	17 05.4
	17	12 33.5	14 50.6	02♐59.9	23 38.0
	27	15 43.1	20 18.3	06 35.1	00♑34.4
DEC	7	19 10.0	25 52.3	10 11.4	07 57.2
	17	22 51.7	01♒32.3	13 47.5	15 49.5
	27	26 45.8	07 18.3	17 22.7	24 15.4
JAN	6	00♓50.4	13♒10.2	20♐55.7	03♒18.7
JAN	1	21S19.8	13S01.5	16S41.7	20S54.8
	21	21 10.5	23 13.9	18 34.2	24 46.1
FEB	10	20 34.5	31 57.6	19 55.3	27 59.3
MAR	2	19 35.8	39 05.4	20 37.2	30 30.9
	22	18 20.9	44 46.4	20 29.9	31 58.2
APR	11	16 58.5	48 54.2	19 27.5	31 22.4
MAY	1	15 39.8	50 05.6	17 41.8	27 54.3
	21	14 38.0	46 24.1	15 48.5	22 55.5
JUN	10	14 07.9	39 36.7	14 25.2	18 52.8
	30	14 21.6	33 35.7	13 50.1	16 43.5
JUL	20	15 20.1	29 44.0	14 02.2	16 12.4
AUG	9	16 44.0	27 36.1	14 51.4	16 48.5
	29	18 00.8	26 26.9	16 05.6	18 04.0
SEP	18	18 46.9	25 39.4	17 34.0	19 35.8
OCT	8	18 54.6	24 47.0	19 06.6	21 02.8
	28	18 23.5	23 31.1	20 35.1	22 03.1
NOV	17	17 14.5	21 39.6	21 52.3	22 12.6
DEC	7	15 29.3	19 05.8	22 52.4	21 03.7
	27	13S10.8	15S47.3	23S31.3	18S07.0

1955		Psyche 16	Eros 433	Lilith 1181	Toro 1685
JAN	1	28♒46.9	10♒13.5	19♐09.6	28♑42.2
	11	02♓56.1	16 08.4	22 41.1	08♒05.7
	21	07 13.1	22 09.2	26 08.7	18 12.5
	31	11 36.7	28 16.4	29 31.0	29 05.5
FEB	10	16 05.5	04♓29.9	02♑46.7	10♓44.3
	20	20 38.3	10 50.2	05 54.1	23 05.4
MAR	2	25 14.3	17 17.6	08 51.5	06♈00.4
	12	29 52.2	23 52.5	11 36.7	19 15.9
	22	04♈31.4	00♈35.4	14 07.7	02♉36.9
APR	1	09 11.1	07 27.0	16 21.6	15 47.8
	11	13 50.5	14 27.7	18 15.5	28 34.5
	21	18 28.8	21 38.2	19 46.3	10♊46.3
MAY	1	23 05.5	28 59.1	20 50.4	22 16.3
	11	27 39.5	06♉30.7	21 24.4	03♋01.0
	21	02♉10.5	14 13.7	21R25.4	13 00.9
	31	06 37.5	22 08.3	20 51.5	22 19.1
JUN	10	10 59.6	00♊14.6	19 43.3	00♌59.1
	20	15 15.9	08 32.6	18 04.3	09 05.7
	30	19 25.4	17 01.8	16 01.9	16 43.6
JUL	10	23 26.6	25 41.6	13 47.6	23 56.7
	20	27 18.3	04♋31.3	11 34.7	00♍49.0
	30	00♊58.5	13 29.2	09 36.9	07 23.6
AUG	9	04 25.3	22 34.1	08 05.3	13 43.2
	19	07 36.2	01♌44.4	07 07.0	19 50.2
	29	10 28.1	10 57.8	06 45.8	25 46.7
SEP	8	12 57.8	20 12.5	07D01.8	01♎34.0
	18	15 01.3	29 26.7	07 53.3	07 13.9
	28	16 34.2	08♍37.9	09 17.3	12 47.2
OCT	8	17 32.2	17 44.1	11 10.4	18 14.8
	18	17 51.5	26 43.8	13 29.1	23 37.6
	28	17R29.5	05♎34.8	16 10.3	28 56.2
NOV	7	16 27.2	14 15.7	19 11.1	04♏11.0
	17	14 49.3	22 45.4	22 28.8	09 22.5
	27	12 46.4	01♏02.3	26 01.5	14 30.7
DEC	7	10 33.6	09 05.9	29 46.9	19 35.9
	17	08 27.3	16 55.4	03♒43.6	24 38.3
	27	06 43.4	24 30.3	07 49.9	29 37.7
JAN	6	05♊32.7	01♐50.1	12♒04.6	04♐34.1
JAN	1	12S31.4	14S50.7	23S37.5	17S02.7
	21	09 38.0	10 38.2	23 47.2	11 17.1
FEB	10	06 23.9	05 47.4	23 34.1	03 17.5
MAR	2	02 56.3	00 25.2	23 01.6	05N54.5
	22	00N36.8	05N19.3	22 15.2	14 07.9
APR	11	04 07.6	11 13.7	21 22.3	19 07.7
MAY	1	07 28.5	17 00.4	20 31.8	20 08.9
	21	10 32.7	22 13.4	19 52.2	18 07.5
JUN	10	13 13.8	26 17.0	19 28.8	14 25.6
	30	15 27.0	28 27.0	19 19.6	09 59.7
JUL	20	17 08.7	28 02.9	19 17.3	05 19.0
AUG	9	18 17.7	24 47.5	19 16.7	00 37.2
	29	18 55.1	18 57.8	19 17.0	03S58.9
SEP	18	19 04.5	11 18.2	19 15.9	08 24.4
OCT	8	18 52.2	02 43.1	19 07.0	12 35.3
	28	18 25.0	05S56.4	18 42.0	16 27.2
NOV	17	17 50.3	13 57.8	17 53.3	19 55.3
DEC	7	17 17.5	20 48.8	16 35.3	22 54.2
	27	17N01.2	26S07.5	14S45.0	25S18.7

1956		Psyche 16	Eros 433	Lilith 1181	Toro 1685
JAN	1	06R03.4	28♏12.1	09♒56.3	02♐06.2
	11	05♊11.7	05♐24.4	14 14.7	07 01.2
	21	04D59.9	12 21.2	18 40.0	11 53.0
	31	05 27.3	19 02.1	23 10.9	16 41.4
FEB	10	06 30.6	25 27.1	27 46.7	21 26.3
	20	08 05.6	01♑35.4	02♓26.5	26 07.3
MAR	1	10 07.8	07 26.2	07 09.6	00♑44.0
	11	12 32.7	12 59.1	11 55.5	05 16.4
	21	15 16.7	18 12.2	16 43.3	09 43.5
	31	18 16.2	23 04.0	21 32.4	14 05.0
APR	10	21 28.3	27 32.3	26 22.4	18 20.3
	20	24 50.8	01♒33.4	01♈12.6	22 28.4
	30	28 21.5	05 03.4	06 02.3	26 28.6
MAY	10	01♋58.7	07 57.0	10 51.0	00♒19.9
	20	05 41.1	10 06.7	15 37.8	04 00.7
	30	09 27.3	11 24.6	20 21.9	07 30.5
JUN	9	13 16.3	11R41.2	25 02.6	10 48.3
	19	17 07.3	10 47.5	29 38.5	13 54.2
	29	20 59.3	08 40.1	04♉08.5	16 52.9
JUL	9	24 51.6	05 24.1	08 31.0	19 55.1
	19	28 43.5	01 20.3	12 44.1	23 36.6
	29	02♌34.2	27♑04.0	16 45.6	00♓16.1
AUG	8	06 23.2	23 13.8	20 32.8	26 39.4
	18	10 09.5	20 20.7	24 02.0	12♋50.5
	28	13 52.2	18 39.4	27 09.5	03♌51.6
SEP	7	17 30.8	18D11.2	29 50.2	10 32.3
	17	21 03.8	18 50.2	01♊58.6	15 21.4
	27	24 30.3	20 26.7	03 28.8	20 22.1
OCT	7	27 48.9	22 51.5	04 14.7	26 04.4
	17	00♍57.8	25 56.9	04R12.0	02♍24.8
	27	03 55.3	29 36.0	03 20.2	09 08.9
NOV	6	06 39.3	03♒43.9	01 44.4	15 58.4
	16	09 07.0	08 16.7	29♉38.1	22 37.2
	26	11 15.7	13 11.0	27 21.7	28 54.9
DEC	6	13 02.2	18 24.8	25 17.6	04♎43.5
	16	14 22.8	23 56.5	23 46.2	09 56.6
	26	15 14.4	29 44.4	22 59.8	14 29.2
JAN	5	15♍33.6	05♓48.0	23D03.1	18♎14.5
JAN	1	17N01.4	27S11.2	14S12.4	25S48.8
	21	17 21.7	30 20.2	11 42.1	27 23.7
FEB	10	18 08.6	31 48.3	08 42.7	28 15.1
MAR	1	19 09.8	31 49.9	05 19.0	28 21.7
	21	20 11.5	30 46.5	01 36.9	27 43.1
APR	10	21 02.2	29 03.3	02N16.8	26 19.7
	30	21 33.3	27 05.4	06 14.8	24 09.3
MAY	20	21 39.7	25 16.6	10 09.7	21 01.6
JUN	9	21 18.6	23 56.2	13 53.7	16 22.6
	29	20 30.0	23 06.9	17 19.3	08 25.4
JUL	19	19 15.7	22 16.4	20 19.2	09N16.9
AUG	8	17 39.4	20 46.5	22 47.4	58 30.2
	28	15 45.9	18 55.9	24 39.0	64 37.3
SEP	17	13 41.6	17 13.7	25 50.4	39 40.8
OCT	7	11 33.5	15 35.2	26 16.3	24 06.4
	27	09 30.5	13 42.2	25 46.4	11 47.6
NOV	16	07 42.6	11 18.6	24 13.1	01 30.9
DEC	6	06 21.6	08 14.9	22 00.9	07S04.1
	26	05N40.6	04S27.4	20N09.5	14S12.1

1957		Psyche 16	Eros 433	Lilith 1181	Toro 1685
JAN	1	15♍30.0	03♓20.7	22D55.7	16♎50.6
	11	15R28.6	09 33.3	23♉28.8	20 03.3
	21	14 52.4	16 00.3	24 47.9	22 14.7
	31	13 42.7	22 41.7	26 47.3	23 12.9
FEB	10	12 04.2	29 37.1	29 21.1	22R44.0
	20	10 05.4	06♈46.2	02♊23.0	20 38.0
MAR	2	07 57.7	14 09.1	05 47.8	16 53.1
	12	05 54.1	21 45.7	09 31.3	11 47.8
	22	04 06.5	29 35.4	13 29.4	06 06.4
APR	1	02 43.9	07♉38.3	17 39.2	00 43.6
	11	01 52.1	15 53.7	21 58.3	26♍25.4
	21	01 32.9	24 20.7	26 24.4	23 32.7
MAY	1	01D45.9	02♊58.8	00♋55.8	22 04.8
	11	02 28.9	11 46.5	05 31.4	21D51.7
	21	03 38.8	20 42.4	10 09.6	22 39.2
	31	05 12.3	29 45.1	14 49.8	24 14.6
JUN	10	07 06.4	08♋52.8	19 31.0	26 28.1
	20	09 17.9	18 03.4	24 12.5	29 11.3
	30	11 44.3	27 15.3	28 53.8	02♎18.2
JUL	10	14 23.4	06♌26.3	03♌34.2	05 44.5
	20	17 13.0	15 34.5	08 13.3	09 26.6
	30	20 11.7	24 38.2	12 50.7	13 22.2
AUG	9	23 17.8	03♍35.6	17 25.8	17 29.5
	19	26 29.9	12 25.1	21 58.0	21 46.9
	29	29 47.1	21 05.9	26 27.1	26 13.8
SEP	8	03♎08.2	29 36.5	00♍52.2	00♏49.5
	18	06 32.1	07♎56.4	05 12.8	05 33.4
	28	09 58.1	16 05.3	09 28.2	10 25.5
OCT	8	13 25.0	24 02.8	13 37.3	15 25.8
	18	16 52.0	01♏48.8	17 39.3	20 34.4
	28	20 18.0	09 23.7	21 32.8	25 51.6
NOV	7	23 41.9	16 47.6	25 16.4	01♐17.9
	17	27 02.7	24 00.9	28 48.5	06 53.9
	27	00♏19.1	01♐04.2	02♎07.0	12 40.7
DEC	7	03 29.4	07 57.7	05 09.4	18 38.9
	17	06 32.4	14 42.0	07 53.1	24 50.2
	27	09 26.1	21 17.4	10 14.8	01♑16.2
JAN	6	12♏08.5	27♐44.3	12♎11.0	07♑58.6
JAN	1	05N37.9	03S10.9	19N47.1	16S05.2
	21	06 05.1	01N29.4	19 13.4	21 30.4
FEB	10	07 24.1	06 40.2	19 29.0	25 14.6
MAR	2	09 11.6	12 05.4	20 08.9	26 02.7
	22	10 49.0	17 20.6	20 49.8	22 40.3
APR	11	11 46.3	21 50.9	21 14.3	16 54.6
MAY	1	11 54.2	24 52.7	21 10.9	12 05.5
	21	11 17.3	25 42.6	20 33.3	09 25.5
JUN	10	10 03.7	23 55.2	19 19.5	08 37.9
	30	08 21.4	19 37.9	17 31.0	09 10.7
JUL	20	06 16.9	13 26.9	15 11.6	10 37.9
AUG	9	03 56.2	06 10.9	12 26.7	12 39.9
	29	01 24.8	01S24.2	09 22.5	15 01.8
SEP	18	01S12.0	08 41.3	06 05.5	17 30.5
OCT	8	03 49.0	15 12.9	02 42.7	19 54.0
	28	06 20.7	20 38.7	00S38.9	21 59.4
NOV	17	08 41.9	24 44.8	03 52.0	23 32.7
DEC	7	10 47.3	27 22.7	06 48.8	24 18.1
	27	12S32.1	28S30.4	09S20.4	23S57.9

1958	Psyche 16	Eros 433	Lilith 1181	Toro 1685
JAN 1	10♏48.8	24♐31.9	11♎16.3	04♑35.2
11	13 24.7	00♑54.7	12 58.3	11 26.8
21	15 45.9	07 09.6	14 09.0	18 38.8
31	17 49.4	13 16.6	14 44.4	26 14.2
FEB 10	19 32.4	19 16.1	14R41.9	04♒16.3
20	20 51.9	25 08.4	14 00.2	12 49.4
MAR 2	21 44.4	00♒53.2	12 41.1	21 57.0
12	22 07.4	06 30.7	10 50.6	01♓43.1
22	21R58.5	12 01.0	08 38.8	12 10.7
APR 1	21 17.1	17 23.7	06 19.3	23 20.6
11	20 05.1	22 38.6	04 07.0	05♈11.2
21	18 27.0	27 45.3	02 14.7	17 37.2
MAY 1	16 31.0	02♓43.1	00 52.0	00♉28.4
11	14 27.6	07 31.2	00 03.7	13 31.2
21	12 28.6	12 08.4	29D50.8	26 30.3
31	10 45.1	16 33.0	00♎12.1	09♊10.3
JUN 10	09 25.7	20 43.0	01 04.5	21 19.6
20	08 35.7	24 35.4	02 24.4	02♋51.3
30	08 17.8	28 06.1	04 08.2	13 42.0
JUL 10	08D31.7	01♈10.3	06 12.4	23 51.8
20	09 15.8	03 40.7	08 34.0	03♌23.1
30	10 27.6	05 28.5	11 10.4	12 18.6
AUG 9	12 04.0	06 23.0	13 59.0	20 42.1
19	14 02.2	06R11.1	16 58.2	28 37.1
29	16 19.6	04 42.2	20 06.1	06♍07.0
SEP 8	18 53.5	01 52.3	23 21.2	13 14.9
18	21 41.8	27♓53.0	26 42.3	20 03.5
28	24 42.5	23 19.7	00♏08.2	26 35.0
OCT 8	27 53.8	19 02.4	03 37.8	02♎51.3
18	01♐14.4	15 47.9	07 10.2	08 54.3
28	04 42.8	14 04.7	10 44.3	14 44.8
NOV 7	08 17.7	13D57.8	14 19.2	20 24.0
17	11 58.1	15 20.8	17 54.1	25 52.7
27	15 42.7	18 01.8	21 27.7	01♏11.0
DEC 7	19 30.7	21 48.0	24 59.1	06 19.2
17	23 21.1	26 29.6	28 27.1	11 17.3
27	27 12.7	01♈57.9	01♐50.5	16 04.7
JAN 6	01♑04.6	08♈06.0	05♐08.0	20♏40.9
JAN 1	12S54.6	28S33.5	09S53.2	23S40.4
21	14 07.7	27 55.1	11 37.9	21 31.6
FEB 10	14 51.7	26 03.9	12 29.6	17 34.6
MAR 2	15 04.1	23 13.5	12 14.6	11 34.2
22	14 43.8	19 37.9	10 52.1	03 29.6
APR 11	13 52.6	15 29.4	08 50.1	06N04.3
MAY 1	12 40.3	10 58.2	06 56.5	15 27.1
21	11 28.7	06 11.8	05 47.1	22 00.8
JUN 10	10 43.2	01 15.7	05 32.5	23 52.2
30	10 39.1	03N46.4	06 07.4	21 28.8
JUL 20	11 16.3	08 50.5	07 20.9	16 37.5
AUG 9	12 25.7	13 45.2	09 02.4	10 47.5
29	13 55.8	17 51.3	11 02.3	04 47.6
SEP 18	15 35.3	19 41.6	13 12.2	01S00.3
OCT 8	17 14.5	18 21.6	15 24.6	06 26.6
28	18 44.8	15 36.3	17 32.9	11 26.6
NOV 17	19 58.9	13 42.1	19 31.2	15 57.6
DEC 7	20 51.0	13 26.2	21 14.5	19 56.9
27	21S17.1	14N39.7	22S39.1	23S22.8

1959	Psyche 16	Eros 433	Lilith 1181	Toro 1685
JAN 1	29♐08.6	04♈57.3	03♐30.1	18♏24.2
11	03♑00.5	11 23.5	06 44.1	22 54.4
21	06 51.1	18 22.4	09 49.7	27 11.5
31	10 39.4	25 49.7	12 45.2	01♐14.0
FEB 10	14 24.4	03♉42.1	15 28.7	04 59.7
20	18 04.7	11 56.8	17 57.7	08 25.6
MAR 2	21 39.2	20 30.1	20 09.8	11 28.1
12	25 06.3	29 19.5	22 02.1	14 02.2
22	28 24.3	08♊22.1	23 31.3	16 01.6
APR 1	01♒31.4	17 34.4	24 34.5	17 18.6
11	04 25.5	26 53.7	25 08.2	17R43.6
21	07 04.0	06♋16.9	25R09.8	17 05.8
MAY 1	09 24.2	15 40.2	24 37.9	15 16.3
11	11 22.9	25 01.1	23 32.8	12 10.0
21	12 56.4	04♌16.4	21 57.8	07 55.1
31	14 01.3	13 23.2	20 00.1	02 56.5
JUN 10	14 33.9	22 19.6	17 49.3	27♏53.8
20	14R31.4	01♍03.8	15 38.2	23 30.0
30	13 53.0	09 34.3	13 38.9	20 14.7
JUL 10	12 40.1	17 50.9	12 01.8	18 20.3
20	10 58.6	25 53.4	10 54.5	17D46.3
30	08 58.5	03♎41.8	10 20.5	18 23.9
AUG 9	06 53.0	11 17.2	10D20.6	20 03.9
19	04 57.2	18 40.1	10 53.8	22 37.4
29	03 23.9	25 51.3	11 57.2	25 56.7
SEP 8	02 22.8	02♏52.3	13 28.0	29 57.3
18	01 59.4	09 43.7	15 23.2	04♐35.6
28	02D14.7	16 26.7	17 39.5	09 49.2
OCT 8	03 07.7	23 02.4	20 14.5	15 38.1
18	04 35.5	29 31.4	23 05.6	22 02.5
28	06 34.0	05♐54.7	26 10.6	29 03.4
NOV 7	08 59.8	12 13.0	29 27.7	06♑43.3
17	11 49.1	18 26.9	02♑55.3	15 03.8
27	14 58.5	24 37.0	06 31.7	24 07.1
DEC 7	18 25.3	00♑44.0	10 15.9	03♒55.8
17	22 06.7	06 48.0	14 06.5	14 33.8
27	26 00.5	12 49.5	18 02.4	26 11.6
JAN 6	00♓04.8	18♑49.1	22♑02.7	09♓11.9
JAN 1	21S19.3	15N08.9	22S57.0	24S08.9
21	21 10.8	17 31.5	23 55.3	26 51.9
FEB 10	20 35.8	20 01.0	24 32.8	29 02.4
MAR 2	19 38.3	21 46.0	24 51.7	30 44.3
22	18 24.8	21 57.5	24 56.0	32 03.5
APR 11	17 04.1	20 07.6	24 49.2	33 02.1
MAY 1	15 47.1	16 20.9	24 32.7	33 21.8
21	14 47.1	11 08.1	24 03.6	32 02.0
JUN 10	14 18.6	05 08.5	23 18.7	28 13.0
30	14 33.4	01S03.4	22 24.2	23 28.7
JUL 20	15 32.1	07 02.2	21 37.4	20 02.9
AUG 9	16 54.8	12 30.6	21 11.6	18 23.0
29	18 10.0	17 16.8	21 08.3	17 56.0
SEP 18	18 54.9	21 12.0	21 19.6	18 00.2
OCT 8	19 02.4	24 08.8	21 34.4	17 56.3
28	18 31.9	26 01.3	21 42.0	17 06.2
NOV 17	17 24.2	26 45.8	21 33.3	14 54.5
DEC 7	15 40.6	26 21.1	21 01.4	11 02.7
27	13S23.7	24S50.0	20S02.0	05S52.5

1960	Psyche 16	Eros 433	Lilith 1181	Toro 1685
JAN 1	28♒01.5	15♑49.6	20♑02.1	02♓29.6
11	02♓10.3	21 48.1	24 04.2	16 22.6
21	06 27.0	27 45.0	28 09.2	02♈22.8
31	10 50.2	03♒40.8	02♒16.4	20 31.9
FEB 10	15 18.7	09 35.4	06 24.9	09♉41.2
20	19 51.2	15 29.2	10 33.7	27 49.0
MAR 1	24 26.9	21 22.8	14 42.2	13♊28.8
11	29 04.7	27 16.2	18 49.4	26 26.6
21	03♈43.7	03♓09.9	22 54.4	07♋09.6
31	08 23.3	09 04.4	26 56.5	16 13.7
APR 10	13 02.6	15 00.1	00♓54.5	24 08.5
20	17 40.8	20 57.5	04 47.2	01♌14.1
30	22 17.5	26 57.2	08 33.5	07 45.4
MAY 10	26 51.7	02♈59.8	12 11.6	13 52.4
20	01♉22.7	09 06.1	15 40.0	19 41.3
30	05 49.9	15 17.0	18 56.5	25 17.2
JUN 9	10 12.1	21 32.9	21 58.2	00♍43.4
19	14 28.6	27 55.4	24 42.6	06 02.1
29	18 38.3	04♉25.1	27 05.7	11 15.4
JUL 9	22 39.7	11 03.2	29 03.2	16 24.7
19	26 31.5	17 51.2	00♈30.7	21 30.8
29	00♊11.9	24 50.1	01 22.9	26 34.9
AUG 8	03 38.7	02♊01.2	01R35.4	01♎37.6
18	06 49.5	09 26.1	01 05.6	06 39.3
28	09 41.3	17 05.9	29♓53.5	11 41.0
SEP 7	12 10.6	25 01.4	28 05.6	16 42.7
17	14 13.5	03♋13.9	25 53.7	21 45.0
27	15 45.6	11 43.2	23 35.7	26 48.4
OCT 7	16 42.4	20 28.8	21 31.7	01♏53.1
17	17 00.4	29 30.0	19 58.6	06 59.4
27	16R36.8	08♌43.8	19 08.5	12 07.8
NOV 6	15 32.8	18 07.2	19D06.6	17 18.4
16	13 53.7	27 36.4	19 52.6	22 31.7
26	11 49.9	07♍05.5	21 23.4	27 48.1
DEC 6	09 37.1	16 29.3	23 34.0	03♐07.8
16	07 31.9	25 42.4	26 19.0	08 31.6
26	05 49.8	04♎37.8	29 33.5	13 59.9
JAN 5	04♊41.7	13♎09.7	03♈12.7	19♐33.4
JAN 1	12S44.8	24S17.4	19S42.6	04S27.9
21	09 52.9	21 31.1	18 06.6	01N26.3
FEB 10	06 39.9	17 53.6	16 02.4	06 43.3
MAR 1	03 13.2	13 33.5	13 33.3	09 02.6
21	00N19.6	08 38.9	10 43.9	09 11.5
APR 10	03 50.6	03 17.1	07 39.9	08 23.2
30	07 12.2	02N25.3	04 27.8	06 56.2
MAY 20	10 17.4	08 22.3	01 14.9	04 55.7
JUN 9	13 00.1	14 27.1	01N50.5	02 26.5
29	15 15.0	20 30.9	04 38.0	00S25.4
JUL 19	16 58.6	26 19.5	06 53.6	03 34.4
AUG 8	18 09.3	31 29.6	08 18.2	06 54.1
28	18 48.2	35 23.6	08 29.6	10 18.5
SEP 17	18 58.6	37 07.9	07 18.8	13 41.1
OCT 7	18 46.4	35 45.2	05 16.5	16 55.4
27	18 18.6	30 41.9	03 25.7	19 53.5
NOV 16	17 42.5	22 07.8	02 34.2	22 27.2
DEC 6	17 08.2	10 51.2	02 55.0	24 27.2
26	16N51.4	01S57.9	04N19.7	25S43.2

1961	Psyche 16	Eros 433	Lilith 1181	Toro 1685
JAN 1	05R04.4	09♎48.0	01♈42.4	17♐19.3
11	04♊19.5	18 03.2	05 34.3	22 56.4
21	04D14.7	25 44.1	09 45.0	28 40.5
31	04 49.0	02♏43.1	14 11.0	04♑32.5
FEB 10	05 58.7	08 52.5	18 49.7	10 34.4
20	07 39.6	14 00.7	23 38.9	16 48.1
MAR 2	09 47.0	17 55.3	28 36.6	23 16.1
12	12 16.5	20 22.7	03♉41.0	00♒01.8
22	15 04.4	21 06.8	08 50.9	07 09.3
APR 1	18 07.5	19R59.4	14 04.9	14 43.2
11	21 22.8	17 08.0	19 21.8	22 49.7
21	24 48.2	13 04.2	24 41.0	01♓35.2
MAY 1	28 21.4	08 45.8	00♊01.3	11 06.4
11	02♋00.9	05 09.2	05 22.2	21 29.6
21	05 45.4	02 49.5	10 43.0	02♈48.0
31	09 33.5	01D56.6	16 02.9	14 59.3
JUN 10	13 24.3	02 21.5	21 21.5	27 55.3
20	17 16.8	03 50.8	26 38.4	11♉19.6
30	21 10.3	06 11.2	01♋52.7	24 52.7
JUL 10	25 03.9	09 10.0	07 04.2	08♊17.0
20	28 57.1	12 39.1	12 12.4	21 18.6
30	02♌48.9	16 31.5	17 16.4	03♋48.3
AUG 9	06 38.8	20 41.7	22 16.0	15 40.5
19	10 26.0	25 06.6	27 10.2	26 51.5
29	14 09.6	29 43.3	01♌58.3	07♌19.8
SEP 8	17 48.8	04♐29.5	06 39.6	17 06.8
18	21 22.4	09 24.1	11 12.7	26 14.5
28	24 49.3	14 25.9	15 36.5	04♍46.0
OCT 8	28 08.2	19 33.8	19 49.6	12 45.0
18	01♍17.4	24 47.7	23 50.1	20 14.3
28	04 14.8	00♑06.8	27 35.7	27 16.8
NOV 7	06 58.6	05 30.8	01♍04.1	03♎54.9
17	09 25.9	10 59.7	04 11.9	10 10.1
27	11 34.0	16 33.1	06 55.7	16 03.5
DEC 7	13 19.6	22 11.0	09 11.5	21 35.9
17	14 39.1	27 53.6	10 54.3	26 46.9
27	15 29.2	03♒40.4	11 59.8	01♏36.0
JAN 6	15♍46.8	09♒32.0	12♍23.7	06♏01.9
JAN 1	16N52.0	05S54.7	04N55.3	25S55.9
21	17 14.7	18 48.3	07 19.9	25 59.2
FEB 10	18 04.3	30 31.8	10 11.3	24 53.9
MAR 2	19 07.6	40 23.3	13 13.3	22 28.0
22	20 10.8	47 29.8	16 10.6	18 27.0
APR 11	21 02.3	49 52.6	18 49.2	12 32.8
MAY 1	21 33.7	46 04.1	20 56.9	04 27.3
21	21 39.8	39 01.3	22 23.8	05N45.5
JUN 10	21 18.1	32 51.9	23 03.5	16 45.1
30	20 28.6	28 58.7	22 53.3	25 16.9
JUL 20	19 13.2	27 00.0	21 54.5	28 05.3
AUG 9	17 35.8	26 12.2	20 11.8	24 58.3
29	15 41.3	25 57.8	17 52.8	18 23.7
SEP 18	13 36.0	25 48.4	15 06.7	10 44.4
OCT 8	11 27.4	25 23.5	12 04.2	03 14.5
28	09 24.1	24 28.4	08 56.6	03S38.8
NOV 17	07 36.2	22 53.2	05 56.6	09 48.1
DEC 7	06 15.8	20 32.5	03 18.6	15 12.6
27	05N35.9	17S24.9	01N20.0	19S53.9

1962	Psyche 16	Eros 433	Lilith 1181	Toro 1685
JAN 1	15♍42.2	06♒35.6	12♍17.2	03♏52.0
11	15R42.6	12 29.5	12R19.0	08 05.4
21	15 07.9	18 28.1	11 36.0	11 51.4
31	13 59.6	24 31.6	10 11.0	15 06.7
FEB 10	12 21.9	00♓40.4	08 11.3	17 45.7
20	10 23.6	06 54.7	05 50.6	19 41.7
MAR 2	08 15.9	13 14.9	03 26.0	20 46.9
12	06 11.7	19 41.6	01 14.6	20R51.5
22	04 23.1	26 15.0	29♌31.1	19 46.7
APR 1	02 59.4	02♈56.0	28 23.9	17 27.1
11	02 06.2	09 45.1	27 56.4	13 55.3
21	01 45.8	16 42.9	28D08.1	09 29.1
MAY 1	01D57.6	23 50.1	28 55.5	04 40.8
11	02 39.5	01♉07.6	00♍14.7	00 09.4
21	03 48.6	08 35.6	02 01.0	26♎28.5
31	05 21.4	16 15.1	04 10.0	23 55.5
JUN 10	07 14.8	24 06.3	06 38.3	22 34.5
20	09 25.8	02♊09.3	09 22.4	22D20.3
30	11 51.8	10 24.5	12 19.6	23 03.7
JUL 10	14 30.5	18 51.3	15 27.8	24 35.8
20	17 19.9	27 29.2	18 44.8	26 48.3
30	20 18.2	06♋17.6	22 09.1	29 34.3
AUG 9	23 24.1	15 15.0	25 39.4	02♏49.0
19	26 36.1	24 19.9	29 14.4	06 28.2
29	29 53.1	03♌30.8	02♎53.1	10 29.2
SEP 8	03♎14.1	12 45.5	06 34.6	14 50.1
18	06 37.9	22 01.9	10 17.9	19 29.4
28	10 03.7	01♍18.2	14 02.3	24 26.5
OCT 8	13 30.6	10 31.8	17 47.0	29 41.4
18	16 57.5	19 40.7	21 31.0	05♐14.2
28	20 23.5	28 43.0	25 13.6	11 05.7
NOV 7	23 47.5	07♎36.4	28 53.8	17 17.3
17	27 08.3	16 19.4	02♏30.5	23 50.3
27	00♏24.7	24 50.6	06 02.7	00♑47.3
DEC 7	03 35.3	03♏08.3	09 29.2	08 10.9
17	06 38.4	11 11.6	12 48.5	16 04.2
27	09 32.4	18 59.8	15 59.1	24 31.2
JAN 6	12♏15.1	26♏31.8	18♏59.1	03♒35.9
JAN 1	05N33.7	16S30.8	00N58.8	20S57.7
21	05 59.8	12 27.4	00 16.1	24 48.5
FEB 10	07 18.1	07 44.6	00 46.9	28 01.3
MAR 2	09 05.6	02 28.8	02 14.5	30 32.7
22	10 43.9	03N11.7	03 54.6	32 00.7
APR 11	11 42.2	09 06.5	05 05.3	31 27.1
MAY 1	11 50.9	15 00.8	05 28.5	28 01.4
21	11 14.5	20 33.8	05 04.0	23 03.0
JUN 10	10 01.3	25 14.9	03 58.0	18 59.0
30	08 19.2	28 23.1	02 18.2	16 48.2
JUL 20	06 14.8	29 13.7	00 12.1	16 15.9
AUG 9	03 54.2	27 14.7	02S13.4	16 51.1
29	01 22.9	22 25.7	04 52.1	18 05.9
SEP 18	01S13.9	15 19.8	07 37.8	19 36.9
OCT 8	03 50.8	06 49.5	10 24.9	21 03.1
28	06 22.5	02S09.7	13 07.7	22 02.4
NOV 17	08 43.6	10 48.9	15 41.3	22 10.8
DEC 7	10 49.1	18 29.2	18 00.8	21 00.5
27	12S34.0	24S42.8	20S02.3	18S02.0

1963	Psyche 16	Eros 433	Lilith 1181	Toro 1685
JAN 1	10♏55.3	22♏47.9	17♏30.6	28♑58.6
11	13 31.6	00♐11.6	20 24.5	08♒23.6
21	15 53.2	07 18.5	23 04.8	18 32.0
31	17 57.4	14 07.8	25 28.9	29 26.7
FEB 10	19 41.1	20 38.8	27 34.0	11♓07.3
20	21 01.5	26 51.0	29 17.2	23 30.0
MAR 2	21 55.0	02♑43.1	00♐35.0	06♈26.2
12	22 19.0	08 13.7	01 24.3	19 42.6
22	22R11.4	13 21.3	01 42.1	03♉03.9
APR 1	21 31.2	18 03.1	01R26.2	16 14.8
11	20 20.2	22 16.0	00 36.2	29 01.0
21	18 43.1	25 55.9	29♏14.4	11♊11.9
MAY 1	16 47.4	28 56.7	27 25.7	22 40.7
11	14 44.1	01♒11.6	25 19.5	03♋24.2
21	12 44.6	02 32.2	23 07.1	13 22.8
31	11 00.1	02R48.4	21 00.8	22 39.6
JUN 10	09 39.6	01 52.5	19 12.3	01♌18.3
20	08 48.2	29♑40.7	17 49.7	09 23.8
30	08 28.8	26 19.8	16 58.4	17 00.6
JUL 10	08D41.3	22 13.3	16 40.1	24 12.8
20	09 24.0	17 56.7	16D54.2	01♍04.2
30	10 34.5	14 09.6	17 38.8	07 38.1
AUG 9	12 09.8	11 21.6	18 50.9	13 57.1
19	14 07.0	09 45.2	20 27.4	20 03.6
29	16 23.4	09D21.2	22 25.5	25 59.6
SEP 8	18 56.5	10 02.3	24 42.1	01♎46.6
18	21 44.0	11 38.9	27 14.8	07 26.0
28	24 44.1	14 02.2	00♐01.5	12 59.1
OCT 8	27 54.8	17 03.9	03 00.1	18 26.5
18	01♐14.8	20 37.6	06 08.9	23 49.2
28	04 42.8	24 38.5	09 26.4	29 07.7
NOV 7	08 17.2	29 02.4	12 51.2	04♏22.4
17	11 57.2	03♒46.4	16 22.2	09 33.8
27	15 41.5	08 48.6	19 58.1	14 42.1
DEC 7	19 29.2	14 06.7	23 37.8	19 47.3
17	23 19.2	19 39.9	27 20.4	24 49.8
27	27 10.6	25 27.1	01♑04.9	29 49.4
JAN 6	01♑02.4	01♓27.6	04♑50.1	04♐46.1
JAN 1	12S56.5	26S00.5	20S29.5	16S57.3
21	14 09.8	30 04.7	22 04.5	11 09.7
FEB 10	14 54.1	32 24.7	23 16.4	03 08.6
MAR 2	15 07.0	33 13.2	24 04.0	06N03.1
22	14 47.3	32 53.1	24 24.8	14 13.6
APR 11	13 56.7	31 52.5	24 13.4	19 08.8
MAY 1	12 44.9	30 40.5	23 24.1	20 05.7
21	11 33.2	29 43.0	22 01.2	18 01.8
JUN 10	10 47.2	29 12.2	20 28.5	14 18.9
30	10 42.2	28 41.3	19 16.6	09 53.0
JUL 20	11 18.5	27 08.3	18 42.8	05 12.7
AUG 9	12 27.2	24 33.6	18 47.3	00 31.3
29	13 56.6	22 02.8	19 20.4	04S04.2
SEP 18	15 35.7	20 00.5	20 10.3	08 29.1
OCT 8	17 14.6	18 10.6	21 05.6	12 39.4
28	18 44.8	16 10.4	21 56.3	16 30.8
NOV 17	19 58.8	13 42.4	22 34.0	19 58.1
DEC 7	20 50.9	10 36.4	22 52.2	22 56.3
27	21S17.1	06S48.3	22S46.6	25S19.9

1964	Psyche 16	Eros 433	Lillith 1181	Toro 1685
JAN 1	29♐06.5	28♒25.7	02♑57.5	02♐18.1
11	02♑58.2	04♓32.7	06 42.8	07 13.3
21	06 48.7	10 52.5	10 27.6	12 05.5
31	10 36.9	17 24.8	14 10.6	16 54.3
FEB 10	14 21.9	24 09.6	17 51.0	21 39.7
20	18 02.3	01♈07.0	21 27.4	26 21.4
MAR 1	21 36.7	08 16.8	24 58.7	00♑58.9
11	25 04.0	15 39.2	28 23.6	05 32.2
21	28 22.2	23 14.4	01♒40.4	10 00.6
31	01♒29.5	01♉02.1	04 47.4	14 23.5
APR 10	04 24.0	09 02.2	07 42.8	18 40.7
20	07 02.9	17 14.5	10 24.0	22 51.1
30	09 23.6	25 38.2	12 48.5	26 54.2
MAY 10	11 22.9	04♊12.8	14 53.2	00♒49.4
20	12 57.2	12 57.4	16 34.5	04 35.2
30	14 02.9	21 50.3	17 48.8	08 11.7
JUN 9	14 36.5	00♋50.5	18 32.1	11 39.0
19	14R35.0	09 56.3	18R40.6	14 58.3
29	13 57.6	19 05.6	18 12.1	18 16.8
JUL 9	12 45.6	28 16.8	17 06.5	21 51.3
19	11 04.7	07♌28.0	15 27.0	26 30.8
29	09 05.0	16 36.9	13 22.1	05♓23.1
AUG 8	06 59.4	25 42.2	11 04.3	08♈47.1
18	05 02.9	04♍41.8	08 49.2	08♋15.2
28	03 28.8	13 34.2	06 52.4	00♌47.0
SEP 7	02 26.7	22 18.2	05 26.0	08 43.4
17	02 02.1	00♎52.7	04 38.4	14 16.0
27	02D16.5	09 16.6	04D32.6	19 43.9
OCT 7	03 08.4	17 29.6	05 08.0	25 44.3
17	04 35.3	25 31.2	06 22.5	02♍16.7
27	06 33.2	03♏21.2	08 11.9	09 08.5
NOV 6	08 58.4	10 59.8	10 32.4	16 03.0
16	11 47.3	18 27.1	13 20.2	22 45.2
26	14 56.4	25 43.2	16 31.3	29 05.1
DEC 6	18 22.9	02♐48.8	20 02.9	04♎55.6
16	22 04.2	09 43.8	23 52.1	10 10.4
26	25 57.9	16 28.8	27 56.3	14 44.7
JAN 5	00♓02.2	23♐04.2	02♓13.7	18♎32.1
JAN 1	21S19.4	05S44.7	22S41.1	25S49.8
21	21 11.0	01 06.2	22 02.9	27 23.6
FEB 10	20 36.2	04N05.1	20 59.3	28 13.8
MAR 1	19 38.8	09 36.2	19 33.5	28 18.9
21	18 25.4	15 07.5	17 50.6	27 38.6
APR 10	17 04.6	20 10.1	15 57.5	26 12.9
30	15 47.4	24 05.0	14 03.0	23 59.4
MAY 20	14 47.0	26 07.3	12 17.7	20 47.2
JUN 9	14 17.9	25 39.9	10 54.3	16 01.0
29	14 32.1	22 31.9	10 06.3	07 50.7
JUL 19	15 30.3	17 05.9	10 02.9	10N23.4
AUG 8	16 53.0	10 07.0	10 39.7	60 51.5
28	18 08.6	02 24.8	11 34.9	63 52.5
SEP 17	18 54.1	05S17.2	12 22.0	39 12.6
OCT 7	19 02.1	12 25.1	12 42.8	23 48.1
27	18 32.1	18 33.8	12 28.3	11 34.5
NOV 16	17 24.7	23 25.3	11 34.4	01 20.9
DEC 6	15 41.3	26 48.0	10 00.0	07S11.9
26	13S24.7	28S37.2	07S46.5	14S18.1

1965	Psyche 16	Eros 433	Lillith 1181	Toro 1685
JAN 1	28♒23.3	20♐27.2	00♓29.3	17♎07.3
11	02♓33.1	26 56.8	04 53.7	20 22.5
21	06 50.7	03♑17.1	09 28.3	22 36.9
31	11 14.7	09 28.5	14 11.8	23 39.0
FEB 10	15 43.9	15 31.0	19 03.1	23R15.0
20	20 17.0	21 24.5	24 00.7	21 14.6
MAR 2	24 53.3	27 09.5	29 03.9	17 35.5
12	29 31.6	02♒45.5	04♈11.7	12 34.6
22	04♈11.2	08 12.3	09 23.2	06 54.7
APR 1	08 51.2	13 29.9	14 37.9	01 30.4
11	13 31.0	18 37.5	19 55.1	27♍08.2
21	18 09.7	23 34.4	25 13.8	24 10.7
MAY 1	22 46.8	28 19.7	00♉33.8	22 38.2
11	27 21.4	02♓51.8	05 54.3	22D21.0
21	01♉52.8	07 09.1	11 14.7	23 05.2
31	06 20.3	11 09.0	16 34.5	24 37.9
JUN 10	10 42.9	14 47.9	21 52.9	26 49.3
20	14 59.7	18 01.9	27 09.4	29 30.7
30	19 09.6	20 44.9	02♊23.2	02♎36.3
JUL 10	23 11.2	22 49.1	07 33.5	06 01.5
20	27 03.2	24 05.7	12 39.2	09 42.8
30	00♊43.7	24R23.4	17 39.6	13 37.7
AUG 9	04 10.5	23 30.9	22 33.2	17 44.4
19	07 21.2	21 21.7	27 18.6	22 01.5
29	10 12.8	17 58.1	01♋54.3	26 28.1
SEP 8	12 41.7	13 42.2	06 18.0	01♏03.5
18	14 44.1	09 14.0	10 27.4	05 47.3
28	16 15.5	05 19.7	14 19.7	10 39.4
OCT 8	17 11.4	02 36.7	17 51.0	15 39.7
18	17R28.3	01 21.1	20 57.4	20 48.3
28	17 03.6	01D33.2	23 34.0	26 05.7
NOV 7	15 58.4	03 05.2	25 35.1	01♐32.3
17	14 18.3	05 44.9	26 55.2	07 08.6
27	12 14.0	09 22.3	27 28.6	12 55.7
DEC 7	10 01.0	13 48.6	27R12.2	18 54.5
17	07 56.5	18 56.1	26 06.6	25 06.4
27	06 15.3	24 39.8	24 18.2	01♑33.1
JAN 6	05♊08.6	00♈55.5	22♋01.7	08♑16.4
JAN 1	12S37.8	28S51.9	06S59.4	16S10.9
21	09 44.7	28 44.3	04 01.2	21 35.3
FEB 10	06 30.7	27 19.0	00 36.0	25 20.6
MAR 2	03 03.2	24 50.4	03N08.1	26 13.4
22	00N30.0	21 34.0	07 01.9	22 57.0
APR 11	04 01.2	17 43.9	10 55.2	17 12.5
MAY 1	07 22.6	13 31.9	14 37.7	12 20.4
21	10 27.3	09 07.5	17 58.8	09 37.0
JUN 10	13 09.2	04 38.4	20 48.5	08 46.8
30	15 23.0	00 11.7	22 57.8	09 17.9
JUL 20	17 05.3	04N01.9	24 20.5	10 43.9
AUG 9	18 14.6	07 38.9	24 53.7	12 45.0
29	18 52.1	09 47.6	24 39.1	15 06.0
SEP 18	19 01.4	09 37.5	23 43.7	17 34.0
OCT 8	18 48.6	07 55.8	22 18.8	19 56.6
28	18 20.7	06 30.6	20 40.1	22 01.1
NOV 17	17 45.3	06 19.8	19 06.0	23 33.3
DEC 7	17 12.2	07 32.1	17 54.2	24 17.3
27	16N56.7	09N56.8	17N14.5	23S55.5

1966	Psyche 16	Eros 433	Lillith 1181	Toro 1685
JAN 1	05R37.2	27♓43.9	23R12.3	04♑52.5
11	04♊49.8	04♈14.1	20♋49.0	11 45.0
21	04D42.5	11 11.0	18 28.2	18 58.1
31	05 14.4	18 32.7	16 30.3	26 34.6
FEB 10	06 22.2	26 16.2	15 10.2	04♒38.2
20	08 01.2	04♉19.7	14 34.5	13 12.7
MAR 2	10 07.1	12 41.3	14D44.7	22 22.0
12	12 35.5	21 18.3	15 37.5	02♓09.8
22	15 22.4	00♊08.8	17 07.6	12 39.2
APR 1	18 24.7	09 10.5	19 09.5	23 51.0
11	21 39.4	18 20.5	21 37.8	05♈43.1
21	25 04.2	27 36.5	24 27.7	18 10.3
MAY 1	28 37.1	06♋56.0	27 35.2	01♉02.1
11	02♋16.2	16 16.0	00♌56.8	14 04.9
21	06 00.4	25 34.1	04 29.7	27 03.1
31	09 48.4	04♌47.8	08 11.8	09♊41.8
JUN 10	13 39.0	13 54.3	12 01.0	21 49.4
20	17 31.4	22 52.0	15 55.9	03♋19.1
30	21 24.8	01♍39.2	19 55.2	14 08.0
JUL 10	25 18.3	10 14.2	23 57.7	24 16.0
20	29 11.4	18 36.6	28 02.8	03♌45.6
30	03♌03.3	26 46.0	02♍09.4	12 39.8
AUG 9	06 53.2	04♎42.1	06 16.8	21 01.9
19	10 40.5	12 25.6	10 24.6	28 55.9
29	14 24.2	19 56.9	14 31.9	06♍24.9
SEP 8	18 03.5	27 16.6	18 38.1	13 31.9
18	21 37.4	04♏25.9	22 42.7	20 19.8
28	25 04.5	11 25.4	26 45.0	26 50.8
OCT 8	28 23.7	18 15.9	00♎44.1	03♎06.7
18	01♍33.3	24 58.6	04 39.4	09 09.2
28	04 31.3	01♐34.2	08 29.7	14 59.5
NOV 7	07 15.8	08 03.3	12 14.2	20 38.5
17	09 44.0	14 26.8	15 51.6	26 07.1
27	11 53.0	20 45.1	19 20.3	01♏25.3
DEC 7	13 39.8	26 58.9	22 38.9	06 33.7
17	15 00.8	03♑08.8	25 45.4	11 31.9
27	15 52.5	09 15.0	28 37.6	16 19.5
JAN 6	16♍11.9	15♑17.9	01♏13.0	20♏56.1
JAN 1	16N57.3	10N42.1	17N09.3	23S37.5
21	17 19.4	14 07.7	17 01.9	21 26.5
FEB 10	18 08.1	17 46.2	17 05.9	17 27.0
MAR 2	19 10.6	20 54.3	17 10.9	11 24.0
22	20 13.1	22 42.8	17 06.9	03 17.3
APR 11	21 03.8	22 30.1	16 44.4	06N17.1
MAY 1	21 34.5	20 00.9	15 56.8	15 37.3
21	21 39.9	15 32.2	14 40.8	22 05.0
JUN 10	21 17.5	09 42.7	12 56.4	23 50.1
30	20 27.2	03 14.6	10 45.7	21 22.5
JUL 20	19 11.3	03S16.7	08 12.6	16 29.5
AUG 9	17 33.2	09 25.8	05 21.7	10 39.4
29	15 38.2	14 55.3	02 17.9	04 39.8
SEP 18	13 32.4	19 32.8	00S53.3	01S07.5
OCT 8	11 23.2	23 09.2	04 06.6	06 33.0
28	09 19.3	25 37.6	07 16.4	11 32.4
NOV 17	07 30.7	26 53.5	10 17.3	16 02.6
DEC 7	06 09.4	26 55.8	13 03.7	20 01.1
27	05N28.4	25S47.0	15S30.3	23S26.1

1967		Psyche 16	Eros 433	Lilith 1181	Toro 1685
JAN	1	16♍06.4	12♑16.8	29♎57.5	18♏39.2
	11	16R08.7	18 18.3	02♏23.5	23 09.9
	21	15 35.9	24 17.1	04 28.1	27 27.5
	31	14 29.5	00♒13.4	06 08.1	01♐30.7
FEB	10	12 53.4	06 07.6	07 20.0	05 17.4
	20	10 55.9	12 00.0	08 00.2	08 44.4
MAR	2	08 48.5	17 50.7	08R06.0	11 48.4
	12	06 43.6	23 40.3	07 35.8	14 24.4
	22	04 53.7	29 28.9	06 30.1	16 26.0
APR	1	03 28.2	05♓16.8	04 53.1	17 45.8
	11	02 32.8	11 04.6	02 52.1	18 14.1
	21	02 10.1	16 52.5	00 38.3	17R40.3
MAY	1	02D19.8	22 41.1	28♎25.0	15 55.0
	11	02 59.6	28 30.9	26 24.7	12 52.8
	21	04 06.7	04♈22.3	24 47.9	08 40.7
	31	05 37.8	10 15.9	23 41.4	03 43.0
JUN	10	07 29.6	16 12.6	23 08.1	28♏38.5
	20	09 39.3	22 12.7	23D08.3	24 10.8
	30	12 04.0	28 17.4	23 40.0	20 50.8
JUL	10	14 41.5	04♉27.4	24 40.4	18 51.6
	20	17 29.9	10 43.3	26 06.4	18D13.5
	30	20 27.3	17 06.7	27 54.5	18 47.9
AUG	9	23 32.3	23 38.4	00♏01.9	20 25.3
	19	26 43.6	00♊19.4	02 25.8	22 56.9
	29	29 59.9	07 11.5	05 03.6	26 15.0
SEP	8	03♎20.2	14 15.6	07 53.6	00♐14.7
	18	06 43.5	21 32.8	10 53.7	04 52.5
	28	10 08.7	29 05.0	14 02.4	10 05.9
OCT	8	13 35.2	06♋52.4	17 18.3	15 54.8
	18	17 01.6	14 55.6	20 40.2	22 19.4
	28	20 27.2	23 15.0	24 06.8	29 20.7
NOV	7	23 50.9	01♌48.4	27 37.2	07♑00.8
	17	27 11.4	10 33.1	01♐10.1	15 21.6
	27	00♏27.6	19 25.5	04 44.7	24 24.7
DEC	7	03 38.0	28 17.7	08 20.1	04♒12.9
	17	06 41.0	07♍01.3	11 54.9	14 50.3
	27	09 34.9	15 26.7	15 28.3	26 28.7
JAN	6	12♏17.7	23♍19.6	18♐59.2	09♓33.3

1967		Psyche 16	Eros 433	Lilith 1181	Toro 1685
JAN	1	05N25.8	25S19.4	16S03.2	24S11.9
	21	05 50.4	22 50.7	17 57.4	26 54.0
FEB	10	07 07.6	19 27.8	19 18.3	29 03.4
MAR	2	08 55.1	15 20.1	19 57.0	30 44.1
	22	10 34.4	10 36.4	19 43.2	32 02.1
APR	11	11 34.2	05 24.5	18 32.4	33 00.0
MAY	1	11 44.4	00N09.1	16 41.0	33 20.7
	21	11 09.2	05 59.4	14 47.7	32 04.8
JUN	10	09 57.0	12 01.4	13 29.4	28 19.7
	30	08 15.5	18 10.0	13 01.1	23 34.7
JUL	20	06 11.8	24 18.3	13 19.8	20 05.8
AUG	9	03 51.7	30 14.7	14 14.7	18 23.1
	29	01 20.9	35 38.6	15 34.2	17 53.9
SEP	18	01S15.5	39 54.7	17 07.4	17 56.1
OCT	8	03 52.0	42 08.7	18 44.7	17 50.1
	28	06 23.4	41 15.1	20 18.0	16 57.6
NOV	17	08 44.4	36 22.5	21 40.3	14 43.6
DEC	7	10 49.7	27 10.1	22 45.8	10 51.6
	27	12S34.5	13N44.6	23S30.5	05S45.9

1968		Psyche 16	Eros 433	Lilith 1181	Toro 1685
JAN	1	10♏57.9	19♍28.2	17♐14.1	02♓48.1
	11	13 34.2	26 59.7	20 43.2	16 48.6
	21	15 56.0	03♎38.0	24 07.9	03♈04.7
	31	18 00.5	09 04.9	27 26.8	21 36.6
FEB	10	19 44.6	13 01.1	00♑38.4	11♉06.8
	20	21 05.4	15 10.8	03 41.0	29 23.2
MAR	1	21 59.7	15R21.6	06 32.9	14♊58.8
	11	22 24.4	13 41.5	09 11.8	27 46.7
	21	22R17.5	10 48.8	11 35.3	08♋18.7
	31	21 38.2	07 40.2	13 40.8	17 12.8
APR	10	20 28.0	05 15.4	15 25.1	24 59.2
	20	18 51.5	04 07.2	16 45.0	01♌58.2
	30	16 56.2	04D20.0	17 37.0	08 24.0
MAY	10	14 52.8	05 46.1	17 57.7	14 26.6
	20	12 53.0	08 10.0	17R45.0	20 12.0
	30	11 07.7	11 17.8	16 57.5	25 45.0
JUN	9	09 46.1	14 59.2	15 36.9	01♍08.8
	19	08 53.8	19 04.8	13 48.3	06 25.6
	29	08 33.1	23 28.5	11 40.3	11 37.3
JUL	9	08D44.6	28 06.3	09 25.3	16 45.3
	19	09 26.2	02♏54.1	07 16.8	21 50.3
	29	10 35.7	07 50.1	05 27.3	26 53.5
AUG	8	12 10.2	12 52.5	04 06.7	01♎55.4
	18	14 06.6	17 59.9	03 20.6	06 56.6
	28	16 22.4	23 11.7	03D11.2	11 57.7
SEP	7	18 55.0	28 27.3	03 38.2	16 59.1
	17	21 42.1	03♐46.1	04 39.1	22 01.1
	27	24 41.8	09 08.1	06 10.8	27 04.3
OCT	7	27 52.3	14 33.1	08 10.1	02♏08.8
	17	01♐12.0	20 00.8	10 33.5	07 15.0
	27	04 39.8	25 31.4	13 18.1	12 23.4
NOV	6	08 14.2	01♑04.8	16 21.1	17 34.1
	16	11 54.1	06 40.9	19 40.1	22 47.6
	26	15 38.6	12 20.1	23 13.1	28 04.2
DEC	6	19 26.3	18 02.1	26 58.1	03♐24.3
	16	23 16.5	23 47.1	00♒53.6	08 48.5
	26	27 08.3	29 35.4	04 58.3	14 17.4
JAN	5	01♑00.3	05♒26.8	09♒10.8	19♐51.6

1968		Psyche 16	Eros 433	Lilith 1181	Toro 1685
JAN	1	12S57.0	09N47.8	23S38.2	04S23.2
	21	14 10.4	07S31.9	23 54.3	01N22.1
FEB	10	14 54.9	24 39.3	23 48.1	06 29.2
MAR	1	15 08.1	36 44.3	23 22.9	08 41.0
	21	14 48.8	40 17.8	22 44.0	08 50.3
APR	10	13 58.6	37 03.4	21 58.8	08 05.2
	30	12 47.1	31 46.1	21 15.8	06 41.4
MAY	20	11 35.3	27 26.2	20 42.2	04 43.3
JUN	9	10 48.7	24 51.6	20 21.3	02 16.1
	29	10 43.0	23 49.2	20 09.6	00S34.4
JUL	19	11 18.7	23 49.3	20 00.8	03 42.2
AUG	8	12 26.8	24 22.8	19 53.5	07 01.0
	28	13 56.0	25 05.6	19 49.5	10 24.5
SEP	17	15 34.9	25 38.3	19 47.1	13 46.4
OCT	7	17 13.8	25 45.6	19 39.2	16 59.9
	27	18 44.1	25 15.9	19 17.3	19 57.2
NOV	16	19 58.3	24 01.5	18 33.0	22 29.9
DEC	6	20 50.7	21 58.0	17 20.6	24 28.7
	26	21S17.1	19S05.0	15S36.8	25S43.3

1969		Psyche 16	Eros 433	Lilith 1181	Toro 1685
JAN	1	29♐27.5	03♒05.8	07♒29.0	17♐37.2
	11	03♑19.4	08 59.3	11 45.6	23 15.0
	21	07 10.2	14 56.4	16 08.5	29 00.0
	31	10 58.7	20 57.3	20 36.5	04♑53.1
FEB	10	14 43.8	27 02.1	25 08.9	10 56.1
	20	18 24.4	03♓11.5	29 45.0	17 11.3
MAR	2	21 59.1	09 25.5	04♓23.9	23 41.1
	12	25 26.4	15 44.8	09 04.9	00♒28.9
	22	28 44.7	22 09.9	13 47.7	07 38.7
APR	1	01♒52.0	28 41.3	18 31.3	15 15.4
	11	04 46.4	05♈19.6	23 15.2	23 25.0
	21	07 25.2	12 05.8	27 58.9	02♓14.0
MAY	1	09 45.6	19 00.3	02♈41.6	11 48.8
	11	11 44.5	26 04.0	07 22.6	22 15.7
	21	13 18.3	03♉17.8	12 01.3	03♈37.4
	31	14 23.2	10 42.1	16 36.4	15 51.2
JUN	10	14 55.9	18 17.9	21 07.2	28 48.2
	20	14R53.3	26 05.7	25 32.3	12♉12.4
	30	14 14.5	04♊05.6	29 50.2	25 44.3
JUL	10	13 01.4	12 18.0	03♉59.2	09♊06.6
	20	11 19.5	20 42.7	07 57.0	22 06.0
	30	09 19.1	29 19.0	11 40.9	04♋33.2
AUG	9	07 13.6	08♋06.4	15 07.8	16 22.7
	19	05 17.7	17 03.6	18 13.5	27 31.0
	29	03 45.0	26 08.9	20 53.3	07♌56.5
SEP	8	02 44.7	05♌20.8	23 02.2	17 40.8
	18	02 22.2	14 37.2	24 33.6	26 46.0
	28	02D39.0	23 55.5	25 21.9	05♍15.3
OCT	8	03 33.4	03♍14.0	25R22.9	13 12.3
	18	05 02.6	12 30.0	24 34.7	20 40.1
	28	07 02.9	21 41.1	23 02.8	27 41.2
NOV	7	09 30.2	00♎45.5	20 59.1	04♎18.2
	17	12 21.3	09 40.7	18 43.3	10 32.5
	27	15 32.5	18 24.8	16 38.6	16 25.2
DEC	7	19 00.8	26 56.2	15 04.9	21 57.2
	17	22 44.0	05♏13.1	14 15.8	27 08.1
	27	26 39.6	13 14.2	14D17.0	01♏57.2
JAN	6	00♓45.5	20♏58.6	15♉07.5	06♏23.4

1969		Psyche 16	Eros 433	Lilith 1181	Toro 1685
JAN	1	21S19.6	18S03.7	14S59.4	25S55.5
	21	21 10.0	14 10.2	12 34.5	25 56.9
FEB	10	20 34.0	09 35.8	09 40.6	24 49.3
MAR	2	19 35.5	04 27.0	06 22.1	22 20.4
	22	18 21.0	01N08.4	02 44.7	18 15.8
APR	11	16 59.5	07 01.3	01N05.1	12 17.4
MAY	1	15 41.9	12 59.8	05 00.5	04 07.8
	21	14 41.5	18 46.6	08 54.3	06N06.9
JUN	10	14 13.0	23 56.7	12 39.1	17 02.6
	30	14 28.3	27 54.1	16 07.7	25 23.6
JUL	20	15 27.8	29 53.9	19 12.9	27 59.3
AUG	9	16 51.4	29 14.3	21 47.9	24 44.1
	29	18 07.1	25 36.6	23 46.2	18 07.0
SEP	18	18 52.0	19 18.6	25 00.2	10 28.6
OCT	8	18 58.8	11 06.2	25 17.9	03 00.7
	28	18 26.9	01 56.6	24 23.6	03S50.4
NOV	17	17 17.4	07S15.5	22 20.3	09 57.8
DEC	7	15 31.7	15 44.0	19 59.1	15 20.5
	27	13S12.5	22S54.7	18N24.7	20S00.2

1970	Psyche 16	Eros 433	Lillith 1181	Toro 1685
JAN 1	28♒41.3	17♏08.6	14♉36.3	04♏13.3
11	02♓51.9	24 44.1	15 50.0	08 27.1
21	07 10.4	02♐01.0	17 46.0	12 13.9
31	11 35.3	08 58.5	20 17.8	15 30.2
FEB 10	16 05.5	15 35.6	23 19.4	18 10.8
20	20 39.8	21 50.8	26 45.5	20 09.0
MAR 2	25 17.2	27 43.0	00♊31.2	21 16.9
12	29 56.7	03♑10.0	04 32.7	21 R24.9
22	04♈37.5	08 09.1	08 46.9	20 24.1
APR 1	09 18.8	12 37.3	13 10.8	18 08.8
11	13 59.9	16 29.8	17 42.4	14 40.8
21	18 40.0	19 40.7	22 19.8	10 17.2
MAY 1	23 18.4	22 03.2	27 01.6	05 29.3
11	27 54.5	23 27.8	01♋46.5	00 56.0
21	02♉27.3	23 R44.9	06 33.4	27♎11.6
31	06 56.3	22 46.6	11 21.4	24 34.5
JUN 10	11 20.6	20 29.3	16 10.0	23 09.4
20	15 39.0	17 02.5	20 58.4	22 D51.7
30	19 50.7	12 51.4	25 45.9	23 32.1
JUL 10	23 54.3	08 33.9	00♌32.3	25 01.7
20	27 48.4	04 50.8	05 16.9	27 12.3
30	01♊31.2	02 09.2	09 59.3	29 56.8
AUG 9	05 00.7	00 40.5	14 39.1	03♏10.4
19	08 14.3	00 D23.8	19 15.7	06 48.9
29	11 09.2	01 10.3	23 48.6	10 49.2
SEP 8	13 42.0	02 50.8	28 17.3	15 09.8
18	15 48.6	05 15.8	02♍41.0	19 49.0
28	17 25.0	08 17.2	06 59.0	24 46.2
OCT 8	18 26.4	11 49.1	11 10.4	00♐01.3
18	18 49.0	15 46.4	15 14.0	05 34.5
28	18 R30.4	20 05.0	19 08.8	11 26.7
NOV 7	17 30.6	24 42.5	22 53.0	17 39.1
17	15 54.8	29 36.3	26 24.8	24 13.3
27	13 53.0	04♒44.8	29 42.3	01♑11.6
DEC 7	11 39.8	10 07.0	02♎42.8	08 36.9
17	09 32.8	15 41.6	05 23.5	16 32.3
27	07 47.3	21 28.1	07 41.0	25 01.6
JAN 6	06♊34.7	27♒26.2	09♎31.6	04♒09.2
JAN 1	12 S 33.1	24 S 27.4	18 N 12.1	21 S 03.7
21	09 38.8	29 32.1	18 02.8	24 53.1
FEB 10	06 23.7	32 50.4	18 41.4	28 04.7
MAR 2	02 55.1	34 33.5	19 41.6	30 35.7
22	00 N 39.2	35 04.9	20 40.5	32 05.0
APR 11	04 11.1	34 55.4	21 21.1	31 35.6
MAY 1	07 33.1	34 37.4	21 31.8	28 15.0
21	10 38.1	34 34.2	21 06.2	23 17.5
JUN 10	13 19.9	34 34.5	20 02.1	19 11.0
30	15 33.4	33 28.0	18 20.8	16 57.2
JUL 20	17 15.1	30 29.5	16 06.5	16 22.6
AUG 9	18 23.7	26 58.9	13 24.6	16 56.0
29	19 00.5	24 10.4	10 21.8	18 09.3
SEP 18	19 09.4	22 04.5	07 05.0	19 39.1
OCT 8	18 56.7	20 14.0	03 41.4	21 03.8
28	18 30.1	18 13.9	00 18.5	22 01.5
NOV 17	17 56.9	15 46.6	02 S 56.0	22 07.8
DEC 7	17 26.0	12 42.1	05 53.8	20 54.7
27	17 N 11.1	08 S 56.0	08 S 25.4	17 S 52.7

1971	Psyche 16	Eros 433	Lillith 1181	Toro 1685
JAN 1	07 R 06.3	24♒25.7	08♎39.9	29♑30.4
11	06♊12.9	00♓29.4	10 15.5	08♒58.4
21	05 D 59.4	06 44.0	11 18.3	19 10.2
31	06 25.3	13 09.7	11 44.4	00♓08.5
FEB 10	07 27.7	19 46.5	11 R 31.3	11 52.7
20	09 01.9	26 34.3	10 38.7	24 18.7
MAR 2	11 03.6	03♈33.7	09 09.2	07♈17.5
12	13 28.4	10 44.5	07 10.4	20 35.6
22	16 12.2	18 07.1	04 53.9	03♉57.5
APR 1	19 11.7	25 41.7	02 34.1	17 08.1
11	22 24.1	03♉28.2	00 26.0	29 53.3
21	25 46.7	11 26.7	28♍41.8	12♊02.4
MAY 1	29 17.8	19 37.2	27 29.4	23 28.9
11	02♋55.3	27 58.9	26 52.7	04♋09.7
21	06 38.0	06♊31.4	26 D 51.7	14 05.5
31	10 24.7	15 14.0	27 24.2	23 19.5
JUN 10	14 14.1	24 05.2	28 27.0	01♌55.7
20	18 05.5	03♋03.9	29 56.1	09 58.6
30	21 57.9	12 08.6	01♎48.1	17 33.3
JUL 10	25 50.7	21 17.2	03 59.5	24 43.5
20	29 43.0	00♌28.2	06 27.3	01♍33.2
30	03♌34.3	09 39.6	09 09.0	08 05.6
AUG 9	07 23.6	18 49.3	12 02.4	14 23.2
19	11 10.4	27 55.7	15 05.5	20 28.6
29	14 53.8	06♍57.0	18 16.8	26 23.6
SEP 8	18 32.9	15 51.3	21 34.8	02♎09.7
18	22 06.7	24 37.5	24 58.3	07 48.5
28	25 33.9	03♎14.4	28 26.2	13 21.0
OCT 8	28 53.2	11 40.7	01♏57.4	18 47.9
18	02♍03.2	19 56.2	05 31.1	24 10.2
28	05 01.9	28 00.1	09 06.2	29 28.5
NOV 7	07 47.0	05♏52.2	12 41.6	04♏43.1
17	10 16.3	13 32.5	16 16.7	09 54.4
27	12 26.8	21 01.1	19 50.3	15 02.8
DEC 7	14 15.2	28 17.9	23 21.3	20 08.2
17	15 38.4	05♐23.4	26 48.6	25 11.0
27	16 32.4	12 17.8	00♐10.9	00♐11.0
JAN 6	16♍54.6	19♐01.2	03♐26.8	05♐08.2
JAN 1	17 N 11.5	07 S 53.0	08 S 57.9	16 S 46.9
21	17 32.1	03 16.5	10 40.1	10 55.3
FEB 10	18 18.6	01 N 53.8	11 26.1	02 51.1
MAR 2	19 18.6	07 27.3	11 02.6	06 N 20.1
22	20 18.7	13 07.7	09 32.5	14 24.8
APR 11	21 07.2	18 30.9	07 28.7	19 10.8
MAY 1	21 35.7	23 02.8	05 40.2	19 59.4
21	21 39.2	26 00.6	04 39.3	17 50.7
JUN 10	21 15.0	26 41.4	04 33.4	14 06.0
30	20 23.3	24 40.3	05 15.6	09 40.1
JUL 20	19 06.0	20 04.9	06 35.3	05 00.5
AUG 9	17 26.9	13 32.2	08 22.0	00 20.2
29	15 31.0	05 52.4	10 26.3	04 S 14.2
SEP 18	13 24.4	02 S 06.1	12 40.3	08 38.0
OCT 8	11 14.5	09 43.5	14 56.7	12 47.1
28	09 09.8	16 29.5	17 09.0	16 37.3
NOV 17	07 20.3	22 01.9	19 11.4	20 03.4
DEC 7	05 57.6	26 05.8	20 59.0	23 00.2
27	05 N 14.8	28 S 33.9	22 S 28.0	25 S 22.3

1972	Psyche 16	Eros 433	Lillith 1181	Toro 1685
JAN 1	16♍47.7	15♐40.8	01♐49.8	02♐39.9
11	16 R 52.8	22 18.9	05 01.9	07 35.7
21	16 23.1	28 46.6	08 05.4	12 28.7
31	15 19.4	05♑03.7	10 58.1	17 18.5
FEB 10	13 45.8	11 10.6	13 38.2	22 05.1
20	11 49.8	17 07.3	16 03.1	26 48.3
MAR 1	09 42.8	22 53.5	18 10.3	01♑27.6
11	07 37.3	28 29.3	19 57.0	06 03.0
21	05 45.5	03♒54.3	21 19.7	10 34.0
31	04 17.4	09 07.7	22 15.3	15 00.2
APR 10	03 19.0	14 09.1	22 40.9	19 21.5
20	02 53.0	18 57.3	22 R 33.8	23 37.1
30	02 D 59.6	23 30.7	21 53.0	27 46.7
MAY 10	03 36.4	27 47.6	20 39.7	01♒50.3
20	04 40.8	01♓45.2	18 58.0	05 47.3
30	06 09.5	05 20.1	16 55.9	09 38.7
JUN 9	07 59.2	08 28.0	14 44.1	13 26.8
19	10 07.0	11 02.6	12 34.9	17 15.7
29	12 30.1	12 56.5	10 40.7	21 18.5
JUL 9	15 06.3	14 00.6	09 10.7	26 04.8
19	17 53.5	14 R 03.9	08 11.6	02♓54.1
29	20 49.9	12 57.4	07 46.1	16 30.3
AUG 8	23 54.0	10 35.6	07 D 54.2	28♈02.0
18	27 04.5	07 04.5	08 34.6	02♋21.3
28	00♎20.2	02 48.6	09 44.5	25 22.2
SEP 7	03 40.0	28♒26.4	11 20.7	05♌15.5
17	07 02.9	24 41.6	13 20.3	12 06.1
27	10 27.8	22 06.1	15 40.2	18 26.1
OCT 7	13 54.0	20 52.8	18 17.8	25 01.7
17	17 20.5	21 D 02.0	21 11.0	01♍57.6
27	20 46.0	22 24.9	24 17.4	09 04.3
NOV 6	24 09.8	24 51.0	27 35.3	16 08.3
16	27 30.6	28 10.9	01♑03.2	22 56.5
26	00♏47.1	02♓16.0	04 39.4	29 20.4
DEC 6	03 58.0	06 59.7	08 23.0	05♎13.9
16	07 01.7	12 17.3	12 12.6	10 31.4
26	09 56.4	18 04.4	16 07.1	15 08.4
JAN 5	12♏40.3	24♓18.2	20♑05.6	18♎59.1
JAN 1	05 N 11.7	28 S 55.8	22 S 47.0	25 S 51.8
21	05 34.2	29 25.9	23 50.0	27 23.7
FEB 10	06 49.6	28 32.5	24 32.1	28 11.7
MAR 1	08 36.7	26 30.7	24 55.5	28 13.9
21	10 17.4	23 37.3	25 03.5	27 30.1
APR 10	11 19.5	20 08.7	24 59.1	25 59.7
30	11 31.8	16 18.8	24 42.5	23 39.7
MAY 20	10 58.4	12 19.5	24 09.9	20 17.8
JUN 9	09 47.3	08 21.6	23 19.2	15 15.6
29	08 06.8	04 36.2	22 20.0	06 35.7
JUL 19	06 03.7	01 19.4	21 31.4	12 N 46.8
AUG 8	03 44.1	01 N 01.1	21 06.6	64 04.6
28	01 13.7	01 50.1	21 05.7	61 29.3
SEP 17	01 S 22.4	01 13.6	21 20.2	38 10.7
OCT 7	03 58.6	00 19.8	21 38.8	23 11.5
27	06 29.8	00 07.9	21 50.7	11 09.7
NOV 16	08 50.7	01 00.6	21 46.8	01 03.3
DEC 6	10 56.0	03 01.1	21 20.2	07 S 24.5
26	12 S 40.9	06 N 03.2	20 S 26.6	14 S 27.2

1973		Psyche 16	Eros 433	Lilith 1181	Toro 1685
JAN	1	11♏36.2	21♓45.6	18♑29.7	17♎32.9
	11	14 12.4	28 14.5	22 30.2	20 51.9
	21	16 33.8	05♈06.5	26 33.1	23 11.0
	31	18 38.0	12 19.9	00♒37.6	24 19.4
FEB	10	20 21.8	19 53.5	04 42.9	24R03.4
	20	21 42.2	27 45.5	08 48.1	22 12.2
MAR	2	22 36.1	05♉54.5	12 52.3	18 42.8
	12	23 00.3	14 19.1	16 54.7	13 49.7
	22	22R52.9	22 57.4	20 54.2	08 13.2
APR	1	22 13.2	01♊47.5	24 50.0	02 47.1
	11	21 02.4	10 47.8	28 40.8	28♍18.9
	21	19 25.5	19 55.6	02♓25.4	25 13.7
MAY	1	17 30.0	29 08.9	06 02.4	23 33.6
	11	15 26.4	08♋25.6	09 30.1	23D09.5
	21	13 26.8	17 42.8	12 46.3	23 48.1
	31	11 41.8	26 58.4	15 48.9	25 16.2
JUN	10	10 20.6	06♌10.4	18 34.7	27 23.9
	20	09 28.9	15 16.2	21 00.5	00♎02.4
	30	09 08.9	24 14.1	23 02.5	03 05.6
JUL	10	09D20.9	03♍02.5	24 35.8	06 29.0
	20	10 03.3	11 40.0	25 36.0	10 08.8
	30	11 13.4	20 05.8	25 58.4	14 02.5
AUG	9	12 48.6	28 19.5	25R39.4	18 08.3
	19	14 45.7	06♎20.6	24 38.9	22 24.7
	29	17 02.1	14 09.5	23 00.3	26 50.7
SEP	8	19 35.3	21 46.6	20 53.9	01♏25.9
	18	22 23.0	29 12.2	18 35.5	06 09.5
	28	25 23.3	06♏27.2	16 23.9	11 01.5
OCT	8	28 34.5	13 32.5	14 37.6	16 01.9
	18	01♐54.9	20 28.5	13 30.1	21 10.8
	28	05 23.3	27 16.2	13D08.4	26 28.6
NOV	7	08 58.5	03♐56.4	13 34.6	01♐55.7
	17	12 39.0	10 29.5	14 46.3	07 32.7
	27	16 24.1	16 56.5	16 39.1	13 20.7
DEC	7	20 12.7	23 17.7	19 08.4	19 20.6
	17	24 03.6	29 33.7	22 08.6	25 33.7
	27	27 56.1	05♑45.1	25 35.2	02♑02.0
JAN	6	01♑49.0	11♑52.0	29♓24.3	08♑47.1
JAN	1	13S07.8	07N08.0	20S04.9	16S19.1
	21	14 20.1	11 09.0	18 33.7	21 41.8
FEB	10	15 03.6	15 28.0	16 34.8	25 28.4
MAR	2	15 16.1	19 29.7	14 11.4	26 28.4
	22	14 56.4	22 28.9	11 28.2	23 22.5
APR	11	14 06.4	23 38.7	08 31.0	17 40.9
MAY	1	12 55.5	22 28.2	05 26.6	12 44.4
	21	11 44.5	18 57.6	02 22.6	09 55.6
JUN	10	10 58.9	13 37.1	00N32.1	09 01.3
	30	10 54.0	07 10.7	03 05.9	09 29.5
JUL	20	11 30.1	00 20.8	05 03.3	10 53.3
AUG	9	12 38.4	06S19.4	06 04.2	12 52.8
	29	14 07.2	12 26.1	05 49.6	15 12.4
SEP	18	15 45.5	17 42.8	04 21.8	17 39.2
OCT	8	17 23.4	21 57.6	02 23.5	20 00.5
	28	18 52.1	25 01.9	00 53.6	22 03.5
NOV	17	20 04.5	26 50.2	00 26.5	23 33.8
DEC	7	20 54.7	27 20.7	01 07.4	24 15.6
	27	21S18.6	26S35.6	02N47.2	23S50.8

1974		Psyche 16	Eros 433	Lilith 1181	Toro 1685
JAN	1	29♐52.6	08♑49.1	27♓27.2	05♑22.3
	11	03♑45.3	14 53.9	01♈26.0	12 16.8
	21	07 37.1	20 55.0	05 41.8	19 32.2
	31	11 26.8	26 52.6	10 12.0	27 11.5
FEB	10	15 13.2	02♒46.9	14 54.0	05♒18.1
	20	18 55.3	08 38.3	19 45.7	13 56.2
MAR	2	22 31.7	14 27.0	24 45.5	23 09.5
	12	26 00.9	20 13.1	29 51.6	03♓01.6
	22	29 21.4	25 57.2	05♉02.9	13 35.5
APR	1	02♒31.3	01♓39.3	10 18.3	24 51.7
	11	05 28.4	07 19.6	15 36.4	06♈47.9
	21	08 10.5	12 58.7	20 56.7	19 18.2
MAY	1	10 34.5	18 36.6	26 18.2	02♉12.1
	11	12 37.5	24 13.6	01♊40.1	15 15.1
	21	14 16.0	29 50.4	07 02.0	28 12.0
	31	15 26.0	05♈26.8	12 23.2	10♊47.8
JUN	10	16 04.2	11 03.4	17 43.0	22 51.6
	20	16R07.5	16 40.5	23 01.0	04♋17.0
	30	15 34.3	22 18.2	28 16.6	15 01.5
JUL	10	14 26.2	27 57.0	03♋29.2	25 05.4
	20	12 48.2	03♉37.1	08 38.4	04♌31.1
	30	10 49.6	09 18.3	13 43.5	13 21.7
AUG	9	08 44.1	15 01.2	18 43.8	21 40.8
	19	06 46.0	20 45.6	23 38.7	29 32.0
	29	05 09.4	26 30.8	28 27.2	06♍58.6
SEP	8	04 04.5	02♊17.1	03♌08.4	14 03.6
	18	03 36.9	08 03.4	07 41.1	20 49.8
	28	03D48.7	13 47.9	12 03.9	27 19.3
OCT	8	04 38.7	19 29.8	16 15.2	03♎33.9
	18	06 04.0	25 05.4	20 13.1	09 35.4
	28	08 01.0	00♋30.5	23 55.0	15 24.9
NOV	7	10 25.7	05 40.8	27 18.3	21 03.2
	17	13 14.5	10 27.3	00♍19.6	26 31.3
	27	16 24.0	14 40.4	02 54.8	01♏49.3
DEC	7	19 51.0	18 10.3	04 59.8	06 57.4
	17	23 33.1	20 43.5	06 29.4	11 55.7
	27	27 27.9	22 16.1	07 19.1	16 43.6
JAN	6	01♓33.2	22♋55.9	07R25.1	21♏20.5
JAN	1	21S20.3	26S13.2	03N19.8	23S32.0
	21	21 09.3	24 03.2	05 53.4	21 17.1
FEB	10	20 31.7	20 55.7	08 53.4	17 12.7
MAR	2	19 31.5	17 01.0	12 04.7	11 04.5
	22	18 15.1	12 29.0	15 12.9	02 53.1
APR	11	16 51.4	07 27.8	18 04.5	06N42.8
MAY	1	15 31.2	02 04.1	20 27.1	15 57.6
	21	14 27.9	03N37.2	22 10.7	22 12.8
JUN	10	13 56.2	09 32.4	23 07.7	23 44.3
	30	14 08.7	15 39.1	23 14.7	21 08.5
JUL	20	15 06.8	21 55.5	22 31.7	16 12.7
AUG	9	16 31.7	28 19.5	21 03.0	10 22.7
	29	17 50.4	34 47.6	18 55.7	04 24.6
SEP	18	18 38.2	41 12.1	16 19.0	01S20.9
OCT	8	18 46.6	47 16.1	13 24.1	06 44.6
	28	18 15.2	52 27.8	10 22.8	11 42.2
NOV	17	17 05.4	55 54.5	07 28.9	16 10.7
DEC	7	15 18.8	56 15.6	04 57.9	20 07.6
	27	12S58.7	50N50.2	03N08.4	23S30.9

1975		Psyche 16	Eros 433	Lilith 1181	Toro 1685
JAN	1	29♒29.4	22♋41.8	07♍27.7	19♏03.4
	11	03♓39.4	23 01.7	07R11.0	23 34.6
	21	07 57.6	23 09.8	06 09.2	27 53.0
	31	12 22.3	23 49.2	04 27.4	01♐57.2
FEB	10	16 52.5	25 25.4	02 15.9	05 45.2
	20	21 26.8	28 11.9	29♌50.7	09 14.0
MAR	2	26 04.2	02♌04.4	27 30.1	12 20.0
	12	00♈43.9	06 46.8	25 30.6	14 58.8
	22	05 25.0	12 07.3	24 04.3	17 03.9
APR	1	10 06.5	17 52.9	23 17.6	18 28.0
	11	14 47.8	23 52.5	23D11.2	19 01.6
	21	19 28.2	00♍00.8	23 43.3	18R33.9
MAY	1	24 07.0	06 12.5	24 49.7	16 55.3
	11	28 43.4	12 23.8	26 25.6	13 59.8
	21	03♉16.7	18 34.1	28 26.8	09 52.5
	31	07 46.1	24 41.4	00♍49.1	04 56.3
JUN	10	12 10.9	00♎45.2	03 28.7	29♏49.2
	20	16 30.0	06 45.9	06 22.9	25 15.3
	30	20 42.4	12 42.9	09 28.9	21 47.6
JUL	10	24 46.9	18 36.5	12 44.7	19 40.8
	20	28 42.0	24 27.5	16 08.6	18 55.8
	30	02♊26.1	00♏15.7	19 38.9	19D24.8
AUG	9	05 57.1	06 01.7	23 14.4	20 57.9
	19	09 12.6	11 46.1	26 54.2	23 26.4
	29	12 09.9	17 28.8	00♎36.9	26 42.3
SEP	8	14 45.6	23 10.7	04 22.1	00♐40.4
	18	16 55.6	28 51.9	08 08.6	05 17.2
	28	18 36.1	04♐32.7	11 55.7	10 30.2
OCT	8	19 42.3	10 13.7	15 42.7	16 18.9
	18	20 10.2	15 55.0	19 28.8	22 43.8
	28	19R57.3	21 36.8	23 12.9	29 45.3
NOV	7	19 03.1	27 19.5	26 54.3	07♑25.7
	17	17 31.8	03♑03.3	00♏31.8	15 46.5
	27	15 32.9	08 48.3	04 04.5	24 48.7
DEC	7	13 20.2	14 35.0	07 31.0	04♒35.2
	17	11 11.0	20 23.3	10 49.7	15 10.8
	27	09 21.2	26 13.3	13 59.2	26 49.6
JAN	6	08♊02.6	02♒05.6	16♏57.6	10♓01.6
JAN	1	12S18.9	47N56.9	02N49.8	24S16.3
	21	09 23.7	28 15.7	02 18.7	26 56.6
FEB	10	06 07.8	04 59.8	02 58.6	29 04.0
MAR	2	02 38.6	07S50.9	04 25.9	30 42.7
	22	00N55.9	12 46.9	05 55.3	31 58.7
APR	11	04 27.8	14 25.5	06 51.1	32 55.1
MAY	1	07 49.3	15 06.9	07 00.6	33 17.0
	21	10 53.5	15 52.3	06 25.3	32 07.1
JUN	10	13 34.1	17 02.6	05 11.1	28 28.2
	30	15 46.2	18 37.4	03 24.8	23 42.5
JUL	20	17 26.4	20 26.7	01 13.4	20 08.8
AUG	9	18 33.6	22 17.4	01S16.9	18 21.5
	29	19 09.2	23 56.5	03 59.9	17 48.6
SEP	18	19 17.4	25 11.3	06 49.9	17 47.5
OCT	8	19 04.9	25 51.0	09 41.1	17 38.2
	28	18 39.4	25 46.9	12 28.2	16 42.2
NOV	17	18 08.4	24 52.6	15 06.0	14 25.0
DEC	7	17 39.8	23 05.6	17 29.8	10 33.7
	27	17N25.6	20S26.0	19S35.5	05S37.8

1976	Psyche 16	Eros 433	Lilith 1181	Toro 1685
JAN 1	08 R 37.4	29 ♑ 09.2	15 ♏ 29.9	03 ♓ 11.4
11	07 ♊ 37.5	05 ♒ 02.6	18 21.9	17 25.6
21	07 D 17.4	10 58.2	20 59.5	04 ♈ 12.4
31	07 36.7	16 56.6	23 20.2	23 29.4
FEB 10	08 32.8	22 57.9	25 20.8	13 ♉ 39.7
20	10 01.6	29 02.3	26 58.6	02 ♊ 11.2
MAR 1	11 58.2	05 ♓ 10.5	28 10.0	17 38.4
11	14 18.6	11 22.8	28 51.8	00 ♋ 07.3
21	16 58.5	17 39.5	29 R 01.2	10 19.3
31	19 54.6	24 01.5	28 36.6	18 55.6
APR 10	23 04.0	00 ♈ 29.2	27 37.7	26 27.2
20	26 23.9	07 03.4	26 08.0	03 ♌ 14.2
30	29 52.5	13 44.9	24 13.5	09 30.4
MAY 10	03 ♋ 28.0	20 34.4	22 04.2	15 25.2
20	07 08.8	27 32.8	19 52.1	21 04.4
30	10 53.7	04 ♉ 41.1	17 49.5	26 32.1
JUN 9	14 41.6	12 00.0	16 07.4	01 ♍ 51.8
19	18 31.5	19 30.2	14 53.2	07 05.1
29	22 22.6	27 12.7	14 10.9	12 13.9
JUL 9	26 14.2	05 ♊ 07.7	14 D 01.8	17 19.5
19	00 ♌ 05.5	13 15.7	14 24.7	22 22.5
29	03 55.8	21 36.7	15 17.1	27 23.9
AUG 8	07 44.3	00 ♋ 10.2	16 36.3	02 ♎ 24.5
18	11 30.3	08 55.6	18 18.9	07 24.5
28	15 13.1	17 52.0	20 22.0	12 24.6
SEP 7	18 51.7	26 57.3	22 43.1	17 25.3
17	22 25.0	06 ♌ 10.1	25 19.4	22 26.7
27	25 51.9	15 28.2	28 08.9	27 29.4
OCT 7	29 11.1	24 48.9	01 ♐ 09.9	02 ♏ 33.7
17	02 ♍ 21.0	04 ♍ 10.1	04 20.4	07 39.7
27	05 19.9	13 29.2	07 39.2	12 48.1
NOV 6	08 05.4	22 43.3	11 04.9	17 58.9
16	10 35.2	01 ♎ 50.3	14 36.1	23 12.6
26	12 46.5	10 47.9	18 12.0	28 29.7
DEC 6	14 36.0	19 33.3	21 51.4	03 ♐ 50.3
16	16 00.5	28 05.0	25 33.1	09 15.2
26	16 56.3	06 ♏ 20.9	29 16.4	14 45.0
JAN 5	17 ♍ 20.3	14 ♏ 19.1	03 ♑ 00.1	20 ♐ 20.3
JAN 1	17 N 25.8	19 S 38.2	20 S 03.7	04 S 19.2
21	17 44.7	15 57.7	21 42.5	01 N 07.3
FEB 10	18 28.5	11 34.5	22 57.5	05 56.0
MAR 1	19 25.9	06 35.3	23 46.8	07 57.2
21	20 23.4	01 07.5	24 06.8	08 09.9
APR 10	21 09.6	04 N 40.9	23 51.3	07 31.8
30	21 36.3	10 39.9	22 55.1	06 14.2
MAY 20	21 38.2	16 36.0	21 25.8	04 21.1
JUN 9	21 12.7	22 09.5	19 50.7	01 57.6
29	20 20.0	26 50.8	18 41.0	00 S 50.1
JUL 19	19 02.1	29 59.1	18 11.8	03 55.5
AUG 8	17 22.5	30 47.4	18 21.3	07 12.4
28	15 26.2	28 40.2	18 59.5	10 34.3
SEP 17	13 19.4	23 33.6	19 54.3	13 54.7
OCT 7	11 09.3	16 00.3	20 54.5	17 06.7
27	09 04.2	06 54.6	21 50.1	20 02.5
NOV 16	07 14.2	02 S 44.0	22 33.0	22 33.5
DEC 6	05 50.7	12 01.8	22 56.8	24 30.2
26	05 N 06.6	20 S 16.3	22 S 57.1	25 S 42.5

1977	Psyche 16	Eros 433	Lilith 1181	Toro 1685
JAN 1	17 ♍ 14.7	11 ♏ 10.0	01 ♑ 30.7	18 ♐ 05.4
11	17 R 18.5	18 57.0	05 14.1	23 44.5
21	16 47.5	26 24.1	08 56.6	29 30.9
31	15 42.6	03 ♐ 29.5	12 36.7	05 ♑ 25.7
FEB 10	14 08.3	10 11.7	16 13.4	11 30.8
20	12 11.9	16 29.1	19 45.7	17 48.5
MAR 2	10 04.8	22 19.1	23 12.0	24 21.0
12	07 59.7	27 39.2	26 31.1	01 ♒ 12.1
22	06 08.6	02 ♑ 25.7	29 41.2	08 25.7
APR 1	04 41.3	06 33.6	02 ♒ 40.3	16 06.8
11	03 43.9	09 57.1	05 26.6	24 21.1
21	03 18.8	12 28.1	07 57.4	03 ♓ 15.4
MAY 1	03 D 26.2	13 57.1	10 09.7	12 55.8
11	04 03.7	14 R 14.6	12 00.6	23 27.9
21	05 08.7	13 11.4	13 26.3	04 ♈ 54.1
31	06 37.9	10 46.0	14 22.8	17 10.9
JUN 10	08 28.0	07 10.4	14 46.7	00 ♉ 08.9
20	10 36.1	02 52.6	14 R 34.8	13 32.0
30	12 59.5	28 ♐ 35.3	13 45.8	27 01.2
JUL 10	15 35.9	24 58.5	12 21.7	10 ♊ 20.0
20	18 23.3	22 27.4	10 27.9	23 15.6
30	21 19.9	21 11.6	08 15.1	05 ♋ 38.8
AUG 9	24 24.1	21 D 06.5	05 57.4	17 23.9
19	27 34.8	22 03.4	03 50.0	28 27.6
29	00 ♎ 50.6	23 52.1	02 07.2	08 ♌ 48.7
SEP 8	04 10.4	26 22.7	00 58.6	18 28.7
18	07 33.5	29 27.9	00 29.8	27 30.1
28	10 58.6	03 ♑ 01.4	00 D 42.3	05 ♍ 56.0
OCT 8	14 24.8	06 58.3	01 34.2	13 50.1
18	17 51.4	11 15.1	03 02.5	21 15.5
28	21 17.0	15 49.0	05 03.6	28 14.6
NOV 7	24 40.8	20 37.7	07 33.1	04 ♎ 49.9
17	28 01.7	25 39.9	10 27.8	11 03.1
27	01 ♏ 18.2	00 ♒ 54.1	13 44.2	16 54.9
DEC 7	04 29.1	06 19.4	17 19.2	22 26.2
17	07 32.8	11 55.4	21 10.5	27 37.0
27	10 27.4	17 41.3	25 15.9	02 ♏ 26.2
JAN 6	13 ♏ 11.1	23 ♒ 36.9	29 ♒ 33.2	06 ♏ 52.9
JAN 1	05 N 02.9	22 S 27.5	22 S 52.2	25 S 53.9
21	05 26.5	28 38.8	22 19.1	25 52.2
FEB 10	06 42.8	33 03.7	21 21.1	24 40.7
MAR 2	08 30.2	35 50.9	20 01.5	22 07.1
22	10 10.5	37 24.0	18 25.6	17 56.8
APR 11	11 11.8	38 16.1	16 40.7	11 52.0
MAY 1	11 23.4	38 59.5	14 55.7	03 36.4
21	10 49.2	39 41.1	13 21.6	06 N 40.4
JUN 10	09 37.4	39 22.2	12 11.0	17 28.8
30	07 56.3	36 33.3	11 35.8	25 32.4
JUL 20	05 52.8	32 07.1	11 41.6	27 48.9
AUG 9	03 32.9	28 13.7	12 19.4	24 22.3
29	01 02.3	25 31.0	13 07.1	17 42.4
SEP 18	01 S 33.8	23 34.5	13 43.2	10 05.8
OCT 8	04 09.8	21 51.7	13 54.3	02 41.2
28	06 40.7	19 57.3	13 33.2	04 S 06.7
NOV 17	09 01.0	17 34.8	12 35.8	10 11.0
DEC 7	11 05.6	14 34.8	11 00.2	15 31.2
27	12 S 49.7	10 S 53.3	08 S 47.2	20 S 08.6

1978	Psyche 16	Eros 433	Lilith 1181	Toro 1685
JAN 1	11 ♏ 50.8	20 ♒ 37.8	27 ♒ 23.1	04 ♏ 42.5
11	14 28.2	26 38.3	01 ♓ 46.0	08 57.1
21	16 51.1	02 ♓ 48.4	06 18.6	12 45.1
31	18 56.8	09 07.9	10 59.5	16 03.2
FEB 10	20 42.6	15 37.3	15 47.7	18 46.4
20	22 05.0	22 16.5	20 42.0	20 47.8
MAR 2	23 01.2	29 05.8	25 41.4	21 59.9
12	23 27.9	06 ♈ 05.6	00 ♈ 45.3	22 R 13.3
22	23 R 23.1	13 16.3	05 52.7	21 18.7
APR 1	22 45.9	20 37.9	11 03.0	19 10.0
11	21 37.5	28 11.1	16 15.6	15 48.3
21	20 02.3	05 ♉ 55.9	21 29.8	11 28.6
MAY 1	18 07.9	13 52.4	26 45.0	06 41.6
11	16 04.5	22 00.6	02 ♉ 00.8	02 05.5
21	14 04.1	00 ♊ 20.1	07 16.3	28 ♎ 15.7
31	12 17.8	08 50.5	12 31.0	25 32.3
JUN 10	10 54.7	17 31.1	17 44.4	24 00.8
20	10 00.8	26 20.6	22 55.6	23 D 37.5
30	09 38.7	05 ♋ 18.0	28 04.0	24 13.3
JUL 10	09 D 48.6	14 21.8	03 ♊ 08.6	25 39.2
20	10 29.2	23 30.1	08 08.4	27 46.9
30	11 37.8	02 ♌ 41.1	13 02.3	00 ♏ 29.2
AUG 9	13 11.7	11 53.2	17 49.0	03 41.1
19	15 07.9	21 04.1	22 26.7	07 18.5
29	17 23.5	00 ♍ 12.0	26 53.6	11 18.1
SEP 8	19 56.2	09 15.2	01 ♋ 07.4	15 38.3
18	22 43.6	18 11.8	05 05.2	20 17.6
28	25 43.6	27 00.4	08 43.8	25 15.1
OCT 8	28 54.7	05 ♎ 39.8	11 59.0	00 ♐ 30.9
18	02 ♐ 15.3	14 08.6	14 46.0	06 05.1
28	05 43.8	22 26.3	16 59.7	11 58.5
NOV 7	09 19.3	00 ♏ 32.3	18 33.8	18 12.7
17	13 00.3	08 26.0	19 22.9	24 49.0
27	16 45.8	16 07.4	19 R 22.7	01 ♑ 49.9
DEC 7	20 35.0	23 36.5	18 32.0	09 18.4
17	24 26.7	00 ♐ 53.2	16 56.1	17 17.5
27	28 19.9	07 57.7	14 46.9	25 51.3
JAN 6	02 ♑ 13.8	14 ♐ 50.1	12 ♋ 23.3	05 ♒ 03.9
JAN 1	13 S 12.0	09 S 51.4	08 S 08.4	21 S 11.6
21	14 24.8	05 19.1	05 13.3	24 59.1
FEB 10	15 09.0	00 12.0	01 50.9	28 09.1
MAR 2	15 22.3	05 N 20.8	01 N 51.4	30 39.6
22	15 03.8	11 05.9	05 45.0	32 11.0
APR 11	14 15.2	16 43.1	09 40.5	31 48.1
MAY 1	13 05.3	21 43.4	13 28.0	28 35.4
21	11 54.5	25 28.0	16 57.8	23 39.6
JUN 10	11 08.2	27 12.3	19 59.9	19 29.2
30	11 02.2	26 20.9	22 25.6	17 10.6
JUL 20	11 37.2	22 45.3	24 07.9	16 32.1
AUG 9	12 44.5	16 50.6	25 03.2	17 02.6
29	14 12.6	09 23.7	25 12.1	18 13.7
SEP 18	15 50.3	01 16.3	24 40.3	19 41.4
OCT 8	17 27.6	06 S 46.3	23 38.3	21 04.0
28	18 55.7	14 07.7	22 21.1	21 59.1
NOV 17	20 07.4	20 21.3	21 05.3	22 02.0
DEC 7	20 56.6	25 08.2	20 04.4	20 44.4
27	21 S 19.5	28 S 17.7	19 N 21.9	17 S 36.6

1979	Psyche 16	Eros 433	Lilith 1181	Toro 1685
JAN 1	00♑16.9	11♐25.4	13R35.5	00♒22.5
11	04 10.6	18 11.8	11♋13.3	09 56.0
21	08 03.4	24 46.3	09 09.5	20 13.7
31	11 54.4	01♑09.1	07 40.5	01♓18.2
FEB 10	15 42.2	07 20.1	06 56.2	13 08.5
20	19 25.7	13 19.2	06D58.5	25 39.6
MAR 2	23 03.8	19 06.5	07 45.0	08♈42.1
12	26 34.9	24 41.3	09 11.2	22 02.3
22	29 57.5	00♒03.2	11 10.9	05♉24.5
APR 1	03♒09.8	05 11.6	13 38.6	18 33.7
11	06 09.6	10 05.1	16 29.4	01♊16.1
21	08 54.6	14 42.5	19 38.7	13 21.2
MAY 1	11 22.2	19 01.6	23 03.0	24 42.8
11	13 29.0	22 59.7	26 39.4	05♋18.4
21	15 11.8	26 33.5	00♌25.3	15 08.8
31	16 26.8	29 38.0	04 18.8	24 17.6
JUN 10	17 10.1	02♓07.3	08 18.3	02♌49.1
20	17R19.0	03 54.1	12 22.3	10 47.7
30	16 51.4	04 48.7	16 29.8	18 18.6
JUL 10	15 48.3	04R41.5	20 39.8	25 25.5
20	14 14.3	03 24.0	24 51.4	02♍12.2
30	12 17.9	00 52.3	29 04.1	08 42.1
AUG 9	10 12.5	27♒16.2	03♍17.0	14 57.6
19	08 12.7	23 00.5	07 29.6	21 01.1
29	06 32.4	18 44.1	11 41.4	26 54.5
SEP 8	05 22.8	15 08.0	15 51.7	02♎39.3
18	04 50.1	12 39.4	19 59.8	08 17.0
28	04D56.7	11 29.9	24 05.1	13 48.5
OCT 8	05 42.0	11D38.2	28 06.9	19 14.7
18	07 03.0	12 55.5	02♎04.3	24 36.5
28	08 56.2	15 12.5	05 56.4	29 54.4
NOV 7	11 17.7	18 19.7	09 42.0	05♏08.7
17	14 03.7	22 09.1	13 19.9	10 20.0
27	17 10.8	26 34.8	16 48.7	15 28.5
DEC 7	20 35.9	01♓31.7	20 06.5	20 34.1
17	24 16.2	06 56.2	23 11.5	25 37.3
27	28 09.5	12 45.7	26 01.3	00♐37.9
JAN 6	02♓13.6	18♓57.9	28♎33.2	05♐35.9
JAN 1	21S20.9	28S49.5	19N13.7	16S29.2
21	21 08.6	29 56.2	18 48.4	10 30.7
FEB 10	20 29.6	29 34.3	18 34.7	02 21.7
MAR 2	19 27.7	27 59.3	18 28.6	06N47.7
22	18 09.4	25 29.8	18 19.5	14 42.0
APR 11	16 43.4	22 23.9	17 55.5	19 12.8
MAY 1	15 20.8	18 58.3	17 08.0	19 48.7
21	14 14.7	15 27.7	15 52.7	17 33.3
JUN 10	13 39.9	12 06.1	14 08.8	13 46.9
30	13 49.5	09 08.5	11 58.0	09 21.8
JUL 20	14 46.2	06 52.9	09 24.2	04 43.8
AUG 9	16 12.0	05 37.1	06 31.7	00 05.4
29	17 33.6	05 21.0	03 25.8	04S27.0
SEP 18	18 24.2	05 31.4	00 11.8	08 49.1
OCT 8	18 34.4	05 27.3	03S04.6	12 56.6
28	18 03.8	04 43.3	06 17.8	16 45.1
NOV 17	16 54.0	03 07.2	09 22.1	20 09.6
DEC 7	15 07.2	00 35.2	12 11.9	23 04.6
27	12S46.6	02N50.6	14S41.3	25S24.7

1980	Psyche 16	Eros 433	Lilith 1181	Toro 1685
JAN 1	00♓10.3	15♓49.1	27♎19.6	03♐07.2
11	04 19.1	22 11.9	29 41.5	08 04.0
21	08 36.2	28 55.2	01♏40.9	12 58.1
31	13 00.1	05♈57.8	03 14.2	17 49.4
FEB 10	17 29.3	13 18.5	04 18.0	22 37.8
20	22 02.9	20 56.6	04 48.8	27 23.3
MAR 1	26 39.7	28 51.1	04R44.0	02♑05.3
11	01♈18.7	07♉00.8	04 02.8	06 44.1
21	05 59.2	15 24.7	02 46.3	11 19.2
31	10 40.2	24 01.3	01 00.1	15 50.5
APR 10	15 21.0	02♊49.1	28♎53.2	20 18.1
20	20 01.0	11 46.4	26 37.4	24 41.8
30	24 39.3	20 51.3	24 26.6	29 01.5
MAY 10	29 15.4	00♋01.5	22 32.9	03♒18.3
20	03♉48.5	09 15.4	21 05.6	07 32.8
30	08 17.7	18 30.3	20 10.5	11 47.5
JUN 9	12 42.3	27 44.2	19 49.1	16 08.0
19	17 01.4	06♌55.3	20D00.8	20 43.4
29	21 13.8	16 01.1	20 43.5	25 55.7
JUL 9	25 18.4	24 59.9	21 53.8	02♓34.1
19	29 13.9	03♍50.3	23 28.5	12 40.6
29	02♊58.4	12 30.8	25 24.4	02♈21.0
AUG 8	06 30.3	21 00.4	27 38.3	14♉29.0
18	09 46.8	29 18.7	00♏07.8	28♊30.5
28	12 45.3	07♎25.0	02 50.6	19♋50.1
SEP 7	15 22.7	15 19.4	05 44.6	01♌13.7
17	17 35.0	23 02.3	08 48.2	09 26.9
27	19 18.0	00♏33.8	11 59.8	16 49.1
OCT 7	20 27.5	07 54.6	15 18.0	24 09.0
17	20 59.0	15 05.4	18 41.7	01♍35.3
27	20R49.9	22 06.6	22 09.6	09 01.6
NOV 6	19 59.6	28 59.1	25 40.9	16 17.9
16	18 31.5	05♐43.5	29 14.4	23 13.8
26	16 34.8	12 20.3	02♐49.1	29 42.5
DEC 6	14 22.9	18 50.2	06 24.0	05♎39.6
16	12 12.4	25 13.8	09 58.2	11 00.4
26	10 20.0	01♑31.4	13 30.4	15 40.9
JAN 5	08♊57.6	07♑43.5	16♐59.7	19♎36.0
JAN 1	12S06.8	03N49.5	15S14.8	25S53.6
21	09 11.3	08 09.4	17 10.3	27 23.1
FEB 10	05 55.3	12 52.9	18 30.2	28 08.1
MAR 1	02 26.2	17 31.9	19 04.6	28 06.7
21	01N08.0	21 27.3	18 42.7	27 18.0
APR 10	04 39.2	23 52.8	17 22.4	25 41.0
30	08 00.0	24 06.7	15 25.5	23 11.4
MAY 20	11 03.3	21 50.8	13 34.1	19 34.7
JUN 9	13 42.9	17 20.3	12 22.7	14 07.9
29	15 53.9	11 14.4	12 02.9	04 41.3
JUL 19	17 33.2	04 19.5	12 29.6	16N16.2
AUG 8	18 39.5	02S43.8	13 31.6	63 45.5
28	19 14.4	09 24.8	14 57.3	56 49.9
SEP 17	19 22.3	15 21.4	16 36.1	36 26.6
OCT 7	19 09.9	20 18.0	18 18.8	22 13.2
27	18 45.1	24 03.5	19 57.5	10 31.2
NOV 16	18 15.4	26 30.4	21 25.3	00 36.9
DEC 6	17 48.1	27 35.5	22 36.7	07S42.3
26	17N34.3	27S20.5	23S27.6	14S38.8

1981	Psyche 16	Eros 433	Lilith 1181	Toro 1685
JAN 1	09R26.3	05♑15.3	15♐36.4	18♎07.9
11	08♊26.0	11 24.3	19 03.3	21 32.1
21	08D05.4	17 28.3	22 24.9	23 57.9
31	08 24.1	23 27.6	25 40.2	25 15.3
FEB 10	09 19.5	29 22.6	28 47.4	25R10.9
20	10 47.6	05♒13.4	01♑44.7	23 33.6
MAR 2	12 43.5	11 00.4	04 30.3	20 19.1
12	15 03.0	16 43.7	07 01.8	15 38.5
22	17 42.3	22 23.3	09 16.6	10 08.2
APR 1	20 37.6	27 59.7	11 12.0	04 40.4
11	23 46.2	03♓32.8	12 44.7	00 03.6
21	27 05.6	09 02.8	13 51.4	26♍46.9
MAY 1	00♋33.4	14 29.9	14 28.8	24 54.8
11	04 08.3	19 54.0	14R33.8	24D20.0
21	07 48.4	25 15.1	14 04.7	24 49.5
31	11 32.7	00♈33.4	13 01.6	26 10.3
JUN 10	15 20.0	05 48.4	11 27.4	28 12.0
20	19 09.3	10 59.9	09 29.0	00♎45.9
30	22 59.9	16 07.7	07 16.7	03 45.2
JUL 10	26 51.0	21 10.6	05 03.4	07 05.5
20	00♌41.8	26 07.8	03 02.6	10 42.9
30	04 31.6	00♉58.1	01 25.0	14 34.6
AUG 9	08 19.7	05 38.8	00 18.9	18 39.0
19	12 05.2	10 07.5	29♐48.3	22 54.2
29	15 47.5	14 20.2	29D53.8	27 19.3
SEP 8	19 25.6	18 10.5	00♑34.3	01♏53.8
18	22 58.4	21 31.6	01 47.0	06 37.1
28	26 24.9	24 12.8	03 28.6	11 28.9
OCT 8	29 43.5	25 59.9	05 36.0	16 29.4
18	02♍52.8	26 38.5	08 05.9	21 38.6
28	05 51.0	25R52.9	10 55.3	26 56.8
NOV 7	08 35.9	23 38.5	14 02.0	02♐24.7
17	11 04.9	20 16.0	17 23.4	08 02.6
27	13 15.4	16 33.2	20 57.7	13 51.8
DEC 7	15 03.9	13 38.6	24 43.3	19 53.2
17	16 27.4	12D24.7	28 38.5	26 08.2
27	17 22.1	13 10.8	02♒42.1	02♑38.5
JAN 6	17♍44.8	15♉54.7	06♒52.9	09♑26.3
JAN 1	17N34.7	27S01.2	23S38.5	16S29.2
21	17 53.8	25 11.8	23 59.9	21 48.7
FEB 10	18 37.0	22 21.4	23 59.5	25 36.5
MAR 2	19 33.0	18 41.2	23 40.5	26 46.9
22	20 28.7	14 22.0	23 08.3	23 57.3
APR 11	21 12.9	09 32.9	22 30.2	18 21.6
MAY 1	21 37.4	04 20.9	21 53.9	13 19.3
21	21 37.1	01N08.8	21 25.5	10 22.3
JUN 10	21 09.6	06 53.3	21 05.9	09 21.5
30	20 15.0	12 51.4	20 50.3	09 45.1
JUL 20	18 55.4	19 04.2	20 34.8	11 05.7
AUG 9	17 14.5	25 35.5	20 21.9	13 02.7
29	15 17.2	32 30.4	20 15.3	15 20.4
SEP 18	13 09.6	39 51.7	20 12.6	17 45.4
OCT 8	10 59.1	47 21.9	20 06.0	20 05.0
28	08 54.0	53 32.2	19 46.4	22 06.0
NOV 17	07 04.2	55 03.6	19 05.6	23 34.1
DEC 7	05 41.3	50 12.1	17 57.4	24 12.9
27	04N58.1	41N49.3	16S18.5	23S44.3

1982		Psyche 16	Eros 433	Lillith 1181	Toro 1685
JAN	1	17♍37.6	14♉18.9	04♒46.7	06♑00.1
	11	17R43.5	17 55.9	09 00.6	12 57.4
	21	17 14.8	23 03.2	13 20.2	20 16.0
	31	16 12.1	29 24.4	17 44.6	27 59.2
FEB	10	14 39.5	06♊43.7	22 12.9	06♒10.2
	20	12 44.4	14 45.4	26 44.2	14 53.2
MAR	2	10 37.6	23 19.0	01♓18.1	24 12.2
	12	08 32.1	02♋13.0	05 53.6	04♓10.4
	22	06 39.9	11 16.8	10 30.3	14 50.7
APR	1	05 10.8	20 23.0	15 07.4	26 13.3
	11	04 11.4	29 24.3	19 44.2	08♈15.4
	21	03 44.2	08♌14.6	24 20.2	20 50.4
MAY	1	03D49.5	16 51.4	28 54.6	03♉47.1
	11	04 25.2	25 12.1	03♈26.5	16 50.7
	21	05 28.5	03♍15.5	07 55.2	29 45.7
	31	06 56.2	11 02.5	12 19.6	12♊17.7
JUN	10	08 45.1	18 33.5	16 38.4	24 16.2
	20	10 52.1	25 49.4	20 50.3	05♋35.8
	30	13 14.7	02♎52.2	24 53.5	16 14.3
JUL	10	15 50.3	09 42.9	28 45.8	26 12.4
	20	18 37.1	16 23.0	02♉25.0	05♌32.7
	30	21 33.3	22 54.1	05 47.4	14 18.5
AUG	9	24 37.2	29 17.2	08 49.7	22 33.1
	19	27 47.6	05♏33.5	11 27.3	00♍20.5
	29	01♎03.3	11 44.3	13 34.6	07 43.8
SEP	8	04 23.1	17 50.2	15 06.2	14 45.8
	18	07 46.1	23 52.3	15 56.3	21 29.5
	28	11 11.4	29 51.3	15R59.8	27 56.8
OCT	8	14 37.8	05♐47.6	15 15.8	04♎09.6
	18	18 04.5	11 42.2	13 47.6	10 09.6
	28	21 30.6	17 35.4	11 46.5	15 57.9
NOV	7	24 54.8	23 27.5	09 31.5	21 35.2
	17	28 16.2	29 19.2	07 24.2	27 02.6
	27	01♏33.4	05♑10.7	05 46.0	02♏20.1
DEC	7	04 45.1	11 02.2	04 51.1	07 28.0
	17	07 49.7	16 54.1	04D45.9	12 26.3
	27	10 45.4	22 46.7	05 30.9	17 14.4
JAN	6	13♏30.2	28♑40.1	07♉01.9	21♏51.8
JAN	1	04N55.0	39N33.1	15S48.8	23S24.4
	21	05 16.9	30 28.3	13 30.9	21 04.4
FEB	10	06 31.8	21 49.2	10 44.2	16 53.8
MAR	2	08 18.9	14 07.1	07 32.7	10 38.5
	22	10 00.1	07 40.9	04 01.9	02 20.9
APR	11	11 03.0	02 23.8	00 17.8	07N16.8
MAY	1	11 16.1	02S05.7	03N32.9	16 24.2
	21	10 42.9	06 08.4	07 23.3	22 22.0
JUN	10	09 32.0	09 56.1	11 06.5	23 35.3
	30	07 51.3	13 32.0	14 35.3	20 48.7
JUL	20	05 48.1	16 53.8	17 42.3	15 49.4
AUG	9	03 28.4	19 55.8	20 19.8	10 00.0
	29	00 57.8	22 30.2	22 18.9	04 04.1
SEP	18	01S38.2	24 28.7	23 27.0	01S38.7
OCT	8	04 14.4	25 43.5	23 25.5	06 59.9
	28	06 45.4	26 07.7	22 00.3	11 55.1
NOV	17	09 05.9	25 36.5	19 36.3	16 21.2
DEC	7	11 10.7	24 08.2	17 23.5	20 15.9
	27	12S55.1	21S43.9	16N16.7	23S37.0

1983		Psyche 16	Eros 433	Lillith 1181	Toro 1685
JAN	1	12♏09.3	25♑43.3	06♉11.0	19♏34.5
	11	14 48.0	01♒37.3	08 02.8	24 06.3
	21	17 12.4	07 32.6	10 32.1	28 25.8
	31	19 19.8	13 29.4	13 32.5	02♐31.4
FEB	10	21 07.5	19 28.0	16 58.4	06 21.3
	20	22 32.2	25 28.8	20 45.4	09 52.5
MAR	2	23 30.8	01♓32.0	24 49.1	13 01.7
	12	24 00.3	07 38.2	29 06.1	15 44.4
	22	23R58.2	13 47.9	03♊33.9	17 54.5
APR	1	23 23.7	20 01.4	08 10.0	19 24.7
	11	22 17.9	26 19.6	12 52.4	20 05.9
	21	20 44.7	02♈43.1	17 39.7	19R47.1
MAY	1	18 51.6	09 12.5	22 30.4	18 18.4
	11	16 48.7	15 48.8	27 23.5	15 32.8
	21	14 47.6	22 32.9	02♋18.1	11 33.1
	31	13 00.1	29 25.5	07 13.3	06 39.9
JUN	10	11 35.0	06♉27.9	12 08.4	01 29.7
	20	10 38.8	13 40.9	17 03.0	26♏47.3
	30	10 14.3	21 05.3	21 56.4	23 08.4
JUL	10	10D22.0	28 42.2	26 48.1	20 50.1
	20	11 00.5	06♊32.1	01♌37.8	19 54.9
	30	12 07.3	14 35.6	06 24.9	20D15.7
AUG	9	13 39.5	22 53.0	11 09.0	21 42.3
	19	15 34.3	01♋23.9	15 49.7	24 06.0
	29	17 48.8	10 07.8	20 26.1	27 18.4
SEP	8	20 20.4	19 03.8	24 58.1	01♐14.0
	18	23 07.1	28 10.0	29 24.6	05 49.3
	28	26 06.5	07♌24.6	03♍44.8	11 01.4
OCT	8	29 17.1	16 45.3	07 58.0	16 49.8
	18	02♐37.3	26 09.2	12 02.8	23 14.6
	28	06 05.5	05♍33.7	15 58.0	00♑16.3
NOV	7	09 40.7	14 56.0	19 41.9	07 56.4
	17	13 21.6	24 12.8	23 12.5	16 16.3
	27	17 07.1	03♎21.6	26 27.7	25 16.4
DEC	7	20 56.3	12 19.8	29 24.8	04♒59.1
	17	24 48.0	21 04.2	02♎00.4	15 30.9
	27	28 41.3	29 32.9	04 11.2	27 09.6
JAN	6	02♑35.3	07♏43.4	05♎53.3	10♓33.4
JAN	1	13S17.5	20S59.5	16N11.8	24S21.9
	21	14 30.8	17 31.2	16 32.2	26 59.9
FEB	10	15 15.6	13 18.5	17 36.8	29 04.7
MAR	2	15 29.9	08 28.3	18 59.9	30 40.6
	22	15 12.7	03 07.9	20 19.8	31 53.8
APR	11	14 25.6	02N35.1	21 19.8	32 48.2
MAY	1	13 17.0	08 32.3	21 48.4	33 11.4
	21	12 06.6	14 32.9	21 38.8	32 09.5
JUN	10	11 19.6	20 21.7	20 48.3	28 40.0
	30	11 12.4	25 35.4	19 18.2	23 53.6
JUL	20	11 46.1	29 39.3	17 12.2	20 12.7
AUG	9	12 52.3	31 47.2	14 36.2	18 18.6
	29	14 19.4	31 12.4	11 37.0	17 40.4
SEP	18	15 56.2	27 29.8	08 22.1	17 34.7
OCT	8	17 32.6	20 51.7	04 59.1	17 20.8
	28	18 59.9	12 04.3	01 35.9	16 19.8
NOV	17	20 10.6	02 08.4	01S39.1	13 58.7
DEC	7	20 58.9	07S55.3	04 37.0	10 09.6
	27	21S20.8	17S14.9	07S07.1	05S30.1

1984		Psyche 16	Eros 433	Lillith 1181	Toro 1685
JAN	1	00♑38.3	03♏40.6	05♎06.1	03♓35.2
	11	04 32.3	11 40.9	06 32.2	18 11.6
	21	08 25.3	19 19.4	07 23.3	05♈49.2
	31	12 16.5	26 34.3	07R36.1	26 19.4
FEB	10	16 04.7	03♐22.5	07 08.4	17♉28.7
	20	19 48.6	09 41.7	06 01.1	06♊14.9
MAR	1	23 27.2	15 28.7	04 18.6	21 22.4
	11	26 58.8	20 38.9	02 10.3	03♋19.9
	21	00♒22.0	25 07.4	29♍49.9	13 01.5
	31	03 35.1	28 47.7	27 32.4	21 11.9
APR	10	06 35.9	01♑30.6	25 32.3	28 22.6
	20	09 22.0	03 06.5	24 00.7	04♌53.1
	30	11 50.9	03R24.6	23 03.5	10 56.1
MAY	10	13 59.3	02 15.8	22 43.0	16 40.3
	20	15 44.0	29♐40.6	22D58.0	22 11.0
	30	17 01.2	25 53.6	23 45.3	27 31.8
JUN	9	17 47.0	21 29.1	25 01.7	02♍45.8
	19	17R58.6	17 13.5	26 43.0	07 54.5
	29	17 34.0	13 46.3	28 45.6	12 59.4
JUL	9	16 33.6	11 31.2	01♎06.4	18 01.8
	19	15 01.9	10 32.8	03 42.3	23 02.2
	29	13 07.2	10D44.6	06 31.0	28 01.4
AUG	8	11 02.0	11 56.6	09 30.6	03♎00.1
	18	09 01.3	13 57.4	12 39.0	07 58.6
	28	07 18.9	16 37.7	15 54.8	12 57.5
SEP	7	06 06.3	19 50.2	19 16.8	17 57.2
	17	05 30.2	23 28.5	22 43.6	22 57.8
	27	05D33.0	27 28.3	26 14.4	28 00.0
OCT	7	06 14.6	01♑46.2	29 48.0	03♏03.9
	17	07 32.0	06 19.2	03♏23.5	08 09.8
	27	09 21.8	11 05.6	07 00.1	13 18.2
NOV	6	11 40.3	16 04.0	10 36.6	18 29.3
	16	14 23.4	21 12.8	14 12.3	23 43.4
	26	17 27.8	26 31.5	17 46.1	29 01.0
DEC	6	20 50.4	01♒59.3	21 16.8	04♐22.5
	16	24 28.4	07 35.7	24 43.4	09 48.5
	26	28 19.4	13 20.6	28 04.6	15 19.6
JAN	5	02♓21.5	19♒13.7	01♐18.8	20♐56.5
JAN	1	21S21.8	19S23.2	07S39.0	04S18.1
	21	21 08.5	26 57.4	09 16.2	00N38.4
FEB	10	20 28.4	32 48.6	09 53.3	05 01.0
MAR	1	19 25.4	37 00.8	09 18.2	06 53.1
	21	18 06.1	39 55.9	07 39.3	07 14.3
APR	10	16 39.1	42 06.4	05 35.9	06 47.4
	30	15 15.4	43 53.2	03 56.5	05 38.9
MAY	20	14 08.1	44 40.4	03 08.0	03 52.6
JUN	9	13 31.9	42 37.1	03 13.7	01 34.3
	29	13 40.1	37 35.5	04 05.7	01S09.5
JUL	19	14 35.7	32 24.1	05 33.5	04 12.0
AUG	8	16 01.8	28 43.0	07 26.9	07 26.5
	28	17 24.7	26 22.8	09 37.1	10 46.3
SEP	17	18 17.0	24 45.4	11 56.5	14 04.9
OCT	7	18 28.5	23 17.1	14 18.1	17 15.1
	27	17 58.9	21 34.5	16 35.6	20 09.0
NOV	16	16 49.8	19 22.2	18 43.2	22 38.0
DEC	6	15 03.8	16 31.3	20 36.3	24 32.3
	26	12S44.2	12S58.3	22S10.9	25S41.7

1985		Psyche 16	Eros 433	Lilith 1181	Toro 1685
JAN	1	00♓43.5	16♒51.5	00♐02.0	18♐41.0
	11	04 51.2	22 49.3	03 11.3	24 21.8
	21	09 07.1	28 55.3	06 11.1	00♑10.4
	31	13 29.7	05♓09.6	08 59.2	06 07.8
FEB	10	17 57.7	11 32.1	11 33.6	12 15.9
	20	22 29.9	18 03.3	13 51.9	18 37.0
MAR	2	27 05.2	24 43.5	15 51.1	25 13.8
	12	01♈42.7	01♈32.9	17 28.3	02♒09.5
	22	06 21.7	08 32.2	18 40.2	09 28.8
APR	1	11 01.2	15 41.7	19 23.5	17 16.1
	11	15 40.4	23 01.6	19 R 35.6	25 37.6
	21	20 18.7	00♉32.8	19 14.3	04♓39.5
MAY	1	24 55.4	08 15.3	18 19.3	14 27.9
	11	29 29.7	16 09.2	16 53.4	25 07.5
	21	04♉01.0	24 14.8	15 01.9	06♈40.1
	31	08 28.4	02♊31.9	12 54.2	19 01.2
JUN	10	12 51.0	10 59.9	10 42.0	02♉00.5
	20	17 08.2	19 38.4	08 37.7	15 22.1
	30	21 18.5	28 26.3	06 52.6	28 47.7
JUL	10	25 20.9	07♋22.4	05 34.9	12♊01.6
	20	29 14.1	16 25.4	04 49.3	24 51.6
	30	02♊56.1	25 33.5	04 D 37.5	07♋08.6
AUG	9	06 25.1	04♌44.9	04 58.8	18 47.1
	19	09 38.6	13 57.8	05 50.8	29 44.1
	29	12 33.8	23 10.1	07 11.1	09♌58.6
SEP	8	15 07.3	02♍19.8	08 56.0	19 32.3
	18	17 15.4	11 25.2	11 02.9	28 28.1
	28	18 53.7	20 24.2	13 29.0	06♍49.2
OCT	8	19 58.0	29 15.4	16 11.5	14 39.1
	18	20 24.0	07♎57.4	19 08.5	22 00.9
	28	20 R 09.2	16 28.7	22 17.8	28 57.1
NOV	7	19 13.6	24 48.6	25 37.8	05♎30.0
	17	17 41.3	02♏56.5	29 07.0	11 41.3
	27	15 41.8	10 51.5	02♑44.0	17 31.8
DEC	7	13 29.4	18 33.6	06 27.6	23 02.2
	17	11 20.6	26 02.5	10 16.7	28 12.4
	27	09 31.6	03♐18.0	14 10.2	03♏01.7
JAN	6	08♊14.1	10♐20.3	18♑07.0	07♏28.9
JAN	1	11 S 56.5	11 S 46.1	22 S 35.3	25 S 52.0
	21	09 00.9	07 19.6	23 42.8	25 46.4
FEB	10	05 45.2	02 17.1	24 29.5	24 29.9
MAR	2	02 16.9	03 N 13.3	24 57.1	21 49.9
	22	01 N 16.1	09 00.2	25 08.5	17 31.8
APR	11	04 46.0	14 46.8	25 05.5	11 17.8
MAY	1	08 05.3	20 09.1	24 46.7	02 53.7
	21	11 07.0	24 33.0	24 07.7	07 N 25.9
JUN	10	13 45.0	27 15.6	23 08.8	18 03.9
	30	15 54.5	27 35.0	22 04.6	25 43.3
JUL	20	17 32.5	25 07.8	21 16.1	27 34.0
AUG	9	18 37.7	20 03.8	20 54.8	23 52.4
	29	19 11.8	13 02.0	20 58.6	17 09.5
SEP	18	19 19.1	04 54.6	21 18.1	09 36.0
OCT	8	19 06.2	03 S 27.8	21 41.7	02 16.1
	28	18 40.8	11 23.2	21 58.6	04 S 27.3
NOV	17	18 10.2	18 19.0	21 59.9	10 27.7
DEC	7	17 42.3	23 51.7	21 38.9	15 44.4
	27	17 N 28.7	27 S 47.1	20 S 51.1	20 S 18.9

1986		Psyche 16	Eros 433	Lilith 1181	Toro 1685
JAN	1	08 R 48.4	06♐50.8	16♑08.2	05♏18.1
	11	07♊49.4	13 46.6	20 06.5	09 33.6
	21	07 D 30.1	20 29.0	24 06.9	13 23.0
	31	07 50.1	26 58.0	28 08.3	16 43.2
FEB	10	08 46.7	03♑13.9	02♒10.2	19 29.3
	20	10 15.8	09 16.0	06 11.4	21 34.7
MAR	2	12 12.7	15 04.2	10 11.0	22 52.0
	12	14 33.1	20 38.1	14 08.3	23 R 11.9
	22	17 13.2	25 56.6	18 02.1	22 24.9
APR	1	20 09.3	00♒58.9	21 51.4	20 24.6
	11	23 18.5	05 43.4	25 34.9	17 10.7
	21	26 38.6	10 07.9	29 11.2	12 56.5
MAY	1	00♋07.1	14 09.9	02♓38.7	08 11.0
	11	03 42.5	17 45.7	05 55.7	03 31.9
	21	07 23.3	20 50.4	08 59.6	29♎35.7
	31	11 08.2	23 18.2	11 48.1	26 44.3
JUN	10	14 56.1	25 01.2	14 17.9	25 04.8
	20	18 46.1	25 50.3	16 25.1	24 D 34.3
	30	22 37.2	25 R 36.4	18 05.9	25 04.1
JUL	10	26 28.9	24 11.1	19 15.5	26 25.2
	20	00♌20.3	21 33.0	19 49.2	28 29.1
	30	04 10.7	17 53.4	19 R 43.5	01♏08.6
AUG	9	07 59.4	13 38.1	18 56.4	04 18.3
	19	11 45.6	09 26.6	17 30.2	07 54.2
	29	15 28.4	05 56.6	15 32.3	11 52.9
SEP	8	19 07.2	03 33.2	13 15.9	16 12.6
	18	22 40.6	02 26.7	10 59.2	20 51.9
	28	26 07.7	02 D 33.9	09 00.4	25 49.7
OCT	8	29 27.1	03 47.1	07 34.8	01♐06.3
	18	02♍37.0	05 56.8	06 52.4	06 41.8
	28	05 35.9	08 53.8	06 D 56.6	12 37.0
NOV	7	08 21.4	12 30.7	07 47.0	18 53.4
	17	10 51.1	16 41.6	09 20.3	25 32.5
	27	13 02.3	21 21.6	11 31.4	02♑36.8
DEC	7	14 51.6	26 27.4	14 15.7	10 09.5
	17	16 15.7	01♓56.2	17 28.4	18 13.6
	27	17 11.1	07 45.9	21 05.1	26 53.2
JAN	6	17♍34.5	13♓55.2	25♓02.3	06♒12.7
JAN	1	17 N 29.1	28 S 29.9	20 S 34.7	21 S 21.2
	21	17 48.2	30 18.3	19 11.2	25 06.2
FEB	10	18 31.9	30 32.8	17 20.3	28 14.2
MAR	2	19 28.9	29 29.2	15 05.0	30 43.9
	22	20 25.8	27 27.6	12 30.1	32 17.4
APR	11	21 11.3	24 48.8	09 41.5	32 02.3
MAY	1	21 37.2	21 52.2	06 46.3	28 59.6
	21	21 38.2	18 56.2	03 52.3	24 06.4
JUN	10	21 11.9	16 18.0	01 09.4	19 51.3
	30	20 18.4	14 14.2	01 N 09.9	17 26.7
JUL	20	18 59.7	12 54.4	02 49.0	16 43.5
AUG	9	17 19.4	12 09.2	03 27.9	17 10.4
	29	15 22.5	11 35.1	02 52.7	18 18.8
SEP	18	13 15.1	10 57.2	01 17.3	19 44.1
OCT	8	11 04.5	10 04.0	00 S 29.9	21 04.1
	28	08 59.2	08 41.2	01 38.4	21 56.1
NOV	17	07 09.2	06 37.2	01 44.9	21 54.9
DEC	7	05 45.9	03 45.6	00 48.2	20 31.7
	27	05 N 02.2	00 S 05.5	01 N 03.2	17 S 16.5

1987		Psyche 16	Eros 433	Lilith 1181	Toro 1685
JAN	1	17♍27.0	10♓48.2	23♓01.3	01♒27.8
	11	17 R 33.4	17 06.8	27 07.5	11 08.5
	21	17 05.2	23 43.2	01♈29.2	21 34.3
	31	16 03.0	00♈36.7	06 04.2	02♓47.2
FEB	10	14 30.5	07 46.8	10 50.2	14 45.7
	20	12 35.6	15 12.7	15 45.2	27 24.0
MAR	2	10 28.9	22 54.1	20 47.7	10♈31.8
	12	08 23.2	00♉50.3	25 56.4	23 55.2
	22	06 31.0	09 00.3	01♉09.8	07♉18.3
APR	1	05 01.9	17 23.5	06 27.0	20 26.2
	11	04 02.6	25 58.9	11 47.0	03♊05.4
	21	03 35.6	04♊44.7	17 08.9	15 05.5
MAY	1	03 D 41.1	13 39.8	22 32.0	26 20.9
	11	04 17.2	22 42.4	27 55.5	06♋49.7
	21	05 20.9	01♋50.3	03♊18.9	16 33.2
	31	06 49.0	11 02.0	08 41.5	25 35.2
JUN	10	08 38.4	20 15.3	14 02.8	04♌00.4
	20	10 45.8	29 27.9	19 22.1	11 53.3
	30	13 08.9	08♌38.1	24 39.1	19 19.0
JUL	10	15 45.1	17 43.8	29 53.0	26 21.4
	20	18 32.3	26 43.1	05♋03.2	03♍04.1
	30	21 29.0	05♍34.7	10 09.3	09 30.6
AUG	9	24 33.5	14 17.2	15 10.3	15 43.2
	19	27 44.4	22 49.3	20 05.5	21 44.0
	29	01♎00.6	01♎10.7	24 54.2	27 35.3
SEP	8	04 20.9	09 20.6	29 34.9	03♎18.3
	18	07 44.4	17 18.9	04♌06.7	08 54.4
	28	11 10.2	25 05.9	08 27.9	14 24.6
OCT	8	14 37.2	02♏41.6	12 36.6	19 49.8
	18	18 04.5	10 06.4	16 31.0	25 10.8
	28	21 31.1	17 21.0	20 08.2	00♏28.1
NOV	7	24 55.9	24 25.7	23 25.0	05 42.0
	17	28 17.9	01♐21.3	26 18.1	10 53.1
	27	01♏35.8	08 08.4	28 43.0	16 01.6
DEC	7	04 48.0	14 47.2	00♍34.9	21 07.6
	17	07 53.3	21 18.6	01 49.2	26 11.2
	27	10 49.8	27 42.9	02 20.8	01♐12.6
JAN	6	13♏35.4	04♑00.4	02 R 06.8	06♐11.5
JAN	1	04 N 59.0	00 N 56.5	01 N 38.2	16 S 07.0
	21	05 20.6	05 28.7	04 20.7	09 59.8
FEB	10	06 35.4	10 27.7	07 29.0	01 44.6
MAR	2	08 22.4	15 30.9	10 49.4	07 N 22.3
	22	10 03.7	20 05.5	14 08.4	15 02.8
APR	11	11 06.6	23 28.9	17 12.9	19 13.9
MAY	1	11 19.6	24 55.3	19 50.4	19 33.6
	21	10 46.2	23 53.0	21 50.6	17 09.8
JUN	10	09 34.9	20 20.4	23 05.3	13 21.4
	30	07 54.0	14 47.2	23 29.8	08 57.4
JUL	20	05 50.4	07 59.4	23 03.6	04 21.7
AUG	9	03 30.2	00 42.7	21 49.7	00 S 14.1
	29	00 59.3	06 S 25.3	19 55.1	04 44.1
SEP	18	01 S 37.2	12 57.0	17 29.0	09 03.8
OCT	8	04 13.8	18 32.3	14 42.8	13 09.1
	28	06 45.3	22 57.0	11 49.2	16 55.5
NOV	17	09 06.2	26 01.3	09 02.9	20 17.9
DEC	7	11 11.4	27 40.6	06 40.5	23 10.6
	27	12 S 56.2	27 S 55.2	05 N 01.5	25 S 28.1

1988	Psyche 16	Eros 433	Lillith 1181	Toro 1685
JAN 1	12♏14.1	00♑52.5	02R 19.6	03♐42.3
11	14 53.6	07 06.8	01♍42.6	08 40.2
21	17 19.0	13 15.1	00 21.4	13 35.8
31	19 27.4	19 17.4	28♌23.7	18 28.8
FEB 10	21 16.2	25 14.1	26 03.2	23 19.4
20	22 42.1	01♒05.5	23 37.5	28 07.6
MAR 1	23 41.9	06 51.6	21 25.2	02♑52.9
11	24 12.8	12 32.6	19 41.5	07 35.7
21	24R 12.2	18 08.7	18 35.2	12 15.9
31	23 39.0	23 39.8	18 10.4	16 53.3
APR 10	22 34.6	29 06.0	18D 25.8	21 28.5
20	21 02.4	04♓27.3	19 18.0	26 01.7
30	19 09.9	09 43.4	20 42.8	00♒33.6
MAY 10	17 07.2	14 54.1	22 34.9	05 06.1
20	15 05.8	19 59.2	24 50.2	09 41.2
30	13 17.5	24 57.8	27 24.8	14 23.6
JUN 9	11 51.4	29 49.4	00♍15.1	19 22.2
19	10 53.9	04♈32.8	03 18.5	24 51.9
29	10 28.2	09 06.2	06 32.6	01♓24.6
JUL 9	10D 34.7	13 28.0	09 55.4	10 07.9
19	11 11.9	17 34.9	13 25.4	23 33.0
29	12 17.7	21 23.0	17 01.0	17♈09.4
AUG 8	13 48.9	24 47.2	20 41.2	24♉04.8
18	15 42.8	27 39.6	24 25.0	26♊46.6
28	17 56.6	29 50.9	28 11.3	16♋02.8
SEP 7	20 27.5	01♉09.0	01♎59.4	28 07.7
17	23 13.4	01R 18.2	05 48.6	07♌20.7
27	26 12.4	00 05.3	09 37.8	15 34.3
OCT 7	29 22.4	27♈23.9	13 26.5	23 33.1
17	02♐42.1	23 26.2	17 13.9	01♍26.7
27	06 09.9	18 55.4	20 59.0	09 10.7
NOV 6	09 44.6	14 50.9	24 40.9	16 37.9
16	13 25.1	12 07.7	28 18.6	23 40.7
26	17 10.2	11D 14.5	01♏50.8	00♎13.9
DEC 6	20 58.9	12 11.8	05 16.3	06 14.4
16	24 50.3	14 49.4	08 33.7	11 38.5
26	28 43.3	18 51.7	11 41.1	16 22.7
JAN 5	02♑37.0	24♈03.1	14♏36.8	20♎22.6
JAN 1	13S 18.8	27S 46.3	04N 45.9	25S 56.3
21	14 32.4	26 24.0	04 26.7	27 22.7
FEB 10	15 17.7	23 56.0	05 13.7	28 03.8
MAR 1	15 32.5	20 34.5	06 37.1	27 57.6
21	15 16.0	16 31.6	07 53.4	27 02.7
APR 10	14 29.5	11 57.6	08 34.0	25 17.3
30	13 21.4	07 00.4	08 31.0	22 35.7
MAY 20	12 11.2	01 45.7	07 46.2	18 40.6
JUN 9	11 23.9	03N 42.7	06 24.9	12 43.5
29	11 16.0	09 24.0	04 33.2	02 22.3
JUL 19	11 49.0	15 19.7	02 17.3	19N 51.4
AUG 8	12 54.6	21 32.2	00S 16.9	59 01.8
28	14 21.2	28 00.0	03 03.7	51 49.2
SEP 17	15 57.5	34 14.1	05 57.3	34 30.4
OCT 7	17 33.5	38 26.9	08 52.3	21 06.6
27	19 00.5	38 02.8	11 43.2	09 45.9
NOV 16	20 11.0	33 46.0	14 25.1	00 04.8
DEC 6	20 59.1	29 13.6	16 52.9	08S 04.9
26	21S 20.9	26N 13.5	19S 02.7	14S 54.4

1989	Psyche 16	Eros 433	Lillith 1181	Toro 1685
JAN 1	01♑03.5	21♈51.0	13♏28.1	18♎52.4
11	04 57.1	27 38.4	16 15.6	22 22.3
21	08 49.7	04♉17.6	18 47.5	24 55.8
31	12 40.3	11 38.6	21 01.3	26 23.3
FEB 10	16 27.9	19 35.0	22 53.8	26R 32.1
20	20 11.1	28 00.6	24 21.8	25 10.7
MAR 2	23 48.7	06♊48.8	25 22.0	22 13.5
12	27 19.5	15 54.8	25 51.2	17 48.2
22	00♒41.5	25 13.3	25R 46.9	12 26.4
APR 1	03 53.3	04♋38.4	25 08.1	06 57.8
11	06 52.7	14 05.7	23 55.8	02 12.1
21	09 37.1	23 30.1	22 14.6	28♍41.9
MAY 1	12 04.1	02♌46.9	20 12.4	26 35.7
11	14 10.4	11 53.0	18 00.1	25 47.8
21	15 52.6	20 45.6	15 50.4	26D 06.4
31	17 07.1	29 22.5	13 55.1	27 18.2
JUN 10	17 50.0	07♍43.3	12 23.8	29 12.6
20	17R 58.4	15 47.7	11 22.8	01♎40.7
30	17 30.7	23 35.9	10 54.5	04 35.4
JUL 10	16 27.4	01♎09.3	10D 59.1	07 52.0
20	14 53.3	08 28.7	11 34.8	11 26.5
30	12 57.3	15 35.2	12 38.7	15 15.9
AUG 9	10 51.8	22 30.6	14 07.9	19 18.4
19	08 52.1	29 15.9	15 59.3	23 32.3
29	07 11.7	05♏52.3	18 09.9	27 56.4
SEP 8	06 01.6	12 21.3	20 37.2	02♏30.2
18	05 28.4	18 43.6	23 18.8	07 13.1
28	05D 34.1	25 00.3	26 12.6	12 04.8
OCT 8	06 18.3	01♐12.4	29 17.0	17 05.5
18	07 38.2	07 20.5	02♐30.3	22 15.0
28	09 30.1	13 25.3	05 51.1	27 34.0
NOV 7	11 50.3	19 27.6	09 18.2	03♐02.9
17	14 34.8	25 27.7	12 50.4	08 42.1
27	17 40.4	01♑26.1	16 26.6	14 32.9
DEC 7	21 04.0	07 23.3	20 05.8	20 36.3
17	24 42.7	13 19.5	23 46.9	26 53.7
27	28 34.3	19 15.2	27 29.0	03♑26.9
JAN 6	02♓36.8	25♑10.6	01♑11.1	10♑18.1
JAN 1	21S 21.9	25N 37.0	19S 37.6	16S 43.2
21	21 07.1	24 08.5	21 18.9	21 58.8
FEB 10	20 25.8	22 41.8	22 35.3	25 47.9
MAR 2	19 21.9	20 24.3	23 24.1	27 09.7
22	18 02.1	16 53.7	23 40.4	24 39.5
APR 11	16 35.1	12 20.5	23 16.9	19 11.8
MAY 1	15 11.8	07 10.3	22 10.2	14 02.8
21	14 05.7	01 47.5	20 33.1	10 55.9
JUN 10	13 31.2	03S 30.7	18 57.4	09 47.1
30	13 41.4	08 32.8	17 53.2	10 05.1
JUL 20	14 38.8	13 10.7	17 32.1	11 21.6
AUG 9	16 05.3	17 17.2	17 49.6	13 15.6
29	17 27.3	20 45.7	18 35.0	15 30.9
SEP 18	18 18.1	23 29.5	19 36.2	17 53.7
OCT 8	18 28.0	25 22.0	20 42.2	20 11.1
28	17 57.0	26 17.5	21 43.3	22 09.6
NOV 17	16 46.6	26 12.2	22 31.7	23 34.6
DEC 7	14 59.5	25 05.1	23 01.1	24 09.6
27	12S 39.1	22S 58.2	23S 07.3	23S 36.1

1990	Psyche 16	Eros 433	Lillith 1181	Toro 1685
JAN 1	00♓34.3	22♑12.9	29♐20.1	06♑50.1
11	04 41.6	28 08.2	03♑01.7	13 51.1
21	08 56.9	04♒03.6	06 41.7	21 14.0
31	13 19.1	09 59.5	10 19.0	29 02.1
FEB 10	17 46.7	15 56.0	13 52.4	07♒18.8
20	22 18.5	21 53.5	17 20.6	16 08.1
MAR 2	26 53.5	27 52.5	20 42.4	25 34.1
12	01♈30.8	03♓53.1	23 55.9	05♓39.9
22	06 09.5	09 56.0	26 59.7	16 27.9
APR 1	10 48.8	16 01.7	29 51.7	27 58.1
11	15 27.8	22 10.5	02♒29.5	10♈06.7
21	20 06.0	28 23.4	04 50.6	22 46.6
MAY 1	24 42.6	04♈40.9	06 51.8	05♉45.7
11	29 16.8	11 03.7	08 29.9	18 48.7
21	03♉48.0	17 32.9	09 41.2	01♊40.0
31	08 15.4	24 09.3	10 21.7	14 06.3
JUN 10	12 38.0	00♉53.8	10R 28.3	25 57.8
20	16 55.1	07 47.8	09 58.9	07♋09.6
30	21 05.6	14 52.1	08 53.0	17 40.6
JUL 10	25 08.1	22 07.8	07 14.5	27 31.5
20	29 01.3	29 36.1	05 11.0	06♌45.2
30	02♊43.5	07♊17.8	02 54.4	15 25.1
AUG 9	06 12.6	15 13.7	00 40.0	23 34.5
19	09 26.4	23 24.6	28♑42.0	01♍17.3
29	12 21.8	01♋50.1	27 12.8	08 36.6
SEP 8	14 55.6	10 30.1	26 20.3	15 35.2
18	17 04.0	19 23.9	26D 07.6	22 15.9
28	18 42.6	28 29.7	26 35.1	28 40.8
OCT 8	19 47.2	07♌45.4	27 40.3	04♎51.5
18	20 13.6	17 08.7	29 19.8	10 49.7
28	19R 59.1	26 36.1	01♒29.9	16 36.6
NOV 7	19 03.9	06♍04.4	04 06.8	22 12.9
17	17 31.9	15 30.4	07 06.9	27 39.4
27	15 32.5	24 50.1	10 27.3	02♏56.4
DEC 7	13 20.2	04♎00.4	14 05.2	08 04.1
17	11 11.4	12 58.0	17 58.2	13 02.4
27	09 22.3	21 39.0	22 04.4	17 50.9
JAN 6	08♊04.8	00♏00.8	26♒21.9	22♏29.0
JAN 1	11S 59.3	22S 17.6	23S 04.9	23S 14.7
21	09 04.3	19 03.0	22 39.4	20 47.9
FEB 10	05 49.1	15 01.8	21 49.3	16 29.0
MAR 2	02 21.1	10 21.6	20 38.0	10 04.6
22	01N 11.7	05 09.8	19 10.8	01 39.4
APR 11	04 41.6	00N 26.3	17 35.2	07N 59.7
MAY 1	08 01.0	06 19.5	16 00.2	16 56.3
21	11 02.9	12 21.0	14 37.0	22 32.0
JUN 10	13 41.3	18 19.8	13 37.7	23 23.6
30	15 51.5	23 58.5	13 12.2	20 24.9
JUL 20	17 30.0	28 50.4	13 22.4	15 22.1
AUG 9	18 35.8	32 15.3	13 56.7	09 33.6
29	19 10.4	33 23.0	14 35.0	03 40.2
SEP 18	19 18.0	31 28.5	15 01.1	01S 59.5
OCT 8	19 05.3	26 16.7	15 05.0	07 17.7
28	18 39.8	18 13.9	14 40.1	12 10.1
NOV 17	18 09.0	08 15.4	13 41.8	16 33.6
DEC 7	17 40.6	02S 32.3	12 07.3	20 25.7
27	17N 26.7	13S 07.1	09S 56.6	23S 44.3

1991		Psyche 16	Eros 433	Lilith 1181	Toro 1685
JAN	1	08 R 39.1	25 ♎ 52.5	24 ♒ 11.8	20 ♏ 11.3
	11	07 ♊ 40.1	04 ♏ 03.5	28 34.4	24 43.9
	21	07 D 20.7	11 50.1	03 ♓ 06.2	29 04.7
	31	07 40.8	19 08.7	07 45.9	03 ♐ 12.0
FEB	10	08 37.5	25 56.3	12 32.3	07 04.2
	20	10 06.7	02 ♐ 07.8	17 24.5	10 38.4
MAR	2	12 03.9	07 38.2	22 21.6	13 51.2
	12	14 24.5	12 21.4	27 22.7	16 38.6
	22	17 04.8	16 08.5	02 ♈ 27.3	18 54.5
APR	1	20 01.2	18 49.6	07 34.5	20 31.9
	11	23 10.8	20 13.3	12 43.7	21 22.1
	21	26 31.2	20 R 07.3	17 54.5	21 R 14.0
MAY	1	00 ♋ 00.1	18 25.8	23 06.1	19 57.1
	11	03 35.8	15 15.2	28 17.9	17 23.5
	21	07 17.1	11 01.7	03 ♉ 29.6	13 33.5
	31	11 02.3	06 32.8	08 40.1	08 44.7
JUN	10	14 50.6	02 36.8	13 49.1	03 31.6
	20	18 41.0	29 ♏ 47.9	18 55.8	28 ♏ 39.4
	30	22 32.6	28 19.4	23 59.2	24 47.1
JUL	10	26 24.7	28 D 06.9	28 58.6	22 14.6
	20	00 ♌ 16.5	29 00.4	03 ♊ 52.7	21 06.8
	30	04 07.3	00 ♐ 47.6	08 40.2	21 D 17.4
AUG	9	07 56.4	03 17.4	13 19.8	22 36.0
	19	11 43.1	06 21.5	17 49.5	24 53.7
	29	15 26.4	09 52.8	22 07.1	28 01.9
SEP	8	19 05.6	13 45.8	26 10.2	01 ♐ 54.5
	18	22 39.7	17 57.0	29 55.3	06 27.9
	28	26 07.2	22 23.2	03 ♋ 18.7	11 38.9
OCT	8	29 27.2	27 02.1	06 16.0	17 26.7
	18	02 ♍ 37.8	01 ♑ 52.2	08 41.6	23 51.2
	28	05 37.3	06 52.1	10 30.0	00 ♑ 52.5
NOV	7	08 23.7	12 00.8	11 35.1	08 31.5
	17	10 54.2	17 17.7	11 R 51.8	16 48.8
	27	13 06.2	22 42.1	11 18.0	25 43.9
DEC	7	14 56.6	28 13.6	09 56.3	05 ♒ 19.0
	17	16 21.7	03 ♒ 52.2	07 56.5	15 43.2
	27	17 18.3	09 37.4	05 36.4	27 20.4
JAN	6	17 ♍ 43.0	15 ♒ 29.4	03 ♋ 17.4	11 ♓ 03.0
JAN	1	17 N 27.1	15 S 37.5	09 S 18.5	24 S 28.5
	21	17 46.1	24 49.0	06 26.2	27 03.8
FEB	10	18 30.0	32 24.5	03 06.3	29 05.7
MAR	2	19 27.3	38 22.8	00 N 34.5	30 38.3
	22	20 24.6	43 01.2	04 28.0	31 48.1
APR	11	21 10.5	46 38.1	08 25.5	32 39.9
MAY	1	21 36.8	48 46.2	12 17.7	33 04.2
	21	21 38.2	47 28.7	15 55.1	32 11.2
JUN	10	21 12.2	42 03.4	19 08.0	28 53.0
	30	20 18.9	35 42.6	21 48.0	24 06.3
JUL	20	19 00.3	31 02.6	23 47.7	20 16.9
AUG	9	17 20.0	28 14.1	25 02.9	18 14.1
	29	15 22.9	26 35.9	25 33.2	17 29.1
SEP	18	13 15.3	25 27.8	25 23.3	17 17.4
OCT	8	11 04.4	24 20.3	24 42.7	16 57.3
	28	08 58.7	22 52.8	23 44.8	15 49.7
NOV	17	07 08.1	20 52.2	22 43.2	13 23.8
DEC	7	05 44.0	18 10.9	21 45.9	09 39.6
	27	04 N 59.5	14 S 46.0	20 N 52.7	05 S 26.6

1992		Psyche 16	Eros 433	Lilith 1181	Toro 1685
JAN	1	17 ♍ 34.8	12 ♒ 32.5	04 R 25.3	03 ♓ 51.6
	11	17 R 42.6	18 27.9	02 ♋ 15.2	19 04.8
	21	17 15.7	24 29.8	00 36.5	08 ♈ 09.1
	31	16 14.6	00 ♓ 38.6	29 ♊ 40.8	00 ♉ 39.9
FEB	10	14 43.1	06 54.6	29 D 32.3	23 10.6
	20	12 48.8	13 17.8	00 ♋ 10.1	11 ♊ 59.7
MAR	1	10 42.5	19 48.7	01 29.1	26 25.0
	11	08 36.6	26 27.9	03 24.1	07 ♋ 32.0
	21	06 43.8	03 ♈ 15.5	05 49.0	16 29.3
	31	05 13.9	10 12.2	08 38.3	24 04.0
APR	10	04 13.5	17 18.7	11 47.7	00 ♌ 46.7
	20	03 45.6	24 35.3	15 13.1	06 55.5
	30	03 D 50.0	02 ♉ 02.6	18 51.3	12 41.3
MAY	10	04 25.2	09 41.0	22 39.9	18 12.0
	20	05 28.1	17 30.8	26 36.4	23 31.9
	30	06 55.4	25 32.3	00 ♌ 39.3	28 44.0
JUN	9	08 44.2	03 ♊ 45.4	04 47.1	03 ♍ 50.8
	19	10 51.1	12 09.7	08 58.5	08 53.7
	29	13 13.6	20 44.9	13 12.5	13 53.8
JUL	9	15 49.4	29 30.1	17 28.5	18 52.2
	19	18 36.3	08 ♋ 24.0	21 45.4	23 49.2
	29	21 32.5	17 25.6	26 02.8	28 45.7
AUG	8	24 36.6	26 33.0	00 ♍ 20.1	03 ♎ 42.1
	18	27 47.2	05 ♌ 44.4	04 36.5	08 38.8
	28	01 ♎ 03.1	14 58.2	08 51.6	13 36.1
SEP	7	04 23.2	24 12.0	13 04.8	18 34.6
	17	07 46.4	03 ♍ 23.8	17 15.4	23 34.3
	27	11 11.8	12 32.0	21 22.9	28 35.8
OCT	7	14 38.5	21 34.2	25 26.3	03 ♏ 39.3
	17	18 05.5	00 ♎ 28.8	29 24.9	08 44.9
	27	21 31.8	09 14.3	03 ♎ 17.7	13 53.3
NOV	6	24 56.4	17 49.2	07 03.6	19 04.6
	16	28 18.0	26 12.3	10 41.1	24 19.1
	26	01 ♏ 35.6	04 ♏ 22.9	14 08.8	29 37.4
DEC	6	04 47.6	12 20.1	17 24.8	04 ♐ 59.9
	16	07 52.6	20 03.4	20 27.1	10 27.0
	26	10 48.8	27 32.7	23 13.2	15 59.6
JAN	5	13 ♏ 34.2	04 ♐ 47.3	25 ♎ 40.2	21 ♐ 38.3
JAN	1	04 N 56.0	13 S 48.1	20 N 40.1	04 S 25.2
	21	05 16.7	09 30.5	19 57.3	00 16.7
FEB	10	06 30.7	04 35.7	19 32.4	03 N 33.8
MAR	1	08 17.6	00 N 49.3	19 22.4	05 25.3
	21	09 59.3	06 34.7	19 13.6	06 03.3
APR	10	11 03.0	12 27.0	18 52.1	05 52.4
	30	11 16.7	18 06.5	18 07.9	04 56.0
MAY	20	10 43.9	23 04.9	16 55.7	03 18.4
JUN	9	09 33.1	26 43.8	15 14.3	01 06.4
	29	07 52.5	28 18.9	13 05.3	01 S 32.6
JUL	19	05 49.2	27 14.2	10 32.2	04 31.4
AUG	8	03 29.3	23 20.9	07 39.7	07 42.9
	28	00 58.6	17 04.2	04 32.9	11 00.2
SEP	17	01 S 37.7	09 12.0	01 17.4	14 16.5
OCT	7	04 14.1	00 38.0	02 S 01.1	17 24.6
	27	06 45.3	07 S 49.1	05 16.7	20 16.3
NOV	16	09 06.0	15 30.0	08 23.6	22 42.9
DEC	6	11 11.0	21 55.4	11 15.8	24 34.4
	26	12 S 55.7	26 S 46.0	13 S 47.2	25 S 40.3

1993		Psyche 16	Eros 433	Lilith 1181	Toro 1685
JAN	1	12 ♏ 29.5	01 ♐ 55.2	24 ♎ 43.9	19 ♐ 22.0
	11	15 07.4	09 01.1	26 58.1	25 04.9
	21	17 31.0	15 52.5	28 48.1	00 ♑ 55.9
	31	19 37.5	22 28.8	00 ♏ 10.2	06 56.3
FEB	10	21 23.9	28 49.9	01 00.9	13 07.8
	20	22 47.4	04 ♑ 55.6	01 R 17.0	19 33.0
MAR	2	23 44.4	10 45.1	00 56.3	26 14.6
	12	24 12.2	16 17.7	29 ♎ 59.1	03 ♒ 15.9
	22	24 R 08.6	21 32.5	28 28.3	10 41.6
APR	1	23 32.4	26 27.6	26 30.8	18 36.4
	11	22 25.1	01 ♒ 01.1	24 17.7	27 06.1
	21	20 50.9	05 10.4	22 02.1	06 ♓ 17.1
MAY	1	18 57.0	08 51.4	19 57.4	16 14.8
	11	16 54.0	11 59.7	18 15.0	27 03.3
	21	14 53.4	14 29.0	17 02.2	08 ♈ 43.4
	31	13 06.6	16 11.3	16 23.1	21 09.7
JUN	10	11 42.7	16 58.1	16 D 18.0	04 ♉ 10.9
	20	10 47.6	16 R 39.8	16 45.2	17 31.4
	30	10 24.4	15 09.0	17 42.0	00 ♊ 53.5
JUL	10	10 D 33.1	12 26.1	19 04.9	14 02.2
	20	11 12.4	08 42.8	20 50.5	26 46.0
	30	12 19.8	04 27.6	22 55.9	08 ♋ 56.0
AUG	9	13 52.5	00 19.6	25 18.0	20 26.8
	19	15 47.5	26 ♑ 54.3	27 54.5	01 ♌ 15.7
	29	18 02.1	24 36.1	00 ♏ 43.2	11 22.4
SEP	8	20 33.6	23 32.4	03 42.1	20 48.7
	18	23 19.9	23 D 40.0	06 49.8	29 38.0
	28	26 19.0	24 51.2	10 04.7	07 ♍ 53.3
OCT	8	29 29.0	26 56.0	13 25.5	15 38.2
	18	02 ♐ 48.6	29 45.7	16 51.3	22 55.8
	28	06 16.1	03 ♒ 13.5	20 20.7	29 48.4
NOV	7	09 50.4	07 13.0	23 52.8	06 ♎ 18.4
	17	13 30.4	11 39.9	27 26.7	12 27.4
	27	17 14.9	16 30.9	01 ♐ 01.3	18 16.0
DEC	7	21 02.8	21 42.9	04 35.5	23 45.2
	17	24 53.4	27 14.3	08 08.4	28 54.8
	27	28 45.3	03 ♓ 03.6	11 38.8	03 ♏ 43.8
JAN	6	02 ♑ 37.8	09 ♓ 09.5	15 ♐ 05.5	08 ♏ 11.4
JAN	1	13 S 22.5	27 S 53.0	14 S 27.5	25 S 49.5
	21	14 34.8	30 28.5	16 21.5	25 39.2
FEB	10	15 18.6	31 25.2	17 36.9	24 16.9
MAR	2	15 31.9	30 58.7	18 02.5	21 29.7
	22	15 13.9	29 30.4	17 27.6	17 02.4
APR	11	14 26.2	27 23.9	15 55.0	10 38.1
MAY	1	13 17.5	25 02.4	13 53.6	02 04.4
	21	12 07.8	22 47.7	12 07.8	08 N 17.8
JUN	10	11 21.8	20 59.4	11 07.5	18 43.1
	30	11 15.5	19 48.1	10 59.5	25 54.1
JUL	20	11 49.7	18 59.0	11 36.7	27 14.7
AUG	9	12 56.1	17 56.4	12 47.5	23 16.1
	29	14 22.9	16 34.8	14 20.5	16 30.0
SEP	18	15 59.2	15 11.8	16 05.6	09 00.3
OCT	8	17 34.8	13 44.6	17 54.0	01 46.0
	28	19 01.3	11 57.9	19 38.1	04 S 51.9
NOV	17	20 11.1	09 37.5	21 11.1	10 47.4
DEC	7	20 58.7	06 34.6	22 27.8	16 00.0
	27	21 S 20.0	02 S 46.9	23 S 24.3	20 S 30.8

1994		Psyche 16	Eros 433	Lilith 1181	Toro 1685
JAN	1	00♑41.6	06♓04.5	13♐22.7	06♏00.4
	11	04 34.0	12 18.5	16 47.2	10 16.5
	21	08 25.5	18 48.2	20 06.0	14 07.5
	31	12 14.8	25 33.0	23 17.6	17 29.8
FEB	10	16 01.1	02♈32.7	26 20.6	20 19.2
	20	19 43.1	09 47.0	29 12.8	22 28.9
MAR	2	23 19.3	17 15.5	01♑52.3	23 51.9
	12	26 48.6	24 58.0	04 16.9	24 R19.1
	22	00♒09.2	02♉54.3	06 23.5	23 40.8
APR	1	03 19.3	11 03.6	08 09.5	21 50.0
	11	06 16.9	19 25.4	09 31.5	18 45.4
	21	08 59.4	27 58.8	10 26.1	14 38.0
MAY	1	11 24.3	06♊42.4	10 50.3	09 54.9
	11	13 28.5	15 35.3	10 R41.4	05 13.0
	21	15 08.1	24 35.7	09 58.1	01 09.6
	31	16 20.0	03♋41.7	08 42.1	28♎09.1
JUN	10	17 00.1	12 51.7	06 57.4	26 20.2
	20	17 R05.6	22 03.7	04 52.4	25 41.2
	30	16 35.0	01♌15.5	02 38.8	26 D03.9
JUL	10	15 29.2	10 25.5	00 29.2	27 19.1
	20	13 53.0	19 31.6	28♐36.5	29 18.6
	30	11 55.8	28 31.8	27 10.4	01♏54.6
AUG	9	09 50.1	07♍25.0	26 17.1	05 01.7
	19	07 51.0	16 09.6	25 D59.5	08 35.8
	29	06 12.1	24 44.4	26 17.2	12 33.3
SEP	8	05 04.0	03♎08.7	27 08.4	16 52.4
	18	04 32.9	11 22.0	28 30.4	21 31.6
	28	04 D41.0	19 23.9	00♑19.5	26 29.8
OCT	8	05 27.1	27 14.4	02 32.8	01♐47.3
	18	06 48.9	04♏53.7	05 07.3	07 24.2
	28	08 42.4	12 21.9	08 00.1	13 21.3
NOV	7	11 04.0	19 39.6	11 09.0	19 40.1
	17	13 49.9	26 47.1	14 31.7	26 22.5
	27	16 56.5	03♐44.9	18 06.5	03♑30.7
DEC	7	20 21.1	10 33.7	21 51.7	11 08.1
	17	24 00.8	17 13.6	25 46.0	19 17.9
	27	27 53.3	23 45.2	29 47.9	28 04.2
JAN	6	01♓56.6	00♑09.1	03♒56.6	07♒31.3
JAN	1	21 S 21.0	01 S 43.2	23 S 34.9	21 S 32.2
	21	21 07.6	02 N 55.2	24 03.6	25 14.1
FEB	10	20 27.7	08 02.8	24 10.6	28 19.6
MAR	2	19 25.4	13 21.6	23 59.2	30 48.0
	22	18 07.3	18 24.5	23 34.7	32 23.7
APR	11	16 42.0	22 33.8	23 04.0	32 17.1
MAY	1	15 20.5	25 04.5	22 34.0	29 26.2
	21	14 16.1	25 15.9	22 09.0	24 37.0
JUN	10	13 43.2	22 50.2	21 48.0	20 17.0
	30	13 54.7	18 03.0	21 26.2	17 45.4
JUL	20	14 52.5	11 35.1	21 03.1	16 56.4
AUG	9	16 18.2	04 15.2	20 45.1	17 19.2
	29	17 38.5	03 S 13.3	20 36.6	18 24.3
SEP	18	18 27.9	10 16.5	20 34.8	19 46.6
OCT	8	18 37.3	16 29.3	20 31.1	21 03.5
	28	18 06.5	21 33.9	20 15.8	21 51.9
NOV	17	16 56.9	25 17.7	19 40.5	21 45.8
DEC	7	15 10.7	27 33.8	18 38.8	20 16.2
	27	12 S 51.1	28 S 21.1	17 S 07.1	16 S 52.6

1995		Psyche 16	Eros 433	Lilith 1181	Toro 1685
JAN	1	29♒53.7	26♐58.2	01♒51.5	02♒42.4
	11	04♓01.8	03♑18.2	06 03.0	12 31.4
	21	08 18.0	09 30.8	10 19.7	23 06.1
	31	12 41.0	15 36.4	14 40.6	04♓28.2
FEB	10	17 09.4	21 35.0	19 04.9	16 35.5
	20	21 42.1	27 26.9	23 31.9	29 21.1
MAR	2	26 18.1	03♒12.4	28 00.8	12♈34.3
	12	00♈56.3	08 51.2	02♓30.9	26 00.8
	22	05 35.9	14 23.5	07 01.5	09♉24.6
APR	1	10 16.2	19 49.4	11 32.1	22 30.9
	11	14 56.4	25 08.3	16 01.8	05♊06.2
	21	19 35.6	00♓20.2	20 29.9	17 00.6
MAY	1	24 13.4	05 24.8	24 55.8	28 09.0
	11	28 48.9	10 21.0	29 18.3	08♋30.1
	21	03♉21.3	15 08.3	03♈36.6	18 05.8
	31	07 50.0	19 45.6	07 49.5	27 00.4
JUN	10	12 14.1	24 10.8	11 55.5	05♌18.6
	20	16 32.5	28 22.1	15 53.0	13 05.3
	30	20 44.5	02♈16.4	19 40.1	20 25.3
JUL	10	24 48.4	05 49.5	23 14.0	27 22.9
	20	28 43.2	08 56.5	26 32.0	04♍01.3
	30	02♊27.0	11 29.7	29 30.4	10 24.0
AUG	9	05 57.7	13 19.8	02♉04.6	16 33.3
	19	09 13.1	14 15.8	04 10.0	22 31.4
	29	12 10.3	14 R03.7	05 40.7	28 20.3
SEP	8	14 45.8	12 31.9	06 31.0	04♎01.3
	18	16 56.0	09 37.2	06 R36.6	09 35.6
	28	18 36.5	05 32.4	05 55.0	15 04.5
OCT	8	19 42.7	00 56.7	04 29.7	20 28.6
	18	20 10.9	26♓43.7	02 31.0	25 48.7
	28	19 R57.9	23 41.4	00 16.0	01♏05.3
NOV	7	19 03.8	22 17.1	28♈06.9	06 18.9
	17	17 32.7	22 D33.5	26 24.3	11 29.8
	27	15 33.7	24 22.1	25 23.3	16 38.4
DEC	7	13 21.4	27 30.2	25 D12.0	21 44.7
	17	11 12.4	01♈44.3	25 50.8	26 48.8
	27	09 22.9	06 54.1	27 16.5	01♐51.1
JAN	6	08♊05.0	12♈51.0	29♈23.9	06♐51.2
JAN	1	12 S 11.5	28 S 19.6	16 S 39.3	15 S 40.7
	21	09 17.0	27 23.9	14 29.1	09 24.1
FEB	10	06 02.0	25 17.9	11 50.1	01 03.1
MAR	2	02 33.8	22 15.0	08 46.2	07 N 59.5
	22	00 N 59.7	18 28.5	05 22.5	15 23.5
APR	11	04 30.5	14 10.0	01 44.9	19 12.5
MAY	1	07 51.1	09 28.6	02 N 00.2	19 14.7
	21	10 54.5	04 31.4	05 46.2	16 42.6
JUN	10	13 34.6	00 N 37.3	09 26.1	12 52.4
	30	15 46.2	05 55.1	12 52.6	08 29.9
JUL	20	17 26.1	11 20.4	15 57.9	03 57.1
AUG	9	18 33.1	16 48.5	18 32.7	00 S 35.8
	29	19 08.6	21 54.9	20 24.6	05 02.9
SEP	18	19 16.8	25 20.4	21 15.6	09 19.9
OCT	8	19 04.2	25 14.6	20 43.9	13 22.8
	28	18 38.7	22 13.5	18 47.7	17 06.7
NOV	17	18 07.7	19 10.4	16 17.7	20 26.5
DEC	7	17 39.2	17 42.5	14 28.0	23 16.6
	27	17 N 25.3	17 N 54.7	13 N 55.0	25 S 31.2

1996		Psyche 16	Eros 433	Lilith 1181	Toro 1685
JAN	1	08 R 39.4	09♈47.2	28♈15.4	04♐21.4
	11	07♊40.2	16 04.6	00♉41.2	09 20.5
	21	07 D 20.6	22 59.0	03 39.4	14 17.8
	31	07 40.8	00♉25.7	07 04.5	19 12.9
FEB	10	08 37.8	08 19.8	10 51.6	24 06.1
	20	10 07.3	16 37.6	14 56.5	28 57.4
MAR	1	12 05.0	25 15.8	19 15.9	03♑46.6
	11	14 26.3	04♊10.4	23 46.6	08 34.0
	21	17 07.2	13 18.0	28 26.4	13 20.0
	31	20 04.4	22 35.6	03♊13.3	18 04.4
APR	10	23 14.6	01♋58.8	08 05.5	22 48.4
	20	26 35.7	11 24.5	13 01.6	27 32.7
	30	00♋05.3	20 49.1	18 00.6	02♒18.5
MAY	10	03 41.8	00♌08.8	23 01.2	07 08.9
	20	07 23.6	09 20.8	28 02.8	12 07.6
	30	11 09.6	18 22.4	03♋04.6	17 21.3
JUN	9	14 58.5	27 11.3	08 05.9	23 02.6
	19	18 49.6	05♍46.3	13 06.2	29 32.4
	29	22 41.8	14 06.8	18 05.1	07♓31.1
JUL	9	26 34.4	22 12.1	23 01.9	18 18.8
	19	00♌26.9	00♎03.0	27 56.4	04♈25.7
	29	04 18.3	07 39.9	02♌47.9	29 10.9
AUG	8	08 08.0	15 03.6	07 36.0	00♊11.7
	18	11 55.3	22 15.4	12 20.4	26 11.6
	28	15 39.3	29 16.3	17 00.2	13♋39.7
SEP	7	19 19.1	06♏07.2	21 34.9	25 57.2
	17	22 53.9	12 49.6	26 03.9	05♌50.5
	27	26 22.2	19 24.4	00♍26.1	14 43.9
OCT	7	29 42.9	25 52.4	04 40.6	23 14.2
	17	02♍54.4	02♐14.7	08 46.1	01♍30.1
	27	05 54.9	08 31.9	12 41.1	09 28.4
NOV	6	08 42.3	14 44.8	16 24.0	17 04.2
	16	11 14.1	20 54.2	19 52.7	24 12.2
	26	13 27.5	27 00.4	23 04.6	00♎48.7
DEC	6	15 19.5	03♑03.9	25 57.0	06 51.8
	16	16 46.4	09 05.3	28 26.4	12 18.7
	26	17 44.9	15 04.8	00♎29.0	17 06.1
JAN	5	18♍11.8	21♑02.7	02♎00.9	21♎10.3
JAN	1	17 N 25.7	18 N 09.9	13 N 58.5	25 S 58.6
	21	17 45.0	19 38.4	14 49.2	27 21.4
FEB	10	18 29.2	21 11.8	16 19.8	27 58.3
MAR	1	19 26.8	21 54.5	18 05.8	27 46.6
	21	20 24.4	21 01.3	19 47.0	26 44.6
APR	10	21 10.5	18 15.1	21 07.3	24 49.5
	30	21 36.7	13 50.7	21 55.0	21 54.1
MAY	20	21 37.9	08 22.3	22 02.8	17 37.7
JUN	9	21 11.5	02 25.5	21 27.6	11 06.0
	29	20 17.7	03 S 31.2	20 10.1	00 N 12.9
JUL	19	18 58.4	09 08.1	18 14.0	23 00.0
AUG	8	17 17.4	14 12.0	15 45.3	53 18.6
	28	15 19.7	18 33.5	12 51.0	47 11.8
SEP	17	13 11.4	22 04.9	09 39.0	32 31.9
OCT	7	10 59.7	24 39.5	06 17.5	19 56.7
	27	08 53.1	26 11.8	02 55.0	08 58.1
NOV	16	07 01.4	26 38.2	00 S 19.6	00 S 28.7
DEC	6	05 36.2	25 58.0	03 16.4	08 28.1
	26	04 N 50.3	24 S 13.7	05 S 44.0	15 S 10.1

1997		Psyche 16	Eros 433	Lilith 1181	Toro 1685
JAN	1	18♍05.1	18♑39.7	01♎28.1	19♎38.2
	11	18R11.7	24 37.0	02 39.4	23 13.6
	21	17 43.4	00♒33.2	03 13.1	25 54.4
	31	16 41.2	06 28.6	03R06.6	27 31.8
FEB	10	15 08.7	12 23.7	02 18.8	27R53.7
	20	13 13.6	18 18.7	00 52.3	26 48.3
MAR	2	11 06.9	24 13.8	28♍54.6	24 08.9
	12	09 01.1	00♓09.6	26 37.1	20 00.1
	22	07 08.8	06 06.2	24 15.4	14 48.7
APR	1	05 39.7	12 04.3	22 05.0	09 21.2
	11	04 40.1	18 04.4	20 18.9	04 27.5
	21	04 13.1	24 06.9	19 05.8	00 43.9
MAY	1	04D18.4	00♈12.6	18 29.4	28♍23.1
	11	04 54.2	06 22.1	18D29.6	27 21.3
	21	05 57.8	12 36.2	19 04.5	27D28.1
	31	07 25.7	18 55.8	20 10.0	28 30.1
JUN	10	09 14.8	25 21.8	21 42.4	00♎16.6
	20	11 22.1	01♉55.2	23 37.9	02 38.3
	30	13 44.9	08 37.2	25 52.8	05 28.0
JUL	10	16 20.8	15 29.0	28 24.2	08 40.5
	20	19 07.8	22 31.6	01♎09.4	12 11.8
	30	22 04.1	29 46.6	04 05.9	15 58.6
AUG	9	25 08.2	07♊15.0	07 12.2	19 59.1
	19	28 18.8	14 57.8	10 26.5	24 11.4
	29	01♎34.5	22 56.2	13 47.2	28 34.4
SEP	8	04 54.5	01♋10.7	17 13.4	03♏07.5
	18	08 17.6	09 41.2	20 43.7	07 49.9
	28	11 42.9	18 27.7	24 17.2	12 41.5
OCT	8	15 09.4	27 28.6	27 53.1	17 42.4
	18	18 36.1	06♌41.8	01♏30.3	22 52.5
	28	22 02.1	16 05.1	05 07.9	28 12.2
NOV	7	25 26.4	25 34.3	08 45.1	03♐42.1
	17	28 47.6	05♍05.2	12 20.8	09 22.9
	27	02♏04.7	14 33.9	15 54.0	15 15.5
DEC	7	05 16.3	23 55.0	19 23.7	21 21.2
	17	08 20.7	03♎03.9	22 48.5	27 41.3
	27	11 16.2	11 56.4	26 07.2	04♑17.7
JAN	6	14♏00.9	20♎26.8	29♏18.2	11♑12.7
JAN	1	04N46.0	23S30.6	06S20.6	16S57.0
	21	05 07.8	20 31.2	07 48.5	22 08.5
FEB	10	06 22.9	16 42.8	08 11.5	25 58.1
MAR	2	08 10.3	12 13.6	07 20.5	27 30.8
	22	09 51.9	07 11.4	05 32.3	25 20.9
APR	11	10 54.9	01 43.5	03 32.9	20 03.5
MAY	1	11 07.8	04N03.4	02 06.9	14 48.6
	21	10 34.2	10 02.6	01 34.3	11 31.4
JUN	10	09 22.6	16 06.0	01 54.2	10 14.1
	30	07 41.4	22 01.8	02 57.8	10 25.8
JUL	20	05 37.6	27 31.7	04 34.7	11 37.9
AUG	9	03 17.6	32 05.9	06 35.5	13 28.6
	29	00 46.8	34 59.5	08 52.0	15 41.1
SEP	18	01S49.3	35 18.0	11 16.8	18 01.6
OCT	8	04 25.2	32 16.3	13 43.3	20 16.5
	28	06 55.8	25 45.6	16 05.4	22 12.5
NOV	17	09 15.7	16 19.2	18 17.6	23 34.3
DEC	7	11 19.7	04 58.5	20 15.2	24 05.2
	27	13S03.3	07S04.5	21S54.3	23S26.4

1998		Psyche 16	Eros 433	Lilith 1181	Toro 1685
JAN	1	12♏40.1	16♎14.7	27♏43.7	07♑42.8
	11	15 18.5	24 32.2	00♐50.2	14 47.9
	21	17 42.7	02♏21.1	03 46.5	22 15.7
	31	19 50.1	09 35.3	06 30.4	00♒09.4
FEB	10	21 37.5	16 08.2	08 59.6	08 32.7
	20	23 02.0	21 53.3	11 11.6	17 29.4
MAR	2	24 00.5	26 40.8	13 03.5	27 03.5
	12	24 29.7	00♐19.3	14 32.1	07♓18.2
	22	24R27.7	02 36.7	15 34.3	18 15.2
APR	1	23 53.2	03 18.2	16 06.7	29 54.1
	11	22 47.4	02R14.5	16R06.9	12♈10.4
	21	21 14.4	29♏29.4	15 33.5	24 55.6
MAY	1	19 21.3	25 27.3	14 27.0	07♉57.2
	11	17 18.4	20 59.1	12 51.0	20 59.3
	21	15 17.4	17 00.4	10 52.7	03♊46.4
	31	13 29.4	14 10.4	08 41.9	16 06.1
JUN	10	12 04.1	12 45.0	06 31.3	27 49.5
	20	11 07.3	12D39.3	04 32.8	08♋52.7
	30	10 42.2	13 41.6	02 56.5	19 15.2
JUL	10	10D49.2	15 38.6	01 49.6	28 58.0
	20	11 26.8	18 17.9	01 15.5	08♌04.3
	30	12 32.8	21 30.5	01D14.8	16 37.5
AUG	9	14 04.1	25 09.2	01 46.4	24 41.1
	19	15 57.9	29 08.2	02 47.6	02♍18.6
	29	18 11.5	03♐23.9	04 15.5	09 33.5
SEP	8	20 42.2	07 53.1	06 07.0	16 28.2
	18	23 27.7	12 33.4	08 19.1	23 05.6
	28	26 26.2	17 23.4	10 49.2	29 27.6
OCT	8	29 35.7	22 21.8	13 35.0	05♎35.9
	18	02♐54.7	27 27.6	16 34.1	11 32.1
	28	06 21.9	02♑40.2	19 44.9	17 17.3
NOV	7	09 56.0	07 58.9	23 05.7	22 52.3
	17	13 35.7	13 23.5	26 34.9	28 17.8
	27	17 20.1	18 53.7	00♑11.5	03♏34.2
DEC	7	21 07.9	24 29.3	03 54.0	08 41.5
	17	24 58.4	00♒10.1	07 41.5	13 39.7
	27	28 50.5	05 56.2	11 32.9	18 28.5
JAN	6	02♑43.2	11♒47.5	15♑27.2	23♏07.3
JAN	1	13S25.5	10S03.6	22S15.9	23S03.4
	21	14 37.9	21 26.7	23 29.1	20 29.3
FEB	10	15 22.0	31 28.3	24 21.3	16 01.4
MAR	2	15 35.9	39 51.3	24 53.8	09 27.2
	22	15 18.6	46 27.4	25 08.8	00 53.8
APR	11	14 31.8	50 29.7	25 06.7	08N46.1
MAY	1	13 23.9	49 50.3	24 44.7	17 29.6
	21	12 14.2	44 03.5	23 58.4	22 40.2
JUN	10	11 27.6	36 59.3	22 51.4	23 08.5
	30	11 20.3	31 44.0	21 42.9	19 57.3
JUL	20	11 53.5	28 40.1	20 54.8	14 51.3
AUG	9	12 59.0	27 06.7	20 36.9	09 04.3
	29	14 25.1	26 20.6	20 45.5	03 14.3
SEP	18	16 00.8	25 48.5	21 10.3	02S21.8
OCT	8	17 36.0	25 06.6	21 39.7	07 36.5
	28	19 02.1	23 58.1	22 03.0	12 25.6
NOV	17	20 11.7	22 12.2	22 11.3	16 46.2
DEC	7	20 59.1	19 42.8	21 57.9	20 35.5
	27	21S20.2	16S28.0	21S18.5	23S51.2

1999		Psyche 16	Eros 433	Lilith 1181	Toro 1685
JAN	1	00♑46.8	08♒51.2	13♑29.8	20♏49.2
	11	04 39.4	14 45.2	17 25.2	25 22.6
	21	08 31.2	20 44.6	21 22.2	29 44.7
	31	12 20.9	26 49.6	25 19.8	03♐53.7
FEB	10	16 07.5	03♓00.4	29 17.1	07 48.1
	20	19 50.0	09 17.4	03♒13.3	11 25.3
MAR	2	23 26.9	15 40.8	07 07.2	14 41.9
	12	26 56.9	22 11.1	10 58.0	17 34.0
	22	00♒18.4	28 49.0	14 44.5	19 56.1
APR	1	03 29.4	05♈34.9	18 25.5	21 41.0
	11	06 28.2	12 29.3	21 59.7	22 40.5
	21	09 12.1	19 33.1	25 25.6	22R43.6
MAY	1	11 38.5	26 46.6	28 41.1	21 39.4
	11	13 44.4	04♉10.7	01♓44.4	19 19.0
	21	15 26.2	11 45.8	04 32.9	15 40.3
	31	16 40.1	19 32.3	07 03.4	10 57.4
JUN	10	17 22.8	27 30.5	09 12.8	05 42.6
	20	17R30.8	05♊40.7	10 56.9	00 40.7
	30	17 02.8	14 02.3	12 11.4	26♏33.8
JUL	10	15 59.4	22 35.3	12 51.9	23 45.8
	20	14 24.9	01♋18.8	12R54.2	22 23.6
	30	12 28.7	10 11.5	12 16.3	22D22.3
AUG	9	10 23.1	19 12.5	10 59.2	23 31.6
	19	08 22.9	28 20.0	09 08.2	25 42.1
	29	06 42.4	07♌32.0	06 55.1	28 45.1
SEP	8	05 32.1	16 46.9	04 36.0	02♐33.9
	18	04 58.6	26 02.4	02 28.9	07 04.5
	28	05D04.4	05♍16.2	00 50.3	12 13.6
OCT	8	05 48.4	14 26.7	29♒51.1	17 59.8
	18	07 08.4	23 31.5	29D37.2	24 22.9
	28	09 00.5	02♎28.6	00♓09.3	01♑22.3
NOV	7	11 20.7	11 16.5	01 24.5	08 57.9
	17	14 05.7	19 53.5	03 19.2	17 09.3
	27	17 11.7	28 18.1	05 48.4	25 54.8
DEC	7	20 35.7	06♏29.5	08 47.3	05♒16.3
	17	24 15.2	14 26.7	12 11.9	15 25.6
	27	28 07.5	22 08.8	15 58.2	26 55.7
JAN	6	02♓10.8	29♏35.6	20♓02.9	10♓59.5
JAN	1	21S21.1	15S32.3	21S04.3	24S34.7
	21	21 07.4	11 23.2	19 49.8	27 07.0
FEB	10	20 27.2	06 35.7	18 08.2	29 05.7
MAR	2	19 24.5	01 16.3	16 02.7	30 34.8
	22	18 05.8	04N26.2	13 37.9	31 40.8
APR	11	16 39.8	10 20.3	11 00.1	32 29.4
MAY	1	15 17.4	16 10.1	08 16.4	32 53.9
	21	14 11.7	21 32.0	05 35.4	32 09.3
JUN	10	13 37.4	25 52.9	03 07.7	29 03.8
	30	13 47.4	28 30.2	01 06.9	24 17.9
JUL	20	14 44.3	28 41.1	00N09.5	20 19.4
AUG	9	16 10.2	26 00.8	00 23.7	18 07.3
	29	17 31.8	20 38.2	00S29.9	17 14.7
SEP	18	18 22.6	13 12.6	02 05.7	16 56.6
OCT	8	18 33.0	04 37.8	03 35.4	16 29.9
	28	18 02.7	04S12.8	04 20.7	15 15.7
NOV	17	16 53.3	12 33.5	04 07.3	12 46.0
DEC	7	15 07.0	19 48.4	02 56.2	09 11.2
	27	12S47.1	25S32.7	00S54.6	05S38.3

2000	Psyche 16	Eros 433	Lilith 1181	Toro 1685
JAN 1	00♓07.9	25♏54.1	17♓58.4	03♓31.9
11	04 16.0	03♐13.0	22 11.4	19 33.7
21	08 32.4	10 15.5	26 38.8	10♈47.8
31	12 55.6	17 01.4	01♈18.3	06♉17.0
FEB 10	17 24.4	23 30.4	06 08.1	00♊21.2
20	21 57.6	29 41.4	11 06.3	18 48.6
MAR 1	26 33.9	05♑34.1	16 11.6	02♋08.7
11	01♈12.8	11 07.1	21 22.7	12 11.0
21	05 53.0	16 18.9	26 38.5	20 15.9
31	10 34.0	21 07.6	01♉57.8	27 10.2
APR 10	15 14.9	25 30.4	07 20.0	03♌21.8
20	19 54.9	29 23.4	12 44.0	09 06.7
30	24 33.5	02♒42.3	18 09.2	14 34.0
MAY 10	29 09.9	05 20.5	23 35.1	19 49.9
20	03♉43.3	07 10.5	29 00.7	24 58.1
30	08 13.0	08 03.5	04♊25.6	00♍00.8
JUN 9	12 38.2	07R49.6	09 49.2	05 00.0
19	16 57.8	06 22.4	15 10.9	09 56.6
29	21 11.1	03 41.5	20 30.1	14 51.5
JUL 9	25 16.6	29♑59.2	25 46.4	19 45.5
19	29 12.9	25 44.5	00♋58.8	24 39.0
29	02♊58.5	21 35.7	06 06.8	29 32.5
AUG 8	06 31.3	18 09.3	11 09.7	04♎26.4
18	09 48.9	15 49.0	16 06.4	09 21.1
28	12 48.7	14 41.8	20 56.1	14 16.7
SEP 7	15 27.2	14D45.2	25 37.5	19 13.9
17	17 40.7	15 50.7	00♌09.1	24 12.5
27	19 25.2	17 48.5	04 29.5	29 13.2
OCT 7	20 35.7	20 30.3	08 36.4	04♏16.2
17	21 08.5	23 48.5	12 27.5	09 21.6
27	21R00.5	27 37.2	16 00.1	14 30.0
NOV 6	20 11.0	01♒52.2	19 10.4	19 41.5
16	18 43.8	06 29.6	21 54.7	24 56.5
26	16 47.3	11 26.8	24 08.3	00♐15.5
DEC 6	14 35.5	16 42.1	25 45.9	05 39.0
16	12 25.3	22 13.6	26 42.8	11 07.4
26	10 32.7	28 00.3	26R54.7	16 41.5
JAN 5	09♊10.6	04♓01.7	26♌19.2	22♐22.3
JAN 1	12S07.4	26S42.8	00S17.6	04S53.2
21	09 12.5	30 16.5	02N32.6	02 01.3
FEB 10	05 57.0	32 06.8	05 48.5	01N22.2
MAR 1	02 28.3	32 27.7	09 18.0	03 35.2
21	01N05.7	31 41.6	12 48.3	04 40.7
APR 10	04 37.0	30 15.3	16 06.6	04 50.4
30	07 57.9	28 35.8	19 00.7	04 08.4
MAY 20	11 01.5	27 08.5	21 19.7	02 41.0
JUN 9	13 41.6	26 10.8	22 54.7	00 36.3
29	15 53.0	25 35.1	23 39.7	01S57.4
JUL 19	17 32.6	24 33.4	23 32.9	04 52.0
AUG 8	18 39.2	22 36.8	22 36.4	08 00.2
28	19 14.3	20 26.3	20 56.6	11 14.7
SEP 17	19 22.2	18 32.7	18 42.6	14 28.7
OCT 7	19 09.7	16 47.0	16 06.2	17 34.4
27	18 44.9	14 49.0	13 20.9	20 23.8
NOV 16	18 15.5	12 22.2	10 42.5	22 47.7
DEC 6	17 48.6	09 16.5	08 29.0	24 36.3
26	17N35.4	05S28.2	07N00.7	25S38.5

2001	Psyche 16	Eros 433	Lilith 1181	Toro 1685
JAN 1	09R39.1	01♓35.4	26R39.0	20♐05.1
11	08♊39.3	07 45.1	25♌36.1	25 50.2
21	08D18.9	14 08.3	23 51.9	01♑43.8
31	08 38.3	20 45.1	21 38.0	07 47.3
FEB 10	09 34.6	27 35.0	19 11.6	14 02.5
20	11 03.4	04♈38.0	16 52.0	20 32.0
MAR 2	13 00.3	11 54.3	14 56.2	27 18.5
12	15 20.9	19 23.7	13 36.4	04♒25.7
22	18 01.2	27 06.0	12 57.9	11 58.0
APR 1	20 57.7	05♉01.3	13D01.3	20 00.4
11	24 07.3	13 09.0	13 43.8	28 38.3
21	27 27.7	21 28.7	15 00.6	07♓58.2
MAY 1	00♋56.8	29 59.8	16 47.1	18 05.0
11	04 32.7	08♊41.1	18 58.3	29 01.9
21	08 13.9	17 31.5	21 30.1	10♈48.8
31	11 59.3	26 29.8	24 19.0	23 19.3
JUN 10	15 47.6	05♋34.1	27 21.7	06♉21.7
20	19 38.0	14 42.7	00♍35.7	19 40.4
30	23 29.7	23 53.8	03 59.2	02♊58.7
JUL 10	27 21.7	03♌05.3	07 30.1	16 01.9
20	01♌13.5	12 15.5	11 07.0	28 39.1
30	05 04.4	21 22.4	14 48.8	10♋41.8
AUG 9	08 53.4	00♍24.0	18 34.3	22 04.5
19	12 40.1	09 19.1	22 22.6	02♌45.2
29	16 23.4	18 06.0	26 12.9	12 44.0
SEP 8	20 02.6	26 43.5	00♎04.3	22 03.0
18	23 36.6	05♎10.9	03 56.2	00♍45.8
28	27 04.2	13 27.5	07 47.8	08 55.6
OCT 8	00♍24.1	21 32.6	11 38.2	16 35.6
18	03 34.9	29 26.4	15 26.7	23 49.1
28	06 34.5	07♏08.8	19 12.5	00♎38.4
NOV 7	09 21.0	14 39.9	22 54.5	07 05.6
17	11 51.9	22 00.1	26 31.8	13 12.4
27	14 04.3	29 09.6	00♏03.0	18 59.6
DEC 7	15 55.1	06♐08.9	03 26.8	24 27.6
17	17 21.0	12 58.4	06 41.7	29 36.7
27	18 18.2	19 38.4	09 45.8	04♏25.8
JAN 6	18♍43.9	26♐09.2	12♏37.2	08♏53.9
JAN 1	17N36.0	04S11.5	06N46.0	25S46.4
21	17 55.7	00N28.9	06 40.5	25 31.2
FEB 10	18 39.3	05 40.5	07 33.0	24 02.8
MAR 2	19 35.5	11 08.5	08 48.4	21 07.8
22	20 31.1	16 30.8	09 48.1	16 31.2
APR 11	21 14.7	21 15.4	10 12.0	09 56.2
MAY 1	21 38.3	24 40.6	09 55.2	01 13.5
21	21 36.7	26 01.9	08 59.9	09N09.9
JUN 10	21 07.7	24 48.0	07 30.7	19 20.8
30	20 11.5	20 58.3	05 32.7	26 02.7
JUL 20	18 50.1	15 03.6	03 11.5	26 54.1
AUG 9	17 07.4	07 51.5	00 32.8	22 39.9
29	15 08.4	00 10.2	02S18.0	15 51.5
SEP 18	12 59.2	07S20.1	05 15.3	08 25.7
OCT 8	10 47.1	14 08.9	08 13.8	01 16.8
28	08 40.4	19 53.7	11 08.0	05S15.8
NOV 17	06 49.1	24 18.7	13 52.9	11 06.7
DEC 7	05 24.6	27 14.3	16 23.7	16 15.2
27	04N39.6	28S37.4	18S36.0	20S42.6

2002	Psyche 16	Eros 433	Lilith 1181	Toro 1685
JAN 1	18♍35.2	22♐54.9	11♏13.3	06♏42.5
11	18R44.1	29 21.4	13 57.4	10 59.6
21	18 18.2	05♑39.3	16 25.2	14 52.2
31	17 18.2	11 48.8	18 33.6	18 17.0
FEB 10	15 47.7	17 50.1	20 19.9	21 09.8
20	13 53.9	23 43.4	21 40.4	23 24.3
MAR 2	11 47.6	29 28.5	22 31.9	24 53.2
12	09 41.4	05♒05.7	22 51.5	25 28.0
22	07 47.5	10 34.8	22R36.8	24R58.8
APR 1	06 16.4	15 55.3	21 47.4	23 18.2
11	05 14.2	21 07.2	20 25.5	20 23.6
21	04 44.4	26 09.6	18 36.4	16 23.8
MAY 1	04D47.1	01♓01.8	16 29.5	11 43.8
11	05 20.3	05 43.0	14 16.3	06 59.5
21	06 21.6	10 11.3	12 09.5	02 48.9
31	07 47.4	14 24.9	10 20.6	29♎38.8
JUN 10	09 34.5	18 21.3	08 58.0	27 39.8
20	11 40.2	21 56.4	08 06.9	26 51.6
30	14 01.5	25 06.1	07D48.9	27D06.6
JUL 10	16 36.0	27 43.8	08 03.1	28 15.6
20	19 21.9	29 41.2	08 47.7	00♏10.1
30	22 17.2	00♈48.7	09 59.6	02 42.4
AUG 9	25 20.4	00R54.3	11 35.6	05 46.8
19	28 30.2	29♓46.5	13 32.8	09 18.9
29	01♎45.2	27 19.9	15 48.2	13 15.3
SEP 8	05 04.6	23 40.1	18 19.3	17 33.8
18	08 27.2	19 14.5	21 04.1	22 13.0
28	11 52.0	14 48.4	24 00.3	27 11.8
OCT 8	15 18.1	11 08.8	27 06.5	02♐30.3
18	18 44.6	08 50.1	00♐21.1	08 08.9
28	22 10.4	08D03.9	03 42.6	14 08.2
NOV 7	25 34.5	08 46.8	07 10.0	20 29.9
17	28 55.7	10 49.3	10 42.0	27 16.0
27	02♏12.9	13 58.9	14 17.6	04♑28.7
DEC 7	05 24.6	18 05.0	17 55.8	12 11.4
17	08 29.2	22 59.5	21 35.4	20 27.7
27	11 25.1	28 34.8	25 15.6	29 21.4
JAN 6	14♏10.4	04♈45.8	28♐55.3	08♒57.2
JAN 1	04N36.0	28S44.0	19S05.8	21S43.2
21	04 56.0	28 17.9	20 50.1	25 22.0
FEB 10	06 09.6	26 36.6	22 08.6	28 25.1
MAR 2	07 56.7	23 54.4	22 57.3	30 52.2
22	09 39.3	20 26.0	23 10.5	32 30.0
APR 11	10 44.2	16 24.7	22 40.4	32 32.0
MAY 1	10 58.9	12 01.4	21 25.0	29 53.7
21	10 26.9	07 24.3	19 42.3	25 09.2
JUN 10	09 16.5	02 39.9	18 06.7	20 44.2
30	07 36.1	02N06.5	17 07.0	18 05.2
JUL 20	05 33.1	06 48.2	16 51.8	17 10.0
AUG 9	03 13.6	11 08.0	17 15.4	17 28.3
29	00 43.3	14 17.9	18 06.6	18 29.8
SEP 18	01S52.4	15 00.4	19 13.3	19 49.1
OCT 8	04 28.1	13 15.3	20 24.7	21 02.8
28	06 58.4	11 03.8	21 31.7	21 47.2
NOV 17	09 18.2	10 01.6	22 26.2	21 36.0
DEC 7	11 22.2	10 31.9	23 02.3	19 59.3
27	13S05.9	12N23.4	23S15.7	16S26.5

1931	SAPPHO 80	AMOR 1221	PANDORA 55	ICARUS 1566
JAN 1	21♑52.5	29♓33.2	29♐40.3	25♑51.4
11	27 43.6	01♈50.1	03♑50.7	00♒23.0
21	03♒40.0	04 26.8	08 00.8	05 04.5
31	09 40.8	07 19.9	12 09.5	09 57.2
FEB 10	15 45.4	10 26.9	16 16.0	15 03.3
20	21 53.2	13 45.5	20 19.2	20 26.0
MAR 2	28 03.3	17 14.0	24 17.8	26 09.3
12	04♓15.0	20 50.7	28 10.6	02♓19.0
22	10 27.6	24 34.5	01♒56.2	09 03.6
APR 1	16 40.4	28 24.3	05 33.0	16 34.9
11	22 52.5	02♉19.1	08 59.1	25 10.0
21	29 03.2	06 18.5	12 12.3	05♈13.7
MAY 1	05♈11.6	10 21.8	15 09.9	17 21.5
11	11 16.9	14 28.5	17 49.3	02♉25.0
21	17 18.2	18 38.3	20 06.6	21 48.4
31	23 14.3	22 50.9	21 58.1	17♊13.6
JUN 10	29 04.6	27 06.0	23 19.5	06♋11.6
20	04♉47.7	01♊23.7	24 06.5	26 41.3
30	10 22.3	05 43.5	24R15.3	26♌26.0
JUL 10	15 47.2	10 05.5	23 44.3	28♍07.4
20	21 00.7	14 29.6	22 34.1	20♎25.1
30	26 00.7	18 55.6	20 50.8	04♏23.3
AUG 9	00♊45.0	23 23.6	18 45.5	13 51.1
19	05 10.9	27 53.4	16 33.5	20 59.9
29	09 14.9	02♋24.7	14 32.6	26 53.5
SEP 8	12 53.1	06 57.6	12 57.6	02♐04.1
18	16 00.4	11 31.6	11 59.6	06 49.6
28	18 30.9	16 06.4	11D44.2	11 20.0
OCT 8	20 18.5	20 41.8	12 11.8	15 41.1
18	21 16.1	25 17.0	13 20.4	19 57.1
28	21R18.5	29 51.2	15 06.2	24 10.1
NOV 7	20 23.5	04♌24.0	17 24.5	28 21.9
17	18 34.9	08 53.5	20 11.0	02♑33.7
27	16 06.5	13 18.9	23 21.6	06 46.1
DEC 7	13 19.7	17 38.5	26 52.3	10 59.9
17	10 40.4	21 49.8	00♓40.4	15 15.7
27	08 32.4	25 51.6	04 42.8	19 33.6
JAN 6	07♊10.2	29♌42.1	08♓57.1	23♑54.3
JAN 1	15S59.6	05S34.4	28S39.3	30S25.2
21	13 45.0	03 36.8	28 34.9	28 38.8
FEB 10	10 40.2	01 16.6	28 02.3	26 15.2
MAR 2	06 53.6	01N15.5	27 06.0	23 05.3
22	02 36.8	03 50.8	25 53.1	18 50.1
APR 11	01N56.3	06 21.7	24 33.3	12 46.6
MAY 1	06 31.1	08 41.4	23 18.5	03 16.6
21	10 52.4	10 43.4	22 22.3	13N12.2
JUN 10	14 45.7	12 21.6	21 59.1	32 18.0
30	17 58.0	13 30.4	22 19.2	22 54.0
JUL 20	20 18.7	14 04.3	23 18.4	06S25.4
AUG 9	21 41.1	13 58.1	24 26.3	18 57.6
29	22 03.1	13 07.6	24 55.9	24 21.5
SEP 18	21 27.8	11 29.3	24 21.8	27 20.6
OCT 8	20 02.1	09 01.2	22 51.8	29 10.4
28	17 56.8	05 42.7	20 41.8	30 15.0
NOV 17	15 29.2	01 36.1	18 00.7	30 42.8
DEC 7	13 12.9	03S10.7	14 52.3	30 37.4
27	11N51.1	08S18.5	11S19.3	30S00.6

1932	Sappho 80	Amor 1221	Pandora 55	Icarus 1566
JAN 1	07R45.0	27♌48.4	06♓48.6	21♑43.6
11	06♊48.6	01♍32.4	11 08.2	26 06.0
21	06D44.5	05 04.4	15 36.9	00♒31.9
31	07 29.0	08 29.3	20 12.8	05 02.0
FEB 10	08 55.9	11 55.4	24 54.8	09 37.5
20	10 58.8	15 45.5	29 41.4	14 19.4
MAR 1	13 30.9	20 39.1	04♈31.5	19 09.4
11	16 26.8	27 33.3	09 24.2	24 09.9
21	19 41.9	07♎47.4	14 18.6	29 23.7
31	23 12.0	22 04.0	19 13.7	04♓55.2
APR 10	26 54.2	08♏30.9	24 09.1	10 50.4
20	00♋46.0	23 00.7	29 03.8	17 17.4
30	04 45.2	02♐54.6	03♉57.4	24 28.6
MAY 10	08 50.3	08 24.2	08 49.2	02♈41.2
20	12 59.8	10 59.3	13 38.5	12 19.5
30	17 12.5	12 01.0	18 24.7	23 57.0
JUN 9	21 27.8	12 29.0	23 07.4	08♉12.7
19	25 44.7	13 04.4	27 45.5	25 37.7
29	00♌02.5	14 04.7	02♊18.5	16♊22.5
JUL 9	04 20.8	15 36.3	06 45.6	11♋57.0
19	08 39.0	17 39.7	11 05.5	11♌48.2
29	12 56.5	20 10.0	15 17.2	06♍47.1
AUG 8	17 12.9	23 03.2	19 19.4	28 58.5
18	21 27.7	26 15.4	23 10.1	17♎08.7
28	25 40.4	29 42.3	26 47.8	01♏15.8
SEP 7	29 50.4	03♑21.3	00♋09.7	12 17.9
17	03♍57.0	07 10.1	03 13.0	21 13.1
27	07 59.4	11 06.3	05 54.6	28 43.8
OCT 7	11 56.9	15 08.8	08 10.2	05♐18.0
17	15 48.3	19 16.2	09 55.5	11 13.5
27	19 32.4	23 27.3	11 06.1	16 42.0
NOV 6	23 07.8	27 41.8	11 37.2	21 51.8
16	26 32.6	01♒58.5	11R25.8	26 47.7
26	29 44.9	06 16.8	10 31.2	01♑33.8
DEC 6	02♎42.1	10 36.4	08 57.0	06 12.6
16	05 21.3	14 56.6	06 52.6	10 45.9
26	07 39.2	19 16.9	04 32.2	15 15.3
JAN 5	09♎31.6	23♒37.0	02♋13.5	19♑41.7
JAN 1	11N42.2	09S34.5	10S22.6	29S46.7
21	11 49.1	14 00.5	06 24.4	28 33.2
FEB 10	12 43.3	15 41.7	02 12.4	26 52.1
MAR 1	13 55.8	09 18.3	02N06.6	24 44.5
21	15 04.1	16N23.2	06 25.5	22 08.7
APR 10	15 53.1	36 53.3	10 36.6	18 57.8
30	16 13.7	37 53.9	14 33.1	14 51.7
MAY 20	16 01.3	33 09.4	18 08.4	09 01.1
JUN 9	15 14.6	24 57.5	21 17.2	00N17.7
29	13 54.8	14 48.3	23 55.6	14 33.5
JUL 19	12 04.8	05 03.6	26 02.1	22 56.7
AUG 8	09 49.1	02S46.6	27 38.1	05 23.0
28	07 12.8	08 26.7	28 48.6	10S36.7
SEP 17	04 21.6	12 12.7	29 42.6	19 24.9
OCT 7	01 21.7	14 25.1	30 32.7	24 13.9
27	01S40.1	15 21.5	31 31.7	26 58.3
NOV 16	04 36.3	15 15.9	32 46.0	28 27.1
DEC 6	07 18.5	14 20.3	34 02.0	29 02.6
26	09S36.3	12S45.2	34N43.7	28S56.7

1933	Sappho 80	Amor 1221	Pandora 55	Icarus 1566
JAN 1	08♎50.0	21♒53.0	03R07.6	17♑55.5
11	10 25.1	26 12.6	00♋58.5	22 20.5
21	11 28.1	00♓31.1	29♊16.4	26 43.7
31	11 54.1	04 48.2	28 11.0	01♒06.0
FEB 10	11R39.8	09 03.3	27 46.4	05 27.7
20	10 43.6	13 16.0	28D02.0	09 49.6
MAR 2	09 07.0	17 25.9	28 54.7	14 12.4
12	06 56.9	21 32.6	00♋20.3	18 36.9
22	04 25.3	25 35.6	02 13.8	23 04.2
APR 1	01 47.8	29 34.4	04 30.9	27 35.9
11	29♍22.0	03♈28.3	07 07.6	02♓13.8
21	27 22.0	07 17.0	10 00.2	07 01.0
MAY 1	25 57.7	10 59.7	13 06.2	12 01.3
11	25 13.8	14 35.6	16 22.8	17 20.4
21	25D10.3	18 03.8	19 48.0	23 07.5
31	25 45.0	21 23.3	23 20.3	29 35.9
JUN 10	26 54.2	24 32.7	26 58.0	07♈06.9
20	28 33.3	27 30.5	00♌40.0	16 15.7
30	00♎38.6	00♉14.7	04 25.3	27 56.5
JUL 10	03 06.3	02 42.9	08 12.8	13♉23.9
20	05 53.1	04 52.5	12 01.8	03♊31.8
30	08 56.5	06 39.8	15 51.7	26 53.5
AUG 9	12 14.1	08 00.9	19 41.4	19♋38.4
19	15 44.0	08 51.5	23 30.5	11♌10.2
29	19 24.8	09R06.2	27 18.1	09♍55.5
SEP 8	23 15.0	08 40.8	01♍03.4	04♎44.9
18	27 13.5	07 32.0	04 45.8	23 15.4
28	01♏19.5	05 39.3	08 24.1	07♏33.4
OCT 8	05 31.9	03 07.5	11 57.2	18 55.3
18	09 50.2	00 07.4	15 24.2	28 16.4
28	14 13.7	26♈55.6	18 43.3	06♐14.6
NOV 7	18 41.6	23 52.3	21 53.1	13 14.7
17	23 13.5	21 15.3	24 51.7	19 33.5
27	27 48.7	19 18.1	27 36.8	25 22.3
DEC 7	02♐26.7	18 07.3	00♎05.8	00♑48.5
17	07 06.9	17D43.9	02 15.9	05 57.7
27	11 48.8	18 05.6	04 03.6	10 53.6
JAN 6	16♐31.5	19♈07.8	05♎25.6	15♑38.7
JAN 1	10S11.0	12S10.4	34N44.8	28S48.2
21	11 37.0	09 58.3	34 12.6	28 00.4
FEB 10	12 02.7	07 28.1	33 09.9	26 47.9
MAR 2	11 10.3	04 48.0	32 04.1	25 16.7
22	09 00.0	02 05.6	31 02.9	23 32.9
APR 11	06 10.2	00N32.2	30 01.3	21 41.6
MAY 1	03 41.4	02 58.8	28 51.4	19 46.6
21	02 13.4	05 07.9	27 26.9	17 47.5
JUN 10	01 53.1	06 53.2	25 44.2	15 31.1
30	02 30.9	08 08.2	23 42.7	11 59.8
JUL 20	03 53.0	08 45.4	21 23.6	04 19.7
AUG 9	05 46.8	08 36.3	18 49.8	08N37.1
29	08 00.9	07 31.7	16 05.4	12 02.9
SEP 18	10 25.2	05 25.9	13 15.3	05S12.4
OCT 8	12 50.5	02 29.2	10 25.1	16 12.1
28	15 07.4	00S36.5	07 41.3	22 09.6
NOV 17	17 06.8	02 48.8	05 10.9	25 21.3
DEC 7	18 40.0	03 31.8	03 02.2	26 56.1
27	19S39.2	02S51.8	01N23.8	27S27.9

1934	Sappho 80	Amor 1221	Pandora 55	Icarus 1566
JAN 1	14♐10.1	18♈32.0	04♎48.0	13♑17.4
11	18 53.1	19 52.5	05 55.9	17 57.9
21	23 36.3	21 46.2	06 32.5	22 30.6
31	28 18.6	24 08.4	06R35.2	26 56.4
FEB 10	02♑59.5	26 54.8	06 02.5	01♒16.2
20	07 38.0	00♉02.4	04 54.9	05 30.8
MAR 2	12 13.1	03 28.1	03 16.8	09 40.3
12	16 43.8	07 09.7	01 16.1	13 45.4
22	21 08.7	11 05.5	29♍04.0	17 46.2
APR 1	25 26.1	15 14.1	26 53.9	21 42.6
11	29 34.4	19 34.5	24 58.2	25 35.0
21	03♒31.0	24 06.1	23 27.0	29 23.4
MAY 1	07 13.0	28 48.2	22 26.9	03♓07.7
11	10 37.2	03♊40.8	22 00.2	06 48.3
21	13 39.0	08 44.1	22D07.0	10 25.1
31	16 13.3	13 58.0	22 45.3	13 58.3
JUN 10	18 14.2	19 23.2	23 51.8	17 29.0
20	19 34.8	25 00.2	25 23.6	20 58.1
30	20 09.1	00♋49.7	27 17.3	24 29.0
JUL 10	19R52.4	06 52.9	29 29.6	28 08.7
20	18 44.5	13 10.7	01♎58.3	02♈13.6
30	16 53.6	19 44.5	04 40.7	07 32.9
AUG 9	14 36.3	26 35.7	07 34.9	17 18.2
19	12 17.3	03♌45.5	10 39.2	25♉18.7
29	10 22.8	11 15.5	13 51.9	25♌20.9
SEP 8	09 12.6	19 07.0	17 11.9	14♍04.2
18	08D58.4	27 20.9	20 37.9	19 34.1
28	09 42.7	05♍57.8	24 08.8	23 11.1
OCT 8	11 21.4	14 57.7	27 43.6	05♎30.7
18	13 48.9	24 19.4	01♏21.5	28 29.5
28	16 57.6	04♎00.9	05 01.4	14♏56.8
NOV 7	20 40.6	13 59.0	08 42.4	27 17.1
17	24 51.9	24 08.9	12 23.7	07♐09.9
27	29 26.1	04♏25.2	16 04.0	15 27.2
DEC 7	04♓18.7	14 41.7	19 42.6	22 40.0
17	09 26.3	24 51.7	23 18.1	29 07.0
27	14 45.3	04♐49.0	26 49.3	05♑00.2
JAN 6	20♓13.3	14♐28.5	00♐15.0	10♑27.8
JAN 1	19S47.8	02S31.6	01N05.1	27S28.4
21	19 55.8	00 41.1	00 17.6	27 08.0
FEB 10	19 18.8	01N41.4	00 18.3	26 20.2
MAR 2	17 56.5	04 20.2	01 04.7	25 16.0
22	15 51.7	07 02.9	02 16.4	24 05.9
APR 11	13 10.0	09 38.9	03 19.1	23 01.6
MAY 1	10 00.1	11 59.0	03 43.8	22 17.2
21	06 34.8	13 53.6	03 20.6	22 12.4
JUN 10	03 12.7	15 13.1	02 13.3	23 18.5
30	00 23.8	15 47.3	00 30.6	26 32.5
JUL 20	01N09.5	15 26.2	01S39.1	33 48.9
AUG 9	00 48.2	14 00.3	04 08.4	47 59.6
29	01S17.7	11 22.4	06 50.9	50 22.8
SEP 18	03 58.9	07 30.9	09 40.8	19 22.3
OCT 8	06 06.0	02 34.3	12 32.5	00N23.0
28	07 04.4	03S02.8	15 21.0	12S32.5
NOV 17	06 46.7	08 36.4	18 01.4	20 01.6
DEC 7	05 18.8	13 09.4	20 29.4	23 39.9
27	02S52.8	15S53.6	22S41.9	25S17.0

1935	Sappho 80	Amor 1221	Pandora 55	Icarus 1566
JAN 1	17♓28.3	09♐41.3	28♏32.9	07♑46.7
11	23 00.1	19 10.0	01♐55.1	13 03.7
21	28 37.7	28 14.7	05 09.1	18 02.3
31	04♈19.3	06♑53.3	08 13.2	22 45.8
FEB 10	10 03.7	15 04.4	11 05.2	27 16.4
20	15 49.4	22 47.4	13 42.6	01♒35.3
MAR 2	21 35.6	00♒02.8	16 02.8	05 43.4
12	27 21.3	06 50.9	18 02.5	09 41.1
22	03♉05.7	13 12.0	19 38.3	13 28.3
APR 1	08 48.2	19 07.0	20 46.9	17 04.7
11	14 28.4	24 35.8	21 24.3	20 29.4
21	20 05.6	29 38.3	21R27.8	23 40.9
MAY 1	25 39.6	04♓13.9	20 55.7	26 37.5
11	01♊10.2	08 21.3	19 48.5	29 16.0
21	06 36.7	11 58.6	18 10.5	01♓32.4
31	11 59.1	15 03.3	16 09.8	03 20.8
JUN 10	17 17.2	17 31.6	13 58.1	04 32.2
20	22 30.6	19 19.2	11 49.6	04R54.3
30	27 39.1	20 21.3	09 57.4	04 08.3
JUL 10	02♋42.5	20R32.5	08 32.5	01 46.3
20	07 40.1	19 48.9	07 41.8	27♒11.4
30	12 31.9	18 09.6	07D27.9	19 41.3
AUG 9	17 17.2	15 38.8	07 51.0	09 00.0
19	21 55.3	12 29.4	08 48.9	26♑11.8
29	26 25.6	09 00.7	10 18.3	13 43.6
SEP 8	00♌47.0	05 36.6	12 16.0	03 42.6
18	04 58.4	02 39.3	14 38.3	26♐35.7
28	08 58.5	00 23.6	17 22.2	21 44.5
OCT 8	12 45.2	28♒57.0	20 25.0	18 11.3
18	16 16.6	28 19.7	23 43.8	14 48.3
28	19 30.0	28D28.0	27 16.8	10 02.4
NOV 7	22 22.0	29 16.7	01♑02.0	01 13.2
17	24 49.1	00♓39.5	04 57.7	17♏33.0
27	26 46.7	02 31.0	09 02.6	24D52.4
DEC 7	28 09.8	04 46.4	13 15.2	08♐05.4
17	28 53.7	07 21.3	17 34.4	18 20.0
27	28R53.7	10 12.3	21 59.3	26 41.1
JAN 6	28♌07.3	13♓16.6	26♑28.6	03♑48.7
JAN 1	02S10.5	16S14.8	23S12.4	25S29.0
21	01N02.5	16 22.3	25 03.4	25 43.4
FEB 10	04 34.4	14 47.4	26 38.4	25 21.0
MAR 2	08 08.4	12 05.4	28 00.7	24 39.5
22	11 29.8	08 49.6	29 15.5	23 54.3
APR 11	14 25.6	05 25.8	30 27.0	23 21.4
MAY 1	16 45.8	02 13.7	31 32.9	23 20.9
21	18 23.1	00N30.2	32 18.8	24 21.2
JUN 10	19 13.2	02 29.3	32 24.5	27 06.4
30	19 15.4	03 22.9	31 48.0	32 47.7
JUL 20	18 31.6	02 46.4	30 54.7	42 54.6
AUG 9	17 06.6	00 22.3	30 12.1	56 37.7
29	15 07.2	03S26.1	29 50.5	64 00.3
SEP 18	12 41.5	07 21.1	29 44.5	59 06.2
OCT 8	09 59.1	10 09.5	29 42.8	51 33.4
28	07 10.8	11 30.9	29 32.8	42 37.7
NOV 17	04 30.0	11 37.8	29 03.7	18 07.2
DEC 7	02 13.3	10 48.2	28 07.5	17 21.6
27	00N42.6	09S17.2	26S39.5	21S30.9

1936	Sappho 80	Amor 1221	Pandora 55	Icarus 1566
JAN 1	28R36.3	11♓43.0	24♑13.5	00♑22.4
11	27♌26.9	14 52.8	28 44.7	07 02.5
21	25 34.9	18 12.2	03♒19.2	12 59.7
31	23 09.7	21 39.5	07 56.2	18 24.5
FEB 10	20 27.5	25 12.9	12 34.6	23 23.4
20	17 47.1	28 51.0	17 13.8	28 00.9
MAR 1	15 26.8	02♈32.9	21 53.0	02♒19.3
11	13 40.5	06 17.4	26 31.3	06 20.1
21	12 35.3	10 03.7	01♓08.2	10 03.9
31	12D13.4	13 51.0	05 42.7	13 30.1
APR 10	12 32.5	17 38.4	10 13.8	16 37.6
20	13 28.5	21 25.5	14 40.8	19 24.3
30	14 56.6	25 11.6	19 02.6	21 46.7
MAY 10	16 52.0	28 55.9	23 17.8	23 40.1
20	19 10.2	02♉37.9	27 25.4	24 58.1
30	21 47.7	06 16.9	01♈23.5	25 31.1
JUN 9	24 41.0	09 52.1	05 10.3	25R07.0
19	27 47.7	13 22.6	08 43.6	23 29.9
29	01♍05.5	16 47.3	12 00.6	20 21.6
JUL 9	04 32.5	20 05.0	14 58.2	15 27.2
19	08 07.3	23 14.3	17 32.6	08 45.5
29	11 48.7	26 13.1	19 39.3	00 45.8
AUG 8	15 35.5	28 59.3	21 13.8	22♑30.9
18	19 26.8	01♊29.8	22 11.0	15 10.8
28	23 21.9	03 41.1	22R26.5	09 31.8
SEP 7	27 19.9	05 28.7	21 58.4	05 44.9
17	01♎20.2	06 47.4	20 47.8	03 39.6
27	05 22.1	07 30.7	19 01.5	02 58.7
OCT 7	09 24.9	07R32.0	16 52.9	03D24.7
17	13 28.0	06 44.6	14 39.3	04 44.0
27	17 30.7	05 04.2	12 40.4	06 46.1
NOV 6	21 32.0	02 32.1	11 12.0	09 22.4
16	25 31.2	29♉16.9	10 24.3	12 26.2
26	29 27.2	25 38.3	10D21.7	15 49.2
DEC 6	03♏18.9	22 02.8	11 03.3	19 13.9
16	07 05.1	18 57.1	12 25.5	21 46.3
26	10 44.2	16 41.8	14 23.7	18R56.3
JAN 5	14♏14.5	15♉27.2	16♈52.3	02♑24.9
JAN 1	00N30.1	08S49.4	26S12.3	22S05.9
21	00 30.0	06 42.9	24 03.6	23 21.2
FEB 10	01 50.0	04 18.7	21 25.0	23 33.7
MAR 1	03 58.0	01 44.9	18 21.8	23 16.7
21	06 03.0	00N51.1	15 00.5	22 53.8
APR 10	07 30.8	03 22.9	11 28.4	22 46.4
30	08 10.2	05 44.3	07 53.2	23 19.4
MAY 20	08 02.3	07 49.5	04 22.7	25 06.1
JUN 9	07 12.2	09 33.2	01 04.4	28 53.1
29	05 46.3	10 50.1	01N54.0	35 27.6
JUL 19	03 50.7	11 34.9	04 25.1	44 11.3
AUG 8	01 31.8	11 42.5	06 20.6	50 27.4
28	01S04.5	11 07.7	07 32.4	50 27.3
SEP 17	03 51.9	09 46.0	07 55.0	47 23.0
OCT 7	06 44.2	07 35.1	07 34.7	44 16.7
27	09 35.0	04 42.8	07 01.5	41 38.6
NOV 16	12 17.8	01 42.8	06 56.6	39 03.1
DEC 6	14 45.9	00S20.8	07 42.8	35 36.9
26	16S53.0	00S36.7	09N19.7	27S40.5

1937		Sappho 80	Amor 1221	Pandora 55	Icarus 1566
JAN	1	12♏51.5	15R49.5	15♈49.6	08R06.9
	11	16 15.7	15♉12.4	18 34.2	03D04.1
	21	19 27.5	15D36.0	21 41.9	09♑12.8
	31	22 24.6	16 54.7	25 08.5	15 26.1
FEB	10	25 03.8	19 01.9	28 50.5	21 03.6
	20	27 21.3	21 51.7	02♉45.2	26 07.0
MAR	2	29 13.2	25 18.5	06 49.9	00♒40.8
	12	00♐34.9	29 17.8	11 02.5	04 48.3
	22	01 21.4	03♊46.9	15 21.5	08 30.8
APR	1	01R28.3	08 42.7	19 45.2	11 48.4
	11	00 52.3	14 04.0	24 12.3	14 39.7
	21	29♏33.0	19 49.7	28 42.0	17 01.6
MAY	1	27 35.0	25 59.2	03♊13.1	18 49.5
	11	25 08.2	02♋32.4	07 44.9	19 56.8
	21	22 28.6	09 29.5	12 16.7	20R13.7
	31	19 55.4	16 50.5	16 47.8	19 28.4
JUN	10	17 46.1	24 36.0	21 17.7	17 26.2
	20	16 14.5	02♌45.9	25 45.8	13 52.4
	30	15 27.6	11 19.8	00♋11.4	08 40.3
JUL	10	15D27.1	20 17.2	04 34.0	01 59.9
	20	16 11.6	29 36.2	08 53.0	24♑29.9
	30	17 36.8	09♍14.2	13 07.6	17 09.8
AUG	9	19 38.5	19 07.9	17 17.3	10 54.0
	19	22 12.1	29 12.6	21 20.9	06 13.2
	29	25 13.4	09♎22.4	25 17.5	03 10.8
SEP	8	28 38.9	19 31.4	29 06.0	01 36.4
	18	02♐25.7	29 33.4	02♌44.7	01D15.4
	28	06 31.0	09♏22.2	06 12.2	01 53.2
OCT	8	10 52.8	18 53.6	09 26.3	03 18.8
	18	15 29.4	28 03.8	12 24.6	05 23.6
	28	20 19.1	06♐50.7	15 04.3	08 01.1
NOV	7	25 20.8	15 13.8	17 22.1	11 07.4
	17	00♑33.3	23 13.2	19 14.1	14 39.9
	27	05 55.4	00♑49.7	20 36.5	18 37.3
DEC	7	11 26.5	08 05.0	21 25.0	23 00.0
	17	17 05.5	15 00.4	21R36.1	27 49.8
	27	22 51.6	21 37.4	21 07.9	03♒10.3
JAN	6	28♑44.2	27♑57.7	20♌00.6	09♒08.0
JAN	1	17S26.1	00S20.0	09N57.0	21S08.5
	21	18 57.1	01N31.2	12 21.6	18 32.7
FEB	10	19 54.7	04 18.2	15 06.4	19 56.6
MAR	2	20 14.4	07 30.4	17 58.1	20 22.4
	22	19 51.7	10 45.1	20 44.7	20 30.9
APR	11	18 41.9	13 43.3	23 16.0	20 54.6
MAY	1	16 44.5	16 06.0	25 23.5	22 06.3
	21	14 18.5	17 31.8	27 00.6	24 46.6
JUN	10	12 09.5	17 37.6	28 03.2	29 41.7
	30	10 59.4	16 02.7	28 30.0	36 55.2
JUL	20	10 57.4	12 37.5	28 22.2	43 38.8
AUG	9	11 48.3	07 33.7	27 44.2	45 41.0
	29	13 10.1	01 28.7	26 42.6	44 03.3
SEP	18	14 41.9	04S41.4	25 26.7	41 46.0
OCT	8	16 05.6	09 59.9	24 07.7	39 50.1
	28	17 05.2	13 49.2	22 58.7	38 11.3
NOV	17	17 27.3	15 56.6	22 14.6	36 30.0
DEC	7	17 01.8	16 29.5	22 09.2	34 23.2
	27	15S42.6	15S45.2	22N49.9	31S21.0

1938		Sappho 80	Amor 1221	Pandora 55	Icarus 1566
JAN	1	25♑47.1	24♑49.6	20R38.9	06♒04.0
	11	01♒42.6	01♒01.9	19♌13.5	12 23.5
	21	07 43.2	06 59.2	17 18.0	19 34.7
	31	13 48.3	12 42.7	15 03.5	27 43.5
FEB	10	19 57.1	18 13.1	12 45.0	04♓23.8
	20	26 08.7	23 31.1	10 37.8	19R03.9
MAR	2	02♓22.6	28 37.3	08 54.6	11♒34.9
	12	08 37.8	03♓32.0	07 44.0	11D36.7
	22	14 53.6	08 15.1	07 10.1	13 20.4
APR	1	21 09.3	12 46.8	07D12.6	15 23.0
	11	27 24.0	17 06.9	07 49.6	17 14.9
	21	03♈36.9	21 14.8	08 57.3	18 40.6
MAY	1	09 47.3	25 10.1	10 31.8	19 27.9
	11	15 54.3	28 51.7	12 29.3	19R22.9
	21	21 57.1	02♈18.5	14 46.0	18 10.4
	31	27 54.9	05 29.0	17 19.0	15 32.0
JUN	10	03♉46.5	08 21.1	20 05.6	11 10.0
	20	09 31.2	10 52.5	23 03.4	04 57.8
	30	15 07.9	13 00.2	26 10.7	27♑12.9
JUL	10	20 35.1	14 40.3	29 25.6	18 49.2
	20	25 51.6	15 49.2	02♍46.8	10 58.6
	30	00♊55.8	16 22.1	06 13.2	04 36.6
AUG	9	05 45.5	16R14.7	09 43.6	00 05.0
	19	10 18.5	15 23.9	13 17.1	27♐17.9
	29	14 31.9	13 48.5	16 52.8	25 58.3
SEP	8	18 22.0	11 31.9	20 29.8	25D49.0
	18	21 44.9	08 43.1	24 07.4	26 34.1
	28	24 35.2	05 36.5	27 44.6	28 02.3
OCT	8	26 47.0	02 30.9	01♎20.6	00♑05.1
	18	28 14.0	29♓44.4	04 54.5	02 35.8
	28	28 49.6	27 31.2	08 25.2	05 30.1
NOV	7	28R29.4	26 00.0	11 51.4	08 45.0
	17	27 13.5	25 13.2	15 12.0	12 18.0
	27	25 08.0	25D09.5	18 25.6	16 08.3
DEC	7	22 29.5	25 45.4	21 30.2	20 15.2
	17	19 41.0	26 55.9	24 24.0	24 39.0
	27	17 07.7	28 36.3	27 04.9	29 21.0
JAN	6	15♊10.6	00♈42.1	29♎30.1	04♒23.1
JAN	1	15S14.2	15S24.4	23N06.5	30S21.2
	21	12 47.1	13 31.4	24 25.5	24 40.1
FEB	10	09 31.3	11 03.8	25 31.5	12 20.1
MAR	2	05 36.4	08 16.4	25 49.6	10 45.9
	22	01 15.1	05 21.8	25 15.5	13 42.8
APR	11	03N18.3	02 30.1	24 03.4	15 38.0
MAY	1	07 48.6	00N09.4	22 25.4	18 05.3
	21	12 00.8	02 28.3	20 27.4	22 14.7
JUN	10	15 40.8	04 17.7	18 11.8	29 00.1
	30	18 36.3	05 27.6	15 40.5	37 05.6
JUL	20	20 38.2	05 45.4	12 55.5	41 33.3
AUG	9	21 41.4	04 57.3	09 59.3	41 09.9
	29	21 45.9	02 53.2	06 55.3	39 22.3
SEP	18	20 56.9	00S15.5	03 47.1	37 51.9
OCT	8	19 23.8	03 38.9	00 38.9	36 45.6
	28	17 19.9	06 10.9	02S24.9	35 48.8
NOV	17	15 03.3	07 18.4	05 19.7	34 45.6
DEC	7	13 01.2	07 07.3	08 00.6	33 21.8
	27	11N47.5	05S57.4	10S23.1	31S23.9

1939		Sappho 80	Amor 1221	Pandora 55	Icarus 1566
JAN	1	16R03.6	29♓36.3	28♎19.6	01♒49.3
	11	14♊29.6	01♈53.3	00♏36.1	07 02.6
	21	13 46.0	04 29.9	02 32.6	12 41.9
	31	13D53.3	07 23.0	04 05.7	18 53.4
FEB	10	14 46.9	10 29.9	05 12.1	25 46.7
	20	16 20.5	13 48.5	05 48.4	03♓37.0
MAR	2	18 27.8	17 16.9	05R51.6	12 48.0
	12	21 02.5	20 53.4	05 20.4	23 59.4
	22	23 59.3	24 37.1	04 15.3	08♈12.2
APR	1	27 14.1	28 26.8	02 39.9	18R48.9
	11	00♋43.0	02♉21.5	00 42.0	05 36.9
	21	04 23.3	06 20.7	28♎31.9	23♓28.4
MAY	1	08 12.6	10 23.7	26 22.6	15 02.0
	11	12 08.9	14 30.2	24 26.6	07 54.4
	21	16 10.9	18 39.8	22 53.9	00 08.1
	31	20 17.1	22 52.1	21 51.5	20♒13.4
JUN	10	24 26.4	27 06.9	21 22.6	07 29.2
	20	28 38.2	01♊24.2	21D27.3	22♑56.4
	30	02♌51.6	05 43.6	22 04.2	09 22.0
JUL	10	07 05.8	10 05.2	23 10.3	29♐01.0
	20	11 20.6	14 28.9	24 42.7	22 13.5
	30	15 35.2	18 54.4	26 38.2	18 19.0
AUG	9	19 49.1	23 21.7	28 53.6	16 28.5
	19	24 01.9	27 50.9	01♏26.5	16D05.2
	29	28 13.0	02♋21.4	04 14.4	16 44.4
SEP	8	02♍21.8	06 53.4	07 15.3	18 08.5
	18	06 27.7	11 26.5	10 27.4	20 06.7
	28	10 29.9	16 00.2	13 49.2	22 31.2
OCT	8	14 27.7	20 34.4	17 19.2	25 16.5
	18	18 20.0	25 08.1	20 56.4	28 19.1
	28	22 05.5	29 40.6	24 39.4	01♑36.3
NOV	7	25 43.0	04♌11.2	28 27.4	05 06.0
	17	29 10.9	08 38.3	02♐19.4	08 47.2
	27	02♎27.0	13 00.5	06 14.3	12 38.9
DEC	7	05 29.2	17 16.4	10 11.3	16 40.7
	17	08 14.6	21 23.0	14 09.6	20 52.6
	27	10 39.9	25 18.6	18 08.0	25 14.8
JAN	6	12♎41.6	29♌01.4	22♐05.7	29♑47.9
JAN	1	11N39.3	05S33.1	10S55.2	30S47.4
	21	11 45.7	03 35.5	12 47.9	27 42.5
FEB	10	12 36.8	01 15.4	14 11.2	23 08.2
MAR	2	13 45.1	01N16.6	14 59.5	15 45.4
	22	14 48.5	03 51.7	15 06.8	01 08.6
APR	11	15 32.3	06 22.4	14 32.5	11N38.6
MAY	1	15 47.7	08 41.8	13 31.4	01 10.6
	21	15 30.3	10 43.6	12 34.1	10S01.9
JUN	10	14 39.1	12 21.6	12 08.9	24 50.0
	30	13 15.4	13 30.1	12 27.0	35 45.6
JUL	20	11 22.5	14 03.7	13 25.9	36 44.8
AUG	9	09 04.6	13 57.4	14 56.6	35 24.0
	29	06 26.8	13 06.8	16 49.1	34 30.6
SEP	18	03 34.8	11 28.5	18 53.9	34 06.5
OCT	8	00 34.6	09 00.4	21 02.0	33 54.3
	28	02S27.1	05 42.1	23 05.7	33 39.2
NOV	17	05 23.1	01 35.7	24 57.5	33 10.4
DEC	7	08 05.3	03S10.8	26 31.5	32 19.7
	27	10S24.1	08S18.0	27S43.1	31S00.7

1940	Sappho 80	Amor 1221	Pandora 55	Icarus 1566
JAN 1	11♎44.0	27♌11.8	20♐07.0	27♑29.9
11	13 32.3	00♍47.1	24 04.1	02♒09.0
21	14 50.4	04 07.6	27 58.7	07 01.1
31	15 33.9	07 17.7	01♑50.0	12 08.2
FEB 10	15R38.8	10 25.3	05 36.6	17 33.7
20	15 02.0	13 52.0	09 17.2	23 21.7
MAR 1	13 44.0	18 17.8	12 50.3	29 38.7
11	11 48.5	24 41.3	16 14.2	06♓33.6
21	09 25.2	04♎28.3	19 26.7	14 19.5
31	06 48.6	18 41.2	22 25.9	23 15.4
APR 10	04 15.2	05♏44.9	25 08.9	03♈50.5
20	02 01.5	21 11.5	27 32.7	16 49.3
30	00 19.7	01♐51.0	29 34.0	03♉26.3
MAY 10	29♍16.5	07 48.7	01♒08.7	25 38.3
20	28D54.5	10 40.1	02 12.9	10♊46.5
30	29 12.1	11 52.8	02 42.9	19 18.8
JUN 9	00♎06.1	12 27.8	02R35.4	05♋37.5
19	01 32.5	13 07.9	01 49.5	21♌30.5
29	03 26.9	14 11.5	00 27.7	15♎02.1
JUL 9	05 45.7	15 45.0	28♑36.2	05♏35.6
19	08 25.4	17 49.6	26 27.2	15 03.1
29	11 23.0	20 20.8	24 15.6	21 04.4
AUG 8	14 36.1	23 14.3	22 17.2	25 46.8
18	18 02.8	26 26.8	20 46.2	29 55.2
28	21 41.0	29 53.8	19 51.5	03♐47.9
SEP 7	25 29.7	03♑32.7	19D37.5	07 34.3
17	29 27.4	07 21.4	20 05.0	11 18.8
27	03♏33.2	11 17.5	21 11.4	15 03.7
OCT 7	07 46.3	15 19.8	22 53.3	18 50.7
17	12 05.8	19 27.1	25 06.7	22 40.5
27	16 31.0	23 38.2	27 47.2	26 33.3
NOV 6	21 01.3	27 52.4	00♒51.3	00♑29.7
16	25 36.1	02♒09.0	04 15.7	04 29.8
26	00♐14.9	06 27.2	07 57.1	08 33.7
DEC 6	04 57.2	10 46.7	11 53.4	12 41.7
16	09 42.2	15 06.7	16 02.0	16 53.9
26	14 29.5	19 26.9	20 21.1	21 10.6
JAN 5	19♐18.6	23♒46.8	24♒49.3	25♑32.4
JAN 1	10S53.8	09S33.7	27S57.2	30S35.9
21	12 25.8	13 57.8	28 37.9	28 32.9
FEB 10	13 02.1	15 33.7	28 54.8	25 45.0
MAR 1	12 24.3	08 58.8	28 52.5	21 56.2
21	10 26.9	17N25.9	28 38.5	16 31.4
APR 10	07 39.4	38 23.7	28 23.4	08 09.5
30	05 01.3	38 49.5	28 20.1	06N37.7
MAY 20	03 19.5	33 41.8	28 41.6	30 30.8
JUN 9	02 46.9	25 16.4	29 35.3	41 02.3
29	03 15.5	14 58.7	30 51.6	00S14.8
JUL 19	04 31.1	05 08.9	31 56.3	20 15.6
AUG 8	06 20.0	02S44.2	32 10.3	25 23.5
28	08 30.3	08 25.6	31 25.8	27 57.9
SEP 17	10 51.2	12 12.0	30 02.5	29 36.6
OCT 7	13 12.8	14 24.4	28 17.2	30 41.9
27	15 25.4	15 20.5	26 13.8	31 19.1
NOV 16	17 19.7	15 14.5	23 49.3	31 28.6
DEC 6	18 46.6	14 18.5	21 00.3	31 09.5
26	19S37.9	12S43.0	17S45.4	30S21.0

1941	Sappho 80	Amor 1221	Pandora 55	Icarus 1566
JAN 1	17♐22.8	22♒02.9	23♒01.0	23♑47.1
11	22 12.6	26 22.4	27 33.7	28 11.9
21	27 03.2	00♓40.8	02♓12.9	02♒42.7
31	01♑54.0	04 57.8	06 57.5	07 20.4
FEB 10	06 44.1	09 12.8	11 46.3	12 06.2
20	11 33.0	13 25.5	16 38.3	17 01.9
MAR 2	16 19.9	17 35.4	21 32.8	22 10.0
12	21 03.6	21 42.0	26 28.9	27 33.8
22	25 43.2	25 44.9	01♈25.6	03♓17.9
APR 1	00♒17.3	29 43.7	06 22.5	09 28.8
11	04 44.3	03♈37.7	11 18.8	16 15.5
21	09 02.6	07 26.4	16 13.8	23 51.2
MAY 1	13 09.7	11 09.2	21 06.9	02♈34.2
11	17 02.6	14 45.1	25 57.4	12 50.2
21	20 38.1	18 13.4	00♉44.6	25 13.9
31	23 51.6	21 33.0	05 27.9	10♉26.7
JUN 10	26 37.9	24 42.5	10 06.2	29 11.7
20	28 51.1	27 40.5	14 38.8	23♊00.2
30	00♓23.9	00♉24.9	19 04.7	21♋38.8
JUL 10	01 10.0	02 53.3	23 22.5	15♌57.6
20	01R04.4	05 03.2	27 30.8	10♍44.4
30	00 06.0	06 51.0	01♊28.0	03♎17.9
AUG 9	28♒22.5	08 12.5	05 11.9	20 56.6
19	26 10.2	09 03.6	08 40.3	04♏04.7
29	23 53.7	09R18.9	11 49.9	14 06.8
SEP 8	22 00.1	08 54.2	14 37.3	22 10.5
18	20 50.0	07 46.1	16 58.6	28 58.9
28	20D35.4	05 53.9	18 48.9	04♐59.0
OCT 8	21 19.3	03 22.6	20 03.5	10 27.1
18	22 57.5	00 22.7	20 37.8	15 33.5
28	25 24.1	27♈10.9	20R28.0	20 25.4
NOV 7	28 31.5	24 07.2	19 34.0	25 06.9
17	02♓12.4	21 29.5	17 59.4	29 41.4
27	06 20.9	19 31.5	15 54.2	04♑11.2
DEC 7	10 51.6	18 19.9	13 34.3	08 37.6
17	15 39.7	17D55.7	11 18.2	13 01.9
27	20 41.9	18 16.8	09 23.5	17 25.1
JAN 6	25♓54.8	19♈18.5	08♊03.6	21♑47.7
JAN 1	19S45.3	12S08.1	16S42.0	30S00.7
21	19 41.2	09 55.8	12 56.2	28 33.6
FEB 10	18 50.6	07 25.5	08 51.6	26 36.3
MAR 2	17 13.5	04 45.3	04 34.2	24 06.4
22	14 53.0	02 02.9	00 10.9	20 57.5
APR 11	11 55.1	00N34.8	04N11.4	16 52.5
MAY 1	08 28.6	03 01.3	08 25.9	11 11.0
21	04 45.6	05 10.3	12 26.0	02 24.5
JUN 10	01 03.3	06 55.5	16 06.5	11N44.2
30	02N12.2	08 10.4	19 23.0	27 17.6
JUL 20	04 20.8	08 47.6	22 13.1	14 14.3
AUG 9	04 34.7	08 38.5	24 37.2	06S10.0
29	02 38.6	07 34.1	26 38.8	17 29.2
SEP 18	00S27.7	05 28.7	28 24.4	23 17.9
OCT 8	03 12.8	02 32.3	30 01.3	26 35.1
28	04 42.9	00S33.3	31 30.7	28 29.3
NOV 17	04 46.1	02 45.9	32 36.9	29 27.9
DEC 7	03 31.9	03 29.3	32 51.6	29 43.5
27	01S17.1	02S49.5	32N11.4	29S23.0

1942	Sappho 80	Amor 1221	Pandora 55	Icarus 1566
JAN 1	23♓17.2	18♈42.9	08R38.7	19♑36.5
11	28 34.5	20 02.9	07♊38.8	23 59.0
21	03♈59.0	21 56.2	07D21.6	28 22.2
31	09 28.7	24 18.1	07 46.6	02♒46.2
FEB 10	15 01.9	27 04.3	08 50.0	07 12.0
20	20 37.4	00♉11.7	10 27.1	11 40.3
MAR 2	26 14.0	03 37.4	12 33.1	16 12.0
12	01♉50.5	07 18.9	15 03.0	20 48.6
22	07 26.5	11 14.8	17 52.6	25 31.7
APR 1	13 01.0	15 23.5	20 58.6	00♓23.5
11	18 33.5	19 43.9	24 17.5	05 27.4
21	24 03.7	24 15.7	27 47.0	10 48.0
MAY 1	29 31.0	28 58.0	01♋25.0	16 31.6
11	04♊55.1	03♊50.9	05 09.7	22 47.9
21	10 15.8	08 54.5	08 59.6	29 51.0
31	15 32.7	14 08.7	12 53.5	08♈01.9
JUN 10	20 45.7	19 34.2	16 50.2	17 52.6
20	25 54.4	25 11.7	20 49.0	00♉07.2
30	00♋58.6	01♋01.7	24 49.0	15 35.1
JUL 10	05 57.9	07 05.4	28 49.3	04♊37.2
20	10 52.2	13 23.9	02♌49.6	26 11.2
30	15 40.9	19 58.3	06 48.8	18♋54.5
AUG 9	20 23.6	26 50.1	10 46.6	17♌21.0
19	24 59.7	04♌00.7	14 42.1	15♍14.6
29	29 28.4	11 31.5	18 34.6	06♎50.7
SEP 8	03♌49.0	19 23.7	22 23.3	23 53.0
18	08 00.3	27 38.5	26 07.3	07♏16.4
28	12 00.9	06♍16.1	29 45.5	17 59.8
OCT 8	15 49.3	15 16.7	03♍16.8	26 52.2
18	19 23.3	24 39.1	06 39.6	04♐28.4
28	22 40.6	04♎21.0	09 52.3	11 11.3
NOV 7	25 38.2	14 19.4	12 53.1	17 16.7
17	28 12.4	24 29.5	15 39.5	22 55.0
27	00♍19.3	04♏45.7	18 08.8	28 13.3
DEC 7	01 54.1	15 01.9	20 18.3	03♑16.5
17	02 51.7	25 11.4	22 04.2	08 08.4
27	03R07.7	05♐08.0	23 23.1	12 51.2
JAN 6	02♍38.7	14♐46.6	24♍11.3	17♑26.9
JAN 1	00S36.1	02S29.3	31N56.6	29S12.9
21	02N27.3	00 39.0	30 58.7	28 14.5
FEB 10	05 48.6	01N43.5	30 20.3	26 50.9
MAR 2	09 10.7	04 22.2	30 03.5	25 06.4
22	12 18.7	07 04.8	29 57.5	23 04.3
APR 11	15 00.3	09 40.7	29 48.9	20 46.2
MAY 1	17 05.8	12 00.6	29 27.0	18 08.7
21	18 28.7	13 54.9	28 44.8	14 56.6
JUN 10	19 05.4	15 14.0	27 38.7	10 24.2
30	18 55.6	15 47.7	26 08.1	02 38.4
JUL 20	18 01.7	15 25.8	24 15.1	09N55.6
AUG 9	16 28.6	13 59.0	22 03.2	18 42.2
29	14 23.0	11 20.2	19 37.6	01 54.0
SEP 18	11 52.8	07 27.8	17 04.3	12S11.6
OCT 8	09 07.1	02 30.4	14 30.2	20 04.9
28	06 16.4	03S07.0	12 03.4	24 24.9
NOV 17	03 33.0	08 40.0	09 52.8	26 46.0
DEC 7	01 12.8	13 11.9	08 08.3	27 52.4
27	00S23.4	15S54.6	07N01.0	28S06.7

1943		Sappho 80	Amor 1221	Pandora 55	Icarus 1566
JAN	1	02R59.0	09♐59.8	23♍51.2	15♑09.8
	11	02♍06.8	19 27.7	24 22.7	19 42.6
	21	00 30.6	28 31.6	24R18.8	24 10.0
	31	28♌17.5	07♑09.2	23 38.6	28 33.0
FEB	10	25 40.5	15 19.4	22 23.1	02♒52.4
	20	22 57.9	23 01.7	20 37.9	07 08.5
MAR	2	20 28.3	00♒16.3	18 31.9	11 22.0
	12	18 27.2	07 03.7	16 17.4	15 33.4
	22	17 04.8	13 24.4	14 08.4	19 42.9
APR	1	16 24.8	19 18.9	12 17.1	23 51.3
	11	16D26.6	24 47.4	10 53.0	27 59.4
	21	17 07.1	29 49.6	10 01.6	02♓07.7
MAY	1	18 21.2	04♓25.1	09D44.3	06 18.1
	11	20 04.7	08 32.5	10 00.5	10 32.0
	21	22 12.7	12 09.9	10 47.7	14 52.4
	31	24 41.4	15 14.9	12 02.3	19 23.9
JUN	10	27 27.4	17 43.6	13 41.2	24 13.6
	20	00♍27.9	19 31.8	15 40.9	29 33.9
	30	03 40.4	20 34.7	17 58.3	05♈48.2
JUL	10	07 03.2	20R46.8	20 31.0	13 40.7
	20	10 34.4	20 04.3	23 16.5	24 46.4
	30	14 12.8	18 26.2	26 12.9	12♉29.9
AUG	9	17 57.3	15 56.5	29 18.6	11♊42.1
	19	21 46.9	12 47.8	02♎31.9	16♋42.2
	29	25 40.6	09 19.5	05 51.8	11♌43.4
SEP	8	29 37.8	05 55.2	09 17.0	27 20.6
	18	03♎37.7	02 57.2	12 46.4	13♍14.4
	28	07 39.7	00 40.5	16 19.2	09♎35.0
OCT	8	11 43.0	29♒12.7	19 54.5	29 29.1
	18	15 47.0	28 34.4	23 31.1	14♏06.8
	28	19 51.1	28D41.6	27 08.4	25 33.0
NOV	7	23 54.3	29 29.3	00♏45.4	04♐55.3
	17	27 55.9	00♓51.4	04 20.8	12 54.0
	27	01♏54.9	02 42.2	07 53.9	19 55.0
DEC	7	05 50.3	04 57.0	11 23.3	26 14.4
	17	09 40.8	07 31.5	14 47.7	02♑03.0
	27	13 25.2	10 22.0	18 05.7	07 28.4
JAN	6	17♏01.7	13♓25.9	21♏15.5	12♑35.6
JAN	1	00S37.8	16S15.4	06N51.1	28S03.9
	21	00 45.9	16 21.8	06 43.2	27 32.1
FEB	10	00N28.6	14 46.1	07 24.3	26 34.6
MAR	2	02 38.6	12 03.8	08 37.1	25 20.3
	22	04 52.2	08 47.9	09 46.7	23 57.9
APR	11	06 29.5	05 24.3	10 19.8	22 36.8
MAY	1	07 16.4	02 12.5	10 03.6	21 27.9
	21	07 13.4	00N31.3	09 02.2	20 44.9
JUN	10	06 26.4	02 30.3	07 24.4	20 46.4
	30	05 02.4	03 24.1	05 18.5	21 58.1
JUL	20	03 08.1	02 48.1	02 51.3	24 32.8
AUG	9	00 50.2	00 24.8	00 08.3	24 18.9
	29	01S45.0	03S23.1	02S45.4	08 30.5
SEP	18	04 31.2	07 18.2	05 45.1	06N40.5
OCT	8	07 21.9	10 07.0	08 46.1	07S06.7
	28	10 10.5	11 28.8	11 43.9	17 18.7
NOV	17	12 50.6	11 35.8	14 34.0	22 33.2
DEC	7	15 15.5	10 46.3	17 12.7	25 10.1
	27	17S18.6	09S15.3	19S36.7	26S16.4

1944		Sappho 80	Amor 1221	Pandora 55	Icarus 1566
JAN	1	15♏14.6	11♓52.5	19♏41.7	10♑04.1
	11	18 46.5	15 02.0	22 46.8	15 03.4
	21	22 07.7	18 21.2	25 40.8	19 49.4
	31	25 15.7	21 48.2	28 21.5	24 24.2
FEB	10	28 07.7	25 21.4	00♐46.2	28 49.1
	20	00♐40.7	28 59.5	02 52.1	03♒05.1
MAR	1	02 50.4	02♈41.3	04 35.8	07 12.8
	11	04 32.7	06 25.7	05 53.9	11 12.4
	21	05 42.9	10 11.9	06 43.0	15 04.1
	31	06 15.7	13 59.1	06 59.6	18 47.5
APR	10	06R07.1	17 46.6	06R41.8	22 22.0
	20	05 14.8	21 33.7	05 49.0	25 47.0
	30	03 39.6	25 19.8	04 23.7	29 01.0
MAY	10	01 28.6	29 04.2	02 32.1	02♓02.0
	20	28♏54.3	02♉46.3	00 24.2	04 47.7
	30	26 14.6	06 25.5	28♏12.6	07 13.8
JUN	9	23 49.4	10 00.8	26 11.0	09 14.6
	19	21 55.0	13 31.5	24 30.9	10 41.5
	29	20 42.7	16 56.5	23 21.0	11 20.1
JUL	9	20D17.5	20 14.5	22 45.7	10R48.2
	19	20 39.2	23 24.1	22D46.2	08 26.6
	29	21 45.2	26 23.4	23 21.6	03 06.3
AUG	8	23 31.0	29 09.9	24 29.1	22♒54.4
	18	25 51.7	01♊41.1	26 05.4	05 44.4
	28	28 43.2	03 53.0	28 07.4	13♑11.6
SEP	7	02♐01.3	05 41.5	00♐31.9	22♐36.3
	17	05 42.6	07 01.1	03 15.9	07 52.0
	27	09 44.3	07 45.4	06 16.9	27♏13.0
OCT	7	14 04.0	07R47.9	09 32.6	17 50.0
	17	18 39.5	07 01.8	13 01.2	07 42.1
	27	23 29.4	05 22.6	16 40.9	27♎48.5
NOV	6	28 31.9	02 51.4	20 30.2	05D41.9
	16	03♑46.0	29♉36.8	24 27.8	22♏44.1
	26	09 10.4	25 58.0	28 32.5	05♐16.7
DEC	6	14 44.0	22 21.8	02♑43.2	15 06.1
	16	20 25.9	19 14.8	06 59.0	23 16.0
	26	26 15.4	16 58.0	11 18.8	00♑19.7
JAN	5	02♒11.2	15♉42.0	15♑41.8	06♑36.9
JAN	1	17S45.3	08S47.4	20S10.1	26S23.2
	21	19 13.3	06 41.0	22 13.4	26 22.2
FEB	10	20 08.1	04 16.8	24 00.0	25 49.1
MAR	1	20 26.2	01 43.0	25 31.6	24 58.4
	21	20 04.4	00N53.0	26 49.0	24 03.4
APR	10	18 59.9	03 24.7	27 49.5	23 18.4
	30	17 12.1	05 46.0	28 22.9	23 01.2
MAY	20	14 54.0	07 51.2	28 16.4	23 37.0
JUN	9	12 43.6	09 34.7	27 32.9	25 46.8
	29	11 24.9	10 51.4	26 39.0	30 42.3
JUL	19	11 13.6	11 36.1	26 04.1	40 31.1
AUG	8	11 57.4	11 43.6	26 00.5	57 51.7
	28	13 13.8	11 08.8	26 24.8	77 05.6
SEP	17	14 40.8	09 47.1	27 06.3	65 37.6
OCT	7	15 59.1	07 36.3	27 52.5	45 03.9
	27	16 52.2	04 44.2	28 31.5	15 32.7
NOV	16	17 06.4	01 44.1	28 52.9	13 59.3
DEC	6	16 31.7	00S19.8	28 48.8	20 26.8
	26	15S02.5	00S36.2	28S13.8	23S18.6

1945		Sappho 80	Amor 1221	Pandora 55	Icarus 1566
JAN	1	29♑48.2	16R04.9	13♑56.3	04♑10.7
	11	05♒47.5	15♉26.4	18 20.8	10 06.3
	21	11 52.2	15D48.9	22 47.2	15 32.6
	31	18 01.0	17 06.9	27 14.6	20 35.6
FEB	10	24 13.5	19 13.5	01♒42.1	25 19.5
	20	00♓28.6	22 03.0	06 09.0	29 46.6
MAR	2	06 45.5	25 29.6	10 34.3	03♒58.4
	12	13 03.6	29 29.1	14 57.2	07 56.0
	22	19 21.9	03♊58.3	19 16.8	11 39.2
APR	1	25 39.6	08 54.6	23 31.8	15 07.6
	11	01♈56.1	14 16.4	27 41.4	18 20.2
	21	08 10.4	20 02.8	01♓44.1	21 14.8
MAY	1	14 21.8	26 13.1	05 38.3	23 48.6
	11	20 29.7	02♋47.3	09 22.5	25 57.6
	21	26 33.2	09 45.6	12 54.4	27 35.5
	31	02♉31.3	17 08.0	16 11.6	28 34.4
JUN	10	08 23.6	24 54.9	19 11.3	28R43.0
	20	14 08.8	03♌06.5	21 49.8	27 45.2
	30	19 46.2	11 42.2	24 03.4	25 21.6
JUL	10	25 14.7	20 41.4	25 47.6	21 09.7
	20	00♊33.0	00♍02.3	26 57.3	14 53.6
	30	05 39.7	09 42.2	27 28.6	06 42.8
AUG	9	10 33.2	19 37.6	27R17.9	27♑29.3
	19	15 11.3	29 43.8	26 24.9	18 39.1
	29	19 31.7	09♎54.8	24 54.0	11 25.3
SEP	8	23 31.3	20 04.6	22 54.7	06 16.8
	18	27 06.2	00♏07.0	20 42.8	03 07.9
	28	00♋12.2	09 55.8	18 36.9	01 36.6
OCT	8	02 43.9	19 26.6	16 54.1	01D20.4
	18	04 35.1	28 35.9	15 47.8	01 59.4
	28	05 39.8	07♐21.7	15D24.8	03 15.3
NOV	7	05R51.9	15 43.5	15 46.7	04 49.1
	17	05 08.4	23 41.6	16 51.5	06 10.1
	27	03 31.6	01♑16.7	18 34.9	06R04.1
DEC	7	01 10.9	08 30.6	20 52.0	00 21.2
	17	28♊25.0	15 24.7	23 38.0	14♐38.5
	27	25 38.2	22 00.4	26 48.1	20D39.5
JAN	6	23♊13.9	28♑19.5	00♈18.4	29♐24.4
JAN	1	14S25.0	00S19.5	27S56.9	23S46.2
	21	11 45.8	01N31.7	26 39.3	24 28.9
FEB	10	08 19.8	04 19.1	24 50.8	24 23.6
MAR	2	04 17.8	07 31.7	22 36.3	23 55.1
	22	00N06.7	10 46.7	20 02.5	23 22.8
APR	11	04 38.7	13 45.2	17 17.5	23 05.9
MAY	1	09 02.9	16 08.0	14 30.4	23 27.3
	21	13 04.6	17 33.5	11 51.0	24 58.7
JUN	10	16 30.0	17 38.3	09 30.0	28 26.7
	30	19 08.0	16 01.9	07 39.0	34 50.4
JUL	20	20 50.8	12 34.6	06 29.5	44 19.2
AUG	9	21 35.1	07 28.6	06 09.6	52 53.0
	29	21 22.6	01 22.1	06 35.1	54 13.8
SEP	18	20 20.0	04S48.2	07 18.0	50 40.9
OCT	8	18 38.4	10 05.6	07 34.7	46 45.9
	28	16 32.5	13 52.9	06 56.8	43 25.1
NOV	17	14 21.6	15 58.2	05 22.0	39 52.1
DEC	7	12 30.4	16 29.3	03 00.0	31 30.4
	27	11N26.2	15S43.6	00S02.2	17S48.6

1946	Sappho 80	Amor 1221	Pandora 55	Icarus 1566
JAN 1	24 R 22.0	25 ♑ 12.0	28 ♓ 30.9	25 ♐ 11.0
11	22 ♊ 16.2	01 ♒ 23.2	02 ♈ 10.1	03 ♑ 17.9
21	20 56.5	07 19.5	06 04.3	10 14.4
31	20 26.9	13 02.0	10 10.8	16 19.0
FEB 10	20 D 46.4	18 31.7	14 27.5	21 44.7
20	21 49.8	23 49.0	18 52.1	26 39.3
MAR 2	23 30.5	28 54.5	23 23.1	01 ♒ 08.3
12	25 42.5	03 ♓ 48.6	27 59.1	05 14.0
22	28 20.1	08 31.3	02 ♉ 38.6	08 57.7
APR 1	01 ♋ 18.2	13 02.7	07 20.7	12 19.6
11	04 33.0	17 22.5	12 04.5	15 18.1
21	08 01.1	21 30.3	16 49.0	17 50.6
MAY 1	11 39.8	25 25.5	21 33.7	19 53.5
11	15 27.1	29 07.1	26 17.7	21 20.3
21	19 21.0	02 ♈ 34.0	01 ♊ 00.4	22 03.3
31	23 20.1	05 44.7	05 41.4	21 R 51.6
JUN 10	27 23.5	08 37.1	10 20.0	20 31.0
20	01 ♌ 29.8	11 08.9	14 55.6	17 46.5
30	05 38.4	13 17.2	19 27.7	13 24.9
JUL 10	09 48.7	14 58.2	23 55.5	07 24.7
20	13 59.8	16 08.0	28 18.4	00 09.6
30	18 11.4	16 42.1	02 ♋ 35.7	22 ♑ 30.1
AUG 9	22 22.8	16 R 36.0	06 46.2	15 29.1
19	26 33.4	15 46.7	10 49.0	09 52.7
29	00 ♍ 42.8	14 12.7	14 42.8	05 57.3
SEP 8	04 50.4	11 57.3	18 25.9	03 39.1
18	08 55.5	09 09.4	21 56.6	02 43.4
28	12 57.4	06 03.2	25 12.8	02 D 55.2
OCT 8	16 55.4	02 57.3	28 11.6	04 01.8
18	20 48.3	00 10.0	00 ♌ 50.1	05 52.7
28	24 35.2	27 ♓ 55.5	03 04.7	08 21.0
NOV 7	28 14.7	26 22.8	04 51.2	11 21.7
17	01 ♎ 45.3	25 34.6	06 05.5	14 51.4
27	05 05.1	25 D 29.5	06 43.3	18 49.3
DEC 7	08 11.7	26 04.3	06 R 41.0	23 15.3
17	11 02.9	27 13.7	05 57.8	28 10.9
27	13 35.4	28 53.3	04 35.2	03 ♒ 38.7
JAN 6	15 ♎ 45.6	00 ♈ 58.5	02 ♌ 40.3	09 ♒ 37.0
JAN 1	11 N 19.6	15 S 22.6	00 N 46.6	18 S 40.7
21	11 29.6	13 28.8	04 14.5	20 59.8
FEB 10	12 20.9	11 00.7	07 55.3	21 45.7
MAR 2	13 27.6	08 13.2	11 39.4	21 48.8
22	14 28.0	05 18.5	15 17.6	21 41.8
APR 11	15 08.0	02 26.9	18 41.3	21 51.0
MAY 1	15 19.2	00 N 12.5	21 42.7	22 45.3
21	14 57.7	02 31.3	24 15.3	25 02.1
JUN 10	14 02.8	04 20.8	26 14.2	29 27.6
30	12 36.0	05 30.8	27 36.9	36 26.0
JUL 20	10 40.6	05 49.0	28 23.7	44 01.3
AUG 9	08 20.8	05 01.6	28 37.7	47 30.8
29	05 41.9	02 58.5	28 25.5	46 17.5
SEP 18	02 49.3	00 S 09.4	27 56.9	43 42.1
OCT 8	00 S 10.9	03 32.9	27 24.4	41 22.1
28	03 12.3	06 05.6	27 03.3	39 22.7
NOV 17	06 07.9	07 13.9	27 09.2	37 22.6
DEC 7	08 49.9	07 03.3	27 52.5	34 52.3
27	[illegible]	05 S 52.7	[illegible]	[illegible]

1947	Sappho 80	Amor 1221	Pandora 55	Icarus 1566
JAN 1	14 ♎ 43.5	29 ♓ 53.0	03 R 41.1	06 ♒ 34.6
11	16 41.2	02 ♈ 09.4	01 ♌ 34.3	12 40.6
21	18 10.6	04 45.5	29 ♋ 14.3	17 05.9
31	19 07.0	07 38.3	26 57.5	03 R 12.1
FEB 10	19 26.3	10 45.0	24 59.5	26 D 28.1
20	19 R 05.0	14 03.4	23 31.5	28 ♑ 49.6
MAR 2	18 01.8	17 31.7	22 40.1	02 ♒ 26.5
12	16 19.5	21 08.3	22 D 27.4	06 05.5
22	14 05.1	24 52.0	22 51.4	09 29.0
APR 1	11 31.4	28 41.8	23 49.3	12 29.9
11	08 55.0	02 ♉ 36.6	25 16.5	15 03.6
21	06 32.3	06 36.1	27 08.9	17 05.2
MAY 1	04 37.6	10 39.5	29 22.7	18 27.7
11	03 20.0	14 46.2	01 ♌ 54.1	19 02.4
21	02 42.9	18 56.2	04 40.3	18 R 37.7
31	02 D 46.7	23 09.0	07 38.8	16 58.4
JUN 10	03 28.4	27 24.4	10 47.2	13 49.1
20	04 44.1	01 ♊ 42.3	14 03.8	08 57.9
30	06 29.9	06 02.5	17 27.1	02 28.1
JUL 10	08 41.5	10 24.9	20 55.7	24 ♑ 51.5
20	11 15.4	14 49.5	24 28.6	17 05.6
30	14 08.7	19 16.1	28 04.8	10 13.3
AUG 9	17 18.5	23 44.6	01 ♍ 43.2	04 53.9
19	20 42.7	28 15.2	05 23.2	01 16.8
29	24 19.6	02 ♋ 47.3	09 03.9	29 ♐ 13.4
SEP 8	28 07.5	07 21.1	12 44.5	28 27.8
18	02 ♏ 05.3	11 56.3	16 24.2	28 D 44.6
28	06 11.8	16 32.5	20 02.2	29 51.3
OCT 8	10 26.1	21 09.5	23 37.4	01 ♑ 37.7
18	14 47.4	25 46.8	27 09.0	03 56.7
28	19 15.0	00 ♌ 23.5	00 ♎ 35.8	06 43.1
NOV 7	23 48.2	04 59.2	03 56.4	09 53.1
17	28 26.5	09 32.6	07 09.3	13 24.7
27	03 ♐ 09.2	14 02.6	10 12.9	17 16.4
DEC 7	07 55.9	18 28.2	13 05.1	21 27.7
17	12 46.1	22 47.6	15 43.7	25 59.8
27	17 39.2	26 59.3	18 06.0	00 ♒ 54.1
JAN 6	22 ♐ 34.6	01 ♍ 03.3	20 ♎ 09.2	06 ♒ 14.1
JAN 1	11 S 39.2	05 S 29.4	29 N 27.0	29 S 46.0
21	13 14.1	03 31.9	30 32.0	20 49.0
FEB 10	13 56.4	01 11.8	30 46.9	14 34.6
MAR 2	13 28.4	01 N 20.3	30 09.3	16 32.1
22	11 41.4	03 55.4	28 58.8	17 30.4
APR 11	08 57.5	06 26.1	27 30.2	18 28.1
MAY 1	06 13.8	08 45.4	25 48.1	20 12.1
21	04 22.1	10 47.0	23 52.1	23 32.7
JUN 10	03 40.3	12 24.7	21 41.0	29 18.6
30	04 02.0	13 32.9	19 14.8	36 57.7
JUL 20	05 12.7	14 06.0	16 34.7	42 30.8
AUG 9	06 57.9	13 59.1	13 43.1	43 04.0
29	09 05.1	13 07.8	10 43.2	41 15.3
SEP 18	11 22.7	11 28.8	07 39.0	39 24.3
OCT 8	13 40.3	08 59.9	04 34.8	37 57.9
28	15 48.0	05 40.6	01 35.7	36 44.3
NOV 17	17 35.9	01 33.3	01 S 13.0	35 26.4
DEC 7	18 54.5	03 S 14.5	03 45.5	33 47.3
27	19 S 35.8	08 S 24.4	05 S 55.7	31 S 28.9

1948	Sappho 80	Amor 1221	Pandora 55	Icarus 1566
JAN 1	20 ♐ 06.6	29 ♌ 02.4	19 ♎ 10.2	03 ♒ 30.6
11	25 03.0	03 ♍ 02.1	21 02.6	09 05.3
21	00 ♑ 01.0	06 54.6	22 30.6	15 14.9
31	04 59.9	10 46.9	23 31.0	22 09.5
FEB 10	09 59.4	14 50.2	24 00.4	00 ♓ 05.9
20	14 58.5	19 28.8	23 R 56.0	09 30.6
MAR 1	19 56.6	25 26.8	23 17.0	20 59.4
11	24 53.1	03 ♎ 43.9	22 04.4	00 R 55.7
21	29 46.8	15 31.5	20 22.7	15 ♓ 52.8
31	04 ♒ 36.9	01 ♏ 02.8	18 20.5	05 19.8
APR 10	09 22.1	17 35.4	16 09.0	00 58.9
20	14 00.8	01 ♐ 05.6	14 01.2	28 ♒ 47.2
30	18 31.3	09 49.5	12 09.4	27 01.0
MAY 10	22 51.3	14 19.9	10 42.6	24 45.4
20	26 57.9	16 01.9	09 47.1	21 18.8
30	00 ♓ 47.9	16 16.1	09 25.0	16 06.4
JUN 9	04 17.0	16 00.2	09 D 36.0	08 42.8
19	07 19.6	15 56.8	10 18.4	29 ♑ 15.5
29	09 50.2	16 25.6	11 28.8	18 49.0
JUL 9	11 41.4	17 31.7	13 04.4	09 03.7
19	12 46.0	19 15.2	15 01.9	01 18.8
29	12 R 58.8	21 30.4	17 18.3	25 ♐ 56.9
AUG 8	12 17.0	24 11.7	19 51.1	22 42.5
18	10 46.1	27 14.8	22 38.1	21 09.7
28	08 41.2	00 ♑ 34.6	25 37.2	20 D 53.2
SEP 7	06 25.2	04 07.8	28 46.7	21 34.3
17	04 26.3	07 52.1	02 ♏ 05.2	22 59.4
27	03 07.2	11 44.6	05 31.2	24 58.1
OCT 7	02 D 41.5	15 44.1	09 03.7	27 23.8
17	03 14.1	19 49.1	12 41.5	00 ♑ 11.5
27	04 41.6	23 58.2	16 23.7	03 17.5
NOV 6	06 57.9	28 10.9	20 09.3	06 39.6
16	09 55.9	02 ♒ 26.2	23 57.4	10 15.8
26	13 27.7	06 43.3	27 46.9	14 05.1
DEC 6	17 27.3	11 01.9	01 ♐ 37.2	18 07.1
16	21 49.1	15 21.3	05 26.9	22 21.6
26	26 28.2	19 40.8	09 15.3	26 49.1
JAN 5	01 ♈ 21.3	24 ♒ 00.2	13 ♐ 01.2	01 ♒ 30.7
JAN 1	19 S 39.5	09 S 41.2	06 S 24.0	30 S 45.6
21	19 25.3	14 14.0	07 57.1	27 00.4
FEB 10	18 23.3	16 11.0	08 52.6	20 59.2
MAR 1	16 33.5	10 15.9	09 04.4	09 23.2
21	13 59.5	14 N 35.3	08 31.8	02 N 38.3
APR 10	10 47.5	34 10.9	07 28.8	05 S 28.9
30	07 06.4	36 01.3	06 25.2	11 01.9
MAY 20	03 07.8	32 09.8	05 51.6	17 39.2
JUN 9	00 N 52.7	24 33.9	06 02.7	27 12.5
29	04 32.8	14 41.5	06 58.0	36 33.6
JUL 19	07 18.5	05 01.5	08 29.4	39 18.4
AUG 8	08 22.5	02 S 48.1	10 27.8	38 03.9
28	07 05.0	08 27.8	12 44.4	36 37.3
SEP 17	03 52.0	12 13.1	15 11.1	35 41.5
OCT 7	00 23.9	14 24.6	17 40.8	35 05.3
27	01 S 53.0	15 20.0	20 06.8	34 32.4
NOV 16	02 31.9	15 13.4	22 23.1	33 49.5
DEC 6	01 42.2	14 16.9	24 24.4	32 46.1
26	00 N 15.1	12 S 41.1	26 S 06.8	31 S 13.3

1949	Sappho 80	Amor 1221	Pandora 55	Icarus 1566
JAN 1	29♓22.6	22♒16.5	11♐31.3	29♑36.3
11	04♈22.4	26 35.6	15 15.0	04♒27.0
21	09 31.1	00♓53.6	18 54.3	09 34.9
31	14 46.6	05 10.3	22 27.9	15 03.4
FEB 10	20 07.1	09 25.1	25 53.9	20 57.3
20	25 30.6	13 37.6	29 10.8	27 23.3
MAR 2	00♉56.2	17 47.4	02♑16.6	04♓32.1
12	06 22.8	21 53.9	05 08.9	12 38.7
22	11 49.2	25 56.8	07 45.2	22 06.5
APR 1	17 15.0	29 55.6	10 02.4	03♈33.3
11	22 39.4	03♈49.7	11 57.2	18 02.6
21	28 01.9	07 38.5	13 26.0	07♉12.4
MAY 1	03♊22.1	11 21.4	14 24.7	18R06.4
11	08 39.5	14 57.5	14 49.7	14 02.6
21	13 53.9	18 26.0	14R38.6	06 18.5
31	19 05.1	21 46.0	13 50.2	21♈26.7
JUN 10	24 12.7	24 55.8	12 26.9	00♓00.3
20	29 16.4	27 54.2	10 35.4	26♐02.2
30	04♋16.1	00♉39.2	08 26.3	09 57.2
JUL 10	09 11.4	03 08.2	06 14.3	05 11.8
20	14 02.0	05 18.8	04 14.4	03 57.1
30	18 47.5	07 07.4	02 39.5	04D19.9
AUG 9	23 27.5	08 30.0	01 39.2	05 38.9
19	28 01.3	09 22.1	01D17.6	07 34.0
29	02♌28.5	09R38.8	01 35.8	09 55.0
SEP 8	06 48.0	09 15.4	02 32.0	12 35.8
18	10 58.9	08 08.6	04 02.7	15 31.8
28	15 00.0	06 17.8	06 04.5	18 40.5
OCT 8	18 49.6	03 47.4	08 33.4	21 59.9
18	22 26.0	00 48.0	11 25.8	25 28.4
28	25 46.8	27♈36.1	14 38.7	29 05.2
NOV 7	28 49.2	24 31.6	18 09.0	02♑49.5
17	01♍30.2	21 52.9	21 54.4	06 40.8
27	03 45.5	19 53.5	25 52.9	10 38.8
DEC 7	05 30.8	18 40.5	00♒02.4	14 43.3
17	06 41.4	18 15.1	04 21.3	18 54.2
27	07 12.3	18D35.1	08 48.4	23 12.1
JAN 6	06R59.8	19♈36.0	13♒22.2	27♑37.2
JAN 1	00N59.9	12S06.1	26S33.5	30S38.4
21	03 51.1	09 53.5	27 48.8	28 13.1
FEB 10	07 00.0	07 23.0	28 44.4	24 50.8
MAR 2	10 09.0	04 42.7	29 25.0	20 01.6
22	13 03.0	02 00.1	29 58.2	12 36.6
APR 11	15 30.2	00N37.7	30 34.3	00N35.7
MAY 1	17 21.3	03 04.2	31 23.5	24 50.7
21	18 30.3	05 13.2	32 30.5	28 27.5
JUN 10	18 54.2	06 58.4	33 44.1	05 23.5
30	18 33.2	08 13.4	34 33.8	28S23.8
JUL 20	17 30.0	08 50.7	34 32.1	29 41.2
AUG 9	15 49.5	08 41.8	33 44.2	30 19.5
29	13 38.3	07 37.9	32 36.3	30 59.7
SEP 18	11 04.0	05 33.1	31 24.8	31 37.6
OCT 8	08 15.5	02 37.1	30 10.1	32 06.2
28	05 22.4	00S28.5	28 44.3	32 19.0
NOV 17	02 36.8	02 41.7	26 58.7	32 10.8
DEC 7	00 13.3	03 25.7	24 46.8	31 37.4
27	01S28.5	02S46.3	22S05.7	30S35.7

1950	Sappho 80	Amor 1221	Pandora 55	Icarus 1566
JAN 1	07R11.6	19♈00.8	11♒04.5	25♑23.7
11	06♍36.5	20 20.1	15 41.2	29 52.6
21	05 16.6	22 12.8	20 23.0	04♒30.0
31	03 16.7	24 34.4	25 08.8	09 17.0
FEB 10	00 47.8	27 20.4	29 57.7	14 15.5
20	28♌05.9	00♉27.7	04♓49.0	19 28.2
MAR 2	25 29.7	03 53.4	09 41.7	24 58.2
12	23 16.4	07 35.1	14 35.1	00♓50.6
22	21 37.9	11 31.2	19 28.6	07 12.3
APR 1	20 40.6	15 40.2	24 21.3	14 12.7
11	20D25.4	20 01.1	29 12.6	22 05.6
21	20 49.9	24 33.3	04♈01.9	01♈10.9
MAY 1	21 50.2	29 16.3	08 48.3	11 56.3
11	23 21.4	04♊09.9	13 31.1	25 00.8
21	25 19.0	09 14.2	18 09.4	11♉17.5
31	27 39.0	14 29.4	22 42.2	02♊13.8
JUN 10	00♍17.5	19 55.9	27 08.6	28 57.2
20	03 11.8	25 34.4	01♉27.3	19♋57.6
30	06 19.2	01♋25.7	05 36.6	13♌52.3
JUL 10	09 37.6	07 30.7	09 35.1	12♍19.8
20	13 05.4	13 50.8	13 20.5	07♎28.7
30	16 41.1	20 26.8	16 50.3	25 12.2
AUG 9	20 23.3	27 20.5	20 01.6	07♏21.8
19	24 11.3	04♌33.1	22 50.8	16 17.1
29	28 04.0	12 05.9	25 13.7	23 21.9
SEP 8	02♎00.6	20 00.4	27 05.7	29 21.8
18	06 00.5	28 17.4	28 21.6	04♐42.6
28	10 02.7	06♍57.3	28 56.9	09 38.8
OCT 8	14 06.9	16 00.0	28R48.1	14 19.4
18	18 12.2	25 24.4	27 54.4	18 50.1
28	22 17.9	05♎07.9	26 20.3	23 14.5
NOV 7	26 23.4	15 07.5	24 16.2	27 35.0
17	00♏27.8	25 18.4	21 57.9	01♑53.5
27	04 30.2	05♏34.7	19 45.2	06 10.9
DEC 7	08 29.6	15 50.3	17 55.7	10 28.3
17	12 25.0	25 58.8	16 42.4	14 46.4
27	16 14.9	05♐53.8	16 12.3	19 05.6
JAN 6	19♏58.1	15♐30.4	16D25.9	23♑26.5
JAN 1	01S44.6	02S26.1	21S20.9	30S15.5
21	02 01.2	00 35.7	18 04.4	28 35.0
FEB 10	00 53.9	01N46.9	14 23.9	26 20.0
MAR 2	01N16.4	04 25.7	10 24.9	23 24.2
22	03 37.7	07 08.4	06 14.2	19 33.7
APR 11	05 24.9	09 44.3	01 58.9	14 16.5
MAY 1	06 19.9	12 04.0	02N14.3	06 20.0
21	06 22.5	13 57.9	06 19.0	06N45.4
JUN 10	05 39.0	15 16.3	10 09.2	27 38.6
30	04 17.1	15 49.0	13 40.3	26 16.9
JUL 20	02 24.2	15 25.7	16 49.1	00 48.0
AUG 9	00 07.3	13 57.0	19 34.1	15S21.8
29	02S26.9	11 15.9	21 55.4	22 27.8
SEP 18	05 11.8	07 21.0	23 53.5	26 13.0
OCT 8	08 00.8	02 21.6	25 24.2	28 26.5
28	10 47.3	03S16.8	26 13.3	29 44.4
NOV 17	13 24.6	08 49.2	26 06.5	30 20.3
DEC 7	15 45.7	13 18.5	25 19.9	30 20.3
27	17S44.4	15S57.7	24N37.7	29S47.7

1951	Sappho 80	Amor 1221	Pandora 55	Icarus 1566
JAN 1	18♏07.5	10♐44.7	16D13.7	21♑15.8
11	21 46.6	20 10.5	16♉48.6	25 37.9
21	25 16.1	29 12.0	18 03.0	00♒02.5
31	28 33.9	07♑47.3	19 51.5	04 30.2
FEB 10	01♐37.5	15 55.2	22 09.2	09 02.1
20	04 23.7	23 35.3	24 51.3	13 38.9
MAR 2	06 49.2	00♒47.9	27 53.2	18 22.3
12	08 49.7	07 33.6	01♊11.4	23 14.1
22	10 20.5	13 52.7	04 42.9	28 16.7
APR 1	11 16.8	19 46.0	08 24.7	03♓33.8
11	11R33.5	25 13.5	12 15.1	09 10.2
21	11 07.0	00♓14.9	16 12.0	15 12.8
MAY 1	09 56.2	04 49.9	20 13.9	21 51.7
11	08 04.2	08 57.2	24 19.8	29 21.1
21	05 40.8	12 34.6	28 28.2	08♈01.7
31	03 01.7	15 40.1	02♋38.5	18 23.2
JUN 10	00 26.3	18 09.7	06 49.8	01♉03.9
20	28♏14.3	19 59.1	11 01.3	16 42.5
30	26 39.8	21 03.8	15 12.4	05♊35.0
JUL 10	25 51.5	21R18.1	19 22.6	27 23.3
20	25D51.9	20 38.2	23 31.1	24♋15.9
30	26 39.0	19 03.0	27 37.2	23♌51.5
AUG 9	28 09.3	16 35.9	01♌40.6	18♍03.1
19	00♐17.8	13 29.2	05 40.2	08♎25.4
29	02 59.7	10 01.8	09 35.4	24 39.0
SEP 8	06 10.9	06 37.0	13 25.3	07♏20.8
18	09 47.4	03 37.5	17 08.7	17 28.8
28	13 45.9	01 18.5	20 44.5	25 51.7
OCT 8	18 04.0	29♒48.0	24 11.3	03♐03.8
18	22 39.1	29 07.0	27 27.1	09 27.1
28	27 29.3	29D11.8	00♍30.2	15 16.5
NOV 7	02♑33.2	29 57.3	03 18.1	20 42.0
17	07 49.0	01♓17.4	05 48.0	25 50.0
27	13 15.6	03 06.6	07 56.8	00♑45.2
DEC 7	18 51.9	05 20.1	09 40.7	05 31.1
17	24 36.7	07 53.4	10 56.2	10 09.7
27	00♒28.9	10 43.0	11 39.3	14 42.8
JAN 6	06♒27.8	13♓46.1	11R46.8	19♑11.8
JAN 1	18S09.9	16S17.7	24N32.1	29S34.8
21	19 32.6	16 21.1	24 35.0	28 25.4
FEB 10	20 21.8	14 43.6	25 13.1	26 49.5
MAR 2	20 34.7	12 00.6	26 11.9	24 49.3
22	20 09.6	08 44.6	27 15.5	22 25.0
APR 11	19 05.6	05 21.3	28 10.3	19 32.9
MAY 1	17 23.4	02 09.8	28 46.0	15 59.6
21	15 12.9	00N33.7	28 55.8	11 09.1
JUN 10	13 05.3	02 32.8	28 36.1	03 36.7
30	11 43.2	03 27.2	27 46.6	08N34.6
JUL 20	11 26.5	02 52.5	26 29.2	22 12.5
AUG 9	12 05.6	00 31.3	24 48.2	10 22.3
29	13 17.7	03S15.2	22 49.8	07S05.0
SEP 18	14 39.8	07 10.5	20 41.1	17 27.5
OCT 8	15 51.6	10 00.5	18 30.6	23 06.0
28	16 36.1	11 23.3	16 28.3	26 15.7
NOV 17	16 39.6	11 30.9	14 45.2	27 58.2
DEC 7	15 52.6	10 41.6	13 33.6	28 41.7
27	14S10.7	09S10.7	13N05.4	28S40.9

1952	Sappho 80	Amor 1221	Pandora 55	Icarus 1566
JAN 1	03♒27.6	12♓13.1	11♍47.7	16♑57.8
11	09 29.4	15 21.9	11R36.6	21 25.0
21	15 36.2	18 40.5	10 48.1	25 49.3
31	21 47.3	22 07.0	09 24.2	00♒11.5
FEB 10	28 01.7	25 39.9	07 31.6	04 32.1
20	04♓18.5	29 17.7	05 20.6	08 51.7
MAR 1	10 37.0	02♈59.3	03 04.5	13 11.1
11	16 56.2	06 43.6	00 58.0	17 30.6
21	23 15.3	10 29.7	29♌12.9	21 51.5
31	29 33.7	14 17.0	27 57.8	26 14.6
APR 10	05♈50.3	18 04.5	27 17.2	00♓41.5
20	12 04.6	21 51.7	27D11.5	05 14.3
30	18 15.8	25 38.0	27 39.2	09 55.9
MAY 10	24 23.1	29 22.6	28 37.3	14 50.3
20	00♉26.0	03♉05.0	00♍02.1	20 04.4
30	06 23.7	06 44.5	01 50.1	25 47.7
JUN 9	12 15.3	10 20.2	03 57.8	02♈16.0
19	18 00.2	13 51.4	06 22.3	09 56.0
29	23 37.6	17 16.9	09 01.1	19 32.3
JUL 9	29 06.5	20 35.6	11 51.8	02♉19.3
19	04♊25.9	23 45.9	14 52.5	20 00.7
29	09 34.5	26 46.1	18 01.7	13♊19.8
AUG 8	14 30.9	29 33.7	21 17.9	08♋44.1
18	19 13.5	02♊06.0	24 39.8	00♌54.5
28	23 39.9	04 19.4	28 06.5	20 56.3
SEP 7	27 47.7	06 09.5	01♎36.7	19♍04.2
17	01♋33.8	07 31.2	05 09.8	12♎37.0
27	04 54.1	08 17.8	08 44.8	29 57.5
OCT 7	07 44.1	08R22.9	12 20.6	13♏20.0
17	09 58.4	07 39.8	15 56.6	24 02.8
27	11 30.6	06 03.5	19 31.7	02♐57.4
NOV 6	12 14.9	03 35.0	23 04.9	10 37.4
16	12R06.5	00 22.2	26 35.2	17 25.1
26	11 03.1	26♉44.0	00♏01.4	23 35.1
DEC 6	09 09.7	23 06.9	03 21.9	29 17.3
16	06 38.3	19 57.9	06 35.4	04♑38.5
26	03 49.0	17 38.3	09 40.2	09 43.4
JAN 5	01♋06.4	16♉19.4	12♏34.1	14♑35.4
JAN 1	13S36.7	08S42.9	13N06.2	28S35.0
21	10 48.5	06 36.4	13 40.5	27 52.3
FEB 10	07 15.5	04 12.1	14 52.4	26 44.7
MAR 1	03 09.5	01 38.3	16 07.3	25 19.0
21	01N15.5	00N57.7	16 47.4	23 42.3
APR 10	05 44.2	03 29.4	16 36.9	22 01.3
30	10 01.4	05 50.6	15 40.2	20 22.5
MAY 20	13 52.3	07 55.6	14 07.6	18 50.9
JUN 9	17 04.3	09 39.0	12 07.4	17 26.4
29	19 27.2	10 55.5	09 45.6	15 44.2
JUL 19	20 54.3	11 40.0	07 06.7	11 37.6
AUG 8	21 23.6	11 47.4	04 14.7	00 27.0
28	20 57.9	11 12.8	01 13.7	11N51.5
SEP 17	19 45.0	09 51.5	01S52.3	00S21.6
OCT 7	17 56.3	07 41.6	04 59.1	13 33.9
27	15 47.3	04 50.6	08 02.5	20 43.5
NOV 16	13 37.5	01 51.3	10 58.1	24 30.8
DEC 6	11 50.9	00S12.9	13 41.9	26 24.2
26	[illegible]	[illegible]	[illegible]	[illegible]

1953	Sappho 80	Amor 1221	Pandora 55	Icarus 1566
JAN 1	02R09.2	16R43.4	11♏26.0	12♑40.0
11	29♊41.2	16♉02.1	14 12.4	17 25.3
21	27 51.2	16D22.0	16 44.4	22 01.3
31	26 49.0	17 37.8	18 59.0	26 29.2
FEB 10	26D36.3	19 42.7	20 53.4	00♒49.9
20	27 10.1	22 30.7	22 24.0	05 04.3
MAR 2	28 25.0	25 56.3	23 27.5	09 12.6
12	00♋14.4	29 54.9	24 00.5	13 15.4
22	02 32.7	04♊23.4	24R00.0	17 12.6
APR 1	05 14.4	09 19.2	23 25.0	21 04.1
11	08 15.1	14 40.5	22 16.2	24 50.1
21	11 31.2	20 26.5	20 37.6	28 30.0
MAY 1	14 59.6	26 36.5	18 37.4	02♓03.4
11	18 37.8	03♋10.2	16 26.6	05 30.0
21	22 24.0	10 08.2	14 18.2	08 48.4
31	26 16.5	17 30.2	12 25.2	11 57.5
JUN 10	00♌13.8	25 16.6	10 57.2	14 55.7
20	04 15.2	03♌27.6	10 00.9	17 39.9
30	08 19.4	12 02.7	09 39.4	20 06.1
JUL 10	12 25.8	21 01.1	09D52.2	22 07.7
20	16 33.7	00♍21.2	10 38.0	23 31.3
30	20 42.5	10 00.3	11 53.6	23R49.9
AUG 9	24 51.5	19 54.7	13 35.8	21 37.9
19	29 00.4	29 59.9	15 41.6	08 28.5
29	03♍08.3	10♎10.0	18 07.9	17♏42.5
SEP 8	07 15.0	20 18.9	20 51.9	17♎03.1
18	11 19.6	00♏20.4	23 51.5	10 26.7
28	15 21.3	10 08.4	27 04.5	06 35.6
OCT 8	19 19.7	19 38.5	00♐29.0	05D04.4
18	23 13.6	28 47.4	04 03.8	17 21.8
28	27 02.0	07♐32.7	07 47.0	08♏03.3
NOV 7	00♎43.6	15 54.2	11 37.8	22 49.0
17	04 17.0	23 52.0	15 35.0	04♐05.0
27	07 40.4	01♑27.1	19 37.4	13 14.5
DEC 7	10 51.8	08 40.9	23 44.2	21 01.8
17	13 48.6	15 35.0	27 54.4	27 52.5
27	16 28.0	22 10.8	02♑07.1	04♑02.6
JAN 6	18♎46.8	28♑29.9	06♑21.5	09♑42.4
JAN 1	10N45.9	00S13.5	16S51.8	27S09.2
21	11 01.7	01N37.4	18 57.0	26 53.0
FEB 10	11 56.2	04 24.6	20 42.3	26 08.7
MAR 2	13 03.6	07 37.0	22 06.1	25 08.0
22	14 03.0	10 51.7	23 05.0	24 02.4
APR 11	14 40.7	13 49.5	23 31.4	23 04.5
MAY 1	14 48.8	16 11.2	23 17.6	22 29.7
21	14 24.1	17 35.2	22 29.0	22 40.1
JUN 10	13 26.1	17 38.3	21 32.4	24 11.1
30	11 56.7	16 00.0	20 58.2	28 08.4
JUL 20	09 59.1	12 31.3	21 01.1	36 47.4
AUG 9	07 37.8	07 24.5	21 39.9	54 36.9
29	04 57.9	01 17.8	22 45.5	72 37.4
SEP 18	02 04.8	04S52.1	24 06.2	40 14.6
OCT 8	00S55.5	10 08.9	25 30.7	08 37.0
28	03 56.7	13 55.5	26 48.6	09 40.5
NOV 17	06 51.8	16 00.0	27 50.8	18 37.5
DEC 7	09 33.5	16 30.3	28 29.9	22 52.6
27	11S53.0	15S43.9	28S40.9	24S45.9

1954	Sappho 80	Amor 1221	Pandora 55	Icarus 1566
JAN 1	17♎40.3	25♑22.3	04♑14.1	06♑55.8
11	19 47.2	01♒33.7	08 29.0	12 23.1
21	21 27.3	07 30.1	12 44.2	17 29.1
31	22 36.5	13 12.8	16 58.8	22 18.0
FEB 10	23 09.9	18 42.7	21 12.0	26 52.1
20	23R04.0	24 00.2	25 22.6	01♒13.0
MAR 2	22 16.5	29 06.0	29 29.7	05 22.0
12	20 48.0	04♓00.4	03♒32.2	09 19.3
22	18 44.4	08 43.3	07 28.8	13 04.9
APR 1	16 16.2	13 15.0	11 18.1	16 38.5
11	13 38.6	17 35.2	14 58.4	19 59.0
21	11 09.1	21 43.3	18 27.9	23 04.8
MAY 1	09 02.7	25 38.9	21 44.5	25 53.9
11	07 30.7	29 21.0	24 45.4	28 22.5
21	06 39.0	02♈48.4	27 27.7	00♓26.1
31	06D28.3	05 59.6	29 48.0	01 58.1
JUN 10	06 57.3	08 52.7	01♓41.9	02 48.4
20	08 02.1	11 25.3	03 05.4	02R43.5
30	09 38.5	13 34.4	03 54.1	01 23.4
JUL 10	11 42.7	15 16.3	04R03.9	28♒20.8
20	14 10.8	16 27.2	03 33.2	23 04.5
30	16 59.3	17 02.6	02 23.0	15 09.7
AUG 9	20 05.8	16R57.8	00 39.1	04 52.1
19	23 27.7	16 09.8	28♒33.6	23♑36.8
29	27 03.1	14 37.2	26 21.9	13 24.1
SEP 8	00♏50.4	12 22.9	24 21.9	05 33.3
18	04 48.2	09 35.8	22 49.4	00 12.5
28	08 55.3	06 29.9	21 54.5	26♐51.9
OCT 8	13 11.0	03 23.6	21D42.9	24 52.8
18	17 34.1	00 35.5	22 14.9	23 32.9
28	22 04.2	28♓20.0	23 27.9	22 01.8
NOV 7	26 40.4	26 46.1	25 18.0	18 51.2
17	01♐22.1	25 56.7	27 40.4	10 42.3
27	06 08.9	25D50.5	00♓30.5	26♏12.8
DEC 7	11 00.2	26 24.3	03 44.3	04D17.4
17	15 55.5	27 33.0	07 17.9	15♐48.5
27	20 54.3	29 12.0	11 08.1	25 00.8
JAN 6	25♐56.0	01♈16.7	15♓12.3	02♑40.4
JAN 1	12S23.3	15S22.6	28S38.8	25S00.4
21	14 00.5	13 28.2	28 11.5	25 21.6
FEB 10	14 48.2	10 59.6	27 14.9	25 03.3
MAR 2	14 29.6	08 11.6	25 53.6	24 25.0
22	12 53.2	05 16.5	24 14.5	23 43.3
APR 11	10 14.7	02 24.6	22 26.9	23 15.1
MAY 1	07 27.0	00N15.1	20 41.8	23 21.5
21	05 25.7	02 34.1	19 12.0	24 31.8
JUN 10	04 34.4	04 23.7	18 11.1	27 31.3
30	04 48.8	05 33.8	17 52.0	33 28.5
JUL 20	05 54.3	05 52.4	18 20.1	43 28.6
AUG 9	07 35.8	05 05.5	19 20.7	55 23.3
29	09 39.5	03 03.2	20 12.5	60 02.9
SEP 18	11 53.5	00S04.2	20 13.0	55 49.5
OCT 8	14 06.9	03 27.7	19 10.7	50 09.4
28	16 09.1	06 00.9	17 17.0	44 40.0
NOV 17	17 49.9	07 09.7	14 44.2	33 23.7
DEC 7	18 59.7	06 59.4	11 40.2	15 51.1
27	19S30.2	05S49.8	08S10.1	20S30.6

1955	Sappho 80	Amor 1221	Pandora 55	Icarus 1566
JAN 1	23♐24.8	00♈11.4	13♓08.6	28♐59.9
11	28 27.8	02 27.4	17 18.8	06♑05.6
21	03♑33.1	05 03.1	21 39.3	12 19.7
31	08 40.1	07 55.7	26 08.4	17 56.0
FEB 10	13 48.2	11 02.2	00♈44.3	23 02.6
20	18 57.0	14 20.5	05 25.7	27 45.2
MAR 2	24 05.7	17 48.8	10 11.3	02♒06.7
12	29 13.7	21 25.4	15 00.0	06 08.9
22	04♒20.4	25 09.2	19 50.8	09 52.7
APR 1	09 24.7	28 59.1	24 43.0	13 17.5
11	14 25.5	02♉54.1	29 35.6	16 22.1
21	19 21.9	06 53.7	04♉28.0	19 04.5
MAY 1	24 12.1	10 57.3	09 19.6	21 20.7
11	28 54.4	15 04.4	14 09.7	23 05.9
21	03♓26.6	19 14.7	18 57.7	24 13.1
31	07 45.8	23 27.8	23 43.1	24R32.2
JUN 10	11 48.6	27 43.6	28 25.1	23 50.5
20	15 30.9	02♊01.9	03♊03.2	21 52.3
30	18 47.0	06 22.6	07 36.7	18 20.4
JUL 10	21 31.3	10 45.5	12 04.7	13 04.1
20	23 36.5	15 10.8	16 26.5	06 09.6
30	24 55.0	19 38.0	20 40.8	28♑14.9
AUG 9	25 20.9	24 07.4	24 46.5	20 24.6
19	24R50.8	28 38.8	28 42.2	13 40.9
29	23 28.5	03♋12.0	02♋26.1	08 39.6
SEP 8	21 28.2	07 46.9	05 56.0	05 25.1
18	19 12.2	12 23.6	09 09.6	03 45.3
28	17 08.6	17 01.4	12 03.7	03D24.0
OCT 8	15 41.9	21 40.2	14 35.0	04 05.3
18	15D06.8	26 19.8	16 39.3	05 37.1
28	15 29.3	00♌59.2	18 12.2	07 50.5
NOV 7	16 47.0	05 38.1	19 09.3	10 38.5
17	18 53.5	10 15.7	19R26.2	13 56.8
27	21 41.9	14 50.7	19 00.6	17 41.6
DEC 7	25 04.4	19 22.7	17 53.1	21 47.6
17	28 54.5	23 50.2	16 08.6	26 02.3
27	03♈06.8	28 12.3	13 57.9	29 32.2
JAN 6	07♈36.4	02♍29.9	11♋36.5	26R38.4
JAN 1	19S30.9	05S25.5	07S14.1	21S12.1
21	19 03.8	03 27.9	03 19.3	22 43.6
FEB 10	17 47.4	01 07.6	00N48.1	23 03.7
MAR 2	15 42.5	01N24.5	05 00.7	22 51.3
22	12 53.0	03 59.6	09 10.9	22 32.3
APR 11	09 25.9	06 30.2	13 11.0	22 29.4
MAY 1	05 30.3	08 49.4	16 53.8	23 08.6
21	01 17.9	10 50.6	20 12.9	25 04.3
JUN 10	02N56.7	12 28.0	23 03.0	29 03.0
30	06 54.0	13 35.7	25 20.5	35 45.7
JUL 20	10 05.6	14 08.2	27 04.3	44 09.3
AUG 9	11 50.4	14 00.6	28 16.4	49 27.6
29	11 20.5	13 08.7	29 02.4	48 58.4
SEP 18	08 26.1	11 29.0	29 31.7	46 04.0
OCT 8	04 28.3	08 59.5	29 57.2	43 14.2
28	01 21.9	05 39.9	30 33.9	40 49.4
NOV 17	00 01.1	01 32.4	31 32.7	38 26.1
DEC 7	00 21.6	03S15.6	32 49.7	35 22.9
27	01N58.2	08S26.0	33N54.7	30S02.6

1956	Sappho 80	Amor 1221	Pandora 55	Icarus 1566
JAN 1	05♈19.7	00♍21.7	12R47.5	29R50.4
11	09 56.5	04 37.0	10♋27.1	16♑41.8
21	14 45.5	08 49.8	08 21.6	10D45.0
31	19 43.5	13 08.6	06 44.9	15 37.3
FEB 10	24 48.2	17 47.0	05 45.0	21 02.0
20	29 58.1	23 10.1	05D25.5	26 04.1
MAR 1	05♉11.1	00♎03.8	05 45.2	00♒38.8
11	10 26.3	09 26.3	06 40.7	04 47.3
21	15 42.6	22 13.0	08 08.0	08 30.1
31	20 58.9	08♏04.5	10 02.3	11 47.1
APR 10	26 14.6	23 59.6	12 19.1	14 37.1
20	01♊29.3	06♐26.1	14 55.0	16 56.4
30	06 42.1	14 17.1	17 46.3	18 40.5
MAY 10	11 52.9	18 10.3	20 50.3	19 42.3
20	17 01.2	19 21.0	24 04.9	19R51.6
30	22 06.7	19 05.9	27 27.7	18 56.4
JUN 9	27 09.2	18R22.2	00♌57.4	16 41.6
19	02♋08.3	17D52.9	04 32.6	12 52.9
29	07 03.8	18 00.0	08 11.9	07 25.3
JUL 9	11 55.4	18 48.6	11 54.5	00 32.9
19	16 42.8	20 18.2	15 39.4	22♑58.5
29	21 25.5	22 22.9	19 25.6	15 43.3
AUG 8	26 03.4	24 56.1	23 12.7	09 38.9
18	00♌35.6	27 52.9	26 59.6	05 11.7
28	05 01.6	01♑07.9	00♍45.8	02 22.1
SEP 7	09 20.8	04 37.3	04 30.5	00 58.2
17	13 32.1	08 18.6	08 12.7	00D45.1
27	17 34.3	12 08.9	11 51.7	01 28.7
OCT 7	21 26.2	16 06.4	15 26.4	02 58.2
17	25 05.9	20 09.9	18 55.7	05 05.2
27	28 31.4	24 17.8	22 18.3	07 43.5
NOV 6	01♍40.3	28 29.4	25 32.7	10 49.3
16	04 29.2	02♒43.9	28 37.0	14 19.8
26	06 54.9	07 00.4	01♎29.4	18 13.6
DEC 6	08 53.1	11 18.4	04 07.4	22 31.0
16	10 19.0	15 37.4	06 28.2	27 13.2
26	11 08.2	19 56.6	08 29.1	02♒23.0
JAN 5	11R15.8	24♒15.7	10♎06.4	08♒05.9
JAN 1	02N31.0	09S43.2	34N04.1	27S41.4
21	05 05.1	14 19.7	34 04.4	16 58.1
FEB 10	07 59.1	16 27.3	33 15.9	18 42.4
MAR 1	10 54.2	10 54.8	32 06.6	19 25.6
21	13 34.9	12N42.1	30 53.4	19 43.9
APR 10	15 49.0	31 33.6	29 37.5	20 14.1
30	17 27.9	34 17.2	28 13.5	21 31.6
MAY 20	18 25.5	31 12.1	26 36.2	24 18.7
JUN 9	18 39.5	24 07.3	24 42.4	29 22.3
29	18 10.0	14 30.6	22 31.3	36 40.2
JUL 19	17 00.0	04 56.3	20 04.1	43 10.3
AUG 8	15 14.2	02S51.5	17 23.2	44 53.6
28	12 59.2	08 30.3	14 32.6	43 14.3
SEP 17	10 22.1	12 14.7	11 36.7	41 04.4
OCT 7	07 31.4	14 25.3	08 40.6	39 16.7
27	04 36.4	15 19.9	05 50.4	37 45.0
NOV 16	01 48.0	15 12.6	03 12.4	36 10.9
DEC 6	00S40.0	14 15.4	00 53.8	34 13.7
26	02S29.5	12S39.0	00S57.2	31S28.6

1957	Sappho 80	Amor 1221	Pandora 55	Icarus 1566
JAN 1	11♍18.0	22♒32.1	09♎30.5	05♒44.4
11	10R59.2	26 50.9	10 52.0	11 50.7
21	09 55.8	01♓08.8	11 44.4	18 45.0
31	08 10.6	05 25.3	12 04.3	26 43.3
FEB 10	05 51.6	09 40.1	11R49.5	05♓58.1
20	03 13.5	13 52.5	10 59.5	12R45.2
MAR 2	00 33.6	18 02.3	09 36.6	25♒59.7
12	28♌10.0	22 09.0	07 46.6	18 42.7
22	26 17.0	26 11.9	05 39.3	17D48.3
APR 1	25 02.7	00♈10.8	03 26.9	18 35.7
11	24 30.5	04 05.1	01 22.7	19 42.9
21	24D38.9	07 54.1	29♍38.1	20 36.7
MAY 1	25 24.6	11 37.2	28 21.2	20R56.7
11	26 43.1	15 13.7	27 36.9	20 24.3
21	28 29.8	18 42.5	27D26.3	18 40.9
31	00♍40.3	22 02.8	27 48.1	15 25.1
JUN 10	03 11.2	25 13.2	28 40.2	10 18.1
20	05 58.8	28 12.1	29 59.0	03 17.0
30	09 00.7	00♉57.7	01♎41.5	24♑49.7
JUL 10	12 14.8	03 27.5	03 44.5	16 02.9
20	15 38.8	05 38.9	06 05.1	08 13.5
30	19 11.6	07 28.5	08 40.8	02 09.6
AUG 9	22 51.7	08 52.2	11 29.6	28♐02.8
19	26 37.9	09 45.6	14 29.3	25 39.9
29	00♎29.5	10 03.8	17 38.5	24 41.2
SEP 8	04 25.5	09R42.0	20 55.8	24D48.7
18	08 25.1	08 37.0	24 19.7	25 47.1
28	12 27.8	06 47.7	27 49.4	27 25.5
OCT 8	16 32.7	04 18.6	01♏23.6	29 36.0
18	20 39.2	01 20.0	05 01.3	02♑12.4
28	24 46.8	28♈08.1	08 41.9	05 10.7
NOV 7	28 54.4	25 03.0	12 24.1	08 28.0
17	03♏01.6	22 23.1	16 07.1	12 02.2
27	07 07.4	20 22.1	19 50.0	15 52.4
DEC 7	11 10.7	19 07.6	23 31.6	19 57.8
17	15 10.8	18 40.7	27 11.0	24 18.6
27	19 06.4	18D59.2	00♐47.0	28 55.9
JAN 6	22♏55.9	19♈58.9	04♐18.1	03♒51.1
JAN 1	02S51.5	12S03.9	01S24.0	30S24.4
21	03 16.7	09 50.9	02 26.7	25 27.8
FEB 10	02 17.8	07 19.9	02 43.5	16 03.8
MAR 2	00 09.4	04 39.4	02 13.2	05 24.8
22	02N18.5	01 56.7	01 08.6	10 44.4
APR 11	04 15.9	00N41.2	00 00.1	13 35.3
MAY 1	05 19.9	03 07.7	00N39.6	16 36.0
21	05 28.9	05 16.7	00 33.7	21 18.7
JUN 10	04 49.6	07 02.0	00S18.2	28 43.8
30	03 30.4	08 16.9	01 48.5	37 06.5
JUL 20	01 39.3	08 54.3	03 48.4	41 01.3
AUG 9	00S36.1	08 45.8	06 09.8	40 16.7
29	03 08.9	07 42.4	08 45.4	38 32.9
SEP 18	05 52.2	05 38.5	11 29.1	37 12.2
OCT 8	08 39.3	02 43.4	14 14.8	36 14.4
28	11 23.2	00S21.9	16 57.0	35 24.0
NOV 17	13 57.1	02 35.4	19 30.6	34 26.0
DEC 7	16 14.1	03 20.1	21 51.1	33 07.4
27	18S07.7	02S41.1	23S55.4	31S16.4

1958	Sappho 80	Amor 1221	Pandora 55	Icarus 1566
JAN 1	21♏01.9	19♈24.2	02♐33.3	01♒21.1
11	24 48.0	20 42.5	06 01.5	06 26.3
21	28 25.8	22 34.3	09 22.8	11 54.4
31	01♐53.1	24 55.1	12 35.2	17 50.3
FEB 10	05 07.8	27 40.5	15 37.0	24 21.7
20	08 07.2	00♉47.3	18 26.0	01♓40.3
MAR 2	10 47.8	04 12.6	20 59.4	10 03.9
12	13 06.0	07 54.0	23 14.6	20 01.2
22	14 57.4	11 49.9	25 08.2	02♈21.2
APR 1	16 16.9	15 58.8	26 36.6	18 16.0
11	16 59.7	20 19.5	27 36.4	27 R 06.3
21	17 R 00.9	24 51.6	28 03.8	15 11.8
MAY 1	16 17.3	29 34.6	27 R 56.2	02 53.3
11	14 49.7	04♊28.0	27 12.7	22♓00.0
21	12 43.5	09 32.3	25 54.7	10 33.5
31	10 11.4	14 47.4	24 07.8	26♒16.5
JUN 10	07 31.7	20 13.9	22 01.8	08 12.6
20	05 04.5	25 52.4	19 49.2	19♑03.1
30	03 08.6	01♋43.6	17 44.8	03 33.8
JUL 10	01 55.8	07 48.5	16 01.4	23♐25.7
20	01 D 31.9	14 08.4	14 48.6	17 35.3
30	01 57.5	20 44.3	14 12.0	14 39.4
AUG 9	03 09.2	27 37.6	14 D 13.2	13 37.3
19	05 02.6	04♌50.0	14 51.3	13 D 51.5
29	07 33.0	12 22.5	16 03.7	14 59.1
SEP 8	10 35.1	20 16.5	17 46.8	16 45.0
18	14 05.1	28 33.0	19 57.2	18 59.8
28	17 59.3	07♍12.3	22 31.5	21 37.1
OCT 8	22 14.4	16 14.3	25 26.4	24 32.2
18	26 48.0	25 38.1	28 39.3	27 42.3
28	01♑37.9	05♎20.9	02♑07.9	01♑05.1
NOV 7	06 42.1	15 19.8	05 49.8	04 38.9
17	11 59.1	25 30.1	09 43.5	08 22.9
27	17 27.2	05♏45.8	13 47.2	12 16.2
DEC 7	23 05.2	16 01.0	17 59.5	16 18.5
17	28 52.1	26 09.1	22 19.2	20 29.8
27	04♒46.5	06♐03.9	26 45.1	24 50.1
JAN 6	10♒47.3	15♐40.4	01♒16.2	29♑20.3
JAN 1	18 S 31.8	02 S 21.0	24 S 23.6	30 S 42.1
21	19 48.3	00 30.9	26 05.5	27 50.5
FEB 10	20 30.7	01 N 51.6	27 30.8	23 42.4
MAR 2	20 36.9	04 30.2	28 43.6	17 21.3
22	20 06.4	07 12.6	29 50.1	06 08.0
APR 11	19 00.0	09 48.1	30 57.0	16 N 27.4
MAY 1	17 20.2	12 07.3	32 06.3	11 10.6
21	15 16.0	14 00.5	33 07.9	02 S 36.2
JUN 10	13 12.8	15 18.1	33 38.6	22 36.1
30	11 49.4	15 49.8	33 22.3	34 57.9
JUL 20	11 28.9	15 25.5	32 32.8	35 11.5
AUG 9	12 04.4	13 55.9	31 39.6	34 04.8
29	13 13.1	11 13.9	30 59.8	33 32.8
SEP 18	14 30.9	07 18.6	30 33.0	33 24.7
OCT 8	15 36.7	02 19.0	30 09.5	33 23.2
28	16 12.9	03 S 19.3	29 37.2	33 15.4
NOV 17	16 06.2	08 51.2	28 45.5	32 51.8
DEC 7	15 07.6	13 19.9	27 26.6	32 05.5

1959	Sappho 80	Amor 1221	Pandora 55	Icarus 1566
JAN 1	07♒46.1	10♐54.7	29♑00.0	27♑03.9
11	13 49.9	20 20.4	03♒33.4	01♒39.3
21	19 58.6	29 22.0	08 10.4	06 26.2
31	26 11.2	07♑57.4	12 50.3	11 26.2
FEB 10	02♓27.0	16 05.5	17 32.4	16 42.2
20	08 44.8	23 45.8	22 15.6	22 17.7
MAR 2	15 03.8	00♒58.7	26 59.3	28 17.9
12	21 23.2	07 44.8	01♓42.9	04♓50.4
22	27 42.2	14 04.3	06 25.4	12 05.4
APR 1	03♈59.8	19 58.0	11 06.2	20 18.2
11	10 15.6	25 26.0	15 44.4	29 51.4
21	16 28.7	00♓28.0	20 19.2	11♈17.8
MAY 1	22 38.3	05 03.6	24 49.7	25 27.8
11	28 44.0	09 11.6	29 14.8	13♉46.1
21	04♉45.0	12 50.0	03♈33.3	07♊45.5
31	10 40.7	15 56.4	07 44.0	23 30.8
JUN 10	16 30.5	18 27.2	11 45.2	08♋38.4
20	22 13.6	20 17.9	15 34.9	06♌21.4
30	27 49.4	21 24.2	19 11.1	18♍22.3
JUL 10	03♊17.2	21 R 40.3	22 30.9	18♎50.0
20	08 35.8	21 02.2	25 31.0	04♏46.8
30	13 44.3	19 28.9	28 07.8	14 15.9
AUG 9	18 41.5	17 03.5	00♉16.8	20 58.9
19	23 25.7	13 57.8	01 53.1	26 23.4
29	27 55.2	10 30.8	02 51.9	01♐07.1
SEP 8	02♋07.7	07 05.7	03 R 08.5	05 29.4
18	06 00.2	04 05.0	02 40.9	09 40.1
28	09 29.6	01 44.6	01 30.4	13 44.5
OCT 8	12 31.5	00 12.4	29♈43.5	17 46.3
18	15 01.0	29♒29.8	27 33.9	21 47.3
28	16 52.6	29 D 33.2	25 19.4	25 48.9
NOV 7	17 59.9	00♓17.4	23 19.2	29 52.0
17	18 R 17.6	01 36.6	21 49.8	03♑57.1
27	17 42.1	03 25.0	21 01.2	08 04.6
DEC 7	16 13.9	05 37.8	20 D 57.6	12 15.1
17	14 00.9	08 10.6	21 38.3	16 28.7
27	11 18.7	10 59.8	22 59.3	20 45.8
JAN 6	08♋29.4	14♓02.6	24♈55.9	25♑06.9
JAN 1	12 S 37.0	16 S 18.3	25 S 03.8	30 S 27.6
21	09 38.6	16 21.3	22 33.8	28 31.2
FEB 10	05 58.4	14 43.3	19 35.3	25 53.9
MAR 2	01 48.7	11 59.8	16 13.7	22 23.4
22	02 N 35.6	08 43.6	12 35.3	17 33.1
APR 11	06 59.2	05 20.0	08 47.4	10 23.1
MAY 1	11 06.8	02 08.3	04 57.2	01 N 28.1
21	14 44.6	00 N 35.4	01 11.9	23 54.9
JUN 10	17 40.7	02 34.7	02 N 21.8	36 07.6
30	19 45.8	03 29.5	05 37.4	13 33.7
JUL 20	20 54.9	02 55.6	08 29.1	14 S 38.5
AUG 9	21 07.4	00 35.3	10 51.1	22 50.0
29	20 27.0	03 S 10.7	12 37.0	26 31.7
SEP 18	19 02.3	07 06.6	13 39.1	28 42.3
OCT 8	17 05.1	09 57.3	13 51.1	30 05.0
28	14 51.1	11 20.5	13 22.9	30 52.5
NOV 17	12 39.9	11 28.3	12 50.8	31 08.6
DEC 7	10 55.5	10 38.9	12 54.2	30 54.1

1960	Sappho 80	Amor 1221	Pandora 55	Icarus 1566
JAN 1	09 R 53.4	12♓29.7	23♈53.5	22♑55.8
11	07♋09.5	15 38.3	26 06.0	27 19.0
21	04 52.3	18 56.7	28 46.1	01♒47.0
31	03 16.1	22 23.1	01♉49.3	06 20.7
FEB 10	02 28.4	25 55.9	05 11.6	11 01.0
20	02 D 28.8	29 33.7	08 49.1	15 49.4
MAR 1	03 13.4	03♈15.3	12 39.2	20 48.1
11	04 36.8	06 59.7	16 39.3	25 59.7
21	06 32.5	10 45.9	20 47.2	01♓27.9
31	08 55.0	14 33.4	25 01.3	07 18.1
APR 10	11 39.6	18 21.1	29 20.1	13 37.5
20	14 41.8	22 08.6	03♊42.2	20 36.7
30	17 58.5	25 55.2	08 06.8	28 30.6
MAY 10	21 26.8	29 40.2	12 32.9	07♈40.2
20	25 04.4	03♉23.0	16 59.5	18 34.9
30	28 49.5	07 03.0	21 26.2	01♉52.0
JUN 9	02♌40.7	10 39.2	25 52.2	18 09.7
19	06 36.5	14 11.1	00♋16.9	08♊00.6
29	10 36.2	17 37.4	04 39.7	03♋00.1
JUL 9	14 38.7	20 56.9	09 00.1	02♌13.3
19	18 43.2	24 08.3	13 17.4	27 05.8
29	22 49.3	27 09.7	17 31.1	20♍46.6
AUG 8	26 56.2	29 58.6	21 40.4	10♎57.6
18	01♍03.2	02♊32.6	25 44.4	26 35.1
28	05 10.1	04 48.0	29 42.4	08♏30.4
SEP 7	09 15.9	06 40.3	03♌33.0	17 53.9
17	13 20.3	08 04.6	07 15.3	25 38.3
27	17 22.4	08 54.3	10 47.6	02♐18.3
OCT 7	21 21.6	09 R 02.7	14 08.0	08 15.4
17	25 16.9	08 23.3	17 14.5	13 43.4
27	29 07.4	06 50.7	20 04.6	18 51.4
NOV 6	02♎51.9	04 25.1	22 35.2	23 45.3
16	06 29.0	01 14.3	24 43.2	28 29.2
26	09 57.1	27♉36.2	26 24.4	03♑06.1
DEC 6	13 14.1	23 57.5	27 35.0	07 37.8
16	16 18.1	20 45.4	28 11.1	12 06.0
26	19 06.2	18 22.0	28 R 09.4	16 31.7
JAN 5	21♎35.2	16♉59.2	27♌28.8	20♑55.8
JAN 1	09 N 57.9	08 S 39.8	14 N 09.0	29 S 53.8
21	10 17.9	06 33.0	15 55.8	28 32.5
FEB 10	11 16.9	04 08.6	18 08.1	26 42.5
MAR 1	12 27.7	01 34.6	20 30.9	24 23.2
21	13 29.0	01 N 01.5	22 50.7	21 30.7
APR 10	14 07.3	03 33.2	24 56.2	17 53.3
30	14 15.3	05 54.4	26 38.1	13 02.1
MAY 20	13 49.9	07 59.3	27 50.1	05 49.9
JUN 9	12 51.1	09 42.5	28 28.1	05 N 45.2
29	11 21.0	10 58.9	28 31.1	22 16.8
JUL 19	09 23.0	11 43.3	28 00.8	19 25.8
AUG 8	07 01.4	11 50.6	27 01.7	00 S 47.1
28	04 21.5	11 16.0	25 40.4	14 31.0
SEP 17	01 28.6	09 55.0	24 05.6	21 39.0
OCT 7	01 S 31.4	07 45.6	22 27.7	25 35.5
27	04 32.2	04 55.2	20 58.8	27 50.8
NOV 16	07 27.1	01 55.7	19 52.6	29 02.0
DEC 6	10 08.9	00 S 09.7	19 23.1	29 25.6

1961		Sappho 80	Amor 1221	Pandora 55	Icarus 1566
JAN	1	20♎38.1	17R 24.7	27R 49.7	19♑10.3
	11	22 54.1	16♉39.9	26♌46.3	23 33.8
	21	24 45.1	16D 56.9	25 08.2	27 56.8
	31	26 06.6	18 10.5	23 04.3	02♒19.8
FEB	10	26 54.4	20 13.9	20 47.2	06 43.5
	20	27R 04.1	23 01.0	18 31.8	11 08.7
MAR	2	26 32.7	26 26.2	16 32.7	15 36.1
	12	25 19.9	00♊24.8	15 00.8	20 06.8
	22	23 28.8	04 53.7	14 02.8	24 42.4
APR	1	21 08.4	09 50.3	13 41.3	29 24.5
	11	18 32.5	15 12.8	13D 55.2	04♓16.1
	21	15 57.6	21 00.2	14 41.8	09 20.7
MAY	1	13 40.9	27 11.9	15 57.6	14 43.4
	11	11 54.9	03♋47.7	17 38.4	20 32.3
	21	10 47.6	10 47.8	19 40.9	26 58.7
	31	10 22.0	18 12.3	22 01.5	04♈20.2
JUN	10	10D 36.9	26 01.3	24 37.4	13 04.4
	20	11 29.5	04♌15.1	27 26.1	23 52.1
	30	12 55.8	12 53.0	00♍25.4	07♉39.3
JUL	10	14 51.4	21 54.1	03 33.5	25 18.0
	20	17 12.7	01♍16.9	06 49.0	16♊28.9
	30	19 56.0	10 58.2	10 10.5	08♋56.0
AUG	9	22 58.3	20 54.5	13 36.8	01♌35.9
	19	26 17.3	01♎01.0	17 07.0	01♍03.3
	29	29 50.7	11 11.7	20 40.0	26 52.9
SEP	8	03♏36.8	21 20.3	24 15.0	16♎35.2
	18	07 34.3	01♏20.8	27 51.2	01♏55.6
	28	11 41.8	11 07.1	01♎27.6	14 02.7
OCT	8	15 58.4	20 34.8	05 03.5	23 54.1
	18	20 23.1	29 40.8	08 37.9	02♐12.2
	28	24 55.2	08♐23.1	12 09.6	09 25.4
NOV	7	29 34.0	16 41.4	15 37.8	15 53.0
	17	04♐18.9	24 36.1	19 01.2	21 48.0
	27	09 09.3	02♑08.2	22 18.2	27 18.8
DEC	7	14 04.7	09 19.2	25 27.4	02♑31.6
	17	19 04.7	16 10.8	28 27.0	07 30.6
	27	24 08.5	22 44.2	01♏14.8	12 18.8
JAN	6	29♐16.0	29♑01.3	03♏48.6	16♑58.4

1961		Sappho 80	Amor 1221	Pandora 55	Icarus 1566
JAN	1	13S 06.3	00S 11.7	19N 55.4	29S00.2
	21	14 45.1	01N 39.2	21 06.8	28 05.3
FEB	10	15 37.3	04 27.2	22 23.7	26 45.6
MAR	2	15 27.2	07 40.5	23 05.1	25 06.4
	22	14 01.9	10 55.9	22 53.5	23 12.1
APR	11	11 30.8	13 54.2	21 56.4	21 06.1
MAY	1	08 40.8	16 15.6	20 26.6	18 48.5
	21	06 30.3	17 38.5	18 32.5	16 11.6
JUN	10	05 29.1	17 39.2	16 18.5	12 45.5
	30	05 35.6	15 57.4	13 47.7	06 59.7
JUL	20	06 35.4	12 24.4	11 02.6	03N43.9
AUG	9	08 12.4	07 13.9	08 06.2	15 59.4
	29	10 12.3	01 05.2	05 02.0	06 18.3
SEP	18	12 22.3	05S 04.2	01 53.6	09S28.4
OCT	8	14 31.0	10 18.2	01S 14.8	18 35.8
	28	16 27.2	14 01.0	04 19.0	23 33.2
NOV	17	18 00.5	16 01.9	07 14.6	26 13.1
DEC	7	19 01.0	16 29.4	09 57.1	27 29.5
	27	19S 20.5	15S 41.1	12S 22.2	27S49.7

1962		Sappho 80	Amor 1221	Pandora 55	Icarus 1566
JAN	1	26♐41.8	25♑54.7	02♏33.6	14♑39.5
	11	01♑50.9	02♒04.1	04 59.3	19 15.5
	21	07 02.7	07 58.9	07 06.6	23 45.0
	31	12 16.8	13 40.0	08 52.7	28 09.0
FEB	10	17 32.8	19 08.5	10 13.8	02♒28.4
	20	22 50.0	24 24.9	11 06.6	06 43.6
MAR	2	28 08.0	29 29.7	11 28.1	10 55.2
	12	03♒26.1	04♓23.2	11R 15.6	15 03.5
	22	08 43.6	09 05.5	10 28.6	19 08.8
APR	1	13 59.9	13 36.6	09 09.2	23 11.7
	11	19 14.0	17 56.4	07 22.3	27 12.4
	21	24 24.7	22 04.2	05 17.4	01♓11.4
MAY	1	29 31.1	25 59.6	03 06.2	05 09.6
	11	04♓31.3	29 41.6	01 01.4	09 07.9
	21	09 23.6	03♈09.1	29♎15.1	13 07.7
	31	14 05.9	06 20.6	27 55.8	17 11.8
JUN	10	18 35.0	09 14.1	27 08.7	21 24.0
	20	22 47.5	11 47.2	26D 55.7	25 51.5
	30	26 39.4	13 57.1	27 16.0	00♈47.9
JUL	10	00♈05.0	15 40.1	28 07.4	06 39.5
	20	02 58.3	16 52.3	29 27.1	14 27.4
	30	05 12.3	17 29.2	01♏11.6	26 49.7
AUG	9	06 39.0	17R 26.3	03 18.1	21♉13.3
	19	07 12.2	16 40.2	05 43.5	06♋21.1
	29	06R 48.3	15 09.7	08 25.4	12♌59.4
SEP	8	05 30.1	12 57.2	11 21.7	00♍14.6
	18	03 31.1	10 11.4	14 30.2	10 27.7
	28	01 13.2	07 06.0	17 49.4	26 08.0
OCT	8	29♓04.7	03 59.4	21 17.9	20♎50.8
	18	27 30.9	01 10.1	24 54.1	08♏30.3
	28	26 47.5	28♓52.8	28 37.0	21 41.0
NOV	7	27D 01.1	27 16.8	02♐25.7	02♐08.8
	17	28 09.7	26 25.4	06 18.9	10 51.0
	27	00♈07.1	26D 17.3	10 15.8	18 21.8
DEC	7	02 46.5	26 49.3	14 15.5	25 02.5
	17	05 59.9	27 56.5	18 17.0	01♑06.6
	27	09 40.9	29 34.1	22 19.5	06 43.3
JAN	6	13♈44.1	01♈37.8	26♐21.9	11♑58.9

1962		Sappho 80	Amor 1221	Pandora 55	Icarus 1566
JAN	1	19S 18.1	15S 19.5	12S 55.3	27S47.9
	21	18 38.1	13 24.2	14 53.4	27 19.7
FEB	10	17 07.7	10 55.1	16 25.6	26 25.3
MAR	2	14 48.4	08 07.0	17 27.1	25 14.5
	22	11 44.8	05 11.9	17 51.7	23 56.9
APR	11	08 04.5	02 20.2	17 34.7	22 42.8
MAY	1	03 57.1	00N 19.3	16 43.0	21 44.7
	21	00N 25.6	02 38.1	15 41.9	21 19.3
JUN	10	04 49.4	04 27.7	15 02.9	21 51.4
	30	08 56.5	05 38.0	15 03.9	24 02.9
JUL	20	12 23.2	05 57.0	15 46.2	29 01.7
AUG	9	14 36.3	05 11.1	17 02.2	35 51.7
	29	14 51.3	03 10.0	18 41.7	24 32.0
SEP	18	12 36.2	00 03.7	20 34.2	01 24.2
OCT	8	08 33.5	03S 19.7	22 30.3	03 31.3
	28	04 44.2	05 53.9	24 21.2	15 31.2
NOV	17	02 36.9	07 03.9	25 59.4	21 35.8
DEC	7	02 22.5	06 54.4	27 18.2	24 35.2
	27	03N 34.6	05S 45.3	28S 12.9	25S52.3

1963		Sappho 80	Amor 1221	Pandora 55	Icarus 1566
JAN	1	11♈40.1	00♈33.0	24♐20.8	09♑23.5
	11	15 52.5	02 48.0	28 22.8	14 30.0
	21	20 20.0	05 23.0	02♑23.4	19 21.2
	31	24 59.5	08 15.0	06 21.6	23 59.7
FEB	10	29 48.2	11 21.0	10 16.0	28 26.8
	20	04♉43.5	14 38.9	14 05.6	02♒43.9
MAR	2	09 43.8	18 07.0	17 49.0	06 51.7
	12	14 47.5	21 43.5	21 24.6	10 50.3
	22	19 53.3	25 27.1	24 50.8	14 39.9
APR	1	25 00.3	29 17.1	28 05.5	18 20.1
	11	00♊07.4	03♉12.2	01♒06.4	21 50.1
	21	05 14.2	07 12.0	03 50.9	25 09.0
MAY	1	10 20.0	11 15.9	06 15.7	28 15.0
	11	15 24.2	15 23.3	08 17.3	01♓05.8
	21	20 26.5	19 33.9	09 52.0	03 38.2
	31	25 26.6	23 47.6	10 55.2	05 47.0
JUN	10	00♋24.0	28 04.0	11 23.4	07 25.2
	20	05 18.5	02♊23.0	11R 13.4	08 22.2
	30	10 10.0	06 44.5	10 24.3	08R21.0
JUL	10	14 57.9	11 08.4	08 59.1	06 56.0
	20	19 42.0	15 34.7	07 05.2	03 26.6
	30	24 22.0	20 03.3	04 54.8	26♒51.9
AUG	9	28 57.4	24 34.2	02 44.4	16 05.6
	19	03♌27.7	29 07.4	00 49.7	01 01.1
	29	07 52.4	03♋42.6	29♑24.5	14♑21.3
SEP	8	12 10.6	08 20.0	28 37.6	00 04.1
	18	16 21.7	12 59.6	28D 32.5	19♐34.6
	28	20 24.3	17 40.8	29 09.4	11 54.8
OCT	8	24 17.2	22 23.8	00♒25.4	05 20.7
	18	27 59.0	27 08.4	02 16.6	27♏58.0
	28	01♍27.4	01♌54.0	04 38.9	17 42.8
NOV	7	04 40.3	06 40.5	07 27.9	06 21.8
	17	07 34.9	11 27.5	10 39.9	16D41.7
	27	10 07.6	16 14.4	14 11.7	01♐28.3
DEC	7	12 14.7	21 01.6	18 00.0	12 36.5
	17	13 51.6	25 48.8	22 02.4	21 33.0
	27	14 53.6	00♍36.5	26 16.8	29 06.5
JAN	6	15♍16.2	05♍27.9	00♓41.1	05♑43.6

1963		Sappho 80	Amor 1221	Pandora 55	Icarus 1566
JAN	1	04N 02.4	05S 21.0	28S 22.5	26S00.9
	21	06 19.2	03 23.7	28 44.2	26 04.8
FEB	10	08 58.3	01 03.5	28 40.5	25 35.0
MAR	2	11 39.4	01N 28.5	28 15.8	24 47.3
	22	14 06.4	04 03.5	27 37.5	23 55.7
APR	11	16 07.2	06 34.0	26 56.0	23 15.5
MAY	1	17 33.2	08 52.9	26 24.2	23 05.3
	21	18 18.8	10 53.9	26 15.9	23 51.8
JUN	10	18 21.9	12 30.9	26 43.0	26 17.6
	30	17 43.0	13 38.1	27 45.9	31 35.0
JUL	20	16 25.2	14 10.0	29 01.4	41 37.4
AUG	9	14 33.4	14 01.7	29 45.6	57 29.0
	29	12 13.6	13 08.8	29 28.6	70 07.1
SEP	18	09 33.3	11 28.0	28 16.9	63 27.0
OCT	8	06 40.1	08 57.2	26 29.6	50 58.3
	28	03 43.2	05 35.7	24 17.0	31 46.2
NOV	17	00 52.9	01 25.7	21 40.6	11 59.4
DEC	7	01S 37.9	03S 26.1	18 39.2	19 16.5
	27	03S 32.1	08S 43.6	15S 12.9	22S37.1

1964		Sappho 80	Amor 1221	Pandora 55	Icarus 1566
JAN	1	15♍10.1	03♍01.6	28♒27.8	02♑30.9
	11	15R11.5	07 56.1	02♓56.5	08 46.3
	21	14 28.8	13 01.4	07 32.8	14 26.7
	31	13 02.8	18 30.5	12 15.2	19 39.8
FEB	10	10 58.9	24 44.0	17 02.5	24 31.0
	20	08 28.4	02♎13.9	21 53.8	29 03.3
MAR	1	05 47.7	11 50.2	26 47.9	03♒18.7
	11	03 14.7	24 22.0	01♈44.1	07 18.4
	21	01 05.6	09♏49.4	06 41.5	11 02.7
	31	29♌31.9	26 22.5	11 39.2	14 30.9
APR	10	28 38.8	10♐49.2	16 36.8	17 42.2
	20	28D27.2	21 09.1	21 33.5	20 34.4
	30	28 54.6	27 20.7	26 28.5	23 04.4
MAY	10	29 56.8	00♑04.4	01♉21.5	25 08.2
	20	01♍29.6	00R11.9	06 11.6	26 39.2
	30	03 28.3	28♐45.4	10 58.1	27 29.2
JUN	9	05 49.0	26 41.6	15 40.5	27R26.6
	19	08 28.3	24 49.7	20 17.8	26 15.4
	29	11 23.3	23 41.6	24 49.1	23 37.0
JUL	9	14 31.4	23D26.7	29 13.5	19 11.8
	19	17 50.9	24 04.9	03♊29.6	12 49.4
	29	21 19.8	25 29.5	07 36.0	04 47.3
AUG	8	24 56.8	27 31.3	11 31.2	26♑01.2
	18	28 40.8	00♑03.6	15 12.9	17 50.7
	28	02♎30.6	02 59.6	18 38.7	11 17.3
SEP	7	06 25.5	06 13.9	21 45.8	06 42.6
	17	10 24.7	09 43.1	24 30.4	03 59.8
	27	14 27.3	13 23.7	26 48.7	02 49.3
OCT	7	18 32.8	17 13.2	28 36.0	02D51.5
	17	22 40.5	21 10.2	29 47.5	03 49.9
	27	26 49.5	25 12.7	00♋18.7	05 30.3
NOV	6	00♏59.5	29 19.8	00R06.3	07 41.0
	16	05 09.5	03♒30.5	29♊09.6	10 07.8
	26	09 18.7	07 43.7	27 33.3	12 24.6
DEC	6	13 26.4	11 58.9	25 26.9	13R21.2
	16	17 31.5	16 15.5	23 06.1	08 08.9
	26	21 32.9	20 32.6	20 49.4	22♐34.0
JAN	5	25♏29.6	24♒50.0	18♊53.7	28D00.1

JAN	1	03S52.5	10S03.4	14S17.7	23S04.7
	21	04 30.2	14 57.7	10 23.8	24 00.8
FEB	10	03 44.8	17 41.4	06 13.3	24 02.3
MAR	1	01 42.9	13 06.9	01 52.2	23 38.0
	21	00N50.3	07N52.7	02N32.4	23 08.7
APR	10	02 59.8	24 53.5	06 53.2	22 54.5
	30	04 16.3	29 27.3	11 03.4	23 19.0
MAY	20	04 35.2	28 23.4	14 56.4	24 54.4
JUN	9	04 03.0	22 53.0	18 26.8	28 26.5
	29	02 48.7	14 07.9	21 30.3	34 49.9
JUL	19	01 01.2	04 50.9	24 04.8	43 56.7
AUG	8	01S11.6	02S53.3	26 11.0	51 34.7
	28	03 42.1	08 31.0	27 53.1	52 26.8
SEP	17	06 23.4	12 14.2	29 19.2	49 11.3
OCT	7	09 08.3	14 23.5	30 39.7	45 39.6
	27	11 49.9	15 16.7	32 02.9	42 39.3
NOV	16	14 21.0	15 08.3	33 24.0	39 39.9
DEC	6	16 34.6	14 10.3	34 16.2	35 06.1
	26	[illegible]	[illegible]	[illegible]	18S10.7

1965		Sappho 80	Amor 1221	Pandora 55	Icarus 1566
JAN	1	23♏55.6	23♒07.1	19R36.5	24D55.9
	11	27 48.7	27 24.3	18♊00.2	02♑41.5
	21	01♐34.5	01♓40.8	17 02.7	09 49.8
	31	05 11.4	05 56.1	16D47.2	16 05.3
FEB	10	08 37.1	10 09.9	17 12.9	21 38.6
	20	11 49.4	14 21.5	18 16.1	26 38.3
MAR	2	14 45.2	18 30.6	19 51.9	01♒10.2
	12	17 21.0	22 36.7	21 55.8	05 17.2
	22	19 32.8	26 39.2	24 22.9	09 00.8
APR	1	21 16.0	00♈37.8	27 09.1	12 21.2
	11	22 25.2	04 31.9	00♋11.2	15 16.8
	21	22 55.6	08 20.7	03 26.0	17 45.1
MAY	1	22R42.5	12 03.9	06 51.1	19 41.8
	11	21 43.6	15 40.6	10 24.6	21 00.5
	21	20 01.5	19 09.7	14 04.5	21 32.6
	31	17 44.2	22 30.5	17 49.7	21R06.9
JUN	10	15 07.0	25 41.5	21 38.8	19 28.7
	20	12 30.5	28 41.1	25 30.7	16 23.6
	30	10 14.7	01♉27.8	29 24.8	11 40.3
JUL	10	08 36.8	03 58.8	03♌20.0	05 22.4
	20	07 46.5	06 11.7	07 15.7	28♑00.3
	30	07D46.9	08 03.2	11 11.2	20 28.4
AUG	9	08 37.1	09 29.0	15 05.7	13 47.4
	19	10 12.6	10 25.0	18 58.6	08 36.0
	29	12 28.4	10 46.0	22 49.3	05 04.6
SEP	8	15 19.8	10R27.3	26 36.8	03 06.5
	18	18 41.7	09 25.5	00♍20.2	02 26.5
	28	22 30.0	07 39.3	03 58.8	02D50.3
OCT	8	26 41.6	05 12.4	07 31.1	04 05.6
	18	01♑12.9	02 15.1	10 56.0	06 02.9
	28	06 01.8	29♈03.0	14 12.0	08 35.5
NOV	7	11 06.0	25 56.2	17 17.0	11 39.1
	17	16 23.6	23 13.6	20 09.2	15 10.4
	27	21 52.9	21 09.2	22 46.1	19 08.7
DEC	7	27 32.6	19 51.2	25 04.6	23 34.2
	17	03♒21.0	19 21.1	27 01.9	28 28.7
	27	09 17.2	19D36.9	28 34.3	03♒56.5
JAN	6	15♒19.7	20♈34.3	29♍38.1	10♒02.6

JAN	1	18S51.4	11S58.1	33N58.8	17S40.1
	21	20 01.2	09 44.8	32 59.8	20 03.6
FEB	10	20 36.1	07 13.7	32 00.4	21 02.8
MAR	2	20 34.5	04 33.2	31 15.6	21 13.2
	22	19 56.7	01 50.6	30 41.0	21 11.4
APR	11	18 45.2	00N47.2	30 05.6	21 25.9
MAY	1	17 04.5	03 13.6	29 19.4	22 27.0
	21	15 03.8	05 22.4	28 15.6	24 53.5
JUN	10	13 04.8	07 07.6	26 50.5	29 31.5
	30	11 42.0	08 22.6	25 03.7	36 37.1
JUL	20	11 19.6	09 00.2	22 56.8	43 51.6
AUG	9	11 53.1	08 52.3	20 33.1	46 42.6
	29	12 59.8	07 50.0	17 57.3	45 17.7
SEP	18	14 14.5	05 47.5	15 15.0	42 49.9
OCT	8	15 15.0	02 53.6	12 32.5	40 40.1
	28	15 43.5	00S12.0	09 56.9	38 48.9
NOV	17	15 26.7	02 27.1	07 36.3	36 55.9
DEC	7	14 16.7	03 13.5	05 39.9	34 35.0
	27	12S11.6	02S35.6	04N17.5	31S08.4

1966		Sappho 80	Amor 1221	Pandora 55	Icarus 1566
JAN	1	12♒17.7	20♈00.7	29♍10.0	06♒54.5
	11	18 23.0	21 17.1	29 58.2	13 21.4
	21	24 33.1	23 07.3	00R12.9	20 21.3
	31	00♓46.9	25 27.1	29♍51.8	24R45.1
FEB	10	07 03.2	28 11.9	28 55.1	08 10.9
	20	13 21.4	01♉18.3	27 25.5	03D19.6
MAR	2	19 40.4	04 43.6	25 30.0	05 03.0
	12	25 59.3	08 25.3	23 19.2	07 56.5
	22	02♈17.4	12 21.6	21 06.1	10 55.8
APR	1	08 33.8	16 31.3	19 04.1	13 40.7
	11	14 47.9	20 53.0	17 24.2	16 01.7
	21	20 59.0	25 26.3	16 14.0	17 51.5
MAY	1	27 06.5	00♊10.7	15 37.3	19 01.4
	11	03♉09.7	05 05.9	15D34.5	19R21.5
	21	09 08.2	10 12.2	16 03.9	18 38.6
	31	15 01.3	15 29.6	17 02.8	16 36.5
JUN	10	20 48.5	20 58.5	18 27.7	12 59.2
	20	26 29.3	26 39.9	20 15.3	07 36.1
	30	02♊02.8	02♋34.3	22 22.5	00 36.2
JUL	10	07 28.6	08 42.8	24 46.4	22♑39.7
	20	12 45.8	15 06.6	27 24.5	14 50.4
	30	17 53.4	21 46.9	00♎14.9	08 10.0
AUG	9	22 50.3	28 44.9	03 15.4	03 10.3
	19	27 35.4	06♌02.3	06 24.7	29♐54.3
	29	02♋06.7	13 40.2	09 41.4	28 10.0
SEP	8	06 22.4	21 39.8	13 04.1	27D39.9
	18	10 20.1	00♍02.0	16 32.0	28 09.0
	28	13 56.4	08 47.0	20 03.8	29 25.0
OCT	8	17 08.1	17 54.4	23 38.6	01♑18.4
	18	19 50.4	27 23.0	27 15.6	03 42.4
	28	21 58.1	07♎10.0	00♏53.9	06 32.2
NOV	7	23 25.7	17 11.8	04 32.4	09 44.2
	17	24 07.1	27 23.6	08 10.2	13 16.3
	27	23R57.6	07♏39.4	11 46.3	17 07.2
DEC	7	22 55.8	17 53.1	15 19.5	21 16.3
	17	21 04.7	27 58.4	18 48.7	25 44.6
	27	18 35.9	07♐49.0	22 12.2	00♒33.1
JAN	6	15♋48.0	17♐20.3	25♏28.9	05♒44.7

JAN	1	11S32.0	02S15.6	04N03.4	29S58.8
	21	08 24.3	00 25.6	03 36.9	22 51.7
FEB	10	04 37.8	01N57.0	04 00.3	11 35.7
MAR	2	00 25.8	04 36.0	05 03.7	14 35.7
	22	03N56.3	07 18.6	06 17.7	16 07.1
APR	11	08 13.1	09 54.3	07 06.6	17 23.2
MAY	1	12 09.9	12 13.4	07 09.5	19 22.7
	21	15 33.3	14 06.1	06 24.7	23 02.0
JUN	10	18 12.5	15 22.6	04 59.8	29 11.2
	30	19 59.6	15 52.4	03 03.6	37 02.3
JUL	20	20 50.8	15 25.3	00 43.7	42 10.4
AUG	9	20 46.8	13 51.6	01S53.6	42 18.7
	29	19 52.4	11 04.6	04 42.5	40 29.1
SEP	18	18 16.6	07 03.8	07 37.9	38 45.9
OCT	8	16 11.3	01 59.5	10 34.9	37 27.1
	28	13 52.0	03S40.9	13 28.5	36 19.7
NOV	17	11 38.1	09 10.8	16 14.4	35 06.8
DEC	7	09 53.4	13 33.5	18 48.4	33 33.1
	27	09N[illegible]	16S04.2	21S07.5	31S[illegible]

1967		Sappho 80	Amor 1221	Pandora 55	Icarus 1566
JAN	1	17R13.0	12♐37.3	23♏51.5	03♒05.8
	11	14♋23.8	21 57.6	27 04.0	08 30.5
	21	11 49.4	00♑53.4	00♐06.7	14 25.8
	31	09 48.5	09 22.7	02 57.6	20 59.9
FEB	10	08 31.8	17 25.0	05 34.3	28 26.1
	20	08 03.3	24 59.9	07 54.0	07♓05.1
MAR	2	08D21.0	02♒07.7	09 53.7	17 31.1
	12	09 19.9	08 49.3	11 30.1	00♈29.5
	22	10 54.5	15 04.9	12 39.5	08R00.2
APR	1	12 58.8	20 55.2	13 18.5	22♓13.5
	11	15 27.7	26 20.6	13R24.1	11 57.4
	21	18 16.7	01♓20.5	12 54.5	06 29.1
MAY	1	21 21.9	05 54.7	11 50.2	02 42.3
	11	24 40.3	10 01.9	10 14.8	28♒57.3
	21	28 09.5	13 40.2	08 15.9	24 08.7
	31	01♌47.3	16 47.3	06 05.1	17 26.9
JUN	10	05 32.2	19 19.8	03 55.3	08 21.2
	20	09 22.7	21 13.2	02 00.3	27♑12.2
	30	13 17.5	22 23.0	00 30.9	15 35.0
JUL	10	17 16.0	22R44.0	29♏34.0	05 28.3
	20	21 17.1	22 11.6	29 13.3	27♐59.8
	30	25 20.2	20 44.4	29D28.8	23 09.4
AUG	9	29 24.6	18 25.1	00♐18.6	20 27.6
	19	03♍29.7	15 24.0	01 40.0	19 22.9
	29	07 34.9	11 59.4	03 29.4	19D29.1
SEP	8	11 39.7	08 33.6	05 43.6	20 28.0
	18	15 43.4	05 29.7	08 19.5	22 06.9
	28	19 45.2	03 04.2	11 14.1	24 16.3
OCT	8	23 44.6	01 25.9	14 25.1	26 50.2
	18	27 40.6	00 37.1	17 50.3	29 44.1
	28	01♎32.3	00D34.7	21 27.7	02♑54.6
NOV	7	05 18.7	01 13.7	25 15.9	06 19.8
	17	08 58.1	02 28.4	29 13.3	09 58.0
	27	12 29.4	04 12.9	03♑18.6	13 48.1
DEC	7	15 50.6	06 22.3	07 30.7	17 49.9
	17	18 59.5	08 52.4	11 48.5	22 03.1
	27	21 53.8	11 39.3	16 11.0	26 27.9
JAN	6	24♎30.3	14♓40.1	20♑37.4	01♒05.6
JAN	1	08N59.5	16S22.0	21S39.8	30S42.1
	21	09 25.7	16 18.7	23 38.2	27 14.8
FEB	10	10 31.9	14 37.3	25 20.7	21 55.9
MAR	2	11 48.3	11 52.8	26 49.7	12 38.3
	22	12 52.5	08 37.0	28 08.4	07N13.9
APR	11	13 31.6	05 14.6	29 17.0	00 41.1
MAY	1	13 38.9	02 04.2	30 08.0	07S04.7
	21	13 12.1	00N38.5	30 25.2	15 14.9
JUN	10	12 11.6	02 37.6	29 59.6	26 29.2
	30	10 39.9	03 33.4	29 07.8	36 25.8
JUL	20	08 40.5	03 02.5	28 21.0	38 28.0
AUG	9	06 18.1	00 46.8	27 58.9	37 05.1
	29	03 37.7	02S55.7	28 02.9	35 49.2
SEP	18	00 44.8	06 51.6	28 23.8	35 04.9
OCT	8	02S14.8	09 44.8	28 49.2	34 37.3
	28	05 14.8	11 10.4	29 06.7	34 10.5
NOV	17	08 08.6	11 19.7	29 05.7	33 32.2
DEC	7	10 49.4	10 31.1	28 38.0	32 32.8
	27	13S09.2	09S00.3	27S38.8	31S04.7

1968		Sappho 80	Amor 1221	Pandora 55	Icarus 1566
JAN	1	23♎14.5	13♓08.1	18♑23.8	28♑45.1
	11	25 40.8	16 14.9	22 51.7	03♒29.6
	21	27 44.3	19 31.9	27 22.1	08 29.1
	31	29 20.6	22 57.1	01♒54.3	13 46.6
FEB	10	00♏25.1	26 28.9	06 27.3	19 25.7
	20	00 53.7	00♈05.9	11 00.3	25 31.9
MAR	1	00R42.4	03 46.9	15 32.7	02♓13.7
	11	29♎49.3	07 30.9	20 03.4	09 42.4
	21	28 16.0	11 16.9	24 31.7	18 15.6
	31	26 08.2	15 04.1	28 56.8	28 20.3
APR	10	23 37.6	18 51.9	03♓17.4	10♈38.6
	20	21 00.1	22 39.5	07 32.6	26 23.2
	30	18 32.6	26 26.4	11 41.1	17♉13.3
MAY	10	16 30.7	00♉11.9	15 41.4	28 09.5
	20	15 04.5	03 55.3	19 31.8	28R51.6
	30	14 19.3	07 36.0	23 10.4	29D24.4
JUN	9	14D16.0	11 13.2	26 34.5	05♊38.6
	19	14 52.2	14 46.2	29 41.6	12♏44.7
	29	16 04.3	18 13.9	02♈28.3	21 49.5
JUL	9	17 48.2	21 35.1	04 50.3	24 37.6
	19	19 59.7	24 48.4	06 43.5	26 56.6
	29	22 35.2	27 52.0	08 03.0	29 19.9
AUG	8	25 31.4	00♊43.7	08 43.9	01♐54.3
	18	28 45.6	03 20.9	08R43.0	04 39.6
	28	02♏15.5	05 40.0	07 58.7	07 35.8
SEP	7	05 59.3	07 36.7	06 34.5	10 41.9
	17	09 55.2	09 06.2	04 39.3	13 56.6
	27	14 02.1	10 01.9	02 27.7	17 19.4
OCT	7	18 18.7	10R17.1	00 18.8	20 49.4
	17	22 44.2	09 44.9	28♓30.5	24 26.0
	27	27 17.8	08 19.5	27 16.9	28 08.9
NOV	6	01♐58.6	06 00.0	26 46.4	01♑57.7
	16	06 46.1	02 53.2	27D00.9	05 52.1
	26	11 39.7	29♉15.5	27 58.8	09 52.1
DEC	6	16 38.8	25 33.5	29 36.3	13 57.4
	16	21 42.9	22 15.2	01♈48.0	18 08.4
	26	26 51.7	19 44.0	04 29.0	22 25.2
JAN	5	02♑04.4	18♉13.6	07♈34.7	26♑48.1
JAN	1	13S40.0	08S32.5	27S18.8	30S37.2
	21	15 21.3	06 25.9	25 38.3	28 22.0
FEB	10	16 19.4	04 01.5	23 26.9	25 16.3
MAR	1	16 19.8	01 27.6	20 49.7	20 57.6
	21	15 08.8	01N08.4	17 53.3	14 36.5
APR	10	12 48.7	03 40.0	14 45.2	04 09.7
	30	09 58.5	06 01.0	11 34.0	17N02.2
MAY	20	07 37.6	08 05.7	08 28.2	33 06.1
JUN	9	06 23.1	09 48.7	05 37.2	52 14.9
	29	06 18.4	11 04.8	03 10.3	20S13.4
JUL	19	07 10.1	11 49.0	01 17.8	26 25.6
AUG	8	08 41.2	11 56.2	00 09.6	28 31.4
	28	10 36.4	11 21.7	00N08.7	29 52.1
SEP	17	12 42.3	10 01.1	00S15.1	30 52.3
OCT	7	14 46.5	07 52.4	00 49.9	31 34.4
	27	16 37.7	05 02.6	00 54.4	31 56.2
NOV	16	18 04.9	02 02.3	00 05.3	31 54.4
DEC	6	18 57.9	00S05.9	01N37.7	31 26.3
	26	19S08.5	00S26.8	04N04.1	30S29.6

1969		Sappho 80	Amor 1221	Pandora 55	Icarus 1566
JAN	1	29♐58.9	18R42.1	06♈17.8	25♑02.2
	11	05♑13.8	17♉50.1	09 36.0	29 29.1
	21	10 32.2	18D01.1	13 12.5	04♒03.4
	31	15 53.3	19 10.3	17 04.0	08 46.1
FEB	10	21 16.8	21 10.7	21 07.4	13 38.7
	20	26 42.3	23 56.1	25 20.6	18 43.6
MAR	2	02♒09.1	27 20.8	29 41.6	24 03.5
	12	07 36.7	01♊19.9	04♉08.6	29 42.6
	22	13 04.5	05 50.2	08 40.3	05♓46.8
APR	1	18 31.7	10 49.1	13 15.4	12 24.0
	11	23 57.7	16 14.5	17 52.7	19 45.7
	21	29 21.4	22 05.6	22 31.6	28 08.4
MAY	1	04♓41.7	28 21.8	27 11.0	07♈54.9
	11	09 57.5	05♋02.6	01♊50.2	19 37.8
	21	15 07.0	12 08.5	06 28.9	03♉59.1
	31	20 08.2	19 39.4	11 06.0	21 51.8
JUN	10	24 59.0	27 35.4	15 41.3	14♊58.9
	20	29 36.4	05♌56.6	20 14.1	12♋18.2
	30	03♈56.6	14 42.2	24 43.7	04♌58.4
JUL	10	07 55.8	23 50.9	29 09.7	00♍28.8
	20	11 28.1	03♍21.1	03♋31.4	26 04.5
	30	14 27.6	13 09.5	07 47.9	16♎26.2
AUG	9	16 47.2	23 11.6	11 58.5	01♏01.9
	19	18 18.8	03♎22.7	16 02.2	11 41.1
	29	18 56.0	13 36.3	19 57.8	19 56.8
SEP	8	18R35.1	23 45.7	23 43.9	26 45.8
	18	17 18.1	03♏44.9	27 19.0	02♐41.6
	28	15 18.1	13 28.0	00♌41.0	08 03.4
OCT	8	12 57.2	22 50.8	03 47.7	13 03.0
	18	10 43.0	01♐50.8	06 36.3	17 48.2
	28	09 02.0	10 26.2	09 03.4	22 23.7
NOV	7	08 10.3	18 37.2	11 05.6	26 52.7
	17	08D14.9	26 24.7	12 38.5	01♑17.7
	27	09 14.5	03♑49.6	13 38.0	05 40.1
DEC	7	11 02.9	10 53.8	14 00.4	10 01.1
	17	13 33.1	17 39.1	13R42.6	14 21.7
	27	16 37.6	24 06.9	12 44.7	18 42.4
JAN	6	20♈09.5	00♒18.7	11♌10.2	23♑03.8
JAN	1	19S02.4	00S10.8	04N54.6	30S06.8
	21	18 09.3	01N40.5	07 58.6	28 30.9
FEB	10	16 25.0	04 30.4	11 17.7	26 22.6
MAR	2	13 51.6	07 46.2	14 40.8	23 37.6
	22	10 34.7	11 04.0	17 57.4	20 05.5
APR	11	06 42.3	14 03.9	20 58.5	15 21.9
MAY	1	02 24.7	16 25.9	23 35.8	08 30.5
	21	02N05.8	17 47.2	25 43.0	02N26.3
JUN	10	06 35.1	17 43.5	27 15.4	20 16.5
	30	10 46.6	15 54.0	28 11.3	27 31.2
JUL	20	14 20.2	12 11.2	28 31.4	06 51.9
AUG	9	16 49.1	06 51.2	28 19.6	11S49.1
	29	17 37.7	00 36.9	27 42.6	20 36.7
SEP	18	16 08.7	05S32.0	26 50.2	25 08.6
OCT	8	12 28.0	10 40.2	25 54.4	27 45.6
	28	08 12.7	14 14.4	25 09.7	29 16.5
NOV	17	05 19.2	16 06.9	24 51.5	30 00.1
DEC	7	04 25.5	16 27.7	25 12.7	30 05.0
	27	05N09.6	15S34.9	26N14.7	29S36.0

1970	Sappho 80	Amor 1221	Pandora 55	Icarus 1566
JAN 1	18♈20.5	27♑14.7	12R01.7	20♑52.9
11	22 04.1	03♒19.1	10♌11.5	25 15.1
21	26 07.4	09 09.4	07 59.1	29 38.8
31	00♉25.9	14 46.5	05 39.1	04♒04.7
FEB 10	04 56.2	20 11.5	03 27.3	08 33.8
20	09 35.8	25 24.8	01 38.0	13 06.6
MAR 2	14 21.9	00♓26.8	00 20.7	17 44.6
12	19 13.2	05 18.1	29♋40.2	22 29.4
22	24 07.9	09 58.4	29D37.5	27 23.0
APR 1	29 04.7	14 27.8	00♌10.2	02♓28.5
11	04♊02.9	18 46.3	01 14.9	07 50.0
21	09 01.5	22 53.1	02 47.5	13 33.1
MAY 1	13 59.7	26 47.8	04 43.8	19 46.3
11	18 57.2	00♈29.6	07 00.2	26 41.7
21	23 53.3	03 57.1	09 33.4	04♈36.8
31	28 47.7	07 09.0	12 20.5	13 57.8
JUN 10	03♋40.0	10 03.4	15 19.3	25 20.6
20	08 29.9	12 37.9	18 27.5	09♉28.6
30	13 17.1	14 49.6	21 43.6	26 54.1
JUL 10	18 01.3	16 35.1	25 06.1	17♊20.6
20	22 42.0	17 50.3	28 33.7	10♋05.8
30	27 19.1	18 31.0	02♍05.4	08♌52.5
AUG 9	01♌52.0	18R32.5	05 40.2	07♍00.9
19	06 20.3	17 51.3	09 17.2	29 37.6
29	10 43.4	16 25.7	12 55.5	17♎55.6
SEP 8	15 00.6	14 17.8	16 34.5	02♏19.6
18	19 11.1	11 35.2	20 13.1	13 43.4
28	23 13.8	08 31.4	23 50.7	23 01.0
OCT 8	27 07.6	05 24.0	27 26.2	00♐52.3
18	00♍50.9	02 32.0	00♎58.7	07 44.2
28	04 21.9	00 10.5	04 27.2	13 54.8
NOV 7	07 38.4	28♓29.5	07 50.4	19 36.3
17	10 37.7	27 33.0	11 06.7	24 56.4
27	13 16.8	27D20.2	14 14.8	00♑00.9
DEC 7	15 31.8	27 47.9	17 12.7	04 53.8
17	17 18.6	28 51.6	19 58.2	09 37.7
27	18 32.5	00♈26.3	22 29.0	14 14.8
JAN 6	19♍08.8	02♈27.5	24♎42.3	18♑46.4
JAN 1	05N31.8	15S12.6	26N34.5	29S23.9
21	07 29.5	13 14.9	27 52.1	28 18.0
FEB 10	09 52.8	10 44.9	28 34.4	26 46.3
MAR 2	12 19.7	07 56.6	28 21.6	24 52.1
22	14 33.2	05 01.8	27 24.6	22 37.1
APR 11	16 21.0	02 10.6	26 00.3	20 00.0
MAY 1	17 34.5	00N28.3	24 17.3	16 52.2
21	18 08.6	02 46.7	22 18.0	12 47.8
JUN 10	18 01.4	04 36.2	20 03.1	06 39.9
30	17 13.7	05 46.8	17 33.1	03N36.1
JUL 20	15 48.7	06 07.1	14 49.5	17 17.7
AUG 9	13 51.2	05 23.5	11 54.9	14 34.0
29	11 27.3	03 25.7	08 52.4	03S34.6
SEP 18	08 44.0	00 22.1	05 45.8	15 29.3
OCT 8	05 48.8	03S01.2	02 39.3	21 59.1
28	02 50.4	05 37.8	00S22.4	25 34.8
NOV 17	00S01.4	06 50.7	03 14.2	27 31.0
DEC 7	02 34.4	06 43.2	05 51.0	28 22.1
27	04S32.7	05S35.2	08S07.4	28S26.1

1971	Sappho 80	Amor 1221	Pandora 55	Icarus 1566
JAN 1	18♍55.7	01♈23.8	23♎38.1	16♑31.2
11	19R11.6	03 36.8	25 41.4	21 00.5
21	18 44.8	06 10.1	27 22.5	25 26.0
31	17 34.1	09 00.8	28 37.9	29 48.4
FEB 10	15 43.4	12 06.0	29 24.1	04♒08.2
20	13 21.7	15 23.3	29R38.1	08 26.1
MAR 2	10 43.1	18 51.1	29 17.6	12 42.8
12	08 05.7	22 27.6	28 22.8	16 58.5
22	05 46.5	26 11.6	26 56.3	21 14.1
APR 1	03 58.4	00♉02.0	25 04.1	25 30.6
11	02 49.5	03 57.9	22 56.4	29 48.7
21	02 21.8	07 58.6	20 45.3	04♓10.4
MAY 1	02D34.1	12 03.7	18 43.6	08 37.7
11	03 22.9	16 12.5	17 02.5	13 13.5
21	04 43.8	20 24.9	15 49.8	18 02.9
31	06 32.5	24 40.6	15 09.7	23 13.0
JUN 10	08 44.7	28 59.2	15D03.4	28 55.6
20	11 16.8	03♊20.8	15 29.5	05♈31.3
30	14 05.8	07 45.4	16 25.7	13 35.2
JUL 10	17 09.1	12 12.7	17 48.9	24 12.6
20	20 24.4	16 42.9	19 35.8	09♉19.7
30	23 50.1	21 16.0	21 43.5	01♊24.0
AUG 9	27 24.6	25 51.9	24 09.1	29 24.5
19	01♎06.6	00♋31.0	26 50.2	25♋20.6
29	04 55.2	05 13.1	29 44.7	14♌54.1
SEP 8	08 49.2	09 58.4	02♏50.7	04♍00.1
18	12 48.0	14 47.1	06 06.5	01♎49.6
28	16 50.9	19 39.3	09 30.9	22 50.1
OCT 8	20 56.9	24 35.1	13 02.5	08♏22.6
18	25 05.7	29 35.0	16 40.2	20 29.1
28	29 16.4	04♌39.0	20 22.9	00♐19.7
NOV 7	03♏28.3	09 47.9	24 09.7	08 38.4
17	07 40.9	15 02.5	27 59.6	15 53.5
27	11 53.3	20 23.5	01♐51.8	22 23.5
DEC 7	16 04.6	25 53.2	05 45.1	28 20.3
17	20 14.2	01♍34.5	09 38.8	03♑52.5
27	24 20.9	07 31.1	13 31.9	09 05.6
JAN 6	28♏23.5	13♍51.0	17♐23.2	14♑03.6
JAN 1	04S54.5	05S11.1	08S37.6	28S21.1
21	05 40.0	03 14.0	10 20.4	27 41.8
FEB 10	05 04.1	00 53.9	11 29.5	26 37.3
MAR 2	03 07.9	01N38.2	11 58.5	25 15.6
22	00 31.8	04 13.3	11 43.6	23 44.5
APR 11	01N47.0	06 43.8	10 51.3	22 11.9
MAY 1	03 13.4	09 02.6	09 45.6	20 46.3
21	03 40.0	11 03.2	08 59.3	19 36.9
JUN 10	03 13.1	12 39.6	08 53.4	18 52.6
30	02 02.3	13 45.8	09 32.2	18 33.1
JUL 20	00 17.3	14 16.2	10 49.5	17 30.1
AUG 9	01S53.6	14 05.9	12 36.0	09 53.4
29	04 22.4	13 10.4	14 42.2	05N05.8
SEP 18	07 01.6	11 26.2	16 59.3	03 54.0
OCT 8	09 44.2	08 51.2	19 19.5	11S10.7
28	12 22.8	05 24.6	21 35.5	19 27.9
NOV 17	14 50.1	01 08.0	23 40.7	23 46.9
DEC 7	16 58.9	03S52.7	25 29.6	25 55.7
27	18S42.5	09S24.4	26S58.1	26S46.1

1972	Sappho 80	Amor 1221	Pandora 55	Icarus 1566
JAN 1	26♏22.7	10♍37.6	15♐27.8	11♑36.3
11	00♐23.0	17 12.7	19 17.9	16 27.9
21	04 17.2	24 27.6	23 04.6	21 08.5
31	08 03.8	02♎41.6	26 46.6	25 39.4
FEB 10	11 41.1	12 19.5	00♑22.6	00♒02.1
20	15 06.9	23 44.3	03 51.0	04 17.4
MAR 1	18 18.3	07♏06.8	07 09.9	08 25.5
11	21 12.7	21 56.6	10 17.7	12 27.0
21	23 46.2	06♐47.7	13 11.7	16 22.0
31	25 54.5	20 04.6	15 49.3	20 10.0
APR 10	27 32.9	00♑48.0	18 07.7	23 51.1
20	28 35.8	08 39.2	20 03.2	27 24.5
30	28 58.1	13 46.4	21 32.1	00♓49.4
MAY 10	28R35.7	16 21.2	22 30.6	04 04.8
20	27 26.9	16R34.6	22 54.8	07 08.6
30	25 35.6	14 51.8	22R42.2	09 58.5
JUN 9	23 12.1	11 50.4	21 52.0	12 31.0
19	20 33.5	08 21.0	20 26.6	14 40.0
29	18 01.7	05 15.1	18 33.4	16 16.8
JUL 9	15 56.9	03 03.6	16 23.6	17 06.0
19	14 34.5	01 58.5	14 12.2	16R38.6
29	14 02.7	01D58.0	12 14.8	13 55.9
AUG 8	14D22.7	02 51.8	10 44.1	06 33.3
18	15 32.6	04 30.5	09 49.1	17♒50.8
28	17 27.3	06 44.4	09D34.1	07♑22.8
SEP 7	20 01.5	09 25.5	09 59.2	29♏01.9
17	23 10.3	12 28.2	11 02.6	10 06.2
27	26 48.6	15 47.5	12 40.7	29♎10.8
OCT 7	00♑52.5	19 19.8	14 49.5	20 49.6
17	05 18.6	23 02.7	17 25.4	15 24.4
27	10 03.7	26 53.6	20 24.5	27D15.7
NOV 6	15 05.3	00♒51.0	23 43.6	15♏58.5
16	20 21.6	04 53.6	27 20.0	29 27.9
26	25 50.1	09 00.0	01♒11.0	09♐55.2
DEC 6	01♒29.5	13 09.5	05 14.7	18 31.7
16	07 18.2	17 21.1	09 29.2	25 55.5
26	13 14.6	21 34.1	13 52.7	02♑28.5
JAN 5	19♒17.4	25♒47.9	18♒23.8	08♑24.7
JAN 1	19S03.7	10S49.0	27S16.7	26S50.0
21	20 08.0	16 10.6	28 16.9	26 39.7
FEB 10	20 36.4	19 31.0	28 55.6	25 59.5
MAR 1	20 27.7	15 37.8	29 17.3	25 02.5
21	19 42.8	00 44.8	29 29.8	24 00.7
APR 10	18 25.2	12N28.8	29 43.7	23 07.6
30	16 41.0	19 20.1	30 11.1	22 39.4
MAY 20	14 40.4	21 34.3	31 01.8	22 59.5
JUN 9	12 43.1	19 15.8	32 14.2	24 45.5
29	11 19.6	12 43.1	33 25.4	29 05.9
JUL 19	10 54.5	04 23.8	33 57.9	38 16.0
AUG 8	11 26.1	03S02.3	33 33.7	56 27.3
28	12 32.0	08 33.7	32 29.2	86 32.4
SEP 17	13 45.5	12 13.2	31 06.7	58 47.9
OCT 7	14 43.4	14 19.5	29 34.6	26 45.2
27	15 07.2	15 10.5	27 49.4	06 18.3
NOV 16	14 44.0	15 00.4	25 44.6	16 42.9
DEC 6	13 26.5	14 01.3	23 14.6	21 52.6
26	11S13.8	12S23.6	20S17.1	24S09.8

1973	Sappho 80	Amor 1221	Pandora 55	Icarus 1566
JAN 1	16♒51.6	24♒06.3	16♒34.5	06♑05.9
11	22 57.8	28 20.3	21 09.7	11 44.5
21	29 08.5	02♓34.1	25 50.5	16 58.7
31	05♓22.5	06 47.0	00♓35.9	21 53.2
FEB 10	11 39.1	10 58.8	05 24.9	26 31.2
20	17 56.8	15 08.7	10 16.5	00♒54.5
MAR 2	24 15.0	19 16.4	15 10.1	05 04.5
12	00♈32.9	23 21.4	20 04.7	09 01.8
22	06 49.4	27 23.0	24 59.6	12 46.1
APR 1	13 04.0	01♈21.0	29 54.2	16 17.4
11	19 16.1	05 14.6	04♈47.8	19 34.2
21	25 24.7	09 03.3	09 39.6	22 34.9
MAY 1	01♉29.6	12 46.5	14 29.1	25 17.1
11	07 30.1	16 23.4	19 15.4	27 36.8
21	13 25.7	19 53.0	23 57.8	29 28.9
31	19 16.0	23 14.6	28 35.5	00♓46.1
JUN 10	25 00.4	26 26.6	03♉07.5	01 17.4
20	00♊38.4	29 27.6	07 32.7	00R48.4
30	06 09.6	02♉15.9	11 49.9	28♒59.0
JUL 10	11 33.2	04 49.1	15 57.5	25 23.4
20	16 48.5	07 04.5	19 53.8	19 37.0
30	21 55.0	08 59.0	23 36.8	11 30.8
AUG 9	26 51.3	10 28.5	27 03.6	01 41.2
19	01♋36.4	11 28.7	00♊11.5	21♑37.9
29	06 09.1	11 54.6	02 56.9	12 57.4
SEP 8	10 27.1	11R41.2	05 15.3	06 31.9
18	14 28.6	10 44.9	07 02.2	02 20.5
28	18 10.9	09 03.9	08 12.6	29♐58.1
OCT 8	21 30.4	06 41.3	08 41.6	28 55.8
18	24 23.3	03 46.3	08R26.6	28D44.4
28	26 44.8	00 34.2	07 27.0	28 54.4
NOV 7	28 29.3	27♈25.0	05 47.8	28R43.3
17	29 31.5	24 38.0	03 40.3	26 40.1
27	29R45.7	22 28.2	01 20.7	18 35.4
DEC 7	29 08.6	21 04.6	29♉08.4	04 27.4
17	27 41.0	20 29.3	27 20.9	13D16.1
27	25 29.6	20D40.5	26 10.0	23 17.4
JAN 6	22♋49.1	21♈34.3	25♉42.0	01♑32.1
JAN 1	10S24.0	11S48.3	19S18.5	24S31.0
21	07 08.4	09 34.7	15 47.1	24 59.3
FEB 10	03 17.2	07 03.7	11 54.1	24 45.0
MAR 2	00N55.3	04 23.3	07 45.4	24 09.8
22	05 13.6	01 41.0	03 27.7	23 31.4
APR 11	09 22.4	00N56.5	00N52.2	23 07.5
MAY 1	13 07.2	03 22.6	05 07.3	23 20.1
21	16 15.6	05 31.1	09 11.5	24 39.6
JUN 10	18 37.7	07 16.1	12 59.2	27 51.9
30	20 07.1	08 31.2	16 25.9	34 01.7
JUL 20	20 41.1	09 09.2	19 28.9	43 49.9
AUG 9	20 21.6	09 02.2	22 07.7	54 10.8
29	19 14.1	08 01.7	24 24.5	57 06.4
SEP 18	17 27.9	06 01.5	26 22.8	53 16.1
OCT 8	15 15.0	03 09.6	28 03.9	48 35.1
28	12 50.4	00 03.8	29 18.9	44 25.4
NOV 17	10 32.8	02S13.8	29 46.2	38 50.2
DEC 7	08 45.9	03 03.0	29 17.0	17 22.7
27	07N54.3	02S26.6	28N22.0	19S24.2

1974	Sappho 80	Amor 1221	Pandora 55	Icarus 1566
JAN 1	24R11.7	21♈02.4	25R50.5	27♐36.0
11	21♋24.4	22 15.6	25D44.5	05♑10.0
21	18 39.9	24 03.5	26♉20.6	11 42.5
31	16 19.1	26 21.5	27 35.2	17 31.0
FEB 10	14 37.3	29 05.4	29 23.2	22 45.8
20	13 41.3	02♉11.4	01♊39.4	27 33.7
MAR 2	13D32.3	05 36.9	04 19.3	01♒58.5
12	14 07.0	09 19.2	07 18.5	06 02.3
22	15 19.9	13 16.5	10 33.4	09 46.1
APR 1	17 05.6	17 27.6	14 01.2	13 09.7
11	19 18.3	21 51.2	17 39.1	16 11.6
21	21 53.4	26 26.8	21 25.2	18 49.8
MAY 1	24 46.9	01♊13.8	25 17.8	21 00.1
11	27 55.2	06 12.1	29 15.1	22 37.4
21	01♌15.6	11 21.8	03♋16.3	23 34.1
31	04 46.1	16 43.1	07 20.1	23R39.7
JUN 10	08 24.4	22 16.6	11 25.7	22 41.2
20	12 09.3	28 02.9	15 32.2	20 22.7
30	15 59.5	04♋02.8	19 39.0	16 28.7
JUL 10	19 53.8	10 17.4	23 45.4	10 52.7
20	23 51.4	16 47.9	27 50.7	03 48.2
30	27 51.6	23 35.4	01♌54.4	25♑59.8
AUG 9	01♍53.5	00♌41.4	05 55.7	18 32.1
19	05 56.7	08 07.2	09 54.0	12 19.8
29	10 00.5	15 53.9	13 48.5	07 50.0
SEP 8	14 04.1	24 02.6	17 38.3	05 02.2
18	18 07.2	02♍34.1	21 22.5	03 43.4
28	22 09.0	11 28.0	24 59.9	03D38.1
OCT 8	26 08.7	20 43.6	28 29.1	04 31.5
18	00♎05.5	00♎19.4	01♍48.7	06 12.7
28	03 58.6	10 12.0	04 56.6	08 33.8
NOV 7	07 46.8	20 17.4	07 50.8	11 28.8
17	11 29.0	00♏30.5	10 28.7	14 54.2
27	15 03.5	10 45.1	12 47.3	18 48.0
DEC 7	18 28.9	20 54.9	14 43.4	23 08.8
17	21 43.0	00♐54.1	16 13.2	27 55.1
27	24 43.5	10 36.7	17 12.9	02♒57.4
JAN 6	27♎27.6	19♐58.7	17♍39.1	07♒19.3
JAN 1	07N52.1	02S06.8	28N09.6	20S12.7
21	08 22.9	00 17.1	27 38.6	22 02.5
FEB 10	09 37.0	02N06.0	27 40.3	22 31.3
MAR 2	11 00.8	04 45.6	28 04.8	22 23.9
22	12 10.0	07 28.8	28 37.1	22 09.0
APR 11	12 51.3	10 04.8	29 03.2	22 10.6
MAY 1	12 59.1	12 23.6	29 12.4	22 56.0
21	12 31.7	14 15.4	28 57.8	25 00.6
JUN 10	11 30.1	15 29.8	28 16.0	29 11.0
30	09 57.2	15 56.2	27 06.6	36 01.1
JUL 20	07 56.9	15 23.9	25 31.6	44 04.6
AUG 9	05 33.9	13 43.1	23 35.3	48 33.4
29	02 53.2	10 47.5	21 23.1	47 43.0
SEP 18	00 00.5	06 37.5	19 02.0	44 57.3
OCT 8	02S58.5	01 25.8	16 39.7	42 21.0
28	05 57.5	04S17.2	14 25.1	40 07.0
NOV 17	08 50.2	09 42.6	12 28.4	37 53.1
DEC 7	11 29.7	13 54.3	11 00.9	35 04.8
27	13S48.5	16S11.8	10N14.3	30S37.0

1975	Sappho 80	Amor 1221	Pandora 55	Icarus 1566
JAN 1	26♎07.8	15♐20.5	17♍30.4	05♒22.3
11	28 42.6	24 31.0	17R38.7	07R44.1
21	00♏55.9	03♑16.6	17 09.9	22♑26.6
31	02 43.8	11 35.8	16 04.8	18D24.8
FEB 10	04 02.0	19 28.3	14 27.3	22 22.4
20	04 45.7	26 54.0	12 25.3	26 59.3
MAR 2	04R51.0	03♒53.5	10 11.1	01♒23.4
12	04 15.1	10 27.7	07 58.3	05 25.7
22	02 57.4	16 36.9	06 00.4	09 03.6
APR 1	01 02.4	22 21.7	04 28.0	12 15.8
11	28♎39.1	27 42.5	03 27.5	15 00.2
21	26 02.0	02♓39.0	03 01.8	17 12.8
MAY 1	23 28.5	07 10.6	03D10.4	18 48.4
11	21 14.8	11 16.4	03 50.8	19 39.3
21	19 33.8	14 54.3	05 00.0	19R34.6
31	18 32.9	18 02.2	06 34.2	18 21.3
JUN 10	18D14.0	20 36.8	08 30.1	15 43.9
20	18 36.4	22 33.7	10 44.6	11 29.0
30	19 36.7	23 48.7	13 14.7	05 35.3
JUL 10	21 10.6	24 16.5	15 58.1	28♑23.4
20	23 14.3	23R52.4	18 52.8	20 43.3
30	25 43.5	22 34.5	21 56.8	13 37.7
AUG 9	28 35.0	20 24.3	25 08.8	07 52.9
19	01♏46.0	17 30.7	28 27.4	03 48.3
29	05 13.7	14 10.2	01♎51.4	01 19.7
SEP 8	08 56.2	10 44.5	05 19.8	00 13.2
18	12 52.0	07 36.4	08 51.6	00D13.8
28	16 59.3	05 03.8	12 25.9	01 07.8
OCT 8	21 17.2	03 16.7	16 01.8	02 44.9
18	25 44.6	02 18.8	19 38.3	04 57.3
28	00♐20.5	02D07.7	23 14.6	07 39.2
NOV 7	05 04.4	02 38.8	26 49.7	10 46.9
17	09 55.5	03 46.6	00♏22.5	14 17.8
27	14 53.1	05 25.2	03 51.9	18 10.5
DEC 7	19 56.8	07 29.6	07 16.6	22 25.0
17	25 06.0	09 55.5	10 35.2	27 02.4
27	00♑20.2	12 38.9	13 46.0	02♒04.8
JAN 6	05♑39.0	15♓36.8	16♏47.3	07♒36.9
JAN 1	14S19.1	16S26.5	10N10.2	28S56.5
21	16 00.7	16 13.4	10 25.9	16 25.9
FEB 10	17 01.3	14 26.9	11 26.0	17 12.0
MAR 2	17 08.0	11 41.0	12 43.5	18 18.5
22	16 07.3	08 26.2	13 39.5	18 49.9
APR 11	13 57.3	05 05.8	13 48.8	19 29.9
MAY 1	11 09.4	01 57.6	13 09.0	20 57.8
21	08 41.8	00N43.5	11 48.6	23 58.8
JUN 10	07 17.5	02 42.1	09 56.8	29 20.2
30	07 04.4	03 39.4	07 40.8	36 48.0
JUL 20	07 49.7	03 12.9	05 05.9	42 55.2
AUG 9	09 16.0	01 04.2	02 17.1	44 07.1
29	11 07.1	02S32.3	00S41.4	42 22.6
SEP 18	13 08.6	06 27.7	03 45.2	40 20.4
OCT 8	15 07.7	09 24.5	06 49.9	38 41.2
28	16 52.2	10 53.9	09 51.1	37 16.5
NOV 17	18 11.0	11 05.7	12 44.5	35 48.3
DEC 7	18 53.7	10 18.6	15 26.4	33 58.0
27	18S52.0	08S48.5	17S53.3	31S24.2

1976	Sappho 80	Amor 1221	Pandora 55	Icarus 1566
JAN 1	02♑59.1	14♓06.2	15♏18.0	04♒46.8
11	08 19.9	17 10.3	18 13.7	10 36.0
21	13 44.6	20 25.1	20 56.6	17 06.2
31	19 12.7	23 48.5	23 24.2	24 31.1
FEB 10	24 43.6	27 18.9	25 33.6	03♓11.7
20	00♒16.9	00♈54.8	27 21.6	13 30.1
MAR 1	05 52.2	04 35.0	28 44.9	21 R09.3
11	11 28.8	08 18.4	29 39.8	04 28.2
21	17 06.1	12 04.1	00♐03.3	26♒05.9
31	22 43.6	15 51.3	29 R52.8	23 53.1
APR 10	28 20.5	19 39.3	29♏07.3	23 31.1
20	03♓55.8	23 27.3	27 49.0	23 31.7
30	09 28.8	27 14.8	26 02.7	23 14.1
MAY 10	14 58.1	01♉01.1	23 57.8	22 10.1
20	20 22.4	04 45.5	21 46.3	19 54.7
30	25 40.2	08 27.6	19 41.4	16 02.2
JUN 9	00♈49.3	12 06.5	17 55.4	10 11.3
19	05 47.6	15 41.3	16 37.3	02 21.0
29	10 32.1	19 11.4	15 52.4	23♑09.1
JUL 9	14 59.1	22 35.2	15 D42.8	13 54.8
19	19 04.7	25 51.7	16 07.7	05 59.4
29	22 43.5	28 59.1	17 04.8	00 04.7
AUG 8	25 49.2	01♊55.2	18 31.3	26♐13.5
18	28 15.2	04 37.5	20 23.5	24 06.7
28	29 53.6	07 02.7	22 38.6	23 22.3
SEP 7	00♉37.3	09 06.6	25 13.6	23 D41.4
17	00 R22.4	10 44.4	28 05.7	24 49.0
27	29♈09.8	11 49.9	01♐12.8	26 34.4
OCT 7	27 10.7	12 16.2	04 33.0	28 50.1
17	24 46.5	11 R56.1	08 04.3	01♑30.0
27	22 24.1	10 43.2	11 45.5	04 30.6
NOV 6	20 30.8	08 35.1	15 35.0	07 48.9
16	19 24.7	05 36.4	19 31.7	11 22.8
26	19 D13.7	02 01.6	23 34.6	15 11.6
DEC 6	19 58.1	28♉16.1	27 42.5	19 14.3
16	21 31.8	24 48.9	01♑54.5	23 31.1
26	23 48.0	22 05.7	06 09.8	28 02.7
JAN 5	26♈39.5	20♉22.6	10♑27.4	02♒50.2
JAN 1	18 S 44.0	08 S 20.9	18 S 27.5	30 S 35.6
21	17 39.4	06 14.6	20 33.0	26 18.0
FEB 10	15 43.0	03 50.4	22 20.4	18 56.0
MAR 1	12 57.6	01 16.8	23 49.9	02 38.7
21	09 29.4	01 N 19.1	24 59.8	05 59.0
APR 10	05 27.3	03 50.5	25 44.5	10 37.3
30	01 02.2	06 11.2	25 53.4	14 26.6
MAY 20	03 N 33.1	08 15.7	25 21.8	19 46.7
JUN 9	08 04.5	09 58.4	24 26.6	27 55.4
29	12 16.3	11 14.2	23 39.6	36 45.9
JUL 19	15 50.7	11 58.0	23 23.3	40 23.4
AUG 8	18 27.0	12 05.2	23 42.1	39 27.2
28	19 39.2	11 30.9	24 28.7	37 48.4
SEP 17	18 56.3	10 11.2	25 31.6	36 36.4
OCT 7	16 01.9	08 04.2	26 38.9	35 46.5
27	11 48.5	05 16.1	27 39.5	35 02.5
NOV 16	08 14.2	02 15.6	28 23.7	34 10.2
DEC 6	06 33.4	00 03.6	28 43.9	32 57.8

1977	Sappho 80	Amor 1221	Pandora 55	Icarus 1566
JAN 1	25♈27.2	20 R56.1	08♑44.1	00♒53.1
11	28 36.2	19♉52.1	13 02.7	05 51.2
21	02♉09.9	19 D52.9	17 22.3	11 09.3
31	06 03.5	20 54.2	21 41.9	16 51.6
FEB 10	10 12.2	22 49.1	26 00.8	23 04.1
20	14 33.0	25 30.8	00♒18.0	29 56.2
MAR 2	19 03.0	28 53.8	04 32.5	07♓41.3
12	23 39.8	02♊52.6	08 43.4	16 40.6
22	28 21.8	07 23.9	12 49.6	27 28.4
APR 1	03♊07.4	12 25.0	16 49.6	11♈03.1
11	07 55.4	17 53.6	20 42.3	28 45.1
21	12 44.8	23 48.8	24 25.9	06 R12.1
MAY 1	17 34.9	00♋10.0	27 58.6	26♈39.7
11	22 24.8	06 56.5	01♓18.2	14 40.4
21	27 14.2	14 08.8	04 22.0	00 22.3
31	02♋02.5	21 46.6	07 07.0	10♓02.0
JUN 10	06 49.2	29 49.8	09 29.6	11♒07.1
20	11 34.2	08♌18.4	11 25.8	13♑00.0
30	16 16.9	17 11.4	12 50.9	25♐31.9
JUL 10	20 56.9	26 27.2	13 40.7	16 31.8
20	25 34.2	06♍03.7	13 R51.1	12 14.0
30	00♌08.1	15 57.2	13 20.2	10 34.7
AUG 9	04 38.3	26 03.0	12 09.4	10 D30.0
19	09 04.4	06♎15.8	10 24.7	11 26.7
29	13 25.8	16 28.8	08 18.4	13 05.9
SEP 8	17 41.7	26 35.3	06 06.9	15 15.3
18	21 51.5	06♏29.4	04 08.0	17 48.0
28	25 54.1	16 05.4	02 37.8	20 39.0
OCT 8	29 48.4	25 19.7	01 46.3	23 44.6
18	03♍33.0	04♐10.3	01 D38.4	27 02.8
28	07 06.1	12 36.1	02 14.7	00♑31.7
NOV 7	10 25.7	20 37.5	03 31.8	04 09.9
17	13 29.4	28 15.7	05 25.9	07 57.0
27	16 14.0	05♑32.1	07 52.0	11 52.2
DEC 7	18 36.2	12 28.5	10 45.3	15 55.2
17	20 31.9	19 06.6	14 01.8	20 06.1
27	21 56.6	25 28.0	17 37.7	24 25.0
JAN 6	22♍45.8	01♒34.1	21♓29.5	28♑52.5
JAN 1	06 N 59.8	00 S 06.0	28 S 25.9	30 S 36.5
21	08 36.2	01 N 45.5	27 35.7	27 56.3
FEB 10	10 42.6	04 38.0	26 15.7	24 09.9
MAR 2	12 54.7	07 57.1	24 30.5	18 35.7
22	14 54.6	11 17.8	22 26.9	09 29.1
APR 11	16 29.8	14 19.5	20 13.7	09 N 17.4
MAY 1	17 31.6	16 41.1	18 01.1	21 27.2
21	17 55.1	17 59.0	16 00.4	10 11.9
JUN 10	17 38.6	17 48.0	14 24.3	18 S 01.3
30	16 43.2	15 47.6	13 25.9	33 25.7
JUL 20	15 11.9	11 52.3	13 15.2	33 13.8
AUG 9	13 09.7	06 21.8	13 50.5	32 37.5
29	10 42.4	00 02.8	14 45.6	32 32.2
SEP 18	07 56.7	06 S 03.5	15 15.1	32 41.8
OCT 8	05 00.1	11 03.6	14 47.1	32 51.9
28	02 00.6	14 27.9	13 19.9	32 51.6
NOV 17	00 S 52.2	16 11.5	11 05.0	32 33.3
DEC 7	03 27.0	16 25.8	08 12.9	31 51.4

1978	Sappho 80	Amor 1221	Pandora 55	Icarus 1566
JAN 1	22♍25.9	28♑32.8	19♓31.8	26♑37.6
11	22 55.6	04♒31.9	23 30.7	01♒09.7
21	22 R43.4	10 17.5	27 41.8	05 51.8
31	21 48.1	15 50.5	02♈02.7	10 45.2
FEB 10	20 11.0	21 11.9	06 31.7	15 52.6
20	17 59.3	26 22.1	11 07.1	21 16.7
MAR 2	15 25.5	01♓21.5	15 47.3	27 01.7
12	12 46.1	06 10.5	20 31.5	03♓14.1
22	10 18.9	10 49.0	25 18.4	10 02.0
APR 1	08 18.6	15 17.0	00♉06.9	17 37.8
11	06 54.8	19 34.3	04 56.6	26 19.2
21	06 11.8	23 40.4	09 46.3	06♈31.7
MAY 1	06 D09.5	27 34.6	14 35.6	18 52.2
11	06 44.9	01♈16.3	19 23.9	04♉15.2
21	07 54.2	04 44.1	24 10.3	24 12.7
31	09 32.8	07 56.7	28 54.5	19♊31.4
JUN 10	11 36.5	10 52.2	03♊35.8	07♋20.9
20	14 01.6	13 28.2	08 13.6	28 19.0
30	16 44.7	15 42.1	12 47.2	29♌16.8
JUL 10	19 43.2	17 30.3	17 16.1	01♎16.9
20	22 54.7	18 48.9	21 39.1	22 56.8
30	26 17.3	19 33.6	25 55.5	06♏20.2
AUG 9	29 49.5	19 R39.8	00♋04.3	15 25.9
19	03♎29.9	19 03.8	04 04.0	22 20.4
29	07 17.3	17 43.6	07 53.2	28 04.2
SEP 8	11 10.9	15 40.6	11 30.0	03♐08.2
18	15 09.6	13 01.8	14 52.2	07 49.0
28	19 12.8	09 59.9	17 57.2	12 15.7
OCT 8	23 19.9	06 52.0	20 41.9	16 34.3
18	27 29.9	03 57.5	23 02.5	20 48.2
28	01♏42.4	01 31.8	24 55.2	24 59.6
NOV 7	05 56.7	29♓45.7	26 15.2	29 10.3
17	10 12.0	28 44.0	26 58.3	03♑21.1
27	14 27.8	28 D26.3	27 R00.9	07 32.8
DEC 7	18 43.3	28 49.7	26 21.2	11 46.3
17	22 57.4	29 49.7	25 01.2	16 01.6
27	27 09.5	01♈21.2	23 07.5	20 19.4
JAN 6	01♐18.4	03♈20.0	20♋51.9	24♑40.2
JAN 1	05 S 52.0	15 S 05.8	03 S 57.9	30 S 19.1
21	06 44.7	13 06.4	00 10.9	28 29.0
FEB 10	06 18.6	10 35.6	03 N 48.1	26 01.3
MAR 2	04 29.6	07 47.3	07 51.0	22 47.1
22	01 52.4	04 52.9	11 49.8	18 26.4
APR 11	00 N 34.7	02 02.2	15 36.4	12 14.5
MAY 1	02 10.9	00 N 36.2	19 03.4	02 30.1
21	02 45.5	02 54.2	22 04.2	14 N 29.9
JUN 10	02 24.2	04 43.5	24 33.7	32 39.1
30	01 17.2	05 54.6	26 28.8	21 36.5
JUL 20	00 S 25.3	06 16.1	27 48.7	07 S 59.3
AUG 9	02 34.2	05 34.8	28 36.0	19 50.2
29	05 01.1	03 40.3	28 56.8	24 54.7
SEP 18	07 38.4	00 39.7	29 00.8	27 43.1
OCT 8	10 18.6	02 S 43.2	29 01.1	29 25.8
28	12 54.1	05 22.1	29 13.2	30 24.8
NOV 17	15 17.4	06 37.8	29 51.1	30 48.0
DEC 7	17 21.2	06 32.4	30 58.6	30 38.4

1979		Sappho 80	Amor 1221	Pandora 55	Icarus 1566
JAN	1	29♏14.4	02♈17.5	22R01.5	22♑29.4
	11	03♐21.3	04 28.2	19♋41.1	26 51.8
	21	07 23.2	06 59.8	17 23.7	01♒17.9
	31	11 18.9	09 49.3	15 25.2	05 48.5
FEB	10	15 06.5	12 53.6	13 57.8	10 24.5
	20	18 44.2	16 10.5	13 08.1	15 07.1
MAR	2	22 09.8	19 38.1	12D57.9	19 58.2
	12	25 20.3	23 14.7	13 25.8	24 59.8
	22	28 12.8	26 58.9	14 27.9	00♓15.2
APR	1	00♑43.2	00♉49.9	16 00.0	05 48.9
	11	02 47.0	04 46.7	17 57.7	11 46.6
	21	04 19.2	08 48.5	20 16.7	18 17.3
MAY	1	05 14.0	12 54.9	22 53.7	25 33.2
	11	05R26.4	17 05.3	25 45.3	03♈51.7
	21	04 52.6	21 19.5	28 49.0	13 38.3
	31	03 32.1	25 37.3	02♌02.7	25 26.6
JUN	10	01 30.7	29 58.4	05 24.3	09♉55.2
	20	29♐01.4	04♊22.9	08 52.4	27 35.5
	30	26 23.5	08 50.6	12 25.8	18♊40.2
JUL	10	24 00.1	13 21.6	16 03.2	15♋09.2
	20	22 10.6	17 55.9	19 43.5	14♌27.3
	30	21 08.2	22 33.7	23 26.1	09♍09.4
AUG	9	20D59.1	27 15.1	27 10.0	01♎06.9
	19	21 42.6	02♋00.3	00♍54.5	18 58.5
	29	23 15.3	06 49.6	04 38.8	02♏48.9
SEP	8	25 32.1	11 43.1	08 22.1	13 37.9
	18	28 26.9	16 41.5	12 03.7	22 23.7
	28	01♑54.8	21 44.9	15 42.7	29 47.8
OCT	8	05 51.1	26 53.9	19 17.9	06♐17.0
	18	10 11.5	02♌09.6	22 48.6	12 08.8
	28	14 52.8	07 32.4	26 13.3	17 34.8
NOV	7	19 52.1	13 03.7	29 30.7	22 42.3
	17	25 06.6	18 45.6	02♎39.1	27 36.7
	27	00♒34.4	24 40.1	05 36.7	02♑21.7
DEC	7	06 13.3	00♍50.7	08 21.2	06 59.5
	17	12 01.7	07 22.6	10 50.2	11 32.1
	27	17 58.1	14 21.7	13 00.7	16 01.1
JAN	6	24♒00.8	21♍57.8	14♎49.6	20♑27.1
JAN	1	19S18.1	05S01.4	32N31.3	29S43.0
	21	20 14.4	03 04.5	33 02.7	28 26.0
FEB	10	20 33.9	00 44.3	32 37.4	26 41.6
MAR	2	20 15.3	01N47.9	31 35.0	24 30.6
	22	19 20.0	04 23.2	30 17.1	21 51.3
APR	11	17 52.6	06 53.7	28 51.3	18 36.0
MAY	1	16 00.2	09 12.4	27 16.1	14 24.1
	21	13 55.0	11 12.7	25 28.0	08 24.6
JUN	10	11 56.7	12 48.3	23 24.3	01N07.1
	30	10 33.9	13 53.4	21 04.5	15 31.4
JUL	20	10 10.6	14 22.3	18 29.8	22 25.5
AUG	9	10 45.2	14 09.8	15 42.7	04 16.3
	29	11 53.9	13 11.4	12 46.7	11S26.3
SEP	18	13 08.3	11 23.7	09 45.9	19 57.5
OCT	8	14 04.0	08 44.3	06 45.3	24 35.6
	28	14 22.5	05 12.3	03 50.2	27 12.5
NOV	17	13 51.4	00 49.3	01 06.7	28 35.6
DEC	7	12 24.7	04S19.5	01S18.9	29 06.4
	27	10S03.1	10S00.7	03S19.3	28S56.5

1980		Sappho 80	Amor 1221	Pandora 55	Icarus 1566
JAN	1	20♒58.7	18♍04.3	13♎58.0	18♑14.4
	11	27 04.1	26 03.6	15 34.9	22 39.4
	21	03♓14.0	04♎58.5	16 44.9	27 02.8
	31	09 27.1	15 03.8	17 24.5	01♒25.2
FEB	10	15 42.3	26 31.8	17R31.0	05 47.1
	20	21 58.7	09♏19.5	17 02.5	10 09.4
MAR	1	28 15.2	23 01.0	15 59.5	14 32.5
	11	04♈31.0	06♐46.7	14 25.6	18 57.4
	21	10 45.5	19 36.4	12 28.0	23 25.4
	31	16 57.6	00♑47.2	10 17.6	27 57.7
APR	10	23 06.9	10 01.1	08 07.1	02♓36.4
	20	29 12.9	17 12.0	06 09.1	07 24.5
	30	05♉14.9	22 21.1	04 34.2	12 25.5
MAY	10	11 12.5	25 29.8	03 29.1	17 45.7
	20	17 05.3	26 35.9	02 57.1	23 33.6
	30	22 52.6	25R44.4	02D58.7	00♈02.4
JUN	9	28 34.3	23 12.1	03 31.9	07 33.7
	19	04♊09.9	19 32.5	04 34.1	16 40.8
	29	09 38.7	15 36.2	06 02.2	28 16.7
JUL	9	15 00.4	12 09.8	07 52.6	13♉33.8
	19	20 14.4	09 42.9	10 02.8	03♊24.4
	29	25 19.9	08 26.5	12 29.7	26 30.7
AUG	8	00♋16.2	08D15.8	15 11.0	19♋15.1
	18	05 02.0	09 01.4	18 04.8	11♌00.3
	28	09 36.3	10 32.9	21 09.2	09♍58.9
SEP	7	13 57.4	12 40.1	24 22.6	04♎48.4
	17	18 03.5	15 15.7	27 43.8	23 22.2
	27	21 52.0	18 13.3	01♏11.4	07♏43.3
OCT	7	25 20.3	21 28.0	04 44.4	19 07.7
	17	28 24.6	24 56.4	08 21.8	28 30.6
	27	01♌00.7	28 35.6	12 02.6	06♐29.7
NOV	6	03 03.8	02♒23.1	15 45.8	13 30.5
	16	04 28.1	06 17.4	19 30.7	19 49.8
	26	05 08.3	10 17.0	23 16.0	25 38.8
DEC	6	04R59.9	14 20.6	27 01.1	01♑05.3
	16	04 00.5	18 27.3	00♐44.7	06 14.8
	26	02 13.7	22 36.1	04 25.7	11 10.8
JAN	5	29♋48.8	26♒46.3	08♐03.1	15♑56.3
JAN	1	09S19.8	11S27.7	03S44.6	28S48.7
	21	06 00.0	16 54.5	05 02.9	27 58.8
FEB	10	02 07.3	19 52.1	05 38.9	26 44.3
MAR	1	02N03.5	15 47.2	05 28.1	25 11.0
	21	06 16.5	04 40.5	04 36.3	23 24.7
APR	10	10 16.6	05N44.1	03 26.7	21 30.7
	30	13 50.1	12 38.5	02 32.8	19 32.2
MAY	20	16 45.0	16 12.2	02 19.2	17 28.6
JUN	9	18 52.5	15 53.6	02 52.2	15 06.1
	29	20 07.2	11 14.7	04 06.8	11 28.1
JUL	19	20 27.5	03 56.6	05 54.0	03 47.1
AUG	8	19 56.0	03S09.4	08 05.2	08N56.9
	28	18 38.6	08 34.9	10 32.4	12 02.2
SEP	17	16 44.7	12 11.3	13 08.6	05S19.0
OCT	7	14 25.7	14 15.3	15 47.3	16 20.8
	27	11 56.1	15 04.2	18 22.5	22 17.7
NOV	16	09 33.6	14 52.7	20 48.8	25 27.7
DEC	6	07 40.9	13 52.6	23 01.4	27 00.4
	26	06N43.2	12S14.3	24S56.9	27S30.2

1981		Sappho 80	Amor 1221	Pandora 55	Icarus 1566
JAN	1	00R50.4	25♒06.1	06♐36.6	14♑03.2
	11	28♋10.4	29 16.8	10 11.1	18 43.4
	21	25 22.3	03♓27.8	13 39.6	23 15.6
	31	22 47.4	07 38.4	17 00.6	27 41.1
FEB	10	20 43.7	11 48.2	20 12.3	02♒01.0
	20	19 22.5	15 56.5	23 12.7	06 15.6
MAR	2	18 47.5	20 02.8	25 59.5	10 25.4
	12	18D57.6	24 06.8	28 30.0	14 30.9
	22	19 48.6	28 07.6	00♑41.2	18 32.1
APR	1	21 14.7	02♈04.9	02 29.9	22 29.4
	11	23 10.7	05 58.3	03 52.3	26 22.8
	21	25 31.5	09 46.8	04 44.6	00♓12.3
MAY	1	28 12.5	13 30.1	05 03.7	03 58.4
	11	01♌10.4	17 07.4	04R46.8	07 40.9
	21	04 21.8	20 37.6	03 53.7	11 20.2
	31	07 44.3	24 00.0	02 26.9	14 57.1
JUN	10	11 16.1	27 13.2	00 33.0	18 32.2
	20	14 55.3	00♉15.7	28♐23.4	22 07.7
	30	18 40.5	03 05.8	26 11.7	25 48.0
JUL	10	22 30.7	05 41.3	24 12.4	29 41.4
	20	26 24.7	07 59.5	22 38.1	04♈09.9
	30	00♍21.9	09 57.3	21 37.2	10 14.5
AUG	9	04 21.4	11 30.7	21 14.1	21 47.6
	19	08 22.6	12 35.4	21D29.6	04♊00.5
	29	12 24.9	13 06.6	22 21.7	22♌36.1
SEP	8	16 27.6	12R59.0	23 47.7	12♍03.8
	18	20 30.1	12 08.7	25 43.9	18 24.9
	28	24 31.8	10 33.6	28 06.4	22 58.0
OCT	8	28 31.9	08 15.9	00♑52.1	07♎46.3
	18	02♎29.5	05 24.1	03 57.8	00♏22.3
	28	06 24.0	02 12.6	07 20.9	16 22.5
NOV	7	10 14.2	29♈01.2	10 59.0	28 28.1
	17	13 58.9	26 09.9	14 49.9	08♐11.7
	27	17 36.9	23 54.4	18 52.0	16 23.4
DEC	7	21 06.4	22 24.7	23 03.7	23 32.3
	17	24 25.6	21 43.6	27 23.5	29 56.5
	27	27 32.4	21D49.8	01♒50.4	05♑47.8
JAN	6	00♏23.9	22♈39.4	06♒23.0	11♑14.0
JAN	1	06N39.6	11S38.9	25S27.8	27S29.9
	21	07 12.6	09 25.1	26 58.6	27 05.8
FEB	10	08 33.8	06 54.1	28 12.0	26 14.9
MAR	2	10 06.2	04 13.8	29 12.2	25 07.9
	22	11 21.9	01 31.7	30 06.5	23 55.3
APR	11	12 07.0	01N05.5	31 03.6	22 48.5
MAY	1	12 16.4	03 31.3	32 09.2	22 01.3
	21	11 49.3	05 39.7	33 19.4	21 53.3
JUN	10	10 47.5	07 24.6	34 13.2	22 54.8
	30	09 14.0	08 39.7	34 23.6	26 00.9
JUL	20	07 13.2	09 18.3	33 47.4	33 02.1
AUG	9	04 49.8	09 12.4	32 49.8	46 33.0
	29	02 09.2	08 13.8	31 54.4	47 24.4
SEP	18	00S43.2	06 16.4	31 07.0	17 07.3
OCT	8	03 41.5	03 26.9	30 21.1	00N06.2
	28	06 39.5	00 21.4	29 25.6	13S07.9
NOV	17	09 30.8	01S58.7	28 10.5	20 22.5
DEC	7	12 08.7	02 50.8	26 28.4	23 52.1
	27	14S26.2	02S16.2	24S15.6	25S23.3

1982	Sappho 80	Amor 1221	Pandora 55	Icarus 1566
JAN 1	29♎00.2	22♈09.5	04♒06.1	08♑33.7
11	01♏43.1	23 18.9	08 41.2	13 49.3
21	04 06.2	25 03.9	13 20.6	18 47.1
31	06 05.6	27 19.9	18 03.5	23 30.2
FEB 10	07 37.1	00♉02.4	22 48.9	28 00.3
20	08 36.2	03 07.7	27 36.0	02♒19.1
MAR 2	08 58.3	06 32.9	02♓24.2	06 27.2
12	08 R 40.0	10 15.4	07 12.5	10 25.0
22	07 39.8	14 13.4	12 00.4	14 12.6
APR 1	05 59.5	18 25.5	16 47.1	17 49.5
11	03 46.4	22 50.5	21 31.7	21 14.8
21	01 12.9	27 27.8	26 13.7	24 27.3
MAY 1	28♎35.5	02♊17.0	00♈52.1	27 25.0
11	26 11.9	07 17.7	05 26.0	00♓04.9
21	24 16.5	12 30.2	09 54.4	02 23.3
31	22 59.0	17 54.9	14 16.2	04 14.0
JUN 10	22 24.1	23 31.9	18 30.0	05 28.6
20	22 D 31.3	29 22.2	22 34.2	05 R54.9
30	23 18.4	05♋26.7	26 26.9	05 13.8
JUL 10	24 41.5	11 46.1	00♉05.9	02 58.6
20	26 36.1	18 21.8	03 28.6	28♒30.9
30	28 58.5	25 15.1	06 31.5	21 06.6
AUG 9	01♏44.8	02♌27.1	09 11.1	10 25.2
19	04 51.8	09 59.3	11 22.8	27♑24.0
29	08 17.0	17 52.7	13 01.6	14 34.5
SEP 8	11 58.1	26 07.9	14 02.8	04 11.4
18	15 53.3	04♍45.8	14 21.9	26♐46.1
28	20 01.1	13 45.8	13 R 56.0	21 40.1
OCT 8	24 20.1	23 06.7	12 46.7	17 50.7
18	28 49.3	02♎46.7	11 00.3	14 07.2
28	03♐27.7	12 42.1	08 50.0	08 49.7
NOV 7	08 14.6	22 48.6	06 34.0	29♏12.7
17	13 09.2	03♏01.0	04 31.3	16 14.9
27	18 10.9	13 12.9	02 58.8	26 D09.1
DEC 7	23 19.0	23 18.2	02 06.9	09♐10.7
17	28 33.2	03♐11.2	01 D 59.6	19 16.5
27	03♑52.9	12 46.7	02 36.4	27 32.0
JAN 6	09♑17.4	22♐00.7	03♉53.6	04♑36.2
JAN 1	14 S 56.5	01 S 56.7	23 S 37.6	25 S34.0
21	16 37.6	00 07.3	20 46.7	25 44.3
FEB 10	17 39.8	02 N 16.0	17 28.9	25 18.5
MAR 2	17 51.8	04 56.0	13 49.7	24 34.2
22	17 00.7	07 39.6	09 55.7	23 46.5
APR 11	15 01.5	10 15.7	05 53.8	23 11.6
MAY 1	12 18.0	12 34.2	01 51.2	23 08.9
21	09 45.3	14 24.8	02 N 05.6	24 06.7
JUN 10	08 11.4	15 37.1	05 50.2	26 48.9
30	07 49.3	16 00.1	09 17.2	32 26.7
JUL 20	08 27.8	15 22.8	12 22.0	42 32.0
AUG 9	09 49.1	13 35.7	15 01.1	56 28.8
29	11 35.8	10 32.6	17 11.2	64 26.6
SEP 18	13 32.7	06 15.1	18 47.0	59 34.4
OCT 8	15 26.3	00 57.9	19 38.5	51 43.0
28	17 03.9	04 S 46.3	19 37.5	42 06.6
NOV 17	18 13.9	10 07.2	18 59.5	16 25.9
DEC 7	18 45.8	14 09.9	18 27.1	17 42.8
27	[illegible]	[illegible]	[illegible]	[illegible]

1983	Sappho 80	Amor 1221	Pandora 55	Icarus 1566
JAN 1	06♑34.5	17♐26.5	03♉10.3	01♑11.4
11	12 01.4	26 28.8	04 45.7	07 48.9
21	17 32.5	05♑06.2	06 54.0	13 44.4
31	23 07.3	13 17.3	09 29.9	19 07.9
FEB 10	28 45.4	21 02.2	12 28.5	24 06.2
20	04♒26.3	28 21.0	15 46.0	28 43.2
MAR 2	10 09.3	05♒14.3	19 18.7	03♒01.3
12	15 54.1	11 43.0	23 03.5	07 02.2
22	21 40.0	17 47.6	26 58.3	10 46.2
APR 1	27 26.2	23 28.5	01♊00.8	14 12.7
11	03♓12.3	28 46.2	05 09.3	17 20.8
21	08 57.3	03♓40.3	09 22.4	20 08.2
MAY 1	14 40.1	08 10.3	13 38.8	22 31.6
11	20 20.1	12 15.3	17 57.5	24 26.5
21	25 55.6	15 53.4	22 17.7	25 46.0
31	01♈25.4	19 02.2	26 38.4	26 21.1
JUN 10	06 47.9	21 38.9	00♋59.1	25 R59.8
20	12 00.8	23 39.1	05 19.2	24 25.8
30	17 01.8	24 58.5	09 37.8	21 21.4
JUL 10	21 48.1	25 32.1	13 54.7	16 30.6
20	26 16.0	25 R 15.0	18 09.0	09 51.3
30	00♉21.3	24 04.7	22 20.2	01 51.9
AUG 9	03 59.0	22 02.3	26 27.7	23♑33.4
19	07 02.6	19 15.2	00♌30.6	16 08.1
29	09 25.6	15 58.7	04 28.0	10 23.4
SEP 8	11 00.3	12 33.5	08 19.2	06 31.2
18	11 39.5	09 22.5	12 02.7	04 22.1
28	11 R 19.7	06 44.3	15 37.3	03 37.9
OCT 8	10 02.2	04 50.3	19 01.4	04 D01.3
18	07 57.9	03 44.9	22 13.0	05 18.7
28	05 28.5	03 D 26.6	25 09.8	07 18.6
NOV 7	03 00.8	03 51.2	27 49.2	09 52.9
17	01 01.9	04 53.3	00♍08.0	12 54.2
27	29♈49.9	06 27.0	02 02.8	16 12.7
DEC 7	29 D 32.4	08 27.3	03 29.6	19 29.4
17	00♉09.7	10 49.7	04 24.5	21 39.8
27	01 36.2	13 30.2	04 44.1	17 R20.7
JAN 6	03♉44.7	16♓25.8	04 R 25.6	01♑39.3
JAN 1	18 S 20.1	16 S 29.6	18 N 43.8	22 S16.1
21	17 01.5	16 09.5	19 47.2	23 26.0
FEB 10	14 50.6	14 19.4	21 21.3	23 34.5
MAR 2	11 51.5	11 32.8	23 09.9	23 14.6
22	08 11.0	08 18.8	24 57.9	22 49.3
APR 11	03 59.3	04 59.9	26 33.0	22 39.8
MAY 1	00 N 32.0	01 53.2	27 45.7	23 10.9
21	05 09.7	00 N 46.8	28 29.3	24 55.8
JUN 10	09 39.2	02 45.0	28 40.2	28 40.6
30	13 45.3	03 43.7	28 17.8	35 13.7
JUL 20	17 12.1	03 20.7	27 24.2	44 00.8
AUG 9	19 42.6	01 17.6	26 04.1	50 28.9
29	20 58.3	02 S 14.1	24 23.8	50 37.8
SEP 18	20 37.9	06 09.0	22 31.6	47 33.5
OCT 8	18 23.7	09 08.6	20 36.9	44 23.8
28	14 36.1	10 41.2	18 51.0	41 41.6
NOV 17	10 47.6	10 55.0	17 26.4	39 01.4
DEC 7	08 32.6	10 08.9	16 36.4	35 28.3
27	[illegible]	[illegible]	[illegible]	[illegible]

1984	Sappho 80	Amor 1221	Pandora 55	Icarus 1566
JAN 1	02♉35.6	14♓56.3	04 R 39.7	07 R41.3
11	05 02.4	17 58.3	04♍01.9	02 D49.9
21	08 00.7	21 11.4	02 47.2	09♑08.1
31	11 23.9	24 33.4	01 00.8	15 27.5
FEB 10	15 07.2	28 02.7	28♌52.1	21 09.1
20	19 06.3	01♈37.8	26 34.8	26 15.7
MAR 1	23 17.4	05 17.4	24 23.5	00♒52.6
11	27 38.2	09 00.6	22 31.4	05 02.8
21	02♊06.1	12 46.1	21 08.6	08 48.1
31	06 39.4	16 33.3	20 19.9	12 08.9
APR 10	11 16.6	20 21.6	20 D 07.2	15 03.5
20	15 56.4	24 10.0	20 28.9	17 29.4
30	20 37.9	27 58.1	21 22.0	19 22.3
MAY 10	25 20.4	01♉45.3	22 43.0	20 35.3
20	00♋03.0	05 30.8	24 28.0	20 R59.8
30	04 45.3	09 14.2	26 33.5	20 23.8
JUN 9	09 26.7	12 54.7	28 56.4	18 32.8
19	14 06.8	16 31.4	01♍33.9	15 12.5
29	18 45.3	20 03.6	04 23.7	10 13.6
JUL 9	23 21.8	23 30.1	07 23.8	03 43.5
19	27 55.9	26 49.6	10 32.4	26♑17.3
29	02♌27.2	00♊00.6	13 48.1	18 51.9
AUG 8	06 55.4	03 00.8	17 09.7	12 25.1
18	11 19.8	05 48.1	20 35.9	07 30.7
28	15 40.1	08 19.1	24 05.8	04 15.3
SEP 7	19 55.6	10 29.9	27 38.5	02 30.1
17	24 05.4	12 15.7	01♎13.0	02 D00.0
27	28 08.9	13 30.6	04 48.7	02 30.8
OCT 7	02♍04.8	14 07.6	08 24.4	03 50.9
17	05 51.7	13 R 59.4	11 59.3	05 51.0
27	09 28.3	12 58.8	15 32.5	08 24.9
NOV 6	12 52.5	11 02.2	19 02.9	11 28.1
16	16 02.1	08 12.2	22 29.3	14 57.7
26	18 54.3	04 41.1	25 50.6	18 52.6
DEC 6	21 25.8	00 52.8	29 05.0	23 12.9
16	23 32.9	27♉17.4	02♏11.1	28 00.2
26	25 11.4	24 22.2	05 06.9	03♒18.1
JAN 5	26♍16.6	22♉26.3	07♏50.1	09♒12.5
JAN 1	08 N 17.9	08 S 11.7	16 N 39.7	21 S14.6
21	09 30.3	06 05.5	17 35.5	18 37.9
FEB 10	11 19.0	03 41.3	18 54.9	20 00.8
MAR 1	13 17.1	01 07.6	19 56.8	20 24.4
21	15 05.4	01 N 28.3	20 11.2	20 30.2
APR 10	16 30.3	03 59.6	19 35.1	20 50.3
30	17 23.1	06 20.3	18 19.1	21 56.8
MAY 20	17 38.9	08 24.5	16 33.5	24 29.8
JUN 9	17 15.9	10 07.0	14 24.7	29 15.7
29	16 15.3	11 22.6	11 57.2	36 24.6
JUL 19	14 40.0	12 06.2	09 14.4	43 22.7
AUG 8	12 34.8	12 13.2	06 19.6	45 49.1
28	10 05.3	11 39.1	03 16.5	44 20.4
SEP 17	07 18.2	10 20.0	00 09.0	42 01.2
OCT 7	04 20.3	08 13.9	02 S 59.0	40 01.0
27	01 19.7	05 26.9	06 03.1	38 18.2
NOV 16	01 S 34.8	02 25.5	08 59.0	36 33.8
DEC 6	04 12.6	00 09.3	11 42.6	34 24.7

1985		Sappho 80	Amor 1221	Pandora 55	Icarus 1566
JAN	1	25♍54.8	23R04.9	06♏46.5	06♒45.9
	11	26 37.8	21♉48.7	09 21.1	13 06.2
	21	26R40.8	21D39.0	11 39.2	20 18.4
	31	26 00.8	22 32.2	13 37.6	28 24.1
FEB	10	24 38.5	24 21.6	15 13.2	03R56.8
	20	22 38.6	26 59.9	16 22.5	17♒07.2
MAR	2	20 11.5	00♊21.4	17 01.9	11 11.7
	12	17 32.8	04 20.5	17R08.8	11D41.2
	22	14 59.6	08 53.5	16 41.3	13 36.7
APR	1	12 48.2	13 57.5	15 39.6	15 45.3
	11	11 10.3	19 30.3	14 07.3	17 41.3
	21	10 11.9	25 30.7	12 11.2	19 10.5
MAY	1	09D54.5	01♋58.1	10 01.8	20 00.6
	11	10 16.2	08 51.8	07 51.9	19R59.1
	21	11 13.2	16 12.0	05 53.9	18 50.5
	31	12 41.3	23 58.5	04 18.8	16 16.4
JUN	10	14 36.1	02♌11.0	03 13.7	12 00.3
	20	16 53.7	10 49.1	02 42.1	05 53.9
	30	19 30.8	19 51.8	02D44.9	28♑14.3
JUL	10	22 24.3	29 16.9	03 20.5	19 53.6
	20	25 31.8	09♍01.9	04 26.2	12 02.3
	30	28 51.4	19 02.8	05 59.0	05 38.0
AUG	9	02♎21.1	29 14.0	07 55.5	01 02.8
	19	05 59.8	09♎29.9	10 12.9	28♐12.1
	29	09 46.2	19 43.3	12 48.5	26 49.9
SEP	8	13 39.2	29 47.2	15 39.6	26D37.9
	18	17 37.9	09♏35.8	18 44.4	27 21.2
	28	21 41.7	19 04.3	22 01.0	28 48.2
OCT	8	25 49.6	28 09.2	25 27.7	00♑49.7
	18	00♏01.1	06♐49.4	29 03.3	03 19.7
	28	04 15.5	15 04.4	02♐46.3	06 13.5
NOV	7	08 32.2	22 55.0	06 35.7	09 27.8
	17	12 50.5	00♑22.9	10 30.5	13 00.8
	27	17 09.7	07 29.7	14 29.7	16 51.0
DEC	7	21 29.1	14 17.1	18 32.3	20 57.9
	17	25 48.1	20 47.1	22 37.5	25 22.1
	27	00♐05.5	27 01.2	26 44.2	00♒04.4
JAN	6	04♐20.6	03♒00.7	00♑51.7	05♒07.1
JAN	1	06S49.6	00S05.4	14S50.8	30S08.4
	21	07 49.6	01N46.6	16 52.7	24 18.0
FEB	10	07 33.4	04 42.3	18 31.6	11 35.1
MAR	2	05 53.0	08 05.5	19 44.2	11 10.0
	22	03 16.5	11 30.1	20 25.1	13 55.7
APR	11	00 41.9	14 34.6	20 27.1	15 45.6
MAY	1	01N04.6	16 56.9	19 49.4	18 09.7
	21	01 47.9	18 12.0	18 49.8	22 16.2
JUN	10	01 32.8	17 53.7	18 00.2	28 58.9
	30	00 30.0	15 41.6	17 44.5	37 06.0
JUL	20	01S09.6	11 32.3	18 09.5	41 42.2
AUG	9	03 16.2	05 49.9	19 09.6	41 23.8
	29	05 41.2	00S34.5	20 34.6	39 35.4
SEP	18	08 16.3	06 37.7	22 13.4	38 02.0
OCT	8	10 53.8	11 28.5	23 55.9	36 52.3
	28	13 25.9	14 41.6	25 32.7	35 51.9
NOV	17	15 44.7	16 15.3	26 55.3	34 45.0
DEC	7	17 42.8	16 22.4	27 57.0	33 17.5
	27	19S13.2	15S20.9	28S32.8	31S15.7

1986		Sappho 80	Amor 1221	Pandora 55	Icarus 1566
JAN	1	02♐13.4	00♒02.7	28♐47.9	02♒33.0
	11	06 27.0	05 55.5	02♑55.5	07 47.2
	21	10 36.6	11 35.7	07 02.3	13 27.6
	31	14 41.0	17 03.9	11 07.5	19 40.7
FEB	10	18 38.8	22 21.0	15 10.2	26 36.5
	20	22 28.2	27 27.6	19 09.0	04♓30.3
MAR	2	26 07.3	02♓23.8	23 02.8	13 46.5
	12	29 33.7	07 10.0	26 50.4	25 06.9
	22	02♑44.4	11 46.2	00♒30.1	09♈29.9
APR	1	05 36.3	16 12.2	04 00.3	17R46.2
	11	08 05.2	20 28.0	07 19.0	03 34.4
	21	10 06.1	24 32.9	10 23.7	22♓00.1
MAY	1	11 34.0	28 26.3	13 11.9	14 06.0
	11	12 22.9	02♈07.6	15 40.4	07 23.6
	21	12R27.5	05 35.3	17 45.4	29♒59.4
	31	11 44.9	08 48.3	19 23.0	20 30.5
JUN	10	10 15.5	11 44.6	20 28.9	08 14.7
	20	08 07.2	14 21.9	20 58.9	24♑07.0
	30	05 35.3	16 37.7	20R50.3	10 44.9
JUL	10	03 00.8	18 28.5	20 01.8	00 22.4
	20	00 47.4	19 50.2	18 36.4	23♐28.9
	30	29♐13.5	20 38.9	16 42.2	19 27.2
AUG	9	28 30.2	20R49.8	14 31.8	17 30.6
	19	28D42.1	20 19.0	12 22.0	17D03.0
	29	29 46.8	19 04.3	10 29.5	17 38.3
SEP	8	01♑40.0	17 06.5	09 07.5	18 59.8
	18	04 16.1	14 31.8	08 25.3	20 56.0
	28	07 28.9	11 32.1	08D25.8	23 18.8
OCT	8	11 13.4	08 24.2	09 08.7	26 02.9
	18	15 25.0	05 27.1	10 31.2	29 04.6
	28	19 59.2	02 57.3	12 28.8	02♑21.0
NOV	7	24 53.0	01 05.9	14 57.3	05 50.3
	17	00♒03.4	29♓58.6	17 52.5	09 31.1
	27	05 27.7	29 35.5	21 10.1	13 22.5
DEC	7	11 03.9	29D54.0	24 47.1	17 24.3
	17	16 49.8	00♈49.8	28 40.3	21 36.2
	27	22 43.7	02 17.9	02♓47.0	25 58.5
JAN	6	28♒44.2	04♈13.8	07♓05.2	00♒32.0
JAN	1	19S30.7	14S57.0	28S37.3	30S38.1
	21	20 18.3	12 55.5	28 37.7	27 28.7
FEB	10	20 27.6	10 24.0	28 11.0	22 48.6
MAR	2	19 57.7	07 35.8	27 21.6	15 15.9
	22	18 50.6	04 41.9	26 16.7	00 09.0
APR	11	17 11.1	01 51.9	25 06.4	10N45.5
MAY	1	15 07.8	00N45.8	24 02.7	00 14.2
	21	12 53.7	03 03.3	23 19.6	10S42.7
JUN	10	10 49.8	04 52.4	23 10.9	25 09.8
	30	09 25.2	06 03.9	23 44.8	36 04.8
JUL	20	09 03.9	06 26.6	24 52.3	37 11.1
AUG	9	09 43.9	05 47.7	25 57.1	35 47.2
	29	10 58.9	03 56.7	26 14.1	34 48.8
SEP	18	12 17.4	00 59.3	25 27.4	34 20.0
OCT	8	13 13.5	02S22.9	23 50.0	34 03.5
	28	13 28.7	05 04.2	21 36.9	33 44.4
NOV	17	12 51.5	06 23.2	18 55.0	33 11.8
DEC	7	11 17.5	06 20.2	15 46.6	32 17.5
	27	08S49.2	05S14.5	12S13.7	30S54.9

1987		Sappho 80	Amor 1221	Pandora 55	Icarus 1566
JAN	1	25♒43.3	03♈12.6	04♓54.8	28♑13.8
	11	01♓46.4	05 20.8	09 18.0	02♒53.3
	21	07 53.8	07 50.4	13 49.6	07 45.8
	31	14 04.4	10 38.2	18 28.4	12 53.8
FEB	10	20 16.9	13 41.4	23 12.8	18 20.2
	20	26 30.1	16 57.4	28 01.6	24 09.5
MAR	2	02♈43.5	20 24.5	02♈53.8	00♓28.4
	12	08 55.9	24 00.9	07 48.4	07 25.7
	22	15 06.6	27 45.2	12 44.5	15 14.8
APR	1	21 15.0	01♉36.5	17 41.4	24 15.7
	11	27 20.5	05 33.8	22 38.3	04♈57.7
	21	03♉22.3	09 36.4	27 34.6	18 07.3
MAY	1	09 20.4	13 43.9	02♉29.6	05♉03.2
	11	15 13.9	17 55.6	07 22.7	27 29.5
	21	21 02.7	22 11.3	12 13.3	10♊57.0
	31	26 46.3	26 31.0	17 00.8	18 58.8
JUN	10	02♊24.2	00♊54.3	21 44.4	05♋23.0
	20	07 56.3	05 21.2	26 23.4	24♌57.0
	30	13 22.0	09 51.8	00♊57.2	19♎03.6
JUL	10	18 40.8	14 26.0	05 24.6	08♏04.8
	20	23 52.3	19 04.1	09 44.7	16 49.1
	30	28 55.9	23 46.3	13 56.4	22 28.8
AUG	9	03♋50.6	28 32.6	17 57.9	26 59.0
	19	08 35.6	03♋23.6	21 47.7	00♐59.1
	29	13 10.0	08 19.6	25 23.7	04 46.4
SEP	8	17 31.9	13 20.9	28 43.1	08 29.1
	18	21 40.0	18 28.2	01♋43.4	12 10.6
	28	25 32.0	23 42.3	04 20.6	15 53.5
OCT	8	29 05.2	29 03.7	06 30.7	19 38.9
	18	02♌16.5	04♌34.1	08 09.3	23 27.3
	28	05 01.9	10 14.6	09 11.5	27 19.3
NOV	7	07 16.7	16 07.0	09 33.0	01♑14.9
	17	08 56.1	22 14.3	09R11.4	05 14.4
	27	09 54.2	28 39.5	08 06.4	09 18.0
DEC	7	10R06.1	05♍27.1	06 23.4	13 25.7
	17	09 28.6	12 43.6	04 13.2	17 37.7
	27	08 02.0	20 35.9	01 51.3	21 54.5
JAN	6	05♌53.0	29♍13.8	29♊36.3	26♑16.2
JAN	1	08S04.5	04S50.8	11S16.9	30S29.2
	21	04 40.7	02 54.4	07 18.3	28 22.5
FEB	10	00 47.3	00 34.4	03 05.2	25 30.8
MAR	2	03N20.3	01N57.8	01N15.6	21 37.6
	22	07 26.3	04 33.0	05 36.9	16 07.1
APR	11	11 16.0	07 03.5	09 51.4	07 35.9
MAY	1	14 36.2	09 21.9	13 51.9	07N32.3
	21	17 15.9	11 21.6	17 32.0	30 57.9
JUN	10	19 07.3	12 56.5	20 46.0	41 19.7
	30	20 06.0	14 00.4	23 30.2	02S57.0
JUL	20	20 11.5	14 27.6	25 42.7	21 19.7
AUG	9	19 27.1	14 12.9	27 25.0	26 00.7
	29	17 59.2	13 11.6	28 42.0	28 23.1
SEP	18	15 57.0	11 20.1	29 42.7	29 54.4
OCT	8	13 31.8	08 35.9	30 39.4	30 54.3
	28	10 57.4	04 58.0	31 44.6	31 26.9
NOV	17	08 30.8	00 27.7	33 02.3	31 32.3
DEC	7	06 33.7	04S49.6	34 15.4	31 09.4
	27	05N31.4	10S38.7	34N47.4	30S17.4

1988		Sappho 80	Amor 1221	Pandora 55	Icarus 1566
JAN	1	07 R 02.1	24 ♍ 48.4	00 R 41.9	24 ♑ 04.7
	11	04 ♌ 36.6	03 ♎ 53.2	28 ♊ 36.5	28 29.0
	21	01 51.0	13 58.5	27 00.5	02 ♒ 59.5
	31	29 ♋ 06.6	25 10.1	26 02.8	07 36.8
FEB	10	26 43.7	07 ♏ 25.9	25 D 46.3	12 22.1
	20	24 56.9	20 26.5	26 10.0	17 17.4
MAR	1	23 54.3	03 ♐ 36.4	27 10.6	22 25.0
	11	23 D 37.4	16 15.6	28 43.1	27 48.0
	21	24 03.3	27 48.7	00 ♋ 43.1	03 ♓ 31.3
	31	25 07.6	07 ♑ 55.0	03 06.0	09 40.9
APR	10	26 44.6	16 27.8	05 47.7	16 25.8
	20	28 49.0	23 24.3	08 45.1	23 59.0
	30	01 ♌ 16.3	28 43.0	11 55.1	02 ♈ 38.2
MAY	10	04 02.4	02 ♒ 22.6	15 15.4	12 49.0
	20	07 03.9	04 17.0	18 44.0	25 05.8
	30	10 18.1	04 R 22.9	22 19.2	10 ♉ 09.3
JUN	9	13 42.6	02 44.0	25 59.6	28 44.8
	19	17 15.8	29 ♑ 35.8	29 44.0	22 ♊ 22.0
	29	20 55.9	25 35.1	03 ♌ 31.5	20 ♋ 59.7
JUL	9	24 41.7	21 29.3	07 21.0	15 ♌ 14.1
	19	28 32.2	18 00.6	11 11.9	10 ♍ 06.4
	29	02 ♍ 26.4	15 35.7	15 03.2	02 ♎ 57.9
AUG	8	06 23.5	14 20.7	18 54.4	20 53.7
	18	10 23.0	14 D 10.7	22 44.8	04 ♏ 12.8
	28	14 23.9	14 56.1	26 33.5	14 20.8
SEP	7	18 25.8	16 25.9	00 ♍ 19.8	22 27.2
	17	22 28.0	18 31.1	04 03.0	29 17.2
	27	26 29.8	21 04.3	07 41.9	05 ♐ 17.9
OCT	7	00 ♎ 30.5	23 59.1	11 15.7	10 46.0
	17	04 29.5	27 11.1	14 43.0	15 52.5
	27	08 25.7	00 ♒ 36.8	18 02.4	20 44.1
NOV	6	12 18.4	04 13.1	21 12.4	25 25.4
	16	16 06.4	07 58.0	24 11.0	29 59.8
	26	19 48.3	11 49.7	26 55.8	04 ♑ 29.3
DEC	6	23 22.8	15 46.5	29 24.4	08 55.5
	16	26 48.1	19 47.5	01 ♎ 33.9	13 19.7
	26	00 ♏ 02.1	23 51.4	03 20.8	17 42.7
JAN	5	03 ♏ 02.5	27 ♒ 57.4	04 ♎ 41.8	22 ♑ 05.2
JAN	1	05 N 27.0	12 S 06.8	34 N 45.9	29 S 59.8
	21	05 56.0	17 26.6	34 07.2	28 30.9
FEB	10	07 21.1	19 43.8	33 02.8	26 31.8
MAR	1	09 02.5	15 34.9	31 59.0	24 00.5
	21	10 27.2	06 41.7	31 01.5	20 50.3
APR	10	11 19.1	01 N 51.9	30 03.9	16 44.8
	30	11 33.0	08 16.0	28 57.6	11 04.3
MAY	20	11 08.7	12 14.2	27 36.3	02 22.4
JUN	9	10 08.6	13 05.0	25 56.2	11 N 36.9
	29	08 36.3	09 56.3	23 56.7	27 16.4
JUL	19	06 36.3	03 38.0	21 39.1	14 27.4
AUG	8	04 13.7	03 S 08.4	19 06.4	06 S 13.8
	28	01 33.7	08 30.2	16 22.8	17 40.5
SEP	17	01 S 17.9	12 05.4	13 33.3	23 29.0
OCT	7	04 15.2	14 07.9	10 43.6	26 44.2
	27	07 12.3	14 55.2	08 00.3	28 36.1
NOV	16	10 02.7	14 42.3	05 30.5	29 32.4
DEC	6	12 39.6	13 41.2	03 22.4	29 45.9

1989		Sappho 80	Amor 1221	Pandora 55	Icarus 1566
JAN	1	01 ♏ 52.2	26 ♒ 18.8	04 ♎ 12.8	20 ♑ 20.2
	11	04 43.1	00 ♓ 25.7	05 16.3	24 42.8
	21	07 15.5	04 33.4	05 48.2	29 05.9
	31	09 26.1	08 41.2	05 R 45.8	03 ♒ 30.0
FEB	10	11 10.6	12 48.6	05 07.5	07 56.1
	20	12 24.5	16 54.9	03 54.9	12 24.7
MAR	2	13 03.5	20 59.5	02 12.6	16 56.9
	12	13 R 03.1	25 02.0	00 09.0	21 34.0
	22	12 20.9	29 01.8	27 ♍ 56.1	26 17.7
APR	1	10 57.2	02 ♈ 58.3	25 47.1	01 ♓ 10.5
	11	08 56.5	06 51.1	23 54.4	06 15.6
	21	06 29.5	10 39.3	22 27.6	11 37.6
MAY	1	03 51.3	14 22.6	21 32.3	17 23.2
	11	01 19.5	18 00.1	21 10.8	23 42.0
	21	29 ♎ 10.9	21 30.8	21 D 22.6	00 ♈ 48.1
	31	27 37.3	24 54.0	22 05.3	09 03.5
JUN	10	26 45.3	28 08.3	23 16.0	18 59.9
	20	26 D 36.7	01 ♉ 12.3	24 51.3	01 ♉ 21.3
	30	27 09.6	04 04.3	26 47.8	16 57.1
JUL	10	28 20.7	06 42.2	29 02.7	06 ♊ 04.8
	20	00 ♏ 05.7	09 03.3	01 ♎ 33.4	27 40.7
	30	02 20.3	11 04.7	04 17.4	20 ♋ 34.2
AUG	9	05 00.7	12 42.4	07 12.9	19 ♌ 37.8
	19	08 03.5	13 52.0	10 18.1	17 ♍ 01.0
	29	11 25.8	14 28.9	13 31.6	08 ♎ 20.5
SEP	8	15 05.4	14 R 27.7	16 52.0	25 10.4
	18	19 00.0	13 44.2	20 18.2	08 ♏ 24.2
	28	23 08.0	12 15.7	23 49.1	19 00.7
OCT	8	27 28.2	10 03.6	27 23.7	27 48.5
	18	01 ♐ 59.2	07 15.3	01 ♏ 01.1	05 ♐ 21.0
	28	06 40.1	04 04.7	04 40.4	12 01.4
NOV	7	11 30.1	00 50.9	08 20.7	18 05.1
	17	16 28.3	27 ♈ 54.6	12 00.9	23 41.9
	27	21 34.2	25 32.5	15 40.2	28 59.1
DEC	7	26 47.1	23 55.5	19 17.3	04 ♑ 01.7
	17	02 ♑ 06.3	23 07.7	22 51.1	08 52.9
	27	07 31.4	23 D 07.8	26 20.5	13 35.3
JAN	6	13 ♑ 01.9	23 ♈ 52.6	29 ♏ 43.8	18 ♑ 10.8
JAN	1	15 S 32.6	11 S 26.6	01 N 23.3	29 S 10.4
	21	17 12.7	09 12.6	00 39.7	28 08.8
FEB	10	18 15.5	06 41.6	00 44.8	26 42.2
MAR	2	18 31.2	04 01.6	01 34.7	24 54.8
	22	17 48.4	01 19.8	02 47.5	22 50.1
APR	11	16 00.0	01 N 17.0	03 48.1	20 29.1
MAY	1	13 22.8	03 42.4	04 08.9	17 48.3
	21	10 47.0	05 50.4	03 41.5	14 32.2
JUN	10	09 04.1	07 35.0	02 30.9	09 53.9
	30	08 32.9	08 50.2	00 45.7	02 00.3
JUL	20	09 04.5	09 29.1	01 S 25.9	10 N 32.1
AUG	9	10 20.5	09 24.3	03 56.5	18 23.0
	29	12 02.6	08 27.6	06 39.8	01 09.5
SEP	18	13 54.8	06 32.9	09 30.2	12 S 44.7
OCT	8	15 42.6	03 45.9	12 22.3	20 27.6
	28	17 12.9	00 40.6	15 10.9	24 40.1
NOV	17	18 13.6	01 S 42.4	17 51.4	26 55.5
DEC	7	18 34.3	02 38.1	20 19.6	27 57.2

1990		Sappho 80	Amor 1221	Pandora 55	Icarus 1566
JAN	1	10 ♑ 16.0	23 ♈ 24.9	28 ♏ 03.0	15 ♑ 53.8
	11	15 48.9	24 30.0	01 ♐ 22.7	20 26.2
	21	21 26.4	26 11.8	04 34.0	24 53.5
	31	27 08.0	28 25.4	07 34.9	29 16.5
FEB	10	02 ♒ 53.1	01 ♉ 06.4	10 23.2	03 ♒ 35.8
	20	08 41.2	04 10.9	12 56.5	07 52.1
MAR	2	14 31.8	07 36.0	15 11.8	12 05.9
	12	20 24.3	11 19.1	17 05.9	16 17.5
	22	26 18.0	15 18.1	18 35.6	20 27.5
APR	1	02 ♓ 12.4	19 31.9	19 37.0	24 36.5
	11	08 06.6	23 59.1	20 06.8	28 45.0
	21	14 00.0	28 39.0	20 R 02.3	02 ♓ 54.4
MAY	1	19 51.6	03 ♊ 31.3	19 22.0	07 05.7
	11	25 40.3	08 35.7	18 07.4	11 20.9
	21	01 ♈ 25.2	13 52.5	16 23.6	15 43.2
	31	07 04.8	19 21.9	14 19.2	20 17.0
JUN	10	12 37.6	25 04.4	12 07.0	25 09.7
	20	18 02.0	01 ♋ 00.8	10 00.7	00 ♈ 34.7
	30	23 15.9	07 12.0	08 13.4	06 55.0
JUL	10	28 16.6	13 39.0	06 55.1	14 56.9
	20	03 ♉ 01.7	20 22.9	06 11.5	26 17.6
	30	07 27.1	27 25.2	06 D 05.0	14 ♉ 19.6
AUG	9	11 28.9	04 ♌ 46.8	06 35.0	13 ♊ 33.0
	19	15 02.1	12 29.1	07 38.8	17 ♋ 50.5
	29	18 00.1	20 33.1	09 13.6	12 ♌ 21.8
SEP	8	20 16.6	28 59.2	11 15.7	27 59.6
	18	21 44.0	07 ♍ 47.7	13 41.6	14 ♍ 43.7
	28	22 15.5	16 57.9	16 28.6	11 ♎ 13.0
OCT	8	21 R 47.7	26 27.9	19 33.6	00 ♏ 45.5
	18	20 22.6	06 ♎ 15.4	22 54.4	15 11.6
	28	18 11.7	16 16.4	26 28.9	26 30.8
NOV	7	15 37.0	26 25.7	00 ♑ 15.1	05 ♐ 48.3
	17	13 05.2	06 ♏ 38.1	04 11.6	13 44.1
	27	11 02.6	16 47.1	08 17.0	20 42.9
DEC	7	09 47.0	26 46.7	12 29.8	27 00.7
	17	09 D 25.5	06 ♐ 31.5	16 49.2	02 ♑ 48.3
	27	09 58.0	15 57.1	21 13.9	08 12.9
JAN	6	11 ♉ 19.0	25 ♐ 00.1	25 ♑ 43.0	13 ♑ 19.4
JAN	1	17 S 52.0	01 S 46.4	23 S 02.9	28 S 03.8
	21	16 19.0	00 N 02.7	24 54.4	27 28.6
FEB	10	13 53.8	02 26.4	26 30.1	26 28.2
MAR	2	10 41.1	05 07.2	27 53.3	25 11.1
	22	06 49.4	07 51.4	29 08.8	23 46.3
APR	11	02 29.4	10 27.9	30 20.1	22 23.0
MAY	1	02 N 06.4	12 46.1	31 23.6	21 11.8
	21	06 44.0	14 35.6	32 03.9	20 26.0
JUN	10	11 08.7	15 45.3	32 02.3	20 24.0
	30	15 05.6	16 04.0	31 21.2	21 29.7
JUL	20	18 20.1	15 20.2	30 28.2	23 52.0
AUG	9	20 38.2	13 24.2	29 49.3	23 13.4
	29	21 47.3	10 10.4	29 32.5	07 32.1
SEP	18	21 34.9	05 42.1	29 31.5	06 N 42.0
OCT	8	19 49.5	00 16.8	29 34.4	07 S 40.6
	28	16 36.8	05 S 29.1	29 28.8	17 40.9
NOV	17	12 55.9	10 43.1	29 03.9	22 47.3
DEC	7	10 19.7	14 32.1	28 11.7	25 18.3

1991	Sappho 80	Amor 1221	Pandora 55	Icarus 1566
JAN 1	10♉32.9	20♐31.5	23♑28.0	10♑48.2
11	12 15.4	29 22.4	27 58.9	15 47.0
21	14 35.8	07♑48.2	02♒33.0	20 32.8
31	17 27.2	15 47.9	07 09.3	25 07.3
FEB 10	20 43.2	23 22.0	11 47.0	29 32.0
20	24 19.0	00♒30.9	16 25.5	03♒48.1
MAR 2	28 10.5	07 15.1	21 03.7	07 55.8
12	02♊14.0	13 35.8	25 41.0	11 55.6
22	06 27.0	19 33.4	00♓16.7	15 47.5
APR 1	10 47.2	25 08.4	04 49.7	19 31.2
11	15 12.8	00♓21.2	09 19.3	23 06.3
21	19 42.6	05 11.5	13 44.6	26 31.8
MAY 1	24 15.0	09 38.7	18 04.2	29 46.4
11	28 49.3	13 42.0	22 17.2	02♓48.6
21	03♋24.7	17 19.5	26 21.9	05 35.3
31	08 00.5	20 29.0	00♈16.8	08 02.8
JUN 10	12 36.0	23 07.8	03 59.9	10 05.8
20	17 11.0	25 11.7	07 28.8	11 35.0
30	21 44.8	26 36.5	10 40.6	12 17.3
JUL 10	26 17.2	27 17.2	13 32.1	11R50.4
20	00♌47.7	27R08.9	15 59.1	09 35.0
30	05 15.8	26 08.7	17 57.3	04 23.6
AUG 9	09 41.2	24 16.7	19 22.0	24♒18.8
19	14 03.5	21 38.7	20 07.9	07 02.5
29	18 21.9	18 28.2	20R11.6	13♑55.8
SEP 8	22 36.1	15 04.6	19 31.5	22♐38.3
18	26 45.3	11 50.3	18 10.1	07 30.5
28	00♍48.4	09 05.1	16 16.5	26♏37.0
OCT 8	04 44.7	07 01.6	14 04.8	17 04.4
18	08 32.8	05 45.8	11 53.8	06 53.1
28	12 11.1	05 17.5	10 02.5	27♎26.1
NOV 7	15 38.1	05D32.7	08 45.1	06D55.5
17	18 51.3	06 26.5	08 10.4	23♏47.8
27	21 48.4	07 53.1	08D21.0	06♐11.8
DEC 7	24 26.3	09 47.2	09 14.9	15 56.6
17	26 41.2	12 04.4	10 48.6	24 03.6
27	28 29.3	14 40.6	12 56.7	01♑05.3
JAN 6	29♍46.0	17♓32.5	15♈33.9	07♑21.4
JAN 1	09N31.6	16S33.1	26S21.6	26S25.7
21	10 23.0	16 02.2	24 16.7	26 20.9
FEB 10	11 55.4	14 06.7	21 41.9	25 44.8
MAR 2	13 39.9	11 18.6	18 42.3	24 51.5
22	15 16.0	08 05.6	15 24.4	23 54.2
APR 11	16 29.7	04 48.8	11 55.7	23 07.2
MAY 1	17 12.4	01 44.4	08 24.0	22 48.1
21	17 19.0	00N53.8	04 57.0	23 22.0
JUN 10	16 48.2	02 51.4	01 42.8	25 29.3
30	15 40.9	03 51.5	01N10.9	30 21.6
JUL 20	14 00.4	03 33.0	03 35.9	40 06.9
AUG 9	11 51.2	01 37.5	05 24.0	57 30.0
29	09 19.0	01S47.2	06 26.7	77 27.8
SEP 18	06 29.9	05 40.7	06 39.9	65 49.0
OCT 8	03 31.0	08 44.2	06 14.5	44 31.7
28	00 29.7	10 21.4	05 44.5	14 37.0
NOV 17	02S25.6	10 38.5	05 49.2	14 21.7
DEC 7	05 04.6	09 54.3	06 46.8	20 40.2
27	07S14.6	08S25.7	08N34.1	23S25.7

1992	Sappho 80	Amor 1221	Pandora 55	Icarus 1566
JAN 1	29♍11.9	16♓04.7	14♈11.9	04♑18.2
11	00♎11.1	19 03.4	17 02.1	10 16.2
21	00 32.2	22 13.7	20 14.6	15 44.4
31	00R11.9	25 33.4	23 45.4	20 49.1
FEB 10	29♍08.6	29 01.0	27 31.2	25 34.5
20	27 25.4	02♈34.6	01♉29.2	00♒02.9
MAR 1	25 09.7	06 13.0	05 36.9	04 16.3
11	22 34.7	09 55.3	09 52.3	08 15.3
21	19 57.3	13 40.3	14 13.8	12 00.0
31	17 34.3	17 27.3	18 39.7	15 30.3
APR 10	15 39.8	21 15.6	23 09.1	18 44.9
20	14 22.6	25 04.2	27 40.6	21 41.7
30	13 45.9	28 52.9	02♊13.6	24 18.5
MAY 10	13D49.5	02♉40.9	06 47.2	26 30.8
20	14 30.3	06 27.4	11 20.5	28 13.1
30	15 44.1	10 12.2	15 53.1	29 17.7
JUN 9	17 26.9	13 54.3	20 24.4	29R33.3
19	19 34.4	17 33.1	24 53.7	28 45.0
29	22 02.8	21 07.8	29 20.5	26 33.3
JUL 9	24 49.4	24 37.2	03♋44.2	22 35.5
19	27 51.2	28 00.2	08 04.1	16 34.5
29	01♎06.0	01♊15.3	12 19.7	08 34.4
AUG 8	04 32.3	04 20.4	16 30.1	29♑22.2
18	08 08.1	07 13.4	20 34.3	20 22.5
28	11 52.4	09 51.3	24 31.6	12 52.1
SEP 7	15 44.0	12 10.1	28 20.5	07 27.0
17	19 41.9	14 05.4	01♌59.5	04 03.5
27	23 45.5	15 31.5	05 27.3	02 20.5
OCT 7	27 53.8	16 21.2	08 41.4	01D55.7
17	02♏06.2	16R27.4	11 39.5	02 27.6
27	06 22.0	15 42.3	14 18.9	03 38.1
NOV 6	10 40.7	14 00.4	16 36.1	05 08.0
16	15 01.5	11 22.3	18 27.4	06 26.5
26	19 24.0	07 57.4	19 48.6	06R23.6
DEC 6	23 47.2	04 07.4	20 35.7	01 05.6
16	28 10.5	00 22.7	20R45.3	15♐05.9
26	02♐33.3	27♉12.9	20 15.1	20D26.5
JAN 5	06♐54.5	25♉00.7	19♌05.9	29♐18.8
JAN 1	07S40.7	07S58.3	09N07.2	23S47.9
21	08 50.1	05 52.6	11 38.5	24 29.6
FEB 10	08 47.7	03 28.9	14 29.3	24 22.6
MAR 1	07 20.8	00 55.5	17 26.4	23 52.1
21	04 48.9	01N40.1	20 18.3	23 17.4
APR 10	02 06.9	04 11.1	22 54.8	22 57.3
30	00 07.4	06 31.4	25 07.3	23 14.5
MAY 20	00N48.4	08 35.2	26 49.3	24 40.0
JUN 9	00 42.9	10 17.2	27 56.7	27 59.3
29	00S13.0	11 32.3	28 27.9	34 11.5
JUL 19	01 47.7	12 15.4	28 24.2	43 34.4
AUG 8	03 50.6	12 22.0	27 49.7	52 29.8
28	06 12.5	11 47.7	26 51.2	54 24.0
SEP 17	08 44.8	10 28.9	25 38.0	50 59.7
OCT 7	11 19.3	08 23.8	24 21.4	47 00.8
27	13 48.0	05 37.5	23 14.6	43 35.0
NOV 16	16 02.9	02 34.8	22 32.6	40 00.1
DEC 6	17 56.2	00 13.3	22 29.4	31 57.9
26	19S20.6	00S21.8	23N11.9	17S48.0

1993	Sappho 80	Amor 1221	Pandora 55	Icarus 1566
JAN 1	05♐10.2	25R45.8	19R38.0	25♐54.7
11	09 30.1	24♉13.7	18♌07.6	04♑00.7
21	13 47.0	23D50.2	16 08.1	10 56.4
31	17 59.8	24 32.7	13 51.7	17 00.5
FEB 10	22 07.0	26 14.5	11 33.9	22 25.6
20	26 07.5	28 48.2	09 29.3	27 20.3
MAR 2	29 59.3	02♊07.5	07 50.6	01♒49.1
12	03♑40.4	06 06.8	06 45.7	05 54.8
22	07 08.4	10 41.8	06 17.4	09 38.9
APR 1	10 20.2	15 49.6	06D25.8	13 00.9
11	13 12.4	21 27.8	07 08.2	15 59.7
21	15 40.7	27 35.0	08 20.7	18 32.9
MAY 1	17 39.9	04♋10.7	09 59.5	20 36.1
11	19 04.5	11 13.9	12 00.6	22 03.8
21	19 48.7	18 44.8	14 20.5	22 47.9
31	19R47.0	26 43.2	16 56.2	22R37.1
JUN 10	18 57.2	05♌08.3	19 45.1	21 18.3
20	17 20.9	13 59.6	22 44.9	18 35.6
30	15 07.6	23 15.7	25 53.8	14 15.7
JUL 10	12 35.2	02♍54.0	29 10.0	08 17.6
20	10 06.2	12 51.3	02♍32.4	01 03.0
30	08 04.1	23 02.8	05 59.8	23♑23.2
AUG 9	06 46.5	03♎22.3	09 30.9	16 20.9
19	06D22.4	13 42.9	13 04.9	10 42.0
29	06 54.4	23 57.3	16 41.0	06 44.9
SEP 8	08 19.2	03♏58.2	20 18.3	04 24.8
18	10 31.6	13 40.0	23 55.9	03 27.6
28	13 25.6	22 58.6	27 33.1	03D38.5
OCT 8	16 54.9	01♐51.6	01♎08.8	04 44.1
18	20 54.3	10 18.4	04 42.3	06 34.4
28	25 19.2	18 19.7	08 12.4	09 02.3
NOV 7	00♒05.4	25 56.7	11 37.9	12 02.4
17	05 09.6	03♑11.6	14 57.6	15 32.0
27	10 29.0	10 06.1	18 09.8	19 29.6
DEC 7	16 00.7	16 42.1	21 13.0	23 55.2
17	21 42.8	23 01.8	24 05.1	28 50.6
27	27 33.2	29 06.6	26 43.7	04♒17.6
JAN 6	03♓30.1	04♒57.8	29♎06.5	10♒14.2
JAN 1	19S39.3	00S07.9	23N32.5	18S50.2
21	20 17.6	01N44.8	24 52.1	21 04.6
FEB 10	20 16.2	04 44.9	25 54.7	21 46.5
MAR 2	19 34.4	08 14.0	26 07.5	21 46.7
22	18 14.6	11 44.3	25 29.1	21 37.3
APR 11	16 21.9	14 53.1	24 14.2	21 44.9
MAY 1	14 05.2	17 17.1	22 34.6	22 37.9
21	11 38.6	18 29.5	20 35.6	24 53.5
JUN 10	09 24.0	18 02.5	18 19.3	29 18.1
30	07 52.2	15 35.5	15 47.5	36 16.7
JUL 20	07 30.4	11 07.9	13 02.2	43 55.7
AUG 9	08 17.6	05 09.8	10 05.9	47 32.0
29	09 43.0	01S21.3	07 01.8	46 22.2
SEP 18	11 10.0	07 20.1	03 53.7	43 46.3
OCT 8	12 10.3	11 58.8	00 45.8	41 24.1
28	12 25.2	14 57.5	02S17.5	39 21.6
NOV 17	11 44.4	16 18.6	05 11.5	37 17.9
DEC 7	10 05.4	16 16.4	07 51.4	34 43.8
27	07S32.4	15S09.1	10S12.4	30S52.2

1994	Sappho 80	Amor 1221	Pandora 55	Icarus 1566
JAN 1	00♓31.0	02♒03.8	27♎57.3	07♒12.9
11	06 30.6	07 48.8	00♏11.0	13 15.9
21	12 34.7	13 21.9	02 04.2	17 R23.2
31	18 41.6	18 43.9	03 33.7	02 42.9
FEB 10	24 50.4	23 55.5	04 35.9	26 D47.9
20	01♈00.1	28 57.3	05 07.4	29♑19.8
MAR 2	07 09.4	03♓49.3	05 R05.7	03♒00.1
12	13 17.8	08 31.9	04 29.5	06 41.0
22	19 24.4	13 05.0	03 19.6	10 05.6
APR 1	25 28.6	17 28.5	01 40.5	13 07.3
11	01♉29.8	21 42.2	29♎40.0	15 41.9
21	07 27.6	25 45.6	27 29.3	17 44.2
MAY 1	13 21.3	29 37.9	25 21.3	19 07.7
11	19 10.8	03♈18.6	23 28.1	19 43.7
21	24 55.5	06 46.3	21 59.6	19 R20.0
31	00♊35.2	09 59.7	21 02.0	17 42.6
JUN 10	06 09.6	12 57.2	20 37.8	14 35.4
20	11 38.2	15 36.4	20 D47.3	09 46.2
30	17 00.7	17 54.7	21 28.4	03 18.9
JUL 10	22 16.9	19 48.9	22 38.2	25♑43.3
20	27 25.9	21 15.1	24 13.9	17 57.7
30	02♋27.4	22 09.1	26 12.0	11 04.6
AUG 9	07 20.8	22 R26.4	28 29.7	05 43.3
19	12 05.0	22 02.8	01♏04.4	02 04.8
29	16 39.2	20 55.7	03 53.7	29♐59.8
SEP 8	21 02.0	19 05.2	06 55.7	29 13.0
18	25 11.8	16 36.3	10 08.7	29 D29.0
28	29 06.7	13 40.0	13 30.9	00♑34.8
OCT 8	02♌44.4	10 32.2	17 01.3	02 20.6
18	06 01.7	07 32.0	20 38.5	04 39.3
28	08 55.3	04 56.4	24 21.3	07 25.2
NOV 7	11 20.9	02 57.7	28 09.0	10 35.1
17	13 13.4	01 42.6	02♐00.4	14 06.5
27	14 27.8	01 12.0	05 54.5	17 57.9
DEC 7	14 58.7	01 D23.8	09 50.7	22 09.4
17	14 R41.8	02 13.7	13 47.7	26 41.3
27	13 36.2	03 36.9	17 44.8	01♒35.7
JAN 6	11♌44.8	05♈28.8	21♐41.0	06♒55.9
JAN 1	06 S 46.8	14 S 44.3	10 S 44.2	29 S 31.7
21	03 21.0	12 40.2	12 34.9	20 26.1
FEB 10	00 N 31.1	10 07.8	13 55.6	14 39.4
MAR 2	04 33.9	07 19.7	14 40.5	16 34.0
22	08 31.6	04 26.5	14 43.7	17 29.6
APR 11	12 09.9	01 37.5	14 05.8	18 25.5
MAY 1	15 16.3	00 N 59.2	13 03.5	20 08.4
21	17 40.7	03 15.9	12 07.8	23 28.3
JUN 10	19 16.3	05 04.7	11 46.0	29 13.8
30	19 59.6	06 16.5	12 07.9	36 54.5
JUL 20	19 51.2	06 40.7	13 10.0	42 33.0
AUG 9	18 54.7	06 05.1	14 43.2	43 11.0
29	17 16.9	04 18.8	16 37.7	41 22.8
SEP 18	15 07.1	01 25.9	18 44.0	39 30.1
OCT 8	12 36.1	01 S 55.3	20 53.3	38 00.9
28	09 57.1	04 39.8	22 57.9	36 44.4
NOV 17	07 26.3	06 03.3	24 50.8	35 23.2
DEC 7	05 24.3	06 03.7	26 25.9	33 40.7

1995	Sappho 80	Amor 1221	Pandora 55	Icarus 1566
JAN 1	12 R45.7	04♈29.6	19♐43.1	04♒12.3
11	10♌35.0	06 34.2	23 38.4	09 47.3
21	07 56.8	09 01.0	27 31.0	15 56.9
31	05 10.0	11 46.8	01♑20.1	22 52.0
FEB 10	02 35.4	14 48.5	05 04.1	00♓49.1
20	00 30.6	18 03.6	08 41.7	10 14.6
MAR 2	29♋06.3	21 30.2	12 11.5	21 44.3
12	28 27.1	25 06.6	15 31.4	01 R15.6
22	28 D31.9	28 51.3	18 39.6	15♓44.7
APR 1	29 16.8	02♉43.4	21 33.7	05 30.3
11	00♌36.9	06 41.9	24 10.9	01 19.2
21	02 26.7	10 46.1	26 28.1	29♒13.3
MAY 1	04 41.4	14 55.4	28 21.8	27 31.3
11	07 16.8	19 09.5	29 47.9	25 18.6
21	10 09.1	23 28.0	00♒42.7	21 55.7
31	13 15.5	27 50.9	01 02.4	16 47.0
JUN 10	16 33.4	02♊17.9	00 R44.3	09 27.3
20	20 00.8	06 49.0	29♑48.5	00 04.7
30	23 36.1	11 24.5	28 17.9	19♑40.5
JUL 10	27 17.8	16 04.2	26 20.7	09 55.9
20	01♍04.8	20 48.6	24 09.6	02 10.0
30	04 56.1	25 38.1	21 59.7	26♐45.9
AUG 9	08 51.0	00♋32.6	20 07.1	23 30.1
19	12 48.4	05 33.0	18 44.0	21 55.6
29	16 48.0	10 39.9	17 58.3	21 D37.9
SEP 8	20 48.9	15 53.6	17 D53.9	22 18.3
18	24 50.4	21 15.4	18 29.9	23 42.4
28	28 52.1	26 46.2	19 43.9	25 40.6
OCT 8	02♎53.2	02♌27.1	21 32.3	28 06.0
18	06 52.8	08 20.3	23 50.9	00♑53.2
28	10 50.4	14 27.4	26 35.7	03 59.1
NOV 7	14 44.8	20 51.2	29 43.3	07 20.9
17	18 35.1	27 35.2	03♒10.1	10 56.9
27	22 20.0	04♍43.4	06 53.6	14 46.2
DEC 7	25 58.2	12 20.8	10 51.3	18 48.1
17	29 28.0	20 33.8	15 00.9	23 02.5
27	02♏47.6	29 28.5	19 20.7	27 30.1
JAN 6	05♏54.5	09♎10.8	23♒49.1	02♒11.6
JAN 1	04 N 10.7	04 S 36.4	27 S 53.4	30 S 34.6
21	04 36.7	02 40.7	28 36.0	26 45.8
FEB 10	06 05.5	00 20.9	28 55.5	20 40.4
MAR 2	07 55.7	02 N 11.4	28 56.4	08 57.7
22	09 29.4	04 46.7	28 46.4	02 N 31.6
APR 11	10 27.8	07 17.1	28 36.4	05 S 35.2
MAY 1	10 45.6	09 35.3	28 39.0	11 06.1
21	10 23.2	11 34.5	29 06.9	17 42.6
JUN 10	09 23.9	13 08.3	30 05.7	27 16.2
30	07 51.8	14 10.5	31 22.6	36 41.2
JUL 20	05 51.9	14 35.1	32 21.4	39 31.4
AUG 9	03 29.4	14 16.8	32 26.5	38 17.2
29	00 49.9	13 10.7	31 36.4	36 48.3
SEP 18	02 S 00.9	11 13.0	30 12.1	35 49.6
OCT 8	04 57.1	08 21.0	28 28.6	35 10.3
28	07 52.6	04 33.6	26 28.1	34 34.3
NOV 17	10 40.9	00 S 07.5	24 06.9	33 48.2
DEC 7	13 15.6	05 34.8	21 21.1	32 41.5

1996	Sappho 80	Amor 1221	Pandora 55	Icarus 1566
JAN 1	04♏22.8	04♎13.3	21♒34.0	29♑49.0
11	07 22.6	14 21.5	26 06.1	04♒38.1
21	10 05.8	25 21.1	00♓44.7	09 44.3
31	12 28.9	07♏05.7	05 28.6	15 10.7
FEB 10	14 28.3	19 20.8	10 16.6	21 01.8
20	15 59.6	01♐42.8	15 08.0	27 24.6
MAR 1	16 58.0	13 43.7	20 01.6	04♓28.8
11	17 19.4	25 01.0	24 56.8	12 29.0
21	16 R59.8	05♑18.6	29 52.8	21 48.2
31	15 57.8	14 27.0	04♈48.8	03♈01.8
APR 10	14 15.8	22 23.3	09 44.1	17 10.7
20	12 00.7	29 05.3	14 38.3	05♉55.1
30	09 25.9	04♒29.9	19 30.4	18 29.8
MAY 10	06 48.3	08 34.3	24 19.9	14 R47.0
20	04 25.6	11 12.1	29 06.1	07 10.1
30	02 32.8	12 16.3	03♉48.2	23♈10.0
JUN 9	01 19.4	11 R43.6	08 25.3	08♓06.3
19	00 49.4	09 35.8	12 56.7	00♑41.5
29	01 D03.0	06 10.7	17 20.9	11♐58.5
JUL 9	01 57.1	02 03.2	21 37.1	06 26.3
19	03 27.7	27♑56.3	25 43.5	04 51.3
29	05 30.7	24 29.6	29 38.3	05 D03.5
AUG 8	08 01.7	22 05.5	03♊19.6	06 15.3
18	10 57.2	20 49.1	06 44.8	08 05.7
28	14 14.1	20 D36.5	09 50.6	10 23.6
SEP 7	17 49.5	21 17.6	12 33.6	13 01.6
17	21 41.5	22 42.6	14 49.5	15 55.6
27	25 48.0	24 43.0	16 33.5	19 02.8
OCT 7	00♐07.5	27 10.9	17 40.9	22 20.6
17	04 38.9	00♒01.0	18 06.9	25 48.1
27	09 20.9	03 08.5	17 R48.6	29 23.9
NOV 6	14 12.6	06 29.7	16 46.4	03♑07.3
16	19 13.3	10 02.0	15 04.8	06 57.8
26	24 22.1	13 43.1	12 55.6	10 55.0
DEC 6	29 38.4	17 30.9	10 35.2	14 58.7
16	05♑01.6	21 24.3	08 22.5	19 09.1
26	10 31.1	25 21.8	06 34.7	23 26.2
JAN 5	16♑06.3	29♒22.2	05♊23.5	27♑50.4
JAN 1	15 S 59.6	12 S 52.0	17 S 17.3	30 S 36.0
21	17 39.3	17 38.8	13 35.2	28 10.1
FEB 10	18 43.3	18 54.0	09 33.7	24 48.4
MAR 1	19 03.7	15 02.9	05 18.7	20 02.0
21	18 30.3	08 13.7	00 56.9	12 45.1
APR 10	16 55.2	01 22.0	03 N 24.8	00 N 03.2
30	14 27.6	04 N 18.4	07 39.5	24 20.0
MAY 20	11 49.9	08 18.7	11 40.9	28 12.1
JUN 9	09 56.2	09 56.5	15 23.5	07 13.9
29	09 12.9	08 12.7	18 43.0	29 S 01.6
JUL 19	09 34.6	03 09.8	21 36.9	30 07.7
AUG 8	10 43.3	03 S 04.8	24 05.4	30 37.8
28	12 19.9	08 19.9	26 11.4	31 12.6
SEP 17	14 07.0	11 54.2	28 01.2	31 46.7
OCT 7	15 49.5	13 55.8	29 40.7	32 12.3
27	17 13.6	14 42.1	31 09.4	32 22.7
NOV 16	18 07.0	14 28.2	32 09.8	32 12.3
DEC 6	18 18.9	13 26.4	32 15.5	31 37.1

1997		Sappho 80	Amor 1221	Pandora 55	Icarus 1566
JAN	1	13♑51.5	27♒45.7	05R47.1	26♑03.8
	11	19 30.0	01♓47.6	05♊00.9	00♒32.7
	21	25 13.2	05 51.0	04D58.1	05 10.1
	31	01♒00.7	09 55.1	05 36.5	09 57.1
FEB	10	06 52.0	13 59.4	06 52.2	14 55.7
	20	12 46.5	18 03.1	08 40.5	20 08.3
MAR	2	18 43.5	22 05.5	10 56.0	25 38.4
	12	24 42.6	26 06.2	13 34.2	01♓31.0
	22	00♓42.9	00♈04.6	16 31.2	07 52.7
APR	1	06 43.9	04 00.0	19 43.3	14 53.2
	11	12 44.9	07 52.1	23 07.8	22 46.4
	21	18 44.9	11 40.0	26 42.3	01♈51.7
MAY	1	24 43.2	15 23.1	00♋24.5	12 37.4
	11	00♈38.9	19 00.9	04 13.0	25 42.7
	21	06 30.6	22 32.3	08 06.3	12♉00.3
	31	12 17.5	25 56.5	12 03.1	02♊59.9
JUN	10	17 58.2	29 12.2	16 02.7	29 43.1
	20	23 30.8	02♉18.1	20 03.9	20♋39.7
	30	28 53.9	05 12.6	24 06.1	14♌37.4
JUL	10	04♉05.4	07 53.5	28 08.5	13♍10.2
	20	09 02.5	10 18.2	02♌10.5	08♎19.7
	30	13 42.8	12 24.0	06 11.3	26 00.5
AUG	9	18 02.3	14 06.9	10 10.5	08♏08.1
	19	21 56.8	15 22.8	14 07.2	17 01.8
	29	25 21.5	16 06.8	18 00.7	24 05.1
SEP	8	28 09.8	16R13.7	21 50.2	00♐04.3
	18	00♊15.1	15 38.7	25 34.8	05 24.4
	28	01 30.5	14 18.8	29 13.4	10 20.0
OCT	8	01R49.2	12 14.1	02♍44.7	15 00.3
	18	01 08.6	09 30.9	06 07.3	19 30.7
	28	29♉32.3	06 21.9	09 19.5	23 54.8
NOV	7	27 12.7	03 05.8	12 19.3	28 15.2
	17	24 32.8	00 03.7	15 04.3	02♑33.5
	27	21 59.5	27♈33.6	17 31.9	06 50.8
DEC	7	19 57.6	25 47.6	19 38.8	11 08.2
	17	18 43.7	24 51.2	21 21.7	15 26.1
	27	18D23.6	24D43.8	22 36.8	19 45.3
JAN	6	18♉56.4	25♈22.3	23♍20.4	24♑06.3
JAN	1	17S20.2	11S11.5	31N11.9	30S09.0
	21	15 33.7	08 57.7	30 18.0	28 25.7
FEB	10	12 55.3	06 27.1	29 47.9	26 08.1
MAR	2	09 30.9	03 47.5	29 40.0	23 10.1
	22	05 29.7	01 06.3	29 41.9	19 17.7
APR	11	01 03.6	01N29.9	29 40.0	13 59.0
MAY	1	03N34.2	03 54.7	29 23.7	06 01.9
	21	08 09.2	06 02.2	28 46.0	07N02.1
JUN	10	12 26.6	07 46.5	27 43.5	27 42.1
	30	16 11.8	09 01.6	26 15.7	25 53.5
JUL	20	19 11.2	09 41.0	24 24.8	00 12.9
AUG	9	21 13.5	09 37.5	22 14.6	15S48.6
	29	22 10.0	08 43.1	19 50.3	22 47.3
SEP	18	21 54.7	06 51.8	17 18.1	26 27.3
OCT	8	20 23.6	04 07.9	14 45.3	28 36.5
	28	17 40.3	01 02.9	12 19.9	29 50.5
NOV	17	14 20.2	01S23.6	10 11.2	30 22.9
DEC	7	11 38.6	02 23.7	08 29.4	30 19.6
	27	10N29.8	01S53.9	07N25.6	29S43.9

1998		Sappho 80	Amor 1221	Pandora 55	Icarus 1566
JAN	1	18D33.7	24D57.6	23♍02.8	21♑55.6
	11	19♉31.1	25♈57.2	23 29.4	26 17.6
	21	21 12.1	27 34.8	23R20.3	00♒42.1
	31	23 29.8	29 45.5	22 34.5	05 09.9
FEB	10	26 17.5	02♉24.8	21 14.0	09 41.7
	20	29 29.2	05 28.5	19 24.7	14 18.5
MAR	2	03♊00.0	08 53.6	17 16.2	19 02.0
	12	06 46.0	12 37.6	15 01.5	23 53.7
	22	10 43.7	16 38.2	12 54.5	28 56.3
APR	1	14 50.7	20 54.2	11 07.0	04♓13.5
	11	19 04.9	25 24.3	09 48.2	09 49.8
	21	23 24.3	00♊07.7	09 02.6	15 52.4
MAY	1	27 47.9	05 04.3	08D51.4	22 31.2
	11	02♋14.2	10 13.6	09 13.5	00♈00.3
	21	06 42.4	15 36.0	10 06.0	08 40.8
	31	11 11.9	21 11.8	11 25.5	19 02.0
JUN	10	15 41.8	27 01.4	13 08.7	01♉42.0
	20	20 11.7	03♋05.7	15 12.0	17 20.1
	30	24 41.1	09 25.7	17 32.8	06♊12.5
JUL	10	29 09.4	16 02.4	20 08.2	28 01.2
	20	03♌36.3	22 56.9	22 56.1	24♋56.7
	30	08 01.4	00♌10.5	25 54.6	24♌33.7
AUG	9	12 24.2	07 44.3	29 02.0	18♍44.9
	19	16 44.3	15 39.3	02♎16.8	09♎06.8
	29	21 01.1	23 56.5	05 37.8	25 20.3
SEP	8	25 14.0	02♍35.7	09 03.9	08♏01.5
	18	29 22.4	11 36.9	12 34.1	18 09.0
	28	03♍25.5	20 58.8	16 07.5	26 31.8
OCT	8	07 22.0	00♎39.0	19 43.0	03♐43.5
	18	11 11.1	10 34.2	23 19.8	10 06.6
	28	14 51.2	20 40.1	26 57.0	15 56.0
NOV	7	18 20.6	00♏50.9	00♏33.6	21 21.2
	17	21 37.5	11 01.0	04 08.6	26 29.1
	27	24 39.2	21 04.3	07 41.0	01♑24.4
DEC	7	27 22.9	00♐54.8	11 09.4	06 10.1
	17	29 45.4	10 28.1	14 32.6	10 48.7
	27	01♎42.5	19 40.5	17 49.0	15 21.9
JAN	6	03♎10.1	28♐29.1	20♏57.0	19♑50.8
JAN	1	10N27.2	01S35.0	07N16.8	29S30.2
	21	11 01.7	00N13.8	07 13.2	28 18.1
FEB	10	12 20.4	02 38.2	07 58.2	26 39.7
MAR	2	13 53.3	05 19.9	09 12.5	24 37.3
	22	15 18.9	08 05.2	10 19.7	22 11.2
APR	11	16 23.1	10 42.3	10 48.0	19 17.7
MAY	1	16 56.8	13 00.3	10 26.7	15 43.3
	21	16 55.5	14 48.3	09 20.8	10 52.4
JUN	10	16 17.7	15 54.9	07 39.6	03 21.6
	30	15 04.6	16 07.9	05 31.1	08N44.1
JUL	20	13 19.5	15 15.6	03 02.0	22 07.0
AUG	9	11 07.0	13 08.0	00 17.5	10 00.2
	29	08 32.4	09 40.7	02S37.3	07S27.0
SEP	18	05 41.9	04 59.1	05 37.7	17 45.1
OCT	8	02 42.1	00S35.0	08 39.2	23 19.1
	28	00S19.7	06 21.1	11 37.2	26 24.6
NOV	17	03 15.3	11 24.7	14 27.4	28 03.3
DEC	7	05 55.2	14 56.1	17 05.8	28 43.2
	27	08S07.5	16S29.8	19S29.5	28S39.2

1999		Sappho 80	Amor 1221	Pandora 55	Icarus 1566
JAN	1	02♎30.2	24♐07.8	19♏24.1	17♑36.8
	11	03 41.5	02♑44.2	22 27.2	22 03.9
	21	04 16.2	10 55.5	25 18.9	26 28.4
	31	04R10.7	18 41.4	27 56.7	00♒50.5
FEB	10	03 23.0	26 02.4	00♐18.1	05 11.1
	20	01 53.7	02♒59.4	02 20.1	09 30.8
MAR	2	29♍48.9	09 32.9	03 59.3	13 50.1
	12	27 19.6	15 44.0	05 12.4	18 09.7
	22	24 41.2	21 33.5	05 55.8	22 30.6
APR	1	22 11.3	27 01.5	06R06.4	26 53.7
	11	20 05.2	02♓08.4	05 42.4	01♓20.6
	21	18 33.4	06 54.2	04 43.6	05 53.4
MAY	1	17 41.6	11 18.0	03 13.3	10 34.9
	11	17D30.4	15 19.1	01 18.4	15 29.4
	21	17 57.7	18 55.9	29♏09.0	20 43.3
	31	18 59.9	22 06.0	26 58.5	26 26.2
JUN	10	20 32.5	24 46.9	24 59.9	02♈54.3
	20	22 31.5	26 54.7	23 24.4	10 33.6
	30	24 53.1	28 25.3	22 19.9	20 08.5
JUL	10	27 33.8	29 13.9	21 50.1	02♉53.8
	20	00♎31.1	29R15.4	21D56.0	20 32.1
	30	03 42.5	28 26.6	22 36.0	13♊48.2
AUG	9	07 05.9	26 46.6	23 47.4	09♋13.4
	19	10 39.9	24 19.4	25 27.0	01♌26.4
	29	14 22.9	21 16.8	27 31.6	21 29.0
SEP	8	18 13.8	17 56.3	29 57.9	19♍37.2
	18	22 11.8	14 39.6	02♐43.2	13♎12.5
	28	26 15.8	11 47.3	05 44.9	00♏33.6
OCT	8	00♏25.1	09 33.5	09 00.9	13 56.7
	18	04 39.1	08 06.0	12 29.5	24 40.0
	28	08 56.9	07 26.0	16 08.6	03♐34.7
NOV	7	13 18.2	07D30.3	19 57.1	11 14.9
	17	17 42.1	08 14.3	23 53.7	18 02.8
	27	22 08.1	09 32.5	27 57.0	24 12.9
DEC	7	26 35.5	11 19.4	02♑06.1	29 55.2
	17	01♐03.7	13 30.5	06 20.0	05♑16.5
	27	05 32.0	16 01.6	10 37.7	10 21.4
JAN	6	09♐59.6	18♓49.2	14♑58.4	15♑13.5
JAN	1	08S34.5	16S34.9	20S02.9	28S32.5
	21	09 49.7	15 52.0	22 05.6	27 47.0
FEB	10	09 56.6	13 50.7	23 51.7	26 36.9
MAR	2	08 40.0	11 01.5	25 22.3	25 09.1
	22	06 13.0	07 50.0	26 38.1	23 30.5
APR	11	03 26.6	04 35.8	27 35.8	21 48.0
MAY	1	01 17.2	01 34.0	28 04.5	20 07.9
	21	00 11.5	01N02.1	27 52.8	18 35.4
JUN	10	00 09.5	02 59.0	27 06.3	17 10.2
	30	01 00.2	04 00.7	26 13.2	15 28.6
JUL	20	02 31.2	03 47.3	25 41.3	11 26.3
AUG	9	04 31.4	02 00.4	25 41.5	00 26.7
	29	06 50.8	01S15.7	26 09.3	11N40.3
SEP	18	09 20.5	05 07.0	26 53.8	00S38.8
OCT	8	11 51.9	08 14.7	27 42.7	13 49.3
	28	14 16.7	09 57.5	28 24.4	20 55.0
NOV	17	16 26.6	10 18.9	28 48.7	24 38.3
DEC	7	18 13.4	09 37.2	28 47.8	26 27.9
	27	19S29.9	08S10.0	28S16.8	27S06.8

2000		Sappho 80	Amor 1221	Pandora 55	Icarus 1566
JAN	1	07♐45.9	17♓23.5	12♑47.7	12♑48.9
	11	12 12.8	20 18.3	17 09.6	17 35.5
	21	16 37.7	23 25.5	21 33.0	22 12.3
	31	20 59.6	26 42.6	25 57.3	26 40.9
FEB	10	25 17.5	00♈08.1	00♒21.6	01♒02.5
	20	29 30.0	03 40.1	04 45.0	05 17.5
MAR	1	03♑35.9	07 17.4	09 06.6	09 26.5
	11	07 33.2	10 58.9	13 25.6	13 29.8
	21	11 19.8	14 43.5	17 40.9	17 27.5
	31	14 53.6	18 30.4	21 51.4	21 19.8
APR	10	18 11.3	22 18.8	25 56.0	25 06.3
	20	21 09.4	26 08.1	29 53.2	28 46.8
	30	23 43.6	29 57.6	03♓41.5	02♓21.1
MAY	10	25 48.5	03♉46.7	07 19.0	05 48.3
	20	27 18.6	07 34.9	10 43.5	09 07.5
	30	28 07.7	11 21.5	13 52.6	12 17.7
JUN	9	28R10.2	15 06.1	16 43.0	15 16.9
	19	27 23.6	18 47.6	19 11.1	18 02.4
	29	25 50.0	22 25.6	21 13.1	20 30.6
JUL	9	23 38.9	25 58.9	22 44.1	22 34.4
	19	21 09.2	29 26.4	23 39.7	24 02.3
	29	18 44.4	02♊46.9	23R55.9	24R28.8
AUG	8	16 48.2	05 58.3	23 29.9	22 37.8
	18	15 38.5	08 58.6	22 23.1	11 55.5
	28	15D23.8	11 45.3	20 41.2	00♐53.4
SEP	7	16 06.0	14 14.4	18 35.8	19♎21.1
	17	17 41.5	16 21.9	16 24.0	11 52.3
	27	20 04.4	18 02.4	14 23.6	07 47.1
OCT	7	23 08.4	19 08.9	12 51.0	05D44.5
	17	26 47.2	19 34.1	11 57.6	15 29.9
	27	00♒55.1	19R09.9	11D47.9	06♏46.4
NOV	6	05 27.6	17 49.1	12 22.8	22 03.7
	16	10 20.3	15 29.6	13 39.2	03♐37.6
	26	15 29.8	12 16.9	15 32.7	12 58.5
DEC	6	20 53.3	08 29.1	17 58.5	20 53.4
	16	26 27.8	04 35.6	20 51.7	27 49.4
	26	02♓11.4	01 08.5	24 07.9	04♑03.5
JAN	5	08♓02.1	28♉34.9	27♓43.5	09♑46.3

JAN	1	19S43.5	07S42.8	28S04.0	27S08.5
	21	20 13.7	05 37.9	26 52.7	26 51.1
FEB	10	20 02.9	03 14.5	25 11.1	26 05.3
MAR	1	19 10.3	00 41.4	23 04.0	25 03.0
	21	17 38.2	01N54.0	20 37.9	23 55.6
APR	10	15 32.0	04 24.7	18 01.1	22 55.4
	30	13 00.7	06 44.7	15 22.9	22 17.8
MAY	20	10 18.1	08 48.2	12 53.3	22 24.1
JUN	9	07 45.7	10 29.8	10 43.4	23 48.9
	29	05 55.8	11 44.3	09 05.3	27 35.1
JUL	19	05 22.3	12 27.0	08 10.5	35 52.6
AUG	8	06 11.8	12 33.2	08 05.7	53 04.8
	28	07 50.7	11 58.9	08 42.2	73 24.0
SEP	17	09 33.3	10 40.5	09 26.5	42 33.5
OCT	7	10 45.3	08 36.7	09 35.1	10 22.0
	27	11 06.8	05 51.9	08 45.8	09 14.0
NOV	16	10 28.5	02 48.3	07 00.8	18 28.5
DEC	6	08 49.8	00 20.6	04 30.9	22 49.8
	26	06S17.0	00S22.1	01S26.8	24S44.8

2001		Sappho 80	Amor 1221	Pandora 55	Icarus 1566
JAN	1	05♓41.1	29R28.6	26♓15.2	07♑32.4
	11	11 35.2	27♉35.0	00♈00.6	12 59.9
	21	17 33.6	26 52.0	04 00.2	18 06.2
	31	23 35.3	27D18.8	08 11.5	22 55.3
FEB	10	29 38.6	28 49.2	12 32.2	27 29.5
	20	05♈42.7	01♊15.2	17 00.4	01♒50.6
MAR	2	11 46.6	04 30.4	21 34.6	05 59.7
	12	17 49.4	08 28.6	26 13.4	09 57.0
	22	23 50.4	13 04.8	00♉55.5	13 42.8
APR	1	29 49.1	18 16.1	05 40.1	17 16.5
	11	05♉44.8	23 59.7	10 26.0	20 37.0
	21	11 37.1	00♋14.1	15 12.6	23 43.0
MAY	1	17 25.7	06 58.3	19 59.3	26 32.0
	11	23 09.9	14 11.6	24 45.1	29 00.6
	21	28 49.7	21 53.5	29 29.6	01♓04.4
	31	04♊24.7	00♌03.9	04♊12.2	02 36.3
JUN	10	09 54.4	08 41.6	08 52.3	03 26.8
	20	15 18.8	17 45.8	13 29.3	03R22.0
	30	20 37.5	27 14.6	18 02.6	02 01.8
JUL	10	25 49.9	07♍04.8	22 31.5	28♒59.9
	20	00♋55.9	17 12.3	26 55.4	23 44.2
	30	05 54.8	27 31.7	01♋13.3	15 50.6
AUG	9	10 45.8	07♎55.5	05 24.2	05 35.3
	19	15 28.6	18 16.2	09 27.1	24♑21.3
	29	20 01.8	28 26.2	13 20.5	14 10.4
SEP	8	24 24.4	08♏18.5	17 02.9	06 20.4
	18	28 35.1	17 48.3	20 32.4	00 59.8
	28	02♌31.9	26 52.4	23 46.5	27♐40.2
OCT	8	06 12.6	05♐29.5	26 42.5	25 41.7
	18	09 34.9	13 40.0	29 17.4	24 23.6
	28	12 35.0	21 25.4	01♌27.0	22 56.1
NOV	7	15 09.3	28 47.3	03 07.5	19 51.8
	17	17 13.2	05♑48.0	04 14.4	11 57.1
	27	18 41.6	12 29.7	04 43.4	27♏16.1
DEC	7	19 29.3	18 54.2	04R31.8	04D46.9
	17	19R31.5	25 03.5	03 38.6	16♐20.3
	27	18 45.5	00♒59.2	02 07.0	25 34.2
JAN	6	17♌12.8	06♒42.2	00♌05.5	03♑14.9

JAN	1	05S22.1	00S09.6	00S26.4	25S01.7
	21	01 56.6	01N43.6	03N07.7	25 19.8
FEB	10	01N52.1	04 49.7	06 54.2	24 58.9
MAR	2	05 48.0	08 26.3	10 44.0	24 18.4
	22	09 35.6	12 03.8	14 28.2	23 34.9
APR	11	13 01.1	15 18.0	17 58.2	23 05.3
MAY	1	15 52.8	17 43.6	21 06.5	23 10.6
	21	18 01.4	18 51.8	23 46.3	24 19.9
JUN	10	19 21.2	18 13.2	25 52.8	27 18.6
	30	19 49.8	15 27.7	27 23.1	33 14.6
JUL	20	19 28.1	10 39.2	28 17.4	43 12.9
AUG	9	18 20.7	04 25.2	28 38.6	55 06.8
	29	16 34.3	02S10.3	28 33.5	59 52.1
SEP	18	14 17.9	08 02.0	28 11.7	55 45.3
OCT	8	11 42.1	12 27.0	27 46.2	50 07.7
	28	08 59.5	15 11.4	27 32.5	44 40.5
NOV	17	06 25.1	16 21.0	27 46.0	33 42.9
DEC	7	04 18.9	16 10.9	28 36.0	15 58.2
	27	03N05.1	14S58.9	29N52.8	20S34.2

2002		Sappho 80	Amor 1221	Pandora 55	Icarus 1566
JAN	1	18R04.7	03♒52.2	01R09.3	29♐33.9
	11	16♌10.8	09 29.5	28♋57.4	06♑40.7
	21	13 42.9	14 56.0	26 36.4	12 55.6
	31	10 58.3	20 12.1	24 23.3	18 32.2
FEB	10	08 16.7	25 18.7	22 32.4	23 39.4
	20	05 57.2	00♓16.0	21 14.4	28 22.2
MAR	2	04 13.9	05 04.2	20 34.4	02♒43.9
	12	03 13.5	09 43.6	20D32.9	06 46.4
	22	02D57.5	14 14.1	21 08.1	10 30.3
APR	1	03 23.3	18 35.3	22 16.0	13 55.2
	11	04 26.0	22 47.3	23 52.2	17 00.1
	21	06 00.9	26 49.4	25 52.8	19 42.4
MAY	1	08 02.7	00♈41.0	28 13.5	21 58.8
	11	10 26.9	04 21.3	00♌51.2	23 44.3
	21	13 09.9	07 49.2	03 42.9	24 51.4
	31	16 08.2	11 03.2	06 46.0	25R10.6
JUN	10	19 19.2	14 01.9	09 58.6	24 29.3
	20	22 40.9	16 43.0	13 18.9	22 31.0
	30	26 11.2	19 03.8	16 45.4	18 59.7
JUL	10	29 48.7	21 01.4	20 16.9	13 43.7
	20	03♍32.3	22 31.8	23 52.3	06 49.6
	30	07 20.7	23 31.0	27 30.6	28♑55.8
AUG	9	11 13.1	23 54.4	01♍11.0	21 05.6
	19	15 08.8	23R37.6	04 52.6	14 22.5
	29	19 06.9	22 37.8	08 34.5	09 21.3
SEP	8	23 06.9	20 54.4	12 16.3	06 06.6
	18	27 08.0	18 31.4	15 56.8	04 27.0
	28	01♎09.5	15 38.8	19 35.3	04D05.5
OCT	8	05 11.0	12 31.8	23 11.0	04 46.6
	18	09 11.5	09 29.2	26 42.6	06 18.5
	28	13 10.2	06 48.6	00♎09.1	08 31.7
NOV	7	17 06.5	04 43.3	03 29.2	11 19.7
	17	20 59.1	03 21.0	06 41.3	14 38.2
	27	24 47.0	02 43.5	09 43.6	18 22.9
DEC	7	28 28.9	02D48.8	12 34.3	22 29.7
	17	02♏03.2	03 33.3	15 10.7	26 46.2
	27	05 28.2	04 51.9	17 30.4	00♒22.4
JAN	6	08♏41.8	06♈40.1	19♎30.3	28R05.1

JAN	1	02N57.8	14S33.2	30N12.3	21S14.9
	21	03 18.8	12 27.2	31 10.2	22 43.3
FEB	10	04 48.9	09 54.3	31 14.3	23 00.7
MAR	2	06 46.8	07 06.4	30 28.5	22 46.1
	22	08 29.8	04 14.0	29 14.1	22 25.3
APR	11	09 35.6	01 25.8	27 44.3	22 21.1
MAY	1	09 58.0	01N10.1	26 02.1	22 59.4
	21	09 38.3	03 26.2	24 06.2	24 54.5
JUN	10	08 40.3	05 14.7	21 55.1	28 52.8
	30	07 08.9	06 27.0	19 28.8	35 35.3
JUL	20	05 09.4	06 52.8	16 48.5	43 59.6
AUG	9	02 47.3	06 20.0	13 56.7	49 21.0
	29	00 08.3	04 38.0	10 56.6	48 55.3
SEP	18	02S41.7	01 49.4	07 52.2	46 01.9
OCT	8	05 36.7	01S30.5	04 48.2	43 11.4
	28	08 30.6	04 17.7	01 49.5	40 44.7
NOV	17	11 16.9	05 45.4	00S58.5	38 18.9
DEC	7	13 49.2	05 48.9	03 29.8	35 13.3
	27	16S00.9	04S46.7	05S38.0	29S54.0

1931	Diana 78	Hidalgo 944	Urania 30	Chiron 2060
JAN 1	13♎13.4	07♑12.9	02♒12.7	14R16.3
11	16 14.3	08 52.1	07 11.8	14♉05.2
21	18 43.6	10 30.1	12 15.5	14 00.2
31	20 35.7	12 05.3	17 23.1	14D01.6
FEB 10	21 45.8	13 36.2	22 33.7	14 09.2
20	22 09.0	15 01.2	27 46.9	14 23.0
MAR 2	21R43.0	16 18.8	03♓01.9	14 42.4
12	20 29.8	17 27.4	08 18.2	15 07.0
22	18 36.6	18 25.3	13 35.4	15 36.1
APR 1	16 18.1	19 10.8	18 52.7	16 09.2
11	13 53.3	19 42.5	24 09.6	16 45.3
21	11 41.8	19 59.0	29 25.7	17 23.8
MAY 1	10 00.0	19R59.0	04♈40.1	18 03.9
11	08 57.8	19 41.9	09 52.5	18 44.8
21	08D38.4	19 07.4	15 02.0	19 25.7
31	09 01.3	18 16.3	20 07.7	20 05.8
JUN 10	10 02.2	17 10.3	25 09.0	20 44.4
20	11 36.6	15 51.9	00♉04.6	21 20.7
30	13 39.4	14 25.0	04 53.1	21 54.1
JUL 10	16 05.9	12 54.0	09 33.3	22 23.9
20	18 52.3	11 23.8	14 03.3	22 49.4
30	21 55.0	09 59.6	18 20.5	23 10.0
AUG 9	25 11.1	08 45.5	22 22.6	23 25.3
19	28 38.4	07 45.2	26 05.9	23 34.9
29	02♏14.8	07 01.2	29 26.5	23 38.5
SEP 8	05 58.6	06 34.8	02♊19.6	23R35.9
18	09 48.5	06D26.7	04 39.2	23 27.3
28	13 43.2	06 36.6	06 19.0	23 12.9
OCT 8	17 41.6	07 03.5	07 12.8	22 53.3
18	21 42.9	07 46.4	07R14.9	22 29.0
28	25 46.0	08 43.7	06 23.9	22 01.3
NOV 7	29 50.1	09 53.9	04 44.1	21 31.1
17	03♐54.5	11 15.4	02 28.0	20 59.8
27	07 58.3	12 46.5	29♉57.3	20 28.9
DEC 7	12 00.6	14 25.6	27 36.2	19 59.6
17	16 00.6	16 11.1	25 46.9	19 33.4
27	19 57.3	18 01.5	24 44.2	19 11.3
JAN 6	23♐49.9	19♑55.2	24D33.2	18♉54.3
JAN 1	07S08.5	60S43.4	19S34.7	13N57.1
21	10 34.8	60 41.5	16 53.6	13 53.2
FEB 10	13 18.6	60 55.9	13 37.8	13 56.9
MAR 2	15 03.8	61 28.5	09 53.7	14 07.6
22	15 32.6	62 21.2	05 49.1	14 23.7
APR 11	14 48.1	63 34.3	01 32.5	14 43.3
MAY 1	13 33.7	65 05.3	02N47.5	15 04.4
21	12 43.3	66 46.6	07 02.1	15 25.1
JUN 10	12 43.2	68 23.6	11 02.8	15 43.6
30	13 33.0	69 36.5	14 41.6	15 58.5
JUL 20	15 02.1	70 06.1	17 51.9	16 08.6
AUG 9	16 57.9	69 44.6	20 28.6	16 13.2
29	19 08.6	68 39.8	22 29.5	16 11.7
SEP 18	21 24.1	67 08.6	23 55.1	16 04.2
OCT 8	23 35.3	65 27.6	24 46.0	15 51.4
28	25 34.9	63 47.8	24 57.2	15 34.9
NOV 17	27 16.3	62 15.1	24 18.4	15 16.8
DEC 7	28 34.9	60 52.6	22 59.5	15 00.1
27	29S28.2	59S41.6	21N47.3	14N47.6

1932	Diana 78	Hidalgo 944	Urania 30	Chiron 2060
JAN 1	21♐54.2	18♑58.0	24R32.2	19R02.1
11	25 44.4	20 52.9	24D47.1	18♉48.0
21	29 28.6	22 48.9	25♉51.0	18 40.0
31	03♑05.8	24 44.4	27 37.7	18D38.4
FEB 10	06 34.8	26 38.2	00♊00.6	18 43.4
20	09 53.8	28 28.5	02 53.6	18 54.7
MAR 1	13 01.4	00♒13.8	06 10.8	19 12.1
11	15 55.5	01 52.6	09 47.7	19 35.0
21	18 34.1	03 23.0	13 40.4	20 03.0
31	20 54.7	04 43.4	17 45.5	20 35.3
APR 10	22 54.5	05 52.0	22 00.6	21 11.2
20	24 30.4	06 46.7	26 23.5	21 49.9
30	25 39.6	07 25.9	00♋52.4	22 30.6
MAY 10	26 18.5	07 47.6	05 26.0	23 12.5
20	26R24.6	07R50.1	10 03.2	23 54.9
30	25 56.4	07 32.6	14 42.9	24 36.9
JUN 9	24 53.9	06 54.3	19 24.4	25 17.8
19	23 20.5	05 55.8	24 07.0	25 56.8
29	21 22.8	04 39.1	28 50.1	26 33.2
JUL 9	19 10.7	03 07.2	03♌33.3	27 06.2
19	16 56.7	01 25.0	08 16.0	27 35.2
29	14 53.2	29♑38.5	12 57.8	27 59.5
AUG 8	13 11.1	27 54.1	17 38.4	28 18.6
18	11 58.0	26 18.2	22 17.3	28 32.0
28	11 17.8	24 56.4	26 53.9	28 39.4
SEP 7	11D11.4	23 52.8	01♍28.0	28R40.4
17	11 37.8	23 10.2	05 58.7	28 35.1
27	12 34.1	22 49.7	10 25.7	28 23.6
OCT 7	13 57.5	22D51.5	14 48.0	28 06.4
17	15 44.6	23 14.6	19 04.6	27 43.9
27	17 52.3	23 57.6	23 14.8	27 17.2
NOV 6	20 17.8	24 58.9	27 17.1	26 47.4
16	22 58.3	26 16.5	01♎10.0	26 15.7
26	25 51.7	27 48.2	04 52.0	25 43.5
DEC 6	28 56.0	29 32.5	08 20.6	25 12.3
16	02♒09.3	01♒27.1	11 33.5	24 43.6
26	05 29.9	03 30.5	14 27.9	24 18.6
JAN 5	08♒56.6	05♒40.9	17♎00.0	23♉58.4
JAN 1	29S37.6	59S25.8	21N35.7	14N45.3
21	29 59.7	58 31.3	21 21.6	14 40.7
FEB 10	30 00.8	57 52.8	21 49.5	14 43.4
MAR 1	29 47.2	57 33.5	22 38.0	14 52.8
21	29 27.8	57 37.1	23 25.6	15 07.7
APR 10	29 12.9	58 07.3	23 55.7	15 26.0
30	29 13.1	59 06.4	23 56.9	15 45.9
MAY 20	29 35.2	60 33.7	23 22.9	16 05.4
JUN 9	30 16.1	62 22.5	22 11.5	16 23.0
29	30 56.9	64 17.9	20 24.1	16 37.2
JUL 19	31 10.1	65 56.5	18 04.3	16 46.9
AUG 8	30 43.3	66 51.1	15 17.6	16 51.4
28	29 47.9	66 43.6	12 10.3	16 50.4
SEP 17	28 40.8	65 35.1	08 49.3	16 43.9
OCT 7	27 29.2	63 42.4	05 21.6	16 32.3
27	26 12.1	61 25.6	01 54.7	16 17.2
NOV 16	24 45.1	58 59.7	01S23.8	16 00.3
DEC 6	23 03.7	56 34.1	04 26.2	15 44.4
26	21S05.5	54S13.9	07S03.8	15N32.0

1933	Diana 78	Hidalgo 944	Urania 30	Chiron 2060
JAN 1	07♒33.3	04♒48.0	16♎02.1	24R05.8
11	11 03.0	07 01.8	18 19.0	23♉49.0
21	14 36.4	09 20.1	20 07.3	23 38.3
31	18 12.8	11 41.4	21 22.4	23 34.2
FEB 10	21 50.9	14 04.2	21 59.6	23D36.7
20	25 29.6	16 27.0	21R55.7	23 46.0
MAR 2	29 08.2	18 48.6	21 08.4	24 01.6
12	02♓45.4	21 07.2	19 40.0	24 23.2
22	06 20.5	23 21.6	17 37.2	24 50.2
APR 1	09 52.4	25 30.2	15 11.9	25 22.0
11	13 20.0	27 31.1	12 40.9	25 57.8
21	16 42.3	29 22.7	10 21.2	26 36.8
MAY 1	19 58.0	01♓03.0	08 27.6	27 18.3
11	23 05.6	02 29.6	07 10.1	28 01.3
21	26 03.7	03 40.5	06 32.8	28 45.3
31	28 50.2	04 33.1	06D36.0	29 29.2
JUN 10	01♈23.0	05 04.7	07 17.3	00♊12.4
20	03 39.6	05R13.0	08 32.4	00 54.0
30	05 36.9	04 55.8	10 17.3	01 33.2
JUL 10	07 11.5	04 12.1	12 27.8	02 09.4
20	08 19.9	03 01.8	14 59.9	02 41.8
30	08 57.8	01 27.1	17 50.8	03 09.6
AUG 9	09R02.0	29♒32.6	20 57.4	03 32.4
19	08 29.8	27 25.2	24 17.4	03 49.5
29	07 20.6	25 14.0	27 49.1	04 00.4
SEP 8	05 38.1	23 08.7	01♏30.6	04 05.0
18	03 29.5	21 18.4	05 20.5	04R02.9
28	01 07.2	19 50.4	09 17.9	03 54.3
OCT 8	28♓46.7	18 49.6	13 21.3	03 39.5
18	26 43.0	18 18.1	17 30.1	03 18.9
28	25 09.0	18D16.3	21 43.5	02 53.4
NOV 7	24 12.9	18 43.0	26 00.3	02 24.0
17	23D57.8	19 35.9	00♐20.1	01 52.0
27	24 23.8	20 52.6	04 42.1	01 18.9
DEC 7	25 28.2	22 30.4	09 05.4	00 46.1
17	27 07.2	24 26.6	13 29.5	00 15.2
27	29 17.0	26 38.8	17 53.4	29♉47.5
JAN 6	01♈53.2	29♒04.6	22♐16.4	29♉24.5
JAN 1	20S26.6	53S33.4	07S44.9	15N29.3
21	18 06.0	51 25.5	09 36.3	15 24.6
FEB 10	15 30.0	49 30.6	10 39.3	15 26.7
MAR 2	12 41.9	47 52.7	10 41.8	15 35.3
22	09 45.9	46 36.1	09 39.4	15 49.0
APR 11	06 46.6	45 46.3	07 52.4	16 06.0
MAY 1	03 48.9	45 28.5	06 08.6	16 24.5
21	00 58.2	45 47.8	05 11.0	16 42.6
JUN 10	01N39.9	46 46.9	05 14.2	16 58.7
30	03 58.6	48 23.5	06 11.5	17 11.5
JUL 20	05 49.7	50 25.2	07 50.0	17 20.2
AUG 9	07 02.4	52 26.0	09 56.9	17 24.1
29	07 25.2	53 47.5	12 20.5	17 22.9
SEP 18	06 53.4	53 53.3	14 51.0	17 16.8
OCT 8	05 44.0	52 30.4	17 19.1	17 06.2
28	04 36.1	49 53.5	19 36.4	16 52.3
NOV 17	04 06.7	46 29.6	21 35.1	16 36.8
DEC 7	04 31.5	42 41.8	23 08.3	16 22.1
27	05N49.0	38S44.6	24S10.8	16N10.6

1934	Diana 78	Hidalgo 944	Urania 30	Chiron 2060
JAN 1	00♈32.0	27♒50.2	20♐05.0	29R35.4
11	03 20.1	00♓22.0	24 27.3	29♉15.0
21	06 29.4	03 04.6	28 47.4	29 00.6
31	09 57.0	05 56.1	03♑04.2	28 52.8
FEB 10	13 40.1	08 54.8	07 16.9	28D51.9
20	17 36.7	11 59.6	11 24.3	28 58.0
MAR 2	21 44.8	15 08.9	15 25.0	29 10.9
12	26 02.9	18 21.7	19 17.6	29 30.2
22	00♉29.7	21 36.8	23 00.4	29 55.5
APR 1	05 03.9	24 53.2	26 31.4	00♊26.0
11	09 44.6	28 10.0	29 48.3	01 01.1
21	14 31.2	01♈26.1	02♒48.1	01 40.0
MAY 1	19 22.6	04 40.4	05 27.5	02 21.9
11	24 18.4	07 52.1	07 42.9	03 06.0
21	29 18.1	10 59.8	09 29.5	03 51.5
31	04♊21.0	14 02.3	10 42.6	04 37.5
JUN 10	09 26.8	16 58.2	11 17.5	05 23.1
20	14 34.9	19 45.6	11R09.8	06 07.7
30	19 44.9	22 22.5	10 18.3	06 50.4
JUL 10	24 56.3	24 46.5	08 45.0	07 30.3
20	00♋08.6	26 54.5	06 38.1	08 06.8
30	05 21.1	28 42.9	04 12.8	08 39.1
AUG 9	10 33.4	00♉07.5	01 47.5	09 06.5
19	15 44.5	01 03.1	29♑42.0	09 28.4
29	20 53.6	01 24.5	28 12.0	09 44.2
SEP 8	25 59.8	01R06.1	27 26.6	09 53.5
18	01♌01.8	00 03.5	27D29.3	09R56.1
28	05 58.3	28♈15.7	28 19.0	09 51.7
OCT 8	10 47.6	25 46.4	29 51.5	09 40.6
18	15 27.5	22 47.0	02♒02.4	09 23.1
28	19 55.8	19 36.6	04 46.3	08 59.8
NOV 7	24 09.6	16 37.7	07 58.5	08 31.8
17	28 05.2	14 12.1	11 35.2	08 00.3
27	01♍38.5	12 35.1	15 32.3	07 26.5
DEC 7	04 44.7	11 54.4	19 47.0	06 52.2
17	07 17.7	12D11.6	24 16.7	06 18.9
27	09 11.7	13 23.9	28 59.0	05 48.2
JAN 6	10♍20.0	15♈26.3	03♓52.1	05♊21.5
JAN 1	06N15.6	37S44.8	24S21.2	16N08.4
21	08 26.4	33 46.1	24 41.2	16 03.6
FEB 10	11 07.7	29 50.4	24 27.6	16 05.0
MAR 2	14 08.6	25 59.5	23 44.2	16 12.5
22	17 18.2	22 15.4	22 37.7	16 24.9
APR 11	20 25.7	18 39.4	21 17.9	16 40.4
MAY 1	23 20.4	15 13.2	19 57.3	16 57.1
21	25 51.6	11 57.7	18 50.8	17 13.5
JUN 10	27 48.9	08 53.5	18 14.0	17 27.8
30	29 03.5	06 00.2	18 18.4	17 39.1
JUL 20	29 28.7	03 14.9	18 58.6	17 46.4
AUG 9	29 01.8	00 31.4	19 46.5	17 49.4
29	27 44.3	02N21.7	20 11.9	17 47.8
SEP 18	25 42.4	05 41.2	20 04.1	17 41.8
OCT 8	23 06.5	09 38.7	19 23.6	17 32.1
28	20 09.9	13 58.9	18 09.1	17 19.6
NOV 17	17 08.4	18 07.3	16 17.9	17 05.8
DEC 7	14 19.4	21 58.7	13 48.5	16 52.6
27	12N01.1	25N57.1	10S42.5	16N42.2

1935	Diana 78	Hidalgo 944	Urania 30	Chiron 2060
JAN 1	09♍51.9	14♈19.1	01♓24.3	05R34.2
11	10 35.3	16 45.0	06 22.1	05♊10.0
21	10R26.5	19 53.7	11 28.3	04 51.6
31	09 26.0	23 40.5	16 41.3	04 39.7
FEB 10	07 40.6	28 01.7	22 00.2	04 34.8
20	05 26.5	02♉53.9	27 23.8	04D37.2
MAR 2	03 05.0	08 13.9	02♈51.0	04 46.8
12	00 59.1	13 59.2	08 21.2	05 03.4
22	29♌27.8	20 06.7	13 53.5	05 26.4
APR 1	28 41.5	26 33.4	19 27.1	05 55.3
11	28D43.4	03♊16.2	25 01.6	06 29.4
21	29 31.7	10 11.3	00♉36.1	07 07.9
MAY 1	01♍00.9	17 14.7	06 10.3	07 50.0
11	03 05.4	24 22.4	11 43.6	08 35.0
21	05 39.2	01♋30.2	17 15.3	09 21.8
31	08 36.9	08 34.3	22 45.1	10 09.8
JUN 10	11 54.4	15 31.6	28 12.4	10 58.1
20	15 27.7	22 18.9	03♊36.7	11 45.7
30	19 13.6	28 54.5	08 57.4	12 32.0
JUL 10	23 10.1	05♌16.7	14 13.8	13 16.0
20	27 14.8	11 24.6	19 25.3	13 57.0
30	01♎26.1	17 17.8	24 31.1	14 34.2
AUG 9	05 42.7	22 56.2	29 30.3	15 06.7
19	10 03.4	28 19.6	04♋21.6	15 34.0
29	14 27.2	03♍28.5	09 04.0	15 55.4
SEP 8	18 53.4	08 22.9	13 35.8	16 10.2
18	23 21.0	13 02.9	17 55.0	16 18.1
28	27 49.5	17 28.7	21 59.5	16R18.9
OCT 8	02♏18.2	21 40.0	25 46.3	16 12.5
18	06 46.4	25 36.4	29 12.2	15 59.0
28	11 13.7	29 17.4	02♌13.0	15 39.1
NOV 7	15 39.2	02♎42.1	04 43.8	15 13.3
17	20 02.2	05 49.2	06 39.5	14 43.0
27	24 22.1	08 37.4	07 53.9	14 09.3
DEC 7	28 38.1	11 04.7	08 21.4	13 33.9
17	02♐49.2	13 08.9	07R58.7	12 58.5
27	06 54.5	14 47.7	06 45.5	12 24.8
JAN 6	10♐52.8	15♎58.2	04♌48.0	11♊54.3
JAN 1	11N33.3	27N00.4	09S50.7	16N40.2
21	10 14.9	31 33.3	06 05.8	16 35.7
FEB 10	09 46.1	36 36.9	01 58.5	16 36.8
MAR 2	09 41.5	42 00.2	02N21.7	16 43.5
22	09 23.8	47 18.7	06 44.5	16 54.5
APR 11	08 31.4	51 51.8	10 59.1	17 08.4
MAY 1	07 01.0	54 45.5	14 54.7	17 23.2
21	04 55.8	55 12.4	18 21.1	17 37.4
JUN 10	02 21.0	53 05.4	21 09.4	17 49.6
30	00S37.5	49 03.2	23 12.5	17 58.6
JUL 20	03 53.6	43 58.7	24 26.5	18 03.9
AUG 9	07 20.7	38 34.4	24 51.4	18 05.2
29	10 52.2	33 17.2	24 31.6	18 02.5
SEP 18	14 21.8	28 22.8	23 36.3	17 56.1
OCT 8	17 43.1	23 59.9	22 18.6	17 46.8
28	20 50.1	20 14.4	20 55.5	17 35.4
NOV 17	23 37.5	17 10.3	19 47.1	17 23.4
DEC 7	26 01.1	14 50.6	19 13.5	17 12.1
27	27S58.1	13N17.6	19N25.9	17N03.4

1936	Diana 78	Hidalgo 944	Urania 30	Chiron 2060
JAN 1	08♐54.6	15♎26.6	05R51.5	12R09.0
11	12 49.0	16 22.2	03♌36.8	11♊40.8
21	16 34.7	16 45.9	01 01.1	11 17.8
31	20 10.0	16R36.0	28♋26.1	11 01.3
FEB 10	23 33.3	15 52.2	26 13.6	10 51.9
20	26 42.8	14 35.9	24 38.5	10D49.9
MAR 1	29 36.0	12 51.3	23 49.3	10 55.6
11	02♑10.6	10 45.7	23D47.2	11 08.6
21	04 23.8	08 28.7	24 29.2	11 28.8
31	06 12.3	06 10.9	25 50.2	11 55.5
APR 10	07 32.8	04 02.9	27 44.6	12 28.0
20	08 22.0	02 13.0	00♌06.6	13 05.7
30	08R36.7	00 46.9	02 51.8	13 47.8
MAY 10	08 15.3	29♍47.4	05 55.7	14 33.3
20	07 17.7	29 14.9	09 14.9	15 21.4
30	05 46.8	29D08.4	12 46.9	16 11.3
JUN 9	03 49.6	29 25.4	16 29.0	17 02.1
19	01 36.4	00♎03.5	20 19.5	17 53.0
29	29♐20.0	00 59.8	24 17.0	18 43.0
JUL 9	27 14.1	02 11.8	28 20.0	19 31.3
19	25 29.6	03 37.0	02♍27.6	20 17.2
29	24 14.7	05 13.1	06 38.8	20 59.6
AUG 8	23 33.4	06 58.1	10 52.8	21 37.9
18	23D26.5	08 50.4	15 09.1	22 11.3
28	23 52.7	10 48.2	19 26.9	22 38.9
SEP 7	24 49.2	12 50.1	23 45.6	23 00.2
17	26 12.6	14 54.7	28 04.8	23 14.6
27	27 59.8	17 00.8	02♎23.7	23 21.6
OCT 7	00♑07.3	19 06.8	06 41.8	23R21.0
17	02 32.4	21 11.8	10 58.4	23 12.8
27	05 12.5	23 14.3	15 12.9	22 57.3
NOV 6	08 05.1	25 13.0	19 24.3	22 35.1
16	11 08.3	27 06.6	23 31.8	22 07.1
26	14 20.4	28 53.4	27 34.3	21 34.5
DEC 6	17 39.6	00♏32.0	01♏30.6	20 58.9
16	21 04.7	02 00.9	05 19.3	20 21.9
26	24 34.2	03 18.1	08 58.8	19 45.4
JAN 5	28♑06.9	04♏22.0	12♏27.2	19♊11.2
JAN 1	28S23.2	13N01.7	19N35.5	17N01.8
21	29 47.3	12 25.9	20 24.2	16 58.2
FEB 10	30 48.7	12 27.8	21 01.8	16 59.6
MAR 1	31 34.0	12 49.2	21 09.6	17 05.8
21	32 12.2	13 01.9	20 48.9	17 15.7
APR 10	32 52.6	12 40.0	20 02.6	17 27.8
30	33 40.9	11 34.6	18 50.1	17 40.5
MAY 20	34 31.7	09 52.9	17 10.4	17 52.2
JUN 9	35 03.5	07 47.6	15 03.9	18 01.6
29	34 51.2	05 28.8	12 32.6	18 07.7
JUL 19	33 53.8	03 02.9	09 40.0	18 10.1
AUG 8	32 36.5	00 34.0	06 30.4	18 08.8
28	31 23.5	01S55.2	03 08.7	18 04.0
SEP 17	30 22.5	04 22.4	00S19.6	17 56.3
OCT 7	29 29.7	06 45.4	03 49.2	17 46.6
27	28 36.8	09 02.3	07 14.4	17 35.9
NOV 16	27 36.1	11 11.1	10 29.4	17 25.4
DEC 6	26 21.6	13 09.6	13 28.8	17 16.4
26	24S50.0	14S55.8	16S07.8	17N09.9

1937	Diana 78	Hidalgo 944	Urania 30	Chiron 2060
JAN 1	26♑41.5	03♏58.1	11♏05.3	19R24.5
11	00♒15.6	04 53.3	14 26.0	18♊52.4
21	03 51.3	05 32.4	17 31.8	18 25.2
31	07 27.2	05 54.0	20 19.9	18 04.2
FEB 10	11 02.6	05R57.0	22 47.2	17 50.2
20	14 36.3	05 40.6	24 49.6	17 43.8
MAR 2	18 07.3	05 05.2	26 23.3	17D45.4
12	21 34.6	04 11.7	27 23.8	17 55.0
22	24 57.0	03 02.4	27 46.9	18 12.2
APR 1	28 13.2	01 40.7	27R29.7	18 36.6
11	01♓22.1	00 11.0	26 31.3	19 07.5
21	04 22.0	28♎38.3	24 54.3	19 44.3
MAY 1	07 11.3	27 07.9	22 46.7	20 26.2
11	09 48.2	25 44.6	20 21.0	21 12.2
21	12 10.2	24 32.4	17 53.4	22 01.6
31	14 15.0	23 34.5	15 40.7	22 53.4
JUN 10	15 59.7	22 52.5	13 56.1	23 46.8
20	17 20.9	22 27.4	12 48.6	24 40.8
30	18 15.3	22D19.2	12 21.7	25 34.6
JUL 10	18 39.6	22 27.1	12D35.2	26 27.4
20	18R30.7	22 50.1	13 26.8	27 18.1
30	17 47.3	23 26.9	14 52.3	28 06.0
AUG 9	16 30.0	24 15.9	16 47.7	28 50.2
19	14 43.0	25 15.7	19 09.3	29 29.8
29	12 34.3	26 24.7	21 53.1	00♋04.0
SEP 8	10 15.6	27 41.4	24 56.3	00 32.1
18	08 00.9	29 04.4	28 16.2	00 53.3
28	06 03.4	00♏32.3	01♐50.3	01 07.0
OCT 8	04 33.7	02 03.7	05 37.1	01 12.9
18	03 38.8	03 37.3	09 34.6	01R10.7
28	03D21.4	05 11.7	13 41.6	01 00.5
NOV 7	03 41.2	06 45.6	17 56.8	00 42.7
17	04 36.3	08 17.5	22 19.1	00 17.9
27	06 03.2	09 46.2	26 47.6	29♊47.4
DEC 7	07 58.3	11 10.1	01♑21.5	29 12.4
17	10 18.1	12 27.7	05 59.8	28 34.6
27	12 59.1	13 37.6	10 41.8	27 56.1
JAN 6	15♓58.6	14♏38.3	15♑26.9	27♊18.6

1937	Diana 78	Hidalgo 944	Urania 30	Chiron 2060
JAN 1	24S19.1	15S24.9	16S50.9	17N08.7
21	22 24.6	16 51.6	18 57.6	17 07.1
FEB 10	20 14.9	17 59.6	20 36.8	17 09.8
MAR 2	17 53.5	18 45.2	21 46.7	17 16.3
22	15 25.4	19 05.2	22 24.7	17 25.5
APR 11	12 56.4	18 59.9	22 24.6	17 36.1
MAY 1	10 33.1	18 36.4	21 39.6	17 46.5
21	08 22.6	18 07.5	20 18.1	17 55.1
JUN 10	06 33.3	17 46.7	18 54.1	18 00.9
30	05 14.7	17 43.1	18 04.6	18 03.1
JUL 20	04 36.1	18 00.4	18 03.3	18 01.5
AUG 9	04 43.2	18 38.1	18 43.6	17 56.3
29	05 29.4	19 33.8	19 51.1	17 48.0
SEP 18	06 30.1	20 44.1	21 10.3	17 37.6
OCT 8	07 12.6	22 05.4	22 27.3	17 26.3
28	07 15.8	23 34.4	23 29.7	17 15.4
NOV 17	06 33.8	25 08.0	24 07.3	17 06.0
DEC 7	05 09.4	26 43.5	24 12.0	16 59.4
27	03S07.9	28S18.2	23S38.7	16N56.0

1938	Diana 78	Hidalgo 944	Urania 30	Chiron 2060
JAN 1	14♓26.7	14♏09.2	13♑04.0	27R37.1
11	17 34.4	15 04.6	17 50.4	27♊00.9
21	20 56.6	15 48.6	22 38.7	26 28.6
31	24 31.3	16 19.7	27 28.4	26 01.7
FEB 10	28 16.7	16 36.7	02♒18.8	25 41.7
20	02♈11.2	16R38.7	07 09.1	25 29.2
MAR 2	06 13.5	16 25.4	11 59.0	25D25.0
12	10 22.4	15 56.8	16 47.5	25 29.1
22	14 37.0	15 13.7	21 34.0	25 41.5
APR 1	18 56.4	14 17.7	26 17.7	26 01.9
11	23 19.9	13 11.1	00♓57.8	26 29.8
21	27 46.7	11 57.3	05 33.3	27 04.3
MAY 1	02♉16.5	10 39.8	10 03.2	27 44.8
11	06 48.5	09 22.6	14 25.9	28 30.4
21	11 22.2	08 09.5	18 40.2	29 20.2
31	15 57.3	07 03.9	22 44.2	00♋13.4
JUN 10	20 33.2	06 08.7	26 35.3	01 09.0
20	25 09.3	05 25.7	00♈11.2	02 06.2
30	29 45.1	04 56.3	03 28.2	03 03.9
JUL 10	04♊19.9	04 40.9	06 22.3	04 01.4
20	08 53.0	04D39.5	08 48.9	04 57.6
30	13 23.6	04 51.6	10 42.1	05 51.7
AUG 9	17 50.3	05 16.3	11 56.0	06 42.7
19	22 12.1	05 52.5	12 25.1	07 29.8
29	26 27.3	06 39.1	12R05.2	08 12.1
SEP 8	00♋33.8	07 34.8	10 56.4	08 48.6
18	04 29.3	08 38.2	09 05.6	09 18.6
28	08 10.8	09 48.1	06 47.0	09 41.3
OCT 8	11 34.4	11 03.2	04 22.8	09 56.1
18	14 36.0	12 22.1	02 16.2	10 02.5
28	17 09.8	13 43.5	00 46.6	10R00.3
NOV 7	19 09.9	15 06.2	00 06.2	09 49.6
17	20 29.8	16 28.8	00D18.5	09 30.8
27	21 02.8	17 50.0	01 21.7	09 04.7
DEC 7	20R45.1	19 08.3	03 11.1	08 32.4
17	19 37.2	20 22.3	05 40.0	07 55.6
27	17 46.3	21 30.8	08 42.3	07 16.0
JAN 6	15♋29.6	22♏32.2	12♈12.5	06♋35.8

1938	Diana 78	Hidalgo 944	Urania 30	Chiron 2060
JAN 1	02S32.5	28S41.3	23S24.1	16N55.7
21	00N07.1	30 10.6	22 00.7	16 56.9
FEB 10	03 10.1	31 30.8	19 59.2	17 01.6
MAR 2	06 30.0	32 36.3	17 24.3	17 09.1
22	10 00.4	33 19.9	14 22.8	17 18.3
APR 11	13 34.6	33 35.6	11 02.3	17 27.6
MAY 1	17 05.8	33 22.2	07 31.7	17 35.6
21	20 27.5	32 46.1	04 00.0	17 40.9
JUN 10	23 32.9	32 00.1	00 37.2	17 42.7
30	26 16.0	31 17.6	02N25.8	17 40.3
JUL 20	28 31.5	30 49.0	04 56.3	17 33.7
AUG 9	30 16.0	30 39.5	06 38.5	17 23.4
29	31 29.0	30 50.4	07 14.4	17 10.3
SEP 18	32 14.3	31 20.5	06 33.2	16 55.7
OCT 8	32 40.9	32 07.2	04 56.9	16 41.2
28	33 02.6	33 07.6	03 28.1	16 28.5
NOV 17	33 34.0	34 18.6	03 01.5	16 19.2
DEC 7	34 18.5	35 37.5	03 51.0	16 14.3
27	34N48.4	37S01.4	05N43.8	16N14.0

1939	Diana 78	Hidalgo 944	Urania 30	Chiron 2060
JAN 1	16R39.8	22♏02.4	10♈24.3	06R55.9
11	14♋18.6	22 59.7	14 06.3	06♋16.1
21	12 06.6	23 47.9	18 08.7	05 38.8
31	10 26.5	24 25.4	22 28.0	05 05.9
FEB 10	09 33.1	24 51.2	27 00.6	04 39.0
20	09D32.0	25 04.3	01♉44.1	04 19.3
MAR 2	10 22.9	25R03.8	06 36.1	04 08.0
12	12 00.6	24 49.5	11 34.8	04D05.3
22	14 18.7	24 21.6	16 38.6	04 11.5
APR 1	17 10.8	23 40.7	21 46.2	04 26.5
11	20 30.6	22 48.6	26 56.5	04 49.7
21	24 12.9	21 47.1	02♊08.6	05 20.6
MAY 1	28 13.6	20 39.2	07 21.7	05 58.6
11	02♌28.7	19 28.1	12 35.0	06 42.7
21	06 55.5	18 17.2	17 48.2	07 32.2
31	11 31.5	17 09.8	23 00.5	08 26.0
JUN 10	16 14.8	16 09.0	28 11.5	09 23.2
20	21 03.7	15 17.2	03♋21.0	10 23.0
30	25 57.0	14 36.6	08 28.4	11 24.3
JUL 10	00♍53.5	14 08.1	13 33.3	12 26.3
20	05 52.3	13 52.5	18 35.5	13 28.1
30	10 52.7	13D49.8	23 34.5	14 28.6
AUG 9	15 53.9	13 59.6	28 29.7	15 26.9
19	20 55.5	14 21.4	03♌20.8	16 22.1
29	25 56.7	14 54.2	08 07.2	17 13.1
SEP 8	00♎57.1	15 36.8	12 48.0	17 59.1
18	05 56.3	16 28.3	17 22.7	18 39.2
28	10 53.7	17 27.4	21 50.1	19 12.3
OCT 8	15 48.8	18 32.7	26 09.1	19 37.8
18	20 41.2	19 43.1	00♍18.4	19 54.9
28	25 30.1	20 57.3	04 15.9	20 03.0
NOV 7	00♏15.0	22 14.0	08 00.0	20R02.1
17	04 55.2	23 32.0	11 27.9	19 51.9
27	09 29.7	24 49.8	14 36.6	19 33.1
DEC 7	13 57.8	26 06.1	17 22.8	19 06.4
17	18 18.3	27 19.7	19 42.1	18 33.0
27	22 29.9	28 29.0	21 29.8	17 54.8
JAN 6	26♏31.4	29♏32.8	22♍41.1	17♋13.5

1939	Diana 78	Hidalgo 944	Urania 30	Chiron 2060
JAN 1	34N47.2	37S22.8	06N19.7	16N14.6
21	33 49.7	38 48.8	09 04.2	16 19.7
FEB 10	31 43.8	40 11.8	12 08.8	16 27.8
MAR 2	29 16.1	41 26.0	15 16.6	16 37.7
22	26 49.9	42 23.8	18 12.4	16 47.8
APR 11	24 21.4	42 56.8	20 43.4	16 56.6
MAY 1	21 39.9	42 59.7	22 38.9	17 02.5
21	18 37.8	42 33.6	23 51.2	17 04.5
JUN 10	15 12.3	41 47.1	24 15.9	17 01.8
30	11 24.9	40 53.4	23 52.2	16 54.0
JUL 20	07 19.6	40 05.0	22 42.8	16 41.3
AUG 9	03 01.8	39 30.8	20 53.5	16 24.5
29	01S22.3	39 15.4	18 31.8	16 04.9
SEP 18	05 46.5	39 19.8	15 46.8	15 44.1
OCT 8	10 04.5	39 43.0	12 48.5	15 24.2
28	14 10.2	40 22.7	09 47.6	15 07.6
NOV 17	17 58.2	41 16.4	06 55.8	14 56.2
DEC 7	21 23.8	42 21.5	04 26.1	14 51.5
27	24S23.9	43S35.4	02N33.6	14N53.8

1940	Diana 78	Hidalgo 944	Urania 30	Chiron 2060
JAN 1	24♏32.0	29♏01.7	22♍10.3	17 R34.4
11	28 27.9	00♐02.2	23 01.5	16♋52.5
21	02♐10.9	00 55.0	23 R09.3	16 11.0
31	05 39.3	01 38.7	22 31.4	15 32.2
FEB 10	08 50.7	02 12.3	21 08.8	14 58.0
20	11 42.3	02 34.3	19 07.8	14 30.3
MAR 1	14 11.1	02 44.1	16 41.4	14 10.4
11	16 13.7	02 R41.0	14 06.5	13 59.3
21	17 46.3	02 24.6	11 42.5	13 D57.4
31	18 45.3	01 55.4	09 45.4	14 04.9
APR 10	19 07.2	01 14.1	08 25.7	14 21.6
20	18 R49.8	00 22.2	07 48.5	14 47.2
30	17 53.3	29♏21.9	07 D53.3	15 20.8
MAY 10	16 20.8	28 15.7	08 37.1	16 01.8
20	14 20.0	27 06.9	09 55.8	16 49.3
30	12 02.8	25 58.7	11 44.2	17 42.4
JUN 9	09 43.4	24 54.0	13 58.0	18 40.2
19	07 36.6	23 56.0	16 33.3	19 41.7
29	05 54.1	23 06.9	19 26.4	20 45.9
JUL 9	04 43.5	22 28.5	22 34.7	21 51.9
19	04 08.9	22 02.0	25 55.6	22 58.8
29	04 D09.9	21 47.9	29 27.1	24 05.4
AUG 8	04 44.6	21 D46.4	03♎07.6	25 11.0
18	05 49.9	21 57.2	06 55.7	26 14.5
28	07 21.9	22 19.5	10 50.2	27 14.9
SEP 7	09 17.2	22 52.5	14 50.2	28 11.1
17	11 32.5	23 35.3	18 54.6	29 02.2
27	14 04.6	24 26.6	23 02.6	29 47.2
OCT 7	16 51.0	25 25.3	27 13.7	00♌25.1
17	19 49.5	26 30.2	01♏26.9	00 54.9
27	22 58.0	27 40.0	05 41.7	01 15.9
NOV 6	26 14.9	28 53.5	09 57.3	01 27.6
16	29 38.5	00♐09.2	14 12.9	01 R29.4
26	03♑07.5	01 26.1	18 27.8	01 21.4
DEC 6	06 40.8	02 42.7	22 41.3	01 04.0
16	10 17.0	03 57.6	26 52.3	00 37.9
26	13 55.0	05 09.6	00♐59.9	00 04.4
JAN 5	17♑34.0	06♐17.2	05♐03.0	29♋25.3
JAN 1	25 S 04.8	43 S 55.0	02 N 13.2	14 N55.4
21	27 32.2	45 16.2	01 30.3	15 04.9
FEB 10	29 35.9	46 39.0	01 56.9	15 17.9
MAR 1	31 21.0	47 58.3	03 23.5	15 32.0
21	32 53.7	49 06.5	05 08.5	15 44.9
APR 10	34 15.7	49 54.6	06 21.8	15 54.5
30	35 17.5	50 14.3	06 38.7	15 59.3
MAY 20	35 35.6	50 02.5	05 59.6	15 58.4
JUN 9	34 52.0	49 23.7	04 34.1	15 51.0
29	33 23.6	48 28.7	02 32.4	15 37.3
JUL 19	31 50.9	47 31.0	00 03.5	15 17.6
AUG 8	30 41.8	46 41.6	02 S 44.7	14 53.1
28	30 01.8	46 07.9	05 45.0	14 25.2
SEP 17	29 43.1	45 52.9	08 50.7	13 56.1
OCT 7	29 34.1	45 57.2	11 55.1	13 28.4
27	29 23.8	46 19.5	14 51.7	13 05.0
NOV 16	29 03.6	46 57.8	17 34.3	12 48.6
DEC 6	28 27.4	47 49.8	19 57.1	12 41.4
[illegible]	[illegible]	[illegible]	[illegible]	[illegible]

1941	Diana 78	Hidalgo 944	Urania 30	Chiron 2060
JAN 1	16♑06.4	05♐50.8	03♐26.4	29 R41.5
11	19 45.2	06 55.0	07 26.2	29♋00.0
21	23 23.3	07 52.8	11 19.4	28 16.5
31	26 59.5	08 42.5	15 04.6	27 33.2
FEB 10	00♒32.7	09 23.0	18 40.0	26 52.7
20	04 02.0	09 53.0	22 03.5	26 17.2
MAR 2	07 26.1	10 11.5	25 13.0	25 48.4
12	10 43.8	10 R17.5	28 05.4	25 28.1
22	13 53.7	10 10.6	00♑37.8	25 16.9
APR 1	16 54.5	09 50.7	02 46.5	25 D15.6
11	19 44.2	09 18.1	04 27.1	25 24.3
21	22 21.2	08 33.8	05 35.6	25 42.7
MAY 1	24 43.1	07 39.6	06 07.2	26 10.3
11	26 47.5	06 37.5	05 R58.5	26 46.6
21	28 31.7	05 30.4	05 08.2	27 30.6
31	29 52.6	04 21.4	03 37.6	28 21.6
JUN 10	00♓46.9	03 13.8	01 34.2	29 18.5
20	01 11.6	02 10.5	29♐10.4	00♌20.4
30	01 R04.0	01 14.5	26 42.6	01 26.4
JUL 10	00 22.8	00 27.9	24 29.0	02 35.4
20	29♒08.9	29♏52.4	22 44.3	03 46.4
30	27 25.9	29 29.1	21 38.5	04 58.5
AUG 9	25 21.5	29 18.5	21 D16.3	06 10.7
19	23 06.3	29 D20.4	21 37.5	07 21.9
29	20 53.1	29 34.6	22 39.7	08 31.1
SEP 8	18 54.7	00♐00.3	24 18.9	09 37.4
18	17 21.2	00 36.6	26 30.5	10 39.5
28	16 19.4	01 22.6	29 10.5	11 36.6
OCT 8	15 52.7	02 16.9	02♑14.9	12 27.3
18	16 D01.1	03 18.5	05 40.2	13 10.8
28	16 43.2	04 26.0	09 23.9	13 46.0
NOV 7	17 56.0	05 38.2	13 23.2	14 12.0
17	19 36.0	06 53.8	17 36.0	14 28.2
27	21 40.3	08 11.5	22 00.9	14 33.9
DEC 7	24 05.3	09 29.9	26 35.8	14 R29.1
17	26 48.3	10 47.8	01♒19.7	14 14.1
27	29 46.7	12 03.6	06 11.5	13 49.5
JAN 6	02♓58.2	13♐16.1	11♒09.8	13♌16.7
JAN 1	27 S 11.6	49 S 14.5	22 S 25.5	12 N46.9
21	25 51.1	50 29.8	23 47.6	13 00.9
FEB 10	24 14.1	51 50.7	24 42.1	13 20.0
MAR 2	22 25.2	53 12.7	25 12.3	13 40.3
22	20 30.5	54 28.9	25 24.8	13 58.1
APR 11	18 37.5	55 30.0	25 28.6	14 10.5
MAY 1	16 54.4	56 06.1	25 32.7	14 15.7
21	15 30.6	56 10.3	25 40.7	14 12.7
JUN 10	14 35.8	55 42.8	25 44.5	14 01.1
30	14 18.4	54 51.8	25 30.4	13 41.2
JUL 20	14 39.9	53 50.3	24 59.7	13 13.9
AUG 9	15 28.1	52 51.0	24 30.5	12 40.6
29	16 16.3	52 03.2	24 13.5	12 03.2
SEP 18	16 38.5	51 32.4	24 04.2	11 24.2
OCT 8	16 24.0	51 20.2	23 50.3	10 46.5
28	15 34.1	51 26.5	23 18.3	10 13.7
NOV 17	14 12.6	51 49.8	22 17.7	09 49.3
DEC 7	12 22.3	52 28.4	20 41.2	09 36.3
27	[illegible]	[illegible]	18 S 26.0	09 N36.5

1942	Diana 78	Hidalgo 944	Urania 30	Chiron 2060
JAN 1	01♓20.9	12♐40.3	08♒39.9	13 R34.0
11	04 38.2	13 50.6	13 41.1	12♌57.7
21	08 05.8	14 55.4	18 47.8	12 16.0
31	11 42.0	15 53.3	23 58.9	11 31.2
FEB 10	15 25.3	16 43.0	29 13.6	10 46.1
20	19 14.8	17 23.1	04♓31.5	10 03.0
MAR 2	23 09.1	17 52.3	09 51.7	09 24.6
12	27 07.3	18 09.7	15 13.6	08 53.0
22	01♈08.6	18 R14.4	20 36.9	08 29.7
APR 1	05 12.1	18 05.7	26 00.6	08 16.1
11	09 17.2	17 43.7	01♈24.5	08 D12.7
21	13 23.2	17 08.8	06 48.0	08 19.8
MAY 1	17 29.3	16 22.0	12 10.4	08 37.3
11	21 35.0	15 25.2	17 31.3	09 04.6
21	25 39.6	14 20.6	22 50.0	09 41.3
31	29 42.1	13 11.1	28 05.7	10 26.4
JUN 10	03♉42.0	12 00.1	03♉17.8	11 19.0
20	07 38.3	10 50.8	08 25.4	12 18.3
30	11 29.8	09 46.5	13 27.3	13 23.1
JUL 10	15 15.3	08 50.1	18 22.6	14 32.5
20	18 53.3	08 03.8	23 09.7	15 45.6
30	22 21.7	07 29.3	27 46.9	17 01.2
AUG 9	25 38.4	07 07.5	02♊12.2	18 18.4
19	28 40.5	06 59.0	06 22.9	19 36.2
29	01♊24.5	07 D03.6	10 16.1	20 53.4
SEP 8	03 46.5	07 20.8	13 48.1	22 09.2
18	05 41.3	07 50.0	16 54.1	23 22.3
28	07 03.5	08 30.0	19 29.0	24 31.7
OCT 8	07 47.6	09 19.8	21 26.7	25 36.3
18	07 R48.2	10 18.3	22 40.4	26 34.8
28	07 02.7	11 24.0	23 04.6	27 26.2
NOV 7	05 32.8	12 35.7	22 R35.6	28 09.4
17	03 26.6	13 52.2	21 14.5	28 43.3
27	01 00.8	15 12.0	19 10.5	29 07.1
DEC 7	28♉36.2	16 33.8	16 41.0	29 20.1
17	26 34.9	17 56.3	14 09.5	29 R21.9
27	25 14.2	19 18.0	12 00.3	29 12.7
JAN 6	24♉43.0	20♐37.5	10♊30.8	28♌52.8
JAN 1	09 S 27.9	53 S 35.5	17 S 46.1	09 N38.6
21	06 42.5	54 42.1	14 44.2	09 54.5
FEB 10	03 37.9	55 58.1	11 10.1	10 19.0
MAR 2	00 18.4	57 20.2	07 10.7	10 46.8
22	03 N 11.5	58 43.0	02 54.3	11 12.3
APR 11	06 47.0	59 57.8	01 N 30.1	11 31.0
MAY 1	10 23.5	60 53.7	05 53.4	11 39.9
21	13 56.7	61 19.9	10 06.5	11 37.8
JUN 10	17 22.5	61 11.2	14 00.5	11 24.3
30	20 37.6	60 31.1	17 27.5	11 00.1
JUL 20	23 39.4	59 31.0	20 21.0	10 26.5
AUG 9	26 26.9	58 24.6	22 36.8	09 45.2
29	29 00.6	57 23.8	24 14.9	08 58.4
SEP 18	31 21.7	56 36.4	25 19.5	08 09.0
OCT 8	33 27.9	56 06.1	25 58.6	07 20.2
28	35 03.4	55 53.8	26 19.9	06 35.7
NOV 17	35 32.3	55 58.9	26 21.7	05 59.8
DEC 7	34 28.7	56 20.0	25 51.4	05 36.3
27	32 N 29.5	56 S 56.0	24 N 53.4	05 N28.4

1943	Diana 78	Hidalgo 944	Urania 30	Chiron 2060
JAN 1	24R52.1	19♐58.1	11R09.8	29R04.0
11	24D47.1	21 16.1	10♊04.4	28♌39.3
21	25♉33.6	22 29.7	09D50.4	28 05.8
31	27 07.3	23 37.6	10 26.2	27 25.5
FEB 10	29 22.5	24 38.4	11 47.0	26 40.6
20	02♊13.3	25 30.5	13 46.7	25 54.1
MAR 2	05 33.7	26 12.6	16 18.5	25 08.5
12	09 19.0	26 43.5	19 16.8	24 26.6
22	13 25.0	27 01.8	22 36.5	23 50.8
APR 1	17 47.7	27R06.8	26 13.4	23 23.1
11	22 24.6	26 57.8	00♋04.1	23 05.0
21	27 12.8	26 34.7	04 05.9	22 57.3
MAY 1	02♋10.4	25 57.9	08 16.3	23D00.6
11	07 15.8	25 08.5	12 33.8	23 14.7
21	12 27.3	24 08.3	16 56.6	23 39.5
31	17 43.6	22 59.8	21 23.5	24 14.2
JUN 10	23 03.9	21 46.2	25 53.7	24 58.2
20	28 27.0	20 31.0	00♌26.2	25 50.6
30	03♌52.2	19 17.9	05 00.2	26 50.2
JUL 10	09 18.8	18 10.3	09 35.4	27 56.3
20	14 46.2	17 11.4	14 10.9	29 07.7
30	20 13.7	16 23.6	18 46.5	00♍23.5
AUG 9	25 40.9	15 48.6	23 21.6	01 42.5
19	01♍07.0	15 27.5	27 55.7	03 03.8
29	06 31.9	15D20.6	02♍28.5	04 26.4
SEP 8	11 54.7	15 27.8	06 59.4	05 49.0
18	17 15.0	15 48.5	11 27.7	07 10.8
28	22 32.4	16 21.7	15 53.2	08 30.6
OCT 8	27 46.1	17 06.6	20 14.9	09 47.2
18	02♎55.4	18 01.8	24 31.9	10 59.4
28	07 59.6	19 06.0	28 43.6	12 06.2
NOV 7	12 57.9	20 17.9	02♎48.7	13 06.3
17	17 49.2	21 36.1	06 45.8	13 58.5
27	22 32.5	22 59.2	10 33.6	14 41.6
DEC 7	27 06.4	24 25.8	14 10.0	15 14.7
17	01♏29.3	25 54.5	17 32.9	15 36.9
27	05 39.7	27 23.9	20 39.9	15 47.7
JAN 6	09♏35.1	28♐52.6	23♎27.7	15R46.7

1943	Diana 78	Hidalgo 944	Urania 30	Chiron 2060
JAN 1	31N59.5	57S07.1	24N38.5	05N29.0
21	30 23.1	58 00.3	23 53.6	05 41.7
FEB 10	29 32.7	59 06.1	23 39.9	06 08.0
MAR 2	29 15.4	60 22.9	23 47.6	06 42.2
22	29 07.4	61 47.6	23 58.0	07 16.7
APR 11	28 46.3	63 13.4	23 54.6	07 44.8
MAY 1	27 54.9	64 30.0	23 26.2	08 01.6
21	26 22.5	65 24.0	22 26.4	08 04.6
JUN 10	24 05.1	65 43.7	20 53.3	07 53.2
30	21 04.4	65 25.2	18 48.1	07 28.2
JUL 20	17 25.6	64 35.0	16 14.5	06 51.2
AUG 9	13 16.6	63 26.6	13 17.3	06 04.5
29	08 46.1	62 14.6	10 02.4	05 10.6
SEP 18	04 03.0	61 09.8	06 36.2	04 12.6
OCT 8	00S44.0	60 18.5	03 05.0	03 13.8
28	05 27.0	59 43.4	00S24.2	02 18.3
NOV 17	09 58.7	59 24.7	03 44.9	01 30.3
DEC 7	14 12.9	59 22.0	06 49.8	00 54.1
27	18S04.8	59S34.4	09S32.0	00N33.9

1944	Diana 78	Hidalgo 944	Urania 30	Chiron 2060
JAN 1	07♏39.4	28♐08.5	22♎06.4	15R48.6
11	11 26.6	29 36.3	24 43.4	15♍41.9
21	14 55.3	01♑01.1	26 56.0	15 23.9
31	18 02.4	02 21.7	28 39.8	14 55.9
FEB 10	20 44.2	03 36.3	29 50.4	14 19.3
20	22 57.0	04 43.6	00♏23.5	13 36.5
MAR 1	24 36.2	05 41.9	00R15.5	12 50.0
11	25 37.6	06 29.8	29♎25.1	12 02.7
21	25 57.7	07 05.9	27 54.3	11 17.5
31	25R33.9	07 28.9	25 50.0	10 37.0
APR 10	24 27.4	07 37.5	23 24.8	10 03.7
20	22 43.3	07R31.1	20 54.7	09 39.2
30	20 31.9	07 09.3	18 36.6	09 25.1
MAY 10	18 08.5	06 32.3	16 45.2	09D21.9
20	15 49.8	05 41.1	15 29.6	09 30.0
30	13 51.1	04 37.4	14 54.2	09 49.2
JUN 9	12 23.9	03 24.1	14D59.2	10 19.2
19	11 33.8	02 04.5	15 41.8	10 59.1
29	11D22.5	00 42.6	16 58.3	11 48.2
JUL 9	11 48.4	29♐22.5	18 44.5	12 45.6
19	12 47.8	28 08.4	20 56.2	13 50.2
29	14 16.9	27 03.7	23 29.8	15 01.0
AUG 8	16 11.4	26 11.4	26 22.2	16 17.1
18	18 27.4	25 33.3	29 30.4	17 37.2
28	21 01.7	25 10.7	02♏52.4	19 00.5
SEP 7	23 51.3	25D04.0	06 26.1	20 25.7
17	26 53.7	25 12.9	10 10.0	21 52.0
27	00♐06.8	25 36.9	14 02.6	23 18.1
OCT 7	03 28.7	26 14.7	18 02.6	24 42.9
17	06 57.8	27 05.3	22 09.1	26 05.3
27	10 32.9	28 07.2	26 21.2	27 24.2
NOV 6	14 12.5	29 19.0	00♐37.9	28 38.2
16	17 55.6	00♑39.3	04 58.4	29 46.3
26	21 41.2	02 06.6	09 22.1	00♎47.0
DEC 6	25 28.1	03 39.3	13 48.1	01 39.3
16	29 15.5	05 16.0	18 15.7	02 22.0
26	03♑02.4	06 55.3	22 44.2	02 54.1
JAN 5	06♑47.7	08♑35.7	27♐12.8	03♎14.8

1944	Diana 78	Hidalgo 944	Urania 30	Chiron 2060
JAN 1	18S59.0	59S39.8	10S08.1	00N31.7
21	22 19.3	60 10.8	12 11.1	00 34.9
FEB 10	25 13.5	60 57.0	13 33.0	00 56.4
MAR 1	27 40.9	61 58.6	14 03.4	01 31.6
21	29 36.1	63 15.0	13 32.8	02 12.8
APR 10	30 42.6	64 43.1	12 05.8	02 51.1
30	30 37.9	66 15.5	10 16.2	03 19.0
MAY 20	29 22.2	67 39.7	08 52.9	03 31.9
JUN 9	27 37.7	68 39.5	08 25.1	03 28.0
29	26 14.1	69 00.4	08 55.0	03 07.6
JUL 19	25 34.2	68 37.9	10 11.3	02 32.6
AUG 8	25 36.1	67 40.0	12 00.1	01 45.4
28	26 07.9	66 22.3	14 08.4	00 49.2
SEP 17	26 56.1	65 00.1	16 24.8	00S12.9
OCT 7	27 48.4	63 43.7	18 39.1	01 17.3
27	28 34.5	62 38.7	20 42.0	02 20.0
NOV 16	29 06.6	61 47.3	22 25.1	03 16.9
DEC 6	29 19.4	61 10.0	23 41.0	04 03.7
26	29S09.9	60S46.8	24S24.4	04S36.2

1945	Diana 78	Hidalgo 944	Urania 30	Chiron 2060
JAN 1	05♑17.8	07♑55.5	25♐25.4	03♎07.9
11	09 01.8	09 35.8	29 53.8	03 21.6
21	12 42.7	11 14.9	04♑21.0	03R23.2
31	16 19.3	12 51.2	08 46.2	03 13.0
FEB 10	19 50.6	14 23.3	13 08.7	02 51.8
20	23 15.3	15 49.5	17 27.2	02 20.7
MAR 2	26 32.1	17 08.2	21 40.8	01 41.8
12	29 39.7	18 18.0	25 48.4	00 57.3
22	02♒36.1	19 17.0	29 48.3	00 10.1
APR 1	05 19.5	20 03.7	03♒39.1	29♍23.0
11	07 48.0	20 36.5	07 19.1	28 38.9
21	09 58.9	20 53.9	10 45.6	28 00.5
MAY 1	11 49.7	20R54.8	13 56.3	27 29.9
11	13 17.4	20 38.4	16 47.9	27 08.8
21	14 18.8	20 04.4	19 16.5	26 58.3
31	14 50.8	19 13.6	21 17.9	26D59.1
JUN 10	14R51.0	18 07.4	22 47.2	27 11.1
20	14 17.6	16 48.6	23 39.0	27 34.3
30	13 11.3	15 20.9	23R48.9	28 08.1
JUL 10	11 35.1	13 48.9	23 14.0	28 51.7
20	09 35.6	12 17.7	21 54.8	29 44.4
30	07 23.3	10 52.3	19 58.2	00♎45.0
AUG 9	05 09.8	09 37.1	17 37.0	01 52.7
19	03 07.9	08 35.8	15 10.3	03 06.4
29	01 28.2	07 51.0	12 58.9	04 25.0
SEP 8	00 17.7	07 24.1	11 20.1	05 47.5
18	29♑40.6	07D15.7	10 25.8	07 12.8
28	29D37.7	07 25.5	10D20.8	08 39.7
OCT 8	00♒07.6	07 52.6	11 04.3	10 07.3
18	01 08.1	08 35.9	12 33.2	11 34.4
28	02 35.7	09 33.8	14 42.0	12 59.7
NOV 7	04 27.3	10 44.7	17 25.6	14 22.3
17	06 40.0	12 07.2	20 39.1	15 40.7
27	09 10.5	13 39.3	24 17.6	16 53.8
DEC 7	11 56.4	15 19.5	28 17.4	18 00.3
17	14 55.5	17 06.3	02♓35.3	18 59.0
27	18 05.7	18 58.1	07 08.1	19 48.8
JAN 6	21♒25.1	20♑53.3	11♓53.6	20♎28.6

1945	Diana 78	Hidalgo 944	Urania 30	Chiron 2060
JAN 1	29S02.6	60S42.7	24S30.6	04S42.6
21	28 24.6	60 38.7	24 27.4	04 51.3
FEB 10	27 28.1	60 51.0	23 49.1	04 40.2
MAR 2	26 18.8	61 21.8	22 39.3	04 11.2
22	25 04.3	62 13.0	21 04.7	03 30.3
APR 11	23 53.5	63 25.2	19 14.7	02 46.3
MAY 1	22 56.6	64 56.0	17 20.7	02 08.5
21	22 23.9	66 38.0	15 36.6	01 44.0
JUN 10	22 22.9	68 16.8	14 18.6	01 36.8
30	22 53.2	69 32.2	13 43.7	01 47.7
JUL 20	23 39.5	70 04.6	14 01.6	02 15.3
AUG 9	24 14.3	69 45.1	15 00.0	02 56.9
29	24 16.9	68 40.8	16 00.8	03 49.5
SEP 18	23 45.7	67 08.8	16 28.2	04 49.3
OCT 8	22 48.8	65 25.9	16 09.0	05 52.7
28	21 31.9	63 43.5	15 03.2	06 55.9
NOV 17	19 56.3	62 07.9	13 12.7	07 54.9
DEC 7	18 01.4	60 41.9	10 40.3	08 45.8
27	15S46.4	59S27.4	07S30.3	09S24.8

1946	Diana 78	Hidalgo 944	Urania 30	Chiron 2060
JAN 1	19♒44.3	19♑55.4	09♓29.4	20♎10.0
11	23 07.9	21 51.8	14 20.6	20 44.4
21	26 38.3	23 49.4	19 21.3	21 07.4
31	00♓14.4	25 46.7	24 30.1	21 18.6
FEB 10	03 55.1	27 42.2	29 45.6	21 R17.9
20	07 39.0	29 34.4	05♈06.2	21 05.5
MAR 2	11 25.3	01♒21.8	10 31.1	20 42.4
12	15 13.2	03 02.7	15 59.3	20 09.8
22	19 01.5	04 35.3	21 29.8	19 30.0
APR 1	22 49.6	05 58.1	27 01.8	18 45.2
11	26 36.7	07 09.0	02♉34.8	17 58.2
21	00♈21.7	08 06.3	08 07.9	17 11.9
MAY 1	04 04.0	08 47.9	13 40.8	16 29.0
11	07 42.5	09 12.0	19 12.8	15 52.1
21	11 16.1	09 R16.9	24 43.3	15 23.2
31	14 43.8	09 01.4	00♊12.0	15 03.8
JUN 10	18 04.0	08 24.9	05 38.3	14 55.0
20	21 15.2	07 27.8	11 01.7	14 D57.3
30	24 15.5	06 11.6	16 21.9	15 10.7
JUL 10	27 02.3	04 39.7	21 38.2	15 35.1
20	29 33.1	02 56.8	26 50.0	16 09.8
30	01♉44.6	01 08.8	01♋56.7	16 54.1
AUG 9	03 32.7	29♑22.5	06 57.5	17 47.3
19	04 53.3	27 44.4	11 51.5	18 48.3
29	05 41.6	26 20.2	16 37.8	19 56.1
SEP 8	05 R53.0	25 14.5	21 15.0	21 09.7
18	05 24.5	24 29.9	25 41.5	22 28.0
28	04 14.8	24 07.9	29 55.8	23 50.0
OCT 8	02 27.8	24 D08.6	03♌55.2	25 14.5
18	00 12.9	24 31.0	07 37.4	26 40.5
28	27♈44.7	25 13.9	10 58.9	28 06.7
NOV 7	25 22.3	26 15.4	13 55.7	29 32.1
17	23 23.4	27 33.4	16 23.5	00♏55.5
27	22 01.5	29 06.1	18 16.6	02 15.6
DEC 7	21 24.7	00♒51.5	19 29.6	03 31.3
17	21 D34.9	02 47.6	19 57.3	04 41.3
27	22 30.3	04 52.7	19 R35.8	05 44.4
JAN 6	24♈07.1	07♒05.0	18♌24.9	06♏39.3
JAN 1	15 S 09.7	59 S 10.7	06 S 37.6	09 S32.3
21	12 30.9	58 12.6	02 50.6	09 51.7
FEB 10	09 35.7	57 30.4	01 N 15.8	09 52.9
MAR 2	06 27.1	57 07.4	05 30.9	09 36.0
22	03 09.2	57 07.6	09 43.6	09 03.6
APR 11	00 N 14.0	57 34.7	13 42.7	08 22.3
MAY 1	03 38.3	58 31.4	17 17.1	07 40.5
21	06 59.5	59 57.1	20 16.8	07 06.7
JUN 10	10 14.0	61 45.7	22 33.6	06 47.2
30	13 18.0	63 42.7	24 01.7	06 45.0
JUL 20	16 07.8	65 24.4	24 38.8	07 00.1
AUG 9	18 38.9	66 22.9	24 26.8	07 30.3
29	20 43.7	66 18.7	23 31.5	08 12.7
SEP 18	22 08.2	65 11.5	22 02.8	09 03.6
OCT 8	22 31.2	63 17.8	20 13.3	09 59.3
28	21 41.7	60 58.0	18 19.0	10 56.0
NOV 17	20 08.2	58 27.9	16 38.1	11 50.1
DEC 7	18 48.4	55 57.2	15 30.9	12 38.1
27	[illegible]	[illegible]	[illegible]	13 S16.0

1947	Diana 78	Hidalgo 944	Urania 30	Chiron 2060
JAN 1	23♈13.8	05♒58.0	19 R 06.3	06♏13.0
11	25 09.5	08 13.3	17♌32.5	07 03.5
21	27 38.8	10 33.5	15 20.3	07 44.3
31	00♉37.5	12 57.0	12 45.7	08 14.5
FEB 10	04 00.9	15 22.3	10 10.0	08 33.4
20	07 45.3	17 48.2	07 53.4	08 40.8
MAR 2	11 47.8	20 13.0	06 11.8	08 R36.5
12	16 05.4	22 35.4	05 14.3	08 21.2
22	20 36.0	24 54.0	05 D 02.5	07 55.8
APR 1	25 17.8	27 07.2	05 34.5	07 21.8
11	00♊08.9	29 13.2	06 45.6	06 41.3
21	05 08.1	01♓10.5	08 30.1	05 56.6
MAY 1	10 14.2	02 56.9	10 43.1	05 10.5
11	15 26.2	04 30.5	13 19.5	04 25.6
21	20 43.2	05 48.8	16 15.2	03 44.6
31	26 04.5	06 49.4	19 27.0	03 09.7
JUN 10	01♋29.2	07 29.6	22 51.9	02 42.9
20	06 56.8	07 46.8	26 27.6	02 25.4
30	12 26.7	07 R 38.7	00♍12.3	02 18.2
JUL 10	17 58.2	07 03.6	04 04.2	02 D21.8
20	23 30.8	06 01.0	08 02.3	02 36.1
30	29 03.9	04 32.3	12 05.3	03 01.0
AUG 9	04♌36.9	02 41.5	16 12.4	03 35.8
19	10 09.4	00 34.7	20 22.7	04 19.9
29	15 40.5	28♒21.1	24 35.6	05 12.5
SEP 8	21 09.6	26 10.5	28 50.3	06 12.4
18	26 36.1	24 12.7	03♎06.3	07 18.9
28	01♍58.9	22 36.2	07 23.0	08 30.8
OCT 8	07 17.3	21 26.5	11 39.6	09 47.1
18	12 30.2	20 46.6	15 55.6	11 06.6
28	17 36.3	20 D 37.4	20 10.3	12 28.3
NOV 7	22 34.4	20 57.8	24 22.9	13 51.1
17	27 22.7	21 45.8	28 32.6	15 13.7
27	01♎59.3	22 58.9	02♏38.2	16 35.0
DEC 7	06 22.2	24 34.3	06 38.9	17 53.9
17	10 28.6	26 29.2	10 33.4	19 09.1
27	14 15.2	28 41.1	14 20.1	20 19.4
JAN 6	17♎38.8	01♓07.5	17♏57.6	21♏23.6
JAN 1	18 N 25.4	52 S 56.3	15 N 20.7	13 S24.8
21	19 12.8	50 41.7	16 11.1	13 48.2
FEB 10	20 43.6	48 39.8	17 19.6	13 57.0
MAR 2	22 39.0	46 54.3	18 05.4	13 50.5
22	24 40.3	45 29.6	18 11.6	13 29.7
APR 11	26 29.8	44 31.1	17 39.7	12 57.9
MAY 1	27 51.6	44 04.2	16 33.7	12 20.9
21	28 32.3	44 14.2	14 56.5	11 46.0
JUN 10	28 22.1	45 04.6	12 50.7	11 19.9
30	27 16.1	46 34.2	10 19.8	11 07.4
JUL 20	25 14.4	48 32.6	07 27.8	11 10.0
AUG 9	22 22.0	50 35.3	04 19.5	11 27.3
29	18 47.1	52 03.7	00 59.9	11 56.6
SEP 18	14 40.1	52 18.5	02 S 25.6	12 34.9
OCT 8	10 12.0	51 01.5	05 51.4	13 18.5
28	05 34.0	48 25.1	09 12.0	14 03.9
NOV 17	00 56.6	44 56.8	12 21.7	14 47.8
DEC 7	03 S 30.6	41 01.5	15 15.1	15 27.0
27	07 S 38.5	36 S 54.7	17 S 47.6	15 S59.1

1948	Diana 78	Hidalgo 944	Urania 30	Chiron 2060
JAN 1	16♎00.2	29♒52.6	16♏10.1	20♏52.3
11	19 10.6	02♓25.5	19 42.2	21 53.1
21	21 51.0	05 09.9	23 01.8	22 46.0
31	23 56.7	08 03.9	26 06.6	23 30.1
FEB 10	25 22.2	11 05.9	28 53.8	24 04.5
20	26 02.6	14 14.6	01♐20.0	24 28.3
MAR 1	25 R 54.9	17 28.5	03 21.6	24 41.3
11	24 58.8	20 46.7	04 54.4	24 R43.1
21	23 19.4	24 08.0	05 53.9	24 33.9
31	21 08.7	27 31.3	06 16.3	24 14.6
APR 10	18 43.6	00♈55.8	05 R 58.4	23 46.3
20	16 24.2	04 20.7	04 59.2	23 10.5
30	14 28.6	07 44.9	03 21.8	22 29.4
MAY 10	13 08.7	11 07.7	01 13.8	21 45.3
20	12 30.8	14 27.9	28♏48.1	21 00.6
30	12 D 35.5	17 44.7	26 21.2	20 18.0
JUN 9	13 19.7	20 56.7	24 09.2	19 39.7
19	14 39.3	24 02.6	22 26.2	19 07.7
29	16 29.0	27 00.7	21 20.7	18 43.8
JUL 9	18 44.3	29 49.1	20 56.2	18 29.1
19	21 21.0	02♉25.1	21 D 12.7	18 D24.4
29	24 15.3	04 46.0	22 07.4	18 30.0
AUG 8	27 24.2	06 48.0	23 36.4	18 45.8
18	00♏45.2	08 26.5	25 35.9	19 11.6
28	04 16.1	09 36.4	28 01.4	19 46.8
SEP 7	07 55.1	10 11.4	00♐49.8	20 30.7
17	11 40.9	10 R 05.0	03 57.7	21 22.4
27	15 31.8	09 11.8	07 22.5	22 21.1
OCT 7	19 27.0	07 28.5	11 02.0	23 25.7
17	23 25.4	04 58.3	14 54.2	24 35.2
27	27 26.0	01 53.0	18 57.3	25 48.5
NOV 6	01♐28.0	28♈33.1	23 10.2	27 04.5
16	05 30.5	25 26.2	27 31.4	28 22.1
26	09 32.6	22 57.6	01♑59.9	29 40.2
DEC 6	13 33.7	21 25.6	06 34.9	00♐57.6
16	17 32.7	20 D 59.4	11 15.2	02 13.0
26	21 28.7	21 39.4	16 00.1	03 25.5
JAN 5	25♐20.9	23♈22.3	20♑49.1	04♐33.7
JAN 1	08 S 36.5	35 S 52.4	18 S 22.0	16 S05.7
21	12 08.9	31 42.6	20 23.8	16 26.0
FEB 10	15 01.8	27 34.3	21 59.5	16 35.6
MAR 1	17 00.3	23 29.3	23 09.4	16 33.8
21	17 44.9	19 28.9	23 54.1	16 21.2
APR 10	17 10.2	15 33.8	24 11.8	15 59.5
30	15 51.6	11 44.8	23 55.4	15 31.9
MAY 20	14 46.0	08 01.7	23 00.4	15 03.1
JUN 9	14 27.7	04 23.4	21 43.3	14 38.3
29	15 01.1	00 47.1	20 39.8	14 22.2
JUL 19	16 16.3	02 N 53.3	20 15.1	14 17.4
AUG 8	18 00.3	06 48.6	20 31.2	14 24.5
28	20 00.9	11 16.2	21 16.3	14 42.1
SEP 17	22 07.3	16 37.0	22 14.8	15 08.0
OCT 7	24 10.2	22 54.4	23 11.6	15 38.8
27	26 01.6	29 10.6	23 53.6	16 11.5
NOV 16	27 35.2	33 49.8	24 09.8	16 43.1
DEC 6	28 46.2	36 49.3	23 52.2	17 11.0
26	29 S 32.0	39 N 27.4	22 S 55.7	17 S33.1

1949		Diana 78	Hidalgo 944	Urania 30	Chiron 2060
JAN	1	23♐48.5	22♈34.0	18♑53.1	04♐07.0
	11	27 37.8	24 51.9	23 44.0	05 12.1
	21	01♑21.5	28 02.9	28 37.5	06 11.2
	31	04 58.4	02♉00.7	03♒33.3	07 03.2
FEB	10	08 27.1	06 40.0	08 30.6	07 47.0
	20	11 46.3	11 54.9	13 28.6	08 21.7
MAR	2	14 54.3	17 40.7	18 27.0	08 46.7
	12	17 49.2	23 52.3	23 25.0	09 01.5
	22	20 28.9	00♊24.5	28 22.0	09R05.7
APR	1	22 51.1	07 12.1	03♓17.4	08 59.7
	11	24 52.9	14 10.0	08 10.4	08 43.8
	21	26 31.5	21 12.7	13 00.3	08 19.0
MAY	1	27 43.8	28 15.6	17 46.2	07 46.7
	11	28 26.4	05♋14.5	22 27.0	07 08.6
	21	28R36.9	12 05.5	27 01.8	06 26.9
	31	28 13.1	18 46.4	01♈29.0	05 43.7
JUN	10	27 15.2	25 15.0	05 46.7	05 01.4
	20	25 45.9	01♌30.0	09 53.3	04 22.3
	30	23 51.0	07 31.1	13 46.1	03 48.4
JUL	10	21 40.5	13 17.9	17 21.9	03 21.4
	20	19 26.1	18 50.5	20 37.2	03 02.5
	30	17 20.4	24 09.6	23 27.3	02 52.8
AUG	9	15 34.8	29 15.2	25 46.9	02D52.8
	19	14 17.2	04♍07.9	27 30.2	03 02.4
	29	13 31.9	08 48.2	28 30.6	03 21.8
SEP	8	13D20.7	13 16.1	28R42.9	03 50.4
	18	13 42.1	17 31.9	28 04.5	04 27.6
	28	14 34.1	21 35.6	26 37.4	05 12.7
OCT	8	15 53.5	25 26.9	24 32.4	06 04.8
	18	17 37.1	29 05.3	22 08.0	07 03.0
	28	19 41.7	02♎30.3	19 47.6	08 06.3
NOV	7	22 04.6	05 40.8	17 54.9	09 13.6
	17	24 42.8	08 35.6	16 45.9	10 23.8
	27	27 34.3	11 13.4	16D28.8	11 36.0
DEC	7	00♒36.9	13 32.1	17 04.7	12 48.8
	17	03 48.7	15 29.8	18 29.1	14 01.2
	27	07 08.3	17 04.1	20 36.4	15 12.1
JAN	6	10♒33.9	18♎12.5	23♈20.0	16♐20.2
JAN	1	29S40.8	40N19.9	22S30.9	17S38.4
	21	29 54.6	43 43.7	20 42.1	17 51.2
FEB	10	29 47.6	47 47.9	18 15.7	17 56.0
MAR	2	29 26.6	52 08.9	15 16.9	17 53.1
	22	29 00.1	56 02.2	11 52.6	17 43.2
APR	11	28 38.8	58 25.9	08 10.7	17 27.6
MAY	1	28 33.0	58 24.5	04 19.6	17 08.2
	21	28 50.3	55 48.7	00 27.9	16 47.7
JUN	10	29 28.8	51 19.7	03N15.7	16 29.3
	30	30 11.3	45 52.5	06 42.1	16 16.1
JUL	20	30 29.9	40 08.5	09 41.6	16 10.4
AUG	9	30 09.6	34 32.3	12 03.3	16 13.1
	29	29 18.8	29 17.7	13 33.9	16 23.7
SEP	18	28 13.4	24 31.9	13 56.8	16 40.4
OCT	8	27 01.5	20 19.0	13 03.3	17 00.9
	28	25 42.7	16 41.7	11 20.9	17 22.5
NOV	17	24 13.3	13 42.7	09 56.1	17 42.7
DEC	7	22 29.1	11 23.9	09 38.6	17 59.4
	27	20S28.0	09N47.2	10N33.9	18S11.1

1950		Diana 78	Hidalgo 944	Urania 30	Chiron 2060
JAN	1	08♒50.4	17♎41.7	21♈54.1	15♐46.6
	11	12 18.6	18 36.3	24 53.4	16 52.9
	21	15 51.1	19 01.5	28 19.8	17 54.9
	31	19 26.6	18R55.6	02♉08.6	18 51.4
FEB	10	23 04.1	18 18.2	06 15.1	19 41.3
	20	26 42.6	17 10.1	10 36.1	20 23.8
MAR	2	00♓21.0	15 34.9	15 08.6	20 57.8
	12	03 58.4	13 38.8	19 50.0	21 22.9
	22	07 33.9	11 29.7	24 38.5	21 38.4
APR	1	11 06.5	09 17.6	29 32.5	21 44.2
	11	14 35.1	07 12.1	04♊30.4	21R40.2
	21	17 58.7	05 21.5	09 31.3	21 26.9
MAY	1	21 15.9	03 52.0	14 34.1	21 04.9
	11	24 25.5	02 46.7	19 38.1	20 35.7
	21	27 26.0	02 07.0	24 42.6	20 00.4
	31	00♈15.3	01 52.3	29 46.9	19 21.1
JUN	10	02 51.7	02D00.8	04♋50.7	18 39.8
	20	05 12.4	02 30.4	09 53.4	17 58.6
	30	07 14.5	03 18.4	14 54.7	17 19.7
JUL	10	08 54.9	04 22.4	19 54.1	16 44.9
	20	10 09.8	05 40.1	24 51.4	16 16.0
	30	10 55.2	07 09.2	29 46.0	15 54.3
AUG	9	11R07.5	08 47.7	04♌37.6	15 41.0
	19	10 43.6	10 33.9	09 25.8	15D36.5
	29	09 42.7	12 26.1	14 09.9	15 41.4
SEP	8	08 07.1	14 22.8	18 49.5	15 55.4
	18	06 03.0	16 22.6	23 23.8	16 18.3
	28	03 42.2	18 24.1	27 51.8	16 49.7
OCT	8	01 19.4	20 26.1	02♍12.7	17 28.9
	18	29♓10.3	22 27.2	06 25.3	18 15.1
	28	27 28.7	24 26.2	10 27.9	19 07.4
NOV	7	26 23.5	26 21.7	14 18.9	20 04.9
	17	25 59.4	28 12.3	17 56.2	21 06.5
	27	26D16.8	29 56.5	21 17.2	22 11.3
DEC	7	27 13.4	01♏32.9	24 18.9	23 18.0
	17	28 45.9	02 59.6	26 57.5	24 25.7
	27	00♈49.9	04 15.2	29 09.1	25 33.2
JAN	6	03♈21.4	05♏17.8	00♎49.1	26♐39.3
JAN	1	19S55.0	09N29.7	10N57.2	18S13.2
	21	17 32.3	08 45.0	12 57.2	18 17.6
FEB	10	14 54.5	08 36.2	15 23.2	18 16.2
MAR	2	12 04.6	08 49.4	17 54.9	18 09.6
	22	09 06.7	09 02.5	20 15.4	17 58.9
APR	11	06 05.4	08 52.3	22 10.9	17 45.7
MAY	1	03 05.4	08 06.8	23 30.9	17 31.4
	21	00 12.0	06 48.1	24 08.3	17 17.6
JUN	10	02N29.4	05 04.5	24 00.0	17 05.9
	30	04 52.4	03 04.4	23 06.3	16 58.1
JUL	20	06 49.2	00 54.2	21 30.7	16 55.1
AUG	9	08 09.3	01S21.9	19 19.2	16 57.6
	29	08 40.5	03 40.7	16 39.3	17 05.3
SEP	18	08 15.8	05 59.5	13 39.4	17 16.7
OCT	8	07 08.1	08 15.8	10 28.6	17 30.2
	28	05 55.3	10 27.5	07 16.5	17 43.6
NOV	17	05 17.1	12 32.4	04 13.1	17 55.1
DEC	7	05 33.0	14 28.3	01 29.6	18 02.9
	27	06N42.9	16S13.1	00S41.2	18S06.0

1951		Diana 78	Hidalgo 944	Urania 30	Chiron 2060
JAN	1	02♈02.4	04♏48.2	00♎03.3	26♐06.5
	11	04 46.3	05 43.7	01 25.6	27 11.6
	21	07 52.2	06 23.7	02 08.7	28 13.7
	31	11 16.9	06 46.9	02R09.1	29 11.7
FEB	10	14 57.9	06R51.9	01 24.4	00♑04.7
	20	18 52.9	06 38.2	29♍56.5	00 51.5
MAR	2	22 59.7	06 05.7	27 52.5	01 31.4
	12	27 17.0	05 15.5	25 24.9	02 03.5
	22	01♉43.2	04 09.4	22 51.5	02 27.2
APR	1	06 17.2	02 50.8	20 30.5	02 42.0
	11	10 58.1	01 23.6	18 36.9	02 47.6
	21	15 44.8	29♎52.7	17 21.0	02R44.1
MAY	1	20 36.8	28 23.3	16 46.8	02 31.8
	11	25 33.4	27 00.0	16D53.8	02 11.5
	21	00♊34.0	25 47.1	17 39.4	01 44.0
	31	05 38.0	24 47.5	18 58.8	01 10.9
JUN	10	10 45.2	24 03.4	20 47.6	00 33.6
	20	15 54.8	23 35.7	23 01.6	29♐54.2
	30	21 06.5	23 24.5	25 36.7	29 14.4
JUL	10	26 19.8	23D29.4	28 29.7	28 36.4
	20	01♋34.2	23 49.4	01♎37.8	28 02.0
	30	06 49.2	24 23.1	04 58.5	27 32.7
AUG	9	12 04.0	25 09.2	08 30.0	27 10.0
	19	17 18.0	26 06.2	12 10.7	26 54.9
	29	22 30.5	27 12.6	15 59.1	26 48.1
SEP	8	27 40.3	28 26.9	19 54.1	26D49.9
	18	02♌46.4	29 47.7	23 54.7	27 00.6
	28	07 47.5	01♏13.5	27 59.9	27 19.7
OCT	8	12 42.0	02 43.1	02♏09.0	27 47.1
	18	17 27.9	04 15.0	06 21.2	28 22.0
	28	22 03.1	05 47.9	10 35.7	29 03.7
NOV	7	26 24.8	07 20.6	14 51.9	29 51.4
	17	00♍29.6	08 51.5	19 08.9	00♑44.2
	27	04 13.9	10 19.3	23 26.2	01 41.1
DEC	7	07 32.7	11 42.6	27 42.8	02 41.1
	17	10 20.8	12 59.9	01♐57.9	03 43.1
	27	12 32.1	14 09.8	06 10.7	04 46.0
JAN	6	13♍59.9	15♏10.6	10♐20.2	05♑48.8
JAN	1	07N07.9	16S37.3	01S07.2	18S06.0
	21	09 12.9	18 04.7	02 16.5	18 02.8
FEB	10	11 49.4	19 14.5	02 20.4	17 55.1
MAR	2	14 46.1	20 02.5	01 15.8	17 43.8
	22	17 51.6	20 25.0	00N31.5	17 30.5
APR	11	20 54.9	20 21.5	02 09.9	17 16.9
MAY	1	23 44.8	19 58.1	02 58.8	17 04.4
	21	26 10.2	19 27.2	02 47.5	16 54.6
JUN	10	28 00.8	19 02.4	01 43.1	16 48.1
	30	29 07.4	18 53.7	00S03.0	16 45.5
JUL	20	29 23.5	19 05.5	02 19.9	16 46.9
AUG	9	28 46.5	19 38.0	04 58.0	16 52.0
	29	27 18.1	20 29.0	07 49.3	16 59.9
SEP	18	25 04.9	21 35.1	10 46.0	17 09.7
OCT	8	22 17.0	22 53.0	13 41.0	17 19.6
	28	19 07.6	24 19.1	16 27.3	17 28.1
NOV	17	15 52.0	25 50.5	18 58.1	17 33.6
DEC	7	12 46.9	27 24.4	21 07.6	17 35.1
	27	10N09.7	28S58.0	22S50.6	17S31.7

1952		Diana 78	Hidalgo 944	Urania 30	Chiron 2060
JAN	1	13♍21.9	14♏41.4	08♐16.0	05♑17.5
	11	14 25.8	15 37.1	12 23.3	06 19.9
	21	14 R 38.7	16 21.6	16 25.6	07 20.4
	31	13 58.6	16 53.6	20 21.7	08 18.2
FEB	10	12 29.9	17 11.7	24 09.8	09 12.1
	20	10 25.2	17 R 15.1	27 48.5	10 01.1
MAR	1	08 03.5	17 03.4	01♑15.9	10 44.4
	11	05 48.7	16 36.5	04 29.3	11 21.1
	21	04 01.5	15 55.2	07 26.5	11 50.4
	31	02 55.8	15 00.9	10 04.2	12 11.8
APR	10	02 D 38.1	13 56.0	12 18.6	12 24.8
	20	03 07.5	12 43.6	14 05.9	12 29.2
	30	04 20.2	11 27.0	15 21.4	12 R25.1
MAY	10	06 10.5	10 10.4	16 00.5	12 12.8
	20	08 32.2	08 57.4	15 R 59.7	11 53.0
	30	11 20.0	07 51.4	15 16.3	11 26.5
JUN	9	14 29.1	06 55.3	13 52.1	10 54.6
	19	17 55.2	06 11.2	11 53.0	10 19.0
	29	21 35.5	05 40.4	09 30.9	09 41.1
JUL	9	25 27.0	05 23.4	07 02.9	09 03.0
	19	29 27.4	05 D 20.3	04 46.8	08 26.3
	29	03♎35.2	05 30.6	02 58.8	07 52.8
AUG	8	07 48.8	05 53.6	01 50.0	07 24.2
	18	12 06.8	06 28.1	01 D 25.2	07 01.6
	28	16 28.5	07 13.1	01 45.4	06 46.1
SEP	7	20 52.7	08 07.2	02 47.9	06 38.5
	17	25 18.7	09 09.2	04 28.4	06 D39.0
	27	29 45.9	10 17.8	06 42.6	06 47.8
OCT	7	04♏13.4	11 31.7	09 26.2	07 04.8
	17	08 40.7	12 49.6	12 34.8	07 29.6
	27	13 07.3	14 10.2	16 05.3	08 01.6
NOV	6	17 32.2	15 32.1	19 54.4	08 40.2
	16	21 55.0	16 54.0	23 59.5	09 24.5
	26	26 14.9	18 14.7	28 18.7	10 13.7
DEC	6	00♐31.0	19 32.7	02♒49.8	11 06.9
	16	04 42.6	20 46.7	07 31.4	12 02.9
	26	08 48.7	21 55.1	12 22.0	13 00.9
JAN	5	12♐48.1	22♏56.7	17♒20.3	13♑59.6

JAN	1	09 N 36.9	29 S 21.0	23 S 11.9	17 S30.1
	21	07 57.9	30 49.9	24 18.1	17 20.8
FEB	10	07 13.6	32 10.4	24 55.0	17 07.7
MAR	1	07 07.1	33 16.6	25 05.9	16 52.0
	21	07 01.3	34 01.6	24 58.0	16 35.5
APR	10	06 25.9	34 18.9	24 41.0	16 20.1
	30	05 11.0	34 07.0	24 26.8	16 07.5
MAY	20	03 18.1	33 31.7	24 25.6	15 59.2
JUN	9	00 52.9	32 45.3	24 38.4	15 55.7
	29	01 S 58.0	32 01.4	24 51.8	15 57.1
JUL	19	05 07.5	31 30.6	24 48.7	16 02.5
AUG	8	08 28.6	31 18.6	24 30.1	16 11.0
	28	11 54.4	31 26.9	24 08.0	16 21.1
SEP	17	15 18.1	31 54.5	23 45.3	16 31.4
OCT	7	18 33.3	32 38.9	23 14.2	16 40.3
	27	21 33.7	33 37.3	22 23.5	16 46.5
NOV	16	24 14.1	34 46.7	21 03.4	16 48.6
DEC	6	26 29.9	36 04.2	19 07.6	16 46.0
	26	28 S 19.9	37 S 27.1	16 S 33.9	16 S38.2

1953		Diana 78	Hidalgo 944	Urania 30	Chiron 2060
JAN	1	11♐13.2	22♏33.0	15♒20.1	13♑36.1
	11	15 08.1	23 29.7	20 22.5	14 34.9
	21	18 54.6	24 17.3	25 31.0	15 32.9
	31	22 31.0	24 54.4	00♓44.5	16 29.0
FEB	10	25 55.8	25 19.8	06 02.3	17 22.2
	20	29 07.2	25 32.5	11 23.7	18 11.5
MAR	2	02♑02.9	25 R 31.8	16 47.8	18 56.0
	12	04 40.6	25 17.5	22 14.1	19 34.9
	22	06 57.5	24 49.5	27 41.9	20 07.4
APR	1	08 50.5	24 08.8	03♈10.6	20 32.8
	11	10 16.4	23 16.8	08 39.8	20 50.6
	21	11 11.6	22 15.7	14 08.8	21 00.4
MAY	1	11 33.3	21 08.2	19 37.0	21 R02.1
	11	11 R 19.3	19 57.5	25 04.0	20 55.9
	21	10 28.8	18 47.0	00♉29.3	20 42.1
	31	09 04.5	17 40.1	05 52.0	20 21.4
JUN	10	07 12.1	16 39.6	11 11.7	19 54.7
	20	05 01.1	15 48.2	16 27.5	19 23.2
	30	02 44.4	15 07.8	21 38.6	18 48.4
JUL	10	00 35.0	14 39.5	26 44.2	18 11.8
	20	28♐44.8	14 24.0	01♊42.9	17 35.2
	30	27 22.9	14 D 21.3	06 33.5	17 00.4
AUG	9	26 33.7	14 31.1	11 14.6	16 28.7
	19	26 D 19.0	14 52.8	15 43.8	16 01.9
	29	26 37.8	15 25.3	19 59.1	15 40.9
SEP	8	27 27.4	16 07.8	23 57.6	15 26.8
	18	28 44.9	16 59.0	27 35.7	15 20.1
	28	00♑26.7	17 57.7	00♋49.3	15 D21.2
OCT	8	02 29.7	19 02.8	03 33.4	15 30.3
	18	04 50.9	20 12.9	05 42.1	15 47.1
	28	07 27.5	21 26.7	07 09.3	16 11.2
NOV	7	10 17.2	22 43.1	07 48.7	16 42.2
	17	13 18.1	24 00.6	07 R 35.8	17 19.3
	27	16 28.0	25 18.0	06 30.3	18 01.8
DEC	7	19 45.5	26 34.0	04 37.8	18 48.7
	17	23 09.2	27 47.1	02 12.8	19 39.2
	27	26 37.5	28 56.0	29♊37.2	20 32.3
JAN	6	00♒09.3	29♏59.4	27♊14.4	21♑26.9

JAN	1	28 S 46.2	37 S 52.6	15 S 40.5	16 S34.9
	21	30 00.3	39 17.9	12 20.6	16 21.0
FEB	10	30 51.8	40 40.4	08 31.4	16 03.5
MAR	2	31 27.5	41 54.3	04 20.4	15 44.0
	22	31 56.6	42 51.8	00 N 03.5	15 24.6
APR	11	32 29.1	43 24.7	04 30.8	15 07.2
MAY	1	33 11.8	43 27.6	08 52.0	14 53.7
	21	34 01.3	43 01.4	12 57.4	14 45.7
JUN	10	34 38.2	42 14.9	16 37.9	14 43.7
	30	34 35.5	41 20.9	19 45.4	14 47.7
JUL	20	33 46.8	40 32.1	22 13.8	14 56.3
AUG	9	32 33.3	39 57.4	24 00.1	15 08.0
	29	31 19.3	39 41.4	25 05.4	15 20.8
SEP	18	30 14.7	39 45.0	25 36.2	15 32.8
OCT	8	29 16.9	40 07.4	25 44.2	15 42.2
	28	28 18.3	40 46.3	25 44.5	15 47.7
NOV	17	27 11.6	41 39.2	25 48.7	15 48.1
DEC	7	25 51.1	42 43.6	25 53.7	15 42.9
	27	24 S 13.8	43 S 56.9	25 N 41.3	15 S32.2

1954		Diana 78	Hidalgo 944	Urania 30	Chiron 2060
JAN	1	28♑23.0	29♏28.5	28 R 22.8	20♑59.5
	11	01♒56.2	00♐28.5	26♊14.6	21 54.5
	21	05 31.2	01 20.9	24 47.4	22 49.6
	31	09 06.8	02 04.3	24 09.0	23 43.7
FEB	10	12 42.3	02 37.4	24 D 20.6	24 35.9
	20	16 16.3	02 59.1	25 18.5	25 25.1
MAR	2	19 48.0	03 08.6	26 56.7	26 10.4
	12	23 16.4	03 R 05.2	29 09.1	26 51.0
	22	26 40.1	02 48.6	01♋49.7	27 26.1
APR	1	29 58.3	02 19.3	04 53.2	27 54.9
	11	03♓09.5	01 37.9	08 15.5	28 16.9
	21	06 12.3	00 46.1	11 52.7	28 31.6
MAY	1	09 05.1	29♏46.0	15 41.9	28 38.8
	11	11 46.1	28 40.0	19 40.9	28 R38.3
	21	14 13.0	27 31.5	23 47.5	28 30.4
	31	16 23.6	26 23.6	28 00.3	28 15.4
JUN	10	18 15.0	25 19.3	02♌18.0	27 54.0
	20	19 43.9	24 21.6	06 39.4	27 27.2
	30	20 47.2	23 32.8	11 03.7	26 56.1
JUL	10	21 21.2	22 54.7	15 30.2	26 22.1
	20	21 R 22.9	22 28.5	19 58.1	25 46.9
	30	20 50.2	22 14.7	24 27.0	25 11.8
AUG	9	19 42.8	22 D 13.3	28 56.3	24 38.6
	19	18 04.0	22 24.2	03♍25.5	24 08.7
	29	16 00.4	22 46.5	07 54.2	23 43.5
SEP	8	13 42.8	23 19.6	12 21.7	23 24.0
	18	11 25.0	24 02.3	16 47.6	23 11.1
	28	09 20.6	24 53.6	21 11.3	23 05.4
OCT	8	07 41.5	25 52.2	25 32.2	23 D07.3
	18	06 35.9	26 57.0	29 49.4	23 16.6
	28	06 07.4	28 06.6	04♎02.3	23 33.3
NOV	7	06 D 16.9	29 19.9	08 09.6	23 57.0
	17	07 02.6	00♐35.5	12 10.3	24 27.1
	27	08 21.3	01 52.1	16 03.1	25 02.9
DEC	7	10 09.6	03 08.5	19 46.2	25 43.8
	17	12 23.6	04 23.2	23 17.9	26 28.8
	27	15 00.0	05 34.9	26 35.8	27 17.0
JAN	6	17♓55.7	06♐42.1	29♎37.3	28♑07.5

JAN	1	23 S 46.7	44 S 16.3	25 N 34.4	15 S28.7
	21	21 47.7	45 37.0	24 59.2	15 11.7
FEB	10	19 33.5	46 59.4	24 28.8	14 51.2
MAR	2	17 07.8	48 18.3	24 09.6	14 28.9
	22	14 35.4	49 26.2	23 51.8	14 06.9
APR	11	12 01.8	50 14.0	23 22.1	13 47.4
MAY	1	09 33.2	50 33.6	22 30.2	13 32.4
	21	07 16.7	50 21.7	21 10.2	13 23.5
JUN	10	05 20.2	49 42.8	19 20.3	13 21.7
	30	03 52.7	48 47.8	17 01.8	13 26.6
JUL	20	03 04.0	47 50.0	14 17.9	13 37.1
AUG	9	03 01.5	47 00.5	11 13.4	13 51.3
	29	03 41.9	46 26.5	07 53.5	14 06.6
SEP	18	04 44.1	46 11.2	04 24.3	14 20.7
OCT	8	05 34.7	46 15.0	00 51.5	14 31.6
	28	05 48.1	46 36.8	02 S 38.4	14 37.7
NOV	17	05 15.3	47 14.5	05 59.1	14 38.0
DEC	7	03 58.1	48 06.0	09 04.5	14 31.9
	27	02 S 01.9	49 S 09.1	11 S 48.3	14 S19.7

1955	Diana 78	Hidalgo 944	Urania 30	Chiron 2060
JAN 1	16♓25.6	06♐09.1	28♎08.8	27♑42.0
11	19 30.0	07 13.7	01♏00.9	28 33.2
21	22 49.6	08 11.8	03 32.0	29 25.2
31	26 22.4	09 02.1	05 38.0	00♒17.1
FEB 10	00♈06.4	09 43.3	07 14.7	01 07.7
20	04 00.0	10 14.1	08 18.0	01 56.1
MAR 2	08 01.9	10 33.4	08 43.2	02 41.6
12	12 10.8	10 40.4	08R27.5	03 23.0
22	16 25.8	10R34.5	07 29.9	03 59.8
APR 1	20 45.9	10 15.6	05 53.0	04 31.1
11	25 10.4	09 44.1	03 44.9	04 56.2
21	29 38.6	09 00.9	01 18.3	05 14.7
MAY 1	04♉10.0	08 07.5	28♎49.6	05 26.2
11	08 43.8	07 06.2	26 35.7	05 30.5
21	13 19.9	05 59.6	24 49.7	05R27.6
31	17 57.5	04 50.8	23 40.6	05 17.7
JUN 10	22 36.2	03 43.2	23 11.9	05 01.3
20	27 15.6	02 39.7	23D23.1	04 39.0
30	01♊55.0	01 43.1	24 11.7	04 11.8
JUL 10	06 33.9	00 55.9	25 33.6	03 40.9
20	11 11.6	00 19.5	27 24.7	03 07.6
30	15 47.2	29♏55.3	29 41.2	02 33.4
AUG 9	20 19.8	29 43.6	02♏19.2	01 59.9
19	24 48.2	29D44.6	05 15.7	01 28.5
29	29 10.7	29 57.8	08 28.3	01 00.5
SEP 8	03♋25.8	00♐22.6	11 54.4	00 37.3
18	07 31.3	00 58.0	15 32.3	00 19.7
28	11 24.2	01 43.2	19 20.4	00 08.6
OCT 8	15 01.5	02 36.8	23 17.3	00 04.5
18	18 18.9	03 37.7	27 21.8	00D07.6
28	21 11.3	04 44.7	01♐32.9	00 17.9
NOV 7	23 33.4	05 56.5	05 49.5	00 35.1
17	25 18.2	07 11.7	10 11.0	00 59.0
27	26 19.2	08 29.2	14 36.5	01 28.9
DEC 7	26R31.1	09 47.5	19 05.1	02 04.2
17	25 51.0	11 05.3	23 36.3	02 44.0
27	24 22.5	12 21.2	28 09.1	03 27.6
JAN 6	22♋18.0	13♐33.9	02♑43.0	04♒14.0
JAN 1	01S27.4	49S26.5	12S25.1	14S15.8
21	01N08.6	50 40.9	14 33.5	13 57.0
FEB 10	04 08.9	52 01.2	16 06.3	13 34.5
MAR 2	07 26.5	53 22.9	16 55.7	13 10.1
22	10 54.6	54 39.3	16 52.3	12 46.0
APR 11	14 26.1	55 41.2	15 51.4	12 24.6
MAY 1	17 54.1	56 18.6	14 10.6	12 08.0
21	21 11.3	56 24.4	12 33.5	11 57.9
JUN 10	24 11.0	55 58.2	11 40.5	11 55.3
30	26 46.6	55 08.2	11 44.5	12 00.3
JUL 20	28 52.4	54 06.9	12 38.6	12 11.7
AUG 9	30 24.7	53 07.2	14 08.6	12 27.5
29	31 22.8	52 18.7	16 00.5	12 44.9
SEP 18	31 50.4	51 46.7	18 01.3	13 01.2
OCT 8	31 56.5	51 33.3	19 59.9	13 13.9
28	31 55.0	51 38.3	21 46.0	13 21.3
NOV 17	32 02.6	52 00.4	23 10.5	13 22.3
DEC 7	32 29.2	52 37.7	24 06.1	13 16.3
27	32N59.3	53S28.7	24S27.1	13S03.6

1956	Diana 78	Hidalgo 944	Urania 30	Chiron 2060
JAN 1	23R23.7	12♐58.1	00♑26.0	03♒50.5
11	21♋08.0	14 08.6	05 00.2	04 37.9
21	18 48.3	15 13.8	09 34.3	05 26.8
31	16 49.3	16 12.3	14 07.5	06 16.2
FEB 10	15 29.8	17 02.6	18 39.3	07 05.0
20	15D00.6	17 43.4	23 08.5	07 52.4
MAR 1	15 24.2	18 13.5	27 34.4	08 37.4
11	16 37.3	18 31.9	01♒56.0	09 19.2
21	18 34.3	18R37.5	06 12.1	09 57.0
31	21 08.4	18 30.0	10 21.5	10 30.0
APR 10	24 13.1	18 09.1	14 22.8	10 57.5
20	27 42.9	17 35.2	18 14.2	11 19.0
30	01♌32.9	16 49.5	21 53.6	11 34.1
MAY 10	05 39.0	15 53.5	25 18.7	11 42.3
20	09 58.3	14 49.5	28 26.4	11R43.7
30	14 27.8	13 40.5	01♓13.2	11 38.2
JUN 9	19 05.4	12 29.6	03 35.1	11 26.2
19	23 49.5	11 20.2	05 26.8	11 08.1
29	28 38.4	10 15.6	06 43.5	10 44.8
JUL 9	03♍31.1	09 18.6	07 19.7	10 17.1
19	08 26.6	08 31.5	07R10.9	09 46.3
29	13 23.9	07 56.1	06 16.2	09 13.7
AUG 8	18 22.4	07 33.3	04 38.5	08 40.6
18	23 21.5	07 23.8	02 28.2	08 08.6
28	28 20.5	07D27.4	00 02.6	07 39.1
SEP 7	03♎19.1	07 43.6	27♒42.5	07 13.2
17	08 16.5	08 11.9	25 48.8	06 52.2
27	13 12.4	08 51.1	24 36.4	06 36.9
OCT 7	18 06.3	09 40.1	24D13.1	06 27.9
17	22 57.6	10 37.9	24 40.7	06D25.8
27	27 45.7	11 43.1	25 56.1	06 30.6
NOV 6	02♏30.1	12 54.4	27 54.4	06 42.3
16	07 10.0	14 10.5	00♓30.3	07 00.6
26	11 44.6	15 30.1	03 37.8	07 25.1
DEC 6	16 13.1	16 51.8	07 12.2	07 55.3
16	20 34.3	18 14.2	11 09.3	08 30.3
26	24 47.2	19 36.0	15 25.0	09 09.6
JAN 5	28♏50.6	20♐55.8	19♓56.5	09♒52.1
JAN 1	33N01.9	53S43.4	24S26.6	12S59.5
21	32 28.2	54 49.0	24 00.7	12 39.7
FEB 10	30 41.0	56 04.1	22 58.2	12 16.0
MAR 1	28 17.2	57 25.7	21 22.9	11 50.2
21	25 47.0	58 48.4	19 21.2	11 24.6
APR 10	23 12.7	60 03.7	17 01.9	11 01.5
30	20 26.0	61 00.6	14 35.3	10 43.3
MAY 20	17 20.0	61 28.5	12 13.5	10 31.8
JUN 9	13 52.2	61 21.6	10 11.1	10 28.1
29	10 03.8	60 43.0	08 45.2	10 32.5
JUL 19	05 58.9	59 43.6	08 13.3	10 44.1
AUG 8	01 42.7	58 37.3	08 43.9	11 00.7
28	02S38.7	57 36.0	09 58.4	11 19.6
SEP 17	06 59.2	56 47.6	11 09.2	11 37.8
OCT 7	11 12.7	56 16.1	11 34.3	11 52.5
27	15 13.0	56 02.5	10 59.8	12 01.5
NOV 16	18 54.7	56 06.2	09 28.5	12 03.7
DEC 6	22 13.3	56 25.9	07 07.4	11 58.4
26	25S05.8	57S00.6	04S05.2	11S46.0

1957	Diana 78	Hidalgo 944	Urania 30	Chiron 2060
JAN 1	27♏14.5	20♐24.2	18♓06.2	09♒34.8
11	01♐11.3	21 42.1	22 45.8	10 18.8
21	04 55.8	22 55.6	27 36.8	11 04.8
31	08 26.3	24 03.5	02♈37.4	11 51.7
FEB 10	11 40.4	25 04.007	45.812	38.5
20	14 35.5	25 56.0	13 00.3	13 24.5
MAR 2	17 08.9	26 37.9	18 19.8	14 08.6
12	19 17.0	27 08.5	23 43.1	14 50.1
22	20 56.4	27 26.7	29 09.0	15 28.1
APR 1	22 03.3	27R31.5	04♉36.9	16 01.8
11	22 34.2	27 22.3	10 05.9	16 30.6
21	22R26.7	26 59.0	15 35.2	16 53.9
MAY 1	21 39.9	26 22.0	21 04.5	17 11.2
11	20 16.3	25 32.4	26 33.0	17 22.1
21	18 22.3	24 32.2	02♊00.2	17 26.4
31	16 08.3	23 23.6	07 25.8	17R24.2
JUN 10	13 48.3	22 10.1	12 49.2	17 15.4
20	11 36.9	20 55.0	18 09.9	17 00.7
30	09 46.6	19 42.0	23 27.8	16 40.5
JUL 10	08 26.6	18 34.7	28 42.0	16 15.6
20	07 41.4	17 36.1	03 52.2	15 47.1
30	07D32.0	16 48.6	08 57.9	15 16.2
AUG 9	07 57.1	16 13.9	13 58.4	14 44.2
19	08 53.4	15 53.1	18 52.9	14 12.5
29	10 17.6	15D46.5	23 40.7	13 42.3
SEP 8	12 06.0	15 54.0	28 20.6	13 15.1
18	14 15.2	16 14.9	02♌51.5	12 52.0
28 16	42.116	48.507	119.12	33.9
OCT 8	19 24.2	17 33.6	11 19.7	12 21.7
18	22 18.8	18 29.0	15 13.1	12 15.8
28	25 24.0	19 33.5	18 49.2	12D16.6
NOV 7	28 38.1	20 45.5	22 04.7	12 24.1
17	01♑59.4	22 03.9	24 56.0	12 38.2
27	05 26.5	23 27.2	27 18.2	12 58.5
DEC 7	08 58.1	24 53.9	29 06.4	13 24.5
17	12 32.9	26 22.7	00♍15.4	13 55.7
27	16 10.0	27 52.2	00 39.6	14 31.3
JAN 6	19♑48.1	29♐21.0	00R15.9	15♒10.5
JAN 1	25S52.2	57S13.7	03S03.9	11S40.9
21	28 09.9	58 06.2	00N37.0	11 20.6
FEB 10	30 03.9	59 11.5	04 35.0	10 56.0
MAR 2	31 40.0	60 27.9	08 38.1	10 29.2
22	33 05.0	61 52.3	12 34.4	1002.6
APR 11	34 22.9	63 18.0	16 12.1	09 38.4
MAY 1	35 26.7	64 34.5	19 20.2	09 19.1
21	35 54.2	65 28.7	21 49.4	09 06.5
JUN 10	35 23.3	65 48.7	23 32.2	09 01.9
30	34 02.8	65 30.5	24 24.6	09 05.7
JUL 20	32 29.9	64 40.5	24 25.9	09 17.2
AUG 9	31 15.1	63 32.2	23 39.8	09 34.4
29	30 27.1	62 20.1	22 13.1	09 54.3
SEP 18	29 59.5	61 15.1	20 15.8	10 14.0
OCT 8	29 41.5	60 23.4	18 00.1	10 30.2
28	29 22.3	59 47.7	15 40.1	10 40.7
NOV 17	28 53.3	59 28.3	13 32.1	10 44.0
DEC 7	28 08.5	59 24.8	11 54.7	10 39.4
27	27S04.9	59S36.3	11 07.2	10S27.3

1958	Diana 78	Hidalgo 944	Urania 30	Chiron 2060
JAN 1	17♑59.0	28♐36.800	R33.814	♒50.5
11	21 37.2	00♑04.6	29♌45.9	15 31.2
21	25 15.1	01 29.6	28 11.7	16 14.2
31	28 51.4	02 50.1	26 00.0	16 58.6
FEB 10	02♒25.2	04 04.7	23 26.6	17 43.6
20	05 55.4	05 12.0	20 51.0	18 28.2
MAR 2	09 20.9	06 10.2	18 33.6	19 11.6
12	12 40.3	06 58.1	16 49.8	19 52.8
22	15 52.6	07 34.1	15 48.1	20 31.1
APR 1	18 56.2	07 56.9	15D31.5	21 05.7
11	21 49.5	08 05.5	15 57.9	21 35.9
21	24 30.7	07R59.0	17 02.8	22 01.2
MAY 1	26 57.6	07 37.0	18 41.4	22 20.8
11	29 08.0	06 59.9	20 48.2	22 34.6
21	00♓59.2	06 08.5	23 18.7	22 42.0
31	02 28.1	05 04.8	26 09.1	22R43.2
JUN 10	03 31.6	03 51.5	29 15.6	22 38.0
20	04 06.5	02 31.8	02♍35.6	22 26.8
30	04R09.8	01 09.9	06 06.9	22 09.9
JUL 10	03 39.8	29♐49.9	09 47.4	21 48.1
20	02 36.3	28 35.9	13 35.8	21 22.3
30	01 02.1	27 31.4	17 30.5	20 53.4
AUG 9	29♒03.5	26 39.3	21 30.5	20 22.8
19	26 50.1	26 01.5	25 35.0	19 51.5
29	24 34.5	25 39.2	29 43.0	19 21.1
SEP 8	22 29.8	25D32.8	03♎53.8	18 52.8
18	20 46.9	25 42.0	08 06.8	18 27.8
28	19 34.4	26 06.2	12 21.2	18 07.2
OCT 8	18 56.3	26 44.4	16 36.5	17 51.7
18	18D53.8	27 35.3	20 52.0	17 42.2
28	19 25.9	28 37.5	25 07.0	17D38.9
NOV 7	20 29.8	29 49.6	29 20.7	17 42.2
17	22 02.3	01♑10.2	03♏32.5	17 51.9
27	24 00.1	02 37.7	07 41.3	18 07.9
DEC 7	26 19.8	04 10.6	11 46.2	18 29.7
17	28 58.5	05 47.6	15 46.1	18 56.8
27	01♓53.5	07 27.1	19 39.5	19 28.7
JAN 6	05♓02.3	09♑07.7	23♏25.3	20♒04.5
JAN 1	26S45.9	59S41.5	11N05.0	10S23.2
21	25 18.6	60 11.6	11 36.0	10 03.0
FEB 10	23 35.1	60 57.0	12 53.1	09 38.2
MAR 2	21 39.8	61 57.9	14 11.6	09 10.9
22	19 38.7	63 13.8	14 53.0	08 43.4
APR 11	17 38.7	64 41.6	14 46.4	08 18.2
MAY 1	15 48.0	66 13.9	13 56.0	07 57.6
21	14 15.5	67 38.4	12 28.0	07 43.5
JUN 10	13 11.0	68 38.7	10 27.9	07 37.6
30	12 43.2	69 00.2	08 00.9	07 40.3
JUL 20	12 56.0	68 38.2	05 12.2	07 51.0
AUG 9	13 40.7	67 40.7	02 07.2	08 08.0
29	14 33.1	66 23.1	01S08.7	08 28.6
SEP 18	15 04.8	65 00.5	04 30.0	08 49.4
OCT 8	15 00.4	63 43.5	07 50.8	09 07.2
28	14 18.4	62 37.8	11 05.5	09 19.5
NOV 17	13 02.3	61 45.4	14 08.3	09 24.4
DEC 7	11 15.5	61 06.9	16 53.9	09 21.1
27	09S02.9	60S42.5	19S17.7	09S10.0

1959	Diana 78	Hidalgo 944	Urania 30	Chiron 2060
JAN 1	03♓26.3	08♑17.4	21♏33.5	19♒46.1
11	06 41.3	09 58.0	25 14.8	20 23.6
21	10 07.1	11 37.5	28 45.6	21 03.8
31	13 42.1	13 14.3	02♐03.8	21 45.9
FEB 10	17 25.0	14 47.1	05 07.2	22 29.0
20	21 14.2	16 14.1	07 52.5	23 12.2
MAR 2	25 08.7	17 33.9	10 16.8	23 54.6
12	29 07.6	18 44.8	12 16.1	24 35.4
22	03♈09.9	19 45.1	13 46.2	25 13.8
APR 1	07 14.8	20 33.3	14 42.9	25 49.1
11	11 21.7	21 07.6	15 02.0	26 20.4
21	15 29.8	21 26.7	14R40.6	26 47.2
MAY 1	19 38.5	21R29.4	13 38.1	27 08.8
11	23 47.2	21 14.8	11 57.6	27 25.0
21	27 55.0	20 42.6	09 47.5	27 35.2
31	02♉01.6	19 53.4	07 21.2	27 39.3
JUN 10	06 06.0	18 48.6	04 55.0	27R37.3
20	10 07.2	17 30.8	02 45.9	27 29.3
30	14 04.6	16 03.8	01 07.1	27 15.6
JUL 10	17 56.8	14 31.9	00 06.6	26 56.8
20	21 42.3	13 00.4	29D48.2	26 33.6
30	25 19.6	11 34.1	00♐10.9	26 06.8
AUG 9	28 46.5	10 17.7	01 12.0	25 37.7
19	02♊00.4	09 15.0	02 47.7	25 07.4
29	04 58.4	08 28.5	04 53.5	24 37.2
SEP 8	07 36.4	07 59.9	07 25.7	24 08.2
18	09 50.0	07 49.9	10 20.7	23 41.9
28	11 34.0	07D58.1	13 35.2	23 19.3
OCT 8	12 42.3	08 23.8	17 06.7	23 01.2
18	13 09.5	09 05.8	20 52.9	22 48.6
28	12R51.2	10 02.6	24 51.8	22 41.9
NOV 7	11 45.9	11 12.7	29 01.9	22D41.4
17	09 58.7	12 34.4	03♑21.7	22 47.2
27	07 41.5	14 06.0	07 49.8	22 59.3
DEC 7	05 13.7	15 45.9	12 25.5	23 17.3
17	02 58.3	17 32.5	17 07.4	23 40.7
27	01 15.3	19 24.3	21 54.8	24 09.1
JAN 6	00♊18.7	21♑19.7	26♑47.0	24♒41.7
JAN 1	08S23.4	60S38.6	19S49.9	09S06.0
21	05 38.8	60 32.6	21 42.4	08 46.3
FEB 10	02 34.5	60 42.9	23 09.2	08 21.7
MAR 2	00N45.0	61 11.7	24 12.0	07 54.2
22	04 14.9	62 00.9	24 54.2	07 26.2
APR 11	07 50.3	63 11.4	25 18.1	07 00.1
MAY 1	11 26.4	64 41.0	25 20.9	06 38.4
21	14 58.7	66 22.6	24 54.2	06 23.1
JUN 10	18 22.9	68 02.3	23 57.6	06 15.7
30	21 35.4	69 20.1	22 54.2	06 17.1
JUL 20	24 33.7	69 55.9	22 14.2	06 26.8
AUG 9	27 16.6	69 39.7	22 09.3	06 43.3
29	29 44.9	68 37.7	22 32.7	07 04.1
SEP 18	32 01.2	67 06.6	23 09.6	07 25.8
OCT 8	34 06.6	65 23.3	23 44.6	07 45.0
28	35 51.8	63 39.7	24 04.0	07 58.9
NOV 17	36 45.4	62 02.3	23 56.7	08 05.4
DEC 7	36 09.0	60 34.4	23 14.6	08 03.7
27	34N16.6	59S17.6	21S53.3	07S53.7

1960	Diana 78	Hidalgo 944	Urania 30	Chiron 2060
JAN 1	00R40.6	20♑21.6	24♑20.4	24♒24.9
11	00♊09.9	22 18.3	29 14.6	24 59.4
21	00D31.6	24 16.2	04♒12.3	25 36.9
31	01 43.2	26 14.1	09 13.1	26 16.7
FEB 10	03 39.7	28 10.4	14 16.0	26 57.9
20	06 14.6	00♒03.5	19 20.6	27 39.7
MAR 1	09 22.0	01 51.9	24 26.3	28 21.1
11	12 56.6	03 34.0	29 32.4	29 01.4
21	16 53.5	05 08.2	04♓38.4	29 39.7
31	21 08.9	06 32.6	09 43.8	00♓15.4
APR 10	25 39.6	07 45.3	14 47.9	00 47.5
20	00♋22.5	08 44.6	19 50.0	01 15.6
30	05 15.7	09 28.5	24 49.5	01 39.0
MAY 10	10 17.1	09 55.0	29 45.5	01 57.2
20	15 25.1	10R02.5	04♈37.2	02 09.8
30	20 38.4	09 49.7	09 23.4	02 16.6
JUN 9	25 55.9	09 15.7	14 02.9	02R17.4
19	01♌16.4	08 21.0	18 34.3	02 12.4
29	06 39.4	07 06.8	22 55.7	02 01.6
JUL 9	12 03.8	05 36.4	27 04.7	01 45.6
19	17 29.1	03 54.4	00♉58.9	01 24.9
29	22 54.8	02 06.4	04 34.7	01 00.4
AUG 8	28 20.2	00 19.3	07 47.9	00 32.9
18	03♍44.8	28♑39.7	10 34.0	00 03.7
28	09 08.1	27 13.6	12 47.0	29♒34.0
SEP 7	14 29.6	26 05.5	14 20.5	29 04.9
17	19 48.8	25 18.4	15 08.6	28 37.7
27	25 05.2	24 53.9	15R05.8	28 13.5
OCT 7	00♎18.1	24D52.3	14 11.1	27 53.4
17	05 26.9	25 12.6	12 29.5	27 38.1
27	10 31.0	25 53.6	10 14.0	27 28.4
NOV 6	15 29.3	26 53.5	07 46.7	27 24.6
16	20 21.1	28 10.3	05 31.8	27D27.0
26	25 05.3	29 42.0	03 50.8	27 35.5
DEC 6	29 40.6	01♒26.7	02 57.9	27 50.0
16	04♏05.7	03 22.3	02D57.5	28 10.0
26	08 18.9	05 27.1	03 48.8	28 35.2
JAN 5	12♏18.1	07♒39.4	05♉26.6	29♒04.8
JAN 1	33N44.4	59S00.3	21S26.6	07S50.0
21	31 49.5	57 59.8	19 15.4	07 31.1
FEB 10	30 34.6	57 15.1	16 27.6	07 06.8
MAR 1	29 53.2	56 49.4	13 08.7	06 39.3
21	29 23.0	56 46.9	09 25.9	06 11.0
APR 10	28 41.5	57 11.4	05 27.2	05 44.3
30	27 31.5	58 05.5	01 20.9	05 21.7
MAY 20	25 42.9	59 29.2	02N44.5	05 05.2
JUN 9	23 11.9	61 16.6	06 40.8	04 56.4
29	20 00.2	63 13.7	10 19.7	04 56.4
JUL 19	16 13.5	64 57.4	13 33.6	05 04.9
AUG 8	11 59.1	65 59.5	16 15.1	05 20.8
28	07 25.6	65 59.4	18 17.1	05 41.4
SEP 17	02 41.5	64 55.4	19 30.1	06 03.7
OCT 7	02S04.9	63 03.1	19 41.2	06 24.0
27	06 46.0	60 43.1	18 42.7	06 39.4
NOV 16	11 14.5	58 11.7	17 02.6	06 47.6
DEC 6	15 24.8	55 38.9	15 44.7	06 47.4
26	19S12.1	53S10.7	15N31.2	06S38.8

1961	Diana 78	Hidalgo 944	Urania 30	Chiron 2060
JAN 1	10♏44.2	06♒45.7	04♉42.3	28♒52.4
11	14 34.1	09 01.7	06 44.7	29 24.4
21	18 06.3	11 22.6	09 22.9	29 59.7
31	21 17.9	13 46.9	12 31.0	00♓37.5
FEB 10	24 05.6	16 13.0	16 03.0	01 17.0
20	26 25.6	18 39.8	19 54.5	01 57.3
MAR 2	28 13.7	21 05.6	24 01.7	02 37.7
12	29 25.7	23 29.1	28 21.2	03 17.3
22	29 57.6	25 48.9	02♊50.6	03 55.3
APR 1	29R46.6	28 03.2	07 27.6	04 30.8
11	28 52.8	00♓10.6	12 10.5	05 03.3
21	27 19.5	02 09.3	16 58.0	05 32.1
MAY 1	25 15.6	03 57.3	21 48.7	05 56.5
11	22 54.7	05 32.6	26 41.7	06 16.0
21	20 32.8	06 52.7	01♋36.3	06 30.2
31	18 26.4	07 55.2	06 31.6	06 38.8
JUN 10	16 47.7	08 37.5	11 27.1	06R41.7
20	15 44.5	08 56.8	16 22.4	06 38.7
30	15 19.8	08R50.8	21 16.9	06 30.1
JUL 10	15D32.5	08 17.8	26 10.2	06 16.3
20	16 20.1	07 16.9	01♌02.1	05 57.6
30	17 38.5	05 49.7	05 51.9	05 34.8
AUG 9	19 23.5	03 59.7	10 39.4	05 08.9
19	21 31.5	01 53.1	15 24.2	04 40.8
29	23 58.8	29♒39.0	20 05.7	04 11.7
SEP 8	26 42.2	27 27.3	24 43.4	03 42.7
18	29 39.4	25 28.1	29 16.7	03 15.2
28	02♐48.0	23 49.8	03♍44.8	02 50.2
OCT 8	06 05.9	22 38.3	08 06.9	02 28.7
18	09 31.8	21 56.9	12 21.8	02 11.8
28	13 03.9	21D46.4	16 28.2	02 00.0
NOV 7	16 41.1	22 05.8	20 24.9	01 53.9
17	20 22.3	22 53.3	24 09.7	01D53.8
27	24 06.0	24 06.1	27 40.6	01 59.7
DEC 7	27 51.6	25 41.4	00♎55.1	02 11.5
17	01♑37.9	27 36.7	03 49.9	02 28.9
27	05 24.0	29 49.1	06 21.4	02 51.5
JAN 6	09♑08.8	02♓16.2	08♎25.7	03♓18.7
JAN 1	20S15.5	52S27.7	15N40.4	06S34.6
21	23 29.7	50 10.8	16 45.3	06 16.3
FEB 10	26 18.4	48 06.5	18 24.4	05 52.4
MAR 2	28 42.3	46 18.4	20 14.3	05 25.0
22	30 38.4	44 51.1	21 55.7	04 56.6
APR 11	31 52.8	43 49.7	23 13.8	04 29.5
MAY 1	32 01.7	43 19.9	23 57.9	04 06.3
21	30 57.5	43 27.0	24 01.6	03 49.1
JUN 10	29 14.0	44 14.7	23 22.6	03 39.4
30	27 42.1	45 41.9	22 01.9	03 38.5
JUL 20	26 49.9	47 38.8	20 03.6	03 46.2
AUG 9	26 39.0	49 40.9	17 33.5	04 01.4
29	26 58.7	51 09.5	14 38.7	04 21.9
SEP 18	27 35.4	51 24.7	11 27.1	04 44.5
OCT 8	28 16.6	50 07.3	08 06.8	05 05.6
28	28 52.0	47 29.3	04 46.3	05 22.0
NOV 17	29 13.5	43 58.5	01 34.5	05 31.4
DEC 7	29 15.9	40 00.0	01S19.1	05 32.4
27	28S56.3	35S49.7	03S43.8	05S24.7

1962	Diana 78	Hidalgo 944	Urania 30	Chiron 2060
JAN 1	07♑16.6	01♓00.9	07♎27.3	03♓04.6
11	11 00.5	03 34.8	09 16.1	03 33.9
21	14 41.5	06 20.2	10 30.4	04 06.8
31	18 18.8	09 15.5	11 06.0	04 42.5
FEB 10	21 51.3	12 19.1	10R58.8	05 20.2
20	25 17.6	15 29.5	10 07.5	05 59.2
MAR 2	28 36.6	18 45.4	08 34.5	06 38.6
12	01♒46.7	22 05.7	06 27.1	07 17.5
22	04 46.4	25 29.4	03 59.0	07 55.3
APR 1	07 34.0	28 55.4	01 27.2	08 31.0
11	10 07.3	02♈23.0	29♍09.2	09 04.1
21	12 24.0	05 51.2	27 19.8	09 33.8
MAY 1	14 21.7	09 19.2	26 07.9	09 59.5
11	15 57.3	12 46.2	25 37.2	10 20.6
21	17 07.7	16 11.2	25D47.4	10 36.7
31	17 50.0	19 33.3	26 35.0	10 47.6
JUN 10	18R01.2	22 51.4	27 56.2	10 52.8
20	17 39.3	26 04.2	29 46.4	10R52.4
30	16 44.0	29 10.3	02♎01.1	10 46.3
JUL 10	15 17.3	02♉07.8	04 37.1	10 35.0
20	13 25.0	04 54.4	07 30.7	10 18.6
30	11 15.7	07 27.6	10 39.4	09 58.0
AUG 9	09 01.1	09 43.8	14 00.9	09 33.8
19	06 54.0	11 38.8	17 33.2	09 07.0
29	05 05.6	13 07.7	21 14.8	08 38.7
SEP 8	03 44.6	14 04.1	25 04.4	08 10.0
18	02 56.2	14R21.5	29 00.6	07 42.2
28	02D41.9	13 53.1	03♏02.6	07 16.3
OCT 8	03 01.4	12 33.7	07 09.4	06 53.4
18	03 52.2	10 23.4	11 20.2	06 34.6
28	05 11.5	07 29.4	15 34.2	06 20.5
NOV 7	06 56.1	04 10.0	19 50.8	06 11.8
17	09 02.6	00 52.6	24 09.0	06D08.9
27	11 28.1	28♈05.9	28 28.3	06 11.8
DEC 7	14 10.0	26 13.9	02♐47.9	06 20.6
17	17 05.7	25 29.7	07 06.9	06 35.1
27	20 13.2	25D56.5	11 24.6	06 54.8
JAN 6	23♒30.7	27♈31.9	15♐40.0	07♓19.4
JAN 1	28S47.9	34S46.4	04S14.0	05S21.5
21	28 01.2	30 32.5	05 45.2	05 04.2
FEB 10	26 56.4	26 19.5	06 17.8	04 41.0
MAR 2	25 38.8	22 09.2	05 42.1	04 14.0
22	24 15.8	18 02.4	04 07.7	03 45.5
APR 11	22 56.2	13 59.9	02 16.2	03 18.2
MAY 1	21 49.7	10 01.7	00 58.0	02 54.3
21	21 06.8	06 07.4	00 38.8	02 36.0
JUN 10	20 55.8	02 15.2	01 18.1	02 25.1
30	21 18.7	01N39.1	02 44.9	02 22.8
JUL 20	22 03.8	05 42.7	04 46.8	02 29.2
AUG 9	22 45.3	10 08.9	07 12.5	02 43.4
29	22 58.6	15 17.5	09 52.7	03 03.4
SEP 18	22 36.9	21 32.1	12 38.7	03 26.1
OCT 8	21 46.2	28 53.6	15 22.6	03 48.0
28	20 32.6	36 06.0	17 56.8	04 05.6
NOV 17	18 58.2	41 02.1	20 14.1	04 16.5
DEC 7	17 03.1	43 36.4	22 08.2	04 19.0
27	14S47.3	45N34.2	23S34.1	04S12.7

1963	Diana 78	Hidalgo 944	Urania 30	Chiron 2060
JAN 1	21♒50.9	26♈36.0	13♐32.7	07♓06.6
11	25 12.6	28 43.5	17 46.5	07 33.3
21	28 41.9	01♉49.4	21 56.7	08 03.9
31	02♓17.3	05 47.0	26 02.0	08 37.6
FEB 10	05 57.6	10 29.2	00♑01.1	09 13.6
20	09 41.6	15 49.2	03 52.7	09 51.3
MAR 2	13 28.5	21 40.9	07 35.1	10 29.6
12	17 17.1	27 58.0	11 06.3	11 07.9
22	21 06.7	04♊34.1	14 24.2	11 45.4
APR 1	24 56.5	11 23.5	17 26.2	12 21.2
11	28 45.5	18 19.9	20 09.0	12 54.7
21	02♈33.0	25 18.2	22 29.4	13 25.2
MAY 1	06 18.2	02♋13.7	24 22.9	13 52.1
11	10 00.0	09 02.4	25 45.1	14 14.7
21	13 37.6	15 41.4	26 31.5	14 32.6
31	17 09.8	22 08.7	26R37.4	14 45.4
JUN 10	20 35.2	28 22.9	26 00.8	14 52.8
20	23 52.6	04♌23.4	24 42.1	14R54.7
30	26 59.9	10 10.1	22 46.8	14 51.1
JUL 10	29 55.0	15 43.0	20 26.7	14 42.1
20	02♉35.5	21 02.5	17 58.4	14 28.0
30	04 58.1	26 09.2	15 40.8	14 09.4
AUG 9	06 59.3	01♍03.4	13 51.1	13 47.0
19	08 34.9	05 45.7	12 40.5	13 21.7
29	09 40.1	10 16.4	12D15.4	12 54.3
SEP 8	10 10.4	14 35.6	12 36.4	12 26.0
18	10R01.4	18 43.7	13 40.8	11 58.1
28	09 11.0	22 40.4	15 24.8	11 31.5
OCT 8	07 40.6	26 25.4	17 43.4	11 07.6
18	05 36.8	29 58.4	20 31.9	10 47.1
28	03 12.3	03♎18.6	23 46.5	10 31.0
NOV 7	00 45.1	06 25.0	27 23.1	10 20.0
17	28♈33.8	09 16.5	01♒18.8	10 14.4
27	26 54.7	11 51.5	05 30.9	10D14.6
DEC 7	25 58.5	14 08.3	09 56.9	10 20.7
17	25D49.1	16 04.9	14 35.0	10 32.4
27	26 26.7	17 38.8	19 23.6	10 49.5
JAN 6	27♈47.6	18♎47.8	24♒20.9	11♓11.5
JAN 1	14S10.2	46N07.8	23S50.7	04S09.9
21	11 30.0	48 53.4	24 37.4	03 53.7
FEB 10	08 33.1	52 23.7	24 52.9	03 31.3
MAR 2	05 22.7	56 08.5	24 40.9	03 04.8
22	02 02.9	59 13.6	24 08.4	02 36.5
APR 11	01N22.2	60 30.7	23 25.6	02 08.9
MAY 1	04 48.3	59 13.9	22 45.4	01 44.4
21	08 11.5	55 35.3	22 21.6	01 25.2
JUN 10	11 28.2	50 27.3	22 23.9	01 13.2
30	14 34.8	44 40.9	22 48.8	01 09.5
JUL 20	17 28.2	38 50.2	23 15.2	01 14.6
AUG 9	20 04.6	33 14.2	23 22.8	01 27.7
29	22 18.1	28 02.6	23 10.8	01 47.1
SEP 18	23 56.9	23 20.7	22 44.5	02 09.7
OCT 8	24 39.6	19 11.3	22 01.9	02 32.1
28	24 07.6	15 36.7	20 55.6	02 50.8
NOV 17	22 37.4	12 38.8	19 17.9	03 03.1
DEC 7	21 05.2	10 19.7	17 04.1	03 07.1
27	20N19.5	08N41.0	14S13.2	03S02.3

1964		Diana 78	Hidalgo 944	Urania 30	Chiron 2060
JAN	1	27♈02.0	18♎16.6	21♒51.2	10♓59.9
	11	28 42.8	19 12.2	26 52.5	11 24.2
	21	00♉59.8	19 39.4	02♓00.9	11 52.6
	31	03 48.0	19R36.4	07 15.1	12 24.4
FEB	10	07 02.6	19 02.5	12 34.2	12 58.8
	20	10 40.0	17 58.7	17 57.4	13 35.0
MAR	1	14 36.4	16 28.0	23 23.9	14 12.4
	11	18 48.9	14 35.9	28 52.8	14 50.0
	21	23 15.2	12 30.2	04♈23.7	15 27.2
	31	27 53.2	10 20.4	09 55.7	16 03.0
APR	10	02♊41.1	08 15.7	15 28.3	16 36.9
	20	07 37.5	06 24.4	21 01.1	17 08.1
	30	12 41.1	04 53.0	26 33.3	17 35.9
MAY	10	17 50.8	03 44.9	02♉04.5	17 59.9
	20	23 05.8	03 01.8	07 34.2	18 19.4
	30	28 25.0	02 43.4	13 01.7	18 34.0
JUN	9	03♋47.9	02D48.0	18 26.5	18 43.5
	19	09 13.8	03 13.8	23 48.0	18 47.6
	29	14 41.9	03 58.2	29 05.4	18R46.2
JUL	9	20 11.8	04 58.8	04♊18.1	18 39.5
	19	25 42.9	06 13.3	09 24.9	18 27.6
	29	01♌14.4	07 39.5	14 24.9	18 11.1
AUG	8	06 46.2	09 15.3	19 17.1	17 50.5
	18	12 17.3	10 59.0	23 59.6	17 26.5
	28	17 47.2	12 48.9	28 30.8	17 00.2
SEP	7	23 15.4	14 43.6	02♋48.7	16 32.5
	17	28 40.9	16 41.6	06 50.4	16 04.6
	27	04♍03.1	18 41.4	10 32.9	15 37.7
OCT	7	09 21.3	20 42.0	13 52.4	15 12.8
	17	14 34.1	22 41.8	16 44.0	14 50.9
	27	19 40.6	24 39.7	19 02.6	14 33.1
NOV	6	24 39.5	26 34.3	20 42.1	14 19.9
	16	29 29.2	28 24.1	21 36.2	14 12.0
	26	04♎07.9	00♏07.8	21R40.2	14D09.7
DEC	6	08 33.7	01 43.7	20 51.6	14 13.1
	16	12 43.8	03 10.3	19 13.7	14 22.3
	26	16 35.6	04 25.8	16 57.7	14 36.8
JAN	5	20♎05.6	05♏28.7	14♋21.7	14♓56.5
JAN	1	20N17.7	08N22.8	13S24.9	02S59.8
	21	20 46.0	07 34.4	09 52.1	02 44.8
FEB	10	21 59.9	07 21.4	05 52.7	02 23.3
MAR	1	23 39.9	07 31.6	01 35.0	01 57.3
	21	25 26.4	07 44.8	02N51.6	01 29.3
APR	10	27 01.1	07 38.6	07 16.9	01 01.6
	30	28 07.8	07 00.2	11 30.9	00 36.6
MAY	20	28 33.2	05 49.6	15 23.6	00 16.7
JUN	9	28 08.2	04 13.8	18 45.7	00 03.5
	29	26 48.4	02 20.4	21 29.2	00N01.4
JUL	19	24 34.8	00 15.8	23 28.5	00S02.3
AUG	8	21 32.6	01S55.8	24 41.7	00 14.3
	28	17 50.1	04 10.9	25 11.3	00 32.8
SEP	17	13 37.6	06 26.7	25 04.8	00 55.2
OCT	7	09 05.7	08 40.8	24 35.2	01 18.0
	27	04 25.1	10 50.8	24 00.0	01 37.6
NOV	16	00S14.3	12 54.5	23 37.8	01 51.2
DEC	6	04 43.0	14 49.7	23 41.1	01 56.7
	26	08S53.0	16S34.2	24N01.4	01S53.4

1965		Diana 78	Hidalgo 944	Urania 30	Chiron 2060
JAN	1	18♎44.4	05♏05.2	15R25.0	14♓48.0
	11	21 59.3	05 59.6	12♋48.3	15 10.5
	21	24 45.8	06 38.6	10 28.9	15 37.1
	31	26 58.9	07 00.8	08 44.7	16 07.3
FEB	10	28 33.4	07R05.1	07 46.6	16 40.4
	20	29 24.4	06 50.7	07D37.7	17 15.5
MAR	2	29R28.2	06 17.8	08 15.2	17 51.9
	12	28 43.6	05 27.4	09 34.5	18 28.9
	22	27 14.6	04 21.4	11 29.3	19 05.6
APR	1	25 10.6	03 03.1	13 53.7	19 41.3
	11	22 47.7	01 36.4	16 42.6	20 15.2
	21	20 25.5	00 06.3	19 51.3	20 46.8
MAY	1	18 22.0	28♎37.7	23 16.1	21 15.2
	11	16 51.5	27 15.3	26 54.0	21 39.9
	21	16 01.7	26 03.3	00♌42.4	22 00.5
	31	15D54.1	25 04.5	04 39.3	22 16.4
JUN	10	16 27.1	24 21.0	08 43.2	22 27.2
	20	17 36.4	23 53.9	12 52.5	22 32.9
	30	19 17.1	23 43.1	17 06.2	22R33.1
JUL	10	21 24.7	23D48.3	21 23.5	22 28.1
	20	23 54.7	24 08.4	25 43.3	22 17.8
	30	26 43.3	24 42.1	00♍05.1	22 02.8
AUG	9	29 47.4	25 28.1	04 28.4	21 43.6
	19	03♏04.2	26 24.9	08 52.3	21 20.8
	29	06 31.6	27 31.1	13 16.7	20 55.4
SEP	8	10 07.7	28 45.1	17 40.8	20 28.3
	18	13 50.8	00♏05.4	22 04.0	20 00.6
	28	17 39.6	01 30.9	26 25.9	19 33.5
OCT	8	21 33.1	03 00.0	00♎45.8	19 08.1
	18	25 29.9	04 31.4	05 03.0	18 45.4
	28	29 29.2	06 03.8	09 16.8	18 26.4
NOV	7	03♐30.2	07 35.9	13 26.1	18 11.8
	17	07 31.9	09 06.1	17 30.0	18 02.3
	27	11 33.6	10 33.3	21 27.4	17 58.2
DEC	7	15 34.3	11 55.9	25 16.5	17D59.7
	17	19 33.1	13 12.5	28 55.9	18 06.9
	27	23 29.2	14 21.6	02♏23.7	18 19.6
JAN	6	27♐21.6	15♏21.6	05♏37.3	18♓37.4
JAN	1	10S03.2	17S03.2	24N06.9	01S50.7
	21	13 37.4	18 30.0	24 11.7	01 36.5
FEB	10	16 34.3	19 39.4	23 57.0	01 15.7
MAR	2	18 40.3	20 27.2	23 33.0	00 50.3
	22	19 35.1	20 49.3	23 01.4	00 22.5
APR	11	19 08.3	20 45.5	22 15.3	00N05.2
MAY	1	17 48.6	20 21.6	21 07.6	00 30.4
	21	16 33.2	19 50.1	19 33.6	00 50.8
JUN	10	16 01.9	19 24.6	17 32.1	01 04.5
	30	16 22.9	19 15.1	15 04.4	01 10.3
JUL	20	17 27.3	19 26.0	12 13.9	01 07.4
AUG	9	19 01.9	19 57.6	09 04.8	00 56.3
	29	20 54.0	20 47.7	05 42.4	00 38.3
SEP	18	22 52.3	21 52.9	02 12.0	00 16.2
OCT	8	24 47.2	23 09.9	01S20.5	00S06.8
	28	26 30.4	24 35.4	04 49.3	00 27.0
NOV	17	27 55.4	26 06.1	08 08.4	00 41.4
DEC	7	28 57.6	27 39.4	11 12.0	00 47.9
	27	29S34.5	29S12.4	13S54.7	00S45.5

1966		Diana 78	Hidalgo 944	Urania 30	Chiron 2060
JAN	1	25♐26.0	14♏52.8	04♏02.4	18♓27.9
	11	29 16.1	15 47.8	07 08.1	18 48.1
	21	03♑01.1	16 31.5	09 55.7	19 12.7
	31	06 39.6	17 02.6	12 21.5	19 41.1
FEB	10	10 10.4	17 20.0	14 22.1	20 12.6
	20	13 32.1	17R22.8	15 53.0	20 46.5
MAR	2	16 43.2	17 10.4	16 49.8	21 22.0
	12	19 41.7	16 43.0	17 08.6	21 58.2
	22	22 25.8	16 01.3	16R46.4	22 34.6
APR	1	24 53.1	15 06.8	15 42.7	23 10.3
	11	27 01.0	14 01.9	14 01.1	23 44.5
	21	28 46.6	12 49.6	11 49.8	24 16.6
MAY	1	00♒06.8	11 33.5	09 22.4	24 45.9
	11	00 58.5	10 17.4	06 55.5	25 11.8
	21	01 18.7	09 05.0	04 45.1	25 33.8
	31	01R05.1	07 59.7	03 04.4	25 51.3
JUN	10	00 17.3	07 04.4	02 01.3	26 04.0
	20	28♑56.8	06 21.0	01D38.6	26 11.6
	30	27 08.7	05 50.9	01 56.0	26R13.9
JUL	10	25 01.7	05 34.6	02 50.3	26 10.9
	20	22 47.0	05D32.0	04 17.6	26 02.8
	30	20 37.5	05 42.8	06 13.9	25 49.7
AUG	9	18 44.9	06 06.1	08 35.2	25 32.2
	19	17 18.3	06 40.9	11 18.0	25 11.0
	29	16 23.3	07 26.0	14 19.3	24 46.7
SEP	8	16 02.1	08 20.2	17 36.4	24 20.4
	18	16D14.3	09 22.2	21 07.3	23 53.0
	28	16 58.0	10 30.8	24 50.0	23 25.8
OCT	8	18 10.0	11 44.5	28 42.9	22 59.7
	18	19 47.2	13 02.2	02♐44.8	22 36.0
	28	21 46.6	14 22.5	06 54.3	22 15.5
NOV	7	24 04.9	15 44.1	11 10.5	21 59.2
	17	26 39.5	17 05.8	15 32.5	21 47.6
	27	29 28.1	18 26.0	19 59.4	21 41.3
DEC	7	02♒28.3	19 43.5	24 30.3	21D40.6
	17	05 38.4	20 56.9	29 04.6	21 45.4
	27	08 56.6	22 04.8	03♑41.4	21 55.8
JAN	6	12♒21.4	23♏05.7	08♑20.2	22♓11.4
JAN	1	29S39.7	29S35.3	14S31.5	00S43.6
	21	29 45.6	31 03.7	16 41.3	00 30.7
FEB	10	29 30.7	32 23.6	18 19.9	00 10.9
MAR	2	29 01.5	33 29.3	19 22.4	00N13.9
	22	28 26.6	34 13.5	19 41.7	00 41.3
APR	11	27 56.6	34 30.2	19 09.5	01 08.9
MAY	1	27 42.1	34 17.6	17 49.0	01 34.4
	21	27 51.5	33 42.0	16 10.3	01 55.4
JUN	10	28 25.3	32 55.5	14 57.4	02 10.1
	30	29 09.3	32 11.7	14 35.8	02 17.1
JUL	20	29 36.0	31 41.0	15 05.7	02 15.5
AUG	9	29 25.8	31 29.0	16 14.8	02 05.6
	29	28 42.1	31 37.3	17 48.1	01 48.6
SEP	18	27 39.8	32 04.8	19 31.5	01 26.9
OCT	8	26 28.0	32 49.0	21 12.4	01 03.8
	28	25 07.7	33 47.2	22 39.9	00 42.9
NOV	17	23 35.8	34 56.3	23 44.3	00 27.4
DEC	7	21 48.7	36 13.5	24 17.8	00 19.6
	27	19S44.4	37S36.1	24S15.0	00N20.5

1967	Diana 78	Hidalgo 944	Urania 30	Chiron 2060
JAN 1	10♒38.2	22♏36.2	06♑00.6	22♓03.0
11	14 05.9	23 33.2	10 40.1	22 21.0
21	17 38.1	24 21.0	15 20.5	22 43.7
31	21 13.8	24 58.6	20 00.9	23 10.3
FEB 10	24 51.9	25 24.5	24 40.9	23 40.3
20	28 31.2	25 37.8	29 19.5	24 12.9
MAR 2	02♓10.9	25R37.9	03♒56.1	24 47.4
12	05 50.0	25 24.2	08 29.8	25 23.0
22	09 27.5	24 57.1	12 59.7	25 59.0
APR 1	13 02.5	24 17.2	17 24.8	26 34.6
11	16 34.0	23 26.0	21 43.9	27 09.1
21	20 00.9	22 25.6	25 55.7	27 41.7
MAY 1	23 22.1	21 18.8	29 58.7	28 11.8
11	26 36.4	20 08.5	03♓51.0	28 38.8
21	29 42.1	18 58.3	07 30.1	29 02.1
31	02♈37.6	17 51.5	10 53.7	29 21.2
JUN 10	05 21.0	16 50.9	13 58.2	29 35.6
20	07 49.8	15 59.3	16 39.5	29 45.1
30	10 01.4	15 18.4	18 53.3	29 49.5
JUL 10	11 52.7	14 49.6	20 34.1	29R48.5
20	13 19.7	14 33.4	21 36.0	29 42.4
30	14 19.0	14D30.1	21R54.4	29 31.3
AUG 9	14 46.2	14 39.2	21 25.3	29 15.6
19	14R38.1	15 00.1	20 09.7	28 55.8
29	13 52.7	15 32.0	18 14.7	28 32.8
SEP 8	12 30.5	16 13.8	15 54.3	28 07.3
18	10 36.5	17 04.4	13 29.9	27 40.4
28	08 20.4	18 02.5	11 23.5	27 13.1
OCT 8	05 55.9	19 07.0	09 53.5	26 46.6
18	03 39.4	20 16.6	09 11.6	26 22.0
28	01 45.7	21 30.0	09D21.4	26 00.3
NOV 7	00 26.1	22 46.0	10 21.5	25 42.3
17	29♓46.9	24 03.2	12 07.5	25 28.8
27	29D49.9	25 20.3	14 33.1	25 20.5
DEC 7	00♈33.8	26 36.2	17 32.8	25 17.5
17	01 55.3	27 49.2	21 01.1	25D20.1
27	03 50.1	28 58.1	24 53.0	25 28.2
JAN 6	06♈14.2	00♐01.5	29♓04.6	25♓41.7
JAN 1	19S10.6	37S57.2	24S08.3	00N22.1
21	16 44.6	39 22.2	23 17.1	00 33.7
FEB 10	14 03.3	40 44.5	21 48.3	00 52.5
MAR 2	11 09.9	41 58.4	19 46.2	01 16.5
22	08 08.3	42 56.2	17 17.3	01 43.5
APR 11	05 03.0	43 29.7	14 29.8	02 11.0
MAY 1	01 58.7	43 33.3	11 33.1	02 36.7
21	00N59.8	43 08.0	08 37.9	02 58.3
JUN 10	03 47.3	42 22.0	05 56.4	03 13.9
30	06 18.0	41 28.2	03 43.3	03 22.0
JUL 20	08 24.6	40 39.3	02 15.9	03 21.7
AUG 9	09 57.5	40 04.1	01 52.0	03 13.0
29	10 44.1	39 47.3	02 38.2	02 57.0
SEP 18	10 33.6	39 50.3	04 07.4	02 35.9
OCT 8	09 31.9	40 11.9	05 22.1	02 12.8
28	08 13.3	40 50.0	05 37.9	01 51.4
NOV 17	07 21.9	41 42.3	04 44.2	01 34.9
DEC 7	07 23.1	42 46.0	02 49.2	01 25.7
27	08N20.5	43S58.8	00S06.0	01N25.3

1968	Diana 78	Hidalgo 944	Urania 30	Chiron 2060
JAN 1	04♈58.7	29♏30.6	26♓56.5	25♓34.3
11	07 36.0	00♐30.7	01♈16.7	25 50.3
21	10 36.7	01 23.3	05 51.3	26 11.1
31	13 57.4	02 07.0	10 37.9	26 36.0
FEB 10	17 35.4	02 40.5	15 34.2	27 04.5
20	21 28.1	03 02.8	20 38.2	27 35.8
MAR 1	25 33.6	03 12.8	25 48.5	28 09.4
11	29 50.0	03R10.0	01♉03.5	28 44.3
21	04♉15.7	02 54.2	06 21.9	29 19.9
31	08 49.8	02 25.6	11 43.0	29 55.4
APR 10	13 31.0	01 45.0	17 05.7	00♈30.1
20	18 18.3	00 54.0	22 29.2	01 03.2
30	23 11.1	29♏54.5	27 53.0	01 34.1
MAY 10	28 08.7	28 49.1	03♊16.5	02 02.1
20	03♊10.5	27 41.0	08 38.9	02 26.6
30	08 15.9	26 33.3	14 00.1	02 47.2
JUN 9	13 24.4	25 29.2	19 19.5	03 03.3
19	18 35.5	24 31.4	24 36.5	03 14.7
29	23 48.8	23 42.4	29 51.0	03 21.0
JUL 9	29 03.8	23 03.9	05♋02.4	03R22.1
19	04♋19.9	22 37.2	10 10.3	03 18.0
29	09 36.7	22 22.7	15 14.4	03 08.8
AUG 8	14 53.4	22D20.8	20 13.8	02 54.8
18	20 09.5	22 31.0	25 08.2	02 36.7
28	25 24.1	22 52.7	29 56.8	02 14.9
SEP 7	00♌36.3	23 25.1	04♌38.7	01 50.3
17	05 45.1	24 07.2	09 13.0	01 24.0
27	10 49.4	24 57.9	13 38.4	00 56.8
OCT 7	15 47.3	25 55.9	17 53.3	00 30.0
17	20 37.6	27 00.1	21 56.3	00 04.6
27	25 17.9	28 09.3	25 44.9	29♓41.8
NOV 6	29 45.6	29 22.2	29 16.4	29 22.3
16	03♍58.2	00♐37.4	02♍28.0	29 07.1
26	07 51.8	01 53.8	05 15.7	28 56.7
DEC 6	11 22.2	03 09.8	07 35.1	28 51.7
16	14 24.6	04 24.3	09 21.4	28D52.1
26	16 53.0	05 35.9	10 29.1	28 58.1
JAN 5	18♍41.4	06♐43.2	10♍53.6	29♓09.4
JAN 1	08N42.7	44S18.1	00N40.7	01N26.5
21	10 38.3	45 38.2	04 04.6	01 36.9
FEB 10	13 06.9	47 00.3	07 45.4	01 54.6
MAR 1	15 56.2	48 19.0	11 29.6	02 17.8
21	18 54.1	49 27.0	15 04.1	02 44.2
APR 10	21 48.9	50 15.1	18 16.7	03 11.6
30	24 28.6	50 35.4	20 56.4	03 37.4
MAY 20	26 42.0	50 24.4	22 54.4	03 59.6
JUN 9	28 18.3	49 46.2	24 04.5	04 16.0
29	29 08.7	48 51.8	24 23.9	04 25.1
JUL 19	29 07.2	47 54.2	23 53.8	04 26.0
AUG 8	28 12.1	47 04.6	22 38.7	04 18.6
28	26 26.0	46 30.1	20 46.0	04 03.6
SEP 17	23 55.9	46 14.3	18 25.5	03 43.2
OCT 7	20 52.3	46 17.5	15 48.4	03 20.3
27	17 27.9	46 38.6	13 07.2	02 58.5
NOV 16	13 57.2	47 15.6	10 36.1	02 41.0
DEC 6	10 35.9	48 06.5	08 31.2	02 30.7
26	07N40.3	49S09.0	07N10.3	02N28.9

1969	Diana 78	Hidalgo 944	Urania 30	Chiron 2060
JAN 1	18♍03.2	06♐16.9	10♍49.3	29♓04.3
11	19 24.8	07 20.9	10R46.0	29 18.7
21	19 57.0	08 18.4	09 55.2	29 38.0
31	19R36.8	09 08.1	08 19.6	00♈01.6
FEB 10	18 26.2	09 48.5	06 08.0	00 29.0
20	16 33.4	10 18.6	03 35.1	00 59.4
MAR 2	14 15.6	10 37.2	01 00.5	01 32.2
12	11 54.9	10 43.5	28♌43.6	02 06.6
22	09 52.9	10R37.0	26 59.0	02 41.8
APR 1	08 27.2	10 17.5	25 55.9	03 17.2
11	07 46.8	09 45.5	25D36.6	03 51.9
21	07D53.8	09 01.9	25 59.5	04 25.3
MAY 1	08 45.7	08 08.4	27 00.6	04 56.7
11	10 17.0	07 07.1	28 34.9	05 25.4
21	12 22.2	06 00.6	00♍37.5	05 50.8
31	14 55.7	04 52.3	03 04.0	06 12.4
JUN 10	17 52.2	03 45.1	05 50.2	06 29.8
20	21 07.6	02 42.3	08 53.0	06 42.5
30	24 38.4	01 46.5	12 09.6	06 50.2
JUL 10	28 21.5	01 00.0	15 37.6	06R52.7
20	02♎14.7	00 24.5	19 15.4	06 50.1
30	06 16.1	00 01.0	23 01.1	06 42.3
AUG 9	10 23.8	29♏50.0	26 53.5	06 29.8
19	14 36.8	29D51.6	00♎51.6	06 12.8
29	18 53.8	00♐05.4	04 54.4	05 52.0
SEP 8	23 13.9	00 30.6	09 00.9	05 28.2
18	27 36.2	01 06.4	13 10.6	05 02.3
28	02♏00.0	01 51.8	17 22.6	04 35.3
OCT 8	06 24.5	02 45.6	21 36.3	04 08.4
18	10 49.1	03 46.6	25 51.1	03 42.5
28	15 13.2	04 53.6	00♏06.0	03 18.9
NOV 7	19 35.9	06 05.2	04 20.7	02 58.4
17	23 56.9	07 20.3	08 34.2	02 42.0
27	28 15.0	08 37.5	12 45.7	02 30.2
DEC 7	02♐29.7	09 55.5	16 54.3	02 23.6
17	06 40.1	11 12.9	20 59.0	02D22.5
27	10 45.1	12 28.3	24 58.6	02 27.0
JAN 6	14♐43.9	13♐40.5	28♏51.9	02♈36.8
JAN 1	06N55.3	49S29.7	06N57.4	02N30.0
21	04 57.9	50 44.0	06 58.4	02 39.5
FEB 10	03 58.8	52 04.0	08 03.2	02 56.4
MAR 2	03 50.5	53 25.2	09 38.7	03 19.0
22	03 59.3	54 41.0	10 54.7	03 45.1
APR 11	03 46.5	55 42.0	11 21.2	04 12.2
MAY 1	02 53.3	56 18.4	10 54.8	04 38.0
21	01 18.3	56 23.3	09 42.8	05 00.3
JUN 10	00S52.7	55 56.7	07 53.5	05 17.2
30	03 32.1	55 06.5	05 34.2	05 26.9
JUL 20	06 31.8	54 05.5	02 51.6	05 28.6
AUG 9	09 44.2	53 06.3	00S07.9	05 22.0
29	13 01.7	52 18.4	03 18.4	05 07.8
SEP 18	16 17.4	51 46.9	06 33.8	04 47.9
OCT 8	19 24.5	51 33.9	09 48.2	04 25.2
28	22 16.8	51 39.3	12 55.4	04 03.2
NOV 17	24 48.7	52 01.5	15 49.6	03 45.3
DEC 7	26 55.9	52 39.0	18 25.4	03 34.2
27	28S36.1	53S29.9	20S38.2	03N31.5

1970	Diana 78	Hidalgo 944	Urania 30	Chiron 2060
JAN 1	12♐45.4	13♐04.9	26♏56.1	02♈31.2
11	16 40.6	14 14.9	00♐45.7	02 43.7
21	20 27.6	15 19.4	04 26.6	03 01.1
31	24 05.1	16 17.1	07 57.0	03 23.1
FEB 10	27 31.6	17 06.7	11 14.8	03 49.0
20	00♑45.1	17 46.7	14 17.5	04 18.2
MAR 2	03 43.7	18 16.1	17 02.3	04 50.0
12	06 25.1	18 33.6	19 25.7	05 23.8
22	08 46.4	18 R 38.4	21 24.0	05 58.6
APR 1	10 44.9	18 30.2	22 53.1	06 33.9
11	12 17.2	18 08.6	23 48.5	07 08.8
21	13 19.9	17 34.2	24 06.0	07 42.6
MAY 1	13 50.1	16 48.2	23 R 42.9	08 14.7
11	13 R 44.9	15 51.9	22 38.5	08 44.4
21	13 03.7	14 48.0	20 56.3	09 11.1
31	11 47.8	13 39.2	18 44.9	09 34.2
JUN 10	10 02.0	12 28.8	16 17.9	09 53.1
20	07 55.2	11 20.0	13 52.6	10 07.6
30	05 39.0	10 16.2	11 45.3	10 17.2
JUL 10	03 26.6	09 20.0	10 09.4	10 21.7
20	01 30.8	08 33.8	09 13.3	10 R 21.1
30	00 00.9	07 59.3	08 D 59.6	10 15.3
AUG 9	29♐02.9	07 37.4	09 27.8	10 04.5
19	28 39.2	07 28.6	10 34.9	09 49.2
29	28 D 49.2	07 D 32.8	12 16.5	09 29.8
SEP 8	29 31.0	07 49.7	14 28.8	09 07.1
18	00♑41.5	08 18.3	17 07.6	08 41.9
28	02 17.2	08 57.9	20 09.2	08 15.2
OCT 8	04 15.1	09 47.2	23 30.7	07 48.1
18	06 31.8	10 45.1	27 09.2	07 21.7
28	09 04.8	11 50.3	01♑02.5	06 57.2
NOV 7	11 51.5	13 01.5	05 08.7	06 35.4
17	14 49.8	14 17.4	09 26.1	06 17.4
27	17 57.8	15 36.7	13 53.2	06 03.8
DEC 7	21 13.9	16 58.0	18 29.0	05 55.2
17	24 36.4	18 20.0	23 12.0	05 52.0
27	28 04.0	19 41.3	28 01.5	05 D 54.3
JAN 6	01♒35.5	21♐00.4	02♒56.6	06♈02.2
JAN 1	28 S 56.9	53 S 44.6	21 S 07.4	03 N 32.2
21	30 03.7	54 50.1	22 47.7	03 40.3
FEB 10	30 47.7	56 05.1	24 01.9	03 56.2
MAR 2	31 15.9	57 26.3	24 52.6	04 17.9
22	31 37.6	58 48.4	25 25.1	04 43.4
APR 11	32 03.1	60 02.8	25 45.6	05 10.2
MAY 1	32 40.1	60 58.8	25 56.7	05 36.1
21	33 27.6	61 25.6	25 53.1	05 58.7
JUN 10	34 08.4	61 17.8	25 24.6	06 16.3
30	34 15.1	60 38.8	24 35.6	06 27.0
JUL 20	33 35.8	59 39.5	23 50.6	06 29.9
AUG 9	32 27.0	58 33.6	23 29.3	06 24.5
29	31 13.3	57 32.9	23 32.2	06 11.5
SEP 18	30 06.2	56 45.2	23 47.7	05 52.4
OCT 8	29 04.8	56 14.3	24 00.6	05 30.0
28	28 02.2	56 01.1	23 57.2	05 07.8
NOV 17	26 51.4	56 05.2	23 26.1	04 49.1
DEC 7	25 26.8	56 25.2	22 19.6	04 36.9
27	23 S 45.4	57 S 00.0	20 S 34.0	04 N 33.0

1971	Diana 78	Hidalgo 944	Urania 30	Chiron 2060
JAN 1	29♑49.3	20♐21.2	00♒28.4	05♈57.6
11	03♒22.3	21 38.8	05 25.9	06 08.1
21	06 57.3	22 52.1	10 27.7	06 23.7
31	10 33.5	23 59.7	15 33.2	06 44.0
FEB 10	14 09.6	25 00.2	20 41.6	07 08.5
20	17 44.7	25 52.2	25 52.3	07 36.4
MAR 2	21 17.9	26 34.2	01♓04.8	08 07.3
12	24 47.9	27 05.0	06 18.3	08 40.4
22	28 13.8	27 23.5	11 32.5	09 14.8
APR 1	01♓34.5	27 R 28.6	16 46.7	09 50.0
11	04 48.7	27 19.9	22 00.3	10 25.0
21	07 55.0	26 57.2	27 12.9	10 59.3
MAY 1	10 51.9	26 20.9	02♈23.8	11 32.1
11	13 37.5	25 32.1	07 32.2	12 02.8
21	16 10.0	24 32.6	12 37.5	12 30.6
31	18 26.8	23 24.8	17 38.9	12 55.1
JUN 10	20 25.4	22 11.9	22 35.1	13 15.7
20	22 02.7	20 57.4	27 25.4	13 32.0
30	23 15.2	19 44.8	02♉08.0	13 43.5
JUL 10	23 59.5	18 37.8	06 41.4	13 50.0
20	24 R 12.3	17 39.2	11 03.7	13 R 51.3
30	23 50.8	16 51.5	15 12.2	13 47.5
AUG 9	22 54.4	16 16.6	19 03.8	13 38.6
19	21 24.8	15 55.4	22 35.2	13 25.0
29	19 27.6	15 D 48.2	25 41.3	13 07.0
SEP 8	17 12.7	15 55.1	28 17.2	12 45.5
18	14 53.1	16 15.3	00♊16.8	12 21.1
28	12 42.9	16 48.2	01 33.2	11 54.8
OCT 8	10 55.2	17 32.5	02 00.8	11 27.8
18	09 39.1	18 27.1	01 R 35.5	11 00.9
28	09 00.0	19 30.8	00 18.3	10 35.5
NOV 7	08 D 59.3	20 42.0	28♉18.3	10 12.6
17	09 35.8	21 59.6	25 52.5	09 53.0
27	10 46.7	23 22.1	23 24.9	09 37.6
DEC 7	12 28.3	24 48.2	21 19.9	09 27.1
17	14 37.0	26 16.3	19 55.6	09 21.9
27	17 09.3	27 45.2	19 22.0	09 D 22.2
JAN 6	20♓01.8	29♐13.3	19 D 40.9	09♈28.0
JAN 1	23 S 17.2	57 S 10.9	20 S 01.3	04 N 33.3
21	21 14.2	58 02.9	17 26.9	04 40.2
FEB 10	18 56.0	59 07.5	14 17.4	04 55.0
MAR 2	16 26.2	60 23.4	10 39.0	05 15.8
22	13 49.5	61 47.0	06 39.4	05 40.6
APR 11	11 11.2	63 12.2	02 26.7	06 07.1
MAY 1	08 37.3	64 28.4	01 N 50.5	06 33.0
21	06 14.6	65 22.6	06 03.6	06 55.9
JUN 10	04 10.6	65 43.1	10 04.1	07 14.1
30	02 34.1	65 25.7	13 44.3	07 25.7
JUL 20	01 34.9	64 36.6	16 57.1	07 29.7
AUG 9	01 21.7	63 29.1	19 37.3	07 25.6
29	01 54.8	62 17.6	21 41.8	07 13.7
SEP 18	02 56.5	61 12.8	23 09.1	06 55.5
OCT 8	03 53.8	60 21.2	23 56.2	06 33.6
28	04 17.1	59 45.4	23 54.5	06 11.3
NOV 17	03 53.5	59 25.9	22 56.5	05 52.0
DEC 7	02 43.4	59 22.2	21 27.9	05 38.8
27	00 S 52.3	59 S 33.5	20 N 23.6	05 N 33.6

1972	Diana 78	Hidalgo 944	Urania 30	Chiron 2060
JAN 1	18♓33.2	28♐29.4	19 D 25.1	09♈24.4
11	21 34.7	29 56.7	20♉09.0	09 32.9
21	24 52.5	01♑21.1	21 39.0	09 46.6
31	28 24.0	02 41.2	23 48.9	10 05.3
FEB 10	02♈07.3	03 55.4	26 31.6	10 28.2
20	06 00.8	05 02.3	29 41.5	10 55.0
MAR 1	10 03.0	06 00.3	03♊13.3	11 24.9
11	14 12.6	06 48.0	07 02.6	11 57.3
21	18 28.6	07 23.9	11 06.0	12 31.3
31	22 50.1	07 46.8	15 20.6	13 06.3
APR 10	27 16.2	07 55.5	19 43.8	13 41.5
20	01♉46.4	07 R 49.3	24 14.0	14 16.2
30	06 19.9	07 27.7	28 49.4	14 49.7
MAY 10	10 56.2	06 51.2	03♋28.8	15 21.3
20	15 35.0	06 00.5	08 11.2	15 50.4
30	20 15.5	04 57.6	12 55.5	16 16.3
JUN 9	24 57.4	03 45.0	17 41.2	16 38.5
19	29 40.3	02 26.2	22 27.7	16 56.5
29	04♊23.4	01 05.1	27 14.3	17 10.0
JUL 9	09 06.4	29♐45.7	02♌00.5	17 18.5
19	13 48.6	28 32.1	06 46.1	17 21.8
29	18 29.0	27 28.0	11 30.4	17 R 20.0
AUG 8	23 07.0	26 35.9	16 13.3	17 13.1
18	27 41.3	25 57.9	20 54.1	17 01.2
28	02♋10.5	25 35.3	25 32.4	16 44.8
SEP 7	06 33.3	25 D 28.4	00♍07.9	16 24.5
17	10 47.3	25 37.1	04 39.9	16 01.0
27	14 50.2	26 00.6	09 07.5	15 35.3
OCT 7	18 39.2	26 37.9	13 30.4	15 08.3
17	22 10.2	27 27.9	17 47.3	14 41.2
27	25 18.9	28 29.2	21 57.1	14 15.0
NOV 6	28 00.1	29 40.4	25 58.9	13 50.9
16	00♌07.2	01♑00.0	29 50.7	13 29.9
26	01 34.0	02 26.5	03♎30.9	13 12.8
DEC 6	02 14.0	03 58.4	06 57.3	13 00.4
16	02 R 02.5	05 34.5	10 07.1	12 53.1
26	01 00.1	07 13.0	12 57.4	12 D 51.4
JAN 5	29♋13.4	08♑52.6	15♎24.6	12♈55.1
JAN 1	00 S 18.9	59 S 38.6	20 N 15.9	05 N 33.7
21	02 N 13.8	60 08.5	20 19.4	05 39.3
FEB 10	05 11.6	60 53.6	21 04.5	05 52.8
MAR 1	08 27.1	61 54.1	22 08.0	06 12.7
21	11 52.9	63 09.4	23 08.4	06 36.9
APR 10	15 21.5	64 36.5	23 49.5	07 03.0
30	18 45.6	66 08.1	24 00.1	07 28.7
MAY 20	21 57.5	67 31.8	23 33.8	07 52.0
JUN 9	24 49.9	68 31.6	22 28.8	08 10.6
29	27 15.9	68 53.2	20 46.2	08 23.1
JUL 19	29 09.6	68 31.8	18 30.1	08 28.2
AUG 8	30 27.1	67 35.1	15 46.0	08 25.3
28	31 07.7	66 18.4	12 40.5	08 14.6
SEP 17	31 15.2	64 56.7	09 20.6	07 57.4
OCT 7	30 58.5	63 40.4	05 53.7	07 36.0
27	30 31.9	62 35.2	02 27.5	07 13.7
NOV 16	30 13.0	61 43.4	00 S 50.4	06 54.0
DEC 6	30 16.3	61 05.5	03 51.6	06 39.8
26	30 N 37.6	60 S 41.6	06 S 27.2	06 N 33.4

1973		Diana 78	Hidalgo 944	Urania 30	Chiron 2060
JAN	1	00R00.6	08♑12.7	14♎28.8	12D52.9
	11	27♋54.6	09 52.4	16 40.0	13♈00.0
	21	25 34.0	11 30.7	18 21.3	13 12.4
	31	23 22.9	13 06.3	19 28.2	13 29.8
FEB	10	21 43.4	14 37.6	19 56.0	13 51.8
	20	20 50.3	16 03.1	19R41.5	14 17.7
MAR	2	20D48.7	17 21.3	18 43.9	14 46.9
	12	21 38.2	18 30.4	17 05.7	15 18.7
	22	23 13.8	19 28.8	14 55.6	15 52.4
APR	1	25 28.9	20 15.1	12 26.9	16 27.4
	11	28 17.2	20 47.4	09 56.7	17 02.7
	21	01♌32.7	21 04.5	07 42.3	17 37.8
MAY	1	05 10.0	21R05.3	05 57.0	18 11.8
	11	09 05.3	20 48.8	04 49.6	18 44.2
	21	13 14.7	20 15.1	04 23.1	19 14.1
	31	17 35.4	19 24.6	04D36.6	19 41.1
JUN	10	22 05.3	18 19.0	05 27.2	20 04.6
	20	26 42.1	17 01.0	06 50.7	20 24.0
	30	01♍24.5	15 34.3	08 42.7	20 38.9
JUL	10	06 11.3	14 03.3	10 59.3	20 48.9
	20	11 01.1	12 33.1	13 36.7	20 53.9
	30	15 53.3	11 08.5	16 31.7	20R53.6
AUG	9	20 47.1	09 54.1	19 41.9	20 48.1
	19	25 41.7	08 53.4	23 04.8	20 37.6
	29	00♎36.6	08 08.9	26 38.8	20 22.4
SEP	8	05 31.3	07 42.2	00♏22.2	20 03.1
	18	10 25.1	07D33.8	04 13.5	19 40.4
	28	15 17.7	07 43.3	08 11.8	19 15.0
OCT	8	20 08.5	08 10.1	12 16.1	18 48.1
	18	24 56.8	08 52.8	16 25.2	18 20.8
	28	29 42.3	09 50.0	20 38.6	17 54.1
NOV	7	04♏24.2	11 00.3	24 55.3	17 29.2
	17	09 01.8	12 21.9	29 14.6	17 07.1
	27	13 34.5	13 53.1	03♐35.8	16 48.8
DEC	7	18 01.1	15 32.5	07 58.2	16 35.0
	17	22 20.8	17 18.3	12 20.9	16 26.2
	27	26 32.5	19 09.1	16 43.3	16 22.9
JAN	6	00♐34.8	21♑03.3	21♐04.4	16D25.2
JAN	1	30N42.5	60S37.3	07S07.6	06N33.2
	21	30 26.5	60 32.6	08 55.1	06 38.0
FEB	10	29 02.0	60 44.3	09 52.1	06 50.7
MAR	2	26 51.1	61 14.4	09 46.4	07 09.9
	22	24 24.8	62 04.9	08 35.9	07 33.5
APR	11	21 50.6	63 16.3	06 45.8	07 59.2
MAY	1	19 03.3	64 46.2	05 06.1	08 24.8
	21	15 57.2	66 27.2	04 16.6	08 47.9
JUN	10	12 30.2	68 05.0	04 28.0	09 06.8
	30	08 43.9	69 19.8	05 32.2	09 19.8
JUL	20	04 42.1	69 52.0	07 16.2	09 25.5
AUG	9	00 29.9	69 33.1	09 27.3	09 23.4
	29	03S46.7	68 29.9	11 54.5	09 13.5
SEP	18	08 01.9	66 59.0	14 28.1	08 57.1
OCT	8	12 09.4	65 17.0	16 59.3	08 36.2
	28	16 03.4	63 35.3	19 19.7	08 14.1
NOV	17	19 38.4	62 00.2	21 21.7	07 54.1
DEC	7	22 50.0	60 34.6	22 58.7	07 39.4
	27	25S35.3	59S20.4	24S05.4	07N32.3

1974		Diana 78	Hidalgo 944	Urania 30	Chiron 2060
JAN	1	28♏34.9	20♑05.8	18♐54.1	16D23.3
	11	02♐31.9	22 01.2	23 14.2	16♈28.4
	21	06 17.2	23 57.7	27 31.9	16 38.9
	31	09 48.9	25 53.9	01♑46.0	16 54.6
FEB	10	13 04.8	27 48.3	05 55.4	17 15.0
	20	16 02.7	29 39.3	09 59.1	17 39.6
MAR	2	18 39.3	01♒25.5	13 55.5	18 07.8
	12	20 51.7	03 05.2	17 43.1	18 38.9
	22	22 36.5	04 36.7	21 20.3	19 12.2
APR	1	23 49.6	05 58.2	24 44.6	19 47.0
	11	24 27.8	07 07.9	27 53.6	20 22.5
	21	24R28.3	08 04.0	00♒44.5	20 58.0
MAY	1	23 49.6	08 44.4	03 13.4	21 32.7
	11	22 33.8	09 07.5	05 16.6	22 06.0
	21	20 45.9	09R11.6	06 49.3	22 37.2
	31	18 35.6	08 55.4	07 46.6	23 05.7
JUN	10	16 16.4	08 18.5	08R04.1	23 30.8
	20	14 02.2	07 21.2	07 38.5	23 52.0
	30	12 06.6	06 05.4	06 29.4	24 08.9
JUL	10	10 39.5	04 34.2	04 41.5	24 21.0
	20	09 46.2	02 52.3	02 25.3	24 28.1
	30	09D28.8	01 05.7	29♑57.4	24R30.0
AUG	9	09 46.1	29♑20.9	27 37.4	24 26.5
	19	10 35.3	27 44.3	25 43.0	24 18.0
	29	11 53.3	26 21.5	24 28.1	24 04.5
SEP	8	13 36.3	25 17.0	23 59.4	23 46.6
	18	15 40.7	24 33.2	24D18.0	23 25.0
	28	18 03.8	24 11.8	25 22.1	23 00.4
OCT	8	20 42.3	24D12.7	27 07.0	22 33.8
	18	23 34.1	24 35.1	29 28.0	22 06.3
	28	26 37.0	25 17.7	02♒20.3	21 39.0
NOV	7	29 49.1	26 18.6	05 39.2	21 13.1
	17	03♑08.9	27 36.0	09 20.9	20 49.7
	27	06 34.8	29 07.8	13 22.2	20 29.7
DEC	7	10 05.4	00♒52.1	17 40.0	20 13.9
	17	13 39.8	02 47.0	22 12.1	20 03.2
	27	17 16.5	04 50.8	26 56.2	19 57.7
JAN	6	20♑54.5	07♒01.7	01♓50.5	19D57.9
JAN	1	26S12.3	59S03.8	24S17.0	07N31.9
	21	28 24.2	58 06.1	24 42.0	07 35.4
FEB	10	30 12.4	57 24.4	24 34.1	07 47.0
MAR	2	31 43.0	57 01.9	23 57.0	08 05.2
	22	33 03.2	57 02.5	22 57.6	08 28.0
APR	11	34 17.9	57 30.1	21 45.9	08 53.2
MAY	1	35 22.3	58 26.9	20 34.5	09 18.5
	21	35 55.8	59 52.5	19 38.4	09 41.8
JUN	10	35 34.3	61 40.3	19 12.7	10 01.1
	30	34 20.6	63 36.0	19 25.6	10 14.8
JUL	20	32 48.9	65 15.8	20 06.9	10 21.5
AUG	9	31 31.3	66 12.7	20 47.2	10 20.5
	29	30 38.6	66 07.6	21 02.3	10 11.9
SEP	18	30 06.0	65 00.8	20 47.6	09 56.5
OCT	8	29 43.1	63 08.3	20 04.2	09 36.4
	28	29 19.2	60 50.2	18 49.6	09 14.5
NOV	17	28 45.6	58 22.1	16 59.9	08 54.2
DEC	7	27 56.5	55 53.5	14 32.8	08 38.8
	27	26S48.8	53S29.9	11S29.0	08N30.5

1975		Diana 78	Hidalgo 944	Urania 30	Chiron 2060
JAN	1	19♑05.4	05♒55.5	29♒22.2	19D57.1
	11	22 43.8	08 09.3	04♓21.0	20♈00.1
	21	26 21.9	10 28.0	09 27.9	20 08.7
	31	29 58.8	12 49.9	14 41.4	20 22.6
FEB	10	03♒33.5	15 13.5	20 00.5	20 41.4
	20	07 04.9	17 37.6	25 24.2	21 04.7
MAR	2	10 31.7	20 00.5	00♈51.4	21 31.9
	12	13 53.0	22 20.9	06 21.4	22 02.2
	22	17 07.4	24 37.4	11 53.6	22 35.0
APR	1	20 13.4	26 48.2	17 27.0	23 09.6
	11	23 09.7	28 52.0	23 01.2	23 45.2
	21	25 54.2	00♓46.7	28 35.5	24 21.1
MAY	1	28 25.2	02 30.5	04♉09.3	24 56.6
	11	00♓40.2	04 01.2	09 42.3	25 30.8
	21	02 36.6	05 16.6	15 13.8	26 03.3
	31	04 11.5	06 14.1	20 43.2	26 33.2
JUN	10	05 21.8	06 51.2	26 10.2	27 00.0
	20	06 04.0	07 05.3	01♊34.0	27 23.1
	30	06R15.5	06R54.4	06 54.2	27 42.0
JUL	10	05 53.7	06 16.8	12 10.0	27 56.3
	20	04 58.1	05 12.2	17 20.7	28 05.6
	30	03 30.9	03 42.5	22 25.4	28 09.6
AUG	9	01 37.1	01 51.4	27 23.3	28R08.4
	19	29♒26.0	29♒45.7	02♋13.0	28 01.9
	29	27 09.7	27 34.1	06 53.2	27 50.3
SEP	8	25 01.1	25 26.3	11 22.3	27 34.0
	18	23 12.5	23 31.9	15 38.0	27 13.6
	28	21 52.7	21 58.7	19 38.1	26 49.8
OCT	8	21 06.9	20 52.0	23 19.6	26 23.7
	18	20D57.1	20 14.8	26 38.4	25 56.1
	28	21 22.3	20D07.5	29 30.7	25 28.4
NOV	7	22 20.2	20 29.2	01♌51.0	25 01.5
	17	23 47.8	21 18.1	03 33.7	24 36.8
	27	25 41.4	22 31.4	04 33.0	24 15.1
DEC	7	27 57.8	24 06.4	04R43.5	23 57.5
	17	00♓33.9	26 00.6	04 02.6	23 44.7
	27	03 26.9	28 11.4	02 32.5	23 37.1
JAN	6	06♓34.4	00♓36.4	00♌21.9	23D35.1
JAN	1	26S28.8	52S55.3	10S37.8	08N29.8
	21	24 57.4	50 43.0	06 54.8	08 32.1
FEB	10	23 09.8	48 43.5	02 48.5	08 42.5
MAR	2	21 10.4	47 00.6	01N31.8	08 59.6
	22	19 04.9	45 38.6	05 56.0	09 21.6
APR	11	17 00.2	44 42.9	10 13.5	09 46.2
MAY	1	15 04.1	44 18.9	14 13.6	10 11.3
	21	13 25.5	44 31.7	17 46.2	10 34.6
JUN	10	12 13.8	45 24.5	20 42.2	10 54.2
	30	11 38.4	46 55.6	22 54.3	11 08.4
JUL	20	11 44.4	48 54.2	24 18.2	11 16.1
AUG	9	12 25.5	50 55.2	24 53.3	11 16.2
	29	13 19.5	52 20.5	24 44.0	11 08.8
SEP	18	13 57.1	52 32.5	23 58.8	10 54.5
OCT	8	13 59.6	51 14.8	22 51.2	10 35.3
	28	13 23.2	48 40.2	21 38.5	10 13.7
NOV	17	12 11.0	45 15.6	20 40.9	09 53.3
DEC	7	10 26.5	41 25.0	20 17.5	09 37.2
	27	08S13.2	37S23.7	20N36.2	09N27.9

1976	Diana 78	Hidalgo 944	Urania 30	Chiron 2060
JAN 1	04♓59.0	29♒22.2	01 R 31.4	23 R35.4
11	08 12.9	01♓53.6	29♋06.4	23 D36.3
21	11 38.1	04 36.0	26 28.6	23♈42.8
31	15 12.9	07 27.9	24 00.0	23 54.9
FEB 10	18 55.8	10 27.6	22 00.7	24 12.1
20	22 45.5	13 33.6	20 43.6	24 34.0
MAR 1	26 40.8	16 44.7	20 13.7	25 00.0
11	00♈40.8	19 59.6	20 D 30.7	25 29.5
21	04 44.4	23 17.3	21 30.3	26 01.8
31	08 51.0	26 36.8	23 06.8	26 36.2
APR 10	12 59.7	29 57.2	25 14.8	27 11.9
20	17 09.9	03♈17.4	27 48.6	27 48.2
30	21 21.0	06 36.5	00♌43.6	28 24.3
MAY 10	25 32.3	09 53.6	03 56.2	28 59.5
20	29 43.2	13 07.6	07 22.9	29 33.2
30	03♉53.0	16 17.3	11 01.1	00♉04.6
JUN 9	08 01.0	19 21.4	14 48.9	00 33.2
19	12 06.4	22 18.3	18 44.3	00 58.2
29	16 08.4	25 06.3	22 45.9	01 19.2
JUL 9	20 05.6	27 42.9	26 52.6	01 35.7
19	23 57.0	00♉05.8	01♍03.4	01 47.3
29	27 40.9	02 11.4	05 17.4	01 53.7
AUG 8	01♊15.3	03 55.8	09 33.9	01 R54.7
18	04 38.0	05 14.5	13 52.2	01 50.4
28	07 46.0	06 01.8	18 11.9	01 40.8
SEP 7	10 35.6	06 R 11.7	22 32.1	01 26.2
17	13 02.8	05 39.1	26 52.5	01 07.2
27	15 02.5	04 19.7	01♎12.4	00 44.5
OCT 7	16 28.9	02 13.8	05 31.2	00 18.9
17	17 16.3	29♈28.7	09 48.3	29♈51.5
27	17 R 19.2	26 19.3	14 03.0	29 23.3
NOV 6	16 35.0	23 08.7	18 14.2	28 55.6
16	15 05.7	20 21.2	22 21.2	28 29.6
26	12 59.9	18 17.4	26 23.0	28 06.3
DEC 6	10 34.8	17 10.6	00♏18.1	27 46.8
16	08 12.3	17 D 05.2	04 05.2	27 31.9
26	06 14.4	18 00.1	07 42.6	27 22.1
JAN 5	04♊58.3	19♈51.3	11♏08.2	27♈17.9
JAN 1	07 S 35.8	36 S 22.7	20 N 45.9	09 N26.9
21	04 51.5	32 18.7	21 28.6	09 28.0
FEB 10	01 47.1	28 16.7	21 53.7	09 37.1
MAR 1	01 N 32.7	24 18.7	21 51.1	09 53.2
21	05 02.8	20 26.1	21 24.9	10 14.3
APR 10	08 38.3	16 40.0	20 36.3	10 38.3
30	12 14.1	13 01.6	19 23.2	11 02.9
MAY 20	15 45.4	09 31.2	17 43.4	11 26.1
JUN 9	19 07.9	06 08.5	15 36.8	11 45.9
29	22 17.7	02 51.6	13 05.4	12 00.7
JUL 19	25 12.0	00 N 23.8	10 12.5	12 09.2
AUG 8	27 49.7	03 46.5	07 02.3	12 10.4
28	30 11.6	07 30.4	03 40.0	12 04.2
SEP 17	32 21.0	11 53.2	00 10.7	11 51.1
OCT 7	34 21.3	16 59.7	03 S 19.9	11 32.8
27	36 08.2	22 11.4	06 46.1	11 11.7
NOV 16	37 16.1	26 27.2	10 02.2	10 51.2
DEC 6	37 02.4	29 46.9	13 02.8	10 34.6
26	35 N 22.4	33 N 00.8	15 S 42.8	10 N24.4

1977	Diana 78	Hidalgo 944	Urania 30	Chiron 2060
JAN 1	05 R 23.0	19♈00.4	09♏47.5	27 R18.9
11	04♊36.6	21 22.6	13 05.1	27 D18.1
21	04 D 42.4	24 32.0	16 07.1	27♈23.2
31	05 39.3	28 23.7	18 50.5	27 33.8
FEB 10	07 22.5	02♉52.6	21 12.1	27 49.8
20	09 45.7	07 54.5	23 07.8	28 10.7
MAR 2	12 43.2	13 25.8	24 33.5	28 35.9
12	16 09.0	19 22.2	25 24.8	29 04.9
22	19 58.2	25 40.1	25 R 37.8	29 36.9
APR 1	24 06.9	02♊15.6	25 09.8	00♉11.2
11	28 31.3	09 04.0	24 00.9	00 47.1
21	03♋08.6	16 01.3	22 14.9	01 23.8
MAY 1	07 56.6	23 02.9	20 01.0	02 00.5
11	12 52.9	00♋04.4	17 33.2	02 36.7
21	17 56.2	07 02.2	15 07.8	03 11.5
31	23 05.0	13 52.9	13 01.3	03 44.2
JUN 10	28 18.0	20 33.8	11 25.7	04 14.2
20	03♌34.4	27 03.0	10 28.4	04 40.8
30	08 53.1	03♌19.2	10 D 12.1	05 03.6
JUL 10	14 13.5	09 21.6	10 35.5	05 21.9
20	19 34.9	15 10.0	11 35.7	05 35.4
30	24 56.7	20 44.1	13 08.9	05 43.7
AUG 9	00♍18.2	26 04.2	15 10.7	05 46.7
19	05 39.2	01♍10.7	17 37.4	05 R44.1
29	10 59.0	06 03.6	20 25.7	05 36.1
SEP 8	16 17.0	10 43.2	23 32.2	05 23.0
18	21 32.9	15 09.8	26 54.7	05 05.1
28	26 46.0	19 23.1	00♐30.9	04 43.2
OCT 8	01♎55.7	23 23.0	04 19.0	04 18.1
18	07 01.6	27 09.1	08 17.5	03 50.7
28	12 02.6	00♎40.6	12 24.9	03 22.3
NOV 7	16 58.2	03 56.7	16 40.1	02 53.9
17	21 47.5	06 56.2	21 02.3	02 26.9
27	26 29.1	09 37.3	25 30.1	02 02.3
DEC 7	01♏02.2	11 58.5	00♑03.0	01 41.3
17	05 25.2	13 57.4	04 40.1	01 24.7
27	09 36.2	15 31.5	09 20.6	01 13.2
JAN 6	13♏33.8	16♎38.6	14♑03.9	01♉07.2
JAN 1	34 N 43.7	34 N 04.0	16 S 26.2	10 N22.8
21	32 40.3	37 58.9	18 33.6	10 23.1
FEB 10	31 10.3	42 29.4	20 12.8	10 31.5
MAR 2	30 12.4	47 18.3	21 21.6	10 46.7
22	29 26.1	51 52.1	21 56.3	11 07.1
APR 11	28 29.6	55 20.4	21 49.8	11 30.5
MAY 1	27 06.2	56 46.9	20 56.7	11 54.6
21	25 06.4	55 40.3	19 29.8	12 17.5
JUN 10	22 26.8	52 19.0	18 06.9	12 37.2
30	19 09.2	47 32.5	17 23.0	12 52.1
JUL 20	15 19.0	42 08.8	17 28.5	13 00.9
AUG 9	11 03.5	36 40.6	18 15.3	13 02.8
29	06 30.6	31 27.4	19 28.3	12 57.4
SEP 18	01 48.6	26 40.1	20 52.5	12 45.2
OCT 8	02 S 54.6	22 25.3	22 14.3	12 27.6
28	07 31.7	18 47.1	23 21.5	12 07.1
NOV 17	11 55.9	15 48.8	24 04.3	11 46.8
DEC 7	16 01.3	13 33.2	24 14.5	11 30.0
27	19 S 43.9	12 N 02.3	23 S 47.1	11 N19.3

1978	Diana 78	Hidalgo 944	Urania 30	Chiron 2060
JAN 1	11♏36.8	16♎08.6	11♑41.9	01 R09.5
11	15 26.7	17 01.1	16 26.4	01 D06.4
21	18 59.3	17 22.7	21 12.5	01♉09.3
31	22 11.9	17 R 12.1	25 59.6	01 17.9
FEB 10	25 01.3	16 28.6	00♒47.2	01 32.0
20	27 23.6	15 13.9	05 34.4	01 51.4
MAR 2	29 15.0	13 32.2	10 20.7	02 15.3
12	00♐31.0	11 30.1	15 05.4	02 43.3
22	01 07.7	09 16.8	19 47.6	03 14.7
APR 1	01 R 02.3	07 02.8	24 26.6	03 48.7
11	00 14.1	04 57.6	29 01.4	04 24.7
21	28♏46.1	03 09.7	03♓31.0	05 01.7
MAY 1	26 46.3	01 44.6	07 54.2	05 39.2
11	24 27.3	00 45.1	12 09.6	06 16.4
21	22 05.2	00 11.8	16 15.3	06 52.5
31	19 56.1	00 D 03.8	20 09.7	07 26.8
JUN 10	18 13.0	00 19.0	23 49.9	07 58.6
20	17 04.5	00 54.9	27 12.8	08 27.4
30	16 33.9	01 48.9	00♈15.2	08 52.4
JUL 10	16 D 40.9	02 58.5	02 52.2	09 13.2
20	17 23.3	04 21.3	04 58.7	09 29.2
30	18 36.8	05 54.9	06 29.3	09 40.2
AUG 9	20 17.7	07 37.6	07 17.6	09 45.7
19	22 22.1	09 27.5	07 R 19.1	09 R45.6
29	24 46.1	11 23.0	06 31.7	09 39.9
SEP 8	27 27.0	13 22.7	04 58.3	09 28.9
18	00♐21.9	15 25.1	02 50.2	09 12.8
28	03 28.5	17 28.9	00 25.7	08 52.3
OCT 8	06 45.0	19 32.8	28♓07.6	08 28.1
18	10 09.5	21 35.6	26 18.3	08 01.1
28	13 40.5	23 36.0	25 12.8	07 32.5
NOV 7	17 16.9	25 32.7	24 D 59.0	07 03.5
17	20 57.3	27 24.1	25 37.6	06 35.3
27	24 40.6	29 08.8	27 04.6	06 09.1
DEC 7	28 26.0	00♏45.4	29 14.5	05 46.2
17	02♑12.1	02 12.1	02♈01.1	05 27.3
27	05 58.2	03 27.3	05 18.1	05 13.4
JAN 6	09♑43.2	04♏29.2	09♈00.6	05♉05.1
JAN 1	20 S 35.6	11 N 46.6	23 S 34.1	11 N17.8
21	23 46.6	11 10.5	22 17.2	11 17.0
FEB 10	26 32.4	11 10.8	20 22.4	11 24.1
MAR 2	28 54.2	11 30.6	17 54.5	11 38.2
22	30 49.6	11 44.0	15 00.0	11 57.6
APR 11	32 06.1	11 26.4	11 46.9	12 20.2
MAY 1	32 20.3	10 28.2	08 23.9	12 43.7
21	31 21.4	08 54.9	05 00.5	13 06.3
JUN 10	29 39.8	06 57.7	01 46.9	13 25.9
30	28 05.9	04 46.0	01 N 05.1	13 41.1
JUL 20	27 09.6	02 26.1	03 21.5	13 50.5
AUG 9	26 54.5	00 02.3	04 45.4	13 53.3
29	27 10.2	02 S 22.5	04 59.1	13 49.0
SEP 18	27 43.4	04 45.8	03 58.5	13 38.0
OCT 8	28 21.5	07 05.5	02 18.9	13 21.6
28	28 54.0	09 19.4	01 05.2	13 01.9
NOV 17	29 12.8	11 25.3	01 00.7	12 41.8
DEC 7	29 12.5	13 21.3	02 09.7	12 24.7
27	28 S 50.3	15 S 05.1	04 N 18.0	12 N13.3

1979	Diana 78	Hidalgo 944	Urania 30	Chiron 2060
JAN 1	07♑50.9	04♏00.0	07♈06.4	05R08.5
11	11 35.0	04 54.6	10 59.9	05♉03.1
21	15 16.5	05 33.5	15 12.0	05D03.6
31	18 54.5	05 55.2	19 39.4	05 10.0
FEB 10	22 27.7	05R58.4	24 19.2	05 22.2
20	25 55.0	05 42.7	29 08.8	05 39.8
MAR 2	29 15.2	05 08.1	04♉06.3	06 02.4
12	02♒26.7	04 15.7	09 10.0	06 29.4
22	05 28.1	03 07.8	14 18.2	07 00.0
APR 1	08 17.6	01 47.5	19 29.9	07 33.7
11	10 53.1	00 19.2	24 44.1	08 09.6
21	13 12.5	28♎47.8	29 59.7	08 47.1
MAY 1	15 13.1	27 18.4	05♊16.1	09 25.3
11	16 52.0	25 55.9	10 32.7	10 03.5
21	18 06.4	24 44.3	15 48.7	10 40.9
31	18 52.9	23 46.4	21 03.9	11 16.9
JUN 10	19 08.6	23 04.3	26 17.6	11 50.6
20	18R51.5	22 38.8	01♋29.5	12 21.5
30	18 00.7	22 29.9	06 39.3	12 49.0
JUL 10	16 38.2	22D37.1	11 46.5	13 12.3
20	14 48.9	22 59.2	16 50.6	13 31.0
30	12 41.1	23 34.9	21 51.5	13 44.7
AUG 9	10 26.6	24 22.9	26 48.3	13 53.0
19	08 17.8	25 21.5	01♌40.9	13R55.7
29	06 26.4	26 29.4	06 28.4	13 52.6
SEP 8	05 01.7	27 45.0	11 10.2	13 43.9
18	04 08.9	29 06.9	15 45.4	13 29.8
28	03D50.5	00♏33.7	20 13.1	13 10.9
OCT 8	04 06.2	02 04.0	24 31.8	12 47.8
18	04 53.5	03 36.6	28 40.3	12 21.5
28	06 10.0	05 10.0	02♍36.7	11 52.9
NOV 7	07 52.1	06 42.8	06 18.6	11 23.4
17	09 56.6	08 13.9	09 43.7	10 54.1
27	12 20.6	09 41.6	12 48.6	10 26.4
DEC 7	15 01.3	11 04.7	15 29.6	10 01.5
17	17 56.1	12 21.6	17 42.5	09 40.4
27	21 03.2	13 30.8	19 22.2	09 24.1
JAN 6	24♒20.3	14♏30.9	20♍23.8	09♉13.2
JAN 1	28S41.3	15S28.9	04N57.1	12N11.5
21	27 52.0	16 54.1	07 53.4	12 09.6
FEB 10	26 44.5	18 00.9	11 08.5	12 15.5
MAR 2	25 24.1	18 45.5	14 26.1	12 28.5
22	23 58.2	19 04.9	17 32.0	12 46.8
APR 11	22 35.2	18 59.4	20 13.3	13 08.4
MAY 1	21 25.1	18 36.0	22 19.2	13 31.3
21	20 38.0	18 07.2	23 41.8	13 53.4
JUN 10	20 22.9	17 46.1	24 16.3	14 12.8
30	20 42.5	17 42.0	24 01.5	14 28.1
JUL 20	21 26.5	17 58.4	22 59.9	14 38.0
AUG 9	22 09.8	18 35.2	21 17.0	14 41.5
29	22 26.9	19 29.8	19 00.4	14 38.3
SEP 18	22 08.9	20 38.9	16 19.6	14 28.5
OCT 8	21 20.7	21 59.0	13 24.8	14 13.2
28	20 08.5	23 26.7	10 27.1	13 54.4
NOV 17	18 34.6	24 59.1	07 38.8	13 34.8
DEC 7	16 39.5	26 33.2	05 13.6	13 17.6
27	14S23.2	28S06.4	03N27.2	13N05.6

1980	Diana 78	Hidalgo 944	Urania 30	Chiron 2060
JAN 1	22♒40.6	14♏02.1	19♍58.1	09R17.9
11	26 02.1	14 57.0	20 38.9	09♉09.9
21	29 31.5	15 40.6	20R35.1	09D07.8
31	03♓07.2	16 11.4	19 44.9	09 11.9
FEB 10	06 47.9	16 28.3	18 10.9	09 22.0
20	10 32.7	16R30.4	16 01.1	09 37.8
MAR 1	14 20.3	16 17.3	13 30.0	09 58.8
11	18 10.0	15 49.0	10 56.1	10 24.6
21	22 00.8	15 06.5	08 37.9	10 54.4
31	25 51.9	14 11.2	06 50.8	11 27.7
APR 10	29 42.5	13 05.5	05 43.5	12 03.5
20	03♈31.8	11 52.6	05 19.1	12 41.3
30	07 18.9	10 36.0	05D36.5	13 20.2
MAY 10	11 03.0	09 19.7	06 31.8	13 59.4
20	14 43.2	08 07.4	08 00.5	14 38.2
30	18 18.3	07 02.5	09 57.8	15 15.8
JUN 9	21 47.1	06 07.7	12 19.2	15 51.6
19	25 08.1	05 25.0	15 00.9	16 24.8
29	28 19.6	04 55.7	17 59.6	16 54.7
JUL 9	01♉19.7	04 40.3	21 12.4	17 20.8
19	04 05.8	04D38.7	24 37.2	17 42.4
29	06 34.8	04 50.4	28 12.0	17 59.1
AUG 8	08 43.4	05 14.6	01♎55.2	18 10.4
18	10 27.4	05 50.2	05 45.6	18 16.0
28	11 42.1	06 36.2	09 41.9	18R15.8
SEP 7	12 22.9	07 31.1	13 43.3	18 09.8
17	12R25.0	08 33.8	17 48.8	17 58.0
27	11 45.8	09 42.9	21 57.7	17 41.0
OCT 7	10 25.5	10 57.1	26 09.2	17 19.4
17	08 29.0	12 15.3	00♏22.6	16 53.9
27	06 08.3	13 35.9	04 37.3	16 25.7
NOV 6	03 39.8	14 57.7	08 52.5	15 55.8
16	01 23.0	16 19.5	13 07.5	15 25.6
26	29♈35.5	17 39.9	17 21.4	14 56.5
DEC 6	28 28.9	18 57.4	21 33.6	14 29.6
16	28D09.4	20 10.8	25 43.0	14 06.2
26	28 37.4	21 18.5	29 48.6	13 47.3
JAN 5	29♈49.8	22♏19.2	03♐49.4	13♉33.6
JAN 1	13S45.9	28S29.3	03N08.6	13N03.6
21	11 04.9	29 57.0	02 34.4	13 00.6
FEB 10	08 07.0	31 15.8	03 10.0	13 05.4
MAR 1	04 55.5	32 19.8	04 41.2	13 17.2
21	01 34.5	33 02.4	06 22.6	13 34.3
APR 10	01N51.9	33 17.5	07 26.5	13 55.0
30	05 19.3	33 04.1	07 33.5	14 17.0
MAY 20	08 43.9	32 28.7	06 46.5	14 38.4
JUN 9	12 02.0	31 43.5	05 15.0	14 57.5
29	15 10.2	31 01.8	03 08.8	15 12.7
JUL 19	18 05.6	30 33.7	00 36.5	15 22.8
AUG 8	20 44.8	30 24.6	02S14.4	15 26.9
28	23 02.8	30 35.6	05 17.0	15 24.7
SEP 17	24 48.9	31 05.4	08 24.7	15 16.0
OCT 7	25 42.6	31 51.7	11 31.1	15 02.0
27	25 21.7	32 51.5	14 29.8	14 44.2
NOV 16	23 55.7	34 01.7	17 14.7	14 25.3
DEC 6	22 18.4	35 19.6	19 39.9	14 08.2
26	21N22.9	36S42.4	21S41.0	13N55.8

1981	Diana 78	Hidalgo 944	Urania 30	Chiron 2060
JAN 1	29♈15.7	21♏55.8	02♐13.7	13R38.4
11	00♉52.9	22 51.7	06 10.9	13♉28.2
21	03 07.0	23 38.2	10 01.0	13 24.1
31	05 52.9	24 14.2	13 42.5	13D26.3
FEB 10	09 06.0	24 38.5	17 13.6	13 34.6
20	12 42.2	24 49.9	20 31.9	13 48.9
MAR 2	16 37.8	24R48.1	23 35.4	14 08.8
12	20 49.9	24 32.5	26 20.9	14 33.7
22	25 16.0	24 03.4	28 45.0	15 03.0
APR 1	29 53.8	23 21.9	00♑44.2	15 36.0
11	04♊41.7	22 29.2	02 13.9	16 11.9
21	09 38.1	21 27.7	03 09.9	16 50.1
MAY 1	14 41.8	20 20.2	03 28.1	17 29.8
11	19 51.6	19 09.8	03R05.1	18 10.1
21	25 06.5	18 00.0	02 00.7	18 50.2
31	00♋25.7	16 53.9	00 18.2	19 29.5
JUN 10	05 48.6	15 54.6	28♐06.3	20 07.2
20	11 14.2	15 04.6	25 39.3	20 42.5
30	16 42.1	14 25.5	23 14.1	21 14.8
JUL 10	22 11.7	13 58.5	21 08.0	21 43.3
20	27 42.3	13 44.4	19 34.5	22 07.6
30	03♌13.4	13D42.9	18 41.4	22 27.0
AUG 9	08 44.5	13 53.8	18D31.9	22 41.0
19	14 14.8	14 16.4	19 05.1	22 49.3
29	19 44.1	14 49.7	20 17.5	22R51.7
SEP 8	25 11.3	15 32.9	22 05.4	22 48.0
18	00♍36.0	16 24.5	24 24.2	22 38.4
28	05 57.3	17 23.6	27 09.8	22 23.2
OCT 8	11 14.4	18 28.8	00♑18.7	22 02.8
18	16 26.2	19 38.9	03 47.4	21 38.2
28	21 31.9	20 52.6	07 33.4	21 10.3
NOV 7	26 29.8	22 08.7	11 34.6	20 40.2
17	01♎18.6	23 25.8	15 48.5	20 09.2
27	05 56.7	24 42.7	20 13.8	19 38.8
DEC 7	10 21.8	25 58.0	24 49.0	19 10.3
17	14 31.7	27 10.4	29 32.7	18 44.9
27	18 23.5	28 18.4	04♒23.8	18 23.7
JAN 6	21♎53.7	29♏20.8	09♒21.4	18♉07.8
JAN 1	21N17.9	37S07.8	22S12.1	13N53.3
21	21 38.8	38 32.4	23 37.7	13 49.8
FEB 10	22 45.3	39 53.7	24 36.1	13 53.8
MAR 2	24 17.8	41 05.8	25 10.7	14 04.7
22	25 56.0	42 01.2	25 27.9	14 20.9
APR 11	27 21.1	42 31.9	25 36.3	14 40.5
MAY 1	28 17.1	42 32.9	25 43.6	15 01.6
21	28 30.9	42 05.8	25 51.1	15 22.1
JUN 10	27 53.9	41 19.5	25 49.0	15 40.4
30	26 22.8	40 26.8	25 26.2	15 55.1
JUL 20	23 59.0	39 40.0	24 50.2	16 04.9
AUG 9	20 48.4	39 07.6	24 21.2	16 09.1
29	16 59.6	38 53.7	24 07.9	16 07.3
SEP 18	12 42.7	38 59.4	24 03.7	15 59.5
OCT 8	08 08.2	39 23.5	23 55.4	15 46.4
28	03 26.4	40 03.8	23 29.5	15 29.7
NOV 17	01S12.8	40 57.6	22 35.1	15 11.7
DEC 7	05 40.6	42 02.6	21 04.9	14 55.1
27	09S49.2	43S16.1	18S56.0	14N42.8

1982		Diana 78	Hidalgo 944	Urania 30	Chiron 2060
JAN	1	20♎11.6	28♏50.4	06♒51.9	18 R15.1
	11	23 29.6	29 49.4	11 52.3	18♉02.0
	21	26 20.3	00♐40.6	16 57.7	17 55.0
	31	28 38.7	01 22.8	22 07.5	17 D54.3
FEB	10	00♏19.8	01 54.6	27 20.8	18 00.1
	20	01 18.7	02 15.1	02♓37.0	18 12.1
MAR	2	01 R31.0	02 23.2	07 55.6	18 30.0
	12	00 55.5	02 R18.6	13 15.7	18 53.4
	22	29♎34.7	02 00.9	18 37.0	19 21.6
APR	1	27 36.6	01 30.6	23 58.9	19 53.9
	11	25 16.4	00 48.5	29 20.6	20 29.7
	21	22 52.4	29♏56.2	04♈41.9	21 08.1
MAY	1	20 43.5	28 55.9	10 02.2	21 48.4
	11	19 04.9	27 50.2	15 20.6	22 29.7
	21	18 05.2	26 42.3	20 36.8	23 11.3
	31	17 D47.7	25 35.2	25 49.9	23 52.5
JUN	10	18 11.1	24 32.1	00♉59.0	24 32.4
	20	19 11.4	23 35.7	06 03.5	25 10.2
	30	20 44.4	22 48.3	11 02.0	25 45.4
JUL	10	22 45.1	22 11.6	15 53.3	26 17.1
	20	25 08.9	21 46.8	20 35.9	26 44.7
	30	27 52.4	21 34.2	25 07.9	27 07.5
AUG	9	00♏51.8	21 D34.0	29 27.0	27 25.2
	19	04 04.6	21 45.9	03♊30.6	27 37.1
	29	07 28.5	22 09.1	07 15.1	27 43.0
SEP	8	11 01.4	22 42.7	10 36.5	27 R42.7
	18	14 41.8	23 25.9	13 30.0	27 36.3
	28	18 28.3	24 17.4	15 49.5	27 23.7
OCT	8	22 19.5	25 16.1	17 29.1	27 05.6
	18	26 14.4	26 20.8	18 22.0	26 42.6
	28	00♐12.2	27 30.2	18 R23.0	26 15.5
NOV	7	04 11.7	28 43.1	17 30.8	25 45.6
	17	08 12.1	29 58.1	15 49.4	25 14.1
	27	12 12.7	01♐14.1	13 31.8	24 42.4
DEC	7	16 12.3	02 29.6	10 59.4	24 12.0
	17	20 10.4	03 43.3	08 36.3	23 44.2
	27	24 05.9	04 53.9	06 45.0	23 20.2
JAN	6	27♐57.8	06♐00.0	05♊39.7	23♉01.2
JAN	1	10 S 47.5	43 S 35.5	18 S 17.7	14 N40.7
	21	14 22.1	44 55.7	15 21.5	14 36.4
FEB	10	17 20.8	46 17.2	11 52.5	14 39.4
MAR	2	19 30.9	47 34.6	07 57.4	14 49.1
	22	20 32.8	48 40.5	03 44.3	15 04.1
APR	11	20 12.6	49 26.0	00 N 38.1	15 22.5
MAY	1	18 53.7	49 43.3	05 00.9	15 42.3
	21	17 32.6	49 29.9	09 14.9	16 01.8
JUN	10	16 52.5	48 50.5	13 11.5	16 19.2
	30	17 04.6	47 56.1	16 42.8	16 33.3
JUL	20	18 01.3	46 59.8	19 42.0	16 42.8
AUG	9	19 29.5	46 12.3	22 04.9	16 47.1
	29	21 16.1	45 40.4	23 50.8	16 45.8
SEP	18	23 09.6	45 27.1	25 03.2	16 38.9
OCT	8	25 00.3	45 32.8	25 48.3	16 27.2
	28	26 39.6	45 56.1	26 10.3	16 11.8
NOV	17	28 01.1	46 35.0	26 03.1	15 54.8
DEC	7	28 59.9	47 27.4	25 16.8	15 39.0
	27	29 S 33.6	48 S 31.1	24 N 09.4	15 N26.8

1983		Diana 78	Hidalgo 944	Urania 30	Chiron 2060
JAN	1	26♐02.4	05♐27.6	06 R06.1	23 R10.1
	11	29 52.2	06 31.0	05♊26.1	22♉53.8
	21	03♑36.9	07 27.8	05 D37.8	22 43.6
	31	07 15.4	08 16.6	06 37.9	22 39.9
FEB	10	10 46.4	08 56.3	08 20.3	22 D42.8
	20	14 08.5	09 25.6	10 38.6	22 52.2
MAR	2	17 20.0	09 43.4	13 26.6	23 07.9
	12	20 19.5	09 R48.9	16 38.6	23 29.5
	22	23 04.7	09 41.7	20 10.1	23 56.3
APR	1	25 33.3	09 21.6	23 57.1	24 27.8
	11	27 43.0	08 49.1	27 56.5	25 03.1
	21	29 30.8	08 05.2	02♋05.9	25 41.7
MAY	1	00♒53.5	07 11.5	06 23.1	26 22.5
	11	01 48.2	06 10.2	10 46.3	27 04.8
	21	02 11.6	05 04.1	15 14.3	27 48.0
	31	02 R01.7	03 56.2	19 45.9	28 31.0
JUN	10	01 17.5	02 49.6	24 20.1	29 13.2
	20	00 00.2	01 47.5	28 56.3	29 53.8
	30	28♑14.9	00 52.5	03♌33.6	00♊31.9
JUL	10	26 09.4	00 06.8	08 11.7	01 07.0
	20	23 55.0	29♏32.1	12 49.9	01 38.2
	30	21 44.5	29 09.4	17 27.7	02 04.9
AUG	9	19 49.5	28 59.0	22 04.9	02 26.5
	19	18 19.8	29 D01.2	26 40.8	02 42.5
	29	17 21.3	29 15.3	01♍15.0	02 52.4
SEP	8	16 56.3	29 40.8	05 47.2	02 56.0
	18	17 D04.9	00♐16.8	10 16.6	02 R53.2
	28	17 45.2	01 02.2	14 42.7	02 43.9
OCT	8	18 54.3	01 55.9	19 04.9	02 28.5
	18	20 29.1	02 56.8	23 22.2	02 07.6
	28	22 26.2	04 03.4	27 33.7	01 42.0
NOV	7	24 42.7	05 14.7	01♎38.3	01 12.7
	17	27 15.9	06 29.3	05 34.5	00 41.0
	27	00♒03.2	07 45.9	09 20.8	00 08.3
DEC	7	03 02.5	09 03.2	12 55.3	29♉36.1
	17	06 11.9	10 19.9	16 15.7	29 05.9
	27	09 29.6	11 34.5	19 19.4	28 39.0
JAN	6	12♒54.1	12♐45.8	22♎03.1	28♉16.7
JAN	1	29 S 38.1	48 S 48.5	23 N 54.3	15 N24.6
	21	29 41.0	50 02.9	23 15.3	15 19.8
FEB	10	29 23.3	51 22.6	23 12.7	15 21.9
MAR	2	28 51.3	52 43.2	23 31.7	15 30.4
	22	28 13.7	53 57.7	23 52.1	15 44.1
APR	11	27 40.7	54 57.2	23 57.3	16 01.1
MAY	1	27 23.2	55 31.9	23 36.0	16 19.6
	21	27 29.7	55 35.2	22 42.0	16 37.8
JUN	10	28 01.6	55 07.8	21 13.4	16 54.0
	30	28 45.6	54 17.5	19 11.6	17 07.0
JUL	20	29 15.0	53 17.3	16 40.3	17 15.9
AUG	9	29 08.5	52 19.4	13 44.7	17 19.9
	29	28 27.8	51 33.0	10 30.9	17 18.8
SEP	18	27 27.0	51 03.2	07 05.2	17 12.6
OCT	8	26 15.7	50 52.0	03 34.4	17 02.0
	28	24 55.3	50 58.9	00 05.3	16 48.0
NOV	17	23 22.9	51 22.6	03 S 15.1	16 32.4
DEC	7	21 35.1	52 01.4	06 19.5	16 17.6
	27	19 S 30.0	52 S 53.5	09 S 00.6	16 N05.9

1984		Diana 78	Hidalgo 944	Urania 30	Chiron 2060
JAN	1	11♒11.1	12♐10.7	20♎44.0	28 R27.2
	11	14 38.5	13 19.7	23 16.4	28♉07.6
	21	18 10.7	14 23.3	25 23.3	27 53.9
	31	21 46.5	15 20.0	27 00.4	27 46.7
FEB	10	25 24.8	16 08.5	28 02.9	27 D46.4
	20	29 04.5	16 47.5	28 26.9	27 52.8
MAR	1	02♓44.8	17 15.8	28 R09.2	28 05.9
	11	06 24.6	17 32.2	27 08.7	28 25.4
	21	10 03.0	17 R36.1	25 29.1	28 50.5
	31	13 39.1	17 26.9	23 18.3	29 20.8
APR	10	17 11.9	17 04.6	20 49.9	29 55.6
	20	20 40.2	16 29.6	18 21.1	00♊34.0
	30	24 03.2	15 43.1	16 08.1	01 15.3
MAY	10	27 19.3	14 46.8	14 24.5	01 58.6
	20	00♈27.3	13 43.0	13 18.6	02 43.2
	30	03 25.4	12 34.6	12 53.0	03 28.1
JUN	9	06 11.7	11 24.8	13 D07.5	04 12.7
	19	08 44.0	10 17.0	13 58.8	04 56.1
	29	10 59.5	09 14.1	15 22.9	05 37.5
JUL	9	12 55.1	08 19.0	17 15.6	06 16.2
	19	14 27.3	07 33.9	19 32.8	06 51.3
	29	15 32.1	07 00.3	22 10.9	07 22.2
AUG	8	16 05.5	06 39.3	25 07.1	07 48.2
	18	16 R03.9	06 31.3	28 18.4	08 08.7
	28	15 24.9	06 D36.2	01♏42.8	08 23.2
SEP	7	14 08.6	06 53.5	05 18.5	08 31.3
	17	12 19.2	07 22.4	09 03.8	08 R32.7
	27	10 05.4	08 02.0	12 57.4	08 27.4
OCT	7	07 40.9	08 51.3	16 58.2	08 15.5
	17	05 21.9	09 48.9	21 05.1	07 57.4
	27	03 23.6	10 53.8	25 17.2	07 33.8
NOV	6	01 58.4	12 04.5	29 33.7	07 05.8
	16	01 13.4	13 19.8	03♐53.8	06 34.4
	26	01 D10.7	14 38.4	08 16.7	06 01.0
DEC	6	01 49.8	15 58.9	12 41.7	05 27.3
	16	03 07.1	17 19.9	17 08.0	04 54.7
	26	04 58.7	18 40.2	21 35.1	04 24.9
JAN	5	07♈20.5	19♐58.2	26♐01.9	03♊59.1
JAN	1	18 S 56.0	53 S 08.4	09 S 36.3	16 N03.7
	21	16 29.1	54 14.7	11 36.8	15 58.8
FEB	10	13 46.7	55 30.0	12 54.5	16 00.2
MAR	1	10 52.2	56 50.9	13 18.4	16 07.6
	21	07 49.3	58 12.0	12 39.7	16 20.0
APR	10	04 42.5	59 24.9	11 06.5	16 35.5
	30	01 36.5	60 18.6	09 16.9	16 52.5
MAY	20	01 N 24.0	60 43.0	07 59.3	17 09.0
JUN	9	04 13.9	60 33.4	07 39.2	17 23.6
	29	06 47.7	59 53.4	08 16.2	17 35.2
JUL	19	08 58.3	58 54.2	09 38.4	17 42.8
AUG	8	10 36.4	57 49.3	11 31.8	17 46.1
	28	11 29.3	56 50.2	13 43.9	17 44.7
SEP	17	11 25.1	56 04.5	16 03.7	17 38.9
OCT	7	10 26.9	55 35.6	18 21.2	17 29.2
	27	09 06.8	55 24.7	20 27.4	17 16.5
NOV	16	08 10.5	55 30.9	22 14.0	17 02.5
DEC	6	08 06.1	55 53.0	23 34.0	16 49.1
	26	08 N 58.6	56 S 29.8	24 S 21.9	16 N38.4

1985	Diana 78	Hidalgo 944	Urania 30	Chiron 2060
JAN 1	06♈20.4	19♐27.4	24♐15.2	04R08.9
11	08 58.2	20 43.4	28 41.5	03♊46.2
21	11 59.6	21 55.0	03♑06.5	03 29.2
31	15 21.4	23 00.6	07 29.1	03 18.8
FEB 10	19 00.6	23 58.9	11 48.3	03D15.4
20	22 54.7	24 48.5	16 03.4	03 19.2
MAR 2	27 01.7	25 28.0	20 13.0	03 29.9
12	01♉19.7	25 56.1	24 15.9	03 47.4
22	05 47.3	26 11.9	28 10.6	04 11.0
APR 1	10 23.3	26R14.3	01♒55.4	04 40.4
11	15 06.3	26 03.0	05 28.2	05 14.7
21	19 55.7	25 37.8	08 46.7	05 53.1
MAY 1	24 50.6	24 59.4	11 47.9	06 34.9
11	29 50.3	24 08.9	14 28.6	07 19.3
21	04♊54.2	23 08.3	16 44.6	08 05.4
31	10 01.7	22 00.1	18 31.3	08 52.3
JUN 10	15 12.4	20 47.5	19 43.9	09 39.4
20	20 25.7	19 33.9	20 17.3	10 25.6
30	25 41.2	18 22.9	20R07.4	11 10.2
JUL 10	00♋58.3	17 17.9	19 13.1	11 52.4
20	06 16.6	16 21.7	17 36.7	12 31.5
30	11 35.5	15 36.7	15 27.7	13 06.6
AUG 9	16 54.3	15 04.4	13 01.8	13 37.0
19	22 12.5	14 45.7	10 38.5	14 02.0
29	27 29.1	14D41.0	08 37.8	14 21.1
SEP 8	02♌43.4	14 50.0	07 15.0	14 33.6
18	07 54.3	15 12.0	06 38.5	14 39.4
28	13 00.5	15 46.4	06D51.2	14R38.1
OCT 8	18 00.7	16 31.9	07 51.0	14 29.8
18	22 53.3	17 27.3	09 33.6	14 14.8
28	27 35.9	18 31.5	11 54.3	13 53.5
NOV 7	02♍06.6	19 42.9	14 47.4	13 27.0
17	06 22.3	21 00.4	18 08.4	12 56.2
27	10 19.4	22 22.5	21 53.0	12 22.5
DEC 7	13 54.3	23 47.7	25 57.6	11 47.6
17	17 01.8	25 14.9	00♓19.1	11 13.1
27	19 36.4	26 42.5	04 55.0	10 40.6
JAN 6	21♍32.3	28♐09.1	09♓42.7	10♊11.7
JAN 1	09N24.5	56S43.5	24S29.5	16N36.0
21	11 18.4	57 37.7	24 31.7	16 31.5
FEB 10	13 45.6	58 44.3	23 59.1	16 32.9
MAR 2	16 33.1	60 01.3	22 55.8	16 39.7
22	19 28.5	61 25.1	21 28.4	16 51.0
APR 11	22 19.5	62 48.7	19 46.5	17 05.1
MAY 1	24 54.0	64 01.8	18 01.8	17 20.2
21	27 00.3	64 51.2	16 28.7	17 34.7
JUN 10	28 27.7	65 06.4	15 23.6	17 47.1
30	29 07.5	64 44.6	15 02.3	17 56.5
JUL 20	28 54.3	63 53.1	15 30.4	18 02.2
AUG 9	27 46.9	62 45.4	16 29.5	18 03.7
29	25 48.6	61 35.5	17 21.1	18 01.2
SEP 18	23 07.1	60 33.5	17 36.6	17 55.0
OCT 8	19 53.0	59 45.4	17 08.9	17 45.7
28	16 19.2	59 13.5	15 58.6	17 34.2
NOV 17	12 39.9	58 58.0	14 06.4	17 21.8
DEC 7	09 10.1	58 58.4	11 33.6	17 10.3
27	06N05.7	59S13.8	08S23.8	17N01.2

1986	Diana 78	Hidalgo 944	Urania 30	Chiron 2060
JAN 1	20♍39.6	27♐26.0	07♓17.4	10R25.6
11	22 13.8	28 51.6	12 10.5	09♊59.0
21	23 00.0	00♑14.0	17 12.9	09 37.8
31	22R54.8	01 31.8	22 22.8	09 23.1
FEB 10	21 57.9	02 43.5	27 39.1	09 15.4
20	20 15.8	03 47.6	03♈00.6	09D15.1
MAR 2	18 03.2	04 42.6	08 26.0	09 22.2
12	15 40.2	05 27.1	13 54.6	09 36.5
22	13 29.8	05 59.7	19 25.6	09 57.7
APR 1	11 50.9	06 19.0	24 57.9	10 25.0
11	10 54.6	06R24.3	00♉31.2	10 58.0
21	10D45.5	06 14.6	06 04.7	11 35.8
MAY 1	11 21.9	05 49.9	11 37.8	12 17.6
11	12 39.3	05 10.5	17 10.1	13 02.7
21	14 32.4	04 17.6	22 41.0	13 50.1
31	16 55.0	03 13.1	28 09.9	14 39.0
JUN 10	19 42.2	01 59.9	03♊36.6	15 28.5
20	22 49.6	00 41.3	09 00.3	16 17.9
30	26 13.2	29♐21.3	14 20.6	17 06.2
JUL 10	29 50.1	28 04.0	19 37.0	17 52.6
20	03♎37.9	26 53.1	24 48.8	18 36.3
30	07 34.2	25 52.0	29 55.3	19 16.4
AUG 9	11 37.6	25 03.3	04♋55.8	19 52.2
19	15 46.7	24 28.8	09 49.1	20 23.0
29	20 00.1	24 09.4	14 34.4	20 48.0
SEP 8	24 16.9	24D05.5	19 10.1	21 06.5
18	28 36.3	24 16.8	23 34.7	21 18.2
28	02♏57.3	24 42.4	27 46.2	21 22.6
OCT 8	07 19.4	25 21.6	01♌42.2	21R19.6
18	11 41.8	26 13.0	05 19.7	21 09.3
28	16 03.8	27 15.2	08 35.4	20 52.0
NOV 7	20 24.8	28 26.8	11 24.9	20 28.4
17	24 44.0	29 46.5	13 43.2	19 59.5
27	29 00.6	01♑12.7	15 25.1	19 26.5
DEC 7	03♐14.1	02 44.1	16 24.6	18 51.0
17	07 23.3	04 19.0	16R36.9	18 14.7
27	11 27.5	05 56.2	15 59.1	17 39.4
JAN 6	15♐25.5	07♑34.2	14♌32.5	17♊06.7
JAN 1	05N25.5	59S19.9	07S31.2	16N59.6
21	03 15.9	59 53.8	03 44.2	16 55.9
FEB 10	02 05.4	60 42.5	00N22.8	16 57.3
MAR 2	01 52.3	61 46.3	04 39.7	17 03.6
22	02 07.6	63 03.9	08 55.5	17 13.7
APR 11	02 08.9	64 31.7	12 59.1	17 26.1
MAY 1	01 30.7	66 01.7	16 39.7	17 39.2
21	00 08.6	67 21.3	19 47.1	17 51.3
JUN 10	01S52.0	68 14.5	22 12.8	18 01.2
30	04 22.9	68 28.7	23 50.7	18 07.9
JUL 20	07 15.5	68 01.1	24 38.0	18 11.0
AUG 9	10 21.6	67 01.3	24 36.1	18 10.4
29	13 33.6	65 44.5	23 50.4	18 06.1
SEP 18	16 44.2	64 25.1	22 30.6	17 58.9
OCT 8	19 46.5	63 12.7	20 49.7	17 49.5
28	22 34.3	62 12.4	19 04.0	17 38.8
NOV 17	25 01.9	61 26.1	17 32.3	17 28.1
DEC 7	27 05.2	60 54.0	16 35.4	17 18.6
27	28S41.5	60S36.2	16N29.8	17N11.7

1987	Diana 78	Hidalgo 944	Urania 30	Chiron 2060
JAN 1	13♐27.4	06♑45.2	15R21.6	17R22.6
11	17 21.9	08 22.9	13♌33.2	16♊51.9
21	21 08.5	09 59.2	11 11.2	16 26.2
31	24 45.9	11 32.6	08 33.6	16 06.6
FEB 10	28 12.3	13 01.5	06 02.4	15 53.9
20	01♑26.2	14 24.4	03 57.3	15 48.9
MAR 2	04 25.5	15 39.8	02 31.4	15D51.5
12	07 07.8	16 46.0	01 51.5	16 02.0
22	09 30.5	17 41.3	01D57.5	16 19.8
APR 1	11 30.8	18 24.3	02 45.9	16 44.5
11	13 05.3	18 53.4	04 11.8	17 15.6
21	14 10.9	19 07.3	06 09.4	17 52.2
MAY 1	14 44.2	19R04.8	08 33.4	18 33.6
11	14R42.7	18 45.4	11 19.5	19 19.0
21	14 05.3	18 09.1	14 23.5	20 07.5
31	12 53.0	17 16.6	17 42.4	20 58.2
JUN 10	11 10.3	16 09.6	21 13.5	21 50.2
20	09 05.5	14 51.2	24 54.5	22 42.7
30	0649.813	24.828	43.723	34.8
JUL 10	04 36.7	11 55.1	02♍39.8	24 25.7
20	02 38.5	10 27.0	6 41.3	25 14.3
30	01 05.3	09 05.0	10 47.4	26 00.0
AUG 9	00 03.5	07 53.7	14 57.1	26 41.8
19	29♐35.7	06 56.1	19 09.7	27 18.9
29	29D41.8	06 14.6	23 24.5	27 50.6
SEP 8	00♑19.9	05 50.7	27 40.9	28 16.1
18	01 27.0	05D44.6	01♎58.2	28 34.8
28	02 59.8	05 56.0	06 15.9	28 46.1
OCT 8	04 55.0	06 24.3	10 33.3	28R49.7
18	07 09.5	07 07.9	14 49.8	28 45.4
28	09 40.5	08 05.7	19 04.8	28 33.5
NOV 7	12 25.6	09 16.0	23 17.2	28 14.3
17	15 22.5	10 37.2	27 26.5	27 48.6
27	18 29.4	12 07.8	01♏31.6	27 17.5
DEC 7	21 44.5	13 46.0	05 31.2	26 42.5
17	25 06.2	15 30.4	09 24.2	26 05.2par
27 28	33.417	19.513	09.025	27.5
JAN 6	02♒04.4	19♑11.6	16♏43.9	24♊51.4
JAN 1	29S01.4	60S34.0	16N36.9	17N10.5
21	30 04.5	60 34.7	17 29.9	1708.3
FEB 10	30 45.2	60 51.8	18 31.1	17 10.5
MAR 2	31 10.1	61 26.9	19 04.8	17 16.7
22	31 28.7	62 21.7	19 01.017	25.9
APR 11	31 51.1	63 36.4	18 22.7	17 36.8
MAY 1	32 25.6	65 08.0	17 12.9	17 47.6
21	33 11.8	66 48.2	15 33.3	17 56.2
JUN 10	33 53.8	68 22.3	13 25.8	18 03.3
30	34 04.3	69 30.5	10 53.5	18 12.7
JUL 20	33 29.1	69 54.9	08 00.3	18 20.0
AUG 9	32 22.9	69 29.4	04 50.7	18 18.5
29	31 09.8	68 23.0	01 29.8	18 11.1
SEP 18	30 02.1	66 52.5	01S57.0	18 01.9
OCT 8	28 59.5	65 13.7	05 24.3	17 51.8
28	27 55.6	63 37.1	08 46.3	17 41.6
NOV 17	26 43.5	62 08.3	11 57.3	17 32.5
DEC 7	25 17.6	60 49.9	14 52.2	17 25.4
27	23S35.0	59S43.3	17S26.2	17N21.2

1988		Diana 78	Hidalgo 944	Urania 30	Chiron 2060
JAN	1	00♒18.5	18♑15.3	14♏57.8	25R09.1
	11	03 51.1	20 08.4	18 27.1	24♊34.4
	21	07 26.0	22 02.5	21 43.4	24 03.7
	31	11 02.1	23 55.9	24 44.0	23 38.7
FEB	10	14 38.4	25 47.2	27 26.2	23 20.4
	20	18 13.9	27 34.9	29 46.4	23 09.7
MAR	1	21 47.4	29 17.4	01♐40.8	23D07.0
	11	25 18.0	00♒53.0	03 05.2	23 12.5
	21	28 44.8	02 20.2	03 55.3	23 26.0
	31	02♓06.4	03 37.0	04R07.0	23 47.2
APR	10	05 21.7	04 41.7	03 38.1	24 15.4
	20	08 29.4	05 32.4	02 28.1	24 50.1
	30	11 27.8	06 07.3	00 41.5	25 30.5
MAY	10	14 15.4	06 24.8	28♏27.4	26 15.6
	20	16 50.0	06R23.2	25 59.5	27 04.7
	30	19 09.3	06 01.6	23 34.9	27 56.8
JUN	9	21 10.9	05 19.8	21 29.5	28 51.0
	19	22 51.4	04 18.5	19 55.5	29 46.6
	29	24 07.6	02 59.8	19 00.4	00♋42.4
JUL	9	24 56.1	01 27.2	18D46.3	01 37.8
	19	25 13.2	29♑45.6	19 12.5	02 31.7
	29	24R56.4	28 01.0	20 15.9	03 23.2
AUG	8	24 04.5	26 19.6	21 52.3	04 11.5
	18	22 38.7	24 47.4	23 57.7	04 55.8
	28	20 44.4	23 29.9	26 28.4	05 35.0
SEP	7	18 30.8	22 30.7	29 20.6	06 08.4
	17	16 10.6	21 52.1	02♐31.5	06 35.2
	27	13 58.5	21 35.4	05 58.7	06 54.7
OCT	7	12 07.3	21D40.2	09 39.7	07 06.5
	17	10 47.1	22 05.9	13 32.9	07R10.0
	27	10 03.8	22 50.8	17 36.7	07 05.1
NOV	6	09D59.0	23 53.4	21 49.6	06 52.2
	16	10 31.9	25 11.6	26 10.6	06 31.5
	26	11 39.8	26 43.6	00♑38.5	06 04.1
DEC	6	13 18.9	28 27.5	05 12.5	05 31.1
	16	15 25.8	00♒21.5	09 51.6	04 54.1
	26	17 56.7	02 23.8	14 35.1	04 15.1
JAN	5	20♓48.3	04♒32.7	19♑22.2	03♋35.9
JAN	1	23S06.6	59S28.6	18S00.9	17N20.7
	21	21 02.3	58 38.8	20 04.1	17 20.7
FEB	10	18 42.9	58 05.0	21 40.8	17 24.2
MAR	1	16 11.8	57 50.4	22 51.0	17 30.7
	21	13 33.6	57 58.8	23 34.6	17 39.2
APR	10	10 53.6	58 33.4	23 48.4	17 48.3
	30	08 17.8	59 36.5	23 24.9	17 56.5
MAY	20	05 52.8	61 06.3	22 22.3	18 02.6
JUN	9	03 45.9	62 55.6	21 02.0	18 05.5
	29	02 05.9	64 48.9	20 01.2	18 04.6
JUL	19	01 02.5	66 22.3	19 42.3	17 59.8
AUG	8	00 44.9	67 09.8	20 04.7	17 51.5
	28	01 14.6	66 55.8	20 55.6	17 40.5
SEP	17	02 15.6	65 43.8	21 59.4	17 27.9
OCT	7	03 15.1	63 51.1	23 01.3	17 15.2
	27	03 42.1	61 37.1	23 48.4	17 03.9
NOV	16	03 22.2	59 15.9	24 10.1	16 55.2
DEC	6	02 15.0	56 55.9	23 58.3	16 50.1
	26	00S25.7	54S42.0	23S08.1	16N49.0

1989		Diana 78	Hidalgo 944	Urania 30	Chiron 2060
JAN	1	19♓37.4	03♒40.4	17♑26.9	03R51.5
	11	22 40.0	05 52.6	22 15.9	03♋13.2
	21	25 58.9	08 08.8	27 07.4	02 38.1
	31	29 31.6	10 27.7	02♒00.7	02 07.7
FEB	10	03♈16.4	12 47.8	06 55.3	01 43.7
	20	07 11.4	15 07.6	11 50.4	01 27.2
MAR	2	11 15.1	17 25.6	16 45.5	01 18.8
	12	15 26.4	19 40.6	21 40.1	01D18.9
	22	19 44.2	21 50.7	26 33.2	01 27.7
APR	1	24 07.5	23 54.6	01♓24.4	01 44.9
	11	28 35.6	25 50.4	06 12.9	02 09.9
	21	03♉07.8	27 36.3	10 57.8	02 42.2
MAY	1	07 43.5	29 10.4	15 38.2	03 21.1
	11	12 22.2	00♓30.4	20 13.0	04 05.7
	21	17 03.2	01 34.0	24 40.7	04 55.1
	31	21 46.3	02 18.7	29 00.3	05 48.4
JUN	10	26 30.9	02 42.1	03♈09.4	06 44.7
	20	01♊16.4	02R41.9	07 06.0	07 43.1
	30	06 02.6	02 16.5	10 47.4	08 42.7
JUL	10	10 48.7	01 24.9	14 09.9	09 42.6
	20	15 34.0	00 08.1	17 09.7	10 41.7
	30	20 17.9	28♒28.7	19 41.9	11 39.3
AUG	9	24 59.5	26 31.9	21 40.5	12 34.3
	19	29 37.6	24 25.2	22 59.8	13 25.8
	29	04♋11.1	22 17.5	23 33.7	14 12.9
SEP	8	08 38.3	20 18.2	23R17.8	14 54.7
	18	12 57.2	18 35.7	22 12.2	15 30.2
	28	17 05.6	17 16.1	20 23.1	15 58.7
OCT	8	21 00.5	16 23.7	18 05.0	16 19.4
	18	24 38.2	16 00.1	15 40.3	16 31.7
	28	27 54.7	16D05.1	13 32.3	16R35.3
NOV	7	00♌44.4	16 37.4	12 01.4	16 30.0
	17	03 01.6	17 34.7	11 19.7	16 16.0
	27	04 39.6	18 54.6	11D30.9	15 53.9
DEC	7	05 31.6	20 34.5	12 33.3	15 24.6
	17	05R33.1	22 31.9	14 21.8	14 49.7
	27	04 42.6	24 44.2	16 49.6	14 10.7
JAN	6	03♌05.2	27♒09.6	19♈50.8	13♋29.8
JAN	1	00N14.2	54S03.6	22S45.2	16N49.4
	21	02 47.3	52 02.5	21 03.0	16 53.0
FEB	10	05 45.5	50 14.9	18 43.3	16 59.6
MAR	2	09 01.2	48 44.6	15 51.2	17 08.1
	22	12 26.9	47 36.3	12 33.4	17 17.1
APR	11	15 54.7	46 55.0	08 57.8	17 25.3
MAY	1	19 17.1	46 46.1	05 13.0	17 31.2
	21	22 26.2	47 14.3	01 27.4	17 33.8
JUN	10	25 14.5	48 21.5	02N09.9	17 32.1
	30	27 34.7	50 03.9	05 29.2	17 25.9
JUL	20	29 20.8	52 07.8	08 20.2	17 15.2
AUG	9	30 28.8	54 05.5	10 30.6	17 00.8
	29	30 58.3	55 19.3	11 44.7	16 43.8
SEP	18	30 53.2	55 16.5	11 46.1	16 25.8
OCT	8	30 22.6	53 48.5	10 33.6	16 08.6
	28	29 41.2	51 11.8	08 49.3	15 54.3
NOV	17	29 06.9	47 52.6	07 41.2	15 44.7
DEC	7	28 56.0	44 12.4	07 46.7	15 40.8
	27	29N08.5	40S24.5	09N02.8	15N42.7

1990		Diana 78	Hidalgo 944	Urania 30	Chiron 2060
JAN	1	03R59.0	25♒55.4	18♈16.4	13R50.3
	11	02♌03.3	28 26.4	21 32.0	13♋09.3
	21	29♋45.2	01♓07.3	25 12.1	12 29.5
	31	27 28.4	03 56.5	29 12.4	11 53.2
FEB	10	25 36.8	06 52.4	03♉29.1	11 22.1
	20	24 27.1	09 53.5	07 58.7	10 57.9
MAR	2	24D08.0	12 58.8	12 38.7	10 41.6
	12	24 40.6	16 06.8	17 27.0	10 34.2
	22	26 00.6	19 16.4	22 21.4	10D35.8
APR	1	28 02.2	22 26.8	27 20.9	10 46.4
	11	00♌38.8	25 36.5	02♊23.8	11 05.9
	21	03 44.1	28 44.8	07 29.1	11 33.7
MAY	1	07 13.0	01♈50.4	12 36.2	12 09.1
	11	11 00.7	04 52.0	17 44.0	12 51.3
	21	15 03.5	07 48.5	22 52.0	13 39.5
	31	19 18.5	10 38.3	27 59.8	14 32.8
JUN	10	23 43.1	13 19.5	03♋06.7	15 30.2
	20	28 15.2	15 50.4	08 12.3	16 30.7
	30	02♍53.5	18 08.4	13 16.3	17 33.6
JUL	10	07 36.3	20 10.6	18 18.2	18 37.7
	20	12 22.5	21 53.8	23 17.6	19 42.1
	30	17 11.4	23 13.7	28 14.4	20 45.9
AUG	9	22 02.0	24 06.0	03♌07.7	21 48.2
	19	26 53.7	24 25.9	07 57.5	22 47.9
	29	01♎45.9	24R08.2	12 42.9	23 44.0
SEP	8	06 37.9	23 09.7	17 23.5	24 35.7
	18	11 29.3	21 29.1	21 58.5	25 21.8
	28	16 19.6	19 09.8	26 27.0	26 01.5
OCT	8	21 08.2	16 21.8	00♍47.8	26 33.7
	18	25 54.6	13 20.7	05 00.0	26 57.8
	28	00♏38.2	10 26.6	09 01.7	27 13.1
NOV	7	05 18.3	07 58.9	12 51.2	27 19.0
	17	09 54.4	06 12.0	16 26.3	27R15.4
	27	14 25.6	05 14.7	19 44.2	27 02.4
DEC	7	18 51.0	05D09.2	22 41.8	26 40.6
	17	23 09.7	05 53.9	25 15.5	26 11.1
	27	27 20.5	07 25.2	27 20.6	25 35.2
JAN	6	01♐22.1	09♈38.4	28♍52.7	24♋54.9
JAN	1	29N12.2	39S27.2	09N30.7	15N44.0
	21	29 04.4	35 39.3	11 46.8	15 52.0
FEB	10	27 54.6	31 55.5	14 26.4	16 03.0
MAR	2	25 53.7	28 18.1	17 10.3	16 14.9
	22	23 31.7	24 49.3	19 42.1	16 25.9
APR	11	20 59.0	21 31.4	21 48.4	16 34.3
MAY	1	18 12.7	18 26.4	23 18.6	16 38.7
	21	15 07.7	15 36.8	24 05.6	16 38.0
JUN	10	11 42.3	13 04.6	24 05.8	16 31.7
	30	07 58.2	10 51.2	23 19.5	16 19.6
JUL	20	03 59.1	08 56.6	21 50.0	16 02.3
AUG	9	00S10.0	07 17.9	19 43.3	15 40.6
	29	04 23.3	05 45.9	17 07.2	15 16.0
SEP	18	08 34.7	04 01.9	14 10.2	14 50.5
OCT	8	12 38.4	01 39.0	11 01.8	14 26.4
	28	16 28.4	01N39.5	07 51.8	14 06.5
NOV	17	19 59.5	05 43.3	04 50.9	13 53.1
DEC	7	23 07.1	10 12.6	02 10.7	13 47.9
	27	25S48.4	15N00.9	00N04.5	13N51.4

1991		Diana 78	Hidalgo 944	Urania 30	Chiron 2060
JAN	1	29♏22.5	08♈26.9	28♍11.1	25R15.5
	11	03♐19.0	10 59.2	29 24.8	24♋33.8
	21	07 04.1	14 07.1	29 58.0	23 50.9
	31	10 35.8	17 46.7	29R47.3	23 09.3
FEB	10	13 52.2	21 54.8	28 51.4	22 31.2
	20	16 50.7	26 29.3	27 12.9	21 58.6
MAR	2	19 28.6	01♉27.8	25 01.0	21 33.3
	12	21 42.8	06 48.7	22 29.9	21 16.5
	22	23 29.8	12 30.6	19 57.5	21 08.8
APR	1	24 45.8	18 31.7	17 42.2	21D10.9
	11	25 27.6	24 50.3	15 57.9	21 22.5
	21	25R31.9	01♊24.5	14 53.1	21 43.5
MAY	1	24 57.6	08 11.6	14D30.5	22 13.3
	11	23 45.9	15 09.0	14 48.7	22 51.2
	21	22 01.4	22 13.6	15 44.3	23 36.3
	31	19 53.6	29 21.7	17 12.8	24 27.8
JUN	10	17 34.9	06♋29.7	19 09.4	25 24.7
	20	15 19.6	13 34.3	21 29.9	26 26.2
	30	13 21.4	20 32.0	24 10.7	27 31.1
JUL	10	11 50.2	27 20.3	27 08.3	28 38.6
	20	10 52.4	03♌57.0	00♎20.3	29 47.6
	30	10 30.2	10 20.1	03 44.3	00♌57.2
AUG	9	10D42.8	16 28.8	07 18.5	02 06.4
	19	11 27.8	22 22.2	11 01.4	03 14.2
	29	12 41.8	27 59.8	14 51.5	04 19.6
SEP	8	14 21.2	03♍21.4	18 47.9	05 21.6
	18	16 22.6	08 26.8	22 49.5	06 19.0
	28	18 42.9	13 15.7	26 55.4	07 10.9
OCT	8	21 19.1	17 48.2	01♏04.9	07 56.3
	18	24 08.9	22 03.6	05 17.2	08 34.1
	28	27 09.9	26 01.3	09 31.6	09 03.4
NOV	7	00♑20.5	29 40.5	13 47.3	09 23.4
	17	03 39.0	02♎59.8	18 03.7	09 33.5
	27	07 03.7	05 57.8	22 20.0	09R33.5
DEC	7	10 33.4	08 32.5	26 35.4	09 23.4
	17	14 07.0	10 41.4	00♐49.0	09 03.6
	27	17 43.0	12 22.1	04 59.9	08 35.2
JAN	6	21♑20.6	13♎31.6	09♐07.2	07♌59.5
JAN	1	26S24.5	16N16.3	00S20.0	13N53.6
	21	28 32.5	21 31.9	01 22.2	14 06.0
FEB	10	30 17.1	27 10.7	01 17.1	14 22.6
MAR	2	31 44.3	33 07.6	00 04.9	14 40.0
	22	33 01.4	39 09.5	01N43.6	14 55.1
APR	11	34 14.0	44 51.6	03 15.9	15 05.6
MAY	1	35 18.0	49 34.8	03 55.6	15 09.9
	21	35 54.3	52 29.2	03 35.8	15 06.9
JUN	10	35 37.8	52 55.5	02 24.6	14 56.4
	30	34 28.2	50 53.2	00 33.5	14 38.4
JUL	20	32 57.7	47 01.9	01S47.1	14 13.8
AUG	9	31 38.9	42 13.1	04 28.3	13 43.8
	29	30 43.9	37 08.4	07 22.0	13 10.1
SEP	18	30 08.8	32 14.5	10 21.0	12 35.2
OCT	8	29 43.4	27 48.2	13 18.2	12 01.9
	28	29 17.4	23 59.5	16 06.7	11 33.4
NOV	17	28 41.9	20 55.0	18 40.1	11 12.8
DEC	7	27 51.1	18 39.5	20 52.4	11 02.9
	27	26S41.8	17N15.8	22S38.8	11N04.9

1992		Diana 78	Hidalgo 944	Urania 30	Chiron 2060
JAN	1	19♑31.7	13♎00.9	07♐04.1	08R18.1
	11	23 09.6	13 53.8	11 09.1	07♌39.5
	21	26 47.5	14 11.6	15 08.5	06 56.8
	31	00♒24.2	13R52.8	19 01.3	06 12.3
FEB	10	03 58.9	12 57.3	22 45.6	05 28.5
	20	07 30.3	11 27.7	26 19.7	04 48.1
MAR	1	10 57.4	09 29.7	29 41.8	04 13.1
	11	14 19.1	07 12.1	02♑49.2	03 45.5
	21	17 34.0	04 46.5	05 39.1	03 26.6
	31	20 40.8	02 24.7	08 08.4	03 17.4
APR	10	23 37.9	00 17.4	10 13.1	03D18.4
	20	26 23.6	28♍32.9	11 49.1	03 29.7
	30	28 55.9	27 15.5	12 52.0	03 50.8
MAY	10	01♓12.5	26 27.1	13 17.0	04 21.4
	20	03 10.8	26 07.0	13R01.2	05 00.6
	30	04 48.0	26D13.0	12 03.2	05 47.7
JUN	9	06 00.7	26 42.6	10 25.7	06 41.7
	19	06 45.9	27 32.7	08 17.2	07 41.7
	29	07R00.5	28 40.2	05 51.1	08 46.7
JUL	9	06 41.9	00♎02.6	03 24.8	09 55.7
	19	05 49.6	01 37.2	01 16.4	11 07.7
	29	04 25.1	03 22.0	29♐39.9	12 21.8
AUG	8	02 33.4	05 14.9	28 44.4	13 36.8
	18	00 23.4	07 14.3	28D33.5	14 51.8
	28	28♒06.9	09 18.5	29 06.3	16 05.8
SEP	7	25 57.0	11 26.2	00♑20.0	17 17.6
	17	24 06.2	13 35.9	02 10.2	18 26.3
	27	22 43.3	15 46.5	04 32.2	19 30.8
OCT	7	21 54.5	17 56.6	07 22.1	20 29.9
	17	21D41.6	20 05.1	10 35.8	21 22.5
	27	22 03.9	22 10.7	14 10.1	22 07.6
NOV	6	22 59.4	24 11.9	18 02.3	22 44.0
	16	24 24.7	26 07.5	22 09.7	23 10.9
	26	26 16.6	27 56.0	26 30.3	23 27.6
DEC	6	28 31.7	29 35.7	01♒02.6	23 33.5
	16	01♓06.6	01♏05.1	05 44.7	23R28.5
	26	03 58.8	02 22.4	10 35.5	23 13.0
JAN	5	07♓05.8	03♏25.8	15♒33.8	22♌47.7
JAN	1	26S21.4	17N03.0	23S01.0	11N07.2
	21	24 48.7	16 42.1	24 11.2	11 22.7
FEB	10	22 59.7	16 59.7	24 52.6	11 45.1
MAR	1	20 58.9	17 30.7	25 08.8	12 09.6
	21	18 51.9	17 40.1	25 06.7	12 31.5
APR	10	16 45.6	17 00.1	24 55.9	12 47.0
	30	14 47.6	15 27.4	24 47.8	12 53.7
MAY	20	13 06.8	13 17.1	24 50.8	12 50.5
JUN	9	11 52.5	10 46.1	25 03.3	12 37.2
	29	11 14.1	08 05.8	25 10.0	12 14.2
JUL	19	11 17.2	05 22.6	24 58.2	11 42.8
AUG	8	11 56.7	02 39.8	24 35.0	11 04.4
	28	12 51.1	00S00.2	24 13.1	10 21.2
SEP	17	13 30.9	02 35.7	23 53.4	09 35.9
OCT	7	13 36.2	05 05.0	23 26.6	08 51.6
	27	13 02.3	07 26.2	22 40.9	08 11.9
NOV	16	11 51.8	09 37.4	21 26.1	07 40.8
DEC	6	10 08.5	11 36.8	19 35.6	07 21.8
	26	07S55.8	13S22.3	17S07.0	07N17.6

1993		Diana 78	Hidalgo 944	Urania 30	Chiron 2060
JAN	1	05♓49.4	03♏02.2	13♒33.7	22R58.9
	11	09 04.1	03 56.4	18 35.9	22♌28.4
	21	12 30.1	04 34.1	23 43.9	21 50.5
	31	16 05.8	04 53.7	28 56.9	21 07.4
FEB	10	19 49.6	04R54.0	04♓13.9	20 21.7
	20	23 40.3	04 34.6	09 34.4	19 36.1
MAR	2	27 36.6	03 55.7	14 57.6	18 53.1
	12	01♈37.5	02 58.7	20 22.7	18 15.3
	22	05 42.2	01 45.9	25 49.4	17 44.9
APR	1	09 49.9	00 21.0	01♈17.0	17 23.3
	11	13 59.8	28♎48.9	06 44.8	17 11.7
	21	18 11.3	27 14.6	12 12.5	17D10.7
MAY	1	22 23.8	25 43.5	17 39.4	17 20.5
	11	26 36.4	24 20.6	23 04.9	17 40.8
	21	00♉48.9	23 09.7	28 28.6	18 11.2
	31	05 00.4	22 13.8	03♉49.7	18 50.9
JUN	10	09 10.2	21 34.5	09 07.6	19 39.1
	20	13 17.6	21 12.4	14 21.5	20 34.8
	30	17 21.6	21D07.4	19 30.5	21 37.2
JUL	10	21 21.1	21 18.6	24 33.5	22 45.1
	20	25 15.0	21 44.8	29 29.5	23 57.6
	30	29 01.6	22 24.6	04♊16.8	25 13.6
AUG	9	02♊39.0	23 16.5	08 53.8	26 32.2
	19	06 05.1	24 18.9	13 18.5	27 52.2
	29	09 16.7	25 30.3	17 28.1	29 12.8
SEP	8	12 10.6	26 49.2	21 19.8	00♍32.7
	18	14 42.5	28 14.1	24 49.6	01 51.0
	28	16 47.3	29 43.7	27 52.9	03 06.5
OCT	8	18 19.6	01♏16.5	00♋24.7	04 18.0
	18	19 13.2	02 51.3	02 18.5	05 24.6
	28	19R22.6	04 26.6	03 28.0	06 24.8
NOV	7	18 44.9	06 01.1	03R47.8	07 17.6
	17	17 20.9	07 33.5	03 14.1	08 01.9
	27	15 19.0	09 02.3	01 49.0	08 36.5
DEC	7	12 55.3	10 26.1	29♊41.8	09 00.7
	17	10 31.5	11 43.5	27 10.0	09 13.8
	27	08 30.6	12 52.7	24 37.5	09R15.4
JAN	6	07♊10.0	13♏52.5	22♊27.5	09♍05.6
JAN	1	07S10.8	13S50.9	16S15.1	07N19.3
	21	04 25.6	15 15.0	12 59.7	07 34.4
FEB	10	01 20.3	16 19.3	09 14.2	08 00.9
MAR	2	02N00.3	17 00.5	05 06.0	08 32.7
	22	05 31.0	17 16.4	00 43.7	09 03.2
APR	11	09 06.8	17 08.6	03N43.2	09 26.5
MAY	1	12 42.7	16 45.3	08 05.5	09 38.9
	21	16 13.6	16 19.7	12 13.4	09 38.4
JUN	10	19 35.2	16 04.3	15 58.1	09 24.8
	30	22 43.5	16 07.3	19 11.4	08 59.0
JUL	20	25 35.7	16 31.2	21 47.1	08 22.3
AUG	9	28 10.6	17 15.2	23 41.9	07 36.8
	29	30 29.3	18 16.2	24 56.5	06 45.1
SEP	18	32 35.4	19 30.8	25 37.1	05 50.0
OCT	8	34 32.9	20 55.5	25 54.8	04 55.0
	28	36 19.3	22 26.9	26 02.9	04 03.8
NOV	17	37 31.0	24 02.0	26 10.0	03 20.8
DEC	7	37 24.0	25 38.1	26 08.2	02 50.3
	27	35N47.9	27S12.5	25N42.0	02N35.8

1994	Diana 78	Hidalgo 944	Urania 30	Chiron 2060
JAN 1	07 R 44.5	13♏23.9	23 R 28.5	09 R 11.9
11	06♊48.1	14 18.3	21♊36.7	08♍56.6
21	06 D 44.1	15 01.0	20 30.5	08 31.1
31	07 31.9	15 30.4	20 D 14.9	07 56.7
FEB 10	09 07.0	15 45.6	20 48.3	07 15.6
20	11 23.8	15 R 45.6	22 06.1	06 30.1
MAR 2	14 15.9	15 30.1	24 02.0	05 43.0
12	17 37.2	14 59.3	26 29.4	04 57.2
22	21 23.1	14 13.9	29 23.0	04 15.4
APR 1	25 28.8	13 15.8	02♋37.6	03 40.1
11	29 50.9	12 07.6	06 09.2	03 13.1
21	04♋26.4	10 52.5	09 54.6	02 56.0
MAY 1	09 12.7	09 34.3	13 50.9	02 49.6
11	14 07.7	08 16.9	17 55.9	02 D 54.4
21	19 10.0	07 04.2	22 07.9	03 10.2
31	24 17.6	05 59.6	26 25.4	03 36.8
JUN 10	29 29.8	05 05.7	00♌47.2	04 13.4
20	04♌45.3	04 24.4	05 12.3	04 59.4
30	10 03.2	03 57.0	09 39.8	05 53.8
JUL 10	15 22.9	03 43.6	14 09.2	06 55.6
20	20 43.6	03 D 44.3	18 39.7	08 03.9
30	26 04.6	03 58.3	23 10.7	09 17.4
AUG 9	01♍25.5	04 24.9	27 42.0	10 35.4
19	06 45.8	05 02.9	02♍12.9	11 56.7
29	12 04.9	05 51.0	06 42.9	13 20.2
SEP 8	17 22.3	06 48.0	11 11.6	14 45.0
18	22 37.6	07 52.7	15 38.5	16 09.9
28	27 50.1	09 03.5	20 02.8	17 33.7
OCT 8	02♎59.4	10 19.4	24 24.2	18 55.6
18	08 04.8	11 38.9	28 41.5	20 14.1
28	13 05.5	13 00.8	02♎54.1	21 28.2
NOV 7	18 00.9	14 23.7	07 01.1	22 36.7
17	22 49.9	15 46.3	11 00.9	23 38.3
27	27 31.7	17 07.3	14 52.4	24 31.8
DEC 7	02♏05.0	18 25.2	18 33.8	25 16.1
17	06 28.2	19 38.7	22 03.1	25 50.1
27	10 40.1	20 46.4	25 18.1	26 13.0
JAN 6	14♏38.6	21♏46.8	28♎15.9	26♍24.2
JAN 1	35 N 15.7	27 S 35.5	25 N 31.9	02 N 35.0
21	33 07.8	29 03.4	24 50.0	02 43.2
FEB 10	31 29.3	30 21.6	24 21.5	03 07.7
MAR 2	30 22.2	31 24.3	24 08.0	03 43.4
22	29 27.2	32 04.7	23 56.7	04 22.2
APR 11	28 22.9	32 17.4	23 32.9	04 56.1
MAY 1	26 52.5	32 01.8	22 46.1	05 18.6
21	24 46.5	31 25.1	21 30.2	05 26.1
JUN 10	22 01.7	30 40.2	19 43.5	05 17.7
30	18 40.2	30 00.4	17 27.2	04 54.1
JUL 20	14 47.1	29 35.2	14 44.9	04 16.9
AUG 9	10 29.8	29 29.5	11 41.4	03 28.7
29	05 56.2	29 44.0	08 22.1	02 32.3
SEP 18	01 14.2	30 17.3	04 53.1	01 30.9
OCT 8	03 S 28.2	31 06.6	01 20.4	00 27.9
28	08 03.9	32 09.0	02 S 09.6	00 S 32.6
NOV 17	12 26.2	33 21.4	05 30.4	01 26.4
DEC 7	16 29.5	34 41.0	08 35.7	02 09.3
27	20 S 09.5	36 S 05.1	11 S 18.9	02 S 36.8

1995	Diana 78	Hidalgo 944	Urania 30	Chiron 2060
JAN 1	12♏41.2	21♏17.6	26♎49.4	26♍20.1
11	16 32.2	22 13.8	29 37.4	26 R 25.3
21	20 06.4	23 00.6	02♏03.3	26 18.7
31	23 21.3	23 36.7	04 03.3	26 00.8
FEB 10	26 13.3	24 00.8	05 32.8	25 32.6
20	28 39.1	24 12.1	06 27.6	24 55.9
MAR 2	00♐34.7	24 R 09.7	06 R 43.5	24 12.9
12	01 55.7	23 53.5	06 17.7	23 26.2
22	02 38.2	23 23.7	05 10.2	22 38.8
APR 1	02 R 39.2	22 41.1	03 24.7	21 53.4
11	01 57.4	21 47.4	01 10.5	21 12.9
21	00 35.5	20 44.8	28♎41.8	20 39.6
MAY 1	28♏40.2	19 36.2	26 15.0	20 15.3
11	26 23.4	18 24.8	24 06.6	20 01.4
21	24 00.9	17 14.1	22 29.2	19 D 58.5
31	21 48.5	16 07.3	21 29.6	20 07.0
JUN 10	20 00.2	15 07.6	21 D 10.9	20 26.7
20	18 45.2	14 17.3	21 31.5	20 57.2
30	18 07.5	13 38.2	22 28.4	21 37.8
JUL 10	18 D 07.8	13 11.5	23 57.8	22 27.6
20	18 43.5	12 57.6	25 55.1	23 25.7
30	19 51.1	12 D 56.7	28 16.7	24 31.2
AUG 9	21 26.8	13 08.3	00♏59.1	25 43.0
19	23 26.4	13 31.6	03 59.1	26 59.9
29	25 46.4	14 05.7	07 14.4	28 21.1
SEP 8	28 23.8	14 49.6	10 42.8	29 45.5
18	01♐15.5	15 42.1	14 22.4	01♎11.8
28	04 19.4	16 42.0	18 11.7	02 39.1
OCT 8	07 33.5	17 48.0	22 09.5	04 06.3
18	10 55.8	18 58.8	26 14.4	05 32.2
28	14 25.0	20 13.3	00♐25.6	06 55.7
NOV 7	17 59.8	21 30.1	04 42.1	08 15.5
17	21 38.7	22 48.0	09 03.1	09 30.5
27	25 20.8	24 05.5	13 27.9	10 39.4
DEC 7	29 05.0	25 21.4	17 55.5	11 40.8
17	02♑50.2	26 34.3	22 25.3	12 33.8
27	06 35.5	27 42.8	26 56.7	13 17.0
JAN 6	10♑19.8	28♏45.6	01♑28.7	13♎49.6
JAN 1	21 S 00.5	36 S 26.5	11 S 55.6	02 S 40.9
21	24 08.7	37 51.8	14 02.4	02 45.0
FEB 10	26 52.0	39 13.4	15 32.3	02 29.5
MAR 2	29 12.0	40 25.6	16 16.7	01 57.5
22	31 07.2	41 20.7	16 05.8	01 15.7
APR 11	32 26.5	41 50.8	14 57.1	00 33.4
MAY 1	32 47.0	41 51.1	13 12.8	00 N 00.7
21	31 54.6	41 23.2	11 38.8	00 20.3
JUN 10	30 15.1	40 36.3	10 52.6	00 22.4
30	28 38.5	39 43.7	11 04.1	00 07.0
JUL 20	27 37.1	38 57.5	12 04.5	00 S 24.5
AUG 9	27 16.4	38 26.1	13 39.8	01 09.3
29	27 26.9	38 13.6	15 35.9	02 04.4
SEP 18	27 55.5	38 20.9	17 40.6	03 06.1
OCT 8	28 29.4	38 46.5	19 42.8	04 11.0
28	28 58.2	39 28.3	21 32.6	05 15.1
NOV 17	29 13.6	40 23.6	23 01.2	06 14.5
DEC 7	29 10.2	41 29.8	24 01.3	07 05.0
27	28 S 45.2	42 S 44.4	24 S 27.3	07 S 42.6

1996	Diana 78	Hidalgo 944	Urania 30	Chiron 2060
JAN 1	08♑27.8	28♏15.0	29♐12.7	13♎34.7
11	12 11.3	29 14.3	03♑44.8	14 01.7
21	15 52.4	00♐05.9	08 16.6	14 16.9
31	19 30.0	00 48.2	12 47.2	14 R 20.0
FEB 10	23 03.0	01 20.0	17 15.8	14 11.3
20	26 30.3	01 40.4	21 41.7	13 51.5
MAR 1	29 50.5	01 48.3	26 03.7	13 21.6
11	03♒02.3	01 R 43.3	00♒20.8	12 43.6
21	06 04.2	01 25.1	04 31.9	11 59.8
31	08 54.3	00 54.1	08 35.6	11 12.9
APR 10	11 30.7	00 11.2	12 30.2	10 25.8
20	13 51.3	29♏18.1	16 14.1	09 41.3
30	15 53.3	28 16.8	19 44.8	09 02.1
MAY 10	17 34.2	27 10.3	22 59.9	08 30.5
20	18 50.7	26 01.4	25 56.0	08 08.0
30	19 39.6	24 53.6	28 29.3	07 56.1
JUN 9	19 58.3	23 49.9	00♓35.5	07 D 55.2
19	19 R 44.2	22 53.1	02 09.5	08 05.6
29	18 56.5	22 05.5	03 05.8	08 27.1
JUL 9	17 36.9	21 28.8	03 R 20.1	08 59.3
19	15 49.7	21 04.0	02 48.7	09 41.4
29	13 43.3	20 51.8	01 32.4	10 32.7
AUG 8	11 28.9	20 D 51.9	29♒37.7	11 32.1
18	09 18.8	21 04.3	27 17.4	12 38.6
28	07 25.2	21 28.0	24 51.3	13 51.4
SEP 7	05 57.4	22 02.3	22 40.2	15 09.2
17	05 01.1	22 46.1	21 02.3	16 31.0
27	04 39.2	23 38.3	20 09.9	17 55.7
OCT 7	04 D 51.3	24 37.7	20 D 07.2	19 22.2
17	05 35.5	25 43.1	20 54.0	20 49.5
27	06 49.0	26 53.1	22 26.6	22 16.3
NOV 6	08 28.5	28 06.7	24 39.3	23 41.5
16	10 30.8	29 22.4	27 27.0	25 04.0
26	12 52.9	00♐38.9	00♓44.4	26 22.4
DEC 6	15 31.9	01 55.0	04 26.6	27 35.6
16	18 25.5	03 09.3	08 30.0	28 42.4
26	21 31.3	04 20.4	12 50.9	29 41.3
JAN 5	24♒47.4	05♐27.0	17♓26.4	00♏31.5
JAN 1	28 S 35.5	43 S 04.0	24 S 28.1	07 S 49.5
21	27 43.7	44 25.1	24 08.0	08 06.2
FEB 10	26 33.9	45 47.2	23 11.7	08 03.6
MAR 1	25 11.4	47 05.1	21 43.2	07 42.3
21	23 43.2	48 11.2	19 49.0	07 06.4
APR 10	22 18.0	48 56.4	17 38.0	06 23.2
30	21 05.4	49 13.2	15 20.8	05 41.9
MAY 20	20 15.6	48 59.0	13 10.1	05 10.9
JUN 9	19 57.6	48 18.8	11 21.0	04 55.6
29	20 14.8	47 23.8	10 11.0	04 58.4
JUL 19	20 57.9	46 27.4	09 56.1	05 18.4
AUG 8	21 42.6	45 40.2	10 39.5	05 53.5
28	22 02.7	45 09.1	11 54.6	06 40.5
SEP 17	21 47.9	44 56.8	12 53.8	07 35.6
OCT 7	21 02.2	45 03.7	13 04.2	08 35.2
27	19 51.5	45 28.3	12 18.5	09 35.6
NOV 16	18 18.7	46 08.5	10 40.0	10 32.9
DEC 6	16 24.2	47 02.2	08 14.6	11 23.5
26	14 S 08.3	48 S 07.0	05 S 09.5	12 S 04.0

1997		Diana 78	Hidalgo 944	Urania 30	Chiron 2060
JAN	1	23♒27.8	05♐01.0	15♓34.6	00♏12.6
	11	26 49.4	06 04.2	20 17.8	00 56.9
	21	00♓18.8	07 00.6	25 12.0	01 30.7
	31	03 54.4	07 48.9	00♈15.0	01 53.3
FEB	10	07 35.3	08 27.7	05 25.6	02 04.1
	20	11 20.1	08 55.9	10 42.0	02R03.2
MAR	2	15 07.8	09 12.5	16 03.1	01 50.7
	12	18 57.7	09R16.6	21 27.8	01 27.6
	22	22 48.6	09 07.7	26 55.2	00 55.4
APR	1	26 40.0	08 45.9	02♉24.3	00 15.9
	11	00♈30.9	08 11.5	07 54.6	29♎31.5
	21	04 20.5	07 25.8	13 25.3	28 45.0
MAY	1	08 08.0	06 30.4	18 55.7	27 59.1
	11	11 52.7	05 27.5	24 25.4	27 16.5
	21	15 33.4	04 20.2	29 53.9	26 39.6
	31	19 09.1	03 11.4	05♊20.6	26 10.6
JUN	10	22 38.7	02 04.4	10 45.2	25 50.8
	20	26 00.5	01 02.3	16 07.1	25 41.4
	30	29 13.1	00 07.7	21 25.9	25D42.9
JUL	10	02♉14.2	29♏22.8	26 41.1	25 55.4
	20	05 01.4	28 49.1	01♋52.2	26 18.7
	30	07 31.9	28 27.7	06 58.6	26 52.2
AUG	9	09 41.9	28 18.8	11 59.6	27 35.3
	19	11 27.5	28D22.5	16 54.4	28 27.1
	29	12 44.1	28 38.3	21 42.2	29 26.7
SEP	8	13 26.5	29 05.4	26 21.8	00♏33.2
	18	13R30.4	29 43.0	00♌51.9	01 45.3
	28	12 52.9	00♐29.9	05 10.9	03 02.2
OCT	8	11 33.6	01 25.0	09 16.8	04 22.6
	18	09 38.0	02 27.2	13 07.2	05 45.6
	28	07 17.3	03 35.1	16 39.5	07 09.9
NOV	7	04 48.3	04 47.5	19 50.0	08 34.5
	17	02 30.8	06 03.0	22 34.6	09 58.2
	27	00 42.1	07 20.5	24 48.7	11 19.7
DEC	7	29♈34.8	08 38.5	26 26.6	12 38.0
	17	29D14.9	09 55.7	27 23.2	13 51.7
	27	29 42.6	11 10.7	27R33.7	14 59.6
JAN	6	00♉55.6	12♐22.2	26♌54.9	16♏00.7
JAN	1	13S23.6	48S28.3	04S07.5	12S13.7
	21	10 41.9	49 44.2	00 24.1	12 36.5
FEB	10	07 43.2	51 05.1	03N36.9	12 43.2
MAR	2	04 31.1	52 26.3	07 43.9	12 33.2
	22	01 09.6	53 40.8	11 45.5	12 08.0
APR	11	02N17.1	54 39.5	15 29.8	11 32.1
MAY	1	05 44.9	55 12.4	18 46.1	10 52.5
	21	09 09.7	55 13.5	21 24.5	10 17.2
JUN	10	12 28.0	54 43.6	23 17.4	09 53.1
	30	15 36.5	53 51.7	24 20.2	09 44.3
JUL	20	18 32.3	52 50.6	24 31.7	09 51.8
AUG	9	21 12.4	51 52.9	23 55.1	10 14.4
	29	23 31.7	51 07.6	22 37.0	10 49.2
SEP	18	25 19.9	50 39.4	20 47.3	11 32.9
OCT	8	26 16.3	50 30.0	18 38.5	12 21.7
	28	25 57.7	50 38.9	16 25.3	13 12.1
NOV	17	24 31.8	51 04.7	14 24.7	14 00.5
DEC	7	22 52.5	51 45.5	12 56.0	14 43.8
	27	21N54.3	52S39.6	12N18.4	15S19.3

1998		Diana 78	Hidalgo 944	Urania 30	Chiron 2060
JAN	1	00♉13.7	11♐47.0	27R20.5	15♏31.1
	11	01 47.5	12 56.1	26♌17.5	16 28.2
	21	03 59.0	13 59.6	24 30.1	17 16.7
	31	06 43.2	14 56.1	22 09.1	17 55.5
FEB	10	09 55.3	15 44.1	19 32.4	18 23.9
	20	13 30.8	16 22.3	17 00.8	18 41.2
MAR	2	17 26.5	16 49.6	14 53.2	18 47.1
	12	21 39.0	17 04.9	13 23.5	18R41.7
	22	26 05.8	17R07.4	12 38.1	18 25.7
APR	1	00♊44.7	16 56.6	12D37.6	17 59.8
	11	05 33.9	16 32.5	13 19.3	17 25.8
	21	10 31.7	15 55.7	14 38.0	16 45.5
MAY	1	15 37.1	15 07.3	16 28.6	16 01.3
	11	20 48.6	14 09.2	18 46.0	15 15.9
	21	26 05.4	13 03.8	21 25.5	14 31.7
	31	01♋26.6	11 54.1	24 23.5	13 51.3
JUN	10	06 51.4	10 43.3	27 36.7	13 16.9
	20	12 19.1	09 34.9	01♍02.4	12 50.4
	30	17 49.2	08 31.9	04 38.7	12 32.9
JUL	10	23 20.8	07 37.1	08 23.5	12 25.6
	20	28 53.5	06 52.7	12 15.4	12D28.7
	30	04♌26.8	06 20.1	16 13.3	12 42.3
AUG	9	09 59.9	06 00.4	20 16.0	13 06.3
	19	15 32.5	05D53.9	24 22.7	13 39.9
	29	21 03.8	06 00.3	28 32.7	14 22.7
SEP	8	26 33.2	06 19.3	02♎45.1	15 13.7
	18	02♍00.0	06 49.9	06 59.3	16 12.0
	28	07 23.6	07 31.2	11 14.8	17 16.7
OCT	8	12 42.9	08 22.1	15 30.7	18 26.7
	18	17 57.2	09 21.4	19 46.6	19 40.8
	28	23 05.3	10 27.7	24 01.8	20 58.2
NOV	7	28 05.9	11 39.8	28 15.4	22 17.5
	17	02♎57.8	12 56.4	02♏26.7	23 37.7
	27	07 39.2	14 16.2	06 34.7	24 57.7
DEC	7	12 08.1	15 37.7	10 38.4	26 16.2
	17	16 22.4	16 59.7	14 36.8	27 32.1
	27	20 19.1	18 20.7	18 28.5	28 44.1
JAN	6	23♎55.3	19♐39.4	22♏11.8	29♏51.2
JAN	1	21N49.1	52S54.9	12N18.7	15S26.6
	21	22 04.7	54 03.0	12 57.6	15 49.0
FEB	10	23 06.7	55 20.0	14 14.8	15 59.3
MAR	2	24 35.1	56 42.3	15 24.3	15 56.7
	22	26 09.1	58 04.3	15 54.0	15 41.7
APR	11	27 29.7	59 17.2	15 38.0	15 16.5
MAY	1	28 20.3	60 09.9	14 41.1	14 45.3
	21	28 27.9	60 32.3	13 08.6	14 13.6
JUN	10	27 44.1	60 20.1	11 05.3	13 47.6
	30	26 05.6	59 37.7	08 35.9	13 32.1
JUL	20	23 34.5	58 36.8	05 45.2	13 29.6
AUG	9	20 17.0	57 31.2	02 38.4	13 40.1
	29	16 21.8	56 32.4	00S39.2	14 02.0
SEP	18	11 59.4	55 47.6	04 02.0	14 32.4
OCT	8	07 20.3	55 20.3	07 24.5	15 08.0
	28	02 34.7	55 11.1	10 40.8	15 45.6
NOV	17	02S07.6	55 19.3	13 45.2	16 21.9
DEC	7	06 38.0	55 43.5	16 32.6	16 54.3
	27	10S49.0	56S22.4	18S58.3	17S20.5

1999		Diana 78	Hidalgo 944	Urania 30	Chiron 2060
JAN	1	22♎10.0	19♐00.4	20♏21.2	29♏18.4
	11	25 34.6	20 17.4	23 59.8	00♐22.5
	21	28 32.8	21 29.8	27 27.4	01 19.9
	31	01♏00.1	22 36.3	00♐41.7	02 09.5
FEB	10	02 51.6	23 35.4	03 40.3	02 50.3
	20	04 02.1	24 25.7	06 20.1	03 21.5
MAR	2	04 27.4	25 05.7	08 37.5	03 42.3
	12	04R05.1	25 34.4	10 29.0	03 52.5
	22	02 56.1	25 50.4	11 50.0	03R52.0
APR	1	01 07.2	25R52.9	12 36.3	03 40.9
	11	28♎51.4	25 41.5	12R44.1	03 20.3
	21	26 25.9	25 15.9	12 10.8	02 51.0
MAY	1	24 10.5	24 36.9	10 57.0	02 14.9
	11	22 21.1	23 45.6	09 07.1	01 34.0
	21	21 08.4	22 43.8	06 50.7	00 50.4
	31	20 37.5	21 34.4	04 22.7	00 06.6
JUN	10	20D47.7	20 20.4	01 59.6	29♏25.0
	20	21 36.1	19 05.5	29♏57.4	28 47.9
	30	22 58.5	17 53.3	28 28.4	28 17.1
JUL	10	24 49.7	16 47.1	27 38.9	27 54.2
	20	27 05.6	15 50.0	27D31.2	27 40.3
	30	29 42.0	15 04.4	28 04.0	27D36.1
AUG	9	02♏35.3	14 31.6	29 13.8	27 41.9
	19	05 42.8	14 12.8	00♐56.9	27 57.7
	29	09 02.1	14D08.2	03 09.0	28 23.1
SEP	8	12 30.9	14 17.5	05 46.1	28 57.7
	18	16 07.7	14 40.1	08 45.0	29 40.6
	28	19 50.9	15 15.1	12 02.6	00♐31.1
OCT	8	23 39.3	16 01.4	15 36.2	01 28.3
	18	27 31.8	16 57.9	19 24.1	02 31.2
	28	01♐27.2	18 03.1	23 24.0	03 38.6
NOV	7	05 24.7	19 15.7	27 34.6	04 49.7
	17	09 23.4	20 34.4	01♑54.5	06 03.2
	27	13 22.4	21 57.7	06 22.4	07 18.0
DEC	7	17 20.8	23 24.3	10 57.4	08 33.1
	17	21 17.8	24 52.9	15 38.5	09 47.2
	27	25 12.3	26 21.9	20 24.7	10 59.1
JAN	6	29♐03.6	27♐49.9	25♑15.5	12♐07.8
JAN	1	11S48.0	56S34.2	19S31.0	17S25.9
	21	15 25.7	57 30.0	21 25.6	17 42.3
FEB	10	18 29.0	58 38.0	22 54.4	17 49.8
MAR	2	20 46.9	59 56.5	23 58.9	17 48.4
	22	22 00.0	61 21.9	24 41.9	17 38.6
APR	11	21 50.9	62 47.0	25 04.6	17 21.7
MAY	1	20 34.8	64 01.1	25 02.7	16 59.9
	21	19 06.0	64 51.1	24 28.1	16 36.4
JUN	10	18 13.2	65 06.0	23 24.9	16 15.2
	30	18 12.4	64 43.1	22 20.5	16 00.1
JUL	20	18 57.7	63 50.2	21 44.4	15 53.7
AUG	9	20 16.2	62 41.1	21 45.3	15 57.1
	29	21 54.5	61 30.2	22 14.6	16 09.4
SEP	18	23 40.6	60 27.8	22 57.2	16 28.8
OCT	8	25 24.4	59 39.7	23 37.7	16 52.6
	28	26 57.4	59 08.3	24 02.8	17 17.9
NOV	17	28 12.7	58 53.6	24 01.3	17 42.1
DEC	7	29 05.7	58 54.8	23 25.4	18 02.9
	27	29S33.9	59S11.3	22S10.4	18S18.6

2000	Diana 78	Hidalgo 944	Urania 30	Chiron 2060
JAN 1	27♐08.4	27♐06.1	22♑49.6	11♐33.9
11	00♑57.7	28 33.1	27 42.3	12 40.6
21	04 42.0	29 57.0	02♒38.3	13 42.2
31	08 20.3	01♑16.3	07 36.9	14 37.8
FEB 10	11 51.5	02 29.4	12 37.7	15 26.3
20	15 13.9	03 34.9	17 39.9	16 06.7
MAR 1	18 26.3	04 31.3	22 42.9	16 38.2
11	21 26.8	05 17.0	27 46.3	17 00.2
21	24 13.4	05 50.6	02♓49.2	17 12.2
31	26 44.1	06 10.9	07 51.2	17R14.1
APR 10	28 56.3	06R16.7	12 51.7	17 06.1
20	00♒47.0	06 07.4	17 49.8	16 48.8
30	02 13.6	05 42.7	22 45.0	16 23.2
MAY 10	03 12.5	05 02.8	27 36.4	15 50.5
20	03 40.8	04 09.1	02♈22.8	15 12.5
30	03R36.2	03 03.5	07 03.4	14 31.3
JUN 9	02 57.4	01 48.7	11 36.5	13 48.9
19	01 45.4	00 28.4	16 00.6	13 07.8
29	00 04.3	29♐06.5	20 13.8	12 29.8
JUL 9	28♑01.4	27 47.2	24 13.4	11 57.1
19	25 47.7	26 34.5	27 56.4	11 31.2
29	23 35.6	25 31.9	01♉19.5	11 13.2
AUG 8	21 37.1	24 41.9	04 17.7	11 04.2
18	20 02.5	24 06.5	06 46.0	11D04.5
28	18 58.0	23 46.7	08 38.5	11 14.2
SEP 7	18 27.0	23D42.7	09 48.4	11 33.3
17	18D29.7	23 54.2	10 10.3	12 01.3
27	19 04.4	24 20.5	09R40.7	12 37.7
OCT 7	20 08.6	25 00.5	08 20.8	13 21.6
17	21 38.9	25 52.9	06 20.3	14 12.3
27	23 32.0	26 56.5	03 56.4	15 08.8
NOV 6	25 45.2	28 09.7	01 33.0	16 10.1
16	28 15.5	29 31.0	29♈34.2	17 15.2
26	01♒00.3	00♑59.1	28 17.3	18 22.9
DEC 6	03 57.5	02 32.4	27D52.0	19 32.3
16	07 05.1	04 09.4	28 19.7	20 42.2
26	10 21.3	05 48.8	29 36.5	21 51.4
JAN 5	13♒44.6	07♑29.0	01♉36.9	22♐58.8
JAN 1	29S37.0	59S17.7	21S45.4	18S21.6
21	29 34.8	59 52.7	19 40.7	18 29.5
FEB 10	29 12.1	60 42.7	16 59.1	18 31.1
MAR 1	28 35.4	61 47.9	13 46.2	18 26.7
21	27 53.1	63 07.1	10 09.0	18 17.3
APR 10	27 15.3	64 36.8	06 15.3	18 04.2
30	26 52.9	66 09.0	02 13.5	17 48.8
MAY 20	26 55.0	67 30.7	01N48.0	17 33.1
JUN 9	27 23.7	68 25.5	05 40.9	17 19.0
29	28 07.6	68 40.0	09 16.8	17 08.7
JUL 19	28 40.8	68 11.6	12 27.6	17 04.0
AUG 8	28 40.2	67 10.1	15 05.1	17 05.6
28	28 04.4	65 51.6	17 00.3	17 13.2
SEP 17	27 06.4	64 30.6	18 01.2	17 25.6
OCT 7	25 56.1	63 17.0	17 53.6	17 40.8
27	24 35.6	62 15.9	16 37.2	17 56.6
NOV 16	23 02.7	61 29.1	14 54.9	18 10.8
DEC 6	21 14.2	60 56.6	13 52.3	18 21.6
26	19S08.2	60S38.5	14N00.1	18S27.8

2001	Diana 78	Hidalgo 944	Urania 30	Chiron 2060
JAN 1	12♒22.6	06♑48.9	00♉44.0	22♐32.1
11	15 49.4	08 29.0	03 07.2	23 37.9
21	19 21.2	10 07.5	06 03.2	24 40.2
31	22 56.8	11 43.0	09 26.2	25 37.7
FEB 10	26 34.9	13 14.0	13 11.1	26 29.6
20	00♓14.5	14 38.8	17 13.5	27 14.8
MAR 2	03 54.9	15 56.0	21 30.2	27 52.5
12	07 34.7	17 03.7	25 58.0	28 21.8
22	11 13.4	18 00.5	00♊34.5	28 42.2
APR 1	14 49.9	18 44.6	05 17.9	28 53.3
11	18 23.1	19 14.5	10 06.6	28R55.0
21	21 52.1	19 28.8	14 59.0	28 47.4
MAY 1	25 15.8	19R26.3	19 54.4	28 31.0
11	28 32.9	19 06.3	24 51.6	28 06.8
21	01♈42.0	18 28.8	29 49.9	27 35.9
31	04 41.5	17 34.5	04♋48.7	26 59.9
JUN 10	07 29.3	16 25.4	09 47.4	26 20.6
20	10 03.5	15 04.2	14 45.5	25 40.0
30	12 21.0	13 34.9	19 42.6	25 00.1
JUL 10	14 19.0	12 02.3	24 38.3	24 23.0
20	15 54.0	10 31.4	29 32.2	23 50.5
30	17 01.7	09 07.3	04♌24.0	23 24.0
AUG 9	17 38.5	07 54.2	09 13.1	23 04.9
19	17R40.3	06 55.6	13 59.3	22 54.0
29	17 04.5	06 14.0	18 42.0	22D51.8
SEP 8	15 51.2	05 50.5	23 20.5	22 58.6
18	14 03.9	05D45.4	27 54.4	23 14.3
28	11 51.1	05 58.5	02♍22.8	23 38.5
OCT 8	09 26.4	06 28.8	06 44.7	24 10.8
18	07 05.7	07 14.9	10 59.3	24 50.4
28	05 05.1	08 15.5	15 04.9	25 36.6
NOV 7	03 37.1	09 28.8	19 00.1	26 28.4
17	02 49.0	10 53.3	22 43.0	27 25.0
27	02D44.0	12 27.2	26 11.2	28 25.2
DEC 7	03 20.9	14 09.0	29 22.2	29 28.1
17	04 36.7	15 57.1	02♎12.6	00♑32.6
27	06 27.5	17 49.9	04 38.6	01 37.5
JAN 6	08♈48.7	19♑45.9	06♎36.0	02♑41.8
JAN 1	18S26.9	60S35.9	14N15.4	18S28.7
21	15 58.2	60 37.1	15 39.0	18 28.1
FEB 10	13 14.2	60 54.7	17 33.6	18 22.8
MAR 2	10 18.1	61 30.6	19 36.9	18 13.5
22	07 13.8	62 26.6	21 30.2	18 01.7
APR 11	04 05.7	63 43.0	22 59.0	17 48.9
MAY 1	00 58.3	65 17.1	23 52.8	17 36.6
21	02N03.7	67 00.3	24 05.2	17 26.0
JUN 10	04 55.3	68 37.5	23 33.7	17 18.1
30	07 31.2	69 48.1	22 19.3	17 13.8
JUL 20	09 44.6	70 13.2	20 25.9	17 13.5
AUG 9	11 26.3	69 46.1	17 59.7	17 17.1
29	12 23.6	68 36.7	15 07.9	17 24.3
SEP 18	12 23.6	67 02.8	11 58.6	17 33.9
OCT 8	11 27.3	65 20.7	08 40.1	17 44.2
28	10 05.8	63 41.0	05 21.3	17 53.7
NOV 17	09 05.7	62 09.2	02 11.4	18 00.7
DEC 7	08 57.3	60 47.8	00S39.7	18 03.8
27	09N46.4	59S38.0	03S00.8	18S02.3

2002	Diana 78	Hidalgo 944	Urania 30	Chiron 2060
JAN 1	07♈34.6	18♑47.6	05♎41.1	02♑09.8
11	10 09.4	20 44.6	07 22.5	03 13.4
21	13 08.9	22 42.7	08 28.0	04 14.7
31	16 29.3	24 40.2	08 53.3	05 12.7
FEB 10	20 07.7	26 35.7	08R35.2	06 06.3
20	24 01.6	28 27.6	07 32.6	06 54.5
MAR 2	28 08.8	00♒14.4	05 49.6	07 36.4
12	02♉27.3	01 54.4	03 35.1	08 11.3
22	06 55.8	03 25.9	01 03.7	08 38.3
APR 1	11 32.9	04 47.0	28♍33.6	08 57.0
11	16 17.4	05 56.1	26 21.8	09 07.0
21	21 08.5	06 50.9	24 41.5	09R08.1
MAY 1	26 05.2	07 29.7	23 40.7	09 00.6
11	01♊07.0	07 50.5	23D21.3	08 44.8
21	06 13.2	07R51.7	23 42.2	08 21.7
31	11 23.1	07 32.2	24 39.8	07 52.3
JUN 10	16 36.4	06 51.4	26 09.5	07 18.0
20	21 52.5	05 49.8	28 07.1	06 40.5
30	27 10.8	04 29.6	00♎28.3	06 01.6
JUL 10	02♋31.0	02 54.2	03 09.4	05 23.2
20	07 52.5	01 08.7	06 07.6	04 47.1
30	13 14.6	29♑19.4	09 20.0	04 15.2
AUG 9	18 37.0	27 32.9	12 44.5	03 48.7
19	23 58.8	25 56.0	16 19.5	03 29.1
29	29 19.2	24 34.3	20 03.1	03 17.1
SEP 8	04♌37.7	23 31.7	23 54.3	03D13.2
18	09 52.9	22 51.1	27 51.9	03 17.9
28	15 03.7	22 33.3	01♏54.7	03 31.0
OCT 8	20 09.1	22D38.3	06 02.2	03 52.2
18	25 07.1	23 05.1	10 13.4	04 21.2
28	29 56.0	23 52.1	14 27.4	04 57.3
NOV 7	04♍33.7	24 57.6	18 43.8	05 39.7
17	08 57.2	26 19.4	23 01.6	06 27.6
27	13 03.7	27 55.6	27 20.1	07 20.1
DEC 7	16 49.2	29 44.2	01♐38.8	08 16.1
17	20 09.2	01♒43.3	05 56.5	09 14.7
27	22 58.6	03 51.1	10 12.6	10 14.7
JAN 6	25♍11.6	06♒06.0	14♐26.2	11♑15.3
JAN 1	10N06.9	59S22.5	03S29.9	18S01.2
21	11 56.4	58 29.3	04 55.1	17 53.8
FEB 10	14 20.0	57 52.1	05 19.5	17 42.5
MAR 2	17 04.4	57 34.2	04 34.7	17 28.5
22	19 56.6	57 39.5	02 55.0	17 13.5
APR 11	22 43.8	58 11.9	01 05.8	16 59.3
MAY 1	25 13.7	59 13.7	00N04.5	16 47.5
21	27 14.1	60 44.1	00 14.6	16 39.3
JUN 10	28 34.0	62 36.2	00S32.6	16 35.4
30	29 04.8	64 34.5	02 05.5	16 35.7
JUL 20	28 41.2	66 14.3	04 12.0	16 39.8
AUG 9	27 22.4	67 07.5	06 41.4	16 46.8
29	25 12.2	66 55.9	09 24.7	16 55.6
SEP 18	22 18.7	65 42.0	12 13.6	17 05.0
OCT 8	18 52.6	63 44.0	15 00.2	17 13.5
28	15 06.9	61 22.5	17 37.2	17 19.7
NOV 17	11 15.1	58 52.5	19 57.7	17 22.3
DEC 7	07 31.7	56 23.0	21 55.3	17 20.4
27	04N11.7	53S59.0	23S25.1	17S13.6

Bibliography

Abetti, Giorgio. *The History of Astronomy*. Translated by Betty Burr Abetti. New York: Henry Schuman, 1952.

Aeschylus. "The Eumenides." In *The Oresteian Trilogy*. Translated by Phillip Vellacott. Maryland: Penguin Books, 1956.

Apuleius. *The Golden Ass*. Translated by William Adlington. New York: Collier Books, 1972.

Athanassakis, Apostolis N., trans. *The Homeric Hymns*. Baltimore: Johns Hopkins University Press, 1976.

Bach, Eleanor. *Ephemerides of The Asteroids*. New York: Celestial Communications, Inc., 1973.

Bach, Eleanor, Zipporah Dobyns, Rique Pottenger and Neil Michelsen. *The Asteroid Ephemeris 1883-1999*. Los Angeles: TIA Publications, 1977.

Bachofen, J. J. *Myth, Religion and Mother Right*. Princeton, New Jersey: Princeton University Press, 1967.

Berry, Patricia. "The Rape of Demeter/Persephone and Neurosis." *Spring* (1975).

Boer, Charles, trans. *The Homeric Hymns*. Irving, Texas: Spring Publications, Inc., 1979.

Bolen, Jean Shinoda. *Goddesses in Everywoman*. San Francisco: Harper and Row, 1984.

Bradley, Marion Zimmer. *The Forbidden Tower*. and other Darkover novels. New York: Daw Books, Inc., 1977.

Briffault, Robert. *The Mothers: A Study of the Origins of Sentiments and Institutions*. New York: MaMillan, 1927.

Brindel, June Rachey. *Ariadne*. New York: St. Martins Press, 1980.

Bulfinch. *Bulfinch's Mythology*. New York: Doubleday and Co., 1948.

Campbell, Joseph. *The Masks of God: Occidental Mythology*. Maryland: Penguin Books, 1964.

Castillejo, Irene Claremont de. *Knowing Woman: A Feminine Psychology*. New York: Harper and Colophon Books, 1973.

Chapman, Clark R. "The Nature of the Asteroids." *Scientific American*, vol. 232, no. 1 (January 1975).

Chapman, Clark R., James G. Williams, and William K. Hartman. "The Asteroids." *Annual Review of Astronomy and Astrophysics*, vol. 16 (1978).

Chesler, Phyllis. *Women and Madness*. New York: Doubleday, 1972.

Chicago, Judy. *Through the Flower*. New York: Doubleday, 1977.

Christ, Carol P. and Judith Plaskau, eds. *Womanspirit Rising: A Feminist Reader in Religion*. San Francisco: Harper and Row, 1979.

Ciaccio, Edward J. "Celestial Bodies." *Astronomy*, vol. 11, no. 5 (May 1983).

Conrad, Jack Randolph. *The Horn and the Sword: The History of the Bull as a Symbol of Power and Fertility*. New York: E. P. Dutton and

Co., Inc., 1957.
Daly, Mary. *Beyond God the Father: Towards a Philosophy of Women's Liberation*. Boston: Beacon Press, 1973.
Davis, Elizabeth Gould. *The First Sex*. New York: Penguin Books, 1971.
Davis, Joel. "The Flying Mountains." *Astronomy*, vol. 8, no. 5 (May 1980).
de Beauvoir, Simone. *The Second Sex*. Translated and edited by H. M. Parshley. New York: Bantam Books, 1953.
Demetrakopoulous, Stephanie A. "Hestia, Goddess of the Hearth: Notes on an Oppressed Archetype." *Spring* (1979).
Diner, Helen. *Mothes and Amazons: The First Feminine History of Culture*. New York: Anchor Books, 1973.
Dinnerstein, Dorothy. *The Mermaid and the Minotaur: Sexual Arrangements and Human Malaise*. New York: Harper and Row, 1976.
Dowling, Christine. *The Goddess: Mythological Images of the Feminine*. New York: The Crossroad Publishing Co., 1981.
Evans, Sir Arthur. *The Earlier Religion of Greece in the Light of Cretan Discoveries*. London: Macmillan and Co., Ltd., 1931.
Farmer, Penelope. *The Story of Persephone*. New York: Wm. Morrow and Co., 1973.
Farnell, Lewis R. *The Cults of the Greek States*. London: Oxford University Press, 1907.
Frazer, James G. *The Golden Bough: The Roots of Religion and Folklore*. New York: Avenel Books, 1981.
Friday, Nancy. *My Mother Myself: The Daughter's Search for Identity*. New York: Dell Publishing Co., 1977.
Friedman, Louis and Carl Sagan. "Mission to the Asteroids." *Science Digest*, vol. 92, no. 3 (March 1984).
Friedrich, Paul. *The Meaning of Aphrodite*. Chicago: University of Chicago Press, 1978.
Gilbert, Lucy and Webster, Paula. *Bound by Love: The Sweet Trap of Daughterhood*. Boston: Beacon Press, 1982.
Gimbutas, Marija. *The Gods and Goddeses of Old Europe, 7000 to 3500 bc*. Berkeley: University of California Press, 1974.
Grant, Michael. *Myths of the Greeks and Romans*. New York: Mentor Books, 1964.
Graves, Robert. *The White Goddess*. New York: Farrar, Straus and Giroux, 1978.
______. *The Greek Myths, Vols. 1 and 2*. Maryland: Penguin Books, 1964.

Graves, Robert and Raphael Patai. *Hebrew Myths: The Book of Genesis*. New York: McGraw-Hill Book Co., 1963.

The Great Goddess. *Heresies: A Feminist Publication on Art and Politics*. (Spring 1978).

Greene, Liz. *Relating: An Astrologer's Guide to Living with Others on a Small Planet*. New York: Samuel Weiser, 19___.

Griffin, Susan. *Woman and Nature: The Roaring Inside Her*. New York: Harper and Row, 1978.

Guerber, H. A. *Myths of Greece and Rome*. New York: American Book co., 1893.

Hall, Nor. *The Moon and the Virgin: Relfections of the Archetypal Feminine*. New York: Harper and Row, 1980.

Hallett, Judith P. "Sappho and Her Social context: Sense and Sensuality". *Signs*. (Spring 1979): 447-64.

Harding, M. Esther. *The Way of All Women*. New York: Putnam's, 1973.

Hartman, William K. "Vesta, A World of Its Own." *Astronomy*, vol. 77, no. 2 (February 1983).

Harrison, Jane Ellen. *Epilogomena to the Study of Green Religion and Themis*. New York: University Books, 1962.

______. *Mythology*. Boston: Marshall Jones Co., 1924.

______. *Myths of Greece and Rome*. London: Ernest Benn, Ltd., 1927.

______. *Prolegomena to the Study of Green Religion*. Massachusetts: Cambridge University Press, 1922.

______. *The Religion of Ancient Greece*. London: Archibald Constable and Co., 1905.

Hays, H. R. *The Dangerous Sex: The Myth of Feminine Evil*. New York: Putnam, 1964.

Heilbrun, Carolyn G. *Towards a Recognition of Androgeny*. New York: Albert A. Knopf, 1973.

______. *Reinventing Womanhood*. New York: Norton, 1979.

Hill, P. Maurice, tr. *The Poems of Sappho*. New York: Philosophical Library, 1954.

Hillman, James, ed. *Facing the Gods*. Irving, Texas: Spring Publications, Inc., 1980.

Hesiod. *Theogony*. Translated by Norman O. Brown. New York: The Liberal Arts Press, 1953.

Homer. *The Iliad*. Translated by E. V. Reiu. Maryland: Penguin Books, 1950.

Homer. *The Odyssey*. Translated by W. H. D. Rouse. New York: Mentor Books, 1949.

Johnson, Robert A. *She: Understanding Feminine Psychology*. New York: Harper and Row, 1977.

Joseph, Anthony M. "Chiron: Archetypal Image of Teacher and Healer." In *Ephemeris of Chiron 1890-2000*. Toronto, Canada: Phenomena Publications, 1978.

Jung, Emma. *Animus and Anima*. New York, Spring 1969.

Jung, Carl G. and Carl Kerenyi. *Essays on a Science of Mythology: The Myth of the Divine Child and the Mysteries of Eleusis*. Bollingen Series XXII, translated by R. F. C. Hull. Princeton, New Jersey: Princeton University Press, 1949.

Jung, Carl G. *Mandala Symbolism*. Princeton, New Jersey: Princeton University Press, 1972.

______. "On the Psychology of the Unconscious." In *Two Essays on Analytic Psychology*. Cleveland: Meridian Books, 1965.

Kerenyi, Carl. *The Gods of the Greeks*. translated by Norman Cameron. Great Britain: Billings and Sons, Ltd., 1982.

______. *Zeus and Hera: Archetypal Image of Father, Husband and Wife*. Translated by Christopher Holme. Princeton, New Jersey: Princeton University Press, 1975.

______. *Athene: Virgin and Mother in Greek Religion*. Translated by Murray Stein. Zurich, Swtz: Spring Publications, 1978.

______. *Eleusis: Archetypal Image of Mother and Daughter*. Translated by Ralph Manheim. New York: Schocken, 1977.

Kerr, Richard A. "Asteroid Theory of Extinctions Strengthened." *Science*, vol. 210 no. 4469 (October 31, 1980).

Kirksey, Barbara. "Hestia: A Background of Psychological Focusing." In *Facing the Gods*. Edited by James Hillman. Irving, Texas: Spring Publications, Inc., 1980.

Koltov, Barbara. "Hestia/Vesta." *Quadrant*. vol. 10, no. 2 (Winter, 1977).

Lantero, Ermine. *The Continuing Discovery of Chiron*. Maine: Samuel Weiser, Inc., 1983.

Lederer, Wolfgang, M.D. *The Fear of Women*. New York: Harvest/Harcourt Brace Jovanovich, 1968.

Leinbach, Esther V. *Planets and Asteroids: Relationships in Conjunctions*. Vulcan Books, 1984.

Levy, Rachel G. *Religious Concepts of the Stone Age*. New York: Harper Torchbooks, 1963.

Lewis, C. S. *Till We Have Faces: A Myth Retold*. New York: Harcourt Brace and World, 1956.

Ley, Willy. *Watchers of the Skies*. New York: The Viking Press, 1963.

MacDonald, George. *Phantasies and Lilith*. Michigan: Wm. B.

Eardmans Publishing Co., 1964.
Millett, Kate. *Sexual Politics*. New York: Ballantine Books, 1969.
Monoghan, Patricia. *The Book of Goddesses and Heroines*. New York: E. P. Dutton, 1981.
Morrison, David. "Asteroids." *Astronomy*, vol. 4, no. 6 (June 1976).
Murray, Alexander S. *Manual of Mythology*. New York: Tudor Publishing Co., 19____.
Murray, Gilbert. *Five Stages of Greek Religion*. New York: Doubleday Anchor Books, 1955.
Mylonas, George E. *Eleusis and the Eleusinian Mysteries*. Princeton, New Jersey: Princeton University Press, 1961.
Neslen, Kristie. *The Origin*. San Francisco: Venusian Propaganda, 1979.
Neumann, Erich. *The Great Mother: An Analysis of the Archetype*. Bollingen Series XLVII, translated by Ralph Manheim. Princeton, New Jersey: Princeton Univesity Press, 1974.
______. *Amor and Psyche: The Psychic Development of The Feminine*. Bollingen Series LVI. Princeton, New Jersey: Princeton University Press, 1973.
______. *The Origins and History of Consciousness*. Bollingen Series XLII. Princeton, New Jersey: Princeton University Press, 1973.
New Larousse Encyclopedia of Mythology. Translated by Richard and Ames D. Aldington. New York and London: Hamlyn Publishing Group, Ltd., 1983.
Nilsson, Martin P. *A History of Greek Religion*. Translated by F. J. Fielden. New York: W. W. Norton, 1964.
______. *Greek Folk Religion*. New York: Harper Torchbooks, 1961.
Noelle, Richard. *Chiron: New Planet on The Horoscope*. Tempe, Arizona: American Federation of Astrologers, 1983.
Ochs, Carol. *Behind the Sex of God: Towards a New Consciousness: Transcending Matriachry and Patriarchy*. Boston: Beacon Press, 1977.
Orbach, Susie. *Fat is a Feminist Issue*. New York: Berkley Publishing Corp., 1978.
Ovid. *Metamorphosis*. Translated by Mary M. Innes. Maryland: Penguin Books, 1955.
Panofsky, Dora and Erwin. *Pandora's Box*. Bollingen Series LII. Princeton, New Jersey: Princeton University Press, 1956.
Patai, Raphael. *The Hebrew Goddess*. New York: Avon Books, 1978.
Perera, Sylvia Brinton. *Descent to the Goddess: A Way of Initiation for Women*. Toronto, Canada: Inner City Books, 1981.

Reed, Evelyn. *Woman's Evolution: From Matriarchal Clan to Patriarchal Family*. New York and Toronto, Canada: Pathfinder Press, 1975.

Rich, Adrienne. *Of Woman Born*. New York: Bantam Books, 1976.

Richardson, Robert S. "The Discovery of Icarus." *Scientific American* vol. 212, no. 4 (April 1965).

Rivlin, Lily. "Lilith." In *Ms.* Vol. 6. (December 1972).

Robinson, David M. *Sappho and Her Influence*. Massachusetts: Marshal Jones Co., 1924.

Robinson, James M., ed. *The Nag Hammadi Library in English*. San Francisco: Harper and Row, 1977.

Rodden, Lois M. *The American Book of Charts*. San Diego: Astro Computing Services, 1980.

______. *Profiles of Women*. Tempe, Arizona: American Federation of Astrologers, 1979.

Rose, H. J. *Religion in Greece and Rome*. New York: Harper Torchbooks, 1959.

______. *A Handbook of Greek Mythology*. New York: E. F. Dutton and Co., Inc., 1959.

Rush, Anne Kent. *Moon, Moon*. New York: Random House; Berkeley: Moon Book, 1976.

Sappho: A New Translation. Translated by Mary Barnard. Berkeley and Los Angeles, California: University of California Press, 1958.

Schure, Edouard. *The Mysteries of Ancient Greece: Orpheus/Plato*. New York: Rudolf Steiner Publications, 1971.

Sherfey, Mary Jane. *The Nature and Evolution of Female Sexuality*. New York: Vintage Books, 1966.

Singer, June. *Androgeny: Toward a New Theory of Sexuality*. New York: Anchor Press, Doubleday, 1977.

Sjoo, Monica and Barbara Mor. *The Ancient Religion of the Great Cosmic Mother of All*. Trondheim, Norway: Rainbow Press, 1981.

Slater, Philip E. *The Glory of Hera: Greek Mythology and the Greek Family*. Boston: Beacon Press, 1968.

Smith, William, ed. *A Smaller Classical Mythology*. London: John Murray, 1875.

Spignesi, Angelyn. *Starving Women: A Psychology of Anorexia Nervosa*. Irving, Texas: Spring Publications, Inc., 1983.

Spretnak, Charlene. *Lost Goddesses of Early Greece*. Berkeley: Moon Books, 1978.

______, ed. *The Politics of Women's Spirituality*. New York: Anchor Press/Doubleday, 1982.

Starhawk. *The Spiral Dance: A Rebirth of the Ancient Religion*

of the Great Goddess. San Francisco: Harper and Row, 1979.
Stein, Murray. "Hera: Bound and Unbound." *Spring* (1977).
Stone, Merlin. *Ancient Mirrors of Womanhood Vols. I and II*. New York: New Sybylline Books, 1979.
______. *When God Was a Woman*. New York: Harvest/Harcourt Brace Jovanovich, 1976.
Tenzin, Gyatso, The Fourteenth Dalai Lama. *Kindness, Clarity and Insight*. Translated by Jeffrey Hopkins and Elizabeth Napper. New York: Snow Lions Publications, 1984.
Thompson William, Irwin. *The Time Falling Bodies Take to Light: Mythology, Sexuality and the Origins of Culture*. New York: St. Martins Press, 1981.
Three Initiates. *The Kyblion: Hermetic Philosophy*. Chicago: The Yogi Publication Society, 1912.
Thorsten, Geraldine. *God Herself: The Feminine Roots of Astrology*. New York: Doubleday and Co., 1980.
Tripp, Edward. *The Meridian Book of Classical Mythology*. New York: New American Library, 1970.
Van Flandern, Thomas. "Exploding Planets." *Science Digest*. (April 1982).
Von Franz, Maria-Louise. *The Interpretation of Apuleius' Golden Ass*. Irving, Texas: Spring Publications, Inc., 1980.
Walker, Barbara G. *The Woman's Encyclopedia of Myths and Secrets*. San Francisco: Harper and Row, 1983.
Walton, Evangeline. *The Sword is Forged*. New York: Simon and Schuster, 1984.
Wasson, R. Gordon, Carl A. Ruck and Albert Hofmann. *The Road to Eleusis: Unveiling the Secret of the Mysteries*. New York: Harcourt Brace Jovanovich, Inc., 1978.
Weigall, Arthur. *Sappho of Lesbos*. New York: Frederick A. Stokes Co., 1932.
Weigle, Marta. *Spiders and Spinsters: Women and Mythology*. Albuquerque: University of New Mexico Press, 1982.
Weinberg, Judy. "Lilith Sources." In *Lilith* vol. 1, no. 1. (June 1976).
Wolkstein, Diane and Samuel N. Kramer. *Inanna: Queen of Heaven and Earth*. New York: Harper and Row, 1983.
Woodman, Marion. *Addiction to Perfection: The Still Unravished Bride*. Toronto, Canada: Inner City Books, 1982.
Zabriski, Philip T. "Goddesses in Our Midst." *Quadrant* no. 17. (Fall 1974).
Zuckoff, Avina Cantor. "The Lilith Question." *Lilith* vol. 1, no. 1. (June 1966).

Also by ACS Publications

All About Astrology Series of booklets
The American Atlas, Expanded Fifth Edition: US Latitudes & Longitudes, Time Changes and Time Zones (Shanks)
The American Book of Tables (Michelsen)
The American Ephemeris Series 1901-2000
The American Ephemeris for the 20th Century [Noon or Midnight] 1900 to 2000, Revised Fifth Edition
The American Ephemeris for the 21st Century 2001-2050, Revised Second Edition
The American Heliocentric Ephemeris 1901-2000
The American Midpoint Ephemeris 1991-1995
The American Sidereal Ephemeris 1976-2000
Asteroid Goddesses: The Mythology, Psychology and Astrology of the Reemerging Feminine (George & Bloch)
Astro-Alchemy: Making the Most of Your Transits (Negus)
Astro Essentials: Planets in Signs, Houses & Aspects (Pottenger)
Astrological Games People Play (Ashman)
Astrological Insights into Personality (Lundsted)
Basic Astrology: A Guide for Teachers & Students (Negus)
Basic Astrology: A Workbook for Students (Negus)
The Book of Jupiter (Waram)
The Book of Neptune (Waram)
The Changing Sky: A Practical Guide to the New Predictive Astrology (Forrest)
Complete Horoscope Interpretation: Putting Together Your Planetary Profile (Pottenger)
Cosmic Combinations: A Book of Astrological Exercises (Negus)
Dial Detective: Investigation with the 90° Dial (Simms)
Easy Tarot Guide (Masino)
Expanding Astrology's Universe (Dobyns)
Hands That Heal (Burns)
Healing with the Horoscope: A Guide To Counseling (Pottenger)
Houses of the Horoscope (Herbst)
The Inner Sky: The Dynamic New Astrology for Everyone (Forrest)
The International Atlas, Revised Third Edition: World Latitudes & Longitudes, Time Changes and Time Zones (Shanks)
The Koch Book of Tables (Michelsen)
Midpoints: Unleashing the Power of the Planets (Munkasey)
New Insights into Astrology (Press)
The Night Speaks: A Meditation on the Astrological Worldview (Forrest)
The Only Way to... Learn Astrology, Vols. I-VI (March & McEvers)
- Volume I - Basic Principles
- Volume II - Math & Interpretation Techniques
- Volume III - Horoscope Analysis
- Volume IV- Learn About Tomorrow: Current Patterns
- Volume V - Learn About Relationships: Synastry Techniques
- Volume VI - Learn About Horary and Electional Astrology

Planetary Heredity (M. Gauquelin)
Planetary Planting (Riotte)
Planets in Solar Returns: A Yearly Guide for Transformation and Growth (Shea)
Planets in Work: A Complete Guide to Vocational Astrology (Binder)
Psychology of the Planets (F. Gauquelin)
Skymates: The Astrology of Love, Sex and Intimacy (S. & J. Forrest)
Spirit Guides: We Are Not Alone (Belhayes)
Tables of Planetary Phenomena (Michelsen)
Twelve Wings of the Eagle: Our Spiritual Evolution through the Ages of the Zodiac (Simms)
The Way of the Spirit: The Wisdom of the Ancient Nanina (Whiskers)

Titles from Steven Forrest

The Inner Sky

The Dynamic New Astrology For Everyone

Forrest's New Astrology encourages free choice—not fate. The author provides directions for uncovering your hidden potential. Nothing is "carved-in-stone" when it comes to your personality—you can change. Forrest skillfully guides you while you seek out and find new areas of inner strength and personal growth. **(B131X) $12.95**

The Changing Sky

A Practical Guide to the New Predictive Astrology

In this sequel to *The Inner Sky* Forrest dispels the myths and misconceptions that surround predictive astrology. In no uncertain terms the author describes what predictive astrology can do for you and what it cannot. Forrest states ... "What modern predictive astrology can do is inform you in advance of the natural rhythms of your life—and moods—thereby helping you arrange your outward experiences in the happiest, most harmonious and efficient manner." **(B122X) $12.95**

Skymates

The Astrology of Love, Sex and Intimacy

Steven and Jodie Forrest have taken pen in hand to put years of their own practical experience about *synastry*—the astrology of intimacy, sex and partnership— into this book. The authors discuss how best to use astrology in your relationship(s) ... as "a wise counselor, an all knowing third party who loves both of us with supernatural clarity, insight, and caring." Steven and Jodie use astrology in a most creative and unique way to help you discover the emotional needs of yourself and your lover. **(B143X) $14.95**

The Night Speaks

A Meditation on the Astrological Worldview

The Night Speaks, written with Steven Forrest's wonderfully evocative style, elicits awe and inspiration in the reader. He traces the wonder of astrology and the human/cosmos connection. He discusses some scientific information as to why and how we might explain astrology, but keeps throughout a mystical, transcendent feel. If you've wanted a book to explain "why you believe in that stuff" to doubting friends, this is it!

(B149X) $12.95

Credit Card Orders call Toll-Free: OR Send your check or money order to:

1 800 888 9983

Monday - Friday, 9 AM to 5 PM Pacific Time
We accept VISA, MasterCard and AMEX

ACS Publications
P.O. Box 34467, Dept.AG94
San Diego, CA 92163-4487

Shipping & Handling fees: up to $30=$3; up to $50=$5; up to S75=$6; up to $100=$7
(Outside the US: up to $30=$5; up to $50=$9; up to $75=12; up to $100=$15)

International Orders: Payment must be in US Dollars only by International Money Order or Credit Card.

Prices subject to change without notice

THE AMERICAN EPHEMERIS for the 20th CENTURY 1900 TO 2000
THE AMERICAN EPHEMERIS for the 21st CENTURY 2001 TO 2050 at Midnight
THE AMERICAN HELIOCENTRIC EPHEMERIS
Tables of Planetary Phenomena